Principles of Marketing

Visit the

Principles of Marketing,

Fourth European edition

Companion Website at

www.pearsoned.co.uk/

kotler to access a rich

resource of valuable

learning materials for

students, including:

■ Chapter objectives for you to quickly check the learning outcomes of each topic

■ Multiple choice questions for every chapter, with instant feedback

■ Annotated weblinks to relevant specific Internet resources to facilitate in-depth independent research

■ Additional case studies that allow you to apply theory to recognisable real-world brands and products

■ Searchable online glossary

■ Flashcards to test your knowledge of key terms and definitions

FOURTH EUROPEAN EDITION

Principles of Marketing

PHILIP KOTLER

VERONICA WONG

JOHN SAUNDERS

GARY ARMSTRONG

 Prentice Hall
FINANCIAL TIMES

An imprint of **Pearson Education**
Harlow, England • London • New York • Boston • San Francisco • Toronto • Sydney • Singapore • Hong Kong
Tokyo • Seoul • Taipei • New Delhi • Cape Town • Madrid • Mexico City • Amsterdam • Munich • Paris • Milan

Pearson Education Limited
Edinburgh Gate
Harlow
Essex CM20 2JE
England

and Associated Companies throughout the world

Visit us on the World Wide Web at:
www.pearsoned.co.uk

First European Edition published 1996
Second European Edition published 1999 by Prentice Hall Europe
Third European Edition published by Pearson Education
Fourth European Edition published 2005

ISBN 0 273 68456 6

British Library Cataloguing-in-Publication Data
A catalogue record for this book is available from the British Library

10 9 8 7 6 5 4 3 2 1
09 08 07 06 05

Typeset in 10/12.5pt Minion by 35
Printed and bound by Mateu-Cromo Artes Graficas, Spain

The publisher's policy is to use paper manufactured from sustainable forests.

To Peter Doyle and Jim Lynch:
Two late, great marketing educators, colleagues and friends.

BRIEF CONTENTS

CONTENTS

Contents

Part four Core strategy

Chapter ten Segmentation and positioning

Chapter eleven Relationship marketing

Contents

Supporting resources

Visit **www.pearsoned.co.uk/kotler** to find online resources

Companion Website for students

- Chapter objectives for you to quickly check the learning outcomes of each topic
- Multiple choice questions for every chapter, with instant feedback
- Annotated weblinks to relevant specific Internet resources to facilitate in-depth
- independent research
- Additional case studies that allow you to apply theory to recognisable real-world
- brands and products
- Searchable online glossary

For instructors

- A secure, password-protected area offering downloadable teaching support
- Customisable PowerPoint slides, including key figures and tables from the main text
- Instructor's Manual, including sample answers for all question material in the book
- Sample answers to the questions from the *Marketing in Practice* DVD, which contains video case studies from Lancôme, Fruitella and Bacardi Breezer

For more information about the *Marketing in Practice* DVD and other Marketing-related resources, please contact your local Pearson Education sales representative.

OneKey: All you and your students need to succeed

OneKey is an exclusive new resource for instructors and students, giving you access to the best online teaching and learning tools 24 hours a day, 7 days a week.

OneKey means all your resources are in one place for maximum convenience, simplicity and success.

A OneKey product is available for *Principles of Marketing, Fourth European edition* for use with BlackBoard™, WebCT and CourseCompass. It contains over 40 hours of fully interactive learning materials including:

- Online Study Guide
- Flashcards to test your knowledge of key terms and definitions

For more information about the OneKey product please contact your local Pearson Education sales representative or visit **www.pearsoned.co.uk/onekey**.

GUIDED TOUR

Great **colour photography** from real, high-profile European marketing campaigns is used to open each chapter and raise the thought-provoking issue the chapter will go on to explore

Business is like riding a bicycle. Either you keep moving or you fall down.

JAMES KEASLEY SIMPSON

Marketing in the Internet age

Chapter objectives

After reading this chapter, you should be able to:

- Identify the major forces shaping the new digital age.
- Explain how businesses have responded to the Internet and other powerful new technologies with e-business strategies and how these strategies are beneficial to both buyers and sellers.
- Describe the four major e-commerce domains.
- Discuss how marketers conduct e-commerce in ways that profitably deliver value to customers.
- Overview the promise and challenges that e-commerce presents for the future.

Mini Contents List

- Prelude case – Cool Diamonds: are they forever?
- Introduction
- Major forces shaping the Internet age
- Marketing Insights 4.1 – The new dotcom landscape
- Marketing strategy in the new digital age
- E-commerce domains
- Conducting e-commerce
- Marketing Insights 4.2 – Viral boosters for Ragu
- The promise and challenges of e-commerce
- Summary
- Concluding concept 4 – eBay: connecting in China

◄ SOURCE: Expedia.com

Chapter objectives enable you to focus on what you should have achieved by the end of the chapter

The **chapter openers** concisely introduce the themes and issues explored in the chapter by including a **Mini Contents List**, so you can assess the importance of the chapter at this specific point in your study

Key terms are highlighted throughout the text: definitions are listed within a full Glossary at the back of the book. This is a particularly useful revision purposes tool

Prelude case NSPCC: misunderstood

When the National Society for the Prevention of Cruelty to Children (NSPCC) released its year-end and annual accounts in December 2003, it promptly received condemnation.

The revelation that the charity spent more on fundraising, publicity, campaigning and administration than on direct services to children (£43 m or £70.5 m compared with £20 m) was a sign of complete incompetence, according to Gerald Howarth, Conservative MP for Aldershot. He vowed to stop backing the NSPCC's high-profile Full Stop campaign.

According to Quentin Anderson, chief executive of Addison, the corporate marketing arm of WPP Group, such swift dismissal of the NSPCC strategy is unwise and fails to recognise the professional makeover many charities have undertaken in recent years. Charities are now highly organised operations. In line with environmental and social pressure groups they have adopted a more businesslike approach, which is essential if they are to survive in a crowded sector. When arguing how big the various components of the NSPCC's budget should be, detractors must remember that there is a total of £75 m to disburse. Charities need highly skilled staff to manage such funds.

The NSPCC's campaign makes sense. The charity has stated that its long-term objectives are to raise social awareness of child cruelty and to raise £250 m through the 'Full Stop' initiative. If people do not understand what the charity's directors are trying to achieve in the long term, they will judge them on short-term results. With the NSPCC, these include a £13.5 m overspend for the last financial year. The NSPCC needs to ensure that people understand what it is trying to achieve because it needs their help. It needs to show that it is aware, reacting to change and anticipating it. Despite the furor, the NSPCC sticks to their guns and kept campaigning. The advertising is central to NSPCC's mission: 'to end cruelty to children for ever'. With help from the campaign, 690,000 people had pledged their support for their campaign to achieve a better future for all children.

Marketing is ideally suited to the task the charity has set itself. In crude terms, its route to market is not so obvious as those of other charities. For example, it is comparatively easy for 'Meals on Wheels' to identify where its services are needed and to dedicate the majority of its expenditure to staff and the resources they require. By contrast, the NSPCC has defined its audience as the whole population. By communicating clearly with all communities, it hopes, no doubt, to enlist many more foot soldiers than direct action ever would.

And the campaign has got a lot right. To achieve its aim the NSPCC decided to use celebrities to back its central message that to reduce cruelty to children you need to raise awareness of child cruelty and challenge social attitudes. To reach those at risk it has focused on teenage media. This translates to television, radio, magazines and the Internet.

As a result, visitors to its website will find messages from Kylie Minogue and Ms Dynamite. Other male and female icons, such as Diana Ross, David Beckham and Pelé, have also been highly visible in their support for the 'Full Stop' campaign.

Matching your brand to a superstar is a successful marketing technique and need not be a cause for controversy. Nike pays Tiger Woods handsomely but obviously believes it gets value for money. The NSPCC would be foolish not to exploit celebrities willing to donate their time free of charge. Without Kylie, would the Full Stop campaign receive their-page exposure in the magazines teenagers read?

Because the charity has advertised its brand effectively, victims are more likely to know they can go direct to the 'Kidszone' at its website and obtain professional advice.

So, why should the NSPCC be criticised for spending money and talking about it? The charity understands that dissemination of better information creates confidence in the community. This leads to many benefits, including greater loyalty from donors and a more secure position in the sector. It also avoids the accusation of hoarding funds that has been levelled at many charities.

The negative reaction to the publication of the NSPCC accounts is a sign not that its marketing strategy is failing but that its communications policy is. A first principle for all good communicators is to evoke messages defining what the organisation does and what its aims are. The NSPCC, it appears, has simply released its annual figures and allowed the public to draw its own conclusions.

The annual report, like every communication, should have a specific goal and add value to what has already been done. The NSPCC should have explained better the rationale behind its spending on marketing. It should have made clear that a high level of set-up costs in terms of administration and training is inevitably associated with a campaign such as Full Stop.

It should have demonstrated in donors and opinion-formers that it understands its campaign is expensive. But it should also have left them in no doubt that it thinks raising awareness is the only way to lobby for legislative change and – what really counts – to reach more victims of abuse.

Questions

You should attempt these questions only after completing your reading of this chapter.

1. Who are the charity's target market and what are the roots aspects of the service offered by a charity organisation such as the NSPCC?
2. Assess the role of marketing in assisting the charity to achieve its goals. Should the charity spend more on fundraising, publicity, campaigning and administration than on direct services to children?
3. Evaluate the NSPCC's current marketing strategy. Has the charity got its current marketing strategy wrong? Or are the problems due to its communication policy?

168

Prelude cases concentrate on specific products, brands or organisations to introduce theories of marketing in practice

Part 1 Marketing now

What is marketing?

What does the term *marketing* mean? Many people think of marketing only as selling and advertising. And no wonder, for every day we are bombarded with television commercials, newspaper ads, direct mail campaigns, Internet pitches and sales calls. Although they are important, they are only two of many marketing functions and are often not the most important ones.

Today, marketing must be understood not in the old sense of making a sale – 'telling and selling' – but in the new sense of *satisfying customer needs*. Selling occurs only after a product is produced. By contrast, marketing starts long before a company has a product. Marketing is the homework that managers undertake to assess needs, measure their extent and intensity and determine whether a profitable opportunity exists. Marketing continues throughout the product's life, trying to find new customers and keep current customers by improving product appeal and performance, learning from product sales results and managing repeat performance.

Everyone knows something about 'hot' products. When Sony designed PlayStation, when Nokia introduced fashionable mobile phones, when The Body Shop introduced animal-cruelty-free cosmetics and toiletries, these manufacturers were swamped with orders. Like Swatch and Smart Car, they were 'right' products offering new benefits; not 'me-too' products. Peter Drucker, a leading management thinker, has put it this way: 'The aim of marketing is to make selling superfluous. The aim is to know and understand the customer so well that the product or service fits . . . and sells itself.'[2] If the marketer does a good job of identifying customer needs, develops products that provide superior value, distributes and promotes them effectively, these goods will sell very easily. This does not mean that selling and advertising are unimportant. Rather, it means that they are part of a larger marketing mix – a set of marketing tools that work together to affect the marketplace.

We define **marketing** as a *social and managerial process by which individuals and groups obtain what they need and want through creating and exchanging products and value with others*. To explain this definition, we examine the following important terms: *needs, wants and demands; products and services; value, satisfaction and quality; exchange, transactions and relationships;* and *markets*. Figure 1.1 shows that these core marketing concepts are linked, with each concept building on the one before it.

Marketing—A social and managerial process by which individuals and groups obtain what they need and want through creating and exchanging products and value with others.

Figure 1.1 **Core marketing concepts**

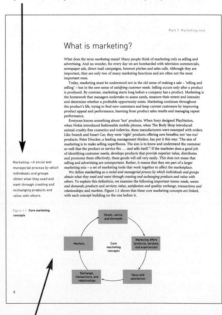

6

Figures and tables illustrate key points, concepts and processes visually to reinforce your learning

xx

If you want to explore topics further, **Discussing the issues** encourages stimulating debates and class exercises

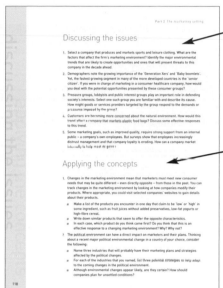

Every chapter ends with **Applying the concepts**, that test your understanding and help you to track your progress

Snappy **Marketing insight** boxes improve your understanding by expanding on the central concepts of the chapter

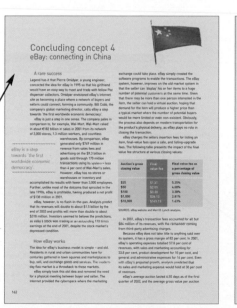

Longer, colourfully illustrated and up-to-date **Concluding concept cases** at the end of every chapter. This helps you consolidate the major themes by encouraging you to apply what you have learnt to real-life marketing scenarios

Each chapter is supported by a list of **References**, directing your independent study to both printed and electronic sources

GUIDED TOUR: STUDENT RESOURCES ON THE WEBSITE

Principles of Marketing is supported by a fully interactive Companion Website, available at **www.pearsoned.co.uk/ kotler**, that contains a wealth of additional teaching and learning material

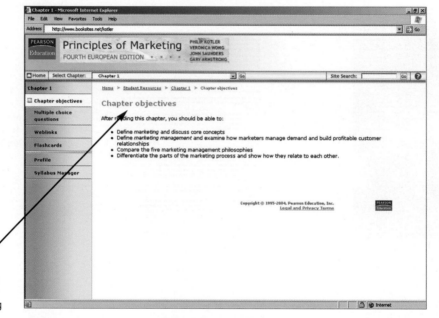

Chapter objectives are designed to summarise the main points for you to refer to when studying or revising

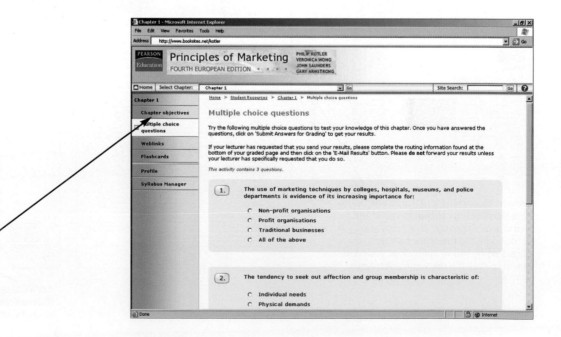

Extensive **Multiple choice questions**, all with helpful feedback on incorrect answers, help develop your subject knowledge and improve your understanding

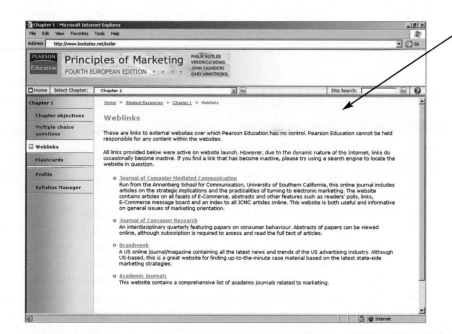

Clickable **Weblinks**, with details of how they can help your study, support each chapter and direct your independent learning

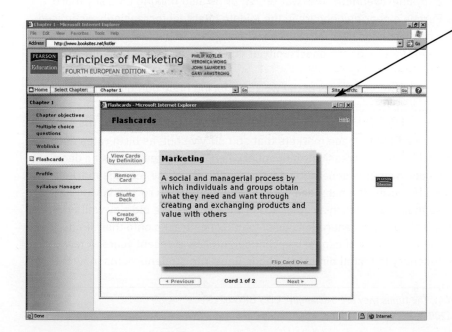

Interactive Flashcards help you to check and learn key concepts, and can be used as a revision tool

PREFACE

'The times they are a-changin'[A]   Bob Dylan (1964)

Forty years after Bob Dylan recorded this eponymous song, times are indeed changing. Among the changes is this one-time anti-establishment singer enrobing to receive an honorary degree at Scotland's ancient St Andrew's University. Maybe he has taken up golf! In considering marketing, a more fitting line is 'Times they are forever a-changin', and ever faster'. As *The Darkness*[B] recognise, get 'stuck in a rut' and you have had it.

Some of the changes are political, such as the enlarged European Union, and some failed politics, such as 'the war on terror'. The European Union's move east to embrace Cyprus, the Czech Republic, Estonia, Hungary, Latvia, Lithuania, Malta, Poland, Slovakia and Slovenia increases the EU's geographical area by a quarter and its population by a fifth. The move also increases the diversity in the EU since most of the accession countries are much less wealthy than the rest of the EU, so it increases the EU's gross domestic product by one-twentieth. The 'war on terror' is also making diversity more pronounced as Europe's near neighbours in the Middle East feel increasingly victimised by the West. The tension spills over into Europe where Islam is the fastest growing religion. Europe therefore faces the opportunity of an enlarged market but with increased diversity.

Europe, like other developed areas of the world, is facing huge demographic changes that will increasingly challenge the minds of politicians and marketers alike. The post-World War 2 generation of baby boomers who listen to Bob Dylan are ageing. The shock of that generation created the teenage markets that still survive but, as birth rates decline, the grey market will become increasingly influential when making key marketing decisions.

Already the people-over-fifty generation dominates the one-time teenage market for popular music. However, the baby-boomers' domination of pop record buying has occurred because they are 'stuck in a rut' of acquiring music in the old way while the technologically adept younger generations download iTunes tracks onto their iPods. The electronic interconnectedness of people has changed hugely in recent years. A few years ago, it was revolutionary to install direct telephone lines into student rooms; now the

---

[A] Bob Dylan (1964), *The times they are a-changin'*, CBS BPG 62251
[B] The Darkness (2004), *Permission to land*, Atlantic 5050466-7452-2-4

technology is redundant as younger generations keep in touch by texting, mobile phone or by email. One outcome of this personal interconnectedness is the decline in visits to Student Guilds or Unions that were once the only places in which to meet and spend time.

It is befitting our increasingly global reach that the personal interconnectedness is not distance related – communications are only a little more expensive across the world than across the corridor. Globalisation remains a controversial issue but its pace is quickening. Two major forces are accelerating globalisation and both have China and India at their core. With their markets now more free, the growth of these two economies (China 9.8% and India 10.4% GNP growth in 2004) is far outstripping Western growth (EU 1.3% and US 4.9%). As the huge and increasingly wealthy populations of China and India continue to grow, it is success in their markets that will dominate competition. Simultaneously, the huge supply of well-qualified, skilled and inexpensive labour in India and China makes them attractive for creating as well as supplying goods and services.

The Fourth European Edition

The Fourth European Edition of *Principles of Marketing* offers significant improvements in perspective, in organisation, content and style. Recognising Europe's internationalism and the growth of globalisation, examples and cases are drawn, not from Europe alone, but from the US, Japan, South-east Asia and Africa. Some examples and cases concentrate on national issues, but even these have been selected to reflect issues of interest to students worldwide. Many involve developments in e-commerce, mobile communications, fashion and entertainment. Although such cases cover many markets and products, the brands and customers used are close to the experience or aspiration of readers.

This book has eight parts. The first four cover marketing concepts and strategy and the last four the marketing mix.

Part 1 Marketing Now introduces marketing in a changing world and then immediately introduces Strategic Marketing as a way of integrating all marketing's activities. Besides providing an early framework for marketing thinking, the chapter shows the links between the chapters that follow and sets the stage for the remainder of the text.

Part 2 The Marketing Setting begins with Chapter 3 which examines the dimensions of the environment in which modern firms compete. Unlike most other texts which treat major environmental trends such as the Internet revolution, globalisation and marketing's role in the wider society as end-of-book afterthoughts, *Principles of Marketing* presents these topics up-front. The new Chapter 4 considers how marketing strategies and practices should adapt to take advantage of the Internet, which has become an important part of the underlying fabric of modern marketing. Chapter 5 addresses the important issues of socially responsible marketing, while Chapter 6 covers marketing in the global marketplace.

Part 3 Markets covers customer behaviour and how to gather market information. Chapters 7 examines consumer behaviour and the consumer markets where we, the final consumer, reside. Chapter 8 then studies business-to-business (B2B) marketing, including selling to international government agencies. Although less conspicuous in the High Street, B2B markets are where most marketing activity takes place. Chapter 9 provides a comprehensive coverage of marketing research and covers a wide range of methods of gathering information to guide marketing decisions.

Part 4 Core Strategy begins with a chapter on how to break markets down into market segments, choose target markets and position products and services in the customers' mind. Next, Chapter 11 shows how to build relationships with customers through customer satisfaction, quality, value and service, while Chapter 12 explores ways of creating competitive advantage and competing effectively.

The final four parts cover the marketing mix.

Part 5 Product has three chapters. Chapter 13 on product and branding strategy gives an expanded coverage of contemporary issues such as brand equity, brand positioning, brand management and rebranding. Chapter 14 addresses new product and brand development and how to manage the product over its life-cycle. The final chapter in this part offers full and separate coverage of the extremely important area of marketing services.

Part 6 Price is presented by a single and streamlined Chapter 16 which discusses key pricing considerations and approaches and the determination of pricing strategies in an increasingly value-driven and dynamic pricing environment.

Part 7 Promotion comprises three chapters. Chapter 17 considers the importance of developing an integrated marketing communications strategy. Advertising, sales promotion and public relations are covered in Chapter 18. The part concludes with Chapter 19 on personal selling and other forms of direct marketing.

Part 8 Place represents the last stage in getting products or services to the buyer. Chapter 20, the final chapter of this text, considers the traditional flow of goods and services through marketing channels and logistics management to wholesaling and retailing.

Classic features

- Practical, managerial approaches to marketing from the top gurus in the field prepare students for business challenges in the real world.
- Rich topical examples and applications explain the major decisions that marketing managers face.
- Prelude Cases open each chapter with a major example describing a distinctive and thought-provoking market situation.
- Marketing Insight boxes explore short examples and company cases.
- Full-colour adverts bring to life the powerful importance of marketing in our everyday lives.

New to this edition

- Completely revised and updated Prelude Cases, Marketing Insights and end-of-chapter cases (Concluding concepts) reflect the growing influence of e-commerce.
- Enhanced full-colour tables, adverts and figures highlight key ideas and marketing strategies.
- A comprehensive Companion Website, containing a wealth of teaching material for lecturers and learning materials for students, is available at www.pearsoned.co.uk/kotler. Completely updated, this site boasts great additions, such as more case studies, more multiple choice questions, and sample answers to the questions from the Marketing in Practice DVD.

ACKNOWLEDGEMENTS

No book is the work only of its authors. We owe much to the pioneers of marketing who identified its major issues and developed its concepts and techniques and how to communicate them. We are particularly indebted to the two great marketing educators, Peter Doyle (Warwick) and Jim Lynch (Leeds), to whom we dedicate this book. Also, among the pioneers who greatly influenced our work and academic lives are Michael Baker (Strathclyde), Malcolm Cunningham (UMIST) and Malcolm MacDonald (Cranfield).

Our thanks also go to our colleagues at the J. L. Kellogg Graduate School of Management, Northwestern University; the Kenan-Flagler Business School, University of North Carolina at Chapel Hill; and Aston Business School, for ideas, encouragement and suggestions. Also thanks to all our friends in the Academy of Marketing, European Marketing Academy, Informs, the American Marketing Association, the Chartered Institute of Marketing and the European Foundation for Management Development who have stimulated and advised us over the years. It has been an honour to work with so many people who have helped pioneer marketing in Europe.

Thanks to Maria del Mar Souza Fontan, Sylvie Laforet, Andy Hirst, Pedro Quelhas Brito, Ann Torres, Thomas Helgesson, Robert A. Van der Zwart, Samual Pronk, and Kevin Done who have contributed excellent cases to this edition. Also many thanks to Brigitte Nicolaud for her enthusiasm and expertise in updating and expanding the robust supplements package.

We were aided in our revision of this edition by many reviewers from universities and colleges throughout Europe who responded to Pearson Education's questionnaires and to whom we extend our thanks.

We also owe a great deal to the people at Pearson Education who have done a wonderful job in helping us develop and produce this book: Thomas Sigel, Acquisitions Editor; David Cox, Development Editor; Tina Cadle-Bowman, Editorial Manager; Peter Hooper, Editorial Assistant; Maggie Wells, Deputy Design Manager; Bridget Allen, Pre-Press Manager and Kay Holman, Senior Project Controller. We should also thank Patrick Bonham, freelance copy editor and proof-reader and Sue Williams, freelance picture researcher. A special mention should also go to Maggie Wells for producing such a wonderful text design, and to Katherine Harding, the exciting young artist whose original art adorns our cover.

PHILIP KOTLER
VERONICA WONG
JOHN SAUNDERS
GARY ARMSTRONG

Publisher's acknowledgements

We are grateful to the following for permission to reproduce copyright material:

Figures, exhibits and tables: Exhibits 1.2 and 1.4 from *CBCL Manufacturer Performance* and *CBCL Brand Performance, AGB Superpanel*, Taylor Nelson Sofres (1994); Exhibit 1.5 from data by kind permission of ACNielsen Corporation (1994); Figure 3.8 from chart on p. 150 from 'Emerging market indicators', in 'The Economist', 29 January 2000, copyright © The Economist Newspaper Ltd., London, 2000; Table 4.1 from Internet World Stats, www.internetworldstats.com; p. 178, Figure 5.1 reprinted by permission of *Harvard Business Review*, figure of 'The Sustainability Portfolio', from 'Beyond Greening: Strategies for a Sustainable World', by Stuart Hart, Jan–Feb 1997, p. 74. Copyright © 1996 by the Harvard Business School Publishing Corporation; all rights reserved; Table 6.1 from table in 'Approaches to assessing international opportunities for small and medium-sized businesses', *Columbia Journal of World Business*, Fall 1982, pp. 26–32, (Douglas S.P., Craig C.S. and Keegan, W., 1982). Copyright © 1982, 1999, *Columbia Journal of World Business*. Reprinted with permission; Table 7.1 from Office of National Statistics *Socioeconomic Classification*, (ONS). Crown copyright material is reproduced under class Licence Number C01W0000039 with the permission of the Controller of HMSO; Table 7.2 adapted from table on p. 16 from 'A modernised family life cycle', in *Journal of Consumer Research*, June 1979, University of Chicago Press, (Murphy, P.E. and Staples, W.A., 1979), copyright © 1979 *Journal of Consumer Research*; Figure 7.3 adapted from figure on p. 185 in 'Reference group influence product and brand purchase decisions', in *Journal of Consumer Research*, Sept. 1982, University of Chicago Press, (William O. Bearden and Michael J. Etzel, 1982), copyright © Journal of Consumer Research, Inc., 1982; Table 7.3 from table on p. 34 from 'The concept and application of lifestyle segmentation', reprinted with permission from *Journal of Marketing*, January 1974, published by the American Marketing Association, (Plummer, J.T.); Figure 7.4 adapted from *Motivation and Personality*, 2nd Edition, Pearson Education, Inc. (Maslow, A.H., 1970); Figure 7.5 adapted from *Consumer Behavior and Marketing Action*, 6th Edition, p. 67, South-Western College Publishing, reprinted with permission from the author (Assael, H., 1998); Figure 7.8 redrawn from Figure 7.2 on p. 262 reprinted with the permission of The Free Press, a Division of Simon and Schuster, Inc., from *Diffusion of Innovations*, Fourth Edition, by Everett M. Rogers. Copyright © 1995 by Everett M. Rogers. Copyright © 1962, 1971, 1983 by The Free Press; Table 8.1 adapted from table on p. 14 from *Industrial Buying and Creative Marketing*, Allyn & Bacon, (Robinson, P.J., Faris, C.W. And Wind, Y., 1967); Figure 8.3 from *Marketing Principles*, 3rd Edition, Scott, Foresman & Co. (Enis, B.M., 1980), Copyright © 1980 Scott, Foresman & Co.; Figure 8.3 from *Marketing Principles*, 3rd Edition, Scott, Foresman & Co. (Enis, B.M., 1980), copyright © 1980 Scott, Foresman & Co.; Table 9.2 adapted from *Market Research: Measurement and Method*, 6th Edition, Macmillan Publishing Company, (Tull, D.S. and Hawkins, D.I., 1993), reprinted with permission from the estate of Donald S. Tull; Exhibit 9.2 from table from *Visitors to Galway City for 1996*, reproduced with permission of Galway Chamber of Commerce, (1996); Table 9.3 adapted from Tables 9 and 10 from *Trade Association estimates of expenditure*, in ESOMAR's *Annual Study of the Market Research Industry*, www.esomar.nl/press/industryreport01.htm, reprinted with permission from ESOMAR (European Society for Opinion and Marketing Research), www.esomar.org; Figure 10.2 from figure on p. 324 from 'Systemic Positioning', in *European Marketing Academy Proceedings*, 26th April to 9th May 1992, Aarhus, (Dreher, A., Ritter, A., and Mühlbacher, H.,

1992), reproduced by kind permission of Hans Mühlbacher; Exhibits 10.3 and 10.4 from *National Food Survey*, pub. MAFF. Crown copyright material is reproduced under class Licence Number C01W0000039 with the permission of the Controller of HMSO; Table 10.4 adapted from table from *Segmenting the Industrial Market*, Lexington Books, (Bonoma, T.V. and Shapiro, B.P., 1983); Figure 11.2 from Fig. 2.2 on p. 37 reprinted with the permission of The Free Press, a Division of Simon and Schuster, Inc., from *Competitive Advantage: Creating and Sustaining Superior Performance* by Michael E. Porter. Copyright © 1985, 1998 by Michael E. Porter; Figure 11.3 from Fig. on p. 39 from '*Quality as a strategic weapon: measuring relative quality, value and market differentiation*', in *European Business Journal*, Vol. 2, No. 4, 1990, Whurr Publishers Ltd. (Luchs, R., 1990); Table 12.2 adapted from FORTUNE Global 500, FORTUNE Magazine, copyright © 2004 Time Inc., All rights reserved (July 26, 2004); Table 1 in Case 12, Ch. 12 from table from '*Prijvergelijkingen mobile bellen*', in Zembla-documentaire *Mobiele Miljarden*, 4th February 1999, http://www.omroep.nl/vara/tv/zembla/gsm.html, PriceWaterhouseCoopers Management Consultants, (1999); Table 2 in Case 12, Ch. 12 from table from '*Wireless Data Evolution White Paper*', in *Nokia Wireless Data Library*, April 1998, No. 12, Nokia Telecommunications Oy, (1998); Table 14.2 from table on p. 340 from *Marketing Management: Analysis, Planning, Implementation, and Control*, 11th Edition, by Philip Kotler, Copyright © 2003, reprinted by permission of Pearson Education, Inc., Upper Saddle River, NJ 07548; Figure 16.7 from Fig. on p. 5 from *The Strategy and Tactics of Pricing*, 3rd Edition, Prentice-Hall, Inc. (Pearson Education, Inc.), (Nagle T.T. and Holden, R.K., 1995); Table 19.1 adapted from table from '*Sales compensation: In search of a better solution*', in *Compensation & Benefits Review*, November–December 1993, pp. 53–60. Copyright © 1998 American Management Association, (http://www.amanet.org), (Johnson, S.T., 1993); Figure 19.2 reprinted with permission from *Dartnell Corporation, 30th Sales Force Compensation Survey*, copyright © 1998 by Dartnell Corporation, 360 Hiatt Drive, Palm Beach Gardens, FL 33418. All rights reserved. For more information please call 1-800-621-5463 or visit our Web site at http://www.dartnellcorp.com.

Financial Times Limited: Chapter 3 Prelude Case 'Big food has a lot on its plate' by Richard Tomkins, FT.com, © *Financial Times*, 12 February 2003; Marketing Insight box 3.1 'Diageo defends policy on thalidomide', © *Financial Times*, 9 March 2000 and 'Improving quality of life and profits', © *Financial Times*, 13 August 2002; Marketing Insight box 3.2 'Big designs on practicality', Finland supplement, © *Financial Times*, 10 July 2000; Chapter 6 Prelude Case 'Schnapps goes to college' by Bettina Wassener, © *Financial Times*, 4 September 2003; Chapter 14 Prelude Case 'Nokia tries to learn a new game' by Christopher Brown-Humes and Robert Budden, FT.com, © *Financial Times*, 5 February 2004; Marketing Insight box 14.2 'A camera focused on luxury', © *Financial Times*, 31 March 2003; Marketing Insight box 15.1 'British Airways. Claire cuts the long haul for callers', FT.com, © *Financial Times*, 16 April 2003; Chapter 17 Prelude Case 'Cadbury hits a purple patch' adapted from EmikoTerazono, FT Creative Business, FT.com, © *Financial Times*, 1 March 2004; Marketing Insight box 18.1 'The decline of hard cash', © *Financial Times*, 28 October 2002; Marketing Insight box 18.2 'Fun and games', FT Creative Business, © *Financial Times*, 9 September 2003; Chapter 20 Prelude Case 'Bytes to order' by Geoff Wheelwright, © *Financial Times*, 26 November 2003; Marketing Insight box 20.1 'Mail box etc: New network of one-stop-shops', Financial Times Special Report: 'Franchising', © *Financial Times*, 4 June 2003.

Other text extracts: Chapter 4 Prelude Case based on company data provided by Cool Diamonds; Chapter 15 Prelude Case, 'Stena Line: Sailing out of troubled waters' reprinted and adapted with permission of Anna-Lena Ackfeldt, Aston Business School; Chapter 18 Concluding concept 'In search of a mission', from *The Financial Times Limited*, 5 February 2004, © David Bowen; Chapter 19 Prelude Case based on Mogens Bjerre, MD Foods AMBA, 'A new world of sales and marketing', in *Understanding Marketing*: A European casebook, Celia Philips, Ad Pruyn and Marie-Paule Kestemont (eds), pp. 30–41, reproduced with permission © John Wiley & Sons Limited, Chichester, UK, 2000.

Plates (old editions): Michelin and Hjemmet Mortenson (left) and 3M (right) p. 52; Mont Blanc and The Advertising Archives p. 59; Volkswagen of America, Inc. and Arnold Worldwide p. 103; Joseph Van Os, Getty Images, Inc. / Image Bank p. 108; Marks & Spencer p. 113 Chapter 4 Prelude Case image supplied by Molly McKellar Public Relations, London p. 127; NSPCC, photographer: Matt Harris p. 169; ASA London p. 171; Inchon International Airport Corporation, Korea, Agency: Dentsu, Young and Rubicam, Korea p. 188; L'Oréal, USA courtesy of Bernard Matussiere p. 221; Associated Press p. 223; Guy Laroche advert, courtesy of Bernaud Matussiere p. 237; American Honda Motor Co., Inc. p. 275, reprinted with permission; Packard Bell, agency: Fred Fisher Associates p. 277; Nikon, Inc. p. 284; Corbis, photographer: Jon Feingersh p. 313; SAS, agency Mason Zimbler p. 319; Infineon, agency J. Walter Thompson p. 341; Integrated Media Systems Center p. 359; Twin Vision Productions, Inc. p. 369; NOP Research Group Ltd. p. 368; Vans, Inc. p. 394, Copyright © 2001 Vans, Inc., reprinted with permission; Duck Head Apparel Co. p. 404; Jeff Baker, Getty Images, Inc. – Hulton Archive Photos (left) p. 411; SW Productions, Getty Images, Inc. (right) on p. 411; Smirnoff, Lowe Howard-Spinks Agency, illustrator: Bob Hersey p. 415; KPNQwest, agency PPGH JWL Colors, photographer Jan Willem Scholten p. 426; Regent International Hotels p. 427; Lacoste, agency: Pentland Group p. 429; Philips Consumer Electronics, agency: Interface Marketing Communications p. 429; Pillsbury UK Ltd., agency: Euros p. 430; Porsche, Boxster and the Porsche Crest are registered trademarks and the distinctive shapes of PORSCHE automobiles are trade dress of Fr. Ing, h.c.F. Porsche AG, reprinted with permission of Porsche Cars North America, Inc. Copyrighted by Porsche Cars North America, Inc. p. 433; Playtex Ltd. p. 435; Diageo Ireland p. 435. The KALIBER word and UNICORN device are trademarks. Copyright © Guinness & Co. Created by Euro RSCG agency; Breitling SA p. 436; Mann (Norway), Oct. 2000 p. 441; Diageo Ireland p. 442. The GUINNESS word is a trademark. Copyright © Guinness & Co.; Courtesy Unilever plc p. 444; Triumph International Ltd. p. 462; Unilever and The Advertising Archives p. 495; Encyclopedia Britannica p. 497; Bartle Bogle Hegarty (BBH) p. 497; Airbus, agency: Euro RSCG WNEK Gosper p. 517; Lofthouse of Fleetwood p. 524; Image reprinted with kind permission of Rockwell Automation, agency: Chilworth Communications p. 543; MCC Smart GmbH, www.media.smart.com p. 552; Interbrand p. 560; 3M p. 592, used with permission; DaimlerChrysler Corporation p. 593, copyright © DaimlerChrysler/Liaison Agency; Swatch AG p. 608; Scandinavian Airlines, agency: Admaker p. 634; Munshi Ahmed Photography p. 647; Swatch ad. Courtesy of Swatch Ltd. p. 669; Advertising Archives p. 670; Image on p. 676, courtesy of Gibson Guitar; Image on p. 692, images courtesy of Nintendo America, Inc, agency: Leo Burnett; Volkswagen of America, Inc. and Arnold Worldwide, photographer: Steve Bronstein ©, for image "Snow Angel" image on p. 736; Jon Feingersh/Stock Boston p. 743; V&S Vin & Sprit AB (publ). Absolut Country of Sweden Vodka and logo, Absolut, Absolut bottle design and Absolut calligraphy are trademarks owned by V&S Vin & Sprit AB (publ), copyright © 2004 V&S Vin & Sprit AB p. 754; V&S Vin & Sprit AB. Absolut Country of Sweden Vodka and logo, Absolut, Absolut bottle design and Absolut calligraphy are trademarks owned by V&S Vin & Sprit AB (publ), copyright © 2003 V&S Vin & Sprit AB (publ) p. 767; The Image Works p. 795; American Express

Acknowledgements

Incentive Services p. 822; Walter Hodges and Tony Stone Images p. 825, reproduced courtesy of GettyOne; Stock Boston, photographer: Charles Gupton p. 881.

Plates (new edition): © Apple Computers, Inc. use with permission. All rights reserved. Apple ® and the Apple logo are registered trademarks of Apple Computer, Inc. Image supplied by the Advertising Archive p. 2; DaimlerChrysler UK Ltd p. 7; DaimlerChrysler AG Stuttgart/Auburn Hills p. 18; Bear Design Ltd. p. 28; Becton, Dickinson and Company © 2003. Photo © Richard Lord p. 32; HMV UK Ltd p. 35; Advertising Archives/www.fashionmall.com p. 46; Siemens VDO Automotive AG p. 55; Corbis/S Henchoz p. 84; DaimlerChrysler AG Stuttgart/Auburn Hills p. 94; Shell International, agency: J Walter Thompson p. 116; Expedia.com p. 124; Cooldiamonds.com p.127; Worldbid.com p. 139; Priceline.com p. 141; ABB Ltd p. 146; Clarins UK Ltd p. 147; Cadbury Trebor Bassett p. 148; Manager of http:groups.msn.com.harrypotteruk p. 152; Dutch Foundation on Smoking and Health, agency: BVH Communicatie-adviesbureau, Netherlands. Photo © Gerdjan van der Lugt p. 166; *Agency*: Eni/Grey Worldwide Italy, *photographer*: Peter Lavery, www.peterlavery.com p. 176; Advertising Archives p. 185; CAN Corporate Angel Network/French Blitzer Scott p. 193; HSBC Holdings Plc., agency: Lowe Worldwide, photographer: Richard Pullar p. 208; Virgin Cosmetics Company p. 218; Fritz Hoffman/The Image Works, Inc p. 221; McDonald's Europe Limited p. 231; HSBC Holdings Plc. agency: Lowe Worldwide, photographer: Richard Pullar p. 234; Pirelli & C. SpA p. 235; Levi Strauss Jeans, agency BBH p. 252; Leapfrog Day Nurseries p. 263; Patek Philippe *agency*: Geneva/Leagas Delaney, *photographer*: Peggy Sirota represented by E.M. Managed p. 272; Lavazza SpA. Designer: Armando Testa, photographer: Baptiste Mondino for Lavazzo Calendar 2003/Advertising Archives p. 298; NetJets Management Ltd p. 301; INVISTA/McCann Erikson p. 304; British Airways/M&C Saatchi p. 310, *photographer*: Gary Simpson; Corbis Sygma, *photographer*: Dean Francis p. 334; Cereal Partners UK/Courtesy Société des Produits Nestlé S.A, trademark owners p. 349; General Mills and General Mills UK/Advertising Archives p. 388 and p. 430; Breitling SA p. 441; Audi UK p. 438; Renault UK/Publicis p. 439; American Express Germany, 2003, agency: Ogilvy&Mather, Frankfurt for p. 458; PeopleSoft UK & Ireland p. 482; McDonald's Europe Limited p. 490; Eurex/Karyn Hieronymi p. 513; Freeserve/M&C Saatchi p. 536; Institut do turismo de Portugal p. 544; Lexus (GB) Ltd. Photographer: Mathias Bauman, Defrance, Düsseldorf, Germany p. 547; Omega SA/Photo copyright NASA p. 548; Microsoft Corporation p. 578; Logitech® io™ p. 584; Johnson and Johnson/Liquorice p. 586; Wirtschafts Woche, agency: Jung von Matt/Spree, illustration: René Borst p. 620; Chewton Glen p. 627; Shangri-La International Hotel Management Limited/TBWA Hong Kong p. 636; Associated Press/Wide World Photos/Hasan Jamali p. 646; Iceland Foods Plc/Advertising Archives p. 660; BMW (GB) Ltd/Saatchi and Saatchi, *agency*: WCRS p. 666; priceline.com p. 668; Dvdcompare.net/rewind.com p. 697 (left); Pricescan.com, Inc p. 697 right; DoH/Crown Copyright p. 716; Raffles International Hotels and Resorts p. 721; Adsa p. 722 (top left); New Crane Ltd p. 722 (top centre); Profile Pursuit Ltd p. 722 (top right); BBC Worldwide for p. 722 (bottom left); Health and Fitness p. 722 (bottom right); F 1 Racing p. 722 (bottom centre); Lever Fabergé from originals in Unilever Archives p. 725; Royal Mail 'Desperately Seeking Generous Partner' advertisement © Royal Mail Group plc, Royal Mail and the Royal Mail Cruciform are registered trademarks of Royal Mail Group plc, 'With US It's Personal' is a trademark of Royal Mail Group plc., reproduced by permission of Royal Mail p. 728; Savoir Beds Agency: Large, Smith and Walford Partnership p. 733; Courtesy Société des Produits Nestlé S.A, trademark owners p. 734; Home Office/Crown Copyright p. 758; Virgin Atlantic p. 765; DaimlerChrysler AG Stuttgart/Auburn Hills p. 770; BMW (GB) Ltd/Saatchi & Saatchi, *agency*: WCRS p. 771; HSBC Holdings Plc., agency:

Lowe Worldwide, photographer: Richard Pullar p. 782; www.ericsson.com for p. 798; Avon Cosmetics Ltd p. 806; Shangri-La International Hotel Management Limited/TBWA Hong Kong p. 811; Digital Vision Limited p. 819; Nokia.com p. 830; SAP Global Marketing. Agency: OgilvyOne Worldwide p. 834; www.3suisses.fr for p. 839 (left); www.redoute.co.uk p. 839 (right); H&M p. 854; The Body Shop International plc. p. 869; Birmingham Photo Library/Jonathan Berg p. 878 (both); Robocom Systems International p. 886; DHL Worldwide Network/Jung von Matt p. 890.

In some instances we have been unable to trace the owners of copyright material, and we would appreciate any information that would enable us to do so.

ABOUT THE AUTHORS

Philip Kotler is S. C. Johnson & Son Distinguished Professor of International Marketing at the J. L. Kellogg Graduate School of Management, Northwestern University. He received his master's degree at the University of Chicago and his PhD at MIT, both in Economics. Dr Kotler is author of Marketing Management: Analysis, Planning, Implementation and Control (Prentice Hall). He has authored several other successful books and he has written over 100 articles for leading journals. He is the only three-time winner of the Alpha Kappa Psi award for the best annual article in the Journal of Marketing. Dr Kotler's numerous major honours include the Paul D. Converse Award given by the American Marketing Association to honour 'outstanding contributions to the science of marketing' and the Stuart Henderson Brit Award as Marketer of the Year. In 1985, he was named the first recipient of two major awards: the Distinguished Marketing Educator of the Year Award, given by the American Marketing Association, and the Philip Kotler Award for Excellence in Health Care Marketing. Dr Kotler has served as a director of the American Marketing Association. He has consulted with many major US and foreign companies on marketing strategy.

Veronica Wong, BSc, MBA (Bradford), PhD (Manchester), Fellow of the Royal Society of Arts, Fellow of the Chartered Institute of Marketing, is Professor of Marketing and Head of the Marketing Group at Aston Business School. She is Vice-President (Conferences) of the European Marketing Academy and a member of the UK's Economic and Social Research Council (ESRC) Virtual College for Management, Psychology, Linguistics and Education. She was born in Malaysia where she studied until her first degree. Previously, Dr Wong worked at the Universities of Loughborough and Warwick. She has also taught in Malaysia and worked for Ciba Laboratories, UK. She has worked with a wide range of international firms and government and private bodies concerned with product innovation and its management, including Britain's Department of Trade and Industry (DTI) Innovation Advisory Unit and the Marketing Council. She has also published over sixty articles for leading journals, including publications in the *Journal of International Business Studies*, the *Journal of Product Innovation Management*, *Technovation* and *Industrial Marketing Management*.

John Saunders, BSc (Loughborough), MBA (Cranfield), PhD (Bradford), FEMAC, FBAM, FCIM, FRSA is Professor of Marketing, Head of Aston Business School and Pro-Vice Chancellor of Aston University. Previously, he worked for Hawker Siddeley and British Aerospace and has acted as a consultant for many leading organisations, including Rolls-Royce, Unilever, Nestlé, Ford, the European Commission, the Cabinet Office and the Singapore Government. He is Dean of the CIM's senate and a member of the steering committee of the EFMD and AACS International's initial accreditation committee. His international experience includes work as a business school accreditor for EQUIS and AACSB, and he assisted in the national research assessment exercises of the United Kingdom, the Netherlands and New Zealand. His publications include *The Marketing Initiative* and co-authorship of *Marketing Strategy* and *Competitive Positioning*. He has published over eighty refereed journal articles, including publications in the *Journal of Marketing*, *Journal of Marketing Research*, *Marketing Science*, *Journal of International Business Studies*, *Journal of Product Innovation Management* and *International Journal of Research in Marketing*.

Gary Armstrong is Professor and Chair of Marketing in the Kenan-Flagler Business School at the University of North Carolina at Chapel Hill. He received his PhD in marketing from Northwestern University. Dr Armstrong has contributed numerous articles to leading research journals and consulted with many companies on marketing strategy; however, his first love is teaching. He has been very active in Kenan-Flagler's undergraduate business programme and he has received several campus-wide and business schools teaching awards. In 2004, Dr Armstrong received for the fourth time the UNC Board of Governors Award for Excellence in Teaching, the highest teaching honour bestowed at the University of North Carolina at Chapel Hill.

No profit grows where is no pleasure taken.

WILLIAM SHAKESPEARE

Marketing now

Chapter 1 Marketing now ■ Chapter 2 Strategic marketing

PART ONE OF PRINCIPLES OF MARKETING examines marketing's role in an organisation, the activities that constitute marketing and how the parts are integrated into a marketing plan.

Chapter 1 shows how marketing is everywhere. It also tells how marketing has grown with the belief that organisations do best by caring for their customers. It then looks at the marketing activities appearing elsewhere in Principles of Marketing and shows how they combine to make modern marketing.

Chapter 2 takes the discussion from what marketing does to how marketing is done. In developing the strategic marketing planning process, it looks at how marketing fits with other business activities, the making of a marketing plan and how the plans become actions.

iPod min

Marketing is to selling
What seduction is to abduction.

Marketing now

Chapter objectives

After reading this chapter, you should be able to:

- Define *marketing* and discuss its core concepts.
- Define marketing management and examine how marketers manage demand and build profitable customer relationships.
- Compare the five *marketing management philosophies*.
- Differentiate the parts of the *marketing process* and show how they relate to each other.

Mini Contents List

Prelude case Nike

Nike has built the ubiquitous 'SWOOSH' (which represents the wing of Nike, the Greek goddess of victory) into one of the best-known brand symbols on the planet.

The power of its brand and logo speaks loudly to Nike's superb marketing skills. The company's strategy of building superior products around popular athletes and its classic 'Just do it!' ad campaign have forever changed the face of sports marketing. Nike spends hundreds of millions of dollars annually on big-name endorsements, splashy promotional events and many attention-getting ads. Nike has associated itself with some of the biggest names in sports: heroic images of Tiger Woods, Renaldo, Ronaldinho and Kelly Holmes made many people who wear the swoosh feel as if they were winners!

> But Nike's biggest obstacle may be its own incredible success.

Nike's initial success resulted from the technical superiority of its running and basketball shoes. But Nike gives its customers more than just good athletic gear. As the company notes on its Web page (www.nike.com): 'Nike has always known the truth – it's not so much the shoes but where they take you.' Beyond shoes, apparel and equipment, Nike markets a way of life, a sports culture, a 'Just do it!' attitude. The company was built on a genuine passion for sports, a maverick disregard for convention, hard work and serious sports performance. Nike is athletes, athletes are sports, *Nike is sports*.

Over the past decade, Nike's revenues grew at an incredible annual rate of 21 per cent. Nike, with a 27 per cent share internationally, dominates the world's athletic footwear market.

Nike also moved aggressively into new markets, from baseball and golf to inline skating and rock climbing. Its familiar swoosh logo is now found on everything from sports apparel, sunglasses and footballs to batting gloves and hockey sticks.

In 1998, however, Nike stumbled and its sales slipped. Many factors contributed to the company's woes. The 'brown shoe' craze for hiking and rugged, outdoor styles such as Timberland, Hush Puppies and Doc Martens ate into the athletic footwear business. Nike also faced increasing competition from Adidas,

Germany's venerable sporting goods company, and from clothing designers such as Tommy Hilfiger and Ralph Lauren. In Europe, Nike and Adidas maintain a fierce battle for leadership with about 24 per cent market share each. To make matters worse, college students and consumer groups at home have protested against Nike for its alleged exploitation of child labour in Asia and its commercialisation of sports.

But Nike's biggest obstacle may be its own incredible success. A Nike executive admits that Nike has moved from maverick to mainstream, and the swoosh is becoming too common to be cool. How can a swoosh be cool when mums, dads and grandmas wear them? According to one analyst, 'When Tiger Woods made his debute in Nike gear, there were so many logos on him he looked as if he'd got caught in an embroidering machine.' The world was over swooshed!

To address these problems, Nike went back to basics – focusing on innovation and introducing new sub-brands: 'jumping man' logo and the ACG [All Condition Gear] line of outdoor and hiking styles. Recent advertising de-emphasises the swoosh, refocusing on product performance and using only the Nike script logo name.

However, to win globally, Nike must dominate in soccer, the world's most popular sport. Elbowing its way to the top in soccer will not be easy. Adidas has long dominated, with an 80 per cent global market share in football gear. Moreover, Nike must deliver worldwide quality, innovation and value and earn consumers' respect on a country-by-country basis. No longer the rebellious, anti-establishment upstart, huge Nike must continually reassess its relationships with customers. Says its founder and chief executive, Phil Knight, 'Now that we've [grown so large], there's a fine line between being a rebel and being a bully. [To our customers,] we have to be beautiful as well as big.'[1]

Questions

1. What would you consider Nike's 'superb marketing skills'?
2. Why does Nike require these skills to compete in the marketplace?
3. Show how marketing principles and practices will enable Nike to satisfy these needs, bearing in mind the company's diverse range of product and geographic markets.

Introduction

Today's successful companies have one thing in common. Like Nike, their success comes from a strong customer focus and heavy commitment to marketing. These companies share an absolute dedication to sensing, serving and satisfying the needs of customers in well-defined target markets. They motivate everyone in the organisation to deliver high quality and superior value for their customers, leading to high levels of customer satisfaction. These organisations know that if they take care of their customers, market share and profits will follow.

Marketing is about customers. Customers are an essential component of a marketing system. Each one of us is a customer in every area of human interrelation, from the consumption of education and health care and the queue in the post office to flying in a discount airline, and in every financial transaction, from the buying of biscuits to the purchase of a mobile phone. Creating customer value and satisfaction is at the very heart of modern marketing thinking and practice. Although we will explore more detailed definitions of marketing later in this chapter, perhaps the simplest definition is this one: marketing is the delivery of customer satisfaction at a profit. The goal of marketing is to attract new customers by promising superior value, and to keep current customers by delivering satisfaction.

Many people think that only large companies operating in highly developed economies use marketing, but sound marketing is critical to the success of every organisation, whether large or small, domestic or global. In the business sector, marketing first spread most rapidly in consumer packaged-goods companies, consumer durables companies and industrial equipment companies. Within the past few decades, however, consumer service firms, especially airline, insurance and financial services companies, have also adopted modern marketing practices. Business groups such as lawyers, accountants, medical practitioners and architects, too, have begun to take an interest in marketing and to advertise and price their services aggressively. Marketing has also become a vital component in the strategies of many non-profit organisations, such as schools, charities, churches, hospitals, museums, performing arts groups and even police departments.

Today, marketing is practised widely all over the world. Most countries in North and South America, Western Europe and Asia have well-developed marketing systems. Even in Eastern Europe and the former Soviet republics, where marketing has long had a bad name, dramatic political and social changes have created new opportunities for marketing. Business and government leaders in most of these nations are eager to learn everything they can about modern marketing practices.

You already know a lot about marketing – it is all around you. You see the results of marketing in the abundance of products that line the store shelves in your nearby shopping centre. You see part of marketing in TV advertising, in magazines and on Internet pages. At home, at college, where you work, where you play – you are exposed to marketing in almost everything you do. Yet, there is much more to marketing than meets the consumer's casual eye. Behind it is a massive network of people and activities competing for your attention, trying to understand what you want, and striving to fulfil that want. As Jeff Boz, the founder of Amazon, explains, 'If you focus on what customers want and build a relationship, they will allow you to make money.'

This book will give you an introduction to the basic concepts and practices of today's marketing. In this chapter, we begin by defining marketing and its core concepts, describing the major philosophies of marketing thinking and practice, and the range of activities that make up marketing.

What is marketing?

What does the term *marketing* mean? Many people think of marketing only as selling and advertising. And no wonder, for every day we are bombarded with television commercials, newspaper ads, direct mail campaigns, Internet pitches and sales calls. Although they are important, they are only two of many marketing functions and are often not the most important ones.

Today, marketing must be understood not in the old sense of making a sale – 'telling and selling' – but in the new sense of *satisfying customer needs*. Selling occurs only after a product is produced. By contrast, marketing starts long before a company has a product. Marketing is the homework that managers undertake to assess needs, measure their extent and intensity and determine whether a profitable opportunity exists. Marketing continues throughout the product's life, trying to find new customers and keep current customers by improving product appeal and performance, learning from product sales results and managing repeat performance.

Everyone knows something about 'hot' products. When Sony designed PlayStation, when Nokia introduced fashionable mobile phones, when The Body Shop introduced animal-cruelty-free cosmetics and toiletries, these manufacturers were swamped with orders. Like Swatch and Smart Car, they were 'right' products offering new benefits; not 'me-too' products. Peter Drucker, a leading management thinker, has put it this way: 'The aim of marketing is to make selling superfluous. The aim is to know and understand the customer so well that the product or service fits . . . and sells itself.'[2] If the marketer does a good job of identifying customer needs, develops products that provide superior value, distributes and promotes them effectively, these goods will sell very easily. This does not mean that selling and advertising are unimportant. Rather, it means that they are part of a larger marketing mix – a set of marketing tools that work together to affect the marketplace.

We define **marketing** as *a social and managerial process by which individuals and groups obtain what they need and want through creating and exchanging products and value with others*. To explain this definition, we examine the following important terms: *needs*, *wants and demands*; *products* and *services*; *value, satisfaction and quality*; *exchange, transactions and relationships*; and *markets*. Figure 1.1 shows that these core marketing concepts are linked, with each concept building on the one before it.

Marketing—A social and managerial process by which individuals and groups obtain what they need and want through creating and exchanging products and value with others.

Figure 1.1 Core marketing concepts

This ad is selling the product, but the Smart Car is the result of marketing from the ground up where the innovative vehicle was designed for an emergent market of fashionable, urban living, young drivers.
SOURCE: Smart – a brand of DaimlerChrysler. DaimlerChrysler UK Ltd.

Each part of the marketing definition defines what marketing is and how it is practised. In business-to-business marketing, where professional organisations *exchange products of value to each other*, marketing can be an *exchange* between similar *individuals and groups*. This contrasts with consumer markets where marketing is not an *exchange* between similar *individuals and groups*. In consumer markets, for one group marketing is a *managerial process* pursued to fulfil their *needs and wants*, while the other group is just going through life fulfilling their *needs and wants*. With this difference identified, the definition of marketing identifies marketing's unique contribution to an organisation and the demands it imposes.

What is marketing?	A *managerial process* deployed by an organisation (*individual or group*).
What is its objective?	To fulfil the *needs and wants* of the deploying organisation. These could be anything. They could be to maximise profits, although the objective of commercial marketers is usually to achieve sales targets or market share objectives. More generally, the objective for a profit or non-profit organisation could be to change the *needs and wants* of *other individuals or groups*, for example to increase the *want* of *individuals* for protection against AIDS.
How is this achieved?	A *social process* whereby *other individuals or groups* obtain needs and wants by *creating and exchanging products and value*. This limits how the deploying organisation behaves. It has to understand the *needs and wants* of *other individuals or groups* and change itself so that it can *create products and value* that it can *exchange*.

The essence of marketing is a very simple idea that extends to all walks of life. Success comes from understanding the needs and wants of others and creating ideas, services or products that fulfil those needs and wants. Most organisations, from Boo.com to WorldCom, fail because they fail to fulfil the wants and needs of others.

Needs, wants and demands

Human need—A state of felt deprivation.

The most basic concept underlying marketing is that of human needs. **Human needs** are states of felt deprivation. They include basic *physical* needs for food, clothing, warmth and safety; *social* needs for belonging and affection; and *individual* needs for knowledge and self-expression. Marketers did not invent these needs; they are a basic part of the human make-up. When a need is not satisfied, a person will do one of two things:

1. look for an object that will satisfy it; or
2. try to reduce the need.

People in industrial societies may try to find or develop objects that will satisfy their desires. People in less developed societies may try to reduce their desires and satisfy them with what is available.

Human want—The form that a human need takes as shaped by culture and individual personality.

Wants are the form human needs take as they are shaped by culture and individual personality. A hungry person in Mauritius may want a mango, rice, lentils and beans. A hungry person in Eindhoven may want a ham and cheese roll and a beer. A hungry person in Hong Kong may want a bowl of noodles, 'char-siu' pork and jasmine tea. A British drinker may want an Indian curry after leaving the pub. Wants are shaped by one's society and are described in terms of objects that will satisfy needs. As a society evolves, the wants of its members expand. As people are exposed to more objects that arouse their interest and desire, producers try to provide more want-satisfying products and services.

Demands—Human wants that are backed by buying power.

People have narrow, basic needs (e.g. for food or shelter), but almost unlimited wants. However, they also have limited resources. Thus, they want to choose products that provide the most satisfaction for their money. When backed by an ability to pay – that is, buying power – wants become **demands**. Consumers view products as bundles of benefits and choose products that give them the best bundle for their money. Thus, a Toyota Yaris gives basic safe and reliable transport, low price and fuel economy. A Jaguar gives sportiness, comfort, luxury and status. Given their wants and resources, people demand products with the benefits that add up to the most satisfaction.

Outstanding marketing companies go to great lengths to learn about and understand their customers' needs, wants and demands. They conduct consumer research about consumer likes and dislikes. They analyse customer complaint, enquiry, warranty and service data. They observe customers using their own and competing products and train salespeople to be on the lookout for unfulfilled customer needs. Understanding customer needs, wants and demands in detail provides important input for designing marketing strategies.

The market offering – products, services and experiences

Companies address needs by putting forth a *value proposition*, a set of benefits that they promise to consumers to satisfy their needs. The value proposition is fulfilled through a **marketing offer** – some combination of products, services, information, or experiences offered to a market to satisfy a need or want. Marketing offers are not limited to physical *products*. In addition to tangible products, marketing offers include *services*, activities or benefits offered for sale that are essentially intangible and do not result in the ownership of anything. Examples include banking, airline, hotel, tax preparation, and home repair services. More broadly, marketing offers also include other entities, such as *persons*, *places*, *organisations*, *information* and *ideas*.

Marketing offer—Some combination of products, services, information, or experiences offered to a market to satisfy a need or want.

Many sellers make the mistake of paying more attention to the specific products they offer than to the benefits and experiences produced by these products. They see themselves as selling a product rather than providing a solution to a need. A manufacturer of drill bits may think that the customer needs a drill bit. But what the customer is after is a hole. Or, more likely, the real *need* is to fix things together. These sellers may suffer from 'marketing myopia'. They are so taken with their products that they focus only on existing wants and lose sight of underlying customer needs. They forget that a product is only a tool to solve a consumer problem. These sellers will have trouble if a new product comes along that serves the customer's need better or less expensively. The customer with the same *need* will *want* the new product.

Thus, smart marketers look beyond the attributes of the products and services they sell. They create brand *meaning* and brand *experiences* for consumers. For example, Absolut Vodka means much more to consumers than just white alcoholic spirit – it has become an icon rich in style and meaning. A Fender is more than just a guitar, it is B.B. King, Jimi Hendrix, Eric Clapton, Keith Richards – it is Rock'n'Roll.

By orchestrating several services and products, companies can create, stage and market brand experiences. DisneyWorld is an experience; so is a ride in a Porsche. You experience a visit to a West End show in London, browsing in Galeries Lafayette or surfing Sony's playstation.com website. As products and services increasingly become commodities, experiences have emerged for many firms as the next step in differentiating the company's offer. Consider, for example, a restaurant that does not even serve food:

> [One] entrepreneur in Israel has entered the experience economy with the opening of Café Ke'ilu, which roughly translates as 'Cafe Make Believe'. Manager Nir Caspi told a reporter that people come to cafés to be seen and to meet people, not for the food; Café Ke'ilu pursues that observation to its logical conclusion. The establishment serves its customers empty plates and mugs and charges guests $3 during the week and $6 on weekends for the social experience.[3]

'What consumers really want is [offers] that dazzle their senses, touch their hearts, and stimulate their minds', declares one expert. 'They want [offers] that deliver an experience.'[4]

Value, satisfaction and quality

Consumers usually face a broad array of products and services that might satisfy a given need. How do they choose among these many products? Consumers make buying choices based on their perceptions of the value that various products and services deliver.

The guiding concept is **customer value**. Customer value is the difference between the values the customer gains from owning and using a product and the costs of obtaining the product. For example, Mercedes-Benz customers gain a number of benefits. The most obvious is a well-engineered and reliable car. However, customers may also receive some status and image values. Owning or driving a Mercedes-Benz may make them feel more important. When deciding whether to buy the desired model, customers will weigh these and other values against what it costs to buy the car. Moreover, they will compare the value of owning a Mercedes against the value of owning other comparable manufacturers' models – Lexus, Jaguar, BMW – and select the one that gives them the greatest delivered value.

Customers often do not judge product values and costs accurately or objectively. They act on *perceived* value. Customers perceive Mercedes-Benz to provide superior performance, and are hence prepared to pay the higher prices that the company charges. **Customer satisfaction** depends on a product's perceived performance in delivering value relative to a buyer's expectations. If the product's performance falls short of the customer's expectations, the buyer is dissatisfied. If performance matches expectations, the buyer is satisfied. If performance exceeds expectations, the buyer is delighted. Outstanding marketing companies go out of their way to keep their customers satisfied. They know that satisfied customers make repeat purchases and tell others about their good experiences with the product. The key is to match customer expectations with company performance. Smart companies aim to delight customers by promising only what they can deliver, then delivering more than they promise.[5]

Exchange, transactions and relationships

Marketing occurs when people decide to satisfy needs and wants through exchange. **Exchange** is the act of obtaining a desired object from someone by offering something in return. Exchange is only one of many ways people can obtain a desired object. For example, hungry people can find food by hunting, fishing or gathering fruit. They could beg for food or take food from someone else. Finally, they could offer money, another good or a service in return for food.

As a means of satisfying needs, exchange has much in its favour. People do not have to prey on others or depend on donations. Nor must they possess the skills to produce every necessity for themselves. They can concentrate on making things they are good at making and trade them for needed items made by others. Thus, exchange allows a society to produce much more than it would with any alternative system.

Exchange is the core concept of marketing. For an exchange to take place, several conditions must be satisfied. Of course, at least two parties must participate and each must have something of value to offer the other. Each party must also want to deal with the other party and each must be free to accept or reject the other's offer. Finally, each party must be able to communicate and deliver.

These conditions simply make exchange *possible*. Whether exchange actually *takes place* depends on the parties coming to an agreement. If they agree, we must conclude that the act of exchange has left both of them better off or, at least, not worse off. After all, each was free to reject or accept the offer. In this sense, exchange creates value just as production creates value. It gives people more consumption choices or possibilities.

Whereas exchange is the core concept of marketing, a transaction is marketing's unit of measurement. A **transaction** consists of a trading of values between two parties: one party gives X to another party and gets Y in return. For example, you pay a retailer €5,000 for a

Customer value—The consumer's assessment of the product's overall capacity to satisfy his or her needs.

Customer satisfaction—The extent to which a product's perceived performance matches a buyer's expectations. If the product's performance falls short of expectations, the buyer is dissatisfied. If performance matches or exceeds expectations, the buyer is satisfied or delighted.

Exchange—The act of obtaining a desired object from someone by offering something in return.

Transaction—A trade between two parties that involves at least two things of value, agreed-upon conditions, a time of agreement and a place of agreement.

plasma TV or a hotel €120 a night for a room. This is a classic monetary transaction, but not all transactions involve money. In a barter transaction, you might trade your old refrigerator in return for a neighbour's second-hand television set. Or a lawyer writes a will for a doctor in return for a medical examination.

In the broadest sense, the market tries to bring about a response to some offer. The response may be more than simply 'buying' or 'trading' goods and services. A political candidate, for instance, wants a response called 'votes', a church wants 'membership', and a social-action group wants 'idea acceptance'. Marketing consists of actions taken to obtain a desired response from a target audience towards some product, service, idea or other object.

Transaction marketing is part of the larger idea of **relationship marketing**. Beyond creating short-term transactions, smart marketers work at building long-term relationships with valued customers, distributors, dealers and suppliers. They build strong economic and social connections by promising and consistently delivering high-quality products, good service and fair prices. Increasingly, marketing is shifting from trying to maximise the profit on each individual transaction to maximising mutually beneficial relationships with consumers and other parties. In fact, ultimately, a company wants to build a unique company asset called a marketing network. A marketing network consists of the company and all of its supporting stakeholders: customers, employees, suppliers, distributors, retailers, ad agencies, and others with whom it has built mutually profitable business relationships. Increasingly, competition is not between companies but rather between whole networks, with the prize going to the company that has built the best network. The operating principle is simple: build a good network of relationships with key stakeholders, and returns will follow.[6] Chapter 11 will further explore relationship marketing and its role in creating and maintaining customer satisfaction.

Relationship marketing—The process of creating, maintaining and enhancing strong, value-laden relationships with customers and other stakeholders.

Markets

The concepts of exchange and relationships lead to the concept of a market. A **market** is the set of actual and potential buyers of a product. These buyers share a particular need or want that can be satisfied through exchanges and relationships. Thus, the size of a market depends on the number of people who exhibit the need, have resources to engage in exchange, and are willing to offer these resources in exchange for what they want.

Originally, the term *market* stood for the place where buyers and sellers gathered to exchange their goods, such as a village square. Economists use the term to refer to a collection of buyers and sellers who transact in a particular product class, as in the housing market or the grain market. Marketers, however, see the sellers as constituting an industry and the buyers as constituting a market. The relationship between the *industry* and the *market* is shown in Figure 1.2. The sellers and the buyers are connected by four flows. The sellers send products, services and communications to the market; in return, they receive money and information. The inner loop shows an exchange of money for goods; the outer loop shows an exchange of information.

Market—The set of all actual and potential buyers of a product or service.

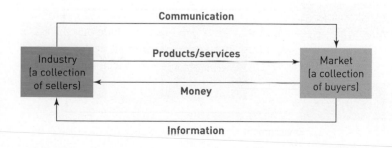

Figure 1.2 A simple marketing system

Modern economies operate on the principle of division of labour, where each person specialises in producing something, receives payment, and buys needed things with this money. Thus, modern economies abound in markets. Producers go to resource markets (raw material markets, labour markets, money markets), buy resources, turn them into goods and services, and sell them to intermediaries, who sell them to consumers. The consumers sell their labour, for which they receive income to pay for the goods and services they buy. The government is another market that plays several roles. It buys goods from resource, producer and intermediary markets, it pays them, it taxes these markets (including consumer markets) and it returns needed public services. Thus, each nation's economy and the whole world economy consist of complex interacting sets of markets that are linked through exchange processes.

In advanced societies, markets need not be physical locations where buyers and sellers interact. With modern communications and transportation, a merchant can easily advertise a product on a late evening television programme, take orders from thousands of customers over the phone, and mail the goods to the buyers on the following day without having had any physical contact with them.

Marketing

Considering *market* brings us full circle to the concept of *marketing*. Marketing means managing markets to bring about exchanges and relationships for the purpose of creating value and satisfying needs and wants. Thus, we return to our definition of marketing as a process by which individuals and groups obtain what they need and want by creating and exchanging products and value with others.

Exchange processes involve work. Sellers must search for buyers, identify their needs, design good products and services, promote them, and store and deliver them. Activities such as product development, research, communication, distribution, pricing and service are core marketing activities. Although we normally think of marketing as being carried on by sellers, buyers also carry on marketing activities. Consumers do marketing when they search for the goods they need at prices they can afford. Company purchasing agents do marketing when they track down sellers and bargain for good terms. A *sellers' market* is one in which sellers have more power and buyers must be the more active 'marketers'. In a *buyers' market*, buyers have more power and sellers have to be more active 'marketers'.

Figure 1.3 shows the main elements in a modern marketing system. In the usual situation, marketing involves serving a market of end users in the face of competitors. The company and the competitors send their respective products and messages directly to consumers or through marketing intermediaries to the end users. All of the actors in the system are affected by major environmental forces – demographic, economic, physical, technological, political/legal, social/cultural. We will address these forces that affect marketing decisions in Chapter 5.

Each party in the system adds value for the next level. Thus, a company's success depends not only on its own actions, but also on how well the entire value chain serves the needs of final consumers. IKEA, the Swedish furniture retailer, cannot fulfil its promise of low prices

Figure 1.3 Main actors and forces in a modern marketing system

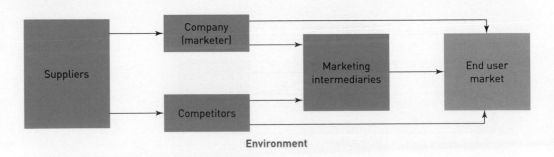

12

unless its suppliers provide merchandise at low costs. Neither can Toyota deliver high quality to car buyers unless its dealers provide outstanding service.

Marketing management

We define **marketing management** as the art and science of choosing target markets and building profitable relationships with them. This involves obtaining, retaining and developing customers through creating and delivering and communicating superior customer value. Thus, marketing management involves managing demand, which in turn involves managing customer relationships.

Marketing management— The art and science of choosing target markets and building profitable relationships with them.

Demand management

Most people think of marketing management as finding enough customers for the company's current output, but this is too limited a view. The organisation has a desired level of demand for its products. At any point in time, there may be no demand, adequate demand, irregular demand or too much demand, and marketing management must find ways to deal with these different demand states. Marketing management is concerned not only with finding and increasing demand, but also with changing or even reducing it.

For example, the Eden Project is an ecologically appealing attraction in the west of England that has a series of huge 'biomes' with climates and plants from deserts to rainforests. Unfortunately, in summertime it has trouble meeting demand during peak usage periods that typically occur when holidaymakers try to escape a rainy day at the coast. In these and other cases of excess demand, the needed marketing task, called **demarketing**, is to reduce demand temporarily or permanently. The aim of demarketing is not to destroy demand, but only to reduce or shift it. Thus, marketing management seeks to affect the level, timing and nature of demand in a way that helps the organisation achieve its objectives. Simply put, marketing management is *demand management*.

Demarketing—Marketing to reduce demand temporarily or permanently – the aim is not to destroy demand, but only to reduce or shift it.

Building profitable customer relationships

Managing demand means managing customers. A company's demand comes from two groups: new customers and repeat customers. Traditional marketing theory and practice have focused on attracting new customers and creating transactions – making the sale. In today's marketing environment, however, changing demographic, economic and competitive factors mean that there are fewer new customers to go around. The costs of *attracting* new customers are rising. In fact, it costs five times as much to attract a new customer as it does to keep a current customer satisfied. Thus, although finding new customers remains very important, the emphasis is shifting towards *retaining* profitable customers and building lasting *relationships* with them.

Companies have also discovered that losing a customer means losing not just a single sale, but also a lifetime's worth of purchases and referrals. For example, the *customer lifetime value* of a supermarket customer might well exceed €1,000,000. Thus, working to retain customers makes good economic sense. A company can lose money on a specific transaction, but still benefit greatly from a long-term relationship. The key to customer retention is superior customer value and satisfaction.

Marketing management practice

All kinds of organisations use marketing, and they practice it in widely varying ways. Many large firms apply standard marketing practices in a formalised way. However, other companies use marketing in a less formal and orderly fashion. Companies such as easyJet and Dyson achieved success by seemingly breaking all the rules of marketing. Instead of commissioning expensive marketing research, spending huge sums on mass advertising and operating large marketing departments, these companies practised *entrepreneurial marketing*. Their founders, typically, live by their wits. They visualise an opportunity and do what it takes to gain attention. They build a successful organisation by stretching their limited resources, living close to their customers and creating more satisfying solutions to customer needs. It seems that not all marketing must follow in the footsteps of marketing giants such as Procter & Gamble.[3]

However, entrepreneurial marketing often gives way to *formulated marketing*. As small companies achieve success, they inevitably move towards more formulated marketing. They begin to spend more on television advertising in selected markets. They may also expand their sales force and establish a marketing department that carries out market research. They embrace many of the tools used in so-called professionally run marketing companies. Before long, these companies grow to become large and, eventually, mature companies. They get stuck in formulated marketing, poring over the latest Nielsen numbers, scanning market research reports and trying to fine-tune dealer relations and advertising messages. These companies sometimes lose the marketing creativity and passion that they had at the start. They now need to re-establish within their companies the entrepreneurial spirit and actions that made them successful in the first place. They need to practise *entrepreneurial marketing*, that is, to encourage more initiative and 'entrepreneurship' at the local level. Their brand and product managers need to get out of the office, start living with their customers and visualise new and creative ways to add value to their customers' lives.

The bottom line is that effective marketing can take many forms. There will be a constant tension between the formulated side of marketing and the creative side. It is easier to learn the formulated side of marketing, which will occupy most of our attention in this book. However, we will also see how real marketing creativity and passion operate in many companies – whether small or large, new or mature – to build and retain success in the marketplace.

Marketing management philosophies

We describe marketing management as carrying out tasks to achieve desired exchanges with target markets. What *philosophy* should guide these marketing efforts? What weight should be given to the interests of the organisation, customers and society? Very often these interests conflict. Invariably, the organisation's marketing management philosophy influences the way it approaches its buyers.

There are five alternative concepts under which organisations conduct their marketing activities: the *production*, *product*, *selling*, *marketing* and *societal marketing* concepts.

The production concept

Production concept—The philosophy that consumers will favour products that are available and highly affordable, and that management should therefore focus on improving production and distribution efficiency.

The **production concept** holds that consumers will favour products that are available and highly affordable, and that management should therefore focus on improving production and distribution efficiency. This concept is one of the oldest philosophies that guide sellers.

The production concept is a useful philosophy in two types of situation. The first occurs when the demand for a product exceeds the supply. Here, management should look for ways to increase production. The second situation occurs when the product's cost is too high and improved productivity is needed to bring it down. For example, in the early years of the Ford Motor Company, Henry Ford's whole philosophy was to perfect the production of the

Model T so that its cost could be reduced and more people could afford it. He joked about offering people a car of any colour as long as it was black. The company won a big share of the automobile market with this philosophy. However, companies operating under a production philosophy run a big risk of focusing too narrowly on their own operations. After some time, Ford's strategy failed. Although its cars were priced low, customers did not find them very attractive. In its drive to bring down prices, the company lost sight of something else that its customers wanted – namely, *attractive*, affordable vehicles. The gap left by Ford gave rise to new market opportunities that rival General Motors was quick to exploit.

The product concept

Another important concept guiding sellers, the **product concept**, holds that consumers will favour products that offer the most quality, performance and innovative features, and that an organisation should thus devote energy to making continuous product improvements. Some manufacturers believe that if they can build a better mousetrap, the world will beat a path to their door.[4] But they are often rudely shocked. Buyers may well be looking for a better solution to a mouse problem, but not necessarily for a better mousetrap. The solution might be a chemical spray, an exterminating service or something that works better than a mousetrap. Furthermore, a better mousetrap will not sell unless the manufacturer designs, packages and prices it attractively, places it in convenient distribution channels, and brings it to the attention of people who need it and convinces them that it is a better product. A product orientation leads to obsession with technology because managers believe that technical superiority is the key to business success.

The product concept also can lead to 'marketing myopia'. For instance, railway management once thought that users wanted *trains* rather than *transportation* and overlooked the growing challenge of airlines, buses, trucks and cars. Building improved trains would not satisfy consumers' demand for transportation, but creating other forms of transportation and extending choice would.

> **Product concept**—The idea that consumers will favour products that offer the most quality, performance and features, and that the organisation should therefore devote its energy to making continuous product improvements.

The selling concept

Many organisations follow the **selling concept**, which holds that consumers will not buy enough of the organisation's products unless it undertakes a large-scale selling and promotion effort. The concept is typically practised with *unsought goods* – those that buyers do not normally think of buying, such as Readers Digest and double glazing. These industries must be good at tracking down prospects and convincing them of product benefits.

The selling concept is also practised in the non-profit area. A political party, for example, will vigorously sell its candidate to voters as a fantastic person for the job. The candidate works hard at selling him or herself – shaking hands, kissing babies, meeting supporters and making speeches. Much money also has to be spent on radio and television advertising, posters and mailings. Candidate flaws are often hidden from the public because the aim is to get the sale, not to worry about consumer satisfaction afterwards.

Most firms practise the selling concept when they have overcapacity. Their aim is to sell what they make rather than make what the market wants. Such marketing carries high risks. It focuses on creating sales transactions in the short term, rather than on building long-term, profitable relationships with customers. It assumes that customers who are coaxed into buying the product will like it. On the other hand, if they do not like it, they may forget their disappointment and buy it again later. These are usually poor assumptions to make about buyers. Most studies show that dissatisfied customers do not buy again. Worse yet, while the average satisfied customer tells three others about good experiences, the average dissatisfied customer tells 10 others of his or her bad experiences.[7]

> **Selling concept**—The idea that consumers will not buy enough of the organisation's products unless the organisation undertakes a large-scale selling and promotion effort.

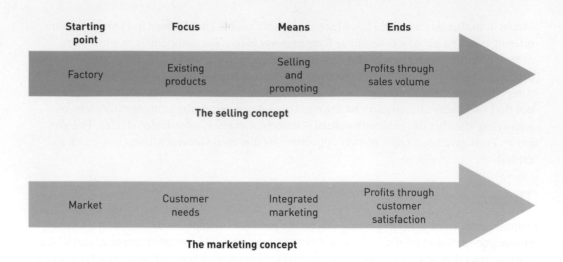

Figure 1.4 The selling and marketing concepts contrasted

Starting point	Focus	Means	Ends
Factory	Existing products	Selling and promoting	Profits through sales volume

The selling concept

Starting point	Focus	Means	Ends
Market	Customer needs	Integrated marketing	Profits through customer satisfaction

The marketing concept

The marketing concept

Marketing concept—The marketing management philosophy which holds that achieving organisational goals depends on determining the needs and wants of target markets and delivering the desired satisfactions more effectively and efficiently than competitors do.

The **marketing concept** holds that achieving organisational goals depends on determining the needs and wants of target markets and delivering the desired satisfactions more effectively and efficiently than competitors do.

The selling concept and the marketing concept are frequently confused. Figure 1.4 compares the two concepts. The selling concept takes an *inside-out* perspective. It starts with the factory, focuses on the company's existing products and calls for heavy selling and promotion to obtain profitable sales. It focuses on customer conquest – getting short-term sales with little concern about who buys or why.

In contrast, the marketing concept takes an *outside-in* perspective. It starts with a well-defined market, focuses on customer needs, coordinates all the marketing activities affecting customers and makes profits by creating long-term customer relationships based on customer value and satisfaction. Under the marketing concept, customer focus and value are the paths to sales and profits.

Many successful and well-known global companies have adopted the marketing concept. IKEA, Procter & Gamble, Marriott, Nordström and Wal-Mart follow it faithfully. Toyota, the highly successful Japanese car manufacturer, is also a prime example of an organisation that takes a customer- and marketing-oriented view of its business.

Toyota is intent on getting deep into the hearts and minds of its customers, to establish precisely what they want and subsequently find ways to fulfil their wishes. In Japan, Toyota's 14-storey Amlux building, resembling a blue and black striped rocket, attracts millions of visitors. These could be potential customers or people with ideas on how the company should respond to consumers' vehicle requirements. These visitors are allowed to spend as much time as they want designing their own vehicles on computer/TV screens in the vehicle-design studio. Visitors can obtain specific information about the company, its dealers or products. The visitors are also allowed to expound, at length, on what they think Toyota should be doing or making. Meanwhile, Toyota's attentive note-taking staff ensure that the entire Amlux complex is dedicated to involving potential customers who can give them close insights into how their car needs can be satisfied.

In marketing-led organisations, real customer focus has to work from the top down and the bottom up and it has to be totally accepted by the whole workforce. This organisation-wide belief ensures that customer retention becomes a priority and all staff are committed to building lasting relationships with the customer. To achieve successful implementation of the marketing concept, the organisation therefore focuses on how best to tap and channel the knowledge and understanding, the motivation, the inspiration and the imagination of all staff to deliver products and services that meet exactly what the customer requires from the organisation.

Many companies claim to practise the marketing concept but do not. They have the *forms* of marketing – such as a marketing director, product managers, marketing plans and marketing research – but this does not mean that they are *market-focused* and *customer-driven* companies. The question is whether they are finely tuned to changing customer needs and competitor strategies. Great companies – Philips, Marks & Spencer, Fiat, IBM – have lost substantial market share in the past because they failed to adjust their marketing strategies to the changing marketplace.

Implementing the marketing concept often means more than simply responding to customers' stated desires and obvious needs. Customer-driven companies research current customers to learn about their desires, gather new product and service ideas and test proposed product improvements. Such customer-driven marketing usually works well when there exists a clear need and when customers know what they want. In many cases, however, customers do not know what they want or even what is possible. Such situations call for *customer-driving* marketing – understanding customer needs even better than customers do themselves, and creating products and services that will meet existing and latent needs now and in the future.

Customers are notoriously lacking in foresight. Twenty years ago, how many of us were asking for mobile phones, fax machines and copiers at home, cars with on-board navigation systems, hand-held global satellite positioning receivers, cyber-cafés or interactive television shopping networks? As the late Akio Morita, Sony's visionary leader, once said: 'Our plan is to lead the public with new products rather than ask them what kinds of products they want. The public does not know what is possible, but we do. So, instead of doing a lot of market research, we refine our thinking on a product and its use and try to create a market for it by educating and communicating with the public.'[8]

Years of hard work are needed to turn a sales-oriented company into a marketing-oriented company. The goal is to build customer satisfaction into the very fabric of the firm. However, the marketing concept does not mean that a company should try to give *all* consumers *everything* they want. The purpose of marketing is not to *maximise* customer satisfaction, but to meet customer needs profitably. Marketers must therefore seek to achieve the very delicate balance between creating more value for customers and making profits for the company.

The societal marketing concept

The **societal marketing concept** holds that the organisation should determine the needs, wants and interests of target markets. It should then deliver the desired satisfactions more effectively and efficiently than competitors in a way that maintains or improves both the consumer's *and society's* well-being. The societal marketing concept is the newest of the five marketing management philosophies.

The societal marketing concept questions whether the pure marketing concept is adequate in an age of environmental problems, resource shortages, worldwide economic problems and neglected social services. It asks whether the firm that senses, serves and satisfies individual wants is always doing what is best for consumers and society in the long run. According to the societal marketing concept, the pure marketing concept overlooks possible conflicts between short-run consumer *wants* and long-run consumer *welfare*.

Societal marketing concept—The idea that the organisation should determine the needs, wants and interests of target markets and deliver the desired satisfactions more effectively and efficiently than competitors in a way that maintains or improves both the consumer's and society's well-being.

People don't always see accidents coming. But their cars will.

'Accidents will happen', as the saying goes. Especially when people lose concentration. In fact, inattentiveness is one of the most frequent causes of mishaps, both at home and on the road. Which is why we're developing cars that can actually recognise obstacles independently. The car will then alert the driver to a potential hazard and help to avoid it. DaimlerChrysler Research is already creating intelligent technologies like this today, for the automobile of tomorrow. Because one day we hope there will be a new saying: 'Accidents won't happen'.

To obtain more detailed information on the 'Vision of Accident-free Driving' visit
www.daimlerchrysler.com

DAIMLERCHRYSLER
Answers for questions to come.

DaimlerChrysler exhibit societal marketing by investing in technology that reduces accidents. This often means systems such as BAS (Brake Assist), Electronic Stability Programme (ESP) and Sensotronic Brake Control that take control away from the driver.
SOURCE: DaimlerChrysler AG Stuttgart/Auburn Hills.

18

The citizen brands

marketing insights

Consumer activism and government vigilance in monitoring the impact of business on society are on the rise. Many companies, particularly the very large ones, have to reflect a greater sense of corporate responsibility, ensuring that they are readily accountable to consumers, employees, shareholders and society. Corporate citizenship is cast as a new model for today's businesses. Many companies are thinking hard about how to build and maintain strong *citizen* brands. Companies whose business strategies include corporate citizenship activities will realise their investment in the form of reinforcement of brand values and enhanced customer loyalty.

This is what London's Capital Radio, with a long history of corporate citizenship, believe will sustain the popularity of their brand. Capital Radio, launched over two decades ago, offered a service to the community through help-lines, flat-share and support services. Partnering their *citizen* brand – *Capital* – in doing good is *Floodlight*, an educational publication that is a market leader in the further education and part-time education directories market. Capital Radio and a sister station, Capital Gold, run commercials that encourage listeners to pick up a copy of the publication. The idea behind the publication was to help listeners advance themselves through education.

Other companies are addressing the need to build social, including employee, welfare and ethical considerations into their business practices. Oil company Shell suffered two blows to its reputation in 1995. One was from its attempt to dispose of the Brent Spar oilrig in the North Sea, and the other was over its failure to oppose the Nigerian government's execution of Ken Saro-Wiwa, a human-rights activist in a part of Nigeria where Shell had extensive operations. Since then, the company has rewritten its business principles and created an elaborate mechanism to implement them. Surveys now invariably rank Shell among the most environmentally friendly and socially aware companies in the world.

The trend towards corporate citizenship is further illustrated by NatWest Bank's *Community Bond*. A NatWest customer contributes (a loan) and becomes a bondholder. The money funds charitable projects. The loan is repaid to the bondholder who can choose a lower rate of return, triggering a donation from NatWest to a network of regional charitable loan funds. The NatWest Community Bond creates 'social capital' for the brand. It helps the bank to promote and sustain relationships with its customers and partners in the charity sector. In addition, by aligning corporate and community values, it gives NatWest status as a citizen brand.

SOURCES: 'Doing well by doing good', *The Economist* (22 April 2000), pp. 83–6; Linda Bishop, 'The corporate citizen', *Marketing Business* (April 2000), pp. 16–19; Carole Hoyos and Sheila McNulty, 'The oil company the greens love to hate', *Financial Times* (11 June 2003), p. 12; also see: Wally Ollins, 'Trading identities: why countries and companies are taking on each other's roles', available from **www.un.org/partners/business**.

Figure 1.5 Three considerations underlying the societal marketing concept

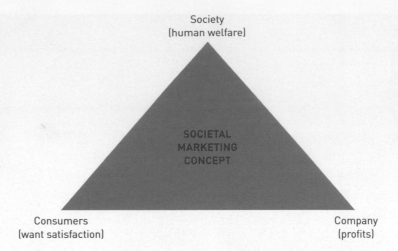

Consider the fast-food industry. Most people see today's giant fast-food chains as offering tasty and convenient food at reasonable prices. Yet certain consumer and environmental groups have voiced concerns. Critics point out that hamburgers, fried chicken, French fries and most other foods sold by fast-food restaurants are high in fat and salt. The products are wrapped in convenient packaging, but this leads to waste and pollution. Thus, in satisfying consumer wants, the highly successful fast-food chains may be harming consumer health and causing environmental problems.

Such concerns and conflicts led to the societal marketing concept. As Figure 1.5 shows, the societal marketing concept calls upon marketers to balance three considerations in setting their marketing policies: company profits, consumer wants and society's interests. Originally, most companies based their marketing decisions largely on short-run company profit. Eventually, they began to recognise the long-run importance of satisfying consumer wants, and the marketing concept emerged. Now many companies are beginning to think of society's interests when making their marketing decisions.

Increasingly, firms also have to meet the expectations of society as a whole. For example, society expects businesses genuinely to uphold basic ethical and environmental standards. Not only should they have ethics and environmental policies, they must also back these with actions (see Marketing Insights 1.1).

Marketing in the noughties

In the 1980s Japan was pre-eminent as the world champion marketer with its global manufacturing and consumer electronics. In the nineties Japan stumbled but Europe remained strong with its luxury brands and liberated East European markets. Through the two decades, the US remained strong, trading upon its technological leadership and global consumer products. Now, in the 'noughties', some of Europe's leading economies are stagnating, along with Japan, and the engines for growth are the economic giants at the extremes of the wealth spectrum. At one end, the wealthy US benefits from its leadership of the hardware (Dell and Intel), software (Microsoft) and services (Amazon and eBay) of the e-revolution. At the other end, less wealthy China and India achieve double-digit growth, as their newly unshackled economies became global leaders in services and manufacturing.[9]

As the world spins through the first decade of the twenty-first century, dramatic changes are occurring in the world of marketing. Business pundits and politicians are referring to a new economy (see Marketing Insights 1.2) within which firms have to think afresh about their

A new dawn?

marketing insights

Western Europe's material prosperity has soared more in the past 250 years than in the previous 1,000 (see Exhibit 1.1), thanks to industrialisation. Arguably, this remarkable phenomenon may not live on forever, given that the frontiers of technology and science are moving closer. Or, natural or man-made environmental disasters may intervene. Nonetheless, scientific progress today seems certain to continue, harnessing technological progress that, in turn, sustains economic growth and improves living standards. For example, America's recent economic 'miracle' – rapid growth, subdued inflation and low unemployment – has been attributed to the information technology revolution. In the new century, will western Europe also partake of a 'new economy' and, if so, what is the shape of things to come?

Knowledge? Service? Digital? E-economy? M-economy?

Business pundits and politicians say that our countries' economic welfare will increasingly rely on wealth creation in knowledge-based, high value-added industries, such as computing, software and telecommunications, and those employing highly skilled workers, such as finance and education. Many talk about the 'knowledge economy', driven by skyrocketing investment in knowledge. Witness the acceleration in the number of patents filed in the last decade. Thanks to landmark legal battles, businesses across Europe and the US can now patent a raft of new areas of technology, from biotechnology, genes and financial services, to consulting, software, business methods and the Internet.

The European Union's measures of knowledge investment show that Sweden, which currently spends 3.8 per cent of GDP on R&D, tops the international league table, just followed by Finland (3.7 per cent), then Japan (3.0), the US (2.7) and Germany (2.5). Austria, Britain, Denmark, France, Iceland and the Netherlands all spent close to the EU average (1.9 per cent). Moreover, the EU's burgeoning knowledge economy is evident from the 49 per cent of *total* business output accounted for by knowledge-based industries. In spending on R&D, investment in software and both public and private spending on education, Sweden tops the list again, with an investment reaching 10.6 per cent of its GDP, followed by France (10.0 per cent), Britain (8.3) and the US (8.0). Japan's investment of 6.6 per cent is puny compared to the EU's average spend of just under 8.0 per cent of GDP.

Notwithstanding the inevitable imperfection in definition and measurement, the OECD suggests that the proportion of business R&D spending accounted for by services rose nearly five-fold to 20 per cent over the past two decades. Moreover, nearly 20 per cent of global trade is now in services, rather than manufactured goods. According to the World Trade Organisation (WTO), global exports of commercial services totalled $1.4 trillion in 2002, of which the EU accounted for some 40 per cent,

...1.2

compared to the US with a 20 per cent share. Western Europe is advancing towards not only a knowledge economy, but also an increasingly dominant service economy.

What of the Internet and 'E'-economy? Although western European firms are increasing their investment in information technology (IT), the EU investment of nearly 4.2 per cent of GDP lags behind America's 5.3 per cent. However, Sweden (6.8 per cent), the UK (5.6) and Luxembourg (5.4) outspend the US. At the end of the last decade the US had five times as many households per 1,000 population with access to the Internet. Now the gap is closing, with the percentage of EU households with access to the Internet increasing to 40.4 per cent in 2002. Nevertheless, there is high variation across the EU, from 65.5 per cent in the Netherlands to 9.2 per cent in Greece. The EU is ahead of the US in 'wireless technology'. With a much higher use of mobile phones, which are touted to become the most widely used link to the Internet, M (mobile)-commerce is expected to flourish.

New digital products are showing signs of pulling Japan out of its long recession. World sales of DVD players and DVDs overtook those of VCRs in 2002, and satellite digital TV reception is already the dominant technology. Other substitutions are occurring. Digital camcorders and cameras are expected to overtake sales of their conventional brethren in 2003 and 2004. Plasma TV and in-car GPS navigation are currently expensive, but prices will come down as production capacity rises and the products become less exclusive. Just

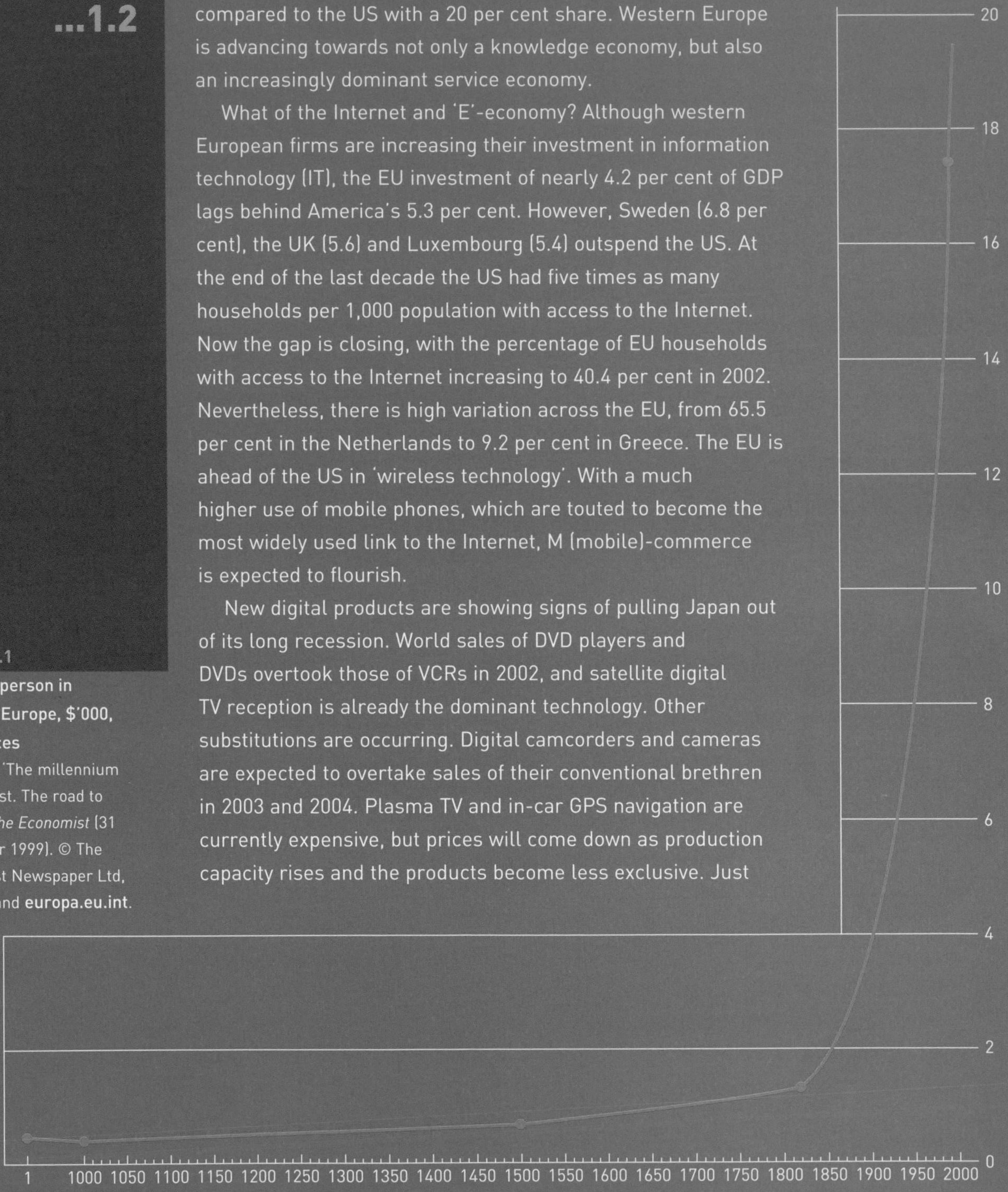

Exhibit 1.1

GDP per person in Western Europe, $'000, 1990 prices
SOURCE: 'The millennium of the West. The road to riches', *The Economist* (31 December 1999). © The Economist Newspaper Ltd, London, and **europa.eu.int**.

breaking are digital radios and active GPS systems that warn drivers of hazards and speed restrictions.

To reap the benefits of the E, M and digital economies, EU politicians have to make far-reaching structural, tax, labour market and capital market reforms. These will try to create flexible, open and efficient markets where business entrepreneurship and innovation can flourish. Europe itself is changing, for that matter. The euro zone creates a big single capital market, facilitating business's efforts to raise money for investment. *Slowly*, things are moving in the right direction: tax cuts in Germany, France and the Netherlands; deregulation of industries, such as utilities and telecommunications; and countries like Spain making their labour markets more flexible, although the effectiveness of these policies is not showing in the larger euro economies.

Many forces are working together to direct the EU's business revolution. From the Internet and information technology, to the pressures for restructuring and deregulation, responsive countries and businesses will emerge the winners. Whether in terms of knowledge, service, E, M or digital economy, Europe's economic transformation may hope to yield a capitalism that is more transparent, more efficient and, most importantly, more rewarding for all that partake in it.

SOURCES: Adapted from **www.wto.org** (World Trade Organisation); **www.europa.eu.int** (European Union); Chris Anderson, 'The great crossover' in *The World in 2003*, *The Economist*, London.

marketing objectives and practices. Rapid changes can quickly make yesterday's winning strategies out of date. As management thought-leader Peter Drucker observed, a company's winning formula for the last decade would probably be its undoing in the next decade. The rapid pace of change means that the firm's ability to change will become a competitive advantage.

From time immemorial people have seen their era as being one of uncertainty, discontinuity, turbulence and threat. 'Everything flows and nothing stays', said the Greek philosopher Heraclitus in 513 BC. Heraclitus also anticipated Peter Drucker's call for continuous change, explaining 'You can't step twice into the same river'. The popularity of retro-look products, such as the VW Beetle, Mini, Chrysler PT Cruiser and Ford Thunderbird, shows consumers a yearning for the security, simplicity and certainty of the past. A romantic view of the 1950s and 1960s forgets the Cold War, a Europe divided, Vietnam, Korea, race riots and fear over the emergence of heroes who terrified the establishment: Elvis Presley, Chuck Berry, James Dean, The Rolling Stones, The Who, Jimi Hendrix, Mohammed Ali and Bob Dylan. In reality, times are always changing and marketing is the interface between organisations and that ever-changing environment.

Ever-changing markets are not a threat, but the lifeblood of marketing. They create opportunities for existing brands to refresh, opportunities for new products, new ways of communicating to customers and completely new markets:

- **An exiting brand**: rather than resisting change, the BBC, Britain's not-for-profit national broadcaster, championed digital radio, broadcasting an increased range of high sound quality digital channels to stimulate digital radio manufacture.

- **New products**: seeing a market shift to small cars and retro appeal, BMW relaunched the Mini. With Europe's stagnant market, the Mini has become BMW's saviour in recent years. It is even succeeding in the USA where the 1960s Mini was never marketed.

- **Communications**: globalisation has allowed companies to keep in touch with their customers 24 7. Make an early morning telephone enquiry or book an airline ticket and the odds are you will be talking to someone in India. Do not expect a local accent to give you a clue; training takes care of that.

- **New markets**: not long ago few had heard of Nokia. The company grew with the emergence of mobile telecommunications and recognising mobile phones as a fashion accessory. Meanwhile, VW's dominant share (38 per cent) of China's motor vehicle market – growing at 40 per cent a year – is keeping it in profits while other car makers suffer.[10]

The remainder of this chapter examines the components of marketing activity that link the world's changing environment to marketing strategies and actions that fulfil the needs of tomorrow's customers. It introduces each chapter of this book and shows how they follow a sequence that builds from an understanding of the environment surrounding marketing to creating marketing activities.

The marketing process

'Business has only two basic functions – marketing and innovation', says the leading business guru, Peter Drucker. Such claims can seduce marketers into seeing themselves as superior to or independent of other business functions. That view is incorrect. Marketing exists as part of an organisation whose parts are interdependent. Drucker emphasises the importance of selling and inventing what people want, rather than taking the production or sales concept of marketing and trying to sell what the producer wants. For an organisation to survive, all its parts must work together for the good of all.

Strategy, marketing and planning

Marketing process—The process of (1) analysing marketing opportunities; (2) selecting target markets; (3) developing the marketing mix; and (4) managing the marketing effort.

Marketing is one part of the strategy of an organisation where marketing of the strategic plan drives the company forward. The **marketing process** in Figure 1.6 shows marketing's role and activities in organisations and the forces influencing marketing strategy. The numbers in the figure refer to chapters covering the issues in this text.

The marketing activities that most people manage concern a small part of a large organisation with many other products and markets. For example, Anglo-Dutch Unilever has business units ranging from spreads and cooking products, marketing Rama, Flora Pro-activ and others, to prestige fragrances including Very Valentino and House of Curreti. All share the company's purpose: '. . . to serve consumers in a unique and effective way'. Subsidiary to Unilever's overall strategy are strategies for each business unit and each part of the world. Within those will be plans for 'I Can't Believe It's Not Butter' and Calvin Klein fragrances.

Chapter 2 starts by looking at the broad strategy of an organisation and works down from a company's overall strategy to the construction of marketing plans for individual products or brands. Marketing plans exist alongside an organisation's other plans. Operational plans set production levels for the mix of products made. Many marketing activities, such as 'buy

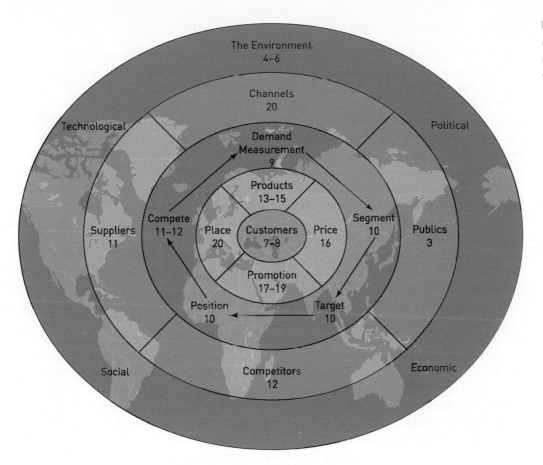

Figure 1.6 Influences on marketing strategy, showing the numbers of the chapters in which they appear in this text

one, get one free' price promotions, lead to hugely changed sales volumes and so need coordinating with production and distribution schedules so that shelves are stocked when campaigns run. Meeting increased production schedules will need extra staff and raw materials, hence influencing personnel plans and raw materials purchasing. More strategic marketing issues, such as developing new products to fit changing market needs, influence a company's research and development effort and financial strategy if a new product needs new production facilities or an expensive launch.

With limited resources and overlapping demand, the promotion of one product, such as cholesterol-reducing Flora Pro-activ, could influence the sales of Becel, another spread with a health appeal. These interactions form an important part of strategy, marketing and planning. Two particular issues are the relationship of marketing to other business functions and the various new ways in which marketing is organised.

The marketing setting

Since marketing is about making and selling what people want to buy, the most important first stage in marketing planning is understanding the marketing environment: the setting where marketing takes place. This has two levels: first, the macroenvironment of broad societal forces that influence a business; and second, the microenvironment of forces closer to the company that affects its ability to serve its customers. These are the subject of Part Two of this book. Part Three focuses on customers, an exceptionally important group within marketing's microenvironment.

Macro- and microenvironment

The macro- and microenvironment are largely issues that a company cannot control, but they can have a huge influence on an organisation's performance. They are the subject of Chapter 3 of this book.

PEST analysis systematises an examination of the Political, Economic, Social and Technological elements of the macroenvironment. Marketers, like most groups of people, play a part in setting the PEST agenda, but in most cases their influence is small. The exception is organisations whose contributions to national economies are very large, such as food or extraction companies in the Third World, or lobby groups, such as French farmers or the American gun lobby.

Most organisations need to observe the macroenvironment to understand how they need to adjust to it. For example, the economic macroenvironment is causing many charities difficulties. Stock market declines are reducing their earnings from their investments and the economic pinch is influencing large donors, including governments, who are less willing to give. This is throwing the charities back onto campaigns based on small donors or profits from charity shops whose contribution is less cyclical.

Several features of the PEST environment are having a huge influence on many markets. The economics of high house prices, available technology for planned parenting and a social change in the number of career women mean that people are setting up home later and having fewer children. The combined influence of these macroenvironmental factors will hugely change our world in the coming decades as populations age, children become rarer and dependency ratios increase. More immediately, many markets are changing as young adults are lingering with their parents until they are in their thirties and many people choose to be DINKYs (Double Income, No Kids Yet) rather than face the social and economic costs of parenting: big cars, big houses, child care fees, etc. This substitution of personal consumption for the costs of bringing up children is driving the demand for many luxury products (two-seat cars, designer clothes, clubs, loft living, restaurants, long-haul holidays).

As the macroenvironment shifts, so does the microenvironment. The media are changing in order to provide channels that serve young wealthy consumers; food retailers move into town to serve the YUPPY (Young Urban Professionals) market. In many cases, the huge, steady changes in the marketing environment are conspicuous but still too fast for those marketers who do not respond quickly to those changes. Hence the rapid decline of Toys 'R' Us and the steady decline of Mothercare. Other organisations such as Saga, which provides holidays, radio stations, insurance, etc. for older people, are doing well.

E-marketing, society and globalisation

E-marketing, social issues and globalisation are three great macroenvironmental trends that are having a huge impact upon marketing, business and communities. Chapters 4, 5 and 6 take these in turn.

E-marketing: marketing in the Internet age

E-marketing is now so established that it does not seem new. It appears to have gone through a life-cycle of excessive exuberance and investment, crashing decline and failure, to more staid maturity. This is true of dot.com bubble companies, such as boo.com and pet.com, though this shakeout had no influence on the inexorable growth in e-business. E-commerce has not only changed the way we do business but also created new business. Three purely online retailers – Amazon, eBay and Expedia – now have sales of over €1bn. Other businesses have grown as e-marketing allows more convenient, low-cost means of distribution. Consumers across the world are benefiting from Ryanair and easyJet's pioneering of low-cost flying that uses Internet-only selling. Meanwhile, innovative 'bricks and bits' companies have embraced e-marketing. Tesco's low-tech approach to e-retailing has allowed it to grow to become the world's largest online grocery retailer. US supermarket chain Safeway has now licensed Tesco's low-tech approach.

The US is the world leader in e-commerce and online retailing. Between 1997 and 2002, the number of online shoppers grew from 5m to 37m households, spending $72bn. Outside the US, poor PC penetration or low credit card use hampers the adoption of online retailing. In Europe, the pace is increasing with 17 per cent of Europeans buying online over the last three months of 2002. So far, there are few Europe-wide online retailers, although there are some significant national successes. Otto, the German catalogue dealer, is a close second to Amazon in the German market, and Ahold's Albert.nl sales have grown by 30–40 per cent year on year.

With penetration of online retailing well into double figures, growth will not remain as meteoric as in the early years, but the average growth rate of online business is 15 per cent compared with 3 per cent for conventional channel users. Whether a retailer adopts a purely online operation or not, consumers increasingly use the Internet to check out products, services and prices before they buy. Many people visit the Jamjar site to check out new car prices and discounts before seeing a car dealer, but increasing numbers of people also buy through such sites. Before going to a concert or the theatre, hiring a car, booking a hotel or a flight, increasing numbers of customers are recognising that lastminute.com is quicker, easier and cheaper than buying direct or through an agent. E-business and online retailing are still small compared with conventional trade, but for how long?[11]

Marketing and society: social responsibility and marketing ethics

Marketing is most often associated with capitalism, an often questioned socio-economic philosophy that took several knocks in the first few years of this millennium. In particular, the stock market collapses across the world, the flawed governance that allowed WorldCom, Enron and Vivendi to fail so catastrophically, and worldwide best sellers, such as *No Logo* and *Fast Food Nation*, question the foundation of modern business and marketing.[12]

The stock market collapse is not a marketing issue, although many small investors and savers probably suffered because of the overselling of risky investments. Similarly, marketing was not a central contributor to the most conspicuous corporate collapses. However, the business failures and the popular questioning of marketing make even more important an understanding of the relationship between business and society. The societal marketing concept starts to address the social dimensions of marketing. Additionally, the very definition of marketing, '*a social and managerial process by which individuals and groups obtain what they need and want through creating and exchanging products and value with others*', emphasises that the process should be an exchange that fulfils wants and needs. Furthermore, we know that the best marketing performance comes from satisfying customers so that they return to buy more and pass on the good news to their friends. Social responsibility is not just important to marketing: it is central to marketing.

A second dimension of marketing goes beyond commercial exchange. Marketing is increasingly used to achieve ends that are not commercial. Non Governmental Organisations (NGOs) use marketing to draw attention to causes, to raise money to support their cause and to distribute to those in need. Both NGOs and government agencies use marketing to promote their activities. The Samaritans use advertising to alert those in need that there is someone to talk to and willing to help when they are desperate, and advertising is used to try to reduce accidents from drinking and driving. Besides reducing suffering, campaigns that reduce accidents are far more economical than the medical emergency and repair costs of accidents.

Globalisation: the global marketplace

Globalisation influences the marketing environment in two ways: firstly, in the continued growth in the proportion of a country's trade that is traded internationally; and secondly, in

Gambling is one of many activities that is highly regulated or banned in many countries. The Internet is giving companies in countries with more relaxed laws global reach as well as using scale and operational economies to give the punters more of a chance of winning.
SOURCE: Bear Design Ltd.

the disquiet many people feel about globalisation. In the decade up to 2002, world trade in merchandise and services each increased by an average of 6.5 per cent per annum – close to doubling over 10 years! Simultaneously, each region's trade was becoming less concentrated. Over the 10-year period, the proportion of international trade between European Union partners increased in total, but declined from 72 per cent to 67 per cent of EU trade. The main regions taking up the increased proportion of EU trade were the USA, the ex-Soviet bloc countries and China. The implications for marketers of this growing international trade are changed competition as marketers from the world's regions compete, global supply chains as products chase low-cost suppliers, and an increasing proportion of trade with people outside one's own culture. Advances in information and communications technology are making marketing operations global as call centres and product development move offshore.

With the rate of change, it is no wonder that special-interest groups, from trade unions seeking to protect local jobs to eco-warriors seeking to save the world, find globalisation disturbing. Globalisation is shifting wealth across the world but not in the way that many people fear. The annual average growth per head of population in less developed economies that are 'more globalised' averaged 4 per cent plus between 1990 and 2001. This compares with growth rates averaging 2 per cent for rich countries and 1 per cent for 'less globalised', less developed countries. As a consequence, the proportion of the world's population in poverty has declined from 56 per cent in 1980 to 23 per cent in 2000. There remains a very large tail of 1.1 billion people in poverty (down from 1.9 billion in 1980), mostly in sub-Saharan Africa, but the world is developing a huge, technologically sophisticated middle class as world incomes even out.

The more even distribution of the world's income adds an extra globalisation pressure facing marketers. Since the colonial era, world trade involved selling sophisticated goods to less developed countries in exchange for raw materials. Increasingly, marketing success means selling to countries that are technological equals and who have their own enterprises and innovations.[13]

Markets

To succeed in today's competitive marketplace, companies must be customer centred – winning customers from competitors by delivering greater value. However, before it can satisfy consumers, a company must first understand their needs and wants. Sound marketing requires analysis and understanding of customers' wants and needs. Understanding customer behaviour and the research used to uncover this information is the subject of Part Three of this book.

Consumer markets

All marketing ends with consumers and the study of consumers is the subject of Chapter 7. Commercial organisations survive when enough people exchange enough of their assets for the product or service that an organisation offers. Often the asset is money, but it could also be debt to a credit company or products given in part exchange. This transaction gives suppliers the revenue they need to survive, and without it marketing has failed, but marketers are involved in streams of decisions, actions and behaviour before and after that transaction. The same is true for marketers in non-profit organisations, although in those cases an action, such as visiting a doctor or not drinking and driving, is the pivotal point.

To develop marketing strategies and plans, and to get ideas for new offerings, marketers explore the whole of consumer behaviour from well before to well after the pivotal trans-action. Buyer behaviour starts with a consumer's social position, lifestyle and preferences even before there is a glimmer of a need or want for the product being marketed. Then, even if the purchase is as simple as a drink, there is a process of awareness of a product, interest in some more than others, desire for a particular form of need fulfilment, and only then, action. During this same process, consumers make decisions about where to get the drink. The cold water tap, the fridge, a convenience store or a bar? Marketers can fail anywhere in this process.

The richness of marketing stems from its central involvement in two of the most complex entities that we know of: the human brain and the society in which we live. In trying to understand consumers, marketers draw on all sources of knowledge: from psychology in understanding how we perceive objects to physics in understanding how we can make drink containers we can use on the move; from sociology in understanding how our friends influence our purchases to semiotics in understanding how we respond to symbols.

The result of this diversity is no one model of consumer behaviour but a vast wealth of ways of informing our thinking. Any of these can help us see why marketing campaigns are failing to reveal radical new marketing ideas. For example, recent years have seen two new products that invigorated orange drinks, a tired old commodity. Sunny Delight gave orange drinks a new sweeter, smoother taste that appealed to children and for a while outsold Coca-Cola in many markets. Tango's success came from advertising that made the product appealing to young men.

The study of consumer behaviour does not end with a purchase. What makes people satisfied or dissatisfied? Increasingly marketers are drawing on anthropology to understand how we relate to products.[14] We need to know how they are used. Gift purchases are very different from products purchased for self use. Companies want to know how to establish long-lasting relationships with consumers. This interest in the period after a purchase makes the study of consumers a circular rather than linear activity. People's attitudes and lifestyles are influenced by past purchases, and each passage through awareness, interest, desire and action influences all other purchase decisions.

Business-to-business markets

All marketing ends with consumers, yet most marketing and sales are from business to business. Chapter 8 examines such markets. The reason why business-to-business markets are greater than consumer markets is the number of stages a product goes through from being a raw material or produce to the final consumer. Even a simple product, such as a magazine bought at a kiosk, has passed through several stages. Foresters sell logs to a paper maker; the paper maker sells to a printer working under contract to a publisher. The magazines then go to a specialist wholesaler who delivers them to the retailer. Until the final purchase, all the transactions are business-to-business. Moreover, the number of business-to-business transactions does not end there. The forester will hire contract loggers and pay a company to transport the logs to the paper maker; lawyers draw up contracts between the businesses involved. Each business will use commercial banks and maybe consultants to help them perform better.

Business-to-business marketing is not solely about commercial enterprise. Buyers and sellers are often governments and public-sector organisations, like schools or hospitals or charities. All share the same features in having complex buying processes involving many people with different motives who may come and go as the buying process continues. There are professional buyers and negotiators in the buying process, but many other actors play a role and the desires of the individuals concerned vary. Additionally, business-to-business markets are often international and involve overseas governments. Each person in a business-to-business market has the same emotions, needs and wants as a consumer, but they are overlaid with an extra layer of complexity.

Market research

Market research is a wide range of methods and tools used to help marketers understand markets. It is the subject of Chapter 9. Market research follows the breadth of consumer behaviour and business-to-business marketing in having a huge armoury of techniques to help with marketing questions. These range from anthropological studies where observers track a household's behaviour to routine mass surveys of thousands of retailers. The output can vary from descriptive analyses of a few customers' responses to a new product concept to mathematical models that forecast advertising effects or future demand.

Market research is such a specialised part of marketing that it is usually done by specialists, within either a marketer's organisation or an agency. Like advertising, market research is such a distinctive and important part of marketing that it has professional bodies, qualification and an industry of its own. Within that industry, marketers can choose among a whole range of suppliers with different skills. Marketers may not conduct their own market research but they commission it and act upon its results. The quality of the marketing decisions depends upon the quality of the marketing research on which they are based and its interpretation. It is, therefore, essential that marketers appreciate market research and what it can do.

Strategic marketing

Strategic marketing, the process of aligning the strengths of an organisation with groups of customers it can serve, is the subject of Part Four of this text. It affects the whole direction and future of an organisation, so knowledge of the macro- and microenvironments and the markets served needs to inform the process. Markets are also busy so that competitors are also trying to find ways of capturing more customers or retaining their own. Marketing strategy, therefore, has three interdependent parts: segmenting markets into groups that can be served, ways of developing advantageous relations with those customers, and strategies to handle competitors.

Segmentation and positioning

Customers are people, so differ considerably. Companies know that they cannot satisfy all consumers in a given market – at least, not all consumers in the same way. There are too many kinds of consumer with too many kinds of need, and some companies are in a better position than others to serve some groups of customers better. Consequently, companies use **market segmentation** to divide the total market. They then choose **market segments** and design strategies for profitably serving chosen segments. This process involves market segmentation, targeting and positioning. These are the subject of Chapter 10.

From the complexity of humans, it follows that there are many ways in which markets segment, and finding a new way of segmenting markets or a new segment can be the breakthrough that creates a market success. Simple criteria, like age, gender and social class, do little to inform marketers, since even among middle-class teenage boys there is a huge variety in interest: sporty football fanatics, video junkies, punk musicians, etc. Only multi-criteria approaches reveal segments such as GUPPYs (gay urban professionals), high-spending groups who start and nurture many new trends in music, fashion and entertainment and whose presence in a community is a measure of its creative potential.

Market targeting involves evaluating each market segment's attractiveness and selecting one or more segments to enter. An organisation evaluates its strengths relative to the competition and considers how many segments it can serve effectively. Finally, **market positioning** gives a product a clear, distinctive and desirable place in the minds of target consumers compared with competing products. A **product's position** is the place the product occupies in consumers' minds. If a product is perceived to be exactly like another product on the market, consumers would have no reason to buy it. Market positioning can be the key to success, such as a toy shop being marketed as the Early Learning Centre. Clearly, such an offering has to be more than just a name. To appeal to parents and their children, the store concentrates on educational toys and books, avoiding heavily merchandised (Barbie or Disney products) or electrical toys.

The company can position a product on only one important differentiating factor or on several. However, positioning on too many factors can result in consumer confusion or disbelief. Once the company has chosen a desired position, it must take steps to deliver and communicate that position to target consumers.

Market segmentation— Dividing a market into distinct groups of buyers with different needs, characteristics or behaviour, who might require separate products or marketing mixes.

Market segment—A group of consumers who respond in a similar way to a given set of marketing stimuli.

Market targeting— The process of evaluating each market segment's attractiveness and selecting one or more segments to enter.

Market positioning— Arranging for a product to occupy a clear, distinctive and desirable place relative to competing products in the minds of target consumers. Formulating competitive positioning for a product and a detailed marketing mix.

Product's position—The way the product is defined by consumers on important attributes – the place the product occupies in consumers' minds relative to competing products.

Relationship marketing

Marketing management's crucial task is to create profitable relationships with customers. Chapter 11 explores how to build those relationships. Until recently, customer relationship management was defined narrowly as a customer database management activity. By this definition, it involves managing detailed information about individual customers and carefully managing customer contacts in order to maximise customer loyalty. More recently, however, relationship management has taken on a broader meaning. In this broader sense, relationship management is the overall process of building and maintaining profitable customer relationships by delivering superior customer value and satisfaction. Thus, today's companies are going beyond designing strategies to *attract* new customers and create

This BD business-to-business ad shows many aspects of marketing at work. It positions the company and its social responsibility awareness of AIDS in Africa and the company's relationship with the International AIDS Vaccine Initiative (IAVA).
SOURCE: Becton, Dickinson and Company © 2003. Photo © Richard Lord.

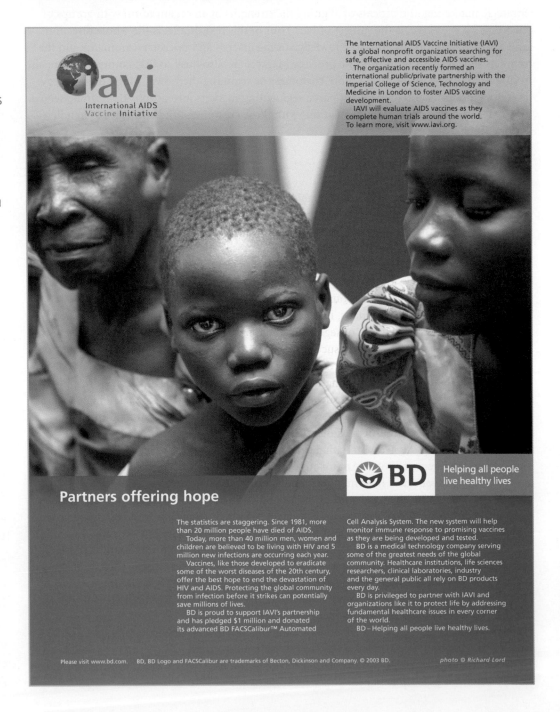

transactions with them. They are using customer relationship management to *retain* current customers and build profitable, long-term *relationships* with them. The new view is that marketing is the science and art of finding, retaining, *and* growing profitable customers. Companies are also realising that losing a customer means losing more than a single sale. It means losing the entire stream of purchases that the customer would make over a lifetime of patronage.

The key to building lasting customer relationships is to create superior customer value and satisfaction. To gain an advantage, the company must offer greater value to chosen target segments, either by charging lower prices than competitors or by offering more benefits to justify higher prices. However, if the company positions the product as *offering* greater value, it must *deliver* greater value. Effective positioning begins with actually *differentiating* the company's marketing offer so that it gives consumers more value than is offered by the competition. Satisfied customers are more likely to be loyal customers, and loyal customers are more likely to give the company a larger share of their business.

Competitive strategy

Providing excellent value and customer service is a necessary but not sufficient means of succeeding in the marketplace. Besides embracing the needs of consumers, marketing strategies must build an advantage over the competition. The company must consider its size and industry position, and then decide how to position itself to gain the strongest possible competitive advantage. Chapter 12 explains how to do this.

The design of competitive marketing strategies begins with competitor analysis. The company constantly compares the value and customer satisfaction delivered by its products, prices, channels and promotion with those of its close competitors. In this way, it can discern areas of potential advantage and disadvantage. The company must formally or informally monitor the competitive environment to answer these and other important questions: Who are our competitors? What are their objectives and strategies? What are their strengths and weaknesses? How will they react to different competitive strategies we might use?

Which competitive marketing strategy a company adopts depends on its industry position. A firm that dominates a market can adopt one or more of several **market leader** strategies. Well-known leaders include Nescafé, Perrier, Swatch, Chanel, Johnnie Walker, Coca-Cola, McDonald's, Marlboro, Komatsu (large construction equipment), Sony, Nokia, Lego and Shell.

Market challengers are runner-up companies that aggressively attack competitors to get more market share. For example, Lexus challenges Mercedes, Adidas challenges Nike, and Airbus challenges Boeing. The challenger might attack the market leader, other firms of its own size, or smaller local and regional competitors. Some runner-up firms will choose to follow rather than challenge the market leader. Firms using **market follower** strategies seek stable market shares and profit by following competitors' product offers, prices and marketing programmes. Smaller firms in a market, or even larger firms that lack established positions, often adopt **market nicher** strategies. They specialise in serving market niches that large competitors overlook or ignore. Market nichers avoid direct confrontations with the big companies by specialising along market, customer, product or marketing-mix lines. Through clever niching, low-share firms in an industry can be as profitable as their large competitors. Two regions of Europe are particularly strong in cultivating strong niche players: Germany for medium-sized specialist engineering firms and northern Italy's fashion industry.

The marketing mix

Once the company has chosen its overall competitive marketing strategy, it is ready to begin planning the details of the marketing mix. The marketing mix, one of the dominant ideas in modern marketing, is covered in Parts Five to Eight of this book.

Market leader—The firm in an industry with the largest market share; it usually leads other firms in price changes, new product introductions, distribution coverage and promotion spending.

Market challenger—A runner-up firm in an industry that is fighting hard to increase its market share.

Market follower—A runner-up firm in an industry that wants to hold its share without rocking the boat.

Market nicher—A firm in an industry that serves small segments that the other firms overlook or ignore.

Figure 1.7 The four Ps:
the marketing mix

Marketing mix			
Product	**Promotion**	**Price**	**Place**
Variety	Advertising	List price	Channels
Quality	Promotions	Discounts	Coverage
Design	Personal selling	Allowances	Assortments
Features	Publicity	Payment period	Locations
Brand name		Credit terms	Inventory
Packaging			Transport
Services			
Warranties			

Target market

Marketing mix—The set of controllable tactical marketing tools – product, price, place and promotion – that the firm blends to produce the response it wants in the target market.

Product—Anything that can be offered to a market for attention, acquisition, use or consumption that might satisfy a want or need. It includes physical objects, services, persons, places, organisations and ideas.

Price—The amount of money charged for a product or service, or the sum of the values that consumers exchange for the benefits of having or using the product or service.

Promotion—Activities that communicate the product or service and its merits to target customers and persuade them to buy.

Place—All the company activities that make the product or service available to target customers.

The **marketing mix** is the set of controllable tactical marketing tools that the firm blends to produce the response it wants in the target market. The marketing mix consists of everything the firm can do to influence the demand for its product. The many possibilities gather into four groups of variables known as the 'four Ps': product, price, place and promotion.[15] Figure 1.7 shows the marketing tools under each P.

Product means the totality of 'goods and services' that the company offers the target market. The product is the subject of the three chapters in Part Five of this book. The Honda Civic 'product' is nuts, bolts, spark plugs, pistons, headlights and many other parts. Honda offers several Civic styles and dozens of optional features. The car comes fully serviced, with a comprehensive warranty and financing that is as much a part of the product as the exhaust pipe. Increasingly, the most profitable part of the business for car companies is the loan that they offer to car buyers.

Price is what customers pay to get the product. It is covered in this book's Part Six. Honda suggests retail prices that its dealers might charge for each car, but dealers rarely charge the full asking price. Instead, they negotiate the price with each customer. They offer discounts, trade-in allowances and credit terms to adjust for the current competitive situation and to bring the price into line with the buyer's perception of the car's value.

Promotion means activities that communicate the merits of the product and persuade target customers to buy it. Part Seven of this book devotes three chapters to marketing communications. Honda spends millions on advertising each year to tell consumers about the company and its products. Dealership salespeople assist potential buyers and persuade them that a Honda is the car for them. Honda and its dealers offer special promotions – sales, cash rebates, low financing rates – as added purchase incentives.

Place includes company activities that make the product available to target consumers. Place is covered in the final Part Eight of this book. Honda maintains a body of independently owned dealerships that sell the company's cars. They select dealers carefully and support them strongly. The main dealers keep a stock of Hondas, demonstrate them to potential buyers, negotiate prices, close sales, arrange finance, and service the cars after the sale.

An effective marketing programme blends the marketing mix elements into a coordinated programme designed to achieve the company's marketing objectives. The marketing mix constitutes the company's tactical toolkit for establishing strong positioning in target markets. However, note that the four Ps represent the sellers' view of the marketing tools available for influencing buyers. From a consumer viewpoint, each marketing tool must deliver a customer benefit. One marketing expert suggests that companies should view the four Ps as the customer's four Cs:[16]

Four Ps	Four Cs
Product	Customer needs and wants
Price	Cost to the customer
Place	Convenience
Promotion	Communication

Winning companies are those that meet customer needs economically and conveniently and with effective communication.

This campaign presents the whole marketing mix: the promotion shows the product, its price and the place to buy it.
SOURCE: HMV Group Ltd.

Summary

Today's successful companies – whether large or small, for-profit or non-profit, domestic or global – share a strong focus and a heavy commitment to marketing. Many people think of marketing as only selling or advertising. However, marketing combines many activities – marketing research, product development, distribution, pricing, advertising, personal selling and others – designed to sense, serve and satisfy consumer needs while meeting the organisation's goals. Marketing seeks to attract new customers by promising superior value, and to keep current customers by delivering satisfaction.

We defined marketing as *a social and managerial process by which individuals and groups obtain what they need and want through creating and exchanging products and value with others*. The core concepts of marketing are *needs*, *wants* and *demands*; *products* and *services*; *value*, *satisfaction* and *quality*; *exchange*, *transactions* and *relationships*; and *markets*. Wants are the form assumed by human needs when shaped by culture and individual personality. When backed by buying power, wants become demands. People satisfy their needs, wants and demands with products and services.
A product is anything that can be offered to a market to satisfy a need, want or demand. Products also include services and other entities such as persons, places, organisations, activities and ideas.

We explained the relationships between customer value, satisfaction and quality. In deciding which products and services to buy, consumers rely on their perception of relative value. *Customer value* is the difference between the values the customer gains from owning and using a product and the costs of obtaining and using the product. *Customer satisfaction* depends on a product's perceived performance in delivering value relative to a buyer's expectations. Customer satisfaction is closely linked to *quality*, leading many companies to adopt *total quality management (TQM)* practices. Marketing occurs when people satisfy their needs, wants and demands through exchange. Beyond creating short-term exchanges, marketers need to build long-term relationships with valued customers, distributors, dealers and suppliers.

We then defined marketing management and examined how marketers manage demand and build profitable customer relationships. *Marketing management* is the analysis, planning, implementation and control of programmes designed to create, build and maintain beneficial exchanges with target buyers for the purpose of achieving organisational objectives. Marketing is at times also concerned with changing or even reducing demand. Beyond designing strategies to *attract* new customers and create *transactions* with them, today's companies are focusing on *retaining* current customers and building lasting relationships through offering superior customer value and satisfaction.

The five marketing management philosophies were compared. The *production concept* holds that consumers favour products that are available and highly affordable; management's task is to improve production efficiency and bring down prices. The *product concept* holds that consumers favour products that offer the most quality, performance and innovative features; thus, little promotional effort is required. The *selling concept* holds that consumers will not buy enough of the organisation's products unless it undertakes a large-scale selling and promotion effort. The *marketing concept* holds that achieving organisational goals depends on determining the needs and wants of target markets and delivering the desired satisfactions more effectively and efficiently than competitors do. The *societal marketing concept* holds that the company should determine the needs, wants and interests of target markets. Generating customer satisfaction *and* long-run societal well-being are the keys to achieving both the company's goals and its responsibilities.

Finally, the marketing process linked together the full range of marketing activities covered in the remainder of this book. *Strategy, marketing and planning* views marketing as part of a wider organisation where marketing is just one activity that helps deliver customer value. Marketing, and all other functions, are driven by an organisation's mission and vision. Chief among strategic marketing decisions is the choice among the portfolio of activities that a company can pursue. The relationship between marketing and other business functions is as critical to success as is the organisation of marketing.

Marketing exists within a *macroenvironment* of political, economic, social and technological issues that greatly influence markets. Closer to a marketer is the *microenvironment* that is particular to a company. Although the macro- and microenvironments are always in flux and changing, there are three major trends that are hugely important to marketing. These are the development of the Internet and *e-marketing, globalisation,* and *the social environment and social responsibility.*

Customers are central to marketing activity. All marketing activity ends with the consumers. In trying to understand them, marketers draw on ideas from all areas of human knowledge. The study flows from understanding lifestyles, attitudes and behaviour before there is the *need* or *want* for a product or service. It examines the processes that lead to an *exchange* and behaviour after a purchase.

Most marketing is from *business to business.* Business-to-business buying is more complex than consumer buying because of the number of influences on corporate decisions. This variety and complexity of business-to-business buying is made greater by government and international involvement.

Marketing research is a wide range of analysis tools. The variety of these activities is huge and the technical requirements are so varied that marketing research is a distinct sub-profession of marketing.

Marketing strategy aligns an organisation with a group of customers whom it can serve better than its competitors do. *Market segmentation* breaks a market into groups of similar customers. *Target markets* are chosen from among the market segments and *market positioning* is used to form favourable associations in customers' minds. No longer does marketing focus on a single transaction but now it seeks to establish relationships. *Relationship marketing* depends upon knowing customers and providing value. *Competitive strategy* recognises that an organisation needs to address competitors' reactions in developing a marketing strategy. Successful marketing strategy gives customers value in ways that competitors find hard to match.

Marketing is implemented through the four Ps of the *marketing mix*: *product, promotion, price* and *place.* Each of the Ps has many facets and poses a myriad of alternatives. The marketing strategy guides the choice among the marketing mix so that it provides customer value.

Discussing the issues

1. Discuss why you should study marketing.

2. As the preview case implies, the marketing efforts of organisations seek to fulfil consumer needs. How genuine are the needs targeted by Nike's marketing efforts? Critically evaluate the role that marketing plays in satisfying human desires.

3. What is the single biggest difference between the marketing concept and the production, product and selling concepts? Which concepts are easiest to apply in the short run? Which concept can offer the best long-term success?

4. Using practical examples, discuss the key challenges facing companies in the twenty-first century. What actions might marketers take to ensure they continue to survive and thrive in the new connected world of marketing?

5. According to economist Milton Friedman, 'Few trends could so thoroughly undermine the very foundations of our free society as the acceptance by corporate officials of a social responsibility other than to make as much money for their stockholders as possible.' Do you agree or disagree with Friedman's statement? What are some drawbacks of the societal marketing concept?

Applying the concepts

1. Go to a fast food restaurant and order a meal. Note the questions you are asked, and observe how special orders are handled. Next, go to a restaurant on your college or university campus and order a meal. Note the questions you are asked here, and observe whether special orders are handled the same way as they are at the fast food restaurant.

    ■ Did you observe any significant differences in how orders are handled?
    ■ Consider the differences you saw. Do you think the restaurants have different marketing management philosophies? Which is closest to the marketing concept? Is one closer to the selling or production concept?
    ■ What are the advantages of closely following the marketing concept? Are there any disadvantages?

2. Take a trip to a shopping centre. Choose a category of store, such as department stores, shoe shops, bookshops, women's clothing shops and so forth. List the competing shops in each category, walk past them and quickly observe their merchandise and style. Note how the shops are decorated and how well they are located. Note what other shops are close to them and how close they are to their competitors.

    ■ Are the competing shops unique, or could one pretty much substitute for another? What does this say about the overall goals that the shopping centre is fulfilling?
    ■ Consider the attitudes of the shoppers you saw. Did some apparently find shopping a pleasure, while others found it a bother?
    ■ A major goal for marketing is to maximise consumer satisfaction. Discuss the extent to which the shopping centre serves this goal.

    Now, visit online retailers in the same category as the bricks and mortar shop you chose.

    ■ Note the categories of merchandise and store layout and comment on the overall goals that the online retailer is fulfilling. What are the major differences between a traditional and an electronic retailer?
    ■ To what extent is the shopping experience similar or different across the traditional and online shopping environments?
    ■ Contrast the ways in which the two shopping formats seek to maximise consumer satisfaction. What advantages have they over one another?

References

1. Ore Beaverton, 'Nike battles backlash from overseas sweatshops', *Marketing News* (9 November 1999), p. 14; Uta Harnischfeger, 'Adidas reports sharp nine-month profit fall', *Financial Times* (3 November 2000), p. 28; 'Thanks, Mike: Phil Knight on Michael Jordan's retirement', Nike press release, www.nikebiz.com (2004); and Nike's Web page at www.nike.com (September 2004).

2. Peter F. Drucker, *Management: Tasks, responsibilities, practices* (New York: Harper & Row, 1973), pp. 64–5.

3. Sam Hill and Glenn Rifkin, *Radical Marketing* (New York: Harper Business, 1999).

4. Ralph Waldo Emerson offered this advice: 'If a man . . . makes a better mousetrap . . . the world will beat a path to his door.' Several companies, however, have built better mousetraps yet failed. One was a laser mousetrap costing $1,500. Contrary to popular assumptions, people do not automatically learn about new products, believe product claims, or willingly pay higher prices.

5. For more on customer satisfaction see Regina Fazio Marcuna, 'Mapping the world of customer satisfaction', *Harvard Business Review* (May–June), p. 30; David M. Szymanski, 'Customer satisfaction: a meta-analysis of the empirical evidence', *Academy of Marketing Science Journal* (Winter 2001), pp. 16–35; Claes Fornell, 'The science of satisfaction', *Harvard Business Review* (March–April 2001), pp. 120–1.

6. See Mary M. Long and Leon G. Schiffman, 'Consumption values and relationships', *Journal of Consumer Marketing* (2000), p. 241; Naras V. Eechambadi, 'Keeping your existing customers loyal', *Interaction Solutions* (February 2002).

7. Barry Farber and Joyce Wycoff, 'Customer service: evolution and revolution', *Sales and Marketing Management* (May 1991), p. 47; Kevin Lawrence, 'How to profit from customer complaints', *The Canadian Manager* (Fall 2000), pp. 25, 29.

8. Gary Hamel and C.K. Prahalad, 'Seeing the future first', *Fortune* (5 September 1994), pp. 64–70. Also see Anthony W. Ulwick, 'Turning customer input into innovation', *Harvard Business Review* (January 2002), pp. 91–7.

9. Stanley Fischer, 'Globalisation and its challenges', *American Economic Review*, **93**, 2 (May 2003).

10. For some insights see 'Digital radio: boxing clever', *The Economist* (28 June 2003), p. 32; 'Outsourcing in India', *The Economist* (23 August 2003), pp. 53–4; Khozem Merchant, 'Outsourcing', *Financial Times* (3 June 2003), p. 9; James Mackintosh and Richard McGregor, 'A leap over the cliff: are the big profits to be made in China blinding foreign carmakers to the risks ahead?', *Financial Times* (25 August 2003), p. 15.

11. Susanna Voyle, 'Online, instore, in profit and now in the US', *Financial Times* (30 June 2001); Geoffrey Nain, 'Customers become a reality in web based shopping malls', *Financial Times* (5 February 2003).

12. Naomi Klein, *No Logo: Taking aim at the brand bullies* (Flamingo, 2001); Eric Schlosser, *Fast Food Nation: What the all American meal is doing for the world* (Penguin, 2002).

13. World Trade Organisation (www.wto.com); 'Liberty's great advance – special supplement: a survey of capitalism and democracy', *The Economist* (28 June 2003), pp. 4–7.

14. Mark Ritson and Richard Elliott, 'Social issues of advertising: an ethnographic study of adolescent advertising audiences', *Journal of Consumer Research*, **24** (December 1999).

15. The four-P classification was first suggested by E. Jerome McCarthy, *Basic Marketing: A managerial approach* (Homewood, IL: Irwin, 1960). For more discussion of this classification scheme, see T.C. Melewar and John Saunders, 'Global corporate visual identity systems: using an extended marketing mix', *European Journal of Marketing*, **34**, 5/6 (2000), pp. 538–50; Christian Gronroos, 'Keynote paper: From marketing mix to relationship marketing – towards a paradigm shift in marketing', *Management Decision*, **35**, 4 (1997), pp. 322–39.

16. Robert Lauterborn, 'New marketing litany: four Ps passé; C-words take over', *Advertising Age* (1 October 1990), p. 26.

WEB RESOURCES

For additional classic case studies and Internet exercises, visit www.pearsoned.co.uk/kotler

Concluding concept 1
KitKat: Have a break . . .

SYLVIE LAFORET
Sheffield University

ANDY HIRST
Loughborough University

Sonia Ng sat down to have a cup of tea with her friend, David Johnson, in the company's dimly lit canteen in York, England. She unwrapped the bright red paper band from a KitKat, then ran a finger down the foil between the two biscuits. She snapped the biscuits apart, handed one to David and sighed: 'This KitKat is not going to be like any I have eaten before.' As a new assistant brand manager, Sonia had to prepare the brand plan for KitKat. It was a great break for her as KitKat was the company's top confectionery brand. Her first action was to gather what information she could about the brand, then talk to managers who knew about it.

Rowntree launched KitKat in August 1935 as 'Chocolate Crisp'. Renamed twice – in 1937 as 'KitKat Chocolate Crisp' and in 1949 as 'KitKat' – by 1950 it was Rowntree's biggest brand and it has remained so ever since. The name KitKat has favourable onomatopoeic qualities that help the association of the wafer biscuit with a dry, soft snapping or cracking, as of the biscuit being broken or bitten. Other Rowntree brands include Rowntree's Fruit Pastilles (launched 1881), Rowntree's Fruit Gums (1893), Black Magic (1933), Aero (1935), Dairy Box (1936), Smarties (1937), Polo (1948) and After Eight (1962).

Rowntree is a large exporter of chocolate and sugar confectionery, selling to over 120 countries. The most important markets are Europe and the Middle East. Besides the UK, the European markets include France, Germany, Belgium, Holland, Italy and Ireland. The chocolate biscuit countline (CBCL) market is not as large in the rest of Europe as it is in the UK. The proportions of KitKat volume sales are 67 per cent for the UK, 10.6 for Germany and 5.6 for France. And over the last decade overseas markets have grown by more than 50 per cent.

> 'This KitKat is not going to be like any I have eaten before', she said.

Net operating profits, return on capital employed (ROCE) and market shares drive the company. Each product group has objectives. The company has a cascade system so that each brand has its objectives as well. Each has a brand plan – business plans for each brand. One of the strategic objectives is to increase sales across the European markets. Often the marketing managers are not always able to put in capital to supply across Europe. To do this the company has a penetration strategy, which means that the margins are lower, and this has a depressing effect on the group's ROCE.

The company's long-term aims are to become the clear leader in the UK confectionery industry and to generate real growth in the profitability and productivity of its confectionery business. It also aims to increase the efficiency of its supply chain and so improve customer service.

Business strategy

The company's strategy is to pursue the company's objectives rather than to defend its position against competitors. For example, some countlines are 'below threshold size'. The objective for these is to improve the performance up to the threshold level. Rod Flint, the director of J. Walter Thompson, which is responsible for KitKat's advertising, comments: 'Their objective is not always driven by the stock market. They are highly global in their approach now, since they are also organising their European marketing department.'

Basic principles drive the company's brand strategy. It believes in offering the consumer value for money. It also believes in developing long-term brands and aims to differentiate its products from one another within the brand portfolio, which the company thinks will offer a competitive advantage over those of its competitors. The company works to ensure that its brands maintain clear positions in order to prevent cannibalisation. Up to now, the best way to achieve this has been stand-alone product brands, as opposed to umbrella brands. More recently, however, the cost of establishing new brands has increased very dramatically. The company is continually looking for ways to leverage the brand across the confectionery business and other product

Chapter 1 Marketing now

categories. Part of the company's brand policy is also to dedicate significant sums of money to advertising and promotions. This helps to build customer loyalty and block the entrance of new competitors. On average, 10 per cent of the sales value of the brand goes on advertising and promotions.

KitKat

When launched, KitKat entered a market already dominated by Cadbury's Dairy Milk. In fact KitKat's white and red end-to-end wrapping was designed to differ from Dairy Milk's side-to-side purple wrapping. From its beginning, KitKat was positioned as both a confectionery and a snack. It is now positioned halfway between a snack and an indulgence. In the consumers' eyes, however, KitKat is essentially a snack product, and its slogan 'Have a break, have a KitKat' is widely known through long-running ads on TV and in other media.

The KitKat brand has two formats in the UK. The two-finger format is bought in multipacks (packs of eight or more) at large grocers by parents for their children. In contrast, the four-finger format is bought individually by 16–24-year-olds for their consumption (Exhibit 1.2). The two-finger format's £112m (€184m) annual sales is part of the £535m per annum CBCL sector whose sales are for non-personal and 'family' consumption, as well as for snack and kids' consumption. The four-finger format is part of the £1,865m per annum general chocolate countline sector whose products are for personal consumption, broad usage and the 'adults' and 'self-eats' categories. The four-finger format was the main volume format, but its £96m sales have been overtaken by the two-finger format as the grocery sector rose at the expense of the CTNs (confectioner/tobacconist/newsagent). About 18 per cent of KitKat two-finger's volume goes through cash-and-carry to CTN, compared with 80 per cent of the four-finger format.

The company divides the chocolate market into three categories: chocolate box assortments (a gift-oriented marketplace), the countline market (a 'self-eat' market, e.g. KitKat four-finger) and CBCL, a sector that the company created. KitKat is marketed as a countline product in its four-finger format and as a CBCL in its two-finger format. This helped KitKat cover two sections in stores, one selling confectionery and the other selling biscuits.

Exhibit 1.2 **CBCL competitor performance**

Manufacturer	% share	% change year on year
Rowntree	25.3	−2.6
United Biscuits	17.4	−15.7
Jacobs Bakery	12.0	−1.5
Mars Confectionery	3.3	−14.0
Burtons	7.1	−14.3
Thomas Tunnocks	3.8	−3.5
Fox's	7.8	51.8
Others	5.7	3.6
Cadbury	2.2	n/a
Private label	15.3	25.6
Total market		0.9

SOURCE: AGB Superpanel.

Exhibit 1.3 **KitKat sales by pack and sector: tonnes (change over last five years)**

	Two-finger			Four-finger	
	Singles	Multipacks	Other	Singles	Multipacks
Multiple retail	50 (0%)	21,200 (13%)	50 (−50%)	1,900 (6%)	3,600 (31%)
Wholesale/ independent	650 (−41%)	1,950 (−2%)	50 (−75%)	13,950 (15%)	150 (−40%)

SOURCES: Internal.

The reason for the promotion of KitKat as a CBCL is the growing power of the multiple grocers (Exhibit 1.3). There has been a shift from a less structured retail sector into multiple businesses that are sophisticated and powerful. The company produces different packs for the multiple grocers and the independent sector. This avoids direct price and value comparison by the consumer and, therefore, restricts the power of the multiple retailers in their negotiations to increase their profitability.

KitKat two-finger is market leader with 19.5 per cent of the CBCL market (Exhibit 1.4). KitKat's nearest competitors are Mars Bars and Twix, both Mars products. Twix was launched as a countline product, but is now marketed as single fingers in the multipack format in the CBCL category. KitKat two-finger's main CBCL competitors are United Biscuits and Jacobs; in the general chocolate countline category, KitKat four-finger's main competitors are Mars and Cadbury.

Exhibit 1.4 CBCL brand performance

	% share (expenditure)	% change (year on year)
KitKat 2-finger	19.5	2.5
Penguin	8.8	7.4
Club	9.0	−7.7
Twix	3.3	−13.6
Rocky	4.1	159.3
Blue Riband	2.7	−4.0
Breakaway	2.7	−7.9
Wagon Wheel	4.7	−15.3
Tunnocks CW	3.4	−2.1
Classic	2.4	−11.2
Trio	2.2	−5.3
Private label	15.3	25.6

SOURCE: AGB Superpanel.

Exhibit 1.5 Countline brand performance

	% share (expenditure)	% change (year on year)
Mars Bar	13.9	0.8
Snickers	7.5	−0.3
KitKat 4-finger	6.7	−0.1
Twix	4.9	0
Twirl	3.3	−0.2
Time Out	2.7	−0.3
Drifter	1.3	0

SOURCE: AC Nielsen (countlines and filled blocks excluding CBCL multis).

The market

The chocolate confectionery market is concentrated, stable and very competitive. The leading suppliers are Cadbury (28 per cent market share), Rowntree (25), Mars (21) and Terry's Suchard (5). KitKat has the biggest advertising expenditure in the UK confectionery market. The £1.5 billion confectionery snack market, including countlines and chocolate blocks, is 38 per cent of the confectionery market. This market has grown by 20 per cent over the past five years, following the rise in popularity of snacking. Growth in both the countline market and the CBCL sector has now stabilised. As market leader, KitKat has retained a price premium and set prices for its competitors to follow. There is a risk to volume if the market does not follow. The market share for KitKat four-finger was 7 per cent of the general countline market. KitKat four-finger had lost some of its market share to Mars Bar (Exhibit 1.5) and is a weak no. 3, competing with three strong Mars products: Mars Bars, Twix and Snickers.

New-product development, which fuelled countline growth, has seen a number of new entrants. Firstly, the CBCL market has seen the entrance of Fox's Rocky bar. Rocky has claimed 4.1 per cent of the market. Cadbury has made the second major new-product development. It launched the Fuse bar – a mixture of chocolate, fudge and raisins. It cost £7 million to create, sold 40 million bars in its first week and was becoming the second most popular chocolate bar in the UK.

Pressure will continue to be on the countline market as the population of 15–24-year-olds declines. The KitKat two-finger sales are biased towards the C1 and C2 socio-economic and the 35–44 age groups. There is also a high penetration of very young consumers, particularly in the 12–15 age group. The four-finger format has a smarter image, inclines more towards 'chocolate occasions' consumption, and is consumed on the street. Consumption is heavily biased towards female buyers. The two-finger format ads aim at the 35–44-year-olds through morning television. Children are not specifically targeted. The four-finger format ads target the 16–24-year-olds through TV and youth press. The ad strategy for this format is different from that of the two-finger. The company puts an emphasis on updating KitKat's brand image by making it appeal to the younger generation through advertising in trendy and young people's magazines and independent radio.

The promotions for the two-finger format are value- and grocery-trade-oriented (for example, 'one bar free' activity, or repeat purchase incentives). For the four-finger format, the promotions are different because of the different segments targeted (for example, 1p off). However, there is an annual pan-promotion for KitKat as a whole that consists of big promotions, price and emphasis on brand awareness. There is a price differentiation between the two formats. KitKat four-finger is 'twin-priced' in parallel with Twix, and 2p below the Mars Bar. This is because KitKat is 'snacky' and not as hunger satisfying as the Mars Bar. If the company deviated from this pricing strategy, its volume share might drop. The two-finger format is not as price-sensitive as the four-finger. As a market leader within the CBCL category, it can more or less dictate price. Thus its competitor Penguin is priced 2p below KitKat two-finger. According to KitKat's brand managers, 'The objective for KitKat is to maintain customer loyalty by being innovative, and to remain *the* number one UK confectionery brand.' There is evidence of relative brand loyalty for KitKat. However, people who buy KitKat two-finger will also be likely to buy other brands, such as Classic, Club Orange, Penguin, Twix, Blue Riband and Gold. According to Brian Ford, the brand manager for the KitKat two-finger: 'Although they have tried to differentiate the two formats of KitKat in its segmentation and positioning strategies, the consumer sees no difference in the total brand.'

In light of the recent developments, KitKat has worked hard to maintain its position as the market leader. When KitKat Orange was launched as a limited edition, the first flavour variant in its 59-year history, the success of the product was so phenomenal that customers were writing letters to have the product re-released. A second new mint variant has been even more popular in trials.

Competition

Competition is likely to come from small brands, grocery retailers' own labels and other lines coming into the UK. There is also a crossover between the chocolate countline and the CBCL sector. Cadbury has recently encroached into KitKat's 'Have a break' territory with Time Out – a bar aimed at the CBCL sector. Time Out aims to bridge the gap between chocolate snack bars, such as Twirl, and wafer-based snacks, such as KitKat. It will compete with KitKat and Twix and should take sales away from brands with a 'heavy sweet' product image, like Spira and Twix.

Competition from other European confectioners has intensified with the growth of discounters such as Aldi and Netto. This might lead to a price-cutting war in the multiple grocery sector, especially among KwikSave, Lo-Cost and Asda. Aldi is a particular concern because it is importing bags of KitKat minis from Germany. Although Rowntree sells many of its countlines as minis, it does not make or sell KitKat in that format. Besides losing it revenue, Aldi's KitKat minis cause other problems: first, large grocers, like Sainsbury and Tesco, now want supplies of minis like Aldi's; second, the biscuit and chocolate used to make the German KitKat are distinctly different from those used in Britain.

Outside the UK, the four-finger format sells more than the two-finger format. European retailers outside the UK also emphasise minis (Aldi imports only that form). Rowntree does sell minis in the UK, but these are very low-volume products and appear only in variety packs with other minis. The company does not see them as a threat to its existing brands as the volume of minis is relatively low in comparison.

The company is now producing to capacity. The problem is managing demand in the marketplace. 'We can't give them any more, so we use price to limit demand and to get maximum profit return on the amount we produce', explains Ford. In his opinion, this is easier for the two-finger format because it is the market leader in the CBCL category, but is less easy in the four-finger case. 'It is not the market leader in the chocolate count-line sector, therefore we cannot dictate price.'

Brand pressures

For generations Rowntree had succeeded in the marketplace by making highly differentiated products that the competition found hard to copy. This contrasted with Mars whose products were strong brands but easy to make. Recently the company's confidence had been battered by the failure of Secret, a countline that used a new process to spin chocolate threads round a caramel core. After two new production lines were built and the product heavily advertised using a highly atmospheric campaign based on a Secret Agent theme, the product failed in the marketplace and proved too expensive to make. As a failure, the Secret story came very close to the flop of an equally differentiated Savanna, a pyramid-shaped boxed chocolate, that had occurred a few years earlier. The company had also failed in their launch of the Italian market-leading boxed chocolate Baci on to the UK market. Targeted head-on against the successful Ferrero Rocher chocolates and given a powerful Italian theme (Verdi . . . Ferrari . . . Baci), customers had stuck to the established brand.

Following the failures, the new product emphasis had shifted to levering existing brands rather than developing new ones. One idea was to follow Mars' lead and launch a KitKat iced confectionery. Another was to launch KitKat Chunky, a thick, single finger of KitKat about the size of a Snickers bar. This would be a 'hunger satisfier' like Mars' market-leading countlines.

To fit the regulations across Europe, some KitKats produced have different chocolate from others. Although they taste different, most consumers cannot tell the difference. The management of so many internationally important brands limits the company's freedom of action outside the UK. The pricing relationships between, say, France, Germany and the UK need careful controlling. At the same time, the company needs to achieve its UK business objectives. The marketing of brands will be different because these brands are at different product life-cycle states in different markets. 'The UK is probably the most sophisticated confectionery market in Europe', claims Robertson. 'Therefore, for example, the company's advertising style for KitKat is not directly transferable to Germany. The German consumer does not understand the British sense of humour', explains Robertson. 'So, from the business perspective, there is a pulling together in Europe, while from the consumer perspective, there are still marked differences between different types of consumers, and that is the biggest problem.'

The packing used for KitKat in the UK is different from that used elsewhere. So KitKat exported to Germany does not have UK packaging and vice versa. Germany's KitKat is flow-wrapped, whereas the UK has a foil and band. This relatively expensive format appeared because of the early competition with Cadbury, whose market-leading milk chocolate bars had blue foil and a blue wrapper. To differentiate it from Cadbury, the KitKat pack is a silver foil with a visually strong red band wrapped end to end.

Standardisation to less expensive flow wrap had been resisted in the UK because of the ritualistic way that UK consumers eat KitKat. Often they eat KitKat socially over a cup of tea. When eating KitKat, many consumers first take off the red wrapper, then run a finger down the foil between two biscuits. With the top of the foil broken, the KitKat fingers are snapped off and then eaten one by one, just as KitKat's new assistant brand manager, Sonia Ng, did. Her job was to develop a brand plan for KitKat while the whole tradition of KitKat was being challenged. After a series of product failures top management had decided to revitalise the business by:

- focusing more on major brands, reducing the overall brand portfolio;
- using existing brands for innovation where possible;
- making sure that much more emphasis went into meeting customers' expectations, through improving performance versus price;
- boosting trade cooperation and becoming more category focused.

KitKat was one of five brands identified for innovation. After years of relatively minor development of KitKat, a senior product manager and the ad agency had 'dug out ideas from the drawers'. Among them was KitKat Chocolate, a bar made of pure chocolate but in the shape of a KitKat. The variant would be a direct attack on the Cadbury's Dairy Milk that was the market leader when KitKat was launched. As Sonia ritualistically consumed her KitKat she pondered that her new job was a great break, but not an easy one.

Questions

1. Has KitKat taken a marketing-oriented approach to developing its confectionery brand? What elements of marketing orientation, if any, are missing?
2. What is the situation facing KitKat: the strengths and weaknesses of the brand and the opportunities and threats it faces?
3. How and why are the KitKat two-fingers and four-fingers marketed differently?
4. What are the barriers to the brand's standardisation across Europe and should the company now move towards standardising its brand and packaging across Europe?
5. How would you describe the organisational structure of the company and its marketing department? In what alternative ways could the company organise the management of its wide range of confectionery?
6. Should the launch of KitKat Chocolate be once again rejected?

SOURCES: Adapted and prepared with assistance from: the advertising agency J. Walter Thompson, London; Nestlé Rowntree, York; and Nestec, Vevey, Switzerland and reference to Nicholas Whitaker, *Sweet Talk: A secret history of confectionery* (Victor Gollancz, London, 1988); Kamran Kashani (ed.), *A Virtuous Cycle: Innovation, consumer value, and communication* (European Brands Association, London, 2000); Nicholas Kochan (ed.), *The World's Greatest Brands* (Interbrand/ Macmillan Business, London, 2003) and kitkat.co.uk; names, statistics and some details have been changed for commercial reasons.

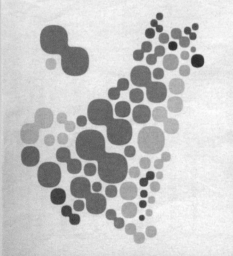
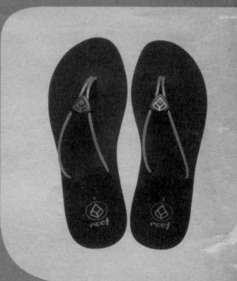

Click
to get back to boo

You have reached a static printed page.
You can bookmark it and save it as a favourite,
or download it for recycling. Or you can use
this link to www.boo.com where you'll find our
entire spring summer collection – and where
you can zoom, spin and try on the latest sports
and streetwear online.

Go to boo.com now
and we'll take £20
off your purchase.*

Enter code BCAD0018 at checkout.

boo.com
Spring Summer 2000

> In action, be primitive: in foresight, a strategist.

RENE CHAR

Strategic marketing

CHAPTER TWO

Chapter objectives

After reading this chapter, you should be able to:

- Explain company-wide strategic planning and its principal steps.
- Describe how companies develop mission statements and objectives.
- Explain how companies evaluate and develop their business portfolios.
- Explain marketing's role in strategic planning.
- Describe the marketing management process.
- Show how marketing organisations are changing.

Mini Contents List

◄ SOURCE: Advertising Archives
www.fashionmall.com.

Prelude case Poor little rich brands

'We prefer the Blue Circle Café to the Sotto Vento', exclaims Sten, the son of a Norwegian millionaire. The Sotto Vento is on the exclusive Costa Smeralda, and is Sardinia's most famous disco but, says Sten, 'is already being invaded by "the Rolex crowd".'

Sten has a point. While most people never aspire to owning a pair of €2,000 Gucci crocodile skin loafers, some do. According to Sten, those who want to show off such belongings go to Antibes or St Tropez. Costa Smeralda is different. The likes of Sylvester Stallone, Tom Cruise and Nicole Kidman go there so as not to be seen. They do not wear Gucci, Prada or Versace to display their success but because that is what their local store sells. Whereas luxury brands bestow glamour to ordinary mortals, the super rich who holiday at Costa Smeralda bestow glamour to the luxury brands.

> While most people never aspire to owning a pair of €2,000 Gucci crocodile skin loafers, some do.

Costa Smeralda retains its exclusivity by staying small, being well guarded and being accessible only by helicopter or cabin cruiser. However, life has recently not been so easy for the luxury brands that adorn its visitors. Many of the luxury-brand makers were founded in the 1950s by mainly Italian entrepreneur designers who are now ageing and whose families lack the design and management skills to run an increasingly competitive business. Luxury-goods sales have also been hit hard by the worldwide economic slowdown.

The 'new idea' for luxury-goods makers is to control the whole value chain, from manufacture to distribution, retailing and marketing. This comes expensive where advertising costs approach 35 per cent of sales and the rental of the prime retail site they need can cost up to €10,000 per square metre. Covering such costs requires the sales volume and working capital that many of the family firms lack. According to Cedric Magnelia, of Credit Suisse First Boston, gaining sales by brand extensions into such obvious areas as perfumes has been 'done to death'. There also seems little further to gain from the 'old idea' of designers creating stunning but hugely loss-making *haute couture* while money was made from licensees selling perfumes, handbags and scarves. Down-market associations easily taint luxury brands. TAG Heuer and Porsche both tried stretching their product ranges down-market. Both increased sales, tarnished their luxury brand names and retreated back up-market.

The formation of luxury conglomerates has become part of the 'new idea'. These offer negotiating power in obtaining retail space, skills in areas where brands could be extended, access to capital and managerial skills. Two of the biggest of these are French LVHM, who own Louis Vuitton, Christian Dior, Givenchy and others, and Swiss Richemont, whose brands include Cartier, Dunhill and Piaget. The recognition of the conglomerate strategy has led to a feeding frenzy as Gucci consume Italian shoemaker Sergio Rossi, and LVHM and Prada jointly share out Fendi with its famous Baguette handbag. Laurent Paichot, of the Federation of Swiss Watch Makers, thinks being bought by a conglomerate is the only alternative for many small watchmakers: 'Due to globalisation everything is expensive – especially advertising.' He continues, 'Bigger companies have the economic power to really push the product and consumers will buy from a brand they know well.'

However, in this industry, synergy is hard to find. Morgan Stanley Dean Witter's Claire Kent says 'cost savings in a takeover in this industry are spurious'. How can synergy be achieved in a market where the appeal is the idiosyncratic way products are designed, made and marketed? Hermès boasts that it takes them longer to make their Kelly bags than it takes BMW to assemble a car! Even where cost savings are easy and logical to find, they can endanger brands. Richemont is eager to clarify that Mont Blanc factories do not make Cartier pens.

LVHM's broad range and strength in the Japanese market have helped it weather the economic storm better than many of its competitors. Its performance contrasts with that of Gucci whose sales are heavily down because of merchandising errors and excessive time turning round Yves St Laurent, a struggling acquisition.

A few luxury-goods makers, such as Rolex, Mondane Watch and Prada, are holding out against the force of the 'new idea'. Mondane intends to remain a speciality watchmaker while Rolex is adamant that it will remain independent, although it seems unlikely that Sten will be wearing one.[1]

Questions

1. What makes a luxury good or service desirable?
2. Is the economic drive for scale inconsistent with consumers' desires in the €60 billion luxury-goods industry?
3. Does Sten's sneering at 'the Rolex crowd' suggest that Rolex is failing in its desire to remain an independent luxury-goods maker?

Introduction

Just like the luxury-goods makers in the prelude case, all companies need strategies to meet changing markets. No one strategy is best for all companies. Each company must find the way that makes most sense, given its situation, opportunities, objectives and resources. Marketing plays an important role in strategic planning. It provides information and other inputs to help prepare the strategic plan. Strategic planning is also the first stage of marketing planning and defines marketing's role in the organisation. The strategic plan guides marketing, which must work with other departments in the organisation to achieve strategic objectives.

Here we look at the three stages of strategic market planning: first, the strategic plan and its implications for marketing; second, the marketing process; and third, ways of putting the plan into action.

Strategic planning

Overview of planning

Many companies operate without formal plans. In new companies, managers are sometimes too busy for planning. In small companies, managers may think that only large corporations need planning. In mature companies, many managers argue that they have done well without formal planning, so it cannot be very important. They may resist taking the time to prepare a written plan. They may argue that the marketplace changes too fast for a plan to be useful – that it would end up collecting dust.[2]

Failing to plan means planning to fail. Moreover, formal planning yields benefits for all types of company, large and small, new and mature. It encourages systematic thinking. It forces the company to sharpen its objectives and policies, leads to better coordination of company efforts, and provides clearer performance standards for control. The argument that planning is less useful in a fast-changing environment makes little sense. The opposite is true: sound planning helps the company to anticipate and respond quickly to environmental changes, and to prepare better for sudden developments. Such planning could have helped Carrefour,[3] Europe's largest retailer, avoid their share price collapse after they were first dismissive of the impact of the Internet on their business and then announced a vague, €1 billion e-commerce strategy.[4]

Companies usually prepare annual plans, long-range plans and strategic plans:

- The **annual plan** is a short-term plan that describes the current situation, company objectives, the strategy for the year, the action programme, budgets and controls. For an oil company, such as BP, this is about maintaining profitability through the continuing Middle East crises and Europe's continued slow growth.

- The **long-range plan** describes the primary factors and forces affecting the organisation during the next several years. It includes the long-term objectives, the main marketing strategies used to attain them and the resources required. This long-range plan is reviewed and updated each year so that the company always has a current long-range plan. The company's annual and long-range plans deal with current businesses and how to keep them going. For BP the long-range plan looks at future oil supplies and strategies for emerging markets, such as China.

- The **strategic plan** involves adapting the firm to take advantage of opportunities in its constantly changing environment. It is the process of developing and maintaining a strategic fit between the organisation's goals and capabilities and its changing marketing

Annual plan—A short-term plan that describes the company's current situation, its objectives, the strategy, action programme and budgets for the year ahead, and controls.

Long-range plan—A plan that describes the principal factors and forces affecting the organisation during the next several years, including long-term objectives, the chief marketing strategies used to attain them and the resources required.

Strategic plan—A plan that describes how a firm will adapt to take advantage of opportunities in its constantly changing environment, thereby maintaining a strategic fit between the firm's goals and capabilities and its changing market opportunities.

opportunities. BP's use of its initials to represent Beyond Petroleum reflects that company's strategic view of its future, in which environmental issues are important and the era of the internal combustion engine declines.[5]

Strategic planning sets the stage for the marketing plan. It starts with its overall purpose and mission. These guide the formation of measurable corporate objectives. A corporate audit then gathers information on the company, its competitors, its market and the general environment in which the firm competes. A SWOT analysis gives a summary of the strengths and weaknesses of the company together with the opportunities and threats it faces. Next, headquarters decides what portfolio of businesses and products is best for the company and how much support to give each one. This helps to provide the strategic objectives that guide the company's various activities. Then each business and product unit develops detailed marketing and other functional plans to support the company-wide plan. Thus marketing planning occurs at the business-unit, product and market levels. It supports company strategic planning with more detailed planning for specific marketing opportunities. For instance Nestlé, the world's largest food manufacturer, develops an overall strategic plan at its headquarters in Vevey, Switzerland. Below that, each strategic group, such as confectionery, develops subordinate strategic plans. These feed into the strategic plan's national operations. At each level, marketing and other functional plans will exist. At the final level, brand plans cover the marketing of brands such as KitKat, Nescafé and Friskies Felix in national markets.

The planning process

Putting plans into action involves four stages: analysis, planning, implementation and control. Figure 2.1 shows the relationship between these functions, which are common to strategic planning, marketing planning or the planning for any other function.

■ *Analysis.* Planning begins with a complete analysis of the company's situation. The company must analyse its environment to find attractive opportunities and to avoid environmental threats. It must analyse company strengths and weaknesses, as well as current and possible marketing actions, to determine which opportunities it can best pursue. Analysis feeds information and other inputs to each of the other stages.

Figure 2.1 Market analysis, planning, implementation and control

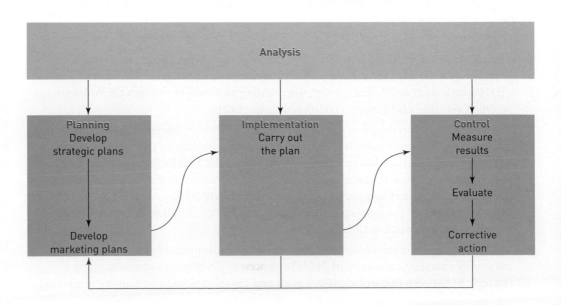

- *Planning.* Through strategic planning, the company decides what it wants to do with each business unit. Marketing planning involves deciding marketing strategies that will help the company attain its overall strategic objectives. Marketing, product or brand plans are at the centre of this.

- *Implementation.* Implementation turns strategic plans into actions that will achieve the company's objectives. People in the organisation who work with others, both inside and outside the company, implement marketing plans.

- *Control.* Control consists of measuring and evaluating the results of plans and activities, and taking corrective action to make sure objectives are being achieved. Analysis provides information and evaluations needed for all the other activities.

The strategic plan

The strategic plan contains several components: the mission, the strategic objectives, the strategic audit, SWOT analysis, portfolio analysis, objectives and strategies. All of these feed from and feed into marketing plans.

The mission

A mission states the purpose of a company. Firms often start with a clear mission held within the mind of their founder. Then, over time, the mission fades as the company acquires new products and markets. A mission may be clear, but forgotten by some managers. An extreme case of this was the Anglican Church Commissioners, who thought they had the 'Midas touch' when they started speculating on the international property market. They found out that markets go down as well as up and lost a third of the Church's ancient wealth in the process.[6] Other problems can occur when the mission may remain clear but no longer fits the environment. The luxury-goods firms in the prelude case are struggling with that problem.

When an organisation is drifting, the management must renew its search for purpose. It must ask, What business are we in? What do consumers value? What are we in business for? What sort of business are we? What makes us special? These simple-sounding questions are among the most difficult that the company will ever have to answer. Successful companies continuously raise these questions and answer them. Asking such basic questions is a sign of strength, not uncertainty.

Many organisations develop formal mission statements that answer these questions. A **mission statement** is a statement of the organisation's purpose – what it wants to accomplish in the larger environment. A clear mission statement acts as an 'invisible hand' that guides people in the organisation, so that they can work independently and yet collectively towards overall organisational goals.

Traditionally, companies have defined their business in product terms ('we manufacture furniture'), or in technological terms ('we are a chemical-processing firm'). But mission statements should be *market-oriented*.

What business are we in?

Asking this question helps. Market definitions of a business are better than product or technological definitions. Products and technologies eventually become outdated, but basic market needs may last for ever. A market-oriented mission statement defines the business based on satisfying basic customer needs. Thus Rolls-Royce is in the power business, not the aero-engine business. Visa's business is not credit cards, but allowing customers to exchange value – to exchange assets, such as cash on deposit or equity in a home, for virtually anything,

Mission statement—
A statement of the organisation's purpose – what it wants to accomplish in the wider environment.

Setting company objectives and goals. Michelin defines its mission as 'service to people and their transportation', rather than reducing its purpose to the mere production of tyres. This mission leads to specific business and marketing objectives. 3M has held on to its mission to be innovative through product generations.

SOURCE: (left) Michelin and Hjemmet Mortensen AS; (right) Advertising courtesy of 3M.

anywhere in the world. Creative 3M does more than just make adhesives, scientific equipment and healthcare products; it solves people's problems by putting innovation to work for them.

Who are our customers?

This is a probing question. Who are the customers of Rolls-Royce's new Trent aero-engine? At one level it is the airframers, like Boeing and European Airbus. If Rolls-Royce can get an airframer to launch a new aircraft with a Rolls-Royce engine, this saves development costs and makes early orders likely. Is it the airline or leasing companies that eventually buy the engines? They will certainly have to sell to them as well. Is it the pilot, the service crew or even the passenger? Unlike the competition, Rolls-Royce has a brand name that is synonymous with prestige and luxury.

What are we in business for?

This is a hard question for non-profit-making organisations. Do universities exist to educate students or to train them for industry? Is the pursuit of knowledge by the faculty the main reason for their existence? If so, is good research of economic value or is pure research better?

What sort of business are we?

This question guides the strategy and structure of organisations. Companies aiming at *cost leadership* seek efficiency. These firms, like Aldi or KwikSave, run simple, efficient organisations with careful cost control. These contrast with *differentiators*, like Sony, who aim to make profits by inventing products, such as the Walkman, whose uniqueness gives a competitive edge. *Focused* companies concentrate upon being the best at serving a well-defined target market. They succeed by tailoring their products or services to customers they know well. In Britain, Coutts & Co., a Royal Bank of Scotland subsidiary, does this by providing 'personal banking' to the very wealthy. Michael Porter[7] describes a fourth option that occurs if firms do not define how they are to do business: *stuck in the middle*.

Management should avoid making its mission too narrow or too broad. A lead-pencil manufacturer that says it is in the communication equipment business is stating its mission too broadly. A mission should be:

- *Realistic.* Singapore International Airlines is excellent, but it would be deluding itself if its mission were to become the world's largest airline.

- *Specific.* It should fit the company and no other. Many mission statements exist for public-relations purposes, so lack specific, workable guidelines. The statement 'We want to become the leading company in this industry by producing the highest-quality products with the best service at the lowest prices' sounds good, but it is full of generalities and contradictions. Such motherhood statements will not help the company make tough decisions.

- Based on *distinctive competencies.* Bang & Olufsen has the technology to build microcomputers, but an entry into that market would not take advantage of its core competencies in style, hi-fi and exclusive distribution.

- *Motivating.* It should give people something to believe in. It should get a 'Yeah!', not a yawn or a 'Yuck!'. A company's mission should not say 'making more sales or profits' – profits are only a reward for undertaking a useful activity. A company's employees need to feel that their work is significant and that it contributes to people's lives. Contrast the mission of Greenpeace, 'to ensure the ability of the Earth to nurture life in all its diversity', with the strategy of ABB, '[to] offer more value for customers while building a linear organization'.

Visions guide the best missions. A vision is a contagious dream, a widely communicated statement or slogan that captures the needs of the time. Sony's president, Akio Morita, wanted everyone to have access to 'personal portable sound', and his company created the Walkman. Richard Branson thought 'flying should be fun', so he founded Virgin Airlines. Julian Richer has become a business guru after making his Richer Sounds hi-fi dealer the 'Friendliest, cheapest, busiest', most profitable and productive in the industry.[8]

The company's mission statement should provide a vision and direction for the company for the next 10–20 years. It should not change every few years in response to each new turn in the environment. Still, a company must redefine its mission if that mission has lost credibility or no longer defines an optimal course for the company.[9] The hostile environment caused Siemens, the German electronics giant, to review its strategy. Its seven core statements (Figure 2.2) provided strong communications to drive its strategy, structure and style of management.

From mission to strategic objectives

The company's mission needs to be turned into strategic objectives to guide management. Each manager should have objectives and be responsible for reaching them. For example, its fertiliser business unit is one of International Minerals & Chemical Corporation's many activities. The fertiliser division does not say that its mission is to produce fertiliser. Instead, it says that its mission is to 'increase agricultural productivity'. This mission leads to a hierarchy of objectives, including business objectives and marketing objectives. The mission of

Figure 2.2 Siemens' seven core statements

Strategy	Competitive strength	Achieve a sustained leading position worldwide
Identity	Progress	Technological, social and marketing competences focused on progress
Entrepreneurial style	Will to lead	Agree on clear objectives and vigorously transform them into competitive advantage
Managers	Entrepreneurship	Managers and employees think and act as if it were their own company
Executive decision making	Speed	Faster decision making through integrated business functions
New organisation	Close to the customer	Marketing-oriented business functions create entrepreneurial freedom
Strength	Systems integration	Integrate competitive products into problem-solving systems

increasing agricultural productivity leads to the company's business objective of researching new fertilisers that promise higher yields. Unfortunately, research is expensive and requires improved profits to plough back into research programmes. So improving profits becomes another key business objective. Profits are improved by increasing sales or reducing costs. Sales increase by improving the company's share of the domestic market, or by entering new foreign markets, or both. These goals then become the company's current marketing objectives. The objective to 'increase our market share' is not as useful as the objective to 'increase our market share to 15 per cent in two years'. The mission states the philosophy and direction of a company, whereas the strategic objectives are measurable goals.

Strategic audit

'Knowledge is power': so stated Francis Bacon, the sixteenth-century philosopher, while according to the ancient Chinese strategist Sun Zi, 'The leader who does not want to buy information is inconsiderate and can never win.' The strategic audit covers the gathering of this vital information. It is the intelligence used to build the detailed objectives and strategy of a business. It has two parts: the external audit and the internal audit.

The **external audit** or marketing environment audit examines the macroenvironment and task environment of a company. EuroDisney's problems can be partly explained by an excessive faith in company strengths and too little attention being paid to the macroenvironment. French labour costs make the park much more expensive than in America, Europe's high travel costs add to guests' total bill, and the north European climate takes the edge off all-year-round operations. EuroDisney contrasts with the success of Center Parcs. This Dutch company's resort hotels offer north Europeans undercover health and leisure facilities that they can enjoy all year round.

The **internal audit** examines all aspects of the company. It covers the whole *value chain* described by Michael Porter.[10] It includes the primary activities that follow the flow of goods or services through the organisation: inbound logistics, operations, outbound logistics, sales and marketing, and after-sales services. In addition, it extends to the support activities on which the primary activities depend: procurement, technology development, human resource management and the infrastructure of the firm. These go beyond traditional marketing activities, but marketing strategy depends on all of them. A key to the Italian Benetton's

External audit—A detailed examination of the markets, competition, business and economic environment in which the organisation operates.

Internal audit—An evaluation of the firm's entire value chain.

54

Siemens pursues its mission by providing totally integrated automation technology to its business customers in the automotive industry.
SOURCE: Siemens VDO Automotive AG.

international success is a system that allows it to change styles and colours rapidly. Unlike traditional mass-clothing manufacturers, which have to order fabrics in colours and patterns over a year ahead of seasons, Benetton's design and manufacturing technology allows it to change within a season.

Reading financial statements is basic to understanding the state of a company and seeing how it is developing. The operating statement and the balance sheet are the two main financial statements used. The **balance sheet** shows the assets, liabilities and net worth of a

Balance sheet—A financial statement that shows assets, liabilities and net worth of a company at a given time.

marketing insights

2.1 Albumart.com: But will we make money?

Exhibit 2.1 shows the 2003 operating statement for Albumart.com, a start-up that has avoided the big bucks and bust of Boo.com and others. They market specialised picture frames designed to display 'album art'. They enable people to make a wall decoration by slotting an old favourite vinyl album or CD cover directly into the frame. This statement is for a retailer; the operating statement for a manufacturer would be somewhat different. Specifically, the section on purchases within the 'Cost of goods sold' area would be replaced by 'Cost of goods manufactured'.

Exhibit 2.1 Operating statement for Albumart.com for year ending 31 December 2003 (€)

Gross sales			325,000
less: Sales returns and allowances			25,000
Net sales			300,000
Cost of goods sold			
Beginning inventory, 1 January 2000, at cost		60,000	
Purchases	150,000		
plus: Freight-in	10,000		
Net cost of delivered purchases		160,000	
Cost of goods available for sale		220,000	
less: Ending inventory, 31 December 2000, at cost		45,000	
Total cost of goods sold			175,000
Gross margin			125,000
Expenses			
Selling expenses		50,000	
Administrative expenses		30,000	
General expenses		20,000	
Total expenses			100,000
Net profit			25,000

The outline of the operating statement follows a logical series of steps to arrive at the firm's €25,000 net profit figure:

Net sales	€300,000
Cost of goods sold	−€175,000
Gross margin	€125,000
Expenses	−€100,000
Net profit	€25,000

The first part details the amount that Albumart.com received for the goods sold during the year. The sales figures consist of three items: gross sales, returns or allowances, and net sales. *Gross sales* is the total amount charged to customers

...2.1

during the year for merchandise purchased from Albumart.com. Some customers returned merchandise. If the customer gets a full refund or full credit on another purchase, we call this a return. Other customers may decide to keep the item if Albumart.com will reduce the price. This is called an allowance. By subtracting returns and allowances from gross sales:

Gross sales	€325,000
Returns and allowances	−€25,000
Net sales	€300,000

The second part of the operating statement calculates the amount of sales revenue that Albumart.com retains after paying the costs of the merchandise. We start with the inventory in the store at the beginning of 2003. During the year, Albumart.com aim to buy €150,000 worth of frames. Albumart.com also has to pay an additional €10,000 to get the products delivered, giving the firm a net cost of €160,000. Adding the beginning inventory, the cost of goods available for sale amounted to €220,000. The €45,000 ending inventory on 31 December 2003 is then subtracted to come up with the €175,000 *cost of goods sold*.

The difference between what Albumart.com paid for the merchandise (€175,000) and what it sold it for (€300,000) is called the *gross margin* (€125,000).

In order to show the profit Albumart.com 'cleared' at the end of the year, we must subtract from the gross margin the expenses incurred while doing business. *Selling expenses* included two employees, advertising in music magazines and the cost of mailing the merchandise. Selling expenses totalled €50,000 for the year. *Administrative expenses* included the salary for an office manager, office supplies such as stationery and business cards, and miscellaneous expenses including an administrative audit conducted by an outside consultant. Administrative expenses totalled €30,000 in 1995. Finally, the *general expenses* of rent, utilities, insurance, and depreciation came to €20,000. Total expenses were therefore €100,000 for the year. By subtracting expenses (€100,000) from the gross margin (€125,000), we arrive at the *net profit* of €25,000 for Albumart.com during 2000. Not a lot, but not a loss.

company at a given time. The **operating statement** (also called profit-and-loss statement or income statement) is the more important of the two for marketing information. It shows company sales, cost of goods sold, and expenses during a specified time period. By comparing the operating statement from one time period to the next, the firm can spot favourable or unfavourable trends and take appropriate action. Marketing Insights 2.1 describes these statements in more detail and explains their construction.

Operating statement (profit-and-loss statement or income statement)— A financial statement that shows company sales, cost of goods sold and expenses during a given period of time.

SWOT analysis

SWOT analysis—A distillation of the findings of the internal and external audits which draws attention to the critical organisational strengths and weaknesses and the opportunities and threats facing the company.

SWOT analysis draws the critical strengths, weaknesses, opportunities and threats (SWOT) from the strategic audit. The audit contains a wealth of data of differing importance and reliability. SWOT analysis distils these data to show the critical items from the internal and external audits. The number of items is small for forceful communications, and they show where a business should focus its attention.

Opportunities and threats

Managers need to identify the main threats and opportunities that their company faces. The purpose of the analysis is to make the manager anticipate important developments that can have an impact on the firm. A large pet food division of a multinational company could list the following.

Opportunities

- *Economic climate.* Because of improved economic conditions, pet ownership is increasing in almost all segments of the population.
- *Demographic changes.* (1) Increasing single parenthood, dual-income families and ageing will increase the trend towards convenient pet foods (from wet to dry); and (2) the aged population will grow and increasingly keep pets as company.
- *Market.* The pet food market will follow the human market in the concern for healthy eating and pre-prepared luxury foods.
- *Technology.* New forms of pet food that are low in fat and calories, yet highly nutritious and tasty, will soon emerge. These products will appeal strongly to many of today's pet food buyers, whose health concerns extend to their pets.

Threats

- *Competitive activity.* A large competitor has just announced that it will introduce a new premium pet food line, backed by a huge advertising and sales promotion blitz.
- *Channel pressure.* Industry analysts predict that supermarket chain buyers will face more than 10,000 new grocery product introductions next year. The buyers accept only 38 per cent of these new products and give each one only five months to prove itself.
- *Demographic changes.* Increasing single parenthood and dual-income families will encourage the trends towards (1) pets that need little care (cats rather than dogs), and (2) smaller pets that eat less.
- *Politics.* European Union legislation will force manufacturers to disclose the content of their pet food. This will adversely affect the attractiveness of some ingredients like kangaroo and horsemeat.

Not all threats call for the same attention or concern – the manager should assess the likelihood of each threat and the potential damage each could cause. The manager should then focus on the most probable and harmful threats and prepare plans in advance to meet them.

Opportunities occur when an environmental trend plays to a company's strength. The manager should assess each opportunity according to its potential attractiveness and the company's probability of success. Companies can rarely find ideal opportunities that exactly fit their objectives and resources. The development of opportunities involves risks. When evaluating opportunities, the manager must decide whether the expected returns justify these risks. A trend or development can be a threat or an opportunity, depending on a company's

New Look. New Mood. New Times.

New: Meisterstück Sport
Chronograph Stainless Steel
Automatic with Rubber Strap
and Security Clasp

Meisterstück Solitaire
Stainless Steel
Doué Ballpoint Pen

THE ART OF WRITING YOUR LIFE
Writing Instruments · Watches · Leather · Jewellery · Eyewear

Montblanc Boutiques. 60/61 Burlington Arcade. 10/11 Royal Exchange. Canada Place, Canary Wharf.
Harrods, Knightsbridge. Selfridges, Oxford Street. Call 020 7663 4830 for further details and national stockists.

Mont Blanc competes in the
exquisite accessories market,
capitalising on its strength as a
maker of exclusive pens, to add
watches, men's fragrances and
other products to its range.
SOURCE: Mont Blanc and the
Advertising Archives.

strengths. The development of the steel-braced radial tyre was an opportunity for Michelin, which used its technological lead to gain market share. To the rest of the industry, the new technology was a threat because the tyre's longer life reduced total demand and the new technology made their plant obsolete.

Strengths and weaknesses

The strengths and weaknesses in the SWOT analysis do not list all features of a company, but only those relating to **critical success factors**. A list that is too long betrays a lack of focus and an inability to discriminate what is important. The strengths or weaknesses are *relative*, not absolute. It is nice to be good at something, but it can be a weakness if the competition is stronger. Mercedes is good at making reliable luxury cars with low depreciation, but this stopped being a strength when Honda's Acura and Toyota's Lexus beat Mercedes on all three fronts in the American market. The Japanese products were not cheap, but they were styled for the American market and came with all the extras that buyers of German luxury cars had to pay for. Finally, the strengths should be *based on fact*. In buying Skoda, VW has acquired a well-known brand name, but is the name a strength? A failure to understand true strengths can be dangerous. A well-known aircraft manufacturer for years promoted the quality of its after-sales service. Only after another company acquired it did it find out that its reputation was the worst in the industry.

A major pet food manufacturer could pitch the following strengths and weaknesses against the opportunities and threats.

Critical success factors—
The strengths and
weaknesses that most
critically affect an
organisation's success.
These are measured
relative to competition.

Strengths

- Market leader in the dry cat food market.
- Access to the group's leading world position in food technology.
- Market leader in luxury pet foods.
- The group's excellent worldwide grocery distribution.
- Pet food market leader in several big markets, including France, Italy, Spain and South America.

Weaknesses

- Number three in the wet pet food market.
- Excessive product range with several low-volume brands.
- Most brand names are little known, and are cluttered following acquisitions.
- Relatively low advertising and promotions budget.
- Product range needs many manufacturing skills.
- Poor store presence in several large markets: Germany, UK, USA and Canada.
- Overall poor profit performance.

The pet food company shows how some parts of the SWOT balance. The strengths in dry and luxury pet foods match demographic trends, so this looks like an opportunity for growth. Access to food technology should also help the company face changing consumer tastes and legislation. The weaknesses suggest a need for more focus. Dropping some uneconomic lines in the mass wet pet food market, simplifying the brand structure and concentrating on fewer manufacturing processes could release resources for developing the dry and luxury markets. By using its access to worldwide grocery distribution, the company could become profitable and focused.

The business portfolio

The **business portfolio** is the collection of businesses and products that make up the company. It is a link between the overall strategy of a company and those of its parts. The best business portfolio is the one that fits the company's strengths and weaknesses to opportunities in the environment. The company must (1) analyse its *current* business portfolio and decide which businesses should receive more, less or no investment, and (2) develop growth strategies for adding *new* products or businesses to the portfolio.

Analysing the current business portfolio

Portfolio analysis helps managers evaluate the businesses making up the company. The company will want to put strong resources into its more profitable businesses and phase down or drop its weaker ones. Financial Times-owned publishers Dorling Kindersley needed 'remedial surgery' to allow them to concentrate on their core business of illustrated books. In doing so they scaled back activities such as CD-ROM publishing, video production and door-to-door sales network.[11]

Management's first step is to identify the key businesses making up the company. These are strategic business units. A **strategic business unit** (SBU) is a unit of the company that has a separate mission and objectives, and which can be planned independently from other company businesses. An SBU can be a company division, a product line within a division, or sometimes a single product or brand.

The next step in business portfolio analysis calls for management to assess the attractiveness of its various SBUs and decide how much support each deserves. In some companies, this

Business portfolio— The collection of businesses and products that make up the company.

Portfolio analysis— A tool by which management identifies and evaluates the various businesses that make up the company.

Strategic business unit (SBU)— A unit of the company that has a separate mission and objectives and that can be planned independently from other company businesses. An SBU can be a company division, a product line within a division, or sometimes a single product or brand.

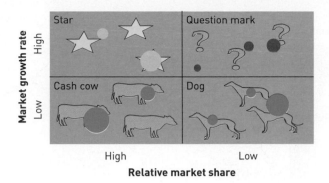

Figure 2.3 The BCG
growth–share matrix

occurs informally. Management looks at the company's collection of businesses or products and uses judgement to decide how much each SBU should contribute and receive. Other companies use formal portfolio-planning methods.

The purpose of strategic planning is to find ways in which the company can best use its strengths to take advantage of attractive opportunities in the environment. So most standard portfolio-analysis methods evaluate SBUs on two important dimensions: the attractiveness of the SBU's market or industry, and the strength of the SBU's position in that market or industry. The best-known portfolio-planning methods are from the Boston Consulting Group, a leading management consulting firm, and by General Electric and Shell.

The Boston Consulting Group box

Using the Boston Consulting Group (BCG) approach, a company classifies all its SBUs according to the *growth–share matrix* shown in Figure 2.3. On the vertical axis, *market growth rate* provides a measure of market attractiveness. On the horizontal axis, *relative market share* serves as a measure of company strength in the market. By dividing the growth–share matrix as indicated, four types of SBU can be distinguished:

1. **Stars.** Stars are high-growth, high-share businesses or products. They often need heavy investment to finance their rapid growth. Eventually their growth will slow down, and they will turn into cash cows.

2. **Cash cows.** Cash cows are low-growth, high-share businesses or products. These established and successful SBUs need less investment to hold their market share. Thus they produce cash that the company uses to pay its bills and to support other SBUs that need investment.

3. **Question marks.** Question marks are low-share business units in high-growth markets. They require cash to hold their share, let alone increase it. Management has to think hard about question marks – which ones they should build into stars and which ones they should phase out.

4. **Dogs.** Dogs are low-growth, low-share businesses and products. They may generate enough cash to maintain themselves, but do not promise to be large sources of cash.

The 10 circles in the growth–share matrix represent a company's 10 current SBUs. The company has two stars, two cash cows, three question marks and three dogs. The areas of the circles are proportional to the SBUs' sales value. This company is in fair shape, although not in good shape. It wants to invest in the more promising question marks to make them stars, and to maintain the stars so that they will become cash cows as their markets mature. Fortunately, it has two good-sized cash cows whose income helps finance the company's question marks, stars and dogs. The company should take some decisive action concerning its dogs and its question marks. The picture would be worse if the company had no stars, or had too many dogs, or had only one weak cash cow.

Stars—High-growth, high-share businesses or products that often require heavy investment to finance their rapid growth.

Cash cows—Low-growth, high-share businesses or products; established and successful units that generate cash that the company uses to pay its bills and support other business units that need investment.

Question marks—Low-share business units in high-growth markets that require a lot of cash in order to hold their share or become stars.

Dogs—Low-growth, low-share businesses and products that may generate enough cash to maintain themselves, but do not promise to be large sources of cash.

Figure 2.4 GE's strategic
business-planning grid

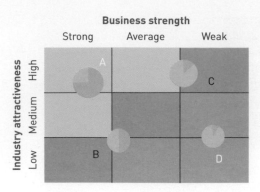

Figure 2.4 GE's strategic business-planning grid

Once it has classified its SBUs, the company must determine what role each will play in the future. There are four alternative strategies for each SBU. The company can invest more in the business unit to *build* its share. It can invest just enough to *hold* the SBU's share at the current level. It can *harvest* the SBU, milking its short-term cash flow regardless of the long-term effect. Finally, the company can *divest* the SBU by selling it or phasing it out and using the resources elsewhere.

As time passes, SBUs change their positions in the growth–share matrix. Each SBU has a life-cycle. Many SBUs start out as question marks and move into the star category if they succeed. They later become cash cows as market growth falls, then finally die off or turn into dogs towards the end of their life-cycle. The company needs to add new products and units continuously, so that some of them will become stars and, eventually, cash cows that will help finance other SBUs.

The General Electric grid

General Electric introduced a comprehensive portfolio planning tool called a *strategic business-planning grid* (see Figure 2.4). It is similar to Shell's *directional policy matrix*. Like the BCG approach, it uses a matrix with two dimensions – one representing industry attractiveness (the vertical axis) and one representing company strength in the industry (the horizontal axis). The best businesses are those located in highly attractive industries where the company has high business strength.

The GE approach considers many factors besides market growth rate as part of *industry attractiveness*. It uses an industry attractiveness index made up of market size, market growth rate, industry profit margin, amount of competition, seasonality and cycle of demand, and industry cost structure. Each of these factors is rated and combined in an index of industry attractiveness. For our purposes, an industry's attractiveness is high, medium or low. As an example, the Dutch chemical giant Akzo Nobel has identified speciality chemicals, coatings and pharmaceuticals as attractive. Its less attractive bulk chemical and fibre businesses are being sold.

For *business strength*, the GE approach again uses an index rather than a simple measure of relative market share. The business strength index includes factors such as the company's relative market share, price competitiveness, product quality, customer and market knowledge, sales effectiveness and geographic advantages. These factors are rated and combined in an index of business strengths described as strong, average or weak.

The grid has three zones. The green cells at the upper left include the strong SBUs in which the company should invest and grow. The amber diagonal cells contain SBUs that are medium in overall attractiveness. The company should maintain its level of investment in these SBUs. The three red cells at the lower right indicate SBUs that are low in overall attractiveness. The company should give serious thought to harvesting or divesting these SBUs.

The circles represent four company SBUs; the areas of the circles are proportional to the relative sizes of the industries in which these SBUs compete. The pie slices within the circles represent each SBU's market share. Thus circle A represents a company SBU with a 75 per cent market share in a good-sized, highly attractive industry in which the company has strong business strength. Circle B represents an SBU that has a 50 per cent market share, but the industry is not very attractive. Circles C and D represent two other company SBUs in industries where the company has small market shares and not much business strength. Altogether, the company should build A, maintain B and make some hard decisions on what to do with C and D.

Management would also plot the projected positions of the SBUs with and without changes in strategies. By comparing current and projected business grids, management can identify the primary strategic issues and opportunities it faces. One of the aims of portfolio analysis is to direct firms away from investing in markets that look attractive, but where they have no strength:

> In their rush away from the declining steel market, four of Japan's 'famous five' big steel makers (Nippon, NKK, Kawasaki, Sumitomo and Kobe) diversified into the microchip business. They had the misplaced belief that chips would be to them in the future what steel had been to the 1950s and that they had to be part of it. The market was attractive but it did not fit their strengths. So far, none have made money from chips. The misadventure also distracted them from attending to their core business.
>
> The 'famous five's' failure contrasts with Eramet, a focused French company who are the world's biggest producer of Ferro-nickel and high-speed steels. They owe their number one position to their decision to invest their profits in a 'second leg' that would be a logical industrial and geographical diversification for them. They bought French Commentryene and Swedish Kloster Speedsteel. They quickly integrated them and, according to Yves Rambert, their chairman and chief executive, 'found that the French and the Swedes can work together'.[12]

Problems with matrix approaches

The BCG, GE, Shell and other formal methods revolutionised strategic planning. However, such approaches have limitations. They can be difficult, time consuming and costly to implement. Management may find it difficult to define SBUs and measure market share and growth. In addition, these approaches focus on classifying *current* businesses, but provide little advice for *future* planning. Management must still rely on its judgement to set the business objectives for each SBU, to determine what resources to give to each and to work out which new businesses to add.

Formal planning approaches can also lead the company to place too much emphasis on market-share growth or growth through entry into attractive new markets. Using these approaches, many companies plunged into unrelated and new high-growth businesses that they did not know how to manage – with very bad results. At the same time, these companies were often too quick to abandon, sell or milk to death their healthy, mature businesses. As a result, many companies that diversified in the past are now narrowing their focus and getting back to the industries that they know best (see Marketing Insights 2.2).

marketing insights

2.2 | **KISS (Keep It Simple Stupid)**

When times are good, many businesses catch expansion fever. 'Big is beautiful' and everyone wanted to get bigger and grow faster by broadening their business portfolios. Companies like Vivendi and Warner Bros. neglected their stodgy core businesses to acquire glamorous businesses in more attractive industries. It did not seem to matter that many of the acquired businesses fitted poorly with old ones, or that they operated in markets unfamiliar to company management.

Many firms exploded into conglomerates, sometimes containing hundreds of unrelated products and businesses. Extreme cases involved French banks and Japanese electronics companies buying Hollywood film studios. Managing these 'smorgasbord' portfolios proved difficult. Eventually managers realised that it was tough to run businesses they knew little about. Many newly acquired businesses were also bogged down under added layers of corporate management and administrative costs. Meanwhile, the profitable core businesses wither from lack of investment and management attention.

Encumbered with the burden of their scattergun diversification, acquisition fever gave way to a new philosophy of keeping things simple: 'narrowing the focus', 'sticking to your knitting', 'the urge to purge'. They all mean narrowing the company's market focus and returning to the idea of serving one or a few core industries that the firm knows. Companies are shedding businesses that do not fit their narrowed focus and rebuilding by concentrating resources on other businesses that do. Examples are Royal Dutch/Shell's sale of their coal division or Lucas selling swathes of peripheral and underperforming activities to refocus on its core of automotive, aerospace and electronic components. The result is a smaller, but more focused company: a stronger firm serving fewer markets, but serving them much better.

When Cor Boonstra joined Philips, as their first outsider to become President, he was horrified at what he found. Philips was the world's number one in lighting, number two in television tubes and number eight in semiconductors, but had lots of other activities bleeding cash and managerial time. Its lighting and tubes were under pressure from manufacturers from South Korea and Taiwan, but the ability to compete was being swamped by numerous unconnected and loss-making businesses. Boonstra also inherited a 'hopelessly bureaucratic' business with layers and layers of management between factory and consumer. His strategy was to take the company back to its core strengths in 'high-volume consumer electronics'. Marketing expenditure in the core businesses was to increase while the strategy was to 'close, fix or sell' the 'bleeders'. Among the non-core businesses sold are Polygram, a music and film business, a chain of video stores and loss-making Grundig. In his first two years Boonstra sold off 40 businesses, losing 28,000 workers but bringing in €8bn to

...2.2

invest in the core. The company shrunk to a less bloated eight divisions with 80 businesses from 120 businesses in 11 divisions, but many more factories have to go. However, all is not gloom. While becoming a less complex company, Philips is gaining market share in its major markets and profits are growing.

Philips is now facing a dilemma that concentration forces on many businesses. Should it sell the very business on which it was founded? Reckitt & Colman did that when they sold Colman's mustard. Lighting is profitable and strong business but it is far from its chosen future in consumer electronics.

Now boom has turned to bust, many companies are wondering how to manage themselves through the hard times. There are excellent examples of how to do so. Even in such depressed economies as Germany and Japan, Kao, VW, Honda, Siemens and Canon continue to gain strength while all about them are floundering. Their secret is to gain from global-scale economies, process and product innovation, keeping their eyes on cash flows and the bottom line, and stick to their core businesses. In other words, come boom or bust, there is one strategy: keep it simple, stupid.

SOURCES: *The Economist*, 'Oil and coal: downcast' (4 September 1999), p. 81; Barbara Smirt, 'Philips to focus on consumer electronics', *Financial Times* (13 February 1998), p. 29; *The Economist*, 'Philips: the shrinking company' (8 May 1999), pp. 98–9; *The Economist*, 'Vivendi Universal: messier's mess' (8 June 2002), pp. 69–71; *The Economist*, 'Media conglomerates: tangled web' (25 May 2002), pp. 81–3; *The Economist*, 'Rising above the sludge' (15 April 2003), pp. 77–9.

Despite these and other problems, and although many companies have dropped formal matrix methods in favour of customised approaches better suited to their situations, most companies remain firmly committed to strategic planning.

Such analysis is no cure-all for finding the best strategy. Conversely, it can help management to understand the company's overall situation, to see how each business or product contributes, to assign resources to its businesses, and to orient the company for future success. When used properly, strategic planning is just one important aspect of overall strategic management, a way of thinking about how to manage a business.[13]

Developing growth strategies

The product/market expansion grid,[14] shown in Figure 2.5, is a useful device for identifying growth opportunities. This shows four routes to growth: market development, new markets, new products and diversification. We use the grid to explain how Mercedes-Benz, the luxury car division of DaimlerChrysler, hoped to return to profits after its €1bn loss in mid-1990.[15]

Market penetration

The new C-class (medium-sized family saloon) and E-class (executive saloon) helped Mercedes-Benz increase its sales by 23 per cent, besides costing less to produce. Sales were up 40 per cent in western Europe (excluding Germany), 34 per cent in the United States and 30 per cent in Japan. In Germany, the 38 per cent growth gave a 2 per cent rise in market share.

Figure 2.5 Product/market expansion grid

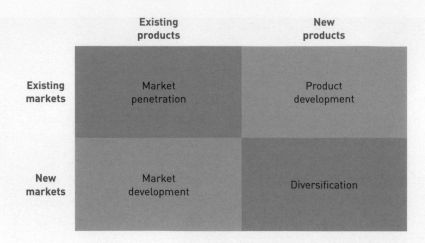

Market development

With its A-class small family saloon and Smart Car, Mercedes entered the small car market, while the relaunch of the Maybach brought the company back into the super luxury price bracket. Besides offering cost savings, the formation of DaimlerChrysler in 1998 gave the company a chance to develop lower-price brands worldwide through products like the Chrysler Neon and Voyager. However, there is some worry that the build quality and association with such down-market products is tarnishing Mercedes' reputation for safety and quality. Additionally, executing the merger between the two companies with such strong but different cultures has proved as difficult as could be expected.

The company's global coverage and small car skills have more recently been extended by deals with troubled Asian car makers: Japan's Mitsubishi Motors and South Korea's Hyundai.

Diversification

Diversification was an option taken by Mercedes. After rapidly moving into aerospace, its DASA defence subsidiary is now merged into the Franco-German EADS (European Aeronautic Defence and Space Company). The company is also selling loss-making subsidiaries, such as rail equipment maker Adtranz.[16]

Marketing within strategic planning

Planning functional strategies

The company's strategic plan establishes what kinds of business the company will be in and its objectives for each. Then, within each business unit, more detailed planning takes place. The main functional departments in each unit – marketing, finance, accounting, buying, manufacturing, personnel and others – must work together to accomplish strategic objectives.

Each functional department deals with different publics to obtain resources such as cash, labour, raw materials, research ideas and manufacturing processes. For example, marketing brings in revenues by negotiating exchanges with consumers. Finance arranges exchanges with lenders and stockholders to obtain cash. Thus the marketing and finance departments must work together to obtain needed funds. Similarly, the personnel department supplies labour, and the buying department obtains materials needed for operations and manufacturing.

Marketing's role in strategic planning

There is much overlap between overall company strategy and marketing strategy. Marketing looks at consumer needs and the company's ability to satisfy them; these factors guide the company mission and objectives. Most company strategic planning deals with marketing variables – market share, market development, growth – and it is sometimes hard to separate strategic planning from marketing planning. Some companies refer to their strategic planning as 'strategic marketing planning'.

Marketing plays a key role in the company's strategic plans in several ways. First, marketing provides a guiding *philosophy* – company strategy should revolve around serving the needs of important consumer groups. Second, marketing provides *inputs* to strategic planners by helping to identify attractive market opportunities and by assessing the firm's potential to take advantage of them. Finally, within individual business units, marketing designs *strategies* for reaching the unit's objectives.

Within each business unit, marketing management determines how to help achieve strategic objectives. Some marketing managers will find that their objective is not to build sales. Rather, it may be to hold existing sales with a smaller marketing budget, or even to reduce demand. Thus marketing management must manage demand to the level decided upon by the strategic planning prepared at headquarters. Marketing helps to assess each business unit's potential, set objectives for it and then achieve those objectives.

Marketing and the other business functions

In some firms, marketing is just another function – all functions count in the company and none takes leadership. At the other extreme, some marketers claim that marketing is the *principal* function of the firm. They quote Drucker's statement: 'The aim of the business is to create customers.' They say it is marketing's job to define the company's mission, products and markets, and to direct the other functions in the task of serving customers.

Enlightened marketers put the *customer*, not their department, at the centre of the company. Firms cannot succeed without customers, so the crucial task is to attract and hold them. Customers are attracted by promises and held by satisfaction. Marketing defines the promise and ensures its delivery. However, consumer satisfaction is affected by the performance of other departments, so *all* functions should work together to sense, serve and satisfy customer needs.

Each business function has a different view of which publics and activities are most important. Manufacturing focuses on suppliers and production; finance addresses stockholders and sound investment; marketing emphasises consumers and products, pricing, promotion and distribution. Ideally, all the different functions should blend to achieve consumer satisfaction. In practice, departmental relations are full of conflicts and misunderstandings. The marketing department takes the consumer's point of view. But when marketing tries to develop customer satisfaction, it often causes other departments to do a poorer job *in their terms*. Marketing department actions can increase buying costs, disrupt production schedules, increase inventories and create budget headaches. Thus the other departments may resist bending their efforts to the will of the marketing department.

Despite the resistance, marketers must champion all departments' 'thinking consumer' and put the consumer at the centre of the company. Customer satisfaction requires a total company effort to deliver superior value to target customers.

Creating value for buyers is much more than a 'marketing function'; rather, it is 'analogous to a symphony orchestra in which the contribution of each subgroup is tailored and integrated by a conductor – with a synergistic effect. A seller must draw upon and integrate effectively . . . its entire human and other capital resources . . . [Creating superior value for buyers] is the proper focus of the entire business and not merely of a single department in it.'[17]

The marketing plan

Within an organisation's strategic plan are marketing plans for each business, product or brand. A series of separate plans is necessary because even within a well-focused company product classes can face hugely different circumstances.

> In Europe's super-hot summer of 2003 Nestlé gave out profit warnings because the high temperature reduced people's consumption of some processed food while the popularity of the Atkins diet hit diet and slimming lines. Meanwhile, ice cream and mineral water sales skyrocketed. Elsewhere, the usually hot and humid north-east coast of the US hardly had a day without rain and clouds.

What does a marketing plan look like? Our discussion focuses on product or brand plans that are a development of the general planning process in Figure 2.1. A product or brand plan should have an executive summary, the current marketing situation, threats and opportunities, objectives and issues, marketing strategies, action programmes, budgets and controls (see Table 2.1).[18]

Table 2.1 **Contents of a marketing plan**

Section	Purpose
Executive summary	Presents a quick overview of the plan for quick management review.
Current marketing situation	The marketing audit that presents background data on the market, product, competition and distribution.
SWOT analysis	Identifies the company's main *strengths* and *weaknesses* and the main *opportunities* and *threats* facing the product.
Objectives and issues	Defines the company's objectives in the areas of sales, market share and profits, and the issues that will affect these objectives.
Marketing strategy	Presents the broad marketing approach that will be used to achieve the plan's objectives.
Action programmes	Specifies *what* will be done, *who* will do it, *when* it will be done and *what* it will cost.
Budgets	A projected profit-and-loss statement that forecasts the expected financial outcomes from the plan.
Controls	Indicates how the progress of the plan will be monitored.

Executive summary

The marketing plan should open with a short summary of the main goals and recommendations in the plan. Here is a short example:

> The 2003 Marketing Plan outlines an approach to attaining a significant increase in company sales and profits over the preceding year. The sales target is €24 million – a planned 20 per cent sales gain. We think this increase is attainable because of the improved economic, competitive, and distribution picture. The target operating margin is €2.5 million, a 25 per cent increase over last year. To achieve these goals, the sales promotion budget will be €500,000, or 2 per cent of projected sales. The advertising budget will be €720,000, or 3 per cent of projected sales . . . [more details follow]

The executive summary helps top management to find the plan's central points quickly. A table of contents should follow the executive summary.

Marketing audit

The **marketing audit** is a systematic and periodic examination of a company's environment, objectives, strategies and activities to determine problem areas and opportunities. The first main section of the plan describes the target market and the company's position in it (Table 2.2 gives the questions asked). It should start with the strategic imperatives: the pertinent objectives, policies and elements of strategy passed down from broader plans. In the **current marketing situation** section, the planner provides information about the market, product performance, competition and distribution. It includes a *market description* that defines the market, including chief market segments. The planner shows market size, in total and by segment, for several past years, and then reviews customer needs together with factors in the marketing environment that may affect customer purchasing. Next, the *product review* shows sales, prices and gross margins of the principal products in the product line. A section on *competition* identifies big competitors and their individual strategies for product quality, pricing, distribution and promotion. It also shows the market shares held by the company and each competitor. Finally, a section on *distribution* describes recent sales trends and developments in the primary distribution channels.

Managing the marketing function would be hard enough if the marketer had to deal only with the controllable marketing-mix variables. Reality is harder. The company is in a complex marketing environment consisting of uncontrollable forces to which the company must adapt. The *environment* produces both threats and opportunities. The company must carefully analyse its environment so that it can avoid the threats and take advantage of the opportunities.

The company's marketing environment includes forces close to the company that affect its ability to serve its consumers, such as other company *departments*, *channel members*, *suppliers*, *competitors* and other *publics*. It also includes broader *demographic* and *economic* forces, *political* and *legal* forces, *technological* and *ecological* forces, and *social* and *cultural* forces. The company must consider all of these forces when developing and positioning its offer to the target market.

SWOT analysis

The SWOT analysis section draws from the market audit. It is a brief list of the critical success factors in the market, and rates strengths and weaknesses against the competition. The SWOT analysis should include costs and other non-marketing variables. The outstanding opportunities and threats should be given. If plans depend upon assumptions about the market, the economy or the competition, they need to be explicit.

Marketing audit—A comprehensive, systematic, independent and periodic examination of a company's environment, objectives, strategies and activities to determine problem areas and opportunities, and to recommend a plan of action to improve the company's marketing performance.

Current marketing situation—The section of a marketing plan that describes the target market and the company's position in it.

Table 2.2 Marketing audit
questions

Marketing environment audit

The macroenvironment

1. *Demographic*. What primary demographic trends pose threats and opportunities for this company?
2. *Economic*. What developments in income, prices, savings and credit will impact on the company?
3. *Natural*. What is the outlook for costs and availability of natural resources and energy? Is the company environmentally responsible?
4. *Technology*. What technological changes are occurring? What is the company's position on technology?
5. *Political*. What current and proposed laws will affect company strategy?
6. *Cultural*. What is the public's attitude towards business and the company's products? What changes in consumer lifestyles might have an impact?

The task environment

1. *Markets*. What is happening to market size, growth, geographic distribution and profits? What are the large market segments?
2. *Customers*. How do customers rate the company on product quality, service and price? How do they make their buying decisions?
3. *Competitors*. Who are the chief competitors? What are their strategies, market shares, and strengths and weaknesses?
4. *Channels*. What main channels does the company use to distribute products to customers? How are they performing?
5. *Suppliers*. What trends are affecting suppliers? What is the outlook for the availability of key production resources?
6. *Publics*. What key publics provide problems or opportunities? How should the company deal with these publics?

Marketing strategy audit

1. *Mission*. Is the mission clearly defined and market-oriented?
2. *Objectives*. Has the company set clear objectives to guide marketing planning and performance? Do these objectives fit with the company's opportunities and strengths?
3. *Strategy*. Does the company have a sound marketing strategy for achieving its objectives?
4. *Budgets*. Has the company budgeted sufficient resources to segments, products, territories and marketing-mix elements?

Marketing organisation audit

1. *Formal structure*. Does the chief marketing officer have adequate authority over activities affecting customer satisfaction? Are activities optimally structured along functional, product, market and territory lines?
2. *Functional efficiency*. Do marketing, sales and other staff communicate effectively? Are the staff well trained, supervised, motivated and evaluated?
3. *Interface efficiency*. Do staff work well across functions: marketing with manufacturing, R&D, buying, personnel, etc.?

Table 2.2 (cont'd)

Marketing systems audit

1. *Marketing information system.* Is the marketing intelligence system providing accurate and timely information about developments? Are decision makers using marketing research effectively?
2. *Planning system.* Does the company prepare annual, long-term and strategic plans? Are they used?
3. *Marketing control system.* Are annual plan objectives being achieved? Does management periodically analyse the sales and profitability of products, markets, territories and channels?
4. *New-product development.* Is the company well organised to gather, generate and screen new-product ideas? Does it carry out adequate product and market testing? Has the company succeeded with new products?

Productivity audit

1. *Profitability analysis.* How profitable are the company's different products, markets, territories and channels? Should the company enter, expand or withdraw from any business segments? What would be the consequences?
2. *Cost-effectiveness analysis.* Do any activities have excessive costs? How can costs be reduced?

Marketing function audit

1. *Products.* Has the company developed sound product-line objectives? Should some products be phased out? Should some new products be added? Would some products benefit from quality, style or feature changes?
2. *Price.* What are the company's pricing objectives, policies, strategies and procedures? Are the company's prices in line with customers' perceived value? Are price promotions used properly?
3. *Distribution.* What are the distribution objectives and strategies? Does the company have adequate market coverage and service? Should existing channels be changed or new ones added?
4. *Advertising, sales promotion and publicity.* What are the company's promotion objectives? How is the budget determined? Is it sufficient? Are advertising messages and media well developed and received? Does the company have well-developed sales promotion and public relations programmes?
5. *Sales force.* What are the company's sales force objectives? Is the sales force large enough? Is it properly organised? Is it well trained, supervised and motivated? How is the sales force rated relative to those of competitors?

Objectives and issues

Having studied the strengths, weaknesses, opportunities and threats, the company sets objectives and considers issues that will affect them. The objectives are goals that the company would like to attain during the plan's term. For example, the manager might want to achieve a 15 per cent market share, a 20 per cent pre-tax profit on sales and a 25 per cent pre-tax profit on investment. If current market share is only 10 per cent, the question needs answering: Where are the extra sales to come from? From the competition, by increasing usage rate, by adding, and so on?

Marketing strategy

In this section of the marketing plan, the manager outlines the broad marketing strategy or 'game plan' for attaining the objectives. Marketing strategy is the marketing logic by which the business unit hopes to achieve its marketing objectives. It shows how strategies for target markets and positioning build upon the firm's differential advantages. It should detail the market segments on which the company will focus. These segments differ in their needs and wants, responses to marketing, and profitability. The company should put its effort into those market segments it can best serve from a competitive point of view. It should develop a marketing strategy for each targeted segment.

Marketing mix

The manager should also outline specific strategies for such marketing mix elements in each target market: new products, field sales, advertising, sales promotion, prices and distribution. The manager should explain how each strategy responds to the threats, opportunities and critical issues described earlier in the plan.

Action programmes

Marketing strategies become specific action programmes that answer the following questions: *What* will be done? *When* will it be done? *Who* is responsible for doing it? *How much* will it cost? For example, the manager may want to increase sales promotion as a key strategy for winning market share. A sales promotion action plan should outline special offers and their dates, trade shows entered, new point-of-purchase displays and other promotions. The action plan shows when activities will start, be reviewed and be completed.

Budgets

Action plans allow the manager to make a supporting marketing budget that is essentially a projected profit and loss statement. For revenues, it shows the forecast unit sales and the average net price. On the expense side, it shows the cost of production, physical distribution and marketing. The difference is the projected profit. Higher management will review the budget and either approve or modify it. Once approved, the budget is the basis for materials buying, production scheduling, personnel planning and marketing operations. Budgeting can be very difficult and budgeting methods range from simple 'rules of thumb' to complex computer models.

Controls

The last section of the plan outlines the controls that will monitor progress. Typically, there are goals and budgets for each month or quarter. This practice allows higher management to review the results of each period and to spot businesses or products that are not meeting their goals. The managers of these businesses and products have to explain these problems and the corrective actions they will take.

Marketing implementation—
The process that turns marketing strategies and plans into marketing actions in order to accomplish strategic marketing objectives.

Implementation

Planning good strategies is only a start towards successful marketing. A brilliant marketing strategy counts for little if the company fails to implement it properly. **Marketing implementation** is the process that turns marketing strategies and *plans* into marketing *actions* to accomplish strategic marketing objectives. Implementation involves day-to-day, month-to-month activities that effectively put the marketing plan to work. Whereas marketing planning addresses the *what* and *why* of marketing activities, implementation addresses the *who*, *where*, *when* and *how*.

Marketing organisation

The company must have people who can carry out marketing analysis, planning, implementation and control. If the company is very small, one person might do all the marketing work – research, selling, advertising, customer service and other activities. As the company expands, organisations emerge to plan and carry out marketing activities. In large companies there can be many specialists: brand managers, salespeople and sales managers, market researchers, advertising experts and other specialists.

Modern marketing activities occur in several forms. The most common form is the *functional organisation*, in which functional specialists head different marketing activities – a sales manager, an advertising manager, a marketing research manager, a customer service manager, a new-product manager. A company that sells across the country or internationally often uses a *geographic organisation*, in which its sales and marketing people run specific countries, regions and districts. A geographic organisation allows salespeople to settle into a territory, get to know their customers, and work with a minimum of travel time and cost.

Companies with many very different products or brands often create a *product management* or *brand management* organisation. Using this approach, a manager develops and implements a complete strategy and marketing programme for a specific product or brand. Product management first appeared in Procter & Gamble in 1929. A new soap, Camay, was not doing well, and a young P&G executive was assigned to give his exclusive attention to developing and promoting this brand. He was successful, and the company soon added other product managers. Since then, many firms, especially consumer products companies, have set up product management organisations. However, recent changes in the marketing environment have caused many companies to rethink the role of the product manager. Many companies are finding that today's marketing environment calls for less brand focus and more customer focus. They are shifting towards *customer equity management* – moving away from managing just product profitability and towards managing *customer* profitability.[19]

For companies that sell one product line to many different types of markets and customers who have different needs and preferences, a *market* or *customer management organisation* might be best. A market management organisation is similar to the product management organisation. Market managers are responsible for developing marketing strategies and plans for their specific markets or customers. This system's main advantage is that the company is organised around the needs of specific customer segments.

Large companies that produce many different products flowing into many different geographic and customer markets usually employ some *combination* of the functional, geographic, product, and market organisation forms. This ensures that each function, product and market receives its share of management attention. However, it can also add costly layers of management and reduce organisational flexibility. Still, the benefits of organisational specialisation usually outweigh the drawbacks.

Marketing control

Because many surprises occur during the implementation of marketing plans, the marketing department must engage in constant marketing control. **Marketing control** is the process of measuring and evaluating the results of marketing strategies and plans and taking corrective action to ensure the achievement of marketing objectives. It involves the four steps shown in

Marketing control—
The process of measuring and evaluating the results of marketing strategies and plans, and taking corrective action to ensure that marketing objectives are attained.

Figure 2.6 **The control process**

Figure 2.6. Management first sets specific marketing goals. It then measures its performance in the marketplace and evaluates the causes of any differences between expected and actual performance. Finally, management takes corrective action to close the gaps between its goals and its performance. This may require changing the action programmes or even changing the goals.

Operating control involves checking ongoing performance against the annual plan and taking corrective action when necessary. Its purpose is to ensure that the company achieves the sales, profits and other goals set out in its annual plan. It also involves determining the profitability of different products, territories, markets and channels. **Strategic control** involves looking at whether the company's basic strategies match its opportunities and strengths. Marketing strategies and programmes can quickly become outdated and each company should periodically reassess its overall approach to the marketplace. Besides providing the background for marketing planning, a *marketing audit* can also be a positive tool for strategic control. Sometimes it is conducted by an objective and experienced outside party who is independent of the marketing department. Table 2.2 showed the kind of questions the marketing auditor might ask. The findings may come as a surprise – and sometimes as a shock – to management. Management then decides which actions make sense and how and when to implement them.

Operating control—Checking ongoing performance against annual plans and taking corrective action.

Strategic control—Checking whether the company's basic strategy matches its opportunities and strengths.

Implementing marketing

Implementation is difficult – it is easier to think up good marketing strategies than it is to carry them out.

Many managers think that 'doing things right' (implementation) is as important as, or even more important than, 'doing the right things' (strategy). The fact is that both are critical to success.[20] However, companies can gain competitive advantages through effective implementation. One firm can have essentially the same strategy as another, yet win in the marketplace through faster or better execution.

In an increasingly connected world, people at all levels of the marketing system must work together to implement marketing plans and strategies. At Bosch, for example, marketing implementation for the company's power tool products requires day-to-day decisions and actions by thousands of people both inside and outside the organisation. Marketing managers make decisions about target segments, branding, packaging, pricing, promoting, and distributing. They connect with people elsewhere in the company to get support for their products and programmes. They talk with engineering about product design, with manufacturing about production and inventory levels, and with finance about funding and cash flows. They also connect with outside people, such as advertising agencies to plan ad campaigns and the media to obtain publicity support. The sales force urges retailers to advertise Bosch products, provide ample shelf space, and use company displays.

Successful marketing implementation depends on how well the company blends its people, organisational structure, decision and reward systems, and company culture into a cohesive action programme that supports its strategies. At all levels, the company must be staffed by people who have the needed skills, motivation and personal characteristics. Before a company can hope to obtain and retain its customers, it must learn how to gain, train and retain its staff. A major recent study shows, within industries, human resource management and the quality of management training (particularly to MBA level) to be the largest indicator of company performance.

Another factor affecting successful implementation is the company's **decision-and-reward systems** – formal and informal operating procedures that guide planning, budgeting, compensation and other activities. For example, if a company compensates managers for short-run results, they will have little incentive to work towards long-run objectives. Companies recognising this are broadening their incentive systems to include more than sales volume. For instance, Xerox rewards include customer satisfaction and Ferrero's the freshness of its chocolates in stores. Effective implementation also requires careful planning. At all levels, the company must fill its structure and systems with people who have the necessary skills, motivation and personal characteristics. In recent years, more and more companies have recognised that long-run human resources planning can give the company a strong competitive advantage.

Finally, for successful implementation, the firm's marketing strategies must fit with its culture. *Company culture* is a system of values and beliefs shared by people in an organisation. It is the company's collective identity and meaning. The culture informally guides the behaviour of people at all company levels. Marketing strategies that do not fit the company's style and culture will be difficult to implement. Because managerial style and culture are so hard to change, companies usually design strategies that fit their current cultures rather than trying to change their styles and cultures to fit new strategies.[21]

Thus successful marketing implementation depends on how well the company blends five elements – action programmes, organisation structure, decision-and-reward systems, human resources and company culture – into a cohesive programme that supports its strategies.

Decision-and-reward systems—Formal and informal operating procedures that guide planning, budgeting, compensation and other activities.

Summary

Strategic planning involves developing a strategy for long-run survival and growth. Marketing helps in strategic planning, and the overall strategic plan defines marketing's role in the company. Not all companies use formal planning or use it well, yet formal planning offers several benefits. Companies develop three kinds of plan: *annual plans*, *long-range plans* and *strategic plans*.

Strategic planning sets the stage for the rest of company planning. The strategic planning process consists of developing the company's mission, understanding a company's strengths and weaknesses, its environment, business portfolio, objectives and goals, and functional plans. Developing a sound *mission statement* is a challenging undertaking. The mission statement should be market-oriented, feasible, motivating and specific, if it is to direct the firm to its best opportunities.

Companies have plans at many levels: global, regional, national and so forth. The higher-level plans contain objectives and strategies that become part of subordinate plans. These *strategic imperatives* are objectives or defined practices. At each level a *strategic audit* reviews the company and its environment. A *SWOT analysis* summarises the main elements of this audit into a statement of the company's strengths and weaknesses and the chief threats and opportunities that exist.

From here, strategic planning calls for analysing the company's *business portfolio* and deciding which businesses should receive more or fewer resources. The company might use a formal portfolio-planning method like the *BCG growth–share matrix* or the *General Electric grid*. However, most companies are now designing more customised portfolio-planning approaches that better suit their unique situations.

This analysis and mission lead to strategic objectives and goals. Management must decide how to achieve growth and profits objectives. The *product/market expansion grid* shows four avenues for market growth: *market penetration*, *market development*, *product development* and *diversification*.

Once strategic objectives and strategies are defined, management must prepare a set of *functional plans* that coordinate the activities of the marketing, finance, manufacturing and other departments. Each of the company's *functional departments* provides inputs for strategic planning. Each department has a different idea about which objectives and activities are most important. The marketing department stresses the consumer's point of view. Marketing managers must understand the point of view of the company's other functions and work with other functional managers to develop a system of plans that will best accomplish the firm's overall strategic objectives.

Each business must prepare marketing plans for its products, brands and markets. The main components of a *marketing plan* are the executive summary, current marketing situation, threats and opportunities, objectives and issues, marketing strategies, action programmes, budgets and controls. To plan good strategies is often easier than to carry them out. To be successful, companies must implement the strategies effectively. *Implementation* is the process that turns marketing strategies into marketing actions. The process consists of five key elements:

1. The *action programme* identifies crucial tasks and decisions needed to implement the marketing plan, assigns them to specific people and establishes a timetable.

2. The *organisation structure* defines tasks and assignments and coordinates the efforts of the company's people and units.

3. The company's *decision-and-reward systems* guide activities such as planning, budgeting, compensation and other activities. Well-designed action programmes, organisation structures and decision-and-reward systems can encourage good implementation.

4. Successful implementation also requires careful *human resources planning*. The company must obtain, maintain and retain good people.

5. The firm's *company culture* can also make or break implementation. Company culture guides people in the company; good implementation relies on strong, clearly defined cultures that fit the chosen strategy.

Most of the responsibility for implementation goes to the company's marketing department. Modern marketing activities occur in a number of ways. The most common form is the *functional marketing organisation*, in which marketing functions are directed by separate managers who report to the marketing director. The company might also use a *geographic organisation*, in which its sales force or other functions specialise by geographic area. After years of stability, market pressures are causing new organisational structures to be tried.

Marketing organisations carry out marketing control. *Operating control* involves monitoring results to secure the achievement of annual sales and profit goals. It also calls for determining the profitability of the firm's products, territories, market segments and channels. *Strategic control* makes sure that the company's marketing objectives, strategies and systems fit with the current and forecast marketing environment. It uses the *marketing audit* to determine marketing opportunities and problems, and to recommend short-run and long-run actions to improve overall marketing performance. The company uses these resources to watch and adapt to the marketing environment.

Discussing the issues

1. What are the benefits of a long-range plan? Does it have any role when forces, such as e-commerce, are changing markets so rapidly?

2. Many companies undertake a marketing audit to identify the firm's strengths and weaknesses relative to competitors, and in relation to the opportunities and threats in the external environment. Why is it important that such an analysis should address relative, not absolute, company strengths and weaknesses?

3. A tour operator has its own charter airline that is also used by other tour operators. The subsidiary is smaller and less profitable than are the competing charter airlines. Its growth rate has been below the industry average during the past five years. Into what cell of the BCG growth–share matrix does this strategic business unit fall? What should the parent company do with this SBU?

4. A consumer electronics company finds that sales in its main product line – CD players – are beginning to stabilise. The market is reaching maturity. What growth strategies might the firm pursue for this product line? How might the strategic-focus tool help managers examine the growth opportunities for this line?

5. The General Electric strategic business-planning grid gives a broad overview that can be helpful in strategic decision making. For what types of decision would this grid be helpful? For what types of strategic decision would it be less useful?

6. Sony's PlayStation is a market leader. Discuss how a competitor would use market-challenger, market-follower and market-nicher strategies to compete effectively with Sony.

Applying the concepts

1. Think of a product or service that has presented you with difficulties in recent weeks (such as late delivery or hard to locate products), then:

   ■ Use the Web to identify Internet-enhanced suppliers of that product or service.

   ■ Evaluate the strengths and weaknesses of Web providers in their ability to overcome the problem you faced.

   ■ Suggest alternative ways in which the Internet could be used to overcome the product or service failure you faced.

2. Take a product or service organisation you are familiar with.

   ■ List the key external environmental opportunities or threats that face the organisation.

   ■ What do you think are the organisation's main strengths and weaknesses?

   ■ Suggest ways in which the organisation might respond to the external forces.

   ■ Recommend a possible marketing strategy which will ensure that the organisation matches its internal capabilities with external opportunities.

References

1. Saskia Sisson, 'Billionaire beach', *The European* (24–30 July 1997), pp. 56–7; Victoria McCubbine, 'Predators stalk the gnomes', *Eurobusiness* (May 2000), pp. 29–30; 'Families out of fashion', *The Economist* (4 March 2000), p. 92; 'Luxury goods: snob appeal', *The Economist* (13 February 1999), pp. 85–6; 'The cashmere revolutionary', *The Economist* (15 July 2000), p. 94; LEX column, 'Luxury goods', *Financial Times* (15 July 2003); Ivar Simensen, 'Trying times for luxury goods', *FT.com* (10 July 2000).

2. Malcolm MacDonald investigates the barriers to marketing planning in his article 'Ten barriers to marketing planning', *Journal of Marketing Management*, **5**, 1 (1989), pp. 1–18; Sean Ennis, 'Marketing planning in the smaller evolving firm: empirical evidence and reflections', *Irish Marketing Review*, **11**, 2 (1998), pp. 49–61.

3. Susanna Voyle, 'Carrefour fails to satisfy its investors' appetites', *Financial Times* (5 April 2000), p. 34.

4. To see how planning and entrepreneurship exist side by side and how the best-performing companies have balanced orientation towards marketing and technology, see Veronica Wong and John Saunders, 'Business orientation and corporate success', *Journal of Strategic Marketing*, **1**, 1 (1993), pp. 20–40.

5. BP's website, bp.com, gives a very comprehensive rolling update of the company's long-range plans and current performance.

6. Florian Gimbel, 'Finding the right path for church funds', *FTfin* (3 May 2003), p. 4.

7. Michael E. Porter, *Competitive Advantage: Creating and sustaining competitive performance* (New York: Free Press, 1985); Nicholas J. O'Shaughnessy, 'Michael Porter's competitive advantage revisited', *Management Decision*, **34**, 6 (1996), pp. 12–20.

8. David Reed, 'Sound advice', *Marketing Business* (November 1997), pp. 24–9.

9. For more on mission statements, see Romauld A. Stone, 'Mission statements revisited', *SAM Advanced Management Journal* (Winter 1996), pp. 31–7; Orit Gadiesh and James L. Gilbert, 'Frontline action', *Harvard Business Review* (May 2001); Digby Anderson, 'Is this the perfect mission statement?', *Across the Board* (May–June 2001), p. 16.

10. Michael Porter popularised his view of value chains through his book *Competitive Advantage*, op. cit.; also see Jim Webb and Chas Gile, 'Reversing the value chain', *Journal of Business Strategy* (March–April 2001), pp. 13–17.

11. Tim Burt, 'A rock and roll reinvention in the bookshops', *Financial Times* (21 October 2002), p. 16.

12. 'Mitsubushi Heavy Industries', *The Economist* (23 October 1999), pp. 119–20; 'Just possibly, something to sing about', *The Economist* (18 March 2000), pp. 97–9; *Le Monde*, 'Eromet in the black' (29 March 2003).

13. For more on developments in strategic planning see Hayley Carter, 'Strategic planning reborn', *Work Study*, **48**, 2 (1999), p. 104; Tom Devane, 'Ten cardinal sins of strategic planning', *Executive Excellence* (October 2000), p. 15; Dave Lefkowith, 'Effective strategic planning', *Management Quarterly* (Spring 2001), pp. 7–11; and Stan Abraham, 'The Association of Strategic Planning: strategy is still management's core challenge', *Strategy & Leadership* (2002), pp. 38–42.

14. H. Igor Ansoff, 'Strategies for diversification', *Harvard Business Review* (September–October 1957), pp. 113–24; Ade S. Olusoga, 'Market concentration versus market diversification and internationalization: implications for MNE performance', *International Marketing Review*, **10**, 2 (1993), pp. 40–59.

15. Information taken from: Guy de Jonquières, 'Pell-mell expansion has sparked controversy', *Financial Times* (11 June 1991), p. 8; Christopher Parkes, 'New car plant will test for "lean production"', *Financial Times* (25 June 1992), p. 4.

16. Haig Simonian, 'Bombardier lined up to buy Adtranz', *Financial Times* (20 July 2000), p. 29; *The Economist*, 'The DaimlerChrysler emulsion' (29 July 2000), pp. 81–2; *The Economist*, 'DaimlerChrysler: revolting' (2 December 2000), p. 102.

17. Nigel Piercy, *Market-led Strategic Change: Transforming the process of going to market* (Oxford: Butterworth-Heinemann, 1997).

18. Harry Macdivitt, 'Plan', Chapter 3 in Chartered Institute of Marketing, *Marketing Means Business for the CEO* (2000), pp. 54–61.

19. See Roland T. Rust, Valerie A. Zeithaml and Katherine N. Lemon, *Driving Customer Equity: How lifetime customer value is reshaping corporate strategy* (New York: Free Press, 2000); and Rust, Lemon and Zeithaml, 'Where should the next marketing dollar go?', *Marketing Management* (September–October 2001), pp. 24–8.

20. For a good discussion of gaining advantage through implementation effectiveness versus strategic differentiation, see Michael E. Porter, 'What is strategy?', *Harvard Business Review* (November–December 1996), pp. 61–78. Also see Charles H. Noble and Michael P. Mokwa, 'Implementing marketing strategies: developing and testing a managerial theory', *Journal of Marketing* (October 1999), pp. 57–73.

21. For more on company cultures, see Rob Goffee and Gareth Jones, *The Character of a Corporation: How your company's culture can make or break your business* (New York: HarperBusiness, 1998); and Thomas A. Atchison, 'What is corporate culture?', *Trustee* (April 2002), p. 11.

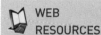

WEB RESOURCES

For additional classic case studies and Internet exercises, visit www.pearsoned.co.uk/kotler

Concluding concept 2
Starbucks

Something was brewing in Seattle in the mid-1980s and it was not just coffee. While travelling in Italy, the popularity of Milan's espresso coffee bars impressed Howard Schultz. At the time, he was director of retail operations and marketing of Starbucks, a provider of coffee to fine restaurants. He concluded that more people needed to join the coffee bar culture – slow down, 'smell the coffee' and enjoy life a little more. From little beans big things grew. The result was Starbucks, the coffeehouse chain that started the trend in America of enjoying coffee to its fullest. Starbucks doesn't sell just coffee, it sells *The Starbucks Experience*. As one Starbucks executive puts it, 'We're not in the business of filling bellies, we're in the business of filling souls.'

Meanwhile, in a trailer park just outside Seattle, Kurt Cobain teamed up with Chris Noveselic to form Nirvana. Kurt Cobain's answer was not to slow down. With a psyche and passion too big for one body, he expressed the pain of a generation. While Howard Schultz wanted to calm things down, Kurt Cobain filled a musical gulf that captured the emptiness felt by his generation. The media captioned them 'Generation X'.

> From little beans big things grew.

Kurt Cobain fulfilled his rock'n'roll destiny and ended his pain by dying young. Generation X continued refilling their souls at Starbucks. Starbucks is now a powerhouse premium brand in a category in which only cheaper commodity products once existed. As the brand has perked, Starbucks' sales and profits have risen like steam off a mug of hot java. Some 20 million customers visit the company's more than 5,500 stores worldwide each week – 10 per cent of them drop by twice a day. Guided by their mission (Exhibit 2.2), Starbucks' sales and earnings have both more than tripled over the last five years.

Starbucks' success, however, has drawn a full litter of copycats, including direct competitors such as Caribou Coffee, Costa Coffee and Coffee Republic. These days it seems that everyone is peddling its own brand of premium coffee. To maintain its phenomenal growth in an increasingly overcaffeinated marketplace, Starbucks has brewed up an ambitious, multipronged growth strategy:

Exhibit 2.2 Mission statement

> **Establish Starbucks as the premier purveyor of the finest coffee in the world while maintaining our uncompromising principles while we grow.**
>
> The following six guiding principles will help us measure the appropriateness of our decisions:
>
> - Provide a great work environment and treat each other with respect and dignity.
> - Embrace diversity as an essential component in the way we do business.
> - Apply the highest standards of excellence to the purchasing, roasting and fresh delivery of our coffee.
> - Develop enthusiastically satisfied customers all of the time.
> - Contribute positively to our communities and our environment.
> - Recognize that profitability is essential to our future success.
>
> Starbucks is committed to a role of environmental leadership in all facets of our business.

■ *More store growth.* Almost 85 per cent of Starbucks' sales comes from its stores. So, not surprisingly, Starbucks is opening new stores at a breakneck pace. Six years ago, Starbucks had just 1,015 stores in total – that's 400 fewer than it built last year alone. Although it may seem that there aren't many places left without a Starbucks, there's still plenty of room to expand. For example, in the US the entire state of Indiana has only one; and the states of Alabama, Arkansas, Mississippi and Tennessee have none at all. Even in crowded markets, such as New York, Paris and London, the company is unconcerned about store saturation. Schultz points to Vancouver, Canada, where competing Starbucks stores are located directly across the street from one another. Both stores generate more than $1 million in annual sales, each well above the sales of a typical Starbucks.

Beyond opening new shops, Starbucks is expanding each store's food offerings, testing everything from Krispy Kreme doughnuts and Fresh Fields gourmet sandwiches to Greek pasta salads and assorted chips.

By offering a beefed-up menu, the company hopes to increase the average customer sales ticket while also boosting lunch and dinner traffic.

- *New retail channels.* The vast majority of coffee is bought in stores and sipped at home. To capture this demand, Starbucks is also pushing into supermarket aisles. However, rather than going head-to-head with giants such as Nestlé (Nescafé) and Kraft (Maxwell House, Sanka), Starbucks struck a co-branding deal with Kraft. Under this deal, Starbucks will continue to roast and package its coffee while Kraft will market and distribute it. Both companies benefit: Starbucks gains quick entry into 25,000 supermarkets, supported by the marketing muscle of 3,500 Kraft salespeople. Kraft tops off its coffee line with the best-known premium brand and gains quick entry into the fast-growing premium coffee segment.

Beyond supermarkets, Starbucks has forged an impressive set of new ways to bring its brand to market. Some examples: Marriott operates Starbucks kiosks in more than 60 airports, and several airlines serve Starbucks coffee to their passengers. Westin and Sheraton hotels offer packets of Starbucks coffee in their rooms. And Starbucks recently signed a deal to operate coffee shops within Waterstones' bookshop superstores. Starbucks also sells gourmet coffee, tea, gifts, and related goods through business and consumer catalogues. And its website, Starbucks.com, has become a kind of 'lifestyle portal' on which it sells coffee, tea, coffeemaking equipment, compact discs, gifts and collectibles.

- *New products and store concepts.* Starbucks has partnered with several firms to extend its brand into new categories. For example, it joined with PepsiCo to stamp the Starbucks brand on bottled Frappuccino drinks and a new DoubleShot espresso drink. Starbucks ice cream, marketed in a joint venture with Breyer's, is now a leading brand of coffee ice cream. Starbucks is also examining new store concepts. It's testing Café Starbucks, a European-style family bistro with a menu featuring everything from huckleberry pancakes to oven-roasted seared sirloin and Mediterranean chicken breast on focaccia. The company is also testing Circadia – a kind of bohemian coffeehouse with tattered rugs, high-speed Internet access, and live music as well as coffee specialities.

- *International growth.* Finally, Starbucks has gone global. In 1996, the company had only 11 coffeehouses outside North America. By 2003, the number had grown in 24 international markets, including more than 1,000 in Asia and 600 in Europe. It is now moving rapidly into Latin America and South America, where it plans to build 900 stores by 2005.

Although Starbucks' growth strategy so far has met with great success, some analysts express strong concerns. What's wrong with Starbucks' rapid expansion? Some critics worry that the company may be overextending the Starbucks brand name. 'People pay up to $3.15 for a caffe latte because it's supposed to be a premium product', asserts one such critic. 'When you see the Starbucks name on what an airline is pouring, you wonder.' Others fear that, by pursuing such a broad-based growth strategy, Starbucks will stretch its resources too thin or lose its focus.

Still others, however, remain true believers. Some even see similarities between Starbucks and a young McDonald's, which rode the humble hamburger to such incredible success. 'The similar focus on one product, the overseas opportunities, the rapid emergence as the dominant player in a new niche', says Goldman Sachs analyst Steve Kent, 'this all applies to Starbucks, too.' Only time will tell whether Starbucks turns out to be the next McDonald's – it all depends on how well the company manages growth. For now, things are really perking. But Starbucks has to be careful that it doesn't boil over.

Questions

1. What has suddenly made people across the world willing to pay three to four times more for a cup of coffee than they used to?
2. Contrast Starbucks' growth strategy with that of McDonald's. How do their growth strategies differ and what could explain the difference?
3. Evaluate the strengths, weaknesses, opportunities and threats of Starbucks. How are such trends as health concerns, the ageing population and anti-globalisation likely to affect the company?
4. Classify Starbucks using the BCG growth–share matrix. What are the implications of its position?
5. Thinking about the future, where do you anticipate Starbucks migrating to on the BCG matrix as the company matures? What strategy would you recommend in the light of Starbucks' future position?
6. To what extent do the elements of Starbucks' strategy concur with its mission?

SOURCES: Adapted from Nelson D. Schwartz, 'Still perking after all these years', *Fortune* (24 May 1999), pp. 203–10; Janice Matsumoto, 'More than mocha – Café Starbucks', *Restaurants and Institutions* (1 October 1998), p. 21; Kelly Barron, 'The cappuccino conundrum',

Forbes (22 February 1999), pp. 54–5; and Stephane Fitch, 'Latte grande, extra froth', *Forbes* (19 March 2001), p. 58. Other information from Richard Papiernik, 'Starbucks still taking bows in long-running coffeehouse show', *Nation's Restaurant News* (12 February 2001), pp. 11, 78; Jacqueline Doherty, 'Make it decaf', *Barrons* (20 May 2002), pp. 20–1; Mary Chung, 'Starbucks: behind the froth of expansion', *FT.com* (27 May 2003); Astrid Wendlandt, 'Brands brew a coffee coup', *Financial Times* (26 June 2003); *Business Wire*, 'Starbucks celebrates milestone' (15 July 2003) and information accessed online at www.starbucks.com, July 2003.

Let the great world spin for ever
down the ringing grooves of change.

ALFRED LORD TENNYSON

The marketing setting

PART TWO OF PRINCIPLES OF MARKETING examines the environment in which
marketing operates. The marketing setting has undergone dramatic change in the
past decade. Technological advances, including the explosion of the Internet,
globalisation and changing societal values, have compelled marketers to rethink
their marketing strategies and processes. In Part Two, we address how marketing
is affected by changes in the environment and what firms must do in order to thrive
in today's new environment. It has four chapters.

Chapter 3 looks at the marketing environment in two parts: the *microenvironment*
that is specific to an organisation's operation, such as suppliers and competitors;
and the *macroenvironment* of wider forces that shape society, such as the natural
and political environment.

In **Chapter 4**, we address the impact of the Internet and new technologies on buyers
and organisations and show how marketers conduct marketing in the digital age.
As a major force, globalisation has also posed new challenges to marketers.

Chapter 5 looks at the global marketplace and examines how marketing strategy
and processes may be adapted to succeed in international markets. Global markets
make it even harder to understand the social environment of marketing.

This understanding is expanded in **Chapter 6**, which looks beyond buying and selling
to examine marketing's role and responsibilities in society. Together these chapters
examine marketing as 'the place where the selfish interests of the manufacturer
coincide with the interest of society', as the advertising guru David Ogilvy put it.

COCKTAIL

Michel
Doux baiser

> The first rule of business: Find out what the man you are dealing with wants, and give it to him.

WARREN TATE

The marketing environment

Chapter objectives

After reading this chapter, you should be able to:

- Describe the environmental forces that affect the company's ability to serve its customers.
- Explain how changes in the demographic and economic environments affect marketing decisions.
- Identify the main trends in the firm's natural and technological environments.
- Explain the key changes that occur in the political and cultural environments.
- Discuss how companies can react to the marketing environment.

Mini Contents List

- Prelude case – Big food has a lot on its plate
- Introduction
- The company's microenvironment
- The company's macroenvironment
- Marketing Insights 3.1 – We have a say!
- Marketing Insights 3.2 – Marimekko: Simplicity sells!
- Responding to the marketing environment
- Summary
- Concluding concept 3 – Toyota Prius: green or geek machine?

◀ SOURCE: Corbis/Design © S. Henchoz.

Prelude case Big food has a lot on its plate

I will always remember the first time I tried to buy a packet of crisps – or potato chips, if you prefer – in a New York supermarket. In vain, I searched for the single-portion packets with which Britons are familiar: all I could see on the shelves were rows and rows of what appeared to be party-sized bags. Then suddenly, I noticed the slogan on one of them. 'Get your own bag!', it screamed, and I realised with amazement and some awe that, in the land of plenty, these enormous bags were intended for a party of one.

Fat, salt and sugar have been the building blocks of success for most of the world's big brand owners.

That was in 1993, and the crisps with the slogan were Frito-Lay's Ruffles. In those days, you could not go to Frito-Lay's website to check the crisps' calorie content. Today, however, you can, and you find that they weigh in at 160 calories to the ounce. On that basis, an 8 oz get-your-own bag would contain 1,280 calories, more than half the average male's total energy needs for a day – and that is before you count the fizzy drinks or beer required to wash the crisps down.

I was thinking of that incident this week as news leaked of Unilever's planned cuts in its sales targets, announced on Thursday. As food companies go, Unilever is better than most: a lot of its products are reasonably nutritious and some, such as its cholesterol-busting spreads, can improve people's health. But even Unilever has been caught up in the sudden panic over obesity. Four years ago, its simultaneous acquisition of SlimFast Foods, the slimming company, and Ben & Jerry's Homemade, the fattening company, looked like a clever each-way bet. However, as people have become fatter and more desperate for a miracle remedy, Atkins has replaced SlimFast as the diet of choice, while Ben & Jerry's high-fat, premium ice-creams have begun to look gross.

Still, things could be worse. It is a curious fact of life that in the food and drink industry, fat, salt and sugar have been the building blocks of success for most of the world's big brand owners. Coca-Cola, PepsiCo, McDonald's, Burger King, Cadbury Schweppes, Mars, Hershey – all are founded on products now blamed for causing obesity; and most of the rest – Kraft Foods, Nestlé, HJ Heinz, Kellogg, General Mills, Campbell Soup – make an unhealthily large contribution to the output of fatty, salty or sugary foods that are accused of contributing to the problem.

Perhaps the food industry's enthusiasm for fattening products mattered less when people's limited means restricted their ability to gorge on them. But evolutionary theory suggests we are programmed to overeat because, through most of human history, food was scarce and over-consumption was an insurance policy against lean times. So as disposable incomes have risen, it has been hard for us to resist the temptation to binge on the food companies' heavily marketed output.

So what happens now? Even among anti-obesity campaigners, few would advocate measures as illiberal as banning undesirable food products or taxing them out of existence, though doubtless we could think of some prime candidates (Velveeta? Spam?).

On the other hand, the industry seems unlikely to get away with the idea that people should simply take more exercise. Even large amounts of physical activity burn off relatively few calories: you would have to do three hours' downhill skiing or spend more than five hours on the golf course to burn off an 8 oz bag of Ruffles.

Obviously, fattening food is not tobacco: consumed in reasonable quantities, it can be a harmless treat. But given our sudden awareness of the growing human and social costs of obesity, I suspect manufacturers of the most obviously unhealthy foods and drinks are now where the tobacco industry was roughly 40 years ago, when studies on both sides of the Atlantic finally established the link between cigarette smoking and cancer.

Those studies did not, of course, lead to a ban on cigarette sales, but they did mark the beginning of the tobacco industry's demonisation. Public health campaigns began warning people of the dangers of smoking, increasing restrictions were placed on manufacturers' ability to advertise, tough new labelling laws were introduced and anti-smoking organisations sprang up to lobby for tobacco controls. Smoking went into decline and eventually, of course, the litigation began.

We should not get too carried away with the parallels: I do not believe there have been any claims yet that passive eating is dangerous, and Michael Bloomberg, New York's mayor, has not yet banned people from consuming fatty foods in the city's bars. Even so, some of the similarities are uncanny. Just as the tobacco industry responded to the health scares by introducing 'light' versions of its top brands, for example, the food industry is producing low-fat, low-sugar or low-salt versions of nearly all its best-known products.

In this context, it is worth noting that light cigarettes are now discredited and Philip Morris is in the process of appealing against a $10.1bn judgement that it deceived Illinois smokers into believing the cigarettes were safer than regular ones. Food companies seem to be leaving themselves open to similar claims, for example by offering reduced-fat or low-fat products that contain nearly as many calories as the regular version.

For food companies, the good news is that, even after 40 years of tobacco's demonisation, people still smoke and the tobacco industry is still making profits. On that basis I confidently predict that even the food industry's most fattening companies can look forward to a secure future, though they may have to forget about growth, and certainly about being much loved.[1]

Questions

1. Is the food industry executive correct in claiming: 'The food industry is nothing like the tobacco industry. Stop smoking and you will live longer; stop eating and you will die sooner.'

2. For decades people have known the impact of an unhealthy diet and what constitutes healthy eating, yet people continue to eat their way to ill health. Since this is not a new problem, what accounts for the sudden upsurge in public and political concern for obesity? Identify the actors and forces in the environment that may work for or against the food industry, showing how these may shape marketing opportunities, pose threats and influence companies' ability to serve target customers well.

3. Why is the focus on the food giants rather than the startlingly unhealthy English fried breakfast, French breakfast of croissant and caffeine-ridden coffee, or continental breakfast of egg, cheese and bread? How should the major food companies, such as Nestlé, Cadbury and Burger King, respond to this surge of concern?

SOURCE: Richard Tomkins, 'Big food has a lot on its plate', FT.com © *Financial Times*, (12 February 2003).

Introduction

Marketing does not operate in a vacuum but, instead, in a complex and changing environment. Indeed, marketers operate in an increasingly connected world. As the prelude case shows, companies today have to be alert and responsive to the interests and concerns of various actors in their marketing environment, not just its immediate customers. In this chapter, you will discover how other *actors* in this environment – suppliers, intermediaries, customers, competitors, publics and others – may work with or against the company. Major environmental forces – demographic, economic, natural, technological, political and cultural – shape marketing opportunities, present threats and influence companies' ability to serve target customers and secure lasting relationships with them. To understand marketing, and to develop and implement effective marketing strategies, you must first understand the environmental context in which marketing operates. Today's marketers must be adept at managing relationships with customers and external partners. However, to do this effectively, marketers must understand the major environmental factors that surround all those relationships.

A company's **marketing environment** consists of the actors and forces outside marketing that affect marketing management's ability to develop and maintain successful relationships with its target customers. The marketing environment offers both opportunities and threats. Successful companies know the vital importance of constantly watching and adapting to the changing environment. Too many other companies, unfortunately, fail to think of change as opportunity. They ignore or resist critical changes until it is almost too late. Their strategies, structures, systems and culture grow increasingly out of date. Corporations as mighty as IBM and General Motors have faced crises because they ignored environmental changes for too long. There are lessons here too for the food giants facing rising public and political concerns for obesity, as intimated in the prelude case.

In the new millennium, both consumers and marketers wonder what the future will bring. The environment continues to change at a rapid pace. For example, think about how you buy groceries today. How will your grocery buying change during the next few decades? What challenges will these changes present for marketers? Some futurists predict that we will not be shopping in multi-aisle supermarkets in 2025. The growth of e-commerce and the rapid speed of the Internet will lead to online ordering of lower-priced, non-perishable products, from strawberry jam to coffee filters. Retailers will become 'bundlers', combining these orders into large packages of goods for each household and delivering them efficiently to their doorsteps. As a result we will see mergers between retailing and home-delivery companies. Consumers will not waste time searching for the best-priced bundle. Online information agents will do it for them, comparing prices among competitors.

Another futuristic view sees computers in 2025 as being as smart as humans. Consumers will use them to exchange information with on-screen electronic agents that ferret out the best deals online. Thanks to embedded-chip technology in the kitchen, products on a continuous household replenishment (CHR) list, like paper towels and pet food, will sense they are running low and reorder themselves automatically. If the information agent finds a comparable but cheaper substitute for a CHR product, the item will be switched instantly.[2]

Such pictures of the future give marketers plenty to think about. More than any other group in the company, marketers must be the trend trackers and opportunity seekers. Although every manager in an organisation needs to observe the outside environment, marketers have two special aptitudes. They have disciplined methods – marketing intelligence and marketing research – for collecting information about the marketing environment. They also normally spend more time in the customer and competitor environment. By carefully and systematically studying the environment, marketers can revise and adapt marketing strategies to meet new marketplace challenges and opportunities.

Marketing environment— The actors and forces outside marketing that affect marketing management's ability to develop and maintain successful relationships with its target customers.

Microenvironment—The forces close to the company that affect its ability to serve its customers – the company, market channel firms, customer markets, competitors and publics, which combine to make up the firm's value delivery system.

Macroenvironment—The larger societal forces that affect the whole microenvironment – demographic, economic, natural, technological, political and cultural forces.

The marketing environment consists of a microenvironment and a macroenvironment. The **microenvironment** consists of the forces close to the company that affect its ability to serve its customers – the company, suppliers, marketing channel firms, customer markets, competitors and publics. The **macroenvironment** consists of the larger societal forces that affect the whole microenvironment – demographic, economic, natural, technological, political and cultural forces. We look first at the company's microenvironment.

The company's microenvironment

Marketing management's job is to attract and build relationships with customers by creating customer value and satisfaction. However, marketing managers cannot accomplish this task alone. Their success will depend on other actors in the company's microenvironment – other company departments, suppliers, marketing intermediaries, customers, competitors and various publics, which combine to make up the company's value delivery network (see Figure 3.1).

The company

In designing marketing plans, marketing management should take other company groups, such as top management, finance, research and development (R&D), purchasing, manufacturing and accounting, into consideration. All these interrelated groups form the internal environment (see Figure 3.2). Top management sets the company's mission, objectives, broad strategies and policies. Marketing managers make decisions within the plans made by top management.

Marketing managers must also work closely with other company departments. Finance is concerned with finding and using funds to carry out the marketing plan. The R&D department focuses on the problems of designing safe and attractive products. Purchasing worries about getting supplies and materials, whereas Operations is responsible for producing the desired quality and quantity of products. Accounting has to measure revenues and costs to help marketing know how well it is achieving its objectives. Together, all of these departments

Figure 3.1 Principal actors in the company's microenvironment

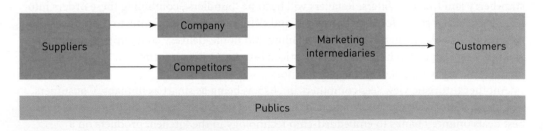

Figure 3.2 The company's internal environment

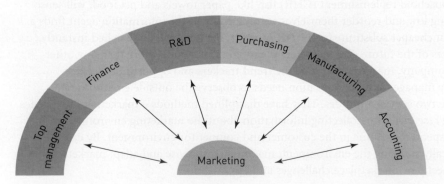

have an impact on the marketing department's plans and actions. Under the marketing concept, all of these functions must 'think customer' and they should work in harmony to provide superior customer value and satisfaction.

Suppliers

Suppliers are an important link in the company's overall customer value delivery system. They provide the resources needed by the company to produce its goods and services. Supplier developments can seriously affect marketing. Marketing managers must watch supply availability – supply shortages or delays, labour strikes and other events can cost sales in the short run and damage customer satisfaction in the long run. Marketing managers also monitor the price trends of their key inputs. Rising supply costs may force price increases that can harm the company's sales volume. Increasingly, today's marketers are treating their suppliers as partners in creating and delivering customer value.

Marketing intermediaries

Marketing intermediaries are firms that help the company to promote, sell and distribute its goods to final buyers. They include *resellers, physical distribution firms, marketing services agencies* and *financial intermediaries*. **Resellers** are distribution channel firms that help the company find customers or make sales to them. These include wholesalers and retailers who buy and resell merchandise. Selecting and working with resellers is not easy. No longer do manufacturers have many small, independent resellers from which to choose. They now face large and growing reseller organisations. These organisations frequently have enough power to dictate terms or even shut the manufacturer out of large markets.

Physical distribution firms help the company to stock and move goods from their points of origin to their destinations. Working with warehouse and transportation firms, a company must determine the best ways to store and ship goods, balancing such factors as cost, delivery, speed and safety.

Marketing services agencies are the marketing research firms, advertising agencies, media firms and marketing consultancies that help the company target and promote its products to the right markets. When the company decides to use one of these agencies, it must choose carefully because the firms vary in creativity, quality, service and price. The company has to review the performance of these firms regularly and consider replacing those that no longer perform well.

Financial intermediaries include banks, credit companies, insurance companies and other businesses that help finance transactions or insure against the risks associated with the buying and selling of goods. Most firms and customers depend on financial intermediaries to finance their transactions. The company's marketing performance can be seriously affected by rising credit costs and limited credit.

Like suppliers, marketing intermediaries form an important component of the company's overall value delivery system. In its quest to create satisfying customer relationships, the company must do more than just optimise its own performance. It must partner effectively with suppliers and marketing intermediaries to optimise the performance of the entire system.

Customers

The company must study its customer markets closely. Figure 3.3 shows six types of customer market. *Consumer markets* consist of individuals and households that buy goods and services for personal consumption. *Business markets* buy goods and services for further processing or for use in their production process, whereas *reseller markets* buy goods and services to resell at a profit. *Institutional markets* are made up of schools, hospitals, nursing homes, prisons and other

Suppliers—Firms and individuals that provide the resources needed by the company and its competitors to produce goods and services.

Marketing intermediaries—Firms that help the company to promote, sell and distribute its goods to final buyers; they include physical distribution firms, marketing-service agencies and financial intermediaries.

Resellers—The individuals and organisations that buy goods and services to resell at a profit.

Physical distribution firms—Warehouse, transportation and other firms that help a company to stock and move goods from their points of origin to their destinations.

Marketing services agencies—Marketing research firms, advertising agencies, media firms, marketing consulting firms and other service providers that help a company to target and promote its products to the right markets.

Financial intermediaries—Banks, credit companies, insurance companies and other businesses that help finance transactions or insure against the risks associated with the buying and selling of goods.

Figure 3.3 Types of customer market

institutions that provide goods and services to people in their care. *Government markets* are made up of government agencies that buy goods and services in order to produce public services or transfer the goods and services to others who need them. Finally, *international markets* consist of buyers in other countries, including consumers, producers, resellers and governments. Each market type has special characteristics that call for careful study by the seller. At any point in time, the firm may deal with one or more customer markets: for example, as a consumer packaged goods manufacturer, Unilever has to communicate brand benefits to consumers as well as maintaining a dialogue with retailers that stock and resell its branded products.

Competitors

The marketing concept states that, to be successful, a company must provide greater customer value and satisfaction than its competitors do. Thus, marketers must do more than simply adapt to the needs of target consumers. They must also gain strategic advantage by positioning their offerings strongly against competitors' offerings in the minds of consumers.

No single competitive marketing strategy is best for all companies. Each firm should consider its own size and industry position compared to those of its competitors. Large firms with dominant positions in an industry can use certain strategies that smaller firms cannot afford. But being large is not enough. There are winning strategies for large firms, but there are also losing ones. And small firms can develop strategies that give them better rates of return than large firms enjoy. We will look more closely at competitor analysis and competitive marketing strategies in Chapter 12.

Publics

Public—Any group that has an actual or potential interest in or impact on an organisation's ability to achieve its objectives.

The company's marketing environment also includes various publics. A **public** is any group that has an actual or potential interest in or impact on an organisation's ability to achieve its objectives. Figure 3.4 shows seven types of public:

1. *Financial publics.* Financial publics influence the company's ability to obtain funds. Banks, investment houses and stockholders are the principal financial publics.

2. *Media publics.* Media publics include newspapers, magazines and radio and television stations that carry news, features and editorial opinion.

3. *Government publics.* Management must take government developments into account. Marketers must often consult the company's lawyers on issues of product safety, truth in advertising and other matters.

4. *Citizen action publics.* A company's marketing decisions may be questioned by consumer organisations, environmental groups, minority groups and other pressure groups (see Marketing Insights 3.1). Its public relations department can help it stay in touch with consumer and citizen groups.

Figure 3.4 **Types of public**

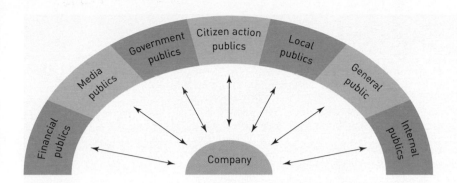

5. *Local publics*. Every company has local publics, such as neighbourhood residents and community organisations. Large companies usually appoint a community-relations officer to deal with the community, attend meetings, answer questions and contribute to worthwhile causes.

6. *General public*. A company needs to be concerned about the general public's attitude towards its products and activities. The public's image of the company affects its buying. Thus, many large corporations invest huge sums of money to promote and build a healthy corporate image.

7. *Internal publics*. These include its workers, managers, volunteers and the board of directors. Large companies use newsletters and other means to inform and motivate their internal publics. When employees feel good about their company, this positive attitude spills over to their external publics.

A company can prepare marketing plans for these publics as well as for its customer markets. Suppose the company wants a specific response from a particular public, such as goodwill, favourable word-of-mouth, or donations of time or money. The company would have to design an offer to this public that is attractive enough to produce the desired response.

We have looked at the firm's immediate or microenvironment. Next we examine the larger macroenvironment.

The company's macroenvironment

The company and all the other actors operate in a larger macroenvironment of forces that shape opportunities and pose threats to the company. Figure 3.5 on page 95 shows the six most influential forces in the company's macroenvironment. The remaining sections of this chapter examine these forces and show how they affect marketing plans.

Demographic environment

Demography is the study of human populations in terms of size, density, location, age, gender, race, occupation and other statistics. The demographic environment is of considerable interest to marketers because it involves people, and people make up markets. Here, we discuss the most important demographic characteristics and trends in the largest world markets.

Demography—The study of human populations in terms of size, density, location, age, sex, race, occupation and other statistics.

marketing insights

3.1   We have a say!

FT

The Irish pop band Westlife, their manager Ronan Keating, together with the lead singer of the group BoyZone, joined celebrities, including footballers Michael Owen, Robbie Fowler and Paul Ince, in a campaign to urge people to boycott Bell's Whisky, Burger King burgers and Häagen-Dazs ice-cream, until the company meets UK thalidomide victims' demands for increased compensation.

Thalidomide, the drug that led to hundreds of children being born without limbs, was withdrawn in 1961, when the side-effects of the drug taken by pregnant women were discovered. Distillers, the company that marketed the drug, has to make annual payments to 450 thalidomide victims until 2009. However, the health of many beneficiaries has been deteriorating. The predicament of these long-suffering victims led to the launch of a consumer boycott by Thalidomide UK, a support group for victims. The target? Distillers parent, Diageo, formed in 1997 after the merger of Grand Metropolitan and Guinness plc, which previously acquired Distillers. Thalidomide UK wanted extra funds to be provided by Diageo to cover the increased costs of victims' deteriorating health and proposed that payments should be extended 10 years, taking most victims up to their retirement age. Frustration with the lack of progress in Diageo's resolve to meet the group's proposals saw an intensification of the campaign, amid claims by Thalidomide UK of Diageo's attempt to dissuade celebrities from backing the offensive.

Publicity of this nature can tarnish a company's image. Even if Diageo is able to defend its policy on thalidomide, as a Diageo spokesperson acknowledges: 'We recognise that there will always be issues of serious concern arising from the tradegy of thalidomide . . . their resolution can be neither swift nor simple.' No matter how these concerns are ultimately resolved, one thing is certain. The company cannot afford to ignore public forces: like a voice from the past, Thalidomide UK will relentlessly knock on its conscience.

Consumer packaged goods manufacturers also face public outcries of one sort or another. One 'voice' that keeps them on their toes is the mounting public criticism for not doing enough to marry product development with environmental sustainability – using less resources and leaving behind less waste to deliver a product's function. Consumer goods giants such as the US group P&G and Anglo-Dutch-owned Unilever remain a constant target for protest groups of all sorts from animal rights activists to environmentalists. Although less in the sustainability spotlight than counterparts in the energy, transport and chemicals industries, companies like P&G and Unilever have to be wary of and responsive to the social and economic concerns of their consumers, shareholders and communities.

Both have a public commitment to sustainability. Both are sustainability leaders. According to the Dow Jones Sustainability index, Unilever tops the food and beverage sector and shares with P&G the pole position for non-cyclical goods and services. Both

...3.1

also have impressive sustainability projects: during the last decade, P&G claims to have reduced CO_2 emissions per tonne of production by two-thirds, while Unilever's have fallen by almost 20 per cent in the last five years. Both firms report big falls in their use of packaging, waste and water use.

However, activists are not always convinced. For example, P&G's recent innovation – convenience food served in plastic packages serving as feeding bowls, complete with scoop bags or litter boxes – does not sound like a committed journey down the sustainable path. Not forgetting the long-running criticism of the environmental impact of Pampers nappies. Unilever is not perfect either. Like its arch-rival P&G, it has paid several fines for violating health, safety and environmental laws in the past. It has also suffered bad publicity following Greenpeace's condemnation of its use of musk in household products and illegal mercury dumping from a factory in India.

Although these incidents question the commitment of these companies and the effectiveness of their sustainability policies, both are trying to live up to public expectations. P&G, for example, are involved in projects that improve water and health/hygiene. Their Recovery Engineering business makes PUR water filters, while NutriDelight, a drink developed with the United Nations Children's Fund, deals with micronutrient deficiency among school-age children. Unilever, meanwhile, is focusing on sustainable agriculture, fisheries and water supplies. With environmental group WWF, it established the Marine Stewardship Council, MSC, which has since become an independent organisation that accredits sustainable fisheries, seeking to make all substantial fish purchases from sustainable sources by 2005.

Peter White, P&G's European head of sustainable development, however, adds that 'sustainability' will not make many consumers choose Ariel (P&G's laundry detergent brand) over Unilever's Persil. Consumers' main priority is still about product performance, value, safety and reliability. These often come at a cost. Hence, it is not a question of which company is ahead in the sustainability index, but of turning pressures for sustainability into an opportunity. Mr White explains that 'It is about providing products that improve people's lives'. He also warns that sustainable development, to be truly sustainable, need to transcend philanthropy, morality, even efficiency (i.e. cost savings from using less resources to deliver the same functions). Any breakthroughs in sustainable development cannot be sustainable by businesses unless these ultimately result in sustained profitability. Commercial businesses have to be driven by profitability. How else can any commercial entity be viable over the long run?

While such arguments will undoubtedly reinforce anti-corporate sentiments, the truth is that environmental challenges pose both threats and opportunities. Sustainability can be viewed as opportunities for creating profitable customer and satisfying societal relationships, rather than a costly responsibility.

SOURCE: Jimmy Burns, 'Diageo defends policy on thalidomide', © *Financial Times* (9 March 2000), p. 6; Roger Cowe, 'Improving quality of life and profits', © *Financial Times* (13 August 2002), p. 12.

Stopping AIDS can save millions of lives.

Just as the red stop sign is an internationally recognized driving symbol, the red ribbon is the worldwide symbol of solidarity against HIV/AIDS. DaimlerChrysler stands shoulder to shoulder with the global community in its efforts to control and stop the spread of HIV/AIDS and to help treat those afflicted with the disease.

Our commitment takes many shapes from our "Workplace initiative on HIV/AIDS" in South Africa, in which we were the first company to provide free anti-retroviral drugs to employees, to Chairman Jürgen Schrempp's leadership role in the Global Business Coalition on HIV/AIDS.

For more information on DaimlerChrysler's initiatives visit www.daimlerchrysler.com

DAIMLERCHRYSLER
Answers for questions to come.

This DaimlerChrysler ad is not about promoting its cars to consumers. Instead, it communicates to the wider public its commitment to the global initiative to control and stop the spread of HIV/AIDS.
SOURCE: DaimlerChrysler AG Stuttgart/Auburn Hills.

94

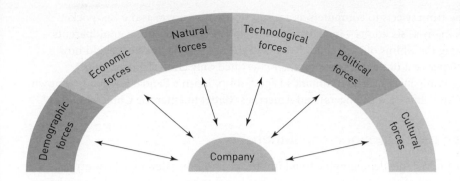

Figure 3.5 Influential forces
in the company's
macroenvironment

Population size and growth trends

In any geographic market, population size and growth trends can be used to gauge its broad potential for a wide range of goods and services. The European Union (EU), together with members of the European Free Trade Area (EFTA), has a population of around 379 million. With another 120 million from eastern Europe and 280 million from the former USSR, the overall European market is significantly larger than the North America Free Trade Area – the United States, Canada and Mexico – with a population of 370 million, and Japan with 130 million. Marketers also view China and India, each with over 1.2 billion people, as potentially lucrative growth markets.[3]

Today, the world has a population of around 6.3 billion people. Recent forecasts from the United Nations Population Division suggest that world population will grow annually at a rate of 1.2 per cent, increasing to about 8.9 billion by 2050. Six countries contribute to half that increase: India for 21 per cent; China for 12 per cent; Pakistan for 5 per cent; Bangladesh, Nigeria and the US for 4 per cent each. India's population increases by more in a week than the EU's in a year! Although these numbers suggest that world population is increasing, the reality is that the population growth rate is falling due largely to higher death rates, mostly attributed to higher projected prevalence of HIV/AIDS, and the forecast reduction in fertility.[4]

Although population over such an extended period is inherently unpredictable, the signs are that the 'humanity of the future will be different from today's', as the following report implies:

> There would be 5.2 billion Asians, up from 3.8 billion in 2004. There would be 1.8 billion Africans, up from 851 million today. There would be 768 million Latin Americans, up from 543 million today. There would be 448 million North Americans, up from 326 million today. But, there would be only 632 million Europeans, down from 726 million today. Within Asia, however, there will be a noteworthy transformation: Japan's population will decline to as little as 110 million. The world's giant will be India, with a population of 1.5 billion, 17.2 per cent of the world's total, ahead even of China's 1.4 billion.[5]

A growing population means growing human needs to satisfy, offering marketers an indication of demand for certain goods and services. Depending on purchasing power, it may also mean growing market opportunities. For example, to curb its skyrocketing population, the Chinese government passed regulations limiting families to one child each. As a result, Chinese children tend to be spoiled and fussed over as never before. They are being showered with everything from sweets to computers as a result of what is known as the 'six-pocket syndrome'. As many as six adults – including parents and two sets of doting grandparents – may be indulging the whims of each child. Parents in the average Beijing household now spend about 40 per cent of their income on their cherished only child. This trend has encouraged toy companies such as Denmark's Lego Group, Japan's Bandai Company (known for its Mighty Morphin Power Rangers) and America's Mattel to enter the Chinese market.[6]

Changing age structure of a population

The single most noticeable demographic trend in Europe and other developed countries, including the US and affluent Asian countries, is the changing age structure of the population. The post-World War II baby boom produced the *baby boomers*, born between 1946 and 1964. The boomers have presented a moving target, creating new markets as they grew from infancy to their pre-adolescent, teenage, young-adult and now middle-age to mature years. Baby boomers cut across all walks of life. But marketers typically have paid the most attention to the smaller upper crust of the boomer generation – its more educated, mobile and wealthy segments. These segments have gone by many names. In the 1980s, they were called 'yuppies' (young urban professionals), 'yummies' (young upwardly mobile mommies), and 'dinkies' (from DINKY, dual-income, no kids yet). In the 1990s, however, yuppies and dinkies gave way to a new breed, with names such as DEWKs (dual-earners with kids) and SLOPPIES (slightly older urban professionals).

The oldest boomers are now in their fifties; the youngest are in their mid-to-late thirties. They are also reaching their peak earning and spending years. Thus, they constitute a lucrative market for housing, furniture and appliances, healthy foods and beverages, physical fitness products, high-priced cars, convenience products and travel and financial services.

The maturing boomers are experiencing the pangs of midlife and rethinking the purpose and value of their work, responsibilities and relationships. They are approaching life with a new stability and reasonableness in the way they live, think, eat and spend. As they continue to age, they will create a large and important seniors market.

The baby boom was followed by a 'birth dearth' creating another generation of people born between 1965 and 1976. The *Generation Xers* tend to be the children of parents who both held jobs. Increasing divorce rates and higher employment for their mothers made them the first generation of latchkey kids. They want to build more traditional families and to be more available to their children. Whereas the boomers created a sexual revolution, the GenXers have lived in the age of AIDS. Having grown up during times of recession and corporate downsizing, they have developed a more cautious economic outlook. As a result, the GenXers are a more sceptical bunch, cynical of frivolous marketing pitches that promise easy success. Their cynicism makes them more savvy shoppers, and their financial pressures make them more value conscious. They like lower prices and a more functional look. The GenXers respond to honesty in advertising. They like irreverence and sass and ads that mock the traditional advertising approach.

GenXers share new cultural concerns. They care about the environment and respond favourably to socially responsible companies. Although they seek success, they are less materialistic; they prize experience, not acquisition. They are cautious romantics who want a better quality of life and are more interested in job satisfaction than in sacrificing personal happiness and growth for promotion.

The GenXers are now growing up and beginning to take over. They are the first generation to have grown up with computers and surf the Net more than other groups, but with serious intent. By 2010, they will have overtaken the baby boomers as a primary market for almost every product category.

Both the baby boomers and GenXers will one day be passing the reins to the latest demographic group, the *echo boomers* (the baby boomlet generation). Born between 1977 and

1994, and ranging from pre-teens to twenties, the echo boomer generation is still forming its buying preferences and behaviours.

The echo boom has created large and growing kid and teens markets. Teens and pre-teens under 20 years of age are high spenders, or at least greatly influence their parents' spending.[7] After years of bust, markets for children's toys and games, clothes, furniture and food are enjoying a boom. For instance, Sony and other electronics firms are now offering products designed especially for children. In recent years, designers and retailers have created new lines, new products and even new stores devoted to children and teens – DKNY, Gap, Naf Naf and Guess, to name just a few. Banks too are offering banking and investment services for kids.

Like the trailing edge of the Generation Xers ahead of them, one distinguishing characteristic of the echo boomers is their utter fluency and comfort with computer, digital and Internet technology. For this reason, one analyst has christened them the Net-Gens (or N-gens). He observes:

> What makes this generation different . . . is not just its demographic muscle, but it is the first to grow up surrounded by digital media. Computers and other digital technologies, such as digital cameras, are commonplace to N-Gen members. They work with them at home, in school, and they use them for entertainment. Increasingly these technologies are connected to the Internet. . . . Constantly surrounded by technology, today's kids are accustomed to its strong presence in their lives. [They] are so bathed in bits that they are no more intimidated by digital technology than a VCR or a toaster. And it is through their use of the digital media that N-Gen will develop and superimpose its culture on the rest of society. Boomers stand back. Already these kids are learning, playing, communicating, working and creating communities very differently than did their parents. They are a force for social transformation.[8]

Do marketers have to create separate products and marketing programmes for each generation? Some experts caution that each generation spans decades of time and many socioeconomic levels. So, they do not constitute meaningful target markets. As such, marketers should form more precise age-specific segments within each group. Others warn that marketers have to be careful about turning off one generation each time they craft a product or message that appeals effectively to another. Marketers should carefully develop their product brands such as to be broadly inclusive, offering each generation something specifically designed for it.

In most rich countries, though, national populations are getting older. The trend is forecast to continue over the next 50 years. Furthermore, this demographic change is not confined to advanced countries. In Latin America and most of Asia, the share of over-60s is set to double between now and 2030, to 14 per cent. In China, it will increase from less than 10 per cent in 2000 to around 22 per cent by 2030.[9]

The ageing population structure reflects two influences. First is a declining birth rate. As mentioned earlier, official forecasts suggest that the world's population is growing more slowly. About half of this slowdown comes from the reduction in the number of babies born per woman (that is, replacement fertility rate, Figure 3.6). However, except for the US, with a fertility rate of 2.11, which is close to replacement, fertility levels are dropping most notably in all the developed, high-income countries. For example, Germany's is 1.35, Japan's is 1.32, Spain's is 1.15 and Hong Kong's is 1.00. All the EU countries rank below the 2.1 fertility level

Figure 3.6 **Total fertility: number of children born per woman in developed and less developed nations**

SOURCE: United Nations. Based on article written by Martin Wolf, published in 'Demography. People, plagues and prosperity: five trends that promise to transform the world's population within 50 years', *Financial Times* (27 February 2003), p. 17.

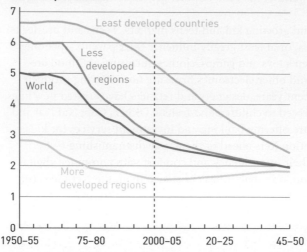

Children per woman

Figure 3.7 **The world's ageing population: life expectancy to 2050**

SOURCE: United Nations. Based on article written by Martin Wolf, published in 'Demography. People, plagues and prosperity: five trends that promise to transform the world's population within 50 years', *Financial Times* (27 February 2003), p. 17.

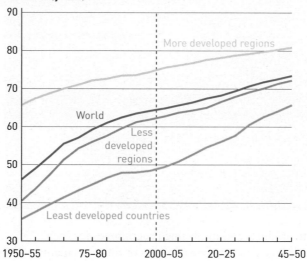

At birth (years)

found in the US. Fertility rates in other developed Asian nations such as Singapore and South Korea also have declined steadily over the past two decades, and all lie below America's 2.1 average. In developing countries, fertility is currently above replacement rate, at nearly 2.92 children per woman. India's fertility rate is currently 3.01, but this represents a rapidly declining trend from 4.5 children per woman back in the 1980s. However, in countries like China, the fertility rate, at 1.83, is already well below replacement. This 'birth-dearth' linked to smaller family sizes is due to people's desire to improve personal living standards, women's desire to work outside the home, and widely available and effective birth control practices.[10] In the case of the least developed nations, fertility rate is over 5 in 2003, and is projected to remain above replacement rates over the next four decades.

Secondly, ageing trends are influenced by life expectancy increases (see Figure 3.7). Life expectancy has risen for the world as a whole, from below 50 half a century ago to 64.6 years in 1995–2000. Life expectancy in the high-income countries is predicted to reach 81.6 years by 2050, up from 74.8 years in 1995–2000. In the developing countries, it is expected to reach 73.1 years, an increase from 62.5 in 1995–2000. Although life expectancy is also projected to rise in the least developed countries in Africa, levels have currently remained at around

50 years, a setback inflicted by HIV/AIDS, whose prevalence has been more serious and prolonged than anticipated according to UN sources.[11]

However, while the world's population is forecast to age faster over the next half century than ever before, countries with lower fertility rates now will be vastly more aged by 2050. Official forecasts for the EU countries suggest that, by 2050, 35 per cent of the population will be over 60 years old, compared to 20 per cent in 2003. Put more colourfully by the historian and demographer Peter Laslett, 'Europe (is) growing older and will never be young again.'

Demographic shifts have important implications for marketing managers. The rising number of elderly customers and a corresponding dearth of younger buyers may not necessarily spell trouble for companies and marketers. Instead, marketers must track demographic trends and moves carefully in order to identify new product and market opportunities for their company.

The rising ageing population, for example, will imply a growing demand for healthcare products, pensions and services tailored to the needs of this group of consumers. According to the charity Help the Aged, 'Today's over-60s are more affluent and active, with lifestyles that are more akin to those of people in their 40s and 50s. Government and industry can no longer ignore this influential group, and must take a closer look at the services and policies that affect the lives of older people.'[12] Indeed, some companies are already grappling with this demographic shift and adapting product marketing and design to cater to older consumers' demands.

> The $600,000 (€495,868) Enzo Ferrari accelerates to 60 mph in under 4 seconds before reaching a top speed of 217 mph. Not a ride to recommend if you're wearing a cardiac pacemaker. But, the Italian car maker is one of the many companies that are now tackling demographic shifts – the ageing population. Climb into the Enzo and, apparently, you will not even notice the modifications designed with 'overweight, arthritic pensioners' in mind. While Ferrari engineers cherish a sporty product whose virile brand depends on images of young drivers haring around Formula One racetracks, the profile of their customers means that they have to pay attention to practicality and functionality without compromising the sportiness. In contrast to F1 drivers Michael Schumacher and Rubens Barrichello, both in their thirties, the average buyer of a Ferrari is close to 50 and will get older. Ferrari designers are responding by enlarging the space to accommodate the driver's expanding backside and sparing the knees with changes to the door height. Part of the roof and the door undermoulding also come away when you open the door to make it easier to enter the car. However, these design changes are done such that no one is able to tell. Ferrari's customers do not want to be patronized and few want to own a car that reminds them of their age. Some companies like Saga, the British holiday operator, magazine publisher and financial services provider, serving the over–50s, so-called 'grey segment', can be rather creative. A recent issue of its magazine shows ads for Bose hi-fi equipment and a red Mazda MX-5 alongside pictures of stairlifts and corn-plasters. Saga Holidays also offers white-water rafting breaks in Canada and jungle trekking in Borneo. It seems Saga knows better – that the new oldies are not ready to be pensioned off.[13]

The changing family

The notion of the ideal family – mum, dad and two kids – has lately been losing some of its lustre. People are marrying later and having fewer children. The specific figures may vary among countries, but the general trend is towards fewer married couples with children. In fact, couples with children under 18 now make up a small proportion of all families. These are worrying trends too for wealthy Asian countries like Singapore, Japan and Hong Kong.

Also, the number of working women, including working mothers, is increasing. This trend has spawned the child day-care business, cleaning and catering services, increased consumption of convenience foods, career-oriented women's clothing and many other business opportunities. Marketers of goods ranging from cars, insurance and travel to financial services are increasingly directing their advertising to working women. For some products such as jewellery, typically bought by men and worn by women, retailers have also seen a move towards more professional women buying jewellery for themselves simply for their own pleasure and interest. Moreover, as a result of the shift in the traditional roles and values of husbands and wives, with male partners assuming more domestic functions such as shopping and child care, more food and household appliance marketers are targeting this group of individuals.

Finally, the number of one-person and non-family households will represent a sizeable proportion of all households. These reflect 'non-traditional' or 'diverse' households consisting of single live-alones, adult live-togethers of one or both sexes, single-parent families, childless married couples or empty-nesters. More married people are divorcing or separating, choosing not to marry, marrying later or marrying without intending to have children. In countries such as Sweden, Germany, Denmark and Switzerland, for example, one-person households now account for over 30 per cent of all homes.[14] Marketers must increasingly consider the special needs of non-traditional households since they are now growing more rapidly than traditional households. Each group has a distinctive set of needs and buying habits. For example, people in the SSWD (single, separated, widowed, divorced) group need smaller apartments, inexpensive and smaller appliances, furniture and furnishings, and food that is packaged in smaller sizes.

Pressures for migration

The next few decades will see the emergence of a world where citizens in the affluent, developed countries have few children while their counterparts in the less wealthy countries have many. These conditions increase the pressures on international migration. As these countries' populations age, there will be many more openings for foreigners in jobs where domestic talent is scarce or to increase the population of economically active young people. Because of the increase in demand for healthcare, pension and welfare provisions, to balance the books, many European countries, including the Nordic countries and Britain, are likely to have to accept high levels of international immigration. According to the Government Actuary Department, nearly two-thirds of the UK's population increase in the next 25 years would be caused by inward migration, with the remainder being due to natural increase – more births than deaths.[15] As one analyst reports:

A world in which people in rich countries have few children and the poor have many is one in which pressures for migration can only grow. . . . The high-income countries are expected to receive an average of only 2 million migrants a year over the next half century or 100 million in total. . . . The UN forecasts that the principal recipients will be the US (1.1 million annual net immigration), Germany (211,000), Canada (173,000), the UK (136,000) and Australia (83,000). Meanwhile, the most important sources are forecast to be China (303,000), Mexico (257,000), India (222,000), the Philippines (184,000) and Indonesia (180,000).

The big question is whether the migration pressure can be contained at what appears relatively low levels. Under the UN's median projections, Europe's population falls by 94 million between 2003 and 2050. But, Africa's population is projected to rise by 952 million, and Asia's population by 1.39 billion. Both will have a large number of young adults desperate for a better life. Given Europe's land borders with Asia and the narrow sea that separates it from Africa, controlling migration is certain to be difficult. It is certain to become an even bigger political issue.

The US is in a very different position. Not only has it been historically more open to immigration, but its neighbours have a less dynamic demographic profile than Europe's. Latin America and the Caribbean are forecast to have only a 225 million increase in population between 2003 and 2050. But the pressure from its closest developing country neighbour will not go away since Mexico's population is forecast to rise to 140 million in 2050, up from 99 million in 2000.[16]

Rising number of educated people

The percentage of a country's population that has been educated – that is, have upper secondary and university-level education – varies across countries, but some trends can be discerned in the EU and other industrialised nations as a whole. According to OECD statistics, there has been a narrowing trend in the gap between the number of men and women who have a university education in member countries. In most countries, equal education has been attained among men and women belonging to the 25–34 age group. Gaps remain in some countries – Britain, Germany and Switzerland, for example – where more men still go to university than women. As economies in eastern Europe and Asia develop, we expect to see rising investment in education and an increasingly educated population. The rising number of educated people will increase the demand for quality products, books, magazines, travel, personal computers and Internet services.[17]

Increasing diversity

The new millennium sees an escalation of efforts towards the enlargement of the European Union, with 10 countries joining the EU in May 2004. The enlarged EU now comprises a family of 25 member states: the 15 members prior to 2004 – France, Luxembourg, Italy, Germany, with East Germany on unification, Netherlands, Belgium, Denmark, Ireland, United Kingdom, Greece, Spain, Portugal, Sweden, Austria and Finland – and the recent, new entrants – Poland, the Czech Republic, Hungary, Slovakia, Lithuania, Latvia, Slovenia, Estonia, Cyprus and Malta. Others including Bulgaria, Romania and Turkey are waiting in the wings, hoping to agree accession treaties before the end of this decade.[18]

The EU, in its present state, and in a potentially enlarged form, presents huge challenges and opportunities for domestic and international marketers. We will discuss international marketing issues in more detail in Chapter 6.

In general, marketers operating in the vastly expanded EU must recognise the great diversity across member states. Unification goes beyond mere economic integration such as the implementation of the single currency, the euro, in January 1999. To date, 11 EU nations have joined the single-currency or 'euro zone'. In the decades ahead, European unification will strive to achieve harmonisation of rules and regulations, which will affect business practices across the Union. Many marketers believe the single European market encourages convergence in consumer tastes, propagating the idea of the 'Euroconsumer'.

Converging lifestyles, values, beliefs, habits and tastes may often not mean converging needs. These may differ across individual country markets, just as spending power and consumption patterns are likely to vary. Europe, like the US, remains a pot-pourri of cultures and systems, which present immense marketing opportunities for sellers. Although social and demographic factors and the marketing strategies of multinational consumer goods companies may combine to make lifestyles of different European (and rising wealthy Asian) nations more alike, diversity will feature just as much as convergence in the new world economy.

Businesses will do well to identify regional, national and local differences, and to develop appropriate marketing strategies that take on board this diversity. Where European consumers display similar cultural values and homogeneous tastes for particular goods and services, then pan-European strategies may be more cost-effective. For example, the internationalism of snob items, such as Rolex watches or Cartier jewellery, which appeal to a small number of like-minded consumers, or high-fashion purchases like Swatch watches and DKNY clothes, which pander to the younger generation of dedicated fashion followers, lend themselves to pan-European marketing or advertising.

In most markets, however, firms have found that the 'one sight, one sound, one sell' dictum loses out to the more effective strategy of customisation. Even Coca-Cola, arch exponent of globalism, tailors the marketing of its drinks to suit different markets. Kronenbourg, France's most popular beer, is sold to a mass market with the eternal images of France, like cafés, boules and Citroën 2CVs. In the UK, Kronenbourg is presented as a drink for 'yuppies'. Unilever customises its advertisements for Impulse, a body spray. In the UK, the handsome young fellow who gets a whiff of Impulse from the woman nearby presents her with a bunch of flowers. In the Italian version, Romeo offers the woman a rose.

Ultimately, marketers must address a marketing basic: identify consumer needs and respond to them. Companies that overlook diversity in favour of pan-European or global strategies must carefully develop and execute their standardised approaches.[19] We discuss pan-European versus standardised marketing practices in greater depth in Chapter 6.

Economic environment

Economic environment— Factors that affect consumer buying power and spending patterns.

Markets require buying power as well as people. The **economic environment** consists of factors that affect consumer purchasing power and spending patterns. Nations vary greatly in their levels and distribution of income. Some countries have *subsistence economies* – they consume most of their own agricultural and industrial output, hence offer few market opportunities. At the other extreme are *industrial economies*, which constitute rich markets for different kinds of goods. Marketers must pay close attention to major trends and consumer spending patterns both across and within their world markets.

Income distribution and changes in purchasing power

Global upheavals in technology and communications in the last decade brought about a shift in the balance of economic power from the West (mainly North American, Canadian and western European nations) towards the rapidly expanding economies of Asia and the Pacific Rim. Up until the Asian economic and financial crisis in 1997, many of the Asian 'tiger'

We build cars for people who love to drive. Some of them happen to use wheelchairs. For these drivers, and for families who transport someone in a wheelchair, we present the Volkswagen Mobility Access Program.

This is our way of lending a hand to anyone who needs to make a new Volkswagen* more accessible. If you need to add hand controls, we'll refund up to $500! If you need to add a lift, we'll refund up to $1000!

After all, when we say "Drivers wanted", we mean every one of them.

Volkswagen targets people with disabilities who want to travel. It offers a Mobility Access Programme and has even modified its catchy 'Drivers Wanted' tag line to appeal to motorists with disabilities: 'All Drivers Wanted'.
SOURCE: Volkwagen.

economies, notably South Korea, Taiwan, Thailand, Malaysia, Indonesia and Singapore, were enjoying annual growth rates in excess of 7 per cent, compared to the 2–3 per cent found in western Europe and the USA.[20]

Official statistics have adjusted downwards the annual growth rates of these economies, in the first decade of the 2000s. However, rapid economic recovery in Singapore, Taiwan and South Korea means purchasing power income per head will exceed that of the US and western Europe.[21]

In view of the rising importance of overseas markets as a source of growth for many western businesses, the uncertain economic climate in the Asian economies has important implications for international marketers. They must determine how changing incomes affect purchasing power and how they translate into marketing threats and opportunities for the firm.

Where consumer purchasing power is reduced, as in countries experiencing economic collapse or in an economic recession, financially squeezed consumers tend to spend more carefully and seek greater value in the products and services they buy. For example, 'thrift shops' have been booming in Japan, whose economy has been in recession. *Value marketing* becomes the watchword for many marketers. Rather than offering high quality at a high price, or lesser quality at very low prices, marketers have to look for ways to offer the more financially cautious buyers greater value – just the right combination of product quality and good service at a fair price.

Marketers should also pay attention to *income distribution* as well as average income. Consumers with the greatest purchasing power are likely to belong to the higher socioeconomic groups, whose rising incomes mean that their spending patterns are less susceptible to economic downturns than those of lower-income groups. The *upper* economic strata of a society become primary targets for expensive luxury goods. The comfortable, *middle* income groups are more careful about their spending, but can usually afford the good life some of the time. The *lower* strata will stick close to the basics of food, clothing and shelter needs. In some countries, an *underclass* exists – people permanently living on state welfare and/or below the poverty line – which has little purchasing power, often struggling to make even the most basic purchases.

Changing consumer spending patterns

Generally, the total expenditures made by households tend to vary for essential categories of goods and services, with food, housing and transportation often using up most household income. However, consumers at different income levels have different spending patterns. Some of these differences were noted over a century ago by Ernst Engel, who studied how people shifted their spending as their income rose. He found that as family income rises, the percentage spent on food declines, the percentage spent on housing remains constant (except for such utilities as gas, electricity and public services, which decrease), and both the percentage spent on other categories and that devoted to savings increase. **Engel's laws** have generally been supported by later studies.

Changes in major economic variables such as income, cost of living, interest rates, and saving and borrowing patterns have a large impact on the marketplace. Companies watch these variables by using economic forecasting. Businesses do not have to be wiped out by an economic downturn or caught short in a boom. With adequate warning, they can take advantage of changes in the economic environment.

Engel's laws—Differences noted over a century ago by Ernst Engel in how people shift their spending across food, housing, transportation, health care, and other goods and services categories as family income rises.

Natural environment—Natural resources that are needed as inputs by marketers or that are affected by marketing activities.

Natural environment

The **natural environment** involves the natural resources that are needed as inputs by marketers or that are affected by marketing activities. Environmental concerns have grown steadily during the past three decades. Protection of the natural environment will remain a crucial worldwide issue facing business and the public. In many cities around the world, air and water pollution have reached dangerous levels. World concern continues to mount about the depletion of the earth's ozone layer and the resulting 'greenhouse effect', a dangerous warming of the earth. And many of us fear that we will soon be buried in our own rubbish. Marketers should be aware of four trends in the natural environment.

Shortages of raw materials

Air and water may seem to be infinite resources, but some groups see long-run dangers. Air pollution chokes many of the world's large cities and water shortages are already a big problem in some parts of the world. Renewable resources, such as forests and food, also have to be used wisely. Non-renewable resources such as oil, coal and various minerals pose a serious problem. Firms making products that require these scarce resources face large cost increases, even if the materials do remain available. They may not find it easy to pass these costs on to the consumer. However, firms engaged in research and development and in exploration can help by developing new sources and materials.

Increased cost of energy

One non-renewable resource – oil – has created the most serious problem for future economic growth. The large industrial economies of the world depend heavily on oil, and until economical energy substitutes can be developed, oil will continue to dominate the world political and economic picture. Many companies are searching for practical ways to harness solar, nuclear, wind and other forms of energy. Others are directing their research and development efforts to produce high energy-efficient technologies to meet customers' needs. For example, the tyre company Michelin introduced *Energy* low-resistance tyres that offer a 5 per cent reduction in fuel consumption. Car makers such as Ford, Volkswagen, Opel and Peugeot-Citroën have introduced new, sophisticated compact cars with small dimensions and low weight that meet the environmentalists' 'year-2000 holy grail' – fuel consumption of just 3 litres per 100 km. And, the chemical group BASF has developed new thermal insulation technologies that help to reduce energy consumption in old buildings to 3 litres per square metre per year.[22]

Increased pollution

Industry has been largely blamed for damaging the quality of the natural environment. The 'green' movement draws attention to industry's 'dirty work': the disposal of chemical and nuclear wastes, the dangerous mercury levels in the ocean, the quantity of chemical pollutants in the soil and food supply, and the littering of the environment with non-biodegradable bottles, plastics and other packaging materials.

Many companies, especially those at the 'grubbier' ends of manufacturing, often complain about the cost of fulfilling their obligations to 'clean up' regulations or to produce new greener technologies.[23] On the other hand, more alert managers are responding to public environmental concerns with more ecologically sensitive goods, recyclable or biodegradable packaging, improved pollution controls and more energy-efficient operations.

Environmental pressures may be one firm's expensive obligation, but another's chance for profit. The increase in demand for waste management – collecting, transporting and disposal of solid rubbish – and recycling has also led to a growing industry worth billions of euros. Europe's environmental industry has been growing at 7 per cent a year over the last decade, the industry attracting big players, including America's Waste Management, Asea Brown Boveri's Flakt, and Lurgi, a part of Germany's Metallgesellschaft. Some big operators in sewage treatment, like France's Générales des Eaux, Lyonnaise des Eaux Dumez and Saur, Bouygues's subsidiary, have expanded abroad and give public authorities in European countries a one-stop shop: that is, they finance, build and operate water-treatment plants.

The complexity of EU green directives and national laws has created a booming business in environmental consultancy, particularly in the areas of environmental auditing and risk management. As the green business grows, with it will flourish clever companies that have learnt to turn trash into cash![24]

In consumer markets, niche green segments, where environmentally sensitive consumers are prepared to pay a premium price for green benefits, have emerged in categories ranging from cosmetics, toiletries and detergents to passenger cars. However, most consumers worldwide are more likely to make trade-offs between green advantages and product quality and performance benefits in their purchasing decision.

For example, in a recent international poll, two-thirds of respondents in Venezuela and half those in China, India and Egypt agreed strongly that they were willing to pay a 10 per cent premium for a greener product. Though consumers may tell pollsters they will pay a premium to support the environment, getting them to do so at the shop may be trickier. The Body Shop, the British firm known for its ecologically sensitive beauty products, has used green strategies in overseas markets with mixed success.[25] Customers still consider non-green attributes more important in making purchase decisions. So, although environmental pressures upon businesses in the decade ahead are expected to escalate, firms must seek to balance both the ecological and performance benefit expectations of the mass of consumers.[26]

Government intervention in natural resource management

The governments of different countries vary in their concern and efforts to promote a clean environment. Some countries have adopted policies that have a stronger, positive impact on environmental sustainability than others. One report which ranks countries by five criteria of environmental sustainability, such as whether their main environmental systems are flourishing and how well they cooperate with other countries in managing common environmental problems, places the Nordic countries at the top of the league. Belgium, Italy and Greece, by contrast, do remarkably badly (Figure 3.8).[27] Whereas some governments vigorously pursue environmental quality, others, especially many poorer nations, do little about it, largely because they lack the needed funds or political will. Even the richer nations lack the vast funds and political accord needed to mount a worldwide environmental effort.

Figure 3.8 Environmental sustainability index
SOURCE: 'Emerging-market indicators', *The Economist* (29 January 2000), p. 150. Copyright © The Economist Newspaper Ltd, London, 2000.

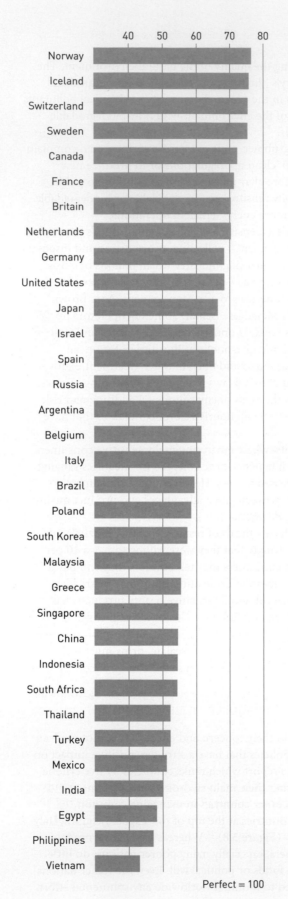

The general hope is that companies around the world will accept more social responsibility, and that less expensive devices can be found to control and reduce pollution.

In most countries, industry has been pressured rather than persuaded to 'go green'. Environment protection agencies of one sort or another have been established to enforce pollution standards and to conduct pollution research. Environmental legislation has toughened up in recent years and businesses can expect this to continue in the foreseeable future. Governments have also looked at the potential of voluntary agreements with industry. The idea is to help industry meet environmental standards cost-effectively.

> Consider Holland's National Environmental Policy Plan (NEPP), which set tight targets for pollution reduction. Some industries agreed to tougher pollution controls in return for greater government flexibility over their implementation. Although firms knew that failure to cooperate meant harsher laws would follow, the NEPP provided a channel for government–industry dialogue and cooperation. Detailed plans were agreed with sectors accounting for 60–70 per cent of Holland's environmental pollution. Deals with oil refineries in Rotterdam helped to cut smog and sulphur dioxide emissions. Agreements with packaging firms have led to a decline in the volume of municipal waste. Ammonia output also declined sharply.[28]

In most developed western nations, well-organised sectors, such as oils, chemicals, pharmaceuticals and food, are more likely to reach common agreements with government agencies and their plans for environmental control. Enlightened companies, however, go beyond what government regulations dictate. They are developing *environmentally sustainable* strategies and practices in an effort to create a world economy that the planet can support indefinitely. They are responding to consumer demands with ecologically safer products, recyclable or biodegradable packaging, better pollution controls and more energy-efficient operations. Many of these companies, from IKEA, Lego and McDonald's to 3M, IBM and BMW, are recognising the link between a healthy economy and a healthy ecology.[29]

Technological environment

The **technological environment** is perhaps the most dramatic force now shaping our destiny. Technology has released such wonders as penicillin, organ transplants, notebook computers and the Internet. It has also released such horrors as nuclear missiles, chemical weapons and assault rifles, and such mixed blessings as cars, televisions and credit cards. Our attitude towards technology depends on whether we are more impressed with its wonders or its blunders.

The technological environment is changing rapidly. Marketers should watch the following trends in technology.

Technological environment—Forces that create new technologies, creating new product and market opportunities.

Fast pace of technological change

Many of today's common products were not available 100 years ago: televisions, home freezers, automatic dishwashers, contraceptives, earth satellites, personal computers, compact disc players, digital video discs, facsimile machines, mobile phones. The list is unending! New technologies create new markets and opportunities. However, every new technology replaces an older technology. Transistors hurt the vacuum-tube industry, xerography killed the carbon-paper business, cars and roads hurt the railways, and compact discs hurt vinyl records. When old industries fought or ignored new technologies, their business declined. Companies that fail to anticipate and keep up with technological change soon find their products outdated.

Technological environment: technology is perhaps the most dramatic force shaping the environment. Here, a herder makes a call on his mobile phone.
SOURCE: Joseph Van OS, Getty Images, Inc./Image bank.

But keeping pace with technological change is becoming more challenging for firms today. *Technology life cycles* are getting shorter. Take the typewriter. The first-generation modern mechanical typewriter dominated the market for 25 years. Subsequent generations had shorter lives – 15 years for electromechanical models, seven years for electronic versions and five years for first-generation microprocessor-based ones. And today, the average life span of some computer software products, for example, is now well under one year.

Moreover, technology trends can be very fickle. Consider the ever-changing world of children's games consoles. At first, kids of all ages were clamouring for a Sega Dreamcast. Then, Sony's PlayStation 2 became the next hit. By Christmas 2000, the craze turned to Nintendo's Dolphin and Microsoft's X-Box systems. One thing's for sure – many of these will end up as obsolete appliances before the next Christmas season!

Firms must track technological trends and determine whether or not these changes will affect their products' continued ability to satisfy customers' needs. Technologies arising in unrelated industries can also affect the firm's fortunes. The mechanical watch industry was overtaken by manufacturers of electronic components seeking new applications and growth opportunities for their quartz technology. Businesses must assiduously monitor their technological environment to avoid missing new product and market opportunities.

High R&D budgets

Technology and innovations require heavy investments in research and development. It is not uncommon for pharmaceuticals companies, for example, to spend as much as €500 million to develop a new drug. High R&D spending is also a feature of many industries, including cars, communications, computers, aerospace, engineering, entertainment and consumer electronics. The soaring cost of R&D increases the difficulty, even for big companies, to master a wide range of technologies. To overcome the barrier, firms have sought to collaborate with other firms to develop new products and technologies; they may license inventions developed by other firms or even acquire smaller, innovative firms that may not have sufficient financial resources to develop and commercialise new technologies.

Concentration on minor improvements

As a result of the high cost of developing and introducing new technologies, many companies are tinkering – making minor product improvements – instead of gambling on substantial innovations. The high costs and risks of commercialisation failure make firms take this cautious approach to their R&D investment. Most companies are content to put their money into copying competitors' products, making minor feature and style improvements, or offering simple extensions of current brands. Thus much research is in danger of being defensive rather than offensive.

Increased regulation

As products and technology become more complex, the public needs to know that these are safe. Thus, government agencies investigate and ban potentially unsafe products. In the EU and America, complex regulations exist for testing new drugs. The US Federal Food and Drug Administration, for example, is known for its strict enforcement of drug testing and safety rules. Statutory and industry regulatory bodies exist to set safety standards for consumer products and penalise companies that fail to meet them. Such regulations have resulted in much higher research costs and in longer times between new-product ideas and their introduction. Marketers should be aware of these regulations when seeking and developing new products.

Marketers need to understand the changing technological environment and how new technologies can serve customer and human needs. They need to work closely with R&D people to encourage more market-oriented research. They must also be alert to the possible negative aspects of any breakthroughs (like the sequencing of the human genome[30]) or innovations (like Viagra, the anti-impotence drug) that might harm users or arouse opposition from pressure groups.

Political environment

Marketing decisions are strongly affected by developments in the political environment. The **political environment** consists of laws, government agencies and pressure groups that influence and limit various organisations and individuals in a given society.

Political environment— Laws, government agencies and pressure groups that influence and limit various organisations and individuals in a given society.

Legislation regulating business

Even the most liberal advocates of free-market economies agree that the system works best with at least some regulation. Well-conceived regulation can encourage competition and ensure fair markets for goods and services. Thus governments develop *public policy* to guide commerce – sets of laws and regulations that limit business for the good of society as a whole. Almost every marketing activity is subject to a wide range of laws and regulations.

Legislation affecting business around the world has increased steadily over the years. The European Commission has a framework of laws covering competitive behaviour, product standards, product liability and commercial transactions for the nations of the EU. Similarly, the US has many laws covering issues such as competition, fair trade practices, environmental protection, product safety, truth in advertising, packaging and labelling, pricing and other important areas. Several countries have passed strong consumer legislation. For example, Norway bans several forms of sales promotion – trading stamps, contests, premiums – as being inappropriate or unfair ways of promoting products. Thailand requires food processors selling national brands to market low-price brands also, so that low-income consumers can find economy brands on the shelves. In India, food companies must obtain special approval to launch brands that duplicate those already existing on the market, such as additional cola drinks or new brands of rice.

Understanding the public policy implications of a particular marketing activity is not a simple matter. First, there are many laws created at different levels: for example, in the EU, business operators are subject to European Commission, individual member state and specific local regulations; in the USA, laws are created at the federal, state and local levels, and these regulations often overlap. Second, the regulations are constantly changing – what was allowed last year may now be prohibited, and what was prohibited may now be allowed. In the single European market, deregulation and ongoing moves towards harmonisation are expected to take time, creating a state of flux, which challenges and confuses both domestic and international marketers. They must therefore work hard to keep up with changes in regulations and their interpretations.

In many countries, business legislation has been enacted for a number of reasons. The first is to *protect companies* from each other. Although business executives may praise competition, they sometimes try to neutralise it when it threatens them. Antitrust agencies, competition authorities and monopolies and mergers commissions have surfaced to enforce laws, typically passed to define and prevent unfair competition. For example, the European Commission recently introduced new competition laws to promote a level playing field for firms in the telecommunications sector. These laws have several goals, from seeking to establish a better pricing balance, to forcing incumbent telecoms operators to open up local markets to new market entrants. The EU's competition authorities have also been known to block many merger deals, one example being the decision to veto Volvo's proposal to merge with Scania, its Swedish truck rival.[31]

The second purpose of government regulation is to *protect consumers* from unfair and unscrupulous business practices. Some firms, if left alone, would make shoddy products, tell lies in their advertising and deceive consumers through their packaging and pricing. Unfair and unscrupulous business practices have been defined and are enforced by various agencies. For example, the EU Directive on Privacy and Electronic Communications, enforced in October 2003, intends to crack down on 'spam' by giving government agencies the power to prosecute firms that send unsolicited e-mails.[32]

The third purpose of government regulation is to *protect the interests of society* against unrestrained business behaviour. Profitable business activity does not always create a better quality of life. Regulation arises to ensure that firms take responsibility for the social costs of their production or products.

New laws and their enforcement are likely to continue or increase. Business executives must watch these developments when planning their products and marketing programmes. International marketers will additionally encounter dozens, even hundreds, of agencies set up to enforce trade policies and regulations. Importantly, they need to understand these laws at the local, country, regional and international levels.

Growth of public interest groups

The number and power of public interest groups have increased during the past two decades. Consumerism, a powerful force that has its roots in the US, has spilled over to countries in western Europe and other developed market economies such as Australia. Hundreds of other consumer interest groups, private and governmental, operate at all levels – regional, national and local. Other groups that marketers need to consider are those seeking to protect the environment, to campaign against animal cruelty and to advance the rights of various groups such as women, children, gays and lesbians, ethnic minorities, senior citizens and the handicapped. As we saw in Marketing Insights 3.1 and the prelude case, global companies cannot ignore the views of public interest groups.

Increased emphasis on ethics and socially responsible actions

Written regulations cannot possibly cover all potential marketing abuses, and existing laws are often difficult to enforce. However, beyond written laws and regulations, business is also governed by social codes and rules of professional ethics. Enlightened companies encourage their managers to look beyond what the regulatory system allows and simply to 'do the right thing'. These socially responsible firms actively seek out ways to protect the long-run interests of their consumers and the environment.

The recent rash of business scandals and increased concerns about the environment have created fresh interest in the issues of ethics and social responsibility. Almost every aspect of marketing involves such issues. Unfortunately, because these issues usually involve conflicting interests, well-meaning people can disagree honestly about the right course of action in a particular situation. Thus many industrial and professional trade associations have suggested codes of ethics, and many companies are now developing policies and guidelines to deal with complex social responsibility issues.

The boom in e-commerce and Internet marketing has created a new set of social and ethical issues. Privacy issues are the primary concern. For example, website visitors often provide extensive personal information that might leave them open to abuse by unscrupulous marketers. Moreover, both Intel and Microsoft have been accused of covert, high-tech computer chip and software invasions of customers' personal computers to obtain information for marketing purposes.

Another cyberspace concern is that of access by vulnerable or unauthorised groups. For example, marketers of adult-oriented materials have found it difficult to restrict access by minors. In a more specific example, sellers using eBay.com, the online auction website, recently found themselves the victims of a 13-year-old boy who had bid on and purchased more than €3 million worth of high-priced antiques and rare art works on the site. eBay has a strict policy against bidding by anyone under 18 but works largely on the honour system. Unfortunately, this honour system did little to prevent the teenager from taking a cyberspace joy ride.[33]

In Chapter 5, we will discuss in greater depth the public and social responsibility issues surrounding major marketing decisions, the legal issues that marketers should understand, and the common ethical and societal concerns that marketers face.

Cultural environment

The **cultural environment** is made up of institutions and other forces that affect society's basic values, perceptions, preferences and behaviours. People grow up in a particular society that shapes their basic beliefs and values. They absorb a world-view that defines their relationships with others. The following cultural characteristics can affect marketing decision making. Marketers must be aware of these cultural influences and how they might vary across societies within the markets served by the firm.

Cultural environment—
Institutions and other forces that affect society's basic values, perceptions, preferences and behaviours.

Persistence of cultural values

People in a given society hold many beliefs and values. Their core beliefs and values have a high degree of persistence. For example, most of us believe in working, getting married, giving to charity and being honest. These beliefs shape more specific attitudes and behaviours found in everyday life. *Core* beliefs and values are passed on from parents to children and are reinforced by schools, religious groups, business and government.

Secondary beliefs and values are more open to change. Believing in marriage is a core belief; believing that people should get married early in life is a secondary belief. Marketers have some chance of changing secondary values, but little chance of changing core values. For example, family-planning marketers could argue more effectively that people should get married later than that they should not get married at all.

Shifts in secondary cultural values

Although core values are fairly persistent, cultural swings do take place. Consider the impact of popular music groups, movie personalities and other celebrities on young people's hair styling, clothing and sexual norms. Marketers want to predict cultural shifts in order to spot new opportunities or threats. Such information helps marketers cater to trends with appropriate products and communication appeals.

The principal cultural values of a society are expressed in people's views of themselves and others, as well as in their views of organisations, society, nature and the universe.

People's views of themselves

People vary in their emphasis on serving themselves versus serving others. Some people seek personal pleasure, wanting fun, change and escape. Others seek self-realisation through religion, recreation or the avid pursuit of careers or other life goals. People use products, brands and services as a means of self-expression and buy products and services that match their views of themselves.

In the last decade or so, personal ambition and materialism increased dramatically, with significant marketing implications. In a 'me-society', people buy their 'dream cars' and take their 'dream vacations'. They tend to spend to the limit on self-indulgent goods and services. Today, people are adopting more conservative behaviours and ambitions. They are more cautious in their spending patterns and more value-driven in their purchases. Moving into the new millennium, materialism, flashy spending and self-indulgence have been replaced by more sensible spending, saving, family concerns and helping others. This suggests a bright future for products and services that serve basic needs and provide real value rather than those relying on glitz and hype.

People's views of others

More recently, observers have noted a shift from a 'me-society' to a 'we-society', in which more people want to be with and serve others. Notes one trend tracker, 'People want to get out, especially those . . . working out of their home and feeling a little cooped-up [and] all those shut-ins who feel unfulfilled by the cyberstuff that was supposed to make them feel like never leaving home.'[34] Other surveys showed that more people are becoming involved in charity, volunteer work and social service activities.[35] These trends suggest greater demand for 'social support' products and services that improve direct communication between people, such as health clubs, family vacations and games.

People's views of organisations

People vary in their attitudes towards corporations, government agencies, trade unions, universities and other organisations. By and large, people are willing to work for big organisations and expect them, in turn, to carry out society's work. In recent years, there has been a decrease in confidence in, and loyalty towards, business and political organisations and institutions. Recent high-profile corporate scandals surrounding once-admired companies such as Enron and WorldCom in the US, and Lernout & Hauspie and Ahold in Europe,[36] have only but fuelled this public distrust in mighty corporations. In the workplace, there has been an overall decline in organisational loyalty. Recent waves of company downsizing, for example, have bred cynicism and distrust. Many people today see work not as a source of satisfaction, but as a necessary chore to earn money to enjoy non-work hours.

This trend suggests that organisations need to find new ways to win consumer confidence and employee confidence. They need to review their advertising communications to make sure their messages are honest. Also, they need to review their various activities to make sure that they are coming across as 'good corporate citizens'. More companies are linking themselves to worthwhile causes, measuring their images with important publics and using public relations to build more positive images.[37]

Companies are increasingly seeking to improve their positive impact on society. Here, Marks & Spencer's award-winning Children's Promise campaign reinforces the company's commitment to supporting the local community.
SOURCE: Marks & Spencer.

People's views of society

People vary in their attitudes towards their society – from patriots who defend it, to reformers who want to change it, and malcontents who want to leave it. People's orientation to their society influences their consumption patterns, levels of savings and attitudes towards the marketplace.

In the more affluent, industrialising Asian nations, consumers aspire to achieve the high living standards and lifestyles of people in the more advanced western countries. The display of conspicuous consumption and fondness for expensive western brands – the common label for achievement and westernisation – are highly acceptable behaviour. Consumer patriotism, for example, is not an issue, since locally made goods are often viewed as inferior or less desirable than foreign imported brands. Consumers' predispostion towards western brands suggest a greater demand for goods marketed by companies of western origin, hence creating new marketing opportunities for these firms. By contrast, in the western developed countries, the last two decades saw an increase in consumer patriotism. European consumers reckoned that sticking to locally produced goods would save and protect jobs. Similarly, many US companies also responded to American patriotism, which has been increasing gradually for the past two decades but has experienced a surge following the 11 September 2001 terrorist attacks.[38]

People's views of nature

People vary in their attitudes towards the natural world. Some feel ruled by it, others feel in harmony with it and still others seek to master it. A long-term trend has been people's growing mastery over nature through technology and the belief that nature is bountiful. More recently, however, people have recognised that nature is finite and fragile – that it can be destroyed or spoiled by human activities.

Love of nature is leading to more camping, hiking, boating, fishing and other outdoor activities. Business has responded by offering more products and services catering to these interests. Tour operators are offering more tours to wilderness areas and retailers are offering more fitness gear and apparel. Food producers have found growing markets for 'natural' products like natural cereal, natural ice-cream, organically farmed produce and a variety of health foods. Marketing communicators are using appealing natural backgrounds in advertising their products. Yet others have succeeded in building their fortunes by emphasising simplicity and inspiration drawn from nature (see Marketing Insights 3.2).

People's views of the universe

Finally, people vary in their beliefs about the origin of the universe and their place in it. While the practice of religion remains strong in many parts of the world, religious conviction and practice have been dropping off through the years in certain countries, notably in the United States and Europe where, for example, church attendance is on the decline. However, some

marketing insights

3.2 Marimekko: Simplicity sells!

Back in the 1960s Marimekko, a small Finnish company that sells clothing, bags, interior textiles and accessories, made sensational news in the US. The reason? Jacqueline Kennedy, then First Lady, had chosen to buy some maternity dresses from the little-known clothing designer over an American one. The company, however, suffered six years of losses after being taken over by Amer, the Finnish conglomerate, in 1985.

In 1991, Marimekko was bought back by Kirsti Paakkanen. Over the last decade, Ms Paakkanen steadily rebuilt Marimekko's financial strength, capitalising on its trademark of bold colours, bright patterns and distinctive stripes. Marimekko sees itself as a lifestyle company, synonymous with the best of Finnish design, with an emphasis on simplicity and inspiration drawn from Finnish nature. The simple, horizontally striped T-shirts epitomise Marimekko's quality, functionality and practicality. According to Ms Paakkanen, the secrets of the company's success today are a clear set of values: community spirit, respect and caring – values that are set out clearly in the company's annual report. There is also a steadfast support of employees, particularly a refusal to stifle the creativity of its designers. Maybe this is one reason why the company enjoys exceptionally strong employee loyalty – some 40 per cent of employees who joined in the 1950s and 1960s were still with the company in 2000. Marimekko celebrates its 50th anniversary in 2001, against a forecast of steady growth, both at home and in markets across the EU, US and Japan. What is remarkable is that the company is achieving higher sales abroad, despite the problems that have afflicted so many international retailers when expanding outside their own countries. Bright and breezy, big and bold, Marimekko is set to remain one of Finland's best known international brands, after Nokia. There is no better reminder of that than a recent headline on a *New York Times* article about Scandinavian design: 'Marimekko, I think I love you'.

SOURCE: Christopher Brown-Humes, 'Big designs on practicality' in supplement on Finland, © *Financial Times* (10 July 2000), p. vi. More information on the company can be accessed at www.marimekko.com.

futurists have noted an emerging renewal of interest in religion, perhaps as part of a broader search for a new inner purpose. People have been moving away from materialism and dog-eat-dog ambition to seek more permanent values and a more certain grasp of right and wrong. The 'new realists' reflect a move away from overt consumerism. Some experts observe that this trend reflects a 'new spiritualism' which is affecting consumers in everything, from the television shows they watch and the books they read, to the products and services they buy. 'Since consumers don't park their beliefs and values on the bench outside the marketplace', adds one expert, 'they are bringing this awareness to the brands they buy. Tapping into this heightened sensitivity presents a unique marketing opportunity for brands.'[39]

However, in many overseas markets where western companies seek to expand, such as India, China and south-east Asia, society's value systems place great importance on economic achievement and material possession. The values of these 'enthusiastic materialists' are also shared by the developing markets of Europe, such as Turkey, and some Latin American countries.[40]

Responding to the marketing environment

Many companies view the marketing environment as an 'uncontrollable' element to which they must adapt. They passively accept the marketing environment and do not try to change it. They analyse the environmental forces and design strategies that will help the company avoid the threats and take advantage of the opportunities the environment provides.

Other companies take an **environmental management perspective**.[41] Rather than simply watching and reacting, these firms take aggressive actions to affect the publics and forces in their marketing environment. Such companies hire lobbyists to influence legislation affecting their industries and stage media events to gain favourable press coverage. They run 'advertorials' (ads expressing editorial points of view) to shape public opinion. They take legal action and file complaints with regulators to keep competitors in line. They also form contractual agreements to better control their distribution channels.

Often, companies can find positive ways to overcome seemingly uncontrollable business environmental constraints. For example:

Environmental management perspective—A management perspective in which the firm takes aggressive actions to affect the publics and forces in its marketing environment rather than simply watching it and reacting to it.

> Cathay Pacific Airlines . . . determined that many travelers were avoiding Hong Kong because of lengthy delays at immigration. Rather than assuming that this was a problem they could not solve, Cathay's senior staff asked the Hong Kong government how to avoid these immigration delays. After lengthy discussions, the airline agreed to make an annual grant-in-aid to the government to hire more immigration inspectors – but these reinforcements would service primarily the Cathay Pacific gates. The reduced waiting period increased customer value and thus strengthened [Cathay's competitive advantage].[42]

Marketing management cannot always affect environmental forces. In many cases, it must settle for simply watching and reacting to the environment. For example, a company would have little success in trying to influence geographic population shifts, the economic environment or important cultural values. But whenever possible, smart marketing managers will take a *proactive* rather than *reactive* approach to the marketing environment.

WHERE YOU DEMAND WE SUPPLY.

Behind Sam Singh, captain of a Shell G Class carrier, sit 135,000 cubic metres of liquefied natural gas (LNG).

On deck, it's a balmy 25 degrees. In the insulated LNG containers, it's minus 160°C.

Sam's carrier is just one of our specialised fleet that carries over nine million tonnes of LNG around the world every year.

They bridge the gap between places like Brunei, Oman and Nigeria, with an abundance of natural gas, and markets with a rapidly rising demand like Asia, the Americas and Europe.

We have been investing in our LNG operations for over forty years. Now these efforts are paying off handsomely.

Within ten years, the number of our LNG plants will have doubled. So too will the number of countries we supply.

Why? Because by 2025 gas, the cleanest fossil fuel, could well have overtaken oil as the world's predominant source of energy.

Developing and connecting the gas markets of the world is an increasingly crucial business in which no one matches our expertise and commitment.

And if people like Sam have anything to do with it, no one ever will.

To find out more about our Gas & Power business visit www.shell.com

Businesses face great pressure to balance economic progress with social responsibility. Here, the multinational company Shell articulates the need for striking a balance between the need to protect people's way of life and the environment and to provide sustainable, affordable energy.

SOURCE: Shell International. Agency: J. Walter Thompson.

Summary

Companies must constantly watch and adapt to the *marketing environment* in order to seek opportunities and ward off threats. The marketing environment comprises all the actors and forces that affect the company's ability to transact effectively with its target market.

The company's marketing environment can be divided into the microenvironment and the macroenvironment. The *microenvironment* consists of other actors close to the company that combine to form the company's value delivery network. It includes the company's *internal environment* – its departments and management levels, which influence marketing decision making. *Marketing channel firms* – the firm's suppliers and marketing intermediaries, including resellers, physical distribution firms, financial intermediaries and marketing services agencies – cooperate to create customer value. Another set of forces include five types of customer *markets* in which the company can sell: the consumer, producer, reseller, government and international markets. *Competitors* vie with the company in an effort to serve customers better. Finally, various *publics* – financial, media, government, citizen action, local, general and internal publics – have an actual or potential interest in or impact on the organisation's ability to achieve its objectives.

The company's *macroenvironment* consists of six forces that shape opportunities and pose threats to the company. These include demographic, economic, natural, technological, political and cultural forces that affect the entire microenvironment.

We addressed how changes in the demographic and economic environments affect marketing decisions. In the more developed western economies, today's *demographic environment* shows a changing age structure, shifting family profiles, trends towards a better educated, international migration and increasing diversity. The *economic environment* includes factors that influence consumers' buying power and spending patterns. The trends are towards greater value, with consumers seeking just the right combination of good quality and service at the right price.

We looked at the major trends in the firm's natural and technological environments. The *natural environment* shows these major trends: shortages of certain raw materials, increased energy costs, higher pollution levels, more government intervention in natural resource management and higher levels of citizen concern and activism about these issues. The *technological environment* reveals rapid technological change, high R&D budgets, the concentration by companies on minor product improvements and increased government regulation.

Key changes are also observed in the political and cultural environments. The *political environment* consists of laws, agencies and groups that influence or limit marketing actions. The political environment has undergone three changes that affect marketing actions: increasing legislation regulating business, the rising importance of public interest groups, and increased emphasis on ethics and socially responsible actions. The *cultural environment* suggests trends towards a 'we-society', a cautious trust of institutions, increasing conservatism, greater appreciation for nature, a new realism and the search for more meaningful and enduring values.

Companies can passively accept the marketing environment as an uncontrollable element to which they must adapt, avoiding threats and taking advantage of opportunities as they arise. Or they can take an *environmental management perspective*, proactively working to change the environment rather than simply reacting to it.

Discussing the issues

1. Select a company that produces and markets sports and leisure clothing. What are the factors that affect the firm's marketing environment? Identify the major environmental trends that are likely to create opportunities and ones that will present threats to this company in the decade ahead.

2. Demographers note the growing importance of the 'Generation Xers' and 'Baby boomlets'. Yet, the fastest growing segment in many of the more developed countries is the 'senior citizen'. If you were in charge of marketing in a consumer healthcare company, how would you deal with the potential opportunities presented by these consumer groups?

3. Pressure groups, lobbyists and public interest groups play an important role in defending society's interests. Select one such group you are familiar with and describe its cause. How might goods or services providers targeted by the group respond to the demands or pressures imposed by the group?

4. Customers are becoming more concerned about the natural environment. How would this trend affect a company that markets plastic food bags? Discuss some effective responses to this trend.

5. Some marketing goals, such as improved quality, require strong support from an internal public – a company's own employees. But surveys show that employees increasingly distrust management and that company loyalty is eroding. How can a company market internally to help meet its goals?

Applying the concepts

1. Changes in the marketing environment mean that marketers must meet new consumer needs that may be quite different – even directly opposite – from those in the past. You can track changes in the marketing environment by looking at how companies modify their products. Where appropriate, you could visit selected companies' websites to gain details about their products.

   ▪ Make a list of the products you encounter in one day that claim to be 'low' or 'high' in some ingredient, such as fruit juices without added preservatives, low-fat yogurts or high-fibre cereal.
   ▪ Write down similar products that seem to offer the opposite characteristics.
   ▪ In each case, which product do you think came first? Do you think that this is an effective response to a changing marketing environment? Why? Why not?

2. The political environment can have a direct impact on marketers and their plans. Thinking about a recent major political environmental change in a country of your choice, consider the following:

   ▪ Name three industries that will probably have their marketing plans and strategies affected by the political changes.
   ▪ For each of the industries that you named, list three potential strategies to help adapt to the coming changes in the political environment.
   ▪ Although environmental changes appear likely, are they certain? How should companies plan for unsettled conditions?

References

1. Richard Tomkins, 'Big food has a lot on its plate', *Financial Times* (12 February 2004); accessed at www.ft.com, 12 February 2003.

2. Jennifer Lach, 'Dateline America: May 1, 2025', *American Demographics* (May 1999), pp. 19–20.

3. Martin Wolf, 'Why Europe was the past, the US is the present and a China-dominated Asia the future of the global economy', *Financial Times* (22 September 2003), p. 21; the *UN World Population Prospects* gives population details for individual countries; also, for continuously updated projections of the world population, consult the UN world population and US Census Bureau's websites: www.un.org/esa/population/unpop, and www.census.gov.

4. See www.un.org/esa/population/unpop; Martin Wolf, 'Demography: people, plagues and prosperity: five trends that promise to transform the world's population within 50 years', *Financial Times* (27 February 2003), p. 17.

5. Wolf, op. cit.

6. Lorien Holland, 'Baby boom', *Far Eastern Economic Review* (24 June 1999), p. 61; Sally D. Goll, 'Marketing: China's (only) children get the royal treatment', *Wall Street Journal* (8 February 1995), pp. B1, B3.

7. See Philip Kotler, *Marketing Management: Analysis, planning, implementation, and control*, 11th edn (Upper Saddle River, NJ: Pearson Education, 2003), p. 163.

8. Accessed online from www.growingupdigital.com/flecho.html, October 1999. Also see Diane Summers, 'Generation X comes of age', *Financial Times* (16 February 1998), p. 16; and Douglas Tapscott, *Growing Up Digital: The rise of the Net generation* (New York: McGraw-Hill, 1999).

9. Stephen Fidler, 'Problem of ageing "underestimated"', *Financial Times* (17/18 June 2000), p. 7; 'Fewer and wrinklier Europeans', *The Economist* (15 January 2000), p. 42; European Commission, *Demographic Statistics* in addition to UN Population Division and OECD are further sources of information on population statistics and projections.

10. 'A survey of the 20th century. On the yellow brick road', *The Economist* (11 September 1999), p. 6; 'Too many or too few', *The Economist* (25 September 1999), p. 19; 'Like herrings in a barrel', *The Economist* (31 December 1999), pp. 13–14.

11. 'Out of Africa', *The Economist* (14 June 2003), p. 32; Wolf, op. cit.

12. Simon Briscoe, 'Women with degrees "more likely to reject motherhood"', *Financial Times* (25 April 2003), p. 4; Paul Bettes, 'Ageing Europe faces up to need for pension reform', *Financial Times* (28 August 2003), p. 18; 'Krybbe to grave', in 'Dancing to a new tune: a survey of the Nordic region', *The Economist* (14 June 2003), pp. 10–13.

13. Dan Roberts, 'The ageing business: companies and marketers wrestle with adapting their products to older consumers' demands', *Financial Times* (20 January 2004), p. 19.

14. David Short, 'A different taste of things to come', *The European* (14–20 October 1994), p. 21; data on household composition available online at http://europa.eu.int/comm/eurostat/Public/datashop/; also, information on changing US household composition accessed online at www.census.gov/population/projections/nation/hh-fam/, August 2003.

15. 'Mix and match', in 'Dancing to a new tune: a survey of the Nordic region', *The Economist* (14 June 2003), pp. 7–10; Kevin Brown, 'Ageing process likely to prove costly for next generation', *Financial Times* (24–25 August 2002), p. 4; details accessed at www.ft.com/changingbritain.

16. Wolf, op. cit.

17. 'Education. The uses of literacy', *The Economist* (17 June 2000), pp. 34–5; 'Dorothy's dream', The Economist 20th Century Survey, *The Economist* (11 September 1999), pp. 34–8.

18. For a more detailed discussion and analysis of EU enlargement, see 'When east meets west' in 'A survey of the EU enlargement', *The Economist* (22 November 2003); also see Stefan Wagstyl, 'Opening the door: as Europe prepares to end the divisions of the past, the disputes of the present cast a shadow', *Financial Times* (2 January 2004); 'Enlarging the European Union', *The Economist* (12 October 2002), p. 42.

19. Alan Mitchell, 'Brands play for global domination', *Marketing Week* (2 February 1996), pp. 26–7; 'The myth of the Euro-consumer', *The Economist* (4 November 1989), pp. 107–8.

20. 'The day the miracle came to an end', *Financial Times* (12 January 1998), p. 8; John Ridding and James Kynge, 'Complacency gives way to contagion', *Financial Times* (13 January 1998), p. 8.

21. See 'Can Europe compete? Balance of economic power begins to shift', *Financial Times* (9 March 1994), p. 14; 'Emerging-market indicators', *The Economist* (18 May 1999), p. 142; data on Gross Domestic Product (GDP) of countries, including GDP at purchasing power parity, are obtained from the following sources: Eurostat (National Statistics Office) (data accessible at: http://europa.eu.int/), World Bank, International Monetary Fund. Data are also available to subscribers to *The Economist* at www.economist.com.

22. Tony Lewin, 'Car makers line up for next baby boom', *The European* (30 May 1996), p. 30.

23. Michael Smith and Leyla Boulton, 'Oil v. autos in fight over cost of pollution', *Financial Times* (17 February 1998), p. 2; Casper Henderson, 'Might PVC be PC after all?', *Financial Times* (7 June 2000), p. 17.

24. John-Paul Flintoff, 'Stinking rich in Holland Park', *The Business Weekend FT Magazine* (29 April 2000), pp. 28–31; 'Pollution: the money in Europe's muck', *The Economist* (20 November 1993), pp. 109–10.

25. 'How green is your market?', *The Economist* (8 January 2000), p. 77.

26. For more discussion, see Veronica Wong, William Turner and Paul Stoneman, 'Marketing strategies and market prospects for environmentally-friendly consumer products', *British Journal of Management* (1996), pp. 263–81.

27. 'Emerging-market indicators. Green growth', *The Economist* (29 January 2000), p. 150.

28. 'Going Dutch', *The Economist* (20 November 1993), p. 110.

29. For more discussion, see Michael E. Porter and Claas van der Linde, 'Green *and* competitive: ending the stalemate', *Harvard Business Review* (September–October 1995), pp. 120–34; Stuart L. Hart, 'Beyond greening: strategies for a sustainable world', *Harvard Business Review* (January–February 1997), pp. 67–76; and Forest L. Reinhardt, 'Bringing the environment down to earth', *Harvard Business Review* (July–August 1999), pp. 149–57.

30. David Pilling, Clive Cookson and Victoria Griffith, 'Human blueprint is revealed', *Financial Times* (27 June 2000), p. 1; Clive Cookson, 'Book of life that rewrites existence', *Financial Times* (27 June 2000), p. 15; Victoria Griffith, 'Advance is a mixed blessing', *Financial Times* (27 June 2000), p. 15.

31. Michael Smith, 'Brussels acts over telecoms pricing and unveils competition blueprint', *Financial Times* (13 April 2000), p. 1; Christopher Brown-Humes, 'Volvo attacks Brussels over Scania ruling', *Financial Times* (9 March 2000), p. 33.

32. 'EU rules aim to outlaw spam', *Marketing Business* (May 2003), p. 6; for more information on the new EU directive on consumer privacy and electronic communications, visit www.informationcommissioner.gov.uk.

33. '13-year-old bids over $3M for items in eBay auctions', *USA Today* (30 April 1999), p. 10B.

34. See Cyndee Miller, 'Trendspotters: "Dark Ages" ending; so is cocooning', *Marketing News* (3 February 1997), pp. 1, 16.

35. Adrienne Ward Fawcett, 'Lifestyle study', *Advertising Age* (18 April 1994), pp. 12–13.

36. Robert Howell, 'How accounting executives looked the wrong way', *Financial Times*, *FT Summer School Day 7: Finance Part I* (13 August 2002), p. 11.

37. For more information on ethics and sustainability, visit the Chartered Institute of Marketing's (CIM) Knowledge Centre at www.cim.co.uk.

38. See 'A run on patriotism', *Warehousing Management* (November 2001), p. 5; Bill McDowell, 'New DDB Needham report: consumers want it all', *Advertising Age* (November 1996), pp. 32–3.

39. Myra Stark, 'Celestial season', *Brandweek* (16 November 1998), pp. 25–6; also see David B. Wolfe, 'The psychological center of gravity', *American Demographics* (April 1998), pp. 16–19; and Richard Cimino and Don Lattin, 'Choosing my religion', *American Demographics* (April 1999), pp. 60–5.

40. Dyan Machan, 'A more tolerant generation', *Forbes* (8 September 1997), pp. 46–7; William Davis, 'Opinion', *Marketing Business* (March 1996), p. 6.

41. See Carl P. Zeithaml and Valerie A. Zeithaml, 'Environmental management: revising the marketing perspective', *Journal of Marketing* (Spring 1984), pp. 46–53.

42. Howard E. Butz Jr. and Leonard D. Goodstein, 'Measuring customer value: gaining the strategic advantage', *Organizational Dynamics* (Winter 1996), pp. 66–7.

WEB RESOURCES

For additional classic case studies and Internet exercises, visit www.pearsoned.co.uk/kotler

Concluding concept 3
Toyota Prius: green or geek machine?

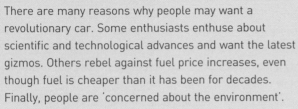

There are many reasons why people may want a revolutionary car. Some enthusiasts enthuse about scientific and technological advances and want the latest gizmos. Others rebel against fuel price increases, even though fuel is cheaper than it has been for decades. Finally, people are 'concerned about the environment'.

Hoping that all of the above was true, and looking to grab a technological advantage over other car manufacturers, in 2000 Toyota introduced Prius, their first hybrid car. Prius means 'to go before', so is a name that may be very prophetic. The Prius and the Honda Insight are the first in a wave of hybrid family cars coming out ahead of similar vehicles from GM, Ford and DaimlerChrysler.

At first glance, the Prius seems to have a lot going for it. It combines a 1.5 litre, four-cylinder petrol engine and a 33-kilowatt electric motor. It comfortably seats five, if the three in the back aren't too tall or too big, and has 0.34 m^3 of luggage space. The electric motor starts the car and operates at low speeds, using a nickel metal-hydride battery. At higher speeds, the Prius automatically switches to the internal combustion engine. Under normal motorway driving conditions, it should get 28 km per litre.

The downside is that the Prius is no muscle car. It also costs about €4,000 more than the Toyota Echo, although they are nearly the same car. Of course, getting twice as many kilometres per litre of petrol will help to offset the price differential. Assuming the range and a typical 2002 price of €1.00/litre, the Prius owner would have to buy 4,000 litres of petrol, enough fuel for 112,000 km, which could take years. Of course, if prices were to rise drastically, that could change. But even if prices doubled – which is not likely – you'd have to drive more than 50,000 km to make up the initial price difference.

The picture gets even gloomier when you realise that no one is going to get the estimated fuel consumption anyway. The Environmental Protection Agency (EPA) has admitted that its testing procedure overstates petrol mileage by as much as 15 per cent. It tests cars on a chassis dynamometer, where the driven wheels turn freely on a set of rotating drums – far from normal driving conditions. In addition, hybrids use regenerative braking to recharge their batteries, with the result that braking during the EPA driving cycle is feeding more energy back into the system, boosting estimated petrol mileage.

Although this offers a fuel saving, the overall cost of ownership looks less attractive. Compared with the family 'Car of the Year 2004', the conventionally powered Toyota Avensis 1.8 T3-S, the Prius looks poor value. Although the Prius saves on fuel, its overall running cost comes out higher than that of the equivalent Avensis. The reason is its 25 per cent higher service or contract hire cost.

On the brighter side, Toyota and its competitors believe that costs will decrease once production of hybrids begins to yield economies of scale. The benefits of scale would not stop with the producer. For example, a major part of the cost of the car is the nickel metal-hydride batteries. A company such as Panasonic could reduce the cost of producing batteries through research and development, if the market merited such an investment, and could further reduce the price of batteries through its own economies of scale.

However, realising that cost reductions are a way off and that fuel savings aren't going to be the key to convincing people to purchase the Prius, car manufacturers have asked for tax incentives to stimulate purchase of clean-fuel and high-mileage cars.

Several governments are providing incentives to people to buy hybrid cars. The US government offers $2,000 federal income-reduction and the UK government offers reduced car tax on initial purchase. Electric car drivers can also avoid London's £5 per day Congestion Charge.

Are consumers ready for hybrids? Do improved gas mileage and emissions standards affect their buying decision? A glance at car sales in the last 10 years would suggest not. The biggest sales growth was in gas-guzzling 4 × 4s. After all, we rarely saw Range Rovers 10 years ago; now they're a fairly common sight. People, it seems, think it's a good idea for their neighbours to drive 'green machines', not themselves.

Actually, when the Prius was introduced, it flew out of dealers' showrooms. Between July and October 2000, Toyota sold 2,610 Priuses and had difficulty keeping up with demand. By the end of October 2000, the cars were

> Are consumers ready for hybrids?

waitlisted until January. Of course, much of that sales success is attributable to Toyota's clever marketing. Two years before introduction, Toyota began educating consumers about the Prius. The company established a website to distribute information and also sent e-brochures to 40,000 likely buyers just before the introduction. Within two weeks. Toyota sold 1,800 cars based on the email message.

In all, Toyota spent €15 million in 2002 promoting the Prius. There were print ads in magazines, but the bulk of the campaign was in television advertising. Ads running before the actual introduction used the tag line 'A car that sometimes runs on gas power and sometimes runs on electric power, from a company that always runs on brain power'. These ads helped to position Toyota as an 'environmentally concerned' company and more subtly stressed the technology aspect of the car. After introduction, the ads appealed more to emotion, with tag lines such as 'When it sees red, it charges' – a reference to the car's recharging at traffic lights. The headline captured the consumer's attention through ambiguity. Only through focusing on the ad could the consumer learn why the headline was accurate. Again, the appeal is based on the technology of the car. Finally, Toyota took advantage of Earth Day to send out green seed cards shaped like Toyota's logo to prospective buyers, wrapped some Priuses in green, and gave away cars at Earth Day events.

Of course, €15 million is just a drop in the ocean compared to Toyota's overall marketing budget of €200 million in 2002, but Toyota was satisfied with the effectiveness of the campaign, given the 'newness' of the car and the need to explain its technology.

Much of this success can also be attributed to the narrow targeting of the ads. The company expected the first hybrid car buyers to be 'techies' and early adopters (people who are highly likely to buy something new). They were right. Many Prius owners are immersed in the technology. They flood chatrooms with discussion of the car. The Priusenvy.com website urges owners to 'Kick some gas'.

Owners immediately began tinkering with the car's computer system. One owner was able to add cruise control (an option not offered by Toyota) by wiring in a few switches in the car's computer system. The founder of priusenvy.com worked out how to use the car's dashboard display screen to show files from his laptop, play video games, and look at rear-view images from a video camera pointed out of the back of the car. One Austrian consumer installed a sniffer – a device on the car's computer network that monitors electronic messages. With the sniffer, he

will be able to hook up add-ons such as a MiniDisc Player, an MP3 player, a laptop computer and a TV tuner. In the past, owners using mechanical skills customised cars with paint, lowered bodies, and souped-up engines. In the future, customisation may rely on being computer savvy.

Even though the Internet was a major part of the Prius launch, Toyota does not sell the car from its website. Buyers go to prius.toyota.com online to pick a colour and decide whether they want a CD player and floor mats – the only options available from Toyota. After that, the dealers get involved, but it takes specially trained salespeople to explain and promote the Prius. Consequently, only 75 per cent of Toyota dealers handle the car. Many of them are not happy about the need to train salespeople. And why should they be? Margins are higher on gas-guzzlers, which are also easier to sell.

Given dealer reluctance and consumer resistance, why have Toyota and Honda spent so much on their hybrids? While part of the answer is government regulations, a bigger part of the answer is competition. All car manufacturers concede that they will eventually have to move to hybrids to raise petrol mileage and lower emissions, and all of them have plans to do so. Ford, for example, plans to introduce an Escape SUV that will get 17 km/litre. DaimlerChrysler says that 15 per cent of its sport-utility vehicles will be hybrids that will get 20 per cent better fuel efficiency than conventional vehicles. General Motors is betting on hybrid buses and trucks. Toyota hopes, however, that its early entry will be the basis for a system of hybrids from ultracompact 'minicars' to luxury saloons, sport-utility vehicles, and even commercial trucks.

The mass market, however, values space, comfort, and power. Although hybrids may have space and comfort, power would appear to be more elusive. Without greater power, it will be interesting to see whether consumers, who like speed on those open autobahns and acceleration on alpine roads, will settle for a hybrid.

Questions

1. What microenvironmental factors affect the introduction and sales of the Toyota Prius? How well has Toyota dealt with these factors?

2. Outline the major macroenvironmental factors – demographic, economic, natural, technological, political, and cultural – that have affected the introduction and sales of the Toyota Prius. How has Toyota dealt with each of these factors?

3. Evaluate Toyota's marketing strategy so far. What has Toyota done well? How might it improve its strategy?

4. In your opinion, what are the advantages of Toyota's early entry into the hybrid market? What are the disadvantages? Should Toyota have waited – like Ford, GM and DaimlerChrysler?

SOURCES: 'Hit the road, tech', *Fortune* (Winter 2001), pp. 37–8; Jeffrey Ball, 'Hybrid gas–electric car owners can get income-tax deductions', *Wall Street Journal* (22 May 2002), p. D8; Jeff Green, 'Attention techies and assorted geniuses: Toyota Prius wants you', *Brandweek* (15 May 2000), p. 113; Karl Greenberg, 'A wildflower grows in Torrance as Toyota gets environmentally aware', *Brandweek* (20 May 2002), p. 42; Margaret Littman, 'Hybrid engine cars do better with hybrid marketing tactics', *Marketing News* (25 September 2000), p. 42; John McElroy, 'A long time coming', *Ward's Auto World* (July 2001), p. 21; Margot Roosevelt, 'Hybrid power', *Time* (11 December 2000), pp. 94–5; Norihiko Shirouzu, 'Ford aims to sell a gas–electric SUV that will offer sizable fuel efficiency', *Wall Street Journal* (7 March 2000), p. A2; Sherri Singer, 'Toyota Prius', *Machine Design* (28 January 1999), pp. S52–3; Emily Thornton, 'Enviro-Car: the race is on', *Business Week* (8 February 1999), p. 74; Thomas Weber, 'Hacking your car: how auto buffs use the Net to reprogram vehicles', *Wall Street Journal* (2 July 2001), p. B1; David Welch, '46 miles per gallon 47 48', *Business Week* (14 August 2000), p. 68, 'Toyota prices', *What Car? Road Test Directory* (February/March 2004), p. 113; *What Car Buyer Guide* (March 2004), p. 253.

check in

check out

check out

check out

check out

Check out your hotel before you check in. Expedia.co.uk has a variety of hotels to choose from whatever your budget. We provide photos, a detailed list of facilities and even a map of where you'll be staying. So whether you know where you want to stay or you're just looking for inspiration, we'll help you create and plan every aspect of your trip, just the way you want it.

Expedia.co.uk
What's your perfect trip?

> Business is like riding a bicycle. Either you keep moving or you fall down.

JAMES BEASLEY SIMPSON

Marketing in the Internet age

CHAPTER four

Chapter objectives

After reading this chapter, you should be able to:

- Identify the major forces shaping the new digital age.
- Explain how businesses have responded to the Internet and other powerful new technologies with e-business strategies and how these strategies are beneficial to both buyers and sellers.
- Describe the four major e-commerce domains.
- Discuss how marketers conduct e-commerce in ways that profitably deliver value to customers.
- Overview the promise and challenges that e-commerce presents for the future.

Mini Contents List

◀ SOURCE: Expedia.com.

Prelude case Cool Diamonds: are they forever?

The company

Turning Cool Diamonds into the largest Internet-based jewellers in Europe has been an incredible journey for the Einhorn family. The glamorous world of diamond trading is in the blood of the founder of Cool Diamonds' Michel Einhorn. But it was the spilling of blood that prompted his father, Kurt, to become a diamond trader and later inspired his son to follow him into the family business, based in Antwerp.

At the age of 12, Kurt had escaped with his mother from a train bound for Auschwitz. He was hiding among the sacks on a coal merchant's cart, when a border guard began prodding the pile with his bayonet and struck Kurt's hand. But Kurt did not move a muscle and the pair escaped over the border into Switzerland. His mother had used a diamond ring worth £5,000 (€7,500) in today's money, hidden in her hair, to bribe the coal merchant – this saved their lives.

With 300 members of his family now working in the diamond business based in Belgium, Michel Einhorn has the right credentials when it comes to selling diamond jewellery, as well as a ready supply of high quality gems.

Based in London's Hatton Garden, Michel came up with the innovative idea of selling diamonds on the Web. Together with partner Chris O'Farrell, they formed Cool Diamonds in 1999.

E-diamonds: luxury that won't cost the earth

Diamonds are the ultimate statement of ardour and affection. Diamond jewellery makes a breathtaking gift. But they're not just a girl's best friend. Today, young trendies – from Britney Spears and Mel C to David Beckham and Denise Van Outen – are flashing their belly-button studs and ear studs.

The Internet is changing the face of diamond purchasing. By keeping abreast with the most up-to-date technology supporting the Web, and using the latest JSP-xml language, information loads twice as fast as that of their main US competitor, Bluenile, while remaining accessible to large companies using protective computer firewalls. The cooldiamonds.com site gives customers a three-dimensional view of a piece of jewellery. According to Michel, 'With just one click of the mouse, you can drag the piece from the left and to the right as it rotates before your eyes – the only thing you cannot do is touch it!'. The site now attracts more than 3.1 million hits a month and sells thousands of euros worth

of beautiful designer pieces at the click of a button – without the purchaser ever having set eyes on the jewel before it drops on to their doormat. However, it is also possible for the potential customer to make an appointment to visit the Hatton Garden offices if a personal viewing is preferred.

On cooldiamonds.com, visitors can choose from an ever-expanding range of jewellery, including navel studs and toe rings as well as the more conventional bracelets, rings, earrings and pendants. All combine classic elegance with modern design. Cool Diamonds takes the mystique out of diamond buying. Customers can select a design they like and then separately specify the stone according to the four Cs: cut (shape), clarity (from flawless to severely blemished), colour (from white to dirty yellow) and carat (size). There is a fifth C – cost. If they click on 'more expensive', it will go up first by size. If it is too expensive, they can change the clarity or the colour. Customers have more choice because they can select a piece of diamond jewellery 'off-the-peg' or have Cool Diamonds create a bespoke piece just for them.

However, choice is not the only benefit that Cool Diamonds offers customers. A purchase from Cool Diamonds offers good value for money because prices are kept low as there are no expensive overheads, such as prestigious retail premises to maintain. In addition, traditional retail prices carry a huge mark-up, typically reflecting the cost of centrally located outlets, massive stocks and the long chain of middlemen (dealers, cutters, jewellery manufacturers) involved in the trade (also called the diamond pipeline). Moreover, the stock does not need to be duplicated as it is kept in one central location. As such, it can offer the public better value – about 40 per cent of high-street prices. Customers can pay with a credit card over the Internet, which is simple and secure, or they can make a purchase by telephoning Cool Diamonds direct. All diamonds are independently certified, and purchasers have a 10-day money-back guarantee if they change their mind.

Cool Diamonds bucks the trend . . .

While doom and gloom surrounds the luxury goods market, Cool Diamonds is experiencing a huge growth in hits on the site with sales to match. Within three years of setting up online, Cool Diamonds became profitable and has since added to its credibility as the leading designer diamond jewellery site by linking up with well-known names in the world of fashion.

The company is always looking for fresh talent to design for the site. When it undertook a commission from Jasper Conran, the British designer of 'modern classicism', to design stunning

Diamonds are the ultimate statement of ardour and affection.

accessories for the site, hits on the site shot up to an incredible 853,000 a month, with increased sales. Cool Diamonds also works in partnership with the prestigious Central Saint Martins College of Art and Design. In 2002, the Cool Diamonds Award was launched: an annual presentation aimed at rewarding the best of the up-and-coming British design talent. In 2003, the award went to 22-year-old design student Franky Wongkar of Indonesia for his 'organically' inspired design for a pair of diamond earrings. In 2004, the award focused on pendants. Winning designs are available for sale from the Cool Diamonds website. In addition, since it purchased the *Atelier* collection of haute couture diamond jewellery designed by the late Gianni Versace, the site has attracted more than 1.3 million hits a month, providing an innovative sales outlet for a superb collection of rings, bracelets, necklaces and earrings, retailing from £3,000 to £30,000.

Cool Diamonds forever

Cool Diamonds appears to be doing a good job persuading people that diamonds are forever. They have used a unique combination of skills that underpin their business rather than the millions of pounds of venture funding behind other, now failed, Internet sites. 'We are thriving', says Michel Einhorn.

Cool Diamonds grew the business naturally and has seen a steady increase in hits and sales, which have trebled over the past two years. Creative use of public relations has enabled the company to expand consumer awareness as well as fostering

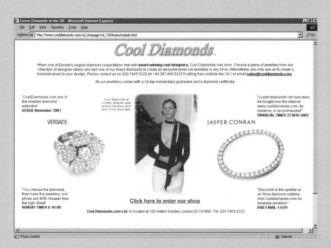

Cool Diamonds have revolutionised the way in which diamond jewellery can be purchased.
SOURCE: Molly McKellar Public Relations, London.

excellent relations with the fashion press. In the past, Cool Diamonds benefited from the positive endorsement given by the UK's Consumers' Association in its *Which*? magazine. However, Cool Diamonds had restricted their advertising spend, relying mainly on word-of-mouth (or word-of-Web) recommendations and PR to communicate their 'sparkle' to the public. It is highly rewarding from the company's perspective to have *Vogue*, *Tatler* and the FT writing features about Cool Diamonds. As the business is growing, the company has recently decided to reinvest all profits in a serious advertising campaign to drive future growth.

In a bid to replicate its success in the UK, Cool Diamonds has also opened an office in France. However, the Cool Diamonds French operation has yet to make a strong impact, with the site attracting around 150,000 hits a month. The founding partners believe that there are lessons to be learnt from the rapid decline of pan-European e-tailer Boo.com – mismanagement as well as trying to expand too quickly without taking time to build local teams. In the UK, customers seem to have developed a strong taste for diamonds, and many are happy to buy through the Internet. However, French consumers appear less than enthusiastic about buying diamond jewellery online.

In the last few years, the company has revolutionised the way in which diamonds are bought. Gone is the mystique. In its place, customers are offered an Internet site that is design-led, fast, friendly and safe, offering an unprecedented amount of choice to a worldwide client base. Meanwhile, as business in the UK booms, Michel Einhorn has to determine how best to proceed to ensure Cool Diamonds, like their stones, will be forever.[1]

Questions

1. Evaluate Cool Diamonds' marketing approach to date. Identify the major factors that have influenced its success. What problems do you see with their current approach?
2. What are the major challenges facing Cool Diamonds in the future?
3. What marketing recommendations would you make to Cool Diamonds, taking into account the ways in which Cool Diamonds can attract people to visit their website and to eventually buy expensive diamond jewellery through their site?
4. Is it a good idea for Cool Diamonds to reinvest all profits in a serious advertising campaign to compound its future growth? Explain your answer. What steps might the company take to sustain planned growth in the UK and its overseas markets?

Introduction

In Chapter 3, we addressed the major environmental forces that affect marketing strategy and practice. We saw why and how marketing strategy and practice have undergone dramatic change during the past decade. One of the major forces in the macroenvironment that challenges marketing strategy and practice is technological change. Indeed, major technological advances, including the explosion of the Internet, have had a major impact on buyers and the marketers who serve them. To thrive in this new Internet age – even to survive – marketers must rethink their strategies and adapt them to today's new environment. Our prelude case – Cool Diamonds – shows how companies have responded to the sweeping changes in the marketing landscape that are affecting marketing thinking and practice.

Recent technological advances, including the widespread use of the Internet, have created what some call a New Economy. Although there has been widespread debate in recent years about the nature and even the existence of such a New Economy, few would disagree that the Internet and other powerful new connecting technologies are having a dramatic impact on marketers and buyers. Many standard marketing strategies and practices of the past – mass marketing, product standardisation, media advertising, store retailing, and others – were well suited to the so-called Old Economy. These strategies and practices will continue to be important in the New Economy. However, marketers will also have to develop new strategies and practices better suited to today's new environment.

In this chapter, we first describe the key forces shaping the new Internet age. Then we examine how marketing strategy and practice are changing to meet the requirements of this new age.

Major forces shaping the Internet age

Many forces are reshaping the world economy, including technology, globalisation, environmentalism and others. Here, we address four specific forces that underlie the new digital era (see Figure 4.1): digitalisation and connectivity, the explosion of the Internet, new forms of intermediaries, and customisation and customerisation.

Figure 4.1 **Forces shaping the Internet age**

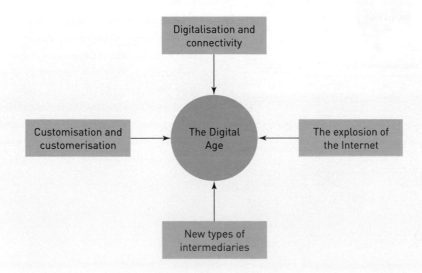

Digitalisation and connectivity

Many appliances and systems in the past – ranging from telephone systems, wrist watches and musical recordings to industrial gauges and controls – operated on analogue information. Analogue information is continuously variable in response to physical stimuli. Today a growing number of appliances and systems operate on *digital information*, which comes as streams of zeros and ones, or *bits*. Text, data, sound and images can be converted into *bitstreams*. A laptop computer manipulates bits in its thousands of applications. Software consists of digital content for operating systems, games, information storage and other applications.

For bits to flow from one appliance or location to another requires *connectivity*, a telecommunications network. Much of the world's business today is carried out over networks that connect people and companies. *Intranets* are networks that connect people within a company to each other and to the company network. *Extranets* connect a company with its suppliers, distributors, and other outside partners. And the **Internet**, a vast public web of computer networks, connects users of all types all around the world to each other and to an amazingly large information repository. The Internet makes up one big 'information highway' that can dispatch bits at incredible speeds from one location to another.

The Internet explosion

With the creation of the World Wide Web and Web browsers in the 1990s, the Internet was transformed from a mere communication tool into a certifiably revolutionary technology. During the final decade of the twentieth century, the number of Internet users worldwide grew to almost 400 million. By 2003, Internet penetration in the United States had exceeded 66 per cent. Although the dot-com crash in 2000 led to cutbacks in technology spending, research suggests that the growth of Internet access among the world's population will continue to explode. Internet penetration in the European Union countries varies as shown in Table 4.1. It is highest in Sweden, reaching 76.9 per cent by January 2004, followed by The Netherlands with 66.0 per cent penetration and Denmark with a penetration rate of 62.5 per cent. Internet use in the old 15-nation EU has grown 97.2 per cent between 2000 and 2004, while the new EU members report a whopping increase of 155.1 per cent over the same period. As Table 4.1 shows, there are now over 184 million Internet users in the expanded EU, representing an overall growth of 102.3 per cent between 2000 and 2004. According to Internet World Stats, the number of Web surfers worldwide reached nearly 700 million by 2004 and is expected to approach 1.5 billion by 2007.[2]

Internet access via mobile phones is also growing in popularity, with mobile terminal access in Europe increasing to 300 million users by 2004, compared to 200 million users using PC-based access.[3]

Internet (the Net)—A vast public web of computer networks connecting users of all types all around the world to each other and to a large 'information repository'. The Internet makes up one big 'information highway' that can dispatch bits at incredible speeds from one location to another.

Mobile marketing is taking off as forward-thinking companies have begun to use short messaging service (SMS) to promote their products and services. Examples include HarperCollins (books), Twentieth Century Fox (films), Cadbury's (confectionery) and McDonald's (fast food). Independent research carried out for the UK's Mobile Marketing Association (MMA) suggests that, far from being annoyed by advertising on their phone, consumers like it. According to the research, carried out among a sample of 705 respondents in the UK, Germany and Italy, 43 per cent of respondents said they felt that the messages they received via SMS have a positive impact on the advertised

Table 4.1 Internet usage, growth and penetration in the European Union (March 2004)
SOURCE: Reproduced from Internet World Stats (www.internetworldstats.com); p. 178. Demographic data from World Gazetter, www.gazettezer.de; usage from Nielsen/NetRatings, www.nielsen-netratings.com, ITU, www.itu.net, and local NICs.

European Union	Internet users, latest data	Use growth (2000–2004)	Penetration (% population)
Austria	3,340,000	59.0%	41.6%
Belgium	3,769,123	88.5%	36.4%
Denmark	3,375,850	73.1%	62.5%
Finland	2,650,000	37.5%	50.7%
France	22,199,080	161.2%	37.3%
Germany	44,842,759	86.8%	54.3%
Greece	1,704,900	70.5%	15.2%
Ireland	1,319,608	68.3%	32.8%
Italy	19,900,000	50.8%	35.4%
Luxembourg	165,000	65.0%	36.0%
Netherlands	10,806,328	177.1%	66.0%
Portugal	2,000,000	−20.0%	19.2%
Spain	13,600,467	152.4%	32.5%
Sweden	6,913,676	70.8%	76.9%
United Kingdom	34,765,774	125.8%	58.8%
10 new Member States of the EU			
Cyprus	210,000	75.0%	22.1%
Czech Republic	2,600,000	160.0%	25.3%
Estonia	444,000	21.1%	35.9%
Hungary	1,600,000	123.8%	15.8%
Latvia	310,000	106.7%	13.7%
Lithuania	500,000	122.2%	14.3%
Malta	82,900	107.3%	21.6%
Poland	8,800,000	217.1%	23.3%
Slovakia	862,800	32.7%	16.0%
Slovenia	750,000	150.0%	38.4%
European Union	168,012,565	98.4%	44.2%
New members EU	16,239,700	155.1%	21.9%
Total EU (May 2004)	184,252,265	102.3%	40.6%

brand, with only 7 per cent expressing a negative opinion. Sixty-eight per cent of respondents would most likely or definitely recommend that friends receive such messages, and 43 per cent said they would be likely to respond by viewing an ad or visiting the website. But the key to mobile marketing success is to ensure that permission is gained from potential customers who have opted in to receive SMS ads from marketers. Companies who have successfully deployed mobile marketing acknowledge that another ingredient for success is to ensure two-way advertising through implementing interactive campaigns.[4]

The proportion of Internet users who conduct online shopping remains relatively low compared to those using conventional sales outlets at the moment, but e-commerce is growing very fast. The proportion of Internet sales to total retail sales varies across the

European markets. According to figures from IMRG, the e-tailing trade body in the UK, the UK online retailing sector outperforms that of its European rivals. In the UK, Internet retail sales grew by 7 per cent between 2002 and 2003, compared to 3.6 per cent reported for all retail sales. Data collected by Visa, the credit card company, suggests that the UK had the lion's share of goods bought online with the credit card.[5]

This explosive worldwide growth in Internet usage forms the heart of the so-called New Economy. The Internet has been *the* revolutionary technology of the new millennium, empowering consumers and businesses alike with blessings of connectivity. For nearly every New Economy innovation to emerge during the past decade, the Internet has played a starring – or at the very least a 'best supporting' – role. The Internet enables consumers and companies to access and share huge amounts of information with just a few mouse clicks. Recent studies have shown that consumers are accessing information on the Internet before making major life decisions. One in three consumers relies heavily on the Internet to gather information about choosing a school, buying a car, finding a job, dealing with a major illness or making investment decisions. As a result, to be competitive in today's new marketplace, companies must adopt Internet technology or risk being left behind.[6]

New forms of intermediaries

New technologies have led thousands of entrepreneurs to launch Internet companies – the so-called dotcoms – in hopes of striking gold. The amazing success of early Internet-only companies, such as AOL, Amazon.com, Yahoo!, eBay, E*Trade, and dozens of others, struck terror in the hearts of many established manufacturers and retailers. For example, computer manufacturers such as Compaq Computer, which sold its computers only through retailers, worried when Dell Computer grew faster by selling online. Established store-based retailers of all kinds – from bookstores, music stores and florists to travel agents, stockbrokers and car dealers – began to doubt their futures as competitors sprung up selling their products and services via the Internet. They feared, and rightly so, being *disintermediated* by the new e-tailers – being cut out by this new type of intermediary.

The formation of new types of intermediaries and new forms of channel relationships caused existing firms to re-examine how they served their markets. At first, the established *brick-and-mortar* firms, such as Tesco, Marks & Spencer, Barnes & Noble and NatWest Bank, dragged their feet, hoping that the assaulting *click-only* firms would falter or disappear. Then they wised up and started their own online sales channels, becoming *click-and-mortar* competitors. Ironically, many click-and-mortar competitors have become stronger than the click-only competitors that pushed them reluctantly onto the Internet (see Marketing Insights 4.1). In fact, although some click-only competitors are surviving and even prospering in today's marketplace, many once-formidable dotcoms, such as eToys, Webvan, Pets.com, Garden.com, and Mothernature.com, have failed in the face of poor profitability and plunging stock values. Other notable dotcom casualties include Swedish-founded Letsbuyit.com, the pan-European business-to-consumer (B2C) retailer selling a comprehensive range of goods from diamond necklaces to electronic equipment, and Intershop, the much-hyped German software company.[7]

Customisation and customerisation

The Old Economy revolved around *manufacturing companies* that mainly focused on standardising their production, products and business processes. They invested large sums in brand building to promote the advantages of their standardised market offerings. Through standardisation and branding, manufacturers hoped to grow demand and take advantage of economies of scale. As a key to managing their assets, they set up command-and-control systems that would run their businesses like machines.

In contrast, the New Economy revolves around *information businesses*. Information has the advantages of being easy to differentiate, customise, personalise and send at incredible speeds

marketing insights

4.1 The new dotcom landscape

It's summer 2003, five years on from the launch of Internet service provider Freeserve and the first meetings of the First Tuesday dotcom networkers, and only about 40 people have shown up at a London hotel for Upstart Europe, an annual conference on start-ups and trends.

The absence of dotcoms on the agenda is also instructive. There are only two venture capitalists in the audience and the scope of the conference is widened to include more biotech and life sciences. 'If you look at the VC [venture capital] scene, it's like a hurricane has passed and there's a lot of debris', says Jerome Mol, entrepreneur and conference organiser.

Eventually, 160 people turn up and Mr Mol draws a parallel with the first stirrings of summer. 'The number of deals and financing was extremely low in the first five months of the year but since then it has been ramping up tremendously', he says. 'It's definitely bottomed out. It's been a rollercoaster but we've survived.'

Elsewhere, Mark Rogers, a dotcom chief executive, is giving his annual speech to school leavers at Westminster School. Even the mood of the sixth-formers reflects a sea change in their expectations. 'A year ago, they were still asking me about valuations but today it was not so much about making a fortune – it was more about doing useful things.'

The utilitarian approach has become predominant – whether it is the focus on solid technologies such as search engines and wi-fi wireless Internet connections, or on websites that just do their job well and produce real profits. Futuristic business plans have been replaced by a return to basics, and inexperienced chief executives have been swept away by conventional companies exploiting a medium whose acceptance among users has quietly accelerated.

Rebecca Jennings, of Forrester Research, says: 'There's been continued growth in the market since the beginning and it will top $10bn (£6.3bn) in the UK this year: $200m was spent in the UK last year on online advertising and 55 per cent of adults, about 30m people, now have regular Internet access.'

Familiarity has bred confidence among users about buying online and their increasing sophistication has led to the popularity of sites that improve their searching, compare prices and aggregate offers.

'Before they bought books and DVDs', says Mrs Jennings. 'Now that's been extended to higher-ticket items such as travel.'

A campaign in July to promote Internet shopping saw consumers spend £1.15bn online that month – up 208 per cent on July 2002, according to IMRG, the e-retail industry body.

The Internet is looking more like the traditional high street, says Nigel Reynolds, who was involved in two of the first four dotcom flotations for PwC, the accounting firm. 'It's very much the old, traditional businesses that are starting to trade as dotcoms', he says. What were once labelled the dinosaurs are now rethinking their

...4.1

Internet strategies. Old brick-and-mortar retailers such as Sainsbury's and Tesco are cleaning up amid the rubble of the fallen dotcoms. Tesco learnt the lessons from the Internet meltdown. By 2002, it became the world's biggest Web grocer. But, unlike fallen dotcom star Webvan in the US, the British retailer decided to initially fill Web orders from existing Tesco supermarkets rather than dedicated, money-guzzling warehouses. Webvan failed because of reckless spending.

Simon Chamberlain, general manager of Hitwise, which monitors net use, says there are dominant players in some sectors, such as Autotrader in the automotive category or eBay in auctions, but small players can survive as users become more familiar with Web tools and comparison sites such as search engine Google and the French online shopping web site Kelkoo, recently acquired by Yahoo!.

'There are almost 2,000 travel sites in the UK and more than 500 online recruitment sites. We have seen some consolidation but the good news is that there are a lot of niche players getting business because people are searching for very specific things', says Chamberlain. Sites that have built a community and attained a critical mass of users are most likely to endure. For example, Friendsreunited, Faceparty and dating sites are thriving, as are betting exchanges, while travel hubs such as cheapflights.co.uk are essential destinations for their aggregation of what is on offer.

Two founders still running their self-financed travel business are Richard Coundley and Marcelle Speller, a husband and wife team that set up holiday-rentals.com before the bubble in 1996. It puts holidaymakers in direct contact with private property owners and was a winner at the New Media Age industry awards this year.

Ms Speller says: 'It took six years to break even and venture capitalists would have given up on it. But founding it ourselves, we weren't going to do that. We've now reached critical mass. It's very hard to become another eBay but we feel we are offering something of real benefit.'

The Internet is a fast, exciting world. No one can deny that, not least yesterday's dotcom stars. 'Here today, gone tomorrow' seems to best describe the pace of cyber activity and the lifespan of many of Europe's once optimistic Internet start-ups.

The e-revolution may not be completely over. The venture capital scene may never feel like the good old days of the dotcom boom either. But, as the storm calms, the dotcom industry wakes up to a new challenge. This time the battle will be fought and won where real and virtual worlds unite.

The late arrivals at the Internet party – the so-called Old Economy companies – are set to dominate the e-commerce landscape. And, as the rubble is cleared, investors can now tell good clicks from bad.

SOURCES: Based on Chris Nuttall, 'Dotcom takes on the bustle of the high street', *Financial Times* (1 September 2003), p. 3. Information on successful dotcom pioneers based on 'Internet pioneers', *The Economist* (3 February 2001), pp. 91–3; 'Party like it's 1999', *The Economist* (23 February 2002), pp. 87–8; and 'Off their trolleys', *The Economist* (23 November 2002), pp. 80–1; see also Andrew Edgecliffe-Johnson, 'E-revolution shelved', *Financial Times* (3 August 2000), p. 16; Susanna Voyle, 'E-tailers find their perfect partner on the high street', *Financial Times* (7 April 2000), p. 25; 'Europe's dot.bombs', *The Economist* (5 August 2000), p. 20; 'Only the strong survive after the storm', in 'The Internet revolution, Special report', *Financial Times* (16 October 2000), p. 14.

over networks. With rapid advances in Internet and other connecting technologies, companies have grown skilled in gathering information about individual customers and business partners (suppliers, distributors, retailers). In turn, they have become more adept at individualising their products and services, messages and media.

Dell Computer, for example, lets customers specify exactly what they want in their computers and delivers customer-designed units in only a few days. On its Reflect.com website, Procter & Gamble allows people to reflect their needs for, say, a shampoo by answering a set of questions. It then formulates a unique shampoo for each person.[8]

Customisation differs from *customerisation*. Customisation involves taking the initiative to customise the market offering. For example, a Levi's salesperson takes the person's measurements and the company customises the jeans at the factory. In **customerisation**, the company leaves it to individual customers to design the offering. For example, jeans customers may take their own measurements and add specific features that they may want in their jeans, such as colourful patches. Such companies have become facilitators and their customers have moved from being consumers to being *prosumers*.[9]

Customerisation—Leaving it to the individual customers to design the marketing offering – allowing customers to be prosumers rather than only consumers.

Marketing strategy in the new digital age

For many companies, conducting business in the new digital age will call for a new model for marketing strategy and practice. According to one strategist: 'Sparked by new technologies, particularly the Internet, the corporation is undergoing a radical transformation that is nothing less than a new industrial revolution. . . . To survive and thrive in this century, managers will need to hard-wire a new set of rules into their brains. The 21st century corporation must adapt itself to management via the Web.'[10] Suggests another, the Internet is 'revolutionizing the way we think about . . . how to construct relationships with suppliers and customers, how to create value for them, and how to make money in the process; in other words, [it's] revolutionizing marketing.'[11]

Some strategists envisage a day when all buying and selling will involve direct electronic connections between companies and their customers. The new model will fundamentally change customers' notions of convenience, speed, price, product information, and service. This new consumer thinking will affect every business. Comparing the adoption of the Internet and other new marketing technologies to the early days of the aeroplane, Amazon.com CEO Jeff Bezos says 'It's the Kitty Hawk era of electronic commerce.' Even those offering more cautious predictions agree that the Internet and e-business will have a tremendous impact on future business strategies.

The fact is that today's economy requires a mixture of Old Economy and New Economy thinking and action. Companies need to retain most of the skills and practices that have worked in the past. But they will also need to add major new competencies and practices if they hope to grow and prosper in the new environment. Marketing should play the lead role in shaping new company strategy.

E-business, e-commerce and e-marketing

E-business or electronic business—The use of electronic platforms – intranets, extranets and the Internet – to conduct a company's business.

E-business involves the use of electronic platforms – intranets, extranets and the Internet – to conduct a company's business. The Internet and other technologies now help companies to carry on their business faster, more accurately, and over a wider range of time and space. Countless companies have set up websites to inform about and promote their products and services. They have created intranets to help employees communicate with each other and access information found in the company's computers. They have set up extranets with their major suppliers and distributors to assist information exchange, orders, transactions and payments. Companies such as Cisco, Microsoft and Oracle run almost entirely as e-businesses, in which memos, invoices, engineering drawings, sales and marketing information – virtually everything happen over the Internet instead of on paper.[12]

Electronic commerce is more specific than e-business. E-business includes all electronics-based information exchanges within or between companies and customers. In contrast, e-commerce involves buying and selling processes supported by electronic means, primarily the Internet. *E-markets* are 'market*spaces*' rather than physical 'market*places*'. Sellers use e-markets to offer their products and services online. Buyers use them to search for information, identify what they want, and place orders using credit or other means of electronic payment.

E-commerce includes *e-marketing* and *e-purchasing* (*e-procurement*). **E-marketing** is the marketing side of e-commerce. It consists of company efforts to communicate about, promote and sell products and services over the Internet. Thus, easyJet.com, Nokia.com and Dell.com conduct e-marketing at their websites. The flip side of e-marketing is e-purchasing, the buying side of e-commerce. It consists of companies purchasing goods, services and information from online suppliers.

In business-to-business buying, e-marketers and e-purchasers come together in huge e-commerce networks. Examples include e-cement.com which operates a business-to-business e-commerce network for the cement making industry; milkquota.com for the agricultural sector; efoodmanager.com, the pan-European online purchasing network for the food industry; and GE Global eXchange Services (GXS). The latter represent one of the world's largest business-to-business e-commerce networks (www.gegxs.com). More than 100,000 trading partners in 58 countries, including giants such as 3M, DaimlerChrysler, Sara Lee, and Kodak, use the GXS network to complete some 1 billion transactions each year, accounting for $1 trillion (€0.83 trillion) worth of goods and services.[13]

E-commerce and the Internet bring many benefits to both buyers and sellers. Let's review some of these major benefits.

Benefits to buyers

Internet buying benefits both final buyers and business buyers in many ways. It can be convenient: customers don't have to battle traffic, find parking spaces and trek through stores and aisles to find and examine products. They can do comparative shopping by browsing through mail catalogues or surfing websites. Direct marketers never close their doors. Buying is easy and private: customers encounter fewer buying hassles and don't have to face salespeople or open themselves up to persuasion and emotional pitches. Business buyers can learn about and buy products and services without waiting for and tying up time with salespeople.

In addition, the Internet often provides buyers with greater *product access and selection*. For example, the world's the limit for the Web. Unrestrained by physical boundaries, cybersellers can offer an almost unlimited selection. Compare the incredible selections offered by Web merchants such as Amazon.com or eBay to the more meagre assortments of their counterparts in the brick-and-mortar world.

Beyond a broader selection of sellers and products, e-commerce channels also give buyers access to a wealth of comparative *information* about companies, products and competitors. Good sites often provide more information in more useful forms than even the most solicitous salesperson can. For example, Amazon.com offers top-10 product lists, extensive product descriptions, expert and user product reviews and recommendations based on customers' previous purchases.

Finally, online buying is *interactive* and *immediate*. Buyers often can interact with the seller's site to create exactly the configuration of information, products or services they desire, then order or download them on the spot. Moreover, the Internet gives consumers a greater

Electronic commerce— A general term for a buying and selling process that is supported by electronic means.

Electronic marketing— The marketing side of e-commerce – company efforts to communicate about, promote and sell products and services over the Internet.

measure of control. Like nothing else before it, the Internet has empowered consumers. For example, computer or car buyers can go online before showing up at a retailer or dealership, arming themselves with both product and cost information. This is the new reality of consumer control.

Benefits to sellers

E-commerce also yields many benefits to sellers. First, the Internet is a powerful tool for *customer relationship building*. Because of its one-to-one, interactive nature, the Internet is an especially potent marketing tool. Companies can interact online with customers to learn more about specific needs and wants. With today's technology, an online marketer can select small groups or even individual consumers, personalise offers to their special needs and wants and promote these offers through individualised communications.

In turn, online customers can ask questions and volunteer feedback. Based on this ongoing interaction, companies can increase customer value and satisfaction through product and service refinements. One expert concludes: 'Contrary to the common view that Web customers are fickle by nature and will flock to the next new idea, the Web is actually a very sticky space in both business-to-consumer and business-to-business spheres. Most of today's online customers exhibit a clear [tendency] toward loyalty.'[14]

The Internet and other electronic channels yield additional advantages, such as *reducing costs* and *increasing speed and efficiency*. As seen in the case of Cool Diamonds, e-marketers avoid the expense of maintaining a store and the related costs of rent, insurance and utilities. E-tailers such as Amazon.com reap the advantage of a negative operating cycle: Amazon.com receives cash from credit card companies just one day after customers place an order. Then it can hold on to the money for 46 days until it pays suppliers, book distributors, and publishers.

By using the Internet to link directly to suppliers, factories, distributors and customers, businesses such as Dell Computer and Cool Diamonds are cutting costs and passing savings on to customers. Because customers deal directly with sellers, e-marketing often results in lower costs and improved efficiencies for channel and logistics functions such as order processing, inventory handling, delivery, and trade promotion. Finally, communicating electronically often costs less than communicating on paper through the mail. For instance, a company can produce digital catalogues for much less than the cost of printing and mailing paper ones.

E-marketing also offers greater *flexibility*, allowing the marketer to make ongoing adjustments to its offers and programmes. For example, once a paper catalogue is mailed to final consumer or business customers, the products, prices and other catalogue features are fixed until the next catalogue is sent. However, an online catalogue can be adjusted daily or even hourly, adapting product assortments, prices and promotions to match changing market conditions.

Finally, the Internet is a truly *global* medium that allows buyers and sellers to click from one country to another in seconds. GE's GXS network provides business buyers with immediate access to suppliers in 58 countries, ranging from the United States and the United Kingdom to Hong Kong and the Philippines. A Web surfer from Paris or Hong Kong can access an online Marks & Spencer catalogue as easily as someone living in London, the international retailer's home town. Thus, even small e-marketers find that they have ready access to global markets.

E-commerce domains

The four major Internet domains are shown in Figure 4.2 and discussed below. They include B2C (business to consumer), B2B (business to business), C2C (consumer to consumer) and C2B (consumer to business).

Figure 4.2 E-marketing domains

	Targeted to consumers	Targeted to businesses
Initiated by business	B2C (business to consumer)	B2B (business to business)
Initiated by consumer	C2C (consumer to consumer)	C2B (consumer to business)

B2C (business to consumer)

The popular press has paid the most attention to **B2C (business-to-consumer) e-commerce** – the online selling of goods and services to final consumers. Despite some gloomy predictions, online consumer buying continues to grow at a healthy rate. As we saw in Marketing Insights 4.1, online retail sales in countries such as the UK are growing steadily, while consumers are shifting purchases from lower-value items such as books, videos and DVDs to higher-ticket items such as travel. In this chapter's opening case, we also saw how consumers have taken to the Internet to buy expensive items costing thousands of euros, such as diamond jewellery. In the US, consumers spent more than $112 billion (€92.6 billion) online in 2002, up 56 per cent from the previous year. The largest categories of consumer online spending include travel services, clothing, computer hardware and software, consumer electronics, books, music and video, health and beauty, home and garden, flowers and gifts, sports and fitness equipment, and toys.[15]

B2C (business-to-consumer) e-commerce—The online selling of goods and services to final consumers.

Online consumers

When people think of the typical Internet user, some still mistakenly envisage a pasty-faced computer nerd or 'cyberhead', others a young, techy, up-market male professional. Such stereotypes are sadly outdated. As more and more people find their way onto the Internet, the cyberspace population is becoming more mainstream and diverse. 'The Internet was, at first, an elitist country club reserved only for individuals with select financial abilities and technical skills', says an e-commerce analyst. 'Now, nearly every socioeconomic group is aggressively adopting the Web.'[16] The Internet provides e-marketers with access to a broad range of demographic segments. In recent research conducted among 3,600 individuals who play online games, the US Digital Marketing Services found that American females over 40 years old spend the most time per week playing online games (e.g., word and puzzle, casino, trivia and arcade games) at 9.1 hours, which accounts for 41 per cent of their connection time. By contrast, female teenagers spend 7.4 hours per week playing games, while females under 40 years log 6.2 hours. Although findings from comparable research among their European counterparts are not to hand, the American survey sheds light on the evolving nature of the contemporary Web user.[17]

Growing Internet diversity will open new e-commerce targeting opportunities for marketers. For example, the Web now reaches consumers in all age groups including children and teens. Thus, these 'net kids' and teens segments have attracted a host of e-marketers. America Online offers a Kids Only area featuring homework help and online magazines along with the usual games, software and chatrooms. The Microsoft Network site carries Disney's Daily Blast, which offers kids games, stories, comic strips with old and new Disney characters, and current events tailored to pre-teens. BeingGirl.com is a site for teens, offering information on relationships, boys, periods and much more. Leading girls' entertainment software publishers also joined forces to offer a special website (just4girls.com) that promotes stories, games, dolls and accessories targeted at 8–12-year-old girls.[18]

Although Internet users are still younger on average than the population as a whole, consumers aged 50 and older make up almost 20 per cent of the online population. Whereas younger groups are more likely to use the Internet for entertainment and socialising, older Internet surfers go online for more serious matters. For example, 24 per cent of people in this age group use the Internet for investment purposes, compared with only 3 per cent of those aged 25–29. Thus, older 'Netizens' make an attractive market for Web businesses, ranging from florists and automotive retailers to financial services providers.[19]

Internet consumers differ from traditional offline consumers in their approaches to buying and in their responses to marketing. The exchange process in the Internet age has become more customer initiated and customer controlled. People who use the Internet place greater value on information and tend to respond negatively to messages aimed only at selling. Traditional marketing targets a somewhat passive audience. In contrast, e-marketing targets people who actively select which websites they will visit and what marketing information they will receive about which products and under what conditions.

Internet directories, such as Yahoo! NodeWorks and Lycos, and 'search engines', such as Google, AltaVista, Excite, AlltheWeb and many others, give consumers access to vast and varied information sources, making them better informed and more discerning shoppers. AlltheWeb, developed by Finnish firm Fast Search & Transfer and touted to be a serious rival to the US-spawned Google, was able at the time of writing to index some 2,112,188,990 Web pages on its home page on a day, running neck to neck with Google, with a listing of 2,469,940,685 Web pages! As technology advances, these search engines are able to take the information from several billion of these Web pages, integrating them with hot-off-the-press news from thousands of news sources across the globe and hundreds of millions of multimedia, video, software and compressed MP3 sound files, all in a single search result![20]

In fact, online buyers are increasingly creators of product information, not just consumers of it. As greater numbers of consumers join Internet interest groups that share product-related information, 'word-of-Web' is joining 'word-of-mouth' as an important buying influence. Thus, the new world of e-commerce will require new marketing approaches.

B2C websites

Consumers can find a website for buying almost anything. The Internet is most useful for products and services when the shopper seeks greater ordering convenience or lower costs. The Internet also provides great value to buyers looking for information about differences in product features and value. However, consumers find the Internet less useful when buying products that must be touched or examined in advance. Still, even here there are exceptions. For example, who would have thought that people would order expensive jewellery from cooldiamonds.com or computers from Dell or Gateway without seeing and trying them first?

B2B (business-to-business) e-commerce—Using B2B trading networks, auction sites, spot exchanges, online product catalogues, barter sites and other online resources to reach new customers, serve current customers more effectively and obtaining buying efficiencies and better prices.

B2B (business to business)

Although the popular press has given the most attention to business-to-consumer (B2C) websites, consumer goods sales via the Web are dwarfed by **B2B (business-to-business) e-commerce**. One study estimates that B2B e-commerce will reach $4.3 trillion (€3.6 trillion) in 2005, compared with just $282 billion (€233 billion) in 2000. Another estimates that by 2005, more than 500,000 enterprises will use e-commerce as buyers, sellers, or both.[21] B2B exchanges are now found in a host of industries ranging from motor car, aerospace and petroleum, to chemicals, food, energy, pharmaceuticals and many others. Firms are using B2B trading networks, auction sites, spot exchanges, online product catalogues, barter sites and other online resources to reach new customers, serve current customers more effectively and obtain buying efficiencies and better prices.

Most major business-to-business marketers now offer product information, customer purchasing, and customer support services online. B2B exchanges enable buyers to gain efficiencies on many levels, from the identification of new sources of supply and negotiations, to carrying out transactions and payments and supply chain management functions such as production line planning and collaborative product design and development. An increasing number of manufacturers, for example, have been able to accelerate the product development process by using the Internet to share designs for component or assemblies with suppliers or to pass design work on from teams in one time zone to another.[22]

Much B2B e-commerce takes place in **open trading networks** – huge e-marketspaces in which buyers and sellers find each other online, share information and complete transactions efficiently. For example, ECeurope (www.eceurope.com) is part of a huge business-to-business trading trading network and there are almost 100 trade sites in this network including eceurope.com, worldbid.com, the Fita Buy/Sell Exchange etc. It represents one of the largest sources of international trade leads and tender opportunities from companies and government organisations around the world. Over 300,000 businesses have registered with the site in the hope of increasing their sales, reducing supplier costs and finding new business contacts. Other international e-trading networks include Global Business Web (www.globalbusinessweb.com), a free global site where companies from hosts of industries can make contact, conduct research, promote their business and trade. A host of barter exchange sites have also emerged in recent years. Examples include BarterNet Corp, iBart and Barter Directory. Others include Antwerpes (www.antwerpes.com), an Internet services company that operates one of Germany's largest online shopping sites for medical products. Through its DocCheck® Shop (www.doccheck.com), it offers pharmaceutical companies the opportunity to set up buying groups for their sales departments or to integrate complete shops with an individual product range into their Internet operation.[23]

Open trading networks— Huge e-marketspaces in which B2B buyers and sellers find each other online, share information and complete transactions efficiently.

Trading networks: Worldbid.com offers businesses the chance to search for qualified B2B trade leads in their industry.
SOURCE: Worldbid.com.

Private trading networks (PTNs)—B2B trading networks that link a particular seller with its own trading partners.

Despite the increasing popularity of such e-marketspaces, one Internet research firm estimates that 93 per cent of all B2B e-commerce is conducted through private sites. Increasingly, online sellers are setting up their own **private trading networks** (PTNs).

Open trading networks facilitate transactions between a wide range of online buyers and sellers. In contrast, private trading networks link a particular seller with its own trading partners. Rather than simply completing transactions, PTNs give sellers greater control over product presentation and allow them to build deeper relationships with buyers and sellers by providing value-added services.

The firm can set up its own private exchange, which allows its customers to browse, buy equipment, schedule deliveries and process warranties.

> For example, ChemConnect assists customers in optimising their purchasing and sales processes for chemicals, plastics and related products through a unique combination of exchanging market information, industry expertise, e-commerce solutions and an active network of trading partners. More than 7,500 member companies in multiple industries around the world can use ChemConnect's highly efficient tools and services to streamline transactions and lower costs.[24]

A PTN of this sort may enable the firm to operate with greater efficiency and trim processing costs, without losing control of the presentation of its brand name or running the risk of rubbing elbows with competitors in an open exchange.

C2C (consumer to consumer)

C2C (consumer-to-consumer) e-commerce—Online exchanges of goods and information between final consumers.

Much C2C (**consumer-to-consumer**) **e-commerce** and communication occurs on the Web between interested parties over a wide range of products and subjects. In some cases, the Internet provides an excellent means by which consumers can buy or exchange goods or information directly with one another. Such C2C sites give people access to much larger audiences than the local flea market or newspaper classifieds (which, by the way, are now also going online). For example, QXL, Alando, eBay, auctions.Amazon, bid-up and other auction sites offer popular marketspaces for displaying and selling almost anything, from art and antiques, coins, stamps and jewellery to computers and consumer electronics. eBay's C2C online trading community of more than 42 million registered users worldwide transacted more than €7 billion ($9 billion) in trades last year. The company's website hosts more than 2 million auctions each month for items in more than 18,000 categories. eBay maintains auction sites in several countries, including Japan, the United Kingdom and Germany.[25]

In other cases, C2C involves interchanges of information through forums and Internet newsgroups that appeal to specific special-interest groups. Such activities may be organised for commercial or non-commercial purposes. *Forums* are discussion groups located on commercial online services such as Freeserve, AOL and CompuServe. A forum may take the form of a library, a 'chatroom' for real-time message exchanges, and even a classified ad directory. For example, AOL boasts some 14,000 chatrooms, which account for a third of its members' online time. It also provides 'buddy lists' which alert members when friends are online, allowing them to exchange instant messages.

Newsgroups are the Internet version of forums. However, such groups are limited to people posting and reading messages on a specified topic, rather than managing libraries or conferencing. Internet users can participate in newsgroups without subscribing. There are tens of thousands of newsgroups dealing with every imaginable topic, from healthy eating and caring for your Bonsai tree to collecting antique cars or exchanging views on the latest soap opera happenings.

C2C means that online visitors don't just consume product information – increasingly, they create it. They join Internet interest groups to share information, with the result that 'word of Web' is joining 'word of mouth' as an important buying influence. Word about good companies and products travels fast. Word about bad companies and products travels even faster.

C2B (consumer to business)

The final e-commerce domain is **C2B** (**consumer-to-business**) **e-commerce**. Thanks to the Internet, today's consumers are finding it easier to communicate with companies. Most companies now invite prospects and customers to send in suggestions and questions via company websites. Beyond this, rather than waiting for an invitation, consumers can search out sellers on the Web, learn about their offers, initiate purchases and give feedback. Using the Web, consumers can even drive transactions with businesses, rather than the other way around. For example, using Priceline.com, would-be buyers can name their own price for airline tickets, hotel rooms, rental cars, and even home mortgages, leaving the sellers to decide whether to accept their offers.

Consumers can also use websites such as PlanetFeedback.com to ask questions, offer suggestions, lodge complaints or deliver compliments to companies. The site provides letter templates for consumers to use based on their moods and reasons for contacting the company. The site then forwards the letters to the customer service manager at each company and helps to obtain a response. Last year, PlanetFeedback.com forwarded more than 330,000 consumer letters composed on their site. Not all of the letters were complaints. One-quarter of them offered compliments, while another one-fifth made suggestions for product or service improvements.[26]

C2B (consumer-to-business) e-commerce—Online exchanges in which consumers search out sellers, learn about their offers, and initiate purchases, sometimes even driving transaction terms.

C2B e-commerce: services such as Priceline enable consumers to 'name their own price' when building a holiday, resulting in huge savings on hotels and flights.
SOURCE: www.priceline.co.uk.

Conducting e-commerce

Companies of all types are now engaged in e-commerce. In this section, we first discuss the different types of e-marketers. Then we examine how companies go about conducting marketing online.

Click-only versus click-and-mortar e-marketers

The Internet gave birth to a new species of e-marketers – the *click-only* dotcoms – which operate only online without any brick-and-mortar market presence. In addition, most traditional *brick-and-mortar* companies have now added e-marketing operations, transforming themselves into *click-and-mortar* competitors.

Click-only companies

Click-only companies—The so-called dotcoms which operate only online without any brick-and-mortar market presence.

Click-only companies come in many shapes and sizes. They include *e-tailers*, dotcoms that sell products and services directly to final buyers via the Internet. Examples include Amazon.com, Egg (financial services) and eBookers (travel). The click-only group also includes *search engines and portals* such as Yahoo!, Google and Excite, which began as search engines and later added services such as news, weather, stock reports, entertainment and storefronts, hoping to become the first port of entry to the Internet.

Internet service providers (ISPs) such as AOL, Freeserve, Earthlink and others are click-only companies that provide Internet and email connections for a fee. *Transaction sites*, such as auction site eBay, take commissions for transactions conducted on their sites. Various *content sites*, such as Financial Times (www.ft.com), New York Times on the Web (www.nytimes.com) and ESPN.com (www.ESPN.com), provide financial, research and other information. Finally, *enabler sites* provide the hardware and software that enable Internet communication and commerce.

The hype surrounding such click-only Web businesses reached astronomical levels during the 'dotcom gold rush' of the late 1990s, when avid investors drove dotcom stock prices to dizzying heights. However, the investing frenzy collapsed in 2000 and many high-flying, overvalued dotcoms came crashing back to earth. Boo.com (sportswear), Boxman.com and Clickmango (healthcare) were among the high-profile e-tail casualties. Other such as World Online (Internet service provider) faced disastrous flotations in the wake of disinterested financial markets. Survivors such as Amazon.com and Priceline.com saw their stock values plunge.

Dotcoms failed for many reasons. Some rushed into the market without proper research or planning. Often, their primary goal was simply to launch an initial public offering (IPO) while the market was hot. Many relied too heavily on spin and hype instead of developing sound marketing strategies. Flush with investors' cash, the dotcoms spent lavishly offline on mass marketing in an effort to establish brand identities and attract customers to their sites. For example, during the fourth quarter of 1999, prior to the dotcom crash, the average e-tailer spent an astounding 109 per cent of sales on marketing and advertising.[27] As one industry watcher concluded, many dotcoms failed because they 'had dumb-as-dirt business models, not because the Internet lacks the power to enchant and delight customers in ways hitherto unimaginable.'[28]

The dotcoms tended to devote too much effort to acquiring new customers instead of building loyalty and purchase frequency among current customers. In their rush to cash in, many dotcoms went to market with poorly designed websites that were complex, hard to navigate and unreliable. When orders did arrive, some dotcoms found that they lacked the well-designed distribution systems needed to ship products on time and handle customer

Table 4.2 Sources of e-commerce revenue

Product and service sales income	Many e-commerce companies draw a good portion of their revenues from markups on goods and services they sell online.
Advertising income	Sales of online ad space can provide a major source of revenue. At one point, Buy.com received so much advertising revenue that it was able to sell products at cost.
Sponsorship income	A dotcom can solicit sponsors for some of its content and collect sponsorship fees to help cover its costs.
Alliance income	Online companies can invite business partners to share costs in setting up a website and offer them free advertising on the site.
Membership and subscription income	Web marketers can charge subscription fees for use of their site. Many online newspapers (*Wall Street Journal* and *Financial Times*) require subscription fees for their online services. Auto-By-Tel receives income from selling subscriptions to auto dealers who want to receive hot car buyer leads.
Profile income	Websites that have built databases containing the profiles of particular target groups may be able to sell these profiles if they get permission first. However, ethical and legal codes govern the use and sale of such customer information.
Transaction commissions and fees	Some dotcoms charge commission fees on transactions between other parties who exchange goods on their websites. For example, eBay puts buyers in touch with sellers and takes from 1.25 to 5 per cent commission on each transaction.
Market research and information fees	Companies can charge for special market information or intelligence. For example, NewsLibrary charges a dollar or two to download copies of archived news stories. LifeQuote provides insurance buyers with price comparisons from approximately 50 different life insurance companies, then collects a commission of 50 per cent of the first year's premium from the company chosen by the consumer.
Referral income	Companies can collect revenue by referring customers to others. Edmunds receives a 'finder's fee' every time a customer fills out an Auto-By-Tel form at its Edmunds.com website, regardless of whether a deal is completed.

enquiries and problems. Finally, the ease with which competitors could enter the Web, and the ease with which customers could switch to websites offering better prices, forced many dotcoms to sell at margin-killing low prices.

No doubt, many click-only dotcoms are surviving and even prospering in today's marketspace. Others are showing losses today but promise profits tomorrow. Leading online retailers such as Amazon.com took six years from inception to make a pro forma profit – profit excluding losses on investments in other Internet companies and other items. But Amazon has grown and expanded relatively quickly, dominating the online e-tailing sector it has entered and earning over $3 billion of sales a year. Thus, for many dotcoms, including Internet giants such as Amazon.com, the Web is not an instant, vast moneymaking proposition. Companies engaging in e-commerce need to describe to their investors how they will eventually make profits. They need to define a revenue and profit model. Table 4.2 shows that a dotcom's revenues may come from any of several sources.

Click-and-mortar companies

Many established companies moved quickly to open websites providing information about their companies and products. However, most resisted adding e-commerce to their sites. They felt that this would produce *channel conflict* – that selling their products or services online would be competing with their offline retailers and agents. For example, computer manufacturers such as Compaq Computer, Toshiba and Acer feared that their retailers would drop their computers if they sold the same computers directly online. Store-based booksellers including Waterstones and Barnes & Noble delayed opening their online site to challenge Amazon.com.

These companies struggled with the question of how to conduct online sales without cannibalising the sales of their own stores, resellers or agents. However, they soon realised that the risks of losing business to online competitors were even greater than the risks of angering channel partners. If they didn't cannibalise these sales, online competitors soon would. Thus, many established brick-and-mortar companies are now prospering as **click-and-mortar companies**. For example, the British Tesco, a traditional brick-and-mortar grocery retailer, became the world's biggest web-grocer in late 2002. Its success is a stark contrast to the first generation of hopeful Internet start-ups in the American food business, such as Webvan, Peapod and Streamline – all now spectacularly bust or reduced to a marginal existence.[29]

Most click-and-mortar marketers have found ways to resolve the resulting channel conflicts.[30] For example, in its home and overseas markets, Avon worried that direct online sales might cannibalise the business of its Avon representatives, who had developed close relationships with their customers. Fortunately, Avon's research showed little overlap between existing customers and potential Web customers. Avon shared this finding with the reps and then moved into e-marketing. As an added bonus for the reps, Avon also offered to help them set up their own websites.

What gives the click-and-mortar companies an advantage? Established companies have known and trusted brand names and greater financial resources. They have large customer bases, deeper industry knowledge and experience and good relationships with key suppliers. By combining e-marketing and established brick-and-mortar operations, they can offer customers more options. For example, consumers can choose the convenience and assortment of 24-hour-a-day online shopping, the more personal and hands-on experience of in-store shopping, or both. Customers can buy merchandise online, then easily return unwanted goods to a nearby store. For example, those wanting to buy diamond jewellery from Cool Diamonds can call the London office on the phone, go online to the company's website or visit the company's premises in London. In the final analysis, customers can call, click or visit.

Click-and-mortar companies—Traditional brick-and-mortar companies that have added e-marketing to their operations.

Setting up an e-marketing presence

Clearly all companies need to consider moving into e-marketing. Companies can conduct e-marketing in any of the four ways shown in Figure 4.3: creating a website, placing ads online, setting up or participating in Web communities or using online e-mail or webcasting.

Figure 4.3 Setting up for e-marketing

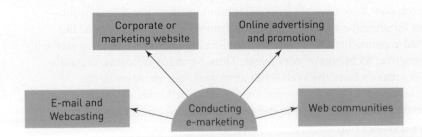

Creating a website

For most companies, the first step in conducting e-marketing is to create a website. However, beyond simply creating a website, marketers must design attractive sites and find ways to get customers to visit the site, stay around and come back to the site frequently.

Types of website

Websites vary greatly in purpose and content. The most basic type is a **corporate website**. These are designed to handle interactive communication *initiated by the consumer*. They seek to build customer goodwill and to supplement other sales channels rather than to sell the company's products directly. For example, the corporate websites of Nokia and IKEA typically offer a rich variety of information and other features in an effort to answer customer questions, build closer customer relationships and generate excitement about the company. Corporate websites generally provide information about the company's history, its mission and philosophy, and the products and services that it offers. They might also tell about current events, company personnel, financial performance and employment opportunities. Many corporate websites also provide exciting entertainment features to attract and hold visitors. Finally, the site might also provide opportunities for customers to ask questions or make comments through email before leaving the site.

Other companies create a **marketing website**. These sites engage consumers in an interaction that will move them closer to a purchase or other marketing outcome. With a marketing website, communication and interaction are *initiated by the marketer*. Such a site might include a catalogue, shopping tips and promotional features such as coupons, sales events or contests. Companies aggressively promote their marketing websites in traditional, offline, print and broadcast advertising, and through 'banner-to-site' ads that pop up on other websites.

> For example, Toyota operates a marketing website at www.toyota.com. Once a potential customer clicks in, the carmaker wastes no time trying to turn the enquiry into a sale. The site offers plenty of entertainment and useful information, from cross-country trip guides and tips for driving with kids, to golf and outdoor events. But the site is also loaded with more serious selling features, such as detailed descriptions of current Toyota models and information on dealer locations and services, complete with maps and dealer Web links. Visitors who want to go further can use the Shop@Toyota feature to choose a Toyota, select equipment and price it, then contact a dealer and apply for credit. Or they fill out an online order form for brochures and a free interactive CD-ROM that shows off the features of Toyota models. The chances are good that before the CD-ROM arrives, a local dealer will call to invite the prospect in for a test drive.[31]

B2B marketers also make good use of marketing websites. For example, customers visiting ABB's website (www.abb.com) can draw on pages and pages of information to get answers about the company's products anytime and from anywhere in the world. FedEx's website (www.fedex.com) allows customers to schedule their own shipments, request a courier and track their packages in transit.

Corporate website—A site set up by a company on the Web, which carries information and other features designed to answer customer questions, build customer relationships and generate excitement about the company, rather than to sell the company's products or services directly. The site handles interactive communication initiated by the consumer.

Marketing website—A site on the Web created by a company to interact with consumers for the purpose of moving them closer to a purchase or other marketing outcome. The site is designed to handle interactive communication initiated by the company.

145

B2B companies have adopted Web marketing. Customers visiting ABB's website (www.abb.com) can draw on thousands of pages of information to get answers about the company's products anytime and from anywhere in the world. SOURCE: www.abb.com.

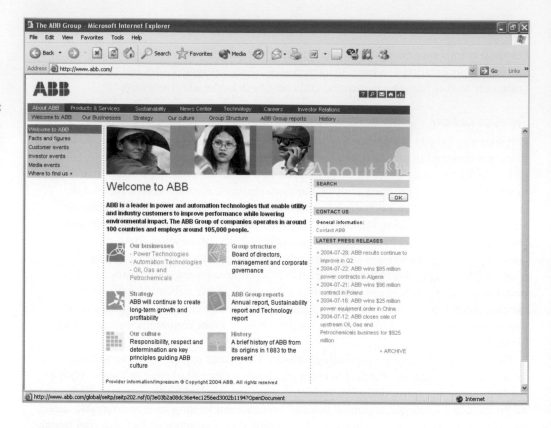

Designing attractive websites

Creating a website is one thing; getting people to *visit* the site is another. The key is to create enough value and excitement to get consumers to come to the site, stick around and come back again.

A recent survey of fervent online surfers shows that people's online expectations have skyrocketed over the last few years. Today's Web users are quick to abandon any website that doesn't measure up. 'Whether people are online for work reasons or for personal reasons', says the chairman of the firm that ran the survey, 'if a website doesn't meet their expectations, two-thirds say they don't return – now or ever. They'll visit you and leave and you'll never know. We call it the Internet death penalty.'[32]

This means that companies must create sites that are easy to read and navigate as well as constantly update their sites to keep them current, fresh and exciting. Doing so involves time and expense, but the expense is necessary if the online marketer wishes to cut through the increasing online clutter. In addition, many online marketers believe that they cannot build a brand simply on the Internet, but have to spend heavily on good old-fashioned advertising and other offline marketing avenues to attract visitors to their sites. At the same time, one study reported that 37 per cent of online purchases were through referred websites and 13 per cent through email marketing, compared to only 6 per cent being inspired by offline advertisements. These results imply that marketers need to create a core of Net users who can spread the word about the company or its brands through the Internet itself.[33]

For some types of product, attracting visitors is easy. Consumers buying new cars, computers or financial services will be open to information and marketing initiatives from sellers. Marketers of lower-involvement products, however, may face a difficult challenge in attracting website visitors. As one veteran notes: 'If you're shopping for a computer and you see a banner that says, "We've ranked the top 12 computers to purchase", you're going to click on the banner. [But] what kind of banner could encourage any consumer to visit dentalfloss.com?'[34] For such low-interest products, the company should create a corporate website to answer customer questions and build goodwill, using it only to supplement selling efforts through other marketing channels.

A key challenge is designing a website that is attractive on first view and interesting enough to encourage repeat visits. The early text-based websites have largely been replaced in recent years by graphically sophisticated websites that provide text, sound and animation (for examples, see www.sonystyle.com, www.cadbury.com or www.disney.com). To attract new visitors and to encourage revisits, suggests one expert, e-marketers should pay close attention to the seven Cs of effective website design:[35]

- *Context*: site layout and design
- *Content*: text, pictures, sound, and video that the website contains
- *Community*: the ways in which the site enables user-to-user communication
- *Customisation*: the site's ability to tailor itself to different users or to allow users to personalise the site
- *Communication*: the ways in which the site enables site-to-user, user-to-site, or two-way communication
- *Connection*: the degree to which the site is linked to other sites
- *Commerce*: the site's capabilities to enable commercial transactions.

At the very least, a website should be easy to use and physically attractive. Beyond this, however, websites must also be interesting, useful and challenging. Ultimately, it's the value of the site's *content* that will attract visitors, get them to stay longer and bring them back for more.

Effective websites contain deep and useful information, interactive tools that help buyers find and evaluate products of interest, links to other related sites, changing promotional offers and entertaining features that lend relevant excitement. For example, in addition to convenient online purchasing, Clarins.com offers in-depth information about Clarins products and treatments, the latest product launches, beauty tips and advice, an interactive tool for determining the browser's skin type and promotional treats.

Effective websites offer more than just a directory of products and pricing information. Instead, like this Clarins website, visitors are presented with deep and useful information and interactive tools for finding and evaluating the company's offerings.
SOURCE: Clarins UK Ltd.

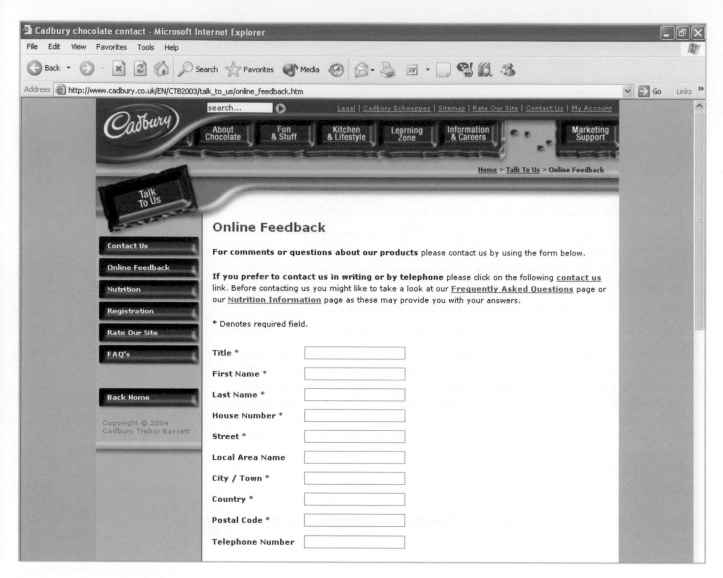

Here, companies such as Cadbury's seek to improve their website by getting visitors to rate their satisfaction with it.
SOURCE: Cadbury Trebor Bassett.

Online advertising—
Advertising that appears while consumers are surfing the Web, including banner and ticker ads, interstitials, skyscrapers and other forms.

From time to time, a company needs to reassess its website's attractiveness and usefulness. One way is to invite the opinion of site design experts. But a better way is to have users themselves evaluate what they like and dislike about the site. For example, visitors to the following websites are invited to rate their satisfaction with the company's website by completing an online questionnaire: construction equipment manufacturer JCB (www.jcb.com); car manufacturer Peugeot (www.Peugeot.com); insurance company Direct Line (www.directline.com); and Cadbury's (www.cadbury.com).

Placing ads and promotions online

E-marketers can use **online advertising** to build their Internet brands or to attract visitors to their websites. Here, we discuss forms of advertising promotion and their future.

Forms of online advertising and promotion

Online ads pop up while Internet users are surfing online services or websites. Such ads include banner ads and tickers (banners that move across the screen). For example, a Web user who is looking up airline schedules or fares might find a flashing banner on the screen exclaiming 'Rent a car from Europcar and get up to two days free!'. To attract visitors to its own website, Toyota sponsors Web banner ads on other sites, such as ESPN SportZone (www.espn.com).

New online ad formats include *skyscrapers* (tall, skinny ads at the side of a Web page) and rectangles (boxes that are much larger than a banner). *Interstitials* are ads that pop up between changes on a website. You may have noticed these ads, which appear as a separate window displaying a different product or service, when you visit a particular website. For example, at the UCAS website (www.ucas.co.uk), students viewing information about university applications and placements in the UK would confront pop-up ads featuring product offers and advice from banks and insurance companies. Visitors to www.msnbc.com's sports area may suddenly be viewing a separate window featuring wireless video cameras. Or, when you visit www.msm.com, you may find yourself suddenly browsing a separate window linked to handbag.com, which advertises women's handbags, as well as offering fun advice for females! Sponsors of *browser ads* pay viewers to watch them. For example, in the US, Alladvantage.com downloads a view bar to users where ads are displayed to targeted users. Viewers earn 20 cents to $1 per hour in return.

Content sponsorships are another form of Internet promotion. Companies can gain name exposure on the Internet by sponsoring special content on various websites, such as news or financial information. The sponsor pays for showing the content and, in turn, receives recognition as the provider of the particular service on the website. Sponsorships are best placed in carefully targeted sites where they can offer relevant information or service to the audience.

E-marketers can also go online with *microsites*, limited areas on the Web managed and paid for by an external company. For example, an insurance company might create a microsite on a car-buying site, offering insurance advice for car buyers and at the same time offering good insurance deals. Internet companies can also develop alliances and affiliate programmes in which they work with other online companies to 'advertise' each other. For example, BT Openworld and AOL have created many successful alliances with other companies and mention their names on their site. Amazon.com has more than 350,000 affiliates across the globe who post Amazon.com banners on their websites.

Finally, e-marketers can use **viral marketing**, the Internet version of word-of-mouth marketing. Viral marketing involves creating an e-mail message or other marketing event that is so infectious that customers will want to pass it on to their friends. Because customers pass the message or promotion on to others, viral marketing can be very inexpensive. And when the information comes from a friend, the recipient is much more likely to open and read it. The aim is to get the company's customers to do your marketing for you (see Marketing Insights 4.2).[36]

The future of online advertising

Online advertising serves a useful purpose, especially as a supplement to other marketing efforts. However, the Internet will not soon rival the major television and print media, in spite of its early promise. Neither will it be a substitute for these traditional advertising channels. Many marketers still question the value of Internet advertising as an effective tool. Costs are reasonable compared with those of other advertising media but Web surfers can easily ignore such advertising and often do. Although many firms are experimenting with Web advertising, it plays only a minor role in most promotion mixes.

As a result, online advertising expenditures still represent only a small fraction of overall advertising media expenditures. In the UK, annual online marketing amounted to

Viral marketing—
The Internet version of word-of-mouth marketing – e-mail messages or other marketing events that are so infectious that customers will want to pass them on to friends.

marketing insights

4.2   Viral boosters for Virgin

When we hear about a virus spreading online, we often think about those awful blaster worms, sobig viruses and the like that spread like wildfire, infecting hundreds and thousands of PC systems at the click of a mouse. However, online viral phenomena can take a very different form – one of which is claimed to have lain at the heart of many B2C dotcom marketing successes. The phenomenon is called viral marketing – an activity that facilitates and encourages people to pass along a marketing message. Taking advantage of the speed and global reach afforded by Internet communications, companies have begun to tap the enormous potential of viral marketing. At the heart of the B2C boom, it seemed as if every online start-up had a viral component to its strategy, or, at least, claimed to have one.

Viral marketing depends on a high pass-along rate from person to person. If a large percentage of recipients forward the message to a large number of friends, the overall growth snowballs very quickly. If the pass-along numbers get too low, the overall growth quickly fizzles.

Consider the following examples. Digital Media Communications (DMC) was commissioned to help Virgin Mobile plan, seed and track its new Virgin Mobile online viral and buzz marketing campaign. The campaign supported the 'Flash-It' in-store promotion that enabled Virgin Mobile customers to gain £1 of free airtime for every £10 they spend in any Virgin Megastore or Virgin Megastore Xpress, simply by flashing their Virgin Mobile phones at the till when they pay. James Kydd, brand director for Virgin Mobile, explains: 'The Flash-It promotion has been running for several months and is proving such a success that we've decided to give it further support. We're using DMC's online viral marketing expertise to widen awareness of the promotion with this booster viral campaign targeted at the culture-driving, technology-savvy online audience.'

The entertaining campaign features two digital film clips created by Rainey Kelly Campbell Roalfe/Y&R. The films encourage Virgin Mobile customers to stop trying to impress Virgin Megastore staff with their flashing antics, and simply show them their phones for free airtime. The first film, 'Bendy Babe', shows an attractive blonde customer displaying her flexible skills to a bewildered store assistant who doesn't quite know where to look. The second film, 'Deep Throat', shows a second customer swallowing a coat hanger in an attempt to impress the same poor store assistant. Both films urge viewers to forget their flashing antics and 'Just show us your phone!'. They also invite viewers to click through to the Virgin Mobile website where they can find out more about the promotion.

The viral campaign is being seeded as *advertainment* content via our DMC's online influencer network, as well as being featured on sports, music and lifestyle websites.

...4.2

The online film-tracking system also provides real-time accountability of the films' views and hotlinks in order to quantify the impact the campaign has on brand awareness. Footage showing Virgin Mobile customers behaving badly was put out as three viral executions at the end of October 2003, distributed by DMC, rather than on television. Word of mouth has worked to the extent that the 'bendy babe' spot tops the chart of Lycos' most viewed viral ads.

Another example of successful viral marketing is provided by MTV's 'Gift' campaign which was run in 2001. The campaign aimed to cut through all the Christmas 'noise' and produce a high-profile MTV viral Christmas card, to promote and generate goodwill for the MTV brand over the Christmas season and to provide entertainment value to MTV fans and non-fans alike. A clip based on a Christmas setting and using advanced special effects was developed. Along with an MPEG file, a QuickTime version of the clip was released. Once released, the viral spread was tracked. In the first three weeks after release, 30,000 people downloaded the clip from two seed sites; 280,585 people watched the QuickTime file. An estimated 6.6 million watched the MPEG file. By summer 2002, the MPEG file became world famous and MTV brand and attitude was spread by fans to millions of other fans worldwide.

Viral marketing is not new. Offline, it has been referred to as word-of-mouth influence, creating a buzz, leveraging the media, network marketing and so forth. Not all viral marketing strategies work and some may offend. However, on the Internet, experts suggest that effective viral marketing campaigns bear many if not all of the following hallmarks:

- they give away free products or services;
- they provide for effortless transfer of messages to others;
- the transmission method must be rapidly scalable from small to very large (i.e. mail servers must be added rapidly to facilitate the exponential growth of message exposure);
- they exploit common human motivations and behaviour that drive the urge to communicate messages;
- they place messages into recipients' existing communication networks; and
- they leverage others' resources such as affiliate programmes to place text or graphic links and news releases onto other websites.

SOURCES: 'DMC helps Virgin Mobile encourage flashers', accessed at www.dmc.co.uk, 27 March 2004; Ralph F. Wilson, 'The six principles of viral marketing', *Web Marketing Today*, 70 (1 February 2000), accessed at www.wilsonweb.com, 27 March 2004; MTV Case Study: Gift, accessed at www.theviralfactory.com/casestudyMTV.htm, 27 March 2004.

£200 million (€300 million) in 2002, or 2 per cent of overall spend; in Europe, the total spend of nearly €800 million accounts for an even smaller proportion – 1.3 per cent. Even in the US, online advertising spending amounted to just $7.2 billion (€5.95 billion), a mere 3.1 per cent of overall spend offline. Experts argue that the industry has yet to develop good measures of advertising impact – of who clicks on Web ads and how the ads affect them. Thus, although many firms are experimenting with Web advertising, it still plays only a minor role in their promotion mixes.[37] Despite the recent setbacks, some industry insiders remain optimistic about the future of online advertising. Although the growth of online advertising spending has slowed after the burst of the dotcom bubble in 2000, more recently the signs are that Internet advertising is steadily making a come-back.

Whatever its future, companies are now seeking more effective forms and uses for Web advertising and marketing. Nonetheless, to make the best use of the Internet as a communications tool, marketers and advertisers alike have to devise ways to harness fully the Internet's interactivity and potential for ultra-precise targeting – two of its most potent qualities.[38] More importantly, online advertising should not be a mere 'add-on', but an integrated part of the firm's marketing efforts.

Creating or participating in Web communities

The popularity of forums and newsgroups has resulted in a rash of commercially sponsored websites called **Web communities**, which take advantage of the C2C properties of the Internet. Such sites allow members to congregate online and exchange views on issues of common interest. They are the cyberspace equivalent to a Starbucks coffeehouse, a place where everybody knows your email address.

Online communities have mushroomed in the last few years. Today, people, irrespective of their age, gender and interests, can join online communities, ranging from sites focusing on entertainment, movies and health, to ones devoted to home and families, lifestyles, and

Web communities— Websites upon which members can congregate online and exchange views on issues of common interest.

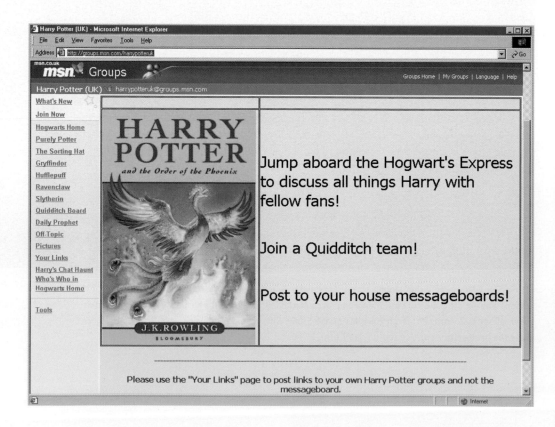

Web communities: at sites such as these, fans re-live the magic in Harry Potter's online world. SOURCE: http://groups.msn.com. harrypotteruk.

money and investments. For example, mymovies.net is a forum for people who like movies, and where they can cruise the net for online movie trailers and share views on films. Scores of sites are now available where Harry Potter fans can 'hang out' online (e.g. www.groups.msn.com/harrypotteruk/), not to mention the communities of 'Elven Realm' where anyone who is interested in *Lord of the Rings* can join to recapture a spot of magic on the Net (e.g. Follow the Quest, and the Elven Realm of Mirkwood, accessed at www.MSNGroups.com). Others include iVillage.com, a Web community in which women can exchange views and obtain information, support, and solutions on families, food, fitness, relationships, relaxation, home and garden, news and issues, or just about any other topic. The site draws 393 million page views per month, putting it in a league with magazines such as *Cosmopolitan*, *Glamour* and *Vogue*.[39]

Visitors to these Internet neighbourhoods develop a strong sense of community. Such communities are attractive to advertisers because they draw consumers with common interests and well-defined demographics. Moreover, cyberhood consumers visit frequently and stay online longer, increasing the chance of meaningful exposure to the advertiser's message. For example, iVillage provides an ideal environment for the Web ads of companies such as Procter & Gamble, Revlon, Kimberly-Clark, Clairol and others who target women consumers.

Using email and webcasting

Email has exploded onto the scene as an important e-marketing tool and is becoming a mainstay for both B2C and B2B marketers. The company can encourage prospects and customers to send questions, suggestions and complaints to the company via email. Customer service representatives can quickly respond to such messages. The company may also develop Internet-based electronic mailing lists of customers or prospects. Such lists provide an excellent opportunity to introduce the company and its offerings to new customers and to build ongoing relationships with current ones. Using the lists, online marketers can send out customer newsletters, special product or promotion offers based on customer purchasing histories, reminders of service requirements or warranty renewals, or announcements of special events. Emailing is becoming one of the cheapest and most effective means of bringing an offer or product information direct to customers, with response rates of between 5 and 10 per cent. Forrester Research estimates that emails account for around 15 per cent of US and European online marketing spend in 2001; the proportion is forecast to reach some 30 per cent by 2006.[40]

However, to compete effectively in this increasingly cluttered email environment, marketers are designing 'enriched' email messages – animated, interactive and personalised messages full of streaming audio and video. Then they are targeting these attention-grabbers more carefully to those who want them and will act upon them.

Companies can also sign on with any of a number of **webcasting** services which automatically download customised information to recipients' PCs. An example is Internet Financial Network's Infogate, which sends up-to-date financial news, market data and real-time stock quotes to subscribers in the financial services industry for a fee. Infogate frames the top and bottom inch of subscribers' computer screens with personalised news and other information tailored to their specific interests. Rather than spending hours scouring the Internet, subscribers can sit back while Infogate automatically delivers information of interest to their desktops.[41] The major commercial online services also offer webcasting to their members. For example, AOL offers a feature called Driveway that will fetch information, Web pages and email-based articles on members' preferences and automatically deliver it to their PCs.

Also known as 'push' programming, webcasting affords an attractive channel through which online marketers can deliver their Internet advertising or other information content. However, as with other types of online marketing, companies must be careful that they do not cause resentment among Internet users who are already overloaded with 'junk email' or

Webcasting (push programming)—The automatic downloading of customised information of interest to recipients' PCs, affording an attractive channel for delivering Internet advertising or other information content.

'spam', offering anything from 'prescription-free Viagra' and cheap loans to pornography and get-rich-quick schemes. Spam as a percentage of total email traffic has jumped from 8 per cent in September 2001 to 45 per cent by early 2003, according to one source.[42]

Hence, email marketers walk a fine line between adding value for consumers and being intrusive. Companies must beware of irritating consumers by sending unwanted email to promote their products. Netiquette, the unwritten rules that guide Internet etiquette, suggests that marketers should ask customers for permission to email marketing pitches. They should also tell recipients how to 'opt-in' or 'opt-out' of email promotions at any time. This approach, known as permission-based marketing, has become a standard model for email marketing. However, as spam has become an increasing nuisance, there is growing pressure from anti-spammers for government action to curb it. Although legal remedies will not present the ultimate solution to spam, new rules are currently enforced to curb this unsavoury marketing practice. For example, from October 2003, all EU nations have to implement legislation which bans the sending of email unless the recipient has specifically 'opted in' to receive it, in line with an EU directive passed in July 2003.

The promise and challenges of e-commerce

E-commerce continues to offer both great promise and many challenges for the future. We now look at both the promises of e-commerce and the 'darker side' of the Web.

The continuing promise of e-commerce

Its most ardent apostles still envisage a time when the Internet and e-commerce will replace magazines, newspapers and even stores as sources for information and buying. However, such 'dotcom fever' has cooled recently and a more realistic view has emerged. 'It's time for Act II in the Internet revolution', suggests one analyst. 'The first act belonged to dotcoms with big visions and small bank accounts. Now the stages will be taken by big companies that move their factories, warehouses and customers onto the Web.'[43]

To be sure, online marketing will become a successful business model for some companies, Internet firms such as Amazon.com, eBay and Egg, and direct-marketing companies such as Dell Computer. Michael Dell's goal is one day 'to have *all* customers conduct *all* transactions on the Internet, globally'. And e-business will continue to boom for many B2B marketers – companies such as Cisco Systems, General Electric and IBM.

However, for most companies, online marketing will remain just one important approach to the marketplace that works alongside other approaches in a fully integrated marketing mix. Eventually, as companies become more adept at integrating e-commerce with their everyday strategy and tactics, the 'e' will fall away from e-business or e-marketing. 'The key question is not whether to deploy Internet technology – companies have no choice if they want to stay competitive – but how to deploy it', says business strategist Michael Porter. He continues: 'We need to move away from the rhetoric about "Internet industries", "e-business strategies", and a "new economy", and see the Internet for what it is: . . . a powerful set of tools that can be used, wisely or unwisely, in almost any industry and as part of almost any strategy.'[44]

The Web's darker side

Along with its considerable promise, there is a 'darker side' to Internet marketing. Here, we examine two major sets of concerns: Internet profitability and legal and ethical issues.

Internet profitability

One major concern is profitability, especially for B2C dotcoms. For many online marketers, including Internet superstars such as Amazon.com, the Web is not an instant money-making proposition. According to one report, fewer than half of the websites surveyed at the height of the dotcom boom were profitable.[45] In another study, of the 456 Internet companies that went public since 1994, only 11 per cent are still in business and profitable. Of those still in business and not acquired by another company, only 25 per cent are profitable.[46]

One problem is that the Internet still offers limited consumer exposure and skewed user demographics. Although expanding rapidly, online marketing still reaches only a limited marketspace. And although the Web audience is becoming more mainstream, online users still tend to be somewhat more upmarket and better educated than the general population. This makes the Internet ideal for marketing financial services, travel services, computer hardware and software and certain other classes of products. However, it makes online marketing less effective for selling mainstream products. Moreover, in most product categories, users still do more window browsing and product research than actual buying.

Finally, the Internet offers millions of websites and a staggering volume of information. Thus, navigating the Internet can be frustrating, confusing and time consuming for consumers. In this chaotic and cluttered environment, many Web ads and sites go unnoticed or unopened. Even when noticed, marketers will find it difficult to hold consumer attention. One study found that a site must capture Web surfers' attention within eight seconds or lose them to another site. That leaves very little time for marketers to promote and sell their goods.

Legal and ethical issues

From a broader societal viewpoint, Internet marketing practices have raised a number of ethical and legal questions. In previous sections, we've touched on some of the negatives associated with the Internet, such as unwanted email and the annoyance of pop-up ads. Here we examine concerns about consumer online privacy and security and other legal and ethical issues.

Online privacy and security

Online privacy is perhaps the number-one e-commerce concern. Most e-marketers have become skilled at collecting and analysing detailed consumer information. Marketers can easily track website visitors, and many consumers who participate in website activities provide extensive personal information. This may leave consumers open to information abuse if companies make unauthorised use of the information in marketing their products or exchanging databases with other companies. Many consumers and policy makers worry that marketers have stepped over the line and are violating consumers' right to privacy.[47]

Many consumers also worry about *online security*. They fear that unscrupulous snoopers will eavesdrop on their online transactions or intercept their credit card numbers and make unauthorised purchases. In turn, companies doing business online fear that others will use the Internet to invade their computer systems for the purposes of commercial espionage or even sabotage. There appears to be an ongoing competition between the technology of Internet security systems and the sophistication of those seeking to break them.

In response to such online privacy and security concerns, governments in countries such as the US and in the EU have passed legislation to regulate how Web operators obtain and use consumer information. For example, online privacy legislation being passed in the US would require online service providers and commercial websites to get customers' permission before they disclose important personal information. That would include financial, medical, ethnic, religious, and political information, along with Social Security data and sexual orientation. In the EU, an anti-spam and online privacy directive passed in May 2002 establishes 'opt-in' as the default rule for commercial email – consumers must give prior permission to marketers before being sent e-communications. All commercial email communications also must have an 'opt-out' feature. The directive also states that Web surfers must be told ahead of time about sites' cookie procedures, giving consumers the right to refuse cookie-based data collection. It also specifies that users must give explicit permission for their personal data to be included in public directories. Although the directive has been approved by the EU Parliament, it still remains for the EU member states to individually pass the regulation as part of their own national laws – a process that no doubt can take years.[48]

Of special concern are the privacy rights of children. Many websites directed towards children collect personal information from children, but not all such sites may include any disclosure of their collection and use of such information. As a result, governments have passed online privacy protection laws, which require website operators targeting children to post privacy policies on their sites. In most cases, they must also notify parents about the information they're gathering and obtain parental consent before collecting personal information from children under 13.[49] In addition, smart companies must respond to consumer privacy and security concerns with actions of their own. For example, they can conduct voluntary audits of their privacy and security policies. They can also strive to exceed any government-mandated privacy regulations, for example by giving away so-called personal firewall software to online customers.

Still, examples of companies aggressively protecting their customers' personal information are few and far between. However, Jupiter Media Metrix forecasts that in 2006 almost $25 billion (€20.6 billion) in revenues will be lost as a result of US consumers' privacy concerns. Moreover, they predict, online sales in 2006 would be as much as 25 per cent higher if consumers' concerns were adequately addressed.[50] Comparable figures for the European Union member states are not available, but, if the US findings are anything to go by, it becomes clear that the costs of inaction could be astronomical on a global scale. Finally, if Web marketers don't act to curb privacy abuses, legislators most probably will.

Other legal and ethical issues

Beyond issues of online privacy and security, consumers are also concerned about *Internet fraud*, including identity theft, investment fraud and financial scams. There are also concerns about *segmentation and discrimination* on the Internet. Some social critics and policy makers worry about the so-called *digital divide* – the gap between those who have access to the latest Internet and information technologies and those who don't. They are concerned that, in this information age, not having equal access to information can be an economic and social handicap. The Internet currently serves the socio-economically better-off consumers. However, poorer consumers still have less access to the Internet, leaving them increasingly less informed about products, services and prices. Some people consider the digital divide to be a national crisis; others see it as an overstated non-issue.[51]

A final Internet marketing concern is that of *access by vulnerable or unauthorised groups*. For example, marketers of adult-oriented materials have found it difficult to restrict access by minors. In a more specific example, sellers using eBay.com, the online auction website, recently found themselves the victims of a 13-year-old boy who'd bid on and purchased more than $3 million worth of high-priced antiques and rare artworks on the site. eBay has a strict policy against bidding by anyone under 18 but works largely on the honour system. Unfortunately, this honour system did little to prevent the teenager from taking a cyberspace joyride.[52]

Despite these challenges, companies large and small are quickly integrating online marketing into their marketing mixes. As it continues to grow, online marketing will prove to be a powerful tool for building customer relationships, improving sales, communicating company and product information, and delivering products and services more efficiently and effectively.

Summary

This chapter introduces the forces shaping the new Internet environment and how marketers are adapting. Four major forces underlie the Internet age: digitalisation and connectivity, the explosion of the Internet, new types of intermediaries, and customisation and customerisation. Much of today's business operates on digital information, which flows through connected networks. Intranets, extranets and the Internet now connect people and companies with each other and with important information. The Internet has grown explosively to become *the* revolutionary technology of the new millennium, empowering consumers and businesses alike with the benefits of connectivity.

The Internet and other new technologies have changed the ways in which companies serve their markets. New Internet marketers and channel relationships have arisen to replace some types of traditional marketers. The new technologies are also helping marketers to tailor their offers effectively to targeted customers or even to help customers customerise their own marketing offers.

Conducting business in the digital age will call for a new model of marketing strategy and practice. Companies need to retain most of the skills and practices that have worked in the past, but must also add major new competencies and practices if they hope to grow and prosper in the New Economy. E-business is the use of electronic platforms to conduct a company's business. E-commerce involves buying and selling processes supported by electronic means, primarily the Internet. It includes e-marketing (the selling side of e-commerce) and e-purchasing (the buying side of e-commerce).

E-commerce benefits both buyers and sellers. For buyers, e-commerce makes buying convenient and private, provides greater product access and selection, and makes available a wealth of product and buying information. It is interactive and immediate and gives the consumer a greater measure of control over the buying process. For sellers, e-commerce is a powerful tool for building customer relationships. It also increases the sellers' speed and efficiency in addition to offering greater flexibility and better access to global markets.

Companies can practise e-commerce in any or all of four domains. B2C (business-to-consumer) e-commerce is initiated by businesses and targets final consumers. Despite recent setbacks following the 'dotcom gold rush' of the late 1990s, B2C e-commerce continues to grow at a healthy rate. Although online consumers are still somewhat higher in income and more technology-oriented than traditional buyers, the cyberspace population is becoming much more mainstream and diverse. This growing diversity opens up new e-commerce targeting opportunities for marketers.

B2B (business-to-business) e-commerce dwarfs B2C e-commerce. Most businesses today operate websites or use B2B trading networks, auction sites, spot exchanges, online product catalogues, barter sites or other online resources to reach new customers, serve current customers more effectively and obtain buying efficiencies and better prices. Business buyers and sellers meet in huge marketspaces, or open trading networks, to share information and complete transactions efficiently, or they set up private trading networks that link them with their own trading partners.

Through C2C (consumer-to-consumer) e-commerce, consumers can buy or exchange goods and information directly from or with one another. Examples include online auction sites, forums and Internet newsgroups. Finally, through C2B (consumer-to-business) e-commerce, consumers are now finding it easier to search out sellers on the Web, learn about their products and services, and initiate purchases. Using the Web, customers can even drive transactions with companies, rather than the other way around.

The Internet gave birth to the *click-only* dotcoms, which operate only online. In addition, many traditional brick-and-mortar companies have now added e-marketing operations, transforming themselves into *click-and-mortar* competitors. Many click-and-mortar companies are now having more online success than their click-only competitors.

Companies can conduct e-marketing in any of four ways: creating a website, placing ads and promotions online, setting up or participating in Web communities or using online email or webcasting. The first step typically is to set up a website. Corporate websites are designed to build customer goodwill and to supplement other sales channels, rather than to sell the company's products directly. Marketing websites engage consumers in an interaction that will move them closer to a direct purchase or other marketing outcome. Beyond simply setting up a site, companies must make their sites engaging, easy to use, and useful in order to attract visitors, hold them, and bring them back again.

E-marketers can use various forms of online advertising to build their Internet brands or to attract visitors to their websites. Beyond online advertising, other forms of online marketing include content sponsorships, microsites, and viral marketing, the Internet version of word-of-mouth marketing. Online marketers can also participate in Web communities, which take advantage of the C2C properties of the Web. Finally, email marketing has become a hot new e-marketing tool for both B2C and B2B marketers.

We reviewed the promise and challenges that e-commerce presents for the future. E-commerce continues to offer great promise for the future. For most companies, online marketing will become an important part of a fully integrated marketing mix. For others, it will be the major means by which they serve the market. However, e-commerce also faces many challenges. One challenge is Web profitability – surprisingly few companies are using the Web profitably. The other challenge concerns legal and ethical issues – issues of online privacy and security, Internet fraud and the 'digital divide'. Despite these challenges, companies large and small are quickly integrating online marketing into their marketing strategies and mixes.

Discussing the issues

1. List and discuss the four major forces that are shaping the Internet age.

2. Make a list of products or services that you have purchased via the Internet. What were the factors that influenced your decision to make the purchases online? If these products or services could also be purchased from an offline reseller or retail outlet, would the buying experience be different? How?

3. Imagine that you are the information services manager for a company that develops customised tours for senior citizens interested in visiting exotic, foreign locations. Explain how you could use intranets, extranets and the Internet to increase your company's communication with its target market segment and expand its business.

4. The growth of the Internet has spawned click-only and click-and-mortar e-tailers. Which type of e-marketer do you think will be the more successful in the future? Explain.

5. In the past year there has been a dramatic increase in the number of Web communities. If you were (a) Adidas, (b) Nokia, (c) British Airways or (d) Sony, what type of Web communities would you be interested in sponsoring? What would be the possible advantages and disadvantages of doing this? Find a Web community and evaluate its site. Discuss your conclusions.

Applying the concepts

1. Pick a favourite website. Visit your selected site. While you have logged on to the site, take some time to explore the site.

   ■ Analyse the site and rate it on the seven Cs of effective website design.

   ■ How might the site be improved? Be specific, please.

   ■ Justify your recommendations.

2. Firms in the new digital era will increasingly use open and private trading networks and electronic exchanges. B2B purchasing managers will need to be more 'Web smart' to stay even with competitors.

   ■ List the advantages and disadvantages of using open and private trading networks and electronic exchanges for purchasing goods and services.

   ■ Consider a consumer appliances retailer of your choice and the electronic exchanges and trading networks that the selected firm potentially purchases goods and services from. What type of companies found on these trading networks and electronic exchanges might want to sell to the consumer appliance retailer? Explain.

   ■ Among the usual items that firms initially purchase through trading networks and electronic exchanges are operational supplies and services. Why?

   ■ Would open networks be a good place for this retailer to buy goods?

   ■ Would a handshake with a long-time vendor be more important than a cyber exchange or open trading network? Explain.

References

1. Based on company data provided by Cool Diamonds; materials supplied by Molly McKellar Public Relations, London; more information about the company's products available at www.cooldiamonds.com; see also Simon London, 'Don't let diamonds get you down', *Financial Times* (31 May 2000), p. 18; John-Paul Flintoff, 'Diamond geezers', *Weekend FT* (18 August 2000), pp. 18–22; David Andrews, 'A discount on screen gems', *Daily Express* (14 June 2000), p. 19; Sarah Williams, 'Diamonds are forever', *Internet Investor* (October 2000), pp. 76–7.

2. Internet usage for the European Union and new members of the EU joining in May 2004, as well as world Internet statistics, are based on data provided by Internet World Stats, accessed at www.internetworldstats.com, March 2004; see also data published in 'Internet penetration and use 2000–2003', in *The European Marketing Pocket Book* (Henley-on-Thames: World Advertising Research Centre, 2004). Data on Internet usage in European countries are also available from Internet Software Consortium accessed at www.isc.org; Internet usage numbers are also published by Nielsen-NetRatings and a variety of local, country sources including IWS (accessed at www.internetworldstats.com); see also Humphrey Taylor, 'Internet penetration at 66% of adults (137 million) nationwide', *The Harris Poll* (17 April 2002); and 'Internet users will top 1 billion in 2005', press release, Computer Industry Almanac, Inc. (12 March 2002), and accessed online at www.c-i-a.com.

3. Figures given by The Gartner Group and reported in *FT Telecommunications Survey, Financial Times* (21 June 2000), p. X.

4. David Murphy, 'RU ready to buy?', *Marketing Business* (June 2002), p. 35; see also Joia Shillingford, 'Plenty more to come for mobile net enthusiasts', FT Telecoms, Financial Times Survey, *Financial Times* (21 June 2000), p. XVII; George Cole, 'Word of mouth spreads the net of m-commerce', *Financial Times* (12 April 2000), p. 15; information obtained at CIM website www.cim.co.uk, 'Get ready for m-commerce' (January 2000).

5. Susanna Voyle, 'Shoppers spend record £1.17bn over internet', *Financial Times* (12 December 2003), p. 3; Kim Benjamin, 'Internet technologies grow in Europe', *e.business* (February 2000), pp. 18–19; statistics provided by Forrester Research.

6. Robyn Greenspan, 'The Web as a way of life', accessed online at cyberatlas.internet.com, 21 May 2002.

7. 'Letsbinit.com', *The Economist* (6 January 2001), p. 62; 'Is there life in e-commerce?', *The Economist* (3 February 2001), pp. 19–20.

8. Jaime Wold, 'Your very own breakfast cereal', *The New York Times* (9 December 2001), p. 6.10. For other examples, including B2B examples, see Stefan Thomke and Eric Von Hippel, 'Customers as innovators', *Harvard Business Review,* April 2002, pp. 74–81.

9. See Jerry Wind and Arvid Rangaswamy, 'Customerization: the next revolution in mass customization', *Journal of Interactive Marketing* (Winter 2001), pp. 13–32; and Yoram Wind and Vijay Mahajan, 'Convergence marketing', *Journal of Interactive Marketing* (Spring 2002), pp. 64–79.

10. John A. Byrne, 'Management by the Web', *Business Week* (28 August 2000), pp. 84–96.

11. Alan Mitchell, 'Internet zoo spawns new business models', *Marketing Week* (21 January 1999), pp. 24–5. Also see Philip Kotler, *Marketing Moves: A new approach to profits, growth, and renewal* (Boston: Harvard Business School Press, 2002).

12. Paola Hjelt, 'Flying on the Web in a turbulent economy', *Business Week* (30 April 2001), pp. 142–8.

13. Information accessed online at http://www.specials.ft.com/connectis/, September 2003; www.gegxs.com/gxs/aboutus, June 2002.

14. Frederick F. Reichheld and Phil Schefter, 'E-loyalty: your secret weapon on the Web', *Harvard Business Review* (July–August 2000), pp. 105–13.

15. See 'Party like it's 1999', *The Economist* (23 February 2002), pp. 87–8; 'We have lift off', *The Economist* (3 February 2001), pp. 91–3; Robert D. Hof, 'How E-Biz rose, fell, and will rise anew', *Business Week* (13 May 2002), pp. 64–72; and Beth Cox, 'E-commerce goes on a roll' (26 April 2002), accessed online at www.atnewyork.com/news/article.php/1016561.

16. 'Blue collar occupations moving online', accessed online at www.cyberatlas.internet.com, 12 April 2001.

17. Robyn Greenspan, 'Girl gamers grow up', *ClickZ Stats Demographics* (12 February 2004), accessed at http://www.clickz.com/stats/big_picture/demographics/article.php/3312301, March 2004; 'Females lead online growth spurt', *CommerceNet and Nielsen Media Research* (17 June 1999), accessed online at www.cyberatlas.com.

18. Richard Tomkins, 'Long arm of commerce touches the newsroom', *Financial Times* (16 October 2000), p. 18; B.G. Yovovich, 'Girls in cyberspace', *Marketing News* (8 December 1997), pp. 8, 12; Paul M. Eng, 'Cybergiants see the future and it's Jack and Jill', *Business Week* (14 April 1997), p. 44.

19. See Joanne Cleaver, 'Surfing for seniors', *Marketing News* (19 July 1999), pp. 1, 7; Sara Teasdale Montgomery, 'Senior surfers grab Web attention', *Advertising Age* (10 July 2000), p. S4; Hassan Fattah, 'Hollywood, the Internet, & kids', *American Demographics* (May 2001), pp. 51–6; and Michael Pastore, 'Online seniors enthusiastic about Internet use' (10 September 2001), accessed online at cyberatlas.internet.com.

20. Paul Taylor, 'Searching questions', *Financial Times* (13 August 2002), p. 12.

21. See Steve Hamm, 'E-Biz: down but hardly out', *Business Week* (26 March 2001), pp. 126–30; and 'B2B e-commerce headed for trillions' (6 March 2002), accessed online at cyberatlas.internet.com.

22. Emma Charlton, 'Business-to-business online exchanges. A case of first come, first served', FT-IT Review, Manufacturing in the Internet age, *Financial Times* (1 November 2000), p. II; Andrew Baxter, 'Internet heralds new era of collaboration', FT-IT Review, Manufacturing in the Internet age, *Financial Times* (1 November 2000), p. V; additional information on B2B exchanges accessed at www.ft.com/ftit.

23. Information based on *Internet World Stats*, Trade exchanges – B2B, accessed at www.internetworldstats.com, and information accessed at www.antwerps.com, March 2004; see also Liz Bassett, 'e-business websites', *Connectis* (October 2000), p. 25.

24. Michael Rappa, 'ChemConnect', *Managing the Digital Enterprise* (16 July 2003), accessed online at http://digitalenterprise.org/cases/chemconnect.html, 11 March 2004.

25. 'Define and sell', in 'A survey of e-commerce', *The Economist* (26 February 2000), p. 9; eBay facts from eBay annual reports and other information accessed at www.ebay.com, July 2002.

26. 'Define and sell', op. cit.; Gary M. Stern, 'You got a complaint?', *Link-Up* (September–October 2001), p. 28; and Bob Tedeschi, 'In the current Internet wilderness, some consumer community sites are hanging on, and even making money', *New York Times* (7 January 2002), p. C6.

27. Bradley Johnson, 'Out-of-sight spending collides with reality', *Advertising Age* (7 August 2000), pp. S4–S8.

28. Gary Hamel, 'Is this all you can build with the Net? Think bigger', *Fortune* (30 April 2001), pp. 134–8.

29. 'Off their trolleys', *The Economist* (23 November 2002), pp. 80–1.

30. See Chuck Martin, *Net Future* (McGraw-Hill, 1999), p. 33.

31. See Kathy Rebello, 'Making money on the Net', *Business Week* (23 September 1996), pp. 104–18; Melanie Berger, 'It's your move', *Sales & Marketing Management* (March 1998), pp. 45–53.

32. Sharon Gaudin, 'The site of no return', *DataMation*, accessed at www.internet.com, 28 May 2002.

33. Robert McLuhan, 'Target marketing', *e.business* (June 2000), pp. 34–8.

34. John Deighton, 'The future of interactive marketing', *Harvard Business Review* (November–December 1996), pp. 151–62.

35. Jeffrey F. Rayport and Bernard J. Jaworski, *e-Commerce* (New York: McGraw Hill, 2001), p. 116.

36. For these and other examples, see William M. Bulkeley, 'E-commerce (a special report): Cover story – pass it on: Advertisers discover they have a friend in "viral" marketing', *Wall Street Journal* (14 January 2002), p. R6.

37. Emiko Terazono, 'The rebirth of online marketing', *Financial Times FT Creative Business* (1 July 2003), pp. 10–11.

38. Fiona Harvey, 'Across the digital divide', *Financial Times FT Creative Business* (17 December 2002), pp. 4–5; 'Advertising that clicks', *The Economist* (9 October 1999), pp. 101–2, 105; Rob Norton, 'The bright future of Web advertising', *Ecompany Now* (June 2001), pp. 50–60; 'Summit participants agree online poised for growth', *Advertising Age* (1 April 2002), p. C6.

39. Information from the iVillage Metrics section of www.ivillage.com, April 2002.

40. Information based on figures reported in Fiona Harvey, 'Across the digital divide', op. cit.

41. See Robert Sales, 'IFN launches Infogate, targets online equities market data users', *Wall Street & Technology* (May 2000), p. 84.

42. 'Junk e-mail: stopping spam', *The Economist* (26 April 2003), p. 66.

43. Elizabeth Corcoran, 'The E Gang', *Fortune* (24 July 2000), p. 145.

44. Michael Porter, 'Strategy and the Internet', *Harvard Business Review* (March 2001), pp. 63–78.

45. Lisa Bransten, 'E-commerce (a special report) – A new model – the bottom line: if they built it, will profits come?', *Wall Street Journal* (12 July 1999), p. R8; see also Shikhar Ghosh, 'Making business sense of the Internet', *Harvard Business Review* (March–April 1998), pp. 126–35.

46. Timothy J. Mullaney, 'Break out the black ink', *Business Week* (13 May 2002), pp. 74–6.

47. See Peter Han and Angus Maclaurin, 'Do consumers really care about online privacy?', *Marketing Management* (January–February 2002), pp. 35–8.

48. See Christopher Saunders, 'EU OKs spam ban, online privacy rules' (31 May 2002), article accessed at www.clickz.com/news/article.php/115439, 28 March 2004; see also Adam Clymer, 'Senator prevents action on online privacy bill', *New York Times* (17 May 2002), p. A16; for more details on online privacy protections visit www.cdt.org/privacy/guide/protect/.

49. See Jennifer DiSabatino, 'FTC OKs self-regulation to protect children's privacy', *Computerworld* (12 February 2001), p. 32.

50. See 'Seventy percent of US consumers worry about online privacy, but few take protective action, reports Jupiter Media Metrix', Jupiter Media Metrix press release, 3 June 2002, accessed online at www.jmm.com.

51. See Benjamin M. Compaine, *The Digital Divide: Facing a crisis or creating a myth?* (Boston: MIT Press, 2001); Lisa J. Servon, *Bridging the Digital Divide: Technology, community, and public policy* (Oxford, UK: Blackwell Publishers, 2002), and Blaise Cronin, 'The Digital Divide', *Library Journal* (15 February 2002), p. 48.

52. '13-year-old bids over $3M for items in eBay auctions', *USA Today* (30 April 1999), p. 10B.

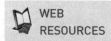

WEB RESOURCES

For additional classic case studies and Internet exercises, visit www.pearsoned.co.uk/kotler

Concluding concept 4
eBay: connecting in China

A rare success

Legend has it that Pierre Omidyar, a young engineer, concocted the idea for eBay in 1995 so that his girlfriend would have an easy way to meet and trade with fellow Pez dispenser collectors. Omidyar envisioned eBay's Internet site as becoming a place where a network of buyers and sellers could connect, forming a community. Bill Cobb, the company's global marketing director, calls eBay a step towards 'the first worldwide economic democracy'.

eBay is just a step in one sense. The company pales in comparison to, for example, Wal-Mart. Wal-Mart raked in about €182 billion in sales in 2001 from its network of 3,000 stores, 1.3 million workers, and countless warehouses. By comparison, eBay generated only $749 million in revenue from sales fees and advertising on the $9.3 billion in goods sold through 170 million transactions using its system – less than 4 per cent of Wal-Mart's sales. However, eBay has no stores or warehouses or inventory and accomplished its results with fewer than 3,000 employees. Further, unlike most of the dotcoms that sprouted in the late 1990s, eBay is profitable, having produced a net profit of $138 million in 2001.

> eBay is a step towards 'the first worldwide economic democracy'.

eBay, however, is no flash-in-the-pan. Analysts predict that its revenues will double to about $1.5 billion by the end of 2003 and profits will more than double to about $318 million. Investors seemed to believe the predictions, as eBay's stock was trading at an astounding 113 times earnings at the end of 2001, despite the stock market's depressed condition.

How eBay works

The idea for eBay's business model is simple – and old. Residents in rural and urban communities have for centuries gathered in town squares and marketplaces to buy, sell, and exchange goods and services. The modern-day flea market is a throwback to these markets.

eBay simply took this old idea and removed the need for a physical meeting between buyer and seller. The Internet provided the cyberspace where the marketing exchange could take place. eBay simply created the software programs to enable the transactions. The eBay system, however, improves on the old market system in that the seller can 'display' his or her items to a huge number of potential customers at the same time. Given that there may be more than one person interested in the item, the seller can hold a virtual auction, hoping that demand for the item will produce a higher price than a typical market where the number of potential buyers would be more limited or even non-existent. Obviously, the process also depends on modern transportation for the product's physical delivery, as eBay plays no role in closing the transaction.

eBay charges the sellers insertion fees for listing an item, final-value fees upon a sale, and listing-upgrade fees. The following table presents the impact of the final value fee structure at various closing values:

Auction's gross closing value	Final value fee	Final value fee as a percentage of gross closing value
$25	$1.31	5.25%
$50	$2.00	4.00%
$100	$3.38	3.38%
$1,000	$28.13	2.81%
$10,000	$163.13	1.63%

SOURCE: eBay website and Merrill Lynch analysis.

In 2001, eBay's transaction fees accounted for all but $84 million of its revenues, with the remainder coming from third-party advertising charges.

Because eBay does not take title to anything sold over its system, it has a gross margin of 82 per cent. In 2001, eBay's operating expenses totalled 57.8 per cent of revenues, with sales and marketing accounting for 33.8 per cent, product development for 10 per cent, and general and administrative expenses for 14 per cent. Even with eBay's projected growth, analysts predicted that its sales and marketing expense would hold at 30 per cent of revenues.

eBay's average auction lasted 6.55 days as of the first quarter of 2002, and the average gross value per auction was $22.50. As of early 2002, the average seller sponsored three auctions and produced $1.72 in net revenue for eBay per auction. eBay classified its offerings into 18,000 categories, with high-priced merchandise, like cars and computers, continuing to grow as a percentage of total sales value. In fact, eBay Motors was the company's fastest-growing category in early 2002. Collectibles, like the Pez dispensers, accounted for only about one-third of eBay's items.

eBay's members, or users (never called customers), would tell you that one reason the system has been so successful is that they feel like 'winners' whenever they are successful at an auction. The members police themselves, providing feedback points to each other so that disreputable buyers and sellers are quickly identified. Members also communicate directly with eBay's staff to point out problems and suggest solutions. In addition, it is very easy for members to use eBay's system.

A new CEO

In 1997, eBay recruited Meg Whitman to become the company's CEO. Whitman had worked at Disney and Hasbro, but was not an Internet junkie. She had degrees from Princeton and Harvard and brought with her a marketing background built on a commitment to customer satisfaction. When Whitman took over, the company had only $49 million in merchandise sales. She helped the company go public in 1998.

Whitman has led eBay through many changes. Recently, the company instituted a 'buy-it-now' pricing system that lets a seller set a fixed price at which a buyer can purchase the item without going through the traditional auction process. Whitman estimates that this type of purchase will increase from 20 per cent to 33 per cent of eBay's sales.

Although the company began as a way for individuals to buy and sell, many people have realised that it is a perfect vehicle for their own businesses. As a result, analysts estimate that there are over 200,000 businesses that exist only on eBay.

New frontiers

eBay has announced that its goal is to achieve sales of $3 billion by 2005. To reach this lofty target, Whitman realises that eBay must develop international markets – especially in the light of analysts' suggestions that the company's core US market growth rate is slowing and advertising revenues are down due to the economic slowdown.

eBay has already ventured into international markets. It has operations in Australia, Austria, Canada, France, Germany, Ireland, Italy, New Zealand, Switzerland, and the United Kingdom. In the first quarter of 2002, international revenues accounted for 21 per cent of eBay's revenues, up from 18 per cent in the last quarter of 2001; and its 2001 international revenue reached $115 million, up from $34 million a year earlier.

Despite eBay's progress in international markets, all has not gone well. Yahoo! Japan beat eBay to the punch by offering online auctions in Japan in September 1999. eBay entered Japan five months later, but those five months were critical. eBay charged a fee for each transaction, which Yahoo! did not, and required users to provide a credit card number. Many young Japanese do not use credit cards, preferring to pay by cash or bank draft. Further, although many observers thought online auctions would not work in Japan due to Japanese reluctance to buy used goods from strangers, its economic recession and the emergence of environmental awareness helped to overcome this reluctance. Plus, Yahoo! users could adopt Internet nicknames for their transactions, removing some of the stigma. Then, observers suggested, eBay was slow to adopt local touches, like horoscopes and newsletters, that it needed to attract users. eBay compounded all this by taking a low-key approach to promotion, while Yahoo! bought billboards and opened an Internet café with Starbucks.

All these missteps, analysts argue, resulted in the 'network effect'. Sellers want to go where there are buyers, and buyers want to go where there is a large selection, i.e. sellers. Once this network reaches a critical mass, it becomes very difficult for a competitor to succeed. Sellers and buyers flocked to Yahoo!, and by mid-2001 Yahoo! had captured 95 per cent of the $1.6 billion online market – eBay had only 3 per cent. By early 2002, eBay threw in the towel and announced its withdrawal from Japan.

Within weeks, however, eBay announced it had purchased 33 per cent of a Chinese Internet auction site, EachNet, for $30 million. Two young entrepreneurs who met at Harvard Business School started EachNet in 1999. Shao Yibo and Tan Haiyin studied Internet businesses as part of a class project and decided that the eBay model was the only one that would work in Asia. With support from Asian venture capitalists, they launched their site, which by 2002 had 3.5 million registered users and 50,000 items listed for sale.

Although eBay executives argue that the eBay model has universal application, the company's experiences in

Japan and China highlight key differences as companies move from one national market to another. In China, for example, EachNet's customers hurried to the site to trade practical items like apparel or cellular phones, not the collectibles that fuelled growth in the US market. Rather than use the postal or courier systems to make payment, as one might do in the United States, Chinese traders mostly sell within their own cities. Although transportation systems are improving, they are still creaky by US standards, so shipping an item is not easy or reliable. Many Chinese still don't feel comfortable doing business online, especially when they are dealing with other individuals rather than companies. Moreover, e-commerce companies have also been concerned about regulation by the Chinese government. In early 2002, the government blocked access to foreign-based news and information sites.

China represents the world's fifth largest online economy, with 27 million Internet users. Of these, some 32 per cent indicate they made purchases online in the past year. Yet 30 per cent of users say they rarely visit an e-commerce site. With a population of over 1 billion people, however, there certainly is plenty of room for growth.

Meg Whitman and eBay's other executives know that to meet their sales and revenue targets, they must be successful in international markets – especially in China. eBay is the world's largest person-to-person trading community. Whitman hopes that China, with the world's largest population, will be a perfect fit for eBay's business model.

Questions

1. What are the forces shaping the development of Internet businesses like eBay in the United States? How are these forces similar or different in the EU and in other countries, such as Japan or China?
2. How do the text's terms 'customisation' and 'customerisation' apply to eBay's marketing strategy?
3. How does eBay create value for the members of its community?
4. What marketing recommendations would you make to eBay to help it be successful as it enters the Chinese market?

SOURCES: Jerry Adler, 'The eBay way of life', *Newsweek* (17 June 2002), pp. 51–9; Brad Stone, 'Meg gets on the line', *Newsweek* (17 June 2002), p. 56; J Baldauf, 'eBay, Inc.', Lehman Brothers (24 April 2002); 'eBay in China', *China E-Business* (1 April 2002), p. 4; Nick Wingfield and Connie Ling, 'Unbowed by its failure in Japan, eBay will try its hand in China', *Wall Street Journal* (18 March 2002), p. B1; Ina Steiner, 'eBay regroups in Asia: goodbye Japan, hello China', www.auctionbytes.com, NewsFlash No. 255, 27 February 2002; Ken Belson, Rob Hoff and Ben Elgin, 'How Yahoo! Japan beat eBay at its own game', *Business Week Online* (4 June 2001); Bruce Einhorn, 'Can EachNet become an eBay in China's image?', *BusinessWeek Online* (27 March 2000); www.ebay.com.

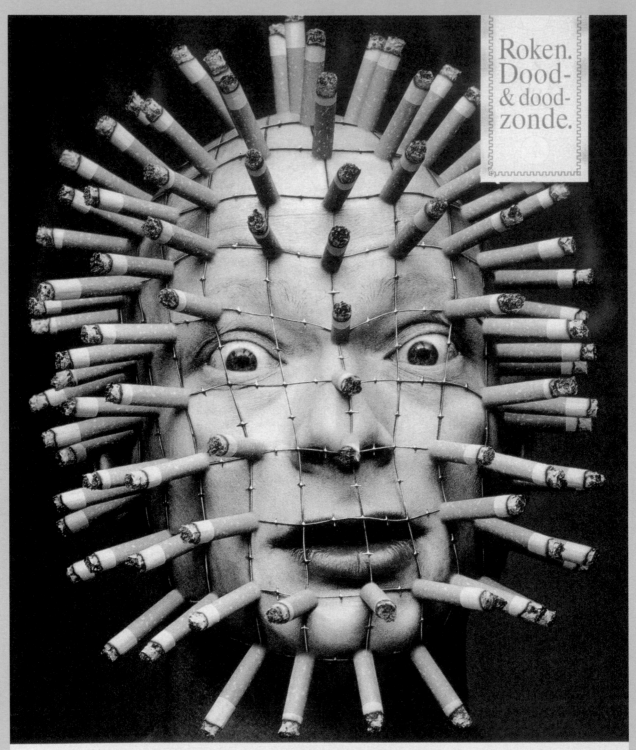

Roken.
Dood-
& dood-
zonde.

ALS JE MEER INFORMATIE WILT, BEL DAN DE STICHTING
VOLKSGEZONDHEID EN ROKEN: 0900-5002025 (20 CT P/M)

We are in a system of 'fouling our own nest', so long as we behave as independent, rational, free-enterprises.

GARRETT HARDING

Marketing and society:
social responsibility and marketing ethics

Chapter objectives

After reading this chapter, you should be able to:

- Identify the major social criticisms of marketing.
- Define *consumerism* and *environmentalism* and explain how they affect marketing strategies.
- Describe the principles of socially responsible marketing.
- Explain the role of ethics in marketing.

Mini Contents List

◀ **SOURCE: STIVORO-Dutch Foundation on Smoking and Health.**
Agency: BVH Communicatie-adviesbureau, Netherlands.
Photographer: © Gerdjan van der Lugt.

Prelude case NSPCC: misunderstood

When the National Society for the Prevention of Cruelty to Children (NSPCC) released its year-end annual accounts in December 2000, it promptly received condemnation.

The revelation that the charity spent more on fundraising, publicity, campaigning and administration than on direct services to children (£43 m or €70.5 m compared with £32 m) was a sign of complete incompetence, according to Gerald Howarth, Conservative MP for Aldershot. He vowed to stop backing the NSPCC's high-profile Full Stop campaign.

According to Quentin Anderson, chief executive of Addison, the corporate marketing arm of WPP Group, such swift dismissal of the NSPCC strategy is unwise and fails to recognise the professional makeover many charities have undertaken in recent years. Charities are now highly organised operations. In line with environmental and social pressure groups they have adopted a more businesslike approach, which is essential if they are to survive in a crowded sector. When arguing how big the various components of the NSPCC's budget should be, detractors must remember that there is a total of £75 m to disburse. Charities need highly skilled staff to manage such funds.

The NSPCC's campaign makes sense. The charity has stated that its long-term objectives are to raise social awareness of child cruelty and to raise £250 m through the 'Full Stop' initiative. If people do not understand what the charity's directors are trying to achieve in the long term, they will judge them on short-term results. With the NSPCC, these include a £13.5 m overspend for the last financial year. The NSPCC needs to ensure that people understand what it is trying to achieve because it needs their help. It needs to show that it is awake, reacting to change and anticipating it. Despite the furor, the NSPCC stuck to their guns and kept campaigning. The advertising is central to NSPCC's mission: '**to end cruelty to children for ever**'. With help from the campaign, 650,000 people had pledged their support for their campaign to achieve a better future for all children.

Marketing is ideally suited to the task the charity has set itself. In crude terms, its route to market is not so obvious as those of other charities. For example, it is comparatively easy for 'Meals on Wheels' to identify where its services are needed and to dedicate the majority of its expenditure to staff and the resources they require. By contrast, the NSPCC has defined its audience as the whole population. By communicating clearly with all communities, it hopes, no doubt, to enlist many more foot soldiers than direct action ever would.

And the campaign has got a lot right. To achieve its aim the NSPCC decided to use celebrities to back its central message that to reduce cruelty to children you need to raise awareness of child cruelty and challenge social attitudes. To reach those at risk it has focused on teenage media. This translates to television, radio, magazines and the Internet.

> The NSPCC would be foolish not to exploit celebrities willing to donate their time free of charge.

As a result, visitors to its website will find messages from Kylie Minogue and Ms Dynamite. Other male and female icons, such as Diana Ross, David Beckham and Pelé, have also been highly visible in their support for the 'Full Stop' campaign.

Matching your brand to a superstar is a successful marketing technique and need not be a cause for controversy. Nike pays Tiger Woods handsomely but obviously believes it gets value for money. The NSPCC would be foolish not to exploit celebrities willing to donate their time free of charge. Without Kylie, would the Full Stop campaign receive front-page exposure in the magazines teenagers read?

Because the charity has advertised its brand effectively, victims are more likely to know they can go direct to the 'Kidszone' at its website and obtain professional advice.

So, why should the NSPCC be criticised for spending money and talking about it? The charity understands that dissemination of better information creates confidence in the community. This leads to many benefits, including greater loyalty from donors and a more secure position in the sector. It also avoids the accusation of hoarding funds that has been levelled at many charities.

The negative reaction to the publication of the NSPCC accounts is a sign not that its marketing strategy is failing but that its communications policy is. A first principle for all good communicators is to evolve messages defining what the organisation does and what its aims are. The NSPCC, it appears, has simply released its annual figures and allowed the public to draw its own conclusions.

The annual report, like every communication, should have a specific goal and add value to what has already been done. The NSPCC should have explained better the rationale behind its spending on marketing. It should have made clear that a high level of set-up costs in terms of administration and training is inevitably associated with a campaign such as Full Stop.

It should have demonstrated to donors and opinion-formers that it understands its campaign is expensive. But it should also have left them in no doubt that it thinks raising awareness is the only way to lobby for legislative change and – what really counts – to reach more victims of abuse.[1]

Questions

You should attempt these questions only after completing your reading of this chapter.

1. Who are the charity's target market and what are the main aspects of the service offered by a charity organisation such as the NSPCC?
2. Assess the role of marketing in assisting the charity to achieve its goals. Should the charity spend more on fundraising, publicity, campaigning and administration than on direct services to children?
3. Evaluate the NSPCC's current marketing strategy. Has the charity got its current marketing strategy wrong? Or are the problems due to its communication policy?

Introduction

Responsible marketers discover what consumers want and respond with marketing offers that give satisfaction and value to buyers and profit to the producer. The *marketing concept* is a philosophy of customer service and mutual gain. Its practice leads the economy by an invisible hand to satisfy the many and changing needs of millions of consumers.

Not all marketers follow the marketing concept, however. In fact, some companies use questionable marketing practices, and some marketing actions that seem innocent in themselves strongly affect the larger society. Consider the sale of cigarettes. On the face of it, companies should be free to sell cigarettes and smokers should be free to buy them. But this transaction affects the public interest. First, the smokers are harming their health and may be shortening their own lives. Second, smoking places a financial burden on the smoker's family and on society at large. Third, other people around smokers may suffer discomfort and harm from secondhand smoke. Finally, marketing cigarettes to adults might also influence young people to begin smoking. Not surprising, the marketing of tobacco products has sparked substantial debate and negotiation in recent years.[2] This example shows that private transactions may involve larger questions of public policy.

Marketers face difficult decisions when choosing to serve customers profitably, on the one hand, and seeking to maintain a close fit between consumers' wants or desires and societal welfare, on the other. This chapter examines the social effects of private marketing practices. We focus on marketing as a social institution. We examine several questions: What are the most frequent social criticisms of marketing? What steps have private citizens taken to curb marketing ills? What steps have legislators and government agencies taken to curb marketing

The NSPCC's 'Full Stop' campaign. To reach its various target audiences, the charity organisation has to spend huge sums on fundraising and marketing campaigns. Critics, however, question whether the organisation should spend more on marketing campaigns and administration than on direct services to children.
SOURCE: NSPCC. *Photographer*: Matt. Harris.

ills? What steps have enlightened companies taken to carry out socially responsible and ethical marketing? We examine how marketing affects and is affected by each of these issues. You will see that social responsibility and ethical actions are more than just the right thing to do; they are also good for business. In addition, as the prelude case suggests, the issues of public accountability, social responsibility and ethical behaviour are also relevant for not-for-profit organisations.

Social criticisms of marketing

Marketing receives much criticism. Some of this criticism is justified; much is not. Social critics claim that certain marketing practices hurt individual consumers, society as a whole and other business firms.

Marketing's impact on individual consumers

Consumers have many concerns about how well marketing and businesses, as a whole, serve their interests. Consumers, consumer advocates, government agencies and other critics have accused marketing of harming consumers through high prices, deceptive practices, high-pressure selling, shoddy or unsafe products, planned obsolescence and poor service to disadvantaged consumers.

High prices

Many critics charge that marketing practices raise the cost of goods and cause prices to be higher than they would be under more 'sensible' systems. They point to three factors: *high costs of distribution*, *high advertising and promotion costs* and *excessive mark-ups*.

High costs of distribution
A long-standing charge is that greedy intermediaries mark up prices beyond the value of their services. Critics charge either that there are too many intermediaries, or that intermediaries are inefficient and poorly run, or that they provide unnecessary or duplicated services. As a result, distribution costs too much and consumers pay for these excessive costs in the form of higher prices.

How do resellers answer these charges? They argue that intermediaries do work which would otherwise have to be done by manufacturers or consumers. Mark-ups reflect services that consumers themselves want – more convenience, larger stores and assortment, longer store opening hours, return privileges and others. Moreover, the costs of operating stores keep rising, forcing retailers to raise their prices. In fact, they argue, retail competition is so intense that margins are actually quite low: for example, after taxes, supermarket chains are typically left with barely 1 per cent profit on their sales. If some resellers try to charge too much relative to the value they add, other resellers will step in with lower prices. Low-price stores and other discounters pressure their competitors to operate efficiently and keep their prices down.

High advertising and promotion costs
Modern marketing is also accused of pushing up prices because of heavy advertising and sales promotion. For example, a dozen tablets of a heavily promoted brand of aspirin sell for the same price as 100 tablets of less promoted (often termed 'generic') brands. Differentiated products – cosmetics, detergents, toiletries – include promotion and packaging costs that can amount to 40 per cent or more of the manufacturer's price to the retailer. Critics charge that much of the packaging and promotion adds only psychological value to the product rather

than real functional value. Retailers use additional promotion – advertising, displays and sweepstakes – that add even more to retail prices.

Marketers respond by saying that consumers can usually buy functional versions of products at lower prices. However, they *want* and are willing to pay more for products that also provide psychological benefits – that make them feel wealthy, attractive or special. Brand-name products may cost more, but branding gives buyers assurances of consistent quality. Heavy advertising adds to product costs but is needed to inform millions of potential buyers of the availability and merits of a brand. If consumers want to know what is available on the market, they must expect manufacturers to spend large sums of money on advertising. Also, heavy advertising and promotion may be necessary for a firm to match competitors' efforts. The business would lose 'share of mind' if it did not match competitive spending. At the same time, companies are cost conscious about promotion and try to spend their money wisely.

Excessive mark-ups

Critics also charge that some companies mark up goods excessively. They point to the drug industry, where a pill costing 10 cents to make may cost the consumer €4 to buy. They point to the pricing tactics of perfume manufacturers, who take advantage of customers' ignorance of the true worth of a 50 g bottle of Chanel perfume, while preying on their desire to fulfil emotional needs.

Marketers respond that most businesses try to deal fairly with consumers because they want repeat business. Most consumer abuses are unintentional. When shady marketers do take advantage of consumers, they should be reported to industry watchdogs and to other consumer-interest or consumer-protection groups. Marketers also stress that consumers often don't understand the reason for high mark-ups. For example, pharmaceutical mark-ups must cover the costs of purchasing, promoting and distributing existing medicines, plus the high research and development costs of formulating and testing new medicines.

Deceptive practices

Marketers are sometimes accused of deceptive practices that lead consumers to believe they will get more value than they actually do. Deceptive marketing practices fall into three groups: *deceptive pricing*, *promotion* and *packaging*. Deceptive pricing includes practices such as falsely advertising 'factory' or 'wholesale' prices or a large price reduction from a phoney high retail list price. Deceptive promotion includes practices such as overstating the product's features or performance, luring the customer to the store for a bargain that is out of stock, or running

The ASA advertises its services to those it seeks to protect – the consumers, offering them the opportunity to terminate advertising campaigns if they are in conflict with views of acceptability as perceived by the general public.
SOURCE: ASA, London.

rigged contests. Deceptive packaging includes exaggerating package contents through subtle design, not filling the package to the top, using misleading labelling, or describing size in misleading terms.

Deceptive practices have led to legislation and other consumer-protection actions. For example, European directives such as the Council Directive 93/35/EEC paved the way for far-reaching changes to cosmetics laws. The legislation controls the constituents of cosmetic products and accompanying instructions and warnings about use. It also specifies requirements for marketing of cosmetic products, including product claims, labelling, information on packaging and details about the product's intended function. Where a product claims to remove 'unsightly cellulite' or make the user look '20 years younger', proofs must be documented and made available to the enforcement authorities. These laws also require clear details specifying where animal testing has been carried out on both the finished product and/or its ingredients. In recognition of the increased public resistance to animal testing, a limited EU ban on animal testing for cosmetic ingredients has been in force since 1 January 1998.

Similar directives are found to regulate industry practices in the United States. The Federal Trade Commission (FTC), which has the power to regulate 'unfair or deceptive acts or practices', has published several guidelines listing deceptive practices. The toughest problem is defining what is 'deceptive'. For example, some years ago, Shell Oil advertised that Super Shell petrol with platformate gave more mileage than did the same fuel without platformate. Now this was true, but what Shell did not say is that almost *all* petrol includes platformate. Its defence was that it had never claimed that platformate was found only in Shell petroleum fuel. But even though the message was literally true, the FTC felt that the ad's *intent* was to deceive.

Marketers argue that most companies avoid deceptive practices because such practices harm their business in the long run. If consumers do not get what they expect, they will switch to more reliable products. In addition, consumers usually protect themselves from deception. Most consumers recognise a marketer's selling intent and are careful when they buy, sometimes to the point of not believing completely true product claims. One noted marketing thinker, Theodore Levitt, claims that some advertising puffery is bound to occur – and that it may even be desirable:

> There is hardly a company that would not go down in ruin if it refused to provide fluff, because nobody will buy pure functionality. . . . Worse, it denies . . . people's honest needs and values. Without distortion, embellishment and elaboration, life would be drab, dull, anguished and at its existential worst . . .[3]

High-pressure selling

Salespeople are sometimes accused of high-pressure selling that persuades people to buy goods they had no thought of buying. It is often said that cars, insurance, property and home improvement plans are *sold*, not *bought*. Salespeople are trained to deliver smooth, canned talks to entice purchase. They sell hard because commissions and sales contests promise big prizes to those who sell the most.

Marketers know that buyers can often be talked into buying unwanted or unneeded things. A key question is whether industry self-regulatory or trading standards bodies, consumer-protection laws and consumer-interest groups are sufficiently effective in checking and curbing unsavoury sales practices. In this modern era, it is encouraging to note that one or more of these can work to the advantage of consumers. Or, where deceptive practices are carried out, regulators will catch out wrongdoers, who will invariably pay the penalties for irresponsible marketing. In most cases, marketers have little to gain from high-pressure selling. Such tactics may work in one-time selling situations for short-term gain.

As a result of the Financial Services Authority (FSA) investigations into sales practices at life assurance companies in the late 1980s and during the 1990s, hosts of life assurance firms are facing penalties for mis-selling products ranging from endowment mortgages to personal pension funds. Oral persuasion was used by sales forces to entice clients to buy unsuitable products. Amongst the headline-grabbing penalties imposed by the FSA is Abbey Life's £1m (€1.5m) fine. Up to 46,000 people were mis-sold Abbey Life endowment mortgages, while a further 4,000 customers mis-sold other financial products are expected to receive compensation. Lloyds TSB, which owns Abbey Life, is known to have set aside £165m to cover these compensation costs. At least a dozen other life assurance companies have been fined a total of nearly £1 million for failing to ensure that potential customers were fully informed about different policies. Those singled out, including Scottish Widows, Guardian Royal Exchange, General Accident, Commercial Union and Norwich Union, were severely reprimanded for mis-selling, offering poor value to customers who surrender their policies early and exploiting customers' ignorance. One industry source states that endowment mortgage mis-selling has prompted 50,000 complaints up until 2003, and could cost the industry more than the £14bn cost of personal pensions mis-selling. The Consumers' Association, however, believes that up to 5 million people have been sold endowments and has been encouraging policyholders to make complaints.[4]

However, most selling involves building long-term relationships with valued customers. High-pressure or deceptive selling can do serious damage to such relationships. For example, imagine a Lever account manager trying to pressure a Tesco buyer, or an IBM salesperson trying to browbeat a Siemens information technology manager. It simply wouldn't work.

Shoddy or unsafe products

Another criticism is that products lack the quality they should have. One complaint is that products are not made well and services not performed well. A second complaint is that some products deliver little benefit. For example, some consumers are surprised to learn that many of the 'healthy' foods being marketed today, such as cholesterol-free salad dressings, low-fat frozen dinners and high-fibre bran cereals, may have little nutritional value.[5]

In order to persuade customers to buy their brand rather than any other, manufacturers sometimes make claims that are not fully substantiated.

The recent spate of food scares, the rise in obesity and the increasing popularity of functional food products that claim to have beneficial effects on consumer health have spurred the European Commission into action. Planned legislation would ban companies from using claims 'that make reference to general, non-specific benefits to overall good health, well-being and normal functioning of the body'. So, slogans such as '90 per cent fat-free' and 'strengthens your body natural defences' would be prohibited. According to David Byrne, EU Commissioner for health and consumer safety, there is a need to ensure that consumers are not fooled by information provided on the products. A fundamental requirement is that consumers are protected. The Commission's proposals for new legislation have been welcomed by consumers' associations across EU countries. These proposals would ban food companies from making 'misleading' claims about the effects of their products. Jim Murray, director of BEUC, the European consumer association, adds 'We are strongly in favour of regulation. With all these claims there is the danger that people see food products as magic bullets, and move away from a balanced diet – which is the best guarantee of good health and good nutrition.'

The food industry, however, is less enthusiastic. They welcome regulations that would allow companies to use the same labelling across the EU, but fear that the Commission may be overstepping the mark. It may be easy to see why. The new regulations would mean that Nestlé LCI yoghurts, Danone Actimel drinkable yoghurt range and Unilever's Latta margarine would not be able to claim to stimulate, help or strengthen your body's natural defences. Neither would Kellogg's, the breakfast cereal giant, be allowed to use the little symbols to indicate the health benefits that it puts on cereals in its range.[6]

A third complaint concerns product safety. Product safety has been a problem for several reasons, including manufacturer indifference, increased production complexity, poorly trained labour and poor quality control. Consider the following cases of costly and image-damaging crises brought upon several car manufacturers:

In the late 1990s, Chrysler issued one of the largest product recall notices in the history of the motoring industry, calling back 900,000 vehicles, ranging from pick-ups to a selection of 'people carriers' including the Voyager, Wrangler and Jeep Cherokee models, for a variety of reasons in seven different recalls. Another example is provided by VW which recalled 350,000 of its models worldwide because of a potentially faulty electric cable, as well as some 950,000 Golfs, Jettas, Passats and Corrados because of problems, including a cooling system fault, which could potentially damage engines and injure passengers. Even Rolls-Royce was forced to check some of its Bentley Continental T sports coupés (at €360,000 apiece) because of concerns that airbags were firing unexpectedly.[7]

For years, consumer protection groups or associations in many countries have regularly tested products for safety, and have reported hazards found in tested products, such as electrical dangers in appliances, and injury risks from lawnmowers and faulty car design. The testing and reporting activities of these organisations have helped consumers make better buying decisions and have encouraged businesses to eliminate product flaws. Marketers may sometimes face dilemmas when seeking to balance consumer needs and social responsibility. For example, no amount of test results can guarantee product safety in cars if consumers value speed and power more than safety features. Buyers might choose a less expensive chainsaw without a safety guard, although society or a government regulatory agency might deem it irresponsible and unethical for the manufacturer to sell it.

However, most responsible manufacturers *want* to produce quality goods. The way a company deals with product quality and safety problems can damage or help its reputation. Companies selling poor-quality or unsafe products risk damaging conflicts with consumer groups and regulators. Moreover, unsafe products can result in product liability suits and large awards for damages. Consumers who are unhappy with a firm's products may avoid future purchases and talk other consumers into doing the same. Consider what happened to Bridgestone/Firestone following its recent recall of 6.5 million flawed Firestone tyres. Product liability and safety concerns have driven the company to the edge of bankruptcy.[8]

Thus, quality missteps can have severe consequences. Today's marketers know that customer-driven quality results in customer satisfaction, which in turn creates profitable customer relationships.

Planned obsolescence

Critics have charged that some producers follow a programme of **planned obsolescence**, causing their products to become obsolete before they need replacement. For example, some critics charge that some producers continually change consumer concepts of acceptable styles in order to encourage more and earlier buying. An obvious example is constantly changing clothing fashions.

Other producers are accused of holding back attractive functional features, then introducing them later to make older models obsolete. Critics claim that this practice is frequently found in the consumer electronics and computer industry. For example, Intel and Microsoft have been accused in recent years of holding back their next-generation computer chips or software until demand is exhausted for the current generation. Consumers have also expressed annoyance with Japanese camera, watch and consumer electronics companies' policy of rapid and frequent model replacement. Rapid obsolescence has created difficulties in obtaining spare parts for old models. Moreover, dealers refuse to repair outdated models and planned obsolescence rapidly erodes basic product values. Still other producers are accused of using materials and components that will break, wear, rust, or rot sooner than they should.

Marketers respond that consumers *like* style changes; they get tired of the old goods and want a new look in fashion or a new design in cars. No one has to buy the new look, and if too few people like it, it will simply fail. For most technical products, customers *want* the latest innovations, even if older models still work. Companies that withhold new features do so when these features are not fully tested, when they add more cost to the product than consumers are willing to pay, and for other good reasons. But they do so at the risk that a competitor will introduce the new feature and steal the market. Moreover, companies often put in new materials to lower their costs and prices. Thus, companies do not design their products to break down earlier, because they do not want to lose their customers to other brands. Instead, they seek constant improvement to ensure that products will consistently meet or exceed customer expectations. Much of so-called planned obsolescence is the working of the competitive and technological forces in a free society – forces that lead to ever-improving goods and services.[9]

Poor service to disadvantaged consumers

Finally, marketing has been accused of poorly serving disadvantaged consumers. Critics claim that the urban poor often have to shop in smaller stores that carry inferior goods and charge higher prices. Marketing's eye on profits also means that disadvantaged consumers are not viable segments to target. The high-income consumer is the preferred target. Or, that

Planned obsolescence—
A strategy of causing products to become obsolete before they actually need replacement.

Eni demonstrates its commitment to improving the living conditions of local communities through its anti-malaria programme in Nigeria, where over 90 per cent of the population lives with the disease and the mortality rate is the highest in the world.
SOURCE: *Agency*: Eni/Grey Worldwide Italy. *Photographer*: Peter Lavery, www.peterlavery.com.

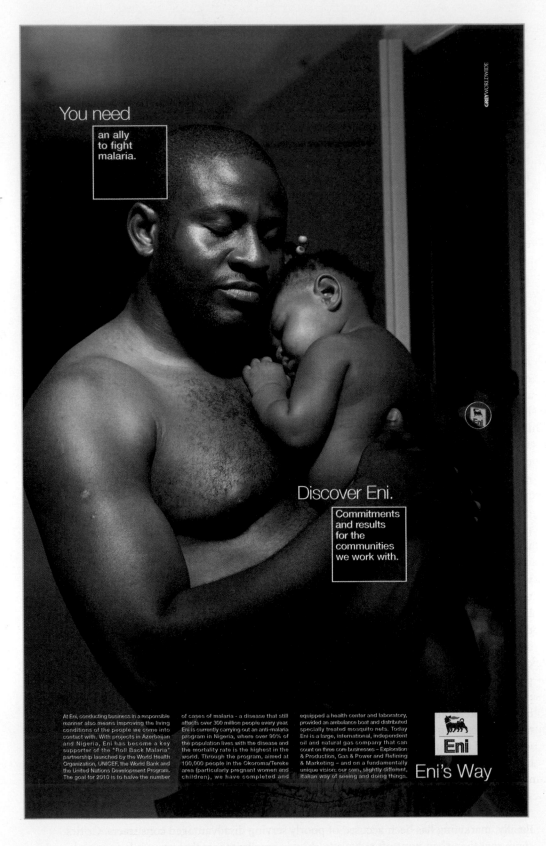

corporations, for all their might and power, are not doing enough to enhance the quality of life or living conditions of the local communities their businesses depend on.

Clearly, better marketing systems must be built in low-income areas – one measure is to get large retailers to open outlets in low-income areas. Moreover, low-income people often need consumer protection. Consumer-protection agencies should take action against suppliers who advertise false values, sell old merchandise as new, or charge too much for credit. Offenders who deliver poor value should be expected to compensate customers, as we have seen in the case of endowment and pension products mis-selling in the UK financial services industry.

We now turn to social critics' assessment of how marketing affects society as a whole.

Marketing's impact on society as a whole

The marketing system, as we – in Europe and other developed economies such as North America – are experiencing it, has been accused of adding to several 'evils' in our society at large. Advertising has been a special target. It has been blamed for creating false wants, fostering greedy aspirations and urging too much materialism in our society.

False wants and too much materialism

Critics have charged that the marketing system urges too much interest in material possessions. People are judged by what they *own* rather than by who they *are*. To be considered successful, people must own a large home or smart-looking apartment in a prime residential area, expensive cars, the latest (or best) designer clothing and high-tech gadgets. This drive for wealth and possessions hit new highs in the 1980s, when phrases such as 'greed is good' and 'shop till you drop' seemed to characterise the times. In the new millennium, even though many social scientists have noted a reaction against the opulence and waste of the previous decades and a return to more basic values and social commitment, our infatuation with material things continues.

The critics do not view this interest in material things as a natural state of mind, but rather as a matter of false wants created by marketing. Businesses spend huge sums of money to hire advertising agencies to stimulate people's desires for goods, and advertisers use the mass media to create materialistic models of the good life. People work harder to earn the necessary money. Their purchases increase the output of the nation's industry, and industry, in turn, uses the advertising industry to stimulate more desire for the industrial output. Thus marketing is seen as creating false wants that benefit industry more than they benefit consumers.

These criticisms overstate the power of business to create needs. People have strong defences against advertising and other marketing tools. Marketers are most effective when they appeal to existing wants rather than when they attempt to create new ones. Furthermore, people seek information when making important purchases and often do not rely on single sources. Even minor purchases that may be affected by advertising messages lead to repeat purchases only if the product performs as promised. Finally, the high failure rate of new products shows that companies are not able to control demand.

On a deeper level, our wants and values are influenced not only by marketers, but also by family, peer groups, religion, ethnic background and education. If modern societies, wherever they exist, are highly materialistic, these values arose out of basic socialisation processes that go much deeper than business and mass media could produce alone. The importance of wealth and material possessions to the overseas Chinese, for example, is explained more by cultural and socialisation factors than by sustained exposure to western advertising influences. Moreover, in affluent economies such as America, some social critics see materialism as a positive and rewarding force:

When we purchase an object, what we really buy is meaning. Commercialism is the water we swim in, the air we breathe, our sunlight and our shade. . . . Materialism is a vital source of meaning and happiness in the modern world. . . . We have not just asked to go this way, we have demanded. Now most of the world is lining up, pushing and shoving, eager to elbow into the mall. Getting and spending has become the most passionate, and often the most imaginative, endeavor of modern life. While this is dreary and depressing to some, as doubtless it should be, it is liberating and democratic to many more.[10]

Too few social goods

Business has been accused of overselling private goods at the expense of public goods. As private goods increase, they require more public services that are usually not forthcoming. For example, an increase in car ownership (private good) requires more roads, traffic control, parking spaces and police services (public goods). The overselling of private goods results in 'social costs'. For cars, the social costs include excessive traffic congestion, air pollution, and deaths and injuries from car accidents.

A way must be found to restore a balance between private and public goods. One option is to make producers bear the full social costs of their operations. For example, the government could require car manufacturers to build cars with even more safety features and better pollution-control systems. Car makers would then raise their prices to cover extra costs. If buyers found the price of some cars too high, however, the producers of these cars would disappear, and demand would move to those producers that could support both the private and social costs.

A second option is to make consumers pay the social costs. For example, highway authorities around the world are starting to charge 'congestion tolls' in an effort to reduce traffic congestion.

Countries such as Norway, the UK, France, Singapore and the US are managing traffic with varying tolls. For example, traffic congestion has been reported to have been reduced by some 40 per cent in inner city London, since the introduction of the £5-a-day congestion charge in 2003. In Singapore and southern California, drivers are being charged premiums to travel in underused car pool lanes. Peak surcharges are being studied for roads around New York, San Francisco, Los Angeles and other American cities. Economists point out that traffic jams are caused when drivers are not charged the costs they impose on others, such as delays. The solution: Make 'em pay![11]

More generally, if the costs of driving rise high enough, consumers will travel at non-peak times or find alternative transportation modes.

Cultural pollution

Critics charge the marketing system with creating *cultural pollution*. Our senses are being assaulted constantly by advertising. This devious practice is inflicted on our kids every day. Commercials interrupt serious programmes; pages of ads obscure printed matter; billboards mar beautiful scenery. These interruptions continuously pollute people's minds with messages of materialism, sex, power or status. Children's constant exposure to advertising, the protectionists argue, creates mercenary kids, experts in 'pester power', who force their downtrodden and beleaguered parents into spending enormous sums of money on branded goods and the latest crazes. Although most people do not find advertising overly annoying (some even think it is the best part of television programming), some critics call for sweeping changes.

Marketers answer the charges of 'commercial noise' with the following arguments. First, they hope that their ads reach primarily the target audience. But because of mass-communication channels, some ads are bound to reach people who have no interest in the product and are therefore bored or annoyed. As for TV advertising's influence on children, free marketers point to European research that shows that parents and peers influence children more than advertising. Trend products like yoyos, Beanie Babies and Furbies have reached the top without a penny spent on TV commercials. Children are not empty vessels helplessly vulnerable to marketers' wiles. They are capable of absorbing and assimilating advertising messages, approaching commercials with a critical mind and to draw their own verdict.[12] People who buy magazines slanted towards their interests – such as *Vogue, Bliss, Loaded, Heat* or *Fortune* – rarely complain about the ads because the magazines advertise products of interest. Second, ads make much of television and radio free, and keep down the costs of magazines and newspapers. Most people think commercials are a small price to pay for these benefits. Finally, consumers have alternatives: they can zip and zap TV commercials or avoid them altogether on many cable and satellite channels. Thus to hold consumer attention, advertisers are making their ads more entertaining and informative.

Too much political power

Another criticism is that business wields too much political power. 'Oil', 'tobacco', 'pharmaceuticals', 'financial services' and 'alcohol' have the support of important politicians and civil servants, who look after an industry's interests against the public interest. Advertisers are accused of holding too much power over the mass media, limiting their freedom to report independently and objectively.

The setting up of citizens' charters and greater concern for consumer rights and protection over the 1990s have put more pressure on business accountability in the twenty-first century. Fortunately, many powerful business interests once thought to be untouchable have been tamed in the public interest. For example, in western Europe and the United States, consumerism campaigns have resulted in legislation requiring the car industry to build more safety into its cars and cigarette companies to put health warnings on their packages. More recently, giants such as Coca-Cola, Microsoft and Intel have felt the impact of regulators seeking to balance the interests of big business against those of the public. Moreover, because the media receive advertising revenues from many different advertisers, it is easier to resist the influence of one or a few of them. Too much business power tends to result in counterforces that check and offset these powerful interests.

Let us now take a look at the criticisms that business critics have levelled at companies' marketing practices.

Marketing's impact on other businesses

Critics also charge that companies' marketing practices can harm other companies and reduce competition. Three problems are involved: acquisition of competitors, marketing practices that create barriers to entry, and unfair competitive marketing practices.

Critics claim that firms are harmed and competition reduced when companies expand by acquiring competitors rather than by developing their own new products. The large number of acquisitions and rapid pace of industry consolidation over the past two decades have caused concern that vigorous young competitors will be absorbed and that competition will be reduced. In virtually every major industry – retailing, financial services, utilities, transportation, motor vehicles, telecommunications, entertainment – the number of major competitors is shrinking. Consider the glut of acquisitions in the food industry during the past few years – Unilever's buying Bestfoods, Philip Morris's snatching Nabisco, General Mills' swallowing Pillsbury, Kellogg's taking over Keebler and PepsiCo's seizing of Quaker Oats.[13]

Acquisition is a complex subject. Acquisitions can sometimes be good for society. The acquiring company may gain economies of scale that lead to lower costs and lower prices. A well-managed company may take over a poorly managed company and improve its efficiency. An industry that was not very competitive might become more competitive after the acquisition. But acquisitions can also be harmful and are therefore closely regulated by some governments and competition (or mergers and monopolies) commissions.

Critics have also claimed that marketing practices bar new companies from entering an industry. The use of patents and heavy promotion spending can tie up suppliers or dealers to keep out or drive out competitors. Those concerned with antitrust regulation recognise that some barriers are the natural result of the economic advantages of doing business on a large scale. Other barriers could be challenged by existing and new laws. For example, some critics have proposed a progressive tax on advertising spending to reduce the role of selling costs as a substantial barrier to entry.

Finally, some firms have in fact used unfair competitive marketing practices with the intention of hurting or destroying other firms. They may set their prices below costs, threaten to cut off business with suppliers, or discourage the buying of a competitor's products. Various laws work to prevent such predatory competition. It is difficult, however, to prove that the intent or action was really predatory.

Take Microsoft, for example. Competitors and regulators have accused Microsoft of predatory 'bundling' practices – the term describes Microsoft's practice of continually adding new features to its Windows operating system that is installed in a majority of the world's desktop computers. Because customers are essentially locked in to Windows, it's easy for the company to get them to use its other software – even if competitors make better products. That dampens competition, reduces choice, and could retard innovation.[14] (See Marketing Insights 5.1.)

Another example which reminds us of the vulnerability of firms, particularly dominant, global companies, to competition authorities is Coca-Cola's recent experience. Spurred by its acquisition of Cadbury's soft-drinks brands outside America, competition authorities from Chile to Australia to Europe scrutinised Coke's market share and business practices. In Europe, the European Commission had launched an investigation into Coke's alleged anti-competitive practices in Germany, Denmark and Austria: one common anti-competitive practice is to give retailers and restaurants free fridges or soda fountains if they refuse to sell soft drinks from rival firms. Another is to offer them special prices if they stock the complete

Microsoft: a giant against the world

marketing insights

Microsoft is no stranger to PC users. But the world's biggest software company has a reach that extends beyond the PC into everything from computerised toys, smart-phones and TV set-top boxes to selling cars and airline tickets over the Internet. In its zeal to become a leader not just in operating systems but on the Internet, the company bundled its Internet Explorer browser into its Windows software. This move sparked an antitrust suit by the US government, much to the delight of Microsoft's rivals. After all, Web-browsing innovator Netscape has seen its market share plummet as it tries to sell what Microsoft gives away for free. After a two-year trial, the antitrust authorities emerged victors, when the judge who heard the landmark case against the software giant ruled that Microsoft broke antitrust laws and behaved illegally by tying its Web browser to its best-selling Windows operating system. The antitrust officials demanded Microsoft to be broken up into two separate businesses – one to run its Windows operating system and the other to manage its application software products such as word processing and spreadsheets. The company was also required to implement a host of measures aimed at curbing any abuse of its dominant position. Microsoft protested its innocence. On appeal, the remedy to break up the giant corporation was rejected by the higher court, although the ruling that the company illegally maintained its monopoly was upheld. Nine US states that brought charges against Microsoft and the Justice Department settled with Microsoft before new remedy hearings took place. Nine other state regulators pressed for harder remedies, but their efforts were thwarted on 1 November 2002 by Judge Colleen Kollar-Kotelly who ruled that the company's settlement with the Department of Justice and the nine US states was an adequate remedy for the group's antitrust violations.

Meanwhile, in Brussels, the company was being investigated by the European Commission for anti-competitive behaviour. The Commission was looking into the implications of the US ruling on Microsoft for its own investigations into the company's dominant position in the EU. At the time of the appeal hearings in the US, the European Commission was investigating five enquiries into different aspects of Microsoft's behaviour. These range from its monopoly of the PC operating system market, following complaints from rival firms such as Sun Microsystems, and predatory behaviour associated with Windows 2000, to the company's pricing policy for French software, where the firm allegedly sold software more cheaply in Canada than in France. Meanwhile, problems brew further afield for the global firm, with lawyers seeking to expand the case against Microsoft by claiming damages for worldwide customers. They argue that international curbs against anti-competitive commercial activity have become so prevalent that they must be deemed to rise to the level of the law of nations. They also claim to have the support from a mixture of United Nations

...5.1

statements of principles on competition and recommendations from the Organisation for Economic Cooperation and Development (OECD). Not surprisingly, the European Commission had come under pressure from the US to drop its investigation following Judge Kollar-Kotelly's ruling.

Nonetheless, the Commissioner argues that while the US case was about Microsoft's abuse of monopoly power to drive out competitors like Netscape, the European Commission's investigations concern later events: the bundling of Media Player in the Windows operating system to squeeze out competitors and the design of Windows to favour its own server. Among others, RealNetworks, the streaming media group, have filed antitrust lawsuits against Microsoft, alleging the software giant had illegally used its market clout to monopolise the digital media field. The Commission has consistently emphasised its intention to find Microsoft guilty of abusing its dominant position. It is unlikely that the Commission will take a final decision before mid-2004. No doubt, the Commission's enquiries follow submissions of complaints made by Microsoft's rivals – with little evidence that consumers have been damaged by its practices. The Commission emphasises it has to substantiate these allegations. In March 2004, the Commission, however, scaled down its demands for Microsoft to change its business practices. Although the Commission had wanted both home users and corporate customers to be offered Windows without Media Player or, alternatively, force Microsoft to include rival programs in Windows, it jettisoned both these options. Instead, it proposes to give computer manufacturers the choice of whether to sell Windows with Media Player, with a rival product or without any such program. The pressure from Brussels is on Microsoft, but a final verdict by the EU court could take four or five years!

SOURCES: 15 + Daniel Dombey, 'Brussels back-pedals over Microsoft ruling', *Financial Times* (15 March 2004), p. 25; Scott Morrison and Daniel Dombey, 'Antitrust suit piles pressure on Microsoft', *Financial Times* (19 December 2003), p. 34; Daniel Dombey, 'Microsoft on antitrust attack', *Financial Times* (12 November 2003), p. 25; Daniel Dombey, 'Brussels puts pressure on Microsoft', *Financial Times* (30 October 2003), p. 30; Paul Abrahams and Richard Waters, 'Microsoft tries to play down antitrust court triumph', *Financial Times* (4 November 2002), p. 8; Francesco Guerrera, 'Microsoft to take tough line with EU', *Financial Times* (4 November 2002), p. 1; 'Breaking up Microsoft', *The Economist* (10 June 2000), p. 20.

range of Coke's products, including Sprite and Fanta. A third offers retailers rebates and volume discounts for sales growth.[15]

Although competitors and governments charge that the actions of companies such as Coca-Cola and Microsoft are predatory and illegal, the fundamental question remains: is this unfair competition or the healthy competition of a more efficient company against the less efficient?

Citizen and public actions to regulate marketing

Because some people view business as the cause of many economic and social ills, grassroots movements have arisen from time to time to keep business in line. The two main movements have been consumerism and environmentalism.

Consumerism

Western business firms have been the targets of organised consumer movements on three occasions. Consumerism has its origins in the United States. The first consumer movement took place in the early 1900s. It was fuelled by rising prices, Upton Sinclair's writings on conditions in the meat industry, and scandals in the drug industry. The second consumer movement, in the mid-1930s, was sparked by an upturn in consumer prices during the Great Depression and another drug scandal.

The third movement began in the 1960s. Consumers had become better educated, products had become more complex and potentially hazardous, and people were unhappy with western (usually meaning American) institutions. Ralph Nader appeared on the scene in the 1960s to force many issues, and other well-known writers accused big business of wasteful and unethical practices. President John F. Kennedy declared that consumers have the right to safety and to be informed, to choose and to be heard. The American Congress investigated certain industries and proposed consumer-protection legislation. Since then, many consumer groups have been organised and several consumer laws have been passed. The consumer movement has spread internationally and has become very strong in Europe.[16]

But what is the consumer movement? **Consumerism** is an organised movement of citizens and government agencies to improve the rights and power of buyers in relation to sellers. Traditional sellers' rights include the following:

- The right to introduce any product in any size and style, provided it is not hazardous to personal health or safety; or, if it is, to include proper warnings and controls.
- The right to charge any price for the product, provided no discrimination exists among similar kinds of buyer.
- The right to spend any amount to promote the product, provided it is not defined as unfair competition.
- The right to use any product message, provided it is not misleading or dishonest in content or execution.
- The right to use any buying incentive schemes, provided they are not unfair or misleading.

Traditional buyers' rights include the following:

- The right not to buy a product that is offered for sale.
- The right to expect the product to be safe.
- The right to expect the product to perform as claimed.

Comparing these rights, many believe that the balance of power lies on the sellers' side. True, the buyer can refuse to buy. But critics feel that the buyer has too little information, education and protection to make wise decisions when facing sophisticated sellers. Consumer advocates call for the following additional consumer rights:

Consumerism—An organised movement of citizens and government agencies to improve the rights and power of buyers in relation to sellers.

■ The right to be well informed about important aspects of the product.

■ The right to be protected against questionable products and marketing practices.

■ The right to influence products and marketing practices in ways that will improve the 'quality of life'.

Each proposed right has led to more specific proposals by consumerists. The right to be informed includes the right to know the true interest on a loan (truth in lending), the true cost per unit of a brand (unit pricing), the ingredients in a product (ingredient labelling), the nutrition in foods (nutritional labelling), product freshness (open dating) and the true benefits of a product (truth in advertising). Proposals related to consumer protection include strengthening consumer rights in cases of business fraud, requiring greater product safety and giving more power to government agencies. Proposals relating to quality of life include controlling the ingredients that go into certain products and packaging, reducing the level of advertising 'noise' and putting consumer representatives on company boards to protect consumer interests.

Consumers have not only the *right* but also the *responsibility* to protect themselves instead of leaving this function to someone else. Consumers who believe that they got a bad deal have several remedies available, including contacting the company or the media, contacting government or private consumer-interest/protection bodies or agencies, and going to small-claims courts.

Environmentalism

Environmentalism—An organised movement of concerned citizens and government agencies to protect and improve people's living environment.

Whereas consumerists consider whether the marketing system is efficiently serving consumer wants, environmentalists are concerned with marketing's effects on the environment and the costs of serving consumer needs and wants. **Environmentalism** is an organised movement of concerned citizens and government agencies to protect and improve people's living environment. Environmentalists are not against marketing and consumption; they simply want people and organisations to operate with more care for the environment. They assert that the marketing system's goal is not to maximise consumption, consumer choice or consumer satisfaction, but rather to maximise life quality. 'Life quality' means not only the quantity and quality of consumer goods and services, but also the quality of the environment. Environmentalists want environmental costs to be included in both producer and consumer decision making.

The first wave of modern environmentalism was driven by environmental groups and concerned consumers in the 1960s and 1970s. They were concerned with damage to the ecosystem caused by strip mining, forest depletion, acid rain, loss of the atmosphere's ozone layer, toxic wastes and litter. They were also concerned with the loss of recreational areas and with the increase in health problems caused by bad air, polluted water and chemically treated food.

The second wave was driven by governments, which passed laws and regulations during the 1970s and 1980s governing industrial practices impacting the environment. This wave hit some industries hard. Heavy industry, public utilities, and chemical and steel companies had to spend heavily on clean-up technology, waste management and other pollution-control equipment. The car industry had to introduce expensive emission controls in cars. In some countries, governments have introduced tough regulations on car makers to deal with environmental problems, as in the case of Germany, which introduced laws to create a car recycling system.[17] The petroleum industry has had to create new low-lead and unleaded petrols. The packaging industry has had to find ways to reduce litter and energy consumption. In some sectors, innovative recycling schemes are being pioneered by private companies.

Environmental campaigns are gaining popularity. This campaign urges the British public to make the effort to recycle their glass bottles and jars by disposing them at bottle banks.
SOURCE: Advertising Archives.

Putting up some new wallpaper in your apartment? Perhaps, you'd never think to use some dirty nappies. The city of Santa Clarita in California recently piloted a nappy recycling scheme for collecting used nappies from families which will be turned into materials for shoe insoles, roof shingles and, you guessed right, wallpaper. Why start in Santa Clarita? Three out of four inhabitants in the city are under 44. More than 150 babies are born every month. Each of these new residents typically produce one tonne of dirty nappies before she or he is potty-trained. Most of these 'poopy' nappies end up in landfills. Coming to the rescue lately is Knowaste, a New-York based company specializing in recycling absorbent hygiene products and turning them into pulp and plastic. The state of California and Santa Clarita each contributed $250,000 to pilot a scheme for recycling Santa Claritans' nappies. The city's rubbish-collecting company is responsible for picking up piles of nappies from the kerb, delivering them to the recycling plant and selling the recycled products.

The business is not new to Knowaste. In 1999, the company opened a plant in the Netherlands, which now processes 35,000 or more tonnes of dirty nappies a year. But, the raw material comes from incontinent aged folks, not babies, consistent with the demographic trends in the country. The plant works with local retirement homes and is paid €100 for every tonne of soiled trash it takes from the delivery lorries and a payment – €200–300 – for each tonne of the plastic and pulp at the other end. The rewards are lucrative – it has presold all its 2003 production. Unlike in the US, with so much empty space, landfills are getting less popular and more expensive in Europe. So, the recycling market is a serious option. However, Knowaste argues that nappies are still one of the main bits of rubbish still landing in landfills, and, as tougher green laws are being imposed, so recycling's the way to go. Comforting thought or not? Let's face it – do you really want to stay dry under a nappy umbrella or ease into a nappy pair of slippers?[18]

These industries often resent environmental regulations, especially when they are imposed too rapidly to allow companies to make proper adjustments. Many of these companies claim they have had to absorb large costs that have made them less competitive.

The first two environmentalism waves are merging into a third and stronger wave in which companies are accepting responsibility for doing no harm to the environment. They are shifting from protest to prevention, and from regulation to responsibility. More and more companies are adopting **environmental sustainability** – developing strategies that both sustain the environment and produce profits for the company.

Sustainability is a crucial but difficult goal. John Browne, chairman of giant oil company BP, recently asked this question: 'Is genuine progress still possible? Is development sustainable? Or is one strand of progress – industrialisation – now doing such damage to the environment that the next generation won't have a world worth living in?'[19] Browne sees the situation as an opportunity. Five years ago, BP broke ranks with the oil industry on environmental issues. 'There are good commercial reasons to do right by the environment',

Environmental sustainability—A third environmentalism wave in which companies seek to produce profits for the company while sustaining the environment.

says Browne. Under his leadership, BP has become active in public forums on global climate issues and has worked to reduce emissions in exploration and production. It has begun marketing cleaner fuels and invested significantly in exploring alternative energy sources, such as photovoltaic power and hydrogen. At the local level, BP recently opened 'the world's most environmentally friendly service station' near London:

> The new BP Connect service station features an array of innovative green initiatives that show BP's commitment to environmental responsibility. The station runs entirely on renewable energy and generates up to half of its own power, using solar panels installed on the roofs and three wind turbines. More than 60 per cent of the water needed for the restrooms comes from rainwater collected on the shop roof and water for hand washing is heated by solar panels. The site's vapour recovery systems collect and recycle even the fuel vapour released from customers' tanks as pump gas. BP has planted landscaping around the site with indigenous plant species. And, to promote biodiversity awareness, the company has undertaken several initiatives to attract local wildlife to the area, such as dragonflies and insect-feeding birds. The wild-flower turf under the wind farm will even provide a habitat for bumble bees.[20]

Figure 5.1 shows a grid that companies can use to gauge their progress towards environmental sustainability. At the most basic level, a company can practise *pollution prevention*. This involves more than pollution control – cleaning up waste after it has been created. Pollution prevention means eliminating or minimising waste *before* it is created. Companies emphasising prevention have responded with 'green marketing' programmes – developing ecologically safer products, recyclable and biodegradable packaging, better pollution controls and more energy-efficient operations. They are finding that they can be both green and competitive. Consider how the Dutch flower industry has responded to its environmental problems:

	Internal	External
Tomorrow	**New environmental technology** Is the environmental performance of our products limited by our existing technology base? Is there potential to realise major improvements through new technology?	**Sustainability vision** Does our corporate vision direct us towards the solution of social and environmental problems? Does our vision guide the development of new technologies, markets, products and processes?
Today	**Pollution prevention** Where are the most significant waste and emission streams from our current operations? Can we lower costs and risks by eliminating waste at the source or by using it as useful input?	**Product stewardship** What are the implications for product design and development if we assume responsibility for a product's entire life cycle? Can we add value or lower costs while simultaneously reducing the impact of our products?

Figure 5.1 The environmental sustainability grid
SOURCE: Harvard Business School Publishing. Reprinted by permission of *Harvard Business Review*, figure of The Sustainability Portfolio, from 'Beyond Greening: strategies for a sustainable world', by Stuart Hart, Jan–Feb 1997. Copyright © 1996 by the Harvard Business School Publishing Corporation; all rights reserved.

> Intense cultivation of flowers in small areas was contaminating the soil and groundwater with pesticides, herbicides and fertilizers. Facing increasingly strict regulation, the Dutch growers understood that the only effective way to address the problem would be to develop a closed-loop system. In advanced Dutch greenhouses, flowers now grow in water and rock wool, not soil. This lowers the risk of infestation, reducing the need for fertilizers and pesticides, which are delivered in water that circulates and is re-used. The closed-loop system also reduces variation in growing conditions, thus improving product quality. Handling costs have reduced because the flowers are cultivated on specially designed platforms. The net result is not only dramatically lower environmental impact but also lower costs, better quality and enhanced global competitiveness.[21]

At the next level, companies can practise *product stewardship* – minimising not just pollution from production but all environmental impacts throughout the full product life cycle. Many companies are adopting design for environment (DFE) practices, which involve thinking ahead in the design stage to create products that are easier to recover, reuse or recycle. DFE not only helps to sustain the environment; it can be highly profitable:

> Consider Xerox Corporation's Asset Recycle Management (ARM) programme, which uses leased Xerox copiers as sources of high-quality, low-cost parts and components for new machines. A well-developed [process] for taking back leased copiers combined with a sophisticated re-manufacturing process

The boom in environmentalism has reached such dimensions that even Seoul's International Airport claims to be environmentally friendly.
SOURCE: Inchon International Airport Corporation, Korea.
Agency: Dentsu Young and Rubicam, Korea.

allows components to be reconditioned, tested and then reassembled into 'new' machines. Xerox estimates that ARM savings in raw materials, labour and waste disposal fall in the €300-million to €400-million range. By redefining product-in-use as part of the company's asset base, Xerox has discovered a way to add value and lower costs. It can continually provide lease customers with the latest product upgrades, giving them state-of-the-art functionality with minimum environmental impact.[22]

At the third level of environmental sustainability, companies look to the future and plan for *new environmental technologies*. Many organisations that have made good headway in pollution prevention and product stewardship are still limited by existing technologies. To develop fully sustainable strategies, they will need to develop new technologies. For example, detergent manufacturers have developed laundry products for low-temperature washing. Some have embarked on a 'wash right' campaign which promotes the virtues of low temperature washing by emphasising the benefits to the clothes as well as energy savings.

Finally, companies can develop a *sustainability vision*, which serves as a guide to the future. It shows how the company's products and services, processes and policies must evolve and what new technologies must be developed to get there. This vision of sustainability provides a framework for pollution control, product stewardship and environmental technology.

Most companies today focus on the lower-left quadrant of the grid in Figure 5.1, investing most heavily in pollution prevention. Some forward-looking companies practise product stewardship and are developing new environmental technologies. Few companies have well-defined sustainability visions. Emphasising only one or a few cells in the environmental sustainability grid in Figure 5.1 can be shortsighted. For example, investing only in the bottom half of the grid puts a company in a good position today but leaves it vulnerable in the future. In contrast, a heavy emphasis on the top half suggests that a company has good environmental vision but lacks the skills needed to implement it. Thus, companies should work at developing all four dimensions of environmental sustainability. Hewlett-Packard is doing just that:

Hewlett-Packard has evolved through three distinct phases of environmental sustainability over the past two decades. In the 1980s, the environmental concerns were primarily pollution control and prevention, with a focus on reducing emissions from existing manufacturing processes. . . . In the 1990s, the focus shifted to . . . a product stewardship function, which focused on developing global processes for tracking and managing regulatory compliance issues, customer inquiry response systems, information management, public policy shaping, product take-back programs, green packaging, and integrating 'design for the environment' and life cycle analysis into product development processes. Today, sustainability is about developing technologies that actually contribute a positive impact to environmental challenges. [However,] HP has recognized that pollution prevention and product stewardship have become baseline market expectations. To be an environmental leader in the 21st century, HP needs to integrate environmental sustainability into its fundamental business [vision and] strategy.[23]

Environmentalism creates special challenges for global marketers. As international trade barriers come down and global markets expand, environmental issues will continue to have an ever-greater impact on international trade. Global companies have to operate in accordance with stringent environment regulations that are being developed in countries across North America, Western Europe and other developed regions. For example, the European Union's Eco-Management and Audit Regulation has provided guidelines for environmental self-regulation. The EU has also recently passed 'end-of-life' regulations that require car makers to recycle or reuse at least 80 per cent of their old cars by 2006. Similarly, in the United States, for example, more than two dozen major pieces of environmental legislation have been enacted since 1970, and recent events suggest that more regulation is on the way. A side accord to the North American Free Trade Agreement (NAFTA) set up a commission for resolving environmental matters.[24]

Marketers' lives will become more complicated. They must raise prices to cover environmental costs, knowing that the product will be harder to sell. Yet environmental issues have become so important in our society that there is no turning back to the time when few managers worried about the effects of product and marketing decisions on environmental quality.[25]

However, environmental policies still vary widely from country to country, and uniform worldwide standards are not expected for many years. Although countries such as Denmark, Germany, Japan and the United States have fully developed environmental policies and high public expectations, major countries such as China, India, Brazil and Russia are in only the early stages of developing such policies. Moreover, environmental factors that motivate consumers in one country may have no impact on consumers in another. For example, PVC soft-drink bottles cannot be used in Switzerland or Germany. However, they are preferred in France, which has an extensive recycling process for them. Thus, international companies are finding it difficult to develop standard environmental practices that work around the world. Instead, they are creating general policies, and then translating these policies into tailored programmes that meet local regulations and expectations.

Figure 5.2 Legal issues facing marketing management

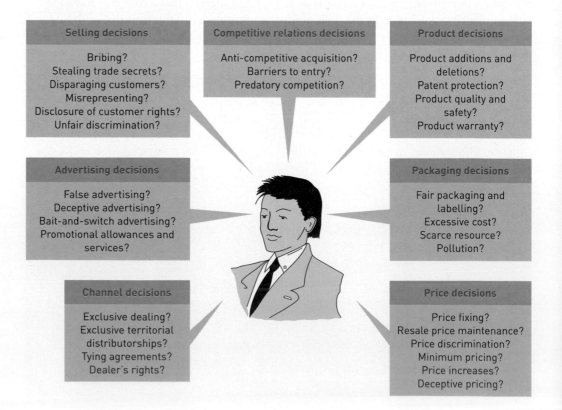

Selling decisions	Competitive relations decisions	Product decisions
Bribing? Stealing trade secrets? Disparaging customers? Misrepresenting? Disclosure of customer rights? Unfair discrimination?	Anti-competitive acquisition? Barriers to entry? Predatory competition?	Product additions and deletions? Patent protection? Product quality and safety? Product warranty?

Advertising decisions		Packaging decisions
False advertising? Deceptive advertising? Bait-and-switch advertising? Promotional allowances and services?		Fair packaging and labelling? Excessive cost? Scarce resource? Pollution?

Channel decisions		Price decisions
Exclusive dealing? Exclusive territorial distributorships? Tying agreements? Dealer's rights?		Price fixing? Resale price maintenance? Price discrimination? Minimum pricing? Price increases? Deceptive pricing?

Public actions to regulate marketing

Citizen concerns about marketing practices will usually lead to public attention and legislative proposals. New bills will be debated – many will be defeated, others will be modified and a few will become workable laws.

Figure 5.2 illustrates the principal legal issues facing marketing management. Individual country laws exist which affect marketing. The task is to translate these laws into the language that marketing executives understand as they make decisions about competitive relations, products, price, promotion and channels of distribution.

Having discussed citizen and public actions to regulate marketing, consumerism, environmentalism and regulation – and the way they affect marketing – we will next examine the business actions towards socially responsible marketing that lead to different philosophies of enlightened marketing and the fostering of marketing ethics.

Business actions towards socially responsible marketing

Today, most companies have grown to accept the new consumer rights, at least in principle. They might oppose certain pieces of legislation as inappropriate ways to solve specific consumer problems, but they recognise the consumer's right to information and protection. Many of these companies have responded positively to consumerism and environmentalism in order to serve consumer needs better.

Enlightened marketing

The philosophy of **enlightened marketing** holds that a company's marketing should support the best long-run performance of the marketing system. Enlightened marketing consists of five principles: consumer-oriented marketing, innovative marketing, value marketing, sense-of-mission marketing and societal marketing.

Consumer-oriented marketing

Consumer-oriented marketing means that the company views and organises its marketing activities from the consumer's point of view. It works hard to sense, serve and satisfy the needs of a defined group of customers. Good marketing companies tend to have one thing in common – an all-consuming passion for delivering superior value to carefully chosen customers. Only by seeing the world through its customers' eyes can the company build lasting and profitable customer relationships.

Innovative marketing

The principle of **innovative marketing** requires that the company continuously seek real product and marketing improvements. The company that overlooks new and better ways to do things will eventually lose customers to another company that has found a better way.

As the environmental director at Scandic Hotels, Ola Ivarsson's aim was to transform the chain into an eco-friendly business, a move that began to revolutionize Europe's leisure industry.

Under Ivarsson's direction, Scandic Hotels made design improvements that drastically improved the company's environmental impact. The hotel chain's

Enlightened marketing—
A marketing philosophy holding that a company's marketing should support the best long-run performance of the marketing system; its five principles are consumer-oriented marketing, innovative marketing, value marketing, sense-of-mission marketing and societal marketing.

Consumer-oriented marketing—A principle of enlightened marketing which holds that a company should view and organise its marketing activities from the consumers' point of view.

Innovative marketing—
A principle of enlightened marketing which requires that a company seek real product and marketing improvements.

annual consumption of plastic, metal usage, and the discharge of harmful chemicals has fallen dramatically in recent years; the quantity of unsorted waste produced by the chain has been reduced by a whopping 50 per cent. Ivarsson's programme served to boost the chain's popularity, helping to lift Scandic out of the difficulties it experienced in the early 1990s.

The centrepiece of this design revolution is the 'recyclable room' that Ivarsson created with the help of his team of in-house architects. They managed to make the room a remarkable 97 per cent recyclable, and since then Scandic has built 2,700 more worldwide.

Ivarsson explains, 'We identified our customers' most repetitive activities and found ways of making these less damaging to the environment.' Ivarsson found that many of the best solutions were the least complicated. 'The most creative ideas were deceptively simple', he says. 'For example, we used to provide soap in miniature bars and shampoo in 50 ml bottles. But most customers only use a tiny fraction of these quantities during their stay, so we decided to offer soap and shampoo using dispensers instead. It saves us more than 25 tonnes of soap and shampoo each year.'

Scandic's dispenser system and other innovations, such as the chain's use of natural, renewable materials (wood, wool and cotton), are catching on among European hoteliers, and the benefits of these materials have been both environmental and economic.

'But customers don't have to be less comfortable', Ivarsson says. 'Our recyclable rooms are at least as comfortable as the others, and they are always booked up first. It's not difficult to see why they're popular. If you look at all that wood, you get a lovely homey, hearty, welcoming feeling – it is beautiful.' On this front, Scandic's philosophy is in sync with the message of the United Nations Environment Programme's (UNEP) campaign of sustainable consumption: more environmentally friendly consumption does not result in taking away comfort and choice from consumers. Rather, sustainable consumption can be cool and fashionable – 'it's about consuming differently, consuming efficiently, and having an improved quality of life.'[26]

Value marketing

Value marketing—A principle of enlightened marketing which holds that a company should put most of its resources into value-building marketing investments.

According to the principle of **value marketing**, the company should put most of its resources into value-building marketing investments. Many things marketers do – one-shot sales promotions, minor packaging changes, advertising puffery – may raise sales in the short run, but add less *value* than would actual improvements in the product's quality, features or convenience. Enlightened marketing calls for building long-run consumer loyalty, by continually improving the value that consumers receive from the firm's marketing offer.

Sense-of-mission marketing

Sense-of-mission marketing—A principle of enlightened marketing which holds that a company should define its mission in broad social terms rather than narrow product terms.

Sense-of-mission marketing means that the company should define its mission in broad *social* terms rather than narrow *product* terms. When a company defines a social mission, employees feel better about their work and have a clearer sense of direction. For example,

Cancer Patients Fly Free

Photography by Susi Dugaw

Here, big corporations work with charity Corporate Angel Network to realise an important mission – to get cancer patients to critical cancer treatment centres using empty seats on corporate jets.
SOURCE: CAN, Corporate Angel Network.

So near, yet so far.

Critical treatment centers, often thousands of miles away, are frequently a cancer patient's best chance for survival. But costly airfare, stressful delays, and unnecessary exposure to crowds are the last thing these patients need.

We give cancer patients a lift.

We are Corporate Angel Network, the nationwide public charity with only one mission—to arrange passage for cancer patients to treatment centers using the empty seats on corporate jets.

Our five employees and 60 highly involved and compassionate volunteers work directly with patients and families to coordinate their travel needs with the regularly scheduled flight plans of our Corporate Angels—500 major corporations, including 56 of the top 100 in the *Fortune 500*®, who generously make empty seats on their aircraft available to our patients.

To date, they've flown more than 15,000 flights with Corporate Angel Network patients onboard.

Need a lift?
Just give us a call. We'll do the rest.

Corporate Angel Network, Inc.
Westchester County Airport, One Loop Road, White Plains, NY 10604
Phone (914) 328-1313   Fax (914) 328-3938
Patient Toll Free — (866) 328-1313
Info@CorpAngelNetwork.org   www.CorpAngelNetwork.org

defined in narrow product terms, the British Co-operative Bank's mission might be to sell banking services, but the company has taken a firm decision to promote a broader mission – to be an ethical bank, refraining from doing business with those companies that engage in so-called unsavoury business practices, from companies that are involved in the fur trade to tobacco product manufacturers. Organisations like Corporate Angel Network, a public charity, can realise their mission – to arrange air passage for cancer patients to treatment centres thousands of miles away using the empty seats on corporate jets. Some 500 major corporations, including 56 of the top 100 in the *Fortune 500*, have generously made empty seats on their aircraft available to the charity.

Societal marketing

Societal marketing—
A principle of enlightened marketing which holds that a company should make marketing decisions by considering consumers' wants, the company's requirements, consumers' long-run interests and society's long-run interests.

Following the principle of **societal marketing**, an enlightened company makes marketing decisions by considering consumers' wants and long-run interests, the company's requirements and society's long-run interests. The company is aware that neglecting consumer and societal long-term interests is a disservice to consumers and society. In many cases customer needs, customer wants and customer long-run interests are the same things, and customers are the best judges of what is good for them. However, customers do not invariably choose to do what's good for them. People want to eat fatty food, which is bad for their health; some people want to smoke cigarettes knowing that smoking can kill them and damage the environment for others; many enjoy drinking alcohol despite its ill effects. To control some of the potential evils of marketing, there has to be access to the media for the counter-argument – against smoking, against fatty foods, against alcohol. There is also a need for regulation – self if not statutory – to check unsavoury demand.

A second problem is that what consumers want is sometimes at odds with societal welfare. If marketing's job is to fulfil customers' wants, unsavoury desires leave marketers with a dilemma. Consumers want the convenience and prestige of hardwood window frames, doors and furniture, but society would also like to keep the Amazon rainforest; consumers want the comfort of central heating and air-conditioning, yet we need to conserve energy; the growing number of cars on the road, not least a fast-rising source of carbon emissions, overwhelm the benefits of improved fuel efficiency, but few bother to reduce car ownership per household. Marketing has to be more alert to the inconsistencies between consumer wants and society's welfare. Where there is insufficient drive from within the consumer movement and consumers' own sense of responsibility, marketers would do better to control or regulate their own behaviour in providing undesirable goods or services for society at large. If not, legislation is likely to do that for them.

Desirable products—
Products that give both high immediate satisfaction and high long-run benefits.

Pleasing products—
Products that give high immediate satisfaction but may hurt consumers in the long run.

Salutary products—Products that have low appeal but may benefit consumers in the long run.

Deficient products—
Products that have neither immediate appeal nor long-term benefits.

A sociately oriented marketer wants to design products that are not only pleasing but also beneficial. The difference is shown in Figure 5.3. Products can be classified according to their degree of immediate consumer satisfaction and long-run consumer benefit. **Desirable products** such as a tasty and nutritious breakfast food give both high immediate satisfaction and high long-run benefits. **Pleasing products** give high immediate satisfaction, but may hurt consumers in the long run. Examples are indulgence goods like confectionery, alcohol and cigarettes. **Salutary products** have low appeal, but benefit consumers in the long run, for instance seat belts and airbags in cars. Finally, **deficient products**, such as bad-tasting and ineffective medicines, have neither immediate appeal nor long-run benefits.

Examples of desirable products abound. Philips Lighting's Earth Light compact fluorescent light bulb provides good lighting while giving long life and energy savings. Maytag's front-loading Neptune washer provides superior cleaning along with water savings and energy

Figure 5.3 Societal classification of new products

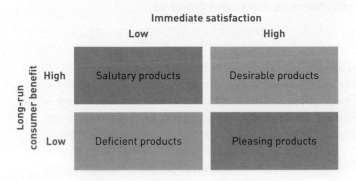

efficiency. And the international office furniture maker Herman Miller has won numerous awards for its ecologically friendly products and business practices: its Avian office chair, for example, has the lowest possible environmental impact and is 100 per cent recyclable.

Companies should try to turn all of their products into desirable products. The challenge posed by pleasing products is that they sell very well, but may end up hurting the consumer. The product opportunity, therefore, is to add long-run benefits without reducing the product's pleasing qualities. The challenge posed by salutary products is to add some pleasing qualities so that they will become more desirable in the consumers' minds. For example, synthetic fats and fat substitutes, such as NutraSweet's Simplesse and P&G's Olese, improve the appeal of low-calorie and low-fat foods.

Marketing ethics

Ethics, in the broadest sense of the word, is rising to the top of the corporate agenda. Scarcely a week goes by without a leading company accused, rightly or wrongly, of unethical business practices, whether it is Ahold's fraudulent accounting practices, Schering-Plough's promotion of drugs for uses not approved by regulators, or Boeing, the NYSE and the US mutual fund industry defiance of trading rules to enable big investors to profit at the expense of small ones.[27]

However far from reality the accusations of manufacturers' unethical business practices are, companies under attack risk tarnishing their reputation. And those found guilty of wrongdoing face hefty legal penalties, as in the recent cases of Swiss and German companies that were sued for Holocaust compensation and the world's largest vitamin companies for price-fixing. High-publicity scandals, which made international news, such as the case of Union Carbide's plant in Bhopal, India, which negligently released toxic fumes, killing 25,000 people, serve to remind society of the pressing imperatives for corporations to act in an ethical manner.

Conscientious marketers, however, face many moral dilemmas. The best thing to do is often unclear. Because not all managers have fine moral sensitivity, companies need to develop *corporate marketing ethics policies* – broad guidelines that everyone in the organisation must follow. They cover distributor relations, advertising standards, customer service, pricing, product development and general ethical standards.

The finest guidelines cannot resolve all the difficult ethical situations the marketer faces. However, managers need a set of principles that will help them figure out the moral importance of each situation and decide how far they can go in good conscience.

But *what* principle should guide companies and marketing managers on issues of ethics and social responsibility? One philosophy is that such issues are decided by the free market and legal system. Under this principle, companies and their managers are not responsible for making moral judgements. Companies can in good conscience do whatever the system allows.

A second philosophy puts responsibility not in the system, but in the hands of individual companies and managers. This more *enlightened philosophy* suggests that a company should have a 'social conscience'. Companies and managers should apply high standards of ethics and morality when making corporate decisions, regardless of 'what the system allows'. They must work out a philosophy of socially responsible and ethical behaviour. Consistent with the societal marketing concept, each manager must look beyond what is legal and allowed, and develop standards based on personal integrity, corporate conscience and long-run consumer welfare. A clear and responsible philosophy will help the marketing manager deal with the many knotty questions posed by marketing and other human activities.

In searching for ethical standards for marketing, marketing managers may also draw upon postmodernist thinking and philosophies that date back well beyond marketing itself. Marketing Insights 5.2 introduces some of this.[28]

As with environmentalism, the issue of ethics provides special challenges for international marketers. Business standards and practices vary a great deal from one country to the next.

marketing insights

5.2 From Plato's *Republic* to supermarket slavery

There is good reason to search a long way back for the ethics to guide marketing. As the British philosopher Alfred North Whitehead (1861–1947) commented, 'all Western philosophy is really no more than a footnote to Plato's (428–354 BC) great work *The Republic*'. If that were true, our thinking on 'marketing ethics' is little more than a smudge on that footnote.

The ancients were also practical, as Plato's student explained:

> Ethics is a rough and ready business determined by ordinary practical men of common sense, not by inbred ascetic 'experts' with their heads in a remote and austere world.
>
> Aristotle (384–322 BC)

Thinking's the thing

A lot of thinking went on in ancient Athens, a city state of about 400,000 people. Socrates (469–399 BC) thought that the most important thing about human beings is that they ask questions. He also thought that real moral knowledge existed and was worth pursuing. He did not think morality could be tough, but said that it was more than just obeying the law. The newly democratic Athenians did not like this questioning of state morality, so they condemned him to death by poisoning.

Good for the state and good for you too

Plato thought that Athens' experiments with democracy were a shambles and left town. He believed in moral absolutes that were separate from the more sordid world. This led him to idealise regimes where right and wrong were well defined. He thought militaristic and disciplined Sparta was a much better place than freethinking Athens and that people should do what is good for the state. Lots of leaders have tried this and very nasty it is too.

Choosing the happy medium

Aristotle rejected his teachers' concern for absolute truths, suggesting that people take a middle road and learn how to behave from experience. People learn to become good citizens, and from that achieve contentment. Well, most people! And how about being a good citizen of a gang of hooligans?

It was a long time before Western philosophy recovered from these Greeks, but the Renaissance got things going again. Machiavelli was born in another city state: Florence.

He may be dung, but at least he's our dung

Machiavelli (1469–1527) was an observer rather than a philosopher. After he saw what succeeded, he recognised that politics and morality mix badly. This is a convenient view for business leaders who think there should be two sets of moral standards: one for public life and one for private life. In political and business life it is necessary to be pragmatic and prudent – in other words, unethical – while retaining a different private ethic. As recent politicians have found, life does not always divide so easily.

Solitary, poor, nasty, brutish and short

The English Royalist Hobbes (1588–1678) is even more depressing than Machiavelli. People are awful and are prevented from degenerating into our natural brutish behaviour only by realising that everyone behaving that way would make life unbearable. People therefore establish a 'social contract' (which parents call 'bringing up') that has to be enforced by a neutral third party (government contract). Franco-Swiss Rousseau (1712–78) had the opposite view that humanity is essentially good, but is corrupted by society to want things like smart clothes, carriages and Nike trainers.

Sum happiness

English Utilitarians Bentham (1748–1832) and Mill (1806–73) invented a form of moral calculus. Bentham thought his country's laws were in a mess because they lacked a scientific foundation. He saw human beings as pleasure–pain machines, so he suggested that law makers should balance the sum of the pain and pleasure to achieve 'the greatest happiness of the greatest number'. This has two consequences: means justifying ends, and problems for minority groups. Mills worried about this 'tyranny of the majority'. He preferred talking about happiness rather than pleasure, tolerated individual lifestyles and thought that the 'happiness sums' varied and were for individuals as well as law makers.

Bah, happiness

Kant (1724–1804) had little time for happiness. The German idealist's ethics had categorical imperatives. He believed that a moral action was one done out of a sense

5.2...

...5.2

of duty. Ethics was about finding out our duties and living by them. Kant deduced a 'universality test' to find the compulsory rules. He asked people to imagine what it would be like if everybody did what they themselves wanted to do. Using this mind model, we deduce that if people sold shoddy goods habitually, life would be chaotic and, therefore, people have a duty not to sell shoddy goods.

And justice for all

The American John Rawls (1921–2002) has greatly influenced modern liberal thinking. He has a mind model based on imagining a group of people brought together with no knowledge of what place they will have in society. They have to invent a series of rules that will make their community just and fair. Then they have to live in it.

Don't know; can't know

This rationalist claim to understanding 'truths' started being undermined by Scotsman David Hume (1711–76). His 'meta-ethics' does not offer any advice, but recognises an 'is–ought gap' between what we experience (is) and the conclusion we try to draw from that (ought). Even though we know that bull bars on cars kill children (is), we can only produce a false argument that they should not be sold (ought). Developing similar insights, it follows that any moral argument between people is 'utterly futile, unsolvable and irrational' (A.J. Ayers, 1910–89).

The age of unreason

Postmodernists have pursued this ethical scepticism to new levels. Reason fails because of its dependence on language. What passed as reason in the past has caused so much human suffering. This level of ethical uncertainty is not new; it is close to the Sophist views that Plato argued against. Postmodernists despair at the society they see coming: a kaleidoscope of consumerist images that hypnotise citizens into accepting the morality of capitalism; where individual morality ceases to exist, where all that remains is supermarket slavery and where the only choice is by consumers between products – marketing.

Meanwhile Alisdair MacIntyre looks back to the Aristotelian idea that we should concentrate less on the individual and more on people and what is good for the society.

SOURCES: J. Ackrill, *Aristotle and the Philosophers* (Oxford, 1981); G. Kerner, *Three Philosophical Moralists* (Oxford, 1990); A. MacIntyre, *A Short History of Ethics* (Routledge, 1987); D. Robinson and C. Garratt, *Ethics for Beginners* (Icon, 1996); B. Russell, *A History of Western Philosophy* (Oxford, 1945); P. Singer, *Practical Ethics* (Oxford, 1993); Lynn Sharp Paine, *Value Shift* (McGraw-Hill, 2003).

Imagine you are trying to win a big public contract in a developing country. The minister in charge makes unmistakable references to the disgracefully low pay of local civil officials and the benefits his own children would enjoy if they could study abroad. The cost of providing this (concealed as a 'scholarship' paid for by your company) is minute compared with the value of the contract. Your competitors, given the chance, would assuredly find the money. Do you pull out, or pay up?

Most businesspeople in such situations find that their scruples are soon swallowed. So do most governments. Germany is one of several European countries where bribes paid abroad are tax-deductible (although the tax office may want proof that the person paid is not liable for German income tax). The United States is harsher – under the Foreign Corrupt Practices Act, executives can face jail for paying bribes. But it is hard to prove; and many firms may get third-party consultancies to do their bribing for them. So, across the globe, national cultures naturally impose different standards of behaviour on individuals and organisations. In the European Union, each market sector in each country is still characterised by a mixture of accepted commercial practices, codes of practice and formalised legislation. What is considered an acceptable practice in one country may be illegal in another. True, the EU seeks to move towards a pan-European business ethics policy and codes of conduct, but that day is still some way off.[29]

One recent study found that companies from some nations were much more likely to use bribes when seeking contracts in emerging-market nations. The most flagrant bribe-paying firms were from Russia and China, with Taiwan and South Korea close behind. The least corrupt were companies from Australia, Sweden, Switzerland, Austria and Canada.[30] The question arises as to whether a company must lower its ethical standards to compete effectively in countries with lower standards. In a recent study, two researchers posed this question to chief executives of large international companies and got a unanimous response: no.[31]

For the sake of all the company's stakeholders – customers, suppliers, employees, shareholders and the public – it is important to make a commitment to a common set of standards worldwide. Some Western firms have already done so. For example, the ethical code of jeans manufacturer Levi Strauss forbids bribes, whether or not prevalent or legal in the foreign country involved.

Many industrial and professional associations have suggested codes of ethics. Efforts have also been made to develop 'global' standards. One example is the Social Accountability standard called SA8000, launched in 1998 by an independent US-based agency, the Council on Economic Priorities. SA8000 verifies the ethical stance of businesses in the production and sourcing of goods from the developing countries. Businesses applying for the standard are accredited by SGS-ICS, the Swiss company that is the world's largest certification agency. Many companies are now adopting their own codes of ethics.[32] Companies have set up ethics committees and are also developing programmes, workshops and seminars to teach managers about important ethics issues and help them find the proper responses.[33] Further, more and more international companies have appointed high-level ethics officers to champion ethics issues and to help resolve problems and concerns facing employees.

Still, compliance rules, written codes and ethics training programmes do not guarantee ethical behaviour. It is not uncommon to find corporate pledges to work for the good of the company's shareholders, customers and staff. For example, the code of the Prudential Corporation, a life-insurance-to-property group, notes that 'in providing its business, the Prudential aims are to abide by the spirit of laws as well as their letter and to be a significant contributor to the development and well-being of the wider community in which we operate'. The guidelines are well meaning but too abstract to direct action when the interests of the company diverge sharply from those of its employees, customers or the local community. There have to be precise statements that spell out what employees must do in specific dilemmas, such as bribes and gifts, whether being offered or asked for. There should also be sanctions to enforce the code, so that ethical pledges are more than mere PR 'puff'.

Ethics and social responsibility require a total corporate commitment. They must be components of the overall corporate culture. Ethics programmes or seminars for employees help to imbue corporate ethics and codes of conduct among staff, while ethical and social audits may be used to monitor and evaluate business conduct and to use the lessons to guide both policy and behaviour:

> In the final analysis, 'ethical behaviour' must be an integral part of the organization, a way of life that is deeply ingrained in the collective corporate body. . . . In any business enterprise, ethical behaviour must be a tradition, a way of conducting one's affairs that is passed from generation to generation of employees at all levels of the organization. It is the responsibility of management, starting at the very top, to both set the example by personal conduct and create an environment that not only encourages and rewards ethical behaviour, but which also makes anything less totally unacceptable.[34]

The future holds many challenges and opportunities for marketing managers as they move into the twenty-first century. Technological advances in every area, from telecommunications information technology and the Internet to healthcare and entertainment, provide abundant marketing opportunities. However, forces in the socioeconomic, cultural and natural environments increase the limits under which marketing can be carried out. Companies that are able to create new customer value in a socially responsible way will have a world to conquer.

Summary

In this chapter, we have examined many important concepts involving marketing's sweeping impact on individual consumers, other businesses and society as a whole. Responsible marketers discover what consumers want and respond with the right products, priced to give good value to buyers and profit to the company. A marketing system should sense, serve and satisfy consumer needs and improve the quality of consumers' lives. In working to meet consumer needs, marketers may take some actions that are not to everyone's liking or benefit. Marketing managers should be aware of the main *criticisms of marketing*.

Marketing's *impact on individual consumer welfare* has been criticised for its *high prices*, *deceptive practices*, *high-pressure selling*, *shoddy or unsafe products*, *planned obsolescence* and *poor service to disadvantaged consumers*. Marketing's *impact on society* has been criticised for *creating false wants* and *too much materialism*, *too few social goods*, *cultural pollution* and *too much political power*. Critics have also criticised marketing's *impact on other businesses* for *harming competitors* and *reducing competition* through acquisitions, practices that create barriers to entry, and unfair competitive marketing practices.

Concerns about the marketing system have led to *citizen action movements*. *Consumerism* is an organised social movement intended to strengthen the rights and power of consumers relative to sellers. Alert marketers view it as an opportunity to serve consumers better by providing more consumer information, education and protection.

Environmentalism is an organised social movement seeking to minimise the harm done to the environment and quality of life by marketing practices. The first wave of modern environmentalism was driven by environmental groups and concerned consumers, whereas the second was driven by government, which passed laws and regulations governing practices impacting the environment. Moving into the twenty-first century, the first two environmentalism waves are merging into a third and stronger wave in which companies are accepting responsibility for doing no environmental harm. Companies now are adopting policies of environmental sustainability – developing strategies that both sustain the environment and produce profits for the company.

Many companies originally opposed these social movements and laws, but most of them now recognise a need for positive consumer information, education and protection. Some companies have followed a policy of enlightened marketing based on the principles of *consumer orientation*, *innovation*, *value creation*, *social mission* and *societal marketing*.

Increasingly, companies are responding to the need to provide company policies and guidelines to help their employees deal with questions of *marketing ethics*. Of course, even the best guidelines cannot resolve all the difficult ethical decisions that individuals and firms must make. However, there are some principles that marketers can choose among. One principle states that such issues should be decided by the free market and legal system. A second, and more enlightened, principle puts responsibility not in the system but in the hands of individual companies and managers. Each firm and marketing manager must work out a philosophy of socially responsible and ethical behaviour. Under the societal marketing concept, managers must look beyond what is legal and allowable and develop standards based on personal integrity, corporate conscience and long-term consumer welfare.

Discussing the issues

1. Marketing receives much criticism, some justified and much not. Which of the major criticisms of marketing discussed in the chapter do you think are most justified? Which are least justified? Explain.

2. You have been invited to appear along with an economist on a panel assessing marketing practices in the soft-drink industry. You are surprised when the economist opens the discussion with a long list of criticisms (focusing especially on the unnecessarily high marketing costs and deceptive promotional practices). Abandoning your prepared comments, you set out to defend marketing in general and the beverage industry in particular. How would you respond to the economist's attack?

3. Comment on the state of consumers' rights on the Internet and in e-commerce. Design a 'Bill of Rights' that would protect consumers while they shop for products and services on the Internet. Consider such issues as government regulation, ease and convenience of use, solicitation, privacy and cost-efficient commerce.

4. You are the marketing manager for a small firm that makes kitchen appliances. While conducting field tests, you discover a design flaw in one of your best-selling ovens that could potentially cause harm to a small number of consumers. However, a product recall is likely to bankrupt your company, leaving all of the employees (including you) jobless. What would you do?

5. The issue of ethics provides special challenges for international marketers as business standards and practices vary a great deal from one country to the next. Should a company adapt its ethical standards to compete effectively in countries with different standards? (Bribes, use of child labour, low wages, positive discrimination against female workers and members from ethnic minorities might be examples of values/practices which vary across countries/cultures in different corners of the globe and can be used to focus your discussion.)

Applying the concepts

1. Changes in consumer attitudes, especially the growth of consumerism and environment-alism, have led to more societal marketing – and to more marketing that is *supposedly* good for society, but is actually close to deception.

   ■ List three examples of marketing campaigns that you feel are genuine societal marketing. If possible, find examples of firm communications, including advertising or packaging that support these campaigns. You may also visit relevant websites of companies of your choice to gather more specific information on these campaigns.

   ■ Find three examples of deceptive or borderline imitations of societal marketing. How are you able to tell which campaigns are genuine and which are not?

   ■ What remedies, if any, would you recommend for this problem?

2. As a small child you were probably taught that 'it is better to give than to receive'. This advice is one of the cornerstones of philanthropy, including corporate philanthropy. Given the new environmentalism and social responsibility in Western societies today, explain what should be an organisation's view towards charitable giving. What are the marketing ramifications of an organisation's philanthropic activities? Many corporations support worthy causes and contribute generously to their communities. Check out the websites of one of the following or some other company of your choice and report on its philanthropic and socially responsible activities: Nestlé (www.nestlé.com), Johnson & Johnson (www.jnj.com), Nike (www.nikebiz.com), Coca-Cola (www.cocacola.com) and Prudential Life Insurance (www.prudential.com). How does philanthropy by corporations relate to the social criticisms of marketing?

References

1. Quentin Anderson, 'Inside track: In defence of the NSPCC. Viewpoint Quentin Anderson: The furore over the charity's allocation of funds rests on a misunderstanding of its long-term goals', *Financial Times* (14 December 2000), p. 19; NSPCC's website: www.nspcc.org.uk (February 2004).

2. See Richard Tomkins, 'Smoke signals out as cigarette adverts meet their match', *Financial Times* (9 February 2003), p. 3; Deborah L. Vence, 'Match game', *Marketing News* (11 November 2002), pp. 1, 11–12; and Neil Buckley, 'Philip Morris case brings threst of fresh tobacco suits', *Financial Times* (24 March 2003), p. 30; Gordon Fairclough, 'Study slams Philip Morris ads telling teens not to smoke – how a market researcher who dedicated years to cigarette sales came to create antismoking ads', *Wall Street Journal* (29 May 2002), p. B1.

3. Excerpts from Theodore Levitt, 'The morality(?) of advertising', *Harvard Business Review* (July–August 1970), pp. 84–92; Ben Abrahams, 'The ASA: older and wiser', *Marketing* (10 July 2000), p. 3.

4. Isabel Berwick, 'City watchdog warns of further mis-selling fines', *Financial Times* (5 December 2002), p. 3; Kate Burgess, 'Scandal to hit more sectors', *Financial Time. Money: Mis-selling* (20–21 September 2003), p. M29.

5. Karolyn Schuster, 'The dark side of nutrition', *Food Management* (June 1999), pp. 34–9.

6. Tobias Buck, 'Brussels gets teeth into food groups' "misleading" claims', *Financial Times* (1/2 February 2003), p. 7.

7. 'When quality control breaks down', *The European* (6–12 November 1997), p. 29. For more discussion on managing product recalls, see N. Craig Smith, Robert J. Thomas and John A. Quelch, 'A strategic approach to managing product recalls', *Harvard Business Review* (September–October 1996), pp. 102–12.

8. David Welch, 'Firestone: Is this brand beyond repair?', *Business Week* (11 June 2001), p. 48.

9. For a thought-provoking short case involving planned obsolescence, see James A. Heely and Roy L. Nersesian, 'The case of planned obsolescence', *Management Accounting* (February 1994), p. 67. Also see Joel Dreyfuss, 'Planned obsolescence is alive and well', *Fortune* (15 February 1999), p. 192.

10. James Twitchell, 'Two cheers for materialism', *The Wilson Quarterly* (Spring 1999), pp. 16–26; *Lead Us into Temptation: The triumph of American materialism* (New York: Columbia University Press, 1999); and *Living It Up: Our love affair with luxury* (New York: Columbia University Press, 2002).

11. Kim Clark, 'Real-World-O-Nomics: How to make traffic jams a thing of the past', *Fortune* (31 March 1997), p. 34; Roger Blitz, 'Congestion charge zone "is harming" business', *Financial Times* (14–15 February 2004), p. 3.

12. Gail Kemp, 'Commercial break: Should kids' TV ads be banned?', *Marketing Business* (September 1999), pp. 16–18; John Clare, 'Marketing's "material girls" aged only three', *The Daily Telegraph* (23 November 1999), p. 9; Martin Lindstrom and Patricia B. Seybold, *Brandchild* (Kogan Page, 2003); see also Jonathan Hall, 'Children and the money machine', *Financial Times FT Creative Business* (18 March 2003), p. 6.

13. Greg Winter, 'Hershey is put on the auction block', *New York Times* (26 July 2002), p. 5.

14. Dan Carney and Mike France, 'The Microsoft case: tying it all together', *Business Week* (3 December 2001), pp. 68–9; Richard Wolffe, 'Lawyers try to expand case against Microsoft', *Financial Times* (17/18 June 2000), p. 9; Deborah Hargreaves, 'European Commission to continue inquiry', *Financial Times* (9 June 2000), p. 11; Richard Wolffe and Fiona Harvey, 'Door left open for Microsoft talks', *Financial Times* (9 June 2000), p. 11; Richard Wolffe, Andrew Hill and Lesia Ruda Kewych, 'Judge rules against Microsoft', *Financial Times* (4 April 2000), p. 1; Steve Hamm, 'Microsoft's future', *Business Week* (19 January 1998), pp. 58–68; Ronald A. Cass, 'Microsoft, running scared', *The New York Times* (28 June 1999), p. 17.

15. 'Going for Coke', *The Economist* (14 August 1999), pp. 55–6; 'Coke is hit again', *The Economist* (24 July 1999), pp. 70–1.

16. For more details, see Paul N. Bloom and Stephen A. Greyser, 'The maturing of consumerism', *Harvard Business Review* (November–December 1981), pp. 130–9; Douglas A. Harbrecht, 'The second coming of Ralph Nader', *Business Week* (6 March 1989), p. 28; George S. Day and David A. Aaker, 'A guide to consumerism', *Marketing Management* (Spring 1997), pp. 44–8; Benet Middleton, 'Consumerism: a pragmatic ideology', *Consumer Policy Review* (November/December 1998), pp. 213–7; Colin Brown, 'Consumer activism in Europe', *Consumer Policy Review*, **8**, 6 (1998), pp. 209–12.

17. Michael Lindemann, 'Green light begins to flash for recyclable cars in Germany', *Financial Times* (3 August 1994), p. 2; Udo Mildenberger and Anshuman Khare, 'Planning for an environmentally-friendly car', *Technovation*, **20**, 4 (2000), pp. 205–14.

18. Adapted from 'Many nappy returns', *The Economist* (23 November 2003), p. 56.

19. Peter M. Senge, Goran Carstedt and Patrick L. Porter, 'Innovating our way to the next industrial revolution', *MIT Sloan Management Review* (Winter 2001), pp. 24–38.

20. Based on information from 'BP Launches World's Greenest Service Station', BP press release, 25 April 2002, accessed online at www.bp.com/centres/press/media_resources/press_release/index.asp; and www.bp.com/centres/press/hornchurch/index.asp, September 2002.

21. Michael E. Porter and Claas van der Linde, 'Green and competitive: ending the stalemate', *Harvard Business Review* (September–October 1995), pp. 120–34. See also Andrea Prothero,

'Green marketing: the "fad" that won't slip away', *Journal of Marketing Management*, **14**, 6 (1998), pp. 507–12.

22. See 'Environment, Health, and Safety 2000 Progress Report', Xerox Corporation, accessed online at http://www2.xerox.com/downloads/ehs2000pdf; Stuart L. Hart, 'Beyond greening: strategies for a sustainable world', *Harvard Business Review* (January–February 1997), pp. 66–76; and Jacquelyn Ottman, 'Environmental winners show sustainable strategies', *Marketing News* (27 April 1998), p. 6.

23. Lynelle Preston, 'Sustainability at Hewlett-Packard: from theory to practice', *California Management Review* (Spring 2001), pp. 26–36.

24. 'EMAS-Newsletter: The Eco-Management and Audit Scheme', June 2002, accessed online at http://europa.eu.int/comm/environment/emas; Michelle Conlin and Paul Raeburn, 'Industrial evolution', *Business Week* (8 April 2002), pp. 70–2; Lars K. Hallstrom, 'Industry versus ecology: environment in the New Europe', *Futures* (February 1999), pp. 25–38; Andreas Diekmann and Axel Frannzen, 'The wealth of nations and environmental concern', *Environment and Behavior* (July 1999), pp. 540–9; John Audley, *Green Politics and Global Trade: NAFTA and the future of environmental politics* (Georgetown University Press, 1997).

25. For more details on the 'green' debate, see R. Schuster, *Environmentally Oriented Consumer Behaviour in Europe* (Hamburg: Kovac, 1992); R. Worcester, *Public and Elite Attitudes to Environmental Issues* (London: MORI, 1993); Ian Hamilton Fazey, 'Paints and the environment', survey, *Financial Times* (8 April 1994); Stavros P. Kalafatis, Michael Pollard, Robert East and Markos H. Tsogas, 'Green marketing and Azjen's theory of planned behaviour: a cross-market examination', *Journal of Consumer Marketing*, **16**, 5 (1999), pp. 441–60.

26. Scandic Hotel example and quotes taken from Nathan Yates, 'Now recycle your room', *The European Magazine* (24–30 April 1997), p. 13; UNEP sustainable consumption campaign based on Vanessa Houlder, 'Guilt is no solution', *Financial Times* (16 October 2003), p. 5.

27. Christopher Bowe, 'Schering-Plough might face charges', *Financial Times Money & Business* (31 May/1 June 2003), p. M5; Simon London, 'Climate change: corporate scandals push the need for ethical standards to the top of the business agenda', *Financial Times* (31 December 2003), p. 13.

28. 'Who will listen to Mr Clean?', *The Economist* (2 August 1997), p. 58.

29. See Susan Norgan, *Marketing Management: A European perspective* (Wokingham, Berks: Addison-Wesley, 1994), p. 49; David Murphy, 'Cross-border conflicts', *Marketing* (11 February 1999), pp. 30–3.

30. Barbara Crossette, 'Russia and China top business bribers', *New York Times* (17 May 2002), p. A10.

31. John F. Magee and P. Ranganath Nayak, 'Leaders' perspectives on business ethics', *Prizm* (Arthur D. Little, Inc., Cambridge, MA, first quarter, 1994), pp. 65–77; see also Kumar C. Rallapali, 'A paradigm for development and promulgation of a global code of marketing ethics', *Journal of Business Ethics* (January 1999), pp. 125–37.

32. Simon Buckby, 'Standard to verify business ethics launched', *Financial Times* (11 June 1998), p. 9; Bodo Schlegelmilch, 'A review of marketing ethics: an international perspective', *International Marketing Review*, **16**, 3 (1999), pp. 1–7.

33. 'Good takes on greed', *The Economist* (17 February 1990), pp. 87–9; Patrick Maclagan, 'Education and development for corporate ethics: an overview', *Industrial and Commercial Training*, **26**, 4 (1994), pp. 3–7.

34. From 'Ethics as a practical matter', a message from David R. Whitman, chairman of the board of Whirlpool Corporation, as reprinted in Ricky E. Griffin and Ronald J. Ebert, *Business* (Englewood Cliffs, NJ: Prentice Hall, 1989), pp. 578–9. For more discussion, see Thomas Donaldson, 'Values in tension', *Harvard Business Review* (September–October 1996), pp. 48–62.

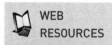

WEB RESOURCES

For additional classic case studies and Internet exercises, visit www.pearsoned.co.uk/kotler

Concluding concept 5
Nestlé: singled out again and again

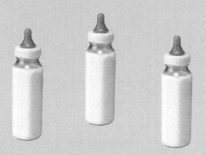

> During the first few months, the mother's milk will always be the most natural nutriment, and every mother able to do so, should herself suckle her children.
>
> Henri Nestlé, 1869

The corporate affairs department at Nestlé UK's headquarters were bracing themselves for another burst of adverse publicity. At the forthcoming General Synod of the Church of England a motion would call for a continued ban on Nescafé by the Church. They also wanted the Church Commissioners to disinvest their £1.1m (€1.8m) in Nestlé. The Church's much publicised boycott of Nescafé first occurred, amid much ridicule, in 1991, as a protest against the use of breast milk substitutes in the Third World countries. In the aftermath of the 1991 vote, Nescafé claimed that its sales increased, although many churchgoers said they stopped using the brand-leading coffee. The new protest would be one of many the company had faced from Baby Food Action (BFA) protesters over decades although, according to Nestlé, the protesters' complaints had no foundation.

Nestlé SA, whose headquarters are in Vevey, Switzerland, is the world's largest food company, with annual sales of CHF89 billion (€59bn), 508 factories and 254,200 employees worldwide in 2002. Henri Nestlé invented manufactured baby food 'to save a child's life' and the company have been suppliers ever since. Then, in the late 1970s and early 1980s, Nestlé came under heavy fire from activists who charged the company with encouraging Third World mothers to give up breast feeding and use a company-prepared formula. In 1974 the British charity War on Want published a pamphlet, *The Baby Killer*, that criticised Unigate and Nestlé's ill-advised marketing efforts in Africa. While War on Want criticised the entire infant formula industry, the German-based Third World Action Group issued a 'translation' of the original pamphlet retitled *Nestlé Kills Babies*, which singled out the company for 'unethical and immoral behaviour'. The pamphlets generated much publicity. Enraged at the protest, Nestlé sued the activists for defamation. The two-year case kept media attention on the issue. 'We won the legal case, but it

was a public-relations disaster', commented a Nestlé executive.

In 1977, two American social-interest groups, the Interfaith Center on Corporate Responsibility and the Infant Formula Action Coalition (INFACT), spearheaded a worldwide boycott against Nestlé. The campaign continued despite the fact that many organisations rejected the boycott. The US United Methodist Church concluded that the activists were guilty of 'substantial and sometimes gross misrepresentation', of 'inflammatory rhetoric', and of using 'wildly exaggerated figures'. The boycott was called off in 1984 when the activists accepted that the company was complying with an infant formula marketing code adopted by the World Health Organisation (WHO). Since then, church, university, local government and other action groups periodically rediscover the controversy and create publicity by calling for a boycott.

> 'Every day 4,000 babies die from unsafe bottle feeding', explain BMA.

The main accusation now is that Nestlé's use of promotions persuaded hundreds of thousands of poverty-stricken, poorly educated mothers that formula feeding was better for their children. 'Every day 4,000 babies die from unsafe bottle feeding', explain BMA. They continue, 'Donations of infant formula can do more harm than good.' Their concern is the donation of free or low-cost supplies of infant formula to maternity wards and hospitals in developing countries. Formula feeding is usually an unwise practice in such countries because of poor living conditions and habits; people cannot or do not clean bottles properly and often mix formula with impure water. Income level does not permit many families to buy sufficient quantities of formula. The protesters hit out at industry practices generally but keep Nestlé as their prime target:

- Promotional baby booklets ignoring or de-emphasising breast feeding.
- Misleading advertising encouraging mothers to bottle-feed their babies and showing breast feeding to be old-fashioned and inconvenient.
- Gifts and samples inducing mothers to bottle feed their infants.

- Posters and pamphlets in hospitals.
- Endorsements of bottle feeding by milk nurses.
- Formula so expensive that poor customers dilute to non-nutritious levels.

A WHO code eliminates all promotional efforts, requiring companies to serve primarily as passive 'order takers'. It prohibits advertising, samples and direct contact with consumers. Contacts with professionals (such as doctors) occur only if professionals seek such contact. Manufacturers can package products with some form of visual corporate identity, but they cannot picture babies. The WHO code effectively allows almost no marketing. However, the code contains only *recommended* guidelines. They become *mandatory* only if individual governments adopt national codes through their own regulatory mechanisms.

WHO allows the donation of free or low-cost supplies of infant formulas for infants who cannot be breast-fed. However, the International Association of Infant Food Manufacturers (IFM) is working with WHO and UNICEF to secure country-by-country agreements with countries to end free and low-cost supplies.

Nestlé itself has a policy on low-cost supplies in developing countries, as follows:

- Where there is government agreement, Nestlé will strictly apply the terms of that agreement.
- Where there is no agreement Nestlé, in cooperation with others, will be active in trying to secure early government action.
- Where other companies break an agreement, Nestlé will work with IFM and governments to stop the breach.
- Nestlé will take disciplinary measures against any Nestlé personnel or distributors who deliberately violate Nestlé policy.

Given the repeated public relations problems that Nestlé faces, why does it not take unilateral action in ending free supplies? Since the Third World infant formula market is so small compared with Nestlé's worldwide interests, why bother with it? Part of the answer is in Henri Nestlé's desire 'to save a child's life'. The European Commission's directive on baby food concludes that infant formula is 'the only processed foodstuff that wholly satisfies the nutritional requirements of infants' first four to six months of life'.

Few mothers in countries with very high infant mortality rates use anything other than breast milk. However, Kenya is probably typical of what happens when mothers do supplement breast milk with something else:

- 33 per cent use uji, a local food made from maize;
- 33 per cent use cow's milk;
- 28 per cent use water;
- 14 per cent use glucose;
- 11 per cent use milk powder, of which some is infant formula;
- 3 per cent use tea.

A study in the Ivory Coast shows the sort of problems that arise when Nestlé withdraws unilaterally. Other companies replaced the supplies to the affluent private nurseries, but supplies for mothers in need collapsed. As a result the main hospital was not able to 'afford to buy enough to feed abandoned babies or those whose mothers are ill'.

Questions

1. Was and is Nestlé's and the other IFM members' marketing of infant formula 'unethical and immoral'?
2. Is it the case that ethical standards should be the responsibility of organisations such as WHO and UNESCO, and that the sole responsibility of firms is to work within the bounds set?
3. Is Nestlé just unlucky or did its actions precipitate its being singled out by activists? Is the activists' focus on Nestlé unjust and itself dangerous? What accounts for Nestlé's continuing in the infant formula market despite the protests?
4. Did Nestlé benefit from confronting the activists directly in court and winning? Should firms ever confront activists directly? What other forms of action are available to the company? Should firms withdraw from legitimate markets because of the justified or unjustified actions of pressure groups?
5. The WHO code is a recommendation to government. Is it Nestlé's responsibility to operate according to the national legislation of any given country, or to follow WHO's recommendations to that country? Do international bodies setting international standards, such as WHO and UNICEF, have a moral responsibility to make those standards clearly understood by all parties and to demand action by national governments to enact them?
6. How should Nestlé respond to the threats from the General Synod? Since Nestlé claimed sales increased after the Nescafé boycott in 1991, should it just ignore the problem?

SOURCES: John Sparks, 'The Nestlé controversy – anatomy of a boycott', Public Policy Education Fund, Inc. (June 1981); European Commission, Commission Directive on Infant Formula and Follow-on Formula, 91/321/EEC; UNICEF, *The State of the World's Children* (1992); RBL, *Survey of Baby Feeding in Kenya* (1992); Nestlé, *Nestlé and Baby Milk* (1994); Andrew Brown, 'Synod votes to end Nestlé boycott after passionate debate', *The Times* (12 July 1994); World Health Assembly Resolution 54.2 'Infant and young child nutrition' (2001); Nestle.com (February 2004), competing websites babymilk.nestle.com (2003) and babymilkaction.org (February 2004).

BELGIUM
Festive treat

UK
Festive treat

SWEDEN
Festive treat

Never underestimate the importance of local knowledge.

Mince pies or rice pudding at
Christmas? It's just something you know
when you're a local.

At HSBC, we have banks in more
countries than anyone else. And each one
is staffed by local people.

We have offices in 79 countries and
territories; Europe, Asia-Pacific, the
Americas, the Middle East, and Africa.

Being local enables them to offer
insights into financial opportunities and
create service initiatives that would
never occur to an outsider.

It means our customers get the kind
of local knowledge and personal service
that you'd expect of a local bank.

And a level of global knowledge and
widely sourced expertise that you wouldn't.

HSBC
The world's local bank

The world is a stage, but the play
is badly cast.

OSCAR WILDE

The global marketplace

Chapter objectives

After reading this chapter, you should be able to:

- Discuss how the international trade system, economic, political–legal and cultural environments affect a company's international marketing decisions.
- Describe three key approaches to entering international markets.
- Explain how companies adapt their marketing mixes for international markets.
- Distinguish between the three major forms of international marketing organisation.

Mini Contents List

◀ SOURCE: HSBC Holdings Plc.
Agency: Lowe Worldwide
Photographer: Richard Pullar.

Prelude case Jägermeister: Schnapps goes to college

Hasso Kaempfe and his team at Jägermeister face the unenviable task of surviving as a medium-sized family-owned outfit, in a difficult economic environment, with the help of a single product that is hardly a 'must-have'. Yet Mr Kaempfe has no reason to regret his decision, five years ago, to leave his job on the board of Tchibo, the Hamburg-based coffee roasting empire, and head to the town of Wolfenbüttel to take on the task of managing Jägermeister, the liqueur maker. At the very least, the job has provided the pleasant challenge of selling a product whose image has traditionally been more closely associated with hunting and grandmothers' after-dinner tipples than the up-and-coming, free-spending group most beverages companies like to woo. Jägermeister, which is sold in chunky green bottles emblazoned with a stag, is made to a closely guarded recipe using 56 herbs and spices. Its tangy, herbal taste and brown colour are more reminiscent of cough syrup than the fashionable alcopops and flavoured vodkas currently in vogue in student bars and trendy restaurants across the world. Yet the Jägermeister name is now better known than ever before in the company's 125-year history.

Mr Kaempfe's approach has differed from that generally seen in the industry. Rather than trying to enforce a single, blanket image across all its geographical markets, the company has adapted the Jägermeister brand and marketing strategy for each country. Most companies try to market products with a single image that makes them instantly recognisable anywhere in the world. 'Becks, Campari, Sol, Corona, Jack Daniels, all have a single global image carefully nurtured and pushed by their respective owners. Country-specific advertising exists, but the overall image is the same', says Mr Kaempfe. This approach is not without merits, he says, but impractical for a niche company such as Jägermeister.

Rather than fearing that diversity could dilute brand recognition, Mr Kaempfe insists it is a vital factor in Jägermeister's success and future survival in the face of shifting tastes. 'We have slightly different images in our various key markets. This hedges the risk we have as a single-product company and means we see no need to diversify by buying in other brands', he says.

Fifty-eight per cent of sales now go abroad (up from 46 per cent in 1998), and group sales in 2002 have risen to €222 m (£153 m) last year from DM365 m (€182 m) in 1998. Nearly 30 per cent goes to the US, despite a name that hardly trips off the tongue and the fact that the US has little tradition of drinking schnapps. Jägermeister's initial success in the US is based on its positioning in bars in the late 1990s. Jägermeister managed to

> Jägermeister's tangy, herbal taste and brown colour are more reminiscent of cough syrup than fashionable alcopops and flavoured vodkas.

build on its popularity via product promotions and sponsorship. As a result, any college student in the US is likely to know the drink as something they have got drunk on at least once in the past year. Jägermeister spends no money on media advertising in the US. Instead, 'Jägerettes' girls dispense samples with a touch of raunchiness and its garish orange banners and T-shirts are common at US music events. In this way, it has become a 'college dorm joy-juice' with Jack Daniels and José Cuervo as its main competitors.

Ironically, few Europeans are aware that Jägermeister has attained cult status among US students, because their image of the liqueur is very different. In Italy, Jägermeister's second biggest export market, the drink is considered an upmarket, elegant version of local digestivi (after-dinner drinks) such as Ramazzotti and Averna, rather than the stuff of wild college parties. In the UK, Jägermeister is slowly gaining a foothold by targeting young adults in their twenties. Germans, meanwhile, continue to see Jägermeister as a traditional schnapps, albeit one with an increasingly cool image. The company uses Jägerettes, promotion activities and give-aways in its home country but it focuses less on universities and music sponsorship. It can also afford classic media advertising. Backed by a cheeky campaign featuring two talking wall-mounted stags, Jägermeister has undergone one of the most successful brand rejuvenations ever seen in Germany.

Beyond that, Mr Kaempfe plans to promote the brand in central and eastern Europe, Spain and Finland and, longer term, in Australia and Brazil. Judging by the speed of its growth over the past five to six years, those countries may not have long to wait. 'But we can afford to be patient', says Mr Kaempfe. 'That is one of the advantages about being family-owned; we do not constantly have to produce rapid growth for each quarterly report.'[1]

Questions

You should attempt these questions only after completing your reading of this chapter.

1. What are the key factors that Jägermeister should consider when deciding on which new country-markets to enter?
2. What modes of market entry might Jägermeister consider when expanding into new foreign markets? Assess their merits and disadvantages.
3. What constitutes an effective global marketing programme for a company such as Jägermeister?

SOURCE: Bettina Wassener, 'Schnapps goes to college', *Financial Times* (4 September 2003), p. 15.

Introduction

With faster communication, transportation and financial flows, the world is rapidly shrinking. Brands or products originating from one country – Gucci handbags, Mont Blanc pens, German BMWs, Japanese sushi, McDonald's hamburgers – are finding enthusiastic acceptance in others.

International trade is booming. Since 1969, the number of multinational corporations in the world's 14 richest countries has more than tripled from 7,000 to 24,000. These companies control one-third of all private-sector assets and enjoy world sales of $6 trillion (€4.96 trillion). Imports of goods and services now account for 24 per cent of gross domestic product worldwide, double that of 40 years ago. World trade now accounts for 29 per cent of world GDP, a 10 per cent increase since 1990.[2] The US exported more than any other single country, with foreign sales of $695 bn (€781 bn) or 12.4 per cent of world exports in 1999. However, the EU, with exports of nearly €800 bn in 1999, took a bigger share (18.9 per cent) of world trade.[3] Increasingly, every firm, large or small, faces global marketing issues.

Because of its special importance, we will focus exclusively on this topic in this chapter. We will address the key decisions marketers make in going global: analysing the global environment; deciding whether or not to go international; deciding which markets to enter and how to enter; deciding the global marketing programme; and determining the global marketing organisation.

Global marketing in the twenty-first century

Companies pay little attention to international trade when the home market is big and teeming with opportunities. The home market is also much safer. Managers do not need to learn other languages, deal with strange and changing currencies, face political and legal uncertainties or adapt their products to different customer needs and expectations.

Today, however, the situation is different. The business environment is changing and firms cannot afford to ignore international markets. Countries around the world increasingly rely on each other's goods and services. And companies once protected from foreign competition now have to adopt a more global outlook in their approach to business.

True, many companies have been carrying on international activities for decades. Across Europe and North America, names such as Toyota, Sony, Panasonic and Toshiba have become household words in the same way as Kodak, McDonald's, Gillette, Nestlé, Nokia, Mercedes and IKEA are familiar names to most consumers in Asian countries like Japan, Singapore and Thailand. But today global competition is intensifying. Foreign firms are expanding aggressively into new international markets and home markets are no longer as rich in opportunity. Local companies that never thought about foreign competitors suddenly find these competitors in their own backyards. The firm that stays at home to play it safe not only misses the opportunity to enter other markets, but also risks losing its home market.

Although some nations and companies would like to stem the tide of foreign imports through protectionism, in the long run this would only raise the cost of living and protect inefficient domestic firms. The better way for companies to compete is to improve their products continuously at home and expand into foreign markets.

Companies that delay taking steps towards internationalising risk being shut out of growing markets around the world. Firms that stay at home to play it safe may not only lose their chances to enter other markets, but also risk losing their sales to companies from neighbouring countries who have invaded their home markets.

Ironically, although the need for companies to go abroad is greater today than in the past, so are the risks. Companies that go global confront several major problems. High debt, inflation and unemployment in many countries have resulted in highly unstable governments and currencies, which limit trade and expose foreign firms to many risks. Governments are placing more regulations on foreign firms, such as requiring joint ownership with local partners, mandating the hiring of foreign nationals, and limiting profits that can be taken from the country. Moreover, some governments often impose high tariffs or trade barriers in order to protect their own industries. Finally, corruption is an increasing problem – officials in several countries often award business not to the best bidder, but to the highest briber.

Global industry—An industry in which the strategic positions of competitors in given geographic or national markets are affected by their overall global positions.

Still, companies selling in global industries have no choice but to internationalise their operations and strive to be a global firm. A **global industry** is one in which the strategic positions of competitors in given geographic or national markets are affected by their overall global positions. A **global firm** is one that, by operating in more than one country, gains research and development, production, marketing and financial advantages that are not available to purely domestic competitors. The global company sees the world as one market. It minimises the importance of national boundaries, and raises capital, obtains materials and components, and manufactures and markets its goods wherever it can do the best job. For example, Ford's 'world truck' sports a cab made in Europe and a chassis built in North America. It is assembled in Brazil and imported to the United States for sale. Thus global firms gain advantages by planning, operating and coordinating their activities on a worldwide basis. These gains are a key reason behind the recent global restructuring programmes undertaken by leading German car producers BMW and Mercedes-Benz. **Global marketing** is concerned with integrating or standardising marketing actions across a number of geographic markets. This does not rule out adaptation of the marketing mix to individual countries, but suggests that firms, where possible, ignore traditional market boundaries and capitalise on similarities between markets to build competitive advantage.

Global firm—A firm that, by operating in more than one country, gains R&D, production, marketing and financial advantages that are not available to purely domestic competitors.

Global marketing— Marketing that is concerned with integrating or standardising marketing actions across different geographic markets.

Because firms around the world are globalising at a rapid rate, domestic firms in global industries must act quickly before the window closes. This does not mean that small and medium-sized firms must operate in a dozen countries to succeed. These firms can practise global niching. In fact, companies marketing on the Internet may find themselves going global whether they intend it or not. In many cases, they may run up against unexpected problems, especially governmental or cultural restrictions. Even established Internet marketers are only beginning to discover the reality of global cyber marketing.

For example, in Germany, a vendor cannot accept payment via credit card until two weeks after an order has been sent. It is also illegal for credit card companies and direct-marketing firms to gather certain types of data on potential applicants. Such restrictions, sometimes combined with underdeveloped banking systems, have limited credit-card and direct-mail usage in many countries. Consider another example. Recently, two French anti-racism groups sued Yahoo! to remove collectibles such as swastika flags and Nazi uniforms from its American website, as it is illegal in France to display or sell objects that incite racial hatred. A French judge subsequently ruled that Yahoo!, the leading Web portal, must block French users from viewing and buying Nazi memorabilia on its American auction site, or else pay a fine. Although there was a remote chance that such a ruling will ever be enforced for technical as well as legal reasons, the decision sets a precedent for the way in which national governments might impose their own laws in an online world that has seemingly transcended country borders. Although some are quick to dismiss the ruling against Yahoo! as an amusing French attempt to defy commercial reality, many fear that the decision will incite other countries to try to impose laws on foreign Web services. This could mean costly reprogramming of sites to comply with many different jurisdictions.[4]

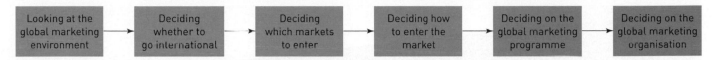

Figure 6.1 **Major decisions in international marketing**

Despite the barriers, however, global Internet enterprise is growing rapidly. For companies that wish to go or stay global, the Internet and online services can represent an easy way to get started, or to reinforce other marketing efforts. Moreover, the world is becoming smaller and every business operating in a global industry – whether large or small, online or offline – must assess and establish its place in world markets.

Increasing globalisation means that all companies have to answer some basic questions. What market position should we try to establish in our country, in our economic region (e.g. western Europe, eastern Europe, North America, Asia, Pacific Rim) and globally? Who will our global competitors be, and what are their strategies and resources? Where should we produce or source our products? What strategic alliances should we form with other firms around the world?

As shown in Figure 6.1, a company faces six major decisions in international marketing. Each decision will be discussed in detail.

Looking at the global marketing environment

Doing international business successfully requires firms to take a broad market perspective.

Understanding the global environment

Before deciding whether or not to sell abroad, a company must thoroughly understand the international marketing environment. That environment has changed a great deal in the last two decades, creating both new opportunities and new problems. The world economy has globalised. World trade and investment have grown rapidly, with many attractive markets opening up in western and eastern Europe, China, the Pacific Rim, Russia and elsewhere.[5] There has been a growth of global brands in motor vehicles, food, clothing, cosmetics, electronics, computers and software and many other categories. The number of global companies has grown dramatically. The international financial system has become more complex and volatile. In some country markets, foreign companies face increasing trade barriers, erected to protect domestic markets against outside competition.

The international trade system

Companies looking abroad must develop an understanding of the international trade system. When selling to another country, the firm faces various trade restrictions. The most common is the **tariff**, which is a tax levied by a foreign government against certain imported products. The tariff may be designed either to raise revenue or to protect domestic firms: for example, those producing motor vehicles in Malaysia and whisky and rice in Japan. The exporter also may face a **quota**, which sets limits on the amount of goods the importing country will accept in certain product categories. The purpose of the quota is to conserve foreign exchange and to protect local industry and employment. An **embargo** or boycott, which totally bans some kinds of import, is the strongest form of quota.

Tariff—A tax levied by a government against certain imported products. Tariffs are designed to raise revenue or to protect domestic firms.

Quota—A limit on the amount of goods that an importing country will accept in certain product categories; it is designed to conserve on foreign exchange and to protect local industry and employment.

Embargo—A ban on the import of a certain product.

213

Many companies have made the world their market: opening megastores in Milan, London, Los Angeles, Vienna and Tokyo.
SOURCE: Virgin Cosmetics Company

Exchange controls—
Government limits on the amount of its country's foreign exchange with other countries and on its exchange rate against other currencies.

Non-tariff trade barriers—
Non-monetary barriers to foreign products, such as biases against a foreign company's bids or product standards that go against a foreign company's product features.

Firms may face **exchange controls** that limit the amount of foreign exchange and the exchange rate against other currencies. The company may also face **non-tariff trade barriers**, such as biases against company bids or restrictive product standards that favour or go against product features.[6]

At the same time, certain forces help trade between nations. Examples are the General Agreement on Tariffs and Trade and various regional free trade agreements.

The World Trade Organisation and GATT

The General Agreement on Tariffs and Trade (GATT) is a 56-year-old treaty designed to promote world trade by reducing tariffs and other international trade barriers. Since the treaty's inception in 1948, member nations (currently numbering 144) have met in eight rounds of GATT negotiations to reassess trade barriers and set new rules for international trade. The first seven rounds of negotiations reduced average worldwide tariffs on manufactured goods from 45 per cent to just 5 per cent.

The most recently completed GATT negotiations, called the Uruguay round, dragged on for seven long years before concluding in 1993. The benefits of the Uruguay round will be felt for many years as the accord promotes long-term global trade growth. It reduced the world's remaining manufactured goods tariffs by 30 per cent, boosting global merchandise trade by up to 10 per cent, or nearly €320 billion in 2002. The new round also extended GATT to cover trade in agriculture and a wide range of services, and it toughened international protection of copyrights, patents, trademarks and other intellectual property.[7]

Beyond reducing trade barriers and setting international standards for trade, the Uruguay Round established the World Trade Organisation (WTO) to enforce GATT rules. One of the WTO's first major tasks was to host negotiations on the General Agreement on Trade in Services, which deals with worldwide trade in banking, securities and insurance services. In general, the WTO acts as an umbrella organisation, overseeing GATT, the General Agreement on Trade in Services and a similar agreement governing intellectual property. In addition, the WTO mediates global disputes and imposes trade sanctions, authorities that the previous GATT organisation never possessed.[8] Top decision makers from the WTO meet once every two years to discuss matters relating to all WTO agreements. A fresh round of talks began in Cancún, Mexico, in late 2003.[9]

Regional free-trade zones

Some countries have formed free-trade zones or economic communities – groups of nations organised to secure common goals in the regulation of international trade. One such community is the European Union, which seeks to create a single European market by reducing barriers to the free flow of products, services, finances and labour among member countries and developing policies on trade with non-member nations. Today, the European Union represents one of the world's single largest markets. Up until 2004, the 15 member countries in the EU contained more than 374 million consumers and accounted for some 20 per cent of the world's exports. With 10 new eastern and southern European countries – Cyprus, the Czech Republic, Estonia, Hungary, Lithuania, Latvia, Malta, Poland, Slovakia and Slovenia – joining the EU in 2004, and with more European nations gaining admission over the next decade, the EU could contain as many as 450 million people in over 25 countries.[10]

European unification offers tremendous trade opportunities for non-European firms. However, it also poses threats. As a result of increased unification, European companies will grow bigger and more competitive. Perhaps an even bigger concern, however, is that lower barriers *inside* Europe will only create thicker *outside* walls. Some observers envisage a 'Fortress Europe' that heaps favours on firms from EU countries but hinders outsiders by imposing obstacles such as stiffer import quotas, local content requirements and other non-tariff barriers.

Progress towards European unification, however, has been slow – many doubt that complete unification will ever be achieved. Nonetheless, on 1 January 1999, 11 of the 15 member nations (that is, all but the UK, Greece, Denmark and Sweden) took a significant step towards unification by adopting the euro as a common currency. These 11 nations represent 290 million people and a €7.7 trillion market. In January 2001, Greece became the twelfth member nation to adopt the euro. Currencies of the individual euro-zone countries were phased out gradually until 1 January 2002, when the euro became the only currency. Adoption of the euro will decrease much of the currency risk associated with doing business in Europe, making member countries with previously weak currencies more attractive markets. In addition, by removing currency conversion hurdles, the switch is likely to increase cross-border trade and highlight differences in pricing and marketing from country to country.[11]

Even with the adoption of the euro as a standard currency, from a marketing viewpoint creating an economic community will not create a homogeneous market. As one international analyst suggests, 'Even though you have fiscal harmonisation, you can't go against 2,000 years of tradition.' With 15 different languages and distinctive national customs, it is unlikely that the EU will ever become the 'United States of Europe'.[12] Although economic and political boundaries may fall, social and cultural differences will remain, and companies marketing in Europe will face a daunting mass of local rules. Still, even if only partly successful, European unification will make a more efficient and competitive Europe a global force with which to reckon.[13]

In North America, the United States and Canada phased out trade barriers in 1989. In January 1994, the *North American Free Trade Agreement (NAFTA)* established a free-trade zone among the United States, Mexico and Canada. The agreement created a single market of 360 million people who produce and consume $6.7 trillion (€5.53 trillion) worth of goods and services. As it is implemented over a 15-year period, NAFTA will eliminate all trade barriers and investment restrictions among the three countries. Prior to NAFTA, tariffs on American products entering Mexico averaged 13 per cent, whereas US tariffs on Mexican goods averaged 6 per cent.

Thus far, the agreement has allowed trade between the countries to flourish. Each day the United States exchanges more than $1 billion (€0.83 billion) in goods and services with Canada, its largest trading partner. Since the agreement was signed in 1993, exports from the United States to Mexico have increased 170 per cent, while Mexican exports to the United States grew some 241 per cent. In 1998, Mexico passed Japan to become America's second largest trading partner. Given the apparent success of NAFTA, talks are now underway to investigate establishing a Free Trade Area of the Americas (FTAA). This mammoth free trade zone would include 34 countries stretching from the Bering Strait to Cape Horn, with a population of 800 million and a combined gross domestic product of more than $11 trillion (€9.09 trillion).[14]

Other free trade areas have formed in Latin America and South America. For example, MERCOSUR now links six members: Argentina, Brazil, Paraguay, Uruguay, Bolivia and Chile. With a population of more than 200 million and a combined economy of more than $1 trillion (€0.83 trillion) a year, these countries make up the largest trading bloc after NAFTA and the European Union. There is talk of a free trade agreement between the EU and MERCOSUR, and MERCOSUR's member countries are considering adopting a common currency, the merco.[15]

Other free-trade communities exist (see Figure 6.2). In fact, almost every member of the WTO is also a member of one or more such communities. And of the 100 or so free-trade arrangements listed by the WTO, over half came into being in the 1990s.

Each nation has unique features that must be understood. A country's readiness for different products and services and its attractiveness as a market to foreign firms depend on its economic, political–legal and cultural environments. We address these environmental influences next.

Economic environment

The international marketer must study each country's economy. Two economic factors reflect the country's attractiveness as a market: the country's *industrial structure* and its *income distribution*.

The country's industrial structure shapes its product and service needs, income levels and employment levels. Four types of industrial structure should be considered:

1. *Subsistence economies.* In a subsistence economy, the vast majority of people engage in simple agriculture. They consume most of their output and barter the rest for simple goods and services. They offer few market opportunities.

2. *Raw-material-exporting economies.* These economies are rich in one or more natural resources, but poor in other ways. Much of their revenue comes from exporting these resources. Examples are Chile (tin and copper), The Democratic Republic of Congo (formerly Zaïre) (copper, cobalt and coffee) and Saudi Arabia (oil). These countries are good markets for large equipment, tools and supplies, and trucks. If there are many foreign residents and a wealthy upper class, they are also a market for luxury goods.

3. *Industrialising economies.* In an industrialising economy, manufacturing accounts for 10–20 per cent of the country's economy. Examples include Egypt, the Philippines, India,

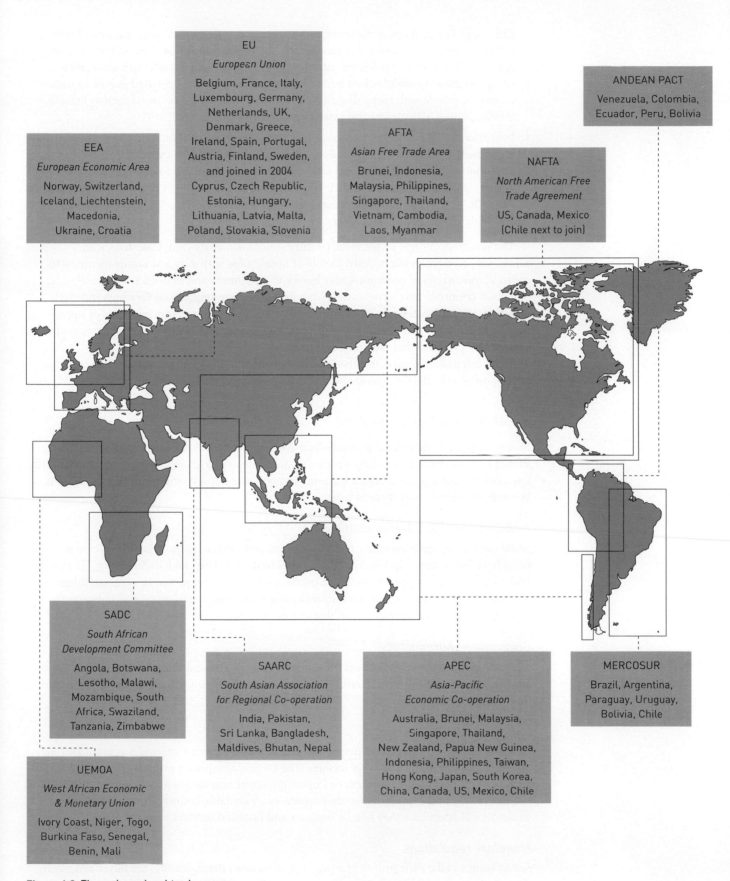

EEA
European Economic Area
Norway, Switzerland, Iceland, Liechtenstein, Macedonia, Ukraine, Croatia

EU
European Union
Belgium, France, Italy, Luxembourg, Germany, Netherlands, UK, Denmark, Greece, Ireland, Spain, Portugal, Austria, Finland, Sweden, and joined in 2004 Cyprus, Czech Republic, Estonia, Hungary, Lithuania, Latvia, Malta, Poland, Slovakia, Slovenia

AFTA
Asian Free Trade Area
Brunei, Indonesia, Malaysia, Philippines, Singapore, Thailand, Vietnam, Cambodia, Laos, Myanmar

NAFTA
North American Free Trade Agreement
US, Canada, Mexico (Chile next to join)

ANDEAN PACT
Venezuela, Colombia, Ecuador, Peru, Bolivia

SADC
South African Development Committee
Angola, Botswana, Lesotho, Malawi, Mozambique, South Africa, Swaziland, Tanzania, Zimbabwe

SAARC
South Asian Association for Regional Co-operation
India, Pakistan, Sri Lanka, Bangladesh, Maldives, Bhutan, Nepal

APEC
Asia-Pacific Economic Co-operation
Australia, Brunei, Malaysia, Singapore, Thailand, New Zealand, Papua New Guinea, Indonesia, Philippines, Taiwan, Hong Kong, Japan, South Korea, China, Canada, US, Mexico, Chile

MERCOSUR
Brazil, Argentina, Paraguay, Uruguay, Bolivia, Chile

UEMOA
West African Economic & Monetary Union
Ivory Coast, Niger, Togo, Burkina Faso, Senegal, Benin, Mali

Figure 6.2 The main regional trade groups

China and Brazil. As manufacturing increases, the country needs more imports of raw textile materials, steel and heavy machinery, and fewer imports of finished textiles, paper products and motor vehicles. Industrialisation typically creates a new rich class and a small but growing middle class, both demanding new types of imported goods. In these countries, people with rising disposable income want to spend on items such as fashion, mobile phones, CD players and instant coffee.

4. *Industrial economies*. Industrial economies are large exporters of manufactured goods and investment funds. They trade goods among themselves and also export them to other types of economy for raw materials and semi-finished goods. The varied manufacturing activities of these industrial nations and their large middle class make them rich markets for all sorts of goods. Asia's newly industrialised economies, such as Taiwan, Singapore, South Korea and Malaysia, fall into this category.

The second economic factor is the country's income distribution. Countries with subsistence economies may consist mostly of households with very low family incomes. In contrast, industrialised economies may have low-, medium- and high-income households. Still other countries may have households with only either very low or very high incomes. However, in many cases, poorer countries may have small but wealthy segments of upper-income consumers. Also, even in low-income and developing countries, people may find ways to buy products that are important to them.

Thus, international marketers face many challenges in understanding how the economic environment will affect decisions about which global markets to enter and how.

Political–legal environment

Nations differ greatly in their political–legal environments. At least four political–legal factors should be considered in deciding whether to do business in a given country: attitudes towards international buying, government bureaucracy, political stability and monetary regulations. We will consider each of these in turn.

Attitudes towards international buying

Some nations are quite receptive to foreign firms, and others are quite hostile. Western firms have found newly industrialised countries in the Far East, such as Singapore, Thailand, Malaysia and the Philippines, attractive overseas investment locations. In contrast, others like India are bothersome with their import quotas, currency restrictions and limits on the percentage of the management team that can be non-nationals.

Government bureaucracy

This is the extent to which the host government runs an efficient system for helping foreign companies: efficient customs handling, good market information, and other factors that aid in doing business.

Political stability

Governments change hands, sometimes violently. Even without a change, a government may decide to respond to new popular feelings. The foreign company's property may be taken, its currency holdings may be blocked, or import quotas or new duties may be set. International marketers may find it profitable to do business in an unstable country, but the unsteady situation will affect how they handle business and financial matters.

Monetary regulations

Sellers want to take their profits in a currency of value to them. Ideally, the buyer can pay in the seller's currency or in other world currencies. Short of this, sellers might accept a blocked currency – one whose removal from the country is restricted by the buyer's government – if they can buy other goods in that country that they need themselves or can sell elsewhere for a needed currency. Besides currency limits, a changing exchange rate, as mentioned earlier, creates high risks for the seller.

Most international trade involves cash transactions. Yet many nations have too little hard currency to pay for their purchases from other countries. They may want to pay with other items instead of cash, which has led to a growing practice called **countertrade**. Countertrade now accounts for an estimated 20 per cent of all world trade.[16]

Countertrade takes several forms. *Barter* involves the direct exchange of goods or services. For example, British coalmining equipment has been 'sold' for Indonesian plywood; Volkswagen cars were swapped for Bulgarian dried apricots; and Boeing 747s, fitted with Rolls-Royce engines, were exchanged for Saudi oil. Another form is *compensation* (or *buyback*), whereby the seller sells a plant, equipment or technology to another country and agrees to take payment in the resulting products. Thus, Goodyear provided China with materials and training for a printing plant in exchange for finished labels. Another form is *counterpurchase*. Here the seller receives full payment in cash, but agrees to spend some portion of the money in the other country within a stated time period. For example, Pepsi sells its syrup to Russia for roubles, and agrees to buy Russian vodka for reselling in the United States.

Countertrade deals can be very complex. For example, DaimlerChrysler recently agreed to sell 30 trucks to Romania in exchange for 150 Romanian jeeps, which it then sold to Ecuador for bananas, which were in turn sold to a German supermarket chain for German currency. Through this roundabout process, DaimlerChrysler finally obtained payment in German money.[17]

> **Countertrade**—International trade involving the direct or indirect exchange of goods for other goods instead of cash. Forms include barter compensation (buyback) and counterpurchase.

Cultural environment

Culture is defined simply as *the learned distinctive way of life of a society*. The dimensions of culture include the social organisation of society, religion, customs and rituals, values and attitudes towards domestic and international life, education provision and literacy levels, political system, aesthetic systems (e.g. folklore, music, arts, literature) and language. Each country has its own traditions, cultural norms and taboos. When designing global marketing strategies, companies must understand how culture affects consumer reactions in each of its international markets. In turn, they must also understand how their strategies affect culture.

> **Culture**—The set of basic values, perceptions, wants and behaviours learned by a member of society from family and other important institutions.

How culture impacts marketing strategy

Companies must examine the ways consumers in different countries think about and use certain products or services before planning a marketing programme. There are often surprises.

For example, the average Frenchman uses almost twice as many cosmetics and beauty aids as does his female partner. The Germans and the French eat more packaged, branded spaghetti than do Italians. Italian children like to eat chocolate bars between slices of bread as a snack. In Belgium, don't be surprised to find that clothes for baby girls are trimmed with blue and those for baby boys with pink.

Business norms and behaviour also vary from country to country. Business executives need to be briefed on these factors before conducting business in another country. Here are some examples of different global business behaviour:

- In face-to-face communications, Japanese business executives rarely say 'no' to the western business executive. Thus westerners tend to be frustrated and may not know where they stand. Where westerners come to the point quickly, Japanese business executives may find this behaviour offensive.

■ In France, wholesalers don't want to promote a product. They ask their retailers what they want and deliver it. If a foreign company builds its strategy around the French wholesaler's cooperation in promotions, it is likely to fail.

■ When British executives exchange business cards, each usually gives the other's card a cursory glance and stuffs it in a pocket for later reference. In Japan, however, executives dutifully study each other's cards during a greeting, carefully noting company affiliation and rank. They hand their card to the most important person first.

■ In the United Kingdom and the United States, business meals are common. In Germany, these are strictly social. Foreigners are rarely invited to dinner and such an invitation suggests a very advanced association. The opposite applies in Italy where entertaining is an essential part of business life (guests should offer to pay but, in the end, should defer to their Italian host). In France, watch out. There are two kinds of business lunch – one for building up relations, without expecting anything in return, and the other to discuss a deal in the making or to celebrate a deal afterwards. Deals, however, should be concluded in the office, never over a lunch table.

■ Shaking hands on meeting and on parting is common in Germany, Belgium, France and Italy. Ignoring this custom, especially in France, causes offence. In France, it is advisable to shake hands with everyone in a crowded room.

By the same token, companies that understand cultural nuances can use them to advantage when positioning products internationally. For example, consider French cosmetics giant L'Oréal:

> It's a sunny afternoon outside Parkson's department store in Shanghai, and a marketing battle is raging for the attention of Chinese women. Tall, pouty models in beige skirts and sheer tops pass out flyers promoting Revlon's new spring colours. But their effort is drowned out by L'Oréal's eye-catching show for its Maybelline brand. To a pulsing rhythm, two gangly models in shimmering lycra tops dance on a podium before a large backdrop depicting the New York City skyline. The music stops, and a makeup artist transforms a model's face while a Chinese saleswoman delivers the punch line. 'This brand comes from America. It's very trendy', she shouts into her microphone. 'If you want to be fashionable, just choose Maybelline'. Few of the women in the crowd realize that the trendy 'New York' Maybelline brand belongs to French cosmetics giant L'Oréal. . . .
>
> Blink an eye and L'Oréal has just sold 85 products around the world, from Redken hair care and Ralph Lauren perfumes to Helena Rubinstein cosmetics. In the battle for global beauty markets, L'Oréal has developed a winning formula: . . . conveying the allure of different cultures through its many products. Whether it's selling Italian elegance, New York street smarts, or French beauty through its brands, L'Oréal is reaching out to a vast range of people across incomes and cultures.[18]

Thus, the key to success for the international marketer lies in assiduously researching and understanding a country's cultural traditions, preferences and behaviours. Building *cultural empathy* in this way helps companies to avoid embarrassing mistakes and to take advantage of cross-cultural opportunities.

The impact of marketing strategy on culture

While marketers worry about the impact of culture on their global marketing strategies, others may be concerned with the impact of marketing strategies on global cultures. In recent years, some critics argue that 'globalisation' is nothing more than 'Americanisation'. They worry that the more people around the world are exposed to the American culture and lifestyle in the food they eat, the stores in which they shop, and television shows and movies they watch, the more they will lose their individual cultural identities.

These critics contend that exposure to American values and products erodes other cultures and westernises the world. They point out that teenagers around the world watch MTV and ask their parents for more westernised clothes and other symbols of American pop culture and values. Grandmothers in small villas in northern Italy no longer spend each morning visiting local meat, bread and produce markets to gather the ingredients for dinner. Instead, they now shop at Wal-Mart Supercentres. Women in Saudi Arabia see American films and question their societal roles. In China, most people never drank coffee before Starbucks entered the market. Now Chinese consumers rush to Starbucks stores 'because it's a symbol of a new kind of lifestyle.' Similarly in China, where McDonald's operates 80 restaurants in Beijing alone, nearly half of all children identify the chain as a domestic brand.[19]

Recently, such concerns have led to a backlash against American globalisation. For example, as a symbol of American capitalism, McDonald's has been singled out by anti-globalisation protestors all over the world. Its restaurants are also targeted when anti-American sentiment peaks. For example, almost immediately after US armed forces unleashed their attack on Afghanistan following the 11 September 2001 terrorist attacks, McDonald's stores in Pakistan, India and elsewhere around the world came under attack. Local protestors burned American flags outside the restaurants and vandalised McDonald's storefronts.

Despite the concerns, most studies reveal that, although globalisation may bridge culture gaps, it does not eliminate them. Instead, the cultural exchange goes both ways. Western childhood has also increasingly been shaped by Asian cultural imports, ranging from the Power Rangers and Tamagotchi to Pokémon, Sega and Nintendo. Because English remains the Web's dominant language, having Web access means that, by default, many youths around the world have greater exposure to western (often meaning American) pop culture. But these very technologies also enable students, say from the Balkans, who are studying abroad to listen to webcast news and music from their own mother country.[20]

In the final analysis, companies doing global marketing have to learn that, to succeed abroad, they must adapt to local cultural values and traditions rather than trying to force their own.

Deciding whether to go international

Not all companies need to venture into international markets to survive. Many local businesses need to market well only in the local marketplace. Operating domestically is easier and safer. Managers would not need to learn other languages and laws, deal with volatile currencies, face political and legal uncertainties, or redesign their products to suit different customer needs and expectations. However, companies that operate in global industries, where their strategic positions in specific markets are affected strongly by their overall global positions, must compete on a worldwide basis if they are to succeed.

Several factors might draw a company into the international arena. Global competitors offering better products or lower prices might attack the company's domestic market. The company might want to counterattack these competitors in their home markets to tie up their resources. Or the company might discover foreign markets that present higher profit opportunities than the domestic market does. The company's domestic market might be stagnant or shrinking, or the company might need an enlarged customer base in order to achieve economies of scale. The company might want to reduce its dependence on any one market so as to reduce its risk. Finally, the company's customers might be expanding abroad and require international servicing.

Before going abroad, the company must weigh several risks and answer many questions about its ability to operate globally. Can the company learn to understand the preferences and buyer behaviour of consumers in other countries? Can it offer competitively attractive products? Will it be able to adapt to other countries' business cultures and deal effectively with foreign nationals? Do the company's managers have the necessary international experience? Has management considered the impact of regulations and the political environments of other countries?

Because of the risks and difficulties of entering international markets, most companies do not act until some situation or event thrusts them into the global arena. Someone – a domestic exporter, a foreign importer, a foreign government – may ask the company to sell abroad. Or the company may be saddled with overcapacity and must find additional markets for its goods.

Deciding which markets to enter

Before going abroad, the company should define its international *marketing objectives* and *policies*. It should decide what *volume* of foreign sales it wants. Most companies start small when they go abroad. Some plan to stay small, seeing foreign sales as a small part of their business. Other companies have bigger plans, seeing foreign business as equal to or even more important than their domestic business.

The company must decide *how many* countries it wants to market in and *how fast* to expand. Generally, it makes better sense to operate in fewer countries with deeper penetration

in each. The company must also decide on the *types* of country to enter. A country's attractiveness depends on the product, geographical factors, income and population, political climate and other factors. The seller may prefer certain countries or parts of the world. In recent years, many major new markets have emerged, offering both substantial opportunities and daunting challenges. The latent needs of consumers in the developing world present huge potential markets for food, clothing, shelter, household appliances, consumer electronics and other goods. As such, many companies are now rushing into Eastern Europe, China and India with hopes of tapping the unmet needs of these consumers (see Marketing Insights 6.1).

After listing possible international markets, the company must screen and rank each one on several factors, including market size, market growth, cost of doing business, competitive advantage and risk level. The goal is to determine the potential of each market, using indicators like those shown in Table 6.1. Then the marketer must decide which markets offer the greatest long-run return on investment.

Making the 'go' or 'no-go' decision requires management to invest time and effort in researching the potential challenges and opportunities facing the company. Increasingly, a vast array of resources is available on the Internet. These resources offer managers a way to research prospective target markets and customers as well as gain critical information about doing business in unfamiliar countries and market environments. Market research, therefore, is key to understanding how the company may break into overseas markets or improve their existing international marketing practices and contacts.[21]

marketing insights

6.1 Emerging markets: going east

China and India each have over a billion consumers, presenting tempting prospects for international companies. The experience of international companies suggests that, despite the attractiveness of these emerging markets, their consumers remain an elusive target. Many dominant brands – from Unilever, Sony and Mercedes to Levi, Kellogg and Ford – have all struggled to deliver on the promise of the 'billion-consumer' markets.

A common fallacy lies in the thinking that there are huge margins to be gained from skimming the 3 or 5 per cent of affluent consumers in emerging markets who have global preferences for 'luxury goods' and purchasing power. In India, Coca-Cola came in at the top and tried to trickle down. It launched pricey 350 ml bottles instead of offering cheaper smaller ones. Rather than concentrating on the main towns, it went for the whole of India with a single size and price, using expensive and flawed distribution and advertising. Ford and other motor manufacturers also misjudged the Indian market. They started with medium-sized cars in a market dominated by small ones, and expected to compete with nearly 70 per cent overcapacity in medium-sized car manufacturing. Kellogg's offered premium-priced cereals supported by expensive marketing. They soon learnt that, although market research showed that India was the largest cereal-eating nation on earth, consumers were choosing to buy Champion's products costing a fifth the price of Kellogg's. By contrast, Akai, the Japanese consumer electronics producer, stole a march on global giant Sony, by offering cheaper televisions and taking customers' old sets in part-exchange.

Analysts argue that it is important to define the Indian market not by income alone, but by consumption. A disaggregation will yield a demographic pyramid of five layers: the destitute, climbers, aspirants, consumers and the rich – who are the 1 million households earning more than Rs 1 million (€25,600) a year. The 30m people normally identified as consumers have less disposable income than the groups below them, because they tend to spend more on education. The bottom of the pyramid, especially the aspirants, is more attractive because of rising incomes. Unilever's Indian subsidiary, Hindustan Lever, designed products for each of the five tiers. It began moving goods by road instead of rail, building a network of 40,000 wholesalers and 500,000 retailers and supplying it with credit. Levi initially aggregated the 156m people aged 12 to 19, but 111m of these live in rural India. Targeting the top tier leaves a meagre 500,000 rich urban consumers, potentially yielding slim pickings.

The key to success lies in developing products for each or most of the five consumption segments, instead of targeting the 'affluent global consumer'. But segmentation of this nature is costly and only justified if consumers are able and willing to pay for specialised products. The experience of SmithKline Beecham (SB)

...6.1

in India points to the power of targeting local consumers. But fine segmentation does not have to come at a cost. Horlicks, its flagship product in India, has long been positioned as 'the great family nourisher'. It caught on because of milk shortages and poor health conditions and people saw a need for a nutritional supplement. SB built its own supply chain, worked hard at paring costs and pricing, and markets its drink as a nutrient for all seasons and all types. Its supply chain now reaches 375,000 outlets across India. Horlicks refill packages and Horlicks biscuits give consumers the same nutrition at a fraction of the cost of a jar. The Horlicks brand has also been launched into new areas, from Junior Horlicks and Mothers' Horlicks for pregnant or breast-feeding women, to Horlicks for sports, convalescence, the elderly or kids during the monsoon fever period.

Unilever's early, troubled decade and a half in China culminated in recent sweeping restructuring of its Chinese operations, and careful adaptation to the vagaries of operating in this populous market. Its 14 joint ventures with local companies in sectors ranging from detergents, food and wine to ice-creams, toothpaste and chemicals are now brought under three companies: home and personal care; ice-cream; and food and beverages. A crucial change has been to become more local. R&D is adapted to Chinese tastes and local remedies. Drawing from Hindustan Lever's considerable expertise on selling in rural India, Unilever now targets consumers well beyond China's largest cities and has been increasing the range of prices for its various brands, tapping particularly the lower end of the market. For example, Unilever sells pricier Omo laundry detergents to the wealthy, urban consumer who has a washing machine and is prepared to pay a premium for the detergent. To compete with low-priced mass market offerings from local upstarts, it also offers its cheaper Sunlight soap to consumers with more modest means.

Increasingly, multinational companies such as Unilever, Procter & Gamble, Nestlé and Coca-Cola are discovering that consumers in emerging markets such as India and China will remain hard to get unless they develop value propositions that appeal to the mass market. Products transplanted from affluent, developed nations tend to appeal to a relatively small élite. International companies have to delve deeper into the local consumer base in order to tap the potential of the 'billion-consumer' markets.

SOURCES: Gordon Redding, 'China: rough but ready for outsiders', *Financial Times, FT Summer School*, (26 August 2003), p. 11; Niraj Dawar and Amitava Chattopadhyay, 'The new language of emerging markets', *Financial Times, Mastering Management* (13 November 2000), pp. 6–7; David Gardner, 'Slim pickings for the international brand in India', *Financial Times* (10 October 2000), p. 19; 'How Horlicks won an empire', *Financial Times* (10 October 2000), p. 19; Rahul Jacob, 'A Chinese clean-up operation', *Financial Times* (18 May 2000), p. 18; Niraj Dawar and Tony Frost, 'Competing with giants: Survival strategies for emerging market companies', *Harvard Business Review* (March–April 1999), pp. 119–29.

Table 6.1 Indicators of market potential

1. Demographic characteristics Size of population Rate of population growth Degree of urbanisation Population density Age structure and composition of the population	**4. Technological factors** Level of technological skills Existing production technology Existing consumption technology Education levels
2. Geographic characteristics Physical size of a country Topographical characteristics Climate conditions	**5. Sociocultural factors** Dominant values Lifestyle patterns Ethnic groups Linguistic fragmentation
3. Economic factors GDP per capita Income distribution Rate of growth of GNP Ratio of investment to GNP	**6. National goals and plans** Industry priorities Infrastructure investment plans

SOURCE: Susan P. Douglas, C. Samuel Craig and Warren Keegan, 'Approaches to assessing international marketing opportunities for small and medium-sized businesses', *Columbia Journal of World Business* (Fall 1982), pp. 26–32. © 1982, 1999, *Columbia Journal of World Business*. Reprinted with permission. Also see Pankaj Ghemawat, 'Distance still matters', *Harvard Business Review* (September–October 2001), pp. 137–47.

Deciding how to enter the market

Once a company has decided to market in a foreign country, it must determine the best mode of entry. Its choices are exporting, joint venturing and direct investment. Figure 6.3 shows these routes to servicing foreign markets, along with the options that each one offers. As we can see, each succeeding strategy involves more commitment and risk, but also more control and potential profits.

Exporting

The simplest way to enter a foreign market is through exporting. The company may passively export its surpluses from time to time, or it may make an active commitment to expand exports to a particular market. In either case, the company produces all its goods in its home country. It may or may not modify them for the export market. Exporting involves the least change in the company's product lines, organisation, investments or mission.

Figure 6.3 Market entry strategies

Indirect exporting

Companies typically start with indirect exporting, working through independent international marketing intermediaries. Indirect exporting involves less investment because the firm does not require an overseas sales force or set of contacts. It also involves less risk. International marketing intermediaries – home-based export merchants or agents, cooperative organisations, government export agencies and export-management companies – bring know-how and services to the relationship, so the seller normally makes fewer mistakes.

Direct exporting

Sellers may eventually move into direct exporting, whereby they handle their own exports. The investment and risk are somewhat greater in this strategy, but so is the potential return. A company can conduct direct exporting in several ways. It can set up a domestic export department that carries out export activities. Or it can set up an overseas sales branch that handles sales, distribution and perhaps promotion. The sales branch gives the seller more presence and programme control in the foreign market and often serves as a display centre and customer service centre. Or the company can send home-based salespeople abroad at certain times in order to find business. Finally, the company can do its exporting either through foreign-based distributors that buy and own the goods or through foreign-based agents that sell the goods on behalf of the company.

Today, electronic communication via the Internet enables companies, particularly small ones, to extend their reach to worldwide markets. No longer is it necessary for firms to attend overseas trade shows to exhibit their products to overseas buyers and distributors. The Internet has become an effective medium for attaining exporting information and guidelines, doing market research and enabling overseas customers to order and pay for goods.

Joint venturing

A second method of entering a foreign market is **joint venturing** – joining with foreign companies to produce or market products or services. Joint venturing differs from exporting in that the company joins with a partner to sell or market abroad. It differs from direct investment in that an association is formed with someone in the foreign country. There are four types of joint venture: licensing, contract manufacturing, management contracting and joint ownership.

Joint venturing—Entering foreign markets by joining with foreign companies to produce or market a product or service.

Licensing

Licensing is a simple way for a manufacturer to enter international marketing. The company enters into an agreement with a *licensee* in the foreign market. For a fee or royalty, the licensee buys the right to use the company's manufacturing process, trademark, patent, trade secret or other item of value. The company thus gains entry into the market at little risk; the licensee gains production expertise or a well-known product or brand name without having to start from scratch.

East European brewers such as Czech Republic's Pilsner Urquell and the Budvar Company have sought to strengthen their international market positions through licensing the production of their beer brands in breweries abroad. Coca-Cola markets internationally by licensing bottlers around the world and supplying them with the syrup needed to produce the product. And in an effort to bring online retail investing to people abroad, online brokerage E*Trade has set up E*Trade-branded websites under licensing agreements in France, Norway, Denmark, Sweden, Germany, Canada, Australia, Hong Kong, Korea, Japan and South Africa.[22]

Licensing—A method of entering a foreign market in which the company enters into an agreement with a licensee in the foreign market, offering the right to use a manufacturing process, trademark, patent, trade secret or other item of value for a fee or royalty.

Licensing has potential disadvantages, however. The firm has less control over the licensee than it would over its own production facilities. Furthermore, if the licensee is very successful, the firm has given up these profits, and if and when the contract ends, it may find it has created a competitor.

Contract manufacturing

Contract manufacturing—A joint venture in which a company contracts with manufacturers in a foreign market to produce the product.

Another option is **contract manufacturing**. The company contracts with manufacturers in the foreign market to produce its product or provide its service. Many western firms have used this mode for entering Taiwanese and South Korean markets.

The drawbacks of contract manufacturing are the decreased control over the manufacturing process and the loss of potential profits on manufacturing. The benefits are the chance to start faster, with less risk, and the later opportunity either to form a partnership with or to buy out the local manufacturer.

Management contracting

Management contracting—A joint venture in which the domestic firm supplies the management know-how to a foreign company that supplies the capital; the domestic firm exports management services rather than products.

Under **management contracting**, the domestic firm supplies management know-how to a foreign company that supplies the capital. The domestic firm exports management services rather than products. Hilton uses this arrangement in managing hotels around the world. Management contracting is a low-risk method of getting into a foreign market, and it yields income from the beginning. The arrangement is even more attractive if the contracting firm has an option to buy a share in the managed company later on. The arrangement is not sensible, however, if the company can put its scarce management talent to better uses or if it can make greater profits by undertaking the whole venture. Management contracting also prevents the company from setting up its own operations for a period of time.

Joint ownership

Joint ownership—A joint venture in which a company joins investors in a foreign market to create a local business in which the company shares joint ownership and control.

Joint-ownership ventures consist of one company joining forces with foreign investors to create a local business in which they share joint ownership and control. A company may buy an interest in a local firm, or the two parties may form a new business venture. Joint ownership may be needed for economic or political reasons. A foreign government may require joint ownership as a condition for entry. Or the firm may lack the financial, physical or managerial resources to undertake the venture alone.

Joint ownership has certain drawbacks. The partners may disagree over investment, marketing or other policies. To enjoy partnership benefits, collaborators must clarify their expectations and objectives and work hard to secure a win–win outcome for all parties concerned.

Direct investment

Direct investment—Entering a foreign market by developing foreign-based assembly or manufacturing facilities.

The biggest involvement in a foreign market comes through **direct investment** – the development of foreign-based assembly or manufacturing facilities. If a company has gained experience in exporting and if the foreign market is large enough or growing rapidly, foreign production makes economic sense. For example, Nokia, the Finnish mobile handset manufacturer, initially entered the Chinese market through joint ventures. In 2003, it sought to strengthen its position in China, the world's fastest growing mobile-phone market, by merging its joint venture operations and to start local production of CDMA handsets.[23] Foreign production facilities offer many advantages:

1. The firm may have lower costs in the form of cheaper labour or raw materials, foreign government investment incentives and freight savings.

2. The firm may improve its image in the host country because it creates jobs.

3. Generally, a firm develops a deeper relationship with government, customers, local suppliers and distributors, allowing it to adapt its products better to the local market.

4. Finally, the firm keeps full control over the investment and therefore can develop manufacturing and marketing policies that serve its long-term international objectives.

The main disadvantage of direct investment is that the firm faces many risks, such as restricted, devalued or sharply rising currencies, worsening markets or government takeovers. For example, early investors in Hungary's automotive industry, such as Opel, the German subsidiary of General Motors, had to make substantial adjustments to their business plans as the economic conditions in the country proved much worse than originally anticipated. More recently, the strengthening of the Hungarian currency, the forint, has pushed labour costs up while reducing productivity growth. In response, foreign direct investors such as Philips of The Netherlands has reduced its workforce in Hungary, while others, like IBM, have closed their factories altogether.[24] In some cases, a firm has no choice but to accept these risks if it wants to operate in the host country.

There are therefore direct and indirect ways of entering a foreign market. Firms seeking to market goods and services in a foreign market should evaluate the alternative modes of entry and decide upon the most cost-effective path that would ensure long-term performance in that market.

Firms typically move through four stages of internationalisation: no regular exporting activity, exporting through independent agents, setting up one or more sales subsidiaries and establishing production facilities abroad.[25] The first step is to move from stage 1 to stage 2. Having had some experience of exporting via an independent agent in a nearby or familiar country, the firm then engages more agents to enter additional countries. It then sets up an export department to manage its agent relationships. Later, it may replace these agents with its own sales subsidiary(ies) in its largest export market(s). Eventually, the firm establishes an international department to manage its overseas subsidiaries. If sales are large and stable, or if the host country requires local production, the firm takes the next step of establishing production facilities in these markets. By this stage, the firm has become internationalised, engaging in coordinating worldwide sourcing, financing, production and marketing.[26]

Deciding on the global marketing programme

The marketing programme for each foreign market must be carefully planned. Managers must first decide on the precise customer target or targets to be served. Then managers have to decide how, if at all, to adapt the firm's marketing mix to local conditions. To do this requires a good understanding of country market conditions as well as cultural characteristics of customers in that market. We have already addressed the need for cultural sensitivity. This section will discuss reasons for standardisation versus adaptation for the global market before highlighting specific international marketing mix decisions.

Standardisation or adaptation for international markets?

At one extreme are companies that use a **standardised marketing mix** worldwide, selling largely the same products and using the same marketing approaches worldwide. At the other extreme is an **adapted marketing mix**. In this case, the producer adjusts the marketing mix elements to each target, bearing more costs but hoping for a larger market share and return.

Standardised marketing mix—An international marketing strategy for using basically the same product, advertising, distribution channels and other elements of the marketing mix in all the company's international markets.

Adapted marketing mix— An international marketing strategy for adjusting the marketing-mix elements to each international target market, bearing more costs but hoping for a larger market share and return.

The question of whether to adapt or standardise the marketing mix has been much debated in recent years. The marketing concept holds that marketing programmes will be more effective if tailored to the unique needs of each targeted customer group. If this concept applies within a country, it should apply even more in international markets. Consumers in different countries have widely varied cultural backgrounds, needs and wants, spending power, product preferences and shopping patterns. Because these differences are hard to change, most marketers adapt their products, prices, channels and promotions to fit consumer desires in each country.

However, some global marketers are bothered by what they see as too much adaptation, which raises costs and dilutes global brand power. As a result, many companies have created so-called world brands – more or less the same product sold the same way to all consumers worldwide. Marketers at these companies believe that advances in communication, transportation and travel are turning the world into a common marketplace. These marketers claim that people around the world want basically the same products and lifestyles. Despite what consumers say they want, all consumers want good products at lower prices.

Moreover, the development of the Internet, the rapid spread of cable and satellite TV around the world, and the creation of telecommunications networks linking previously remote places have all made the world a smaller place. For instance, the disproportionately American programming beamed into homes in the developing nations has sparked a convergence of consumer appetites, particularly among youth. Fashion trends spread almost instantly, propelled by TV and Internet chat groups. Around the world, news and comment on almost any topic or product is available at the click of a mouse or twist of a dial. The resulting convergence of needs and wants has created global markets for standardised products, particularly among the young middle class.

Proponents of global standardisation claim that international marketers should adapt products and marketing programmes only when local wants cannot be changed or avoided. Standardisation results in lower production, distribution, marketing and management costs, and thus lets the company offer consumers higher quality and more reliable products at lower prices. In fact, some companies have successfully marketed global products – for example, Starbucks coffee, Philips razors and Sony Walkmans.

However, even for these 'global' brands, companies make some adaptations. Moreover, the assertion that global standardisation will lead to lower costs and prices, causing more goods to be snapped up by price-sensitive consumers, is debatable. Consider, for example, MTV.

Pummelled by dozens of local music channels in Europe, such as Germany's *Viva*, Holland's *The Music Factory*, and Scandinavia's *ZTV*, MTV Europe dropped its pan-European programming. Rather than featuring a large amount of American and British pop along with local European favourites, the division created regional channels broadcast by four separate MTV stations – MTV: UK & Ireland; MTV: Northern Europe; MTV: Central Europe; and MTV: Southern Europe. Each of the four channels shows programmes tailored to music tastes of its local market, along with more traditional pan-European pop selections. Within each region, MTV further subdivides its programming. For example, within the United Kingdom, MTV offers sister stations M2 and VH–1, along with three new digital channels: MTV Extra, MTV Base and VH–1 Classic. Says the head of MTV Europe, 'We hope to offer every MTV fan something he or she will like to watch any time of the day.'[27]

In these cases, incremental revenues from adapting products far exceeded the incremental costs.

Clearly, global standardisation is not an all-or-nothing proposition but rather a matter of degree. Companies should look for more standardisation to help keep down costs and prices and to build greater global brand power. But they must not replace long-run marketing thinking with short-run financial thinking. Although standardisation saves money, marketers must make certain that they offer what consumers in each country want.[28]

Many possibilities exist between the extremes of standardisation and complete adaptation. For example, although Philips dishwashers, clothes washers and other major appliances share the same interiors worldwide, their outer styling and features are designed to meet the preferences of consumers in different countries.

Similarly, global companies such as McDonald's have adapted to local cultural values and traditions rather than trying to implement a standard approach across the world. The company uses the same basic operating formula in its restaurants around the world but adapts its menu to local tastes (see Marketing Insights 6.2). CEO Jack Greenberg notes that McDonald's is 'a decentralized entrepreneurial network of locally owned stores that is very flexible and adapts very well to local conditions. We offer an opportunity to entrepreneurs to run a local business with local people supplied by a local infrastructure.' This concept is echoed on the McDonald's website and throughout its corporate culture. Not just in France, as intimated in Marketing Insights 6.2, the company encourages franchisees in other countries to introduce menu items that reflect local tastes, including 'McCafés' in Vienna, which offer coffee blended to local tastes, the Maharaja Mac (made of mutton) in India, the Tatsuta Burger in Japan, the McPork Burger with Thai Basil in Thailand and the McTempeh Burger (made from fermented soybeans) in Indonesia. In fact, McDonald's restaurants in Bombay and Delhi feature a menu that is more than 75 per cent locally developed.[29]

In France, McDonald's do as the French do!
SOURCE: McDonald's Europe Limited

marketing insights

6.2   McDonald's French-style!

Given the state of Franco–US relations, it may come as a surprise that McDonald's, an American icon, should be borrowing ideas from France as it tries to revitalise its brand.

It is, after all, only four years since José Bové, the moustachioed farmer, became a French folk hero after leading an assault that demolished a partially built McDonald's restaurant in a protest against punitive US tariffs on Roquefort cheese.

But France is McDonald's best-performing European subsidiary in terms of operating income per outlet and is in the global vanguard in redesigning restaurants and launching products. In 2003, the country will account for 10 per cent of McDonald's reduced worldwide restaurant openings programme.

French management attributes some of its success to the autonomy it has from US headquarters. French executives also say that working in a difficult environment has forced them to adapt to local tastes and habits.

'We have certainly tried hard to build trust and give the image of a real French company and not an entity that gets its orders from Chicago', says Jean-Pierre Petit, deputy managing director for France.

Denis Hennequin, chief executive of McDonald's France, says the chain tends to get used in France more as a restaurant than a 'snacking place', earning 80 per cent of daily revenues in four hours, around lunch and dinner time. The company has spent €1,200–€1,500 ($1,452–$1,815) a square metre transforming and upgrading many outlets into what it calls 'casual restaurants', using a team of French architects and interior designers. The aim has been to make the seating space more comfortable and improve the décor – notably by using stone, wood and leather. There are lounge chairs in place of hard, fixed, plastic seats. Some restaurants have Apple iPod digital music players installed around the walls, so diners can don headphones and listen to music of their choice.

McDonald's France was also a pioneer in adapting its offering to local tastes by including a range of salads and fresh fruit, as well as some dairy products and Evian mineral water supplied by Danone, the French food group. Following a recent promotional campaign, a quarter of customer visits included the purchase of a Croque McDo, McDonald's version of the croque monsieur, the classic French grilled sandwich.

'The French market is very fragmented and has an atypical structure, which has led us to make some different choices from what McDonald's has done elsewhere', says Mr Hennequin.

Charlie Bell, McDonald's chief executive officer, who previously headed the European division, says he admired and learnt from the French management's

...6.2

'holistic' approach. 'The French team did a particularly good job. They had a focus on the modernity of McDonald's', he says. 'We're getting rid of the NIH factor – Not Invented Here. We're going to take good ideas, wherever they came from, and scale them up fast.'

However, Mr Hennequin says Franco-American tensions will continue to affect McDonald's in France. 'The French will always have a love–hate relationship with Americans because they come from two cultures that both believe they have a predominant role to play in the shaping of the world', he says.

Still, he cannot resist a final dig at those who claim to be France's flag-bearers in the fight against American invaders. 'José Bové drives a John Deere tractor and wears Levi's [jeans]', he notes.

SOURCE: Adapted from Raphael Minder, 'Croques, leather and headphones put France in the vanguard', *Financial Times* (29 August 2003), p. 15.

The decision about which aspects of the marketing mix to standardise and which to adapt should be taken on the basis of target market conditions. Firms are often unwilling to modify their product offering for foreign markets because of 'cultural arrogance'. German and American machine-tool manufacturers, for example, saw their world market shares dive over the 1980s due, in part, to their reluctance to adapt products and marketing approaches in the face of changing customer needs in their home and foreign markets. 'What's good for Germany is good enough for the world market' was the view typifying a large proportion of German machine-tool producers which formed the focus of a study into international marketing strategies in the UK market. This cultural arrogance has been termed the 'self-reference criterion' and has been a significant factor in accounting for poor export performance.[30]

Some international marketers suggest that companies should 'think globally but act locally'. They advocate a 'glocal' strategy in which the firm standardises certain core marketing elements and localises others. The corporate level gives strategic direction; local units focus on the individual consumer differences. They conclude: global marketing, yes; global standardisation, not necessarily.

Let us now examine marketing mix decisions with regard to global marketing planning.

Product

Five strategies allow for adapting product and promotion to a foreign market (see Figure 6.4).[31] We first discuss the three product strategies and then turn to the two promotion strategies.

Straight product extension means marketing a product in a foreign market without any change. Straight extension has been successful in some cases. Philips shavers, Kellogg cereals, Heineken beer, Coca-Cola and Black & Decker tools are all sold successfully in about the same form around the world. Straight extension is tempting because it involves no additional product-development costs, manufacturing changes or new promotion. But it can be costly in the long run if products fail to satisfy foreign consumers.

Straight product extension— Marketing a product in a foreign market without any change.

Operating in 79 countries and regions across the world, HSBC advocates the importance of 'thinking globally, but acting locally'.
SOURCE: HSBC Holdings Plc.
Agency: Lowe Worldwide.
Photographer: Richard Pullar.

CHINA
Delicacy

NETHERLANDS
Delicacy

FRANCE
Delicacy

Never underestimate the importance of local knowledge.

Real, authentic, local cuisine? It's something you tend to know when you're from a particular area.

At HSBC, we have banks in more countries than anyone else. And each one is staffed by local people.

We have offices in 79 countries and territories; Europe, Asia-Pacific, the Americas, the Middle East, and Africa. Being local enables them to offer insights into financial opportunities and create service initiatives that would never occur to an outsider.

It means our customers get the kind of local knowledge and personal service that you'd expect of a local bank.

And a level of global knowledge and widely sourced expertise that you wouldn't.

HSBC
The world's local bank

Product adaptation—
Adapting a product to meet local conditions or wants in foreign markets.

Product adaptation involves changing the product to meet local conditions or wants. For example, Philips began to make a profit in Japan only after it reduced the size of its coffee makers to fit into smaller Japanese kitchens and its shavers to fit smaller Japanese hands. Komatsu, the Japanese construction machinery maker, had to alter the design of the door handles of earthmovers sold in Finland: drivers wearing thick gloves in winter found it impossible to grasp the door handles, which were too small (obviously designed to fit the fingers of the average Japanese, but not the double-cladded ones of larger European users!). And Nokia customised its 6100 series mobile phone for every major market. It built in rudimentary voice recognition for Asia where keyboards are a problem and raised the ring volume so the phone could be heard on crowded Asian streets.[32]

	Product		
	Don't change product	Adapt product	Develop new product
Don't change promotion	1. Straight extension	3. Product adaptation	
			5. Product invention
Adapt promotion	2. Communication adaptation	4. Dual adaptation	

Promotion

Figure 6.4 **Five international product and promotion strategies**

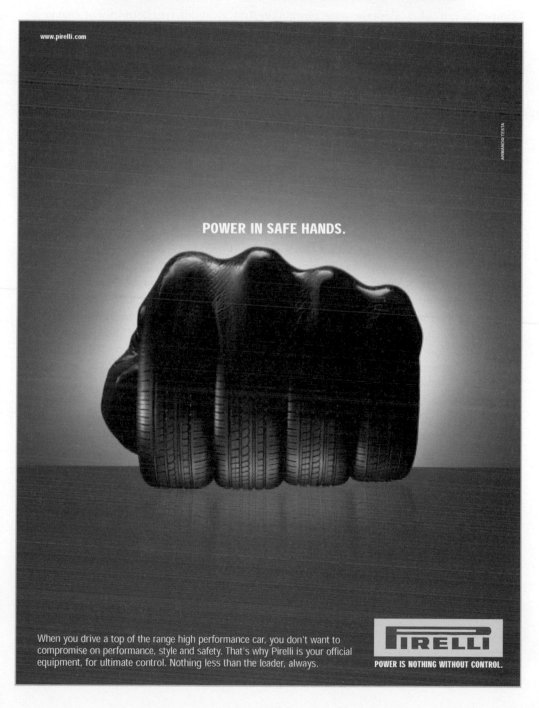

The Italian execution of a Pirelli campaign shows the global application of many of today's ads.
SOURCE: Pirelli & C. SpA.

Product invention—Creating new products or services for foreign markets.

Product invention consists of creating something new for the foreign market. This strategy can take two forms. It might mean reintroducing earlier product forms that happen to be well adapted to the needs of a given country. Or a company might create a new product to meet a need in another country. For example, an enormous need exists for low-cost, high-protein foods in less developed countries. Companies such as Quaker Oats, Swift and Monsanto are researching the nutrition needs of these countries, creating new foods, and developing advertising campaigns to gain product trial and acceptance. Product invention can be costly, but the pay-offs are worthwhile.

Promotion

Companies can either adopt the same promotion strategy in different countries or change it for each local market.

Consider advertising messages. Some global companies use a standardised advertising theme around the world. For example, IBM Global Services runs virtually identical 'People Who Think. People Who Do. People Who Get It.' ads in dozens of countries around the world.

Sometimes the copy is varied in minor ways to adjust for language differences. Colours may also be changed to avoid taboos in other countries. For example, in Spain, packaging that uses red and yellow, the colours of the Spanish flag, may be seen as an offence to Spanish patriotism. In Greece, purple should be avoided as it has funeral associations. Black is an unlucky colour for the Chinese, white is a mourning colour in Japan, and green is associated with jungle sickness in Malaysia.

Indeed, many global companies have had difficulty crossing the language barrier, with results ranging from mild embarrassment to outright failure. Seemingly innocuous brand names and advertising phrases can take on unintended or hidden meanings when translated into other languages. Careless translations can make a marketer look downright foolish to foreign consumers. The classic language blunders in international marketing involve standardised brand names that do not translate well. In Sweden, Helene Curtis changed the name of its 'Every Night Shampoo' to 'Every Day' because Swedish consumers usually wash their hair in the morning. When Coca-Cola first marketed Coke in China in the 1920s, it developed a group of Chinese characters that, when pronounced, sounded like the product name. Unfortunately, the characters actually translated to mean 'bite the wax tadpole'. Now, the characters on Chinese Coke bottles translate as 'happiness in the mouth'.

Car-maker Rolls-Royce avoided the name Silver Mist in German markets, where *Mist* means 'manure'. Sunbeam, however, entered the German market with its Mist Stick hair curling iron. As should have been expected, the Germans had little use for a 'manure wand'. A similar fate awaited Colgate when it introduced a toothpaste in France called Cue, the name of a notorious porno magazine. One well-intentioned firm sold its shampoo in Brazil under the name Evitol. It soon realised it was claiming to sell a 'dandruff contraceptive'.

Interbrand of London, the firm that created household names such as Prozac and Acura, recently developed a brand-name 'hall of shame' list, which contained these and other foreign brand names that are unlikely to cross the English language barrier: Krapp toilet paper (Denmark), Crapsy Fruit cereal (France), Happy End toilet paper (Germany), Mukk yogurt (Italy), Zit lemonade (Germany), Poo curry powder (Argentina) and Pschitt lemonade (France).

Travellers often encounter well-intentioned advice from service firms that takes on meanings very different from those intended. The menu in one Swiss restaurant proudly stated: 'Our wines leave you nothing to hope for.' Signs in a Japanese hotel pronounced: 'You are invited to take advantage of the chambermaid.' At a laundry in Rome, it was: 'Ladies, leave your clothes here and spend the afternoon having a good time.' The brochure at a Tokyo car rental offered this sage advice: 'When passenger of foot heave in sight, tootle the horn. Trumpet him melodiously at first, but if he still obstacles your passage, tootle him with vigour.' And a Chinese grocery retailer in Kuala Lumpur offers to sell all sorts of sundry goods, although foreign visitors may be somewhat wary about stepping into the store. Why? Because it is called 'Sin Tit'.

Advertising themes often lose – or gain – something in the translation. The Coors beer slogan 'get loose with Coors' in Spanish came out as 'get the runs with Coors'. Coca-Cola's 'Coke adds life' theme in Japanese translated into 'Coke brings your ancestors back from the dead'. In Chinese, the KFC slogan 'finger-lickin' good' came out as 'eat your fingers off'. Even when the language is the same, word usage may differ from country to country. Thus, the British ad line for Electrolux vacuum cleaners – 'Nothing sucks like an Electrolux' – would capture few customers in the United States.[33]

Other companies follow a strategy of **communication adaptation**, fully adapting their advertising messages or techniques to local markets. Mass media communications are less effective in emerging markets such as China or India. Their vast rural population is dispersed and has limited access to broadcast media. Unilever used video vans that toured the villages screening films in the local language, interspersed with advertising for Unilever products.

Media also need to be adapted internationally because media use and media availability vary from country to country. For example, Austria and Italy regulate TV advertising to children. In Saudi Arabia, advertisers have to refrain from using women in ads. TV advertising time varies across Europe, for instance, ranging from four hours a day in France to none in Scandinavian countries, where print advertising is preferred to TV ads. Advertisers must buy time months in advance, and they have little control over air times. The types of print media also vary in effectiveness. For example, magazines are a popular medium in Italy and a minor one in Austria. Newspapers are national in the United Kingdom, but are only local in Spain.[34]

Companies adopt a dual adaptation strategy when both the product and communication messages have to be modified to meet the needs and expectations of target customers in different country markets.

Communication adaptation— A global communication strategy of fully adapting advertising messages to local markets.

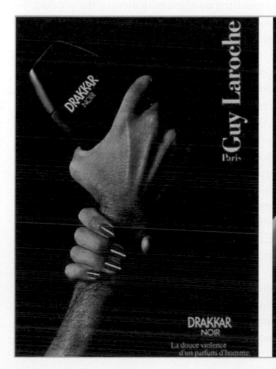 

Some companies standardise their advertising around the world, adapting only to meet cultural differences. Guy LaRoche uses similar ads in Europe (left) and Arab countries (right), but tones down the sensuality in the Arab version – the man is clothed and the woman barely touches him.
SOURCE: Courtesy of Bernard Malussiere.

> For example, the French food multinational, Danone, not only had to bring its products closer to consumer tastes, but also adapted advertising messages to suit different European market expectations. In France, yoghurt is typically sold as a plain yoghurt, a symbol of good health. Fruit and flavourings come later. Advertising emphasises the health logic. In the UK, the product is associated with pleasure, of a sort enjoyed by adults. Fruits add to the pleasure of eating yoghurt. Plain, flavoured yoghurt (without the fruit) is considered a lesser yoghurt, one without the pleasure. In Spain or Portugal, where fruit is abundant, consumers prefer plain yoghurt, eaten as much by children as by adults. In Italy, consumers prefer blended yoghurt, while flavoured varieties are positioned for very young children. Advertising messages are therefore adjusted accordingly to reflect these preferences.

Even sales promotion techniques have to be adapted to different countries. For example, in Germany, companies cannot advertise money-back guarantees and laws limit price discounts to 3 per cent of price. Several European countries also have regulations preventing or restricting the use of sales promotion tools such as rebates, coupons, premiums and games of chance.

Price

Companies also face several problems when setting their international prices.

Companies selling their products abroad may face a *price escalation* problem due to the need to add the cost of transportation, tariffs, importer margin, wholesaler margin and retailer margin to their factory price. For example, a Gucci handbag may sell for €150 in Italy and the equivalent of €350 in Singapore. Depending on these added costs, the product may have to sell for two to five times as much in another country to make the same profit.

Another problem involves setting a *transfer price* – that is, the price that a company charges for goods that it ships to its foreign subsidiaries. If the company charges a foreign subsidiary too much, it may end up paying higher tariff duties even while paying lower income taxes in the foreign country. If the company charges its subsidiary too little, it can be charged with *dumping* – that is, pricing exports at levels less than their costs or less than the prices charged in its home market. For example, the EU imposed anti-dumping duties of as much as 96.0 per cent on imports of broadcasting cameras made by some Japanese companies after an investigation by the European Commission found that Japanese exporters had, through unfair pricing, increased their share of the EU studio video camera market in the early 1990s.[35]

Recent economic and technological forces have had an impact on global pricing. For example, in the euro-zone, the adoption of a single currency is reducing the amount of price differentiation. As consumers recognise price differentiation by country, companies are being forced to harmonise prices throughout the countries that have adopted the single currency. Companies and marketers that offer the most unique or necessary products or services will be least affected by such 'price transparency'.

The Internet will also make global price differences more obvious. When firms sell their wares over the Internet, customers can see how much products sell for in different countries. They might even be able to order a given product directly from the company location or dealer offering the lowest price. This will force companies towards more standardised international pricing.[36]

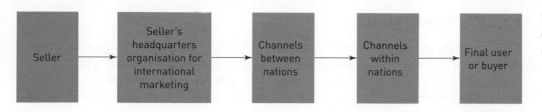

Figure 6.5 Whole-channel concept for international marketing

Distribution channels

The international company must take a *whole-channel* view of the problem of distributing products to final consumers. Figure 6.5 shows the three main links between the *seller* and the *final buyer*. The first link, the *seller's headquarters organisation*, supervises the channels and is part of the channel itself. The second link, *channels between nations*, moves the products to the borders of the foreign nations. The third link, *channels within nations*, moves the products from their foreign entry point to the final consumers. Some manufacturers may think their job is done once the product leaves their hands, but they would do well to pay more attention to its handling within foreign countries.

Channels of distribution within countries vary greatly from nation to nation. First, there are the large differences in the *numbers and types of intermediaries* serving each foreign market.

For example, a European company marketing in China must operate through a frustrating maze of state-controlled wholesalers and retailers. Chinese distributors often carry competitors' products and frequently refuse to share even basic sales and marketing information with their suppliers. Hustling for sales is an alien concept to Chinese distributors, who are used to selling all they can obtain. Working with or getting around this system sometimes requires substantial time and investment.[37] When Coke first entered China, for example, customers bicycled up to bottling plants to get their soft drinks. Many shopkeepers still don't have enough electricity to run soft-drink coolers. Now, Coca-Cola sets up direct-distribution channels, investing heavily in refrigerators and trucks, and upgrading wiring so that more retailers can install coolers.[38]

Another difference lies in the size and character of retail units abroad. Whereas large-scale retail chains dominate the British and US scene, most retailing in the rest of Europe and other countries, such as Japan and India, is done by many small independent retailers. Getting to grips with a foreign country's distribution structure is often crucial to achieving effective market access. The international firm must therefore invest in acquiring knowledge about each foreign market's channel features and decide on how best to break into complex or entrenched distribution systems. In addition, when first entering a foreign market, the company must select the most appropriate distributors, working with them to determine and agree on mutually beneficial distribution targets and performance goals.[39]

Deciding on the global marketing organisation

The key to success in any marketing strategy is the firm's ability to implement the chosen strategy. Because of the firm's distance from its foreign markets, international marketing strategy implementation is particularly difficult. The firm must have an organisation structure that fits with the international environment.

Companies manage their international marketing activities in at least three different ways. Most companies first organise an export department, then create an international division and finally become a global organisation.

Export department

A firm normally gets into international marketing by simply shipping out its goods. If its international sales expand, the company organises an **export department** with a sales manager and a few assistants. As sales increase, the export department can then expand to include various marketing services, so that it can actively go after business. If the firm moves into

joint ventures or direct investment, the export department will no longer be adequate.

International division

Many companies get involved in several international markets and ventures. A company may export to one country, license to another, have a joint-ownership venture in a third and own a subsidiary in a fourth. Sooner or later it will create an **international division** or subsidiary to handle all its international activities.

The international division's corporate staff consists of marketing, manufacturing, research, finance, planning and personnel specialists. They plan for and provide services to various operating units. Operating units may be organised in one of three ways. They may be *geographical* organisations, with country managers who are responsible for salespeople, sales branches, distributors and licensees in their respective countries. Or the operating units may be *world product groups*, each responsible for worldwide sales of different product groups. Finally, operating units may be *international subsidiaries*, each responsible for its own sales and profits.

Global organisation

Several firms have passed beyond the international division stage and become truly **global organisations**. They stop thinking of themselves as national marketers that sell abroad and start thinking of themselves as global marketers. The top corporate management and staff plan worldwide manufacturing facilities, marketing policies, financial flows and logistical systems. The global operating units report directly to the chief executive or executive committee of the organisation, not to the head of an international division. Executives are trained in worldwide operations, not just domestic or international. The company recruits management from many countries, buys components and supplies where they cost the least, and invests where the expected returns are greatest.

In the twenty-first century, major companies must become more global if they hope to compete. As foreign companies successfully invade the domestic market, domestic companies must move more aggressively into foreign markets. They will have to change from companies that treat their foreign operations as secondary concerns, to companies that view the entire world as a single borderless market.[40]

Summary

In this chapter, we looked at why companies today can no longer afford to pay attention only to their domestic market, regardless of its size. Many industries are global industries, and those firms that operate globally achieve lower costs and higher brand awareness. At the same time, *global marketing* is risky because of variable exchange rates, unstable governments, protectionist tariffs and trade barriers, and several other factors. Given the potential gains and risks of international marketing, companies need to adopt a systematic approach to making international marketing decisions. Here, we review the major global marketing concepts covered in this chapter.

Managers must understand the *global marketing environment*, especially the *international trade system*. The company must assess each foreign market's *economic*, *political–legal* and *cultural characteristics*. It must then decide whether to go international based on a consideration of the potential risks and benefits. Next, the company must decide on the volume of international sales it wants, how many countries it wants to market in, and which specific *country markets* it *wants to enter*. This decision calls for weighing the probable rate of return on investment against the level of risk.

The company has to *decide how to enter* each chosen market – whether through *exporting*, *joint venturing* or *direct investment*. Many companies start as exporters, move to joint ventures and finally make a direct investment in foreign markets. Increasingly, however, firms – domestic or international – use joint ventures and even direct investments to enter a new country market for the first time. In *exporting*, the company enters a foreign market by sending and selling products through international marketing intermediaries (indirect exporting) or the company's own department, branch, or sales representative or agents (direct exporting). When establishing a *joint venture*, a company enters foreign markets by joining with foreign companies to produce or market a product or service. In *licensing*, the company enters a foreign market by contracting with a licensee in the foreign market, offering the right to use a manufacturing process, trademark, patent, trade secret, or other item of value for a fee or royalty. In *direct investment*, the company enters a foreign market by developing foreign-based assembly or production facilities.

When selling goods or services abroad, the company must decide on its global marketing programme. Managers must decide on the level of *adaptation* or *standardisation* of their *product*, *promotion*, *price* and *distribution channels* for each foreign market. At one extreme, global companies use a *standardised marketing mix* worldwide. Others use an *adapted marketing mix*, in which they adjust the marketing mix to each target market, bearing more costs but hoping for a larger market share and return.

Finally, the firm must develop an effective organisation for international marketing. Most firms start with an *export department* and graduate to an *international division*. A few become *global organisations*, with worldwide marketing planned and managed by the top officers of the company, who view the entire world as a single borderless market.

Discussing the issues

1. The world is shrinking rapidly with the advent of faster communication, transportation and financial flows. The terms *global industry* and *global firm* are becoming more common. Define these terms and provide an example of each. Explain your examples.

2. When exporting goods to a foreign country, a marketer may be faced with various trade restrictions. Discuss the effects these restrictions might have on an exporter's marketing mix: (a) tariffs, (b) quotas and (c) embargoes.

3. With all the problems facing companies that 'go global', why are so many companies choosing to expand internationally? What are the advantages of expanding beyond the domestic market?

4. Imported products are usually more expensive, but not always: a Nikon camera is cheaper in London than in Tokyo. Why are foreign prices sometimes higher and sometimes lower than domestic prices for exports?

5. Before going abroad, a company should try to define its international marketing objectives, policies and modes of entry. Assume that you are a product manager for Dyson, a manufacturer of domestic vacuum cleaners and washing machines. Outline a plan for expanding your operations and marketing efforts into the United States.

6. Which type of international marketing organisation would you suggest for the following companies: (a) Adidas selling a wide range of sports and athletic clothing and footwear across the globe; (b) DaimlerChrysler's expansion into China; and (c) Ericsson selling its full line of products in the Far East? Explain.

Applying the concepts

1. It used to be that free trade and globalisation talks involved mostly discussions about tariffs and quotas. Now the two equate with culture, sovereignty and power. Trade talks were once held in smoke-filled rooms by diplomats. Today, they are conducted via television and the World Wide Web, with anti-globalisation protesters often dominating the scenes. These protesters argue that globalisation is about exploitation and environmental destruction. They feel that it will result in the assimilation of people, markets and cultures into a more generic whole. For more information, visit the following websites: the International Trade Association (www.ita.doc.gov), the 2003 *World Fact Book*, a CIA publication (www.odic.gov/cia/publications/factbook/index.html), The World Bank (www.worldbank.org) and the World Trade Organisation (www.wto.org); also visit www.paris21.org/betterworld, for more information on 'A better world for all', a report prepared jointly by the UN, World Bank, IMF and OECD.

    - What is the World Trade Organisation? Who are the member nations?
    - What have you learned about the anti-globalisation movement and their protests against globalisation at previous WTO conferences? How should the WTO proceed in the face of such protests?
    - Write a short position paper either defending or rejecting globalisation.
    - What are the implications for multinational companies seeking to protect and defend their position in the face of anti-globalisation sentiments?

2. Nowhere is international competition more apparent than in the digital camera market. Overnight, the advent of digital cameras has changed the way many photographers view their equipment. Digital cameras offer opportunities for reproduction and Internet viewing unrivalled by more traditional products. However, the market is also uncharted, chaotic, and increasingly crowded, with more than 20 manufacturers worldwide. The latest entrant is film giant Fuji (www.fujifilm.com). As the world's number-two producer, Fuji now plans to meet or beat Kodak (www.kodak.com), Sony (www.sony.com), Olympus (www.olympus.com), and Konica (www.konica.com) in digital camera products. Fuji introduced its first digital cameras in its own backyard – Japan, which is also a Sony stronghold. One factor motivating the move into digital cameras was its inability to erode Kodak's worldwide share of the film market. If the wave of the future turns out to be digital, Fuji plans to ride the wave's crest for as long as it can.

- Analyse Fuji's strategy of entering the digital camera market. What challenges is Fuji most likely to face in the digital camera market? How might Fuji's traditional strengths in film aid its efforts in the new digital camera market?
- What world markets should Fuji consider after Japan? Explain.
- If you were the marketing manager of Fuji, what advertising strategy would you suggest for Fuji's new product venture in Europe? What distribution strategy would you use?
- What actions will Kodak, Olympus, Konica and Sony probably take to counter Fuji's entry?

References

1. This case is a reproduction of Bettina Wassener, 'Schnapps goes to college', *Financial Times* (4 September 2003), p. 15; article accessed at FT.com site, 3 September 2003.

2. International Trade Statistics 2001, GTO, p. 1, accessed online at www.wto.org/english/res_e/statis_e/its02_toc_e.htm, September 2002.

3. 'Financial indicators. Top exporters', *The Economist* (15 April 2000), p. 145.

4. Anna Chalmers, 'Feelings run high on Nazi issue', *Financial Times IT Review* (6 December 2000), p. xxiii; 'The Internet: Vive la liberté', *The Economist* (25 November 2000), pp. 120, 125; Shannon Oberndorf, 'Europe jumps online', *Catalog Age* (June 1999), p. 10; and Bill Spindle, 'E-commerce (a special report)', *Wall Street Journal* (12 July 1999), p. R22; 'First America, then the world', *The Economist. E-Commerce Survey* (26 February 2000), pp. 35–6, 41.

5. 'WTO predicts global trade to rise 6.5%', *Financial Times* (14 April 2000), p. 12.

6. For more on non-tariff and other barriers, see Carla Rapoport, 'The big split', *Fortune* (6 May 1991), pp. 38–48; Mark Maremont, 'Protectionism is king of the road', *Business Week* (13 May 1991), pp. 57–8.

7. Douglas Harbrecht and Owen Ullmann, 'Finally GATT may fly', *Business Week* (29 December 1993), pp. 36–7; Jon Marks, 'New kids on the Eurotrading bloc', *Financial Times, FT Exporter*, 11 (Spring 1996), p. 7; 'Special article: World trade: Fifty years on', *The Economist* (16 May 1998), pp. 21–3; and Helene Cooper, 'The millennium – Trade & commerce: Trading blocks', *Wall Street Journal* (11 January 1999), p. R50; Michael Finger and Julio J. Nogues, 'The unbalanced Uruguay outcome: the new areas in future WTO negotiations', *The World Economy* (March 2002), pp. 321–40; and *WTO Annual Report 2002*, accessed online at www.wto.org.

8. Supachai Panitchpakdi, 'Cancún must keep Doha on track', *Financial Times* (5 September 2003), p. 21; Martin Wolf, 'Welcoming China to the world', *Financial Times* (17 May 2000), p. 23; James Kynge, 'Rising giant "enters the world"', *Financial Times Survey* (13 November 2000), p. I; 'Fifty years on', *The Economist* (16 May 1998), pp. 21–5; 'School's brief: trade winds', *The Economist* (8 November 1997), pp. 124–5; 'All free traders now', *The Economist* (7 December 1996), pp. 25–7.

9. Guy de Jonquières, 'Modest goals in Cancún: Trying to achieve liberalisation in a group of 146 countries is well-nigh impossible', *Financial Times* (4 September 2003), p. 19; see also 'Economic focus: Weighing up the WTO', *The Economist* (23 November 2002), p. 96.

10. Information about the European Union from *The European Union at a Glance*, accessed online at http://europa.eu.int, August 2003; For more information about EU enlargement, see *EU Enlargement Survey* (22 November 2003), accessed online at www.Economist.com/surveys.

11. Stanley Reed, 'We have lift off! The strong launch of the euro is hailed around the world', *Business Week* (18 January 1999), pp. 34–7; Quentin Peel, 'Mapping Europe's future', *Financial Times* (19 June 2000), p. 26; 'Finance and economics: Up for adoption; Central Europe and the euro', *The Economist* (1 June 2002), pp. 69–70.

12. James Welsh, 'Enter the euro', *World Trade* (January 1999), pp. 34–8.

13. See 'Around Europe in 40 years', *The Economist* (31 May 1999), p. S4; Colin Egan and Peter McKiernan, *Inside Fortress Europe: Strategies for the single market*, the EIU series (Wokingham, Berks: Addison-Wesley, 1994); Brian Rothery, *What Maastricht Means for Business* (Aldershot: Gower, 1993).

14. Charles J. Whalen, 'NAFTA's scorecard: so far, so good', *Business Week* (9 July 2001), pp. 54–6; Geri Smith, 'Betting on free trade: will the Americas be one big market?', *Business Week* (23 April 2001), pp. 60–2; Ernesto Zedillo, 'Commentary: free trade is the best diplomacy', *Forbes* (23 July 2001), p. 49; and Fay Hansen, 'World trade update', *Business Finance* (March 2002), pp. 9–11.

15. Larry Rohter, 'Latin America and Europe to talk trade', *New York Times* (26 June 1999), p. 2; and Bernard Malamud and Wayne A. Label, 'The merco: a common currency for Mercosur and Latin America', *American Business Review* (June 2002), pp. 132–9.

16. Dan West, 'Countertrade', *Business Credit* (April 2001), pp. 64–7; Dan West, 'Countertrade', *Business Credit* (April 2002), pp. 48–51.

17. See Louis Kraar, 'How to sell to cashless buyers', *Fortune* (7 November 1988), pp. 147–54; 'Pepsi to get ships, vodka in $3 billion deal', *Durham Morning Herald* (10 May 1990), p. B5; Cyndee Miller, 'Worldwide money crunch fuels more international barter', *Marketing News* (2 March 1992), p. 5; Darren McDermott and S. Karen Witcher, 'Bartering gains currency', *Wall Street Journal* (6 April 1998), p. A10; Anne Millen Porter, 'Global economic meltdown boosts barter business', *Purchasing* (11 February 1999), pp. 21–5; S. Jayasankaran, 'Fire-fighting', *Far Eastern Economic Review* (31 May 2001), p. 52; and Dalia Marin and Monika Schnitzer, 'The economic institution of international barter', *The Economic Journal* (April 2002), pp. 293–316.

18. Gail Edmondson, 'The beauty of global branding', *Business Week* (28 June 1999), pp. 70–5.

19. Elisabeth Rosenthal, 'Buicks, Starbucks and fried chicken. Still China?', *New York Times* (25 February 2002), p. A4.

20. Henry Jenkins, 'Culture goes global', *Technology Review* (July–August 2001), p. 89.

21. Websites such as these may be of use to exporters and international marketers seeking market information about exporting. Some are officially sanctioned by government agencies; others are commercial in nature, offering research material and contact opportunities on a subscription basis. The British Chambers of Commerce (www.britishchambers.org.uk/exportzone), British Trade International (www.brittrade.com/emic), Trade UK (www.tradeuk.com), The United States–Asia Environmental Partnership (www.usaep.org/export/index.htm/), Asia Market Research Dot Com (www.asiamarketresearcg.com), and Cyberatlas (http://cyberatlas.internet.com) give a global overview of the state of the online marketplace.

22. Robert Neff, 'In brief: e-trade licensing deal gives it an Israeli link', *American Banker* (11 May 1998); www.etrade.com.

23. Christopher Brown-Humes, 'Nokia plans to launch new Chinese venture', *Financial Times* (1 April 2003), p. 27.

24. Robert Wright, 'Fresh investors sought', *Financial Times, Special Report Hungary* (27 May 2003), p. VI.

25. Jan Johanson and Finn Wiedersheim-Paul, 'The internationalization of the firm', *Journal of Management Studies* (October 1975), pp. 305–22.

26. Somkid Jatusripitak, *The Exporting Behavior of Manufacturing Firms*, Ann Arbor: University of Michigan Press, 1986.

27. Sally Beatty and Carol Hymowitz 'Boss Talk: How MTV stays tuned into teens', *Wall Street Journal* (21 March 2000), p. 81, Kerry Capell, 'MTV's World: Mando-Pop. Mexican Hip Hop. Russian Rap. It's all fueling the global channel', *Business Week* (18 February 2002), pp. 81–84. For more discussion on the advantages of a global strategy and potential pitfalls, see Kevin Lane and Sanjay Sood, 'The ten commandments of global branding', *Asian Journal of Marketing* (Volume 8, No. 2, 2001), pp. 72–84.

28. See Theodore Levitt, 'The globalization of markets', *Harvard Business Review* (May–June 1983), pp. 92–102; David M. Szymanski, Sundar G. Bharadwaj and Rajan Varadarajan, 'Standardization versus adaptation of international marketing strategy: An empirical investigation', *Journal of Marketing* (October 1993), pp. 1–17; Ashish Banerjee, 'Global campaigns don't work; multinationals do', *Advertising Age* (18 April 1994), p. 23; Jeryl Whitelock and Carole Pimblett, 'The standardization debate in international marketing', *Journal of Global Marketing* (1997), p. 22; and David A. Aaker and Ericj Joachimsthaler, 'The lure of global branding', *Harvard Business Review* (November–December 1999), pp. 137–44.

29. Moises Naim, 'McAtlas shrugged', *Foreign Policy* (May–June 2001), pp. 26–37; and Suh-Kyung Yoon, 'Look who's going native', *Far Eastern Economic Review* (1 February 2001), pp. 68–9.

30. See George S. Yip, 'Global strategy . . . in a world of nations?', *Sloan Management Review* (Fall 1989), pp. 29–41; Kamran Kashani, 'Beware the pitfalls of global marketing', *Harvard Business Review* (September–October 1989), pp. 91–8; Saeed Saminee and Kendall Roth, 'The influence of global marketing standardization on performance', *Journal of Marketing* (April 1992), pp. 1–17.

31. See Warren J. Keegan, *Global Marketing Management*, 7th edition, Upper Saddle River, NJ: Prentice Hall, 2002, pp. 346–51. See also Warren J. Keegan and Bodo B. Schlegelmilch, *Global Marketing Management: A European Perspective*, Harlow, Essex: FT/Prentice Hall, 2001; Peter G. P. Walters and Brian Toyne, 'Product modification and standardization in international markets: strategic options and facilitating policies', *Columbia Journal of World Business* (Winter 1989), pp. 37–44.

32. See Andrew Kupfer, 'How to be a global manager', *Fortune* (14 March 1988), pp. 52–8; Jack Neff, 'Test it in Paris, France, launch it in Paris, Texas', *Advertising Age* (31 May 1999), p. 28.

33. See Matt Forney, Dimon Fluendy and Emily Thornton, 'A matter of wording', *Far Eastern Economic Review* (10 October 1996), pp. 72–3; David A. Ricks, 'Perspectives: Translation blunders in international business', *Journal of Language for International Business*, **7**, 2 (1996), pp. 50–5; Ken Friedenreich, 'The lingua too Franca', *World Trade* (April 1998), p. 98; and Richard P. Carpenter, 'What they meant to say was . . .', *Boston Globe* (2 August 1998), p. M6; Lara L. Sowinski, 'Ubersetzung, traduzione, or traduccion', *World Trade* (February 2002), pp. 48–9.

34. Alicia Clegg, 'One ad one world', *Marketing Week* (20 June 2002), pp. 51–2.

35. See Guy de Jonquières, 'High duties against Japan', *Financial Times* (4 May 1994), p. 7.

36. Ram Charan, 'The rules have changed', *Fortune* (16 March 1998), pp. 159–62.

37. See Maria Shao, 'Laying the foundation for the great mall of China', *Business Week* (25 January 1988), pp. 68–9; and Mark L. Clifford and Nicole Harris, 'Coke pours into China', *Business Week* (28 October 1996), p. 73.

38. Richard Tomlinson, 'The China card', *Fortune* (25 May 1998), p. 82; and Paul Mooney, 'Deals on wheels', *Far East Economic Review* (20 May 1999), p. 53.

39. David Arnold, 'Seven rules of international distribution', *Harvard Business Review* (November–December 2000), pp. 131–7.

40. See Kenichi Ohmae, 'Managing in a borderless world', *Harvard Business Review* (May–June 1989), pp. 152–61; William J. Holstein, 'The stateless corporation', *Business Week* (14 May 1990), pp. 98–105; John A. Byrne and Kathleen Kerwin, 'Borderless management', *Business Week* (23 May 1994), pp. 24–6; see also Christopher A. Bartlett and Sumantra Goshal, *Managing Across Borders*, Cambridge, MA: Harvard Business School Press, 1989.

WEB RESOURCES

For additional classic case studies and Internet exercises, visit www.pearsoned.co.uk/kotler

Concluding concepts 6
Making the global tipple: soil, climate, aspect and mystique

'A few decades ago it was not difficult to know about wine', explained Ivor Trink, one of Australia's new breed of flash, flying wine makers. 'There was claret, burgundy, champagne, port, sherry and loads of gut rot.' Dr Trink had been invited, and paid a fat fee, to talk to a gathering of some of Bordeaux's 12,000 wine producers. He continued, 'You are the guardians of the *terrier*, that combination of soil, climate and aspect shaped by two millennia of expertise that signal a wine's excellence. Australian wine producers are resigned to French producers continuing to dominate the great heights of wine making, trophy wines selling for hundreds of euros a bottle.' 'Of course', heckled one distinguished wine grower, 'but we don't need you to tell us that.'

Undeterred, Dr Trink continued and started to win over his sceptical audience. He projected a chart (Exhibit 6.1) that showed how the main European suppliers, which he called the 'old world', are still forecast to dominate the world's wine production. 'You have the advantage', he continued, 'as your own Baroness Philippine de Rothschild told me, "Winemaking is easy. Only the first 200 years are difficult." And you certainly have experience. The museum at Château Mouton Rothschild traces wine making back to Roman times and has a cellar devoted to mid-nineteenth-century vintages. The whole place reeks as much of history as wine.

'In a market that is very fragmented, the world market leader – France's luxury goods giant LVHM – has less than 1 per cent of the world market, and the number of "old world" winemakers swamp those from the new world. Italy alone has 1 million winemakers and this region, Bordeaux, makes more wine than the whole of Australia.

'You have the mystique beloved of wine enthusiasts. As the author and wine guru Hugh Johnson proclaims: "Why is wine so fascinating? Because there are so many different kinds, and every single one is different." The prices of the world's most costly wines show France's dominance. While Château d'Yquem (1811) sauternes has

> "Winemaking is easy. Only the first 200 years are difficult."

Exhibit 6.1 Forecast regional share of world production (2006)

Region	% share
Main European exporters: France, Italy, Portugal and Spain	51
Second-tier European producers (Germany, Portugal, Romania)	9
Other major southern hemisphere exporters: Argentina, Chile, New Zealand and South Africa	10
Australia	5
US	8
Rest of world	17

sold for $26,500 (€30,000), Moët & Chandon Esprit de Siècle champagne for $10,000 and Château Mouton Rothschild (1945) for $4,200, the best that the rest of the world can manage is $1,400 for Australian Grange (1955) and $1,000 for Californian Screaming Eagle (1995).

'In addition you have the *appellation contrôlée* that protects your wine's identity through a plethora of rigidly enforced regulations covering the grapes that can be used in a region's blend, the way they are picked, the way the wines are planted, their irrigation, the wine's alcoholic content, the labelling and much more. Your "brands", if you will excuse my use of the word, are the most protected in the world.

'You also have amazingly loyal customers. For example, France is one of the world's greatest consumers of wine and yet imports account for less than 5 per cent of sales. As Françoise Brugière, of the Office National Introprofessionel des Vins, explained to me, "It's no accident that Chauvin was a Frenchman." And the French are not alone in their loyalty. Italian and Spanish wine drinkers are just as loyal to wine made in their own country. Even in Australia over 90 per cent of the wine consumed is home grown.

'Your position in the wine world is pre-eminent. Through your combined strength you have already given bloody noses to the big conglomerates moving into your markets. Remember the fanfare when Coca-Cola introduced their new beverage category, wine, in 1976. It took them four years of losses to learn that Coke is no Grand Cru and make an ignominious exit in 1980. Having not learned from your victory over Coca-Cola, Nestlé, Philip Morris and RJR Nabisco all entered the wine trade, lost their shirts and quit the wine trade in the 1980s. True, some global companies are still dabbling in wine but they are finding it tough. Seagram has just sold off its champagne brands. Only Diageo is hanging on but they are dismissive of the role of wine in their overall strategy. As one manager joked: "Two millennia ago a miracle changes water into wine. We're still waiting for the second miracle: turning wine into profits!".'

The audience was getting to like Dr Tipple but their mood was about to change. 'Yes, you are confidently on top of the pile now but, unless you shape up, Bordeaux will be as much a wine-making joke as Britain. For too long you have ignored customers. You think you are so special, custodians of a grand heritage that defines your nation. You are wrong. You are mostly outdated business, yes business, who for generations have operated more for your own convenience than that of the customers.

'You may have 95 per cent of the French market but the market is, literally, dying on you and you are losing ground elsewhere. Over the past 30 years France's wine consumption has halved and the average age of the regular wine consumer, who drinks at least a glass a day, has risen from 35 to 55. You have lost touch with the youth market. Go to Paris and you will find the bars full of young people drinking. Drinking, yes, but not French wine or wine from any other country. Their drink is foreign beer or whisky.

'The situation in your traditional export markets is equally dire. In the late 1980s, France and Europe's other three big exporters accounted for 85 per cent of the world's exports. They are now down to about 70 per cent. The British market is a good example of what is happening outside the wine-producing countries. Only six years ago, French, German and Italian wines accounted for two-thirds of the wine the Brits consumed. Their combined share is now less than 50 per cent and declining. In 2003 Australia overtook France as Britain's largest wine supplier.

'France, Italy and Spain may be holding onto their share of their declining markets but, elsewhere, new-world wines are driving out the old. And it is in these non-wine-growing areas that wine consumption is growing. While the share of world exports, excluding intra-EU trade, of the main European exporters has slipped from 75 per cent to 55 per cent over the last 10 years, sales of new-world

Exhibit 6.2 **Forecast change in wine production (2001–2006)**

Region	% point change in share
Chile	+24
Australia	+20
Spain	+14
US	+11
France	+6
Italy	−4

exporters have soared. This table (Exhibit 6.2) shows how percentage points in world production is forecast to change.

'Your political parties are now competing in thinking of ways of bolstering up your flagging industry. The Socialists have proposed classing wine as an agricultural product so that it avoids the ban on advertising on alcoholic beverages. Your agriculture minister is also proposing to rationalise the numerous national and regional committees that control wine research. This government assistance may help but it is you, the wine makers, who have to change or wither on the vine with your unwanted grapes.

'You may claim that the new world's gains have been made because of their heavy advertising but that is only part of the story. New-world wine producers are producing brands but a large part of their success is because they understand what brands are. For a brand to succeed consumers have got to recognise and enjoy what they are getting. For a long time, that has not been true of old-world wines. The quality of old-world wines can be outstanding but often it is not. One old-world wine buff was close to the truth when he joked: "It costs £20 (€33) for a good bottle of burgundy, but to enjoy a great bottle of burgundy it cost £200 plus £1800 for the other nine bottles that were not."

'The old world are still trying to use the old SCAM of Soil, Climate, Aspect and Mystique but are losing out to the new world's appliance of science and professionalism. That is what accounted for the "Judgement of Paris" as long ago as 1976. On that occasion the Paris-based wine merchant Steven Spurrier brought together 15 of the most influential French wine critics to compare Californian and French wines in a blind test. These critics were shocked and there was a national outcry when, without the benefit of labels and bottles to guide them, the critics chose the Californian wine over the French. After cries that the test was rigged it was rerun two years later and, once again, gave the same results!

'It seems that your great wine heritage now accounts for little, according to the world's leading wine critics. Australia's Grange, first produced in 1950, "has replaced Bordeaux's Pétrus as the world's most exotic and concentrated wine" and it is argued that New Zealand sauvignon blanc, first produced in 1970, is "arguably, the best in the world". Price comparisons in the UK market show how consumers are voting. Besides gaining sales, new-world wines carry higher prices than European producers: the average price paid for a bottle of New Zealand wine is over £5, for Australian and US wines over £4 a bottle, the average French bottle is about £3.50 and the average German bottle a little over £2.50.

'How has the new world achieved this success? The answer is the appliance of science in wine making and marketing. As John Worontschak, a fellow Australian who lives in Bordeaux, so eloquently explains: "It's because we're open to new ideas, and we're not full of pretentious bullshit." Australia, California and New Zealand do not strive to uphold wine-making traditions supported by state subsidies, but strive to make good, consistent, keenly priced wines, carefully crafted to fit consumers' tastes and expectations. An indication of their scientific endeavour is the production of scientific papers on wine making. Although Australia and New Zealand have only a fraction of the world market they already produce 20 per cent of the scientific papers on wine making. That investment has made them good but also means they are getting better.

'The new world's more enlightened regulations enable them to make both consistent and excellent wines in a way that your *appellation contrôlée* blocks. Their wines are consistent because they can use different irrigation methods and take grapes from different areas to make the taste right. If in one year the conditions are perfect to produce an excellent strong vintage, they will do it and win international prizes for their efforts; your *appellation contrôlée* would prevent you making the superb wines above the regulated strength. If the vintage needs it, they will put oak chips in a barrel to bring out the flavour while you would have to hope for the vagaries of the oak barrel and your variable climate. Yes, your love of the old ways, cottage industries and *appellation contrôlée* are great gifts to the new world.

'Our final great advantage is marketing, but that is more than big budgets. It is finding out what people want and respecting their views. For instance we know that, once people have decided not to buy the cheapest wine, their choice is influenced by four main factors: past experience of wines, the country of origin of the wine, the variety of grape and brand. Too often the wine labels in the

old world are designed to look grand and regulate, rather than elucidate. As Hugh Johnson comments on German wine labels: ". . . laws have introduced ambiguities which only the most dogged use of a reference book can elucidate. Whether there was a publisher on the committee that framed them I don't know. But there can't have been a customer."

'In pandering to customers, not custom, new-world growers understand the importance of consistency and rewarding customers with a taste they like. You may find it amazing but many potential customers are attracted to the sophistication of wine drinking but don't like the taste. Rather than rejecting these lost causes, Californians have invested in wine coolers (a mixture of wine and fruit juices) and fruit-flavoured wines. It is consistently giving customers what they want that allows inexpensively produced new-world wines to sell at a higher price than old-world bottles.

'It is also important to recognise the importance of country of origin. Many of the new-world wines come from young countries with a youthful, fun-loving image. There are also linguistic and historic links with the new world. To English-speaking people, Screaming Eagle is a lot easier to remember and sounds more fun than Veuve Clincquot-Ponsardin or Regierungsbezirk. These links really do matter in the wine trade. For example, the historical links are helping South African wines in the Netherlands while "brand Australia" is struggling in Germany. Eventually Australia will have to do in Germany what they did for the UK market, use focus groups to come up with attractive Australian-sounding names – like Barramundi – that appeal to the local consumer.

'Certainly some French producers have responded with English-sounding names, but are they the right names to build an attack against the young competition? Names like Fat Bastard, Old Git and Old Tart are certainly Anglo-Saxon and memorable, but they sound to me more like an expression of disdain for modern wine consumers than names that will build loyalty and prestige.

'Californians started putting grape varieties on their wine to help give consumers a clue to taste. It is a trick that has since been adopted from New Zealand's superb sauvignon blanc to Chile's merlot. The grape variety constrains the taste that can be constructed but is a useful shorthand valued by mid-range consumers. South Africa is even marketing a Goats do Roam but I believe your Institut National des Appellations d'Origine is trying to ban it since it sounds too similar to Côtes du Rhône!

'Branding is the real spirit of new-world wines. It demands the simple labelling, consistency and quality that new-world wines give. In using these marketing techniques, the scale of new-world wine makers gives them an advantage. Although globally no single winegrower has the dominance of Diageo in the spirits market or Coca-Cola in soft drinks, new-world producers are huge compared with Europe's fragmented industry. In Australia four companies have 80 per cent of wine production and in the huge US market the five biggest producers account for 62 per cent of the market. Like it or not, the big brands are coming. Yes, wine is special to the producers and drinkers, but no more special than globally marketed Highland Park malt whisky or Guinness beer. As the wine journalist Andrew Jefford complained, Australian brands, like Jacob's Creek and Nottage Hill, are "becoming the equivalent of cans of lager; standardised, consistent, reliable, risk-free, challenge-free". Why does he complain? What's wrong with that? The longer you and he fight the march of progress, the sooner you'll die.'

Questions

1. What accounts for the new world's recent success over the old world's wine producers?

The remaining questions for this case ask you to evaluate alternative courses of action suggested in a discussion by the Bordeaux winemakers following Dr Tipple's presentation.

2. Stick to what we have always been doing and build upon our unique *terrier*. Great wines are beyond the marketing babble of the multinationals. We have defeated Coca-Cola, Nestlé and the like, and will defeat this new challenge from much smaller new-world wine makers who are a fraction of the

size of those we have already beaten. After all, the world's wine critics, wine enthusiasts the world over and our local customers remain discerning and are loyal to our wines.

3. Adopt Australian methods of wine production and branding for international markets, like several local wine-makers have done. We must be humble and learn from British Diageo in developing an accessible French brand, such as their Le Piat d'Or, or American Australian Southcorp with Vichon.

4. Follow the lead taken by France's LVHM and Pernod Ricard and buy into the new-world wines' positioning and expertise. LVHM own Australian Green Point and Californian Domaine Chandon while Pernod Ricard owns Australian Jacob's Creek and South African Long Mountain.

5. Seek the disestablishment of *appellation contrôlée* for many of our wine-growing areas so that we can develop the global French brands we need.

6. Follow the lead shown by our farming colleagues to protect our consumers from practices that undermine our European heritage. We have fought against hormones in American beef, genetically modified soya beans and bananas from the Windward Islands. We need to use our political clout in the EU as well as our own parliament.

SOURCES: 'The globe in a glass', *The Economist* (18 December 1999), pp. 107–23; John Apthorp, 'Lord of the wines', *EuroBusiness* (August 2000), pp. 76–7; Giles MacDonogh, 'French take to terrier in battle with brands', *Financial Times Survey: World Wine Industry* (15 December 2000), p. I; Stephen Brook, 'The long road from Hirondelle to here', *Financial Times Survey: World Wine Industry* (15 December 2000), p. IV; Adam Jones, 'Rivalries bubble out in the world of wine', *Finamcial Times* (19 August 2003), p. 24; *La Tribune*, 'French socialists propose wine-advertising rescue' (19 February 2004); *La Tribune*, 'French wine sector: New World challenge (24 November 2003).

The secret of business is to know something that nobody else knows.

ARISTOTLE ONASSIS

Markets

PART THREE OF PRINCIPLES OF MARKETING looks at the most important part of any marketing activity: the people who buy and how to find out about them.

Chapter 7 explores ways of understanding consumer markets: individuals and households who buy goods and services for final consumption. The many ways of doing this give insights that can help in the design of marketing research and guide marketing decision making.

Although consumer marketing is the most visible, the majority of marketing is to other organisations. These include retailers that sell on to final consumers, and sellers of capital equipment – such as trucks, raw materials, components or business services. **Chapter 8** reviews this wide range of business markets.

As Gunther Grass recognised, 'Information networks straddle the world. Nothing remains concealed. But the sheer volume of information dissolves the information. We are unable to take it all in.' **Chapter 9** shows how *marketing research* and marketing information systems help sift through this information, gather further information, process and present results to support marketing decision making.

PART
three

501®
JEANS MIT ANTI-FORM

Rick

"NIEMALS, ICH PASS EINFACH NICHT IN EUREN CLUB"

501@eu.levi.com

What do I want? Everything!
When do I want it? Now!

GRAFFITI

Consumer markets

Chapter objectives

After reading this chapter, you should be able to:

- Define the consumer market and construct a simple model of consumer buying behaviour.
- Tell how culture, subculture and social class influence consumer buying behaviour.
- Describe how consumers' personal characteristics and primary psychological factors affect their buying decisions.
- Discuss how consumer decision making varies with the type of buying decision.
- Explain the stages of the buyer decision and adoption processes.

Mini Contents List

◀ SOURCE: Levi Strauss Jeans.
Agency: BBH.

Prelude case Sheba: the pets' St Valentine's Day

PEDRO QUELHAS BRITO
Universidado do Porto, Portugal

Several years of growth averaging 22 per cent year on year have attracted more than 60 new brands from both local and multinational companies to Portugal's €350 million pet food market. EFFEM-Portugal, whose brands include Sheba, Whiskas and Pedigree Pal, has over half of the pet food market but not all its brands were doing well.

EFFEM had played an important role in developing the market. Much of its success came from understanding the behaviour of both pets and their owners. For example, cats are resolved animals. They eat what they like and leave what they dislike. A cat is selective and sensitive regarding its nutritional needs and taste. If given food it dislikes, a cat seeks an alternative. Dogs are different. A hungry dog will eat almost anything, and eats it quickly. For cat food the main concern is to give pleasure and to provide variety. For dogs it is volume and ease of consumption.

> The Valentine's card showed two cats, probably lovers . . .

Sheba is EFFEM's super-premium brand for cats. With its exceptional quality and its high price, it aims to delight the most discerning cats and is particularly appropriate for special occasions. But Sheba was in trouble. After initial advertising and sales promotional support during its launch, it had been left to fend for itself in the increasingly competitive pet food market. After several years of trading, Sheba's market position and even its commercial existence were threatened by the absence of marketing support and the entrance of new competitors into its market niche. Only 9 per cent of the total market had ever bought a can of Sheba at least once. Sheba's low market share of just 2 per cent justified little promotional expenditure, but for Sheba it was fight back or die.

EFFEM's answer was a two-stage point of sale promotion, with each stage costing as little as a 30-second prime-time TV commercial. Stage one was during the run-up to Christmas. In-store demonstrators approached consumers and asked them if they owned a cat. If customers answered 'yes', they were offered a greetings card and a 100-gram can of Sheba. In this way both owners and pets received a gift. This sampling raised customers' brand awareness and knowledge of Sheba. Besides giving information, the card encouraged the pet's owners to show their love for their cat by giving it Sheba because 'it deserves it'. The card and its message were designed to generate favourable feelings. After all, it was Christmas time and this 'Santa Claws' gave away 12,000 cans of very special Sheba.

The second stage of the campaign repeated the Christmas promotion, but with St Valentine's Day as the theme. The Valentine's card showed two cats, probably lovers, with the messages: 'Because today is a special day, Sheba has a gift for your cat' and 'Let it know how you love [your cat]'. During the campaign 11,900 cans were given to customers at the point of sale. The Valentine's card also doubled as a cash-back coupon with a face value of €0.50. The refund and the emotional appeal of the message helped customers to confirm their preference for Sheba while showing their love for their cat.

The promotions reversed Sheba's sales decline. The impact on brand awareness/knowledge and repeat purchase was evident and the percentage of consumers who had ever tried Sheba increased to 22 per cent.

Questions

1. Is Sheba based on the tastes of cats or their owners?
2. Does the consumer awareness and knowledge achieved account for the success of the Sheba campaign? If not, what does account for the success?
3. Given that Sheba's sales promotion campaign was so much more successful than conventional advertising, why is it not used more often?

Introduction

EFFEM's success with Sheba shows how consumer buying behaviour has many unexpected dimensions. Since the human mind contains as many interacting neurones as there are leaves in the Amazon jungle, it is not surprising that buying behaviour is not simple. Complicated it is, but understanding buyer behaviour is central to marketing management. Just as marketing ends with consumption, so marketing management must begin with understanding customers.

This chapter explores the dynamics of consumer behaviour and the consumer market. **Consumer buying behaviour** refers to the buying behaviour of final consumers – individuals and households who buy goods and services for personal consumption. All of these final consumers combined make up the **consumer market**. The world consumer market consists of about 6.3 billion people, but the billion people living in North America, Western Europe and Japan make up 70 per cent of the world's spending power.[1] Even within these wealthy consumer markets, consumers vary tremendously in age, income, education level and tastes. They also buy an incredible variety of goods and services. How these diverse consumers make their choices among various products embraces a fascinating array of factors.

Models of consumer behaviour

In earlier times, marketers could understand consumers well through the daily experience of selling to them. But as firms and markets have grown in size, many marketing decision makers have lost direct contact with their customers and must now turn to consumer research. They spend more money than ever to study consumers, trying to learn more about consumer behaviour. Who buys? How do they buy? When do they buy? Where do they buy? Why do they buy?

The central question for marketers is: how do consumers respond to various marketing stimuli that the company might use? The company that really understands how consumers will respond to different product features, prices and advertising appeal has a great advantage over its competitors. Therefore, companies and academics have researched heavily the relationship between marketing stimuli and consumer response. Their starting point is the stimulus–response model of buyer behaviour shown in Figure 7.1. This shows that marketing and other stimuli enter the consumer's 'black box' and produce certain responses. Marketers must figure out what is in the buyer's black box.[2]

Marketing stimuli consist of the four Ps: product, price, place and promotion. Other stimuli include significant forces and events in the buyer's environment: economic,

Consumer buying behaviour—The buying behaviour of final consumers – individuals and households who buy goods and services for personal consumption.

Consumer market—All the individuals and households who buy or acquire goods and services for personal consumption.

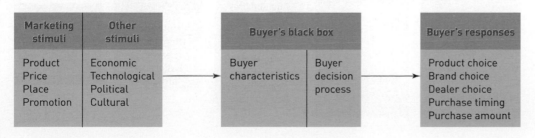

Figure 7.1 Model of buying behaviour

technological, political and cultural. All these stimuli enter the buyer's black box, where they are turned into a set of observable buyer responses (shown on the right-hand side of Figure 7.1): product choice, brand choice, dealer choice, purchase timing and purchase amount.

The marketer wants to understand how the stimuli are changed into responses inside the consumer's black box, which has two parts. First, the buyer's characteristics influence how he or she perceives and reacts to the stimuli. Second, the buyer's decision process itself affects the buyer's behaviour. This chapter first looks at buyer characteristics as they affect buying behaviour, and then examines the buyer decision process. We will never know what exactly is in the black box or be able perfectly to predict consumer behaviour, but the models can help us understand consumers, help us to ask the right questions, and teach us how to influence them.

Characteristics affecting consumer behaviour

Consumer purchases are influenced strongly by cultural, social, personal and psychological characteristics, as shown in Figure 7.2. For the most part, marketers cannot control such factors, but they must take them into account. We illustrate these characteristics for the case of a hypothetical customer, Anna Flores. Anna is a married graduate who works as a brand manager in a leading consumer packaged-goods company. She wants to buy a digital camera to take on holiday. Many characteristics in her background will affect the way she evaluates cameras and chooses a brand.

Cultural factors

Cultural factors exert the broadest and deepest influence on consumer behaviour. The marketer needs to understand the role played by the buyer's culture, subculture and social class.

Culture

Culture—The set of basic values, perceptions, wants and behaviours learned by a member of society from family and other important institutions.

Culture is the most basic cause of a person's wants and behaviour. Human behaviour is largely learned. Growing up in a society, a child learns basic values, perceptions, wants and behaviours from the family and other important institutions. Like most western people, in her childhood Anna observed and learned values about achievement and success, activity and

Figure 7.2 Factors influencing behaviour

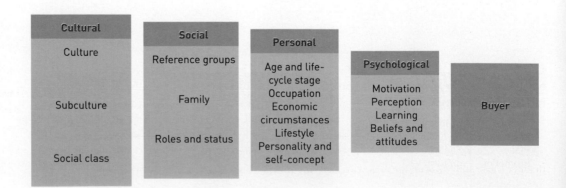

Cultural	Social	Personal	Psychological	
Culture	Reference groups	Age and life-cycle stage	Motivation	
Subculture	Family	Occupation	Perception	Buyer
		Economic circumstances	Learning	
	Roles and status	Lifestyle	Beliefs and attitudes	
Social class		Personality and self-concept		

involvement, efficiency and practicality, progress, material comfort, individualism, freedom, humanitarianism, youthfulness, and fitness and health. Sometimes we take these values for granted, but they are not cultural universals.

> A trade delegation trying to market in Taiwan found this out the hard way. Seeking more foreign trade, they arrived in Taiwan bearing gifts of green baseball caps. Unfortunately, the trip was a month before Taiwan elections, and green was the colour of the political opposition party. Even worse, according to Taiwan culture, a man wears green to signify that his wife has been unfaithful. The head of the delegation noted: 'I don't know whatever happened to those green hats, but the trip gave us an understanding of the extreme differences in our cultures.'[3]

Marketers are always trying to spot *cultural shifts* in order to imagine new products that might be wanted. For example, the cultural shift towards greater concern about health and fitness has created a huge industry for exercise equipment and clothing, lower-calorie and more natural foods, and health and fitness services. Further analysis of this cultural shift shows the complexity of consumer behaviour and how it varies internationally. The 13 per cent of America's population who go to the gym make it the most fitness-conscious nation, although 30 per cent of them are obese and 50 per cent overweight. In contrast, 7 per cent of the less obese British go to the gym while, in much slimmer France and Italy, only 4 per cent of the people take regular vigorous exercise.[4]

The increased desire for leisure time has resulted in more demand for convenience products and services, such as microwave ovens and fast food. Consumers the world over are increasingly concerned about healthy eating. They are also tiring of the shopping and chopping needed to prepare family meals. According to market researchers Taylor Nelson Sofres, over the last 20 years the average time spent preparing a meal has dropped from one hour to 20 minutes. While many consumers express concern about food additives and genetically modified products, one of the fastest-growing markets is for functional foods that scientifically benefit health. For example, Flora Pro.activ is a margarine-like spread that is expensive but 'can dramatically reduce cholesterol to help maintain a healthy heart'.[5]

Besides spending less time preparing food, eating is becoming less of a special event and more a casual activity undertaken while doing something else, such as meeting friends in an informal restaurant or watching TV. Makers of traditional crockery, such as Royal Doulton and Waterford Wedgwood, are shedding workers as they try to adjust to new consumers who no longer buy formal family dinner services but instead buy odd mugs and plates. Doing well out of the trend are craft potters, such as Moorcroft, who make expensive giftable pots, and Alchemy, who make inexpensive items for the catering trade.[6]

Subculture

Each culture contains smaller **subcultures** or groups of people with shared value systems based on common life experiences and situations. Subcultures include nationalities, religions, racial groups and geographic regions. Many subcultures make up important market segments and marketers often design products and marketing programmes tailored to their needs. The huge US market of 260 million people has Hispanic (approaching 40 million) and black (over 30 million) subcultures that are bigger than most national markets. Mass marketers often neglect these subcultures, so these can provide market opportunities for more enterprising businesses.

Subculture—A group of people with shared value systems based on common life experiences and situations.

Islam is the world's fastest growing religion with millions of Muslims living in Europe – 1.3 million in Britain, 3.2 million in Germany and 4.2 million in France. The EU Muslim population is now greater than that of many EU countries, yet some European countries are still struggling over how and whether Muslim students and teachers should wear the headscarves that their beliefs prescribe. Meanwhile HSBC is set to offer Islamic financial products to this growing population. These differ from conventional financial products since they must follow three *sharia* rules:

1. Have no involvement with sinful industries, such as gambling, alcohol or pig meat.

2. A strict ban on *rib* – loosely translated as interest.

3. Avoid *gharar* – excessive risk taking and uncertainty.

Obeying these rules, for products that provide the same benefits as insurance, mortgages or hedge funds, demands creative solutions. For example, instead of providing a loan for a car, *sharia* rules are followed by a supplier of finance buying a car on a customer's behalf and selling it to the customer at a profit. The customer then pays for the car over a fixed period without making any interest.[7]

Like all other people, Anna Flores' buying behaviour will be influenced by her subculture identification. It will affect her food preferences, clothing choices, recreation activities and career goals. Subcultures attach different meanings to picture taking and this could affect both Anna's interest in cameras and the brand she buys.

Social class

Social classes—Relatively permanent and ordered divisions in a society whose members share similar values, interests and behaviours.

Almost every society has some form of social class structure. **Social classes** are society's relatively permanent and ordered divisions whose members share similar values, interests and behaviours. The registrar-general's six social classes have been widely used since the turn of the twentieth century, although all big countries have their own system. In spring 2001 the UK Office of National Statistics adopted a new National Statistics Socio-Economic Classification (NS-SEC) to reflect the social changes of the last century (see Table 7.1). The scheme divides people according to their position in the labour market. Those at the bottom make a short-term exchange of cash for labour while those at the top have long-term contracts and are rewarded by the prospect of career advancement and perks as well as a salary. Although not derived using income, the scale is a good predictor of both income and health, except for the self-employed Class 4 who are as healthy, but not as wealthy, as Classes 1 and 2. Currently there are a number of projects funded by the European Commission that aim to improve the quality of socio-economic and other statistics across Europe.[8]

Not only do class systems differ in various parts of the world: the relative sizes of the classes vary with the relative prosperity of countries. The 'diamond'-shaped classification (few people at the top and bottom with most in the middle) is typical of developed countries, although the Japanese and Scandinavian scales are flatter. In less developed countries, such as in Latin America and Africa, the structure is 'pyramid' shaped with a concentration of poor people at the base. As countries develop, their class structure moves towards the diamond shape,

Classification	Membership
1	Higher managerial and professional occupations
1.1	Employers and managers in large organisations (senior private and public sector employees)
1.2	Higher professionals (partners in law firms, etc.)
2	Lower managerial and professional occupations (middle managers and professionally qualified people)
3	Intermediate occupations (secretaries, policemen, etc.)
4	Small employers and sole traders
5	Lower supervisory, craft and related occupations (skilled manual workers)
6	Semi-routine occupations (shop assistants, etc.)
7	Routine occupations (semi-skilled or unskilled manual workers)

Table 7.1 National statistics – socioeconomic classification

SOURCE: Office of National Statistics. Socioeconomic classification (ONS). Crown copyright material is reproduced under class Licence Number C01W0000039 with the permission of the Controller of HMSO.

although there is evidence that the gap between the richest and poorest in the English-speaking countries is now widening.

Some class systems have a greater influence on buying behaviour than others. In most western countries 'lower' classes may exhibit upward mobility, showing buying behaviour similar to that of the 'upper' classes. But in other cultures, where a caste system gives people a distinctive role, buying behaviour is more firmly linked to social class. Upper classes in almost all societies are often more similar to each other than they are to the rest of their own society. When selecting products and services, including food, clothing, household items and personal-care products, they make choices that are less culture-bound than those of the lower classes. This tendency accounts for the strength of global luxury brands such as Burberry, Tag Heuer and Mont Blanc. Generally, the lower social classes are more culture-bound, although young people of all classes are less so and account for the global youth brands like Nike, Coca-Cola and Swatch.

Anna Flores' occupation puts her in NS-SEC group 2 (lower managerial and professional occupations) although she has set her sights on achieving a 'higher managerial occupation'. Coming from a higher social background, her family and friends probably own expensive cameras and she might have dabbled in photography.

Social factors

A consumer's behaviour is also influenced by social factors, such as the consumer's small groups, family, and social roles and status. Because these social factors can strongly affect consumer responses, companies must take them into account when designing their marketing strategies.

Groups

Groups influence a person's behaviour. Groups that have a direct influence and to which a person belongs are called **membership groups**. Some are *primary groups* with whom there is regular but informal interaction – such as family, friends, neighbours and fellow workers. Children are particularly prone to these social pressures that account for the playground fads that permeate the school year and account for the annual convergence on *a* Christmas toy, such as Cabbage Patch Dolls, Thunderbirds Tracey Island or PlayStation 2.[9] Some are

Membership groups— Groups that have a direct influence on a person's behaviour and to which a person belongs.

Reference groups—Groups that have a direct (face-to-face) or indirect influence on the person's attitudes or behaviour.

Aspirational group—A group to which an individual wishes to belong.

secondary groups, which are more formal and have less regular interaction. These include organisations like religious groups, professional associations and trade unions.

Reference groups are groups that serve as direct (face-to-face) or indirect points of comparison or reference in forming a person's attitudes or behaviour. Reference groups to which they do not belong often influence people. For example, an **aspirational group** is one to which the individual wishes to belong, as when a teenage football fan follows David Beckham or a young girl idolises Britney Spears. They identify with them, although there is no face-to-face contact. Today's parents may be relieved that the modern pop 'heroes' are more agreeable than the rebels, acid freaks and punks that they followed.[10]

Marketers try to identify the reference groups of their target markets. Reference groups influence a person in at least three ways. They expose the person to new behaviours and lifestyles. They influence the person's attitudes and self-concept because he or she wants to 'fit in'. They also create pressures to conform that may affect the person's product and brand choices.

Manufacturers of products and brands subjected to strong group influence must figure out how to reach **opinion leaders** – people within a reference group who, because of special skills, knowledge, personality or other characteristics, exert influence on others. Many marketers try to identify opinion leaders for their products and direct marketing efforts towards them. For example, the hottest trends in teenage music, language and fashion often start in major cities, then quickly spread to more mainstream youth in the suburbs. Thus, clothing companies that hope to appeal to fashion-conscious youth often make a concerted effort to monitor urban opinion leaders' style and behaviour. In other cases, marketers may use *buzz marketing* by enlisting or even creating opinion leaders to spread the word about their brands.

> Frequent the right cafés . . . this summer, and you're likely to encounter a gang of sleek, impossibly attractive motorbike riders who seem genuinely interested in getting to know you over an iced latte. Compliment them on their Vespa scooters glinting in the brilliant curbside sunlight, and they'll happily pull out a pad and scribble down an address and phone number – not theirs, but that of the local 'boutique' where you can buy your own Vespa, just as (they'll confide) the rap artist Sisqo and the movie queen Sandra Bullock recently did. And that's when the truth hits you: this isn't any spontaneous encounter. Those scooter-riding models are on the Vespa payroll, and they've been hired to generate some favorable word of mouth for the recently reissued cult bikes. Welcome to the world of buzz marketing. Similar buzz marketers are now taking to the streets, cafés, nightclubs, and the Internet, in record numbers. Their goal is to seek out the trendsetters in each community and subtly push them into talking up their brand to their friends and admirers.[11]

The importance of group influence varies across products and brands, but it tends to be strongest for conspicuous purchases, like a Vespa scooter.[12] A product or brand can be conspicuous for one of two reasons. First, it may be noticeable because the buyer is one of the few people who own it – luxuries, such as a vintage Wurlitzer juke box or a Breitling Chronomat GT sports watch, are more conspicuous than necessities because fewer people own the luxuries. Second, a product such as Red Bull or Perrier can be conspicuous because the buyer consumes it in public where others can see it. Figure 7.3 shows how group influence

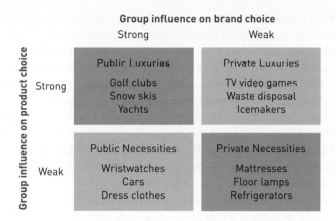

Group influence on brand choice

	Strong	Weak
Strong	Public Luxuries Golf clubs Snow skis Yachts	Private Luxuries TV video games Waste disposal Icemakers
Weak	Public Necessities Wristwatches Cars Dress clothes	Private Necessities Mattresses Floor lamps Refrigerators

Group influence on product choice

Figure 7.3 Extent of group influence on product and brand choice
SOURCE: Adapted from William O. Bearden and Michael J. Etzel, 'Reference group influence on product and brand purchase decisions', *Journal of Consumer Research* (September 1982), p. 185, University of Chicago Press. Copyright © Journal of Consumer Research Inc., 1982.

might affect product and brand choices for four types of product – public luxuries, private luxuries, public necessities and private necessities.

Family

Family members can strongly influence buyer behaviour. We can distinguish between two families in the buyer's life. The buyer's parents make up the *family of orientation*. Parents provide a person with an orientation towards religion, politics and economics, and a sense of personal ambition, self-worth and love. Even if the buyer no longer interacts very much with his or her parents, the latter can still significantly influence the buyer's behaviour. In countries where parents continue to live with their children, their influence can be crucial.

> Procter & Gamble came a cropper in the European market after their €40 million launch of their new Charmin toilet roll. The company found the product's wet strength was wrong so it blocked European drains. Not because of the design of European toilets but because of a mode of consumer behaviour that must be learned in the family – how they use the toilet paper. Europeans fold their toilet paper while Americans scrunch it. 'This leads to different dynamics in the product', says P&G; 'folding paper means you need more strength.'
>
> But even Europeans are not consistent. The British pay more than twice as much as Americans, French and Germans for their toilet rolls. Why? According to Kimberly-Clark the British demand a Rolls-Royce of toilet papers with a softer, more luxurious texture, more sheets per roll, 2 mm wider and 14 mm longer than other countries. The island race is also sensitive to colour, choosing from ranges that include warm pink, breeze blue and meadow green. The reason for this is their desire that the colour of the tissue matches their bathrooms.[13]

The *family of procreation* – the buyer's spouse and children – has a more direct influence on everyday buying behaviour. This family is the most important consumer buying organisation in society and it has been researched extensively. Marketers are interested in the roles and relative influence of the husband, wife and children on the purchase of a large variety of products and services.

Husband–wife involvement varies widely by product category and by stage in the buying process. Buying roles change with evolving consumer lifestyles. Almost everywhere in the world, the wife is traditionally the main purchasing agent for the family, especially in the areas of food, household products and clothing. But with over 60 per cent of women holding jobs outside the home in developed countries and the willingness of some husbands to do more of the family's purchasing, all this is changing. The vast majority of increased car sales in Western Europe is by women for women, hence the market for high-value small cars. At the same time advertising agency Euro RSCG Worldwide have identified a growing group, 'metrosexuals', as the new growth market. These straight men, typified by David Beckham, enjoy such things as shopping and beauty products and are driving the market for male personal care, grooming and cosmetic products.[14]

In the case of expensive products and services, husbands and wives more often make joint decisions. Anna Flores' husband may play an *influencer role* in her camera-buying decision. He may have an opinion about her buying a camera and about the kind of camera to buy. At the same time, she will be the primary decider, purchaser and user.

Consumers' buying roles

Group members can influence purchases in many ways. For example, men normally choose their own newspaper and women choose their own tights. For other products, however, the **decision-making unit** is more complicated with people playing one or more roles:

- **Initiator**. The person who first suggests or thinks of the idea of buying a particular product or service. This could be a parent or friend who would like to see a visual record of Anna's holiday.

- **Influencer**. A person whose view or advice influences the buying decision, perhaps a friend who is a camera enthusiast or a salesperson.

- **Decider**. The person who ultimately makes a buying decision or any part of it – whether to buy, what to buy, how to buy or where to buy.

- **Buyer**. The person who makes an actual purchase. Once the buying decision is made, someone else could make the purchase for the decider.

- **User**. The person who consumes or uses a product or service. Once bought, other members of Anna's family could use her camera.

Roles and status

A person belongs to many groups – family, clubs, organisations. The person's position in each group can be defined in terms of both *role* and *status*. With her parents, Anna Flores plays the role of daughter; in her family, she plays the role of wife; in her company, she plays the role of brand manager. A **role** consists of the activities that people are expected to perform according to the persons around them. Each of Anna's roles will influence some of her buying behaviour.

Each role carries a **status** reflecting the general esteem given to it by society. People often choose products that show their status in society. For example, the role of brand manager has more status in our society than the role of daughter. As a brand manager, Anna will buy the kind of clothing that reflects her role and status.

Personal factors

A buyer's decisions are also influenced by personal characteristics such as the buyer's age and life-cycle stage, occupation, economic situation, lifestyle, and personality and self-concept.

Decision-making unit (DMU)—All the individuals who participate in, and influence, the consumer buying-decision process.

Initiator—The person who first suggests or thinks of the idea of buying a particular product or service.

Influencer—A person whose view or advice influences buying decisions.

Decider—The person who ultimately makes a buying decision or any part of it – whether to buy, what to buy, how to buy, or where to buy.

Buyer—The person who makes an actual purchase.

User—The person who consumes or uses a product or service.

Role—The activities a person is expected to perform according to the people around him or her.

Status—The general esteem given to a role by society.

Age and life-cycle stage

People change the goods and services they buy over their lifetimes. Tastes in food, clothes, furniture and recreation are often age related. Buying is also shaped by the **family life-cycle** – the stages through which families might pass as they mature over time. Table 7.2 lists the stages of the family life-cycle. Although based on the transient love and marriage model of life,[15] marketers often define their target markets in terms of life-cycle stage and develop appropriate products and marketing plans for each stage. For example, Mark Warner offers

Family life-cycle—
The stages through which families might pass as they mature over time.

Table 7.2 Family life-cycle stages

Young	Middle-aged	Older
Single	Single	Older married
Married without children	Married without children	Older unmarried
Married with children	Married with children	
Infant children	Young children	
Young children	Adolescent children	
Adolescent children	Married without dependent children	
Divorced with children	Divorced without children	
	Divorced with children	
	Young children	
	Adolescent children	
	Divorced without dependent children	

SOURCES: Adapted from Patrick E. Murphy and William A. Staples, 'A modernised family life cycle', *Journal of Consumer Research* (June 1979), p. 16, University of Chicago Press; © Journal of Consumer Research, Inc., 1979. See also Janet Wagner and Sherman Hanna, 'The effectiveness of family life cycle variables in consumer expenditure research', *Journal of Consumer Research* (December 1983), pp. 281–91.

family-oriented skiing and watersports holidays with an emphasis on kids' clubs, and 'no kids' holidays for couples wanting to escape from them.

Although life-cycle stages remain the same, shifting lifestyles are causing the decline of some products and growth in others. One product that has almost disappeared in recent years is the baby pram, the one-time status symbol of all mums. Besides there being fewer families with children, many mothers now work, so have less time for strolling the pram, and are more likely to travel by car than on foot. Touring caravans is another product class in decline as families with children become fewer, while single- and double-income, no-kids families spend their money on more exotic holidays. While some markets decline, others grow with changing lifestyles.

> The Japanese call them 'parasite singles', a generation that chooses to linger in their parents' home, rent free, rather than get a steady job and start their own life. Many are also become a 'freeter' – one who drifts from job to job rather than settling down to conventional employment. The same pattern is occurring in western countries where staying with mum is more attractive than being a mum. In most countries men linger at home much longer than women, with Italian men being the world champion lingerers. This shift in life-cycle behaviour is causing a huge shift in demand from home building to single life style consumption.[16]

Psychological life-cycle stages have also been identified. Adults experience certain passages or transformations as they go through life. Thus Anna Flores may move from being a satisfied brand manager and wife to being an unsatisfied person searching for a new way to fulfil herself. In fact, such a change may have stimulated her strong interest in photography. The main stimuli to people taking photographs are holidays, ceremonies marking the progression through the life cycle (weddings, graduations and so on) and having children to take photographs of. Marketers must pay attention to the changing buying interests that might be associated with these adult passages.

Table 7.3 Lifestyle dimensions

Activities	Interests	Opinions	Demographics
Work	Family	Themselves	Age
Hobbies	Home	Social issues	Education
Social events	Job	Politics	Income
Vacation	Community	Business	Occupation
Entertainment	Recreation	Economics	Family size
Club membership	Fashion	Education	Dwelling
Community	Food	Products	Geography
Shopping	Media	Future	City size
Sports	Achievements	Culture	Stage in life cycle

SOURCE: Joseph T. Plummer, 'The concept and application of lifestyle segmentation', reprinted with permission from *Journal of Marketing* published by the American Marketing Association (January 1974), p. 34.

Occupation

A person's occupation affects the goods and services bought. Blue-collar workers tend to buy more work clothes, whereas office workers buy more smart clothes. Marketers try to identify the occupational groups that have an above-average interest in their products and services. A company can even specialise in making products needed by a given occupational group. Thus computer software companies will design different products for brand managers, accountants, engineers, lawyers and doctors.

Economic circumstances

A person's economic situation will affect product choice. Anna Flores can consider buying a professional €5,000 Nikon D1 digital camera if she has enough enthusiasm, disposable income, savings or borrowing power. Marketers of income-sensitive goods closely watch trends in personal income, savings and interest rates. If economic indicators point to a recession, marketers can take steps to redesign, reposition and reprice their products.

Lifestyle

People coming from the same subculture, social class and occupation may have quite different lifestyles. **Lifestyle** is a person's pattern of living as expressed in his or her activities, interests and opinions. Lifestyle captures something more than the person's social class or personality. It profiles a person's whole pattern of acting and interacting in the world. The technique of measuring lifestyles is known as **psychographics**. It involves measuring the primary dimensions shown in Table 7.3. The first three are known as the *AIO dimensions* (activities, interests, opinions). Several research firms have developed lifestyle classifications. The most widely used is the SRI *Values and Lifestyles (VALS)* typology. The original VALS typology classifies consumers into nine lifestyle groups according to whether they were inner directed (for example, 'experientials'), outer directed ('achievers', 'belongers'), or need driven ('survivors'). Using this VALS classification, a bank found that the businessmen they were targeting consisted mainly of 'achievers' who were strongly competitive individualists.[17] The bank designed highly successful ads showing men taking part in solo sports such as sailing, jogging and water skiing.[18]

Everyday-Life Research by SINUS GmbH, a German company, identifies 'social milieus' covering France, Germany, Italy and the UK. This study describes the structure of society with five social classes and value orientations:

Lifestyle—A person's pattern of living as expressed in his or her activities, interests and opinions.

Psychographics—The technique of measuring lifestyles and developing lifestyle classifications; it involves measuring the chief AIO dimensions (activities, interests, opinions).

Table 7.4 Typology of social milieus

Milieu	Germany	France	Italy	UK	Description
Upper conservative	Konservatives-gehobenes	Les Héritiers	Neoconservatori	Upper class	Traditional upper-middle-class conservatives
Traditional mainstream	Floresburgerliches	Les conservateurs installés	Piccola borghesia	Traditional middle class	*Petit bourgeois* group mainly oriented to preserving the status quo
Traditional working class	Traditionsloses Arbeitermilieu	Les laborieux traditionnels	Cultura operaia	Traditional working class	Traditional blue-collar worker
Modern mainstream	Aufstiegsorientiertes	Les nouveaux ambitieux	Rampanti, plus crisaldi	Social climbers, plus progressive working class	Social climber and achievement-oriented white- and blue-collar workers
Trendsetter	Technokratisch-liberales	Les managers moderns	Borghesia illuminata	Progressive middle class	Technocratic-liberals with a postmaterial orientation
Avant-garde	Hedonistisches	Les post-modernistes	Edonisti	'Thatcher's children'	Mainly young pleasure seekers
Sociocritical	Alternatives	Les néo-moralistes	Critica sociale	Socially centred	Pursuing an alternative lifestyle
Under-privileged	Traditionsloses Arbeitermilieu	Les oubliés, plus les rebelles	Sotto-proletariato urbano	Poor	Uprooted blue-collar workers and destitute

- Basic orientation: traditional – *to preserve*
- Basic orientation: materialist – *to have*
- Changing values: hedonism – *to indulge*
- Changing values: postmaterialism – *to be*
- Changing values: postmodernism – *to have, to be and to indulge.*

It distinguishes two types of value: traditional values, emphasising hard work, thrift, religion, honesty, good manners and obedience; and material values concerned with possession and a need for security. From these, SINUS developed a typology of social milieus (see Table 7.4): groups of people who share a common set of values and beliefs about work, private relationships, leisure activities and aesthetics, and a common perception of future plans, wishes and dreams. The size and exact nature of these milieus vary between the countries studied, but there are broad international comparisons.

Knowing the social milieu of a person can provide information about his or her everyday life, such as work likes and dislikes, which helps in product development and advertising. The study finds that the upmarket segments share a similar structure in all four countries, and it identifies trend-setting milieus in each country, containing heavy consumers with comparable attitudinal and sociodemographic characteristics. Important values shared by all these consumers include tolerance, open-mindedness, an outward-looking approach, career and success, education and culture, a high standard of living, hedonistic luxury consumption, individualism and Europe.

The Anticipating Change in Europe (ACE) study, by the RISC research agency of Paris, investigated social changes in 12 European countries, the United States, Canada and Japan.

The objective was to try to understand how social changes influence market trends. RISC describes people using sociodemographic characteristics, socio-cultural profile, activities (sports, leisure, culture), behaviour towards the media (press, radio, television), political inclinations and mood. Using these dimensions, RISC developed six Eurotypes:

1. *The traditionalist* (18 per cent of the European population) is influenced by the culture, socio-economic history and unique situation of his or her country, with a profile reflecting deep-rooted attitudes specific to that country. Consequently, this is the least homogeneous group across countries.

2. *The homebody* (14 per cent) is driven by a strong attachment to his or her roots and childhood environment. Less preoccupied with economic security than the traditionalist, the homebody needs to feel in touch with the social environment. The homebody seeks warm relationships and has difficulty coping with violence in society.

3. *The rationalist* (23 per cent) has an ability to cope with unforeseeable and complex situations, and a readiness to take risks and start new endeavours. Personal fulfilment is more about self-expression than financial reward. The rationalist believes that science and technology will help resolve the challenges facing humanity.

4. *The pleasurist* (17 per cent) emphasises sensual and emotional experiences, preferring non-hierarchically structured groups built around self-reliance and self-regulation and not around leaders or formal decision-making processes.

5. *The striver* (15 per cent) holds the attitudes, beliefs and values that underlie the dynamics of social change. The striver believes in autonomous behaviour and wants to shape his or her life and to exploit mental, physical, sensual and emotional possibilities to the full.

6. *The trend-setter* (13 per cent) favours non-hierarchical social structures and enjoys spontaneity rather than formal procedures. Trend-setters see no need to prove their abilities. Even more individualistic than strivers, they exemplify the flexible response to a rapidly changing environment.

These studies do suggest that there are European lifestyles although, as with social class, there is greater similarity between wealthy Europeans than between poor ones. For this reason, luxury brands and their advertising are often more standardised internationally than other products.[19]

Lifestyle segmentation can also be used to understand Internet behaviour. Forrester developed its 'Technographics' scheme, which segments consumers according to motivation, desire, and ability to invest in technology.[20] The framework splits people into 10 categories, such as:

- *Fast Forwards*: the biggest spenders on computer technology. Fast Forwards are early adopters of new technology for home, office and personal use.

- *New Age Nurturers*: also big spenders but focused on technology for home uses, such as a family PC.

- *Mouse Potatoes*: consumers who are dedicated to interactive entertainment and willing to spend for the latest in 'technotainment'.

- *Techno-strivers*: consumers who use technology primarily to gain a career edge.

- *Handshakers*: older consumers, typically managers, who don't touch computers at work and leave that to younger assistants.

Technographics has been used to better target online airline ticket sales in creating marketing campaigns for time-strapped 'Fast Forwards' and 'New Age Nurturers' while eliminating 'technology pessimists' from its list of targets.

The lifestyle concept, when used carefully, can help the marketer understand changing consumer values and how they affect buying behaviour. Anna Flores, for example, can choose to live the role of a capable homemaker, a career woman or a free spirit – or all three. She plays several roles, and the way she blends them expresses her lifestyle. If she ever became a professional photographer, this would change her lifestyle, in turn changing what and how she buys.

Personality and self-concept

Personality—A person's distinguishing psychological characteristics that lead to relatively consistent and lasting responses to his or her own environment.

Self-concept—Self-image, or the complex mental pictures that people have of themselves.

Each person's distinct personality influences his or her buying behaviour. **Personality** refers to the unique psychological characteristics that lead to relatively consistent and lasting responses to one's own environment. Personality is usually described in terms of traits such as self-confidence, dominance, sociability, autonomy, defensiveness, adaptability and aggressiveness.[21] Personality can be useful in analysing consumer behaviour for certain product or brand choices. For example, coffee makers have discovered that heavy coffee drinkers tend to be high on sociability. Thus Nescafé ads show people together over a cup of coffee.

Many marketers use a concept related to personality – a person's **self-concept** (also called *self-image*). The basic self-concept premise is that people's possessions contribute to and reflect their identities: that is, 'we are what we have'. Thus, in order to understand consumer behaviour, the marketer must first understand the relationship between consumer self-concept and possessions. For example, people buy books to support their self-image:

> People have the mistaken notion that the thing you do with books is read them. Wrong . . . People buy books for what the purchase says about them – their taste, their cultivation, their trendiness. Their aim . . . is to connect themselves, or those to whom they give the books as gifts, with all the other refined owners of Edgar Allen Poe collections or sensitive owners of Virginia Woolf collections. . . . [The result is that] you can sell books as consumer products, with seductive displays, flashy posters, an emphasis on the glamour of the book, and the fashionableness of the bestseller and the trendy author.[22]

Anna Flores may see herself as outgoing, fun and active. Therefore, she will favour a camera that projects the same qualities. In that case the super-compact and stylish Canon Digital IXUS could attract her. 'Everybody smile and say "aaahhhh". The smallest, cutest digicam we've ever fallen for.'[23]

Really, it is not that simple. What if Anna's *actual self-concept* (how she views herself) differs from her *ideal self-concept* (how she would like to view herself) and from her *others self-concept* (how she thinks others sees her)? Which self will she try to satisfy when she buys a camera? Because this is unclear, self-concept theory has met with mixed success in predicting consumer responses to brand images.

Psychological factors

A person's buying choices are further influenced by four important psychological factors: motivation, perception, learning, and beliefs and attitudes.

Motivation

We know that Anna Flores became interested in buying a camera. Why? What is she *really* seeking? What *needs* is she trying to satisfy?

A person has many needs at any given time. Some are *biological*, arising from states of tension such as hunger, thirst or discomfort. Others are *psychological*, arising from the need for recognition, esteem or belonging. Most of these needs will not be strong enough to motivate the person to act at a given point in time. A need becomes a *motive* when it is aroused to a sufficient level of intensity. A **motive** (or *drive*) is a need that is sufficiently pressing to direct the person to seek satisfaction. Psychologists have developed theories of human motivation. Two of the most popular – the theories of Sigmund Freud and Abraham Maslow – have quite different meanings for consumer analysis and marketing.

Motive (drive)—A need that is sufficiently pressing to direct the person to seek satisfaction of the need.

Freud's theory of motivation

Freud assumes that people are largely unconscious of the real psychological forces shaping their behaviour. He sees the person as growing up and repressing many urges. These urges are never eliminated or under perfect control; they emerge in dreams, in slips of the tongue, in neurotic and obsessive behaviour or ultimately in psychoses.

Thus Freud suggests that a person does not fully understand his or her motivation. If Anna Flores wants to purchase an expensive camera, she may describe her motive as wanting a hobby or career. At a deeper level, she may be purchasing the camera to impress others with her creative talent. At a still deeper level, she may be buying the camera to feel young and independent again.

Motivation researchers collect in-depth information from small samples of consumers to uncover the deeper motives for their product choices. They use non-directive depth interviews and various 'projective techniques' to throw the ego off guard – techniques such as word association, sentence completion, picture interpretation and role playing.

Motivation researchers have reached some interesting and sometimes odd conclusions about what may be in the buyer's mind regarding certain purchases. For example, one classic study concluded that consumers resist prunes because they are wrinkled-looking and remind people of sickness and old age. Despite its sometimes unusual conclusions, motivation research remains a useful tool for marketers seeking a deeper understanding of consumer behaviour (see Marketing Insights 7.1).[24]

Maslow's theory of motivation

Abraham Maslow sought to explain why people are driven by particular needs at particular times.[25] Why does one person spend much time and energy on personal safety and another on gaining the esteem of others? Maslow's answer is that human needs are arranged in a hierarchy, from the most pressing to the least pressing. Maslow's hierarchy of needs is shown in Figure 7.4. In order of importance, they are (1) *physiological* needs, (2) *safety* needs, (3) *social* needs, (4) *esteem* needs, (5) *cognitive* needs, (6) *aesthetic* needs and (7) *self-actualisation* needs. A person tries to satisfy the most important need first. When that important need is satisfied, it will stop being a motivator and the person will then try to satisfy the next most important need. For example, a starving man (need 1) will not take an interest in the latest happenings in the art world (need 6), or in how he is seen or esteemed by others (need 3 or 4), or even in whether he is breathing clean air (need 2). But as each important need is satisfied, the next most important need will come into play:

> The wine market shows how the different levels of the need hierarchy can be at play at the same time. Buyers of premium wines are seeking self-esteem and self-actualisation. They may achieve this by showing their knowledge by buying 1986 Chateaux Ausone from a specialist wine merchant. Wine buying makes many other people anxious, particularly if it is a gift. They buy the product to fill a social need but are unable to gauge quality. To be safe they buy from a reputable store (Oddbins) or a brand legitimised by advertising (Le Piat d'Or).

marketing insights

7.1 **'Touchy-feely' research into consumer motivations**

The term *motivation research* refers to qualitative research designed to probe consumers' hidden, subconscious motivations. Because consumers often don't know or can't describe just why they act as they do, motivation researchers use a variety of projective techniques to uncover underlying emotions and attitudes. The techniques range from sentence completion, word association and inkblot or cartoon interpretation tests, to having consumers describe typical brand users or form daydreams and fantasies about brands or buying situations. Some of these techniques verge on the bizarre. One writer offers the following tongue-in-cheek summary of a motivation research session:

> Good morning, ladies and gentlemen. We've called you here today for a little consumer research. Now, lie down on the couch, toss your inhibitions out the window and let's try a little free association. First, think about brands as if they were your *friends* . . . think of your shampoo as an animal. Go on, don't be shy. Would it be a panda or a lion? A snake or a woolly worm? . . . Draw a picture of a typical cake-mix user. Would she wear an apron or a negligée? A business suit or a can-can dress?

Such projective techniques seem dotty, but more and more marketers are turning to these touchy-feely, motivation research approaches to help them probe consumer psyches and develop better marketing strategies.

Many advertising agencies employ teams of psychologists, anthropologists and other social scientists to carry out their motivation research: 'We believe people make choices on a basic primitive level . . . we use the probe to get down to the unconscious.' The agency routinely conducts one-on-one, therapy-like interviews to delve into the inner workings of consumers. Another agency asks consumers to describe their favourite brands as animals or cars (say, Saab versus BMW) in order to assess the prestige associated with various brands.

In an effort to understand the teenage consumer market better, ad agency BSB Worldwide videotaped teenagers' rooms in 25 countries. It found surprising similarities across countries and cultures:

> From the steamy playgrounds of Los Angeles to the stately boulevards of Singapore, kids show amazing similarities in taste, language, and attitude. . . . From the gear and posters on display, it's hard to tell whether the rooms are in Los Angeles, Mexico City, or Tokyo. Basketballs sit alongside soccer balls. Closets overflow with staples from an international, unisex uniform: baggy Levi's or Diesel jeans and rugged shoes from Timberland or Doc Martens.

...7.1

Similarly, researchers at Sega of America's ad agency have learned a lot about video game buying behaviour by hanging around with 150 kids in their bedrooms and by shopping with them. Above all else, they learned, kids do everything fast. As a result, in Sega's most recent 15-second commercials, some images fly by so quickly that adults cannot recall seeing them, even after repeated showings. The kids, weaned on MTV, recollect them keenly.

Some marketers dismiss such motivation research as mumbo jumbo. And these approaches do present some problems. They use small samples, and researchers' interpretations of results are often highly subjective, sometimes leading to rather exotic explanations of otherwise ordinary buying behaviour. However, others believe strongly that these approaches can provide interesting nuggets of insight into the relationships between consumers and the brands they buy. To marketers who use them, motivation research techniques provide a flexible and varied means of gaining insights into deeply held and often mysterious motivations behind consumer buying behaviour.

SOURCES: Excerpts from Annetta Miller and Dody Tsiantar, 'Psyching out consumers', *Newsweek* (27 February 1989), pp. 46–7; G. De Groot, 'Deep, dangerous or just plain dotty?', ESOMAR Seminar on Qualitative Methods of Research, Amsterdam, 1986; Shawn Tully, 'Teens: The most global market of all', *Fortune* (6 May 1994), pp. 90–7; and Tobi Elkin, 'Product pampering', *Brandweek* (16 June 1997), pp. 38–40. Also see 'They understand your kids', *Fortune* (special issue, Autumn/Winter 1993), pp. 29–30; Cyndee Miller, 'Sometimes a researcher has no alternative but to hang out in a bar', *Marketing News* (3 January 1994), pp. 16, 26; Ronald B. Lieber, 'Storytelling: a new way to get close to your customer', *Fortune* (3 February 1997), pp. 102–8; Jerry W. Thomas, 'Finding unspoken reasons for consumers' choices', *Marketing News* (8 June 1998), pp. 10–11; and Michele Marchetti, 'Marketing's weird science', *Sales & Marketing Management* (May 1999), p. 87; Anne Wrangham, 'A question of quality', *Marketing Business* (May 1998), pp. 19–22; Peter Law, 'Warts'n'all', *Marketing Business* (June 1999), pp. 59–61.

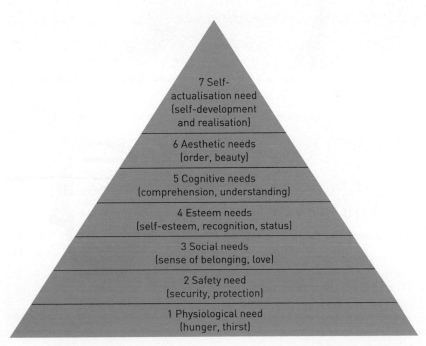

Figure 7.4 Maslow's hierarchy of needs
SOURCE: Adapted from Abraham H. Maslow, *Motivation and Personality*, 2nd edn, 1970 (Prentice Hall, Inc.)

7 Self-actualisation need (self-development and realisation)

6 Aesthetic needs (order, beauty)

5 Cognitive needs (comprehension, understanding)

4 Esteem needs (self-esteem, recognition, status)

3 Social needs (sense of belonging, love)

2 Safety need (security, protection)

1 Physiological need (hunger, thirst)

Maslow's hierarchy is not universal for all cultures. As the heroes of Hollywood movies amply show, Anglo-Saxon culture values self-actualisation and individuality above all else, but that is not universally so. In Japan and German-speaking countries, people are most highly motivated by a need for order (aesthetic needs) and belonging (esteem needs), while in France, Spain, Portugal and other Latin and Asian countries, people are most motivated by the need for security and belonging.[26]

What light does Maslow's theory throw on Anna Flores' interest in buying a camera? We can guess that Anna has satisfied her physiological, safety and social needs; they do not

Patek Philippe of Geneva departs from the usual approach to selling luxury watches by appealing to self-esteem, aesthetic needs or self-actualisation communicated by an association with sport, technology or exquisite design. This 'new man' ad taps into much more basic social and safety needs.
SOURCE: Patek Philippe, *Agency*: Geneva/Leagas Delaney, *Photographer*: Peggy Sirota (represented by. E. M. Managed).

motivate her interest in cameras. Her camera interest might come from an aesthetic need and esteem needs. Or it might come from a need for self-actualisation or cognition – she might want to be a creative person and express herself through photography or explore her potential.

Perception

A motivated person is ready to act. How the person acts is influenced by his or her perception of the situation. Two people with the same motivation and in the same situation may act quite differently because they perceive the situation differently. Anna Flores might consider a fast-talking camera salesperson loud and false. Another camera buyer might consider the same salesperson intelligent and helpful.

Why do people perceive the same situation differently? All of us learn by the flow of information through our five senses: sight, hearing, smell, touch and taste. However, each of us receives, organises and interprets this sensory information in an individual way. Thus **perception** is the process by which people select, organise and interpret information to form a meaningful picture of the world. People can form different perceptions of the same stimulus because of three perceptual processes: selective attention, selective distortion and selective retention.

Perception—The process by which people select, organise and interpret information to form a meaningful picture of the world.

Selective attention

People are exposed to a great number of stimuli every day. For example, the average person may be exposed to more than 1,500 ads a day. It is impossible for a person to pay attention to all these stimuli and some studies show people remembering only three or four.[27] **Selective attention** – the tendency for people to screen out most of the information to which they are exposed – means that marketers have to work especially hard to attract the consumer's attention. Their message will be lost on most people who are not in the market for the product. Moreover, even people who are in the market may not notice the message unless it stands out from the surrounding sea of other ads.

Selective attention—The tendency of people to screen out most of the information to which they are exposed.

Selective distortion

Even noted stimuli do not always come across in the intended way. Each person fits incoming information into an existing mind-set. **Selective distortion** describes the tendency of people to adapt information to personal meanings. Anna Flores may hear the salesperson mention some good and bad points about a competing camera brand. Because she already has a strong leaning towards Fuji, Kodak or Agfa, she is likely to distort those points in order to conclude that one camera is better than the others. People tend to interpret information in a way that will support what they already believe. Selective distortion means that marketers must try to understand the mind-sets of consumers and how these will affect interpretations of advertising and sales information:

Selective distortion—The tendency of people to adapt information to personal meanings.

> Is the €160 billion a year people spend on beauty products not wasted but a sensible investment? Evidence shows that people respond positively to people who are attractive. In sales jobs researchers in the UK found the pay penalty for being unattractive is 15 per cent for men and 11 per cent for women. Even being told a person is attractive or not influences people's judgement. In a recent Norwegian study university students awarded a 20 per cent lighter sentence if they were told criminals were 'handsome' or 'pretty'.[28]

Selective retention

Selective retention—The tendency of people to retain only part of the information to which they are exposed, usually information that supports their attitudes or beliefs.

People will also forget much of what they learn. They tend to retain information that supports their attitudes and beliefs. Because of **selective retention**, Anna is likely to remember good points made about the Fuji and forget good points made about competing cameras. She may remember Fuji's good points because she 'rehearses' them more whenever she thinks about choosing a camera.

Because of selective exposure, distortion and retention, marketers have to work hard to get their messages through. This fact explains why marketers use so much drama and repetition in sending messages to their market. Although some consumers are worried that they will be affected by marketing messages without even knowing it, most marketers worry about whether their offers will be perceived at all.

Learning

Learning—Changes in an individual's behaviour arising from experience.

When people act, they learn. **Learning** describes changes in an individual's behaviour arising from experience. Learning theorists say that most human behaviour is learned. Learning occurs through the interplay of *drives*, *stimuli*, *cues*, *responses* and *reinforcement*.

We saw that Anna Flores has a drive for self-actualisation. A *drive* is a strong internal stimulus that calls for action. Her drive becomes a motive when it is directed towards a particular *stimulus object* – in this case, a camera. Anna's response to the idea of buying a camera is conditioned by the surrounding cues. *Cues* are minor stimuli that determine when, where and how the person responds. Seeing cameras in a shop window, hearing a special sale price, and her husband's support are all cues that can influence Anna's *response* to her interest in buying a camera.

Suppose Anna buys the Canon IXUS. If the experience is rewarding, she will probably use the camera more and more. Her response to cameras will be *reinforced*. Then the next time she shops for a camera, binoculars or some similar product, the probability is greater that she will buy a Canon product. We say that she *generalises* her response to similar stimuli.

The reverse of generalisation is *discrimination*. When Anna examines binoculars made by Olympus, she sees that they are lighter and more compact than Nikon's binoculars. Discrimination means that she has learned to recognise differences in sets of products and can adjust her response accordingly.

The practical significance of learning theory for marketers is that they can build up demand for a product by associating it with strong drives, using motivating cues and providing positive reinforcement. A new company can enter the market by appealing to the same drives that competitors appeal to and by providing similar cues, because buyers are more likely to transfer loyalty to similar brands than to dissimilar ones (generalisation). Or a new company may design its brand to appeal to a different set of drives and offer strong cue inducements to switch brands (discrimination).

Beliefs and attitudes

Belief—A descriptive thought that a person holds about something.

Through doing and learning, people acquire their beliefs and attitudes. These, in turn, influence their buying behaviour. A **belief** is a descriptive thought that a person has about something. Anna Flores may believe that an Agfa camera takes great pictures, stands up well under hard use and is good value. These beliefs may be based on real knowledge, opinion or faith, and may or may not carry an emotional charge. For example, Anna Flores' belief that an Agfa camera is heavy may or may not matter to her decision.

Marketers are interested in the beliefs that people formulate about specific products and services, because these beliefs make up product and brand images that affect buying behaviour. If some of the beliefs are wrong and prevent purchase, the marketer will want to launch a campaign to correct them.

People have attitudes regarding religion, politics, clothes, music, food and almost everything else. An **attitude** describes a person's relatively consistent evaluations, feelings and tendencies towards an object or idea. Attitudes put people into a frame of mind of liking or disliking things, of moving towards or away from them. Thus Anna Flores may hold such attitudes as 'Buy the best', 'The Japanese make the best products in the world' and 'Creativity and self-expression are among the most important things in life'. If so, the Canon camera would fit well into Anna's existing attitudes.

Attitudes are difficult to change. A person's attitudes fit into a pattern and to change one attitude may require difficult adjustments in many others. Thus a company should usually try to fit its products into existing attitudes rather than try to change attitudes. Of course, there are exceptions in which the great cost of trying to change attitudes may pay off. For example:

Attitude—A person's consistently favourable or unfavourable evaluations, feelings and tendencies towards an object or idea.

In the late 1950s, Honda entered the US motorcycle market facing a major decision. It could either sell its motorcycles to the small but already established motorcycle market or try to increase the size of this market by attracting new types of consumer. Increasing the size of the market would be more difficult and expensive because many people had negative attitudes toward motorcycles. They associated motorcycles with black leather jackets, switchblades and outlaws. Despite these adverse attitudes, Honda took the second course of action. It launched a major campaign to position motorcycles as good clean fun. Its theme 'You meet the nicest people on a Honda' worked well and many people adopted a new attitude toward motorcycles. In the

1990s, however, Honda faces a similar problem. With the ageing of the baby boomers, the market has once again shifted toward only hard-core motorcycling enthusiasts. So Honda has again set out to change consumer attitudes. Its 'Come Ride With Us' campaign aims to re-establish the wholesomeness of motorcycling and to position it as fun and exciting for everyone.[29]

Consumer decision process

The consumer's choice results from the complex interplay of cultural, social, personal and psychological factors. Although the marketer cannot influence many of these factors, they can be useful in identifying interested buyers and in shaping products and appeals to serve their needs better. Marketers have to be extremely careful in analysing consumer behaviour. Consumers often turn down what appears to be a winning offer. Polaroid found this out when it lost millions on its Polarvision instant home movie system; Ford when it launched the Edsel; RCA on its Selecta-Vision and Philips on its LaserVision video-disc player; TiVo personal video machines; and Bristol Aviation with its trio of the Brabazon, Britannia and Concorde airliners. So far we have looked at the cultural, social, personal and psychological influences that affect buyers. Now we look at how consumers make buying decisions: first, the types of decision that consumers face; then the main steps in the buyer decision process; and finally, the processes by which consumers learn about and buy new products.

Types of buying decision behaviour

Complex buying behaviour— Consumer buying behaviour in situations characterised by high consumer involvement in a purchase and significant perceived differences among brands.

Consumer decision making varies with the type of buying decision. Consumer buying behaviour differs greatly for a tube of toothpaste, a tennis racket, an expensive camera and a new car. More complex decisions usually involve more buying participants and more buyer deliberation. Figure 7.5 shows types of consumer buying behaviour based on the degree of involvement and the extent of the differences among brands.[30]

Complex buying behaviour

Consumers undertake **complex buying behaviour** when they are highly involved in a purchase and perceive significant differences among brands, or when the product is expensive, risky, purchased infrequently and highly self-expressive. Typically, the consumer has much to learn

Figure 7.5 Four types of buying behaviour
SOURCE: Adapted from Henry Assael, *Consumer Behaviour and Marketing Action*, 6th edition, p. 67 (Boston, MA: Kent Publishing Company, 1987) © Wadsworth Inc. 1987. Reprinted by permission of Kent Publishing Company, a division of Wadsworth Inc.

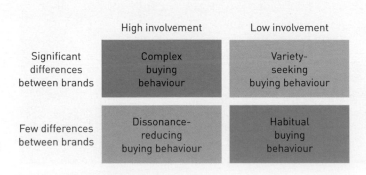

	High involvement	Low involvement
Significant differences between brands	Complex buying behaviour	Variety-seeking buying behaviour
Few differences between brands	Dissonance-reducing buying behaviour	Habitual buying behaviour

Chrom@
The Creation of a
New Lifestyle

Through its unique combination of stunning looks and leading edge technology, Chrom@ represents the ultimate sensory experience in mobile computing. With a Mobile Intel® Pentium® III processor, a brilliant 15" TFT display, 6-way integrated speakers, Dolby Digital audio output and ports for USB and Firewire connectivity, Chrom@ is the optimum mobile platform for creating and enjoying digital media. Using the S-video connector, Chrom@ even gives you the option of enjoying all of your top-quality games and DVD movies on your TV

screen. Fully Internet ready with dedicated Internet keys and including a broad range of quality software titles, Chrom@ offers you a new experience in mobile computing.

Available at PC World and selected Dixons and Currys stores. For more information please phone 01628 508222.

www.packardbell.co.uk

Packard Bell.
Because your computer should understand you.

The purchase of a laptop involves complex buying behaviour. Ads promoting this kind of item should contain long explicative copy to make the customer more comfortable about the product. SOURCE: Packard Bell. *Agency*: Fred Fisher Associates.

about the product category. For example, a personal computer buyer may not know what attributes to consider. Many product features carry no real meaning to the great majority of potential purchasers: an 'Intel 200MHz Pentium II Pro', 'SVGA display', '16Mb Sync DRAM, 256 Kb Cache' or even a '16X Max CD-ROM with 33.6 BPS fax/data (upgradeable to 56K)'.

This buyer will pass through a learning process, first developing beliefs about the product, then developing attitudes, and then making a thoughtful purchase choice. Marketers of high-involvement products must understand the information-gathering and evaluation behaviour of high-involvement consumers. They need to help buyers learn about product-class attributes and their relative importance and about what the company's brand offers on the important attributes. Marketers need to differentiate their brand's features, perhaps by describing the brand's benefits using print media with long copy. They must motivate store salespeople and the buyer's acquaintances to influence the final brand choice. Recognising this problem, Dixons, the electrical retailers, set up the Link chain of stores dedicated to helping baffled buyers on to the information superhighway and multimedia.[31]

Dissonance-reducing buying behaviour

Dissonance-reducing buying behaviour occurs when consumers are highly involved with an expensive, infrequent or risky purchase, but see little difference among brands. For example, consumers buying floor covering may face a high-involvement decision because floor covering is expensive and self-expressive. Yet buyers may consider most floor coverings in a given price range to be the same. In this case, because perceived brand differences are not large, buyers

Dissonance-reducing buying behaviour—Consumer buying behaviour in situations characterised by high involvement but few perceived differences among brands.

277

may shop around to learn what is available, but buy relatively quickly. They may respond primarily to a good price or to purchase convenience. After the purchase, consumers might experience post-purchase dissonance (after-sales discomfort) when they notice certain disadvantages of the purchased carpet brand or hear favourable things about brands not purchased. To counter such dissonance, the marketer's after-sale communications should provide evidence and support to help consumers feel good both before and after their brand choices.

Habitual buying behaviour

Habitual buying behaviour— Consumer buying behaviour in situations characterised by low consumer involvement and few significant perceived brand differences.

Habitual buying behaviour occurs under conditions of low consumer involvement and little significant brand difference. For example, take salt. Consumers have little involvement in this product category – they simply go to the store and reach for a brand. If they keep reaching for the same brand, it is out of habit rather than strong brand loyalty. Consumers appear to have low involvement with most low-cost, frequently purchased products.

Consumers do not search extensively for information about the brands, evaluate brand characteristics and make weighty decisions about which brands to buy. Instead, they passively receive information as they watch television or read magazines. Ad repetition creates *brand familiarity* rather than *brand conviction*. Consumers do not form strong attitudes towards a brand; they select the brand because it is familiar and may not evaluate the choice even after purchase.

Because buyers are not highly committed to any brands, marketers of low-involvement products with few brand differences often use price and sales promotions to stimulate product trial. Gaining distribution and attention at the point of sale is critical. In advertising for a low-involvement product, ad copy should stress only a few key points. Visual symbols and imagery are important because they can be remembered easily and associated with the brand. Ad campaigns should include high repetition of short-duration messages. Television is usually more effective than print media because it is a low-involvement medium suitable for passive learning. Advertising planning should be based on classical conditioning theory, in which buyers learn to identify a certain product by a symbol repeatedly attached to it.

Products can be linked to some involving personal situation. While many expensive watches promote their looks, celebrity or sports associations, Patek Philippe of Geneva show pictures of a 'new man' sleeping, sitting with a male child, and use the slogan: 'You never actually own a Patek Philippe. You merely look after it for the *next* generation.' See page 272.

Variety-seeking buying behaviour

Variety-seeking buying behaviour— Consumer buying behaviour in situations characterised by low consumer involvement, but significant perceived brand differences.

Consumers undertake **variety-seeking buying behaviour** in situations characterised by low consumer involvement, but significant perceived brand differences. In such cases, consumers often do a lot of brand switching. For example, when purchasing confectionery, a consumer may hold some beliefs, choose an item without much evaluation, then evaluate that brand during consumption. But the next time, the consumer might pick another brand out of boredom or simply to try something different. Brand switching occurs for the sake of variety rather than because of dissatisfaction. Confectionery makers know this and compete to have their products in the 'golden arc' from where a person stands to make a purchase and as far as a person can reach.

In such product categories, the marketing strategy may differ for the market leader and minor brands. The market leader will try to encourage habitual buying behaviour by dominating shelf space, avoiding out-of-stock conditions and running frequent reminder advertising. Challenger firms will encourage variety seeking by offering lower prices, deals, coupons, free samples and advertising that presents reasons for trying something new.

The buyer decision process

Most large companies research consumer buying decisions in great detail to answer questions about what consumers buy, where they buy, how and how much they buy, when they buy and why they buy. Marketers can study consumer purchases to find answers to questions about what they buy, where and how much. But learning about the *whys* of consumer buying behaviour and the buying decision process is not so easy – the answers are often locked within the consumer's head.

We will examine the stages that buyers pass through to reach a buying decision. We will use the model in Figure 7.6, which shows the consumer as passing through five stages: *need recognition*, *information search*, *evaluation of alternatives*, *purchase decision* and *postpurchase behaviour*. Clearly the buying process starts long before actual purchase and continues long after. This encourages the marketer to focus on the entire buying process rather than just the purchase decision.

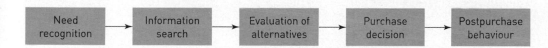

Figure 7.6 Buyer decision process

This model implies that consumers pass through all five stages with every purchase. But in more routine purchases, consumers often skip or reverse some of these stages. A woman buying her regular brand of toothpaste would recognise the need and go right to the purchase decision, skipping information search and evaluation. However, we use the model in Figure 7.6 because it shows all the considerations that arise when a consumer faces a new and complex purchase situation.

To illustrate this model, we return to Anna Flores and try to understand how she became interested in buying a camera and the stages she went through to make the final choice.

Need recognition

The buying process starts with **need recognition** – the buyer recognising a problem or need. The buyer senses a difference between his or her *actual* state and some *desired* state. The need can be triggered by *internal stimuli* when one of the person's normal needs – hunger, thirst, sex – rises to a level high enough to become a drive. From previous experience, the person has learnt how to cope with this drive and is motivated towards objects that he or she knows will satisfy it.

A need can also be triggered by *external stimuli*. Anna passes a bakery and the smell of freshly baked bread stimulates her hunger; she admires a neighbour's new car; or she watches a television commercial for a Caribbean vacation. At this stage, the marketer needs to determine the factors and situations that usually trigger consumer need recognition. The marketer should research consumers to find out what kinds of need or problem arise, what brought them about and how they led the consumer to this particular product. Anna might answer that she felt she needed a camera after friends showed her the photographs they took on holiday. By gathering such information, the marketer can identify the stimuli that most often trigger interest in the product and can develop marketing programmes that involve these stimuli.

Compared with other animals, human beings are most conscious of visual stimulus. However, psychologists and marketers are beginning to recognise that smell is an important stimulus that often operates unconsciously. Marketing Insights 7.2 examines this frontier where marketing is working hand in hand with science.

Need recognition—The first stage of the buyer decision process in which the consumer recognises a problem or need.

7.2 ## Pong: marketing's final frontier

Rolls-Royce Cars hit the headlines recently when it was revealed that they had developed an essence of new car spray to use on their luxurious upholstery after they found out their cars did not smell new enough. Other sellers use similar tricks. There are few people selling houses who have not recognised the trick of percolating coffee when the house is viewed and few stores that have not used the attractive smell of fresh bread. Philosophers from Aristotle to Kant have ranked base smell below the noble senses of seeing, hearing and touching. Yet fragrances are one of the pillars of luxury marketing, with exclusive brands adored by the initiated. Creed is a classic of fragrances, used by Prince Charles and Quincy Jones; Acqua di Parma was adored by Audrey Hepburn and Eva Gardner. Is this obsession an indulgence or does it reflect an insight that few have achieved?

Freud proposes an answer. Smell, he says, is a base sense but one that people have evolved to reject intellectually because of its power. Walking on two legs has taken 1,000 different types of smell receptors in our nose away from the centres of odour that obsess four-legged creatures. With taste, smell was one of the first senses to evolve – it is how amoebas find food.

Old it may be, but neglected it is not. One thousand of our genes relate to our smell receptors in the nose while only three genes control colour vision. Our smell receptors are also well connected. From the nose they first go to the limbic system – a part of the brain that drives mood, sexual urges and fear. Signals then travel to the hippocampus, which controls memories. Only then do the signals travel to the frontal lobes of the brain involved in conscious thought. Your 1,000 smell receptors are always working busily but subliminally.

One example of this subliminal effect is a range of 'odourless' steroids produced by men and women. These directly affect mood. While the masculine version cheers up women, the female version irritates men. Unfortunately, the smell of teenage men also makes people angry. Such a clash of pongs could account for some Saturday night rumbles.

There is more. A granny smell, taken from the armpits of menopausal women, makes people happy while a mummy smell, taken from new mums, can cure depression. Smell also influences perception. Men's regard for how attractive a women smells when they have not seen them corresponds strongly to their perception of a women's visual attractiveness.

Research shows how evolutionary logic drives people's response to smell. Although women have a stronger sense of smell than men, they are not good at identifying physically attractive guys by smell alone. They are attracted instead to the smell of men whose immune system least overlaps with their own. Mating with such partners,

...7.2

they are most likely to sire healthy offspring. This handy sensitivity increases when women are ovulating. Unfortunately this ability is messed up by taking contraceptive pills.

Science is helping remove a smell that no-one finds attractive, body odour (BO). This is caused by Corynebacteria (Coryn), a group of some of the 7,000 bacteria that inhabit all skin. All the bacteria live off the skin's natural fat-laden secretion but, unfortunately for some people, they attract Coryn which is a messy eater that leaves half-digested waste. Quest International, one of the world's largest fragrance houses, is working on long-active deodorants that attack Coryn rather than clogging up the sweat glands like most of the €1.5 billion worth of deodorants do.

The understanding of the science of odour is moving out of the realm of the alchemy of exotic fragrances. Aromatic engineering is a rapidly growing business based on pumping designer smells into offices and stores to make customers feel happier and spend more money. Researchers have found a link between certain genes and the smells that people find attractive. People with HLA-A1 tend to dislike ambergris and musk while those with HLA-A2 like them. This genetic foundation for fragrances explains why perfumes still use the same ingredients as in biblical times. There is also growing evidence that humans have a veromonal nasal organ, a sensor that picks up the pheromones that drive animals sex crazy!

SOURCES: Jerome Burne, 'Why smell gets up your nose', *Financial Times* (8 April 2000), p. 11; Nick Foulkes, 'Have you seen this bottle?', *How to Spend It, Financial Times* (8 April 2000), pp. 31–2; 'Making sense of scents', *The Economist* (13 March 1999), p. 137; 'The sweet smell of success', *The Economist* (25 March 2000), p. 118; 'Cor, you don't half smell', *The Economist* (27 January 2001), p. 114.

Information search

An aroused consumer may or may not search for more information. If the consumer's drive is strong and a satisfying product is near at hand, the consumer is likely to buy it then. If not, the consumer may simply store the need in memory or undertake an **information search** related to the need.

At one level, the consumer may simply enter *heightened attention*. Here Anna becomes more receptive to information about cameras. She pays attention to camera ads, cameras used by friends and camera conversations. Or Anna may go into *active information search*, in which she looks for reading material, phones friends and gathers information in other ways. The amount of searching she does will depend upon the strength of her drive, the amount of information she starts with, the ease of obtaining more information, the value she places on additional information and the satisfaction she gets from searching. Normally the amount of consumer search activity increases as the consumer moves from decisions that involve limited problem solving to those that involve extensive problem solving.

The consumer can obtain information from any of several sources:

- *Personal sources*: family, friends, neighbours, acquaintances
- *Commercial sources*: advertising, salespeople, the Internet, packaging, displays

Information search—
The stage of the buyer decision process in which the consumer is aroused to search for more information; the consumer may simply have heightened attention or may go into active information search.

■ *Public sources*: mass media, consumer-rating organisations

■ *Experiential sources*: handling, examining, using the product.

The relative influence of these information sources varies with the product and the buyer. Generally, the consumer receives the most information about a product from commercial sources – those controlled by the marketer. The most effective sources, however, tend to be personal. Personal sources appear to be even more important in influencing the purchase of services.[32] Commercial sources normally *inform* the buyer, but personal sources *legitimise* or *evaluate* products for the buyer. For example, doctors normally learn of new drugs from commercial sources, but turn to other doctors for evaluative information.

As more information is obtained, the consumer's awareness and knowledge of the available brands and features increases. In her information search, Anna learned about the many camera brands available. The information also helped her drop certain brands from consideration. A company must design its marketing mix to make prospects aware of and knowledgeable about its brand. If it fails to do this, the company has lost its opportunity to sell to the customer. The company must also learn which other brands customers consider so that it knows its competition and can plan its own appeals.

The marketer should identify consumers' sources of information and the importance of each source. Consumers should be asked how they first heard about the brand, what information they received and the importance they place on different information sources.

Evaluation of alternatives

We have seen how the consumer uses information to arrive at a set of final brand choices. How does the consumer choose among the alternative brands? The marketer needs to know about **alternative evaluation** – that is, how the consumer processes information to arrive at brand choices. Unfortunately, consumers do not use a simple and single evaluation process in all buying situations. Instead, several evaluation processes are at work.

Certain basic concepts help explain consumer evaluation processes. First, we assume that each consumer is trying to satisfy some need and is looking for certain *benefits* that can be acquired by buying a product or service. Further, each consumer sees a product as a bundle of *product attributes* with varying capacities for delivering these benefits and satisfying the need. For cameras, product attributes might include picture quality, ease of use, camera size, price and other features. Consumers will vary as to which of these attributes they consider relevant and will pay the most attention to those attributes connected with their needs.

Second, the consumer will attach different *degrees of importance* to each attribute. A distinction can be drawn between the importance of an attribute and its salience. *Salient attributes* are those that come to a consumer's mind when he or she is asked to think of a product's characteristics. But these are not necessarily the most important attributes to the consumer. Some of them may be salient because the consumer has just seen an advertisement mentioning them or has had a problem with them, making these attributes 'top-of-the-mind'. There may also be other attributes that the consumer forgot, but whose importance would be recognised if they were mentioned. Marketers should be more concerned with attribute importance than attribute salience.

Third, the consumer is likely to develop a set of *brand beliefs* about where each brand stands on each attribute. The set of beliefs held about a particular brand is known as the **brand image**. The consumer's beliefs may vary from true attributes based on his or her experience to the effects of selective perception, selective distortion and selective retention.

Fourth, the consumer is assumed to have a *utility function* for each attribute. The utility function shows how the consumer expects total product satisfaction to vary with different levels of different attributes. For example, Anna may expect her satisfaction from a digital camera to increase with better picture quality, to peak with a medium-weight camera as

Alternative evaluation— The stage of the buyer decision process in which the consumer uses information to evaluate alternative brands in the choice set.

Brand image—The set of beliefs that consumers hold about a particular brand.

Table 7.5 A consumer's brand beliefs about cameras

	Attribute			
Camera	Picture quality	Ease of use	Camera size	Price
Agfa	10	6	6	3
Ricoh	6	8	6	6
Canon	8	7	8	6
Mustek	4	6	8	9

opposed to a very light or very heavy one and to be a compact. If we combine the attribute levels at which her utilities are highest, they make up Anna's ideal camera. The camera would also be her preferred camera if it were available and affordable.

Fifth, the consumer arrives at attitudes towards the different brands through some *evaluation procedure*. Consumers have been found to use one or more of several evaluation procedures, depending on the consumer and the buying decision.

In Anna's camera-buying situation, suppose she has narrowed her choice set to four cameras: Agfa ePhoto 1280, Ricoh RDC-300Z, Canon Powershot 350 and the amazingly inexpensive Mustek VDC-100. In addition, let us say she is interested primarily in four attributes – picture quality, ease of use, camera size and price. Table 7.5 shows how she believes each brand rates on each attribute.[33] Anna believes the Agfa will give her picture quality of 10 on a 10-point scale; is not so easy to use, 6; is of medium size, 6; and is expensive, 3. Similarly, she has beliefs about how the other cameras rate on these attributes. The marketer would like to be able to predict which camera Anna will buy.

Clearly, if one camera rated best on all the attributes, we could predict that Anna would choose it. But the brands vary in appeal. Some buyers will base their buying decision on only one attribute and their choices are easy to predict. If Anna wants low price above everything, she should buy the Mustek, whereas if she wants the camera that is easiest to use, she could buy either the Ricoh or the Canon.

Most buyers consider several attributes, but assign different importance to each. If we knew the importance weights that Anna assigns to the four attributes, we could predict her camera choice more reliably. Suppose Anna assigns 40 per cent of the importance to the camera's picture quality, 30 per cent to ease of use, 20 per cent to its size and 10 per cent to its price. To find Anna's perceived value for each camera, we can multiply her importance weights by her beliefs about each camera. This gives us the following perceived values:

Agfa $= 0.4(10) + 0.3(6) + 0.2(6) + 0.1(3) = 7.3$

Ricoh $= 0.4(6) + 0.3(8) + 0.2(6) + 0.1(6) = 6.6$

Canon $= 0.4(8) + 0.3(7) + 0.2(8) + 0.1(6) = 7.5$

Mustek $= 0.4(4) + 0.3(6) + 0.2(8) + 0.1(9) = 5.9$

We would predict that Anna favours the Canon.

This model is called the *expectancy value model* of consumer choice.[34] This is one of several possible models describing how consumers go about evaluating alternatives. Consumers might evaluate a set of alternatives in other ways. For example, Anna might decide that she should consider only cameras that satisfy a set of minimum attribute levels. She might decide that a camera must have a TV connector. In this case, she would choose the Agfa because it is the only one with that facility. This is called the *conjunctive model* of consumer choice. Or she might decide that she would settle for a camera that had a picture quality greater than 7 *or* ease of use greater than 9. In this case, the Agfa, Ricoh or Canon would do, since they all meet at least one of the requirements. This is called the *disjunctive model* of consumer choice.

Once a male preserve, women now buy an increasing proportion of gadgets. Products and promotions are now designed to fulfil the segment's needs.
SOURCE: Nikon Inc.

How consumers go about evaluating purchase alternatives depends on the individual consumer and the specific buying situation. In some cases, consumers use careful calculations and logical thinking. At other times, the same consumers do little or no evaluating; instead they buy on impulse and rely on intuition. Sometimes consumers make buying decisions on their own; sometimes they turn to friends, consumer guides or salespeople for buying advice.

Marketers should study buyers to find out how they actually evaluate brand alternatives. If they know what evaluative processes go on, marketers can take steps to influence the buyer's decision. Suppose Anna is now inclined to buy an Agfa because of its picture quality. What strategies might another camera maker, say Canon, use to influence people like Anna? There are several. Canon could modify its camera to produce a version that has fewer features, but is lighter and cheaper. It could try to change buyers' beliefs about how its camera rates on key attributes, especially if consumers currently underestimate the camera's qualities. It could try to change buyers' beliefs about Agfa and other competitors. Finally, it could try to change the list of attributes that buyers consider or the importance attached to these attributes. For example, it might advertise that to be really useful a camera needs to be small and easy to use. What is the point in having a super-accurate camera if it takes too long to set up and is too awkward to carry around?

Purchase decision—The stage of the buyer decision process in which the consumer actually buys the product.

Purchase decision

In the evaluation stage, the consumer ranks brands and forms purchase intentions. Generally, the consumer's **purchase decision** will be to buy the most preferred brand, but two factors, shown in Figure 7.7, can come between the purchase *intention* and the purchase *decision*. The first factor is the *attitudes of others*. For example, if Anna Flores' husband feels strongly that

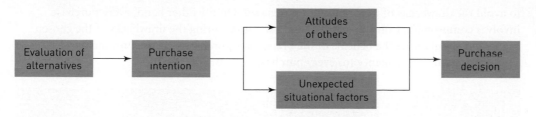

Figure 7.7 Steps between evaluation of alternatives and a purchase decision

Anna should buy the lowest-priced camera, then the chance of Anna buying a more expensive camera is reduced. Alternatively, his love of gadgets may attract him to the Agfa. How much another person's attitudes will affect Anna's choices depends both on the strength of the other person's attitudes towards her buying decision and on Anna's motivation to comply with that person's wishes.

Purchase intention is also influenced by *unexpected situational factors*. The consumer may form a purchase intention based on factors such as expected family income, expected price and expected benefits from the product. When the consumer is about to act, unexpected situational factors may arise to change the purchase intention. Anna may lose her job, some other purchase may become more urgent or a friend may report being disappointed in her preferred camera. Thus preferences and even purchase intentions do not always result in actual purchase choice. They may direct purchase behaviour, but may not fully determine the outcome.

A consumer's decision to change, postpone or avoid a purchase decision is influenced heavily by *perceived risk*. Many purchases involve some risk taking.[35] Anxiety results when consumers cannot be certain about the purchase outcome. The amount of perceived risk varies with the amount of money at stake, the amount of purchase uncertainty and the amount of consumer self-confidence. A consumer takes certain actions to reduce risk, such as avoiding purchase decisions, gathering more information and looking for national brand names and products with warranties. The marketer must understand the factors that provoke feelings of risk in consumers and must provide information and support that will reduce the perceived risk.

Postpurchase behaviour

The marketer's job does not end when the product is bought. After purchasing the product, the consumer will be satisfied or dissatisfied and will engage in **postpurchase behaviour** of interest to the marketer. What determines whether the buyer is satisfied or dissatisfied with a purchase? The answer lies in the relationship between the *consumer's expectations* and the product's *perceived performance*. If the product falls short of expectations, the consumer is disappointed; if it meets expectations, the consumer is satisfied; if it exceeds expectations, the consumer is delighted.

Consumers base their expectations on messages they receive from sellers, friends and other information sources. If the seller exaggerates the product's performance, consumer expectations will not be met – a situation that leads to dissatisfaction. The larger the gap between expectations and performance, the greater the consumer's dissatisfaction. This fact suggests that the seller should make product claims that represent faithfully the product's performance so that buyers are satisfied.

Motoring organisations regularly give pessimistic quotes about how long they will take to reach a customer whose car breaks down. If they say they will be 30 minutes and get there in 20, the customer is impressed. If, however, they get there in 20 minutes after promising 10, the customer is not so happy.

Almost all large purchases result in **cognitive dissonance** or discomfort caused by postpurchase conflict. Consumers are satisfied with the benefits of the chosen brand and glad

Postpurchase behaviour— The stage of the buyer decision process in which consumers take further action after purchase based on their satisfaction or dissatisfaction.

Cognitive dissonance— Buyer discomfort caused by postpurchase conflict.

to avoid the drawbacks of the brands not purchased. On the other hand, every purchase involves compromise. Consumers feel uneasy about acquiring the drawbacks of the chosen brand and about losing the benefits of the brands not purchased. Thus consumers feel at least some postpurchase dissonance for every purchase.

American consumers are having a love affair with luxurious four ton, seven litre engined Sports Utility Vehicles (SUV). Their popularity has propelled the light trucks sector to 48 per cent of vehicles sold in the US. These no-compromise vehicles have the fuel consumption of a truck. According to Jac Nasser, Ford's chief executive: 'They're practical and promise something few other vehicles offer: the just-in-case factor. Just in case you want to buy a dinghy or a tree, you can do it.' SUVs can do it all but some customers are not happy with their purchases. Many have to rebuild their garages in order to house them and they do not fit some parking lots and cannot get into multi-storey car parks. Drivers also neglect to read the instruction behind the sun visor of their Ford Excursion: 'Avoid unnecessary sharp turns or other abrupt manoeuvres'.[36]

Why is it so important to satisfy the customer? Such satisfaction is important because a company's sales come from two basic groups – *new customers* and *repeat customers*. It usually costs more to attract new customers than to retain current ones. Keeping current customers is therefore often more critical than attracting new ones, and the best way to do this is to make current customers happy. A satisfied customer buys a product again, talks favourably to others about the product, pays less attention to competing brands and advertising, and buys other products from the company. Many marketers go beyond merely *meeting* the expectations of customers – they aim to *delight* the customer. A delighted customer is even more likely to purchase again and to talk favourably about the product and company.

A dissatisfied consumer responds differently. Whereas, on average, a satisfied customer tells three people about a good product experience, a dissatisfied customer gripes to 11 people. In fact, one study showed that 13 per cent of the people who had a problem with an organisation complained about that company to more than 20 people.[37] Clearly, bad word-of-mouth travels farther and faster than good word-of-mouth and can quickly damage consumer attitudes about a company and its products.

Therefore, a company would be wise to measure customer satisfaction regularly. It cannot simply rely on dissatisfied customers to volunteer their complaints when they are dissatisfied. In fact, 96 per cent of unhappy customers never tell the company about their problem. Companies should set up suggestion systems to *encourage* customers to complain. In this way, the company can learn how well it is doing and how it can improve. The 3M Company claims that over two-thirds of its new-product ideas come from listening to customer complaints. But listening is not enough – the company must also respond constructively to the complaints it receives.

Thus, in general, dissatisfied consumers may try to reduce their dissonance by taking any of several actions. In the case of Anna – a Canon digital camera purchaser – she may return the camera, or look at Canon ads that tell of the camera's benefits, or talk with friends who will tell her how much they like her new camera. She may even avoid reading about cameras in case she finds a better deal than she got.

Beyond seeking out and responding to complaints, marketers can take additional steps to reduce consumer postpurchase dissatisfaction and to help customers feel good about their purchases. For example, Toyota writes or phones new car owners with congratulations on having selected a fine car. It places ads showing satisfied owners talking about their new cars ('I love what you do for me, Toyota!'). Toyota also obtains customer suggestions for improvements and lists the locations of available services.

Understanding the consumer's needs and buying process is the foundation of successful marketing. By understanding how buyers go through need recognition, information search, evaluation of alternatives, the purchase decision and postpurchase behaviour, the marketer can pick up many clues as to how to meet the buyer's needs. By understanding the various participants in the buying process and the strongest influences on their buying behaviour, the marketer can develop an effective programme to support an attractive offer to the target market.

The buyer decision process for new products

We have looked at the stages that buyers go through in trying to satisfy a need. Buyers may pass quickly or slowly through these stages and some of the stages may even be reversed. Much depends on the nature of the buyer, the product and the buying situation.

We now look at how buyers approach the purchase of new products. A **new product** is a good, service or idea that is perceived by some potential customers as new. It may have been around for a while, but our interest is in how consumers learn about products for the first time and make decisions on whether to adopt them. We define the **adoption process** as 'the mental process through which an individual passes from first learning about an innovation to final adoption',[38] and **adoption** as the decision by an individual to become a regular user of the product.

Stages in the adoption process

Consumers go through five stages in the process of adopting a new product:

1. *Awareness.* The consumer becomes aware of the new product, but lacks information about it.
2. *Interest.* The consumer seeks information about the new product.
3. *Evaluation.* The consumer considers whether trying the new product makes sense.
4. *Trial.* The consumer tries the new product on a small scale to improve his or her estimate of its value.
5. *Adoption.* The consumer decides to make full and regular use of the new product.

This model suggests that the new-product marketer should think about how to help consumers move through these stages. Denon, a leading manufacturer of home cinema equipment, may discover that many consumers in the interest stage do not move to the trial stage because of uncertainty and the large investment. If these same consumers would be willing to use a sound system on a trial basis for a small fee, the manufacturer should consider offering a trial-use plan with an option to buy.

Individual differences in innovativeness

People differ greatly in their readiness to try new products. In each product area, there are 'consumption pioneers' and early adopters. Other individuals adopt new products much later. This has led to a classification of people into the adopter categories shown in Figure 7.8.

New product—A good, service or idea that is perceived by some potential customers as new.

Adoption process—The mental process through which an individual passes from first hearing about an innovation to final adoption.

Adoption—The decision by an individual to become a regular user of the product.

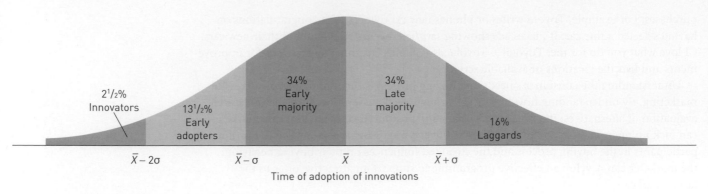

Figure 7.8 Adopter categorisation on the basis of relative time of adoption of innovations
SOURCE: Reprinted with permission of The Free Press, a Division of Simon & Schuster, Inc., by Everett M. Rogers. Copyright © 1995 by Everett M. Rogers from *Diffusion of Innovations*, fourth edition. Copyright © 1962, 1971, 1983 by The Free Press

After a slow start, an increasing number of people adopt the new product. The number of adopters reaches a peak and then drops off as fewer non-adopters remain. Innovators are defined as the first 2.5 per cent of the buyers to adopt a new idea (those beyond two standard deviations from mean adoption time); the early adopters are the next 13.5 per cent (between one and two standard deviations), and so forth.

The five adopter groups have differing values. *Innovators* are adventurous: they try new ideas at some risk. *Early adopters* are guided by respect: they are opinion leaders in their community and adopt new ideas early but carefully. The *early majority* is deliberate: although they are rarely leaders, they adopt new ideas before the average person. The *late majority* is sceptical: they adopt an innovation only after most people have tried it. Finally, *laggards* are tradition-bound: they are suspicious of changes and adopt the innovation only when it has become something of a tradition itself.

> Not all products are targeted at the *early adopters*. Open, owned by BT, BSkyB, HSBC and Matsushita, is an interactive service for digital television aimed at the *late majority* who love television but are scared of new technologies. Using existing televisions, low telephone charges and an inexpensive remote keyboard, Open has lower 'emotional' and financial barriers than Internet adoption. Using their old couch facing their familiar old TV, users can access banking services, shop, gamble or send email.[39]

This adopter classification suggests that an innovating firm should research the characteristics of innovators and early adopters and should direct marketing efforts to them. For example, home computer innovators have been found to be middle-aged and higher in income and education than non-innovators and they tend to be opinion leaders. They also tend to be more rational, more introverted and less social. In general, innovators tend to be relatively younger, better educated and higher in income than later adopters and non-adopters. They are more receptive to unfamiliar things, rely more on their own values and judgement, and are more willing to take risks. They are less brand loyal and more likely to take advantage of special promotions such as discounts, coupons and samples.

Manufacturers of products and brands subject to strong group influence must find out how to reach the opinion leaders in the relevant reference groups. **Opinion leaders** are people within a reference group who, because of special skills, knowledge, personality or other characteristics, exert influence on others. Opinion leaders are found in all strata of

Opinion leaders—People within a reference group who, because of special skills, knowledge, personality or other characteristics, exert influence on others.

society and one person may be an opinion leader in certain product areas and an opinion follower in others. Marketers try to identify the personal characteristics of opinion leaders for the products, determine what media they use and direct messages at them. In some cases, marketers try to identify opinion leaders for their products and direct marketing efforts towards them. This often occurs in the music industry, where clubs and radio DJs are influential. In other cases, advertisements can simulate opinion leadership, showing informal discussions between people and thereby reducing the need for consumers to seek advice from others. For example, in an ad for Herrera for Men cologne, two women discuss the question: 'Did you ever notice how good he smells?' The reason? 'He wears the most wonderful cologne.'

If Anna Flores buys a camera, both the product and the brand will be visible to others whom she respects. Her decision to buy the camera and her brand choice may therefore be influenced strongly by opinion leaders, such as friends who belong to a photography club.

Role of personal influence

Personal influence plays a distinctive role in the adoption of new products. **Personal influence** describes the effect of statements made by one person on another's attitude or probability of purchase. Consumers consult each other for opinions about new products and brands, and the advice of others can strongly influence buying behaviour.

Personal influence is more important in some situations and for some individuals than for others. Personal influence is more important in the evaluation stage of the adoption process than in the other stages; it has more influence on later adopters than on early adopters; and it is more important in risky buying situations than in safe situations.

Personal influence—The effect of statements made by one person on another's attitude or probability of purchase.

Influence of product characteristics on rate of adoption

The characteristics of the new product affect its rate of adoption. Some products catch on almost overnight (such as text messaging), whereas others take a long time to gain acceptance (digital TV). Five characteristics are especially important in influencing an innovation's rate of adoption. For example, consider the characteristics of in-car SatNav (Satellite Navigation) systems in relation to the rate of adoption:

- *Relative advantage*: the degree to which the innovation appears superior to existing products. The greater the perceived relative advantage of using SatNav over maps or taking instructions from a passenger, the sooner SatNav will be adopted.

- *Compatibility*: the degree to which the innovation fits the values and experiences of potential consumers. SatNav, for example, is highly compatible with an active lifestyle. New DVD-based SatNav systems showing maps and giving verbal instruction are more compatible with using maps than the original SatNav systems that just showed direction.

- *Complexity*: the degree to which the innovation is difficult to understand or use. Many customers have great difficulty interfacing with technology, so initial ease of use is critical.

- *Divisibility*: the degree to which the innovation may be tried on a limited basis. SatNav systems have a problem here. They require a big one-off investment if people are to add them to their car.

- *Communicability*: the degree to which the results of using the innovation can be observed or described to others. The benefits of SatNav are easy to demonstrate on a journey.

Other characteristics influence the rate of adoption, such as initial and ongoing costs, risk and uncertainty, social approval and the efforts of opinion leaders. The new-product marketer has to research all these factors when developing the new product and its marketing programme.

Consumer behaviour across international borders

Understanding consumer behaviour is difficult enough for companies marketing in a single country. For companies operating in many countries, however, understanding and serving the needs of consumers is daunting. Although consumers in different countries may have some things in common, their values, attitudes and behaviours often vary greatly. International marketers must understand such differences and adjust their products and marketing programmes accordingly.

Sometimes the differences are obvious. For example, in the UK, where most people eat cereal regularly for breakfast, Kellogg focuses its marketing on persuading consumers to select a Kellogg's brand rather than a competitor's brand. In France, however, where most people prefer croissants and coffee or no breakfast at all, Kellogg's advertising simply attempts to convince people that they should eat cereal for breakfast. Its packaging includes step-by-step instructions on how to prepare cereal. In India, where many consumers eat heavy, fried breakfasts and 22 per cent of consumers skip the meal altogether, Kellogg's advertising attempts to convince buyers to switch to a lighter, more nutritious breakfast diet.[40]

Often, differences across international markets are subtler. They may result from physical differences in consumers and their environments. For example, Remington makes smaller electric shavers to fit the smaller hands of Japanese consumers, and battery-powered shavers for the British market, where some bathrooms have no electrical outlets. Other differences result from varying customs. Consider the following examples:

- Shaking your head from side to side means 'no' in most countries but 'yes' in Bulgaria and Sri Lanka.

- In South America, southern Europe and many Arab countries, touching another person is a sign of warmth and friendship. In the Orient, it is considered an invasion of privacy.

- In Norway or Malaysia, it's rude to leave something on your plate when eating; in Egypt, it's rude *not* to leave something on your plate.

- A door-to-door salesperson might find it tough going in Italy, where it is improper for a man to call on a woman if she is home alone.[41]

Failing to understand such differences in customs and behaviours from one country to another can spell disaster for a marketer's international products and programmes.

Marketers must decide on the degree to which they will adapt their products and marketing programmes to meet the unique cultures and needs of consumers in various markets. On the one hand, they want to standardise their offerings in order to simplify operations and take advantage of cost economies. On the other hand, adapting marketing efforts within each country results in products and programmes that better satisfy the needs of local consumers. The question of whether to adapt or standardise the marketing mix across international markets has created a lively debate in recent years.

Summary

Markets have to be understood before marketing strategies can be developed. The consumer market buys goods and services for personal consumption. Consumers vary tremendously in age, income, education, tastes and other factors. Marketers must understand how consumers transform marketing and other inputs into buying responses. *Consumer behaviour* is influenced by the buyer's characteristics and by the buyer's decision process. *Buyer characteristics* include four main factors: cultural, social, personal and psychological.

Culture is the most basic determinant of a person's wants and behaviour. It includes the basic values, perceptions, preferences and behaviours that a person learns from family and other key institutions. Marketers try to track cultural shifts that might suggest new ways to serve customers. *Social classes* are subcultures whose members have similar social prestige based on occupation, income, education, wealth and other variables. People with different cultural, subculture and social class characteristics have different product and brand preferences.

Social factors also influence a buyer's behaviour. A person's *reference groups* – family, friends, social organisations, professional associations – strongly affect product and brand choices. The person's position within each group can be defined in terms of *role and status*. A buyer chooses products and brands that reflect his or her role and status.

The buyer's age, life-cycle stage, occupation, economic circumstances, lifestyle, personality and other *personal characteristics* and *psychological factors* influence his or her buying decisions. Young consumers have different needs and wants from older consumers; the needs of young married couples differ from those of retired people; consumers with higher incomes buy differently from those who have less to spend.

Before planning its marketing strategy, a company needs to understand its consumers and the decision processes they go through. The number of buying participants and the amount of buying effort increase with the complexity of the buying situation. There are three types of *buying decision behaviour*: *routine response behaviour*, *limited problem solving* and *extensive problem solving*.

In buying something, the buyer goes through a decision process consisting of *need recognition*, *information search*, *evaluation of alternatives*, *purchase decision* and *postpurchase behaviour*. The marketer's job is to understand the buyers' behaviour at each stage and the influences that are operating. This allows the marketer to develop a significant and effective marketing programme for the target market. With regard to new products, consumers respond at different rates, depending on the consumer's characteristics and the product's characteristics. Manufacturers try to bring their new products to the attention of potential early adopters, particularly those with opinion leader characteristics.

A person's buying behaviour is the result of the complex interplay of all these cultural, social, personal and psychological factors. Although marketers cannot control many of these factors, they are useful in identifying and understanding the consumers that marketers are trying to influence.

Discussing the issues

1. Thinking about the purchase of an audio hi-fi system, indicate the extent to which cultural, social, personal and psychological factors affect how a buyer evaluates hi-fi products and chooses a brand.

2. Describe and contrast any differences in the buying behaviour of consumers for the following products: a CD, a notebook computer, a pair of trainers and a breakfast cereal.

3. Why might a detailed understanding of the model of the consumer buying decision process help marketers develop more effective marketing strategies to capture and retain customers? How universal is the model? How useful is it?

4. In designing the advertising for a soft drink, which would you find more helpful: information about consumer demographics or about consumer lifestyles? Give examples of how you would use each type of information.

5. Take, for example, a new method of contraception, which is being 'sold' to young males. It is a controversial, albeit innovative concept. Your firm is the pioneer in launching this device. What are the main factors your firm must research when developing a marketing programme for this product?

6. It has been said that consumers' buying behaviour is shaped more by perception than by reality. Do you agree with this comment? Why or why not?

Applying the concepts

1. Different types of product can fulfil different functional and psychological needs.

   - List five luxury products or services that are very interesting or important to you. Some possibilities are cars, clothing, sports equipment, cosmetics or club membership. List five other necessities that you use which have little interest for you, such as pens, laundry detergent or petrol.

   - Make a list of words that describe how you feel about each of the products/services listed. Are there differences between the types of word you used for luxuries and necessities? What does this tell you about the different psychological needs these products fulfil?

2. Different groups may have different types of effect on consumers.

   - Consider an item you bought which is typical of what your peers (a key reference group) buy, such as a compact disc, a mountain bike or a brand of trainer. Were you conscious that your friends owned something similar when you made the purchase? Did this make you want the item more or less? Why or why not?

   - Now, think of brands that you currently use which your parents also use. Examples may include soap, shaving cream or margarine. Did you think through these purchases as carefully as those influenced by your peers or were these purchases simply the result of following old habits?

3. SRI Consulting, through the Business Intelligence Center online, features the Values and Lifestyles Program (VALS). Visit SRI at www.sri.com and follow links to the VALS questionnaire.

   - Take the survey to determine your type and then read all about your type. Why or why not does it describe you well?

- What four products have high indexes for your type? Do you buy these products?

- Compare the nine Japan-VALS segments with the US VALS. How similar are they and are they likely to explain the European consumer?

- Other than product design, how can marketers use information from Japan-VALS?

References

1. See www.un.org/esa/population/unpop and www.census.gov/main/www/popclock for continuously updated projections of the world's population.

2. Several models of the consumer buying process have been developed by marketing scholars. The most prominent models are those of John A. Howard and Jagdish N. Sheth, *The Theory of Buyer Behaviour* (New York: Wiley, 1969); Francesco M. Nicosia, *Consumer Decision Processes* (Englewood Cliffs, NJ: Prentice Hall, 1966); James F. Engel, Roger D. Blackwell and Paul W. Miniard, *Consumer Behaviour*, 5th edn (New York: Holt, Rinehart & Winston, 1986); James R. Bettman, *An Information Processing Theory of Consumer Choice* (Reading, MA: Addison-Wesley, 1979). For a summary, see Leon G. Schiffman and Leslie Lazar Kanuk, *Consumer Behaviour*, 4th edn (Englewood Cliffs, NJ: Prentice Hall, 1991), Ch. 20.

3. For this and the following example, see Philip R. Cateora, *International Marketing*, 8th edn (Homewood, IL: Irwin, 1993), Ch. 4; Warren J. Keegan and Mark S. Green, *Global Marketing*, 2nd edn (Upper Saddle River, NJ: Prentice Hall, 2000), pp. 129–30; and Warren J. Keegan, *Global Marketing Management*, 7th edn (Upper Saddle River, NJ: Prentice Hall, 2002), pp. 68–9.

4. 'Fat or fit', *The World in 2002* (*The Economist*, 2001).

5. Brian J. Ford, *The Future of Eating* (Thames & Hudson, 2000); Andrew Ward, 'Austin Reed reveals takeover talks as sales suffer 5 per cent fall', *Financial Times* (7 April 2000), p. 23; *The Economist*, 'Blech' (15 January 2000), p. 87; 'Cooking: ready, steady, eat', *The Economist* (8 June 2002), p. 28.

6. 'More industrial decline: the china syndrome', *The Economist* (25 August 2001), p. 33.

7. 'Islam in France', *The Economist* (25 October 2003), pp. 41–2; 'Europe's Muslims', *The Economist* (8 August 2002); 'Muslims in Western Europe', *The Economist* (8 August 2002), pp. 41–2; 'Islamic finance', *The Economist* (25 October 2003), p. 93.

8. Details of NS-SEC and the European initiatives can be found at www.statistics.gov.uk. An introduction to the new scheme is in 'Classification', *The Economist* (3 June 2000), p. 31; and Angela Donkin, Yuan Huang Lee and Barbara Toson, 'Implications of changes in the UK Social and Occupational Classifications in 2001 for Vital Statistics' (*Population Trends*, no. 107, 2002), p. 7.

9. Richard Tomkins, 'The folly of treating children as consumers', *Financial Times* (28 November 2002), p. 23.

10. For a look at the cultural twists and turns over recent generations, see Peter Everett, *You'll Never Want to be 16 Again* (London: BBC Publications, 1994) or Bevis Hillier, *The Style of the Century* (London: Herbert, 1993).

11. Michael Witte, 'Buzz-z-z marketing', *Business Week* (30 July 2001), pp. 50–6.

12 William O. Bearden and Michael J. Etzel, 'Reference group influence on product and brand purchase decisions', *Journal of Consumer Research* (September 1982), p. 185; K. Hogg, M. Bruce and Alexander J. Hill, 'Fashion brand preferences among young consumers', *International Journal of Retail and Distribution Management*, **26**, 8 (1998), pp. 293–300.

13 Sheila Jones, 'Procter & Gamble's bottom line is challenged', *Financial Times* (11 May 2000), p. 1; 'Going soft', *The Economist* (4 March 2000), p. 34.

14 'Real men get waxed', *The Economist* (3 July 2003).

15 'Anti-nuclear reaction', *The Economist* (31 December 1999), pp. 65–6; 'What a lot of sterEUtypes', *The Economist* (23 October 1999), p. 65.

16 Stephanie Armour, 'Slowdown moves more adult kids back home', *USA Today* (24 April 2001), p. 1B; Mariko Sanchanta, 'Youth snubs life as salaryman and seeks its dream', *Financial Times*

(30 September 2002), p. VI; 'Consensus and contraction', *The Economist Special Survey: What Ails Japan?* (20 April 2002), pp. 8–10.

17 Kim Foltz, 'Wizards of marketing', *Newsweek* (22 July 1985), p. 44.

18 For more on VALS and on psychographics in general, see Rebecca Piirto, 'Measuring minds in the 1990s', *American Demographics* (December 1990), pp. 35–9, and 'VALS the second time', *American Demographics* (July 1991), p. 6. For good discussions of other lifestyle topics, see Michael R. Solomon, *Consumer Behavior*, 5th edn (Upper Saddle River, NJ: Prentice Hall, 2002), Ch. 6.

19 Taken from RISC SA, *ACE* (Lyon: RISC SA, 1989); CCA, *CCA Euro-styles* (Paris: CCA, 1989); Norbert Homma and Jorg Uelzhoffer, 'The internationalisation of everyday-life and milieus', *ESOMAR Conference on America, Japan and EC'92: The Prospects for Marketing, Advertising and Research*, Venice, 18–20 June 1990; Marieke de Mooij, *Advertising Worldwide: Concepts, theories and practice of international and global advertising* (Hemel Hempstead: Prentice Hall, 1994).

20. See Paul C. Judge, 'Are tech buyers different?', *Business Week* (26 January 1998), pp. 64–5, 68; Josh Bernoff, Shelley Morrisette and Kenneth Clemmer, 'The Forrester Report', Forrester Research, Inc., 1998; and the Forrester website at www.forrester.com, July 2001.

21. Jennifer Aaker, 'Dimensions of measuring brand personality', *Journal of Marketing Research*, **34** (August 1997), pp. 347–56. Also see Aaker, 'The malleable self: the role of self expression in persuasion', *Journal of Marketing Research* (May 1999), pp. 45–57; and Swee Hoon Ang, 'Personality influences on consumption: insights from the Asian economic crisis', *Journal of International Consumer Marketing* (2001), pp. 5–20.

22. See Myron Magnet, 'Let's go for growth', *Fortune* (7 March 1994), p. 70; Jennifer L. Aaker, 'The malleable self', op. cit.; Leon G. Shiffman and Leslie Lazar Kanuk, *Consumer Behavior*, 7th edn (Upper Saddle River, NJ: Prentice Hall, 2000), pp. 111–18; and Swee Hoon Ang, 'Personality influences on consumption', op. cit.

23. Quote from *Stuff* (September 2000), a magazine for people who lust for hot gadgets.

24. See Annetta Miller and Dody Tsiantar, 'Psyching out consumers', *Newsweek* (27 February 1989), pp. 46–7; Rebecca Piirto, 'Words that sell', *American Demographics* (January 1992), p. 6.

25. Abraham H. Maslow, *Motivation and Personality*, 2nd edn (New York: Harper & Row, 1970), pp. 80–106; E. Wooldridge, 'Time to stand Maslow's hierarchy on its head?', *People Management*, **1**, 25 (1995), pp. 17–19; for examples see Richard Tomkins, 'Luxury for all', *Financial Times* (17 July 2003).

26. S. J. Vittel, S. L. Nwachukwu and J. H. Barnes, 'The effects of culture on ethical decision-making: an application of Hofstede's typology', *Journal of Business Ethics*, **12**, 10 (1993), pp. 753–60; G. Hofstede, 'Cultural constraints in management theories', *International Review of Strategic Management*, **5** (1994), pp. 27–49; M. Sondergaard, 'Hofstede's consequences: a study of reviews, citations and replications', *Organization Studies*, **15**, 3 (1994), pp. 447–56.

27. John Fiske, *Understanding Popular Culture* (London: Routledge, 1989).

28. 'The right to be beautiful', *The Economist* (24 May 2003), p. 9; Joanna Pitman, *On Blondes* (Bloomsbury: London, 2003).

29. See 'Honda hopes to win new riders by emphasizing "fun" of cycles', *Marketing News* (28 August 1989), p. 6.

30. Henry Assael, *Consumer Behaviour and Marketing Action* (Boston, MA: Kent Publishing, 1987), Ch. 4. An earlier classification of three types of consumer buying behaviour – routine response behaviour, limited problem solving and extensive problem solving – can be found in John A. Howard and Jagdish Sheth, *The Theory of Consumer Behaviour* (New York: Wiley, 1969), pp. 27–8. Gordon R. Foxall proposes a more sophisticated Behavioural Perspective Model (BPM) in 'A behavioural perspective on purchasing and consumption' and 'Consumer behaviour as an evolutionary process', *European Journal of Marketing*, **27**, 8 (1993), pp. 7–16 and 46–57 respectively; see also John A. Howard, *Consumer Behaviour in Marketing Strategy* (Englewood Cliffs, NJ: Prentice Hall, 1989).

31. Tom Stevenson, 'Dixons opens shops for baffled buyers', *Independent* (17 October 1994), p. 28.

32. Keith B. Murray, 'A test of services marketing theory: consumer information acquisition theory', *Journal of Marketing* (January 1991), pp. 10–25; W. G. Mangold, F. Miller and G. R. Brockway, 'Word-of-mouth communication in the service marketplace', *Journal of Services Marketing*, **13**, 1 (1999), pp. 73–89.

33. The ratings are based on those given in 'Product test: compact cameras', *Which?* (November 1994), pp. 21–6.

34. This was developed by Martin Fishbein. See Martin Fishbein and Icek Ajzen, *Belief, Attitude, Intention, and Behaviour* (Reading, MA: Addison-Wesley, 1975). For a critical review of this model, see Paul W. Miniard and Joel B. Cohen, 'An examination of the Fishbein–Ajzen behavioral intentions model's concepts and measures', *Journal of Experimental Social Psychology* (May 1981), pp. 309–99; R. Y.-K. Chan and L. Lau, 'A test of Fishbein–Ajzen behavioural intentions model under Chinese cultural settings: are there any differences between PRC and Hong Kong consumers?', *Journal of Marketing Practice: Applied Marketing Science*, **4**, 3 (1998), pp. 85–101.

35. V.-W. Mitchell and Pari Boustani, 'A preliminary investigation into pre- and post-purchase risk perception and reduction', *European Journal of Marketing*, **28**, 1 (1994), pp. 56–71; V.-W. Mitchell, 'Segmenting purchasers of organisational professional services: a risk-based approach', *Journal of Services Marketing*, **12**, 2 (1998), pp. 83–97.

36. See Leon Festinger, *A Theory of Cognitive Dissonance* (Stanford, CA: Stanford University Press, 1957); Schiffman and Kanuk, *Consumer Behaviour*, op. cit., pp. 304–5; Jillian C. Sweeney, Douglas Hausknecht and Geoffrey N. Soutar, 'Cognitive dissonance after purchase: a multidimensional scale', *Psychology and Marketing* (May 2000), pp. 369–85; Patti Williams and Jennifer L. Aaker, 'Can mixed emotions peacefully coexist?', *Psychology and Marketing* (March 2002), pp. 636–49; Tim Burton, 'Cars so big they don't fit the garage', *Financial Times* (16 January 2000), p. 7.

37. See Karl Albrect and Ron Zemke, *Service America!* (Homewood, IL: Dow-Jones Irwin, 1985), pp. 6–7; Frank Rose, 'Now quality means service too', *Fortune* (22 April 1991), pp. 97–108.

38. The following discussion draws heavily from Everett M. Rogers, *Diffusion of Innovations*, 3rd edn (New York: Free Press, 1983). Also see Hubert Gatignon and Thomas S. Robertson, 'A propositional inventory for new diffusion research', *Journal of Consumer Research* (March 1985), pp. 849–67; Rogers, *Diffusion of Innovations*, 4th edn (New York: Free Press, 1995); Marnik G. Dekiple, Philip M. Parker and Milos Sarvary, 'Global diffusion of technological innovations: a coupled-hazard approach', *Journal of Marketing Research* (February 2000), pp. 47–59; Peter J. Danaher, Bruce G. S. Hardie and William P. Putsis, 'Marketing-mix variables and the diffusion of successive generations of a technological innovation', *Journal of Marketing Research* (November 2001), pp. 501–14; Eun-Ju Lee, Jinkook Lee and David W. Schumann, 'The influence of communication source and mode on consumer adoption of technological innovations', *Journal of Consumer Affairs* (Summer 2002), pp. 1–27; G. Antonides, H. B. Amesz and I. C. Hulscher, 'Adoption of payment systems in ten countries – a case study of diffusion of innovations', *European Journal of Marketing*, **33**, 11/12 (1999), pp. 1123–35.

39. 'Open for couch potatoes', *The Economist* (8 January 2000); David Murphy, 'Tomorrow's window of opportunity', *Marketing Business* (June 1999), pp. 43–5; *Sky: the magazine for Sky digital customers* (September 2000); P. Butler and J. Peppard, 'Consumer purchasing on the Internet: processes and prospects', *European Management Journal*, **16**, 5 (1998), pp. 600–10.

40. Mir Maqbool Alam Khan, 'Kellogg reports brisk cereal sales in India', *Advertising Age* (14 November 1994), p. 60.

41. For these and other examples, see William J. Stanton, Michael J. Etzel and Bruce J. Walker, *Fundamentals of Marketing* (New York: McGraw-Hill, 1991), p. 536.

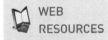

WEB
RESOURCES

For additional classic case studies and Internet exercises, visit www.pearsoned.co.uk/ kotler

Concluding concepts 7
Sony Aibo ERS-7c: Grandma's best friend?

'On the whole, pets are useless, unreliable, messy and expensive', comments *Guardian* writer Justin Hankins. Not so K-9, Dr Who's robo-dog that replaces 'the squelching, oozing yuckiness of the natural world' by sleek, silvery shimmer, adds Mr Hankins.

Sony's Aibo ERS-7c third-generation dog has more tricks up its 32-megapixel memory stick than David Blaine. This is no simple animal or machine. Even the name has many possible meanings. Perhaps it stands for 'artificial intelligence robot'. Perhaps it refers to Aibo's camera eyes, which make it an 'eye bot', or maybe it's just Japanese for companion or pal.

What can you do with Aibo? Well, you can play with it. Aibo has a favourite toy, a pink ball, which it will chase down, pick up in its mouth, and return to you just like any real dog would. If you praise Aibo, its tail wags, its eyes light up green, and it plays a happy melody. It can learn whatever name it is given and even skips across to its recharge station when its batteries run low. It's not exactly like a real dog – it is far less messy and can't jump onto your favourite chair – but close in the sense that Aibo responds visibly to your love and affection.

Aibo can respond to praise and can learn. When you praise Aibo's behaviours, they become stronger and are more likely to be repeated. When scolded, Aibo is sometimes sad and plays a doleful melody. Other times, it responds to scolding by getting agitated and playing an angry melody while its eyes turn red. Although Aibo's responses may be different from a real dog's responses, they do represent the same emotions. Like a real dog, Aibo lets you know that it wants to play by jumping around. In addition to anger, sadness and playfulness, Aibo can show joy (eyes turn green and it plays a happy melody), surprise (eyes light up and it plays a surprised melody and gives a start), discontent (its eyes turn angry red and it moves away), and fear (when it encounters a big hole or rolls onto its back and can't get up, it plays a scared melody).

Voice commands such as 'stay', 'sit' or 'heel' wouldn't work with early Aibos because the puppy had no voice-response mechanism. Instead you gave it commands through a sound controller. Aibo responds only to perfect tones, so the sound controller contains combinations of preset commands in perfect tones. Now, third-generation Abido learns its owner's voice but it can still simply ignore you. When it is in a happy mood, it will perform tricks. Like most temperamental pets, Aibo will play or do tricks only if you're good to it.

When it's time to quit playing, you press the off or the pause button and Aibo lies down and goes to sleep. When not active, Aibo stays in its station, which serves as a battery charger. The robotic puppy comes with two lithium batteries so that one can be charged while the other is in use. A full charge lasts through about 1.5 hours of action.

Aibo comes in three colours (grey, metallic black and silver grey), has stereo microphones for ears, can recognise colours and shapes, and emits a variety of bleeps and chirps. A sensor in its head can distinguish between an amiable pat and a reproachful slap. You can set Aibo to Performance Mode, in which it does tricks, or to Game Mode, in which you control its movements. By making Aibo run and kick, you can even play robot soccer.

Ready to buy an Aibo? You won't find one for sale in any store. It is available only on the Internet at www.world.sony.com/robot/get/meet/html. It's also a little pricey – 250,000 Japanese yen (€2,000). Is anyone willing to pay such a stiff price? When launched in June 1999 Sony offered 5,000 Aibos in Japan and the US and all sold out in only 20 minutes. A second batch of 10,000 in November 1999 received more than 130,000 orders. Facing this greater than anticipated demand, Sony drew lots and selected winners in Japan, the United States and Europe. There appear to be lots of robot-dog's best friends out there!

One of the appealing features of Aibo is its open architecture. Based on experiences with its PlayStation video-game business, Sony decided not to develop everything in-house. Instead, it has invited other developers to create new programs for Aibo. This has resulted in the rapid development of additional memory sticks (programs) that allow you to teach Aibo new tricks or movements.

To test consumer reaction before offering them for sale, Sony demonstrated Aibos at several trade shows. Uniform reaction to the pet was 'That is *so* cute!'. One enthusiastic consumer commented 'I love little robots.

> Like most temperamental pets, Aibo will play or do tricks only if you're good to it.

For me, it would be great. I'm single and I don't have time to keep a dog.' Another said 'This is the coolest thing I've seen all day.' Numerous journalists privileged enough to play with Aibos found them to be lots of fun – even if they can't do anything useful.

Although Aibo isn't likely to fetch your newspaper, bring you your shoes, or scare away burglars, this little puppy does have much promise from a marketing point of view. Sony hopes to create a whole new industry of entertainment robots, an industry that Sony management believe could be larger than the personal computer market. The new Aibo-like entertainment robots have broader appeal. More importantly, they may make people more comfortable with the idea of interacting with humanoid-like machines. Once that happens, robots could become nurses, maids or bodyguards. They might even become partners who will play with and talk to us. There's more than a little bit of *Star Wars'* R2D2 in all this. Back in the eighties, however, R2D2 and his companions seemed a long way off. Now, Aibo and other animal-bots appear to be bringing us into that *Star Wars* world much sooner than we thought.

To many animal lovers Abido is a sad imitation of the real thing. However, like many products, Abido is finding markets that it was not designed for. It has long been understood that dogs are important companions for older couples or single living alone. But expensive, demanding, unreliable, messy dogs can be more than some people can handle. Not so Abido. Increasingly, Abido is being bought as a companion for older people. In that role Abido could have some of the Saint Bernard's life-saving ability about

him. Abido can't run off and get help if Gran's in trouble, but it can be called and it can transmit help messages.

Questions

1. How might personal factors affect the purchase of an Aibo?
2. What cultural and social-class factors might affect the decision to buy an Aibo?
3. How might reference groups affect a consumer's interest in robot pets or robots in general?
4. What motives or needs is an individual likely to be satisfying in purchasing a pet robot?
5. Why, do you think, did Sony choose to sell Aibos only over the Internet? How might this affect a consumer's buying decision process? Was this a wise decision?
6. How could Internet-only selling affect the rate of diffusion of Aibos? In creating its new industry, what could Sony do to speed the diffusion of entertainment robots?

SOURCES: Neil Gross and Irene Kunii, 'Man's best friend – and no scooper needed', *Business Week* (20 July 1998), p. 531; Irene Kunii, 'This cute little pet is a robot', *Business Week* (24 May 1999), pp. 56–7; Peter Landers, 'At last, a dog that barks, wags its tail, and never has to go out', *Wall Street Journal* (12 May 1999), p. B1; Ginny Parker, 'In Japan, robots are not just for factories anymore', *Greensboro News and Record* (2 November 1999), pp. B6 and B7; 'Robots', *The Economist* (5 June 1999), p. 78; Richard Shaffer, 'Can't anyone make a decent robot?', *Fortune* (19 July 1999), pp. 120–1; A. A. Milne, *Winnie the Pooh Collection* (Greenford, Middlesex: Aura, 1998); Justin Hankins, 'When Rover's a robot', *The Guardian* (30 November 2002); J. Mark Lytle, 'Mrs Tanaka with her robot teddy bear', *The Guardian* (11 September 2003); Charlotte Ricca-Smith, 'Gadgets', *The Independent* (24 September 2003).

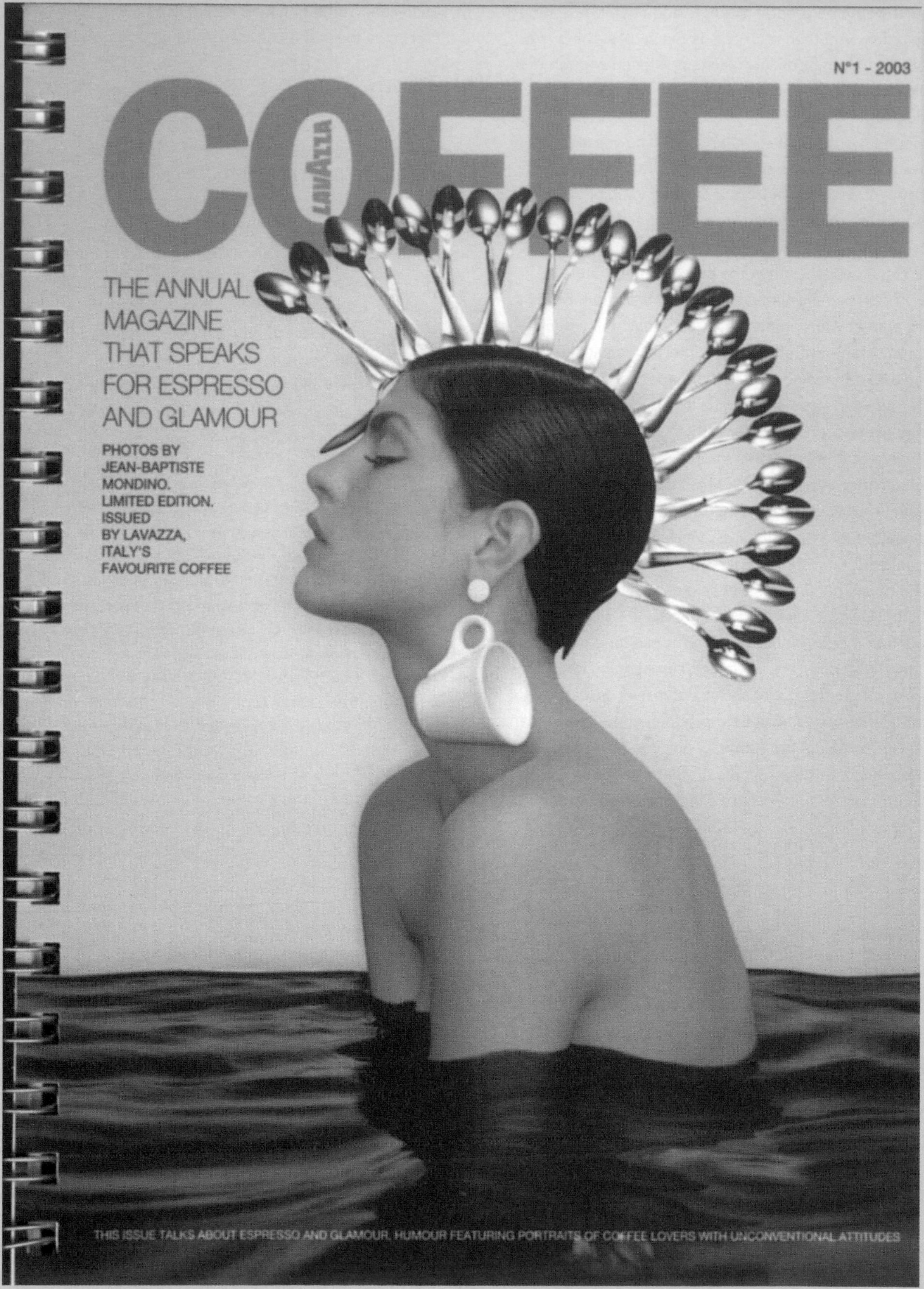
N°1 - 2003
COFFEE
LAVAZZA
THE ANNUAL MAGAZINE THAT SPEAKS FOR ESPRESSO AND GLAMOUR
PHOTOS BY JEAN-BAPTISTE MONDINO. LIMITED EDITION. ISSUED BY LAVAZZA, ITALY'S FAVOURITE COFFEE
THIS ISSUE TALKS ABOUT ESPRESSO AND GLAMOUR, HUMOUR FEATURING PORTRAITS OF COFFEE LOVERS WITH UNCONVENTIONAL ATTITUDES

> Remember, the client's indecision
> is final.
>
> KEN HORNSBY

Business-to-business marketing

Chapter objectives

After reading this chapter, you should be able to:

- Explain how business markets differ from consumer markets.
- Identify the main factors that influence business buyer behaviour.
- List and define the steps in the business buying decision process.
- Explain how institutional and government buyers make their buying decisions.

Mini Contents List

- Prelude case – Concorde is dead. Long live the busjets!
- Introduction
- Business markets
- Business buyer behaviour
- Marketing Insights 8.1 – International marketing manners matter
- Business buying on the Internet
- Institutional and government markets
- Marketing Insights 8.2 – Political graft: wheeze or sleaze?
- Summary
- Concluding concepts 8 – Biofoam: just peanuts?

◀ SOURCE: Lavazza SpA. *Designer*:
Armando Testa. *Photographer*:
Baptiste Mondino for Lavazza
Calendar 2003/Advertising Archives.

Prelude case Concorde is dead. Long live the busjets!

Right until its end, Concorde caught the eye. A supersonic jet loved by celebrities and the super-rich, Concorde outclasses both in being a super celebrity and super expensive. Following its final flight into Heathrow in October 2003, we can now only say 'once we had Concorde'. As the huddle of 100 enthusiasts and media people left Concorde's last flight, not everyone had a tear in their eye.

For the week following the business media was awash with articles about business jets and busjet timeshare. As a NesJets advertorial gloated: 'The days of Concorde may be over, but for those still seeking the luxury of fast-track air travel, there is another option . . .'.

In truth, Concorde's main customers were not celebrities but regular transatlantic travellers for whom time was money. Air France's most frequent Concorde flyer was Pascal La Borge, a medical meeting planner who logged over 400 trips. For such people executive jets were often the quicker choice because they can use smaller airports close to city centres, fly on demand and offer less airport hassle. Now the Atlantic was theirs.

'The jet set' used to refer to the rich and famous who could afford the cost of early jet travel. Now almost everybody flies. Busjet travel retains that exclusive status that 'the jet set' once had as the transport of super-celebrities like Mika Hakkinen, Bill Gates and Madonna, but not for long. Busjet travel is becoming the norm. Sales of busjets, from the 'entry level' €4 m Cessna CJ1 to the €41 m Airbus A319 corporate jetliner, are booming, with order books full three years ahead.

Once looked upon as an executive indulgence, the busjets have become a logical capital investment:

- Busjet travel is down in cost. Typical running cost of the medium-sized, 8–19-seat Dassault Falcon 900EX jet is €1,500 per flying hour based on 1,000 hours per year utilisation. With four passengers the cost is less than €400 each, about the same as a business class fare. Eight people flying brings the cost to that of economy fares; with 16 seats occupied, it comes down to bucket-shop prices.

- Busjets make better use of a firm's most valuable and perishable resource – executive time. As Richard Gaona of Airbus says: 'It's not the speed of the individual aircraft that counts, but the speed at which you can get to where the business is ahead of the competition.'

- Security of flyers and information exist on a busjet in a way that it does not in a first-class lounge or cabin. A busjet is a mobile boardroom as well as a mobile office.

- At the top end of the range an A319 or Boeing BBJ is a mobile hotel that enables the likes of Boeing's Phil Condit to take in New York, Paris, Moscow, Beijing and Tokyo in four days out of his office.

Recognising organisations that can afford to own and operate a business jet is easy. The difficulty is in reaching key decision makers for jet purchases, understanding their motivations and decision processes, analysing what is important to them, and designing marketing approaches.

There are *rational* and *subjective* factors. A company buying a busjet will evaluate the aircraft on quality and performance, prices, operating costs and service. However, having a superior product is not enough: marketers must also consider *human factors* that affect choice. According to Gulfstream, a leading American supplier of business jets: 'The purchase process may be initiated by the chief executive officer (CEO), a board member wishing to increase efficiency or security, the company's chief pilot, or through vendor efforts like advertising or a sales visit. The CEO will be central in deciding whether to buy the jet, but he or she will be heavily influenced by the company's pilot, financial officer and perhaps by the board itself.'

Each party in the buying process has subtle roles and needs. The salesperson who tries to impress both the CEO with depreciation schedules and the chief pilot with runway statistics will almost certainly not sell a plane if he or she overlooks the psychological and emotional components of the buying decision. 'For the chief executive', observes one salesperson, 'you need all the numbers for support, but if you can't find the kid inside the CEO and excite him or her with the raw beauty of the new plane, you'll never sell the equipment. If you sell the excitement, you sell the jet.'

The chief pilot often has veto power over purchase decisions and may be able to stop the purchase of a certain brand of jet by simply expressing a negative opinion. In this sense, the pilot not only influences the decision but also serves as a 'gatekeeper'. Though the corporate legal staff will handle the purchase agreement and the purchasing department will acquire the jet, they usually have little to say about whether, or how, the plane is obtained and which type to select. The users of the jet – management of the buying company, important customers and others – may have an indirect role in choosing the equipment.

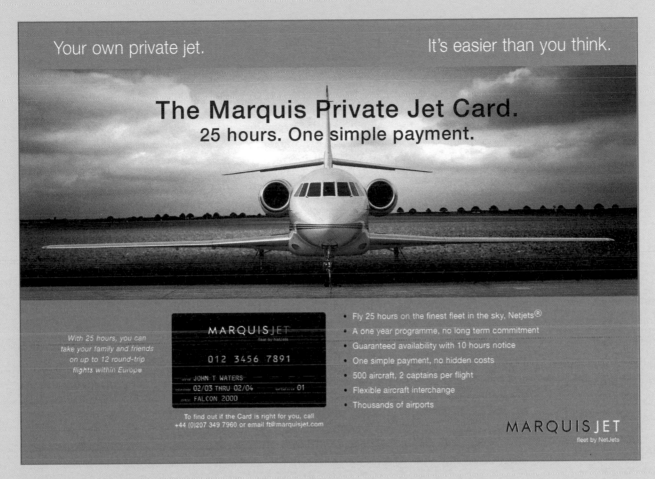

With timeshare you can own as much of an executive jet as you want.
SOURCE: NetJets Management Ltd.

The involvement of many people in the purchase decision creates a group dynamic that the selling company must factor into its sales planning. Who makes up the buying group? How will the parties interact? Who will dominate and who submit? What priorities do the individuals have?

Where is the market going? The answer is bigger and faster. The fastest is the Bombardier Global Express (Gex) BD-700 business jet, capable of carrying eight passengers non-stop from Brussels to Buenos Aires. Cruising close to the speed of sound, it knocks an hour off shorter routes like Berlin–Los Angeles.

The next stop? Gulfstream and Dassault are considering an SSBJ (supersonic busjet). If a €40 m-plus busjet is selling, why not a €55 m SSBJ?[1]

Questions

1. What do you think are the reasons for businesses buying executive jets?
2. Is it correct to say that, unlike people in consumer markets, business buyers are rational?
3. Who are the critical people to influence when selling busjets?

Introduction

In some ways, selling business jets to business buyers is like selling kitchen appliances to families. Busjet makers ask the same questions as consumer marketers: Who are the buyers and what are their needs? How do buyers make their buying decisions and what factors influence these decisions? What marketing programme will be most effective? Nevertheless, the answers to these questions are usually different in the case of the business buyer. Thus, the jet makers face many of the same challenges as consumer marketers – and some additional ones.

In one way or another, most large companies sell to other organisations. Companies such as ABB Asea Brown Boveri (engineering), Norsk Hydro, Akzo Nobel (chemicals) and Arbed (steel) sell *most* of their products to other businesses. Even large consumer-products companies, which make products used by final consumers, must first sell their products to other businesses. For example, Allied Domecq makes many consumer products – La Ina sherry, Presidente brandy, Tetley tea and others. To sell these products to consumers, Allied Domecq must first sell them to wholesalers and retailers that serve the consumer market. Allied Domecq also sells food ingredients directly to other businesses through its Margetts Food and DCA Food Industries subsidiaries.

The **business market** consists of all the organisations that buy goods and services to use in the production of other products and services that are sold, rented or supplied to others. It also includes retailing and wholesaling firms that acquire goods for the purpose of reselling or renting them to others at a profit. The **business buying process** is the decision-making process by which business buyers establish the need for purchased products and services, and identify, evaluate and choose among alternative brands and suppliers.[2] Companies that sell to other business organisations must do their best to understand business markets and business buyer behaviour.

Business market—All the organisations that buy goods and services to use in the production of other products and services, or for the purpose of reselling or renting them to others at a profit.

Business buying process—The decision-making process by which business buyers establish the need for purchased products and services, and identify, evaluate and choose among alternative brands and suppliers.

Business markets

The business-to-business market is *huge*: most businesses just sell to other businesses, and sales to businesses far outstrip those to consumers. The reason for this is the number of times that parts of a consumer product are bought, processed and resold before reaching the final consumer. For example, Figure 8.1 shows the large number of business transactions needed to

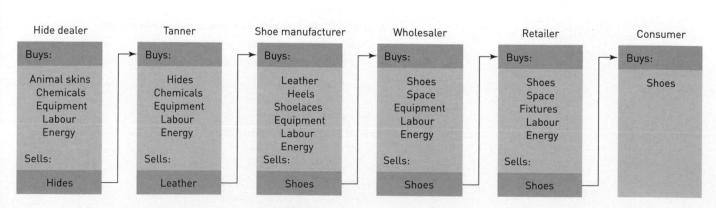

Figure 8.1 Business transactions involved in producing and distributing a pair of shoes

produce and sell a simple pair of shoes. Hide dealers sell to tanners, who sell leather to shoe manufacturers, who sell shoes to wholesalers, who in turn sell shoes to retailers, who finally sell the shoes to consumers. Each party in the chain also buys many other related goods and services. This example shows why there is more business buying than consumer buying – many sets of *business* purchases were made for only one set of *consumer* purchases.

Although the media have given a lot of attention to the booms and busts of business-to-consumer (B2C) dotcom companies, the e-commerce revolution is really business-to-business (B2B). IDC forecast that B2B e-commerce will be worth €500bn by 2003 (up from €12bn in 1997) compared with a forecast of €125bn for B2C. While the leading B2C company Amazon.com is just managing to make a profit, B2B e-commerce has become an established part of doing business practice.[3]

Characteristics of business markets

In some ways, business markets are similar to consumer markets. Both involve people who assume buying roles and make purchase decisions to satisfy needs. However, business markets do differ. The main differences are in market structure and demand, the nature of the buying unit, and the types of decision and the decision process involved.

Market structure and demand

The business marketer normally deals with *far fewer but far larger buyers* than the consumer marketer does. For example, when Michelin sells replacement tyres to final consumers, its potential market includes the owners of cars currently in use. However, Michelin's fate in the business market depends on getting orders from a few large carmakers. These sales of original equipment are doubly important, since many people replace their tyres with the brand already on the car. Even in large business markets, a few buyers normally account for most of the purchasing. As buying power concentrates, the *scale and strategic implications of contracts* escalate. The contract of this decade is for the JSF (Joint Strike Fighter) to equip the USAF, US Navy, US Marines, the Royal Air Force and Royal Navy. Won by Lockheed Martin, in collaboration with BAE Systems, Pratt & Whitney and Rolls-Royce, the initial contract is for 14 flying development aircraft at $US18.9 billion and the final contract will be for approaching 500 planes. While Lockheed Martin celebrates their victory, Boeing is wounded by the failure of their X-32.[4]

Business markets are also more *geographically concentrated*: international financial services in London, petrochemicals and synthetic fibres around Rotterdam and Amsterdam and the movie industry in Hollywood. Further, business demand is **derived demand** – it ultimately derives from the demand for consumer goods. Fokker hopes to sell Glare (GLAss fibre REinforced aluminium) to Airbus for their super jumbo A380 whose demand is forecast because the consumers' demand for air travel is growing and so airlines want more capacity. If consumer demand for air travel drops, so will the demand for the A380, Glare, Rolls-Royce Trent 900 engine and all the other products used to make the aircraft.[5]

Derived demand—Business demand that ultimately comes (derives) from the demand for consumer goods.

INVISTA® sells fibre to the people who sell fabrics, to the people who sell garments, to the retailers who sell them to consumers. Advertising LYCRA® to consumers pulls the fibre through the chain.
SOURCE: INVISTA, McCann Erikson.

LYCRA™ is a registered trademark of DuPont™ for its brand of premium stretch fibres and fabrics under exclusive license to INVISTA Inc. and its affiliates.

Matt Kuchar

HAS IT.

When golf wear has LYCRA®, you get the fit and the swing. (If the tag doesn't say "has it", it doesn't have it.)

You either have it or you don't.

LYCRA®
www.lycra.com

In late 2003 the world's steel industry is awaiting another tumble. European growth looked uncertain, Japan remained in the doldrums and US interest rates are rising. A slight change in consumer demand and industrial confidence has a huge impact on the steel industries' huge plants. That is why the profits, sales and share price of the Anglo Dutch company Corus follow the fortunes of the world's largest roller coaster on Blackpool's Pleasure Beach. Corus provided 2,000 tons of hollow-section steel for its construction. If consumers are short of cash, many will still ride the roller coaster but there will be little demand for new roller coasters and the steel use to make them.[6]

Many business markets have **inelastic demand**: that is, total demand for many business products is not affected much by price changes, especially in the short run. A drop in the price of steel will not cause builders of roller coasters to buy much more steel unless it results in lower construction prices, which, in turn, will increase consumer demand for white-knuckle rides.

Finally, business markets have more *fluctuating demand*. Like the demand for Corus's steel, the demand for many business goods and services changes more than the demand for consumer goods and services. A small percentage increase in consumer demand can cause large increases in business demand. Sometimes a rise of only 10 per cent in consumer demand can cause as much as a 200 per cent rise in business demand during the next period.

Inelastic demand—Total demand for a product that is not much affected by price changes, especially in the short run.

Nature of the buying unit

Compared with consumer purchases, a business purchase usually involves *more buyers* and a *more professional purchasing effort*. Often, business buying is done by trained purchasing agents, who spend their working lives learning how to buy well. The more complex the purchase, the more likely that several people will participate in the decision-making process. Buying committees made up of technical experts and top management are common in the buying of primary goods. Therefore, business marketers must have well-trained salespeople to deal with well-trained buyers.

Types of decision and the decision process

Business buyers usually face *more complex* buying decisions than do consumer buyers. Purchases often involve large sums of money, complex technical and economic considerations, and interactions among many people at many levels of the buyer's organisation. Because the purchases are more complex, business buyers may take longer to make their decisions. For example, the purchase of a large computer system might take many months or more than a year to complete and could involve millions of pounds, thousands of technical details and dozens of people ranging from top management to lower-level users.

The business buying process tends to be *more formalised* than the consumer buying process. Large business purchases usually call for detailed product specifications, written purchase orders, careful supplier searches and formal approval. The buying firm might even prepare policy manuals that detail the purchase process.

Finally, in the business buying process, buyer and seller are often much *more dependent* on each other. Consumer marketers are usually at a distance from their customers. In contrast, business marketers may roll up their sleeves and work closely with their customers during all stages of the buying process – from helping customers define problems, to finding solutions, to supporting after-sales operations. For instance, 60 per cent of the money needed to develop Bombardier's Gex business jet came from suppliers and risk-sharing partners, including engine suppliers BMW/Rolls-Royce. They customise their offerings to meet individual customer needs. In the short run, orders go to suppliers that meet buyers' immediate product and service needs. However, business marketers must also build close *long-run* relationships with customers. In the long run, business marketers keep a customer's orders by meeting current needs *and* thinking ahead to meet the customer's future needs.

Volkswagen is breaking new ground at its Skoda factory by having suppliers' operations directly inside the car plant. Lucas, Johnson Controls and Pelzer are producing rear axles, seats and carpets in the Czech factory. This is one step ahead of Japanese manufacturers, which often have suppliers nearby.[7]

Other characteristics of business markets

Direct purchasing

Business buyers often buy directly from producers rather than through intermediaries, especially for items that are technically complex or expensive. Airlines buy aircraft directly from Boeing or Airbus, Kroger buys packaged goods directly from Procter & Gamble, and universities buy computers directly from IBM, Dell and so on. This process is increasing rapidly with the rapid growth of B2B exchanges.

Reciprocity

Business buyers often practise *reciprocity*, selecting suppliers that also buy from them. For example, a paper company might buy needed chemicals from a chemical company that in turn buys the company's paper.

> Shaken by their failure to win the JSF contract, Boeing is fighting hard to win a $13bn (€18.5bn) contract to supply the Royal Air Force in-flight refuelling fleet with their B767 based tanker. As a sweetener, they are offering a reciprocal arrangement that places £400m with Britain's BAE. The deal could be worth £2bn to BAE if, as expected, the US Air Force also chooses the B767.[8]

Leasing

Business buyers are increasingly leasing equipment instead of buying it outright – everything from printing presses to power plants, business jets to hay balers, and office copiers to offshore drilling rigs. The biggest buyers of airliners, business jets and cars are leasing companies. Some universities have started leasing student halls of residence to release money for investment elsewhere. In this case, they are leasing the facilities they once owned, a strategy often used by large corporations.

The lessee can gain a number of advantages, such as having more available capital, getting the seller's latest products, receiving better servicing and gaining some tax advantages. The lessor gains a larger net income and the chance to sell to customers that might not have been able to afford outright purchase.

A model of business buyer behaviour

At the most basic level, marketers want to know how business buyers will respond to various marketing stimuli. Figure 8.2 shows a model of business buyer behaviour. In this model, marketing and other stimuli affect the buying organisation and produce certain buyer responses. As with consumer buying, the marketing stimuli for business buying consist of the four Ps: product, price, place and promotion. Other stimuli include influential forces in the environment: economic, technological, political, cultural and competitive. These stimuli enter the organisation and are turned into buyer responses: product or service choice; supplier choice; order quantities; and delivery, service and payment terms. In order to design good marketing-mix strategies, the marketer must understand what happens within the organisation to turn stimuli into purchase responses.

Within the organisation, buying activity consists of two main parts: the buying centre, made up of all the people involved in the buying decision, and the buying decision process. Figure 8.2 shows that the buying centre and the buying decision process are influenced by internal organisational, interpersonal and individual factors as well as by external environmental factors.

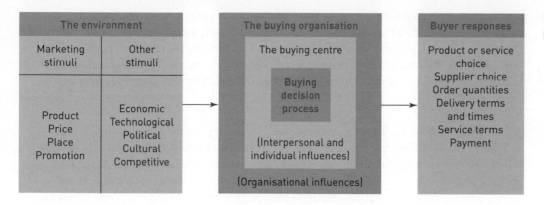

Figure 8.2 A model of business buyer behaviour

Business buyer behaviour

The model in Figure 8.2 suggests four questions about business buyer behaviour: What buying decisions do business buyers make? Who participates in the buying process? What are the strongest influences on buyers? How do business buyers make their buying decisions?

What buying decisions do business buyers make?

The business buyer faces a whole set of decisions in making a purchase. The number of decisions depends on the type of buying situation.

Main types of buying situation

There are three main types of buying situation.[9] At one extreme is the *straight rebuy*, which is a fairly routine decision. At the other extreme is the *new task*, which may call for thorough research. In the middle is the *modified rebuy*, which requires some research. For examples, see Figure 8.3.

Straight rebuy

In a **straight rebuy**, the buyer reorders something without any modifications. It is usually handled on a routine basis by the purchasing department. It is estimated that 90 per cent of these routine B2B transaction will be by e-commerce within a few years.[10] Based on past buying

Straight rebuy—A business buying situation in which the buyer routinely reorders something without any modifications.

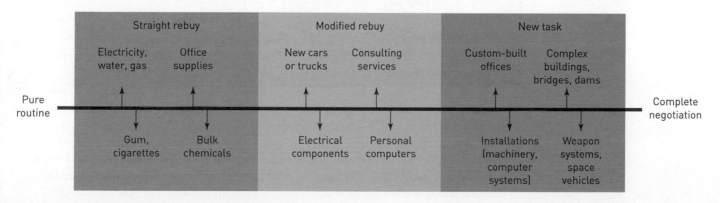

Figure 8.3 **Three types of business buying situation**
SOURCE: Ben M. Enis, *Marketing Principles*, 3rd edn (1980). © 1980 Scott, Foresman & Co.

satisfaction, the buyer simply chooses from the various suppliers on its list. 'In' suppliers try to maintain product and service quality. They often propose automatic reordering systems so that the purchase agent will save reordering time. The 'out' suppliers try to offer something new or exploit dissatisfaction so that the buyer will consider them. 'Out' suppliers try to get their foot in the door with a small order and then enlarge their purchase share over time.

Modified rebuy

Modified rebuy—A business buying situation in which the buyer wants to modify product specifications, prices, terms or suppliers.

In a **modified rebuy**, the buyer wants to modify product specifications, prices, terms or suppliers. The modified rebuy usually involves more decision participants than the straight rebuy. The 'in' suppliers may become nervous and feel pressured to put their best foot forward to protect an account. 'Out' suppliers may see the modified rebuy situation as an opportunity to make a better offer and gain new business.

New task

New task—A business buying situation in which the buyer purchases a product or service for the first time.

A company buying a product or service for the first time faces a **new task** situation. In such cases, the greater the cost or risk, the larger will be the number of decision participants and the greater their efforts to collect information. The new-task situation is the marketer's greatest opportunity and challenge. The marketer not only tries to reach as many key buying influences as possible, but also provides help and information.

Specific buying decisions

The buyer makes the fewest decisions in the straight rebuy and the most in the new-task decision. In the new-task situation, the buyer must decide on product specifications, suppliers, price limits, payment terms, order quantities, delivery times and service terms. The order of these decisions varies with each situation and different decision participants influence each choice.

Systems buying and selling

Systems buying—Buying a packaged solution to a problem and without all the separate decisions involved.

Many business buyers prefer to buy a packaged solution to a problem from a single seller. Called **systems buying**, this practice began with government buying of powerful weapons and communication systems. Instead of buying and putting all the components together, the government asked for bids from suppliers that would supply the components *and* assemble the package or system.

> Intershop is an outstandingly successful company, based in the former East Germany. It is world market leader in software design and licensing for more than 20,000 companies who sell over the Internet. When companies face the need to set up an e-commerce operation, Intershop provides a range of services that they need.[11]

Sellers have increasingly recognised that buyers like this method and have adopted systems selling as a marketing tool. Systems selling is a two-step process. First, the supplier sells a group of interlocking products: for example, the supplier sells not only glue, but also applicators and dryers. Second, the supplier sells a system of production, inventory control, distribution and other services to meet the buyer's need for a smooth-running operation.

Systems selling is a key business marketing strategy for winning and holding accounts. The contract often goes to the firm that provides the most complete system meeting the customer's needs. Consider the following:

The Indonesian government requested bids to build a cement factory near Jakarta. A Western firm's proposal included choosing the site, designing the cement factory, hiring the construction crews, assembling the materials and equipment and turning the finished factory over to the Indonesian government. A Japanese firm's proposal included all of these services, plus hiring and training workers to run the factory, exporting the cement through their trading companies and using the cement to build some needed roads and new office buildings in Jakarta. Although the Japanese firm's proposal cost more, it won the contract. Clearly the Japanese viewed the problem not as one of just building a cement factory (the narrow view of systems selling) but of running it in a way that would contribute to the country's economy. They took the broadest view of the customers' needs. This is true systems selling.

Who participates in the business buying process?

Who buys the goods and services needed by business organisations? The decision-making unit of a buying organisation is called its **buying centre**, defined as all the individuals and units that participate in the business decision-making process.[12]

The buying centre includes all members of the organisation who play any of the following five roles in the purchase decision process.[13]

1. **Users.** Members of the organisation who will use the product or service. In many cases, users initiate the buying proposal and help define product specifications.
2. **Influencers.** People who affect the buying decision. They often help define specifications and provide information for evaluating alternatives. Technical personnel are particularly important influencers.
3. **Buyers.** People with formal authority to select the supplier and arrange terms of purchase. Buyers may help shape product specifications, but they play their most important role in selecting vendors and in negotiating. In more complex purchases, buyers might include high-level officers participating in the negotiations.
4. **Deciders.** People who have formal or informal power to select or approve the final suppliers. In routine buying, the buyers are often the deciders or at least the approvers.
5. **Gatekeepers.** People who control the flow of information to others. For example, purchasing agents often have authority to prevent salespersons from seeing users or deciders. Other gatekeepers include technical personnel and even personal secretaries.

The buying centre is not a fixed and formally identified unit within the buying organisation. It is a set of buying roles assumed by different people for different purchases. Within the organisation, the size and make-up of the buying centre will vary for different products and for different buying situations. For some routine purchases, one person – say a purchasing agent – may assume all the buying centre roles and serve as the only person involved in the buying decision. For more complex purchases, the buying centre may include 20 or 30 people from different levels and departments in the organisation. One survey found that the average number of people involved in a buying decision ranges from about three (for services and items used in day-to-day operations) to almost five (for such high-ticket purchases as construction work and machinery). Another survey detected a trend towards team-based buying – 87 per cent of surveyed purchasing executives expected teams of people from different functions to be making buying decisions in 2000.[14]

Buying centre—All the individuals and units that participate in the business buying-decision process.

Users—Members of the organisation who will use the product or service; users often initiate the buying proposal and help define product specifications.

Influencer—A person whose views or advice carries some weight in making a final buying decision; they often help define specifications and also provide information for evaluating alternatives.

Buyer—The person who makes an actual purchase.

Deciders—People in the organisation's buying centre who have formal or informal powers to select or approve the final suppliers.

Gatekeepers—People in the organisation's buying centre who control the flow of information to others.

Club World. More beds, more places, more often. BRITISH AIRWAYS

Business-class flying is a classic case where the user (the flyer) is not the buyer, decider or gatekeeper. This could be a secretary, a personal assistant or a professional buyer.

SOURCE: British Airways/M&C Saatchi, *Photographer*: Gary Simpson.

Business marketers working in global markets may face even greater levels of buying centre influence. A study comparing the buying decision processes in the United States, Sweden, France and Southeast Asia found that US buyers might be lone eagles compared with their counterparts in some other countries. Sweden had the highest team buying effort, whereas the United States had the lowest, even though the Swedish and US firms had very similar demographics. In making purchasing decisions, Swedish firms depended on technical staff, both their own and suppliers', much more than did the firms in other countries.[15]

The buying centre usually includes some obvious participants who are involved formally in the buying decision. For example, the decision to buy a corporate jet will probably involve the company's chief pilot, a purchasing agent, some legal staff, a member of top management and others formally charged with the buying decision. It may also involve less obvious, informal participants, some of whom may actually make or strongly affect the buying decision. Sometimes, even the people in the buying centre are not aware of all the buying participants. For example, the decision about which corporate jet to buy may actually be made by a corporate board member who has an interest in flying and knows a lot about aircraft. This board member may work behind the scenes to sway the decision. Many business-buying decisions result from the complex interactions of ever-changing buying-centre participants.

The division of roles within the buying centre can cause a conflict of interest. Frequent flyer programmes succeed because a flyer or their secretary books a flight and accumulates frequent flyer points while the company pays. Corporate hospitality uses similar mechanisms to influence demand. Typical examples could include offering an important decider hospitality including a few drinks and tickets for a Wimbledon final (cost €3,000) or a few days' fishing in Norway (€15,000). To some companies spending €15,000 on entertaining is 'peanuts' compared with the potential return. Unsurprisingly, many companies and tax authorities are investigating or banning such benefits.[16]

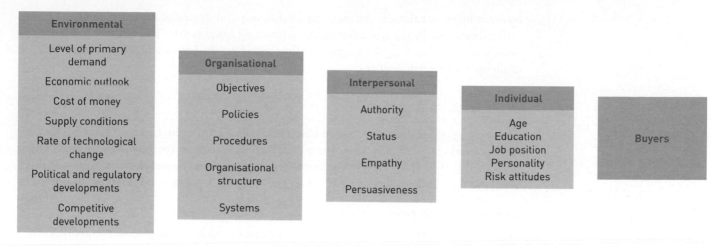

Figure 8.4 **The main influences on business buying behaviour**

What are the main influences on business buyers?

Business buyers are subject to many influences when they make their buying decisions. Some marketers assume that the major influences are economic. They think buyers will favour the supplier who offers the lowest price or the best product or the most service. They concentrate on offering strong economic benefits to buyers. However, business buyers actually respond to both economic and personal factors. Far from being cold, calculating and impersonal, business buyers are human and social as well. They react to both reason and emotion.

Today, most business-to-business marketers recognise that emotion plays an important role in business buying decisions. For example, you might expect that an advertisement promoting large trucks to corporate truck fleet buyers would stress objective technical, performance and economic factors. However, a recent ad for Volvo heavy-duty trucks shows two drivers arm-wrestling and claims: 'It solves all your fleet problems. Except who gets to drive.' It turns out that the type of truck a fleet provides can help it to attract qualified drivers. The Volvo ad stresses the raw beauty of the truck and its comfort and roominess, features that make it more appealing to drivers. The ad concludes that Volvo trucks are 'built to make fleets more profitable and drivers a lot more possessive'.

When suppliers' offers are very similar, business buyers have little basis for strictly rational choice. Because they can meet organisational goals with any supplier, buyers can allow personal factors to play a larger role in their decisions. However, when competing products differ greatly, business buyers are more accountable for their choice and tend to pay more attention to economic factors. Figure 8.4 lists various groups of influences on business buyers – environmental, organisational, interpersonal, and individual.[17]

Environmental factors

Business buyers are influenced heavily by factors in the current and expected *economic environment*, such as the level of primary demand, the economic outlook, and the cost of money. As economic uncertainty rises, business buyers cut back on new investments and attempt to reduce their inventories.

An increasingly important environmental factor is shortages in key materials. Many companies now are more willing to buy and hold larger inventories of scarce materials to ensure adequate supply. Business buyers also are affected by technological, political and competitive developments in the environment. Culture and customs can strongly influence business buyer reactions to the marketer's behaviour and strategies, especially in the international marketing environment (see Marketing Insights 8.1). The business marketer must watch these factors, determine how they will affect the buyer, and try to turn these challenges into opportunities.

Organisational factors

Each buying organisation has its own objectives, policies, procedures, structure and systems. The business marketer must know these *organisational factors* as thoroughly as possible. Questions such as these arise: How many people are involved in the buying decision? Who are they? What are their evaluative criteria? What are the company's policies and limits on its buyers?

Upgraded purchasing

Buying departments have often occupied a low position in the management hierarchy, even though they often manage more than half of the company's costs. In some industries, such as telecommunications, manufacturers buy in items approaching 80 per cent of total cost. With good reason, many companies are upgrading their purchasing activities. Some companies have combined several functions – such as purchasing, inventory control, production scheduling and traffic – into a high-level function called *strategic materials management*. Buying departments in many multinational companies have responsibility for buying materials and services around the world. Many companies are offering higher compensation in order to attract top talent in the buying area. This means that business marketers must also upgrade their salespeople to match the quality of today's business buyers.[18]

Centralised purchasing

In companies consisting of many divisions with differing needs, much of the purchasing is carried out at the division level. Recently, however, some large companies have tried to centralise purchasing. Headquarters identifies materials purchased by several divisions and buys them centrally. Centralised purchasing gives the companies more purchasing clout, which can produce substantial savings.

For the business marketer, this development means dealing with fewer, higher-level buyers. Instead of using regional sales forces to sell a large buyer's separate plants, the seller may use a *national account sales force* to service the buyer. For example, at Xerox, over 250 national account managers each handle one to five large national accounts with many scattered locations. The national account managers coordinate the efforts of an entire Xerox team – specialists, analysts, salespeople for individual products – to sell and service important national customers.[19] National account selling is challenging and demands both a high-level sales force and a sophisticated marketing effort.

Long-term contracts

Business buyers are increasingly seeking long-term contracts with suppliers. For example, GM wants to buy from fewer suppliers that are willing to locate close to its plants and produce high-quality components. Business marketers are also beginning to offer *electronic order interchange* systems to their customers. When using such systems, the seller places terminals hooked to the seller's computers in customers' offices. Then the customer can order needed items instantly by entering orders directly into the computer. The orders are transmitted automatically to the supplier.

Although buyers are seeking closer relations with suppliers, businesses do not always have each other's interests at heart. In all relationships, there is a tension between the comfort of loyalty and the freedom to shop around. Economic and technological changes can make long-term business-to-business relationships inherently unstable.[20] The result is serial monogamy as firms switch between medium-term relationships.

International marketing manners matter

Consolidated Amalgamation, Inc., thinks it's time that the rest of the world enjoyed the same fine products it has offered American consumers for two generations. It dispatches vice-president Harry E. Slicksmile to Europe to explore the territory. Mr Slicksmile stops first in London, where he makes short work of some bankers – he rings them up on the phone. He handles Parisians with similar ease: after securing a table at La Tour d'Argent, he greets his luncheon guest, the director of an industrial engineering firm, with the words, 'Just call me Harry, Jacques.'

In Germany, Mr Slicksmile is a powerhouse. Whisking through a lavish, state-of-the-art marketing presentation, complete with the flip charts and audiovisuals, he shows them that this Georgia boy *knows* how to make a buck. Heading on to Milan, Harry strikes up a conversation with the Japanese businessman sitting next to him on the plane. He flips his card on to the person's tray and, when the two say goodbye, shakes hands warmly and clasps the man's right arm. Later, for his appointment with the owner of an Italian packaging-design firm, our hero wears his comfortable corduroy sport coat, khaki pants and Topsiders. Everybody knows Italians are zany and laid back, right?

Wrong. Six months later, Consolidated Amalgamation has nothing to show for the trip but a pile of bills. There was nothing wrong with Consolidated Amalgamation's products, but the orders probably went to firms whose representative had not antagonised and insulted people as much as Harry did. In Europe, they were not wild about Harry.

In order to succeed in global markets, companies must help their managers to understand the needs, customs and cultures of international business buyers.
SOURCE: (left) Corbis Stock Market/Richard Steedman; (right) Corbis Stock Market/Jon Feingersh

8.1...

This case has been exaggerated for emphasis. People are seldom such dolts as Harry E. Slicksmile, but success in international business has a lot to do with knowing the territory and its people. Poor Harry tried, all right, but in all the wrong ways. The British do not, as a rule, make deals over the phone as much as Americans do. It is not so much a 'cultural' difference as a difference in approach. A proper Frenchman neither likes instant familiarity – questions about family, church or alma mater – nor refers to strangers by their first names.

Harry's flashy presentation was probably also a flop with the Germans, who dislike overstatement and ostentation. According to one German expert, German businesspeople have become accustomed to dealing with Americans. Although differences in body language and customs remain, the past 20 years have softened them. However, calling secretaries by their first names would still be considered rude in Germany: 'They have a right to be called by their surname. You'd certainly ask for – and get – permission first.' In Germany, people address each other formally and correctly: for example, someone with two doctorates (which is quite common) must be referred to as 'Herr Doktor Doktor'.

When Harry Slicksmile grabbed his new Japanese acquaintance by the arm, the executive probably considered him disrespectful and presumptuous. The Japanese, like many others in Asia, have a 'no-contact culture' in which even shaking hands is a strange experience. Harry made matters worse by tossing his business card. Japanese people revere the business card as an extension of self and as an indicator of rank. They do not *hand* it to people; they *present* it – with both hands.

Hapless Harry's last gaffe was assuming that Italians are like Hollywood's stereo-types of them. The flair for design and style that has characterised Italian culture for centuries is embodied in the businesspeople of Milan and Rome. They dress beautifully and admire flair, but they blanch at garishness or impropriety in others' attire.

In order to compete successfully in global markets, or even to deal effectively with international firms in their home markets, companies must help their managers to understand the needs, customs and cultures of international business buyers. Here are a few more rules of social and business etiquette that managers should understand when doing business in another country.

France	Dress conservatively, except in the south where more casual clothes are worn. Do not refer to people by their first names – the French are formal with strangers.
Germany	Be especially punctual. A businessperson invited to someone's home should present flowers, preferably unwrapped, to the hostess. During introductions, greet women first and wait until, or if, they extend their hands before extending yours.

		...8.1
Indonesia	Learn how to sing at least one song. At the end of formal gatherings, people often take turns in singing unaccompanied.	
Italy	Whether you dress conservatively or go native in a Giorgio Armani suit, keep in mind that Italian businesspeople are style conscious. Make appointments well in advance. Prepare for and be patient with Italian bureaucracies.	
Japan	Do not imitate Japanese bowing customs unless you understand them thoroughly – who bows to whom, how many times and when. It is a complicated ritual.	
Saudi Arabia	Although men will kiss each other in greeting, they will never kiss a woman. An American woman should wait for a man to extend his hand before offering hers. If a Saudi offers refreshment, accept – it is an insult to decline it.	
United Kingdom	Toasts are often given at formal dinners. If the host honours you with a toast, be prepared to reciprocate. Business entertaining is done more often at lunch than at dinner.	
United States	Expect to be asked to meet and work at any time, over breakfast, lunch and dinner. Do not be taken in by street attire; American managers' dress code at work is very formal and conservative.	

Do not panic. Most businesspeople you are likely to meet are used to dealing with overseas guests and are used to forgiving their failings. There is, however, a big gap between being forgiven for social transgressions and getting the best deal.

SOURCES: Adapted from Susan Harte, 'When in Rome, you should learn to do what the Romans do', *The Atlanta Journal-Constitution* (22 January 1990), pp. D1, D6; see also Ann Marie Sabath, *International Business Etiquette Europe: What you need to know to conduct business abroad with charm and savvy* (Career Press, 1999); and Wayne A. Conway, Joseph J. Douress and Terri Morrison, *Dun & Bradstreet's Guide to Doing Business Around the World, Revised* (Upper Saddle River, NJ: Prentice Hall, 1999). For a lovely book by a top-selling novelist on the dangers of working in other languages, see Umberto Eco, *Mouse or Rat? Translation as Negotiation* (Weidenfeld & Nicolson, 2003).

Just-in-time production systems

The emergence of *just-in-time (JIT) production systems* has had a considerable impact on business purchasing policies. JIT, in particular, has produced notable changes in business marketing. JIT means that production materials arrive fit for use at the customer's factory exactly when needed for production, rather than being stored in the customer's inventory until used. The goal of JIT is zero inventories with 100 per cent quality. It calls for coordination between production schedules of supplier and customer, so that neither has to carry much inventory. Effective use of JIT reduces inventory and lead times and increases quality, productivity and adaptability to change.

Since JIT involves frequent delivery, many business marketers have set up locations closer to their large JIT customers. Closer locations enable them to deliver smaller shipments more efficiently and reliably. Many firms have set up plants close to Nissan's car plant in the north of England and VW now has suppliers producing inside its Czech Skoda plant. Thus, JIT means that a business marketer may have to make large commitments to important customers. The Biofoam case at the end of this chapter shows a packaging company becoming an on-site supplier to its customers.[21]

Purchasing performance evaluation

Some companies are setting up incentive systems to reward purchasing managers for especially good purchasing performance, in much the same way that salespeople receive bonuses for especially good selling performance. These systems should lead purchasing managers to increase their pressure on sellers for the best terms.

Interpersonal factors

The buying centre usually includes many participants who influence each other. The business marketer often finds it difficult to determine what kinds of *interpersonal factors* and group dynamics enter into the buying process. As one writer notes: 'Managers do not wear tags that say "decision maker" or "unimportant person". The powerful are often invisible, at least to vendor representatives.'[22] Nor does the buying-centre participant with the highest rank always have the most influence. Participants may have influence in the buying decision because they control rewards and punishments, are well liked, have special expertise, or have a special relationship with other important participants. Interpersonal factors are often very subtle. Whenever possible, business marketers must try to understand these factors and design strategies that take them into account.

Individual factors

Each participant in the business buying-decision process brings in personal motives, perceptions and preferences. These individual factors are affected by personal characteristics such as age, income, education, professional identification, personality and attitudes towards risk. In addition, buyers have different buying styles. Some may be technical types who make in-depth analyses of competitive proposals before choosing a supplier. Other buyers may be intuitive negotiators who are adept at pitting the sellers against one another for the best deal.

Secretaries and personal assistants are an important target for DHL, the express courier; they may be told by their boss to send a package but have the discretion to choose the courier. To contact them it advertises in *Executive PA* and other secretarial-type publications and 'always attends the Secretaries Show'. In contrast, UPS, which has a bias towards small business-to-business parcels, finds that traffic, distribution and logistics managers make most decisions. To contact them it schedules its TV advertising around sports events, prime-time films and documentaries.[23]

Stages of the buying process	Buying situations		
	New task	Modified rebuy	Straight rebuy
Problem recognition	Yes	Maybe	No
General need description	Yes	Maybe	No
Product specification	Yes	Yes	Yes
Supplier search	Yes	Maybe	No
Proposal solicitation	Yes	Maybe	No
Supplier selection	Yes	Maybe	No
Order-routine specification	Yes	Maybe	No
Performance review	Yes	Yes	Yes

Table 8.1 Key stages of the business buying process in relation to important buying situations

SOURCE: Adapted from Patrick J. Robinson, Charles W. Faris and Yoram Wind, *Industrial Buying and Creative Marketing* (Boston: Allyn & Bacon, 1967), p. 14.

How do business buyers make their buying decisions?

Table 8.1 lists the eight stages of the business buying process.[24] Buyers who face a new-task buying situation usually go through all stages of the buying process. Buyers making modified or straight rebuys may skip some of the stages. We will examine these steps for the typical new-task buying situation.

Problem recognition

The buying process begins when someone in the company recognises a problem or a need that can be met by acquiring a specific good or a service. **Problem recognition** can result from internal or external stimuli. Internally, the company may decide to launch a new product that requires new production equipment and materials. Alternatively, a machine may break down and need new parts. Perhaps a purchasing manager is unhappy with a current supplier's product quality, service or prices. Externally, the buyer may get some new ideas at a trade show, see an ad or receive a call from a salesperson who offers a better product or a lower price.

General need description

Having recognised a need, the buyer next prepares a **general need description** that describes the characteristics and quantity of the needed item. For standard items, this process presents few problems. For complex items, however, the buyer may have to work with others – engineers, users, consultants – to define the item. The team may want to rank the importance of reliability, durability, price and other attributes desired in the item. In this phase, the alert business marketer can help the buyers define their needs and provide information about the value of different product characteristics. For Fokker to sell Glare, its new aerospace material, for use in the A380 superjumbo it will have to work with Airbus Industries' designers to influence the aircraft's design and the sort of material they specify. Increasingly, new products are designed in conjunction with suppliers whose input influences the product specification.

Product specification

The buying organisation next develops the item's technical **product specifications**, often with the help of a value analysis engineering team. **Value analysis** is an approach to cost reduction in which components are studied carefully to determine whether they can be redesigned,

Problem recognition—The first stage of the business buying process in which someone in the company recognises a problem or need that can be met by acquiring a good or a service.

General need description— The stage in the business buying process in which the company describes the general characteristics and quantity of a needed item.

Product specification—The stage of the business buying process in which the buying organisation decides on and specifies the best technical product characteristics for a needed item.

Value analysis—An approach to cost reduction in which components are studied carefully to determine whether they can be redesigned, standardised or made by less costly methods of production.

standardised or made by less costly methods of production. The team decides on the best characteristics and specifies them accordingly. Sellers, too, can use value analysis as a tool to help secure a new account. By showing buyers a better way to make an object, outside sellers can turn straight rebuy situations into new-task situations that give them a chance to obtain new business.

Supplier search

Supplier search—The stage of the business buying process in which the buyer tries to find the best vendors.

The buyer now conducts a **supplier search** to find the best vendors. The buyer can compile a small list of qualified suppliers by reviewing trade directories, doing a computer search or phoning other companies for recommendations. Today, more and more companies are turning to the Internet to find suppliers. For marketers, this has levelled the playing field – smaller suppliers have the same advantages as larger ones and can be listed in the same online catalogues for a nominal fee:

> Worldwide Internet Solutions Network, better known as WIZnet (www.wiznet.net), has built an 'interactive virtual library of business-to-business catalogues' that is global in coverage. At last report, its database included complete specifications for more than 10 million products and services from 45,000 manufacturers, distributors, and industrial service providers. For purchasing managers, who routinely receive stacks of mail each day, much of it catalogues, this kind of one-stop shopping will be an incredible time-saver (and price-saver, because it allows easier comparison shopping). When told by a management consultant, 'Do a search for 3.5-inch (9 cm) platinum ball valves available from a local source', WIZnet found six local sources for buying the exact product in about 15 seconds. More than just electric Yellow Pages, such as the Thomas Register or Industry.net, WIZnet includes all specifications for the products right in the system and offers secure e-mail to communicate directly with vendors to ask for requests for bids or to place an order. More than 10,000 product specs are added to WIZnet per week, and its database includes catalogues from across the globe.[25]

The newer the buying task, and the more complex and costly the item, the greater the amount of time the buyer will spend searching for suppliers. The supplier's task is to be listed in major directories and build a good reputation in the marketplace. Salespeople should watch for companies in the process of searching for suppliers and make certain that their firm is considered.

Proposal solicitation

Proposal solicitation—The stage of the business buying process in which the buyer invites qualified suppliers to submit proposals.

In the **proposal solicitation** stage of the business buying process, the buyer invites qualified suppliers to submit proposals. In response, some suppliers will send only a catalogue or a salesperson. However, when the item is complex or expensive, the buyer will usually require detailed written proposals or formal presentations from each potential supplier.

Business marketers must be skilled in researching, writing and presenting proposals in response to buyer proposal solicitations. Proposals should be marketing documents, not just technical documents. Presentations should inspire confidence and should make the marketer's company stand out from the competition.

Supplier selection

The members of the buying centre now review the proposals and select a supplier or suppliers. During **supplier selection**, the buying centre will often draw up a list of the desired supplier attributes and their relative importance. In one survey, purchasing executives listed the following attributes as most important in influencing the relationship between supplier and customer: quality products and services, on-time delivery, ethical corporate behaviour, honest communication and competitive prices. Other important factors include repair and servicing capabilities, technical aid and advice, geographic location, performance history and reputation. The members of the buying centre will rate suppliers against these attributes and identify the best suppliers.[26]

As part of the buyer selection process, buying centres must decide how many suppliers to use. Companies once preferred a large supplier base to ensure adequate supplies and to obtain price concessions. These companies would insist on annual negotiations for contract renewal and would often shift the amount of business they gave to each supplier from year to year. Increasingly, however, companies are reducing the number of suppliers. Many have cut the number of suppliers by 20 to 80 per cent. These companies expect their preferred suppliers to work closely with them during product development and they value their suppliers' suggestions.

There is even a trend towards single sourcing, using one supplier for a class of goods over a long period. Not only can using one source translate into more consistent product performance, but also operations can configure themselves for one particular raw material or component rather than changing processes to accommodate different suppliers. Many companies, however, are still reluctant to use single sourcing. They fear that they may become too dependent on the single supplier or that the single-source supplier may become too comfortable in the relationship and lose its competitive edge. Some marketers have developed programmes that address these concerns.

Supplier selection—
The stage of the business buying process in which the buyer reviews proposals and selects a supplier or suppliers.

To better select the most appropriate supplier, companies like SAS offer solutions that increase the level of information about them and improve supplier-relationship management.
SOURCE: SAS. *Agency*: Mason Zimbler.

Order-routine specification

The buyer now prepares an **order-routine specification**. It includes the final order with the chosen supplier or suppliers and lists items such as technical specifications, quantity needed, expected time of delivery, return policies and warranties. In the case of maintenance, repair and operating items, buyers are increasingly using *blanket contracts* rather than periodic purchase orders. A blanket contract creates a long-term relationship in which the supplier promises to re-supply the buyer as needed at agreed prices for a set period. The seller holds the stock and the buyer's computer automatically prints out an order to the seller when stock is needed. A blanket order eliminates the expensive process of renegotiating a purchase each time stock is required. It also allows buyers to write more, but smaller, purchase orders, resulting in lower inventory levels and carrying costs.

Blanket contracting leads to more single-source buying and to buying more items from that source. This practice locks the supplier in tighter with the buyer and makes it difficult for other suppliers to break in unless the buyer becomes dissatisfied with prices or service.

Performance review

In this stage, the buyer reviews supplier performance. The buyer may contact users and ask them to rate their satisfaction. The **performance review** may lead the buyer to continue, modify or drop the arrangement. The seller's job is to monitor the same factors used by the buyer to make sure that the seller is giving the expected satisfaction.

We have described the stages that would typically occur in a new-task buying situation. The eight-stage model provides a simple view of the business buying-decision process. The actual process is usually much more complex. In the modified rebuy or straight rebuy situation, some of these stages would be compressed or bypassed. Each organisation buys in its own way and each buying situation has unique requirements. Different buying-centre participants may be involved at different stages of the process. Although certain buying-process steps usually do occur, buyers do not always follow them in the same order and they may add other steps. Often, buyers will repeat certain stages of the process.

Business buying on the Internet

During the past few years, incredible advances in information technology have changed the face of the business-to-business marketing process. **Electronic data interchange** (EDI) links are particularly common in the food and auto industries. These systems give buyers access to lower purchasing costs, and hasten order processing and delivery. In turn, business marketers are connecting with customers to share marketing information, sell products and services, provide customer support services and maintain ongoing customer relationships. The bespoked EDI systems are now giving way to more flexible and less expensive Internet exchanges whose growth is explosive. While Mitsushita uses its EDI only for ordering its parts, its new Internet-based system will include price negotiations, delivery and payments. The company estimates that the system will allow it to save up to ¥40bn (€300m) on the supplies it has to hold in stock.[27]

In the **Internet exchanges**, buyers post their requirements on the Internet to reach numerous potential suppliers quickly and efficiently. This can be used for both routine and complex products. Japanese Airlines uses the Internet to post orders for in-flight materials, such as plastic cups. Its website carries technical specifications and drawings to show what the company wants, including the airline's logo.[28]

So far, most of the products bought by businesses through Internet or EDI connections are routine MRO materials – maintenance, repair and operations. National Semiconductor has automated almost all of the company's 3,500 monthly requisitions to buy materials ranging from the sterile booties worn in its fabrication plants to state-of-the-art software. The total value of MRO materials pales in comparison to the amount spent for items like aeroplane parts, computer systems and steel tubing. Yet, MRO materials make up 80 per cent of all business orders, and the transaction costs for order processing are high. Thus, companies have much to gain by streamlining the MRO buying process on the Web.

General Electric, the pioneer of Internet buying, planned to be buying *all* of its general operating and industrial supplies online by 2003. Set up in the mid-1990s, its Trading Process Network is a vast Internet bazaar open to its subscribing companies. Other, industry-specific Internet bazaars are taking off and precipitating cross-industry collaboration on a scale once unimaginable:[29]

- Covisint for car components is a joint venture between Ford, General Motors, DaimlerChrysler and Renault/Nissan.
- Orbitz is a travel service owned by five major airlines. It promises to 'Remove the barriers between you and your journey'.
- Chemdex for the exchange of chemicals.
- Paperex for pulp and paper products.

Not all companies or government agencies are happy with Internet exchanges. The European Commission and the American Federal Trade Commission are worried that EDI reduces competition by tying together buyers and suppliers through expensive IT systems. In contrast, Toyota and Honda are reluctant to participate in the open auction-based Covisint because 'Our parts are not purchased through a bidding process. We buy them by building a relationship with our suppliers over time.' They are also concerned about security: 'The other companies are our rivals, and we are competing on parts.' The concerns are not only Japanese. VW do not want to be a junior partner in the site: 'GM is all about driving cost down, whereas Volkswagen sees an advantage in improving response times and increasing its responsiveness to customers.' Some suppliers are also scared about being locked out as Covisint searches for big, low-cost partners.[30]

Institutional and government markets

So far, our discussion of organisational buying has focused largely on the buying behaviour of business buyers. Much of this discussion also applies to the buying practices of institutional and government organisations. However, these two non-business markets have additional characteristics and needs. Thus, in this final section, we will address the special features of institutional and government markets.

Institutional markets

The **institutional market** consists of schools, hospitals, nursing homes, prisons and other institutions that provide goods and services to people in their care. Institutions differ from one another in their sponsors and in their objectives. For example, in the United Kingdom, BUPA hospitals are operated for profit and are predominantly used by people with private medical insurance. National Health Service trust hospitals provide healthcare as part of the welfare state, while charities, such as the Terrence Higgins Trust and many small hospices, run centres for the terminally ill.

Institutional market— Schools, hospitals, nursing homes, prisons and other institutions that provide goods and services to people in their care.

Low budgets and captive patrons characterise many institutional markets. For example, many campus-based students have little choice but to eat whatever food the university supplies. A catering organisation decides on the quality of food to buy for students. The buying objective is not profit because the food is provided as a part of a total service package. Nor is strict cost minimisation the goal – students receiving poor-quality food will complain to others and damage the college's reputation. Thus, the university purchasing agent must search for institutional food vendors whose quality meets or exceeds a certain minimum standard and whose prices are low.

Many marketers set up separate divisions to meet the special characteristics and needs of institutional buyers. For example, Heinz produces, packages and prices its ketchup and other products differently to serve better the requirements of hospitals, colleges and other institutional markets.

Government markets

Government market—
Governmental units – national and local – that purchase or rent goods and services for carrying out the main functions of government.

The **government market** offers large opportunities for many companies. Government buying and business buying are similar in many ways. However, there are also differences that must be understood by companies wishing to sell products and services to governments. To succeed in the government market, sellers must locate key decision makers, identify the factors that affect buyer behaviour and understand the buying decision process.

Government buying organisations are found at national and local levels. The national level is the largest and its buying units operate in both the civilian and military sectors. Various government departments, administrations, agencies, boards, commissions, executive offices and other units carry out buying. Sometimes, the *central buying operation* helps to centralise the buying of commonly used items in the civilian section (for example, office furniture and equipment, vehicles, fuels) and in standardising buying procedures for the other agencies. Defence ministries usually carry out the buying of military equipment for the armed forces.

Strong influences on government buyers

Like consumer and business buyers, government buyers are affected by environmental, organisational, interpersonal and individual factors. One unique thing about government buying is that it is carefully watched by outside publics, ranging from elected representatives to a variety of private groups interested in how the government spends taxpayers' money. Because their spending decisions are subject to public review, government organisations are buried in paperwork. Elaborate forms must be filled in and signed before purchases are approved. The level of bureaucracy and political sensitivities are high and marketers must cut through this red tape. Ways of dealing with governments vary greatly from country to country, and knowledge of local practices is critical to achieving sales successes (see Marketing Insights 8.2).

Non-economic criteria also play a growing role in government buying. Government buyers are asked to favour depressed business firms and areas, small business firms, and business firms that avoid race, sex or age discrimination. Politicians will fight to have large contracts awarded to firms in their area or for their constituency to be the site of big construction projects. EuroDisney is an extreme case, as was Japan's ¥800bn (€6bn) G8 summit meeting in remote Kyushu-Okinawa. Sellers need to keep these factors in mind when seeking government business.

Government organisations typically require suppliers to submit bids and normally award contracts to the lowest bidders. In some cases, however, government buyers make allowances for superior quality or for a firm's reputation for completing contracts on time. Governments will also buy on a negotiated contract basis for complex projects that involve substantial R&D costs and risks or when there is little effective competition. Governments tend to favour

Political graft: wheeze or sleaze?

A Swedish cabinet minister resigned after it was disclosed that she had bought a small toy using an official credit card. Meanwhile in Paris new Members of the European Parliament were invited to an 'official' briefing on the many perks attached to their new status. The subject excited Jean-François Hory. From his place in the front row he turned in his seat, fixed a knowing eye on his new colleagues and addressed them in the manner of an old hand talking down to university freshmen: 'One thing you need to know about travel allowances – they'll want to know your address. If you have one or more second homes, make sure you list the one furthest from Brussels.' Obviously, a return flight from Marseilles to Brussels is worth more than the tram fare from Loos-lès-Lille to Brussels.

"

Political corruption used to be a thing other countries did, but no more. In the United States, United Kingdom, France, Spain, Italy, Japan and elsewhere, accusations of political corruption involving businesses have shaken the countries' leaders. The problem runs deep. In 1999, Paul van Buitenen's 'whistle blowing' precipitated the resignation of all of the EU's commissioners. Eurofraud costs EU taxpayers over €10 billion per year. Sometimes the fiddles are minor, like exaggerating expense claims on Eurojaunts, but often they are not. Antonio Quatraro leapt to his death from a Brussels window. He was a European Commission official responsible for authorising subsidies. A fraud was discovered where he allegedly received backhanders for rigging the auction of Greek-grown tobacco to benefit Italian traders. The oil industry appears particularly dirty and close to governments. The same day in 2003 saw the extending of an investigation into corruption at Yukos, Russia's largest company, and staff at the centre of France's Elf Company gaoled and fined for the diversion of €300 million for personal enrichment.

All governments have codes of practice but they are not consistent. There are also different traditions about obeying rules. In Britain, a Treasury minister had to fight for his political life and was eventually jailed following accusations that a controversial Arab businessperson had paid for a weekend that the minister had had at the Paris Ritz Hotel. The bill was less than €600 and in most other European countries he would not have had to declare such a gift. Meanwhile, Edith Cresson, the former French Prime Minister, had difficulty seeing why she should go when she was at the centre of the storm that ended in the resignation of all the European Commissioners.

In Japan, the attitude towards political corruption is changing slowly. Kiichi Miyazawa resigned as finance minister after being caught up in the Recruit scandal. Recruit, an employment agency, had secretly given large tranches of its own shares to

marketing insights

8.2... politicians, including cabinet ministers, in exchange for political favours. Nevertheless, two years later Mr Miyazawa was sufficiently 'rehabilitated' to become prime minister. This follows the 'traditional' pattern for Japanese politicians caught taking bribes or *o-shoku*, 'defiling one's job'. *O-shoku* carries no moral overtones about wrongdoing; it just means that through carelessness the publicity has dishonoured the politician's honoured position. The usual line of defence in the Diet is that the politicians knew nothing, since their aides took the money. In that way the politician does not lose face, junior aides are not worth prosecuting and everyone is happy.

Transparency International regularly publishes a Corruption Perception Index that focuses on the misuse of public office for private gain. Exhibit 8.1 shows a ranking of Europe's best 20 with their scores on the index. Scandinavian countries have good

Exhibit 8.1 Transparency International's Corruption Perception Index – Europe's best 20

Country	World ranking (1st is least corrupt)	Index
Finland	1	10
Denmark	2	9.8
Sweden	4	9.4
Iceland	6=	9.1
Norway	6=	9.1
Netherlands	9	8.9
UK	10	8.7
Luxembourg	11=	8.6
Switzerland	11=	8.6
USA	14	7.8
Germany	17	7.6
Ireland	19	7.2
Spain	20	7.0
France	21	6.7
Japan	23=	6.4
Portugal	23=	6.4
Belgium	25	6.1
Estonia	27	5.7
Slovenia	28	5.5
Hungary	32	5.2
Greece	35	4.9
Italy	39	4.6
Russia	82	2.1
Yugoslavia	89	1.3
Nigeria	90	1.2

...8.2

reason to be proud of the standards their public servants uphold, but the variation elsewhere in Europe is marked.

The scale of corruption that has destroyed the careers of many European politicians is small beer compared with the 'dash' that lubricates trade in most of the developing world. When selling to governments, marketers face a great dilemma. Should they follow St Ambrose's advice to St Augustine: 'When you are at Rome live in the Roman style; when you are elsewhere live as they live elsewhere'? Or should they behave like a saint?

SOURCES: The leading quotation is from 'An open letter to those unnerved by the little judges', by MEP Thierry Jean-Pierre; other sources are *The Economist* (29 January 2000), pp. 49–55; 'The honeycomb of corruption', *The Economist: China Survey* (8 April 2000), pp. 10–12; Alix Christie and Julie Read, 'Fraud crusader gears up for a fight', *The European* (11–17 November 1994), p. 11; John McBeth, 'Ground zero', *Far Eastern Economic Review* (22 January 1998), pp. 14–17; Paul van Buitenen, 'Corruption at the heart of Europe', *The Times* (14 March 2000), pp. 10–11; *The Economist*, 'Corporate ethics: big oils dirty secrets' (10 May 2003), pp. 61–2; Ankady Ostrovsky, 'Fresh Yukos probe targets oil production site in Siberia' and Robert Graham, 'French court jails Elf officials for corruption', both in *Financial Times* (13 November 2003), p. 12. For the corruption perception index and an analysis of the impact of corruption on economic performance, visit www.transparency.org.

domestic suppliers over foreign suppliers, which is a repeated complaint of multinational businesses. Each country tends to favour its own nationals, even when non-domestic firms make superior offers. The European Commission is trying to reduce such biases.

How do government buyers make their buying decisions?

Government buying practices often seem complex and frustrating to suppliers, who have voiced many complaints about government purchasing procedures. These include too much paperwork and bureaucracy, needless regulations, emphasis on low bid prices, decision-making delays, frequent shifts in buying personnel and too many policy changes. Yet, despite such obstacles, selling to the government can often be mastered. The government is generally helpful in providing information about its buying needs and procedures, and is often as eager to attract new suppliers as the suppliers are to find customers.

Public sector buyers in Europe are required to follow the Official Journal of the European Communities (usually referred to as OJEC). This specifies that when seeking suppliers for a contract over threshold value it is illegal to advertise in national journals and values must be set in euros. The aim is to open the competition for public sector purchases across members of the European Union. OJEC also provides a Common Procurement Vocabulary and provides standards for 'social awareness' and 'green' procurement. The European Commission prosecutes buyers who do not comply with OJEC. Contracts awarded illegally can be nullified and damages awarded.[31]

When the mighty US Fleet edged its way up the Gulf during the Iraq war, five little plastic boats led it. The little Hunt Class MCMVs (Mine Counter-Measure Vessels) were in a league of their own at the dangerous job of clearing a path for the main fleet. They were made by VT, a small British shipbuilding and support services group that is a master at selling to governments around the world. While the world's leading defence contractors seek alliances and mergers to meet the 'peace dividend's' reduced demand, VT has an order book worth £600 million (€900 million) and 14 vessels under construction, 95 per cent of them for export. Part of its strength is VT's dominance in the niche for glass-reinforced plastic (GRP) mine hunters, corvettes and patrol craft. Just the sort of ships that small navies want.

VT's strength extends beyond the vessels. With its vessels it offers a maritime training and support service where it has pioneered computer-based learning. Many clients come from the Middle East and travel with their families, so VT has built an Arabic school for 70 pupils next to the maritime training centre. It now does training for other firms selling to the Middle East, so strengthening its position in the region.

VT also provides services for air forces and navies. Revenues from its US business, VT Griffin, which runs 30 naval, army and air force bases, rose by a third in the first six months of the year. It now plans to quadruple the size of its US operations to capitalise on the huge growth in American defence spending.[32]

For a number of reasons, many companies that sell to the government are not as marketing oriented as VT. Total government spending is determined by elected officials rather than by any marketing effort to develop this market. Government buying has emphasised price, making suppliers invest their effort in technology to bring costs down. When the product's characteristics are specified carefully, product differentiation is not a marketing factor. Nor do advertising or personal selling matter much in winning bids on an open-bid basis.

More companies now have separate marketing departments for government marketing efforts. BAE, Eastman Kodak and Goodyear are examples. These companies want to coordinate bids and prepare them more scientifically, to propose projects to meet government needs rather than just respond to government requests, to gather competitive intelligence, and to prepare stronger communications to describe the company's competence.

Summary

The business market is vast. In many ways, business markets are like consumer markets, but business markets usually have fewer, larger buyers who are more geographically concentrated. Business demand is *derived*, largely *inelastic* and more *fluctuating*. More buyers are usually involved in the business buying decision and business buyers are better trained and more professional than are consumer buyers. In general, business purchasing decisions are more complex and the buying process is more formal than consumer buying.

The *business market* includes firms that buy goods and services in order to produce products and services to sell to others. It also includes retailing and wholesaling firms that buy goods in order to resell them at a profit. Business buyers make decisions that vary with the three types of buying situation: *straight rebuys*, *modified rebuys* and *new tasks*. The decision-making unit of a buying organisation – the *buying centre* – may consist of many people playing many roles. The business marketer needs to know the following: Who are the main participants? In what decisions do they exercise influence? What is their relative degree of influence? Moreover, what evaluation criteria does each decision participant use? The business marketer also needs to understand the primary environmental, interpersonal and individual influences on the buying process. The business buying-decision process itself consists of eight stages: *problem recognition*, *general needs description*, *product specification*, *supplier search*, *proposal solicitation*, *supplier selection*, *order-routine specification* and *performance review*. As business buyers become more sophisticated, business marketers must keep in step by upgrading their marketing accordingly.

The *institutional market* consists of schools, hospitals, prisons and other institutions that provide goods and services to people in their care. Low budgets and captive patrons characterise these markets. The *government market* is also vast. Government buyers purchase products and services for defence, education, public welfare and other public needs. Government buying practices are highly specialised and specified, with open bidding or negotiated contracts characterising most of the buying. Government buyers operate under the watchful eye of politicians and many private watchdog groups. Hence, they tend to require more forms and signatures and to respond more slowly in placing orders.

Discussing the issues

1. Identify the ways in which the fashion clothing market differs from the military uniform market.

2. Which of the main types of buying situation are represented by the following individual circumstances?

   ■ BMW's purchase of computers that go in cars and adjust engine performance to changing driving conditions.

   ■ VW's purchase of spark plugs for its line of Golfs.

   ■ Honda's purchase of light bulbs for a new Civic model.

3. How would a marketer of office equipment identify the buying centre for a law firm's purchase of dictation equipment for each of its partners?

4. Discuss the principal environmental factors that would affect the purchase of radar speed detectors by national and local police forces.

5. Industrial products companies have advertised products to the general public that consumers are not able to buy. How does this strategy help a company sell products to resellers?

6. Assume you are selling a fleet of forklift trucks to be used by a large distribution and warehousing firm. The drivers of the forklift trucks need the latest technology that provides comfort, makes driving easy and improves manoeuvrability. This means more expensive trucks that are more profitable for you. The fleet buyer, however, wants to buy established (not necessarily latest) technology that gives the highest productivity. Who might be in the buying centre? How might you meet the varying needs of these participants?

Applying the concepts

1. Take your college/university as an example of a business customer for books and other educational materials. Imagine that you are a representative from a publisher who intends to establish sales to the college/university. How might you use the model of business buyer behaviour to help you develop a strategy for marketing effectively to this customer? How useful is the model? What (if any) are the limitations? Are there different levels of customers in this situation (e.g. the library as a buying centre; course team members who agree on the textbooks to recommend for student adoption and library stocks; the individual tutor who chooses recommended textbooks and requests the library to stock; or the college/university bookshop)? How might you deal with these different levels of customer?

2. Make a list of the key factors that a local government institution or agency might consider when deciding to purchase new coffee-making machines for users in its offices. Remembering how government buyers make their buying decisions, suggest a scenario that you, as a potential supplier, would use to sell to this institutional buyer.

References

1. Oliver Sutton, 'Buzjet business still buzzing', *Interavia* (September 1999), pp. 30–3; Richard Lofthouse, 'Business jet is business sense', *Interavia* (September 1999), pp. 121–4 and 'If you need to know the price . . .', *Interavia* (September 1999), pp. 127–30; Kevin Cahill, 'Master of the private skies', *Interavia* (September 1999), pp. 138–9; 'Bombadier catches up with itself', *Interavia* (September 1999), pp. 147–8; 'When security is the issue', *Interavia* (September 1999), p. 154; *EuroBusiness* (August 2000); Bill Sweetman, 'Quiet supersonics in sight', *Interavia* (November 2001), pp. 19–20; Kevin Done, 'Business jets "hold key to supersonic travel"', *Financial Times* (28 July 2000), p. 8; *Financial Times Special Report*, 'Corporate aviation' (7 May 2003), pp. I–IV; *The Independent*, 'Concorde Special' (21 October 2003); Ann Treneman, 'The part-time jet set', *The Times Magazine* (8 November 2003), pp. 48–52.

2. This definition is adapted from Frederick E. Webster, Jr and Yoram Wind, *Organizational Buying Behavior* (Englewood Cliffs, NJ: Prentice Hall, 1972), p. 2; also see K. Thompson, H. Mitchell and S. Knox, 'Organisational buying behaviour in changing times', *European Management Journal*, **16**, 6 (1998), pp. 698–705; Michael D. Hutt and Thomas W. Speh, *Business Marketing Management*, 7th edn (Upper Saddle River, NJ: Prentice Hall, 2001), pp. 73–7.

3. Dave Murphy, 'Tomorrow's window of opportunity', *Marketing Business* (June 1999), pp. 43–5; 'E-commerce: the A to Z of B2B', *The Economist* (1 April 2000), pp. 71–4; 'Could B2B B4U', *The Economist* (27 May 2000), p. 113.

4. Bill Sweetman, 'Lift fan carries Lockheed Martin to JSF victory', *Interavia* (November 2002), pp. 9–10.

5. Hans Heerkens, 'Glaring prospect?', *Interavia* (February 2000), p. 17; 'Airbus Industrie: target the 21st century', *Interavia* (March 1999), pp. 13–53; Arthur Leathly, 'Superjumbo brings revolution to the air', *The Times* (14 March 2000), p. 11.

6. 'That sinking feeling', *The Economist* (17 January 1998), pp. 71–2; Peter Marsh, 'Weakened Corus wins a breather to tackle UK sites', *Financial Times* (13 November 2003), p. 27.

7. See Lawrence A. Crosby, Kenneth R. Evans and Deborah Cowles, 'Relationship quality and services selling: an interpersonal influence perspective', *Journal of Marketing* (July 1990), pp. 68–81; Barry J. Farber and Joyce Wycoff, 'Relationships: six steps to success', *Sales and Marketing Management* (April 1992), pp. 50–8; Kevin Done, 'Harmony under the bonnet', *Financial Times* (8 November 1994), p. 17; K. Blois, 'A trust interpretation of business to business relationships: a case-based discussion', *Management Decision*, **36**, 5 (1998), 9 pp.; M.A. Zideldin, 'Towards an ecological collaborative relationship management: a "co-operative" perspective', *European Journal of Marketing*, **32**, 11/12 (1998), 22 pp.; K.J. Blois, 'Trust in business to business relationships: an evaluation of its status', *Journal of Management Studies*, **36**, 2 (1999), pp. 197–215.

8. Peter Spiegel, 'BAE and Boeing target RAF contract through 767 deal', *Financial Times* (13 November 2003), p. 25, and 'UK market is a key battleground for Boeing', *Financial Times* (13 November 2003), p. 34.

9. Patrick J. Robinson, Charles W. Faris and Yoram Wind, *Industrial Buying Behavior and Creative Marketing* (Boston: Allyn & Bacon, 1967). See also Erin Anderson, Weyien Chu and Barton Weitz, 'Industrial purchasing: an empirical exploration of the buyclass framework', *Journal of Marketing* (July 1987), pp. 71–86; K. Thompson, H. Mitchell and S. Knox, 'Organisational buying behaviour in changing times', *European Management Journal*, **16**, 6 (1998), pp. 698–705.

10. Dave Murphy, 'Tomorrow's window of opportunity', *Business Marketing* (June 2000), pp. 43–5.

11. Cait Murphy, 'Will the future belong to Germany?', *Fortune* (2 August 2000), pp. 63–70. For more on systems selling, see Robert R. Reeder, Edward G. Brierty and Betty H. Reeder, *Industrial Marketing: Analysis, planning and control* (Englewood Cliffs, NJ: Prentice Hall, 1991), pp. 264–7.

12. Webster and Wind, *Organizational Buying Behavior*, op. cit., p. 6; P.L. Dawes, G.R. Dowling and P.G. Patterson, 'Factors affecting the structure of buying centers for the purchase of professional business advisory services', *International Journal of Research in Marketing*, **9**, 3 (1992), pp. 269–79; E.J. Wilson and A.G. Woodside, 'A two-step model of influence in group purchasing decisions', *International Journal of Physical Distribution and Logistics Management*, **24**, 5 (1994), pp. 34–44; M. Farrel and B. Schroder, 'Power and influence in the buying centre', *European Journal of Marketing*, **33**, 11/12 (1999), 8 pp.

13. Webster and Wind, *Organizational Buying Behavior*, op. cit., pp. 78–80.

14. For results of both surveys, see 'I think you have a great product, but it's not my decision', *American Salesman* (April 1994), pp. 11–13; and Tim Minahan, 'OEM buying survey – part 2: Buyers get new roles but keep old tasks', *Purchasing* (16 July 1998), pp. 208–9. For more on influence strategies within buying centres, see Philip L. Dawes, Don Y. Lee and Grahame R. Dowling, 'Information control and influence in emergent buying centers', *Journal of Marketing* (July 1998), pp. 55–68; Jeffrey E. Lewin, 'The effects of downsizing on organizational buying behavior: an empirical investigation', *Academy of Marketing Science* (Spring 2001), pp. 151–64.

15. Melvin R. Matson and Esmail Salshi-Sangari, 'Decision making in purchases of equipment and materials: a four-country comparison', *International Journal of Physical Distribution and Logistics Management*, **23**, 8 (1993), pp. 16–30.

16. 'The price of success: losing the lustre', *EuroBusiness* (May 2000), pp. 110–12; 'Corporate hospitality: nice one', *The Economist* (10 June 2000), p. 39; Robin Cobb, 'Let me entertain you', *Marketing Busines* (April 2003), pp. 21–3; Friederike Tiesenhausen Vace, 'Game is up for rugby freebies', *Financial Times* (13 November 2003), p. 6.

17. Webster and Wind, *Organizational Buying Behavior*, op. cit., pp. 33–7. Also R.G. Kauffman, 'Influences on organizational buying choice processes: future research directions', *Journal of Business and Industrial Marketing*, **11**, 3/4 (1996), 11 pp.

18. Peter W. Turnbull, 'Organisational buying behaviour', in Michael J. Baker (ed.), *The Marketing Book* (London: Heinemann, 1994), pp. 147–64.

19. Thayer C. Taylor, 'Xerox's sales force learns a new game', *Sales and Marketing Management* (1 July 1985), pp. 48–51.

20. Keith Blois, 'Are business-to-business relationships inherently unstable?', *Journal of Marketing Management*, **13**, 5 (1997), pp. 367–79.

21. Michiyo Nakamoto, 'Building networks', *Financial Times* (13 November 1992), p. 8; Richard Gourlay, 'From fat to lean enterprises', *Financial Times* (8 November 1994), p. 11; Carlos Cordon, 'Doing justice to just in time', *Financial Times* (9 November 1994), p. 14.

22. Ajay Kohli, 'Determinants of influence in organizational buying: a contingency approach', *Journal of Marketing* (July 1989), pp. 50–65.

23. Malcolm Brown, 'Signed, sealed, delivered', *Marketing Business* (June 1992), pp. 30–2.

24. Robinson, Faris and Wind, *Industrial Buying Behavior*, op. cit., p. 14.; Michael D. Hutt and Thomas W. Speh, *Business Marketing Management,* 7th edn (Upper Saddle River, NJ: Prentice Hall, 2001), pp. 56–66.

25. 'Buying globally made easier', *Industry Week* (2 February 1998), pp. 63–4; *Business Wire,* 'dotlogix to offer WIZNET content management solutions through its "subscription based" service module' (8 November 2001) and online at www.wiznet.net; Jeffrey E. Lewin, 'The effects of downsizing on organizational buying behavior: an empirical investigation', *Academy of Marketing Science* (Spring 2001), pp. 151–64.

26. See 'What buyers really want', *Sales and Marketing Management* (October 1989), p. 30; 'Purchasing managers sound off', *Sales and Marketing Management* (February 1995), pp. 84–5; Thomas Y. Choi and Janet L. Hartley, 'An exploration of supplier selection practices across the supply chain', *Journal of Operations Management* (November 1996), pp. 333–43; Douglas M. Lambert, Ronald J. Adams and Margaret A. Emmelhainz, 'Supplier selection criteria in the healthcare industry: a comparison of importance and performance', *International Journal of Purchasing and Materials Management* (Winter 1997), pp. 16–22; and Craig M. Gustin, Patricia J. Daugherty and Alexander E. Ellinger, 'Supplier selection decisions in systems/software', *International Journal of Purchasing and Materials Management* (Fall 1997), pp. 41–6.

27. 'You'll never walk alone' in 'The net imperative: a survey of business and the Internet', *The Economist* (26 June 1999), pp. 9–17; 'Business-to-business in Japan: no room in the nest', *The Economist* (15 April 2000), pp. 91–2.

28. 'To byte the hand that feeds', *The Economist* (17 January 1998), pp. 75–6; 'A market for monopoly', *The Economist* (17 June 2000), pp. 85–6.

29. Stuart Derrick, 'Market forces', *e.business* (July 2000), pp. 15–16; 'The net imperative: a survey of business and the Internet', *The Economist* (26 June 1999), pp. 1–44.

30. Alexander Harney, 'Toyota set to join online trade exchange' and 'Up close but impersonal', *Financial Times* (10 March 2000), p. 33; 'A market for monopoly', *The Economist* (17 June 2000), pp. 85–6; Stuart Derrick, 'Market forces', *e.business* (July 2000), pp. 15–16.

31. Paul Clarke, 'Public sector purchasing in the European Union: a guide to public procurement, tenders.co.uk/background/pspguide and OJEC.com.

32. Andrew Bolgar, 'Diversifying out of lumpiness', *Financial Times* (2 November 1994), p. 26; Michael Harrison, 'VT aims for $500 m sales in surging US defence sector', *The Independent* (12 November 2003).

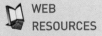

WEB RESOURCES

For additional classic case studies and Internet exercises, visit www.pearsoned.co.uk/ kotler

Concluding concepts 8
Biofoam: just peanuts?

Like diamonds, polystyrene peanuts are forever – their volume is growing at a rate of at least 20 million kg annually. Since their introduction in 1970, they have become one of the most popular forms of packaging material. They are lightweight, inexpensive and resilient. They conform to any shape, protect superbly, resist shifting in transit, leave no dusty residue on the goods they protect and are indestructible. That is the problem. Nearly every one of those peanuts used since 1970 is still with us – blowing in the wind or taking up space in a landfill. Worse yet, they will be with us for another 500 years. They are wonderful but not environmentally sound.

The small firm Biofoam thinks it has solved this problem and helps businesses and governments meet their environmental targets. It sells a peanut made from grain sorghum, a grain now used for animal feed. To make these sorghum peanuts, the company strips the grain of its nutritional value, presses it into pellets, and conveys it through a giant popper. The process creates a product that looks like tan cheese doodles, not so surprising given that the inventors started out to make a snack food. Nevertheless, no one wanted to eat these objects, so the inventors had to find other uses for them. According to Ed Alfke, Biofoam's CEO, the sorghum peanuts do just as good a job as the best foam peanuts and they do not cost any more. Moreover, they hold no electrostatic charge, so they will not cling to nylons or other synthetic fibres (such as your carpet or clothes). Better yet, they are 'absolutely, frighteningly natural', says Tom Schmiegel, a veteran of the plastics industry.

To dispose of a Biofoam peanut, you can: (a) put it in your waste bin, (b) throw it on your front lawn as bird food, (c) compost it, (d) put it in your dog's or cat's bowl, (e) set it out with salsa at your next party, or (f) wash it down your drain. The peanut dissolves in water and has some – although limited – nutritional value. Alfke bought into the company because of its environmentally positive stance. He is convinced that green companies will profit from a global regulatory climate that is increasingly hostile to polluters. 'The writing is on the wall for companies that are not environmentally friendly', he says.

Biofoam initially targeted retailers who wanted to send an environmentally friendly message, helped along by the inclusion of a Biofoam pamphlet explaining the advantages of the Biofoam peanut. It targeted the heaviest users of Styrofoam peanuts who consume up to 20 truckloads of

loose fill a *day*. To date, Biofoam has signed two major accounts – the Fuller Brush Company and computer reseller MicroAge.

Eventually, Biofoam will have to expand beyond environmentally sensitive firms into a broader market. To convince potential users to use Biofoam peanuts, Alfke has come up with a seemingly no-brainer option: to be environmentally responsible without having to pay more or sacrifice convenience. He is willing to install machines on the customer's premises to produce peanuts in-house – an arrangement that would give Biofoam rent-free production sites. He will even provide an employee to operate the machinery. Although this strategy might sound unusual, it has been used by other companies such as Xerox to sell copiers and Tetra Pak to sell juice boxes and milk cartons.

The in-house arrangement has benefits for the customer as well as for Biofoam. Users receive immediate, reliable, just-in-time delivery combined with on-site service and a five-year price guarantee with no intermediaries involved. With Biofoam on-site, users never run out of packaging, and they avoid the expense of stockpiling materials. Lower production costs make Biofoam's product price competitive with that of polystyrene. For Biofoam, the arrangement provides a rent-free network of regional manufacturing facilities and an intimacy with each customer. Because the host company will only consume about one-third of the output, Biofoam plans to sell the excess to smaller firms in the host's area.

However, this in-house production arrangement has disadvantages. From the host's perspective, the machinery takes up 140 m^2 of floor space that could be used to produce something else. Furthermore, some of the output of that 140 m^2 goes to other firms, benefiting Biofoam but doing nothing for the host. Furthermore, the host has a non-employee working in its plant. The peanut-making machinery is also intrusive. It consists of three machines – an extruder, a conditioning chamber and a deduster – joined by ducts and conveyor belts. The machines make lots of noise (like a giant air conditioner), making conversation in the vicinity impossible. The process

> 'The writing is on the wall for companies that are not environmentally friendly'.

creates a smell, rather like the inside of an old barn, and produces heat, a potential problem. Thus, on closer inspection, the in-house arrangement is not entirely desirable. Without this arrangement, however, costs rise considerably. If it had to ship the peanuts to users, Biofoam would have to raise the price 10 to 20 per cent.

Biofoam's competition, the polystyrene loose-fill industry, is a fragmented patchwork of diverse companies. It includes oil companies, chemical producers, fill manufacturers and regional distributors – all of which would suffer from Biofoam's success. One aggressive newcomer is EarthShell that make their packaging out of environmentally friendly natural limestone and potato starch. The industry is much more rough-and-tumble than CEO Alfke anticipated. So far, Biofoam has a microscopic market share. The company's 2000 sales totalled only €3 million – not much in an industry with potential sales of €200 to €600 million a year. Nevertheless, the €3 million represented a five-fold increase over the previous year. Alfke now projects sales of €90 million in 2004, with 30 per cent pre-tax profits. These projections include sales of products other than sorghum peanuts. Alfke plans to add injectible Biofoam and stiff Biofoam packaging materials. Other promising applications have been suggested, such as using Biofoam to absorb oil spills or in medicinal applications, but Alfke does not want to talk about those. For now, 'It's important that we try to stay focused', he claims.

Can Alfke reach his ambitious goals? Many industry observers say no. Environmental claims, say these observers, do not have the impact that they used to have. 'That was something we worried about three years ago', said a purchasing agent. Biofoam's sales representatives are finding the market less environmentally concerned. Others, however, are more optimistic. For example, although she agrees that the novelty of environmentally responsible packaging has worn off, Nancy Pfund, general partner of Hambrecht and Quist's Environmental Technology Fund, thinks that many firms are still interested in environmentally friendly packaging. She notes that companies have 'internalised a lot of environmental procedures without making a lot of noise about it. You also have younger people who grew up learning about the environment in school now entering the consumer market. That's a very strong trend.' Such consumers will demand more responsible packaging.

Are companies that use Biofoam happy with it? Well, some yes, some no. On the positive side is MicroAge Computer. According to Mark Iaquinto, facilities manager,

MicroAge had been searching for an acceptable alternative to polystyrene. Now that it has found Biofoam, he is convinced it can stop searching. On the negative side, Norbert Schneider, president of Fuller Brush Company, has concerns about the way the product crumbles in boxes filled with sharp-pointed brushes. Alfke says that Biofoam is working on a solution, but if it does not find one soon, Fuller Brush may change packaging suppliers.

Other firms have entered the market with biodegradable, water-soluble foams. Made from corn-starch-based thermoplastics, the products can be rinsed down the drain after use. They can be used in loose-fill packaging applications or moulded in place into shaped packaging. They compare favourably with traditional packaging materials for cost and performance.

So, facing a stiffly competitive industry, new competitors and a softening of environmental concerns, Biofoam will find the going hard. However, none of this dents Alfke's enthusiasm. Alfke was a multimillionaire before age 40. 'I've seen a lot of deals', he claims, 'and I've never, *ever* seen a deal as good as this one.' As an experienced businessman, no doubt he *has* seen a lot of deals. He really believes in this one, but is he right?

Questions

1. Outline Biofoam's current marketing strategy.
2. Which elements of the marketing mix are most important for Biofoam to focus on?
3. What is the nature of demand in the loose-fill packaging industry? What factors shape that demand?
4. If you were a buyer of packaging materials, would you agree to Biofoam's offer of machines inside your plant? If not, how could Biofoam overcome your objections?
5. What environmental and organisational factors are likely to affect the loose-fill packaging industry? How will these factors affect Biofoam?
6. Is Alfke right? Is this a good deal? Would you have bought into the firm? Why or why not?

SOURCES: Robert D. Leaversuch, 'Water-soluble foams offer cost-effective protection', *Modern Plastics* (April 1997), pp. 32–5; 'Latest trends in . . . protective packaging', *Modern Materials Handling* (October 2002); Venessa Houlder, 'EU packaging measures: meeting the challenge', FT.com site, 26 May 2003; 'New equipment order increases manufacturing capacity for EarthShell products', *Business Wire* (31 December 2002).

> Research is cheap if you want to stay in business, expensive if you don't.

ANON

Marketing research

Chapter objectives

After reading this chapter, you should be able to:

- Explain the importance of information to the company.
- Define the marketing information system and discuss its parts.
- Describe the four steps in the marketing research process.
- Compare the advantages and disadvantages of various methods of collecting information.
- Discuss the main methods for estimating current market demand.
- Explain specific techniques that companies use to forecast future demand.

Mini Contents List

◀ SOURCE: Corbis Sygma.
Photographer: Dean Francis.

Prelude case Market researching AIDS in Africa: a little achieves the unimaginable

In developed countries the threatened AIDS (acquired immune deficiency syndrome) epidemic is contained, although it is far from eradicated. The link between AIDS and HIV (human immunodeficiency virus) and the fact that HIV is mainly transmitted through unprotected sex and drug abuse are accepted and have changed people's behaviour. Public awareness and scare campaigns accounted for a lot of the success.

The situation in sub-Saharan Africa could not be more different. While the WHO (World Health Organisation) estimates that there are fewer than two million people with HIV/AIDS in the whole of North America, Europe and Central Asia, in sub-Saharan Africa the figure is 32 million and growing. Many of the sufferers are innocents. Mother-to-child infections have grown tenfold. The region now has 40 million AIDS orphans who, according to UNICEF, are 'putty in the hands of warlords'. In worst-hit Botswana, Namibia, Swaziland and Zimbabwe, between 20 and 25 per cent of the sexually active population are infected. A 15-year-old boy in Botswana has an 80 per cent chance of dying of AIDS.

> A 15-year-old boy in Botswana has an 80 per cent chance of dying of AIDS.

South Africa's isolation once protected it from the epidemic, but no more. It now has more HIV/AIDS sufferers than any other country in the world and up to a third of sexually active males are HIV-positive. In 1996 the life expectancy in South Africa was over 60 years. AIDS is likely to bring it down to under 40 years by 2010. Worse is yet to come. HIV/AIDS is hitting the most economically active members of the population. Without AIDS, Botswana's population of 40–49-year-olds would have been 300,000 in 2020. With AIDS it is expected to slump to fewer than 60,000!

Can the catastrophe be stopped? There is hope for drug donations from rich countries and the International AIDS Vaccine Initiative gives some hope. But among the gloom there are some successes. Senegal has remained largely AIDS free as a result of vigorous and unambiguous education programmes.

UNAIDS, the United Nations agency charged with fighting the disease, says the gap between Africa's needs and the donations of rich countries to help fight the disease is rising, but some local research is helping the meagre donations stretch further. Researchers in Tanzania found that spending on diseases did not relate to the disabilities and deaths they cause or the efficacy of treatment. Based on these findings, the inadequate health budget is now spent more effectively.

Uganda is close to the epicentre, but has turned the tide on AIDS. President Museveni acted on the threat as soon as he came to power. Uganda is a poor country but the President commissioned a series of inexpensive surveys (about €25,000 each) into the sexual behaviour of the population. These and other studies uncovered important reasons why AIDS is spreading:

- Sex is fun and an inexpensive recreation.
- Condoms make it less so: 'Would you eat a sweet with a wrapper on it?'
- Some men snip the ends of condoms they are about to use.
- The discussion of sex is often taboo.
- Myths abound: regular infusions of sperm make women grow up beautiful and men can get rid of HIV infection by passing it on to a virgin.
- Wives who ask their husbands to use a condom are in danger of being beaten up.
- Drinking local beers is another form of inexpensive entertainment but the inebriated are prone to unsafe sex.

Realising the scale of the problem and the shortage of funds, the President freed dozens of non-government organisations (NGOs) to educate people about unsafe sex. The NGOs used material and approaches that many other African countries found unacceptable, but within a five-year period the HIV-infected women in urban antenatal clinics fell from 30 to 15 per cent.[1]

Questions

1. What research would you commission to gather an understanding of the behaviour leading to the spread of HIV/AIDS?
2. Is it safe to rely on 'inexpensive research' to guide campaigns as critical as those against AIDS?
3. What are the dangers and benefits of freeing a range of NGOs to drive for a social good rather than a single, well-coordinated campaign?

Introduction

To carry out marketing analysis, planning, implementation and control, managers need information. As Uganda's President Museveni realised in his campaign against AIDS, you need information in order to act effectively. Information is not just an input for making better decisions, but also a marketing asset that gives competitive advantage of strategic importance. Competitors can copy each other's equipment, products and procedures, but they cannot duplicate the company's information and intellectual capital.

All companies start small, knowing their customers personally. Managers picked up marketing information by meeting people, observing them and asking questions. However, with growth they need more and better information. When they become national or international in scope, they need more information on larger, more distant markets. As incomes increase and buyers become more selective, sellers need even better information about how buyers respond to different products and appeals. As sellers use more complex marketing approaches and face more competition, they need information on the effectiveness of their marketing tools. Finally, in today's rapidly changing environments, managers need up-to-date information to make timely decisions. This increased market and customer sophistication has led to the prediction by Sir Martin Sorrell, chief executive of WWP, and the British Market Research Association that the market research industry will grow at twice the rate of marketing generally.[2]

The need for more and better information has been met by an explosion of information technology. The past 30 years have witnessed the emergence of small but powerful computers, text messaging, DVD drives, videoconferencing, broadband Internet access and other advances that have revolutionised information handling. Today's managers often receive too much information. For example, one study found that with all the companies offering data, and with all the information now available through supermarket scanners, a packaged-goods brand manager is bombarded with 1 million to 1 *billion* new numbers each week. Another study found that, on average, office workers spend 60 per cent of their time processing documents; a typical manager reads about a million words a week. Running out of information is not a problem but seeing through the 'data smog' is.[3]

Despite this data glut, marketers frequently complain that they lack enough information of the *right* kind. For example, a recent survey of managers found that although half the respondents said they couldn't cope with the volume of information coming at them, two-thirds wanted even more. The researcher concluded that 'despite the volume, they're still not getting what they want.'[4] Thus, most marketing managers don't need *more* information; they need *better* information. Companies have greater capacity to provide managers with good information, but often have not made good use of it. Many companies are now studying their managers' information needs and designing information systems to meet those needs.

The marketing information system

A **marketing information system (MIS)** consists of people, equipment and procedures to gather, sort, analyse, evaluate and distribute needed, timely and accurate information to marketing decision makers. Figure 9.1 illustrates the marketing information system concept. The MIS begins and ends with marketing managers. First, it interacts with these managers to assess their information needs. Next, it develops the needed information from internal company records, marketing intelligence activities and the marketing research process. Information analysis processes the information to make it more useful. Finally, the MIS distributes information to managers in the right form at the right time to help them in marketing planning, implementation and control.

Marketing information system (MIS)—People, equipment and procedures to gather, sort, analyse, evaluate and distribute needed, timely and accurate information to marketing decision makers.

337

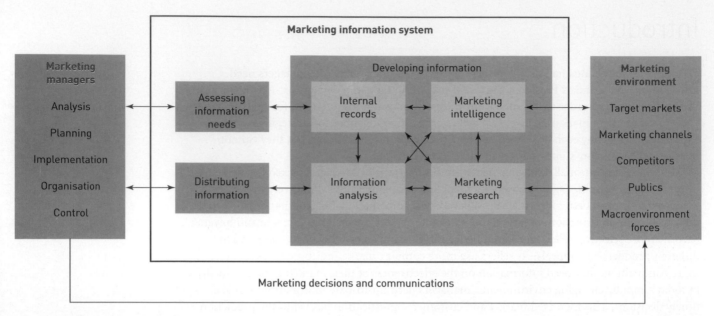

Figure 9.1 The marketing information system

Developing information

The information needed by marketing managers comes from *internal company records*, *marketing intelligence* and *marketing research*. The information analysis system then processes this information to make it more useful for managers.

Internal records

Internal records information—Information gathered from sources within the company to evaluate marketing performance and to detect marketing problems and opportunities.

Most marketing managers use internal records and reports regularly, especially for making day-to-day planning, implementation and control decisions. **Internal records information** consists of information gathered from sources within the company to evaluate marketing performance and to detect marketing problems and opportunities. The company's accounting department prepares financial statements and keeps detailed records of sales, orders, costs and cash flows. Manufacturing reports on production schedules, shipments and inventories. The sales force reports on reseller reactions and competitor activities. The customer service department provides information on customer satisfaction or service problems. Research studies done for one department may provide useful information for several others. Managers can use information gathered from these and other sources within the company to evaluate performance and to detect problems and opportunities.

Here is an example of how companies use internal records information in making better marketing decisions:

Istel is a cross-fertilization scheme set up by AT & T in Europe. The system helps retailers share information about customers. Under the programme customers join the Istel club, which gives them discounts when buying a range of products from member stores. AT & T estimates that its card will save the average customer €100 a year. The retailers then use the information to

> build databases and to target incentives to valuable customers. 'The grocer may like to know who is a high spender in the scheme but is not shopping with them', says Ruth Kemp of Istel. 'Then they can offer incentives to use their store.'[5]

Information from internal records is usually quicker and cheaper to get than information from other sources, but it also presents some problems. Because internal information was intended for other purposes, it may be incomplete or in the wrong form for making marketing decisions. For example, accounting department sales and cost data used for preparing financial statements need adapting for use in evaluating product, sales force or channel performance. In addition, the many different areas of a large company produce great amounts of information, and keeping track of it all is difficult. The marketing information system must gather, organise, process and index this mountain of information so that managers can find it easily and get it quickly.

Marketing intelligence

Marketing intelligence is everyday information about developments in the marketing environment that helps managers prepare and adjust marketing plans. The marketing intelligence system determines the intelligence needed, collects it by searching the environment and delivers it to marketing managers who need it.

Marketing intelligence comes from many sources. Much intelligence is from the company's personnel – executives, engineers and scientists, purchasing agents and the sales force. But company people are often busy and fail to pass on important information. The company must 'sell' its people on their importance as intelligence gatherers, train them to spot new developments and urge them to report intelligence back to the company.

The company must also persuade suppliers, resellers and customers to pass along important intelligence. Some information on competitors comes from what they say about themselves in annual reports, speeches, press releases and advertisements. The company can also learn about competitors from what others say about them in business publications and at trade shows. Or the company can watch what competitors do – buying and analysing competitors' products, monitoring their sales and checking for new patents.

Companies also buy intelligence information from outside suppliers. Dun & Bradstreet is the world's largest research company with branches in 40 countries and a turnover of €1.5 billion. Its largest subsidiary is Nielsen, which sells data on brand shares, retail prices and percentages of stores stocking different brands. Its Info*Act Workstation offers companies the chance to analyse data from three sources on the PCs: Retail Index, which monitors consumer sales and in-store conditions; Key Account Scantrack, a weekly analysis of sales, price elasticity and promotional effectiveness; and Homescan, a new consumer panel. Alliances between marketing research companies allow access to pan-European research. Leading European market research agencies all do more than half their work outside their own country. Among these are The Kanter Group and Taylor Nelson Sofres plc (UK), Nielson Media Research (The Netherlands), GfK and Sample Institut (Germany), Ipos Group SA (France) and Sifo Research (Sweden).[6]

Competitor intelligence

Marketing intelligence can work not only for but also against a company. Companies must sometimes take steps to protect themselves from the snooping of competitors. For example, Kellogg's had treated the public to tours of its plants since 1906, but recently closed its newly upgraded plant to outsiders to prevent competitors from getting intelligence on its high-tech

Marketing intelligence— Everyday information about developments in the marketing environment that helps managers prepare and adjust marketing plans.

Competitor intelligence— Information gathered that informs on what the competition is doing or is about to do.

339

equipment. In Japan corporate intelligence is part of the industrial culture. Everyone from assembly-line workers to top executives considers it their duty to filter intelligence about the competition back to management. In its Bangkok offices one European organisation has a huge poster outside its lavatory saying: 'Wash and hush up! You never know who's listening! Keep our secrets secret.'[7]

Some companies set up an office to collect and circulate marketing intelligence. The staff scan relevant publications, summarise important news and send news bulletins to marketing managers. They develop a file of intelligence information and help managers evaluate new information. These services greatly improve the quality of information available to marketing managers. The methods used to gather competitive information range from the ridiculous to the illegal. Managers routinely shred documents because wastepaper baskets can be an information source. Other firms have uncovered more sinister devices such as Spycatcher's TPR recording system that 'automatically interrogates telephones and faxes. Also a range of tiny microphones.'

European firms lag behind their Japanese and American competitors in gathering competitive intelligence. In Japanese companies it is a long-established practice, for, as Mitsui's corporate motto says: 'Information is the life blood of the company.' In the US, competitive intelligence gathering has grown dramatically as more and more companies need to know what their competitors are doing. Sometimes, when the stakes are high, methods become questionable.

> Procter & Gamble admitted to 'trash diving' at rival Unilever's headquarters. The target was Unilever's hair-care products – Salon Selectives, Finesse, Thermasilk, and Helene Curtis – which competed with P&G's Pantene, Head & Shoulders, and Pert brands. 'Apparently, the operation was a big success', notes an analyst. 'P&G got its mitts on just about every iota of info there was to be had about Unilever's brands.' However, when news of the questionable tactics reached top P&G managers they were shocked. They stopped the project, informed Unilever, and entered negotiations to right whatever competitive wrongs had been done. Although P&G claims it broke no laws, the company reported that the trash raids 'violated our strict guidelines regarding our business policies.'[8]

The techniques used to collect intelligence fall into the following four main groups.

Getting information from published materials and public documents

Keeping track of seemingly meaningless published information can provide competitor intelligence. For instance, the types of people sought in help-wanted ads can indicate something about a competitor's new strategies and products. Government agencies are another good source. Although it is often illegal for a company to photograph a competitor's plant from the air, aerial photos often are on file with geological survey or environmental protection agencies. These are public documents, available for a nominal fee. According to Leonard Fuld, founder of FCI: 'in some countries the government is a rare font of information. France has the Minitel, in the US we have an opus of information databases and networks.'

Competitors themselves may reveal information through their annual reports, business publications, trade show exhibits, press releases, advertisements and Web pages. The Internet is proving to be a vast new source of competitor-supplied information. Most companies now place volumes of information on their websites, providing details to attract customers, partners, suppliers or franchisees, and that same information is available to competitors at the click of a mouse button. Press releases that never made it into the press are posted on websites, letting firms keep abreast of competitors' new products and organisational changes. Help-wanted ads posted on the Web quickly reveal competitors' expansion priorities.

And it's not only company sponsored websites that hold rich competitor intelligence booty. Researchers can also glean valuable nuggets of information from trade association websites.

> Gay Owen, controller of Stone Container's specialty-packaging division, visited a trade association Web site and noticed that a rival had won an award for a new process using ultra-violet resistant lacquers. The site revealed the machines' configuration and run rate, which Stone's engineers used to figure out how to replicate the process.[9]

Using Internet search engines, such as Yahoo! or Google, marketers can search specific competitor names, events or trends and see what turns up. There are thousands of online databases. Companies can subscribe to any of more than 3,000 online databases and information search services such as Dialog, DataStar, Lexis-Nexis, Dow Jones News Retrieval, UMI ProQuest, and Dun & Bradstreet's Online Access. Using such databases, companies can conduct complex information searches in a flash from the comfort of their keyboards.

LACP (www.LACP.com) provides users with a steady stream of intelligence data gleaned from the Internet. It searches the Web and gives users daily email reports detailing the business activities, financial moves and Internet dealings of competitors, prospects and clients, often before the information is officially reported. 'In today's information age, companies are

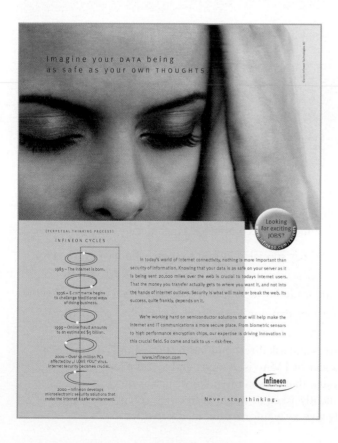

Protection against snooping competitors: the increasing importance of security on the Internet has led to the creation of companies like Infineon, which promotes its concerns about the issue and offers solutions 'to make the Internet and IT communications a more secure place'.
SOURCE: Infineon. *Agency*: J. Walter Thompson.

leaving a paper trail of information online', says Joshua Kopelman, executive vice president of Infonautics, the company that offers the service. 'Company Sleuth uncovers hard-to-find and seemingly hidden business news and information for users so they don't have to simply rely on old news or intuition when making investment and business decisions.'[10]

Getting information by observing competitors or analysing products

Companies can get to know competitors better by buying their products or examining other physical evidence. An increasingly important form of competitive intelligence is benchmarking – taking apart competitors' products and imitating or improving upon their best features. Benchmarking has helped JCB keep ahead in earthmoving equipment. The company takes apart its international competitors' products, dissecting and examining them in detail. JCB also probed the manufacturing operations, the types of machine tools used, their speeds, manning levels, labour costs, quality control and testing procedures, and raw material. It built up a profile of all its main competitors' operations and performance ratios against which to benchmark. In this way, the company knew the extent to which competitors could vary their prices, what their strengths and weaknesses were, and how JCB could exploit these data to its advantage.

Getting information from people who do business with competitors

Key customers can keep the company informed about competitors and their products:

> Gillette told a large account the date on which it planned to begin selling its new Good News disposable razor. The distributor promptly called Bic and told it about the impending product launch. Bic put on a crash programme and was able to start selling its razor shortly after Gillette did.

Intelligence can also be gathered by infiltrating customers' business operations:

> Companies may provide their engineers free of charge to customers . . . The close, cooperative relationship that the engineers on loan cultivate with the customers' design staff often enables them to learn what new products competitors are pitching.

Getting information from recruits and competitors' employees

Companies can obtain intelligence through job interviews or from conversations with competitors' employees. Approaches sometimes recommended include:

- When interviewing people for jobs, pay special attention to those who have worked for competitors, even temporarily.
- Send engineers to conferences and trade shows to question competitors' technical people.
- Advertise and hold interviews for jobs that don't exist in order to entice competitors' employees to spill the beans.
- Telephone competitors' employees and ask direct and indirect questions. 'The rule of thumb', says Jonathan Lax, founder of TMA, 'is to target employees a level below where you think you should start, because that person often knows just as much as his or her senior, and they are not as frequently asked or wary.' Secretaries, receptionists and switchboard operators regularly give away information inadvertently.

Why is Europe different?

Niame Fine, founder of Protec Data, believes there are differences between US and European companies. Language and cultural blocks limit cross-border intelligence gathering. Approaching competitors' employees is a subtle business and people are often put on their guard if approached by someone from a different country. She also says Europeans have greater loyalty than their job-hopping American counterparts.

Although most of these techniques are legal and some are considered to be shrewdly competitive, many involve questionable ethics. The company should take advantage of publicly available information, but avoid practices that might be considered illegal or unethical. A company does not have to break the law or accepted codes of ethics to get good intelligence. So far, many European businesses 'do as they would be done by' and linger at the ethical end of the spectrum of competitive intelligence. However, the European picture is not uniform. Paul Carratu, of Carratu International, put France and Italy alongside the US in their use of industrial espionage. One very high-profile British boss stands accused of sleuthing:

> Bob Ayling, ex-chief executive of British Airways, approached easyJet's founder, Stelios Haji-Ioannou, to ask whether he could visit. Ayling claimed to be fascinated by how the Greek entrepreneur had made the budget airline formula work. Haji-Ioannou not only agreed, but allegedly showed Ayling his business plan. A year later, British Airways announced the launch of Go. 'A carbon copy of easyJet', says easyGroup's director of corporate affairs. 'Same planes, same direct ticket sales, same use of a secondary airport, and same idea to sell on-board refreshments. They succeeded in stealing our business model – it was a highly effective spying job.'[11]

Other European companies are responding to the spying game by developing countermeasures:

> Unilever has begun widespread competitive intelligence training. According to a former Unilever employee, 'We were told how to protect information, as well as how to get it from competitors. We were warned to always keep our mouths shut when traveling. . . . We were even warned that spies from competitors could be posing as drivers at the minicab company we used.' Unilever even performs random checks on internal security. 'At one [internal] conference, we were set up when an actor was employed to infiltrate the group. The idea was to see who spoke to him, how much they told him, and how long it took to realize that no one knew him. He ended up being there for a long time.'[12]

Marketing research

Managers cannot always wait for information to arrive in bits and pieces from the marketing intelligence system. They often require formal studies of specific situations. For example, Apple Computer wants to know how many and what kinds of people or companies will buy its new ultralight personal computer. Or a Dutch pet product firm needs to know the potential market for slimming tablets for dogs. What percentage of dogs are overweight, do their owners worry about it, and will they give the pill to their podgy pooches?[13] In these situations, the marketing intelligence system will not provide the detailed information needed. Because managers normally do not have the skills or time to obtain the information on their own, they need formal marketing research.

Marketing research—
The function that links the consumer, customer and public to the marketer through information that is used to identify and define marketing opportunities and problems, to generate, refine and evaluate marketing actions, to monitor marketing performance, and to improve understanding of the marketing process.

Marketing research is the function linking the consumer, customer and public to the marketer through information that is used to identify and define marketing opportunities and problems, to generate, refine and evaluate marketing actions, to monitor marketing performance, and to improve understanding of the marketing process.[14] Marketing researchers specify the information needed to address marketing issues, design the method for collecting information, manage and implement the data collection process, analyse the results and communicate the findings and their implications.

Marketing researchers engage in a wide variety of activities, ranging from analyses of market potential and market shares to studies of customer satisfaction and purchase intentions. Every marketer needs research. A company can conduct marketing research in its research department or have some or all of it done outside. Although most large companies have their own marketing research departments, they often use outside firms to do special research tasks or special studies. A company with no research department will have to buy the services of research firms.

Many people think of marketing research as a lengthy, formal process carried out by large marketing companies. But many small businesses and non-profit organisations also use marketing research. Almost any organisation can find informal, low-cost alternatives to the formal and complex marketing research techniques used by research experts in large firms.

The marketing research process

The marketing research process (see Figure 9.2) consists of four steps: defining the problem and research objectives; developing the research plan; implementing the research plan; and interpreting and reporting the findings.

Defining the problem and research objectives

The marketing manager and the researcher must work closely together to define the problem carefully and must agree on the research objectives. The manager understands the decision for which information is needed; the researcher understands marketing research and how to obtain the information.

Managers must know enough about marketing research to help in the planning and in the interpretation of research results. If they know little about marketing research, they may obtain the wrong information, accept wrong conclusions, or ask for information that costs too much. Experienced marketing researchers who understand the manager's problem also need involvement at this stage. The researcher must be able to help the manager define the problem and to suggest ways in which research can help the manager make better decisions.

Defining the problem and research objectives is often the hardest step in the research process. The manager may know that something is wrong, without knowing the specific causes. For example, managers of a discount retail store chain hastily decided that poor advertising caused falling sales, so they ordered research to test the company's advertising.

Figure 9.2 **The marketing research process**

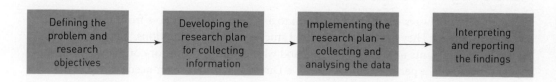

It puzzled the managers when the research showed that current advertising was reaching the right people with the right message. It turned out that the chain stores were not delivering what the advertising promised. Careful problem definition would have avoided the cost and delay of doing advertising research. It would have suggested research on the real problem of consumer reactions to the products, service and prices offered in the chain's stores.

After the problem has been defined carefully, the manager and researcher must set the research objectives. A marketing research project might have one of three types of objective. The objective of **exploratory research** is to gather preliminary information that will help define the problem and suggest hypotheses. The objective of **descriptive research** is to describe things such as the market potential for a product or the demographics and attitudes of consumers who buy the product. The objective of **causal research** is to test hypotheses about cause-and-effect relationships.

> 'Pay as you go' mobile phones evolved from Italian exploratory research. People did not say they wanted 'pay as you go' but expressed anxiety about overspending on calls. Having developed the prepaid mobile phone system, it was tested using descriptive research to gauge consumers' reaction to the concept. Causal research then tested consumers' willingness to pay by testing various pricing options.[15]

The statement of the problem and research objectives guides the entire research process. The manager and researcher should put the statement in writing to be certain that they agree on the purpose and expected results of the research.

Developing the research plan

The second step of the marketing research process calls for determining the information needed, developing a plan for gathering it efficiently and presenting the plan to marketing management. The plan outlines sources of existing data and explains the specific research approaches, contact methods, sampling plans and instruments that researchers will use to gather new data.

Determining information needs

Research objectives need translating into specific information needs.

> Bolswessanen, the Dutch food and drinks company, decides to conduct research to find out how consumers would react to a new breakfast cereal aimed at the adult market. Across Europe young health-conscious people are abandoning croissants in France, rolls in Belgium and lonely espresso in Italy. Since Nestlé and General Mills set up Cereal Partners Worldwide as a joint venture, they have been very active in the market and the project has started to develop. The European breakfast cereal market has been growing fast, but own labels dominate the adult sector.[16] Can Bolswessanen successfully compete with Kellogg's, the market leader, and the aggressive new competitor, Cereal Partners Worldwide? The company's research might call for the following specific information:

Exploratory research— Marketing research to gather preliminary information that will help to better define problems and suggest hypotheses.

Descriptive research— Marketing research to better describe marketing problems, situations or markets, such as the market potential for a product or the demographics and attitudes of consumers.

Causal research—Marketing research to test hypotheses about cause-and-effect relationships.

> 1. The demographic, economic and lifestyle characteristics of current breakfast cereal users. (How do social and demographic trends affect the breakfast cereal market?)
>
> 2. Consumer-usage patterns for cereals: how much do they eat, where and when? (Will all the family eat the cereal or does each family member have their favourite?)
>
> 3. Retailer reactions to the new product. (Failure to get retailer support could hurt its sales.)
>
> 4. Consumer attitudes towards the new product. (Will consumers switch from own brands and is the product attractive enough to compete with Kellogg's?)
>
> 5. Forecasts of sales of the new product. (Will the new packaging increase Bolswessanen's profits?)
>
> Bolswessanen's managers will need this and many other types of information to decide whether to introduce the new product.

Gathering secondary information

Secondary data—
Information that already exists somewhere, having been collected for another purpose.

Primary data—Information collected for the specific purpose at hand.

Secondary data is information that already exists somewhere, having been collected for another purpose. **Primary data** consists of information collected for the specific purpose at hand.

Researchers usually start by gathering secondary data. The company's internal database provides a good starting point. However, the company can also tap a wide assortment of external information sources, ranging from company, public and university libraries to government and business publications.

Commercial data sources

Companies can buy secondary data reports from outside suppliers. For example, Nielsen Media Research sells data on brand shares, retail prices, and percentages of stores stocking different brands. Taylor Nelson Sofres offers TV Audience Measurement using a range of detection techniques to measure cable, satellite, digital and terrestrial TV viewing. Europanel GfK monitors purchases and consumption of over 70,000 households in 23 European countries.[17] These and other firms supply high-quality data to suit a wide variety of marketing information needs.

Online databases and Internet data sources

Most researchers use commercial *online databases*. Marketing researchers can conduct their own searches of secondary data sources. A readily available online database exists to fill almost any marketing information need. General database services such as CompuServe, Dialog and Lexis-Nexis put an incredible wealth of information at the keyboards of marketing decision makers. For example, a company doing business in Germany can check out CompuServe's German Company Library of financial and product information on over 48,000 German-owned firms. Just about any information a marketer might need is available from online databases.[18]

Advantages and disadvantages of secondary data

Secondary data can usually be obtained more quickly and at a lower cost than primary data. For example, an Internet or online database search might provide all the information Danone needs on yoghurt usage, quickly and at almost no cost. A study to collect primary information might take weeks or months and cost tens of thousands of euros. Also, secondary sources sometimes can provide data an individual company cannot collect on its own – information that either is not directly available or would be too expensive to collect. For example, it would be too expensive for Danone to conduct a continuing audit to find out about the market shares, prices and displays of competitors' brands. But it can use the Access Panel service of Ipsos which provides this information on 115,000 households across five European countries.

Secondary data can also present problems. The needed information may not exist – researchers can rarely obtain all the data they need from secondary sources. For example, Danone will not find existing information about consumer reactions to new packaging that it has not yet placed on the market. Even when data can be found, it might not be very usable. The researcher must evaluate secondary information carefully to make certain it is *relevant* (fits research project needs), *accurate* (reliably collected and reported), *current* (up to date enough for current decisions), and *impartial* (objectively collected and reported).

Secondary data provides a good starting point for research and often helps to define problems and research objectives. In most cases, however, the company must also collect primary data.

Planning primary data collection

Good decisions require good data. Just as researchers must carefully evaluate the quality of secondary information they obtain, they must also take great care in collecting primary data to ensure that they provide marketing decision makers with relevant, accurate, current and unbiased information. This could be **qualitative research** that measures a small sample of customers' views, or **quantitative research** that provides statistics from a large sample of consumers. Table 9.1 shows that designing a plan for primary data collection calls for a number of decisions on research approaches, contact methods, sampling plan and research instruments.

Research approaches

Observational research is the gathering of primary data by observing relevant people, actions and situations. For example:

- A French store chain sends *clients mystères* to pose as customers into its stores to check on customer service.
- Microsoft developed OneNote after observing how people make notes on pieces of paper that they often lose.
- Orange, Pace Micro Technology and GWR sponsored the Octagon study – 'reality research' involving 10 households being filmed over a four-week period by researchers who lived with them. It gave a unique insight into people's relationship to household gadgets.[19]

Qualitative research— Exploratory research used to uncover consumers' motivations, attitudes and behaviour. Focus-group interviewing, elicitation interviews and repertory grid techniques are typical methods used in this type of research.

Quantitative research— Research which involves data collection by mail or personal interviews from a sufficient volume of customers to allow statistical analysis.

Observational research— The gathering of primary data by observing relevant people, actions and situations.

Table 9.1 Planning primary data collection

Research approaches	Contact methods	Sampling plan	Research instruments
Observation	Mail	Sampling unit	Questionnaire
Survey	Telephone	Sample size	Electronic instruments
Experiment	Personal	Sampling procedure	
	Internet		

Electronic observation is increasing in use as devices become more powerful, smaller and more intelligent.

■ Nielsen and TNS attach 'people meters' to television sets in selected homes to record who watches what programmes. They provide summaries of the size and demographic make-up of audiences for different television programmes. The television networks use these ratings to judge programme popularity and to set charges for advertising time. Advertisers use the ratings when selecting programmes for their commercials.

■ *Checkout scanners* in retail stores record consumer purchases in detail. Consumer products companies and retailers use scanner information to assess and improve product sales and store performance.

■ **Single-source data systems** electronically monitor both consumers' purchases and consumers' exposure to various marketing activities to evaluate better the link between the two.

Observational research can obtain information that people are unwilling or unable to provide. In some cases, observation is the only way to obtain the needed information. In contrast, some things are simply not observable, such as feelings, attitudes and motives or private behaviour. Long-term or infrequent behaviour is also difficult to observe. Because of these limitations, researchers often use observation along with other data collection methods.

Survey research is the approach best suited for gathering *descriptive* information. A company that wants to know about people's knowledge, attitudes, preferences or buying behaviour can often find out by asking them directly. Survey research is structured or unstructured. *Structured* surveys use formal lists of questions asked of all respondents in the same way. *Unstructured* surveys let the interviewer probe respondents and guide the interview according to their answers.

Survey research may be direct or indirect. In the *direct* approach, the researcher asks direct questions about behaviour or thoughts: for example, 'Why don't you buy clothes at Gap?'. In contrast, the researcher might use the *indirect* approach by asking 'What kinds of people buy clothes at Gap?'. From the response to this indirect question, the researcher may be able to discover why some consumers avoid Gap clothing and why it attracts others. It may suggest reasons the consumer is not conscious of.

Survey research is the most widely used method for primary data collection and is often the only method used in a research study. The principal advantage of survey research is its flexibility. It can obtain many different kinds of information in many different marketing situations. Depending on the survey design, it may also provide information more quickly and at lower cost than observational or experimental research.

However, survey research also presents some problems. Sometimes people are unable to answer survey questions because they do not remember, or never thought about, what they did and why they did it. Or people may be unwilling to respond to unknown interviewers or about things they consider private. Respondents may answer survey questions even when they do not know the answer, simply in order to appear smarter or more informed than they are. Or they may try to help the interviewer by giving pleasing answers. Finally, busy people may not take the time, or they might resent the intrusion into their privacy. Careful survey design can help to minimise these problems.

Experimental research gathers *causal* information. Experiments involve selecting matched groups of subjects, giving them different treatments, controlling unrelated factors and checking for differences in group responses. Thus experimental research tries to explain cause-and-effect relationships. Observation and surveys can collect information in experimental research.

Before extending their product range to include fragrances, researchers at Virgin Megastores might use experiments to answer questions such as the following:

Single-source data systems—Electronic monitoring systems that link consumers' exposure to television advertising and promotion (measured using television meters) with what they buy in stores (measured using store checkout scanners).

Survey research—The gathering of primary data by asking people questions about their knowledge, attitudes, preferences and buying behaviour.

Experimental research—The gathering of primary data by selecting matched groups of subjects, giving them different treatments, controlling related factors and checking for differences in group responses.

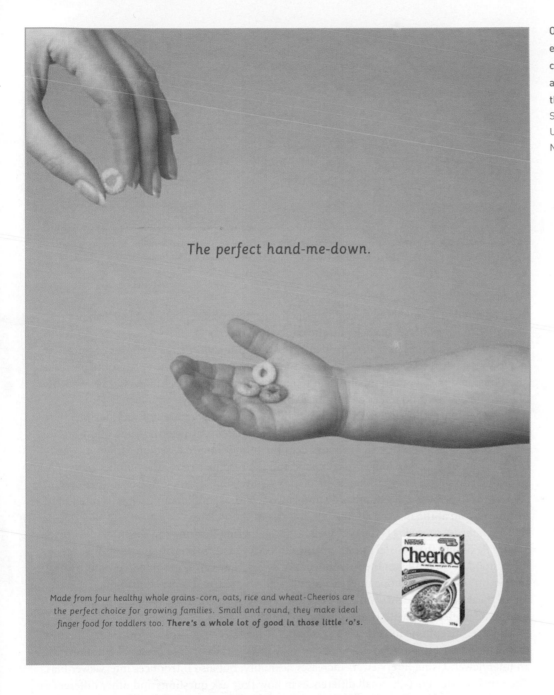

The perfect hand-me-down.

Made from four healthy whole grains-corn, oats, rice and wheat-Cheerios are the perfect choice for growing families. Small and round, they make ideal finger food for toddlers too. **There's a whole lot of good in those little 'o's.**

Observing how young children eat enables Nestlé to run a campaign that suggest an alternative serving method to that illustrated on the pack. SOURCE: Cereal Partners, UK/Courtesy Société des Produits Nestlé S.A., trademark owners.

- How much will the fragrances increase Virgin's sales?
- How will the fragrances affect the sales of other menu items?
- Which advertising approach would have the greatest effect on sales of their fragrances?
- How would different prices affect the sales of the product?
- How will the product affect the stores' overall image?

For example, to test the effects of two prices, Virgin could set up a simple experiment. It could introduce fragrances at one price in one city and at another price in another city. If the cities are similar and if all other marketing efforts for the fragrances are the same, then differences in the price charged could explain the sales in the two cities. More complex experimental designs could include other variables and other locations.

	Mail	Telephone	Personal	Internet
Flexibility	Poor	Good	Excellent	Fair
Quantity of data that can be collected	Good	Fair	Excellent	Good
Control of interviewer effects	Excellent	Fair	Poor	Excellent
Control of sample	Fair	Excellent	Fair	Fair
Speed of data collection	Poor	Excellent	Good	Excellent
Response rate	Poor	Good	Good	Poor
Cost	Good	Fair	Poor	Excellent
Sample frame	Good	Excellent	Fair	Poor

SOURCE: Adapted from *Marketing Research: Measurement and method*, 6th edn, Macmillan Publishing Company, (Tull, D.S. and Hawkins, D.I., 1993). Reprinted with permission from the estate of Donald S. Tull.

Contact methods

Mail, telephone, personal interviews and the Internet can collect data. Table 9.2 shows the strengths and weaknesses of each of these contact methods.

Postal questionnaires have many advantages. They can collect large amounts of information at a low cost per respondent. Respondents may give more honest answers to more personal questions on a postal questionnaire than to an unknown interviewer in person or over the phone, since there is no interviewer to bias the respondent's answers.

However, postal questionnaires also have disadvantages. They are not very flexible: they require simple and clearly worded questions; all respondents answer the same questions in a fixed order; and the researcher cannot adapt the questionnaire based on earlier answers. Mail surveys usually take longer to complete and the response rate – the number of people returning completed questionnaires – is often very low. Finally, the researcher often has little control over the postal questionnaire sample. Even with a good mailing list, it is often hard to control *who* at the mailing address fills out the questionnaire.[20]

Telephone interviewing is the best method for gathering information quickly and provides greater flexibility than postal questionnaires. Interviewers can explain questions that are not understood. Depending on the respondent's answers, they can skip some questions or probe further on others. Telephone interviewing also allows greater sample control. Interviewers can ask to speak to respondents with the desired characteristics, or even by name. Response rates tend to be higher than with postal questionnaires.[21]

However, telephone interviewing also has drawbacks. The cost per respondent is higher than with postal questionnaires and people may not want to discuss personal questions with an interviewer. Using interviewers increases flexibility, but also introduces interviewer bias. The way interviewers talk, small differences in how they ask questions and other differences may affect respondents' answers. Finally, different interviewers may interpret and record responses differently, and under time pressure some interviewers might even cheat by recording answers without asking questions.

Personal interviewing takes two forms – individual and group interviewing. *Individual interviewing* involves talking with people in their homes or offices, in the street, or in shopping malls. The interviewer must gain their cooperation and the time involved can range from a few minutes to several hours. Sometimes people get a small payment in return for their time. *Group interviewing* consists of inviting six to ten people to gather for a few hours with a trained moderator to talk about a product, service or organisation. The moderator needs objectivity, knowledge of the subject and industry, and some understanding of group and consumer behaviour. The participants are normally paid a small sum for attending. The meeting is usually in a pleasant place and refreshments are served to foster an informal setting. The moderator starts with broad questions before moving to more specific issues, and encourages easy-going discussion, hoping that group interactions will bring out actual feelings and thoughts. At the same time, the moderator 'focuses' the discussion – hence the name **focus group** interviewing. The comments are recorded by written notes or on videotapes for study later. Focus group interviewing has become one of the key marketing research tools for gaining insight into consumer thoughts and feelings.[22]

Personal interviewing is quite flexible and can collect large amounts of information. Trained interviewers can hold a respondent's attention for a long time and can explain difficult questions. They can guide interviews, explore issues and probe, as the situation requires. Personal interviews can utilise any type of questionnaire. Interviewers can show subjects actual products, advertisements or packages, and observe reactions and behaviour. In most cases, personal interviews can be conducted fairly quickly.

The main drawbacks of personal interviewing are costs and sampling problems. Personal interviews may cost three to four times as much as telephone interviews. Group interview studies usually employ small sample sizes to keep time and costs down, and it may be hard to generalise from the results. Because interviewers have more freedom in personal interviews, the problem of interviewer bias is greater.

Which contact method is best depends on what information the researcher wants and on the number and types of respondents needed. Advances in computers and communications have had an impact on methods of obtaining information. For example, most research firms now do Computer Assisted Telephone Interviewing (CATI). Professional interviewers call respondents, often using phone numbers drawn at random. When the respondent answers, the interviewer reads a set of questions from a video screen and types the respondent's answers directly into the computer. Although this procedure requires a large investment in computer equipment and interviewer training, it eliminates data editing and coding, reduces errors and saves time. Other research firms set up terminals in shopping centres – respondents sit down at a terminal, read questions from a screen and type their answers into the computer.

Internet data collection can be so quick, easy and inexpensive that some analysts predict that the Internet will soon be the primary marketing research tool.[23] Online researchers recognise that Web surfers are not representative of the population. Online users tend to be better educated, more affluent and younger than the average consumer, and a higher proportion are male. These are important consumers to companies offering products and services online. They are also some of the hardest to reach when conducting a research study. Online surveys are effective in reaching elusive groups, such as teen, single, affluent and well-educated audiences. Although much current Internet data collection is structured, where people complete online questionnaires, chat rooms and on line focus groups provide flexibility:

> Janice Gjersten, director of marketing for an online entertainment company, wants to gauge reaction to a new Web site. She contacts Cyber Dialogue, which provided focus group respondents drawn from its 10,000-person database. The focus group is held in an online chat room, which Gjersten 'looked in on' from her office computer. Gjersten could interrupt the moderator at any time with flash e-mails unseen by the respondents. Although the online focus group lacked voice and body cues, Gjersten says she will never conduct a traditional focus group again. Not only were respondents more honest, but the cost for the online group was one third that of a traditional focus group and a full report came to her in one day, compared to four weeks.[24]

Focus group—A small sample of typical consumers under the direction of a group leader who elicits their reaction to a stimulus such as an ad or product concept.

When appropriate, online research offers marketers two distinct advantages o
traditional surveys and focus groups: speed and cost-effectiveness. Online resea
field quantitative studies and fill response quotas in only a matter of days. Onlin
groups require some advance scheduling, but results are practically instantaneou
on the Internet is also relatively inexpensive. Participants can dial in for a focus g
anywhere in the world, eliminating travel, lodging and facility costs, making onli
cheaper than traditional focus groups. And for surveys, the Internet eliminates mo
postage, phone, labour and printing costs associated with other survey approaches
also no difference in the speed and cost of conducting an international survey rath
domestic one.

Using the Internet to conduct marketing research does have some drawbacks. T
method shares a problem with postal surveys: knowing who's in the sample. Trying
conclusions from a 'self-selected' sample of online users, those who clicked through
questionnaire or accidentally landed in a chat room can be troublesome. Online res
not right for every company or product. For example, mass marketers who need to s
representative cross-section of the population will find online research methodologie
useful, since most low-income consumers do not have online access.

Eye contact and body language are two direct, personal interactions of traditional
group research that are lost online. To overcome such sample and response problems,
and many other firms that offer online services construct panels of qualified Web regu
respond to surveys and participate in online focus groups. NPD's panel consists of 15,0
consumers recruited online and verified by telephone; Greenfield Online picks users fro
its own database, then calls them periodically to verify that they are who they say they a
Another online research firm, Research Connections, recruits in advance by telephone,
taking time to help new users connect to the Internet, if necessary.

Some researchers are wildly optimistic about the prospects for market research on the
Internet. Marketing Insights 9.1 looks into some recent developments in market research
on the Internet.

There is no one best contact method to use. The one chosen depends on the informati
needs, cost, speed and other issues. Table 9.3 shows quantitative data collection methods
across Europe. Rational reasons may account for only part of the variation shown. Face-to
face interview figures are particularly high in southern Europe and the United Kingdom. T
low penetration of telephones in some of these countries may be an influence, but it may a
reflect cultures who like socialising. For example, Ireland's high use of group discussions in
qualitative research may reflect its people's love of conversation. The Scandinavians' use of
telephone interviews is partly explained by their being large countries with small population
In some countries, postal surveys do not work because of low literacy, but another reason is
the unwillingness of people to respond. Research agencies and managers also have preferred
methods, so they will also exert some personal influence on the choice of method. The
relatively lower use of the Internet means that Internet data collection in Europe will lag
behind that in the United States. In addition, the large differences in penetration of the
Internet across Europe mean that its use will not be uniform.

Sampling plans

Marketing researchers usually draw conclusions about large groups of consumers by studying
a small sample of the total consumer population. A **sample** is a segment of the population
selected to represent the population as a whole. Ideally, the sample should be representative,
so that the researcher can make accurate estimates of the thoughts and behaviours of the
larger population.

Designing the sample calls for three decisions. First, *who* is to be surveyed (what *sampling
unit*)? The answer to this question is not always obvious. For example, to study the decision-
making process for a family car purchase, should the researcher interview the husband, wife,

Sample—A segment of the
population selected for market research to represent
the population as a whole.

352

Table 9.2 Strengths and weaknesses of the four contact methods

	Mail	Telephone	Personal	Internet
Flexibility	Poor	Good	Excellent	Fair
Quantity of data that can be collected	Good	Fair	Excellent	Good
Control of interviewer effects	Excellent	Fair	Poor	Excellent
Control of sample	Fair	Excellent	Fair	Fair
Speed of data collection	Poor	Excellent	Good	Excellent
Response rate	Poor	Good	Good	Poor
Cost	Good	Fair	Poor	Excellent
Sample frame	Good	Excellent	Fair	Poor

SOURCE: Adapted from *Marketing Research: Measurement and method*, 6th edn, Macmillan Publishing Company, (Tull, D.S. and Hawkins, D.I., 1993). Reprinted with permission from the estate of Donald S. Tull.

Contact methods

Mail, telephone, personal interviews and the Internet can collect data. Table 9.2 shows the strengths and weaknesses of each of these contact methods.

Postal questionnaires have many advantages. They can collect large amounts of information at a low cost per respondent. Respondents may give more honest answers to more personal questions on a postal questionnaire than to an unknown interviewer in person or over the phone, since there is no interviewer to bias the respondent's answers.

However, postal questionnaires also have disadvantages. They are not very flexible: they require simple and clearly worded questions; all respondents answer the same questions in a fixed order; and the researcher cannot adapt the questionnaire based on earlier answers. Mail surveys usually take longer to complete and the response rate – the number of people returning completed questionnaires – is often very low. Finally, the researcher often has little control over the postal questionnaire sample. Even with a good mailing list, it is often hard to control *who* at the mailing address fills out the questionnaire.[20]

Telephone interviewing is the best method for gathering information quickly and provides greater flexibility than postal questionnaires. Interviewers can explain questions that are not understood. Depending on the respondent's answers, they can skip some questions or probe further on others. Telephone interviewing also allows greater sample control. Interviewers can ask to speak to respondents with the desired characteristics, or even by name. Response rates tend to be higher than with postal questionnaires.[21]

However, telephone interviewing also has drawbacks. The cost per respondent is higher than with postal questionnaires and people may not want to discuss personal questions with an interviewer. Using interviewers increases flexibility, but also introduces interviewer bias. The way interviewers talk, small differences in how they ask questions and other differences may affect respondents' answers. Finally, different interviewers may interpret and record responses differently, and under time pressure some interviewers might even cheat by recording answers without asking questions.

Personal interviewing takes two forms – individual and group interviewing. *Individual interviewing* involves talking with people in their homes or offices, in the street, or in shopping malls. The interviewer must gain their cooperation and the time involved can range from a few minutes to several hours. Sometimes people get a small payment in return for their time. *Group interviewing* consists of inviting six to ten people to gather for a few hours with a trained moderator to talk about a product, service or organisation. The moderator needs objectivity, knowledge of the subject and industry, and some understanding of group and consumer behaviour. The participants are normally paid a small sum for attending. The meeting is usually in a pleasant place and refreshments are served to foster an informal

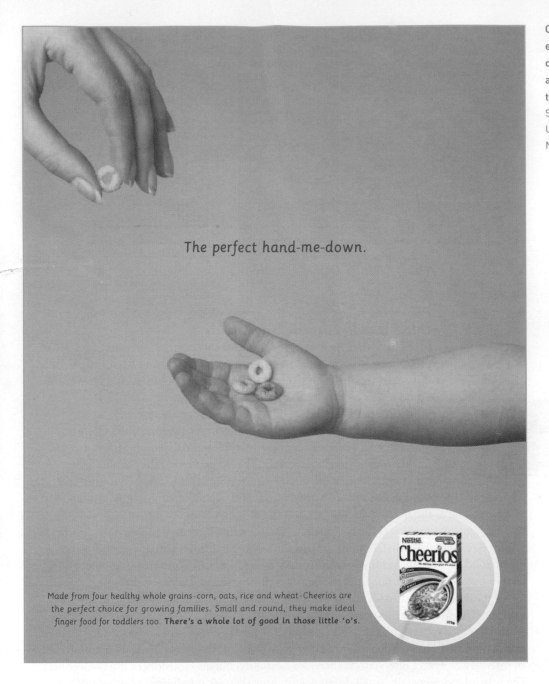

The perfect hand-me-down.

Made from four healthy whole grains-corn, oats, rice and wheat-Cheerios are the perfect choice for growing families. Small and round, they make ideal finger food for toddlers too. **There's a whole lot of good in those little 'o's.**

Observing how young children eat enables Nestlé to run a campaign that suggest an alternative serving method to that illustrated on the pack.
SOURCE: Cereal Partners, UK/Courtesy Société des Produits Nestlé S.A., trademark owners.

■ How much will the fragrances increase Virgin's sales?

■ How will the fragrances affect the sales of other menu items?

■ Which advertising approach would have the greatest effect on sales of their fragrances?

■ How would different prices affect the sales of the product?

■ How will the product affect the stores' overall image?

For example, to test the effects of two prices, Virgin could set up a simple experiment. It could introduce fragrances at one price in one city and at another price in another city. If the cities are similar and if all other marketing efforts for the fragrances are the same, then differences in the price charged could explain the sales in the two cities. More complex experimental designs could include other variables and other locations.

Marketing research on the Internet

As more consumers connect with the Internet, an increasing number of marketers are moving their research onto the Web. Although online research currently makes up less than 5 per cent of all marketing research spending, some say it could account for 50 per cent of all research spending.

Web research offers advantages over traditional surveys and focus groups. The most obvious advantages are speed and low costs. Online focus groups require some advance scheduling, but results are practically instantaneous. Survey researchers routinely complete their online studies in only a matter of days.

> The 10- to 15-minute Internet survey included dozens of questions along with 765 different images of labels, bottle shapes, and such. Some 600 teenagers participated over a three- to four-day period. Detailed analysis from the survey was available five days after all the responses had come in – lightning quick compared to offline efforts.

Internet research is also relatively low in cost. Participants can dial in for a focus group from anywhere in the world, eliminating travel, accommodation and living expenses. The Internet eliminates most of the postage, phone, labour and printing costs associated with other approaches. The cost of Web research 'can be anywhere from 10 per cent to 80 per cent less', says Tod Johnson, head of NPD Group. Moreover, sample size has little influence on costs. The Internet also works well for bringing together people from different parts of the world, especially those in higher-income groups who can't spare the time to travel to a central site.

However, using the Internet in marketing research does have some drawbacks. Many consumers still don't have access to the Internet. That makes it difficult to construct research samples that represent a broad cross-section of people. Still, as Internet usage broadens, many mainstream marketers are now using Web research. UPS uses online research extensively. 'Between 40 per cent and 50 per cent of our customers are online, so it makes sense', says John Gilbert, UPS marketing research manager. He finds little difference in the results of traditional and online studies, and the online studies are much cheaper and faster.

Another major problem of online research is controlling who's in the sample. Tom Greenbaum, president of Groups Plus, recalls a cartoon in which two dogs are seated at a computer: 'On the Internet, nobody knows you are a dog', one says to the other. 'If you can't see a person with whom you are communicating, how do know who they really are?', he says. To overcome such sample and response problems, many online research firms use opt-in communities and respondent panels. Because such

9.1...

respondents opt in and can answer questions whenever they are ready, they yield high response rates. Whereas response rates for telephone surveys have plummeted to less than 14 per cent in recent years, online response rates typically reach 40 per cent or higher.

Even when you reach the right respondents, online surveys and focus groups can lack the dynamics of more personal approaches. 'You're missing all of the key things that make a focus group a viable method', says Greenbaum. 'You may get people online to talk to each other and play off each other, but it's very different to watch people get excited about a concept.' The online world is devoid of the eye contact, body language and direct personal interactions found in traditional focus group research. And the Internet format – running, typed commentary and online 'emoticons' (punctuation marks that express emotion, such as :-) to signify happiness) – greatly restricts respondent expressiveness.

Increasingly, however, advances in technology – such as the integration of animation, streaming audio and video, and virtual environments – will help to overcome these limitations. 'In the online survey of the not-so-distant-future', notes an online researcher, 'respondents will be able to rotate, zoom in on and manipulate (like change the color or size of) three-dimensional products. They'll be able to peruse virtual stores, take items off shelves, and see how they function.'

Just as the impersonal nature of the Web hinders two-way interactions, it can also provide anonymity. This often yields less guarded, more honest responses, especially when discussing topics such as income, medical conditions, lifestyle or other sensitive issues. 'People hiding behind a keyboard get pretty brave', says one researcher. Adds another:

> From those questions that may simply make you squirm a little ('How much money did you lose in the stock market last month?'), to those you most probably don't want to answer to another human being, even if you don't know the person on the other end of the line ('How often do you have sex each week?'), Internet-based surveys tend to draw more honest responses. I once conducted the same survey in a shopping mall and via the Internet. The question was 'How often do you bathe or shower each week?'. The average answer, via the mall interview, was 6.2 times per week. The average via the Internet interview was 4.8 times per week, probably a more logical and honest response. 〞

Perhaps the most explosive issue facing online researchers concerns consumer privacy. Critics worry that online researchers will spam our email boxes with unsolicited emails to recruit respondents. They fear that unethical researchers will use the email addresses and confidential responses gathered through surveys to sell products after the research is completed. They are concerned about the use of electronic agents (called Spambots or Spiders) that collect personal information without the respondents' consent. Failure to address such privacy issues could result in angry, less cooperative consumers and increased government intervention.

Although most researchers agree that online research will never completely replace traditional research, some are wildly optimistic about its prospects. Others, however, are more cautious. 'Ten years from now, national telephone surveys will be the subject of research methodology folklore', proclaims one expert. 'That's a little too soon', cautions another. 'But in 20 years, yes.'

...9.1

SOURCES: Ian P. Murphy, 'Interactive research', *Marketing News* (20 January 1997), pp. 1, 17; 'NFO executive sees most research going to Internet', *Advertising Age* (19 May 1997), p. 50; Kate Maddox, 'Virtual panels add real insight for marketers', *Advertising Age* (29 June 1998), pp. 34, 40; Jon Rubin, 'Online marketing research comes of age', *Brandweek* (30 October 2000), pp. 26-8; 'Web smart', *Business Week* (14 May 2001), p. EB56; Noah Shachtman, 'Web enhanced market research', *Advertising Age* (18 June 2001), p. T18; Thomas W. Miller, 'Make the call: online results are a mixed bag', *Marketing News* (24 September 2001), pp. 30-5; David Jamieson, 'Online research gets fewer Euro votes', *Marketing News* (21 January 2002), p. 15; and Deborah Szynal, 'Gaining steam: big bytes', *Marketing News* (18 March 2002), p. 3.

Table 9.3 Selected European expenditure on ad hoc research

Country	Quantitative				Qualitative		
	Mail	Telephone	Face-to-face	Other	Group	In-depth	Other
Cyprus	1	13	27	4	4	1	–
Czech Republic	1	11	31	7	11	4	1
Denmark	6	20	4	10	12	2	1
Finland	6	18	10	7	4	1	–
France	1	10	20	11	9	3	2
Greece	1	9	26	3	11	3	–
Hungary	1	8	34	8	12	6	–
Ireland	3	15	26	2	16	3	–
Italy	1	21	24	–	8	2	2
Norway	11	39	15	1	6	2	–
Poland	–	6	20	8	13	3	2
Portugal	1	14	24	4	20	6	1
Romania	1	5	32	9	13	3	1
Slovak Republic	–	18	43	1	13	3	–
Spain	2	12	24	5	13	5	–
Switzerland	5	31	11	1	7	3	1
UK	7	19	33	8	9	4	

SOURCE: Adapted from Tables 9 and 10 from *Trade Association estimates of expenditure*, in ESOMAR's Annual Study of the Market Research Industry, www.esomar.nl/press/industryreport01.htm, reprinted with permission from ESOMAR (European Society for Opinion and Market Research), **www.esomar.org**.

Table 9.4 Types of sampling

Probability sample	
Simple random sample	Every member of the population has a known and equal chance of selection.
Stratified random sample	The population is divided into mutually exclusive groups (such as age groups), and random samples are drawn from each group.
Cluster (area) sample	The population is divided into mutually exclusive groups (such as postal districts), and the researcher draws a sample of the groups to interview.
Non-probability sample	
Convenience sample	The researcher selects the easiest population members from which to obtain information.
Judgement sample	The researcher uses his or her judgement to select population members who are good prospects for accurate information.
Quota sample	The researcher finds and interviews a prescribed number of people in each of several categories.

other family members or all of these? The responses obtained from different family members vary, so the researcher must determine the information needed and from whom.[25]

Second, *how many* people are to be surveyed (what *sample size*)? Large samples give more reliable results than small samples. However, it is not necessary to sample the entire target market or even a large portion to get reliable results. If well chosen, samples of less than 1 per cent of a population can often give good reliability.

Third, *how* are the people in the sample *to be chosen* (what *sampling procedure*)? Table 9.4 describes different kinds of sample. Using *probability samples*, each population member has a known chance of being included in the sample, and researchers can calculate confidence limits for sampling error. But when probability sampling costs too much or takes too long, marketing researchers often take *non-probability samples*, even though their sampling error is not measurable. These varied ways of drawing samples have different costs and time limitations, as well as different accuracy and statistical properties. Which method is best depends on the needs of the research project.

Research instruments

In collecting primary data, marketing researchers have a choice of two main research instruments: the *questionnaire* and *mechanical devices*.

The *questionnaire* is by far the most common instrument. Broadly speaking, a questionnaire consists of a set of questions presented to a respondent for his or her answers. The questionnaire is very flexible – there are many ways to ask questions. Questionnaires need to be developed carefully and tested before their large-scale use. A carelessly prepared questionnaire usually contains several errors (see Table 9.5).

In preparing a questionnaire, the marketing researcher must decide what questions to ask, the form of the questions, the wording of the questions and the ordering of the questions. Questionnaires frequently leave out questions that need answering, but include questions that cannot be answered, will not be answered, or need not be answered. Each question should be checked to see that it contributes to the research objectives.

The *form* of the question can influence the response. Marketing researchers distinguish between closed-end and open-end questions. **Closed-end questions** include all the possible answers, and subjects make choices among them. Part A of Table 9.6 shows the most common forms of closed-end questions as they might appear in an SAS survey of airline

Closed-end questions— Questions that include all the possible answers and allow subjects to make choices among them.

Suppose that an adventure holiday director had prepared the following questionnaire to use in interviewing the parents of prospective campers. How would you assess each question?

1. What is your income to the nearest hundred euros?
   People don't usually know their income to the nearest hundred euros, nor do they want to reveal their income that closely. Moreover, a researcher should never open a questionnaire with such a personal question.
2. Are you a strong or a weak supporter of overnight camping for your children?
   What do 'strong' and 'weak' mean?
3. Do your children behave themselves well on adventure holidays?
   Yes ( ) No ( )
   'Behave' is a relative term. Furthermore, are 'yes' and 'no' the best response options for this question? Besides, will people want to answer this? Why ask the question in the first place?
4. How many adventure holiday operators mailed literature to you last April? This April?
   Who can remember this?
5. What are the most salient and determinant attributes in your evaluation of adventure holidays?
   What are 'salient' and 'determinant' attributes? Don't use big words on me!
6. Do you think it is right to deprive your child of the opportunity to grow into a mature person through the experience of adventure holidays?
   A loaded question. Given the bias, how can any parent answer 'yes'?

Table 9.5 A 'questionable questionnaire'

Table 9.6 Types of question

A. Closed-end questions		B. Open-end questions	
Name	**Description**	**Name**	**Description**
Dichotomous	A question offering two answer choices.	Completely unstructured	A question that respondents can answer in an almost unlimited number of ways.
Multiple choice	A question offering three or more choices.	Word association	Words are presented one at a time, and respondents mention the first word that comes to mind.
Likert scale	A statement with which the respondent shows the amount of agreement or disagreement.	Sentence completion	Incomplete sentences are presented one at a time, and respondents complete the sentence.
Semantic differential	A scale is inscribed between two bipolar words, and the respondent selects the point that represents the direction and intensity of his or her feelings.	Story completion	An incomplete story is presented, and respondents are asked to complete it.
Importance scale	A scale that rates the importance of some attribute from 'not at all important' to 'extremely important'.	Picture completion	A picture of two characters is presented, with one making a statement. Respondents are asked to identify with the other and fill in the empty balloon.
Rating scale	A scale that rates some attribute from 'poor' to 'excellent'.	Thematic Apperception Tests (TAT)	A picture is presented, and respondents are asked to make up a story about what they think is happening or may happen in the picture.
Intention-to-buy scale	A scale that describes the respondent's intentions to buy.		

Table 9.6 continued

Table 9.6 (cont'd)

A. Closed-end questions: example

'In arranging this trip, did you personally phone SAS?'   Yes ☐   No ☐

'With whom are you travelling on this flight?'

No one ☐	Children only	☐
Spouse ☐	Business associates/friends/relatives	☐
Spouse and children ☐	An organised tour group	☐

'Small airlines generally give better service than large ones.'

Strongly disagree	Disagree	Neither agree nor disagree	Agree	Strongly agree
1 ☐	2 ☐	3 ☐	4 ☐	5 ☐

SAS Airlines

Large	__x__:____:____:____:____:____	Small
Experienced	____:____:____:____:_x_:____	Inexperienced
Modern	____:____:____:_x_:____:____	Old-fashioned

'Airline food service to me is . . .'

Extremely important	Very important	Somewhat important	Not very important	Not at all important
1 _____	2 _____	3 _____	4 _____	5 _____

'SAS's food service is . . .'

Excellent	Very good	Good	Fair	Poor
1 _____	2 _____	3 _____	4 _____	5 _____

'If in-flight telephone service were available on a long flight, I would . . .'

Definitely buy	Probably buy	Not certain	Probably not buy	Definitely not buy
1 _____	2 _____	3 _____	4 _____	5 _____

B. Open-end questions: example

'What is your opinion of SAS?' _____

'What is the first word that comes to your mind when you hear the following?'

Airline _____

SAS _____

Travel _____

'When I choose an airline, the most important consideration in my decision is

_____ .'

'I flew SAS a few days ago. I noticed that the exterior and interior of the plane had very bright colours. This aroused in me the following thoughts and feelings.' Now complete the story.

Fill in the empty balloon.

Make up a story about what you see.

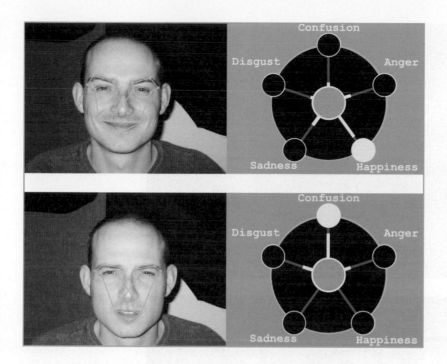

Electronic measures of consumer response allow marketers to look inside the brain or measure facial expressions to examine the response to marketing stimuli.
SOURCE: Integrated Media Systems Centre.

users. **Open-end questions** allow respondents to answer in their own words. The most common forms are shown in part B of Table 9.6. Open-end questions often reveal more than closed-end questions because respondents are not limited in their answers. Open-end questions are especially useful in exploratory research in which the researcher is trying to find out *what* people think, but not measuring *how many* people think in a certain way. Closed-end questions, on the other hand, provide answers that are easier to interpret and tabulate.

Researchers should also use care in the *wording* of questions. They should use simple, direct, unbiased wording. The questions should be pre-tested before use. The *ordering* of questions is also important. The first question should create interest if possible. Ask difficult or personal questions last, so that respondents do not become defensive. The questions should be in a logical order.

Although questionnaires are the most common research instrument, *mechanical instruments* are also used. We discussed two mechanical instruments – people meters and supermarket scanners – earlier in the chapter. Another group of mechanical devices measures subjects' physical responses. For example, a pupilometer tracks a person's eye movements and measures their interest in different stimuli by measuring pupil dilation. These machines are used extensively in the development and testing of Web designs. Once restricted to detecting external indicators of responses to stimuli, researchers are now looking inside the brain to observe responses to stimuli. A MEG (magnetoencephalograph) captures brain functions millisecond by millisecond to record how a brain responds to stimuli, such as an ad or new design, while magnetic resonance imaging (MRI) shows visual portrayals of a brain's responses.[26]

Presenting the research plan

At this stage, the marketing researcher should summarise the plan in a *written proposal*. A written proposal is especially important when the research project is large and complex, or when an outside firm carries it out. The proposal should cover the management problems addressed and the research objectives, the information obtained, the sources of secondary information or methods for collecting primary data, and the way the results will help

Open-end questions— Questions that allow respondents to answer in their own words.

MEG scanner monitoring a
brain's response to stimuli.
SOURCE: (AALS picture)
Twin Vision Productions.

Pupilometer measuring where
eyes land and how long they
linger on a given item.
SOURCE: (ALMIR) picture
Twin Vision Productions.

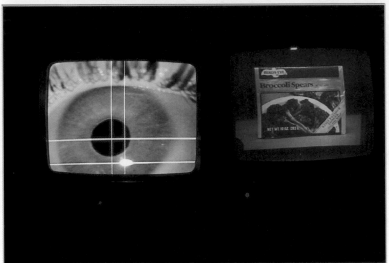

management decision making. The proposal should also include research costs. A written research plan or proposal makes sure that the marketing manager and researchers have considered all the important aspects of the research and that they agree on why and how to do the research.

Implementing the research plan

The researcher next puts the marketing research plan into action. This involves collecting, processing and analysing the information. Data collection can be by the company's marketing research staff or, more usually, by outside firms. The company keeps more control over the collection process and data quality by using its staff. However, outside firms that specialise in data collection can often do the job more quickly and at lower cost.

The data collection phase of the marketing research process is generally the most expensive and the most subject to error. The researcher should watch fieldwork closely to make sure that the plan is implemented correctly and to guard against problems with contacting respondents, with respondents who refuse to cooperate or who give biased or dishonest answers, and with interviewers who make mistakes or take short cuts.

Researchers must process and analyse the collected data to isolate important information and findings. They need to check data from questionnaires for accuracy and completeness, and code it for computer analysis. The researchers then tabulate the results and compute averages and other statistical measures.

Interpreting and reporting the findings

The researcher must now interpret the findings, draw conclusions and report them to management. The researcher should not try to overwhelm managers with numbers and fancy statistical techniques. Rather, the researcher should present important findings that are useful in the important decisions faced by management.

However, interpretation should not be by the researchers alone. They are often experts in research design and statistics, but the marketing manager knows more about the problem and the decisions needed. In many cases, findings can be interpreted in different ways and discussions between researchers and managers will help point to the best interpretations. The manager will also want to check that the research project was conducted properly and that all the necessary analysis was completed. Or, after seeing the findings, the manager may have additional questions that can be answered from the data. Finally, the manager is the one who must ultimately decide what action the research suggests. The researchers may even make the data directly available to marketing managers so that they can perform new analyses and test new relationships on their own.

Interpretation is an important phase of the marketing process. The best research is meaningless if the manager blindly accepts wrong interpretations from the researcher. Similarly, managers may have biased interpretations – they tend to accept research results that show what they expected and to reject those that they did not expect or hope for. Thus managers and researchers must work together closely when interpreting research results and both share responsibility for the research process and resulting decisions.

Demand estimation

When a company finds an attractive market, it must estimate that market's current size and future potential carefully. The company can lose a considerable amount of profit by overestimating or underestimating the market.

Demand is measured and forecast on many levels. Figure 9.3 shows 90 types of demand measurement! Demand might be measured for six different *product levels* (product item, product form, product line, company sales, industry sales and total sales), five different *space levels* (customer, territory, country, region, world), and three different *time levels* (short range, medium range and long range).

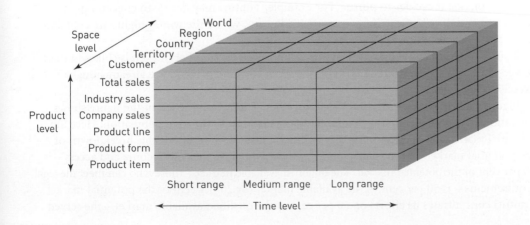

Figure 9.3 Ninety types of demand measurement ($6 \times 5 \times 3$)

Each demand measure serves a specific purpose. A company might forecast short-run total demand for a product as a basis for ordering raw materials, planning production and borrowing cash. Or it might forecast long-run regional demand for a big product line as a basis for designing a market expansion strategy.

Defining the market

Market—The set of all actual and potential buyers of a product or service.

Industry—A group of firms which offer a product or class of products that are close substitutes for each other. The set of all sellers of a product or service.

Potential market—The set of consumers who profess some level of interest in a particular product or service.

Available market—The set of consumers who have interest, income and access to a particular product or service.

Qualified available market—The set of consumers who have interest, income, access and qualifications for a particular product or service.

Served market (target market)—The part of the qualified available market that the company decides to pursue.

Penetrated market—The set of consumers who have already bought a particular product or service.

To economists, a market describes all the buyers and sellers who transact over some good or service. Thus the soft-drink market consists of sellers such as Coca-Cola, Pepsi-Cola, Tango and Lilt and all the consumers who buy soft drinks. The economist's interest is the structure, conduct and performance of each market.

To a marketer, a **market** is the set of all actual and potential buyers of a product or service. A market is the set of buyers and an **industry** is the set of sellers. The size of a market hinges on the number of buyers who might exist for a particular market offer. Potential buyers for something have three characteristics: *interest, income* and *access*.

Consider the consumer market for Finnish Tunturi exercise cycles. To assess its market, Tunturi must first estimate the number of consumers who have a potential interest in owning an exercise bike. To do this, the company could contact a random sample of consumers and ask the following question: 'Do you have an interest in buying and owning an exercise bike?'. If one person out of 10 says yes, Tunturi can assume that 10 per cent of the total number of consumers would constitute the potential market for exercise bikes. The **potential market** is the set of consumers who profess some level of interest in a particular product or service.

Consumer interest alone is not enough to define the exercise bike market. Potential consumers must have enough income to afford the product. They must be able to answer yes to the following question: 'Would you pay €500 for an exercise bike?'. The higher the price, the lower the number of people who can answer yes to this question. Thus market size depends on both interest and income.

Access barriers further reduce exercise bike market size. If Tunturi has no distributors for its products in some areas, potential consumers in those areas are not available as customers. The **available market** is the set of consumers who have interest, income and access to a particular product or service.

Tunturi might restrict sales to certain groups. Excessive repetitive exercise can damage young children, so sales of exercise bikes to anyone under 12 years of age may be discouraged. The remaining adults make up the **qualified available market** – the set of consumers who have interest, income, access and qualifications for the product or service.

Tunturi now has the choice of going after the whole qualified available market or concentrating on selected segments. Tunturi's **served market** is the part of the qualified available market it decides to pursue. For example, Tunturi may decide to concentrate its marketing and distribution efforts in northern Europe, where the winter nights are cold and long. This becomes its served market.

Tunturi and its competitors will end up selling a certain number of exercise bikes in their served market. The **penetrated market** is the set of consumers who have already bought exercise bikes.

Figure 9.4 brings all these market ideas together. The bar on the left of the figure shows the ratio of the potential market – all interested persons – to the total population. Here the potential market is 10 per cent. The bar on the right shows several possible breakdowns of the potential market. The available market – those who have interest, income and access – is 40 per cent of the potential market. The qualified available market – those who can meet the legal requirements – is 50 per cent of the available market (or 20 per cent of the potential market). Tunturi concentrates its efforts on 50 per cent of the qualified available market – the served

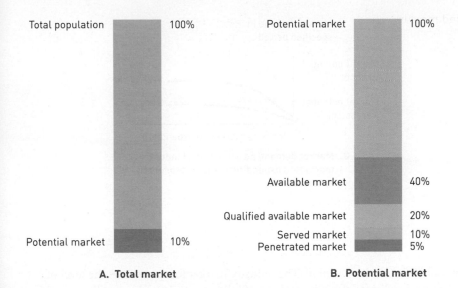

Figure 9.4 **Levels of market definition**

Total population — 100%

Potential market — 10%

A. Total market

Potential market — 100%

Available market — 40%

Qualified available market — 20%

Served market — 10%

Penetrated market — 5%

B. Potential market

market, which is 10 per cent of the potential market. Finally, Tunturi and its competitors have already penetrated 50 per cent of the served market (or 5 per cent of the potential market).

These market definitions are a useful tool for marketing planning. If Tunturi is unsatisfied with current sales, it can take a number of actions. It can expand to other available markets in Europe or elsewhere. It can lower its price to expand the size of the potential market. It can try to attract a larger percentage of buyers from its served market through stronger promotion or distribution efforts to current target consumers. Or it can try to expand the potential market by increasing its advertising to convert non-interested consumers into interested consumers. Concern over heart disease means that many middle-aged people who have avoided exercise for years are being encouraged to do more. Perhaps Tunturi can work through the health industry to attract these.

Measuring current market demand

Marketers need to estimate three aspects of current market demand: total market demand, area market demand, and actual sales and market shares.

Estimating total market demand

The **total market demand** for a product or service is the total volume that would be bought by a defined consumer group in a defined geographic area in a defined time period in a defined marketing environment under a defined level and mix of industry marketing effort.

Total market demand is not a fixed number, but a function of the stated conditions. One of these conditions, for example, is the level and mix of industry marketing effort. Another is the state of the environment. Part A of Figure 9.5 shows the relationship between total market demand and these conditions. The horizontal axis shows different possible levels of industry marketing expenditure in a given period. The vertical axis shows the resulting demand level. The curve represents the estimated level of market demand for varying levels of industry marketing expenditure. Some base sales (called the *market minimum*) would take place without any marketing expenditure. Greater marketing expenditures would yield higher levels of demand, first at an increasing rate and then at a decreasing rate. Marketing expenditures above a certain level would not cause much more demand, suggesting an upper limit to

Total market demand—The total volume of a product or service that would be bought by a defined consumer group in a defined geographic area in a defined time period in a defined marketing environment under a defined level and mix of industry marketing effort.

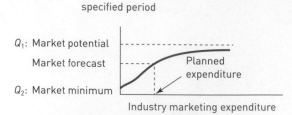

A. **Market demand as a function of industry marketing expenditure (assumes a marketing environment of prosperity)**

B. **Market demand as a function of industry marketing expenditure (under prosperity vs. recession)**

Figure 9.5 **Market demand**

market demand called the *market potential*. The industry market forecast shows the level of market demand corresponding to the planned level of industry marketing expenditure in the given environment.[27]

The distance between the market minimum and the market potential shows the overall sensitivity of demand to marketing efforts. We can think of two extreme types of market: the *expandable* and the *non-expandable*. An expandable market, such as the market for DVD recorders, is one whose size depends upon the level of industry marketing expenditures. For Figure 9.5A, in an expandable market, the distance between Q_1 and Q_2 would be fairly large. In a non-expandable market, such as that for opera, marketing expenditures generate little demand; the distance between Q_1 and Q_2 would be fairly small. Organisations selling in a non-expandable market can take **primary demand** – total demand for all brands of a given product or service – as given. They concentrate their marketing resources on building **selective demand** – demand for *their* brand of the product or service.

Given a different marketing environment, we must estimate a new market demand curve. For example, the market for exercise bikes is stronger during prosperity than during recession. Figure 9.5B shows the relationship of market demand to the environment. A given level of marketing expenditure will always result in more demand during prosperity than it would during a recession. The main point is that marketers should carefully define the situation for which they are estimating market demand.

Companies have developed various practical methods for estimating total market demand. We will illustrate two here. Suppose EMI wants to estimate the total annual sales of recorded compact discs. A common way to estimate total market demand is as follows:

$$Q = n \times q \times p$$

where

Q = total market demand;
n = number of buyers in the market;
q = quantity purchased by an average buyer per year; and
p = price of an average unit.

Thus, if there are 10 million buyers of CDs each year and the average buyer buys six discs a year and the average price is €20, then the total market demand for cassette tapes is €1,200 million (= 10,000,000 × 6 × €20).

A variation on the preceding equation is the *chain ratio method*. Using this method, the analyst multiplies a base number by a chain of adjusting percentages. For example, the United Kingdom has no national service, so the British Army needs to attract 20,000 new male recruits each year. There is a problem here, since the Army is already under strength and the

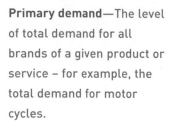

Primary demand—The level of total demand for all brands of a given product or service – for example, the total demand for motor cycles.

Selective demand—The demand for a given brand of a product or service.

population of 16- to 19-year-olds is declining. The marketing question is whether this is a reasonable target in relation to the market potential. The Army estimates market potential using the following method:

Total number of male secondary-school leavers	1,200,000
Percentage who are militarily qualified (no physical, emotional, or mental handicaps)	× 0.50
Percentage of those qualified who are potentially interested in military service	× 0.05
Percentage of those qualified and interested in military service who consider the Army the preferred service	× 0.60

This chain of numbers shows a market potential of 18,000 recruits. Since this is less than the target number of recruits sought, the Army needs to do a better job of marketing itself. They responded by doing motivational research which showed that existing advertising did not attract the target age group, although a military career did give them what they wanted. A new campaign therefore aimed to increase the attractiveness of a military career to both men and women.

Estimating actual sales and market shares

Besides estimating total and area demand, a company will want to know the actual industry sales in its market. Thus it must identify its competitors and estimate their sales.

The industry's trade association will often collect and publish total industry sales, although not listing individual company sales separately. In this way, each company can evaluate its performance against the industry as a whole. Suppose the company's sales are increasing at a rate of 5 per cent a year and industry sales are increasing at 10 per cent. This company is losing its relative standing in the industry.

Another way to estimate sales is to buy reports from marketing research firms that audit total sales and brand sales. For example, Nielsen and other marketing research firms use scanner data to audit the retail sales of various product categories in supermarkets and pharmacies, and sell this information to interested companies. A company can obtain data on total product category sales as well as brand sales. It can compare its performance with that of the total industry or any particular competitor to see whether it is gaining or losing in its relative standing.[28]

Forecasting future demand

Having looked at ways to estimate current demand, we now examine ways to forecast future market demand. **Forecasting** is the art of estimating future demand by anticipating what buyers are likely to do under a given set of conditions. Very few products or services lend themselves to easy forecasting. Those that do generally involve a product with steady sales, or sales growth in a stable competitive situation. But most markets do not have stable total and company demand, so good forecasting becomes a key factor in company success. Poor forecasting can lead to excessively large inventories, costly price markdowns, or lost sales due to being out of stock. The more unstable the demand, the more the company needs accurate forecasts and elaborate forecasting procedures.

Forecasting—The art of estimating future demand by anticipating what buyers are likely to do under a given set of conditions.

Huge investments ride on the back of forecasts. Current forecasts show a huge growth in the European satellite navigation (Sat-Nav) market for private automobiles from over €500 million in 2004. The rest of the Sat-Nav market (recreational marine craft, agriculture, etc.) is also about €500 million. The Europe Space Agency is developing Galileo as an alternative to the American global positioning system (GPS). Galileo will need a minimum of 30 four-tonne satellites in medium Earth orbit (20,000 km altitude) with three additional geostationary relay satellites in higher orbit. Total minimum cost: €3.5 billion. On the back of this the European Space Agency have to forecast how much of the market for launching the satellites they can grab and launch successfully. Meanwhile many consumers are uncertain about the value and usefulness of the €1,000 to €4,000 that in-car Sat-Nav systems cost.[29]

Companies commonly use a three-stage procedure to arrive at a sales forecast. First they make an *environmental forecast* (will the European politico-economy support a Sat-Nav system?), followed by an *industry forecast* (will the total Sat-Nav demand be €4 billion by 2008?) and a *company sales forecast* (what share of the Sat-Nav launch business can the European Space Agency get?). The environmental forecast calls for projecting inflation, unemployment, interest rates, consumer spending and saving, business investment, government expenditures, net exports and other environmental events important to the company. The result is a forecast of gross national product, which is used along with other indicators to forecast industry sales. Then the company prepares its sales forecast assuming a certain share of industry sales.

Companies use several specific techniques to forecast their sales. Table 9.7 lists some of these techniques. All forecasts build on one of three information bases: what people say, what people do, or what people have done. The first basis – *what people say* – involves surveying the opinions of buyers or those close to them, such as salespeople or outside experts. It includes three methods: surveys of buyer intentions, composites of sales force opinions and expert opinion. Building a forecast on *what people do* involves another method, that of putting the product into a test market to assess buyer response. The final basis – *what people have done* – involves analysing records of past buying behaviour or using time-series analysis or statistical demand analysis.

Table 9.7 Common sales forecasting techniques

Based on	Methods
What people say	Surveys of buyers' intentions
	Composite sales force opinions
	Expert opinion
What people do	Test markets
What people have done	Time-series analysis
	Leading indicators
	Statistical demand analysis

Buyers' intentions

One way to forecast what buyers will do is to ask them directly. This suggests that the forecaster should survey buyers. Surveys are especially valuable if the buyers have clearly formed intentions, will carry them out and can describe them to interviewers. A typical intention to buy survey would ask:

Do you intend to buy a car within the next six months?										
0.0 No chance	0.1	0.2 Slight chance	0.3	0.4 Fair chance	0.5	0.6 Good chance	0.7	0.8 Strong chance	0.9	1.0 For certain

This is a *purchase probability scale*. In addition, the various surveys ask about the consumer's present and future personal finances and their expectations about the economy. Consumer durable goods companies subscribe to these indices to help them anticipate significant shifts in consumer buying intentions, so that they can adjust their production and marketing plans accordingly. For *business buying*, various agencies carry out intention surveys about plant, equipment and materials purchases. These measures need adjusting when conducted across nations and cultures. Overestimation of intention to buy is higher in southern Europe than in northern Europe and the United States. In Asia, the Japanese tend to make fewer overstatements than the Chinese.[30]

Composite of sales force opinions

When buyer interviewing is impractical, the company may base its sales forecasts on information provided by the sales force. The company typically asks its salespeople to estimate sales by product for their individual territories. It then adds up the individual estimates to arrive at an overall sales forecast.

Few companies use their sales force's estimates without some adjustments. Salespeople are biased observers. They may be naturally pessimistic or optimistic, or they may go to one extreme or another because of recent sales setbacks or successes. Furthermore, they are often unaware of larger economic developments and do not always know how their company's marketing plans will affect future sales in their territories. They may understate demand so that the company will set a low sales quota. They may not have the time to prepare careful estimates or may not consider it worthwhile.

Accepting these biases, a number of benefits can be gained by involving the sales force in forecasting. Salespeople may have better insights into developing trends than any other group. After participating in the forecasting process, the salespeople may have greater confidence in their quotas and more incentive to achieve them. Also, such grass-roots forecasting provides estimates broken down by product, territory, customer and salesperson.

Expert opinion

Companies can also obtain forecasts by turning to experts. Experts include dealers, distributors, suppliers, marketing consultants and trade associations. Thus motor vehicle companies survey their dealers periodically for their forecasts of short-term demand. Dealer estimates, however, are subject to the same strengths and weaknesses as sales force estimates.

Many companies buy economic and industry forecasts. These forecasting specialists are in a better position than the company to prepare economic forecasts because they have more data available and more forecasting expertise.

Occasionally companies will invite a special group of experts to prepare a forecast. They may exchange views and come up with a group estimate (group discussion method). Or they may supply their estimates individually, with the company analyst combining them into a single estimate (pooling of individual estimates). Or they may supply individual estimates and assumptions reviewed by a company analyst, revised and followed by further rounds of estimation (Delphi method).

Experts can provide good insights upon which to base forecasts, but they can also be wrong (see Marketing Insights 9.2). Where possible, the company should back up experts' opinions with estimates obtained using other methods.

marketing insights

9.2 Sometimes 'expert opinion' isn't all it should be

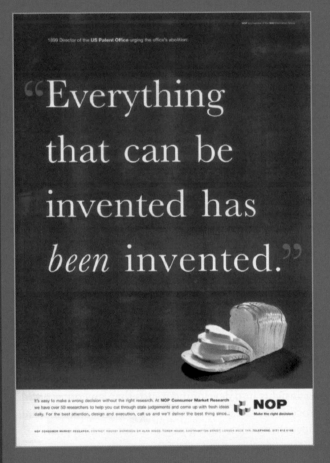

SOURCE: NOP Research Group Ltd.

Before you rely too heavily on expert opinion, you might be interested in learning how some past 'experts' did with their predictions.

Technology:

- 'Everything that can be invented has been invented' (Director of the US Patent Office, 1899).
- 'Rail travel at high speed is not possible, because passengers, unable to breathe, would die of asphyxia' (Dr Dioysy Larder in 1828 – the year Stephenson's *Rocket* commenced service).

9.2...

- 'No large steamship will ever cross the Atlantic, since it would require more coal than it could carry' (Dr Larder again, this time in 1859). Two years later the *Great Eastern* crossed the Atlantic.

- 'Flight by machines heavier than air is unpractical and insignificant, if not impossible' (Simon Newcombe, 1901). Eighteen months later the Wright brothers flew.

- 'Airplanes are interesting toys, but of no military value' (France's Marshal Foch, 1911).

- 'The energy produced by the breaking down of the atom is a very poor kind of thing. Anyone who expects a source of power from the transformation is talking moonshine' (Ernest Rutherford, 1919, after *he* had first split the atom).

- 'I think there's a world market for about five computers' (Thomas J. Watson, IBM Chairman, 1943).

- 'By 1980, all power (electric, atomic, solar) is likely to be virtually costless' (Henry Luce, founder and publisher of *Time*, *Life* and *Fortune*, 1956).

- 'With over 50 foreign cars already on sale here, the Japanese auto industry isn't likely to carve out a big slice of the US market for itself' (*Business Week*, 1958).

SOURCE: NOP Research Group Ltd

Entertainment:

- 'If Beethoven's Seventh Symphony is not by some means abridged, it will soon fall into disuse' (Philip Hale, nineteenth-century music critic).

- 'Who the hell wants to hear actors talk?' (Harry Warner, founder of Warner Bros).

- 'TV won't be able to hold on to any market it captures after the first six months' (Daryl F. Zanuck, head of 20th Century Fox, 1946).

- 'We don't like their sound. Groups of guitars are on the way out' (Decca Recording Company, 1962, when turning down the Beatles). Pye, Columbia and HMV also rejected the Beatles before their signing with EMI.

- 'Unsinkable' (claim made by the *Titanic*'s builders, Harland and Wolff, in 1912, for the ship that cost $7.5 million to build). 'James Cameron has spent $200 million on a movie and it's a dog. He's finally had it!' (Quote repeated by film critic Adam Smith, referring to the blockbuster film *Titanic*).

Environment:

- 'Since populations tend to increase geometrically [1, 2, 4, 8, . . .] and food supply arithmetically [1, 2, 3, 4, . . .], the starvation of Great Britain is inevitable and imminent' (Thomas Robert Malthus, 1798).

- 'Population will soon outstrip food production' (Lester Brown of the Worldwatch Institute, 1973).

- 'Population will increase faster than world food production, so food prices will rise between 35 per cent and 115 per cent by 2000' (*Global 2000*, report to the President of the United States).

...9.2

'We could use up all of the proven reserves of oil in the entire world by the end of the next decade' (Club of Rome, 1972). They also made similar predictions for the reserves of aluminium, copper, lead, natural gas, silver, tin and zinc.

The results so far: known oil reserves are over 1,000 billion barrels, supplies have pushed metals, mineral and food prices down 40 per cent since 1960, and calories consumed per capita in the Third World are 27 per cent higher than in the 1960s!

SOURCES: Patrick McGilligan, *Clint: The Life and Legend* (London: HarperCollins, 1999); 'Sometimes expert opinion isn't all it should be', *Go* (September–October 1985), p. 2; Terry Coleman, *The Liners* (Harmondsworth: Penguin, 1976); Stephen Pile, *The Book of Heroic Failures* (London: Futura, 1980); Charles Gillett, *The Sound of the City: The rise of rock and roll* (London: Souvenir, 1983); 'Environmental scares: plenty of gloom', *The Economist* (20 December 1997); William A. Sherien, *The Fortune Seller: The big business of buying and selling predictions* (John Wiley, 1998); 'We woz wrong', *The Economist* (18 December 1999, pp. 61–2); *Encarta: Multimedia encyclopaedia* (Microsoft, 2000).

Test-market method

Where buyers do not plan their purchases carefully or where experts are not available or reliable, the company may want to conduct a direct test market. This is especially useful in forecasting new-product sales or established-product sales in a new distribution channel or territory. Test marketing is discussed along with new-product development in Chapter 14.

Time-series analysis

Many firms base their forecasts on past sales. They assume that statistical analysis can uncover the causes of past sales. Then analysts can use the causal relations to predict future sales. **Time-series analysis** consists of breaking down the original sales into four components – trend, cycle, season and erratic components – then recombining these components to produce the sales forecast.

Trend is the long-term, underlying pattern of growth or decline in sales resulting from basic changes in population, capital formation and technology. It is found by fitting a straight or curved line through past sales or technical performance.

Time-series analysis— Breaking down past sales into their trend, cycle, season and erratic components, then recombining these components to produce a sales forecast.

Trend—The long-term, underlying pattern of sales growth or decline resulting from basic changes in population, capital formation and technology.

Moore's Law is a technological trend projection based on Intel's founder, Gordon Moore's, observation in the 1970s that the number of transistors on a silicon chip (and hence computing power and speed) doubles every 18 months. He got it slightly wrong: since 1971 it has doubled every 1.96 years. But, as he observes, 'no exponential is forever'. One limit to Moore's Law is the size of electrons. Another is the heat generated by microprocessors. By 2005 microprocessors will be operating at the heat of a nuclear reactor and by 2010 at the heat of a rocket nozzle. And that is in the middle of your lap top![31]

Cycle captures the medium-term, wavelike movement of sales resulting from changes in general economic and competitive activity. The cyclical component can be useful for medium-range forecasting. Cyclical swings, however, are difficult to predict because they do not occur on a regular basis. **Seasonality** refers to a consistent pattern of sales movements within the year. The term *season* describes any recurrent hourly, daily, weekly, monthly or quarterly sales pattern. The seasonal component may relate to weather factors, holidays and trade customs. The seasonal pattern provides a norm for forecasting short-range sales. Finally, *erratic events* include fads, strikes, snow storms, earthquakes, riots, fires and other disturbances. These components, by definition, are unpredictable and should be removed from past data to see the more normal behaviour of sales.

Suppose that ING sells 12,000 new life insurance policies this year and wants to predict next year's December sales. The long-term trend shows a 5 per cent sales growth rate per year. This information alone suggests sales next year of 12,600 ($= 12,000 \times 1.05$). However, a business recession is expected next year, which will probably result in total sales achieving only 90 per cent of the expected trend-adjusted sales. Sales next year are therefore more likely to be 11,340 ($= 12,600 \times 0.90$). If sales were the same each month, monthly sales would be 945 ($= 11,340/12$). However, December is an above-average month for insurance policy sales, with a seasonal index standing at 1.30. Therefore December sales may be as high as 1,228.5 ($= 945 \times 1.3$). The company expects no erratic events, such as strikes or new insurance regulations. Thus it estimates new policy sales next December at 1,228.5 policies.

> **Cycle**—The medium-term wavelike movement of sales resulting from changes in general economic and competitive activity.
>
> **Seasonality**—The recurrent consistent pattern of sales movements within the year.

Leading indicators

Many companies try to forecast their sales by finding one or more **leading indicators**: that is, other time series that change in the same direction but ahead of company sales. For example, a plumbing supply company might find that its sales lag behind the housing starts index by about four months. An index of housing starts would then be a useful leading indicator.

> **Leading indicators**—Time series that change in the same direction but in advance of company sales.

Statistical demand analysis

Time-series analysis treats past and future sales as a function of time, rather than as a function of any real demand factors. But many real factors affect the sales of any product. **Statistical demand analysis** is a set of statistical procedures used to discover the most important real factors affecting sales and their relative influence. The factors most commonly analysed are prices, income, population and promotion.

Statistical demand analysis consists of expressing sales (Q) as a dependent variable and trying to explain sales as a function of a number of independent demand variables $X_1, X_2, \ldots, X_n$. That is:

$$Q = f(X_1, X_2, \ldots, X_n)$$

Using multiple-regression analysis, various equations can be fitted to the data to find the best predicting factors and equation.

For example, the South of Scotland Electricity Board developed an equation that predicted the annual sales of washing machines (Q) to be:[32]

$$Q = 210,739 - 703P + 69H + 20Y$$

where

P = average installed price;
H = new single-family homes connected to utilities; and
Y = per capita income.

> **Statistical demand analysis**—A set of statistical procedures used to discover the most important real factors affecting sales and their relative influence; the most commonly analysed factors are prices, income, population and promotion.

Thus in a year when an average installed price is £387 (€635), there are 5,000 new connected homes and the average per capita income is £4,800, from the equation we would predict the actual sales of washing machines to be 379,678 units:

$$Q = 210{,}739 - 703(387) + 69(5{,}000) + 20(4{,}800)$$

The equation was found to be 95 per cent accurate. If the equation predicted as well as this for other regions, it would serve as a useful forecasting tool. Marketing management would predict next year's per capita income, new homes and prices, and use them to make forecasts.

Statistical demand analysis can be very complex and the marketer must take care in designing, conducting and interpreting such analysis. Yet constantly improving computer technology has made statistical demand analysis an increasingly popular approach to forecasting.

Information analysis

Information gathered by the company's marketing information systems often requires more analysis, and sometimes managers may need more help in applying it to marketing problems and decisions. This help may include advanced statistical analysis to learn more about both the relationships within a set of data and their statistical reliability. Such analysis allows managers to go beyond means and standard deviations in the data. In an examination of consumer non-durable goods in the Netherlands, regression analysis gave a model that forecast a brand's market share (B_t) based upon predicted marketing activity:[33]

$$B_t = -7.85 - 1.45P_t + 0.08A_{t-1} + 1.23D_t$$

where

P_t = relative price of brand;
A_{t-1} = advertising share in the previous period; and
D_t = effective store distribution.

This, and models like it, can help answer marketing questions such as:

- What are the chief variables affecting my sales and how important is each one?
- If I raised my price 10 per cent and increased my advertising expenditures 20 per cent, what would happen to sales?
- How much should I spend on advertising?
- What are the best predictors of which consumers are likely to buy my brand versus my competitor's brand?
- What are the best variables for segmenting my market and how many segments exist?

Information analysis might also involve a collection of mathematical models that will help marketers make better decisions. Each model represents some real system, process or outcome. These models can help answer the questions of *what if?* and *which is best?* During the past 30 years, marketing scientists have developed numerous models to help marketing managers make better marketing-mix decisions, design sales territories and sales-call plans, select sites for retail outlets, develop optimal advertising mixes and forecast new-product sales. One implication of the use of mathematical models and other forms of market measurement is their dependencey on the accuracy of data collected.

Since models are looking for a relationship between, say, advertising exposure and sales, the more accurately advertising exposure is measured, the greater will be the advertising impact revealed. For a long time TV ratings were the most accurately measured media responses, hence skewing expenditure towards TV advertising. More recently, radio and poster advertising have made advances in the measurement of their media responses and grabbed a higher share of advertising spend, so stealing share from commercial TV.[34]

Distributing information

Marketing information has no value until managers use it to make better marketing decisions. The information gathered through marketing intelligence and marketing research must be distributed to the right marketing managers at the right time. Most companies have centralised marketing information systems that provide managers with regular performance reports, intelligence updates, and reports on the results of studies. Managers need these routine reports for making regular planning, implementation and control decisions. But marketing managers may also need non-routine information for special situations and on-the-spot decisions. For example, a sales manager having trouble with a large customer may want a summary of the account's sales and profitability over the past year. Or a retail store manager who has run out of a best-selling product may want to know the current inventory levels in the chain's other stores.

Developments in information technology have caused a revolution in information distribution. With recent advances in computers, software and telecommunications, most companies have decentralised their marketing information systems. In most companies today, marketing managers have direct access to the information network, at any time and from virtually any location.

While working at a home office, in a hotel room, on an aeroplane – any place where they can turn on a laptop computer and phone in – today's managers can obtain information from company databases or outside information services, analyse the information using statistical packages and models, prepare reports using word processing and presentation software, and communicate with others in the network through electronic communications. Such systems offer exciting prospects. They allow managers to get the information they need directly and quickly and to tailor it to their own needs.

International studies

The globalisation of business is extending the task facing managers. Now managers have to manage campaigns across countries and within different countries. International marketing researchers follow the same steps as domestic researchers, from defining the research problem and developing a research plan to interpreting and reporting the results. However, these researchers often face more and different problems. Whereas domestic researchers deal with fairly homogeneous markets within a single country, international researchers deal with markets in many different countries. These different markets often vary dramatically in their levels of economic development, cultures and customs, and buying patterns. Even gathering basic secondary information in many countries is difficult, and primary information can present even more problems. Despite the EU's increased integration and expansion, information gathering across the EU is far from integrated.

In many foreign markets, the international researcher has a difficult time finding good *secondary data*. Whereas many marketing researchers can obtain reliable secondary data on their domestic market, many countries have almost no research services at all. Some international market research firms operate in several large economies, but most countries are not covered by any. Thus, even when secondary information is available, it must usually be obtained from many different sources on a country-by-country basis, making the information difficult to combine or compare.

Because of the scarcity of good secondary data, international researchers must often collect their own primary data. Here again, researchers face problems not encountered domestically. For example, they may find it difficult simply to develop appropriate samples. Whereas researchers in developed countries can use current telephone directories, census data and any of several sources of socio-economic data to construct samples, such information is lacking or unreliable in many countries. Reaching respondents is often not so easy in other parts of the world. In some countries, very few people have private telephones. In other countries, the postal system is notoriously unreliable. In Brazil, for instance, an estimated 30 per cent of the mail is never delivered. In many developing countries, poor roads and transportation systems make certain areas hard to reach, and personal interviews difficult and expensive.[35]

Differences in culture from country to country cause additional problems for international researchers. Language is the most obvious culprit. For example, questionnaires must be prepared in one language and then translated into the languages of each country researched. Responses must then be translated back into the original language for analysis and interpretation. This adds to research costs and increases the risks of error:

> Translating a questionnaire from one language to another is far from easy . . . Many points are [lost], because many idioms, phrases and statements mean different things in different cultures. A Danish executive observed: 'Check this out by having a different translator put back into English what you've translated from the English. You'll get the shock of your life. I remember [an example in which] "out of sight, out of mind" had become "invisible things are insane".'[36]

Buying roles and consumer decision processes vary greatly from country to country, further complicating international marketing research. Consumers in different countries also vary in their attitudes towards marketing research. People in one country may be very willing to respond, while in other countries non-response can be a difficult problem. For example, custom in some Islamic countries prohibits people from talking with strangers – a researcher simply may not be allowed to speak by phone with women about brand attitudes or buying behaviour. In certain cultures, research questions are often considered too personal. For example, in many Latin American countries, people may feel too embarrassed to talk with researchers about their choice of shampoo, deodorant or other personal-care products. Even when respondents are *willing* to respond, they may not be *able* to because of high functional illiteracy rates. And middle-class people in developing countries often make false claims in order to appear well off. For example, in a study of tea consumption in India, over 70 per cent of middle-income respondents claimed that they used one of several national brands. However, the researchers had good reason to doubt these results – more than 60 per cent of the tea sold in India is unbranded generic tea.

Despite these problems, the recent growth of international marketing has resulted in a rapid increase in the use of international marketing research. Global companies have little choice but to conduct such research. Although the costs and problems associated with international research may be high, the costs of not doing it – in terms of missed opportunities and mistakes – might be even higher. Once recognised, many of the problems associated with international marketing research can be overcome or avoided.

Marketing research in small businesses and non-profit organisations

Many of the marketing research techniques discussed in this chapter also can be used by smaller organisations in a less formal manner and at little or no expense. Managers of small businesses and non-profit organisations can obtain good marketing information simply by *observing* things around them. For example, retailers can evaluate new locations by observing vehicle and pedestrian traffic. They can monitor competitor advertising by collecting ads from local media. They can evaluate their customer mix by recording how many and what kinds of customers shop in the store at different times. In addition, many small business managers routinely visit their rivals and socialise with competitors to gain insights.

Managers can conduct informal *surveys* using small convenience samples. The director of an art museum can learn what patrons think about new exhibits by conducting informal focus groups – inviting small groups to lunch and having discussions on topics of interest. Retail salespeople can talk with customers visiting the store; hospital officials can interview patients. Restaurant managers might make random phone calls during slack hours to interview consumers about where they eat out and what they think of various restaurants in the area.

Managers also can conduct their own simple *experiments*. For example, by changing the themes in regular fund-raising mailings and watching the results, a non-profit manager can find out much about which marketing strategies work best. By varying newspaper advertisements, a store manager can learn the effects of things such as ad size and position, price coupons, and media used.

Small organisations can obtain most of the secondary data available to large businesses. In addition, many associations, local media, chambers of commerce and government agencies provide special help to small organisations. Local newspapers often provide information on local shoppers and their buying patterns. Finally, small businesses can collect a considerable amount of information at very little cost on the Internet. They can scour competitor and customer websites and use Internet search engines to research specific companies and issues.

In summary, secondary data collection, observation, surveys and experiments can all be used effectively by small organisations with small budgets. Although these informal research methods are less complex and less costly, they must still be conducted carefully. Managers must think carefully about the objectives of the research, formulate questions in advance, recognise the biases introduced by smaller samples and less skilled researchers, and conduct the research systematically.[37]

> Facing declining congregations, churches are one of many cash-strapped non-profit organisations that have used market research effectively. Recognising that some churches were bucking the trend of falling and ageing church goers, they researched success factors. Some of the conclusions were simple and inexpensive to implement and not a lot to do with God: 'Be welcoming', 'make the building say "Hello!"' and 'make everybody feel important'.[38]

Market research ethics

Increasing consumer resentment has become a major problem for the research industry. This resentment has led to lower survey response rates in recent years – one study found that 38 per cent of consumers now refuse to be interviewed in an average survey, up dramatically from a decade before. Another study found that 59 per cent of consumers had refused to give information to a company because they thought it was not really needed or too personal, up from 42 per cent just five years earlier.[39] There are a number of reasons why this resistance to marketing research is rising. Much of the resistance is to do with how market research has been used and abused.

Intrusions on consumer privacy

Some consumers fear that researchers might use sophisticated techniques to probe our deepest feelings and then use this knowledge to manipulate our buying. Others may have been taken in by previous 'research surveys' that actually turned out to be attempts to sell them something. Other consumers confuse legitimate marketing research studies with telemarketing or database development efforts and say 'no' before the interviewer can even begin. Most, however, simply resent the intrusion. They dislike mail or telephone surveys that are too long or too personal or that interrupt them at inconvenient times.[40]

Misuse of research findings

Research studies can be powerful persuasion tools; companies often use study results as claims in their advertising and promotion. Today, however, many research studies appear to be little more than a search for a sales lead. In fact, in some cases, the research surveys appear to have been designed just to produce the intended effect. Few advertisers openly rig their research designs or blatantly misrepresent the findings; most abuses tend to be subtle 'stretches'. Consider the following examples:[41]

> A study by DaimlerChrysler contends that Americans overwhelmingly prefer Chrysler to Toyota after test-driving both. However, the study included just 100 people in each of two tests. More importantly, none of the people surveyed owned a foreign car, so they appear to be favourably predisposed to US cars.
>
> A poll sponsored by the disposable diaper industry asked: 'It is estimated that disposable diapers account for less than 2 per cent of the content of landfills. In contrast, beverage containers, third-class mail, and yard waste are estimated to account for about 21 per cent of landfill content. Given this, in your opinion, would it be fair to ban disposable diapers?'. Again, not surprisingly, 84 per cent said no.

In some cases, so-called independent research studies are paid for by companies with an interest in the outcome. For example, four studies compare the environmental effects of using disposable diapers to those of using cloth diapers. The two studies sponsored by the cloth diaper industry conclude that cloth diapers are more environmentally friendly while the other two studies, sponsored by the paper diaper industry, conclude just the opposite. Yet both appear to be correct *given* the underlying assumptions used.

To counter the misuse of marketing research the industry has developed broad standards, such as ESOMAR's International Code of Marketing and Social Research Practice (www.esomar.org). This code outlines researchers' responsibilities to respondents and to the general public. For example, it says that researchers should make their names and addresses available to participants, and it bans companies from representing activities like database compilation or sales and promotional pitches as research. However, many of the pseudo-research practices that damage the reputation of legitimate marketing research are conducted by sales organisations that are not committed to the market research profession.[42]

Summary

A well-designed *marketing information system* (MIS) begins and ends with the user. The MIS first *assesses information needs* by interviewing marketing managers and surveying their decision environment to determine what information is desired, needed and feasible to offer. The MIS next *develops information* and helps managers to use it more effectively. *Internal records* provide information on sales, costs, inventories, cash flows and accounts receivable and payable. Such data are quick and cheap, but must often be adapted for marketing decisions. The *marketing intelligence system* supplies marketing executives with everyday information about developments in the external marketing environment. Intelligence can come from company employees, customers, suppliers and resellers, or from monitoring published reports, conferences, advertisements, competitor actions and other activities in the environment.

Marketing research involves collecting information relevant to a specific marketing problem facing the organisation. Marketing research involves a four-step process. The first step consists of *defining the problem and setting the research objectives*. The objectives may be *exploratory*, *descriptive* or *causal*. The second step consists of developing the *research plan* for collecting data from primary and secondary sources. *Primary data collection* calls for choosing a *research approach* (observation, survey, experiment), choosing a *contact method* (mail, telephone, personal), designing a *sampling plan* (whom to survey, how many to survey and how to choose them), and developing *research instruments* (questionnaire, mechanical). The third step consists of *implementing the marketing research plan* by collecting, processing and analysing the information. The fourth step consists of *interpreting and reporting the findings*. Further information analysis helps marketing managers to apply the information, and provides advanced statistical procedures and models to develop more rigorous findings from the information.

Finally, the marketing information system distributes information gathered from internal sources, marketing intelligence and marketing research to the right managers at the right times. More and more companies are decentralising their information systems through networks that allow managers to have direct access to information. To carry out their responsibilities, marketing managers need measures of current and future market size. We define a *market* as the set of actual and potential consumers of a market offer. Consumers in the market have *interest*, *income* and *access* to the market offer. The marketer has to distinguish various levels of the market, such as the *potential market*, *available market*, *qualified available market*, *served market* and *penetrated market*.

One task is to *estimate current demand*. Marketers can estimate total demand through the chain ratio method, which involves multiplying a base number by successive percentages. For *estimating future demand*, the company can use one or a combination of seven possible forecasting methods, based on what consumers say (*buyers' intentions surveys*, *composite of sales force opinions*, *expert opinion*), what consumers do (*market tests*), or what consumers have done (*time-series analysis*, *leading indicators*, *statistical demand analysis*). The best method to use depends on the purpose of the forecast, the type of product and the availability and reliability of data.

Discussing the issues

1. You are a marketing research supplier, designing and conducting studies for a variety of companies. What is the most important thing you may do to ensure your clients will get their money's worth from your services?

2. Companies often face rapidly changing environments. Can market research information go stale? What issues does a manager face in using these research results?

3. What type of research would be appropriate in the following situations and why?

   ■ Nestlé wants to investigate the impact of children on their parents' decisions to buy breakfast foods.

   ■ A college or university bookshop wants to get some insights into how students feel about the shop's merchandise, prices and service.

   ■ L'Oréal wants to determine whether a new line of deodorants for teenagers will be profitable.

   ■ Gap is considering where to locate a new store in a fast-growing suburb.

   ■ Nintendo intends to develop a new range of multimedia products for older children and adults, and wants to test the feasibility of the idea.

4. In market measurement and forecasting, which is the more serious problem: overestimating demand or underestimating it? Give your reasons.

5. What leading indicators might help you predict sales of people carriers? Mobile phones? Baby foods? Describe a general procedure for finding leading indicators of product sales.

Applying the concepts

1. People often make their own judgements about the potential for new products. You may hear someone say a new product will 'never sell' or that it will 'sell like hot cakes'. Recall some recent new products or services that you saw or heard about, and about which you made an informal prediction. What attracted your attention enough to get you to comment on the future of the products or services? What was your forecast? Were you correct?

2. Visit the website www.businessballs.com/demographicclassifications (you will also find the website useful in helping you analyse other marketing problems) and classify yourself and several other people, such as fellow students, on each of the classifications listed.

   ■ Choose a familiar product and consider how marketing data based on each of the classifications could guide marketing activities. Consider which classification you find most useful and explain why.

   ■ Examine the divergence of the classification of people in your group and consider whether the differences suggest different marketing plans for the range.

   ■ These classifications are based on one European country. To what extent could they be applied in another wealthy European country or one of the new east European countries joining the EU?

References

1. 'AIDS in Third World: a global disaster', *The Economist* (2 January 1999), pp. 50–2; 'A turning point for AIDS?', *The Economist* (15 July 2000), pp. 117–19; 'Business and AIDS', *The Economist* (10 February 2001), p. 95; 'AIDS: forty million orphans', *The Economist* (30 November 2002), p. 56; 'For 80 cents more', *The Economist* (17 August 2002), pp. 19–22; 'AIDS: money, money, money', *The Economist* (28 June 2003), p. 117.

2. Danny Rogers, 'Good time to be asking questions', *FT Creative Business* (14 August 2001), pp. 6–7.

3. David Shenk, *Data Smog: Surviving the information glut* (San Francisco: HarperSanFrancisco, 1997); Diane Trommer, 'Information overload – study finds intranet users overwhelmed with data', *Electronic Buyers' News* (20 April 1998), p. 98; Stewart Deck, 'Data storm ahead', *CIO* (15 April 2001), p. 97.

4. Alice LaPlante, 'Still drowning!', *Computer World* (10 March 1997), pp. 69–70; Jennifer Jones, 'Looking inside', *InfoWorld* (7 January 2002), pp. 22–6.

5. Jeffrey Rotfeder and Jim Bartimo, 'How software is making food sales a piece of cake', *Business Week* (2 July 1990), pp. 54–5; Victoria Griffith, 'Smart selling to big spenders', *Financial Times* (1 July 1994), p. 16; Andy Patrizio, 'Home-grown CRM', *Insurance and Technology* (February 2001), pp. 49–50.

6. For more on research firms that supply marketing information, see Jack Honomichl, 'Honomichl 50', special section, *Marketing News* (10 June 2002), pp. H1–H43.

7. Leonard M. Fuld, 'Competitor intelligence: can you plug the leaks?', *Security Management* (August 1989), pp. 85–7; Kate Button, 'Spies like us', *Marketing Business* (March 1994), pp. 7–9; James Curtis, 'Behind enemy lines', *Marketing* (24 May 2001), pp. 28–9.

8. Andy Serwer, 'P&G's covert operation', *Fortune* (17 September 2001), pp. 42–4.

9. 'Spy/counterspy', *Context* (Summer 1998), pp. 20–1.

10. 'Company sleuth uncovers business info for free', *Link-Up* (January–February 1999), pp. 1, 8.

11. For more on competitor intelligence see David B. Montgomery and Charles Weinberg, 'Toward strategic intelligence systems', *Marketing Management* (Winter 1998), pp. 44–52; and Conor Vibert, 'Secrets of online sleuthing', *Journal of Business Strategy* (May–June 2001), pp. 39–42.

12. Curtis, 'Behind enemy lines', op. cit.

13. Isabel Conway, 'Now there's a slimming pill for podgy pooches', *The European – élan* (30 September–6 October 1994), p. 5.

14. The American Marketing Association officially adopted this definition in 1987.

15. David Murphy, 'Marketing research in the dock', *Marketing Business* (July/August 2003), pp. 28–31.

16. Peggy Hollinger, 'Europe reaches for the cereals', *Financial Times* (4 October 1994), p. 21.

17. Honomichl, 'Honomichl 50', op. cit.

18. See Marydee Ojala, 'The daze of future business research', *Online* (January–February 1998), pp. 78–80; and Guy Kawasaki, 'Get your facts here', *Forbes* (23 March 1998), p. 156.

19. Charles Bremmer, 'Curt French asked to join bonjour culture', *The Times* (20 January 2001), p. 17; Paul Abrahams, 'Office pushed the envelope', *Financial Times* (11 December 2002), p. 17; Danny Rogers, 'Good time to be asking questions', *FT Creative Business* (14 August 2001), pp. 6–7.

20. Considerable research has been conducted on how best to increase the response rate of postal interviews. For a review see David Jobber, 'An examination of the effects of questionnaire factors on response to an industrial mail survey', *International Journal of Research in Marketing*, **6**, 2 (1989), pp. 129–40; David Jobber and John Saunders, 'A note on the applicability of the Bruvold–Comer model of mail survey response rates to commercial populations', *Journal of Business Research*, **26**, 3 (1993), pp. 223–36.

21. Jacob Hornik and Tamar Zaig, 'Increasing compliance in costly telephone interviews: a test of four inducement techniques', *International Journal of Research in Marketing*, **8**, 2 (1991), pp. 147–53; William O. Bearden, Charles S. Madden and Kelly Uscategui, 'The pool is drying up', *Marketing Research* (Spring 1998), pp. 26–33; Craig Frazier, 'What are Americans afraid of?', *American Demographics* (July 2001), pp. 43–9; and Steve Jarvis, 'CMOR finds survey refusal rate still rising', *Marketing News* (4 February 2002), p. 4.

22. For more on focus groups, see Holly Edmunds, *The Focus Group Research Handbook* (Lincolnwood, IL: NTC Business Books, 1999); and R. Kenneth Wade, 'Focus groups' research role is shifting', *Marketing News* (4 March 2002), p. 47.

23. Steve Jarvis, 'Two technologies vie for piece of growing focus group market', *Marketing News* (27 May 2002).

24. Sarah Schafer, 'Communications: Getting a line on customers', *Inc. Technology* (1996), p. 102. Also see Alison Stein Wellner, 'I've asked you here because . . .', *Business Week* (14 August 2000), p. F14.

25. For an international review of response differences, see Robert A. Peterson, Dana L. Alden, Mustafa O. Attir and Alain J.P. Jolibert, 'Husband–wife report disagreement: a cross-national investigation', *International Journal of Research in Marketing*, **5**, 2 (1988), pp. 125–36.

26. Jerome Burne, 'A probe inside the mind of a shopper', *Financial Times* (27 November 2003). For more on these machines see the Aston Academy of Life Sciences website: www.aston.ac.uk/lhs.

27. For further discussion, see Gary L. Lilien, Philip Kotler and K. Sridhar Moorthy, *Marketing Models* (Englewood Cliffs, NJ: Prentice Hall, 2002).

28. For a more comprehensive discussion of measuring market demand, see Philip Kotler, *Marketing Management: Analysis, planning, implementation and control*, 10th edn (Englewood Cliffs, NJ: Prentice Hall, 2002).

29. Chris Bullock, 'Europe looks beyond Ariane 5', *Interavia* (April 1999), pp. 42–7; and 'Keeping Europe in the Sat-Nav race', *Interavia* (March 1999), pp. 62–3; Lisa Kelly, 'UK firms aim high in Galileo satellites', *Computing* (20 November 2003); Jim Dunn, 'Satellite navigation: boon or bust?, *The Scotsman* (21 November 2003).

30. Lynn Y.S. Lin, 'Comparison of survey responses among Asian, European and American consumers and their interpretations', ESOMAR Conference, Venice (18–20 June 1990), pp. 120–32.

31. 'Less is Moore', *The Economist* (10 May 2003), p. 10; 'Modifying Moore's Law', *The Economist: A survey of the IT industry* (10 May 2003), p. 6; Simon London, 'Heat becomes computing's hottest topic', *Financial Times* (2 July 2003), p. 13.

32. From Luiz Moutinho, *Problems in Marketing* (London: Chapman, 1991).

33. Karel Jan Alsem, Peter S.H. Leeflang and Jan C. Reuyl, 'The forecasting accuracy of market share models using predicted values of competitive marketing behaviour', *International Journal of Research in Marketing*, **6**, 3 (1989), pp. 183–98.

34. Meg Carter, 'Does TV measure up?', *FT Creative Business* (15 April 2003), p. 6; Nic Hopkins, 'Radio resurgence boosts Chrysalis' (18 November 2003), p. 31.

35. Many of the examples in this section, along with others, are found in Subhash C. Jain, *International Marketing Management*, 3rd edn (Boston: PWS-Kent, 1990), pp. 334–9. See also Ken Gofton, 'Going global with research', *Marketing* (15 April 1999), p. 35; Naresh K. Malhotra, *Marketing Research*, 3rd edn (Upper Saddle River, NJ: Prentice Hall, 1999), Ch. 23; and Tim R.V. Davis and Robert B. Young, 'International marketing research', *Business Horizons* (March–April 2002), pp. 31–8.

36. Jain, *International Marketing Management*, op. cit., p. 338.

37. See Nancy Levenburg and Tom Dandridge, 'Can't afford research? Try miniresearch', *Marketing News* (31 March 1997), p. 19; and Nancy Levenburg, 'Research resources exist for small businesses', *Marketing News* (4 January 1999), p. 19.

38. Margaret Harris, *Organising God* (London: Macmillan Press, 1998); Ruth Glehill, 'Less is more when it comes to worshippers', *The Times* (17 March 2001), p. 10.

39. 'MRA study shows refusal rates are highest at start of process', *Marketing News* (16 August 1993), p. A15; 'Private eyes', *Marketing Tools* (January–February 1996), pp. 31–2. See also John Hagel III and Jeffrey F. Rayport, 'The coming battle for consumer information', *Harvard Business Review* (January–February 1997), pp. 53–65.

40. John Schwartz, 'Chief privacy officers forge evolving corporate roles', *New York Times* (12 February 2001), p. C1; and J. Michael Pemberton, 'Chief privacy officer: your next career?', *Information Management Journal* (May–June 2002), pp. 57–8.

41. See Cynthia Crossen, 'Studies galore support products and positions, but are they reliable?', *Wall Street Journal* (14 November 1991), pp. A1, A9; also see Allan J. Kimmel, 'Deception in marketing research and practice: an introduction', *Psychology and Marketing* (July 2001), pp. 657–61.

42. For example, see Betsy Peterson, 'Ethics revisited', *Marketing Research* (Winter 1996), pp. 47–8; and O.C. Ferrell, Michael D. Hartline and Stephen W. McDaniel, 'Codes of ethics among corporate research departments, marketing research firms, and data subcontractors: an examination of a three-communities metaphor', *Journal of Business Ethics* (April 1998), pp. 503–16. For discussion of a framework for ethical marketing research, see Naresh K. Malhotra and Gina L. Miller, 'An integrated model of ethical decisions in marketing research', *Journal of Business Ethics* (February 1998), pp. 263–80; and Kumar C. Rallapalli, 'A paradigm for development and promulgation of a global code of marketing ethics', *Journal of Business Ethics* (January 1999), pp. 125–37.

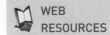

WEB RESOURCES

For additional classic case studies and Internet exercises, visit www.pearsoned.co.uk/kotler

Concluding concepts 9
Judy Greene Pottery

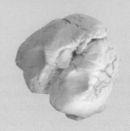

ANN M. TORRES*
National University of Ireland, Galway

Doing something harder is what Judy Greene has done and continues to do. In fact, Paul, Judy's husband and business partner, likens Judy to the blade on an icebreaker ship. 'Judy has to continually break the ice in developing new ideas. Judy never looks back; she is always looking ahead. Like most artists, her *next* piece is the most important.'

Judy is a prominent contemporary potter whose company, *Judy Greene Pottery*, is noted for the quality and design of its output as well as the entrepreneurial qualities of its director. Judy Greene is engaged not only in developing products and designs, but also in managing the manufacturing and retail operations of the firm. Judy's business has been successful, experiencing phenomenal growth rates over the last ten years. Her main concern is to ensure its future prosperity.

'Younger customers are looking for something Irish, but not hackneyed symbols of shamrocks'.

Judy Greene Pottery

When aged 31, Judy left the Irish pottery company *Potaireacht Cléire* in 1981 to start her own business. She had no business plan, no capital and no time to take business-training classes. So, she put key figures on a sheet of paper and went to see the bank manager. An overdraft of €19,000 was approved. By 1998, sales turn-over had reached €1,000,000. Judy's aim was to achieve €1,250,000+ in sales by 2000 and an additional 25 per cent by 2005.

Judy attributes her success, in those years, to having her workshop on the retail site allowing for close, consistent contact with customers. In fact, customers were vital in providing feedback for testing new product ideas. Judy noted that 'if it worked it sold. The customers walking through the workshop were like having a marketing department walking through the door every day.' Judy contemplated what to do next. Her handmade pottery has been extraordinarily successful and she wishes to focus on

developing future strategies to ensure continued prosperity.

The Irish market for giftware and crafts

The Irish crafts/gift market had an estimated annual turnover of €127 million. Handcrafted pottery accounted for approximately 9 per cent of that market, giving a per capita expenditure on pottery of less than €2.50. Pottery made in a studio environment (i.e. handcrafted) has 70 per cent of the Irish market, is usually found at the upper price band for tableware and gift items and is not as price sensitive as other product categories. The craft/gift industry had been a growth market for many years. However, there are signs that growth is beginning to slow.

There are several trends which relate to the Irish craft/gift industry overall:

- The young and more travelled customers are moving away from traditional and safe gifts.
- The influence from the tourist industry continues to be strong.
- The healthy economic climate provides a good foundation for opportunities not only for established firms, but also for new entrants.

Customer profiles

Judy's current customers are mostly female, 25 to 45 years of age and older, coming from mostly middle and upper middle incomes. Many of the younger customers (i.e. mid-twenties to mid-thirties) are newly married couples and/or new homeowners. Exhibit 9.1 gives customer segments. Tourists buy in the retail shop and ship their purchases home, perhaps purchasing again later through mail order. Most of these tourist/mail-order sales are made to customers from the US (90 per cent); smaller proportions are made to tourists from the UK (5 per cent), and other countries (5 per cent). Export sales are made through individual retailers who have sought out *Judy Greene* products or through supplying specialist consumer catalogues. The majority of sales are made to retailers in the US (55 per cent); smaller proportions are made to retailers from Canada (15 per cent), France

Market segment	Oct.–March	April–Sept.
Domestic	90%	80%
Export	2%	5%
Tourist	4%	10%
Mail-order	4%	5%
Total	100%	100%

(10 per cent), the UK (10 per cent) and other countries (10 per cent).

Customer trends

Customer trends are changing and their tastes appear to be moving slowly away from pottery back to china, porcelain and cut glass. Most important for Judy is to identify and stay ahead of the trends. To identify trends, Judy 'devours' interior design magazines and travels abroad to Europe and the United States to see what is popular and selling there. 'Typically what is selling in Frankfurt now, will be in Ireland in two years' time.' For this reason, she finds that the timing of new products and designs is crucial. In fact, the idea for one of her best-selling products, oil burners, was developed as a direct result of a trip to a ceramics fair in Munich, five years ago. While in Germany, she went to numerous chemists' shops to examine the design, function and safety features of various kinds of oil burners. It was one of the most cost-efficient ways to do her R&D work. Thus, when she returned to Galway she wasted little time and resources in developing her final product.

Judy readily admits that reading interior design magazines and examining other markets is no guarantee of success in the Irish market, as design and colour trends may not suit Irish tastes. However, identifying the potential trends and then customising them for the consumers in the home market affords a better chance of success. Judy also relies quite heavily on customer feedback. The retailers and customers who buy *Judy Greene Pottery* are always looking for new designs, so Judy has to stay fresh and respond to their feedback. Judy is aware that she needs to capitalise on ideas for new lines to 'stay fresh' in a highly competitive market. Yet, at the same time, she is also knows it is important to stay true to her own style.

Balancing these two concerns is challenging while trying to satisfy customer demand.

With respect to design preferences, 10 years ago when Judy started, flowers and flowery designs were 'in'. Now she has to consider what the upcoming generations want, as they will be the customers of the future. The younger age groups are more interested in simpler, more classical lines of design. Judy believes that 'younger customers are looking for something Irish, but not hackneyed symbols of shamrocks and shillelaghs'. In response, Judy introduced her *Connemara Collection* to appeal to the younger markets.

Furthermore, Galway being a tourist town, there are the tastes of visitors to consider. Judy has noticed that the English tourists love the flowery designs and will buy everything in the shop. German visitors prefer the simpler designs and buy the larger, exclusive, unique and one-of-a-kind pottery pieces. The American visitors will be one of two types: either ones that buy 'seconds' from the bargain baskets; or ones who buy entire dinner sets, because they like the design and consider money to be no object. Finally, the French and Italian tourists do not buy a lot of pottery and prefer to purchase items in *Design Concourse Ireland*.

As a member of the Galway Chamber of Commerce, Judy does have access to a research report, *Galway Tourism 1997*. According to this report, there were 920,000 visitors to Galway City in 1996 (see Exhibit 9.2) spending an average of €21.34 on gifts.

Focus group research

Although Judy believed she had a good understanding of her loyal customers, she thought it worthwhile to

Exhibit 9.2 Visitors to Galway City, 1996

Country	Percentage
Ireland and N. Ireland (i.e. other than Galway)	42%
United Kingdom	17%
United States of America	15%
Germany	8%
France	7%
Other Europe	7%
Rest of world	4%
Total	100%

SOURCE: Galway Chamber of Commerce.

investigate various other (potential) customer segments. Her objectives in pursuing this research were to learn more about:

- where people got their ideas for fashion, interior design and home furnishings;
- their general perceptions of porcelain, china, and pottery;
- what brands of pottery they knew, liked, and bought (i.e. for themselves or a gift);
- their buying patterns and criteria when buying pottery.

Judy was interested in qualitative information that explained why people think or feel the way they do and so hired a market research firm to organise and facilitate focus group interviews. The researchers identified four customer types.

Young Graduates – future customers

The average age of participants in this focus group was 23 years. All participants had finished their undergraduate studies. At the time of the interviews, they were in the process of postgraduate studies, or in their first job. None of them owned their own home, and they were living either in the family home or in rented accommodation.

The *Young Graduates* described themselves as being very style and fashion conscious. They were very aware of current fashion trends. In addition, many of them liked to buy branded products and perceived that a good brand name added value to their purchases. Most of their influences came from magazines, shop windows or their peers. However, they also had a clear idea of what they liked and the designs and styles they preferred.

Professionals – higher disposable income customers

The average age of participants in this focus group was 36 years. All participants were homeowners and professional women in a full-time job. The majority of these women were married and had children.

The *Professionals* viewed themselves as very practical individuals who preferred comfort, convenience and simplicity in their surroundings and clothing. Terms such as 'very convenient, no thought involved, easy to manage and maintain, comfortable and practical' were mentioned frequently as important factors for purchases to suit their lifestyle. Many of the *Professionals* expressed that they led busy, hectic lives and sought purchases that made their lives easier.

Homemakers – mature customers

The average age of participants in this focus group was 50 years and they had had their home for a number of years. Many of the women identified themselves as homemakers, although many of them work outside the home, or did so at one time. All the women were married and the majority had children.

The *Homemakers* felt that words such as 'casual, functional, traditional and classical' most accurately described themselves and their preferred surroundings. Influences on their choice of style came from themselves and from magazines, as well as from their friends and relatives. However, they did not believe they were influenced by trends in fashion. Essentially, they had developed their own style and preferred to 'stick with it'.

Loyal Customers – core customer base

The fourth focus group was composed of loyal Judy Greene customers. As this was the only criterion, participants' profiles were more diverse than in the other focus groups. The women ranged in age from 35 to 67 years. All the women had their own home. Most of them were married and many of them had children. Half of the participants were professional women in full-time positions, and ranged in age from 37 to 54 years, while the other half identified themselves as homemakers and ranged in age from 35 to 67 years.

The *Loyal Customers* perceived themselves to be independent thinkers. They did not believe they were heavily influenced by trends in fashion and interior design. In general, they favoured clothing and home furnishings that were 'classical, elegant, and of good quality'. Although they appreciated classical styling, they did not view themselves as traditional. Consequently, they clarified that they preferred 'an old style with a modern twist, and a mix of antique and modern furnishings'. Essentially, they liked 'things that won't date, that are smart, but not too trendy'. Many of these women expressed an opinion that 'fashion was for younger people'. Essentially, they felt they were at a stage in their lives where their identities were established and they were comfortable with themselves.

As a whole, the groups preferred pottery to china and porcelain. Still, each group did have distinct characteristics in terms of motivation for purchase, importance of branding, purchase criteria, and preferences for style, design, colour, etc. Exhibit 9.3 summarises the participants' responses from the focus group interviews.

Exhibit 9.3 Summary of customer profiles

	Focus groups			
	Young Graduates	Professionals	Homemakers	Loyal Customers
Customer segment	Future customers	High disposable income customers	Mature customers	Core customer base
Description of personal style	'Classical casuals'	'Practical minimalist'	'Functional traditionalist'	'Timeless modernist'
Purchase motivations	Brand, style and current trends	Convenience, practicality, functionality and value	Function, personal taste and habit (not by brand and fashion)	Quality, function, consistent with own styles – i.e. timeless, smart, won't date
Perception of current fashion	Retro, 1950s style, tailored, classical casual	Space, efficiency, functionality, bright, airy, timeless, simplistic, minimalist	Natural, wood and earth tones, changes slowly over time	Country style, spacious, airy, more for younger people
Pottery preferred (with respect to style, design, colour, etc.)	Simpler, less fussy designs, in bold colours and shapes – like a lot of variety	Clean, simple lines, in white, natural and terracotta tones	Traditional (terracotta) designs and lines in muted colours	Classical lines with a modern twist, but timeless
Q1: Where do you get ideas for fashion, interior design and home furnishings?	Magazines, peers, shop windows, self, 'what I like'	Magazines, peers, friends, i.e. what others did in their homes	Magazines, out of own head, friends and relatives	Irish magazines, visit the shops, own style
Q2: How do you describe your own style and that of your surroundings (i.e. home or accommodation)?	Own style is casual, easy to maintain, comfortable; style, brand and quality conscious, very fashion conscious, very aware of trends	Practical, comfortable, focused, minimalist, simple, convenient, consistent	Casual, functional, individualistic, not too concerned about fashion	Classical, good quality, elegant, independent thinkers, smart styles, not too trendy or dated, old-style with a modern twist
Q3: Words you associate with china and porcelain?	Formal, dainty, dust-collectors, old-fashioned, out of date	Too outdated, costly, expensive, fussy, delicate, irritating	Dainty, impractical, unused, flowery, expensive, not for everyday use	Delicate, lovely, pretty, formal dining room, formal, never used
Q4: Words you associate with pottery?	Earthy, natural, raw/unaffected, in fashion	Functional, chunky, durable, heavy	Chunky, practical, functional, old-fashioned	Warm, earthy, comforting, casual, intimate
Q5: What are important factors when buying pottery?	Colour, shape, design, texture, depends on occasion	Occasion (gift) recipient's taste and preferences, look and design, function, and price	Practicality, function, shape, colour, simplicity, design, style	Shape, colour, functionality

Exhibit 9.3 continued

Exhibit 9.3 (cont'd)

	Focus groups			
	Young Graduates	**Professionals**	**Homemakers**	**Loyal Customers**
Q6: What brands of pottery are you most familiar with (i.e. name recognition)?	Stephen Pearce, Judy Greene, and to lesser extent Nicholas Mosse, Michael Kennedy	Stephen Pearce, Judy Greene and to a lesser extent Nicholas Mosse	Stephen Pearce, Judy Greene and Nicholas Mosse	Stephen Pearce, Jack O'Patsy, Judy Greene, Louis Mulcahy and Nicholas Mosse
Q7: How important is the brand (name) in general and when purchasing pottery?	Very brand and style conscious	Brand not a big issue – more emphasis on function, convenience, comfort, price–value relationship	Brand name is not important	Appreciate value of brand, but brand name is more important for gifts
Q8: How important is price when purchasing pottery?	Brand carries (a lot) more importance, but they also look at price carefully	Value conscious more than price conscious	Price is not very important	Price is not at all important
Q9: How important is in-store service?	Very important	Convenience is very important	Important part of the purchase experience	Extremely important

Questions

1. Classify the types of marketing research used by Judy Greene over her firm's evolution.
2. What market research would you suggest that Judy Greene should have done before starting up her business?
3. To what extent did the qualitative research reported fulfil Judy Greene's research objectives?
4. Based on the research conducted so far, what recommendations would you make to Judy Greene concerning the way ahead for her company?
5. What further research would you recommend she does?

*Based on Ann M. Torres' comprehensive case 'Judy Greene Pottery: Marketing Irish Handcrafted Products', 1999.

The meek shall inherit the earth, but they'll not increase market share.

WILLIAM G. MCGOWAN

Core strategy

PART four

PART FOUR OF PRINCIPLES OF MARKETING covers core strategy, the centre of the marketing process.

Within core strategy, marketing knowledge is made into the strategies that guide marketing action. Businesses mostly succeed by concentrating on a group of customers they can serve better than anyone else. **Chapter 10** explains how markets can be broken down into customer segments and how to choose the ones to target. It then looks at ways to address the target segments by creating mental associations that attract customers to the product or services.

A Levi's ad once claimed that 'quality never goes out of style'. That has become a byword for much of modern marketing, as marketers try to escape from making single transactions with customers to establishing relationships that both enjoy. **Chapter 11** examines how customer satisfaction, quality, value and service contribute to relationship marketing.

Increasingly, it is not enough for marketers to look at customers; they must also look at what their competitors are doing and respond to them. **Chapter 12** shows that success in marketing does not mean direct confrontation with competitors. It is often best to find new ways to please customers that build upon a business's unique strengths.

*Before we knew it
we were having
Häagen~Dazs.*

Fall deeply in Häagen~Dazs.

> I don't know the key to success but the key to failure is trying to please everyone.

BILL CROSBY

Segmentation and positioning

Chapter objectives

After reading this chapter, you should be able to:

- Define market segmentation and market targeting.
- List and discuss the primary bases for segmenting consumer and business markets.
- Explain how companies identify attractive market segments and choose a market-coverage strategy.
- Define differentiation and market positioning.
- Explain why companies seek to differentiate their markets and use positioning strategies.
- List and discuss the principal ways in which companies can differentiate their products.
- Explain how companies can position their products for maximum competitive advantage in the marketplace.

Mini Contents List

Prelude case drivedreamcars.com

Friday night, after a longer and harder week than usual, Gordon drove out of the staff car park onto the expressway in his trusty old diesel estate. It was not the time for speeding. The traffic was heavy, the night closing in and soothing Classic FM on the radio.

'You're wanting the Ferrari Testosterone, yes?'

All was relaxing until a lad in a white van swerved and pushed into the lane two cars up front while gesticulating in a manner consistent with his FCUK sticker in his rear window. A line of drivers' minds were dragged from the FM-induced mood as they slammed on brakes.

The traffic flow restarted and Brahms calmed.

Within minutes, the diesel estate pulled into the garage between a Bentley Mulsanne S and a Porsche 911 Carrera Tiptronic. Rob walked across. 'You're wanting the Ferrari Testosterone, yes?' After a brief familiarisation and swapping of keys, Gordon left the family diesel and delicately eased the Ferrari out of the garage. The 300 bhp engine behind the driver's seat sounded so Ferrari. The car so light; the engine so eager. A slight touch on the accelerator and the car exploded forwards. The machine was eager to go but better to ease into the car's huge potential rather than playing on a busy road.

Classic FM did not fit the enthusiasm and burr of the Ferrari and no radio stations ever played anything remotely appropriate at this time on Friday night. An old Bruce Springsteen album was in the CD player. It kicked off with *Born to Run* – 'Chrome wheeled, fuel injected and steppin' out over the line' – a rising song to blast in the weekend. Life could not get much better than this, but it did.

Out of the city and on to country lanes, there, at the side of the road, was the lad with his white van. This time he was not gesticulating at other road users but at his motor that was not running. Gordon smiled and waved, as Springsteen burst into 'Thunder Road', and let the prancing horse free.

This is not a fairy tale. On Monday morning the Ferrari turned back into a diesel estate and another week of work began. But next Friday it was to be a family car with a difference – a Maserati 3200 GT. The cars are part of the stable of the Classic Car Club, a membership organisation that hires out cars to drool over. For about £1,995 (€3,300) a year, members hire cars based on a points system that varies with time of year, weekend or weekday and make of car. The price includes everything but fuel. Some of the cars are true classics, such as the Triumph TR6, Daimler V8, E-type and Mark II Jaguars. Others, including a Porsche Boxter, TVR and Aston Martin, are more modern but still interesting to drive. All for averaging £50 per driving day – less than a normal car hire and certainly for a lot less than owning a classic car. As the *Independent on Sunday* commented, 'I've scratched my head long and hard to find a catch: there isn't one.'

Whatever the dream that the Classic Car Club offers to its members, the club has its owners scratching their heads too. All members want to hire the same exotic open-topped cars on sunny weekends in summer. Many times the stock of cars is all out while on other occasions most rest in the garage. Downtime can also be a problem. These cars are real classics and some are ageing. Breakdowns can and do occur and take cars off the road for weeks. There are also the speeding fines incurred by members who do not realise they can exceed the speed limit from a standing start in seconds in a car that is designed to attract attention.[1]

Questions

1. What allows a small business, like the Classic Car Club, to succeed against huge global players in the car hire business and is it a business concept that could work elsewhere in the world?
2. Being a small company looking for a membership that is a very small fraction of the total population, how should the club promote itself and what is its target market?
3. How could the club increase its income and even the load on its cars by appealing to additional market segments or segmenting its own customer base?

Introduction

Organisations that sell to consumer and business markets recognise that they cannot appeal to all buyers in those markets or at least not to all buyers in the same way. Buyers are too numerous, too widely scattered and too varied in their needs and buying practices. Companies vary widely in their abilities to serve different segments of the market. Like the Classic Car Club, rather than trying to compete in an entire car hire market, companies identify the parts of the market they can serve best. Segmentation is thus a compromise between mass marketing, which assumes everyone can be treated the same, and the assumption that each person needs a dedicated marketing effort.

Few companies now use mass marketing. Instead, they practise **target marketing** – identifying market segments, selecting one or more of them, and developing products and marketing mixes tailored to each. In this way, sellers can develop the right product for each target market and adjust their prices, distribution channels and advertising to reach the target market efficiently. Instead of scattering their marketing efforts (the 'shotgun' approach), they can focus on the buyers who have greater purchase interest (the 'rifle' approach).

Figure 10.1 shows the major steps in target marketing. **Market segmentation** means dividing a market into distinct groups of buyers with different needs, characteristics or behaviours, who might require separate products or marketing mixes. The company identifies different ways to segment the market and develops profiles of the resulting market segments. **Market targeting** involves evaluating each market segment's attractiveness and selecting one or more of the market segments to enter. **Market positioning** is setting the competitive positioning for the product and creating a detailed marketing mix. We discuss each of these steps in turn.

Market segmentation

Markets consist of buyers, and buyers differ in one or more ways. They may differ in their wants, resources, locations, buying attitudes and buying practices. Through market segmentation, companies divide large, heterogeneous markets into smaller segments that can be reached more efficiently with products and services that match their unique needs. In this section we discuss levels of market segmentation, and in the following six sections we deal with the important topics of segmenting consumer markets, segmenting business markets, segmenting international markets, multivariate segmentation, developing market segments, and requirements for effective segmentation.

Target marketing—Directing a company's effort towards serving one or more groups of customers sharing common needs or characteristics.

Market segmentation—Dividing a market into distinct groups of buyers with different needs, characteristics or behaviour, who might require separate products or marketing mixes.

Market targeting—The process of evaluating each market segment's attractiveness and selecting one or more segments to enter.

Market positioning—Arranging for a product to occupy a clear, distinctive and desirable place relative to competing products in the minds of target consumers. Formulating competitive positioning for a product and a detailed marketing mix.

Market segmentation	Market targeting	Market positioning
1. Identify bases for segmenting the market 2. Develop profiles of resulting segments	3. Develop measures of segment attractiveness 4. Select the target segment(s)	5. Develop positioning for each target segment 6. Develop marketing mix for each target segment

Figure 10.1 Six steps in market segmentation, targeting and positioning

Levels of market segmentation

Because buyers have unique needs and wants, each buyer is potentially a separate market. Ideally, then, a seller might design a separate marketing programme for each buyer. However, although some companies attempt to serve buyers individually, many others face larger numbers of smaller buyers and do not find complete segmentation worthwhile. Instead, they look for broader classes of buyers who differ in their product needs or buying responses. Thus, market segmentation can be carried out at many different levels. Companies can practise no segmentation (mass marketing), complete segmentation (micromarketing) or something in between (segment marketing or niche marketing).

Mass marketing

Mass marketing—Using almost the same product, promotion and distribution for all consumers.

Companies have not always practised target marketing. In fact, for most of the twentieth century, major consumer-products companies held fast to **mass marketing** – mass producing, mass distributing and mass promoting about the same product in about the same way to all consumers. Henry Ford epitomised this marketing strategy when he offered the Model T Ford to all buyers; they could have the car 'in any colour as long as it is black'. That cost Ford the world market leadership that it has never regained.

The traditional argument for mass marketing is that it creates the largest potential market, which leads to the lowest costs, which in turn can translate into either lower prices or higher margins. However, many factors now make mass marketing more difficult. For example, the world's mass markets have slowly splintered into a profusion of smaller segments – from those living near the Arctic to the tropics; from the grey market to the gay market. It is increasingly hard to create a single product or programme that appeals to all of these diverse groups. The proliferation of advertising media and distribution channels has also made it difficult to practise 'one size fits all' marketing.

Not surprisingly, many companies are retreating from mass marketing and turning to segmented marketing.

After pioneering the genre as a rock channel on cable TV, Music Television (MTV) is facing increasingly intensive competition from the likes of BSkyB and Emap's Kiss TV and Kerrang. MTV is fighting back with the military precision of the ex-soldier who runs the European operation. The competition is taking some market share but MTV continues its double digit growth by addressing a series segments in the youth market. While MTV base is becoming a more conventional TV channel showing reality TV shows, such as *The Osbornes*, the company uses its decentralized structure to track twists and turns in national music markets. It then splatters sub-sections of their 16-year to 34-year-old target market with channels covering soul/R&B, pop, rock, hip-hop, indie, and any other music trend that may arrive. Despite the diversity of musical tastes across the world, one of MTV's tricks is to run advertising across a mix of appropriate channels, therefore offering broadcast advertising across narrowcast channels.[2]

Segmenting markets

A company that practises **segment marketing** recognises that buyers differ in their needs, perceptions and buying behaviours. The company tries to isolate broad segments that make up a market and adapts its offers to match more closely the needs of one or more segments.

> At 55 years of age, Roger de Haan retired with a £1bn (€1.66bn) pension from SAGA, the company he created. SAGA's success came from a range of businesses focusing on the needs of the 55-plus age group. Why this focus? Because youth-oriented marketers had neglected Europe's ageing population whose disposable income is 8 per cent above the average (all age groups below 55 have disposable incomes below average!). SAGA products range from holidays through insurance to radio stations. Other marketers are following de Haan's lead. The Aktiv Markt supermarket chain in Austria and Germany is having great success with its stores designed for pensioners and is using a 'third-age suit' that designers don to help them empathise with ageing drivers. There is even a market research agency, Senioragency International, specialising in the needs of the growing segment.[3]

Segment marketing offers several benefits over mass marketing. The company can market more efficiently, targeting its products or services, channels and communications programmes towards only consumers that it can serve best. The company can also market more effectively by fine-tuning its products, prices and programmes to the needs of carefully defined segments. And the company may face fewer competitors if fewer competitors are focusing on this market segment.

Niche marketing

Market segments are normally large identifiable groups within a market – for example, luxury car buyers, performance car buyers, utility car buyers and economy car buyers. **Niche marketing** focuses on subgroups within these segments. A *niche* is a more narrowly defined group, usually identified by dividing a segment into subsegments or by defining a group with a distinctive set of traits who may seek a special combination of benefits. For example, property developers have recognised a niche within the grey market. Further segmenting the grey market, the Palms runs gay and lesbian retirement communities and Rainbow Vision runs retirement homes for the same niche market.[4]

Whereas segments are fairly large and normally attract several competitors, niches are smaller and normally attract only one or a few competitors. Niche marketers have to understand their niches' needs so well that their customers willingly pay a price premium. For example, Ferrari gets a high price for its cars because its loyal buyers feel that no other automobile comes close to offering the product–service–membership benefits as Ferrari.

Niching offers smaller companies an opportunity to compete by focusing their limited resources on serving niches that may be unimportant to, or overlooked by, larger competitors. For example, Mark Warner succeeds by selling to distinct holiday niches: all-inclusive family watersports holidays in southern Europe to northern Europeans, and no-kids holidays for older people who want some peace and quiet. However, large companies also practise niche marketing. For example, Nike makes athletic gear for aerobics, jogging and football, but also for smaller niches such as fell running and street hockey.

Segment marketing— Adapting a company's offerings so they more closely match the needs of one or more segments.

Niche marketing—Adapting a company's offerings to more closely match the needs of one or more subsegments where there is often little competition.

393

Niche marketing: Vans specialises in making thick-soled trainers for skateboarders. SOURCE: Vans Inc. Copyright © 2001 Vans Inc. Reprinted with permission.

In many markets today, niches are the norm. As an advertising agency executive observed: 'There will be no market for products that everybody likes a little, only for products that somebody likes a lot.' Others assert that companies must 'niche or be niched'.

Micromarketing

Micromarketing—A form of target marketing in which companies tailor their marketing programmes to the needs and wants of narrowly defined geographic, demographic, psychographic or behavioural segments.

Segment and niche marketers tailor their offers and marketing programmes to meet the needs of various market segments. At the same time, however, they do not customise their offers to each individual customer. Thus, segment marketing and niche marketing fall between the extremes of mass marketing and micromarketing. **Micromarketing** is the practice of tailoring products and marketing programmes to suit the tastes of specific individuals and locations. Micromarketing includes *local marketing* and *individual marketing*.

Local marketing

Local marketing involves tailoring brands and promotions to the needs and wants of local customer groups – cities, neighbourhoods and even specific stores. Thus, IKEA customises each store's merchandise and promotions to match its local clientele. C&A's difficulties, which have forced it to pull out of some European markets, have been blamed upon the centralisation of their buying in Brussels.

Local marketing has some drawbacks. It can drive up manufacturing and marketing costs by reducing economies of scale. It can also create logistical problems as companies try to meet the varied requirements of different regional and local markets. And a brand's overall image may be diluted if the product and message vary in different localities. Still, as companies face increasingly fragmented markets, and as new supporting technologies develop, the advantages of local marketing often outweigh the drawbacks.

> Having few top US or UK artists in their stable, Bertelsmann Music Group (BMG) has led the pop music industry in signing local European acts. Their early lead is paying off in an otherwise lacklustre industry, although everyone's profits are down. 'It is better for a record company to sell 10m copies of one album than 1m copies of ten', explains Deutsche Morgan Grenfell's Tom Hall. It takes an awful lot of Thrills [Dublin-based country rockers] to match the transatlantic success of White Stripes![5]

Local marketing helps a company to market more effectively in the face of pronounced regional and local differences in community demographics and lifestyles. It also meets the needs of the company's 'first-line customers' – retailers – who prefer more fine-tuned product assortments for their neighbourhoods. It maintains local variety and colour, but at a cost.

Individual marketing

In the extreme, micromarketing becomes **individual marketing** – tailoring products and marketing programmes to the needs and preferences of individual customers. Individual marketing has also been labelled 'markets-of-one marketing', 'customised marketing' and 'one-to-one marketing' (see Marketing Insights 10.1). The prevalence of mass marketing has obscured the fact that for centuries consumers were served as individuals: the tailor custom-made the suit, the cobbler designed shoes for the individual, the cabinet maker made furniture to order.

Individual marketing— Tailoring products and marketing programmes to the needs and preferences of individual customers.

> Customers can still enjoy such 'customised marketing'. Vick Nagle's Constant Tailoring still visits 'gentleman customers' to measure, try and complete tailored clothes made of only the best fabric. Ashby Pine works out of a small workshop-cum-display area in Ashby de la Zouch making made-to-measure furniture. Both owners love their materials and craftsmanship. Ashby Pine has clear objectives: 'We have managed our business down to the level of having a few good customers whom we enjoy working with.'

New technologies are permitting many larger companies to return to customised marketing. More powerful computers, detailed databases, robotic production, and immediate and interactive communication media such as email, fax and the Internet – all have combined to foster 'mass customisation'.[6] **Mass customisation** is the ability to prepare on a mass basis individually designed products and communications to meet each customer's requirements. Consumer marketers are now providing custom-made products in areas ranging from hotel stays and furniture to clothing and bicycles.

Mass customisation— Preparing individually designed products and communication on a large scale.

The move towards individual marketing mirrors the trend in consumer *self-marketing*. Increasingly, individual customers are taking more responsibility for determining which products and brands to buy. Consider two business buyers with two different purchasing styles. The first sees several salespeople, each trying to persuade him to buy their product. The second sees no salespeople but rather logs on to the Internet, searches for information on and evaluations of available products, interacts electronically with various suppliers, users and product analysts, and then makes up her own mind about the best offer. The second purchasing agent has taken more responsibility for the buying process, and the marketer has had less influence over her buying decision.

marketing insights

10.1   If it will digitise, it will customise

Sounds like *Star Wars*; soon in all stores. Suited for Sun, a swimwear manufacturer, uses a computer/camera system in retail stores to design custom-tailored swimsuits for women. The customer puts on an 'off the rack' garment, and the system's digital camera captures her image on the computer screen. The shop assistant applies a stylus to the screen to create a garment with perfect fit. The customer can select from more than 150 patterns and styles, which are re-imaged over her body on the computer screen until she finds the one that she likes best. The system then transmits the measurements to the factory, and the one-of-a-kind bathing suit is mailed to the delighted customer in a matter of days. Such mass customisation is becoming common. Using the Internet, many suppliers are cutting out stores and working directly with customers.

- www.barbie.com enables you to make your own Special Friend of Barbie choosing skin tone, eye colour, hairdo and hair colour, clothes, accessories and name. There is also a questionnaire for detailing your doll's likes and dislikes. When Barbie's Special Friend arrives in the mail, the doll's name is on the packaging along with a computer-generated paragraph about her personality.

- *Make your own CD*. Several Web companies offer the chance to customise a CD. Simply run through their catalogue, sample tracks, submit your list and your CD is in the mail. Customisers include emusic.com and cdj.co.uk.

- *Paris Miki*. At this Tokyo eyeglass store the Mikissimes Custom Designed Eyewear System allows technicians to design lenses and frames that conform to the shape of the customer's face. Using a monitor, styles are superimposed on a scanned image of the person's face. The customer then chooses a style, the glasses are made up and the person walks out with their customised glasses.

- *The watchfactory* website can help you design an almost infinite variety of watches assembled from standard parts and costing the same as off-the-shelf designs.

Although consumer goods are now being marketed one-to-one, business-to-business marketers have been providing customers with tailor-made goods for some time. Often they can supply products and services cheaper and quicker than it used to take to make standardised ones. Particularly for small companies, mass customisation provides a way to stand out against larger competitors. *ChemStation* was a pioneer of this way of doing business.

ChemStation, a small industrial-detergent company, offers its industrial customers individually concocted soap formulas. What cleans a car won't work to clean an aircraft or equipment in a mineshaft. Information collected by ChemStation about a specific customer's cleaning needs is fed into their Tank Management System (TMS)

...10.1

database. Next, they develop a special 'detergent recipe' for the customer, assign it a number, and enter the formula into the TMS. Then, plant workers enter the customer's recipe number into a machine, which mixes up a batch of the special brew. ChemStation then delivers the mixture to a tank installed at the customer's site. The company monitors usage and automatically refills the tank when supplies run low. The customisation system gives customers what they need and reduces costs, resulting in higher margins. Mass customisation also helps ChemStation to lock out competitors. No one – not even the customer – knows what goes into each formula, making it hard for a customer to switch suppliers.

Three trends are behind the growth in one-to-one marketing. The first is the increasing emphasis on customer value and satisfaction. The second is data warehouses allowing companies to store trillions of bytes of customer information. Computer-controlled factory equipment and industrial robots can now quickly readjust assembly lines. Finally, the Internet ties it all together and makes it easy for a company to interact with customers, learn about their preferences and respond. True marketing: giving customers what they want, rather than what the company can produce.

SOURCES: Adapted from Don Peppers, Martha Rogers and Bob Dorf, 'Is your company ready for one-to-one marketing?', *Harvard Business Review* (January–February 1999), pp. 151–60; Angus Kennedy, *The Internet: The Rough Guide* (2003); 'All yours', *The Economist* (1 April 2000), pp. 65–6; 'Mass customisation: a long march', *The Economist* (14 July 2001), pp. 79–81.

Ageing rock band Marillion established a dialogue with their fans prior to completing their as yet unnamed album set for release by EMI. While still recording in their Racket Club Studio, they emailed 30,000 fans on their database. Fans pre-ordering the album will receive an extra CD and additional artwork in which they will be named. Within two weeks of emailing they had 5,500 orders, some offering tremendous support to the band: 'I only want one [CD] but I'm sending 500 quid (€830) because I want to be part of it.' The pre-ordering made the fans happy, and enabled Marillion to cut a good deal with EMI since the record company was guaranteed a hit.[7]

As the trend towards more interactive dialogue and less advertising monologue continues, self-marketing will grow in importance. As more buyers look up consumer reports, join Internet product-discussion forums and place orders, marketers will have to influence the buying process in new ways. They will need to involve customers more in all phases of the product-development and buying process, increasing opportunities for buyers to practise self-marketing.

Segmenting consumer markets

There is no single way to segment a market. A marketer has to try different segmentation variables, alone and in combination, to find the best way to view the market structure. Table 10.1 outlines the major variables used in segmenting consumer markets. Here we look at the major *geographic*, *demographic*, *psychographic* and *behavioural variables*.

Geographic segmentation

Geographic segmentation— Dividing a market into different geographical units such as nations, states, regions, counties, cities or neighbourhoods.

Geographic segmentation calls for dividing the market into different geographical units, such as nations, states, regions, counties, cities or neighbourhoods. A company may decide to operate in one or a few geographical areas, or to operate in all areas but pay attention to geographical differences in needs and wants.

International lifestyles are emerging, but there are counter forces that continue to shape markets. Cross-cultural research has defined five 'mentality fields' for cars in Europe.[8] These show how much language demarcates common cultures and ways of life:

1. The north (Scandinavia).
2. The north-west (the United Kingdom, Iceland, and parts of Norway, Belgium and the Netherlands).
3. The centre (German mentality field extending to Switzerland and parts of Eastern Europe).
4. The west (the French-speaking area, including parts of Switzerland and Belgium).
5. The south (the Mediterranean, covering Spanish, Portuguese, Italian and Greek languages).

Self-expression is important to car buyers in all the geographical regions, but the similarity ends there. The western groups seek quality and practicality, the south want value for money, while the north-western group sees their car in very personal terms. The differences influence the cars they buy and how they are equipped. Although all developed nations worry about the environment, they do so in different ways. In Italy, France and the UK, motorists do not see their car as a source of pollution, while in Germany, demand for environmentally friendly cars is growing fast.

Climatic differences lead to different lifestyles and eating habits. In countries with warm climates, social life takes place outdoors and furniture is less important than in Nordic countries. Not noticing the different sizes of kitchens has caused many marketing mistakes. Philips started making profits in the Japanese market only after it made small coffeemakers to fit the cramped conditions there. In Spain, Coca-Cola withdrew its two-litre bottle after finding it did not fit local refrigerators.[9]

Many companies today have regional marketing programmes within national boundaries – localising their products, advertising, promotion and sales efforts to fit the needs of individual regions, cities and even neighbourhoods. Others are seeking to cultivate yet untapped territory. For example, IKEA expanded globally using its large blue-and-yellow stores and dedicated out-of-town sites that serve countries using a handful of stores. IKEA changed its strategy when acquiring the Habitat furniture chain from Storehouse. The small stores gave it access to passing trade and new customer segments who are less willing to travel. The Habitat chain also serves small towns. In making this significant shift, IKEA is also following the European trend towards town-centre shopping complexes. Having seen American urban decay, European politicians are resisting out-of-town developments.

Table 10.1 Market segmentation
variables for consumer markets

Variable	Typical breakdowns
Geographic	
Region	These can vary in scale from, say, Europe, through groupings of countries (Scandinavia), nations (Finland), to regions within countries (Lapland).
Country size	Giant (USA), large (Germany, Spain), medium (The Netherlands, Australia) or small (Malta, Lithuania).
City size	Under 5,000; 5,000–20,000; 20,000–50,000; 50,000–100,000; 100,000–250,000; 250,000–500,000; 500,000–1,000,000; 1,000,000–4,000,000; 4,000,000 and over.
Density	Urban, suburban, rural.
Climate	Tropical, sub-tropical, temperate, etc.
Demographic	
Age	Under 6, 6–11, 12–19, 20–34, 35–49, 50–64, 65+.
Gender	Male, female.
Family size	1–2, 3–4, 5+.
Family life cycle	Young, single; young, married, no children; young, married, youngest child under 6; young, married, youngest child 6 or over; older, married with children; older, married, no children under 18; older, single; other.
Income	Under €10,000; 10,000–15,000; 15,000–20,000; 20,000–30,000; 30,000–50,000; 50,000–75,000; 75,000–100,000; 100,000 and over.
Occupation	Professional and technical; managers, officials and proprietors; clerical, sales; craftsmen, foremen; operatives; farmers; retired; students; homemakers; unemployed.
Education	Grade school or less; some high school; high school graduate; university; postgraduate; professional.
Religion	Catholic, Protestant, Jewish, Islamic, etc.
Race	White, Black, Polynesian, Chinese, etc.
Nationality	American, British, German, Scandinavian, Latin American, Middle Eastern, Japanese, etc.
Psychographic	
Social class	Lower lowers, upper lowers, working class, middle class, upper middles, lower uppers, upper uppers.
Lifestyle	Achievers, believers, strivers.
Personality	Compulsive, gregarious, authoritarian, ambitious.
Behavioural	
Purchase occasion	Regular occasion, special occasion.
Benefits sought	Quality, service, economy.
User status	Non-user, ex-user, potential user, first-time user, regular user.
Usage rate	Light user, medium user, heavy user.
Loyalty status	None, medium, strong, absolute.
Readiness state	Unaware, aware, informed, interested, desirous, intending to buy.
Attitude towards product	Enthusiastic, positive, indifferent, negative, hostile.

Demographic segmentation

Demographic segmentation
—Dividing the market into
groups based on demo-
graphic variables such
as age, sex, family size,
family life cycle, income,
occupation, education,
religion, race and nationality.

Life-cycle segmentation—
Offering products or
marketing approaches that
recognise the consumer's
changing needs at different
stages of their life.

Demographic segmentation consists of dividing the market into groups based on variables such as age, gender, sexual orientation, family size, family life cycle, income, occupation, education, religion, ethnic community and nationality. Demographic factors are the most popular bases for segmenting customer groups. One reason is that consumer needs, wants and usage rates often vary closely with demographic variables. Another is that demographic variables are easier to measure than most other types of variable. Even when market segments are first defined using other bases – such as personality or behaviour – their demographics need to be known to assess the size of the target market and to reach it efficiently.

Age

Consumer needs and wants change with age. Some companies use age and **life-cycle segmentation**, offering different products or using different marketing approaches for different age and life-cycle groups. For example, Life Stage vitamins come in four versions, each designed for the special needs of specific age segments: chewable Children's Formula for children from 4 to 12 years old; Teen's Formula for teenagers; and two adult versions (Men's Formula and Women's Formula). Johnson & Johnson developed Affinity Shampoo to help women over 40 overcome age-related hair changes. McDonald's targets children, teens, adults and senior citizens with different ads and media.

LEGO's range shows the limits of age-based segmentation. For babies there are Duplo rattles (0 to 3 months), then there are round-edged activity toys made of two or three pieces (3 to 18 months). All these have the familiar LEGO lugs so that they will fit on to LEGO products. Next come Duplo construction kits or toys (2 to 5 years). Duplo bricks look like LEGO bricks, but are twice the size so that young children can manipulate but not swallow them. By the age of 3, children have developed the manipulative skills that allow them to progress to LEGO Basic. The progression is made easy by the small LEGO bricks fitting to Duplo ones.

Age-based segmentation works until children are 5 years old when fewer and fewer girls buy LEGO and boys' interests diversify. In comes LEGO Pirates (6–12 years), Railways (6–12), Technic (7–12), Model Team (9–12) and so on. Lego's product for the new millennium is Mindstorm, intelligent LEGO bricks. The result of a 10-year, DKr100 million (€13.4m) project, the bricks are programmed via an infrared transmitter connected to a PC.[10]

Marketers are continually trying to stretch the age envelope. Teletubbies and Rugrats are entertainment aimed at kids still wearing nappies. Both based on intensive market research, the movies project diametrically opposed views of life. They do, however, share one feature that has always been a feature of teen fads: parents don't like them.[11]

At the other end of childhood Sega and Sony are trying to extend computer gaming technology into business markets. Sega, which has typically focused on the teen market, is now targeting older customers. According to a Sega licensing executive, Sega's core market of 10 to 18-year-olds 'sit in their bedrooms playing games for hours'. Then, however, 'they turn 18 and discover girls . . . and the computer gets locked away'. To retain these young customers as they move into new life-cycle stages, Sega is launching a range of products for adults.[12]

Ethnic segmentation

The multi-ethnic communities within Europe define market segments for all manner of goods: clothes, music, cosmetics and many others. The communities also nurture businesses that appear beyond their own ethnic boundaries.

Gulam Kaderbhoy Noon has expanded his ethnic foods business to a wider community. In just over ten years he has made his Noon Products Europe's largest Indian ready-made meals business. Among his early inventions was Bombay Mix, a spicy nuts and nibbles snack food. He sells 3 million meals a month, many of which are the own-brands of leading grocers. He insists on authentic recipes, methods and ingredients rather than flavourings. Turmeric grows all over India, he explains, '[but] there's one area with a reputation for the very best, and that's the turmeric I want. It's such a small thing in terms of cost, but it's the pains you go to that counts. All good food is in its ingredients.'[13]

Life-cycle stage

Life-cycle stage is important in recreation markets. In the holiday market, for instance, Club 18–30 aims at young singles seeking the four Ss: sun, sand, sea and sex. This boisterous segment does not mix well with the families that the Club Mediterranean caters for. Children's activities and all-day child care are an important part of the latter's provision. Meanwhile, Saga Holidays caters for older people and keeps prices low by offering off-peak holidays.[14]

Gender

Gender segmentation is usual in clothing, hairdressing, cosmetics and magazines. Recently, marketers have noticed other opportunities for gender segmentation. For example, both men and women use most deodorant brands. Procter & Gamble, however, developed Secret as the brand specially formulated for a woman's chemistry, and then packaged and advertised the product to reinforce the female image. In contrast, Gillette's association with shaving makes its deodorant male oriented.

The car industry has also begun to use gender segmentation extensively. Women are a growing part of the car market. 'Selling to women should be no different than selling to men', notes one analyst. 'But there are subtleties that make a difference.'[15] Women have different frames, less upper-body strength and greater safety concerns. To address these issues, car makers are redesigning their cars with bonnets and boots that are easier to open, power steering in small cars, seats and seat belts that fit women better. They have also increased their emphasis on safety, highlighting features such as airbags and remote door locks. In their advertising, some manufacturers target women directly. Indeed, much TV advertising of small cars is now aimed at women and large advertising spreads are designed especially for women consumers in such magazines as *Cosmopolitan* and *Vogue*.

A growing number of websites also target women. For example, Handbag.com promotes itself as 'The Ultimate Accessory – a lifeline for most women. Somewhere to keep everything you need to see you through the day.' With women now representing 45 per cent of Web users – up from 10 per cent five years ago – there is an increasing number of portals dedicated to women. Examples are Charlottestreet.com and Freeserve's Icircle. IPC, publishers of *Marie Claire* and many other magazines, have launched Beme.com. 'The channels on the site are very mood based', according to editor Claire Simmonds. The look of the site betrays its origin in the home of many classy women's magazines. Besides being easy to navigate, the site is stylish, easy on the eyes and only contains ads carefully vetted to fit its ambience.[16]

Income

Income segmentation is often used for products and services such as cars, boats, clothing, cosmetics and travel. Many companies target affluent consumers with luxury goods and convenience services. The brands behind the French LVMH group's initials betray its focus on affluent consumers: Louis Vuitton luggage, Moët & Chandon champagne and Hennessy cognac. Besides its *haute couture* activities, LVMH owns Parfums Christian Dior, has taken control of Guerlain, the French fragrance house, and is stalking Van Clef & Arpels, the Paris-based jeweller. Others aiming at the super luxury market are Vertu's €20,000 mobile phones and high-frill, high-price Bangkok Airways. The mother of all battles is for the super luxury cars where Rolls-Royce's new RR01 (€250,000) from BMW will soon be joined by the Bentley Continental GT (€150,000) from VW, the Maybach (€300,000) from DaimlerChrysler, Lamborghini's LB-140 and Aston Martin's AM305 from Ford.[17]

However, not all companies grow by retaining their focus on the top-income segment. By developing more sophisticated stores with added range and value, established retailers have allowed new entrants to succeed by targeting less affluent market segments. KwikSave, Lidl and Aldi have taken advantage of this opportunity with a lean organisation, narrow product ranges, economically located stores and a no-frills operation that keeps prices down. Similarly, Christine zu Salm turned Germany's unsuccessful TM3 TV channel into Neun Live, a small but profitable operation, by producing low-cost, low-brow interactive programmes that have been criticised by the media establishment.[18]

Geodemographics

Geodemographics is an increasingly used segmentation method. Originally developed by the CACI Market Analysis Group as ACORN (A Classification Of Residential Neighbourhoods), it uses 40 variables from population census data to group residential areas. Geodemographics is developing fast. ACORN has been joined by PIN (Pinpoint Identified Neighbourhoods), Mosaic and Super Profile. Linking them to consumer panel databases is increasing the power of basic geodemographic databases. CCN Marketing has since extended this process to cover the EU using its EuroMOSAIC (Table 10.2).

Table 10.2 CCN EuroMOSAIC households across Europe (%)

Category	Name	B	D	IRL	I	NL	N	E	S	GB
E01	Elite suburbs	8	16	6	4	5	18	1	8	12
E02	Service (sector) communities	22	20	29	12	14	7	17	18	16
E03	Luxury flats	9	7	2	5	8	8	7	3	5
E04	Low-income inner city	5	9	10	8	11	10	1	8	9
E05	High-rise social housing	–	3	–	8	11	4	1	7	5
E06	Industrial communities	12	13	5	19	14	10	18	12	19
E07	Dynamic families	17	8	10	13	14	15	5	9	14
E08	Lower-income families	9	4	12	8	6	7	7	7	8
E09	Rural/agricultural	14	14	21	17	13	17	23	19	6
E10	Vacation/retirement	4	6	4	5	4	3	19	9	6

Psychographic segmentation

Psychographic segmentation divides buyers into groups based on social class, lifestyle or personality characteristics. People in the same demographic group can have very different psychographic make-ups.

Psychographic segmentation—Dividing a market into different groups based on social class, lifestyle or personality characteristics.

Social class

In Chapter 7, we described social classes and showed how they affect preferences in cars, clothes, home furnishings, leisure activities, reading habits and retailers. Many companies design products or services for specific social classes, building in features that appeal to them. In the UK, Butlin's holiday camps cater for working-class families. They cater for the whole family, but prominent attractions are variety shows, bingo, slot machines, discos, dancing and organised entertainment. The camps are very busy and the emphasis is upon fun. Much of the accommodation is basic, regimented, crowded and self-catering. In contrast, Center Parcs has a carless woodland layout with an emphasis on the outdoors and relaxation. Further up-market is Club Med whose ski and sea resorts have an emphasis on exotic locations and good food as well as activities.[19]

Lifestyle

As discussed in Chapter 7, people's interest in goods is affected by their lifestyles. Reciprocally, the goods they buy express their lifestyles. Marketers are increasingly segmenting their markets by consumer lifestyles. For example, General Foods used lifestyle analysis in its successful repositioning of Sanka decaffeinated coffee. For years, Sanka's staid, older image limited the product's market. To turn this situation around, General Foods launched an advertising campaign that positioned Sanka as an ideal drink for today's healthy, active lifestyles. The campaign targeted achievers of all ages, using a classic achiever appeal that Sanka 'Lets you be your best'. Advertising showed people in adventurous lifestyles, such as kayaking through rapids.

Lifestyle segments are either off-the-shelf methods from agencies or customised methods for individual companies. Many companies opt for off-the-shelf methods because of their familiarity and the high cost and complexity of developing their own. The ad agency Young and Rubican's Cross-Cultural Consumer Characterisation (4Cs) is a typical off-the-shelf method. It has three main segments:

- *The constrained*. People whose expenditure is limited by income. It includes the *resigned poor* who have accepted their poverty, and the more ambitious *struggling poor*.
- *The middle majority*. This segment contains *mainstreams* – the largest group of all – *aspirers* and *succeeders*.
- *The innovators*. A segment consisting of *transitionals* and *reformers*.

The *succeeders* are a successful group of people who like to feel in control. By showing travellers in complete control of a situation in which they had lost their American Express traveller's cheques and had them quickly returned, American Express advertising would appeal to this segment. They would be equally attracted to the ability to customise their Mercedes car. In contrast, *mainstreams* need security. They will buy well-known, safe major brands and avoid risk. Highly educated *reformers* would have none of that. They would trust their own judgement and try new ideas. These people are at the forefront of many new trends, such as ecologically friendly products and new tourist destinations.

Lifestyle segments can be superimposed on other segmentation methods. For instance, Third Age Research recognises the different lifestyles of older people. It identifies the *explorers* who like to take up new activities, the *organisers*, the *apathetic*, the *comfortable*, the *fearful*, the *poor me*, the *social lion* and the *status quo*.

Based on a study of over 2,000 respondents and 30,000 'snacking occasions', Nestlé developed its own lifestyle segments of the snacking market. Two major segments it identified were the very different *depressive chocolate lovers* and *energetic males*. The *depressive chocolate lovers* are predominantly young women who buy fast food and eat chocolate. They eat chocolate at any time, but particularly when depressed, to unwind or when bored in the evening at home. For these people taste is important, so they buy expensive products, like boxed chocolates, for themselves. Terry's Chocolate Orange, All Gold, Cadbury's Milk Flake and Black Magic appeal to them. In contrast, *energetic males* are young and disproportionately middle-income lads. They live at a fast pace, work hard, eat fast food and are reckless shoppers. Work tires them, but they exercise regularly and like lively places. They also eat chocolate in a hurry in the evening, at lunch or at mid-morning or afternoon breaks. Boxed chocolates are not for them, but they get their energy fix from countlines like Mars and Snickers.

Being multidimensional, lifestyle segments provide a rich picture of consumers. The *depressive chocolate lovers* and *energetic males* may be of the same age and social class, but their lifestyle segments start to tell us about the people and what appeals to them. An ad for the *energetic males* needs to be lively, social and fast – the product grabbed firmly and eaten.

Personality

Marketers have also used personality variables to segment markets, giving their products personalities that correspond to consumer personalities. Successful market segmentation strategies based on personality work for products such as cosmetics, cigarettes, insurance

Lifestyle segmentation: Duck Head targets a casual student lifestyle, claiming 'You can't get them old until you get them new.'
SOURCE: Duck Head Apparel Co.

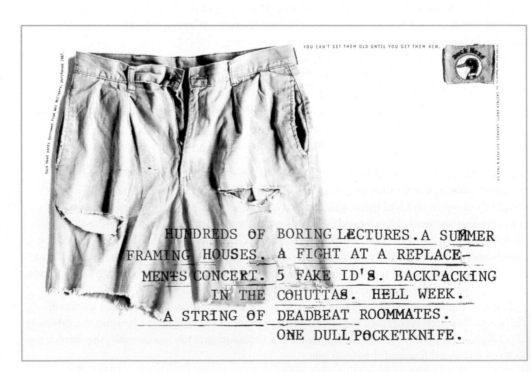

and alcohol. Honda used personality segmentation to power its way into the US market. Now Italian Vespa and British Triumph are following their lead:

> Bikes are about freedom. Honda ads shows a delighted child bouncing up and down on his bed while the announcer says, 'You've been trying to get there all your life.' The ad reminds viewers of the euphoric feelings they got when they broke away from authority and did things their parents told them not to do. The ads appeal to trendsetters and independent personalities in all age groups – 15 per cent are purchased by the over–50 group. Thus, Honda is appealing to the rebellious, independent kid in all of us. Meanwhile, Vespa motor-scooters attract cool individualists and their campaign is backed by Vespa boutiques. That is a different sort of individuality from that portrayed in Triumph motorcycles' product placement in *Mission Impossible 2* or the rebellious images of Marlon Brando's outlaw bikers in *The Wild Ones*.[20]

Behavioural segmentation

Behavioural segmentation divides buyers into groups based on their knowledge, attitudes, uses or responses to a product. Many marketers believe that behaviour variables are the best starting point for building market segments.

Occasions

Buyers can be grouped according to occasions when they get the idea to buy, make their purchase or use the purchased item. **Occasion segmentation** can help firms build up product usage. For example, most people drink orange juice at breakfast, but orange growers have promoted drinking orange juice as a cool and refreshing drink at other times of the day. Mother's Day and Father's Day are promoted to increase the sale of confectionery, flowers, cards and other gifts. The turkey farmer Bernard Matthews fought the seasonality in the turkey market. In some European countries the American bird was as synonymous with Christmas as Santa Claus. He had a problem. In most families, Christmas dinner was the only meal big enough to justify buying such a big bird. His answer was to repackage the meat as turkey steaks, sausages and burgers, and promote them for year-round use. His reformulated turkey is so successful that he is now reformulating New Zealand lamb.

Kodak uses occasion segmentation in designing and marketing its single-use cameras in multi-packs for partygoers or wedding guests. Weddings are such an important ritual in all cultures that whole industries focus on servicing these high-spending events.

Benefits sought

A powerful form of segmentation is to group buyers according to the different *benefits* that they seek from the product. **Benefit segmentation** requires finding the main benefits people look for in the product class, the kinds of people who look for each benefit and the major brands that deliver each benefit. One of the best examples of benefit segmentation was for the toothpaste market (see Table 10.3). Research found four benefit segments: economic, medicinal, cosmetic and taste. Each benefit group had special demographic, behavioural and psychographic characteristics. For example, the people seeking to prevent decay tended to have large families, were heavy toothpaste users and were conservative. Each segment also favoured certain brands. Most current brands appeal to one of these segments. For example, Crest tartar-control toothpaste stresses protection and appeals to the family segment; Aim looks and tastes good and appeals to children.

Behavioural segmentation— Dividing a market into groups based on consumer knowledge, attitude, use or response to a product.

Occasion segmentation— Dividing the market into groups according to occasions when buyers get the idea to buy, actually make their purchase, or use the purchased item.

Benefit segmentation— Dividing the market into groups according to the different benefits that consumers seek from the product.

Table 10.3
Benefit segmentation of the toothpaste market

Benefit segments	Demographics	Behaviour	Psychographics	Favoured brands
Economy (low price)	Men	Heavy users	High autonomy, value oriented	Brands on sale
Medicinal (decay prevention)	Large families	Heavy users	Hypochondriacal, conservative	Crest
Cosmetic (bright teeth)	Teens, young adults	Smokers	High sociability, active	Aqua-Fresh, Ultra Brite
Taste (good tasting)	Children	Spearmint lovers	High self-involvement, hedonistic	Colgate, Aim

SOURCES: Adapted from Russell J. Haley, 'Benefit segmentation: a decision-oriented research tool', *Journal of Marketing* (July 1968), pp. 30–5; see also Haley, 'Benefit segmentation: backwards and forwards', *Journal of Advertising Research* (February–March 1984), pp. 19–25; and Haley, 'Benefit segmentation – 20 years later', *Journal of Consumer Marketing*, **1** (1984), pp. 5–14.

> Colgate-Palmolive used benefit segmentation to reposition its Irish Spring soap. Research showed three deodorant soap benefit segments: men who prefer lightly scented deodorant soap; women who want a mildly scented, gentle soap; and a mixed, mostly male segment that wanted a strongly scented, refreshing soap. The original Irish Spring did well with the last segment, but Colgate wanted to target the larger middle segment. Thus it reformulated the soap and changed its advertising to give the product more of a family appeal.[21]

In short, companies can use benefit segmentation to clarify why people should buy their product, define the brand's chief attributes and clarify how it contrasts with competing brands. They can also search for new benefits and launch brands that deliver them.

User status

Some markets segment into non-users, ex-users, potential users, first-time users and regular users of a product. Potential users and regular users may require different kinds of marketing appeal. For example, one study found that blood donors are low in self-esteem, low risk takers and more highly concerned about their health; non-donors tend to be the opposite on all three dimensions. This suggests that social agencies should use different marketing approaches for keeping current donors and attracting new ones. Britain's voluntary Blood Transfusion Service tapped into the low self-esteem of many blood donors by sending out videos extolling the importance of their blood group: 'your type O blood makes you a universal donor critical to help people of blood groups O, A, B and AB in emergencies' or 'your type AB negative blood group is extremely rare'.

A company's market position will also influence its focus. Market share leaders will aim to attract potential users, whereas smaller firms will focus on attracting current users away from the market leader. Golden Wonder concentrated on regular users to give it a dominant market share with its Pot Noodle and Pot Rice. It was first on the market with its dehydrated snack meals in pots, but new entrants took sales from it. It gained 80 per cent market share by making its brand more appealing to existing users. Kellogg's took a different approach with its Bran Flakes breakfast cereal. Rather than keeping to the original health-conscious users, it aimed at non-users by promoting the superior flavour of the product.

Usage rate

Some markets also segment into light, medium and heavy-user groups. Heavy users are often a small percentage of the market, but account for a high percentage of total buying. For example, the owner of a pub in a mining town knows that 41 per cent of the adult population of the village buy beer. However, the heavy users accounted for 87 per cent of the beer consumed – almost seven times as much as the light users. Clearly, the owner would prefer to attract heavy users to his pub rather than light users.

Airlines' frequent flyer programmes are aimed at heavy users who, because they are business travellers, also buy expensive tickets. British Airways Executive Club blue card members get free AirMiles each time they travel and other priority benefits when booking and checking in. As usage mounts, Club members are upgraded to silver and gold cards, each giving extra benefits and services. Almost all airlines offer similar incentives, but since benefits mount with usage, it pays the frequent flyer to be loyal. Some operators share their schemes to provide wider benefits to the regular traveller.

Several converging new technologies have young people as heavy users. Once stereotyped as heavy users of clothes and pop music, today's young are leading the market in computer games, use of the Internet and mobile phones. The convergence has not been lost on marketers. The latest generation of computer games machines enable Internet access as well as having the ability to play CD music and DVD movies – all media highly used by the young. This convergence explains why Apple's iPod digital jukebox dominated Internet searches and purchases in the run-up to Christmas 2003. It brings together the young market with its heavy Internet use, interest in popular music, an Internet-based product used in downloading and a cute way of storing 10,000 tracks.[22]

Loyalty status

Many firms are now trying to segment their markets by loyalty and are using loyalty schemes to do it. They assume that some consumers are completely loyal – they buy one brand all the time. Others are somewhat loyal – they are loyal to two or three brands of a given product, or favour one brand while sometimes buying others. Still other buyers show no loyalty to any brand. They either want something different each time they buy or always buy a brand on sale. In most cases, marketers split buyers into groups according to their loyalty to their product or service, then focus on the profitable loyal customers.

Loyalty schemes go beyond the continuity programmes that have been used for decades. They seek to build a relationship between the buyer and the brand. In Australia members of Unilever's Omomatic Club – for people with front-loading washing machines – get newsletters, brochures, samples and gift catalogues. 'Front loaders' are rare in Australia, so the club keeps Unilever in touch with a micromarket that its Omomatic detergent is made for. Nestlé's Casa Buitoni Club is for people interested in an Italian lifestyle and cooking. The pasta market is fragmented and penetrated by retailers' own brands, so the club aims to build loyalty and Buitoni's brand heritage of focusing on enthusiasts. The Swatch Club was formed after Swatch studied the market for cult objects. Members are helped to build up their Swatch collection and offered special editions.

The effectiveness of loyalty schemes and segmentation by loyalty is limited by how people buy. Loyal customers are few and very hard to find in most markets. Most customers are promiscuous and polygamous in their relationship with brands. Those with favoured brands will promiscuously try alternatives occasionally, and most customers choose from a repertoire of favourites. But even the polygamous brand users change their repertoires and make opportunistic purchases. There is also a limit to the attention customers devote to some brands, plus the low cost of switching from one brand to another. In many markets, attempts to build brand loyalty will, like most sales promotions, last only as long as the campaign. There is also a danger of loyalty being displaced from the brand to the loyalty scheme – the air miles acquired becoming more important than the airline flown.[23]

Buyer-readiness stage

Buyer-readiness stages—
The stages that consumers normally pass through on their way to purchase, including awareness, knowledge, liking, preference, conviction and purchase.

A market consists of people in different **buyer-readiness stages** of readiness to buy a product. Some people are unaware of the product, some are aware, some are informed, some are interested, some want the product, and some intend to buy. The relative numbers at each stage make a big difference in designing the marketing programme. Car dealers use their databases to increase customer care and to estimate when customers are ready to buy. Guarantees lock customers into having the first few services from a dealer, but after that, the dealer can estimate when services are needed. Close to the due date the customer is sent a reminder or rung to arrange for a service. Some time later the dealer can estimate that the customer is getting ready to buy a new car and can then send out details of new models or deals. Contract publishers, such as Condé Nast and Redwood, now produce contract magazines that fit customers' readiness stage. Usually used to support luxury goods sales, Redwood prepares a 15,000 run of a magazine sent to young people who have initially responded to Army recruitment advertising.[24]

Indiscriminate mailing that does not take into account the buyer-readiness stage can damage relationships. By sending unwanted brochures the dealer becomes a source of junk mail. Even worse, the satisfaction of recent customers reduces if they are told about a better deal or replacement model soon after their purchase.

Attitude towards product

People in a market can be enthusiastic, positive, indifferent, negative or hostile about a product. Door-to-door workers in a political campaign use a given voter's attitude to determine how much time to spend with that voter. They thank enthusiastic voters and remind them to vote; they spend little or no time trying to change the attitudes of negative and hostile voters. They reinforce those who are positive and try to win the votes of those who are indifferent. In such marketing situations, attitudes can be effective segmentation variables.

The world charity Oxfam needs to keep donations up and costs down. Segmentation helps it do this. It values all donors, but treat segments differently. A lot of its income is from *committed givers* who donate regularly, but want low involvement with the charity. They get *Oxfam News*, special appeals and gift catalogues. *Oxfam Project Partners* want and get much more contact with Oxfam. These are further segmented by their choice of project, on which they get regular feedback. Through this scheme, Oxfam, like Action Aid, develops a relationship between the giver and the final recipient. *Leading donors* receive special customer care and information about how their money was spent. Many donors can give little time to Oxfam, but other groups enjoy working in the charity's shops or are enthusiastic *lottery ticket vendors*.[25]

Segmenting business markets

Consumer and business marketers use many of the same variables to segment their markets. Business buyers segment geographically or by benefits sought, user status, usage rate, loyalty status, readiness state and attitudes. Yet business marketers also use some additional variables which, as Table 10.4 shows, include business customer *demographics* (industry, company size), *operating characteristics*, *buying approaches*, *situational factors*, and *personal characteristics*.[26]

Table 10.4 Primary segmentation variables for business markets

Demographics

Industry. **Which industries that buy this product should we focus on?**
Company size. **What size companies should we focus on?**
Location. **What geographical areas should we focus on?**

Operating variables

Technology. **What customer technologies should we focus on?**
User/non-user status. **Should we focus on heavy, medium or light users, or non-users?**
Customer capabilities. **Should we focus on customers needing many services or few services?**

Purchasing approaches

Purchasing function organisations. **Should we focus on companies with highly centralised or decentralised purchasing organisations?**
Power structure. **Should we focus on companies that are engineering dominated, financially dominated or marketing dominated?**
Nature of existing relationships. **Should we focus on companies with which we already have strong relationships or simply go after the most desirable companies?**
General purchase policies. **Should we focus on companies that prefer leasing? Service contracts? Systems purchases? Sealed bidding?**
Purchasing criteria. **Should we focus on companies that are seeking quality? Service? Price?**

Situational factors

Urgency. **Should we focus on companies that need quick delivery or service?**
Specific application. **Should we focus on certain applications of our product rather than all applications?**
Size of order. **Should we focus on large or small orders?**

Personal characteristics

Buyer–seller similarity. **Should we focus on companies whose people and values are similar to ours?**
Attitudes towards risk. **Should we focus on risk-taking or risk-avoiding customers?**
Loyalty. **Should we focus on companies that show high loyalty to their suppliers?**

SOURCES: Adapted from Thomas V. Bonoma and Benson P. Shapiro, *Segmenting the Industrial Market* (Lexington, MA: Lexington Books, 1983); see also John Berrigan and Carl Finkbeiner, *Segmentation Marketing: New methods for capturing business* (New York: Harper Business, 1992).

The table lists important questions that business marketers should ask in determining which customers they want to serve. By going after segments instead of the whole market, companies have a much better chance to deliver value to consumers and to receive maximum rewards for close attention to consumer needs. Thus Pirelli and other tyre companies should decide which *industries* they want to serve. Manufacturers buying tyres vary in their needs. Makers of luxury and high-performance cars want higher-grade tyres than makers of economy models. In addition, the tyres needed by aircraft manufacturers must meet much higher safety standards than tyres needed by farm tractor manufacturers.

Within the chosen industry, a company can further segment by *customer size* or *geographic location*. The company might set up separate systems for dealing with larger or multiple-location customers. For example, Steelcase, a big producer of office furniture, first segments customers into 10 industries, including banking, insurance and electronics. Next, company salespeople work with independent Steelcase dealers to handle smaller, local or regional Steelcase customers in each segment. Many national, multiple-location customers, such as Shell or Philips, have special needs that may reach beyond the scope of individual dealers. So Steelcase uses national accounts managers to help its dealer networks handle its national accounts.

Within a given target industry and customer size, the company can segment by *purchase approaches and criteria*. For example, government, university and industrial laboratories typically differ in their purchase criteria for scientific instruments. Government labs need low prices (because they have difficulty in getting funds to buy instruments) and service contracts (because they can easily get money to maintain instruments). University labs want equipment that needs little regular service because they do not have service people on their payrolls. Industrial labs need highly reliable equipment because they cannot afford downtime.

Table 10.4 focuses on business buyer *characteristics*. However, as in consumer segmentation, many marketers believe that *buying behaviour* and *benefits* provide the best basis for segmenting business markets. For example, a recent study of the customers of Signode Corporation's industrial packaging division revealed four segments, each seeking a different mix of price and service benefits:

1. *Programmed buyers.* These buyers view Signode's products as not very important to their operations. They buy the products as a routine purchase, usually pay full price and accept below-average service. Clearly this is a highly profitable segment for Signode.

2. *Relationship buyers.* These buyers regard Signode's packaging products as moderately important and are knowledgeable about competitors' offerings. They prefer to buy from Signode as long as its price is reasonably competitive. They receive a small discount and a modest amount of service. This segment is Signode's second most profitable.

3. *Transaction buyers.* These buyers see Signode's products as very important to their operations. They are price and service sensitive. They receive about a 10 per cent discount and above-average service. They are knowledgeable about competitors' offerings and are ready to switch for a better price, even if it means losing some service.

4. *Bargain hunters.* These buyers see Signode's products as very important and demand the deepest discount and the highest service. They know the alternative suppliers, bargain hard and are ready to switch at the slightest dissatisfaction. Signode needs these buyers for volume purposes, but they are not very profitable.

This segmentation scheme has helped Signode to do a better job of designing marketing strategies that take into account each segment's unique reactions to varying levels of price and service.[27]

Segmenting international markets

Few companies have either the resources or the will to operate in all, or even most, of the more than 170 countries that dot the globe. Although some large companies, such as Unilever or Sony, sell products in more than 100 countries, most international firms focus on a smaller set. Operating in many countries presents new challenges.[28] The different countries of the world, even those that are close together, can vary dramatically in their economic, cultural and political make-up. Thus, just as they do within their domestic markets, international firms need to group their world markets into segments with distinct buying needs and behaviours.

Companies can segment international markets using one or a combination of several variables. They can segment by *geographic location*, grouping countries by regions such as western Europe, the Pacific Rim, the Middle East or Africa. Countries in many regions have already organised geographically into market groups or 'free-trade zones', such as the European Union, the Association of South-East Asian Nations (ASEAN) and the North American Free Trade Association (NAFTA). These associations reduce trade barriers between member countries, creating larger and more homogeneous markets.

Geographic segmentation assumes that nations close to one another will have many common traits and behaviours. Although this is often the case, there are many exceptions. For example, although the United States and Canada have much in common, both differ culturally and economically from neighbouring Mexico. Even within a region, consumers can differ widely:

> Many marketers think everything between the Rio Grande and Tierra del Fuego at the southern tip of South America is the same, including the 400 million inhabitants. They are wrong. The Dominican Republic is no more like Argentina than Sicily is like Sweden. Many Latin Americans do not speak Spanish, including 140 million Portuguese-speaking Brazilians and the millions in other countries who speak a variety of Indian dialects.

Some world markets segment on *economic factors*. For example, countries might group by population income levels or by their overall level of economic development. Some countries, such as the so-called Group of Eight – the United States, the United Kingdom, France, Germany, Japan, Canada, Italy and Russia – have established highly industrialised economies. Other countries have newly industrialised or developing economies (Singapore, Malaysia, Taiwan, South Korea, Brazil, Mexico and now China). Still others are less developed (India, sub-Saharan Africa). A company's economic structure shapes its population's product and service needs and, therefore, the marketing opportunities it offers.

Intermarket segmentation: teenagers in the developed world show surprising similarity, no matter where they live. Thus, many companies target teenagers with worldwide campaigns.
SOURCE: Jeff Baker, Getty Images, Inc. – Hulton Archive Photos (left); SW Productions, Getty Images, Inc. (right).

Political and legal factors such as the type and stability of government, receptivity towards foreign firms, monetary regulations and the amount of bureaucracy can segment countries. These factors can play a crucial role in a company's choice of which countries to enter and how. *Cultural factors* can also segment markets. International markets can group according to common languages, religions, values and attitudes, customs and behavioural patterns.

Segmenting international markets by geographic, economic, political, cultural and other factors assumes that segments should consist of clusters and countries. However, many companies use a different approach, called *intermarket segmentation*. Using this approach, they form segments of consumers who have similar needs and buying behaviour even though they are from different countries. For example, BMW, Mercedes-Benz, Saab and Volvo target the world's well-to-do, regardless of their country. Similarly, an agricultural chemical manufacturer might focus on small farmers in a variety of developing countries:

> These [small farmers], whether from Pakistan or Indonesia or Kenya or Mexico, appear to represent common needs and behaviour. Most of them till the land using bullock carts and have little cash to buy agricultural inputs. They lack the education . . . to appreciate fully the value of using fertiliser and depend on government help for such things as seeds, pesticides and fertiliser. They acquire farming needs from local suppliers and count on word-of-mouth to learn and accept new things and ideas. Thus, even though these farmers are continents apart and even though they speak different languages and have different cultural backgrounds, they may represent a homogeneous market segment.

Multivariate segmentation

Most of the time companies integrate ways of segmenting markets. We have already mentioned how Lego segments by age until children develop different interests, and how Third Age Research first focuses on older people, then forms lifestyle segments. There are several ways of combining segments.

Simple multivariate segmentation

Many companies segment markets by combining two or more demographic variables. Consider the market for deodorant soaps. Many different kinds of consumer use the top-selling deodorant soap brands, but gender and age are the most useful variables in distinguishing the users of one brand from those of another. In the United States, men and women differ in their deodorant soap preferences. Top men's brands include Dial, Safeguard and Irish Spring – these brands account for over 30 per cent of the men's soap market. Women, in contrast, prefer Dial, Zest and Coast, which account for 23 per cent of the women's soap market. The leading deodorant soaps also appeal differently to different age segments. For example, Dial appeals more to men aged 45 to 68 than to younger men. Women aged 35 to 44, however, are more likely than the average woman to use Dial. Coast appeals much more to younger men and women than to older people – men and women aged 18 to 24 are about a third more likely than the average to use Coast.

Advanced multivariate segmentation

In multivariate segmentation, segments are formed using a number of variables simultaneously. We have already introduced some of these – for example, geodemographic segmentation based on census data, and lifestyle segments based on psychographic variables. Since multivariate segments are composed of several dimensions, they provide a much fuller picture of the consumer.

A multinational drug company used to segment its market geographically until it found that its sales budgets were limited by legislation. That meant that it had to use its detailers (ethical drug salespeople) more carefully. It developed its multivariate segments using the prescribing habits of doctors for numerous drugs. It identified nine segments of doctors with clear marketing implications. Among them were:

■ *Initiators* who prescribed a wide range of drugs in large volumes, but were also eager to try new ones. They were opinion leaders and researchers, but did not have time to see detailers. This group is hard for detailers to see, but critical to the success of new products. They were recognised as 'thought leaders' and had special, research-based promotions and programmes designed for them.

■ *Kinderschrecks* have quite high prescription rates and were willing to see detailers, but had few children patients. They are an accessible and attractive target, but not for children or postnatal products.

■ *Thrifty housewives* were often married women with children who did not run their medical practice full time. They had few patients, prescribed very few drugs and were usually unavailable to detailers. This segment was not attractive.

This allowed the drug company to select target markets for campaigns and help detailers when selling to them.[29]

Multistage segmentation

It is often necessary to segment a market first one way and then another. For example, most multinationals segment their markets first regionally or nationally (macrosegmentation) and then by another means inside each area (microsegmentation). This can reflect the changing needs of geographical areas or the autonomy that is given to local managers to run their businesses. Often the macrosegmentation is demographic while microsegmentation is psychographic or behavioural. A Swedish study of an industrial market shows a clear split.[30] At the macro level, the most commonly used methods are geographical, firm size, organisation (how customer firms are structured), age of firm and age of the chief executive. At the micro level there is more variety: firms' goals, market niches, competition, competitive advantage, expansion plans, personal needs, type of work done, customer type and size of customers.

At times, segmentation may reach to three or more levels. In industrial markets, for instance, a third level could be the individuals within a buying centre – the likely user of a machine tool being approached in a different way to the financial director who would have to pay for it.

Developing market segments

Segmenting markets is a research-based exercise with several stages. These apply irrespective of whether the method used is simple demographics or complex and multivariate.

1. *Qualitative research*. Exploratory research techniques find the motivations, attitude and behaviour of customers. Typical methods are focus-group interviewing, elicitation interviews or repertory grid techniques. At the same time, the researcher can find out the customers' view of competitive products. It is easy for a maker to define the competition in terms of those making similar products, whereas the customers take a broader view. Once brewers realised that people sometimes drank mineral water or soft drinks instead of beer, they knew the structure of their market was changing.

2. *Quantitative research*. Quantitative research identifies the important dimensions describing the market. Data are gathered by mail or personal interviews from enough customers to allow analysis. The sample size will depend upon the level of accuracy needed, the limits of the statistical techniques to be used and the need for sufficient information on each segment. The usual minimum is 100 interviews per segment; if, therefore, there are three or four unequal segments, several hundred completed questionnaires will do. These are used to produce a structured questionnaire measuring:

   - attributes and their importance ratings;
   - brand awareness and brand ratings;
   - product-usage patterns;
   - attitude towards the product category; and
   - demographics, psychology and media habits.

3. *Analysis*. The data collected depend on the sort of analysis to be used. The most common process is the use of *factor analysis* to remove highly correlated variables, then *cluster analysis* to find the segments. Other techniques are available. Practitioners often use *Automatic Interaction Detection* (AID), and *conjoint analysis* is growing in popularity.

4. *Validation*. It is important to check whether the segments are real or have occurred by chance. *Cluster analysis* has an ability to extract interesting-looking clusters from random data, so this stage is critical. Validation can be by analysing the statistics from the analysis, replicating the results using new data, or experimenting with the segments.

5. *Profiling*. Each cluster is profiled to show its distinguishing attitudes, behaviour, demographics and so forth. Usually the clusters get a descriptive name. We saw some of these earlier: *thrifty housewives* and *initiators* among doctors, *organisers* and *explorers* among older people, or the *energetic male* and *depressive chocolate eater*.

Requirements for effective segmentation

Clearly there are many ways to segment a market, but not all segmentations are effective. For example, buyers of table salt may divide into blond and brunette customers, but hair colour obviously does not affect the purchase of salt. Furthermore, if all salt buyers bought the same amount each month, believed all salt is the same and wanted to pay the same price, the company would not benefit from segmenting this market.

To be useful, market segments must have the following characteristics:

■ **Measurability**. The size, buying power and profiles of the segments need measuring. Certain segmentation variables are difficult to measure. For example, there are 30 million left-handed people in Europe – almost equalling the entire population of Canada – yet few firms target them. The crucial problem may be that the segment is hard to identify and measure.

In contrast, the one-time repressed gay market is becoming increasingly important. Some companies, such as Massow Financial Services or the travel agents Sensations and D Tours, are specialising in the gay market. Others, such as the British Tourist Authority, KLM, Royal Shakespeare Company and Absolut Vodka, have products and campaigns tailored to the community. Estimates put the gay market between 6 and 20 per cent of the population and Mintel's Pat Neviani-Aston admits that reliable estimates are few because of people's residual unwillingness to reveal their true sexuality.

■ **Accessibility**. Can market segments be effectively reached and served? Some mainstream campaigns – including, IKEA in Scandinavia and P&G's Lenor in Germany – have used gay themes. However, word of mouth is very important in the often tightly knit gay community. To this can be added the gay media, such as *Blue Magazine*, and gay venues.

■ **Substantiality**. The market segments are large or profitable enough to serve. This is certainly true of the gay market, described by the *Wall Street Journal* as 'the most profitable market in the country'. The gay community shares many of the features of young heterosexuals that makes it very attractive, explains Pat Neviani-Aston: 'dual income, no kids, fairly affluent, higher than average number of holidays, into fashion, cultural events, theatre, good restaurants and hotels'.

■ **Actionability**. Effective programmes need to attract and serve the segments. There are many cases of this being possible within the gay community. Both Absolut Vodka and Bacardi have strong campaigns built around the gay scene. Both British Airways and the British Tourist Authority have partnered with IGLTA (International Gay and Lesbian Travel Association) to attract US gay customers.

Measurability—The degree to which the size, purchasing power and profits of a market segment can be measured.

Accessibility—The degree to which a market segment can be reached and served.

Substantiality—The degree to which a market segment is sufficiently large or profitable.

Actionability—The degree to which effective programmes can be designed for attracting and serving a given market segment.

Market targeting

Marketing segmentation reveals the firm's market-segment opportunities. The firm now has to evaluate the various segments and decide how many and which ones to target. At this point we will look at how companies evaluate and select target segments.

This Smirnoff vodka ad leaves its target market in little doubt.
SOURCE: Smirnoff, Lowe Howard–Spinks Agency, Illustrator: Bob Hersey.

Evaluating market segments

In evaluating different market segments, a firm must look at two dimensions: segment attractiveness and company fit.

Segment attractiveness

The company must first collect and analyse data on current sales value, projected sales-growth rates and expected profit margins for the various segments. Segments with the right size and growth characteristics are interesting. But 'right size and growth' are relative matters. Some companies will want to target segments with large current sales, a high growth rate and a high profit margin. However, the largest, fastest-growing segments are not always the most attractive ones for every company. Smaller companies may find that they lack the skills and resources needed to serve the larger segments, or that these segments are too competitive. Such companies may select segments that are smaller and less attractive, in an absolute sense, but that are potentially more profitable for them.

A segment might have desirable size and growth and still not be attractive from a profitability point of view. The company must examine several significant structural factors that affect long-run segment attractiveness. For example, the company should assess current and potential *competitors*. A segment is less attractive if it already contains many strong and aggressive competitors. The relative *power of buyers* also affects segment attractiveness. If the buyers in a segment possess strong or increasing bargaining power relative to sellers, they will try to force prices down, demand more quality or services, and set competitors against one another. All these actions will reduce the sellers' profitability. Finally, segment attractiveness depends on the relative *power of suppliers*. A segment is less attractive if the suppliers of raw materials, equipment, labour and services in the segment are powerful enough to raise prices or reduce the quality or quantity of ordered goods and services. Suppliers tend to be powerful when they are large and concentrated, when few substitutes exist, or when the supplied product is an important input.

Business strengths

Even if a segment has the right size and growth and is structurally attractive, the company must consider its objectives and resources for that segment. It is best to discard some attractive segments quickly because they do not mesh with the company's *long-run objectives*. Although such segments might be tempting in themselves, they might divert the company's attention and energies away from its main goals. They might be a poor choice from an environmental, political or social-responsibility viewpoint. For example, in recent years, several companies and industries have been criticised for unfairly targeting vulnerable segments – children, the aged, low-income minorities and others – with questionable products or tactics.

Even powerful companies find it hard making headway in markets where they start weak. RTZ is the world's largest mineral extraction company, but when it moved into bulk chemicals and petroleum, it found it could not compete. Before moving into a segment, a firm should consider its current position in that market. A low *market share* indicates weakness. Has the firm the energy, will or resources to build it up to economical levels? A firm's *growing market share* suggests strength, while, conversely, a declining market share suggests a weakness that entering new segments may not help. If a segment uses a firm's *marketing assets*, then it fits the company's strengths. If not, the segment could be costly to develop. This accounts for Whitbread selling off its 'unbranded' pub chains that it sees as low-margin activities that lack the brand-building potential of Marriott hotels, Brewers Fayre restaurants and David Lloyd sports clubs.[31]

Mars' excursion into the iced confectionery market proved difficult. The European iced confectionery market is growing, Mars has the technology and brands that stretched well into ice-cream, but it did not have freezers in shops. Freezers are usually owned by Unilever's Walls or Nestlé's Lyons Maid, both experts in frozen food, who had no reason to let Mars in. However, Mars' *unique products* and *valued reputation* allowed it to gain market share against established competitors.

Non-marketing dimensions influence the ability of a company to succeed in a segment. Has it *low costs*, or has it *underutilised capacity*? Also, does the segment fit the firm's *technology strengths*? DaimlerChrysler has bought high-technology businesses because it believes it will gain from them information and skills it could use in its core car and truck activities. Final considerations are the resources that the firm can bring to the market. These include appropriate *marketing skills*, *general management strengths* and the chance for *forward or backward integration* into the firm's other activities.

Selecting market segments

Royal Dutch/Shell's directional policy matrix plots market attractiveness of segments against business strengths. We introduced the method, along with GE's matrix, in Chapter 3. Originally developed as a way of balancing business portfolios, it is also well suited to decision making about which markets to target. Figure 10.2 shows an application by an Austrian industrial engineering and construction company.

When a segment fits the company's strengths, the company must then decide whether it has the skills and resources needed to succeed in that segment. Each segment has certain success requirements. If the company lacks and cannot readily obtain the strengths needed to compete successfully in a segment, it should not enter the segment. Even if the company possesses the *required* strengths, it needs to employ skills and resources *superior* to those of the competition to really win in a market segment. The company should enter segments only where it can offer superior value and gain advantages over competitors. The company in Figure 10.2 is not very strong in any of the most attractive segments. Segments 13 and 17 look most appealing because they are moderately attractive and fit the firm's strengths. Segment 3 is similar, but the firm needs to build its strengths if it is to compete there. Segments 1, 6 and 9 are attractive, but do not fit the firm's strengths. The firm has to develop new strengths if it is to compete in them. Without the investment the segments are not worth entering, so the firm has to consider the investment needed to enter more than one. Although the firm's strengths are suitable for segments 2 and 12, they are not attractive.

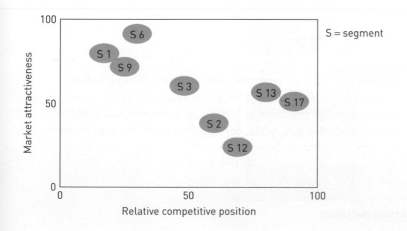

Figure 10.2 Portfolio of customer segments
SOURCE: Reprinted from 'Systematic positioning', in *European Marketing Academy Proceedings*, 26 April to 9 May 1992, Aarhus, (Dreher, A., Ritter, A., and Mühlbacher, H., 1992), reproduced by kind permission of Hans Mühlbacker.

Segment strategy

Target market—A set of buyers sharing common needs or characteristics that the company decides to serve.

Undifferentiated marketing—A market-coverage strategy in which a firm decides to ignore market segment differences and go after the whole market with one offer.

After evaluating different segments, the company must now decide which and how many segments to serve. This is the problem of *target-market selection*. A **target market** consists of a set of buyers who share common needs or characteristics that the company decides to serve. Figure 10.3 shows that the firm can adopt one of three market-coverage strategies: undifferentiated marketing, differentiated marketing and concentrated marketing.

Undifferentiated marketing

Using an **undifferentiated marketing** strategy, a firm might decide to ignore market segment differences and go after the whole market with one offer. This can be because there are weak segment differences or through the belief that the product's appeal transcends segments. The offer will focus on what is *common* in the needs of consumers rather than on what is *different*. The company designs a product and a marketing programme that appeal to the largest number of buyers. It relies on quality, mass distribution and mass advertising to give the product a superior image in people's minds. Advertising and promotions have to avoid alienating segments, and so are often based on product features, like 'Polo, the mint with the hole', or associated with a personality of broad appeal, like Esso's tiger.

Undifferentiated marketing provides cost economies. The narrow product line keeps down production, inventory and transportation costs. The undifferentiated advertising programme keeps down advertising costs. The absence of segment marketing research and planning lowers the costs of market research and product management.

Figure 10.3 Three alternative market-coverage strategies

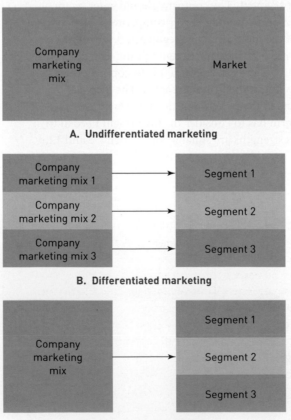

A. Undifferentiated marketing

B. Differentiated marketing

C. Concentrated marketing

418

Most modern marketers, however, have strong doubts about this strategy. Difficulties arise in developing a product or brand that will satisfy all consumers. Firms using undifferentiated marketing typically develop an offer aimed at the largest segments in the market. When several firms do this, there is heavy competition in the largest segments and neglected customers in the smaller ones. The result is that the larger segments may be less profitable because they attract heavy competition. Recognition of this problem has led to firms addressing smaller market segments. Another problem is erosion of the mass market as competitors develop new appeals or segments. For example, Polo mints have faced attacks from competitors aiming at different benefit segments: Extra Strong mints for people who want a strong taste and Clorets as breath fresheners. At the same time, Polo faces direct competition from similarly packaged Trebor Mints in Europe and Duplex in south-east Asia.

Differentiated marketing

Using a **differentiated marketing** strategy, a firm decides to target several market segments and designs separate offers for each. General Motors tries to produce a car for every 'purse, purpose and personality'. By offering product and marketing variations, it hopes for higher sales and a stronger position within each market segment. GM hopes that a stronger position in several segments will strengthen consumers' overall identification of the company with the product category. It also hopes for greater repeat buying because the firm's offer better matches the customer's desire.

Originally Martini products were not marketed separately. Advertising concentrated on the Martini brand and its exciting international lifestyle: 'anytime, anyplace, anywhere'. That changed to having the main Martini brands aimed at clearly defined target markets:

Differentiated marketing— A market-coverage strategy in which a firm decides to target several market segments and designs separate offers for each.

- Martini Rosso, the most popular variety, is aimed at a broad sector of the market. Its ads show it being enjoyed by an attractive young couple with 'Our martini is Rosso' or by a small chic group relaxing in elegant surroundings: 'The bitter sweet sensation'.
- Martini Bianco is targeted at people in their twenties who like light alcoholic drinks. It is shown being casually drunk with ice by a sporty, boisterous set, out of doors: 'The sunny side of life'.
- Martini Extra Dry is for the sophisticated drinker. The advertising focuses on the bottle and the product in an atmosphere of quiet sophistication.

Differentiated marketing typically creates more total sales than does undifferentiated marketing. KLM could fill all the seats on its New York flights charging APEX fares, but its own income and the number of flyers are increased by segmenting the market. In the main cabin or on the upper deck of each Boeing 747–400 taking off from Schiphol Airport, there will be about 300 economy passengers. Some of these, holding restricted APEX tickets costing about €500, will be sitting next to people who have paid over €1,000 for the same flight. They may have booked late or have an open ticket. Forward of them will be about 80 Flying Dutchmen, KLM business-class passengers whose companies paid €3,000 for each seat. In the extreme nose could be about 20 first-class passengers at over €5,000 each. The flight could not operate if everyone paid APEX fares because the Boeing would be full before the airline had covered the operating cost. If only full economy fares were charged, many passengers could not afford to fly, so an economy-class 747–400 could not be justified. Also, some first-class passengers would be deterred from travelling with the crowd. First-class passengers demand big seats, and their catering alone costs over €100 each, but they help maximise the revenue of the airline and the number of people flying.

Concentrated marketing

A third market-coverage strategy, **concentrated marketing**, is especially appealing when company resources are limited. Instead of going after a small share of a large market, the firm goes after a large share of one or a few submarkets. For example, Oshkosh Trucks is the world's largest producer of airport rescue trucks and frontloading concrete mixers. Mills & Boon, which has grown to be one of the world's most successful publishers, targets its inexpensive romantic novels at women in search of romance. The company has researched and knows its market:

- Having the word 'wedding' in a book title guarantees higher sales.
- The heroine is often plain, not gorgeous, to promote reader identification: 'no oil painting in the way of looks'; kind and polite and pleasant and unobtrusive. And best of all, homely.
- The best settings for the story are a hospital or an aircraft (lots of chance for life or death action); doctors and pilots are the best heroes.
- The novels always end happily.[32]

Like Mills & Boon, through concentrated marketing, a firm can achieve a strong market position in the segments (or niches) it serves because of its greater knowledge of the segments and its special reputation. It also enjoys many operating economies because of specialisation in production, distribution and promotion. A firm can earn a high rate of return on its investment from well-chosen segments.

At the same time, concentrated marketing can involve higher than normal risks. A particular market segment can turn sour. For example, when the 1980s boom ended, people stopped buying expensive sports cars and Porsche's earnings went deeply into the red. Another risk is larger competitors entering the segment. High margins, the glamour and lack of competition in the sports car market has attracted Mazda, Toyota and Honda as powerful competitors in that market. Fashion changes can also damage the niche's credibility. The yuppies who made Porsche's fortunes in the 1980s are over the recession, but have grown up and now have kids and a different lifestyle. Big, chunky, luxuriously appointed 4 × 4 land cruisers or people carriers are what they want now.

Choosing a market-coverage strategy

Many factors need considering when choosing a market-coverage strategy. The best strategy depends on *company resources*. Concentrated marketing makes sense for a firm with limited resources. The best strategy also depends on the degree of *product variability*. Undifferentiated marketing is suitable for uniform products such as grapefruit or steel. Products that can vary in design, such as cameras and cars, require differentiation or concentration. Consider the *product's stage in the life cycle*. When a firm introduces a new product, it is practical to launch only one version, and undifferentiated marketing or concentrated marketing therefore makes the most sense. In the mature stage of the product life cycle, however, differentiated marketing begins to make more sense. Another factor is *market variability*. Undifferentiated marketing is appropriate when buyers have the same tastes, buy the same amounts and react in the same way to marketing efforts. Finally, *competitors' marketing strategies* are important. When competitors use segmentation, undifferentiated marketing can be suicidal. Conversely, when competitors use undifferentiated marketing, a firm can gain by using differentiated or concentrated marketing.

Core strategy

Core strategy is at the hub of marketing. It is where company strengths meet market opportunities. It has two parts: first, the identification of a group of customers for whom the firm has a differential advantage; and second, positioning its offerings in the customer's mind. Although Fiat has problems, they spend heavily on Formula 1 racing, and retaining Michael Schumacher as their top driver helps position Ferrari as the world's number one sports car. Similarly, O_2 sponsored the English rugby team in the 2003 World Cup to help position their mobile phone operation with masculine respectability.

> Not all sponsorship helps position a firm's products as successfully as did Mercedes, Cartier, LloydsTSB, Lucozade, Tetley's beer and Hackett men's clothing store in associating themselves with the success, looks and personality of Jonny Wilkinson, the English rugby team's top scorer. In the 2002 World Cup, sponsors achieved an own goal with the fate of the new Renault Clio, as Thierry Henry picked up a red card and France crashed out. 7-Up did even worse in Ireland where their sponsored Ireland and Manchester United captain, Roy Keane, went home in disgrace before a ball was kicked.[33]

Core strategy—The identification of a group of customers for whom the firm has a differential advantage, and then positioning itself in that market.

Differentiation

Consumers typically choose products and services that give them the greatest value. Thus the key to winning and keeping customers is to understand their needs and buying processes better than competitors do, and to deliver more value. To the extent that a company can position itself as providing superior value to selected target markets, either by offering lower prices than competitors do or by providing more benefits to justify higher prices, it gains **competitive advantage**.[34]

Strong positions are not built upon empty promises. If a company positions its product as *offering* the best quality and service, it must then *deliver* the promised quality and service. Positioning therefore begins with *differentiating* the company's marketing offer, so that it will give consumers more value than competitors' offers do. Marketing Insights 10.2 tells how a German company successfully penetrated the US market. It is not just a matter of being different; success comes from being different in a way that customers want.

Not every company can find many opportunities for differentiating its offer and gaining competitive advantage. In some industries it is harder than others. The Boston Consulting Group explains four types of industry based on the number of competitive advantages and the size of those advantages (see Figure 10.4).

Competitive advantage—An advantage over competitors gained by offering consumers greater value, either through lower prices or by providing more benefits that justify higher prices.

Figure 10.4 The new BCG matrix

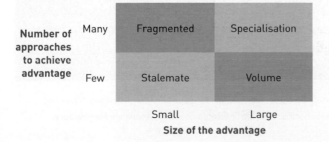

Number of approaches to achieve advantage

Many | Fragmented | Specialisation
Few | Stalemate | Volume

Small | Large
Size of the advantage

10.2 Schott: positioning for success

Positioning came to the help of the German company Schott in marketing Ceran in the US. Ceran, a glass-ceramic material made to cover the cooking surface of electric ranges, seemed to have everything going for it. It was completely non-porous (and thus stain resistant), easy to clean and long-lasting. Also, when one burner is lit, the heat does not spread; it stays confined to the circle directly above the burner. And after 10 years, Ceran hobs still looked and performed like new.

Schott anticipated some difficulty in the US markets. It would have to win over American cooker manufacturers, which would then have to promote Ceran to middle markets – dealers, designers, architects and builders. These middle-market customers would, in turn, influence final consumers. Schott set out to sell Ceran to its target of 14 appliance manufacturers. Schott promoted Ceran's impressive technical and engineering attributes. The appliance companies listened politely to the sales pitch, ordered samples and then . . . nothing.

Market research revealed two problems. First, Schott had failed to position Ceran among the manufacturers' customers. The material was still unknown among final consumers, dealers, designers, architects and builders. Second, the company was attempting to position the product on the wrong benefits. When selecting a hob, customers cared more about appearance and cleanability than sophisticated engineering. Their biggest questions were 'How does it look?' and 'How easy is it to use?'.

Based on these findings, Schott repositioned Ceran, shifting emphasis towards the material's inherent beauty and design versatility. An extensive promotion campaign communicated the new position to middle-market and final buyers. Advertising presented the black hob as 'Formalware for your kitchen', as streamlined and elegant as a tuxedo. As a follow-up, to persuade designers to specify Ceran, Schott positioned Ceran as 'More than a rangetop, a means of expression'. To reinforce this beauty and design positioning, ads featured visuals of a geometric grid of a hob with one glowing red burner.

In addition to advertising, a massive public relations effort resulted in substantial coverage in home improvement publications. It also produced a video news release featuring Ceran that was picked up by 150 local TV stations nationwide. To reinforce a weak link in the selling chain, a video helped retail salespeople show customers the benefits of Ceran in their stores.

Ceran is now selling well. All 14 North American appliance makers are buying production quantities of Ceran and use it in several smooth-top models. Schott is the major smooth-top supplier in the US, and smooth tops now account for more than 15 per cent of the electric stove market. At a recent Kitchen & Bath Show, 69 per cent of all range models on display had smooth tops.

SOURCES: Adapted from Nancy Arnott, 'Heating up sales: formalware for your kitchen', *Sales and Marketing Management* (June 1994), pp. 77–8. See also Richard J. Babyak, 'Tabletop cooking', *Appliance Manufacturer* (February 1997), pp. 65–7.

marketing insights

The four industry types are as follows.

1. **Volume industries,** where there are a few large advantages to be had. The airline industry is one of these. A company can strive for low costs or differentiate by service quality, but can win 'big' on both bases. In these industries, profitability is correlated with company size and market share. As a result, most minor airlines lose money while the main players try to form global alliances to build share. In this case almost all the industry leaders, VW, Hoechst, Hitachi and Unilever are large, low-cost operators providing a high-quality service.

2. **Stalemate industries** produce commodities where there are few potential advantages and each is small. Many old industries like steel and bulk chemicals fall into this category. In these industries it is hard to differentiate products or have significantly lower costs. European firms in these sectors often lose money, since they are unable to compete with products from economies with low-cost labour. Even size and modern plant cannot counter high labour costs.

3. **Fragmented industries** offer many opportunities to differentiate, but each opportunity is small. Many service industries are fragmented. Restaurants are an extreme example: Hard Rock Café has a global reputation and long queues, but its overall share of the market is small. Even market leaders, like McDonald's and KFC, have a small share of the market relative to leaders in other industries. In fragmented industries, profitability is not closely related to size. For many years, global Pizza Hut was not profitable, while every large town has restaurateur millionaires who own few eating places. At the same time, many small restaurants fail each year.

4. **Specialised industries** offer companies many opportunities to differentiate in a way that gives a high pay-off. Pharmaceuticals is a specialised industry. A disproportionately large proportion of the world's most successful companies come from the sector where firms like Novartis, Glaxo Wellcome and Roche are market leaders for particular treatment. Less conspicuous specialised industries are those for scientific instruments and publishing.

Figure 10.5 shows the returns from differentiation using results taken from the Profit Implications of Marketing Strategy (PIMS) study of American and European firms.[35] This study shows that firms with the lowest return on investment (RoI) operate in commodity markets where there is no differentiation on quality or anything else, such as the coal industry. Where there is room for differentiation, losers have inferior quality (Russia's Aeroflot) and more returns than winners (Singapore Airlines). The most highly performing group of companies are 'power companies', which have superior quality in differentiable markets

Volume industry—
An industry characterised by few opportunities to create competitive advantages, but each advantage is huge and gives a high pay-off.

Stalemate industry—
An industry that produces commodities and is characterised by a few opportunities to create competitive advantages, with each advantage being small.

Fragmented industry—
An industry characterised by many opportunities to create competitive advantages, but each advantage is small.

Specialised industry—
An industry where there are many opportunities for firms to create competitive advantages that are huge or give a high pay-off.

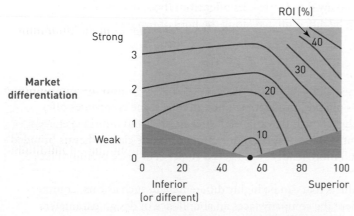

Figure 10.5 How differentiation and quality drive profitability
SOURCE: SPI's Quality/Differentiation Database

(BMW, Lego and Nokia). These are ahead of nichers (such as local airlines), which score lower on quality and RoI than the 'power companies'. According to PIMS, the 'power companies' often have a high market share, since quality, share and RoI are interrelated.

Differentiation may be harder in some industries than others, but creative firms have shown that any market can be differentiated.[36] Few people see the brick market as exciting, but one brick company found a way of getting a competitive advantage. Bricks used to be delivered to building sites in a truck that tipped them on to the ground. In the process many bricks got broken or lost. Workers on the site also had to spend time stacking the bricks. The brick company's idea was to put the bricks on pallets that were lifted off the truck by a small integral crane. The idea was so successful that soon all bricks came that way. The firm's next idea was to carry a small off-the-road fork-lift truck with the bricks, so that it could deliver them to the exact spot where the site manager wanted them.

Oil is a *stalemate industry*, but Royal Dutch/Shell remains the leading petroleum retailer by understanding that fuel is a distress purchase that people do not enjoy. They succeed by making their petrol stations easy to use and paying attention to all the other reasons people stop on a journey: to find their way, get a snack, make a phone call or go to a clean toilet.

Differential advantages can be transient. Some companies find many major advantages that are easily copied by competitors and are, therefore, highly perishable. This is particularly true in financial services, where successful ideas are quickly followed by competitors. The Bank of Scotland's Direct Line insurance company succeeded by offering an economic and high-quality personal insurance service through television advertising and telephone selling. It was so successful that established insurers had to follow. Zurich Insurance intends to attack the conservative German and Italian insurance markets in the same way. Like many online business-to-consumer companies, the Internet financial service providers First-e, Egg and Smile have used price, in the form of high interest on current accounts, to get customers to switch their accounts. However, so far their growth has not produced profitability. One reason is that a low price position is easy for others to follow unless a company has huge cost advantages.[37]

The solution for companies facing the erosion of their advantage is to keep identifying new potential advantages and to introduce them one by one to keep competitors off balance. These companies do not expect to gain a single substantial permanent advantage. Instead, they hope to manage a series of advantages that will increase their share over time. This is how market leaders like Microsoft, Intel, Sony and Gillette have held their position for so long. The true competitive advantage of these firms is their market knowledge, technological expertise, creativity and entrepreneurship, which give them the ability to develop products quickly.

Differentiating markets

In what specific ways can a company differentiate its offer from those of competitors? A company or market offer can be differentiated along the lines of product, services, personnel or image.

Product differentiation

A company can differentiate its physical product. At one extreme, some companies offer highly standardised products that allow little variation: chicken, steel and aspirin. Yet even here, some meaningful differentiation is possible. For example, Perdue claims that its branded chickens are better – fresher and more tender – and gets a 10 per cent price premium based on this differentiation.

Other companies offer products that can be highly differentiated, such as cars, commercial buildings and furniture. Here the company faces an abundance of design parameters. It can offer a variety of standard or optional *features* not provided by competitors. Thus

Volvo provides new and better safety features, while Lufthansa offers wider seats to business-class flyers.

Companies can also differentiate their products on *performance*. Whirlpool designs its dishwasher to run more quietly; Unilever formulates Radion to remove odours as well as dirt from washing. *Style* and *design* can also be important differentiating factors. Both Dyson in vacuum cleaners and Maclaren in pushchairs produced products that performed well but their huge success owes much to their distinctive designs that adhere to the design mantra that 'form follows function'. Similarly, companies can differentiate their products on such attributes as *innovation, consistency, durability, reliability* or *repairability*.[38]

Services differentiation

In addition to differentiating its physical product, the firm can also differentiate the services that accompany the product. Some companies gain competitive advantage through speedy, reliable or careful *delivery*. Harrods, the luxury retailer, delivers to its customers using replica vintage vans – a service particularly popular at Christmas. At the other end of the scale, Domino's Pizza promises delivery in less than 30 minutes or reduces the price.

Installation can also differentiate one company from another. IBM, for example, is known for its quality installation service for its servers. It delivers all pieces of purchased equipment to the site at one time, rather than sending individual components to sit and wait for others to arrive. And when asked to move IBM equipment and install it in another location, IBM often moves competitors' equipment as well. Companies can further distinguish themselves through their *repair services*. Many a car buyer would gladly pay a little more and travel a little further to buy a car from a dealer that provides top-notch repair service.

Some companies differentiate their offers by providing a *customer training* service. For instance, GE not only sells and installs expensive X-ray equipment in hospitals, but also trains the hospital employees who will use the equipment. Other companies offer free or paid *consulting services* – data, information systems and advice services that buyers need. For example, reinsurance company M&G provides information and advice to its customers. It also provides specialist help in developing new products.

Companies can find many other ways to add value through differentiated services. In fact, they can choose from a virtually unlimited number of specific services and benefits through which to differentiate themselves from the competition. Milliken provides one of the best examples of a company that has gained competitive advantage through superior service:

> Milliken sells towels to industrial launderers who rent them out. These towels are similar to competitors' towels yet Milliken charges a higher price for its towels and enjoys the leading market share. How can this be? The answer is that Milliken 'decommoditizes' this product through continuous service enhancement. Milliken trains its customers' salespeople; supplies prospect leads and sales promotional material to them; supplies on-line computer order entry and freight optimization systems; carries on marketing research for customers; sponsors quality improvement workshops; and lends its salespeople to work with customers on Customer Action Teams.[39]

Speed of service is a competitive advantage used by many firms. Fast food is now common on the world's high streets and malls, along with services like one-hour photo processing and Vision Express's one-hour service for spectacles. These services provide a direct benefit to customers by giving rapid gratification and allowing services to be completed within one

Service differentiation: KPN
Qwest's ad focuses on speed as
its main competitive advantage.
SOURCE: KPN Qwest. *Agency*:
PPGH JWT Colors. *Photographer*:
Jan Willem Scholten.

*From **Helsinki** ...*

*... to **Barcelona**, in a flash.*

Not so very long ago, business data communication across Europe seemed to take an age. Low bandwidth connections via networks that were originally designed in the 19th century. Now there's a completely new network, designed and built specifically to meet the needs of today's businesses. A network that operates at the speed of light itself to deliver the bandwidth you need to compete in the 21st century. KPNQwest's EuroRings™ fibre-optic network spans Europe and connects to the world, providing a secure, high-bandwidth platform for e-business. IP connections, intranets, extranets or any other corporate data communications requirement. What are you waiting for? *KPNQwest. Business communications @ the speed of light.*

kpn Qwest

shopping trip. Speed also helps sell more expensive goods. Abbey National found that its success in providing large mortgages depended upon how fast it could confirm that it would give a person a home loan. It responded by allowing local managers to make loan decisions rather than processing applications centrally. In the car market Toyota's two-day policy means that it can supply a well-equipped Lexus within two days, while many other luxury car makers expect prospects to wait several weeks for custom-built cars.

Personnel differentiation:
The Regent Hong Kong's
personnel 'welcome you, move
you, enrich you and delight you'.
SOURCE: Regent International
Hotels.

The success of courier services like TNT and DHL shows that many people are willing to pay extra for a quick, secure service. A study of the importance of service responsiveness to users of small business-computer-based systems shows how speed is valued:

- Eighty-five per cent of users were willing to pay a 10 per cent premium price for same-day service; 60 per cent would pay 20 per cent more; and 40 per cent would pay a 30 per cent premium.

- On average, same-day service was worth twice as much as brand name and distributor reputation, and worth four times more than technical features.

Personnel differentiation

Companies can gain a strong competitive advantage through hiring and training better people than their competitors do. Singapore Airlines enjoys an excellent reputation largely because of the grace of its flight attendants. McDonald's people are courteous, TGI Fridays is fun, Richer Sounds staff are enthusiastic and knowledgeable, and Mark Warner's resort staff arc friendly and upbeat.

Personnel differentiation requires that a company should select its customer-contact people carefully and train them well. These personnel must be competent – they must possess the required skills and knowledge. They need to be courteous, friendly and respectful. They must serve customers with consistency and accuracy. And they must make an effort to understand customers, to communicate clearly with them, and to respond quickly to customer requests and problems.

Allied Breweries relates the type of staff they wish to employ to the market segments served. A segmentation study identified four pub segments in Britain and the managers needed to run them. *Local community pubs* needed a good controller who was mature and experienced. He or she had to be 'one of the crowd', be involved in the local community and be an organiser of pub teams and other events. The personality of the manager is the key to success of *broad-based locals*. They need to maintain a high profile and set the mood of the pub and other staff. *Young persons' circuit pubs* need good organisers who are tolerant but firm. These places are very busy at peak times, so service standards have to be high and efficient. Users of *quality traditional dry pubs* expect attention to detail and high professional standards. Good food is important, so the manager's job is more complicated than for other pubs. The manager may not have a strong personality, but organisational and financial skills are important.

Image differentiation

Even when competing offers look the same, buyers may perceive a difference based on company or brand images. Thus companies work to establish *images* that differentiate them from competitors. A company or brand image should convey a singular and distinctive message that communicates the product's main benefits and positioning. Developing a strong and distinctive image calls for creativity and hard work. A company cannot implant an image in the public's mind overnight using only a few advertisements. If 'IBM means service', this image must be supported by everything the company says and does.

Symbols can provide strong company or brand recognition and image differentiation. Companies design signs and logos that provide instant recognition. They associate themselves with objects or characters that symbolise quality or other attributes, such as the Mercedes star, the Johnnie Walker character, the Michelin man or the Lacoste crocodile. The company might build a brand around some famous person. The perfume Passion is associated with Elizabeth Taylor and Longines watches with an image of Audrey Hepburn from *Breakfast at Tiffany's*. Some companies even become associated with colours, such as Kodak (yellow), Benson & Hedges (gold) or Ferrari (red).

The chosen symbols must be communicated through advertising that conveys the company or brand's personality. The ads attempt to establish a story line, a mood, a performance level – something distinctive about the company or brand. The atmosphere of the physical space in which the organisation produces or delivers its products and services can be another powerful image generator. Hyatt hotels has become known for its atrium lobbies, TGI Friday's restaurants for American memorabilia, and Scruffy Murphy's Pubs with Irish memorabilia. Thus a bank that wants to distinguish itself as the 'friendly bank' must choose the right building and interior design – layout, colours, materials and furnishings – to reflect these qualities. A far cry from the majestic edifices that many banks have inherited.

A company can also create an image through the types of event it sponsors. Perrier, the bottled water company, became known by laying out exercise tracks and sponsoring health sports events. Other organisations have identified themselves closely with cultural events, such as orchestral performances and art exhibits. Still other organisations support popular causes. For example, Heinz gives money to hospitals and Quaker gives food to the homeless.

The crocodile gives instant brand recognition for Lacoste. In the same way, there can be a very strong association between certain colours and companies, like blue for Philips.

SOURCES: (left) Lacoste. *Agency*: Pentland Group. (right) Philips Consumer Electronics. *Agency*: Euro RSCG.

Value positioning

Value positioning offers a range of positioning alternatives based on the value an offering delivers and its price. Consumers typically choose products and services that give them the greatest value. Thus, marketers want to position their brands on the key benefits that they offer relative to competing brands. The full positioning of a brand is called the brand's value proposition – the full mix of benefits upon which the brand is positioned. It is the answer to the customer's question 'Why should I buy your brand?'. Volvo's value proposition hinges on safety but also includes reliability, roominess and styling, all for a price that is higher than average but seems fair for this mix of benefits.

Figure 10.6 shows possible value propositions upon which a company might position its products. In the figure, the five green cells represent winning value propositions – positioning that gives the company competitive advantage. The red cells, however, represent losing value propositions, and the centre cell represents at best a marginal proposition. In the following sections, we discuss the five winning value propositions companies can use to position their products: more for more, more for the same, the same for less, less for much less, and more for less.

More for more

'More for more' positioning involves providing the most upscale product or service and charging a higher price to cover the higher costs. Ritz-Carlton Hotels, Mont Blanc writing

Value positioning—A range of positioning alternatives based on the value an offering delivers and its price.

Figure 10.6 Value positions

		Price		
		Less	Same	More
Benefits	More	More for Less	More for the Same	More for More
	Same	The Same for Less	Me too	
	Less	Less for much Less		

instruments, Bosch-Siemens kitchen appliances or Tod's 133 stud driving shoes[40] – each claims superior quality, craftsmanship, durability, performance or style and charges a price to match. Not only is the marketing offer high in quality, it also offers prestige to the buyer. It symbolises status and a lofty lifestyle. Often, the price difference exceeds the actual increment in quality.

Sellers offering 'only the best' can be found in every product and service category, from hotels, restaurants, food and fashion to cars and kitchen appliances. Consumers are sometimes surprised, even delighted, when a new competitor enters a category with an

More for more value proposition: Häagen-Dazs produces and commercialises super-premium ice-cream at unusually high prices.
SOURCE: Pillsbury UK Ltd.
Agency: Euros.

unusually high-priced brand. Starbucks coffee entered as a very expensive brand in a largely commodity category; Häagen-Dazs came in as a super-premium ice-cream brand at a price never before charged. In general, companies should be on the lookout for opportunities to introduce a 'much more for much more' brand in any underdeveloped product or service category. For example, the €400 Dualit Toaster, a hand-assembled appliance, keeps toast warm for 10 minutes.[41]

Yet 'more for more' brands can be vulnerable. They often invite imitators who claim the same quality but at a lower price. Luxury goods that sell well during good times may be at risk during economic downturns when buyers become more cautious in their spending.

More for the same

Companies can attack a competitor's more for more positioning by introducing a brand offering comparable quality but at a lower price. For example, Toyota introduced its Lexus line with a 'more for the same' value proposition. In the US the headline read: 'Perhaps the first time in history that trading a $72,000 (€81,000) car for a $36,000 car could be considered trading up.' It communicated the high quality of its new Lexus through rave reviews in car magazines, through a widely distributed videotape showing side-by-side comparisons of Lexus and Mercedes-Benz automobiles, and through surveys showing that Lexus dealers were providing customers with better sales and service experiences than were Mercedes dealerships. Many Mercedes-Benz owners switched to Lexus, and the Lexus repurchase rate has been 60 per cent, twice the industry average.[42]

The same for less

Offering 'the same for less' can be a powerful value proposition – everyone likes a good deal. For example, Amazon.com sells the same book titles as its brick-and-mortar competitors but at lower prices. Discount stores such as Matalan and Aldi use this positioning. They don't claim to offer different or better products. Instead, they offer many of the same brands as other stores but at deep discounts based on superior purchasing power and lower-cost operations.

Other companies develop imitative but lower-priced brands in an effort to lure customers away from the market leader. For example, Advanced Micro Devices (AMD) and Cyrix make less expensive versions of Intel's market-leading microprocessor chips. Many personal computer companies make 'IBM clones' and claim to offer the same performance at lower prices.

Less for much less

A market almost always exists for products that offer less and therefore cost less. Few people need, want or can afford 'the very best' in everything they buy. In many cases, consumers will gladly settle for less than optimal performance or give up some of the bells and whistles in exchange for a lower price. For example, many travellers seeking lodgings prefer not to pay for what they consider unnecessary extras, such as a pool, cable television, attached restaurant, or mints on the pillow. Motel chains such as Motel 6 suspend some of these amenities and charge less accordingly.

'Less for much less' positioning involves meeting consumers' lower performance or quality requirements at a much lower price. In Europe low-cost airlines, such as easyJet, Virgin Express and Ryanair, are proliferating where deregulation allows. It is wrong to think that less for less positioning is for people with less money to spend. Many users are business people whose companies are keen to reduce travel budgets. The most regular users are people working away who use budget airlines to get home more often or people owning villas who visit their summer home for short breaks as well as long holidays. Other heavy users are shoppers travelling to global retail centres, such as Paris, London, New York or Chicago, and golfers flying off for a game in Scotland or Spain.[43]

More for less

Of course, the winning value proposition would be to offer 'more for less'. Many companies claim to do this. For example, Dell Computer claims to have better products *and* lower prices for a given level of performance. Procter & Gamble claims that its laundry detergents provide the best cleaning *and* everyday low prices. In the short run, some companies can actually achieve such lofty positions.

Yet in the long run, companies will find it very difficult to sustain such best-of-both positioning. Offering more usually costs more, making it difficult to deliver on the 'for less' promise. Companies that try to deliver both may lose out to more focused competitors.

All said, each brand must adopt a positioning strategy designed to serve the needs and wants of its target markets. 'More for more' will draw one target market, 'less for much less' will draw another, and so on. Thus, in any market, there is usually room for many different companies, each successfully occupying different positions.

The important thing is that each company must develop its own winning positioning strategy, one that makes it special to its target consumers. Offering only 'the same for the same' provides no competitive advantage, leaving the firm in the middle of the pack. Companies offering one of the three losing value propositions – 'the same for more', 'less for more', and 'less for the same' – will inevitably fail. Here, customers soon realise that they've been underserved, tell others, and abandon the brand.

Product positioning

Product position—The way the product is defined by consumers on important attributes – the place the product occupies in consumers' minds relative to competing products.

A **product's position** is the way the product is *defined by consumers* on important attributes – the place the product occupies in consumers' minds relative to competing products. Thus Tide is positioned as a powerful, all-purpose family detergent, Radion removes odours, and Fairy is gentle. Skoda and Subaru are positioned on economy.

> Some say Mark Fields has the best job in the world. He runs Premier Auto Group, Ford's luxury car arm, from his office in a Georgian town house in Berkeley Square, London. Although all his brands are made by Ford, he aims to grow all his brands by positioning that keeps them separate and clear in the customer's mind: 'You try to keep a certain image or profile that makes customers not only buy a car, but join a club.'
>
> The product positions of all the range are not yet sorted. Jaguar is 'The art of performance', Volvo is 'For life', Lincoln is 'American luxury' and Range Rover 'The best 4 × 4 by far'. Still to be determined is the product position of the low-volume, expensive but mouth-watering Aston Martin. His desire is to increase its 651 per year current sales five-fold in five years. And without referring to 007, Goldfinger and ejector seats?

A firm's *competitive advantage* and its *product's position* can be quite different. A competitive advantage is the strength of a company, while a product's position is a prospect's perception of a product. A competitive advantage, like low costs or high quality, could influence a product's position, but in many cases it is not central to it. One of Ford's competitive advantages is the ability of Jaguar to share engineering with Lincoln/Mercury, although the products are far apart in the customers' minds.[44]

What a dog feels
when the leash breaks.

Instant freedom, courtesy of the Boxster S. The 250 horsepower boxer engine launches you forward with its distinctive growl. Any memory of life on a leash evaporates in the wind rushing overhead. It's time to run free. Contact us at 1-800-PORSCHE or porsche.com.

Porsche positions powerfully on performance and the sense of freedom it generates – pure emotion.
SOURCE: Reprinted by permission of Porsche cars North America, Inc.

Consumers are overloaded with information about products and services. They cannot re-evaluate products every time they make a buying decision. To simplify buying decision making, consumers organise products into categories – that is, they 'position' products, services and companies in their minds. A product's position is the complex set of perceptions, impressions and feelings that consumers hold for the product compared with competing products. Consumers position products with or without the help of marketers. But marketers do not want to leave their products' positions to chance. They *plan* positions that will give their products the greatest advantage in selected target markets, and they *design* marketing mixes to create these planned positions.

Positioning was popularised by advertising executives Al Ries and Jack Trout.[45] They saw it as a creative exercise done with an existing product:

Positioning starts with a product, a piece of merchandise, a service, a company, an institution or even a person. . . . But positioning is not about what you do to a product. Positioning is what you do to the mind of the prospect. That is, you position products in the mind of the prospect.

They argue that current products generally have a position in the minds of consumers. Thus Rolex is thought of as the world's top watch, Coca-Cola as the world's largest soft-drink company, Porsche as one of the world's best sports cars, and so on. These brands own those positions and it would be hard for a competitor to steal them.

Ries and Trout show how familiar brands can acquire some distinctiveness in an 'overcommunicated society', where there is so much advertising that consumers screen out most of the messages. A consumer can know only about seven soft drinks, even though there are many more on the market. Even then, the mind often knows them in the form of a *product ladder*, such as Coke > Pepsi > Fanta or Hertz > Avis > Budget. In such a ladder, the second firm usually has half the business of the first firm, and the third firm enjoys half the business of the second firm. Furthermore, the top firm is remembered best.

People tend to remember *no. 1*. For example, when asked 'Who was the first person successfully to fly the Atlantic Ocean?', people usually answer 'Charles Lindbergh'. When asked 'Who was the second person to do it?', they draw a blank. That is why companies fight for the no. 1 position. In reality, the first people to fly the Atlantic were Alcock and Brown, but Charles Lindbergh won the publicity battle.

Ries and Trout point out that the 'size' position can be held by only one brand. What counts is to achieve a no. 1 position along some valued attribute, not necessarily 'size'. Thus 7-Up is the no. 1 'Uncola', Porsche is the no. 1 small sports car and Foster's is Australia's top-selling lager. In the United States, Heineken is 'the' imported beer because it was the first heavily promoted imported beer. The marketer should identify an important attribute or benefit that can convincingly be won by the brand. In that way brands hook the mind in spite of the incessant advertising bombardment reaching consumers.

According to Ries and Trout, there are three positioning alternatives:

1. The first strategy they suggest is to strengthen a brand's *current position* in the mind of consumers. Thus Avis took its second position in the car rental business and made a strong point about it: 'We're number two. We try harder.' This was believable to the consumer. 7-Up capitalised on *not* being a cola soft drink by advertising itself as the Uncola.

2. Their second strategy is to search for a new *unoccupied position* that is valued by enough consumers and grab it: 'Cherchez le creneau', 'Look for the hole'. Find a hole in the market and fill it, they say. Vidal Sassoon's Wash & Go was based on recognising that the fashion for exercise meant that people washed their hair frequently, quickly and away from home. By combining a shampoo and hair conditioner in one the company was able to fill a latent market need. Similarly, after recognising that many housewives wanted a strong washing powder to treat smelly clothes, Unilever successfully launched Radion.

3. Their third strategy is to *deposition* or *reposition* the competition. Most US buyers of dinnerware thought that Lenox china and Royal Doulton both came from continental Europe. Royal Doulton countered with ads showing that Lenox china is from New Jersey, but theirs came from England. In a similar vein, Stolichnaya vodka attacked Smirnoff and Wolfschmidt vodka by pointing out that these brands were made locally, but 'Stolichnaya is different. Similarly, it is Russian.' GUINNESS®, the world's leading stout, has strong Irish associations. However, the focus on individuality in its Rutger Hauer 'Pure Genius' campaign has allowed Murphy's and Beamish to attack GUINNESS® brand's Irish heritage. A final example is KALIBER®, Alcohol Free Premium Lager, drunk by people who want a good time or, as Billy Connolly says in its ads posted next to those for Wonderbra, 'Hello girls!'.

Ries and Trout essentially deal with the psychology of positioning – or repositioning – a current brand in the consumer's mind. They acknowledge that the positioning strategy might call for changes in the product's name, price and packaging, but these are 'cosmetic changes done for the purpose of securing a worthwhile position – in the prospect's mind'.

This award-winning campaign attracted immense attention without offending women. Sales of Wonderbra were reported to have more than doubled as a result.
SOURCE: Playtex.

This poster ad promotes a distinct advantage of no-alcohol beer when meeting the girl in the Wonderbra.
SOURCE: Diageo Ireland, part of the Diageo plc group of companies. The KALIBER word and UNICORN device are trademarks. Copyright © Guinness & Co. Created by Euro RSCG Agency.

Positioning strategies

Marketers can follow several positioning strategies. These strategies use associations to change consumers' perception of products.

Product attributes position many technical products. The positioning of Nokia's 6600 is based on integration: 'Zoom in and take a picture or video. View it in full colour . . . Add text and send a multimedia message . . . Save it . . . Transfer wirelessly over Blootooth . . .'; while much of BMW's advertising promotes individual *technical items*, such as fresh air filters. In the exclusive watch market Breitling, Baume & Mercier and Audemars Piguet's positioning are on their mechanical movements. Some of their designs leave the mechanisms exposed and one ad argues 'Since 1735 there has never been a quartz Blancpain. And there never will be.'

Benefits offered, or the needs they fill, position many products – Crest toothpaste reduces cavities, Aim tastes good and Macleans Sensitive relieves the pain of sensitive teeth. In the confectionery industry, Italian Baci and Ferrero Rocher are gifts, while Mars and Snickers bars satisfy hunger.

Huhtamaki is Finland's largest industrial company but LEAF, its confectionery division, is only tenth in size worldwide. It developed competitive advantage in 'functional chewing and bubble gums'. Its Xylitol Jenkki Xylifresh, probably 'the world's most researched chewing gum', has been used as a reference standard by medical schools measuring dental hygiene. LEAF's other functional gums include BenBits ExtraFresh and Fresh 4 Ever breath fresheners, and vitamin-enriched E.Z.C. Its sugar-based confectionery includes vitamin-enriched +Energi and Läkerol throat soother.

Bentley and Breitling: A true partnership in prestige, technical sophistication and performance. The brands even share the same first letter and corporate logos with wings.
SOURCE: Breitling SA.

Usage occasions position many products. Mentadent Night Action toothpaste, for instance, is for evening use. In the summer, Gatorade is positioned as a drink for replacing athletes' body fluids; in the winter, it can be positioned as the drink to use when the doctor recommends plenty of liquids. KitKat and After Eight mints sell alongside Snickers and Ferrero Rocher, but the positioning is on usage occasion. Internationally, KitKat means 'Have a break', while After Eight is an after-dinner mint to share.

> Red Bull, a soft drink created by a small Austrian company, is a huge success across Europe. According to its sales director: 'We don't want to be compared with the soft drink market. Of course, Red Bull has quite a key position in the market, but it is mainly a sports drink.' Red Bull's origin is in the huge Japanese market for energy drinks. Each can has 80 milligrams of caffeine, a third more than the equivalent amount of Coca-Cola. This has made the drink popular with teetotaller young ravers who can consume several cans a night.[46]

Users help position products. Johnson & Johnson improved the market share for its baby shampoo from 3 per cent to 14 per cent by repositioning the product towards a new *user category* of adults who wash their hair frequently and need a gentle shampoo. Often products are positioned by associating them with their *user class*. Nescafé Gold Blend increased sales dramatically after showing a series of ads romancing thirty somethings, as did Tango soft drinks as a result of the youthful 'You've been Tangoed' campaign.

Activities are often used to sell expensive products. The Geneva-based SMH group positions its watches using sports. Thus Rado has come to specialise in tennis, Omega in sailing and aerospace, 'the first and only watch on the moon', and Longines in skiing and aviation.[47] This positioning activity goes beyond advertising and promotions. Rolex positions its watches using adventurers and backs this with its Sfr450,000 (€298,000) Awards for Enterprise. Over 30 people are Rolex Laureate for their original and creative schemes. The take-off of TAG Heuer as a brand traces back to Steve McQueen wearing a Heuer chronograph and driving the then mythical Heuer-sponsored sports car in the movie *Le Mans*. Since then, TAG Heuer has grown to be Formula 1's official time keeper as it stuck determinedly to its motor sports positioning.[48]

Personalities often help positioning. Prestigious brands are often positioned using successful personalities who can add to a product's character. American Express runs ads showing caricatures of famous businesspeople who are also users; Jameson Irish Whiskey uses sportsmen in its positioning; and Hugo Boss identifies successful people as models in its 'Men at Work' campaign.

> Many argue that Real Madrid bought David Beckham because of his value in the store, rather than his value on the ball. With Tiger Woods and Michael Jordan, David Beckham is a sports and media superstar with access to the world's huge and growing market for sports sponsorship and the worldwide interest they create in the game they play as well as their team. *Fortune Magazine* estimated that Michael Jordan's career brought basketball $10bn (€11bn). So important is catching the stars that Nike has signed promising 13-year-old Freddy Adu for $1 million, gambling that he will be the next Pelé.[49]

Audi is German – 'Vorsprung
durch Technik'.
SOURCE: Audi UK.

Cult positioning is synonymous with children's products. The quiet don, J.R.R. Tolkien, would have gasped at his lifelong work, *Lord of the Rings*, helping sell kids' lunch boxes and potato crisps. However, Time Warner's expected $400 million (€450m) syndication and merchandising income from the trilogy is greater than the film's production cost. Cult positioning helps shift huge volumes on merchandise if associated with a success, but only one or two films a year are blockbusters and the attractiveness of merchandise varies considerably. For example, huge amounts were lost in the toy industry when *Star Wars* prequel merchandise did not shift in the predicted volumes. Contrast that with the phenomenal success of the *Harry Potter* books and movies.

Cult positioning has the ability to shift large volumes of merchandise and add interest to a moribund product, but cults have unpredictable impact and duration. Additionally, the loyalty and awareness is to the cult, not the product, be it *Dr Who*, *Bob the Builder* or Hornby's *Thomas the Tank Engine* and *Harry Potter* model railways. The result is the need for the users of cult positioning to bid for merchandising rights and jump from cult to cult as they go in and out of fashion.[50]

Origin positions product by association with its place of manufacture. Much of Perrier's success depended on the sophistication its French origin gave to it. Similarly, Audi's 'Vorsprung durch Technik' positioned its cars as German, and Renault's 'Créateur d'automobiles' as French. Drinks are often positioned using origin. The positioning of Foster's and Castlemaine XXXX lagers uses their Australian heritage, plus masculine humour to reinforce their character. Marketing Insights 10.3 shows how a leading European company has positioned a whole range of its beers using *origin*.

Other brands can help position products. Clinique's advertising for its 'skin supplies for men' prominently features a Rolex watch. Where firms have traditionally crafted products, such as Wilkinson Sword or Holland & Holland shotguns, these lend glamour to more recent products – in these instances, shaving products and men's clothing respectively. After Volkswagen bought the Czech Skoda company, it used the Volkswagen name to transfer some

of its strong reputation to Skoda. 'Volkswagen were so impressed, they bought the company' ran one press ad. The responsible ad agency, GGK, explains: 'The Volkswagen connection hit the spot. People immediately latched on to it. It allowed susceptible people [who might be persuaded to buy a Skoda] a route into the brand.' Dealers reported an instant 50 per cent sales increase. With VW engineering and Skoda 'more for less' positioning, sales and customer loyalty have continued to grow. Ads still play on Skoda's past reputation but its Fabia 1.4 became the *What Car?* Car of the Year 2000. In 2002 its V8 engined B-plus project will project the company into the executive car market.[51]

Competitors provide two positioning alternatives. A product can be positioned directly *against a competitor*. For example, in ads for their personal computers, Compaq and Dell directly compared their products with IBM personal computers. The direct-selling computer company dan compares its performance with all other suppliers: '1st in repurchase intention,

marketing insights

10.3 | The place is the thing

Towns have long used famous characters to position the locations and give them a theme. Often these have some historical association, having been born, lived or died there. Some of Europe's more conspicuous cases are Mozart's Salzburg, Wagner's Bayreuth and Shakespeare's Stratford-upon-Avon. Other towns have positioned themselves with mythical or literary characters, such as Nottingham's Robin Hood (whose enemy supposedly lived there) or Ashby-de-la-Zouch's Ivanhoe (who fought the Black Knight at Ashby Castle).

Besides using people to position places, places position portfolios of products. Belgian Interbrew is Europe's largest brewer. It retains its hold on the European market by trading on the geographical heritage of its products. The company certainly has plenty of heritage to trade on. First trading in Belgium as Den Hoorn in 1366, it changed its name to Artois 400 years later. Stella Artois remains Belgium's favoured tipple; elsewhere it is marketed as being 'reassuringly expensive'. Another one of Interbrew's brands, Bass, can probably lay claim to the best product placement of all time, having a prominent position in Manet's *A Bar at the Folies Bergère*. Other beers it promotes are Boddingtons, 'the cream of Manchester', Newcastle Brown and Caffrey's Irish beer.

Whitbread, once owner of many of Interbrew's drinks, positions its restaurant chains geographically. Their Pizza Hut and TGI Friday are both positioned as American although the Hut is for families and the TGI is for twenty-somethings. Café Rouge is French, Costa Coffee continental, Brewers Fayre 'Olde Englande' and Beefeaters British and carnivore.

With manufacturers increasingly chasing low wages, there are signs that the 'Made in . . .' label may help keep some jobs in high-wage economies. Consumers shun Prada bags that are not made in Italy, Louis Vuitton from outside France and non-Swiss Cartier. The resistance may stretch beyond luxury goods as local consumers react against the disloyalty of firms. Dyson vacuum cleaner sales dropped sharply in Europe when the firm broadcast that it was switching manufacture from Europe to Malaysia.

SOURCES: Michelin Green Guides to Austria, Germany and Great Britain; Alison Smith, 'Whitbread to shake up restaurants', *Financial Times* (1 November 2000), p. 27; Dan Bilefsky, 'Interbrew offer set to raise €3.3bn', *Financial Times* (9 November 2000), p. 33; Mike Levy, 'Marketing Cinderellas', *Marketing Business* (July/August 2000), pp. 26–7; Fred Kapner, 'The last sector where Made in Europe matters', *Financial Times* (4 December 2003), p. 16; Peter Marsh, 'Dust is settling on the Dyson clean-up', *Financial Times* (12 December 2003), p. 12.

Positioning strategies: Breitling has chosen to position its watches on the attributes of precision and reliability.
SOURCE: Breitling SA.

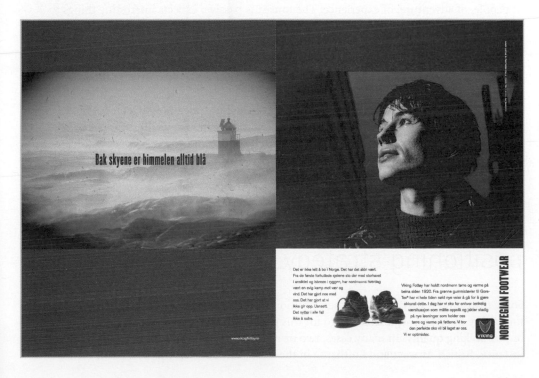

Positioning strategies: the 'Norwegian footwear' slogan used by Viking is an example of a positioning strategy based on *origin*.
SOURCE: Mann (Norway) October 2000.

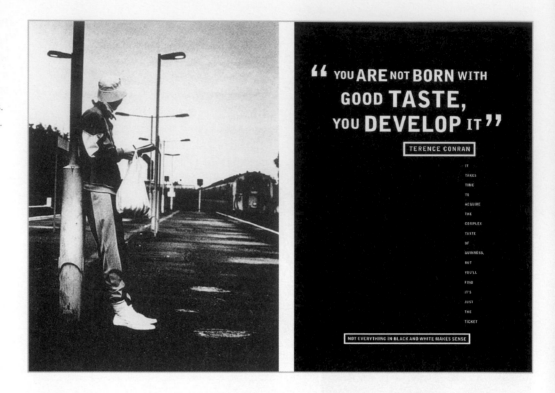

1st in repair satisfaction', and so on. In its famous 'We're number two, so we try harder' campaign, Avis successfully positioned itself against the larger Hertz. A product may also be positioned *away from competitors* – 7-Up became the no. 3 soft drink when it was positioned as the 'Uncola', the fresh and thirst-quenching alternative to Coke and Pepsi. River Island Expeditions positions its holidays, its adventures for travellers, away from package holidays and the tourists who go on them. It says: 'The traveller is active; he goes strenuously in search of people, of adventure, of experience. The tourist is passive; expects interesting things to happen to him. He goes "sight-seeing" (Daniel J. Boorstin, 1962).'

Product class membership is the final means of positioning. For example, Van Den Bergh's I Can't Believe It's Not Butter is clearly positioned against butter, while other yellow fats are promoted as cooking oils. Camay hand soap is positioned with bath oils rather than with soap.

Marketers often use a *combination* of these positioning strategies. Johnson & Johnson's Affinity shampoo is positioned as a hair conditioner for women over 40 (product class *and* user). And in its Christmas campaigns, Martell cognac and Glenlivet malt whisky both neglect the lucrative 18- to 35-year-olds to concentrate on the over-35s (*usage situation* and *user*).

Choosing and implementing a positioning strategy

Some firms find it easy to choose their positioning strategy. For example, a firm well known for quality in certain segments will go for this position in a new segment if there are enough buyers seeking quality. In many cases, two or more firms will go after the same position: for instance, British Airways and Lufthansa in the European business market. Then, each will have to find other ways to set itself apart, such as Lufthansa's promise of reliability and wider seats, and BA's lie-flat seats and executive lounges. Each firm must differentiate its offer by building a unique bundle of competitive advantages that appeal to a substantial group within the segment.

Having identified a set of possible competitive advantages upon which to build a position, the next stages are to select the right competitive advantages and effectively communicate the chosen position to the market.

Selecting the right competitive advantages

Suppose a company is fortunate enough to have several potential competitive advantages. It must now choose the ones upon which it will build its positioning strategy. It must decide *how many* differences to promote and *which ones*.

How many differences to promote?

Many marketers think that companies should aggressively promote only one benefit to the target market. Ad man Rosser Reeves, for example, said a company should develop a **unique selling proposition** (USP) for each brand and stick to it. Each brand should pick an attribute and tout itself as 'no. 1' on that attribute. Buyers tend to remember 'no. 1' better, especially in an over-communicated society. Thus Crest toothpaste consistently promotes its anti-cavity protection, and Mercedes promotes its great automotive engineering. What are some of the 'no. 1' positions to promote? The most significant ones are 'best quality', 'best service', 'lowest price', 'best value' and 'most advanced technology'. A company that hammers away at one of these positions and consistently achieves it will probably become best known and remembered for it.

The difficulty of keeping functional superiority has made firms focus on having a unique **emotional selling proposition** (ESP) instead of a USP. The product may be similar to competitors' products, but it has unique associations for consumers. Leading names like Rolls-Royce, Ferrari and Rolex have done this. Other cars outperform Ferrari on the road and track, but 'the red car with the prancing horse' is the world's no. 1 sports car. Many Formula One racing drivers still dream of racing a Ferrari, and Ferrari pay the 'world's best driver' €40 million a year to make sure he can keep winning for them.[52]

Other marketers think that companies should position themselves on more than one differentiating factor. This may be necessary if two or more firms are claiming to be best on the same attribute. Steelcase, an office furniture systems company, differentiates itself from competitors on two benefits: best on-time delivery and best installation support. Volvo positions its automobiles as 'safest' and 'most durable'. Fortunately, these benefits are compatible – a very safe car is also very durable.

Today, in a time when the mass market is fragmenting into many small segments, companies are trying to broaden their positioning strategies to appeal to more segments. For example, Beecham promotes its Aquafresh toothpaste as offering three benefits: 'anti-cavity protection', 'better breath' and 'whiter teeth'. Clearly, many people want all three benefits, and the challenge is to convince them that the brand delivers all three. Beecham's solution was to create toothpaste that squeezed out of the tube in three colours, thus visually confirming the three benefits. In doing this, Beecham attracted three segments instead of one.

However, as companies increase the number of claims for their brands, they risk disbelief and a loss of clear positioning. Usually, a company needs to avoid three serious positioning errors. The first is **underpositioning** – that is, failing to position the company at all. Some companies discover that buyers have only a vague idea of the brand, or that they do not really know anything special about it. This has occurred with dark spirits – whisky and brandy –

Unique selling proposition (USP)—The unique product benefit that a firm aggressively promotes in a consistent manner to its target market. The benefit usually reflects functional superiority: best quality, best services, lowest price, most advanced technology.

Emotional selling proposition (ESP)—A non-functional attribute that has unique associations for consumers.

Underpositioning—A positioning error referring to failure to position a company, its product or brand.

Unilever positioned its best-selling Lever 2000 soap on three benefits in one: cleansing, deodorising, and moisturising.
SOURCE: Unilever plc.

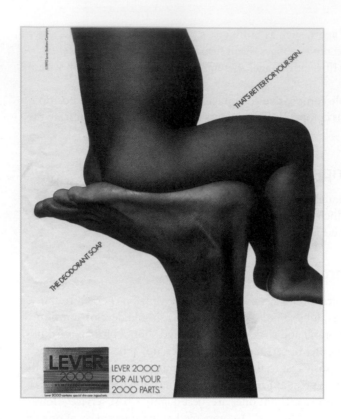

where young drinkers have drifted away from them. United Distillers and Hiram Walker aim to reverse this trend with their Bell's and Teacher's brands by targeting 25- to 35-year-old men. There is much focus on extending the use of both brands as a mixer. This is an anathema to many whisky drinkers, but United Distillers has successfully promoted it as a mixer in both Spain and Greece. The second positioning error is **overpositioning** – that is, giving buyers too narrow a picture of the company. Thus a consumer might think that the Steuben glass company makes only fine art glass costing €1,000 and up, when it also makes affordable fine glass starting at around €50.

Finally, companies must avoid **confused positioning** – that is, leaving buyers with a confused image of the company. For example, Burger King has struggled without success for years to establish a profitable and consistent position. Since 1986, it has undertaken five separate advertising campaigns, with themes ranging from 'Herb the nerd doesn't eat here' and 'This is a Burger King town', to 'The right food for the right times' and 'Sometimes you've got to break the rules'. This barrage of positioning statements has left consumers confused and Burger King with poor sales and profits.[53]

Implausible positioning occurs when the positioning strategy stretches the perception of the buyers too far. Toyota recognised this when it created the Lexus brand rather than try to stretch its highly respected name into the luxury car market. When TiVo personal video recorders were first launched in the US priced from $300 (€337) to $600, customers did not buy. The reason was that people did not believe what the ad showed. It contained a man watching a live game on TV, pausing the game to get a drink, then restarting the 'live' game where he left off. Since TiVo's can digitally record and play back at the same time, the benefit the ad shows is real but people could not believe the claim. TiVo is soon to be relaunched at a lower price and promoting the machines' more believable long recording time per disc (40 hours) and digital quality. Some market positions, while attracting one group of customers, can alienate others and so backfire.

Overpositioning— A positioning error referring to too narrow a picture of the company, its product or a brand being communicated to target customers.

Confused positioning— A positioning error that leaves consumers with a confused image of the company, its product or a brand.

Implausible positioning— Making claims that stretch the perception of the buyers too far to be believed.

Which differences to promote?

Not all brand differences are meaningful or worthwhile. Not every difference makes a good differentiator. Each difference has the potential to create company costs as well as customer benefits. Therefore, the company must carefully select the ways in which it will distinguish itself from competitors. A difference is worth establishing insofar as it satisfies the following criteria:

- *Important*. The difference delivers a highly valued benefit to target buyers.

- *Distinctive*. Competitors do not offer the difference, or the company can offer it in a more distinctive way.

- *Superior*. The difference is superior to other ways by which customers might obtain the same benefit.

- *Communicable*. The difference is communicable and visible to buyers.

- *Pre-emptive*. Competitors cannot easily copy the difference.

- *Affordable*. Buyers can afford to pay for the difference.

- *Profitable*. The company can introduce the difference profitably.

Many companies have introduced differentiations that failed one or more of these tests. The Westin Stamford hotel in Singapore advertises that it is the world's tallest hotel, a distinction that is not important to many tourists – the fact scared many. AT&T's original picturevision phones failed, partly because the public did not think that seeing the other person was worth the phone's high cost. Philips Laservision failed too. Although the laser disks gave excellent picture quality, there were few disks available and the machines could not record. These drawbacks meant that consumers saw Laservision as offering no advantage over videotape machines.

Some competitive advantages are too slight, too costly to develop, or too inconsistent with the company's profile. Suppose that a company is designing its positioning strategy and has narrowed its list of possible competitive advantages to four. The company needs a framework for selecting the one advantage that makes the most sense to develop. Table 10.5 shows a systematic way of evaluating several potential competitive advantages and choosing the right one.

In the table, the company compares its standing on four attributes – technology, cost, quality and service – to the standing of its chief competitor. Let's assume that both companies stand at 8 on technology (1 = low score, 10 = high score), which means that they both have good technology. The company questions whether it can gain much by improving its technology further, especially given the high cost of new technology. The competitor has a better standing on cost (8 instead of 6), and this can hurt the company if the market gets

Competitive advantage	Company standing (1–10)	Competitor standing (1–10)	Importance of improving standing (H-M-L)	Affordability and speed (H-M-L)	Competitor's ability to improve standing (H-M-L)	Recommended action
Technology	8	8	L	L	M	Hold
Cost	6	8	H	M	M	Watch
Quality	8	6	L	L	H	Watch
Service	4	3	H	H	L	Invest

Table 10.5 Finding competitive advantage

more price sensitive. The company offers higher quality than its competitor (8 instead of 6). Finally, both companies offer below-average service (4 and 3).

At first glance, it appears that the company should go after cost or service to improve its market appeal over the competitor. However, it must consider other factors. First, how important are improvements in each of these attributes to the target customers? The fourth column shows that both cost and service improvements would be highly important to customers. Next, can the company afford to make the improvements? If so, how fast can it complete them? The fifth column shows that the company could improve service quickly and affordably. But if the firm decided to do this, would the competitor be able to improve its service also? The sixth column shows that the competitor's ability to improve service is low, perhaps because the competitor does not believe in service or has limited funds. The final column then shows the appropriate actions to take on each attribute. It makes the most sense for the company to invest in improving its service. Service is important to customers; the company can afford to improve its service and can do it fast, and the competitor will probably not be able to catch up.

Communicating and delivering the chosen position

Once it has chosen a position, the company must take strong steps to deliver and communicate the desired position to target consumers. All the company's marketing-mix efforts must support the positioning strategy. Positioning the company calls for concrete action – it is not just talk. If the company decides to build a position on better quality and service, it must first *deliver* that position. Designing the marketing mix – product, price, place and promotion – involves working out the tactical details of the positioning strategy. Thus a firm that seizes upon a 'high-quality position' knows that it must produce high-quality products, charge a high price, distribute through high-quality dealers and advertise in high-quality media. It must hire and train more service people, find retailers that have a good reputation for service, and develop sales and advertising messages that broadcast its superior service. This is the only way to build a consistent and believable high-quality, high-service position.

Companies often find it easier to come up with a good positioning strategy than to implement it. Establishing a position or changing one usually takes a long time. In contrast, positions that have taken years to build can quickly disappear. Once a company has built the desired position, it must take care to maintain the position through consistent performance and communication. It must closely monitor and adapt the position over time to match changes in consumer needs and competitors' strategies. This is how world-leading brands such as Coca-Cola, Nescafé, Snickers, BMW, Rolex, Estée Lauder, Johnnie Walker and Chanel have remained pre-eminent for so long. The company should avoid abrupt changes that might confuse consumers. Coca-Cola forgot this when it introduced its disastrous new Coke, Marlboro's price cuts made the brand fall from being the most highly valued brand to out of the top ten, and Unilever's hasty introduction of the Persil/Omo Power benefited Procter & Gamble. Violent changes rarely succeed – a product's position should evolve as it adapts to the changing market environment.

Summary

Sellers can take three approaches to a market. *Mass marketing* is the decision to mass-produce and mass-distribute one product and attempt to attract all kinds of buyers. *Target marketing* is the decision to identify the different groups that make up a market and to develop products and marketing mixes for selected target markets. Sellers today are moving away from mass marketing and product differentiation towards target marketing because this approach is more helpful in spotting market opportunities and developing more effective products and marketing mixes.

The key steps in target marketing are market segmentation, market targeting and market positioning. *Market segmentation* is the act of dividing a market into distinct groups of buyers who might merit separate products or marketing mixes. The marketer tries different variables to see which give the best segmentation opportunities. For consumer marketing, the chief segmentation variables are geographic, demographic, psychographic and behavioural. Business markets segment by business consumer demographics, operating characteristics, buying approaches and personal character-istics. The effectiveness of segmentation analysis depends on finding segments that are *measurable*, *accessible*, *substantial* and *actionable*.

Next, the seller has to target the best market segments. The company first evaluates each segment's size and growth characteristics, structural attractiveness and compatibility with company resources and objectives. It then chooses one of three market-coverage strategies. The seller can ignore segment differences (*undifferentiated marketing*), develop different market offers for several segments (*differentiated marketing*), or go after one or a few market segments (*concentrated marketing*). Much depends on company resources, product variability, product life-cycle stage and competitive marketing strategies.

The *core strategy* of a company shows how it will address the markets it has targeted. By *differentiation* it develops the strengths of the company, so that they meet the target markets' needs; then, by market positioning, it manages the way consumers view the company and its products. *Differentiation* helps a firm compete profitably. It gives it a *competitive advantage*. If a firm does not differentiate, it will be like 'all the rest' and be forced to compete on price. Differentiation is harder in some industries than others, but it is rare that a creative marketer cannot differentiate a market in some way.

There are four main ways to differentiate: *product differentiation*, *service differentiation*, *personnel differentiation* and *image differentiation*. The ease of following new technological innovations means that the product is becoming an increasingly difficult way to differentiate. Now service and image are the main ways people distinguish between products. As systems and methods become more common, personnel differentiation becomes more important. A firm's functional strengths give it its competitive advantage. Market positioning is about managing customers' view of the company and its products. It is about perception.

Value-based positioning offers a general positioning alternative based on the value delivered for the price charged. Several potentially successful strategies range from *more for more*, where customers are offered superior products or service at a higher price, to *less for less* which offers basic services at discount prices. Combinations of price and value that are the same as those already in the market are unlikely to succeed, as are offerings that deliver less value to customers.

There are several *positioning strategies* for shifting and holding customers' perceptions. Positioning works by associating products with product attributes or other stimuli. Successful firms usually maintain a clear differential advantage and do not make violent changes to their market positions.

Discussing the issues

1. What are the benefits of mass marketing versus market segmentation for a business? Discuss in relation to examples of product and service providers.

2. The European Union, with its member states, is now viewed as an attractive and distinctive geographic market segment. Do you agree with this view? To what extent can businesses market in the same way to different consumers in member states? What does this imply about market segmentation?

3. Financial services providers are looking to segment their markets in the face of greater competition and ever more demanding customers. Would segmentation work for financial services? Show how financial services providers might go about segmenting their markets and implementing selected targeting strategies.

4. Famous personalities are often used in advertising products. Think of examples you know and work out what values the personality brings to the brand.

5. Is positioning helpful to not-for-profit organisations? If so, how should a charity select and implement a positioning strategy? If not, why?

Applying the concepts

1. By looking at advertising and at products themselves, we can often see how marketers are attempting to position their products and what target market they hope to reach.

   - Define the positionings of and target markets for Coca-Cola, Pepsi Cola, Red Bull, Tango and 7-Up.
   - Define the positionings of and target markets for KitKat, Lion Bar, Snickers, Aero, Mars Bars and Twix.
   - Do you think that the soft drinks and confectionery industries achieve distinctive positionings and target markets? Are some more clearly defined than others?

2. Alldays, a convenience store, has located two appropriate properties: one in Appleby Magna (postcode DE12 7AQ) and the other in nearby Measham (postcode DE12 7HR). Visit www.upmystreet.com to view the ACORN geodemographics of the two locations and suggest how Alldays' merchandise and promotions should be adjusted to meet the needs of the alternative communities.

References

1. See www.drivedreamcars.com; Nick Hornby, 'Thunder Road' in *31 Songs* (London: Penguin, 2003); Bruce Springsteen, *Born to Run*, CBS 69170, 1975.

2. MTV.com, Tim Burt, 'Veteran leads MTV's attack', *Financial Times* (12 August 2003), p. 6.

3. Sheed Shah and Matthew Beard, 'Early retirement for the owner of Sagas', *The Independent* (27 November 2003), p. 3; 'Over 60 and overlooked', *The Economist* (10 August 2003), pp. 55–6; Allen Hall and Clare Chapman, 'Supermarkets wise up to their older customers', *The Times* (18 November

2003); Astrid Wendlandt, 'Champion of the "grey pound" calls it a day', *Financial Times* (27 November 2003), p. 23.

4. 'Isn't this gay, dear?', *The Economist* (23 November 2002), p. 54.

5. 'Fifty best albums of the year', *Q* (January 2004), pp. 73–84.

6. For a collection of articles on one-to-one marketing and mass customisation, see James H. Gilmore and B. Joseph Pine, *Markets of One: Creating customer-unique value through mass customization* (Boston: Harvard Business School Press, 2001) and Jerry Wind and Arvid Rangaswamy, 'Customerization: the next revolution in mass customization', *Journal of Interactive Marketing* (Winter 2001), pp. 13–32.

7. Paul Sexton, 'We want to be Marillionaires', *FT Creative Business* (10 October 2000), p. 14.

8. Jocken Pläcking, *Marketing-Kommunikation im Automobilmarkt Europa* (Stuttgart: Motor-Presse, 1990).

9. Marieke De Mooij, *Advertising Worldwide: Concepts, theories and practical multinational and global advertising*, 2nd edn (London: Prentice Hall, 1994).

10. David Blackwell, 'Intelligent as a brick', *Financial Times* (27 January 1998), p. 18; Claire Irvin, *Marketing Business* (September 1999), pp. 36–9.

11. 'Diaper movies: Tommy and Dill', *The Economist* (3 April 1999), p. 99; 'In the crowd', *The Economist* (15 September 2001), p. 36.

12. 'Serious games', *The Economist* (8 July 2000), pp. 129–30.

13. Adam Barnes, 'Nawab of cash and curry', *Business FT Weekend Magazine* (30 September 2000), pp. 26–9; Alicia Clegg, 'Pitch begins for the ethnic pound', *Financial Times* (28 March 2003), p. 14.

14. Rajshekhar G. Javalgi and Paul Dion, 'A life cycle segmentation approach to marketing financial products and services', *Service Industries Journal*, **19**, 3 (1999), pp. 74–96; Wendlandt, 'Champion of the "grey pound" calls it a day', op. cit.

15. See Barbara Beck, 'Women and work: Your money or your time', *The Economist* (18 July 1998), p. S8; Laura Q. Hughes and Alice Z. Cuneo, 'Lowes retools image in push toward women', *Advertising Age* (26 February 2001), pp. 3, 51; Michelle Orecklin, 'What women watch', *Time* (13 May 2002), pp. 65–6; and information accessed online at www.iVillage.com and www.oxygen.com, July 2002.

16. Helene Stapinski, 'Online markets: You go, girls', *Sales and Marketing Management* (January 1999), pp. 47–8; Sarah Bridges, 'World wide women', *e.business* (April 2000), p. 78.

17. 'Is one Rolls-Royce ever enough?', *The Economist* (4 January 2003), p. 51; 'The origins of Vertu', *The Economist* (22 February 2003); 'Rolling out the red carpet', *The Economist* (7 September 2002), p. 76.

18. Bertrand Benoit, 'Neon live on low-brow TV offensive', *Financial Times* (20 December 2002), p. 28; Dan Hogsett, 'Family dollar drives 1Q profits', *Home Textiles Today* (14 January 2002), p. 16.

19. For an insight on the differences between these leisure parks, visit their websites: centerparcs.com and clubmed.com.

20. See 'Vespa takes on Manhattan: Amore', *The Economist* (16 November 2002); 'Triumph: punch power', *The Economist* (24 November 2001), p. 25; Jonathon Welsh, 'Transport: the summer of the scooter: boomers get a new retro toy', *Wall Street Journal* (13 April 2001), p. W1; and Honda's website at www.hondamotorcycle.com/scooter, July 2002.

21. See Schiffman and Kanuk, *Consumer Behavior*, op. cit., p. 48, and for a sophisticated example see Günther Botschen, Eva M. Thelen and Rik Pieters, 'Using means–end structures for benefit segmentation: an application to services', *European Journal of Marketing*, **33**, 1/2 (1999), pp. 38–58.

22. Kim Benjamin, 'Moving with the Internet', *e.business* (April 2000), pp. 18–20; 'Waves of the future', *The Economist* (8 July 2000), pp. 107–9; 'Playing with the big boys', *The Economist* (15 May 1999), pp. 97–8; Sarah Bridges, 'The net generation', *e.business* (May 2000), p. 19; Mark Elliott, 'Net benefits', *Marketing Business* (April 2000), pp. 21–4; Susanne Yoyle, 'Digital music player proves a big hit', *Financial Times* (12 December 2003), p. 3; Brian Wonsink and Sea Bum Park, 'Methods and measures that profile heavy users', *Journal of Advertising Research* (July–August 2000), pp. 61–72.

23. For a comprehensive discussion of loyalty schemes, see Mark Uncles, 'Do you or your customers need a loyalty scheme?', *Journal of Targeting, Measurement and Analysis for Marketing*, **2**, 4 (1994), pp. 335–50; see also F. F. Reichheld, 'Loyalty-based management', *Harvard Business Review* (March–April 1993), pp. 64–73; Andrew S. C. Ehrenberg, 'Locking them in forever', *Admap*, **28**, 11 (1992), p. 14.

24. 'Custom publishing: Voguish', *The Economist* (23 August 2003), p. 55.

25. Martin Howard, 'The practicalities of developing better analysis and segmentation techniques for fine focusing and improving targeting', *Institute for International Research, Conference on Advanced Customer Profiling, Segmentation and Analysis*, London, 10 February 1994.

26. See D. Sudharshan and Frederick Winter, 'Strategic segmentation of industrial markets', *Journal of Business and Industrial Marketing*, **13**, 1 (1998), pp. 8–21; V.-W. Mitchell, 'Segmenting purchasers of organisational professional services: a risk-based approach', *Journal of Services Marketing*, **12**, 2 (1998), pp. 83–97; Bill Merrilees, Rohan Bentley and Ross Cameron, 'Business service market segmentation: the case of electrical and mechanical building maintenance services', *Journal of Business and Industrial Marketing*, **14**, 2 (1999), pp. 151–63; Andy Dexter, 'Egotists, idealists, and corporate animals – Segmenting business markets', *International Journal of Marketing Research* (First Quarter 2002), pp. 31–51.

27. For another interesting approach to segmenting the business market, see Dexter, 'Egotists, idealists, and corporate animals', op. cit.

28. P. G. Walters, 'Global market segmentation and challenges', *Journal of Marketing Management*, **13**, 1–3 (1997), pp. 163–80; V Kumar and Anish Nagpal, 'Segmenting global markets: Look before you leap', *Marketing Research* (Spring 2001), pp. 8–13.

29. Taken from Jens Maier and John Saunders, 'The implementation of segmentation in sales management', *Journal of Personal Selling and Sales Management*, **10**, 1 (1990), pp. 39–48.

30. Gert-Olof Boström and Timothy L. Wilson, 'Market segmentation in professional services – case of CAD adoption amongst architectural firms', *European Marketing Academy Proceedings*, Barcelona, Spain, 25–28 May 1993, pp. 249–60; Carl R. Frear, Mary S. Alguire and Lynn E. Metcalf, 'Country segmentation on the basis of international purchasing patterns', *Journal of Business and Industrial Marketing*, **10**, 2 (1995), pp. 59–68.

31. John Thornhill and Lina Saigol, 'Future Whitbread butterfly emerges from its chrysalis', *Financial Times* (20 October 2000), p. 26.

32. Joseph McAleer, 'A saga of romance, big business and unrequited lust', *The Times* (29 October 1999), pp. 37–8; John Walsh and Jojo Moyes, 'Swoon! Mills & Boon make eyes at male reader' (28 September 2000), p. 1.

33. Richard Tomkins, 'Advertisers lose out on sporting chance', *Financial Times* (21 June 2002), p. 21; Adam Sherwin, 'Payday for rugby as sponsors snub soccer's bad boys', *The Times* (19 November 2003), p. 11.

34. For a discussion of the concepts of differentiation and competitive advantage, and methods for assessing them, see Michael Porter, *Competitive Advantage* (New York: Free Press, 1985), Ch. 2. For more recent discussions, see Leyland Pitt, 'Total e-clipse: five new forces for strategy in the digital age', *Journal of General Management* (Summer 2001), pp. 1–15; and Stanley Slater and Eric Olson, 'A fresh look at industry and market analysis', *Business Horizons* (January–February 2002), pp. 15–22; Grahan Hooley, John Saunders and Nigel Piercy, *Marketing Strategy and Competitive Positioning* (London: Prentice Hall, 2003).

35. For a review of this and other results, see Robert D. Buzzell and Bradley T. Gale, *The PIMS Principle: Linking strategy to performance* (New York: Free Press, 1987).

36. Theodore Levitt, 'Making success through differentiation – of anything', *Harvard Business Review* (January–February 1980).

37. 'Western Europe's insurance tangle', *The Economist* (18 June 1994), pp. 115–16; 'e.Business Report', *e.business* (February 2000), pp. 30–47.

38. John Gapper, 'Wheels of fire', *FT Magazine* (20 September 2003), pp. 16–21; Peter Marsh, 'Dust is settling on the Dyson market clean-up', *Financial Times* (12 December 2003), p. 12.

39. See Tom Peters, *Thriving on Chaos* (New York: Knopf, 1987), pp. 56–7.

40. Bettina von Hase, 'This shoe walks', *Business FT Weekend Magazine* (4 November 2000), pp. 30–4; 'Electrolux: brand challenge', *The Economist* (6 April 2002), p. 68.

41. Mercedes M. Cardona and Jack Neff, 'Everything's at a premium', *Advertising Age* (2 August 1999), pp. 12, 15.

42. Michael Harvey, 'As sport as you want to be', *Weekend FT* (28–29 October 2000), p. XVII.

43. Gillian O'Conner, 'Business opts for no-frills flights', *Financial Times* (13 March 2000), p. 3; Kevin Done, 'EasyJet orders 17 aircraft in expansion drive', *Financial Times* (30 March 2000), p. 26; Kenin Done, 'Web prompts 'huge' savings for Ryanair', *Financial Times* (8 November 2000), p. 34; David Humphries, 'Niche airports for high-flyers', *How To Spend It* (4–5 November 2000), pp. 8–10.

44. Jane Tawbase, 'Jaguar's new dream is a reality', *EuroBusiness* (June 2000), pp. 72–3; Jane Tawbase, 'Filling the garages of families', *EuroBusiness* (July 2000), pp. 70–4; 'Her luxury', *The Economist* (4 November 2000), p. 124.

45. Positioning was introduced in the seminal work by Al Ries and Jack Trout, *Positioning: The battle for your mind* (New York: McGraw-Hill, 1981); see also Al Ries and Jack Trout, *Marketing Warfare* (New York: McGraw-Hill, 1986). For other ideas on positioning see Girish Punj and Junyean Moon, 'Positioning options for achieving brand association: a psychological categorization framework', *Journal of Business Research* (April 2002), pp. 275–83.

46. David Short, 'Red Bull set to lock horns with multinationals', *The European* (19–25 August 1994).

47. Susan Jacquet, 'Ethics and responsibility', *Swiss Quality Timing* (Spring 1994), pp. 40–1.

48. Birna Helgadottir, 'Time has come to realise your dreams', *The European – élan* (16–22 September 1994), p. 6; Tom Rubython, 'Turnaround artist' *EuroBusiness* (April 2000), pp. 38–42; 'Yacht racing: another tack', *The Economist* (22 February 2003), p. 79.

49. 'Branded like Beckham', *The Economist* (5 July 2003), p. 68; 'A Tiger economy', *The Economist* (14 April 2001), p. 94; Denis Campbell and Lawrence Donegan, 'Sold to the highest bidder' *The Observer* (1 June 2003), p. 21.

50. Helen Rumbelow and Sam Lister, 'Rings sequel stuff of nightmare in boy's pyjamas', *The Times* (12 December 2002), p. 3; 'Back on the right track', *Financial Times* (14 March 2003), p. VI.

51. Diane Summers, 'Skoda's sales drive is no joke', *Financial Times* (12 May 1994), p. 11; Paul Mungo, 'Wipe the smile off', *Business Financial Times Weekend Magazine* (29 April 2000), pp. 20–2, 40.

52. Catherine Monk, 'No more red', *EuroBusiness* (April 2000), pp. 68–74; Catherine Monk, 'Ordering up a world champion', *EuroBusiness* (April 2000), pp. 146–8.

53. Mark Landler and Gail DeGeorge, 'Tempers are sizzling over Burger King's new ads', *Business Week* (12 February 1990), p. 33; Philip Stelly, Jr, 'Burger King rule breaker', *Adweek* (9 November 1990), pp. 24, 26.

WEB RESOURCES

For additional classic case studies and Internet exercises, visit www.pearsoned.co.uk/ kotler

Concluding concepts 10
Coffee-Mate

Greg, category manager for coffee creamers, was evaluating his ad agency's proposal for Coffee-Mate (Exhibit 10.1). The £25 million (€42 million) a year coffee creamer market was small with a household penetration of only 18 per cent. Despite the growth of private labels to take 37 per cent of the market, Coffee-Mate's £1.5 million advertising budget had enabled it to hold a 55 per cent market share and squeeze both private label and other brands (Complement, Kenco and Compleat). However, budgets were being squeezed so unless the advertising campaign could show some sales gain, there was a danger that the category could be milked to provide income to invest in food products with more growth potential.

> Powdered or dried milk is a distress product.

Competition in the coffee creamer market

The coffee creamer market is distinct from the declining £43 million instant dry milk market (Marvel, St Ivel Five Pints and Pint Size). Dried or powdered milk had been associated with slimming (e.g. Marvel adopted this positioning). Dried or powdered milk is not a direct substitute for coffee creamers because of its poor mixing qualities. It is used as a whitener in tea or coffee only in 'emergencies' when the household has run out of milk.

The coffee creamer market is undergoing a change in parallel with consumers' developing tastes for skimmed and semi-skimmed milk in their coffee. Milk is the most popular whitener for coffee. Although cream is thought to be the best whitener, consumers perceive cream as reserved, ritualistic and appropriate for special occasions but not for daily use.

Powdered or dried milk is a distress product, creamers are regarded as an indulgence, although non-users did not see creamers as anything like a substitute for cream and were generally suspicious of the product.

Coffee-Mate is a blend of dried glucose and vegetable fat, but cannot be legally defined as non-dairy, since it also contains milk derivatives. Recent improvements to the product include the relaunch of Coffee-Mate 100 g and 200 g in straight-sided glass jars with paper labels, and a 'Nidoll-contoured' jar with shrink-wrapped label. Packs of

Exhibit 10.1 Proposed TV ad to boost sales

Vision	Sound
Jane and John, an affluent thirty-something couple, are entertaining two other similar couples.	Soft soul music playing throughout.
They are ending their meal by drinking coffee out of fine china cups and eating After Eights.	
Jane looks, alarmed, at John. John glances at the empty cream jug.	John (to one of the other guests): 'Do you want another cup?' Guest 1: 'Yes, please.' Guest 2: 'Me, too! With cream!'
Jane rushes into kitchen and frantically looks for cream (there is none) and milk (all gone).	Jane (thinking quickly): 'I'll make it!'
Jane pauses, smiles, then gets out the Coffee-Mate. Jane pours the coffee and adds the Coffee-Mate.	
Jane returns with coffee. Guest sips the coffee containing Coffee-Mate.	Guest 1: 'Lovely, even better than the last one!' Guest 2: 'Yes, how do you do it?'
John smiles quizzically (and admiringly) at Jane. Jane leans back in her chair, smiling knowingly.	Voice: 'Coffee-Mate, never be without it!'

Exhibit 10.2 Reasons for lapsing and rejection (number of respondents)

Spontaneous response	Lapsing	Rejection
Don't drink coffee	11	22
Drink black coffee	5	6
Prefer milk	50	33
Prefer skimmed milk	5	3
Don't like them	10	18
Leaves coffee too hot	2	1
No need to use them	5	5
Don't think to buy them	1	4
Doesn't mix	4	1
Prefer pure things	4	3
Fattening	2	2
Too rich/creamy	1	2
Other	5	3
Don't know	4	9

Exhibit 10.3 Consumption by income group (per person/week)

Weekly income (£)	Weekly expenditure (£)
645+	0.25
475–644	0.19
250–474	0.20
125–249	0.18
0–124	0.17
125+ (no earners)	0.32
0–125 (no earners)	0.19
Old-age pensioners	18.64

SOURCE: National Food Survey, pub. MAFF. Crown copyright material is reproduced under Class Licence Number C01W0000039 with the permission of the Controller of HMSO.

Exhibit 10.4 Consumption by household size (per person/week)

Adults in household	Children in household	Weekly expenditure (£)
1	0	0.27
1	1+	0.15
2	0	0.25
2	1	0.18
2	2	0.15
2	3	0.15
2	4+	0.11
3	0	0.23
3+	1–2	0.16
3+	3+	0.12
4+	0	0.25

SOURCE: National Food Survey, pub. MAFF. Crown copyright material is reproduced under Class Licence Number C01W0000039 with the permission of the Controller of HMSO.

500 g and 1 kg are available in cartons with an inner bag. When Coffee-Mate Lite, a low-fat alternative to Coffee-Mate, was introduced, cannibalisation of volume was minimal. The volume generated by Lite is a key feature in the development of the brand, which has experienced a 10 per cent growth in sales volume in the first three years following Lite's launch.

Coffee-Mate consumer

The average Coffee-Mate consumer buys 1.5 kg annually. There is no *strong* demographic bias among coffee creamer buyers although there is a slight skew towards 45–64-year-olds, two-person households and households without children. Heavy buyers of Coffee-Mate have a slight bias towards lower social class, aged 45+, 2–3-person households with children. Coffee-Mate Lite users have a slight bias towards 45–64-year-olds, full-time working housewives and households without children.

AGB Superpanel data suggest that buyers of Coffee-Mate use all brands and types of coffee. The creamer market has a low interest level since it is not a weekly shopping item. Reasons given for lapsed usage were similar to non-users (Exhibit 10.2).

Because Coffee-Mate and Coffee-Mate Lite are 'consumed' with coffee, popularity and demand will also be affected by the annual coffee consumption, which is static at a low 3 kg per head in the UK (about 1.5 cups per day). The figure for Italy, France and Germany is 5 kg and 11–13 kg in the Benelux region and Scandinavia. The National Food Survey suggests that the higher a household's

income, the more it spends on coffee (Exhibit 10.3). Childless households are the most intense coffee drinkers (Exhibit 10.4).

Dried milk

The image of powdered milk is as a distress product where the *brand* is *bought*, but the *product* is *tolerated*: 'You tend to buy powdered milk thinking that you will need it when you run out, and occasionally you do.' 'Powdered milk is useful if you run out of real milk. You can make it up and use it just like the real thing, but it doesn't taste too good. You have to be a bit desperate to want to use it.'

Other negatives attach to dry milk. Respondents considered it to be inconvenient to prepare. Frequently its performance is seen as disappointing: it is 'lumpy', resulting in 'bits' floating on the top of their coffee. The product also tends to 'congeal' when spooned into tea or coffee. When made up and poured, the product's poor taste qualities are apparent: 'We have had it in our Cornflakes when we've run out, but quite honestly, it tastes so disgusting that in the future I don't think I'd bother.' 'It's all right for baking, but if you want to use it like real milk, it's not really advisable.'

Whiteners/coffee creamers

Coffee creamers have a more polarised image across users and non-users. *Loyal* or *confirmed creamer users* regard creamer as almost a treat. These hedonistic and indulgent properties are sometimes enhanced by the brand (e.g. Coffee-Mate) being perceived as having relaxing or comforting benefits: 'Creamers are a little bit of an indulgence. They make coffee taste so much better. They add something to it which improves the taste.' 'First thing in the morning I tend to have coffee with semi-skimmed milk, but towards 11 o'clock I want something which is more relaxing, more substantial, so I have coffee with Coffee-Mate. It seems to be comforting.'

Creamers' taste is a motivating force behind usage. Loyal users appreciate the thicker, creamier taste. Creamers are considered to supplement the taste of coffee, to complement and improve its flavour. For Coffee-Mate, the perceptions are extremely positive. Users enjoy its sweet delivery, stating that they need not add sugar to it. Fans feel that it does produce a creamy cup of coffee whether or not it is added to instant or freshly brewed 'real' coffee: 'Coffee without Coffee-Mate, just made with milk, tastes like it's got something missing.' 'Coffee-Mate kind of lifts the flavour. It makes a richer, better-tasting cup of coffee, whether it be an instant or a real one.'

Non-users' perceptions of coffee creamers are tainted by their negative attitudes towards dried milk. Creamers are something you have put by for an emergency: 'If someone gave me a cup of coffee with creamer in it, I would think they were doing it because they had run out of milk. I wouldn't have thought it was because they like the taste of it. Surely nobody could like the taste.'

Thus, in marked contrast to the users, non-users describe creamers as changing the taste of coffee, masking its pure taste rather than enhancing it. They also criticised its high sugar content, which the consumers

feel delivers a flavour that is unacceptably sweet. They perceive it to be a poor alternative to cream: 'You can always tell when someone's used creamers, it just tastes powdery. It doesn't taste like cream, it has a taste all of its own.' 'Whiteners taste nothing like cream. They taste powdery. You always know when they're there.'

Lapsed users still see creamers as a bit of an indulgence and a treat. However, they feel an element of guilt in using the product: 'I like coffee creamers – I like the taste. But I stopped using them because I felt I was putting on too much weight and I needed to cut down. I just think there is too much in there, it's just glucose syrup and vegetable fat.' 'My husband had to go on a low-cholesterol diet and I figured that there was just too much fat in the coffee creamers. We've become accustomed now to drinking it black, or with very little skimmed milk.'

Health concerns are having an impact upon milk consumption. This change has been prompted by consumers' concern over health in general, and their level of fat intake in particular. Some consumers found it difficult to wean themselves and their families off milk, initially, and then semi-skimmed milk, in favour of the fully skimmed variety. However, many are persistent in adopting an overall preventative health maintenance regime as well as controlling their weight. So, while a few retained the notion that a cup of real coffee made with cream was the ideal, many others considered their ideal to be coffee drunk with just a dash of milk or black. Coffee-Mate is in danger of being redundant since it is perceived to be too close to cream in its taste and texture while its creamy association is increasingly deemed unhealthy. Coffee-Mate Lite may redeem the situation by offering the same benefits of creamy and rich taste without causing injury to health and weight.

Consumer analyses

TGI User Surveys covering instant/ground coffee and powdered milk/coffee creamer markets yielded five potential consumer groups for Coffee-Mate.

'Sharon and Tracy' – experimentalists (sample proportion: 15.4 per cent)

They like to enjoy themselves and try new things. They enjoy spending money happily and seem to be very materialistic and status conscious. They go out frequently and are uninterested in political or environmental issues. Although they are heavy users of instant coffee, they are low-level users of ground coffee. They claim to use

Nescafé granules and Maxwell House powder most often. They are below-average users of the category and average users of Coffee-Mate, but heavy users of cream.

They are younger (15–44 years) with a mid- to down-market bias (C2D) and children. They are of middle income (£15,000 up to £30,000), but live in state-owned property, in underprivileged areas.

They read many 'low brow' newspapers and the 'mums' magazines such as *Bella*, *Chat* and *Woman*. They are heavy users of commercial terrestrial TV, breakfast programmes and satellite TV and are heavy listeners to pop radio channels. They cannot resist buying magazines and read papers for entertainment rather than for news.

They spend average to high amounts on the main grocery shop. They love shopping for anything, be it food, clothes, kitchen gadgets or whatever. They like to keep up with fashion and believe they are stylish, and feel it is important to try to keep looking young. They will try anything new. They will respond to seeing new things in advertising or in the store.

They are very gregarious and socialise often (heavy users of pubs, wine bars and restaurants). They like to enjoy life and not worry about the future. They holiday abroad (eat, drink and lie in the sun) and like to treat themselves. They tend to spend money without thinking, spend more with their credit card and are no good at saving their money. They feel that it is important for people to think they are doing well. They buy cars for their looks and believe that brands are better than own labels.

They are not really using Coffee-Mate as much as one would have expected.

'Eileen and Mary' – cost constrained, older, conservative (23.6 per cent)

Very price aware, they budget when shopping and look for lowest prices. They are very traditional in their habits (don't like foreign food or foreign holidays). They worry about food ('food is not safe nowadays'), feel safe using products recommended by experts and think fast food is junk. They think it is worth paying more for organic fruit and vegetables and environmentally friendly products, but don't do much about it, perhaps because they can't afford to.

They are light users of instant coffee, using Maxwell House brands most often. They are average users of dried milk but are not really users of Coffee-Mate and never use cream. They are older (55+) and down-market (C2DE). They are not working or are retired in one- or two-person households; hence fewer of this type have children at home. They live in multi-ethnic areas, council areas

and underprivileged areas on a low household income (£5,000–11,000).

They read the tabloid press and *Bella* and *Chat*. They are also heavy users of terrestrial commercial ITV and listen to commercial pop radio stations.

Their expenditure on grocery shopping is low and they tend to shop daily at small grocers. They enjoy shopping, but always look for the lowest prices, decide what they want before they go shopping and budget for every penny. They frequently enter competitions, find saving difficult, save for items they want and like to pay cash.

They are very conservative. They like routine, dislike untidiness, would buy British if they could, have a roast on Sundays and prefer brands to own label. They believe job security is more important than money, would rather have a boring job than no job, and prefer to do rather than take responsibility. Due to both their age and financial constraints, they socialise rarely. Most of this group never entertain friends to a meal, never go to a pub, a wine bar or a restaurant.

'Sarah and Anna' – affluent, young foodies (24.4 per cent)

Unencumbered by children and well off, they love both travelling and food (many claim to be vegetarian). They do not have to budget and can afford to treat themselves to perfume and foreign holidays, preferably more than once a year. They are not interested in additional channels on satellite TV and tend to be light users of all media.

They are heavy users of coffee and ground coffee. They buy decaffeinated, Gold Blend, Alta Rica and Cap Colombie. They are above-average users of creamers, claim to buy Coffee-Mate and Marvel most often, and also use cream.

Aged 35–54, predominantly ABC1, they earn above-average incomes and work full time. They live in areas of affluent minorities, young married suburbs and metro singles, in one- or two-person households.

They read quality newspapers, are light users of commercial radio but they do listen to the radio (usually the BBC) in the car.

They have a high expenditure on their main grocery shop (£71+) but shop infrequently at a large grocery supermarket. They really enjoy cooking and food, read recipes in magazines and like to try out new foods. Their tastes will be varied as they also enjoy travelling abroad on holiday, where they avoid the package trips and like to do as much as possible.

They entertain frequently and invite friends for meals. They also use pubs and wine bars, though not as much as 'Sharon and Tracy', and they are heavy users of restaurants.

They are health conscious (well, they can afford to be) and claim to include fibre in their diet, eat wholemeal bread, have less fat in their diet and eat fewer sweets and cakes. They are prepared to pay more for food without additives and for environmentally friendly products. They also exercise.

They can afford to treat themselves and prefer to buy one good thing rather than many cheap ones. They also like to keep up with technology and want to stand out from the crowd. In their fortunate position they enjoy life and don't worry about the future.

They claim never to buy any product tested on animals, use recycling banks and disapprove of aerosols more than the population at large. They make use of credit cards, especially for business, like to be well insured and consult professional advisers.

'Dawn and Lisa' – cost constrained, young families (13.9 per cent)

This group is severely constrained by their low incomes. But unlike the previous group, they are often young, working part-time or are unemployed or students. They are also not remotely concerned about health or the environment. Many left school at 15 or 16.

They are heavy users of instant coffee but do not use ground coffee. They buy Nescafé granules and Maxwell House powder. They are below-average users of creamers and never use cream.

This group is biased towards the 15–34 age group and is down-market (C2DE) with low incomes (£5,000–11,000). They tend to live in state housing in fading industrial areas. They have young families and there is a slightly greater bias to larger families than in other groups.

They read the tabloid press, *Bella* and *Chat*, and they are heavy viewers of commercial terrestrial and satellite TV, and heavy listeners to independent radio.

Their expenditure on the main grocery shop is low and they shop daily or once a week at discount grocery stores. They always look for the lowest price, watch what they spend, budget for every penny and look out for special offers. They want to save but find it difficult.

As a result of their difficult financial circumstances, they rarely use wine bars, pubs or restaurants. They claim to enjoy going to the pub, but cannot afford to these days. Similarly, when they can afford a holiday, they prefer to do so in the UK.

They have little time or money to worry about the environment or health issues, and claim that health food

is bought by fanatics. They believe that frozen food is as nutritious as fresh foods. They tend to buy own label, presumably because it is cheaper rather than because they believe own-label goods are better than branded goods.

'Dorothy and Amy' – affluent (22.7 per cent)

This group does not have to be price conscious. They are older, sometimes retired or working part-time, and are well off. Often they own their house outright. They are, however, fairly traditional. They are not interested in travelling abroad, they are not health conscious and they are not media aware.

They are the people most likely to be buying Coffee-Mate. They buy instant coffee to the same degree as the rest of the population and are light users of ground coffee. But they use creamers as well as cream.

Dorothy and Amy are older (55+) and are up-market (AB and C1). They still have a reasonable household income despite being retired (£25,000+) and their children have left home. They are clearly a group who have disposable income and are not worried about budgeting. They are to be found in affluent minorities, older suburbs and young married suburbs.

They are readers of quality press, light viewers of ITV and never listen to commercial radio. They are not media aware, claiming to watch little TV and not to notice posters, and do not expect ads to entertain.

Their expenditure on the main grocery shop is above average. They do not enjoy shopping as much as other groups, are not price conscious but are prudent with money (consider themselves good at saving). They do not want to try new things, are not keen to keep up with the latest fashion and are not concerned with their appearance. They buy foreign goods if possible, will pay extra for quality goods, but are not really indulgent.

This is a group whose attitudes tend to lag. They get a great deal of pleasure from gardening and others often ask their advice on the matter. As a group they are happy with their standard of living. They do not often go to pubs, wine bars or restaurants, but they do have people home for meals.

Questions

1. What are the main benefits of Coffee-Mate and what is limiting its sales?
2. Should Coffee-Mate be mass marketed, aimed at one segment or aimed at multiple segments?

3. Evaluate the segments from TGI's user survey for target attractiveness and their fit to Coffee-Mate's strengths. Which of the segments would you target and why?

4. Evaluate the proposed ad for the target market and benefits promoted. Will the ad help propel Coffee-Mate's further growth? Create an alternative ad for your chosen target market.

5. How would the promotion of Coffee-Mate change with the benefits promoted and the competition targeted?

6. Defend your choice of famous personalities who could be used to help position Coffee-Mate in each different segment.

SOURCES: Economist Intelligence Unit, *Retail Business*, no. 418 (December 1992); British Market Research Bureaux, *Instant Powdered Milk and Coffee Creamers* (1992); company sources.

Erst war er heiß auf das schicke Sauna-Set.

Dann auf den kuscheligen Bademantel.

Und diesmal hat er sich gleich ein ganzes

Wellness-Wochenende gegönnt.

Alles aus der neuen **Membership Rewards** Prämienwelt.

LONG LIVE DREAMS

WARNING – Customers are perishable.

NOTICE FOR STAFF IN A FAST FOOD RESTAURANT

Relationship marketing

Chapter objectives

After reading this chapter, you should be able to:

- Define *customer value* and discuss its importance in creating and measuring customer satisfaction and company profitability.
- Discuss the concepts of *value chains* and *value delivery systems* and explain how companies go about producing and delivering customer value.
- Define quality and explain the importance of total quality marketing in building value-laden, profitable relationships with customers.
- Explain the importance of retaining current customers as well as attracting new ones.
- Discuss customer relationship marketing and the main steps in establishing a customer relationship programme.

Mini Contents List

- Prelude case – 'The most important part of a car is the distributor'
- Introduction
- Satisfying customer needs
- Defining customer value and satisfaction
- Marketing Insights 11.1 – Cold turkey has got me on the run
- Delivering customer value and satisfaction
- Customer value
- Relationship marketing
- Marketing Insights 11.2 – Network marketing: we are not alone . . .
- Summary
- Concluding concepts 11 – National Gummi AB

◄ SOURCE: American Express Germany, 2003. *Agency*: Ogilvy & Mather, Frankfurt.

Prelude case 'The most important part of a car is the distributor'

I read this car dealer's poster advertising slogan with some understanding. The copy played on the word distributor: (a) a car dealer, and (b) an electrical component that is the usual cause of old cars not starting on a wet morning. It also resonates with a recent expensive and time-consuming experience buying a luxury car.

The slogan resonates with a recent expensive and time-consuming experience buying a luxury car.

Knowing exactly the car I wanted, I entered the city centre Mercedes dealership in a frame of mind reminiscent of Samuel Johnson's observation on second marriage: 'the triumph of hope over experience'. My last visit, three years ago, ended after an exasperating encounter with the dealer's financial advisor. I asked him the best way of financing a car for a self-employed, top rate of tax payer who was registered for Value Added Tax and drove 16,000 miles (25,600 km) per year. The result of the question was a confusion of down payments, balloon payments, etc.

I tried putting the question simply to the financial advisor: 'What option gives me the lowest cost of ownership of an E230 Estate?'.

Financial advisor: 'We do not do it that way. You will have to ask your accountant.'

I left, asked my accountant, did the sums and leased a car from another dealer 50 minutes drive from where I work.

I had two reasons to believe the city centre dealer would be better this time. I had just bought a second-hand Yaris from Pentagon Toyota and the whole transaction had been quick, efficient and friendly. In addition, Mercedes had just purchased the city centre dealership so now the dealers and their splendid cars would be one.

In summer 2003 I re-entered the city centre dealers, wanting to buy an E270 CDi Estate for cash. The reviews of the new E270 CDi were fantastic – *What Car?* rated it as 'Best Executive Car of the Year'. The Consumer Association's *Which*? surprisingly showed Mercedes plummeting two categories from among Japanese cars rated the 'Best' in reliability to an 'Average' rating. However, other reports mentioned that with the new E-class, Mercedes looked to be overcoming their quality problems.

The dealer's salesman explained to me that since the £1,950 (€3,237) 'Cockpit Management and Navigation Display (COMMAND APS)' used a DVD, I would not be able to play a CD while using the satellite navigation system. I commented that this sounded like a daft 'design feature' for something so expensive, but opted for a 'CD changer in the central console' (another £350) so I could drive and jive. For an agreed price of £36,000, delivery would be on Friday 24 October. The date was after the old Mercedes' lease expired but the Yaris could fill the gap. So far so good, but not for long.

1. Getting rid of the old car was not easy. The contract with DaimlerChrysler Services (DCS) expired on 12 October and the correspondence mentioned they would pick up the car on that day. I rang the Services company to find out when on Sunday the car would be picked up:

DCS: 'We do not pick up cars on Sunday; a driver will be coming on Monday.'

'But I will not be at home on Monday, it is a working day and I already have appointments made. Can they pick it up from work?'

DCS: 'We have no way of contacting the driver now. If you are not at home when the driver arrives on Monday you will have to pay an extra charge.'

'But the contract expires on the 12th.'

DCS: 'We did contact you to arrange the pickup last week.'

'You may have tried but I was in New Zealand and I know nothing about it.'

DCS: 'We will try to contact the driver on Monday but he may have left by the time our office opens.'

After leaving faxes, emails and answerphone messages, I eventually contacted the driver and arranged the Monday pickup at work.

2. Dropping into the city centre dealer on the way in, I went to the sales desk to ask about having a Tracker (a system that tracks stolen cars) fitted to the new car, since a review I had read said the E-series estate would initially be very popular with professional thieves. There was no-one on the sales floor. Snooping round, I found an office where several smartly dressed men stood chatting. One turned to help me: 'Can I help? You will probably want the Service Department. That is the other entrance.'

'No, I'm trying to buy a car. I need to specify a Tracker and check my car's delivery date.'

In a small open office up some stairs a sales clerk asked: 'Which Tracker do you want: Retrieve, Monitor or Horizon?'

After some discussion and being told that the top of the range Horizon was really only appropriate for expensive cars, such as a Ferrari, I opted for the Retrieve system for a one-off payment of about £300.

3. The car was ready on Monday 27 October rather than the 24th. Only three days later than promised, but it did mean that, lacking the larger car, I would have to drive to my daughter's college on both 28 October and 2 November since we could not fit her bike,

grandparents and the rest of the family in another car that we would have to use, instead of the E-series estate.

4. On Monday 27th the car arrived at home and I paid an extra £299 for the Tracker. It was odd that it was not included on the bill for the car, but I assumed the Tracker was from a different company.

While checking over the car with me, the delivery driver showed me the DVD player for the navigator in the luggage compartment. 'Hang on, since the DVD player is in the luggage compartment, does that mean I could play CDs using the normal CD slot while navigating?'

Delivery driver: 'Yes, no problem. And the extra six-disc changer means you will be able to choose between seven CDs.'

'Woops; there goes £350. Never mind, the way the changer flips open does look cool.'

Later that day, at the city centre dealer's Spares Department I buy a set of £130 carrier-bars for the roof of the estate and an £82 bicycle rack. It seems a lot to transport a bike that only cost £100 several years ago but we will probably use it many times in the car's life. I would have to pick them up the next day because they were not in stock.

5. The next Saturday, trying to fix a £40 bike to the £200 rack, I had difficulty following the instructions. With the bike on the roof of the car, I could not 'Insert the anti-theft device (12) and lock the lock of the frame holder (11).' With arms above my head, I could not feel anything like a lock although there was a cable corresponding to 'the anti-theft device'. After taking down bike, bike rack and all, I found there was no lock. 'What awful quality control to leave out the lock', I thought. I was wrong. Still, I did get the bike to my daughter's college but made secure with an old bicycle lock rather than 'the lock of the frame holder'.

6. Next Monday, back to the city centre dealer. 'This bike rack's got no lock.'

Sparesman: 'It should not have one.'

'But the instructions say here "lock the lock of the frame holder".'

The sparesman said: 'See here – this note in the manual "Locks for locking the bicycle carrier are not included and must be ordered separately."'

'Why didn't you tell me when I bought the rack? The system is incomplete without a lock.'

Sparesman: 'It is not standard.'

'Can I have a lock then?'

Sparesman: 'We don't have them in stock but we can order them for you. Do you want two or four?'

'I've only got one bicycle rack; can I have one?'

Sparesman: 'I am sorry but we only sell them in packs and they are £2.70 each, £5.40 for a pack of two.'

Two days later, I get a call to say I can pick up my locks.

7. In December 2003 the legislation changed to make it illegal to use a hand-held mobile phone while driving. I did not like using mobile phones while driving but since the car had numerous buttons with pictures of telephones on, I decided to have one fitted. Among the E-class accessories is listed a 'Mercedes-Benz

hands free system' for £182 or £210 depending on whether the car was with or without 'VDA pre-wiring'. I rang the Service Department of the city centre dealer.

'How much would it cost to fit a mobile phone?'

Service Department: 'Have you got a SatNav System fitted?'

'Yes.'

Service Department: 'I'll ring our Spares Department to check. . . . They say about £1,200 all included.'

'£1,200! What is the £200 system listed in the Accessories Guide?'

Service Department: 'I don't know about that. You had better talk to Spares.'

Spares Department: 'It will be between £1,000 and £1,200 depending upon the wiring needed. You need to bring your car in so we can check.'

'I think I'll wait until after Christmas at that price. Thanks.'

8. I receive a letter from Tracker saying they need a Direct Debit mandate since I opted to pay for my Tracker Network Subscription by annual payment. I rang Tracker.

'When I bought the car I asked for a one-off payment and paid about £299 when the car was delivered.'

Tracker agent: 'Will you check your pink Tracker Order Installation Form to see what network subscription option is ticked and can you give me your TVU Serial Number?'

'There is no box ticked.'

Tracker agent: 'Oh, they are always doing that. They think we know if they leave it blank. You need to contact your dealer.'

Dealer reception: 'Tracker? I'll put you through to Customer Services.'

Customer Services: 'You'll need to speak to Sales. . . . I am sorry there is no one free now. I have left a message with our used car salesman.'

'I don't want to buy a second-hand car but I am getting to understand why I want to sell this one.'

Customer Services: 'He is busy at the moment but he will get back to you in 15 minutes. What is your telephone number?'

Two days later, I am still awaiting his call. The car is great, but the dealer . . .

Questions

1. What do you understand by the slogan 'The most important part of a car is the distributor' and is such a distinction justified when the manufacturer owns the dealership?

2. How are retailers able to survive when providing the levels of customer service described when selling such expensive luxury products? Who is at fault?

3. At what points in the sales and service interaction could the individual contact, the dealer or Mercedes intervene to improve customer satisfaction?

SOURCES: Adapted from www.whatcar.com (March 2003) and sub.which.net (October 2003).

Introduction

Today's companies face tough competition and things will only get harder. In previous chapters, we argued that to succeed in today's fiercely competitive markets, companies have to move from a *product and selling philosophy* to a *customer and marketing philosophy*. This chapter looks in more detail at how companies can win at being better at *meeting and satisfying consumer and customer needs*. As the prelude case shows, even the world's leading companies have difficulty in providing the excellent product and service quality that customers demand.

Satisfying customers is not getting easier. People have come to accept that their consumption experience has become largely adversarial. Customers have got used to having products and services that deliver, so they object when companies fail to deliver the service they promise or fail to achieve what customers anticipate. Much of the frustration experienced by customers is a new *production orientation* that has occurred as firms try to cut costs by de-skilling or automating the customer interface. Few customers have avoided the frustration of having to press a series of digits to ensure their call is directed to the appropriate person, spending minutes listening to awful music while being told 'your call is important to us', then getting through to be told another number to ring.[1] The failure of many companies to give customers what they want is creating new opportunities for effective marketers. Recognising a widening gap between customers' expectations and service, NatWest Bank, a subsidiary of Royal Bank of Scotland, has hired an extra 6,000 staff so that its customers will no longer have to deal with answering machines.[2]

For much of history, there was little need for such concerns for customer relationships or satisfaction. In sellers' markets – characterised by shortages and near-monopolies – companies did not make special efforts to please customers. By contrast, in buyers' markets customers can choose from a wide array of goods and services. In these markets, if sellers fail to deliver acceptable product and service quality, they will quickly lose customers to competitors. In addition, what is acceptable today may not be acceptable to tomorrow's

Triumph communicates specific benefits that target consumers.
SOURCE: Triumph International Ltd.

ever more demanding consumers. Consumers are becoming more educated and demanding, and their quality expectations have been raised by the practices of superior manufacturers and retailers. The decline of many traditional western industries in recent years – cars, cameras, shipping, machine tools, consumer electronics – offers dramatic evidence that firms offering only average quality lose their consumer franchises when attacked by superior competitors.

Satisfying customer needs

To succeed or simply to survive, companies need a new philosophy. To win in today's marketplace, companies must be **customer-centred** – they must deliver superior value to their target customers. They must become adept in *building customer relationships*, not just *building products*. They must be skilful in *market engineering*, not just *product engineering*.

Customer-centred company—A company that focuses on customer developments in designing its marketing strategies and on delivering superior value to its target customers.

Too often, marketing is ignored in the boardroom of companies with the view that the job of obtaining customers is the job of the marketing or sales department. A survey conducted by the Chartered Institute of Marketing found that only 20 per cent of companies in the FTSE 100 had someone with a marketing background on their Board of Directors.[3]

Contrast this with the view of Sir John Browne of BP Amoco:

> We have more than 10 million interactions with customers every day; and more than 100,000 staff in 100 countries. Every action and every activity is an act of marketing.

Like BP Amoco, winning companies have come to realise that marketing cannot do this job alone. Although marketing plays a leading role, it is only a partner in attracting and keeping customers. The world's best marketing department cannot successfully sell poorly made products that fail to meet consumer needs. The marketing department can be effective only in companies in which all departments and employees have teamed up to form a competitively superior *customer value-delivery system*.

This chapter discusses the philosophy of customer-value-creating marketing and the customer-focused firm. It addresses several important questions: What is customer value and customer satisfaction? How do leading companies organise to create and deliver high value and satisfaction? How can companies keep current customers as well as get new ones? How can companies practise total quality marketing?

Defining customer value and satisfaction

Forty years ago, Peter Drucker observed that a company's first task is 'to create customers'. However, creating customers can be a difficult task. Today's customers face a vast array of product and brand choices, prices and suppliers. The company must answer a key question: How do customers make their choices?

The answer is that customers choose the marketing offer that gives them the most value. Customers are value-maximisers, within the bounds of search costs and limited knowledge, mobility and income. They form expectations of value and act upon them. Then they

Figure 11.1 Customer delivered value

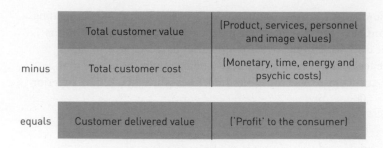

	Total customer value	(Product, services, personnel and image values)
minus	Total customer cost	(Monetary, time, energy and psychic costs)
equals	Customer delivered value	('Profit' to the consumer)

compare the actual value they receive in consuming the product to the value expected, and this affects their satisfaction and repurchase behaviour. We will now examine the concepts of customer value and customer satisfaction more carefully.

Customer value

Customer delivered value— The difference between total customer value and total customer cost of a marketing offer – 'profit' to the customer.

Total customer value—The total of the entire product, services, personnel and image values that a buyer receives from a marketing offer.

Total customer cost—The total of all the monetary, time, energy and psychic costs associated with a marketing offer.

Consumers buy from the firm that they believe offers the highest **customer delivered value** – the difference between *total customer value* and *total customer cost* (see Figure 11.1). For example, suppose that a farmer wants to buy a tractor. He can buy the equipment from either his usual supplier, Massey-Ferguson, or a cheaper east European product. The salespeople for the two companies carefully describe their respective offers to the farmer.

The farmer evaluates the two competing tractors and judges that Massey-Ferguson's tractor provides higher reliability, durability and performance. He also decides that Massey-Ferguson has better accompanying service – delivery, training and maintenance – and views Massey-Ferguson personnel as more knowledgeable and responsive. Finally, the farmer places higher value on Massey-Ferguson's reputation. He adds all the values from these four sources – *product, services, personnel* and *image* – and decides that Massey-Ferguson offers more **total customer value** than does the east European tractor.

Does the farmer buy the Massey-Ferguson tractor? Not necessarily. He will also examine the **total customer cost** of buying the Massey-Ferguson tractor versus the east European tractor product. First, he will compare the prices he must pay for each of the competitors' products. The Massey-Ferguson tractor costs a lot more than the east European tractor does, so the higher price might offset the higher total customer value. Moreover, total customer cost consists of more than just monetary costs. As Adam Smith observed more than two centuries ago: 'The real price of anything is the toil and trouble of acquiring it.' Total customer cost also includes the buyer's anticipated time, energy and psychic costs. The farmer will evaluate these costs along with monetary costs to form a complete estimate of his costs.

The farmer compares total customer value to total customer cost and determines the total delivered value associated with Massey-Ferguson's tractor. In the same way, he assesses the total delivered value for the east European tractor. The farmer then will buy from the competitor that offers the highest delivered value.

How can Massey-Ferguson use this concept of buyer decision making to help it succeed in selling its tractor to this buyer? Massey-Ferguson can improve its offer in three ways. First, it can increase total customer value by improving product, services, personnel or image benefits. Second, it can reduce the buyer's non-monetary costs by lessening the buyer's time, energy and psychic costs. Third, it can reduce the buyer's monetary costs by lowering its price, providing easier terms of sale or, in the longer term, lowering its tractor's operating or maintenance costs.

Suppose Massey-Ferguson carries out a *customer value assessment* and concludes that buyers see Massey-Ferguson's offer as worth €20,000. Further suppose that it costs Massey-Ferguson €14,000 to produce the tractor. This means that Massey-Ferguson's offer potentially generates €6,000 (€20,000 – €14,000) of *total added value*. Massey-Ferguson needs to price its tractor between €14,000 and €20,000. If it charges less than €14,000, it won't cover its costs. If it charges more than €20,000, the price will exceed the total customer value. The price Massey-Ferguson charges will determine how much of the total added value will be delivered to the buyer and how much will flow to Massey-Ferguson. For example, if Massey-Ferguson charges €16,000, it will grant €4,000 of total added value to the customer and keep €2,000 for itself as profit. If Massey-Ferguson charges €19,000, it will grant only €1,000 of total added value to the customer and keep €5,000 for itself as profit. Naturally, the lower Massey-Ferguson's price, the higher the delivered value of its offer will be and, therefore, the higher the customer's incentive to purchase from Massey-Ferguson. Delivered value should be viewed as 'profit to the customer'. Given that Massey-Ferguson wants to win the sale, it must offer more delivered value than the east European tractor does.[4]

Some marketers might rightly argue that this concept of how buyers choose among product alternatives is too rational. They might cite examples in which buyers did not choose the offer with an objectively measured highest delivered value. Consider the following situation:

> The Massey-Ferguson salesperson convinces the farmer that, considering the benefits relative to the purchase price, Massey-Ferguson's tractor offers a higher delivered value. The salesperson also points out that the east European tractor uses more fuel and requires more frequent repairs. Still, the farmer decides to buy the east European tractor.

How can we explain this appearance of non-value-maximising behaviour? There are many possible explanations. For example, perhaps the farmer has a long-term friendship with the east European tractor salesperson. Or the farmer might have a policy of buying at the lowest price. Or perhaps the farmer is short of cash, and therefore chooses the cheaper east European tractor, even though the Massey-Ferguson machine will perform better and be less expensive to operate in the long run.

Clearly, buyers operate under various constraints and sometimes make choices that give more weight to their personal benefit than to company benefit. However, the customer delivered value framework applies to many situations and yields rich insights. The framework suggests that sellers must first assess the total customer value and total customer cost associated with their own and competing marketing offers to determine how their own offers measure up in terms of customer delivered value. If a seller finds that competitors deliver greater value, it has two alternatives. It can try to increase customer value by strengthening or augmenting the product, services, personnel or image benefits of the offer. Or it can decrease total customer cost by reducing its price, simplifying the ordering and delivery process, or absorbing some buyer risk by offering a warranty.[5]

Customer satisfaction

Consumers form judgements about the value of marketing offers and make their buying decisions based upon these judgements. *Customer satisfaction* with a purchase depends upon the product's performance relative to a buyer's expectations. A customer might experience various degrees of satisfaction. If the product's performance falls short of expectations, the customer is dissatisfied. If performance matches expectations, the customer is satisfied. If performance exceeds expectations, the customer is highly satisfied or delighted.

But how do buyers form their expectations? Expectations are based on the customer's past buying experiences, the opinions of friends and associates, and marketer and competitor information and promises. Marketers must be careful to set the right level of expectations.

If they set expectations too low, they may satisfy those who buy, but fail to attract enough buyers. In contrast, if they raise expectations too high, buyers are likely to be disappointed. For example, Holiday Inn ran a campaign a few years ago called 'No Surprises', which promised consistently trouble-free accommodation and service. However, Holiday Inn guests still encountered a host of problems and the expectations created by the campaign only made customers more dissatisfied. Holiday Inn had to withdraw the campaign.

Still, some of today's most successful companies are raising expectations – and delivering performance to match. These companies embrace *total customer satisfaction*. For example, Honda claims, 'One reason our customers are so satisfied is that we aren't' or, as dan Technology puts it, 'We value your business. We want you to buy from us again.' These companies aim high because they know that customers who are *only* satisfied will still find it easy to switch suppliers when a better offer comes along. In one consumer packaged-goods category, 44 per cent of consumers reporting satisfaction later switched brands. In contrast, customers who are *highly satisfied* are much less ready to switch. One study showed that 75 per cent of Toyota buyers were highly satisfied and about 75 per cent said they intended to buy a Toyota again. Thus *customer delight* creates an emotional affinity for a product or service, not just a rational preference, and this creates high customer loyalty.

Today's winning companies track their customers' expectations, perceived company performance and customer satisfaction. They track this for their competitors as well. Consider the following:

> A company was pleased that it continued to find that 80 per cent of its customers said they were satisfied with its new product. However, the product seemed to sell poorly on store shelves next to the leading competitor's product. Company researchers soon learned that the competitor's product attained a 90 per cent customer satisfaction score. Company management was further dismayed when it learned that this competitor was aiming for a 95 per cent satisfaction score.

There are two reasons why historical rates of customer satisfaction do not serve in the long run. As the example shows, once-acceptable levels of customer satisfaction may be overtaken by competitors. This is occurring in the car market where Japanese manufacturers are setting new standards of quality and service. The quality of European cars is better than ever before but does not come close to those of pace-setting Toyota and Honda. At the same time, customers learn from the new levels of quality available in the marketplace and so expect higher standards than before. Unwary companies therefore face 'backward creep' in which their once-acceptable standards fall behind those of the competition and the customers' increased expectations.[6]

For customer-centred companies, customer satisfaction is both a goal and an essential factor in company success. Companies that achieve high customer satisfaction ratings make sure that their target market knows it. These companies realise that highly satisfied customers produce several benefits for the company. They are less price sensitive and they remain customers for a longer period. They buy additional products over time as the company introduces related products or improvements. And they talk favourably to others about the company and its products.

Although the customer-centred firm seeks to deliver high customer satisfaction relative to competitors, it does not attempt to *maximise* customer satisfaction. A company can always increase customer satisfaction by lowering its price or increasing its services, but this may result in lower profits. In addition to customers, the company has many stakeholders, including employees, dealers, suppliers and stockholders. Spending more to increase customer satisfaction might divert funds from increasing the satisfaction of these other 'partners'. Thus the purpose of marketing is to generate customer value profitably. Ultimately, the company must deliver a high level of customer satisfaction, while at the same time delivering at least acceptable levels of satisfaction to the firm's other stakeholders. This requires a very delicate balance: the marketer must continue to generate more customer value and satisfaction, but not 'give away the house'. Many of the world's most successful companies build their strategies on customer satisfaction, but as Marketing Insights 11.1 shows, you do not have to be big to succeed.

Tracking customer satisfaction

Successful organisations are aggressive in tracking both customer satisfaction and dissatisfaction. Several methods are used.

Complaint and suggestion systems

A customer-centred organisation makes it easy for customers to make suggestions or complaints. Hospitals place suggestion boxes in the corridors, supply comment cards to existing patients and employ patient advocates to solicit grievances. Some customer-centred companies may set up free customer hotlines to make it easy for customers to enquire, suggest or complain. Virgin Trains immediately hand out customer complaint forms as soon as there is any reason for passengers to complain, such as a train being delayed.

> Successful companies try very hard. All visitors to Richer Sounds shops get a card showing the shop's team and saying: 'We're listening.' It's a Freepost letter addressed to Julian Richer, the owner of the chain. Inside it reads:
>
> *Thank you* for your support and making us the UK's most successful hi-fi retailer. In order to maintain No. 1 position, we need to know where we've gone wrong. Suggestions or comments regarding customer service, however small, are gratefully received. Every one has Mr Richer's personal attention . . . Please, please, please let us know, as we really do care!

Customer satisfaction surveys

Complaint and suggestion systems may not give the company a full picture of customer satisfaction. One out of every four purchases results in consumer dissatisfaction, but fewer than 5 per cent of dissatisfied customers complain. Rather than complain, most customers simply switch suppliers. As a result, the company needlessly loses customers.

Responsive companies take direct measures of customer satisfaction by conducting regular surveys. They send questionnaires or make telephone calls to a sample of recent customers to find out how they feel about various aspects of the company's performance.

Magazines and consumers' associations often conduct independent surveys. These are invaluable since companies can easily be deluded by their own results.

> Bozell Worldwide's Quality Poll gives a league table and shows how biased local perceptions can be. Gallup conducted a study that asked 20,000 people in 20 countries to rate the quality of manufactured goods from 12 countries.

marketing insights

11.1 Cold turkey has got me on the run

'Oh dear! Am I in trouble now.' It was a week before Christmas as the recalcitrant academic trudged up and down Castle Street trying to buy a goose for Christmas dinner. Long before Charles Dickens' time, when Scrooge sent 'the prize Turkey . . . the big one' to Bob Cratchit's house, goose was the traditional English Christmas fayre. Introduced to Europe from America in the sixteenth century, turkey had displaced goose in all of Castle Street's butchers. Sick of having cold turkey salad, turkey sandwiches and that dreadful turkey curry for days after Christmas, the academic's family had decided to have goose 'for a change'. His job was to get one, but he had left it too late.

Butcher after butcher came out with the worn-out lines: 'You should have ordered one weeks ago', 'We can't get them anywhere' or 'There's no call for them these days.' Even 'A goose? They're so greasy. How about a nice fat turkey? It'll last you for days.' SCREAM!

Defeated, he slumped into his car to drive home. It was dark and on the way through a village he saw the lights of a small shop he had not noticed before – a small independent butcher, well stocked, brightly lit and full of customers. 'Funny', he thought, 'there aren't many of those these days. Still, let's have one last try.'

On joining the festive throng inside, he noticed a sign on the wall. It read:

> *The Ten Commandments of good business*
> 1. The customer is the most important person in my business.
> 2. The customer is not dependent on us; we are dependent on him.
> 3. A customer is not an interruption of our work; he is the purpose of it.
> 4. A customer does us a favour when he calls; we are not doing him a favour by serving him.
> 5. The customer is part of our business, not an outsider.
> 6. The customer is not a cold statistic; he is a flesh and blood human being with feelings and emotions like ours.
> 7. The customer is not someone to argue or match wits with.
> 8. The customer brings us his wants; it is our job to fill those wants.
> 9. The customer is deserving of the most courteous and attentive treatment we can give him.
> 10. The customer is the lifeblood of this, and every other, business.

'Merry Christmas, what can I do for you?', asked the butcher.

'Have you a goose?', the academic asked timidly.

'I haven't got any in, but I'll get one for you. What size do you want?'

Later on, at a local inn, the talk turned to food. 'Have you come across that great butcher in the next village?'

'Great butcher? Come off it. A butcher's a butcher's a butcher!'

'Not this one, he will do anything for you. Nice guy, too.'

Lesson: You do not have to be big to be great.

SOURCES: Charles Dickens, *A Christmas Carol* (London: Hazell, Watson & Viney, 1843); John Lennon, *Cold Turkey* (London: Apple, 1969); Bill Bryson, *Made in America* (London: Black Swan, 1998).

All countries rated themselves higher than other people did. The French put French goods on top, while the Japanese gave themselves twice the rating (76 per cent) that the full sample did (38.5). All other countries were optimistic too: Germans gave themselves 49 per cent against the full sample's 36 per cent and the United Kingdom 39 per cent against 22 per cent.

Ghost shopping

This involves researchers posing as buyers. These 'ghost shoppers' can even present specific problems in order to test whether the company's personnel handle difficult situations well. For example, ghost shoppers can complain about a restaurant's food to see how the restaurant handles this complaint. Research International's Mystery Shopper surveys can measure many dimensions of customer performance. By telephoning it can measure a firm's telephone technique: how many rings it takes to answer, the sort of voice and tone and, if transferred, how many leaps it took before being correctly connected.

Managers themselves should leave their offices from time to time and experience first-hand the treatment they receive as 'customers'. As an alternative, managers can phone their companies with different questions and complaints to see how the call is handled.

Lost customer analysis

Companies should contact customers who have stopped buying or who have switched to a competitor, to learn why this happened. Not only should the company conduct such *exit interviews*, it should also monitor the *customer loss rate*. A rising loss rate indicates that the company is failing to satisfy its customers.[7]

Universities and colleges usually compete by putting on new or improved courses or attracting excellent teachers, but one college's lost customer survey found major reasons for prospective students deciding to study elsewhere that were far from academic. Many prospective students and parents who visited mentioned the unsatisfactory state of the toilets in the Students' Union. Others mentioned the state of the décor in some of the student halls of residence.

Delivering customer value and satisfaction

Customer value and satisfaction are important ingredients in the marketer's formula for success. But what does it take to produce and deliver customer value? To answer this, we will examine the concepts of a *value chain* and *value delivery system*.

Value chain

Michael Porter proposed the **value chain** as the main tool for identifying ways to create more customer value (see Figure 11.2).[8] Every firm consists of a collection of activities performed to design, produce, market, deliver and support the firm's products. The value chain breaks the

Value chain—A major tool for identifying ways to create more customer value.

Figure 11.2 The generic value chain

SOURCE: Reprinted with permission of The Free Press, a Division of Simon & Schuster, Inc., from *Competitive Advantage: Creating and Sustaining Superior Performance* by Michael E. Porter. Copyright © 1985, 1998 by Michael E. Porter.

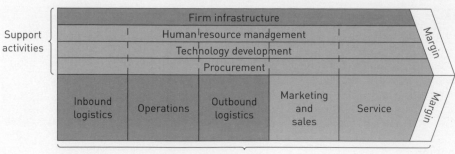

firm into nine value-creating activities in an effort to understand the behaviour of costs in the specific business and the potential sources of competitive differentiation. The nine value-creating activities include five primary activities and four support activities.

The primary activities involve the sequence of bringing materials into the business (inbound logistics), operating on them (operations), sending them out (outbound logistics), marketing them (marketing and sales) and servicing them (service). For a long time, firms have focused on the product as the primary means of adding value, but customer satisfaction also depends upon the other stages of the value chain.[9] The support activities occur within each of these primary activities. For example, procurement involves obtaining the various inputs for each primary activity – only the purchasing department does a fraction of procurement. Technology development and human resource management also occur in all departments. The firm's infrastructure covers the overhead of general management, planning, finance, accounting and legal and government affairs borne by all the primary and support activities.

Under the value-chain concept, the firm should examine its costs and performance in each value-creating activity to look for improvements. It should also estimate its competitors' costs and performances as benchmarks. To the extent that the firm can perform certain activities better than its competitors, it can achieve a competitive advantage.

The firm's success depends not only on how well each department performs its work, but also on how well the activities of various departments are coordinated. Too often, individual departments maximise their own interests rather than those of the whole company and the customer. For example, a credit department might attempt to reduce bad debts by taking a long time to check the credit of prospective customers: meanwhile, salespeople get frustrated and customers wait. A distribution department might decide to save money by shipping goods by rail; again the customer waits. In each case, individual departments have erected walls that impede the delivery of quality customer service.

To overcome this problem, companies should place more emphasis on the smooth management of *core business processes*, most of which involve inputs and cooperation from many functional departments. These core business processes include the following:

■ *Product development process.* All the activities involved in identifying, researching and developing new products with speed, high quality and reasonable cost.

■ *Inventory management process.* All the activities involved in developing and managing the right inventory levels of raw materials, semi-finished materials and finished goods, so that adequate supplies are available while the costs of high overstocks are avoided.

■ *Order-to-payment process.* All the activities involved in receiving orders, approving them, shipping the goods on time and collecting payment.

■ *Customer service process.* All the activities involved in making it easy for customers to reach the right parties within the company to obtain service, answers and resolutions of problems.

Successful companies develop superior capabilities in managing these and other core processes. In turn, mastering core business processes gives these companies a substantial competitive edge.

Many Internet companies have fallen at the final, *customer service,* stage of the value chain. The fear of a faceless company is real among customers, especially in France and Italy, yet a recent survey found that only one-fifth of websites had human contact available through them. Across Europe only a minority of Internet users are willing to make a purchase without some personal contact, even from a well-known company. This reliance on a single, impersonal link with customers is said to account for the slow uptake of Internet shopping in Europe and, according to Datamonitor, is likely to cost European companies €150 billion by 2004.[10]

In its search for competitive advantage, the firm needs to look beyond its own value chain, into the value chains of its suppliers, distributors and, ultimately, customers. More companies today are 'partnering' with the other members of the supply chain to improve the performance of the **customer value delivery system**. For example:

> Online Music Recognition and Searching (OMRS) is a new service that will help record stores find what people want. Many customers enter stores with a snippet of a tune in their mind and depend upon the store's staff to recognise a few lyrics or a half-remembered tune. Unfortunately, few people in record stores have the archivist's memory of the enthusiasts running the record store in Nick Hornby's *Hi-Fidelity.* OMRS overcomes the problem. Customers can hum a part of a tune that is mathematically analysed and compared with a database of recordings. The result: the customer gets the music they want, the record store makes the sale and OMRS gets a reward for their services.[11]

Customer value delivery system—The system made up of the value chains of the company and its suppliers, distributors and ultimately customers, who work together to deliver value to customers.

As companies struggle to become more competitive, they are turning, ironically, to greater cooperation. Companies used to view their suppliers and distributors as cost centres and, in some cases, as adversaries. Today, however, they are selecting partners carefully and working out mutually profitable strategies. Increasingly in today's marketplace, competition no longer takes place between individual competitors. Rather, it takes place between the entire value delivery systems created by these competitors.

Therefore, marketing can no longer be thought of as only a selling department. That view of marketing would give it responsibility only for formulating a promotion-oriented marketing mix, without much to say about product features, costs and other important elements. Under the new view, marketing is responsible for *designing and managing a superior value delivery system to reach target customer segments.* Today's marketing managers must think not only about selling today's products, but also about how to stimulate the development of improved products, how to work actively with other departments in managing core business processes and how to build better external partnerships.[12]

Total quality management

Customer satisfaction and company profitability are linked closely to product and service quality delivered through the whole value chain. Higher levels of quality result in greater customer satisfaction, while at the same time supporting higher prices and often lower costs. Therefore, *quality improvement programmes* normally increase profitability. The Profit Impact of Marketing Strategies studies show similarly high correlation between relative product quality and profitability for Europe and the US (see Figure 11.3).[13]

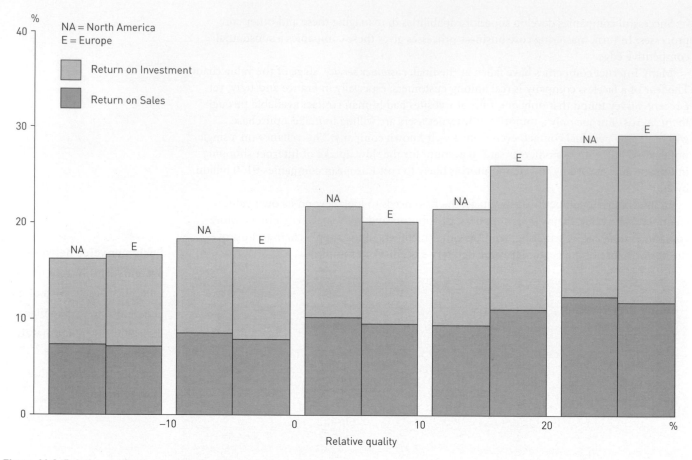

Figure 11.3 **Relative quality boosts rate of return**
SOURCE: Bob Luchs, 'Quality as a strategic weapon: measuring relative quality, value and market differentiation', *European Business Journal*, **2**, 4 (1990), p. 39

The task of improving product and service quality should be a company's top priority. Most customers will no longer tolerate poor or average quality. Companies today have no choice but to adopt total quality management if they want to stay in the race, let alone be profitable. According to GE's chairman, John F. Welch, Jr: 'Quality is our best assurance of customer allegiance, our strongest defense against foreign competition and the only path to sustained growth and earnings.'[14]

Quality—The totality of features and characteristics of a product or service that bear on its ability to satisfy stated or implied needs.

Quality has been variously defined as 'fitness for use', 'conformance to requirements' and 'freedom from variation'.[15] The American Society for Quality Control defines quality as the totality of features and characteristics of a product or service that bear on its ability to satisfy stated or implied needs. This is a customer-centred definition of quality. It suggests that a company has 'delivered quality' whenever its product and service meets or exceeds customers' needs, requirements and expectations.

It is important to distinguish between performance quality and conformance quality. *Performance quality* refers to the *level* at which a product performs its functions. Compare Smart Car and Lexus, Toyota's luxury brand. A Lexus provides higher performance quality than a Smart Car: it has a smoother ride, handles better and lasts longer. It is more expensive and sells to a market with higher means and requirements. *Conformance quality* refers to freedom from defects and the *consistency* with which a product delivers a specified level of performance. Both Lexus and Smart have exceptional reliability records and could offer equivalent conformance quality to their respective markets, since each consistently delivers what its market expects. A €100,000 car that meets all of its requirements is a quality car; so

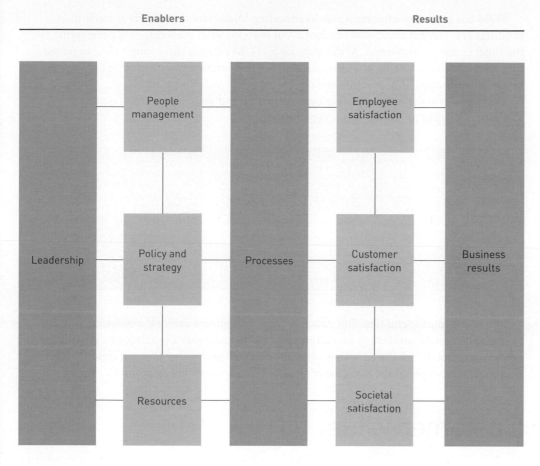

Enablers — Results

Figure 11.4 The European Foundation for Quality Management's model of business excellence

is a €10,000 car that meets all of its requirements. However, if the Lexus handles badly or if the Smart Car gives poor fuel efficiency, then both cars fail to deliver quality, and customer satisfaction suffers accordingly.

In the European Foundation for Quality Management's excellence model (Figure 11.4) marketing shares the responsibility for striving for the highest quality of a company, product or service. Marketing's commitment to the whole process needs to be particularly strong because of the central role of customer satisfaction to both marketing and **total quality management (TQM)**. Within a quality-centred company, marketing management has two types of responsibility. First, marketing management participates in formulating the *strategies and policies* that direct *resources* and strive for quality excellence. Secondly, marketing has to deliver marketing quality alongside product quality. It must perform each marketing activity to consistently high standards: marketing research, sales training, advertising, customer services and others. Much damage can be done to customer satisfaction with an excellent product if it is oversold or is 'supported' by advertising that builds unrealistic expectations.

Within quality programmes, marketing has several roles. Firstly, it has responsibility for correctly identifying customers' needs and wants, and for communicating them correctly to aid product design and to schedule production. Secondly, marketing has to ensure that customers' orders are filled correctly and on time, and must check to see that customers receive proper instruction, training and technical assistance in the use of their product. Thirdly, marketers must stay in touch with customers after the sale, to make sure that they remain satisfied. Finally, marketers must gather and convey customers' ideas for product and service improvement back to the company.

Total quality management (TQM)—Programmes designed to constantly improve the quality of products, services, and marketing processes.

TQM has played an important role in educating businesses that quality is more than products and services being well produced, but is about what marketing has been saying all the time: *customer satisfaction*. At the same time, TQM extends marketing's view to realise that the acquisition, retention and satisfaction of good employees is central to the acquisition, retention and satisfaction of customers.[16]

Total quality is the key to creating customer value and satisfaction. Total quality is everyone's job, just as marketing is everyone's job:

> Marketers who don't learn the language of quality improvement, manufacturing and operations will become as obsolete as buggy whips. The days of functional marketing are gone. We can no longer afford to think of ourselves as market researchers, advertising people, direct marketers, marketing strategists – we have to think of ourselves as customer satisfiers – customer advocates focused on whole processes.[17]

Marketers must spend time and effort not only to improve external marketing, but also to improve internal marketing. Marketers must be the customer's watchdog or guardian, complaining loudly for the customer when the product or the service is not right. Marketers must constantly uphold the standard of 'giving the customer the best solution'.

Customer value

There is no limit to how much a company could spend to improve quality, or in other marketing efforts, to obtain and retain customers. This raises the critical question: how much is a customer worth? Companies are increasingly realising that the answer is a great deal. AOL's Internet acquisitions, and Orange's telecommunications acquisitions, suggest values approaching €10,000 per customer.[18]

Internet companies are willing to pay a high price for prospective customers because they hope to turn them into *profitable customers*. We define a **profitable customer** as a person, household or company whose revenues over time exceed, by an acceptable amount, the company's costs of attracting, selling and servicing that customer. Note that the definition emphasises lifetime revenues and costs, not profit from a single transaction. Here are some dramatic illustrations of **customer lifetime value**:

Profitable customer—
A person, household or company whose revenues over time exceed, by an acceptable amount, the company's costs of attracting, selling and servicing that customer.

Customer lifetime value—
The amount by which revenues from a given customer over time will exceed the company's costs of attracting, selling and servicing that customer.

> Tom Peters, noted author of several books on managerial excellence, runs a business that spends $1,500 a month on Federal Express service. His company spends this amount 12 months a year and expects to remain in business for at least another 10 years. Therefore, he expects to spend more than $180,000 on future Federal Express service. If Federal Express makes a 10 per cent profit margin, Peters' lifetime business will contribute $18,000 to Federal Express's profits. Federal Express risks all of this profit if Peters receives poor service from a Federal Express driver or if a competitor offers better service.

Few companies actively measure individual customer value and profitability. For example, banks claim that this is hard to do because customers use different banking services and transactions are logged in different departments. However, banks that have managed to link customer transactions and measure customer profitability have been appalled by how many unprofitable customers they find. Some banks report losing money on over 45 per cent of their retail customers. It is not surprising that many banks now charge fees for services that they once supplied free.

Customer retention

In the past, many companies took their customers for granted. Customers often did not have many alternative suppliers, or the other suppliers were just as poor in quality and service, or the market was growing so fast that the company did not worry about fully satisfying its customers. A company could lose 100 customers a week, but gain another 100 customers and consider its sales to be satisfactory. Such a company, operating on a 'leaky bucket' theory of business, believes that there will always be enough customers to replace the defecting ones. However, this high *customer churn* involves higher costs than if a company retained all 100 customers and acquired no new ones.

Companies must pay close attention to their customer defection rate and undertake steps to reduce it. First, the company must define and measure its retention rate. For a magazine, it would be the renewal rate; for a consumer packaged-goods firm, it would be the repurchase rate. Next, the company must identify the causes of customer defection and determine which of these can be reduced or eliminated. Not much can be done about customers who leave the region or about business customers who go out of business. But much can be done about customers who leave because of shoddy products, poor service or prices that are too high. The company needs to prepare a frequency distribution showing the percentage of customers who defect for different reasons.

A satisfaction study can show how a company has been misplacing its effort.

> A satisfaction benchmarking study for a restaurant showed that customers rated highly the restaurant's *décor* and the *size of the portions* served. However, the customers did not rate these two criteria as important. In contrast customers thought that the *quality of food* and *cleanliness of toilets* were very important but dimensions on which the restaurant performed poorly. On other dimensions that the customers thought important, the restaurant did fine: *overall cleanliness*, *speed of service* and *helpfulness of staff*. The benchmarking study clearly showed how the restaurant could improve customer satisfaction and, maybe, cut costs by reducing portions.

It is well known in service industries, where de-skilled McJobs abound, that employee satisfaction and retention precede customer satisfaction and retention. The relationship is also strong in rapid growth industries where the poaching of staff drives up wages and in many markets where making sales depends on the continuity of long-term relationships with key accounts. The SAS Institute, the world's largest software company, sees a close relationship between its performance and labour turnover. Its employee-oriented management keeps annual labour turnover at 4 per cent compared with an industry average of 20 per cent. SAS's methods go beyond the €65,000 of M&Ms it doles out to its 7,500 employees each year. The company keeps working hours down, has free healthcare on 'campus', plus gyms, tennis courts, theatres and other benefits. Employees sing the praises of the company and keep customers well satisfied – 98 per cent of them renew their licences on SAS software each year![19]

Customers incur switching costs when they change suppliers. Switching costs are beyond the purchase price and include learning how to use a new product or service, the time selecting a new supplier and the difficulty of operating the new product alongside products already owned. This 'self-incompatibility' or 'weak lock-in' is very common and faced by many consumers when they switch banks, Internet service providers, Microsoft versions, from vinyl or cassette to CDs, or from VCR to DVD. Despite the cost, customers do switch when a better offer comes along. There is little evidence of any 'strong lock-in' where incompatibility gives a leading company a lasting advantage.[20] Having the best product or service is more important than being the first to market, or having a large customer base. Customers accept 'self-incompatibility' and switch when better offers come along.

By reducing customer defections by only 5 per cent, companies can improve profits by anywhere from 25 to 85 per cent.[21] Unfortunately, classic marketing theory and practice centre on the art of attracting new customers rather than retaining existing ones. The emphasis has been on creating *transactions* rather than *relationships*. Discussion has focused on *pre-sale activity* and *sale activity* rather than on *post-sale activity*. Today, however, more companies recognise the importance of retaining current customers by forming relationships with them.

Relationship marketing

Relationship marketing— The process of creating, maintaining and enhancing strong, value-laden relationships with customers and other stakeholders.

Relationship marketing involves creating, maintaining and enhancing strong relationships with customers and other stakeholders. Increasingly, marketing is moving away from a focus on individual transactions and towards a focus on building value-laden relationships and marketing networks. Relationship marketing is oriented more towards the long term. The goal is to deliver long-term value to customers and the measure of success is long-term customer satisfaction. Relationship marketing requires that all of the company's departments work together with marketing as a team to serve the customer. It involves building relationships at many levels – economic, social, technical and legal – resulting in high customer loyalty.

We can distinguish five different levels or relationships that can be formed with customers who have purchased a company's product, such as a car or a piece of equipment:

- *Basic.* The company salesperson sells the product, but does not follow up in any way.
- *Reactive.* The salesperson sells the product and encourages the customer to call whenever he or she has any questions or problems.
- *Accountable.* The salesperson phones the customer a short time after the sale to check whether the product is meeting the customer's expectations. The salesperson also solicits from the customer any product improvement suggestions and any specific disappointments. This information helps the company continuously to improve its offering.
- *Proactive.* The salesperson or others in the company phone the customer from time to time with suggestions about improved product use or helpful new products.
- *Partnership.* The company works continuously with the customer and with other customers to discover ways to deliver better value.

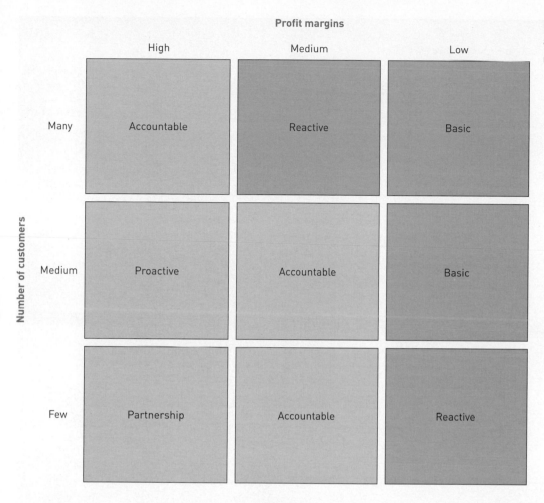

Profit margins

Figure 11.5 shows that a company's relationship marketing strategy will depend on how many customers it has and their profitability. For example, companies with many low-margin customers will practise *basic* marketing. Thus Heineken will not phone all of its drinkers to express its appreciation for their business. At best, Heineken will be reactive by setting up a customer information service. At the other extreme, in markets with few customers and high margins, most sellers will move towards partnership marketing. In exploring the Airbus A340–500 and A340–600, a very large commercial transport, Airbus Industries will work closely with the aero-engine manufacturers as well as with Lufthansa, Virgin Atlantic, Ryanair and KLM, who have shown interest in buying the aircraft. For these businesses, the emphasis has to be on *network marketing*, where the interdependence of firms means they are part of an interdependent network. Marketing Insights 11.2 explores this approach.

What specific marketing tools can a company use to develop stronger customer bonding and satisfaction? It can adopt any of three customer value-building approaches.[22] The first relies primarily on adding *financial benefits* to the customer relationship. For example, airlines offer frequent-flyer programmes, hotels give room upgrades to their frequent guests, and supermarkets give patronage refunds.

Although these reward programmes and other financial incentives build customer preference, they can be easily imitated by competitors and thus may fail to differentiate the company's offer permanently. The second approach is to add *social benefits* as well as financial

marketing insights

11.2 Network marketing: we are not alone . . .

Most companies do not sell to final consumers, but provide products and services to other businesses to which they have to be closely allied. For example, Messier Dowty, makers of landing gear for aircraft, cannot design or market its products in isolation since its landing gear is only of any use if 'designed into' an aircraft. The company, therefore, is part of a *network* including airforces as well as the supplier of tyres for its landing gear. Messier Dowty itself is the result of another network, since it is an Anglo-French joint venture between the TI group and Snecma.

Originating from Scandinavian research, network marketing accepts the influence of a web of interdependencies between firms. Relationship marketing has a clear focus on a business managing the relationship life cycle with its customers, while network marketing recognises interdependencies and a wider range of stakeholders. Exhibit 11.1 compares both network and relationship marketing with the traditional marketing based on discrete transactions. It shows that transaction and relationship marketing are similar in that they are both 'done by the seller to the buyer'. In contrast, network marketing is only prescriptive in emphasising the importance of networks in understanding how firms behave rather than telling of a winning strategy. The alternative use of the term 'markets-as-networks' in place of network marketing gives a better impression of its passive role.

Exhibit 11.1 Comparison of transactional, relationship and network marketing

	Transactional marketing	Relationship marketing	Network marketing
Focus	Profitable transactions	Profitable relationships	Links between organisations
Players	Buyers and sellers in an open market	Buyers and sellers in a relationship	Seller, buyer and other organisations
Communications	Firm to market	Individual to individual	Organisation at many levels
Communications style	Arm's length	Interpersonal	Multipersonal
Duration	Discrete	Life cycle	Continuous but of varying intensity
Formality	Formal	Managed	Interactive
Power	Active seller	Seller manages	Reciprocal relationships

...11.2

Interest in markets-as-networks grew out of the general trend in business for firms to emphasise 'partnership' and 'strategic alliances'. This trend goes beyond marketing to include buying, distribution, R&D and manufacturing. Long before relationship marketing was recognised, leading businesses had developed 'relationship buying', where Japanese companies in particular established very close links with a few preferred suppliers. Many leading companies, including retailers, have now adopted this approach to the extent that the buyer dictates the R&D and product, as well as the sales and marketing of the seller.

When firms and people find relatively simple two-way networks very complicated, it is not surprising that multi-member networks are hard to manage. In high-spending sectors, such as defence and aerospace, Europe's national competitors are failing against the rapidly integrating US industry as reflected in the Boeing–MacDonnell Douglas combine. Airbus hopes to compete with Boeing's 777 and smaller 747 with its Airbus A340–600, but for it to do so the owners of Airbus have to agree. That means obtaining the agreement of Britain's BAe, France's Aérospatiale, Germany's DASA and Spain's Casa, as well as the governments which will have to pay one-third of the development costs. Because of the UK government's reluctance to provide $120 million, BAe is talking to manufacturers in Italy, China, Taiwan, Malaysia and North America, in the hope that their governments will be more generous. As a result of this confusion, European politicians have called for a swift restructuring of Airbus. Some network! No wonder the Eurofighter is struggling to stay in the air!

SOURCES: Roderick J. Bridie, Nicole E. Coviello, Richard W. Brohner and Victoria Little, 'Towards a paradigm shift in marketing? An examination of current marketing practices', *Journal of Marketing Management*, **13**, 5 (1997), pp. 383–406; Lars-Gunnar Mattson, 'Relationship marketing' and 'The markets-as-networks approach – a comparative analysis of two evolving streams of research', *Journal of Marketing Management*, **13**, 5 (1997); 'Eurofighter partner nations want to renegotiate price of aircraft', *AXA Europe (Focus)* (19 September 2003); 'EADS suggest production integration for Eurofighter', *Le Figaro* (12 November 2002); 'Airbus A340–500 gets European take-off permission', *Les Echos* (10 December 2003); 'Airbus appeals for cost cuts', *Le Figaro* (2 June 2003).

benefits. Here company personnel work to increase their social bonds with customers by learning individual customers' needs and wants, and then individualising and personalising their products and services.

The third approach to building strong customer relationships is to add *structural ties* as well as financial and social benefits. For example, a business marketer might supply customers with special equipment or computer linkages that help them manage their orders, payroll or inventory. An investment banker, J.P. Morgan, provides its RiskMetrics financial risk measurement system free of charge to its customers. It has two reasons for doing so. First, says the company, it will promote greater transparency to risk and so help identify problems. Second, J.P. Morgan must also be hoping that the association of its name with a widely accepted benchmarking system will yield long-term commercial advantages, partly through strengthening ties with existing customers. There are clear customer needs here. In the 12 months prior to RiskMetrics' release, estimated derivatives losses by firms, including Metallgesellschaft and Kashima Oil, approached €20 billion.[23]

The main steps in establishing a relationship-marketing programme in a company are as follows.

- *Identify the key customers meriting relationship management.* Choose the largest or best customers and designate them for relationship management. Other customers can be added that show exceptional growth or pioneer new industry developments.

- *Assign a skilled relationship manager to each key customer.* The salesperson currently servicing the customer should receive training in relationship management or be replaced by someone more skilled in relationship management. The relationship manager should have characteristics that match or appeal to the customer.

- *Develop a clear job description for relationship managers.* Describe their reporting relationships, objectives, responsibilities and evaluation criteria. Make the relationship manager the focal point for all dealings with and about the client. Give each relationship manager only one or a few relationships to manage.

- *Have each relationship manager develop annual and long-range customer relationship plans.* These plans should state objectives, strategies, specific actions and required resources.

- *Appoint an overall manager to supervise the relationship managers.* This person will develop job descriptions, evaluation criteria and resource support to increase relationship manager effectiveness.

Volvo's Oncore and Care programmes recognise that the company has multiple relationships with its customers and ensure systematic approaches and consistent treatment across them:[24]

	Corporate clients	Drivers (corporate clients' employees)	Dealers
Volvo	Relationships govern Volvo's inclusion on entitlement list (the make of employee's company cars)	Volvo maintains a direct marketing relationship with all drivers of its cars	Volvo works hard with all its dealer network to maintain and improve its standards
Dealers	Local dealers usually deliver and service the cars	Dealers are the front line of meeting the drivers' expectations	
Drivers	Agreements reached affect which models are available to clients' employees		

When it has properly implemented relationship management, the organisation begins to focus on managing its customers as well as its products. At the same time, although many companies are moving strongly towards relationship marketing, it is not effective in all situations:

> When it comes to relationship marketing . . . you don't want a relationship with every customer. . . . In fact, there are some bad customers. [The objective is to] figure out which customers are worth cultivating because you can meet their needs more effectively than anyone else can.[25]

In the end, companies must judge which segments and which specific customers will be profitable.

Customer relationship management

Companies are awash with information about their customers. Smart companies capture information at every possible customer *touch point*. These touch points include customer purchases, sales force contacts, service and support calls, website visits, satisfaction surveys, credit and payment interactions, market research studies – every contact between the customer and the company.

The trouble is that this information is usually scattered widely across the organisation. It is buried deep in the separate databases, plans and records of many different company functions and departments. To overcome such problems, many companies use customer relationship management (CRM) to manage detailed information about individual customers and carefully manage customer 'touchpoints'. In recent years, there has been an explosion in the number of companies using CRM. One research firm found that 97 per cent of businesses plan to boost spending on CRM technology within the next two years.[26]

CRM consists of sophisticated software and analytical tools that integrate customer information from all sources, analyse it in depth, and apply the results to build stronger customer relationships. CRM integrates everything that a company's sales, service and marketing teams know about individual customers to provide a 360-degree view of the customer relationship. It pulls together, analyses and provides easy access to customer information from all of the various touch points. Companies use CRM analysis to assess the value of individual customers, identify the best ones to target, and customise the company's products and interactions to each customer.

CRM analysts develop data warehouses and use sophisticated data mining techniques to unearth the riches hidden in customer data. A data warehouse is a company-wide electronic storehouse of customer information – a centralised database of finely detailed customer data that needs to be sifted through for gems. The purpose of a data warehouse is not to gather information – many companies have already amassed endless stores of information about their customers. Rather, the purpose is to allow managers to integrate the information the company already has. Then, once the data warehouse brings the data together for analysis, the company uses high-powered data mining techniques to sift through the mounds of data and dig out interesting relationships and findings about customers.

Companies can gain many benefits from customer relationship management. By understanding customers better, they can provide higher levels of customer service and develop deeper customer relationships. They can use CRM to pinpoint high-value customers, target them more effectively, cross-sell the company's products, and create offers tailored to specific customer requirements. Consider the following examples:[27]

- MVC uses CRM in conjunction with its More Card to maintain its market position in the recorded music and video market against discounters and megastores. Besides giving regular customers discounts on purchases, their CRM identifies customer's buying patterns and targets special promotions and deals. A recent European campaign coincided with the annual Country Music Awards in Nashville. This ceremony interests few

European music lovers but MVC knew which of their customers bought country music and anticipated that they would read, hear or see news of the ceremony in the media. Their promotion attracted country music followers to their store by promoting the back catalogue of Lonestar, Alan Jackson, Alison Krauss, and others. Once at the store the country music fan faced the promoted products on a display close to the entrance and many albums available for instore sampling.

- Ping, the golf equipment manufacturer, has used CRM successfully for about two years. Its data warehouse contains customer-specific data about every golf club it has manufactured and sold for the past 15 years. The database, which includes grip size and special assembly instructions, helps Ping design and build golf clubs specifically for each of its customers and allows for easy replacement. If a golfer needs a new nine iron, for

CRM is big business with many companies, such as PeopleSoft, offering to help 'capitalise on every customer interaction across your enterprise'.
SOURCE: People Soft UK & Ireland.

Customers are an investment.
Maximize your return.

PeopleSoft Customer Relationship Management lets you capitalize on every customer interaction across your enterprise.

Only PeopleSoft CRM is fast to implement, easy to use, and delivers smart business processes for managing your customer relationships. It integrates real-time information across your organization to help determine the most profitable ways to manage customers. Simply, PeopleSoft CRM turns every point of customer contact into a profit opportunity. Learn more by visiting us at www.peoplesoft.com/realtime or call 1-888-773-8277.

PeopleSoft® | Customer Relationship Management

example, he can call in the serial number and Ping will ship an exact club to him within two days of receiving the order – a process that used to take two to three weeks. . . . This faster processing of data has given Ping a competitive edge in a market saturated with new products. 'We've been up; the golf market has been down', says Steve Bostwick, Ping's marketing manager. Bostwick estimates the golf market to be down about 15 per cent, but he says Ping has experienced double-digit growth.

CRM benefits do not come without cost or risk, not only in collecting the original customer data but also in maintaining and mining it. Worldwide, companies will spend an estimated €25 billion to €50 billion this year on CRM software alone from companies such as PeopleSoft, Siebel Systems, SAP, Oracle and SPSS. Yet more than half of all CRM efforts fail to meet their objectives. The most common cause of CRM failures is that companies mistakenly view CRM only as a technology and software solution.[28] But technology alone cannot build profitable customer relationships. 'CRM is not a technology solution – you can't achieve . . . improved customer relationships by simply slapping in some software', says a CRM expert. Instead, CRM is just one part of an effective overall *customer relationship strategy*. 'Focus on the *R*', advises the expert. 'Remember, a relationship is what CRM is all about.'[29]

When it works, the benefits of CRM can far outweigh the costs and risks. Based on regular polls of its customers, Siebel Systems claims that customers using its CRM software report an average 16 per cent increase in revenues and 21 per cent increase in customer loyalty and staff efficiency. 'No question that companies are getting tremendous value out of this', says a CRM consultant. 'Companies [are] looking for ways to bring disparate sources of customer information together, then get it to all the customer touch points.' The powerful new CRM techniques can unearth 'a wealth of information to target that customer, to hit their hot button.'[30]

When to use relationship marketing

Relationship marketing is not effective in all situations, although CRM systems are reducing the value threshold at which it becomes appropriate. Transaction marketing, which focuses on one sales transaction at a time, is more appropriate than relationship marketing for customers who have short time horizons and can switch from one supplier to another with little effort or investment. This situation often occurs in 'commodity' markets, such as steel, where various suppliers offer largely undifferentiated products. A customer buying steel can buy from any of several steel suppliers and choose the one offering the best terms on a purchase-by-purchase basis. The fact that one steel supplier works at developing a longer-term relationship with a buyer does not automatically earn it the next sale; its price and other terms still have to be competitive. Global e-procurement systems, like the motor industry's Covisint and aerospace's Exostar, where buyers flag their requirements on the Internet, are tightening profit margins and breaking down close relationships between buyers and suppliers. For example, by using Internet auctions and exchanges BAe decreased its purchasing bill by 5 per cent and its number of suppliers from 14,000 to 2,000.[31]

In contrast, relationship marketing can pay off handsomely with customers that have long time horizons and high switching costs, such as buyers of office automation systems. It can also be part of an e-procurement system, such as Covisint, that will involve suppliers in new product development. When buying complex systems, buyers usually research competing suppliers carefully and choose one from whom they can expect state-of-the-art technology and good long-term service. Both the customer and the supplier invest a lot of money and time in building the relationship. The customer would find it costly and risky to switch to another supplier and the seller would find that losing this customer would be a considerable loss. Thus each seeks to develop a solid long-term working relationship with the other. It is with such customers that relationship marketing has the greatest pay-off.

Figure 11.6 Comparing customer relationship revenues with relationship costs

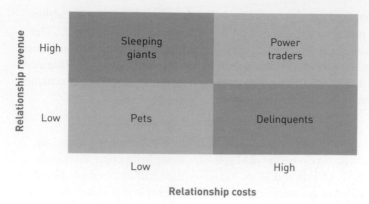

In these situations, the 'in-supplier' and 'out-supplier' face very different challenges. The in-supplier tries to make switching difficult for the customer. It develops product systems that are incompatible with those of competing suppliers and installs its own ordering systems which simplify inventory management and delivery. It works to become the customer's indispensable partner. Out-suppliers, in contrast, try to make it easy and less costly to switch suppliers. They design product systems that are compatible with the customer's system, that are easy to install and learn, that save the customer a lot of money, and that promise to improve through time.

The appropriateness of transaction versus relationship marketing depends on the type of industry and the wishes of the particular customer. Some customers value a high-service supplier and will stay with that supplier for a long time. Other customers want to cut their costs and will switch suppliers readily to obtain lower costs.

Thus relationship marketing is not the best approach in all situations. For it to be worthwhile, relationship revenue needs to exceed relationship costs. Figure 11.6 suggests that some customers are very profitable *sleeping giants*, which generate significant revenue and are profitable but relatively undemanding. Much of the relationship marketing activity is taken up by the *power traders*, which provide significant revenue but are demanding. These are as profitable as the *pets*, which provide little revenue but have appropriately small relationship costs. Transaction marketing is probably adequate for these. The most difficult group is the *delinquents*, which provide little revenue but are demanding. What can a company do about these? One option is to shift the *delinquent* customers to products that are likely to be less difficult to operate or less complicated. Prepaid mobile phone services do this by providing contracts to less well-off customers who prepay for the phone's use. Banks' high charges on unnegotiated overdrafts are a way of doing this. If these actions cause the unprofitable customer to defect, so be it. In fact, the company might benefit by *encouraging* these unprofitable customers to switch to competition.

Summary

Today's customers face a growing range of choices in the products and services they can buy. They base their choices on their perceptions of *quality*, *value* and *service*. Companies need to understand the determinants of *customer value* and *satisfaction*. *Customer delivered value* is the difference between *total customer value* and *total customer cost*. Customers will normally choose the offer that maximises their delivered value.

Customer satisfaction is the outcome felt by buyers who have experienced a company performance that has fulfilled expectations. Customers are satisfied when their expectations are met and delighted when their expectations are exceeded. Satisfied customers remain loyal longer, buy more, are less price sensitive and talk favourably about the company. To be known, customer satisfaction has to be measured and there are several established ways of doing this.

To create customer satisfaction, companies must manage their own *value chains* and the entire *value delivery system* in a customer-centred way. The company's goal is not only to get customers, but, even more importantly, to retain customers. *Total quality management* has become a leading approach to providing customer satisfaction and company profitability across the whole value chain. Delivering quality requires total management and employee commitment as well as measurement and reward systems. Marketers play an especially critical role in their company's drive towards higher quality.

Customer relationship marketing provides the key to retaining customers and involves building financial and social benefits as well as structural ties to customers. *Customer relationship marketing* systems integrate strategy, IT and relationship marketing to deliver value to customers and treat them individually. Companies must decide the level at which they want to build relationships with different market segments and individual customers, from such levels as basic, reactive, accountable and proactive to full partnership. Which is best depends on a customer's lifetime value relative to the costs required to attract and retain that customer.

Discussing the issues

1. Describe a situation in which you became a 'lost customer'. Did you drop the purchase because of poor product quality, poor service quality or both? What should the firm do to 'recapture' lost customers?

2. Recall a purchase experience in which the sales assistant or some other representative of an organisation went beyond the normal effort and 'gave his/her all' to produce the utmost in service quality. What impact did the noticeable effort have on the purchase outcome?

3. Total quality management is an important approach to providing customer satisfaction and company profits. How might total quality be managed for the following product and service offerings: (a) a packaged food product; (b) a restaurant meal; (c) a public utility (such as power supply or garbage collection); (d) a family holiday; (e) a university education?

4. Recall incidents when you have purchased, or tried to purchase, similar items through two or more of the Internet direct marketing call centres or bricks-and-mortar stores. How does the meaning of service quality differ across the three channels and how did they compare in operation?

5. Thinking of the operation of a not-for-profit organisation, such as a charity, propose some ways in which relationship marketing could help them collect money from donors.

Applying the concepts

1. Write a letter of complaint to a firm about one of its products or services. What was the firm's response? Did you receive a refund or replacement product, a response letter or no reply at all? How does the type of response affect your attitude towards the company?

2. Determine two or three relatively obscure subjects on which you could need to purchase a book, for example house prices, the history of puppetry or Portuguese cooking. Then visit several Web book retailers and compare the quality of their service and the mechanisms they use to build relationships into their service (sites could include amazon.com, amazon.co.uk, bol.com, barnesandnoble.com). Compare the best with a search at a local bricks-and-mortar bookstore.

References

1. Shoshana Zuboff and James Maxim's influential book *The Support Economy: Why corporations are failing individuals and the next episode of capitalism* (London: Allen Lane, 2003) is reviewed in 'Face value: Giving people what they want', *The Economist* (10 May 2003), p. 70.

2. This and other examples of how banks have rediscovered being nice to customers are in 'Banking: love me', *The Economist* (23 February 2002), p. 34.

3. 'Hard-edged marketing', Agenda Paper on The Chartered Institute of Marketing's website www.cim.co.uk (2003).

4. For more on measuring customer delivered value, and on 'value/price ratios', see Alan Mitchell, 'Value focused strategy is key to brand growth', *Marketing Week*, **22**, 13 (1999), pp. 36–7.

5. For interesting discussions of value and value strategies, see Albert Caruana and Pierre R. Berthon, 'Service quality and satisfaction – the moderating role of value', *European Journal of Marketing*, **34**, 11/12 (2000), pp. 1338–53; Shirley Daniels, 'Customer value management', *Work Study*, **49**, 2 (2000), pp. 67–70; and Annika Ravald and Christian Grönroos, 'The value concept and relationship marketing', *European Journal of Marketing*, **30**, 2 (1996), pp. 19–30.

6. Armand V. Feigenbaum, 'A challenge creeping up', *Financial Times* (10 January 2001), p. 14.

7. Tor Wallin Anfreassen, 'Antecedents to satisfaction with service recovery', *European Journal of Marketing*, **34**, 1/2 (2000), pp. 156–75; Kate Stewart, 'The customer exit process – A review and research agenda', *Journal of Marketing Management*, **14**, 4 (1998), pp. 235–50.

8. Michael E. Porter, *Competitive Advantage: Creating and sustaining superior performance* (New York: Free Press, 1985); David Walters, 'Implementing value strategy through the value chain', *Management Decision*, **38**, 3 (2000), pp. 160–78.

9. For an analysis of the relative contribution of the product, sales service and after-sales service, see José M. M. Bloemer and Jos G. A. M. Lemmink, 'The importance of customer satisfaction in explaining brand and dealer loyalty', *Journal of Marketing Management*, **8**, 4 (1992), pp. 351–64.

10. Stuart Derrick, 'Saving face', *e.business* (June 2000), pp. 19–20; Stuart Derrick, 'Moving target', *e.business* (July 2000), p. 69; Fletcher Research, 'Multichannel strategies: call centre and web integration' (2000).

11. The enthusiasts in Nick Hornby's *Hi-Fidelity* (London: Indigo, 1995), besides having great knowledge of music, also provide examples of atrocious customer service. See also 'Music-recognition software: om tiddly om pom', *The Economist* (19 October 2002), p. 107.

12. For more discussion, see Shirley Daniels, 'Customer value management', *Work Study*, **49**, 2 (2000), pp. 67–70; Douglas Brownlie, Mike Saren, Robin Wensley and Richard Whittington, 'Rethinking marketing: towards critical marketing accountings', *European Journal of Marketing*, **34**, 1/2 (2000), pp. 223–6.

13. 'Business and Community Annual Report (1997)', *Financial Times* (4 December 1997), p. 5.

14. Specifically, Bob Luchs, 'Quality as a strategic weapon: measuring relative quality, value, and market differentiation', *European Business Journal*, **2**, 4 (1990), pp. 34–47; and generally Robert D. Buzzell and Bradley T. Gale, *The PIMS Principles: Linking strategy to performance* (New York: Free Press, 1987), Ch. 6.

15. Ziaul Huq and Justin D. Stolen, 'Total quality management contrasts in manufacturing and service industries', *International Journal of Quality and Reliability Management*, **15**, 2 (1998), pp. 138–61; T. Thiagarajan and M. Zairi, 'A review of total quality management in practice: understanding the fundamentals through examples of best practice applications – part III', *The TQM Magazine*, **9**, 6 (1997), pp. 414–17.

16. See Joe Folkman, 'Employee surveys that make a difference', *Journal of Services Marketing*, **14**, 5 (2000), pp. 432–6; G. Ronald Gilbert, 'Measuring internal customer satisfaction', *Managing Service Quality*, **10**, 3 (2000), pp. 178–86; and Zoe S. Dimitriades, 'Total involvement in quality management', *Team Performance Management: An International Journal*, **6**, 7/8 (2000), pp. 117–22.

17. J. Daniel Beckham, 'Expect the unexpected in health care marketing future', *The Academy Bulletin* (July 1992), p. 3.

18. Charles Orton-Jones, 'Just how much is a customer worth?', *EuroBusiness* (February 2000), pp. 28–9; Andrew Lorenz, 'Target Germany', *The Sunday Times* (21 November 1999); Christopher Price, 'Upward mobility', *Marketing Business* (March 1999), pp. 36–9; 'A mobile merry-go-round', *The Economist* (23 October 1999), pp. 113–14.

19. Chartered Institute of Marketing, 'Customer retention', in *Marketing Means Business* (Moore Hall: Chartered Institute of Marketing, 1999), pp. 84–8; Fiona Harvey, 'Of chocolates and profit sharing', *Financial Times* (26 July 2000), p. 13; 'Workers of the world, stop moaning', *The Guardian* (16 August 2000); Malcolm McDonald, 'Up close and personal', *Marketing Business* (September 1998), pp. 52–5; Peter Bartram, 'Engineered for growth', *Marketing Business* (February 1999), pp. 24–9.

20. Stan Liebowitz, *Rethinking the Network Economy* (AMACOM, 2002); 'Economic focus: first will be last', *The Economist* (28 September 2002), p. 101.

21. Redrick F. Reicheld and W. Earl Sasser, Jr, 'Zero defections: quality comes to service', *Harvard Business Review* (September–October 1990), pp. 301–7; Mike Page, Leyland Pitt and Pierre Berthon, 'Analyzing and reducing customer defections', *Long Range Planning*, **29**, 6 (1996), pp. 821–34.

22. Leonard L. Berry and A. Parasuraman, *Marketing Services: Competing through quality* (New York: Free Press, 1991), pp. 136–42.

23. Richard Lapper, 'J. P. Morgan offers free use of its toolbox', *Financial Times* (11 October 1994), p. 27.

24. Peter Bartram, 'Engineering for growth', *Marketing Business* (February 2000), pp. 24–7.

25. Y. H. Wong, 'Key to key account management: relationship (guanxi) model', *International Marketing Review*, **15**, 3 (1998), pp. 215–31.

26. Kate Maddox, 'CRM to outpace other IT spending', *B to B* (11 March 2002), pp. 2, 33.

27. For these and other examples see Marc L. Songini, 'Fedex expects CRM system to deliver', *Computerworld* (6 November 2000), p. 10; Leslie Berger, 'Business intelligence: insights from the data pile', *New York Times* (13 January 2002), p. A9; and Geoffrey James, 'Profit motive', *Selling Power* (March 2002), pp. 68–73.

28. Darrell K. Rigby, 'Avoid the four perils of CRM', *Harvard Business Review* (February 2002), pp. 101–9.

29. Michael Krauss, 'At many firms, technology obscures CRM', *Marketing News* (18 March 2002), p. 5.

30. Robert McLuhan, 'How to reap the benefits of CRM', *Marketing* (24 May 2001), p. 35; Sellar, 'Dust off that data', p. 72; Eric Almquist, Carla Heaton and Nick Hall, 'Making CRM make money', *Marketing Management* (May–June 2002), pp. 16–21; Geoff Martin, *Financial Times* (4 July 2001); Malcolm McDonald, 'On the right track', *Marketing Business* (April 2000), pp. 28–9; David Murphy, 'Making CRM work', *Marketing Business* (November 1999), pp. 42–5; 'I want a relationship', *Marketing Business* (e-business: 2000), pp. vi–vii.

31. Kim Benjamin, 'BA's on-line flight path', *e-business* (June 2000), pp. 55–60; Nikki Tait, 'Racing down the electronic highway', *Financial Times: e-procurement* (Winter 2000), pp. 18–19; Geoff Nairn, 'Launching a strike against military costs', *Financial Times: e-procurement* (Winter 2000), pp. 20–1.

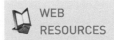

WEB RESOURCES

For additional classic case studies and Internet exercises, visit www.pearsoned.co.uk/kotler

Concluding concepts 11
National Gummi AB

THOMAS HELGASSON
Halmstad University, Sweden

National Gummi has problems. For them it is a new problem, but it is close to that being faced by many small to medium-sized companies these days as their major local customers become part of major multinational companies. Years spent building up relationships with them are in danger of being devalued as their customer's HQ is suddenly centred in a new culture oceans away. What is even more worrying is the standardisation of products; the rationalisation of suppliers and the use of alien e-purchasing systems often follow the consolidation of companies into global giants. All this is happening to National Gummi AB whose major customers, Ford and GM, have swallowed Saab and Volvo, respectively.

National Gummi is a small company situated in the south of Sweden. Founded in 1941, it is now managed by the third generation of the founding family. It has 145 employees and a turnover of SKr 175 m (€20m). National Gummi's main business is making rubber seals that go round the doors and windows of vehicles. Between them Saab and Volvo account for two-thirds of National Gummi's turnover, so to lose their business would be catastrophic. Through close personal relationships over the last 40 years the two Swedish carmakers have learned to trust National Gummi and recognise that the company that can solve their door and window sealing problems.

> National Gummi make rubber seals that go round the doors and windows of vehicles.

The product

Most sealing systems are made of rubber, a material with some drawbacks. Rubber cannot be recycled, it is expensive, complicated to handle in manufacture and is seen by final consumers as being environmentally unfriendly. National Gummi's aim is to change from using rubber to more environmentally friendly Thermo Plastic Elastomers (TPE) that are partly plastic and part rubber. Being a compound, its properties can be changed to fit the needs of doors and windows, while rubber has fixed properties. TPE is also recyclable either as waste material left over from manufacturing or as recovered from a scrapped vehicle, is easy and fast to use in production,

has lower production costs and is generally more environmentally friendly than rubber. TPE's main disadvantage is that it is less 'elastic' than rubber so does not form an effective seal in some parts of all cars, which means that it will have to be used alongside rubber in car assembly.

National Gummi aims to solve TPE's elasticity problem but expects that everyone else in the industry is trying to do the same thing. Following the tradition of past partnerships, in 1998 National Gummi, Saab and Volvo set up a joint project team to develop better TPE seals. After some discussion, the team was made up of two National Gummi engineers, one engineer from each of Saab and Volvo, a polymer-researcher from IFP Research Ltd and a marketer from Halmstad University. Members of the project team all contributed different skills. The National Gummi engineers knew a lot about seals but had little experience with the rest of car assembly. In contrast, the Saab and Volvo engineers had limited experience of seals but knew a lot about cars generally. The IFP researcher had expertise in plastics and rubber generally rather than in their use as seals.

It is common for the Swedish carmakers to work with suppliers on new projects. For components such as floor mats or light bulbs there is little reason to involve suppliers until late in product development. However, with a component such as a seal, which will affect both design and assembly, early participation of all parties in design is very important. The engineers do not have it all their own way in design. The carmakers' marketing people will be championing their customers' requirements, while the purchasing department will be fighting to get costs down.

A relationship without marketing

It is very difficult to become a new supplier to either Saab or Volvo. New 'partners' have to fill all technical requirements, have a low price and be someone that the companies can trust. The relationships are important since the quality and value of the final product are only as good as the components. Of course, National Gummi's 40 years of service and numerous long-standing personal friendships with the carmakers' people give National Gummi a great advantage. Saab and Volvo feel that the people at National Gummi are more than just business partners. They are friends with whom they have worked for many years and who have cooperated in solving many business problems. Through long partnership, National Gummi know the needs of Saab and Volvo and how to work with them.

Of course, National Gummi's relationship with the carmakers has changed over the years. One of National Gummi's early advantages was their extreme proximity to the car plants. When that was the case it was possible to make a visit and solve design or manufacturing problems within hours. Over the years, Saab and Volvo had become more international with operations all over Europe. In some markets National Gummi had to deal with Saab and Volvo through agents and the business had shifted from one with a single language and culture to a multilingual, multicultural entity. IT had started to play a bigger role in routine communications between the carmakers and their suppliers. Meeting the needs of quality management and just-in-time management had also applied pressures, and National Gummi had to establish representation and extra facilities adjacent to car plants. It had become harder and harder for a small independent company to survive in a rapidly changing and increasingly global industry.

Increasingly, communications between National Gummi and the carmakers were electronic: email, telephone, fax and shared software to handle orders and design drawings. However, personal communications remained paramount in maintaining understanding between National Gummi and its customers. Video-conferencing had been used to work with more geographically distant partners and National Gummi knew of several cases of small companies exploiting global markets through the World Wide Web.

The closeness of National Gummi to its customers had allowed the company to develop without the need for conventional marketing skills. Engineers did technical selling and new customers had always found National Gummi rather than the other way round. This worked fine as long as Saab and Volvo remained good partners who respected the profit margins needed by subcontractors. The threat now was the tendency of the industry to seek system solutions rather than components; for example, subcontracting the provision of whole door assemblies, window and door seals included, rather than lots of bits and pieces. These jobs were hard for a small company like National Gummi to tender for and demanded lots of skills that they did not have.

Saab and Volvo were also part of large American companies that put less emphasis on the personal relationships that had been National Gummi's major advantage for so long. Saab and Volvo retained marketing operations in Sweden but these were becoming servants to the global operations, such as Ford's Berkeley Square-based Premier Automobile Group which manages Volvo alongside the Aston Martin, Jaguar, Land Rover, Lincoln and Mercury brands. Covisint, the giant electronic automobile component exchange with its headquarters in Michigan, was also being set up by DaimlerChrysler, Ford, GM, Nissan and Renault. Expected to have a turnover of $250 billion (€280 billion), the Internet exchange would have at least one office in Europe. One of the aims of establishing Covisint is to squeeze margins out of suppliers to the tune of $1,000 to $4,000 per car in the US where costs are already low.

As a small components company with limited potential for systems solutions or advanced research, National Gummi knew it would have to change in order to survive. Advisers had suggested several alternative ways ahead for National Gummi:

1. To become a sub-subcontractor and supply one of the major subcontractors with components. In this case, National Gummi's customers would become the car manufacturer's prime vendors who supplied door assemblies.
2. To specialise in components that are not a part of a system so are sold separately to carmakers.
3. To increase that part of their activities that does not go to Volvo or Saab by finding new customers or selling more to existing customers. Aside from Saab and Volvo, National Gummi has about 2,000 smaller customers.
4. For National Gummi to be more proactive in trying to find customers instead of waiting for customers to find them.

Questions

1. Why is National Gummi facing the problems it is and what could it have done to avoid them?
2. Since National Gummi survived for so long without any marketing activities, would it have been an unnecessary luxury to develop them until recently?
3. How did National Gummi add value to its service to its past clients and how can it continue to do so? Does the development of electronic exchanges mean that relationships between customers and suppliers are history?
4. Since the close relationships between National Gummi and the Swedish carmakers were the foundation of its past success, does the company's present state suggest a danger in relationship marketing? Does relationship marketing differ from what National Gummi has been doing?
5. Examining the strengths and weaknesses of National Gummi, what strategy would you propose for them?

I don't meet competition, I crush it.

CHARLES REVSON

Competitive strategy

Chapter objectives

After reading this chapter, you should be able to:

- Explain the importance of developing competitive marketing strategies that position the company against competitors and give it the strongest possible competitive advantage.
- Identify the steps that companies go through in analysing competitors.
- Discuss the competitive strategies that market leaders use to expand the market and to protect and expand their market shares.
- Describe the strategies that market challengers and followers use to increase their market shares and profits.
- Discuss how market nichers find and develop profitable corners of the market.

Mini Contents List

- Prelude case – PS2 meets the X-box: certainly not all fun and games
- Introduction
- Competitor analysis
- Marketing Insights 12.1 – The singing Swedes
- Competitive strategies
- Marketing Insights 12.2 – Concentrated marketing: nice niches
- Balancing customer–competitor orientations
- Summary
- Concluding concepts 12 – The mobile maelstrom

◄ Source: McDonald's Europe Limited.

Prelude case PS2 meets the X-box: certainly not all fun and games

In the games machine market life is even more challenging than *Tomb Raider*, more aggressive than *Grand Theft Auto* and more brutal than *Resident Evil*. In the early 1980s, no home could be without a video game console and a dozen cartridges. By 1983 Atari, Mattel and a dozen other companies offered some version of a video game system and industry sales topped €3.6 billion worldwide. Then, by 1985, home video game sales had plummeted to €100 million. Game consoles gathered dust, and cartridges, originally priced as high as €40 each, sold for €5. Industry leader Atari was hardest hit. Atari sacked 4,500 employees and sold the subsidiary at a fraction of its 1983 worth. Industry experts blamed the death of the industry on the fickle consumer. Video games, they said, were a passing fad.

In the games machine market life is even more challenging than *Tomb Raider*, more aggressive than *Grand Theft Auto* and more brutal than *Resident Evil*.

However, Nintendo, a 100-year-old toy company from Kyoto, did not agree. In late 1985, on top of the ruins of the video game business, the company introduced its Nintendo Entertainment System (NES). A year later, Nintendo had sold over 1 million NES units. By 1991 Nintendo and its licensees had annual sales of $4 billion in a now revitalised €5 billion video game industry. Nintendo had 80 per cent share of the world market. Forty per cent of Japanese households and about 20 per cent of US and EU households had a NES.

How did Nintendo do it? First, it recognised that video game customers were not so much fickle as bored. The company sent researchers to visit video arcades to find out why alienated home video game fans still spent hours happily pumping arcade machines. The researchers found that Nintendo's *Donkey Kong* and similar games were still mainstays of the arcades, even though home versions were failing. The reason? The arcade games offered better quality, full animation and challenging plots. Home video games, on the other hand, offered only crude quality and simple plots. Despite their exotic names and introductory hype, each new home game was boringly identical to all the others, featuring slow characters that moved through ugly animated scenes to the beat of monotonous, synthesised tones. Kids had outgrown the first-generation home video games.

Nintendo saw the fall of the video game industry as an opportunity. It set out to differentiate itself by offering superior quality – by giving home video games customers a full measure of quality entertainment value for their money. Nintendo designed a basic game system that sold for about €100 yet boasted near arcade-quality graphics. Equally important, it developed innovative and high-quality *Game Paks* to accompany the system. New games constantly appear and mature titles are weeded out to keep the selection fresh and interesting. The games contain consistently high-quality graphics and game plots vary and challenge the user. Colourful, cartoon-like characters move fluidly about cleverly animated screens. The most popular games involved sword-and-sorcery conflicts, or the series of *Super Mario* fantasy worlds, where young heroes battle to save endangered princesses or fight the evil ruler, *Wart*, for peace in the *World of Dreams*.

By differentiating itself through superior products and service, and by building strong relationships with its customers, Nintendo built a seemingly invincible quality position in the video game market. But it soon came under attack. New competitors such as Sony and Sega exploited the opportunities created as Nintendo junkies became bored and sought the next new video thrill. Sony beat Nintendo at its own game – product superiority – when it hit the market with its PlayStation machine, an advanced new system that offered even richer graphics, more lifelike sound and more complex plots. Nintendo countered with the Nintendo 64 and a fresh blast of promotion, but the competition has intensified and, while Nintendos were being discounted, the PlayStation was the Christmas hit toy of 1997.

Meanwhile the computer games world is attacked for being 'violent, destructive, xenophobic, racist and sexist'. Sega Europe has also been attacked for marketing gruesome games such as *Mortal Kombat* and *Murder Death Kill*. The industry has been criticised for cultivating a generation of 'Video Kids' for whom 30 seconds without scoring is boring; moral zombies hooked on worlds where the rules are shot or be shot, consume or be consumed, fight or lose. In Japan, where many of the games come from, consumers are more broad-minded than in most western countries. Nintendo needs to extend its customer range beyond the terminally fickle teenage males. Sega sponsored roadshows with teen magazines, and put girls in its TV ads after complaints from schoolchildren on its 'advisory board' about sexism in advertising. Sega Europe created a new toy division to target 'housewives with children, instead of 14-year-old boys'. The first product was Pico, an electronic learning aid for kids that has taken a 'significant' share of the Japanese high-tech toys market. The €9 million European launch included TV, press and posters with a full below-the-line campaign. Next came an 'electronic

Exhibit 12.1 Peak sales of games consoles

Peak sales year	Format	Games consoles	Peak annual sales
1982	Atari	Atari	10 m
1989	8-bit	NES, Master system	11 m
1993	16-bit	Megadrive/Genesis, SNES, 300	14 m
1997	32/64-bit	PlayStation, N64, Saturn	32 m
2003	128-bit	PS2, X-box, Game cube, Dreamcast	45 m

SOURCES: Sony, Durlacher, *The Economist*.

learning aid that thinks it's a toy' for three- to seven-year-olds. At the older end of the market more cerebral 'stealth games' are taking hold in Japan. *Metal Gear Solid* and *Theft* reward silence, concealment and strategy more than bang and blast. Is this new thrust making gaming more civilised? No way.

While Nintendo and Sega chased the new markets, Sony's PlayStation blasted the 1997 Christmas market with the 'arcade feel' of *Ridge Racer* and *Crash Bindicoot* and 'scary, tension building' *Doom*. It is the kids who drive the games market and what they want is power and the latest cult machine. Three years after PlayStation blasted the competition, their €450 PlayStation 2 (PS2) is aimed to do the same again for Christmas 2000. With Internet access, CD and DVD playability the PS2's 128-bit microprocessor has twice the power of Intel's latest Pentium chip. So powerful is the PS2's processor that its export had to be specially licensed by the Japanese government since it has the performance necessary to guide a cruise missile.

However, Sony is not having it all their own way. Sega launched their Dreamcast a years before PS2 but sales were lacklustre and the machine and its games were soon discounted. The market also attracted the mighty Microsoft whose X-box appeared in late 2001. Unlike other games machines, the X-box is intended for use in a living room using the family TV and operating Microsoft's PC products. Nintendo, too, is fighting back with their Game Cube.

The battle between Sony, Microsoft and Nintendo pushed world games console sales to new heights in 2003 (Exhibit 12.1) but worldwide sales for 2006 are forecast to be less than 10 million. The intense battle is pushing up peak sales but total sales over the life-cycle of 128-bit consoles are little more than those of 64-bit consoles. Each generation of console generates higher peak sales but with a shorter life-cycle.

Along with Sega, Nintendo is the loser in the 128-bit war with worldwide sales totalling 9.63 million compared with PS2's 50 million plus. Sataro Iwata, Nintendo's president, is promising radically new games. He believes that *Tales of Symphonia* and *Pocket Monster Colosseum*, both extensions of their popular *Pokémon* range, 'will have a big impact on the world'. Some industry observers disagree. Takashami Oya, of Credit Suisse First Boston, observes that 'Nintendo is like a boat that has drifted ashore'. In his view, Nintendo have missed the growth market for older, lighter users of games machines. For the time being Nintendo's lead in hand-held machines and the huge margin on games are keeping profits and margins up despite the cube's problems. However, a new round of the console wars is set to open. Off the back of their PS2 success, Sony are launching a hand-held machine in 2005, and 2006 will see 256-bit consoles with undreamt-of multimedia capabilities.[1]

Questions

1. Why do you think Microsoft has chosen to challenge market leader Sony in the computer games market?

2. What are the key ingredients for success in the computer games market?

3. Using information from the case, and your own knowledge, compare the competitive strengths and weaknesses of the competitors in the computer game machine market. Who do you think will be the long-term winners and why?

Introduction

Understanding customers is not enough. As the game console market shows, this is a period of intense competition in local and global markets. Many economies are deregulating and encouraging market forces to operate. The EU is removing trade barriers among European nations and deregulating many previously protected markets. Multinationals are moving aggressively into the south-east Asian markets and competing globally. The result is that companies have no choice but to be 'competitive'. They must start paying as much attention to tracking their competitors as to understanding target customers. Nintendo at first succeeded by being innovative and providing an excellent product that competitors could not match. Their innovativeness revitalised the market, made it grow, made it profitable and large. In doing so they attracted new powerful competitors from other industries, first consumer electronics-based Sony and then super-wealthy Microsoft.

Under the marketing concept, companies gain **competitive advantage** by designing offers that satisfy target-consumer needs better than competitors' offers. They might deliver more customer value by offering consumers lower prices than competitors for similar products and services, or by providing more benefits that justify higher prices. Marketing strategies must consider the strategies of competitors as well as the needs of target consumers. The first step is **competitor analysis**: the process of identifying key competitors; assessing their objectives, strengths and weaknesses, strategies and reaction patterns; and selecting which competitors to attack or avoid. The second step is developing **competitive strategies** that strongly position the company against competitors and give the company the strongest possible competitive advantage.

Competitor analysis

To plan effective competitive marketing strategies, the company needs to find out all it can about its competitors. It must constantly compare its products, prices, channels and promotion with those of close competitors. In this way the company can find areas of potential competitive advantage and disadvantage. It can launch more effective marketing campaigns against its competitors and prepare stronger defences against competitors' actions.

What do companies need to know about their competitors? They need to know: Who are our competitors? What are their objectives? What are their strategies? What are their strengths and weaknesses? What are their reaction patterns? Figure 12.1 shows the main steps in analysing competitors.

Competitive advantage— An advantage over competitors gained by offering consumers greater value, either through lower prices or by providing more benefits that justify higher prices.

Competitor analysis—The process of identifying key competitors; assessing their objectives, strategies, strengths and weaknesses, and reaction patterns; and selecting which competitors to attack or avoid.

Competitive strategies— Strategies that strongly position the company against competitors and that give the company the strongest possible strategic advantage.

Figure 12.1 **Steps in analysing competitors**

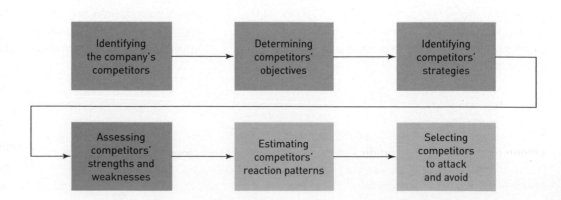

SKIN PROBLEMS?

THE ANSWER'S AT THE SUPERMARKET,
NOT THE CHEMIST.

There's no such thing as beautiful skin, well not on fish anyway. That's why new Birds Eye Simply Fish contains no skin and no bones, just the thickest most succulent cod fillet, cut from the best part of the fish and coated in lightly seasoned breadcrumbs or crispy batter. It's guaranteed to make you even more popular than ever.

FOR THOSE WHO REALLY LOVE FISH.

BIRDS EYE

Under the broadest
consideration, companies that
manufacture certain healthy
foods like fish are competing
with the cosmetics industry.
SOURCE: Unilever/Advertising
Archives.

Identifying the company's competitors

Normally, it would seem a simple matter for a company to identify its competitors. Boeing knows that Airbus is its strongest competitor; and Nokia knows that it competes with Motorola.[2] At the most obvious level, a company can define its *product category competition* as other companies offering a similar product and services to the same customers at similar prices. Thus Volvo might see Mercedes as a foremost competitor, but not Rolls-Royce cars or Reliant (makers of the three-wheeled cars that Mr Bean bullies).

In competing for people's money, however, companies actually face a much wider range of competitors. More broadly, the company can define its *product competition* as all firms making the same product or class of products. Volvo could see itself as competing against all other car manufacturers. Even more broadly, competitors might include all companies making products that supply the same service. Here Volvo would see itself competing against not only other car manufacturers, but also the makers of trucks, motor cycles or even bicycles. Finally and still more broadly, competitors might include all companies that compete for the same consumer's money. Here Volvo would see itself competing with companies that sell major consumer durables, foreign holidays, new homes or extensive home repairs or alterations.

The industry point of view

Many companies identify their competitors from the *industry* point of view. An **industry** is a group of firms that offer a product or class of products that are close substitutes for each other. We talk about the car industry, the oil industry, the pharmaceutical industry or the beverage industry. In a given industry, if the price of one product rises, it causes the demand

Industry—A group of firms
that offer a product or class
of products that are close
substitutes for each other.
The set of all sellers of a
product or service.

for another product to rise. In the beverage industry, for example, if the price of coffee rises, this leads people to switch to tea or lemonade or soft drinks. Coffee, tea, lemonade and soft drinks are substitutes, even though they are physically different products. A company must strive to understand the competitive pattern in its industry if it hopes to be an effective 'player' in that industry.

The market point of view

Instead of identifying competitors from the industry point of view, the company can take a *market* point of view. Here it defines its *task competition* as companies that are trying to satisfy the same customer need or serve the same customer group. From an industry point of view, Heineken might see its competition as Beck's, Carlsberg and other brewers. From a market point of view, however, the task competition may include all 'thirst quenching' or 'social drinking'. Energy drinks, new-age drinks, alcopops, 'designer' water and many other drinks could satisfy the needs. Generally, the market concept of competition opens the company's eyes to a broader set of actual and potential competitors. This leads to better long-run market planning.

The key to identifying competitors is to link industry and market analysis by mapping out product/market segments. Table 12.1 shows a reduced set of product/market segments in the spreads market by product types and competitor battling it out on Tesco's dairy spreads shelf. Market leading Unilever cover almost all product classes with their Flora range augmented by I Can't Believe Its Not Butter and Stork. Tesco's own brands match Unilever in nearly every segment but that expensive and more technically demanding cholesterol lowering segment. Some of the specialist segments in the market are small but these have allowed Pure to establish a health oriented appeal. If Pure wanted to expand, it would need to estimate the market size of each segment, the market shares of the current competitors, and their current capabilities, objectives and strategies. Clearly each product/market segment would pose different competitive problems and opportunities.

Table 12.1 Product market segments for spreads

Product/Market segments	Tesco	Unilever	Others
Buttery taste	Butter Me Up	I Can't Believe Its Not Butter Flora Buttery Vegetable	St Ivel Utterly Butterly
Family spreads	Value	Flora Original	St Ivel Gold, Clover
Reduced fat spreads	Healthy Living Olive Light Only 5% Fat Sunflower	Flora Vegetable Low Fat Flora Diet	St Ivel Gold Light, Diet delight
Olive oil based	Tesco Olive Tesco	Flora Pro Activ Olive	Olivio, Carapelli, Bertolli (Olivio)
Cholesterol lowering	–	Flora Pro-Activ	Benecol
Reduced salt	–	Flora Low Salt	Pure LoSalt
Dairy Free	–	–	Pure Dairy Free Soya
Organic	–	–	Pure Organic Reduced Fat
Cooking	Baking Margarine	White Flora Stork	

SOURCE: The Margarine and Spreads Association's www.margarine.org.uk and www.tesco.com

Taking a customer-oriented view of the market is critical to avoiding 'competitor myopia' where the immediate competition blinds a company to latent competitors who can completely destroy the old ways of doing business.

Encyclopedia Britannica viewed itself as competing with other publishers of printed encyclopedia sets selling for as much as €2,500 per set. However, it learned a hard lesson when Microsoft Encarta, an encyclopedia on CD-ROM, was introduced and sold for only €60. It seems that parents bought the *Britannica* less for its intellectual content than out of a desire to do what's right for their children. Although less comprehensive than the *Britannica*, Encarta and other CD-ROM encyclopedias served this 'do what's right' purpose well. By the time *Britannica* introduced its own CD-ROM and online versions, its sales of its print edition plunged by more than 80 per cent. Thus, Encyclopedia Britannica's real competitor was general databases, in books, on CD-ROM, websites (studyweb.com) or even news groups (comp.infosystems.interpedia).[3]

Determining competitors' objectives

Having identified the main competitors, marketing management now asks: What does each competitor seek in the marketplace? What drives each competitor's behaviour?

The marketer might at first assume that all competitors would want to maximise their profits and choose their actions accordingly. However, companies differ in the emphasis they put on short-term versus long-term profits, and some competitors are oriented towards 'satisfying' rather than 'maximising' profits. They have profit goals that satisfy them, even if the strategies could produce more profits.

Encyclopedia Britannica viewed itself as the world's leading publisher of printed encyclopedias until it discovered that its real competitors were CD-ROM-based software and Internet access.
SOURCE: Encyclopedia Britannica.

Marketers must look beyond competitors' profit goals. Each competitor has a mix of objectives, each with differing importance. The company wants to know the relative importance that competitors place on current profitability, market share growth, cash flow, technological leadership, service leadership and other goals. Knowing a competitor's objectives reveals whether it is satisfied with its current situation and how it might react to competitive actions. For example, a company that pursues low-cost leadership will react much more strongly to a competitor's cost-reducing manufacturing breakthrough than to the same competitor's advertising increase. A company must also monitor its competitors' objectives for attacking various product/market segments. If the company finds that a competitor has discovered a new segment, this might be an opportunity. If it finds that competitors plan new moves into segments now served by the company, it will be forewarned and, hopefully, forearmed.

Identifying competitors' strategies

Strategic group—A group of firms in an industry following the same or a similar strategy.

The more that one firm's strategy resembles another firm's strategy, the more the firms compete. In most industries, the competitors sort into groups that pursue different strategies. A **strategic group** is a group of firms in an industry following the same or a similar strategy in a given target market. For example, in the washing machine industry, Electrolux and Whirlpool belong to the same strategic group producing a full line of medium-price appliances supported by good service. On the other hand, quality-oriented Bosch, Maytag, and innovative new entrant Dyson, belong to a different strategic group. They produce a narrower line of appliances and charge a premium price.

Some important insights emerge from strategic group identification. For example, if a company enters one of the groups, the members of that group become its key competitors. Thus, if the company enters the first group against Electrolux and Whirlpool, it can succeed only if it develops some strategic advantages over these large competitors.

Although competition is most intense within a strategic group, there is also rivalry among groups. First, some of the strategic groups may appeal to overlapping customer segments. For example, no matter what their strategy, all major appliance manufacturers will go after the apartment and home builders segment. Second, the customers may not see much difference in the offers of different groups – they may see little difference in quality between Electrolux and Bosch. Finally, members of one strategic group might expand into new strategy segments, as Whirlpool has done by extending its washing machine range to approach Bosch's prices.[4]

The company needs to look at all the dimensions that identify strategic groups within the industry. It needs to know each competitor's product quality, features and mix, customer services, pricing policy, distribution coverage, sales force strategy, and advertising and sales promotion programmes. It must study the details of each competitor's R&D, manufacturing, buying, financial and other strategies.

Assessing competitors' strengths and weaknesses

Can a company's competitors carry out their strategies and reach their goals? This depends on each competitor's resources and capabilities. Marketers need to identify accurately each competitor's strengths and weaknesses. For example, for a long time American and British acts dominated the popular music industry. Abba signalled a change in the industry structure with an increasing number of Swedish bands or bands recording in Sweden. Marketing Insights 12.1 looks at the marketing strengths underlying this phenomenon.

As a first step, a company gathers key data on each competitor's business over the last few years. It wants to know about competitors' goals, strategies and performance. Admittedly, some of this information will be hard to collect. For example, industrial goods companies find it hard to estimate competitors' market shares because they do not have the same syndicated

The singing Swedes

marketing insights

Why has pop music become one of Sweden's greatest exports and Stockholm one of the hit-making capitals of the world?

Melody makers

'Swedes are very musical people to start with', says Bol Hydena, MD of Nordic MTV. 'Melody-making is important to us and somehow we all seem to be good at it, perhaps because we are exposed to it at such an early age. Most everyone goes to music lessons when they are young. And we all have to sing – the making of song is a national art.' According to Holger Jensen, professor of music at Stockholm University, 'Swedes have an almost inborn ability to create easy, nice-sounding melodies.'

State support

At Sweden's secondary schools, any instrument is easily available to anyone who wants to play. Pupils are strongly encouraged to study musical composition. The immediate result is that thousands of bands, from the awful to the superb, play at weekends in front rooms and garages across the country. Another important tradition, dating back to pre-Woodstock days, is that new and established singers and bands can try out their material in so-called people's or folk parks. Abba, notably, were a product of the circuit that has grown up around these free, government-supported, outdoor venues.

Anglophiles

Swedes pride themselves on their ability to speak and sing in English and, because American and British movies are generally subtitled rather than dubbed, they also have a good grasp of American and English idioms. According to one defiant Swedish-language singer, 'on a certain level, we're all American and English wannabes'. There's nothing particularly Swedish about the chart-topping songs that Max Martin and his musicians whip up for Britney Spears and the Backstreet Boys, but some Swedes argue that Martin's ability to imitate Anglo-American pop and add hummable lyrics is itself thoroughly Swedish.

Market economics

Because the domestic Swedish market is so small, real money-making success requires acts to win fans from abroad. In a country where thousands aspire to a music career, to survive for any length of time one needs to be able to create music for the larger, English listening market. As Sanji Tandan, managing director of Warner Brothers Sweden, puts it: 'They've got to be able to make it out there to make it in here.'

Blonde looks

To really, really make it big requires one more crucial factor. As Professor Jensen slyly observes: 'An interesting feature common to Abba, the A-Teans, the Cardigans and others, is the union of male and female – usually with at least one blonde woman.'

Global competitiveness

The advantage that the Swedish environment gives its musicians is an example of many advantages that a competitor gains from its location. Agencies rate these advantages that are often related to the economic growth of nations. For example, an index of economic freedom shows one advantage that businesses in Hong Kong (first), Singapore (second), the US (third) and the UK (fourth) have over businesses in other countries, while indices of entrepreneurial activity show a wide gap between the G8 and EU member states.

SOURCE: Extract from 'Stockholm syndrome', *The Business FT Weekend* (11 November 2000), pp. 18–22; 'Economic freedom', *The Economist* (12 July 2003), p. 94; Jonathan Guthrie, 'Riding up an enterprise league on a surge in commerce', *Financial Times* (9 January 2004), p. 4.

data services that are available to consumer packaged-goods companies. Still, any information they can find will help them form a better estimate of each competitor's strengths and weaknesses.

Companies normally learn about their competitors' strengths and weaknesses through secondary data, personal experience and hearsay. They can also increase their knowledge by conducting primary marketing research with customers, suppliers and dealers. Recently, a growing number of companies have turned to **benchmarking**, comparing the company's products and processes to those of competitors or leading firms in other industries to find ways of improving quality and performance. Benchmarking has become a powerful tool for increasing a company's competitiveness.

In searching for competitors' weaknesses, the company should try to identify any assumptions they make about their business and the market that are no longer valid. Some companies believe they produce the best quality in the industry when this is no longer true. Many companies are victims of rules-of-thumb such as 'customers prefer full-line companies', 'the sales force is the only important marketing tool' or 'customers value service more than price'. If a competitor is operating on a significant wrong assumption, the company can take advantage of it.

Benchmarking—The process of comparing the company's products and processes to those of competitors or leading firms in other industries to find ways to improve quality and performance.

Estimating competitors' reaction patterns

A competitor's objectives, strategies and strengths and weaknesses explain its likely actions, and its reactions to moves such as a price cut, a promotion increase or a new product introduction. In addition, each competitor has a certain philosophy of doing business, a certain internal culture and guiding beliefs. Marketing managers need a deep understanding of a given competitor's mentality if they want to anticipate how that competitor will act or react.

Each competitor reacts differently. Some do not react quickly or strongly to a competitor's move: they may feel that their customers are loyal; they may be slow in noticing the move; they may lack the funds to react. Some competitors react only to certain types of assault and not to others. They might always respond strongly to price cuts in order to signal that these will never succeed. But they might not respond at all to advertising increases, believing these to be less threatening. Other competitors react swiftly and strongly to any assault. As Unilever has found with its Persil/Omo Power, P&G does not let a new detergent come easily into the market. Many firms avoid direct competition with P&G and look for easier prey, knowing that P&G will fight fiercely if challenged. Finally, some competitors show no predictable reaction pattern. They might or might not react on a given occasion and there is no way to foresee what they will do based on their economics, history or anything else.

In some industries, competitors live in relative harmony; in others, they fight constantly. Knowing how key competitors react gives the company clues on how best to attack competitors or how best to defend the company's current positions.[5]

Selecting competitors to attack and avoid

Management has already largely determined its main competitors through prior decisions on customer targets, distribution channels and marketing-mix strategy. These decisions define the strategic group to which the company belongs. Management must now decide which competitors to compete against most vigorously. The company can focus its attack on one of several classes of competitors.

Strong or weak competitors

Most companies prefer to aim their shots at their weak competitors. This requires fewer resources and less time. Conversely, the firm may gain little. Alternatively, the firm should also compete with strong competitors to sharpen its abilities. Furthermore, even strong competitors have some weaknesses and succeeding against them often provides greater returns.

A useful tool for assessing competitor strengths and weaknesses is **customer value analysis** – asking customers what benefits they value and how they rate the company versus competitors on important attributes. Customer value analysis also points out areas in which the company is vulnerable to competitors' actions.

Customer value analysis— Analysis conducted to determine what benefits target customers value and how they rate the relative value of various competitors' offers.

Close or distant competitors

Most companies will compete with those competitors who resemble them the most. Thus, Citroën/Peugeot competes more against Renault than against Porsche. At the same time, the company may want to avoid trying to 'destroy' a close competitor to avoid accusations of excessive monopolistic power or to keep the known competitors as a bulwark against new competitors.

A company really needs and benefits from competitors. The existence of competitors results in several strategic benefits. Competitors may help increase total demand. They share the costs of market and product development, and help to legitimise new technology. They may serve less attractive segments or lead to more product differentiation. Finally, they may improve bargaining power against labour or regulators.

However, a company may not view all of its competitors as beneficial. An industry often contains 'well-behaved' competitors and 'disruptive' competitors. Well-behaved competitors play by the rules of the industry. They favour a stable and healthy industry, set prices in a reasonable relation to costs, motivate others to lower costs or improve differentiation, and accept a reasonable level of market share and profits. Disruptive competitors, on the other hand, break the rules. They try to buy share rather than earn it, seek subsidies, take large risks, invest in overcapacity and generally shake up the industry.

> Currently several leading European airlines are profitable and growing while their American competitors are suffering. The fallout from 9–11 is one reason for this difference in fortunes. Following the destruction of the Twin Towers the US government gave US airlines a subsidy to help them over the resulting commercial hiatus. In contrast, the EU banned such handouts and so forced Europe's leading airlines to slim to economic levels. The European airlines are now benefiting from the rigorous competition they faced, while their US competitors are loaded with the excess capacity and costs that the subsidy funded.[6]

The implication is that 'well-behaved' companies should try to shape an industry that consists only of well-behaved competitors. Through careful licensing, selective retaliation and coalitions, they can make competitors behave rationally and harmoniously, follow the rules, try to earn share rather than buy it, and differentiate somewhat to compete less directly.

Designing the competitive intelligence system

We have described the main types of information that company decision-makers need to know about their competitors. This information needs collecting, interpreting, distributing and using. Although the cost in money and time of gathering competitive intelligence is high, the cost of not gathering it is higher. Yet the company must design its competitive intelligence system in a cost-effective way.

The competitive intelligence system first identifies the vital types of competitive information and the best sources of this information. Then the system continuously collects information from the field (sales force, channels, suppliers, market research firms, trade associations) and from published data (government publications, speeches, articles). Next, the system checks the information for validity and reliability, interprets it and organises it in an appropriate way. Finally, it sends key information to relevant decision-makers and responds to enquiries from managers about competitors.

With this system, company managers will receive timely information about competitors in the form of phone calls, bulletins, newsletters and reports. In addition, managers can contact the system when they need an interpretation of a competitor's sudden move, or when they require to know a competitor's weaknesses and strengths or how a competitor will respond to a planned company move.

Smaller companies that cannot afford to set up a formal competitive intelligence office can assign specific executives to watch specific competitors. Thus a manager who used to work for a competitor might follow closely all developments connected with that competitor; he or she

BODDINGTONS. THE CREAM OF MANCHESTER.
Boddingtons Draught Bitter. Brewed at the Strangeways Brewery since 1778.

Boddingtons single-mindedly focus on the product's attribute, smoothness – as evidenced by the creamy head – to differentiate it.
SOURCE: Bartle Bogle Hegarty (BBH). *Photography*: Tif Hunter.

would be the 'in-house' expert on that competitor. Any manager needing to know the thinking of a given competitor could contact the assigned in-house expert.

Competitive strategies

Having identified and evaluated the main competitors, the company must now design competitive marketing strategies that best position its offer against competitors' offerings.[7] What broad marketing strategies can the company use? Which ones are best for a particular company or for the company's different divisions and products?

No one strategy is best for all companies. Each company must determine what makes the most sense, given its position in the industry and its objectives, opportunities and resources. Even within a company, different businesses or products need different strategies. Johnson & Johnson uses one marketing strategy for its leading brands in stable consumer markets and a different marketing strategy for its new high-tech healthcare businesses and products. We now look at broad competitive marketing strategies that companies can use.

Competitive positions

Firms competing in a given target market will, at any moment, differ in their objectives and resources. Some firms will be large, others small. Some will have great resources, others will be strapped for funds. Some will be old and established, others new and fresh. Some will strive for rapid market share growth, others for long-term profits. And the firms will occupy different competitive positions in the target market.

Michael Porter suggests four basic competitive positioning strategies that companies can follow – three winning strategies and one losing one.[8] The three winning strategies are:

1. *Overall cost leadership*. Here the company works hard to achieve the lowest costs of production and distribution, so that it can price lower than its competitors and win a large market share. After years of stable industrial structures, changes in the economics of the EU and technology have stimulated a rush for mergers and acquisitions as once nationally dominant firms struggle for scale in the enlarged market. The biggest grab of all has been Vodafone AirTouch's acquisition of Mannesmann. Another major consolidation is aerospace where the aim is to use scale and lean production to drive costs down.[9]

   However, big is not always beautiful. In the steel industry small mini-mills, including Nucor and Chaparral Steel, which use electric furnaces to convert scrap metal, are undercutting the large integrated suppliers, while in retailing big stores are struggling against more nimble and more focused competitors. Scale can sometimes help cut costs but, by itself, it is neither a necessary nor a sufficient way of achieving overall cost leadership.

2. *Differentiation*. Here the company concentrates on creating a highly differentiated product line and marketing programme, so that it comes across as the class leader in the industry. Most customers would prefer to own this brand if its price is not too high. Bose follows this strategy with its ultra-small hi-fi speakers as do Dualit with Alissi with their stylish and fun kitchen utensils.

   Pharmaceutical company GSK claims it has the 'best pipeline in the industry'. That keeps their share prices up when 'the pipeline' is their term for new and unique drugs in various stages of development and testing. For 2006 they anticipate launching their 162 'Better Welburtin' (anti-depressant), 698 (rhinitis/asthma) and dual acting COX2 (pain and schizophrenia). In each of these markets GSK hopes their differentiated treatments will give them an edge on the competition.[10]

3. *Focus*. Here the company focuses its effort on serving a few market segments well rather than going after the whole market. Many firms in northern Italy excel at this. Among them are Luxottica, the world's leading maker of spectacle frames, pasta makers Barilla, and many dynamic small textile firms in the Prato. In an industrial market Domnick Hunter delivers double-digit growth by focusing on its world-beating expertise in industrial filtration products that are essential from nanotechnology to incubators for premature babies.[11]

Companies that pursue a clear strategy – one of the above – are likely to perform well. The firm that carries out that strategy best will make the most profits. Firms that do not pursue a clear strategy – *middle-of-the-roaders* – do the worst. Olivetti, Philips and Marks & Spencer all came upon difficult times because they did not stand out as the lowest in cost, highest in perceived value or best in serving some market segment. Middle-of-the-roaders try to be good on all strategic counts, but end up being not very good at anything.

Examples abound of products and services caught in the middle – adequate but not exciting – losing ground to more clearly positioned competitors at both the high and low ends. For example, swanky stores such as Gap and budget outlets such as Aldi and Matalan are prospering, while long-established high

> street stores flounder. Häagen-Dazs, Ben & Jerry's and other 'super-premium' ice-creams are thriving – as are grocers' own bargain labels – while middle brands such as Crosse & Blackwell are struggling. Travellers want either economy lodging at chains such as Travelodge or to sleep in the lap of luxury; want to fly business class from London Docklands airport or frill-free easyJet. Operations in the 'murky middle' face increasing pressure from competitors at both ends of the spectrum.

Competitive moves

Businesses maintain their position in the marketplace by making *competitive moves* to attack competitors or defend themselves against competitive threats. These moves change with the role that firms play in the target market – that of leading, challenging, following or niching. Suppose that an industry contains the firms shown in Figure 12.2. Some 40 per cent of the market is in the hands of the **market leader**, the firm with the largest market share. Another 30 per cent is in the hands of a **market challenger**, a runner-up that is fighting hard to increase its market share. Another 20 per cent is in the hands of a **market follower**, another runner-up that wants to hold its share without rocking the boat. The remaining 10 per cent is in the hands of **market nichers**, firms that serve small segments not being pursued by other firms.

We now look at specific marketing strategies that are available to market leaders, challengers, followers and nichers. In the sections that follow, you should remember that the classifications of competitive positions often apply not to a whole company, but only to its position in a specific industry. For example, large and diversified companies such as P&G, Unilever, Nestlé, Procordia or Société Générale de Belgique – or their individual businesses, divisions or products – might be leaders in some markets and nichers in others. For example, Procter & Gamble leads in dishwashing and laundry detergents, disposable nappies and shampoo, but it is a challenger to Unilever in hand soaps. Companies' competitive strengths also vary geographically. Buying Alpo from Grand Metropolitan in 1994 made Nestlé the challenger in the US pet-foods market behind Ralston Purina's 18 per cent share. However, in the submarket for US canned cat food, Nestlé has a commanding 39 per cent share. By contrast, in the fragmented European pet-foods market, Nestlé Friskies languishes in fourth place behind Mars' Pedigree (47 per cent), Dalgety and Quaker. However, even with that low base, Nestlé's Go Cat is Europe's top-selling dry cat food.

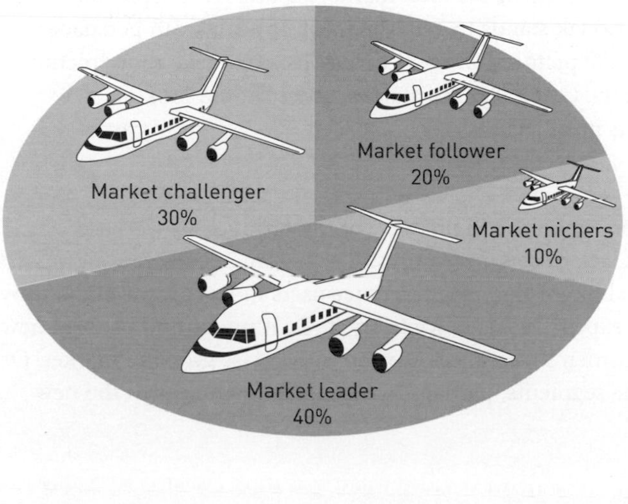

Market leader—The firm in an industry with the largest market share; it usually leads other firms in price changes, new product introductions, distribution coverage and promotion spending.

Market challenger—A runner-up firm in an industry that is fighting hard to increase its market share.

Market follower—A runner-up firm in an industry that wants to hold its share without rocking the boat.

Market nicher—A firm in an industry that serves small segments that the other firms overlook or ignore.

Figure 12.2 **Market structure**

Market challenger
30%

Market follower
20%

Market nichers
10%

Market leader
40%

Market-leader strategies

Most industries contain an acknowledged market leader. The leader has the largest market share and usually leads the other firms in price changes, new product introductions, distribution coverage and promotion spending. The leader may or may not be admired, but other firms concede its dominance. The leader is a focal point for competitors, a company to challenge, imitate or avoid. Some of the best-known market leaders are Boeing (airliners), Nestlé (food), Microsoft (software), L'Oréal (cosmetics), McDonald's (fast food) and De Beer (diamonds).

> Manchester United certainly do not win all football championships but they are overpowering leaders as a world sports brand. The club's global membership and merchandising swamps all other. This generates wealth that allows them to buy players at prices that would make other teams wince. In Britain's high-spending Premier League MUFC is valued at more than all the other teams together![12]

A leader's life is not easy. It must maintain a constant watch. Other firms keep challenging its strengths or trying to take advantage of its weaknesses. The market leader can easily miss a turn in the market and plunge into second or third place. A product innovation may come along and hurt the leader (as when Nokia's and Ericsson's digital phones took the lead from Motorola's analogue models). The leader might grow arrogant or complacent and misjudge the competition. This has resulted in General Motors and Ford losing sales in Europe; after underestimating revitalised competition from VW and Renault, the US giants concentrated their activities in the US. Other leaders might look old-fashioned against new and peppier rivals (as when Britain's Marks & Spencer lost serious ground to more current or stylish brands like Gap, Lees, Tommy Hilfiger, DKNY and Guess).[13]

Remaining an industry leader demands action on four fronts. First, the firm can limit competitive pressures by alliances or mergers. Second, the firm must find ways to expand total demand. Third, the firm can try to expand its market share further, even if market size remains constant. Fourth, a company can retain its strength by reducing its costs. Fifth, the firm must protect its current market share through good defensive and offensive actions (Figure 12.3).

Expanding the total market

The leading firm normally gains the most when the total market expands. If people take more pictures, then as the market leader, Kodak stands to gain the most. If Kodak can persuade more people to take pictures, or to take pictures on more occasions, or to take more pictures on each occasion, it will benefit greatly. Generally, the market leader should look for new users, new uses and more usage of its products.

New users

Every product class can attract buyers who are still unaware of the product, or who are resisting it because of its price or its lack of certain features. A seller can usually find new users in many places. For example, L'Oréal might find new fragrance users in its current markets by convincing women who do not use expensive fragrance to try it. Or it might find users in new demographic segments: for instance, men's fragrances are currently a fast-growing market. Or it might expand into new geographic segments, perhaps by selling its fragrances to the new wealthy in eastern Europe.

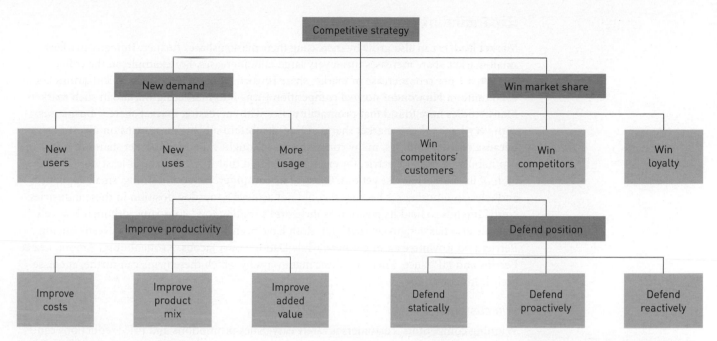

Figure 12.3 **Market leader strategies**

In prudish UK, market leader *Ann Summers* is expanding the market by making 'accessible sex shops' mainstream and by appealing to women. Says owner Jacqueline Gold, '70 per cent of our sales are lingerie. It's the fun element, people, and particularly women, enjoy coming into the store.' Having purchased niche retailer *Knickerbox*, the company aim to have a sex shop on every high street within three years.[14]

New uses

The marketer can expand markets by discovering and promoting new uses for the product. DuPont's nylon is an example of new-use expansion. Every time nylon became a mature product, some new use appeared. Nylon was first used as a fibre for parachutes, then for women's stockings, later as a leading material in shirts and blouses, and still later in vehicle tyres, upholstery and carpeting.

More usage

A third market expansion strategy is to persuade people to use the product more often or to use more per occasion. Campbell encourages people to consume more of its soup by running ads using it as an ingredient in recipes in women's magazines. P&G advises users that its Head & Shoulders shampoo is more effective with two applications instead of one per hair wash.

The Michelin Tyre Company found a creative way to increase usage per occasion. It wanted French car owners to drive more miles per year, resulting in more tyre replacement. Michelin began rating French restaurants on a three-star system and publishing them in its Red Guides. It reported that many of the best restaurants were in the south of France, leading many Parisians to take weekend drives south. Michelin also publishes its Green Guide containing maps and graded sights to encourage additional travel.

Expanding market share

Market leaders can also grow by increasing their market shares further. In many markets, small market-share increases mean very large sales increases. For example, in the coffee market, a 1 per cent increase in market share is worth about €50 million; in soft drinks about €500 million! No wonder normal competition turns into marketing warfare in such markets. Many studies have found that profitability rises with increasing market share.[15] Businesses with very large relative market shares averaged substantially higher returns on investment. Because of these findings, many companies have sought expanded market shares to improve profitability. General Electric, for example, declared that it wants to be at least no. 1 or 2 in each of its markets or else get out. GE shed its computer, air-conditioning, small appliances and television businesses because it could not achieve a top-dog position in these industries. Nestlé intends to hold its position as the world's leading food company, although France's Danone also has designs on that spot. Both have been acquiring businesses, Nestlé buying Perrier and Rowntree among others, while Danone own Jacobs, Kronenbourg, Amora, Lea & Perrins and HP sauce. There are three main ways by which these firms can further increase their leading position.

Win customers

Winning competitors' customers is rarely easy. Sales promotions and price reductions can produce increased share quickly, but such gains are made at the expense of profitability and disappear once the promotion ends. Exceptions to this are price fights stimulated by market leaders with more resources than competitors. Internet businesses are currently absorbing huge losses as they use low price and high advertising expenditure to buy share in the growing market.

In the long term, market share gains are achieved by investment in quality, innovation or brand building. For instance, Mercedes' new C-Class model has helped the company increase its sales by 23 per cent. Sales were up 40 per cent in western Europe (excluding Germany), 34 per cent in the United States and 30 per cent in Japan. In Germany the 38 per cent growth gave a 2 per cent rise in market share.

Win competitors

The forces at play in a company's microenvironment are discussed in Chapter 3. Michael Porter graphically portrayed companies squeezed in a first dimension between suppliers customers who limit the profits a firm can make (shown in Figure 3.1) and market between entrants in a second dimension who can take market share, and makers of substitutes who can replace the market entirely.[16] Take, for example, Kodak. In the Third World markets they are now entering, their profits are limited by how much relatively poor consumers will pay. At the same time the company is forced to pay suppliers at world market rates for the chemicals, components and raw materials it uses to make films. For many years, Kodak has had to fight off Fuji, a Japanese company that had entered many of Kodak's markets. Now Kodak faces the biggest challenge of all, from memory devices in the digital cameras that are replacing the optical cameras that use Kodak films.

Through alliances and mergers, corporations can increase their profitability by changing the competitive environment. Governments realise this and therefore block deals that give companies too much marketing power. One case is the blocking of the proposed merger of American Airlines and British Airways, since the link would give them too much power at London's Heathrow airport.

The 8 Cs framework (Figure 12.4) shows how corporations can increase their marketing power through mergers and alliances. They can have links with:

■ *Competitors.* This automatically increases a company's strength in the market and its buying power. Acquisitions and mergers between one-time competitors are always occurring as firms try to grow to face global competition. The names of many leading

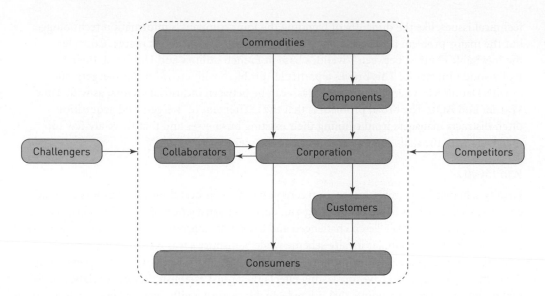

Figure 12.4 **The 8 Cs competitive domain**

companies reflect past mergers: DaimlerChrysler, Vivendi Universal and GSK (GlaxoSmithKline) and Lloyds TSB.

- *Challengers.* It is common for established companies to grow by acquiring small companies that challenge existing products or bring exciting new ideas. Hence the purchase of new-age products, such as Snapple or Ben & Jerry's ice-cream, by food giants.

- *Collaborators.* These can be outside the industry but add some marketing strength to an alliance. One such link-up is between McDonald's, Coca-Cola and Disney; another is between Motorola and Microsoft to provide web-enabled mobile phones.

- *Commodities.* Oil companies own major brands but most of their stock market valuation is based upon their oil reserves. When Royal Dutch/Shell revised their estimated reserves downward their share price immediately fell.

- *Components.* Many car companies own companies that supply them. Many firms have pulled away from the risk of too much vertical integration that compounds the risk of any downturn in sales. Once GM used to own the rubber plantations as a source of raw materials for the tyres they put on their automobiles. An increasing number of global companies, such as Nike, own the brand and little else. Their strength is in design and marketing where most value is added, and not in low value-added activities, such as manufacturing.

- *Customers.* Just as oil companies own their raw material supplier, the refiners also own the petrol stations that sell their branded fuel to consumers. Some luxury goods makers both own their stores and design, market and manufacture their products to keep control of the goods and their customers' experience.

- *Consumers.* It is rare that customers have corporate alliances with the final consumer, although there are some creative exceptions. Bruichladdich, an independent maker of Islay single malt whisky, entices its customers to invest in barrels, hogsheads or butts of their newly distilled spirit that will mature for at least 10 years (£2,295 for 500 litres in a fresh sherry butt!). By this mechanism, by investing in maturing whisky, the customer and the corporation become one.[17]

Big mergers grab headlines but making an acquisition is easier than making it work. Besides raising the wrath of regulatory bodies, most mergers fail. The Boston Consulting Group estimates that 64 per cent of recent US acquisitions actually destroyed value for the acquirer's shareholders. There are several reasons for the high failure rate. These include technical issues, like the difficulty of blending the joint company's information technology, but the major problem is the clash of cultures when two organisations merge. Consider the inevitable contrast between Vivendi's base in French utilities and Universal, their Hollywood film studio. This proves a particular problem with cross-border mergers, such as with DaimlerChrysler, although the clash can be between industrial sectors, as with Time Warner and AOL. The broad problem is that the excitement of mergers and acquisitions often distracts managers from running their existing businesses and that there are few top managers with the skills or interest to manage the merger to success.[18]

Win loyalty

Loyalty schemes have grown hugely in recent years. At their best these are attempts to build customer relationships based on the long-run customer satisfaction discussed in Chapter 11. In the UK grocery market Tesco challenged and overtook Sainsbury's as the market leader by introducing a hugely popular loyalty scheme while Sainsbury's was resisting the trend. Too often these schemes are sales promotions where the customer's loyalty is to the scheme, not the company using it. To have any lasting effects they must establish customer relationships that go beyond collecting points that are redeemable against a gift. Such schemes are easy to follow and once everyone has one, they impose a cost with little benefit.

Gaining increased market share will improve a company's profitability automatically. Much depends on its strategy for gaining increased market share. We see many high-share companies with low profitability and many low-share companies with high profitability. The cost of buying higher market share may far exceed the returns. Higher shares tend to produce higher profits only when unit costs fall with increased market share, or when the company's premium price covers the cost of supplying higher-quality goods.

In addition, many industries contain one or a few highly profitable large firms, several profitable and more focused firms, and a large number of medium-sized firms with poorer profit performance. For example, BMW holds only a small share of the total car market, but it earns high profits because it is a high-share company in its luxury car segment. It achieved this high share in its served market because it does other things right, such as producing high quality, giving good service and holding down its costs.

Improving productivity

Market productivity means squeezing more profits out of the same volume of sales. The size advantage of market leaders can give them lower costs than the competition. Size itself is not sufficient to achieve low costs because this could be achieved by owning unrelated activities that impose extra costs. The lowest costs often occur when a market leader, such as McDonald's, keeps its business simple. The buying and selling of subsidiary businesses often reflects businesses trying to gain strength by simplifying their activities. This explains the sales of Orangina, a soft-drinks business, to Coca-Cola for €760m by the French drinks company Pernod Ricard. By this transaction Coca-Cola gains in efficiency and scale by having more soft drinks to sell globally. With the proceeds from the sale, Pernod Ricard aims to add more wines and spirits brands to its existing range, which includes Wild Turkey, Dubonnet, Havana Club and Jacob's Creek.

Improve costs

To remain competitive, market leaders fight continually to reduce costs. After facing difficulties in the early 1990s, Mercedes used all the classical means of cutting costs:

- *Reduce capital cost.* Firms reduce their capital cost by doing less or doing things quickly. Just-in-time (JIT) methods mean firms have less capital tied up in raw materials, work in progress on the shop floor and finished goods. By accelerating its product development

Mercedes will increase its market responsiveness and accumulated development costs. It will also reduce capital costs by doing less itself. Component manufacturers will provide more preassembled parts and a joint venture with a Romanian company will make car-interior parts.

■ *Reduce fixed costs.* Mercedes acknowledges that Japan's manufacturers have on average a 35 per cent cost advantage over their German competitors. Japan's lower capital costs and longer working hours explain only 10 per cent of the difference. Mercedes responded by cutting 18,000 jobs to save €3 billion. Forced redundancies are almost unknown in Germany, so the deduction is made by the 'social measures' of the non-replacement of people, early retirement and retraining.

■ *Reduce variable cost.* Mercedes' new car plant at Rastatt has pioneered new methods of 'lean production', logistics, total quality and workforce management. Car design has also changed. It will be quicker, and cars are now designed to a target price, rather than the old method of making the best car and then pricing it. The lessons are passed on to Mercedes' suppliers who work closer to Mercedes' research and development. The aim is to reduce the number of parts fitted at the works. The company has also changed its 'Made in Germany' policy, to produce where labour costs are lower.

Change product mix

The aim here is to sell more high-margin vehicles. Mercedes has filled out its range with its M-series sports utility vehicles, the super-luxury Maybach and the Smart sports cars – all growth areas commanding premium prices. Moving into these markets will reduce Mercedes' dependence on its 'lower-priced' models.

Add value

Mercedes makes and sells cars, but its customers want prestige and transport. Mercedes can add value by offering long-term service contracts, leasing deals or other financial packages that make buying easier and less risky for customers. In the past, Mercedes sold basic models that were poorly equipped by modern standards. Customers then paid extra to have a car custom-made for them with the features they wanted. The 'Made in Germany' label that has served the company for so long is no longer enough to command a premium price. The aim is to maintain a price premium by the brand's strength and superior quality across a broad range of products. This contrasts with the Japanese, whose well-equipped luxury Lexus (Toyota), Acura (Honda) and Infiniti (Nissan) brands have tightly targeted small ranges.

Defending its position

While trying to expand total market size, the leading firm must also constantly protect its current business against competitor attacks. AXA must constantly guard against ING in the life assurance market; Exxon against BP; Gillette against Bic; Kodak against Fuji; Boeing against Airbus; Nestlé against Unilever.

What can the market leader do to protect its position? First, it must prevent or fix weaknesses that provide opportunities for competitors. It needs to keep its costs down and its prices in line with the value that the customers see in the brand. The leader should 'plug holes' so that competitors do not jump in. The best defence is a good offence and the best response is *continuous innovation*. The leader refuses to be content with the way things are and leads the industry in new products, customer services, distribution effectiveness and cost cutting. It keeps increasing its competitive effectiveness and value to customers. It takes the offensive, sets the pace and exploits competitors' weaknesses.

Increased competition in recent years has sparked management's interest in models of military warfare. Leader companies can protect their market positions with competitive

Figure 12.5 Defence strategies

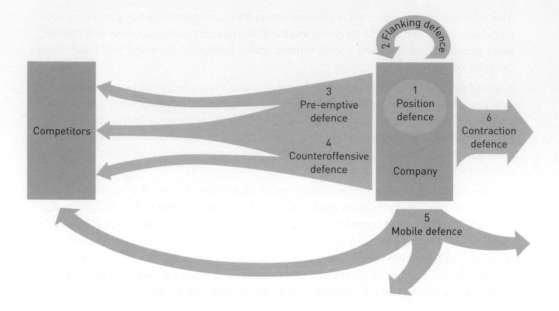

strategies patterned after successful military defence strategies. Figure 12.5 shows six defence strategies that a market leader can use.[19]

Position defence

The most basic defence is a position defence in which a company holds on to its position by building fortifications around its markets. Simply defending one's current position or products rarely works. Henry Ford tried it with his Model T and brought an enviably healthy Ford Motor Company to the brink of financial ruin. Even lasting brands such as Coca-Cola and Nescafé cannot supply all future growth and profitability for their companies. These brands must be improved and adapted to changing conditions and new brands developed. Coca-Cola today, in spite of being the world leader in soft drinks, is aggressively extending its beverage lines and has diversified into desalinisation equipment and plastics.

Flanking defence

When trying to hold its overall position, the market leader should watch its weaker flanks closely. Smart competitors will normally attack the company's weaknesses. Thus the Japanese successfully entered the US small car market because local carmakers left a gaping hole in that submarket. Using a flanking defence, the company carefully checks its flanks and protects the more vulnerable ones. In this way Nestlé's Nescafé and Gold Blend have the support of flanking brands Blend 37, Alta Rica and Cap Colombie. By Unilever acquiring Ben & Jerry's ice-creams and Cadbury Schweppes buying Snapple, the two multinationals are more able to defend their mainstream markets against 'new age' offerings.[20]

Pre-emptive defence

The leader can be proactive and launch a pre-emptive defence, striking competitors before they can move against the company. A pre-emptive defence assumes that an ounce of prevention is worth a pound of cure. Thus, when threatened by the entry of grocery discounters Aldi and Lidl into the UK market, Tesco and Asda fought back with all-time low price budget ranges. These lines took away the discounter's advantage while Tesco and Asda retained their overall value and 'one-stop-shopping' convenience to time-pressed consumers. Aldi did gain a toehold in the market but Tesco and Asda continued to gain market share.[21]

Trading with the market leader has its advantages.

Greater liquidity, in the first place. Eurex is the market leader in European fixed income derivatives with futures and options on the Euro Bund, Euro Bobl and Euro Schatz. Our extensive product range provides you with the right hedging and trading tools to optimize your investments. Small wonder the world's most heavily traded fixed income futures are listed and traded at Eurex. Think big. Think Eurex. www.eurexchange.com

what can we do for you? **E⊃X** eurex

Counteroffensive defence

When attacked, despite its flanking or pre-emptive efforts, a market leader may have to be reactive and launch a counteroffensive defence. When Mars' attack on the ice-cream market, using its brand extensions of Mars Bars, Snickers, Bounty and so on, created a new product class of ice-confectionery. Unilever's Walls ice-cream division, which is market leader in parts of Europe, had difficulty countering this because it had no confectionery brands to use in that way. It overcame the problem by developing brand extensions of Cadbury's products, a competitor of Mars, which has no ice-cream interests.

Sometimes companies hold off for a while before countering. This may seem a dangerous game of 'wait and see', but there are often good reasons for not jumping in immediately. By waiting, the company can understand more fully the competitor's attack and perhaps find a gap through which to launch a successful counteroffensive.

Mobile defence

In a mobile defence a company is proactive in aggressively defending a current market position. The leader stretches to new markets that can serve as future bases for defence and attack. Through *market broadening*, the company shifts its focus from the current product to the broader underlying consumer need. For example, Armstrong Cork redefined its focus from 'floor covering' to 'decorative room covering' (including walls and ceilings) and expanded into related businesses balanced for growth and defence. *Market diversification* into unrelated industries is the other alternative for generating 'strategic depth'. When tobacco companies such as British American Tobacco (BAT) and Philip Morris faced growing curbs on cigarette smoking, they moved quickly into new consumer products industries.

Contraction defence

Large companies sometimes find they can no longer defend all of their positions, since their resources are spread too thinly and competitors are nibbling away on several fronts. So they react with a contracting defence (or strategic withdrawal). The company gives up weaker positions and concentrates its resources on stronger ones.

> The British motorcycle industry showed an extreme case of a contracting defence. Norton, Triumph, BSA, etc. once dominated the world motorcycle market. First challenged by the small bikes made by Honda, Yamaha and others, they contracted into making medium-sized (250 cc) to super-bikes. When the Japanese made 250 cc machines, the British market retreated from entry-level machines to concentrate on larger ones. Eventually only Triumph and Norton super-bikes remained as small, out-of-date specialist manufacturers facing the Japanese giants, and they did not last long. A successful contracting defence must be a retreat into a position of strength.

The American car manufacturers are close to facing the same fate as did the British motorcycle industry. Faced with competition from Japanese and European car manufacturers, GM, Ford and Chrysler retreated to their heartland, selling increasingly large trucks and sports utility vehicles in middle America and the South. Meanwhile Japanese and European carmakers came to dominate passenger car sales, particularly along the East and West coasts. After first resorting to profit squeezing discounts to hold market share, the US manufacturers are now launching a huge range of cars to try to capture the market lost in their contracting defence. The lesson is the need to recognise when a contracting defence leaves a company with too small a base to ensure its survival or allows an attacker to build too dominant a position.[22]

Market-challenger strategies

Firms that are second, third or lower in an industry are sometimes very large. Many European market leaders are in this position relative to their major US or Japanese competitors. Table 12.2 shows some of them. These runner-up firms can adopt one of two competitive strategies: they can attack the leader and other competitors in an aggressive bid

Table 12.2 European leaders' world ranking

Sector	World leader	Revenue (€bn)	European leader	Revenue (€bn)	World ranking
Aerospace	Boeing (US)	54	EABS	26	2
Airlines	AMR (US)	17	Lufthansa	16	3
Beverages	Coca-Cola (US)	20	Diageo	13	4
General merchandisers	Wal-Mart (US)	247	Pinault-Printemps	26	6
Motors	GM (US)	187	DaimlerChrysler	141	3
Petroleum	Exxon Mobil (US)	182	Royal Dutch/Shell	179	2
Pharmaceuticals	Merck (US)	52	GSK	32	4
Telecommunications	Nippon (J)	90	Deutsche Telekom	51	3

SOURCE: Adapted from FORTUNE Global 500, copyright © 2004 Time Inc.; All right reserved. **www.Fortune.com.**

for more market share (market challengers), or they can play along with competitors and not rock the boat (market followers). We now look at competitive strategies for market challengers.

Defining the strategic objective and the competitor

A market challenger must first define its strategic objective. Most market challengers seek to increase their profitability by increasing their market shares. The strategic objective chosen depends on who the competitor is. In most cases, the company can choose which competitors it will challenge.

The challenger can attack the market leader – a high-risk but potentially high-gain strategy that makes good sense if the leader is not serving the market well. To succeed with such an attack, a company must have some sustainable competitive advantage over the leader – a cost advantage leading to lower prices or the ability to provide better value at a premium price.

> For a long time Diageo's Burger King has challenged McDonald's in the US home market on taste, but its recent challenges, including an accelerated programme of building new outlets, better value (with 75 per cent more meat than a Big Mac) and direct taste challenges, have got McDonald's reeling. After 'The taste that beat McDonald's fries' came 'Get ready for a taste that beats Big Mac' and Free FryDay promotions. Meanwhile Mac's new Arch Deluxe burger bombed and a sales promotion deal with too many strings alienated customers.[23]

The challenger can avoid the leader and instead attack firms its own size, or smaller local and regional firms. Many of these firms are underfinanced and will not be serving their customers well. Several of the large beer companies grew to their present size not by attacking large competitors, but by gobbling up small local or regional competitors.

Thus the challenger's strategic objective depends on which competitor it chooses to attack. If the company goes after the market leader, its objective may be to wrest a certain market share. Bic knows that it cannot topple Gillette in the razor market – it simply wants a larger share. Or the challenger's goal might be to take over market leadership. Dell entered the personal computer market late, as a challenger, but quickly became the market leader. If the

Figure 12.6 Attack strategies

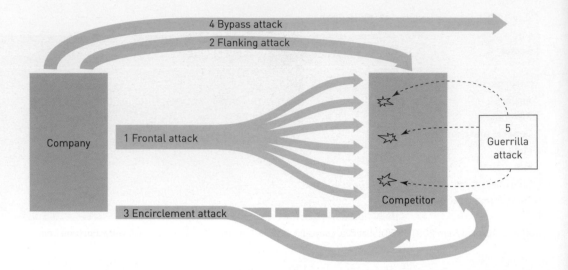

company goes after a small local company, its objective may be to put that company out of business. The important point remains: the company must choose its opponents carefully and have a clearly defined and attainable objective.

Choosing an attack strategy

How can the market challenger best attack the chosen competitor and achieve its strategic objectives? Figure 12.6 shows five possible attack strategies.

Frontal attack

In a full frontal attack, the challenger matches the competitor's product, advertising, price and distribution efforts. It attacks the competitor's strengths rather than its weaknesses. The outcome depends on who has the greater strength and endurance. Even great size and strength may not be enough to challenge a firmly entrenched and resourceful competitor successfully.

> Unilever has twice the worldwide sales of P&G and five times the sales of Colgate-Palmolive, but its American subsidiary trails P&G by a wide margin in the United States. Unilever launched a full frontal assault against P&G in the detergent market while Unilever's Wisk was already the leading liquid detergent. In quick succession, it added a barrage of new products – Sunlight dishwashing detergent, Snuggle fabric softener, Surf laundry powder – and backed them with aggressive promotion and distribution efforts. P&G spent heavily to defend its brands and held on to most of its business. It counter-attacked with Liquid Tide, which came from nowhere in just 17 months to run neck-and-neck with Wisk. Unilever did gain market share, but most of it came from smaller competitors.[24]

If the market challenger has fewer resources than the competitor, a frontal attack makes little sense.

THE AIRBUS FAMILY.
NEXT STOP,
SEVENTH HEAVEN.

The A320 is the world's best selling family of passenger jet. The A330 is the most efficient aircraft in its category. The A340 is the most widely distributed aircraft among airlines in its category. Throughout the Airbus family you'll find the same quality of technology and design. When it comes to improving your fleet, we'll stop at nothing.

AIRBUS
SETTING THE STANDARDS

For many years the challenger in the airlines market, Airbus can now claim to have 'the world's best selling family of passenger jet, the most efficient and widely distributed aircraft in its category'.
SOURCE: Airbus. *Agency*: Euro RSCG WNEK Gosper.

Flanking attack

Rather than attacking head-on, the challenger can launch a flanking attack. The competitor often concentrates its resources to protect its strongest positions, but it usually has some weaker flanks. By attacking these weak spots, the challenger can concentrate its strength against the competitor's weakness. Flank attacks make good sense when the company has fewer resources than the competitor.

> When Airbus Industries started making airliners it was up against Boeing, a company that dominated the industry. Lockheed and McDonnell Douglas had once challenged Boeing as plane makers, but Lockheed had withdrawn from the industry and McDonnell Douglas was reduced to making derivatives of its old aircraft. Airbus's first move was to develop the A300 with range and payload performance different from Boeing's established 727, 737 and 747 range. Airbus is now topping the Boeing range with its super-jumbo and has a healthier order book than Boeing.[25]

Another flanking strategy is to find gaps that are not filled by the industry's products, fill them and develop them into strong segments. European and Japanese carmakers did not compete with American carmakers by producing large, flashy, gas-guzzling contraptions. Instead they recognised an unserved consumer segment that wanted small, fuel-efficient cars and moved to fill this hole. To their satisfaction and Detroit's surprise, the segment grew to be a large part of the market. From that platform the Japanese, in particular, are now attacking America's heartland of large trucks and sports utility vehicles.

Encirclement attack

An encirclement attack involves attacking from all directions, so that the competitor must protect its front, sides and rear at the same time. The encirclement strategy makes sense when the challenger has superior resources and believes that it can break the competitor's hold on the market quickly. An example is Seiko's attack on the watch market. For several years, Seiko has been gaining distribution in every big watch outlet and overwhelming competitors with its variety of constantly changing models. In most markets Seiko offers about 400 models, but its marketing strength is backed by the 2,300 models it makes and sells worldwide.

Bypass attack

A bypass attack is an indirect strategy. The challenger bypasses the competitor and targets easier markets. The bypass can involve diversifying into unrelated products, moving into new geographic markets or leapfrogging into new technologies to replace existing products. Technological leapfrogging is a bypass strategy used often in high-technology industries. Instead of copying the competitor's product and mounting a costly frontal attack, the challenger patiently develops the next technology. When satisfied with its superiority, it launches an attack where it has an advantage.

> After carefully defending its dominant hold on the film market by inventing new and better film formats, Kodak is reeling under the huge decline in film sales as consumers switch to digital. This sudden switch should have been no surprise to Kodak; only a couple of decades ago the company lost huge sales when consumers dumped their cine cameras in favour of video cameras. Kodak's current response to this bypass attack is to retreat into markets, such as India and China, where film sales are rising.

Guerrilla attack

A guerrilla attack is another option available to market challengers, especially smaller or poorly financed ones:

> British Airways is facing Virgin Atlantic run by a much wilier entrepreneur, Richard Branson. He makes guerrilla attacks on his much larger competitors. In these attacks the agile challenger typically makes small, periodic attacks to harass and demoralise the competitor, hoping eventually to establish permanent footholds. It might use selective price cuts, novel products, executive raids, intense promotional outbursts or assorted legal actions. Virgin has been successful so far and taken 22 per cent of the London to New York market. It is also expanding quickly using franchising, an approach new to the airline industry.

Normally, guerrilla actions are by smaller firms against larger ones. The smaller firms need to be aware, however, that continuous guerrilla campaigns can be expensive and must eventually be followed by a stronger attack if the challenger wishes to 'beat' the competitor. A recent

Virgin is one of the world's leading airlines but still plays the part of the challenger. Like this ad, much of its advertising is attackingly comparative.
SOURCE: Virgin Atlantic.

book, *Radical Marketing*, praises companies such as Harley-Davidson and Virgin Atlantic Airways for succeeding by breaking many of the 'rules' of marketing strategy.[26]

Market-follower strategies

Not all runner-up companies will challenge the market leader. The effort to draw away the leader's customers is never taken lightly by the leader. If the challenger's lure is lower prices, improved service or additional product features, the leader can quickly match these to diffuse the attack. The leader probably has more staying power in an all-out battle. A hard fight might leave both firms worse off and this means the challenger must think twice before attacking. Many firms therefore prefer to follow rather than attack the leader.

A follower can gain many advantages. The market leader often bears the huge expenses involved with developing new products and markets, expanding distribution channels, and informing and educating the market. The reward for all this work and risk is normally market leadership. The market follower, on the other hand, can learn from the leader's experience and copy or improve on the leader's products and marketing programmes, usually at a much lower investment. Although the follower will probably not overtake the leader, it can often be as profitable.[27]

In some industries – such as steel, fertilisers and chemicals – opportunities for differentiation are low, service quality is often comparable and price sensitivity runs high. Price wars can erupt at any time. Companies in these industries avoid short-run grabs for market share because the strategy only provokes retaliation. Most firms decide against stealing each other's customers. Instead they present similar offers to buyers, usually by copying the leader. Market shares show a high stability.

This is not to say that market followers are without strategies. A market follower must know how to hold current customers and win a fair share of new ones. Each follower tries to bring distinctive advantages to its target market – location, services, financing. The follower is a primary target of attack by challengers. Therefore, the market follower must keep its manufacturing costs low and its product quality and services high. It must also enter new markets as they appear. Following is not the same as being passive or a carbon copy of the leader. The follower has to define a growth path, but one that does not create competitive retaliation.

The market-follower firms fall into one of three broad types. The *cloner* closely copies the leader's products, distribution, advertising and other marketing moves. It originates nothing – it simply attempts to live off the market leader's investments. IBM's demise started after outsourcing (286 chips from Intel and the MS-DOS operating system from Microsoft) and open architecture allowed low-cost market entrants to copy its PCs.

The *imitator* copies some things from the leader, but maintains some differentiation with packaging, advertising, pricing and other factors. The leader does not mind the imitator as long as the imitator does not attack aggressively. The imitator may even help the leader avoid the charges of monopoly.

> Today's imitators are often retailers making look-alike own brands. The British Producers and Brand Owners Group (BPOG) was formed in response to own brands aping the market leaders too closely. Sainsbury's highly publicised launch of Classic Cola precipitated BPOG's formation and resulted in the retailer backing off. Other confrontations include Sainsbury's Full Roast (based on Nescafé) and Tesco's Unbelievable low-fat spread (close to Van den Bergh's I Can't Believe It's Not Butter).

Finally, the *adapter* builds on the leader's products and marketing programmes, often improving them. The adapter may choose to sell to different markets to avoid direct confrontation with the leader. Many IBM PC lookalikes did this – Amstrad became one of the earliest successful marketers in the PC market when it started selling its ready-for-use machines through conventional electrical goods retailers rather than computer specialists. Now Dell combine direct selling with excellent customer support. Often the adapter grows into a future challenger.

Market-nicher strategies

Almost every industry includes firms that specialise in serving market niches. Instead of pursuing the whole market or even large segments of the market, these firms target segments within segments or niches. This is particularly true of smaller firms because of their limited resources. The main point is that firms with low shares of the total market can be highly profitable through clever niching (see Marketing Insights 12.2).

Concentrated marketing: nice niches

12.2

marketing insights

Jo Brand is a size-challenged comedienne whose act often includes two themes: her size and her love for cakes. The following two niche companies are for her.

Betty's Café Tea Rooms

There are only four Betty's Café Tea Rooms and one Taylor's Tea Room, but they serve 2 million cups of tea a year. They do not advertise, yet year round people queue for a chance to taste their exquisitely expensive tea, coffee and cakes. Inside, a pianist plays light classical music. The rooms are simple, but rich with the atmosphere of times past. Formally dressed waiters, or waitresses wearing black skirt, starched white blouse and apron, serve. Betty's is proud of its heritage and quietly boasts of the York Betty's being built by the same team of craftsmen as the luxury liner, *Queen Mary*.

The first Betty's was opened in Harrogate in 1919 by a Swiss confectioner. He visited the Yorkshire Dales, liked it, stayed and started Betty's. His timing was as good as his patisserie. Harrogate was booming and Betty's was just about the only place an unchaperoned woman could go. Betty's succeeds because of its unique quality and atmosphere. The pastries range from exotic Amadeus torte to local Yorkshire curd tarts and fat rascals. The bakers and confectioners train at Richemont College, Lucerne.

Betty's is a clever multiple nicher. It has diversified into other businesses close to its original business. Each of its Café Tea Rooms retails expensive gift-oriented confectionery, which suits their location in tourist towns. It also has a mail-order business selling cakes, chocolates and speciality teas and coffees by post. Finally, it markets Yorkshire Tea, a brand sold and positioned nationally as a traditional Yorkshire 'cuppa'.

Dawn French fashions

An ouldated study of the contours of 5,000 women links Betty's golden age to Dawn French's fashions. The study's results gave the British Standard Sizes that have pained women for decades. The sizes worked well in the 1950s when food rationing had just ended and people walked a lot, but not now. A recent study of women's contours by J. D. Williams shows that things have changed. For years the company has been selling mail-order clothes to women with a fuller figure who were unable to get suitable clothes from high-street stores. Nigel Green,

...12.2

marketing director of J. D. Williams' Classic Combinations catalogue business, explains:

> Today's woman enjoys a far more self-indulgent lifestyle and is not only taller, but has a noticeably bigger and lower bust, an appreciably larger waist and rib cage, a more rounded tummy, a larger and flatter bottom and far fuller upper arms. And while her hip size may still be 90 cm, the standard British figure [the original size 12] is now more likely to be 95–70–90 than 90–60–90 . . . The old-fashioned dress sizes meant that women . . . had to live with . . . blouses that gape, waistbands that cut and skirts that ride up.

Nigel Green believes these new sizes will give his niche company a unique selling proposition.

Other moves are afoot in the high street. 'Women are no longer prepared to put their lives on hold until they can starve themselves down to size', says Christina Bounce, of Country Casuals Holdings. She continues: 'They are generally feeling happier about their own size, even when it doesn't conform to fashion stereotypes.' D. H. Evans, the Outsize Shop, have long served the outsize market, but the emerging market shows that women no longer feel the need to don masks before entering the premises.

Dawn French's shops, 1647, sell high fashions for the amply proportioned. Few in the trade believe the claim implicit in the shop name that 47 per cent of women are over size 16, but the huge success of the niche retailers shows where the future lies. 'There is correlation between age and increased size and obesity', says Verdict's Clive Vaughan. So, as the middle-aged market grows in number, affluence and girth, the outsize market is a nice niche. But, as Joan Miller of Betty's says, 'If everyone round here decides to get health conscious, we're in real trouble.'

It looks like Joan Miller has little to fret about. According to the European Commission, we are facing an 'obesity epidemic' with several European countries weighing in above the USA, the one-time fat champions. It is easy to see why. Across Europe sedentary leisure and non-physical work are on the increase while wealth is giving us more opportunity to eat the lovely sweet treats that make up so much of our diet – if that is the right word!

SOURCES: **www.bettybypost.com**; Virginia Matthews, 'Oversized and over here', *Marketing Week* (23 September 1994), p. 25; 'Commissioner warns of "obesity epidemic"', *Irish Times* (5 April 2003); Christopher Hirst *et al.*, 'Cake is it', *The Independent* (15 November 2003).

Highly successful mid-size companies found that, in almost all cases, these companies niched within a larger market rather than going after the whole market.

> In *Hidden Champions*, Herman Simon documents the surprising number of German companies that are barely known but have strong profits and global market shares exceeding 50 per cent in their respective niches. Tetra has 80 per cent of the world tropical fish market; Hohner has 85 per cent of the harmonica market; Bechner makes 50 per cent of the world's umbrellas; and Steiner Optical make 80 per cent of the world's military field glasses.

Why is niching profitable? The main reason is that the market nicher ends up knowing the target customer group so well that it meets their needs better than other firms which casually sell to this niche. As a result, the nicher can charge a substantial mark-up over costs because of the added value. Whereas the mass marketer achieves *high volume*, the nicher achieves *high margins*.

Nichers try to find one or more market niches that are safe and profitable. An ideal market niche is big enough to be profitable and has growth potential. It is one that the firm can serve effectively. Perhaps most importantly, the niche is of little interest to large competitors. The firm can build the skills and customer goodwill to defend itself against an attacking big competitor as the niche grows and becomes more attractive.

> Logitech has become a €500 million global success story by focusing on human interface devices – computer mice, game controllers, keyboards, and others. It makes every variation of computer mouse imaginable. Logitech turns out mice for left- and right-handed people, cordless mice that use radio waves, mice shaped like real mice for children, and 3-D mice that let the user appear to move behind screen objects. This year, the company's 200 millionth mouse will roll off the production line. Breeding computer mice has been so successful that Logitech dominates the world market, with Microsoft as its runner-up.[28]

Many nichers do not grow so global but thrive in clusters where the proximity on similar neighbours and local services are positive externalities. **Externalities** are activities or facilities that are external to an organisation but affect its performance. Such a cluster is in the English market town of High Wycombe, where the local furniture college and pool of skilled woodworkers support specialist furniture makers. Among the cluster are Teal, who make tables and chairs for hospitals, Hands, makers of integrated office 'pods' of furniture aimed at the high-tech businesses, and Danish Labofa Antocks Lairn, who make restaurant furniture. The most influential cluster of all is California's Silicon Valley, although northern Italy provides the climate in which such companies abound. Among them are silk from Como, wool from Biella, gold from Vincenza, Ferrari, Ducati and Alfa Romeo.[29]

Externalities—Activities or facilities that are external to an organisation but affect its performance.

The key idea in nichemanship is specialisation. The firm has to specialise along market, customer, product or marketing-mix lines. Here are several specialist roles open to a market nicher:

- *End-use specialist*. The firm specialises in serving one type of end-use customer. For example, Reuters provides financial information and news to professionals and Moss Bros' strength is in clothes hire.

- *Vertical-level specialist.* The firm specialises at some level of the production–distribution cycle. For example, the Dutch-based Anglo-Italian company EVC is Europe's leading manufacturer of polyvinylchloride (PVC), while Country Homes' niche is as an intermediary between owners of country cottages and people who want to hire them for holidays.

- *Customer-size specialist.* The firm concentrates on selling to either small, medium or large customers. Many nichers specialise in serving small customers neglected by the large companies. Fuji gained its initial success in the photocopying market by specialising in small firms neglected by Xerox. Many regional advertising agencies also specialise in serving medium-sized clients.

- *Specific-customer specialist.* The firm limits its selling to one or a few large customers. For example, Teal makes tables and chairs for hospitals.

- *Geographical specialist.* The firm sells only in a certain locality, region or area of the world. Most retail banks stay within their national boundaries. Two odd exceptions to this rule are the European HSBC and Standard & Charter, whose main interest is south-east Asia.

- *Product or feature specialist.* The firm specialises in producing a certain product, product line or product feature. Examples are Rolls-Royce, the only supplier of tilt-thrust jet engines, or Pear Tree, a maker of tree houses.

- *Quality–price specialist.* The firm operates at the low or high end of the market. For example, Hewlett-Packard specialises in the high-quality, high-price end of the hand-calculator market, while Naxos sells inexpensive classical CDs.

- *Service specialist.* The firm offers one or more services not available from other firms: for example, NASA's ability to recover and repair satellites.

Niching carries a very significant risk, in that the market niche may dry up or be attacked. After years alone as a super-luxury carmaker, BMW-owned Rolls-Royce cars is now being attacked by Mercedes, GM and VW extending their range into that exclusive market segment. On a different scale, innovation and intense competition between multinationals and social trends eventually killed off Pollards Cornish Ice Cream. Its niche was selling high-fat dairy ice-cream – an estimated 100 calories per cone – to a declining number of customers in south-west England.

The danger of the disappearing niche is why many companies use **multiple niching**. By developing two or more niches, the company increases its chances of survival. Most of the wealth of successful healthcare companies comes from their each having products in a few niches that they dominate. For instance, Sweden's Gambio concentrates on renal care, cardiovascular surgery, intensive care and anaesthesia, blood compound technology and preventive health services.[30]

Multiple niching—Adopting a strategy of having several independent offerings that appeal to several different subsegments of customer.

Balancing customer–competitor orientations

We have stressed the importance of a company watching its competitors closely. Whether a company is a market leader, challenger, follower or nicher, it must find the competitive marketing strategy that positions it most effectively against its competitors. It must continually adapt its strategies to the fast-changing competitive environment.

This question now arises: can the company spend too much time and energy tracking competitors, damaging its customer orientation? The answer is yes! A company can become so competitor-centred that it loses its even more important customer focus. A **competitor-centred company** is one whose moves are based mainly on competitors' actions and reactions. The company spends most of its time tracking competitors' moves and market shares, and trying to find strategies to counter them.

This mode of strategy planning has some pluses and minuses. On the positive side, the company develops a fighter orientation. It trains its marketers to be on constant alert, watching for weaknesses in their position and watching for competitors' weaknesses. On the negative side, the company becomes too reactive. Rather than carrying out its own consistent customer-oriented strategy, it bases its moves on competitors' moves. As a result, it does not move in a planned direction towards a goal. It does not know where it will end up, since so much depends on what the competitors do.

A **customer-centred company**, in contrast, focuses more on customer developments in designing its strategies. Clearly, the customer-centred company is in a better position to identify new opportunities and set a strategy that makes long-run sense. By watching customer needs evolve, it can decide what customer groups and what emerging needs are the most important to serve, given its resources and objectives.

In practice, today's companies must be **market-centred companies**, watching both their customers and their competitors. They must not let competitor-watching blind them to customer focusing. Figure 12.7 shows that companies have moved through four orientations

Competitor-centred company—A company whose moves are mainly based on competitors' actions and reactions; it spends most of its time tracking competitors' moves and market shares and trying to find strategies to counter them.

Customer-centred company —A company that focuses on customer developments in designing its marketing strategies and on delivering superior value to its target customers.

Market-centred company—A company that pays balanced attention to both customers and competitors in designing its marketing strategies.

Figure 12.7 Evolving company orientations

Customer-centred

	No	Yes
No	Product orientation	Customer orientation
Yes	Competitor orientation	Market orientation

(left axis: **Competitor-centred**)

over the years. In the first stage, they were product-oriented, paying little attention to either customers or competitors. In the second stage, they became customer-oriented and started to pay attention to customers. In the third stage, when they started to pay attention to competitors, they became competitor-oriented. Today, companies need to be market-oriented, paying balanced attention to both customer and competitors. A market orientation pays big dividends – one recent study found a substantial positive relationship between a company's marketing orientation and its profitability, a relationship that held regardless of type of business or market environment.[31]

Summary

To prepare an effective marketing strategy, a company must consider its competitors as well as its actual and potential customers. It must continuously analyse its competitors and develop competitive marketing strategies that effectively position it against competitors and give it the strongest possible *competitive advantage*.

Competitor analysis first involves identifying the company's main competitors, using both an industry and a market-based analysis. The company then gathers information on competitors' objectives, strategies, strengths and weaknesses, and reaction patterns. With this information to hand, it can select competitors to attack or avoid. Competitive intelligence must be collected, interpreted and distributed continuously. Company marketing managers should be able to obtain full and reliable information about any competitor affecting their decisions. The major alternative competitive positions are *cost leadership*, *differentiation* and *focus.* Many firms fail because they do not follow any of these and so become *stuck in the middle.*

Which *competitive marketing strategy* makes the most sense depends on the company's industry position and its objectives, opportunities and resources. The company's competitive marketing strategy depends on whether it is a market leader, challenger, follower or nicher.

A *market leader* faces three challenges: expanding the total market, protecting market share and expanding market share. The market leader wants to find ways to expand the total market because it will benefit most from any increased sales. To expand market size, the leader looks for new users of the product, *new uses* and *more usage.* To protect its existing market share, the market leader has several *defences*: position defence, *flanking defence*, *pre-emptive defence*, *counteroffensive defence*, *mobile defence* and *contraction defence.* The most sophisticated leaders cover themselves by doing everything right, leaving no openings for competitive attack. Leaders can also try to increase their market shares. This makes sense if profitability increases at higher market-share levels.

A *market challenger* is a firm that aggressively tries to expand its market share by attacking the leader, other runner-up firms or smaller firms in the industry. The challenger can choose from a variety of *attack strategies*, including *frontal attack*, *flanking attack*, *encirclement attack*, *bypass attack* and *guerrilla attack.*

A *market follower* is a runner-up firm that chooses not to rock the boat, usually out of fear that it stands to lose more than it might gain. The follower is not without a strategy, however, and seeks to use its particular skills to gain market growth. Some followers enjoy a higher rate of return than the leaders in their industry.

A *market nicher is* a smaller firm that serves some part of the market that is not likely to attract the larger firms. Market nichers often become specialists in some end use, vertical level, customer size, specific customer, geographic area, product or product feature, or service.

A competitive orientation is important in today's markets, but companies should not overdo their focus on competitors. Companies are more likely to be hurt by emerging consumer needs and new competitors than by existing competitors. Companies that balance consumer and competitor considerations are practising a true market orientation.

Discussing the issues

1. Are the Internet banks being 'well behaved' in undercutting the rates charged by established banks? The established banks do not think so, but is the cost cutting good for the customers?

2. Consider Richard Branson's attempts at taking on market leaders in airlines (e.g. British Airways on transatlantic routes), soft drinks (e.g. Coca-Cola) and, more recently, financial services (as seen in the launch of Virgin Direct, which will challenge current providers of traditional and direct insurance products). What market-leader strategies would you recommend for the no. 1 competitor in each of these sectors? Why?

3. A local school faces being closed down as demographics and legislation that allows local competition reduce the number of children attending the school. So far the school has survived on a fixed sum given to the school by the government for each child attending. How could the school increase its chances of survival?

4. The goal of the marketing concept is to satisfy customer wants and needs. What is the goal of a competitor-centred strategy? Discuss whether the marketing concept and competitor-centred strategy are in conflict.

5. Does the global reach and discounting on the Internet mean that the time for nichers or followers is past or does the range of the Internet provide more niching opportunities than ever before? Think of cases for and against the alternative arguments.

Applying the concepts

1. In the rapidly expanding world of the Internet and personal information and communications devices, AOL's plan is to get inside every information appliance. According to AOL's CEO, 'We want to be as pervasive as the telephone or TV, but even more valuable in people's lives.' To this end, AOL is partnering with a broad range of companies. For example, in addition to its already established relationships with Netscape and Sun Systems, AOL will invest approaching $1 billion in Gateway over two years to help develop and co-market Internet appliances. It will partner with 3Com to put its online services on Palm handheld devices. AOL's instant message service will now be part of all new Motorola smart wireless devices, and AOL has joined with DirecTV and Philips Electronics to preload set-top boxes with AOL features and access. However, all will not be easy. AOL is going up against Microsoft with its deep pockets, and its recent moves have attracted Yahoo! All three competitors plan to spread their services to all manner of information devices early in the twenty-first century. For more information, visit www.aol.com.

   ■ What do you see as the major strengths and weaknesses of AOL? How do those strengths and weaknesses match those of Microsoft and Yahoo!?

   ■ What competitive position does AOL hold in its industry? Does this position change as it partners across industry lines?

- Which of the competitive strategies outlined in the chapter is AOL using? How will competitors respond?
- Propose one additional partnership that you think would make sense for AOL. Explain.

2. Yum, yum, yum! chocexpress.com, chocolaterie-stettler.ch, prestat.co.uk and zchocolat.com are battling it out for the fine chocolates market on the Internet.

- Visit the websites and evaluate what each of the providers is doing to get an upper hand in the market.
- Enumerate the features offered by the websites.
- Evaluate the extent to which they are successfully pursuing a niche strategy.
- State which of the websites you think is providing the best service, giving reasons for your choice.
- Do you think the websites have just extended the competition for luxury chocolates by taking sales from the competition or are they likely to expand the market?

References

1. *The Economist* (8 May 1999), pp. 122–3; 'Game wars', *The Economist* (22 April 2000), p. 72; Louise Kehoe, 'Microsoft to take on video game leaders', *Financial Times* (10 March 2000), p. 25; Oliver Edwards, 'X-box is no dog', *EuroBusiness* (May 2000), pp. 35–6; Satham Sanghera, 'Sega moves to increase share of UK market', *Financial Times* (13 October 2000), p. 3; Bryon Acohido, 'Microsoft bets on Xbox, but some skeptical', *USA Today* (24 April 2001), p. 6B; 'Video games: console wars', *The Economist* (22 June 2002), p. 71–2; Michiyo Nakamoto, 'Tie for former champ to lift its game', *Financial Times* (29 August 2003), p. 25.

2. Christopher Brown-Humes, Robert Budden and Andrew Gowers, 'Nokia is the great telecom survivor. But the advent of 3G technology means this is no time for complacency', *Financial Times* (18 November 2002), p. 21; 'Going, Boeing', *The Economist* (19 April 2003), pp. 44–5.

3. See Jonathan Gaw, 'Britannica gives in and gets online', *LA Times* (19 October 2000), p. A1; 'Encyclopaedia Britannica makes some changes', *Link-Up* (July-August 2001), pp. 1, 6; and Peter Jacso, 'Britannica Concise Encyclopaedia', *Link-Up* (May–June 2002), pp. 16–17. For more on identifying competitors, see Bruce H. Clark and David B. Montgomery, 'Managerial identification of competitors', *Journal of Marketing* (July 1999), pp. 67–83.

4. *The Economist*, 'Elecrolux: brand challenge' (6 April 2002), p. 68; Franz Fehrenbach, 'Bosch chief ends the reign of the quiet men', *Financial Times* (9 January 2004), p. 10.

5. For discussions of the underlying rules of competitive interaction and reaction, see Peter S. H. Leeflang and Dick R. Wittink, 'Competitive reaction versus consumer response: Do managers overreact?', *International Journal of Research in Marketing*, **13**, 2 (1996), pp. 103–19; C. Carl Pegels and Yong Il Song, 'Competitive inter-firm interactions: determinants of divergence versus convergence', *Management Decision*, **38**, 3 (2000), pp. 194–208; Jos Lemmink and Hans Kasper, 'Competitive reactions to product quality improvements in industrial markets', *European Journal of Marketing*, **28**, 12 (1994), pp. 50–68.

6. 'Lufthansa: flying high', *The Economist* (9 November 2002), pp. 78–9; Carol Matlack, Joseph Weber and Wendy Zellner, 'In flight trim', *BusinessWeek* (28 April 2003), p. 50.

7. See Michael E. Porter, *Competitive Advantage* (New York: Free Press, 1985), pp. 226–7; George S. Day and Robin Wensley, 'Assessing competitive advantage: a framework for diagnosing competitive superiority', *Journal of Marketing* (April 1988), pp. 1–20; Graham Hooley, John Saunders and Nigel Piercy, *Marketing Strategy and Competitive Positioning* (London: Pearson, 2004).

8. Michael E. Porter, *Competitive Strategy: Techniques for analyzing industries and competitors* (New York: Free Press, 1980), Ch. 2. For other strategy types see Stavros P. Kalafatis, Markos H. Tsogas and Charles Blankson, 'Positioning strategies in business markets', *Journal of Business and Industrial Marketing*, **15**, 6 (2000), pp. 416–37; Harry Vardis and Sandra Vasa-Sideris, 'The PISCESSM Process: guiding clients to creative positioning strategies', *Journal of Business and Industrial Marketing*, **15**, 2/3 (2000), pp. 163–9.

9. Kevin Done, 'Flurry of deals show pace of consolidation', *Financial Times Survey: Aerospace* (24 July 2000), pp. 1–2; Nick Cook, 'The race is on in lean production', *Interavia* (September 1999), pp. 15–17;

Chris Ayers, 'Phone giants play numbers', *The Times* (18 November 1999), p. 41; 'Less mania, more merger', *The Economist* (29 May 1999), pp. 16–17.

10. Mark Court, 'GSK fears new drug shortage', *The Times – Business* (18 November 2002), p. 1; Geoff Dyer and David Firn, 'Jury still out on GSK's claims for having "best pipeline in industry"', *Financial Times* (4 December 2003), p. 27.

11. See Italian Institute for Foreign Trade, 'Spotlighting Italy: focus on clusters', *The Economist* (5 February 2000), promotional supplement; John Kipphoff, 'Domnick Hunter delivers double-digit growth', *The Economist* (21 August 2003), p. 22.

12. 'Footballer's roadshow', *The Economist* (8 April 2000), p. 40; www.manutd.com.

13. Susan Voyle, 'Errors lead to sharp M&S sales fall', *Financial Times* (15 January 2004), p. 1.

14. Anna Minton, 'Changing the knickers of the British high street', *Financial Times* (24 March 2000), p. 30.

15. See Robert D. Buzzell, Bradley T. Gale and Ralph G. M. Sultan, 'Market share – the key to profitability', *Harvard Business Review* (January–February 1975), pp. 97–106. Others suggest that the relationship between market share and profits has been exaggerated. See J. Martin Fraering and Michael S. Minor, 'The industry-specific basis of the market share–profitability relationship', *Journal of Consumer Marketing*, **11**, 1 (1994), pp. 27–37.

16. Porter, *Competitive Strategy*, op cit.

17. Visit www.bruichladdich.com or the Isle of Islay in Scotland.

18. 'After the deal', *The Economist* (7 January 1999); 'Mergers: the return of the deal', *The Economist* (12 July 2003).

19. For more discussion on defence and attack strategies, see Low Sui Pheng, 'Applying the *Thirty-six Chinese Strategies of War* to retail marketing and planning', *Marketing Intelligence and Planning*, **16**, 2 (1998), pp. 124–35; and Hooley, Saunders and Piercy, *Marketing Strategy and Competitive Positioning*, op. cit.

20. Richard Tomkins, 'Cadbury ignores history and buys Snapple', *Financial Times* (19 September 2000), p. 27; 'Unilever: fat and thin', *The Economist* (15 April 2000), p. 85.

21. Susanne Voyle, 'Sainsbury stand still as gap with rivals widens', *Financial Times* (13 January 2004), p. 21.

22. 'Storm clouds over Detroit', *The Economist* (16 November 2002), pp. 75–6; 'The year of the car', *The Economist* (3 January 2004), p. 47.

23. Richard Tomkins, 'Burger King fries harder', *Financial Times* (5 January 2000), p. 21.

24. See 'Easy does it', *The Economist* (18–24 November 2000), pp. 122–5.

25. Kevin Done, 'Airbus overtakes Boeing in aircraft deliveries', *Financial Times* (15 January 2004).

26. Sam Hill and Glenn Rifkin, *Radical Marketing* (New York: HarperBusiness, 1999). Also see Tim Christiansen, 'Radical marketing', *Academy of Marketing Science Journal* (Summer 2000), p. 140.

27. See Kamel Mellahi and Michael Johnson, 'Does it pay to be a first mover in e.commerce? The case of Amazon.com', *Management Decision*, **38**, 7 (2000), pp. 445–52; Marvin B. Lieberman and David B. Montgomery, 'First-mover (dis)advantages: Retrospective and link with the resource-based view', *Strategic Management Journal*, **19**, 12 (1998), pp. 1111–25.

28. 'Logitech Posts Record Q$ to Finish Best Year Ever', Logitech press release, 24 April 2002, accessed online at www.logitech.com.

29. Peter Marsh, 'Adaptability furnishes key to craftsmen's long survival', *Financial Times* (6 September 2000), p. 7; also see a Spanish cluster in Sacha Vaughan, 'Smuggler's legacy', *Weekend FT* (15–16 January 2000), p. XII; 'Cluster analysis', *The Economist* (29 March 2003), pp. 4–7; 'Press the flesh, not the keyboard', *The Economist* (24 August 2003), pp. 56–7.

20. Robert Taylor, 'Gambio: looking forward to a healthy future', *Financial Times: FT500* (10 February 1993), p. 17; Daniel Green, 'Tagamet's US sales fall 76% in quarter', *Financial Times* (19 October 1994), p. 25; Catherine Monk, 'Sprouting in new directions', *EuroBusiness* (July 2000), p. 120. See John C. Narver and Stanley F. Slater, 'The effect of a market orientation on business profitability', *Journal of Marketing* (October 1990), pp. 20–35; Tung-Zong Chang, Rajiv Mehta, Su-Jane Chen, Pia Polsa and Jolanta Mazur, 'The effects of market orientation on effectiveness and efficiency: the case of automotive distribution channels in Finland and Poland', *Journal of Services Marketing*, **13**, 4/5 (1999), pp. 407–18; Tung-Zong Chang and Su-Jane Chen, 'Market orientation, service quality and business profitability: a conceptual model and empirical evidence', *Journal of Services Marketing*, **12**, 4 (1998), pp. 246–64; Wolfgang Fritz, 'Market orientation and corporate success: findings from Germany', *European Journal of Marketing*, **30**, 8 (1996), pp. 59–74.

WEB RESOURCES

For additional classic case studies and Internet exercises, visit www.pearsoned.co.uk/kotler

Concluding concepts 12
The mobile maelstrom

ROBERT A. VAN DER ZWART*
SAMUAL PRONK*

Libertel had been successful in the Dutch mobile phone operator market but the market was hotting up as new technology offered meant that several major strategic choices had to be made. Mobile penetration rates increased from 2 per cent in 1995 to an expected 25–30 per cent in 1999. As the market is changing as it grows, market leader KPN claims that six out of ten new customers now buy a prepaid mobile phone product instead of a mobile subscription contract.

In July 1994, KPN, a former state-owned monopolist, launched 'The Mobile Network' to become the first GSM 900 network in the Netherlands. Libertel, a subsidiary of ING and Vodafone, followed them in September 1995 with their GSM 900 network. For a while the two competitors fought it out alone until the 1998 auction of GSM 1800 frequencies. This allowed Telfort (a joint venture between British Telecom and the Dutch Railways), Dutchtone (an alliance between Rabobank, ABN AMRO and France Télécom), and Ben (an alliance between Belgacom and TeleDanmark) to join the market one after another. Both KPN and Libertel gained GSM 1800 frequencies, but regulatory restrictions inhibit the use of these frequencies until the end of 1999. According to *Het Financieele Dagblad*, €800m was invested in the GSM 1800 licences by four mobile operators, excluding KPN. Of these, Telfort paid €230m in the auction of GSM frequencies. Latecomer Ben, which spent €680m buying licences and operating the network (excluding marketing costs), expects to reach its break-even point by 2003.

The standing and position of each of the competitors is quite different:

■ *KPN* is market leader in wireless communications with 2.2 million customers but expects to lose about 5 per cent market share in 1999. 'We are a Dutch company, we are the biggest and we'd like to keep on being the market leader. We offer the largest variety of subscription contracts. Moreover, we have had experience in the wireless communications market for years.'

■ *Libertel* has a market share of 36 per cent and 1.2 million customers. Since their entrance into the wireless market, call tariffs have dropped by 60 per cent. 'We are the trend setting and the most innovative mobile operator.'

■ *Telfort* has sold 50,000 GSM subscriptions. Telfort wants to attack the market position of Libertel. 'We'd like to keep it simple, so we offer a clear tariff structure. We are also present at many selling points.'

■ *Dutchtone* sells 2,000–3,000 product packages a week, and expects to capture 150,000 customers by the end of 1999. This amounts to a market share of 15–20 per cent. 'We are a new Dutch telecom company – enthusiastic and professional. Our guiding principles are clarity, simplicity, and affordability. No juggling with all kinds of complicated subscriptions and tariff structures, no confusing offers.'

■ *Ben* expects to attract 180,000–230,000 customers by the end of 1999. Within a few years Ben aims for 20 per cent market share in Dutch wireless communications. 'We'd like to meet you in the first place instead of selling you a mobile phone. We'd like to keep it simple and personal. We discuss mobile telephony in common language.'

Although many providers aim to keep things simple, users are faced with a wide range of price options (Exhibit 12.2). After analysing the pricing of the competitors the consultants PriceWaterhouseCoopers concluded that, to remain price competitive, KPN would have to cut its prices by half. However, they also estimated that, if charging the reduced prices, KPN would face a dramatic €450m loss.

All mobile operators offer both prepaid telephone cards and monthly subscription contracts. Since prepaid (PP) telephone cards do not involve any monthly subscription fee, prepaid cards offer flexibility to customers who desire to be wirelessly connected but who do not wish to suffer from high subscription charges. Moreover, a prepaid card disciplines calling behaviour. Although mobile operators receive calling revenues in advance, prepaid cards have a drawback as they induce unpredictable network traffic.

Mobile operators reveal little about their promotional expenditure. According to Ernst Moeksis, a KPN spokesman, venture teams and marketing consultants are deployed in case competitive rivalries release new

> More and more people are on the move, and this time is neither work time nor free time, but mobile time.

Exhibit 12.2 Monthly tariff structures (fees and prepaid tariffs in euros)

Service	Light user (5 min, 20% peak)	Moderate user (65 min, 60% peak)	Heavy user (100 min, 80% peak)
Ben PP	2	34	
Ben Regelnatig		11	20
Ben Vaak		14	14
Dutchtone Consumer	0 (yes, nearly free!)	15	31
Dutchtone PP	2		
Dutchtone Professional		30	36
KPN Allround		42	52
KPN Economy		37	56
KPN Hi	1	32	
KPN PP	3	43	
KPN Premium		37	50
Libertel BelMaar		18	35
Libertel Izi	2	42	
Libertel Personal		43	
Libertel Personal 30		40	60
Libertel Personal 60		36	54
Libertel Pro			57
Libertel Pro 120			51
Telfort 25		19	22
Telfort 50		22	22
Telfort PP	2	33	

SOURCE: PriceWaterhouseCoopers Management Consultants, 'Prijvergelijkingen mobiel bellen' in Zembla-documentaire 'Mobiele Miljarden', 4 February 1999, http://www.omroep.nl/vara/tv/zembla/gsm.html.

information. Nevertheless, there are some indications of promotional efforts. According to BBC, promotional expenses in telecommunications were €340m in 1998. In 1999 mobile communication promotions alone are expected to top €100m. Distribution, via company-owned and other outlets, varies greatly from company to company.

The market

> 'I wish I could split myself in two persons, so I could be in two places at the same time' is a phrase which expresses such a compressed life rhythm.
>
> Popcorn and Marigold (1996): 235

Nokia also acknowledges the compressed life rhythm:

> . . . the division between leisure time and work time is blurring. Lifestyle changes are forcing people to rethink how they spend time on the job, time off the

job and the time in between. The perception of the distance travelled to work and personal locations, the accessibility of transportation and the way to spend the time best are changing rapidly. This creates a situation where more and more people are on the move, and the time spent on the move is neither work time nor free time, but mobile time.

This does not imply an unconditional demand for wireless communications from all people. The young are the heaviest users. A Nokia survey revealed that the Dutch average is 38.5 years, four years below the European average. According to *HP/De Tijd*, further insight into the demographic profile of Dutch mobile customers is hard to obtain. Since nearly one-third of the Dutch mobile customers use prepaid cards, no registered information on mobile calling behaviour is available. A Nokia market study revealed some demographic profiling, although its main concern is adoption of Value Added Services (VAS) (such as

Exhibit 12.3 Value Added Service results

Under 18 years old	19–25	25–36
Heavy SMS users	Heavy SMS users	Moderate SMS users
Are aware of and have used	Are aware of and have used	Are aware of and have used
Gender doesn't play very big role	Male	Male
Monetary issues unlikely to restrain, parents pay the bill	Monetary issues likely to restrain interest in VAS	Monetary issues don't restrain
Live with parents	Students	Highly educated, working on managerial level or as an expert
Quite familiar with Internet technology	Internet and information technology literate	Internet and information technology literate
All very mobile people, participating actively in sports and outdoor activities		

Source: Nokia Telecommunications Oy, 'Wireless Data Evolution White Paper' in *Nokia Wireless Data Library* (April 1998), No. 12 (1998), http://www.forum.nokia.

online consulting of a city navigator on your mobile telephone) amongst early adapters in Finland (Exhibit 12.3).

Whether monetary issues are unlikely to restrain the market or not, Wim Nieuwenhuijse, a consultant of Robert Pino & Company, argues that countries with relatively low cost of ownership experience high penetration rates of mobile customers. Once customers have to pay their own bill (instead of having their employers pay), calling behaviour changes. Thus, mobile calling behaviour can be characterised as price conscious.

Price consciousness also seems to apply to the business segment of the telecommunications market. According to Nokia, the business market can be segmented on the basis of the different business roles:

Although there may be many professionals in a company with different roles, those whose jobs often require working away from the office are the most likely to be the first adopters of wireless data services. . . .

Three main groups emerge:

- *Global Nomads* – 40%: front line professionals who travel on business a lot.

- *Migrators* – 30%: expert support functions – internal movers, trainers, using the same services as Global Nomads, but adopting them somewhat later . . .

- *Settlers* – 30%: less mobile functions – administration, finance. The last group to adopt these services. Office mobility issues are very relevant . . .

As the amount of wireless data products grows and their use becomes widespread, the Global Nomads will be the first mobile professional adopters, with Migrants and Settlers following behind. . . .

Technology

The technological environment of wireless communications is very turbulent. Technology determines what is possible in mobile telephony and five big waves are on the way.

Fixed mobile convergence (FMC)

FMC provides 'one phone for all situations' and comprises a melting together of both fixed and mobile telephony. FMC is an opportunity to attract potential customers of fixed network operators by offering the equivalent of a fixed service on a mobile phone, for example Home Zone Tariffing (HZT), where mobile calls made via the base station close to the customers' home are cheaper than normal mobile calls.

Fixed line operators can fight back by encouraging their customers to use the fixed phone by connecting DECT

(Digital Enhanced Cordless Telecommunications) cordless base stations to existing fixed lines. DECT is an advanced technology that supports wireless telephony at home and in the office and has more capabilities for wireless communication than the existing generation of wireless telephones.

Universal mobile telecommunications system (UMTS)

UMTS, a third-generation mobile telecommunications system, is an initiative to build further on the European success in GSM telephony. UMTS service provision, including Internet and other flexible and personalised services, goes further than the possibilities offered by the current second-generation systems, such as GSM, and enables combined use of terrestrial and satellite components.

From the user's perspective, UMTS is a mobile carrier of new, innovative services, whereby the emphasis will be placed on the supply of information. Mobile multimedia will be made possible within UMTS thanks to transmission speeds of 144–384 kbps up to 2 Mbps in areas with a high level of coverage and a limited mobility. In addition:

1. UMTS services are expected also to be accessible though fixed networks. Using a personal identification, every user will have access to his or her own personal network environment from any fixed or mobile telephone. Personal mobility is guaranteed, even if the user is not carrying his or her mobile telephone or is out of range of a mobile network, concepts which are referred to as the Virtual Home Environment (VHE) and Universal Personal Telecommunications (UPT). This is primarily what distinguishes UMTS from OSM.

2. UMTS offers a far broader range of communication, information and entertainment services than has been the case up to now with mobile networks. The development and availability of online content will determine the success of UMTS. Major opportunities are available in the development of services specific- ally geared towards mobile users by, for example, combining location and route data with online data files.

3. UMTS offers access to communication, information and entertainment services with a video com- ponent, enabling audiovisual, broadcasting and telecommunications sectors to supplement one another.

4. There appear to be at least two market developments under way. First, there is a greater user demand for packages of combined services, whereby the same package of services is available on both the mobile network and the fixed network. The user wants accessibility under one number, irrespective of the network though which communication takes place. In addition, there is a demand for more advanced forms of (mobile) communications than speech, such as electronic mail and Internet applications.

Symbian

This is a consortium of Nokia, Ericsson, Motorola and Psion who are jointly working on the next generation of wireless, handheld computers. For a long time Psion dominated the market in organisers, but sees its position being threatened by Microsoft's Windows CE operating system. Symbian is working on Epoc, an alternative operating system for handheld computers. It has several advantages over Windows CE. Epoc has a less intensive energy use than Windows CE. Epoc can also be customised to fit the needs of the different Epoc licensees. In contrast, Windows CE has a rigorously defined user environment.

Bluetooth

This is an open standard for wireless communications being developed by Ericsson, IBM, Intel, Nokia and Toshiba. It facilitates wireless communication between laptops, printers, scanners, fax machines and mobile telephones by using radio devices that work within a periphery of 10 metres. In creating this standard Ericsson is responsible for developing the radio technology, Toshiba and IBM are jointly specifying the conditions under which Bluetooth technology can be built in mobile equipment, Intel is donating its advanced expertise on software and chips and Nokia is developing software necessary for the radio and handsets.

Satellite communications (SatComs)

SatComs are currently treated as a viable complement to existing terrestrial cellular networks. Employees of multinational companies use SatComs in regions where coverage by a fixed or mobile network is absent or poor. Heavy users of satellite servers could be found in areas such as newsgathering, oil exploration or shipping. High costs, expensive and bulky equipment and annoying delays in voice transmission inhibited mass introduction of satellite services. Nevertheless, organisations such as Iridium, Globalstar and Inmarsat have planned to invest about €40 billion in satellite communications by 2003 as they foresee a growing demand for satellite services in traditional telephony, mobile telephony and broadband Internet traffic.

Should satellite operators be considered a serious competitive threat to terrestrial mobile operators? Views are mixed:

> For cellular companies, the real worry is not that they will be unable to compete with satellite operators, but that they will fail to embrace satellites' capabilities quickly enough. Despite their low call volumes, satellite networks are set to become important additions to terrestrial networks for two reasons. First, by using dual-mode handsets that work on both cellular and satellite networks, wireless companies that enter partnerships with GMPCS operators (GMPCS is a satellite communication standard) will be able to extend their coverage to the whole of the Earth's surface. Those that do not will risk being left behind, especially in the important business segment. As many cellular operators have found, coverage is a key buying factor for customers. Second, satellite calls will be highly profitable. Cellular operators will take a cut on every call customers make when they roam on to a satellite network, just as they do when customers use a GSM network. These calls will be charged at premium rates but incur low marginal costs. In fact, the margins on roamed calls in the GSM world are so attractive that some operators now derive almost one-fifth of their revenue from roaming. Cellular operators should recognise this and promote the adoption of satellite roaming services in their territories.
>
> Evans and Rose (1998): 11

Questions

1. How would you classify the five competitors in the market concerning their competitive positions?
2. What accounts for the large differences in price in the market?
3. Should KNP cut its prices to stay competitive? If so, how can they remain profitable? If not, suggest an alternative defence.

4. Suggest potential competitive strategies for the challenger and followers in the market.
5. What approach should Libertel take concerning the new technologies in the market and why should it differ from that of Dutchtone?

SOURCES: J. C. Arnbak, 'Toespraak 8ᵉ jaarcongres Mobiele Communicatie', *Opta Actueel* (16 December 1998); S. Nold, B. G. August, M. Knickrehm and P. J. Roche, 'Winning in wireless', *The McKinsey Quarterly*, 2 (Spring 1998), pp. 18–31; P. Awde, 'Value-services for fixed networks', *Financial Times* (18 November 1998), FT Telecom p. 10; I. Beijnum, 'Jljitsch GSM-verhaal', *Pagina van Jljitsch van Betinum* (11 February 1999); H. Botman, 'Koopgids voor een GSM-telefoon', *Trouw* (8 February 1999); M. Couzy, 'Voor 80 miljard nieuwe telecomdiensten via satelliet', *Computable on line archief & literatuur* (14 August 1998), p. 25; M. Couzy, 'V&W wil meer aanbod bij opvolger GSM', *Computable on line archief & literatuur* (31 July 1998); A. J. Diepen and K. Gilbert, 'Benchmarkstudie telecommunicatie infrastructuur en diensten', *Rapport aan Hoofddirectie Telecommunicatie en Post* (February 1998), pp. 9–11; A. L. Evans and J. S. Rose, 'The future of satellite communications', *The McKinsey Quarterly* (Spring 1998), pp. 6–17; K. van Gilst, 'Bellen, Bellen, maar geen gehoor', *Adformatie* (24 January 1999), p. 3; M. Houben, 'KPN Telecom moet zich zorgen maken over positie op thuismarkt', *Het Financieele Dagblad* (20 February 1998), p. 13; A. Kantelberg, 'De tienertelefoon', *HP/De Tijd* (4 December 1998), pp. 33–9; J. Libbenga, 'Slimme Telefoon dicteert IT-wereld', *Automatiseringsgids* (4 December 1998), p. 7; W. Nieuwenhuijse, 'Marktturbulentie in mobiel waaiert uit', *Tijdschrift voor Marketing* (February 1998), pp. 46–8; Nokia Telecommunications Oy, 'Wireless Data Evolution White Paper', *Nokia Wireless Data Library* (April 1998); Nokia Telecommunications Oy, 'The demand for value-added services', *Nokia Wireless Data Library* (December 1998); F. Popcorn and L. Marigold, *Clicking* (London: Thorsons, 1996), p. 235; PriceWaterhouseCoopers Management Consultants, 'Prijsvergelijkingen mobiel bellen', *Zembla-documentaire 'Mobiele miljarden'*, 1999; Project Group UMTS, 'Consultation document UMTS', *Ministry of Transport, Public Works and Water Management; Telecommunications and Post Department* (16 July 1998); Redactie Economie, 'Nieuwkomer Ben wordt prijsvechter', *Trouw* (3 February 1999); S. Reeve, 'Direct dialling to success', *The European* (9 November 1998), p. 8; H. Schrameyer, 'Rumour around Dutchtone', *Adformatie* (4 January 1998), p. 20; W. Webb, 'Alternative strategies for fixed mobile convergence', *Motorola Cellular Infrastructure Group* (11 February 1999); www.ben.nl, www.dutchtone.nl, www.kpn.com, www.libertel.nl, www.telfort.nl.

*Robert van der Zwart is a Assistant Professor of Marketing and Samual Pronk is a Research Assistant at the Centre for Supply Chain Management at Nyenrode University, Netherlands.

A hamburger by any other name costs twice as much.

EVAN ESAR (MODERN MARKETER)

Product

IN PART FIVE WE LOOK at the first component in the marketing mix – the product.

Designing good products that customers want to buy is a challenging task. Customers do not buy mere products. They seek product benefits and are often willing to pay more for a brand that genuinely solves their problems. **Chapter 13** explores how marketers can satisfy customer needs by adding value to the basic product; it also shows the complexity arising in product, branding and packaging decisions, and how various forces in the environment pose tough challenges for marketers in the new century.

Markets do not stand still. Companies must adapt their current offerings or create new ones in response to changing customer needs, or to take advantage of new marketing and technological opportunities. **Chapter 14** looks at how to develop and commercialise new products. Importantly, after launch, marketing managers must carefully manage the new product over its lifetime to get the best return from their new-product effort.

While Chapters 13 and 14 deal with products, **Chapter 15** looks more specifically at intangible products or services. It examines the unique characteristics of services and how organisations adapt their approach when marketing them.

PART five

> What's in a name? That which we call a rose by any other name would smell as sweet.

WILLIAM SHAKESPEARE

Product and branding strategy

Chapter objectives

After reading this chapter, you should be able to:

- Define the term *product* including the core, actual and augmented product.
- Explain the main classifications of consumer and industrial products.
- Describe the decisions companies make regarding individual products, product lines and product mixes.
- Discuss branding strategy in relation to the decisions that companies make in building and managing their brands.
- Discuss additional branding issues with respect to socially responsible brand decisions and international marketing.

Mini Contents List

- Prelude case – L'Oréal: are you worth it?
- Introduction
- What is a product?
- Product decisions
- Branding strategy: building strong brands
- Marketing Insights 13.1 – Brands: what are they worth?
- Marketing Insights 13.2 – Trademarks worth fighting for!
- Additional product considerations
- Summary
- Concluding concepts 13 – Colgate: one squeeze too many?

◄ SOURCE: Freeserve.

Prelude case   L'Oréal: are you worth it?

L'Oréal sells cosmetics and toiletries to consumers around the world. One market that has certainly been booming lately is that for hair care products. Brands such as Elvive, Lancôme, Helena Rubenstein and Kérastase, part of the L'Oréal stable, are capitalising on this trend. In one sense, L'Oréal's hair care products – shampoo, conditioners, styling agents – are no more than careful mixtures of chemicals with different smells and colours. But L'Oréal knows that when it sells shampoos and conditioners, it sells much more than a bottle of coloured or fragrant soapy fluids – it sells what the fluids can do for the women who use them.

> **L'Oréal sells much more than a bottle of coloured or fragrant soapy fluids – it sells what the fluids can do for the women who use them.**

Many hair care products are promoted using alluring chat-up lines: 'Your hair is instantly shinier, stronger, healthier, and getting better and better and . . .'. Who would believe that shampoos and conditioners that are designed to rinse away can have any lasting benefits? But women do not see shampoos and conditioners that way. Many things beyond the ingredients add to a shampoo's allure. While hair is dead, it is organic, so will respond to some care and attention. Many consumers believe that their favourite shampoo does more than wash away the grit in their hair; it makes them feel good about themselves.

Thanks to recent scientific breakthroughs, many hair care products can make a difference.

The L'Oréal laboratories in Paris, employing 2,500 employees, dedicate over £180 million a year to R&D. This investment pays. For example, Kérastase, part of the L'Oréal group, developed Ceramide F – a synthetic copy of naturally occurring hair ceramides – which reconstructs the hair's internal structure. Sounds far fetched? But consumers say it works. Kérastase Forcintense revitalises hair that is severely damaged through colouring, overstyling or perming. Other L'Oréal product innovations include colour and conditioning agents – Majirel, Majirouge and Majiblond – for treating fading hair colours due to washing or sunlight, and special formulations – Majimèches – for blondes. All these functional benefits enable L'Oréal to promote the brand's superior performance benefits to consumers.

The wash-in, wash-out nature of hair care suggests that product performance alone may be sufficient to satisfy users. Hairstylist Sam McKnight says that it is an emotionally charged marketplace: a bad hair day means an unhappy woman. There is also a limit to what all the scientific breakthroughs in hair care can do for how a woman feels when she has had a hair wash. McKnight argues that scents and colours must be chosen carefully to match women's desires, moods and lifestyles. His new range of products eschew science and concentrate on the smell. Called 'Sexy', they are expensive, exclusive and smell like no other shampoo has ever smelled before.

Additionally, hair care brands have done well because of the advertising spends that have gone in to promote shampooing as a pleasurable pastime rather than an activity akin to doing a load of washing. L'Oréal and rival firms know just how important this is. Brands such as Elvive, Pantene (by Procter & Gamble) and Organics (by Elida/Lever Fabergé) have advertising spends that will make a girl's hair curl. L'Oréal's leading brand Elvive also tries to capture the essence of pleasure using advertisements that sound tempting: 'Because I'm worth it', says L'Oréal.

Companies also have to play on the shampoo's name, an important product attribute. Names such as Sexy, Dream Hair Sensational and Frizz-Ease suggest that the shampoos and conditioners will do something more than just wash your hair. L'Oréal must also package its hair care products carefully. To consumers, the bottle and package are the most tangible symbols of the product's image. Bottles must feel comfortable, be easy to handle and help to differentiate the product from other brands on the shelf.

So when a woman buys hair shampoos and conditioners, she buys much, much more than simply soapy fluids. The product's image, its promises, its feel, its name and package, even the company that makes it, all become a part of the *total product*.

Hope in a bottle or just so much hype? The answer: it's up to each of us to decide whether we're worth it.[1]

Questions

1. Distinguish between the core, tangible and augmented product that L'Oréal sells.
2. A hair care product's name is a central product attribute. What are the key branding decisions that L'Oréal's marketing managers have to make?
3. L'Oréal markets its hair care products worldwide. What major considerations does the firm face in determining global product decisions?

Introduction

The preview case shows that, clearly, toiletries and cosmetics are more than just toiletries and cosmetics when L'Oréal sells them. This chapter begins with a deceptively simple question: *What is a product?* After answering this question, we look at ways to classify products in consumer and business markets. Then we discuss the important decisions that marketers make regarding individual products, product lines and product mixes. Next, we move from decisions about individual products to the critically important issue of how marketers build and manage brands. Finally, we address socially responsible product decisions and some complex considerations in international product decisions.

What is a product?

A pair of Adidas trainers, a Volvo truck, a Nokia mobile telephone, a Tony & Guy haircut, an Oasis concert, a Club Med vacation, a NatWest e-savings account, advice from your doctor – all are products. We define a **product** as anything that is offered to a market for attention, acquisition, use or consumption and that might satisfy a want or need. Products include more than just tangible goods. Broadly defined, products include physical objects, services, persons, places, organisations, ideas or mixes of these entities. Thus, throughout this text, we use the term *product* broadly to include any or all of these entities.

Services are products that consist of activities, benefits or satisfactions that are offered for sale that are essentially intangible and do not result in the ownership of anything. Examples are banking, hotel, haircuts, tax preparation and home repair services. Because of the importance of services in the world economy, we will look at services marketing in greater detail in Chapter 15.

Levels of product

Product planners need to think about the product on three levels. Each level adds more customer value. The most basic level is the **core product**, which addresses the question: *What is the buyer really buying?* As Figure 13.1 illustrates, the core product stands at the centre of the total product. It consists of the core, problem-solving benefits that consumers seek. A woman buying lipstick buys more than lip colour. Charles Revson of Revlon saw this early: 'In the

Product—Anything that can be offered to a market for attention, acquisition, use or consumption that might satisfy a want or need. It includes physical objects, services, persons, places, organisations and ideas.

Services—Activities, benefits or satisfactions that are offered for sale.

Core product—The problem-solving services or core benefits that consumers are really buying when they obtain a product.

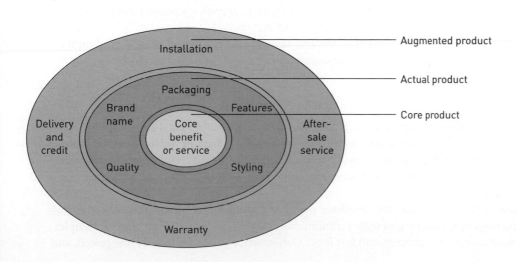

Figure 13.1 **Three levels of product**

factory, we make cosmetics; in the store, we sell hope.' Theodore Levitt has pointed out that buyers 'do not buy quarter-inch drills; they buy quarter-inch holes'. Thus when designing products, marketers must first define the core of *benefits* that the product will provide to consumers.

At the second level, product planners must turn the core benefit into an **actual product**. Actual products may have as many as five characteristics: a *quality level*, product and service *features*, *styling*, a *brand name* and *packaging*. For example, Sony's cam camcorder is an actual product. Its name, parts, styling, features, packaging and other attributes have all been combined carefully to deliver the core benefit – a convenient, high-quality way to capture important moments.

Finally, the product planner must build an **augmented product** around the core and actual products by offering additional consumer services and benefits. Sony must offer more than a camcorder. It must provide consumers with a complete solution to their picture-taking problems. Thus when consumers buy a Sony camcorder, Sony and its dealers might also give buyers a warranty on parts and workmanship, instructions on how to use the camcorder, quick repair services when needed and a freephone number to call if they have problems or questions. To the consumer, all of these augmentations become an important part of the total product.

Therefore, a product is more than a simple set of tangible features. Consumers tend to see products as complex *bundles of benefits* that satisfy their needs. When developing products, marketers must first identify the *core* consumer needs that the product will satisfy. They must then design the *actual* product and finally find ways to *augment* it in order to create the bundle of benefits that will best satisfy consumers.

Today, most competition takes place at the product augmentation level. Successful companies add benefits to their offers that will not only *satisfy*, but also *delight* the customer. However, each augmentation costs the company money, and the marketer has to ask whether customers will pay enough to cover the extra cost. Moreover, augmented benefits soon become *expected* benefits. For example, hotel guests now expect cable television, Internet access, trays of toiletries and other amenities in their rooms. This means that competitors must search for still more features and benefits to differentiate their offers.

Product classifications

Products can be classified according to their durability and tangibility. **Non-durable products** are goods that are normally consumed quickly and used on one or a few usage occasions, such as beer, soap and food products. **Durable products** are products used over an extended period of time and normally survive for many years. Examples are refrigerators, cars and furniture.

Marketers have also divided products and services into two broad classes based on the types of customer that use them – consumer products and industrial products.

Consumer products

Consumer products are those bought by final consumers for personal consumption. Marketers usually classify these goods based on *consumer shopping habits*. Consumer products include *convenience products*, *shopping products*, *speciality products* and *unsought products*. These products differ in the way consumers buy them, so they differ in how they are marketed (see Table 13.1).

Convenience products are consumer goods and services that the consumer usually buys frequently, immediately and with a minimum of comparison and buying effort. Examples are soap, sweets, newspapers and fast food. Convenience goods are usually low priced, and

---

Actual product—A product's parts, quality level, features, design, brand name, packaging and other attributes that combine to deliver core product benefits.

Augmented product— Additional consumer services and benefits built around the core and actual products.

Non-durable product—A consumer product that is normally consumed in one or a few uses.

Durable product—A consumer product that is usually used over an extended period of time and that normally survives many uses.

Consumer product—A product bought by final consumers for personal consumption.

Convenience product— A consumer product that the customer usually buys frequently, immediately, and with a minimum of comparison and buying effort.

Marketing consideration	Type of consumer product			
	Convenience	Shopping	Speciality	Unsought
Customer buying behaviour	Frequent purchase, little planning, little comparison or shopping effort, low customer involvement	Less frequent purchase, much planning and shopping effort, comparison of brands on price, quality, style	Strong brand preference and loyalty, special purchase effort, little comparison of brands, low price sensitivity	Little product awareness or knowledge; if aware, little or even negative interest
Price	Low price	Higher price	High price	Varies
Distribution	Widespread distribution, convenient locations	Selective distribution in fewer outlets	Exclusive distribution in only one or a few outlets per market area	Varies
Promotion	Mass promotion by the producer	Advertising and personal selling by both producer and resellers	More carefully targeted promotion by both producer and resellers	Aggressive advertising and personal selling by producer and resellers
Examples	Toothpaste, magazines, laundry detergent	Major appliances, televisions, furniture, clothing	Luxury goods, such as Rolex watches or fine crystal	Life insurance, blood donations

Table 13.1 Marketing considerations for consumer products

marketers place them in many locations to make them readily available when customers need them.

Shopping products are less frequently purchased and consumers spend considerable time and effort gathering information and comparing alternative brands carefully on suitability, quality, price and style. Examples of shopping products are furniture, clothing, used cars and major household appliances. Shopping products marketers usually distribute their products through fewer outlets but provide deeper sales support to give customers information and advice to help them in their comparison efforts.

Speciality products are consumer goods with unique characteristics or brand identification for which a significant group of buyers is willing to make a special purchase effort. Examples include specific brands and types of car, high-priced home entertainment systems and photographic equipment, luxury goods, designer clothes and the services of medical or legal specialists. A jukebox, for example, is a speciality good because buyers are usually willing to travel great distances to buy one. Buyers normally do not compare speciality goods. They invest only the time needed to reach dealers carrying the wanted products.

Unsought products are consumer goods that the consumer either does not know about or knows about but does not normally think of buying. Most major new innovations are unsought until the consumer becomes aware of them through advertising. Classic examples of known but unsought goods are life insurance, home security systems, funeral services and blood donations. By their very nature, unsought goods require a lot of advertising, personal selling and other marketing efforts.

Shopping product— A consumer product that the customer, in the process of selection and purchase, characteristically compares with others on such bases as suitability, quality, price and style.

Speciality product—A consumer product with unique characteristics or brand identification for which a significant group of buyers is willing to make a special purchase effort.

Unsought product— A consumer product that the consumer either does not know about or knows about but does not normally think of buying.

Figure 13.2 **Classification of industrial goods**

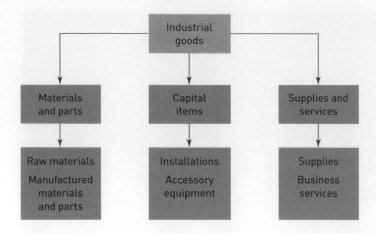

Industrial products

Industrial product—A product bought by individuals and organisations for further processing or for use in conducting a business.

Industrial products are those bought for further processing or for use in conducting a business. Thus the distinction between a consumer product and an industrial product is based on the *purpose* for which the product is purchased. If a consumer buys a lawnmower for home use, the lawnmower is a consumer product. If the same consumer buys the same lawnmower for use in a landscaping business, the lawnmower is an industrial product.

There are three groups of industrial product: *materials and parts*, *capital items* and *supplies and services* (see Figure 13.2).

Materials and parts—Industrial products that enter the manufacturer's product completely, including raw materials and manufactured materials and parts.

Materials and parts are industrial goods that become a part of the buyer's product, through further processing or as components. They include raw materials and manufactured materials and parts.

Raw materials consist of farm products (wheat, cotton, livestock, fruits, vegetables) and natural products (fish, timber, crude petroleum, iron ore).

Manufactured materials and parts include component materials (iron, yarn, cement, wires) and component parts (small motors, tyres, castings). Component materials are usually processed further – for example, pig iron is made into steel, and yarn is woven into cloth. Component parts enter the finished product complete with no further change in form, as when Electrolux puts small motors into its vacuum cleaners and Volvo adds tyres to its automobiles. Most manufactured materials and parts are sold directly to industrial users. Price and service are the most significant marketing factors, while branding and advertising tend to be less important.

Capital items—Industrial goods that partly enter the finished product, including installations and accessory equipment.

Capital items are industrial products that help in the buyers' production or operations. They include installations and accessory equipment. *Installations* consist of buildings (factories, offices) and fixed equipment (generators, drill presses, large computer systems, lifts). *Accessory equipment* includes portable factory equipment and tools (hand tools, lift trucks) and office equipment (fax machines, computers, desks). These products do not become part of the finished product. They have a shorter life than installations and simply aid in the production process.

Supplies and services—Industrial products that do not enter the finished product at all.

Supplies and services are industrial products that do not enter the finished product at all. *Supplies* include operating supplies (lubricants, coal, computer paper, pencils) and repair and maintenance items (paint, nails, brooms). Supplies are the convenience goods of the industrial field because they are usually purchased with a minimum of effort or comparison. *Business services* include maintenance and repair services (window cleaning, computer repair) and business advisory services (legal, management consulting, advertising). Such services are usually supplied under contract.

Organisations, persons, places and ideas

In addition to tangible products and services, in recent years marketers have broadened the concept of a product to include other 'marketable entities' – namely, organisations, persons, places and ideas.

Organisations often carry out activities to 'sell' the organisation itself. *Organisation marketing* consists of activities undertaken to create, maintain or change the attitudes and behaviour of target consumers towards an organisation. Both profit and non-profit organisations practise organisation marketing. Business firms sponsor public relations or corporate advertising campaigns to polish their images. *Corporate image advertising* is a major tool companies use to market themselves to various publics. For example, IBM wants to establish itself as the company to turn to for 'e-Business Solutions'. Similarly, non-profit organisations, such as churches, colleges, charities, museums and performing arts groups, market their organisations in order to raise funds and attract members or patrons.

People can also be thought of as products. *Person marketing* consists of activities undertaken to create, maintain, or change attitudes or behaviour towards particular people. All kinds of people and organisations practise person marketing. Presidents or prime ministers of nations must be skilful in marketing themselves, their parties and their platforms to get needed votes and programme support. Entertainers and sports figures use marketing to promote their careers and improve their impact and incomes. Professionals such as doctors, lawyers, accountants and architects market themselves in order to build their reputations and increase business. Business leaders use person marketing as a strategic tool to develop their companies' fortunes as well as their own. Businesses, charities, sports teams, fine arts groups, religious groups and other organisations also use person marketing. Creating or associating with well-known personalities often helps these organisations achieve their goals better. Thus, brands such as TAG Heuer, Adidas, Nike, Coca-Cola and others have invested millions of euros to link themselves with celebrities.

Place marketing: This ad capitalises on Doura being the host of the UEFA Euro 2004 championship. The campaign was for Portuguese nationals living outside portugal using the Euro 2004 theme.
SOURCE: Institut do turismo de Portugal.

Place marketing involves activities undertaken to create, maintain or change attitudes or behaviour towards particular places. Thus, cities, states, regions and even entire nations compete to attract tourists, new residents, conventions and company offices and factories. For example, today, it is common to find cities, counties and countries marketing their tourist attractions. Many of these also operate industrial development offices that try to sell companies on the advantages of locating new plants in their locations. For example, Ireland is an outstanding place marketer. The Irish Development Board has attracted over 1200 companies to locate their plants in Ireland. At the same time, the Irish Tourist Board has built a flourishing tourism business, and the Irish Export Board has created attractive markets for Irish exports.[2]

Ideas can also be marketed. In one sense, all marketing is the marketing of an idea, whether it be the general idea of brushing your teeth or the specific idea that AquaFresh provides an effective decay prevention. Here, however, we narrow our focus to the marketing of *social ideas*, such as public health campaigns to reduce smoking, alcoholism, drug abuse, child abuse and overeating; environmental campaigns to promote wilderness protection, clean air and conservation; and other campaigns such as education reforms, organ donations, family planning, human rights and racial equality. This area has been called *social marketing*, which includes the design, implementation and control of programmes seeking to increase the acceptability of a social idea, cause or practice among a target group.

But social marketing involves much more than just advertising. Many public marketing campaigns fail because they assign advertising the primary role and fail to develop and use all the marketing mix tools.[3]

Product decisions

Marketers make product decisions at three levels: individual product decisions, product line decisions and product mix decisions. We discuss each in turn.

Individual product decisions

Here, we look at decisions relating to the development and marketing of individual products, namely *product attributes, branding, packaging, labelling* and *product-support services*.

Product attributes

Developing a product involves defining the benefits that the product will offer. These benefits are communicated and delivered by tangible product attributes, such as *quality, features, style* and *design*. Decisions about these attributes are particularly important as they greatly affect consumer reactions to a product. We will now discuss the issues involved in each decision.

Product quality

Quality is one of the marketer's major positioning tools. Quality has a direct impact on product performance; hence, it is closely linked to customer value and satisfaction. In the narrowest sense, quality can be defined as 'freedom from defects'. But most customer-centered companies go beyond this narrow definition. Instead, they define quality in terms of customer satisfaction. For example, Siemens defines quality this way: 'Quality is when our customers come back and our products don't.'[4] This customer-focused definition suggests that quality begins with customer needs, goes beyond customer satisfaction and ends with customer retention.

'Total quality management' (TQM) is an approach in which all the company's people are involved in constantly improving the quality of products, services and business processes. During the past two decades, companies, large and small, have credited TQM with greatly improving their market shares and profits. Recently, however, the total quality movement has drawn criticism. Too many companies viewed TQM as a magic cure-all and created token total quality programmes that applied quality principles only superficially.[5] Still others became obsessed with narrowly defined TQM principles, losing sight of broader concerns for customer value and satisfaction. As a result, many such programmes failed, causing a backlash against TQM.

When applied in the context of creating customer satisfaction, however, total quality principles remain a requirement for success. Although many firms do not use the 'TQM label' any more, for most top companies, customer-driven quality has become a way of doing business. Today, most companies are taking a 'return on quality' approach, viewing quality as an investment and holding quality efforts accountable for bottom-line results.[6]

Product quality has two dimensions – level and consistency. In developing a product, the marketer must first choose a *quality level* that will support the product's position in the target

Product quality—The ability of a product to perform its functions; it includes the product's overall durability, reliability, precision, ease of operation and repair, and other valued attributes.

market. Here, **product quality** stands for the ability of a product to perform its functions. It includes the product's overall durability, reliability, precision, ease of operation and repair, and other valued attributes. Although some of these attributes can be measured objectively, from a marketing point of view, quality should be measured in terms of buyers' perceptions. Companies rarely try to offer the highest possible quality level – few customers want or can afford the high levels of quality offered in products such as a Rolls-Royce, a Sub Zero refrigerator or a Rolex watch. Instead, companies choose a quality level that matches target market needs and the quality levels of competing products.

Beyond quality level, high quality can also mean high levels of quality *consistency*. Here, product quality means *conformance quality* – freedom from defects and *consistency* in delivering a targeted level of performance. In this sense, a Nissan can have just as much quality as a Rolls-Royce. Although a Nissan does not perform as well as a Rolls, it can consistently deliver the quality that customers pay for and expect.

Thus, many companies today have turned customer-driven quality into a potent strategic weapon. They create customer satisfaction and value by consistently and profitably meeting customers' needs and preferences for quality. In fact, quality has now become a competitive necessity – in the twenty-first century, only companies with the best quality will thrive.

Product features

A product can be offered with varying features. A 'stripped-down' model, one without any extras, is the starting point. The company can create more features by adding higher-level models. Features are a competitive tool for differentiating the company's product from competitors' products. Being the first producer to introduce a needed and valued new feature is one of the most effective ways to compete.

How can a company identify new features and decide which ones to add to its product? The company should periodically survey buyers who have used the product and ask these questions: How do you like the product? Which specific features of the product do you like most? Which features could we add to improve the product? How much would you pay for each feature? The answers provide the company with a rich list of feature ideas. Each feature should be assessed on the basis of its *customer value* versus its *company cost*. Features that customers value little in relation to costs should be dropped; those that customers value highly in relation to costs should be added.

Product style and design

Another way to add customer value is through distinctive *product style and design*. Some companies have reputations for outstanding style and design, such as Black & Decker in cordless appliances and tools, Bose in audio equipment and Braun in shavers and small household appliances.

Some companies have integrated style and design with their corporate culture. They recognise that design is one of the most powerful competitive weapons in a company's marketing arsenal.

Consider IKEA, the Swedish home furnishing chain. Its corporate culture is 'småländsk' – thrift is a virtue, no extravagance is allowed. This identity is reflected in IKEA's thrifty (but stylish) designs and the dominance of traditional Scandinavian materials of light wood, linen and cotton textiles. Another company, the carmaker Saab, promotes a design philosophy of simplicity and purity. 'There are few excesses; form follows function. We also believe in fidelity to materials – when it's plastic, we don't try to make it look like wood', says a Saab spokesperson.[7]

Many companies, however, lack a 'design touch'. Their product designs function poorly or are dull or common looking. Some companies like Fiat Auto have learnt that design and style matters.

The Italian car company's European market share had collapsed from 10 per cent in 1990 to 6 per cent in 2003. Part of the problem is that they have alienated drivers by succeeding in making some rather ugly-looking cars: Britain's *Car* magazine has described Fiat's Multipla

Streets ahead.

To develop the most refined 4x4, we've explored every avenue. Sleek aerodynamic design. Best power to weight ratio in its class. 3-litre V6 engine. 4-level air suspension. Motorised tailgate. Steerable headlight system. Sequential control 5-speed transmission. Nine airbag system. And DVD satnav with rear view camera. For more information, call 0845 600 9760 or visit www.lexus.co.uk/rx300 The Lexus RX300. It changes everything.

THE RX300 ⊘ LEXUS

Top Manufacturer for Quality, Reliability and Customer Care in the UK. BBC Top Gear magazine Motoring Survey 2002 and 2003.

Lexus – 1st place, Gold Award J.D. Power and Associates 2001-2004 UK Customer Satisfaction Studies℠

Auto Express Driver Power Survey, Lexus Best Manufacturer 2002-2004

Model shown RX300 SE-L. Specifications listed above apply to RX300 SE-L model. RX300 SE-L £37,825 OTR. RX300 range prices start from £28,995 to £41,200 OTR. Prices correct at time of going to press. BBC Top Gear magazine Motoring Survey 2003 based on the results of questionnaires from over 40,000 motorists spanning 137 models from 35 manufacturers. Auto Express Driver Power Study 2004 based on 37,000 respondents. J.D. Power and Associates 2004 United Kingdom Customer Satisfaction Study℠ based on a total of 23,641 responses from owners of two-year old vehicles. www.jdpower.com
Fuel economy figures: extra-urban 9.4 L/100km (30.1 mpg), urban 16.9 L/100km (16.7 mpg), combined 12.2 L/100km (23.2 mpg). CO_2 emissions 288g/km.

The Lexus RX300 ad highlights product attributes which put the model streets ahead of competitors in the same product class. The RX300 is an example of distinctive product style and design.
SOURCE: Lexus (GB) Ltd.
Photographer: Mathias Bauman.
Agent: Defrance, Düsseldorf, Germany.

people-carrier as having 'bozz-eyed swamp-hog looks' and that its Dobio MPV is a 'Toytown-styled utilo-box' that is 'very big if you're desperate for space. But you'd have to be'. To reverse the falling European sales, Fiat's design director, Humberto Rodriguez, has set out to 'abolish all the strange things' they have done to these vehicles and to spearhead a new design direction for the automotive group – sleeker, family-feeling cars that may not necessarily be head-turners, like the Multipla is; but they will not leave the driver cringing with embarrassment.[8]

Design is a broader concept than style. *Style* simply describes the appearance of a product. A sensational style may grab attention and produce pleasing aesthetics, but it does not necessarily make the product *perform* better. In some cases, it might even result in worse performance. For example, a chair may look great yet be extremely uncomfortable. Unlike style, *design* is more than skin deep – it goes to the very heart of a product. Good design contributes to a product's usefulness as well as to its looks.

The Lexus RX300 as shown in the above advert is an example of distinctive product style and design. The advert features the slogan 'Streets ahead' to promote the RX300's attributes such as technology and styling to suggest that the RX, and hence the driver, is *Streets ahead* of the competition.

As competition intensifies, design will offer one of the most potent tools for differentiating and positioning products of all kinds. That investment in design pays off has certainly been recognised by global companies which have embraced design. Nike, for example, employs some 60 designers and releases over 500 footwear designs each year. Its shoes are worn by athletes, but are aimed primarily at a youthful market for which high-performance footwear is currently fashionable.[9] Apple's iMac computer, introduced in 1998, combined style and content. In response to the project brief – to design a new computer for consumers that was simple, approachable and affordable – Jonathan Ive, Apple's chief designer, produced the award-winning iMac. The computer's cuteness and distinctive colour single-handedly turned the tide for Apple, making it the fastest-selling computer in Apple's history. Others like Canon (cameras), Sony (hi-fis), Philips (compact disc players and shavers), Ford (cars) and Swatch (watches) have also profited from their commitment to product design. Differentiating through design is also a familiar strategy in premium products such as Rolex and Omega watches, Porsche cars and Herman Miller office furniture. These products stand out from the crowd. Good design can attract attention, improve product performance, cut production costs and give the product a strong competitive advantage in the target market.[10]

Branding

Perhaps the most distinctive skill of professional marketers is their ability to create, maintain, protect and enhance brands of their products. A **brand** is a name, term, sign, symbol, design or a combination of these, that identifies the maker or seller of the product or service. Consumers view a brand as an important part of a product, and branding can add value to a product. For example, most consumers would perceive a bottle of Chanel perfume as a high-quality, expensive product. But the same perfume in an unmarked bottle would probably be viewed as lower in quality, even if the fragrance were identical. A brand can provide a guarantee of reliability and quality. For example, a book buyer might not entrust her credit card details with an unknown online book store, but would have little hesitation doing so when buying from Amazon.com as experience had taught her to trust the Amazon brand.

Brand—A name, term, sign, symbol or design, or a combination of these, intended to identify the goods or services of one seller or group of sellers and to differentiate them from those of competitors.

Branding has become so strong that today hardly anything goes unbranded.[11] Salt is packaged in branded containers, common nuts and bolts are packaged with a distributor's label, and automotive parts – spark plugs, tyres, filters – bear brand names that differ from those of the carmakers. Even fruit and vegetables are branded – Sunkist oranges, Del Monte pineapples and Chiquita bananas.

Some products, however, carry no brands. 'Generic' products are unbranded, plainly packaged, less expensive versions of common products ranging from such items as spaghetti to paper towels and canned peaches. They often bear only black-stencilled labels and offer prices as much as 40 per cent lower than those of main brands. The lower price is made possible by lower-quality ingredients, lower-cost packaging and lower advertising costs.

Despite the limited popularity of generics, the issue of whether or not to brand is very much alive today. This situation highlights some key questions: Why have branding in the first place? Who benefits? How do they benefit? At what cost?

Branding helps buyers in many ways:

- Brand names tell the buyer something about product quality. Buyers who always buy the same brand know that they will get the same quality each time they buy.

- Brand names also increase the shopper's efficiency. Imagine a buyer going into a supermarket and finding thousands of generic products.

- Brand names help call consumers' attention to new products that might benefit them. The brand name becomes the basis upon which a whole story can be built about the new product's special qualities.

Branding also gives the supplier several advantages:

- The brand name makes it easier for the supplier to process orders and track down problems.

- The supplier's brand name and trademark provide legal protection for unique production features that otherwise might be copied by competitors.

- Branding enables the supplier to attract a loyal and profitable set of customers.

■ Branding helps the supplier to segment markets. For example, Cadbury offers Dairy Milk, Roses and other brands, not just one general confectionery product for all consumers.

In addition, branding adds value to consumers and society:

■ Those who favour branding suggest that it leads to higher and more consistent product quality.

■ Branding also increases innovation by giving producers an incentive to look for new features that can be protected against imitating competitors. Thus, branding results in more product variety and choice for consumers.

■ Branding helps shoppers because it provides much more information about products and where to find them.

Thus, building and managing brands represents one of the most important marketing tasks. We will discuss branding strategy in more detail later in this chapter.

Packaging

Packaging—The activities of designing and producing the container or wrapper for a product.

Packaging involves designing and producing the container or wrapper for a product. The package may include the product's primary container (the tube holding and protecting Aquafresh toothpaste); a secondary package that is thrown away when the product is about to be used (the cardboard box containing the tube of Aquafresh); and the shipping package necessary to store, identify and ship the product (a corrugated box carrying six dozen tubes of Aquafresh toothpaste). Labelling, printed information appearing on or with the package, is also part of packaging.

In recent times, many factors, beyond containing and protecting the product, have made packaging an important marketing tool. Increased competition and clutter on retail store shelves means that packages must now perform many sales tasks – from attracting attention, to describing the product, to making the sale. Companies are realising the power of good packaging to create instant consumer recognition of the company or brand. For example, in an average supermarket, which stocks 15,000 to 17,000 items, the typical shopper passes by some 300 items per minute, and 53 per cent of all purchases are made on impulse. In this highly competitive environment, the package may be the seller's last chance to influence buyers. It becomes a 'five-second commercial'. Research shows that a sizeable chunk of buyers can be swayed at the last minute from buying their cat's favourite tin of tuna bites if their eye is caught by a well-designed, competitive brand. Hence, manufacturers must use pack design – shape, graphics and texture – to project their brand values and differentiate them in an overcrowded market.

Innovative packaging can give a company an advantage over competitors. For example, Heineken used creative packaging to differentiate the product. In its green-glass bottle, with 'export' on the label, as opposed to the usual brown containers for beer, and priced to match its suggestion of exclusivity, it caught on as a beer for special occasions. According to the company's late founder, Mr Heineken, the firm was selling warmth and happiness, and they had to make the product more distinctive.[12]

Packaging concept—What the package should be or do for the product.

Developing a good package for a new product requires making many decisions. The first task is to establish the **packaging concept**, which states what the package should *be* or *do* for the product. Should the main functions of the package be to offer product protection, introduce a new dispensing method, communicate certain qualities about the product, the brand or the company, or something else? Decisions, then, must be made on package design that cover specific elements of the package, such as size, shape, materials, colour, text and brand mark. These elements must work together to support the product's position and marketing strategy and be consistent with the product's advertising, pricing and distribution.

In recent years, product safety has also become a major packaging concern. We have all learned to deal with hard-to-open 'childproof' packages. And after the rash of product tampering scares during the 1980s, most drug producers and food makers are now putting their products in tamper-resistant packages. In making packaging decisions, the company also must heed growing environmental concerns. Fortunately, many companies have gone 'green'.

For example, Tetra Pak, a Swedish multinational, is noted for its innovative packaging that takes environmental concerns into account. Tetra Pak invented an 'aseptic' package that enables milk, fruit juice and other perishable liquid foods to be distributed without refrigeration. Not only is this packaging more environmentally responsible, it also provides economic and distribution advantages. Aseptic packaging allows dairies to distribute milk over a wider area without investing in refrigerated trucks and facilities. Supermarkets can carry Tetra Pak packaged products on ordinary shelves, allowing them to save expensive refrigerator space. Tetra's motto is 'the package should save more than it cost'. Tetra Pak advertises the benefits of its packaging to consumers directly and even initiates recycling programmes to save the environment.

Labelling

Labels may range from simple tags attached to products to complex graphics that are part of the package. They perform several functions. At the very least, the label *identifies* the product or brand, such as the name 'Sunkist' stamped on oranges. The label might also *grade* the product, or *describe* several things about the product – who made it, where it was made, when it was made, its contents, how it is to be used and how to use it safely. Finally, the label might *promote* the product through attractive graphics.

There has been a long history of legal concerns about packaging and labels. Labels can mislead customers, fail to describe important ingredients or fail to include needed safety warnings. As a result, many countries have laws to regulate labelling. The EU, for example, has comprehensive European Community legislation, which set mandatory labelling requirements and adherence to packaging standards. For drinks, an EU directive has been recently enforced which subjects both non-alcoholic and alcoholic beverages to stringent labelling requirements.[13]

Labelling has also been affected in recent times by *unit pricing* (stating the price per unit of standard measure), *open dating* (stating the expected shelf life of the product) and *nutritional labelling* (stating the nutritional values in the product). In the case of the latter, sellers are required to provide detailed nutritional information on food products. In some countries, the use of health-related terms such as *low-fat*, *light* and *high-fibre* is also regulated. As such, sellers must ensure that their labels contain all the required information and comply with national or international (e.g. US, EU) requirements.

Product-support services

Customer service is another element of product strategy. A company's offer to the marketplace usually includes some services, which can be a minor or a major part of the total offer. In Chapter 15, we will discuss services as products in themselves. Here, we address **product-support services** – services that augment actual products. More and more companies are using product-support services as a major tool in gaining competitive advantage.

Good customer service makes sound business sense. It costs less to keep the goodwill of existing customers than it does to attract new customers or woo back lost customers. A study

Product-support services— Services that augment actual products.

comparing the performance of businesses that had high and low customer ratings of service quality found that the high-service businesses managed to charge more, grow faster and make more profits.[14] Clearly, marketers need to think about their service strategies.

A company should design its product and support services to meet the needs of target customers. Customers vary in the value they assign to different services. Some consumers want credit and financing services, fast and reliable delivery, or quick installation. Others put more weight on technical information and advice, training in product use, or after-sale service and repair. The first step in deciding which product-support services to offer is to determine both the services that target consumer value and the relative importance of these services.

Determining customers' service needs involves more than simply monitoring complaints that come in over freephone lines or on comment cards. The company should periodically survey its customers to assess the value of current services and to obtain ideas for new ones. Once the company has assessed the value of various services to customers, it must next assess the costs of providing these services. It can then develop a package of services that will both delight customers and yield profits to the company.

Many companies are now using the Internet and other modern technologies to provide support services that were not possible before. For example, using the Internet, 24-hour telephone help lines, self-service kiosks and other digital technologies, companies are able to empower consumers to tailor their own service and support experiences.

Product-line decisions

We have looked at decisions about individual products. But product strategy also calls for building a product line. A **product line** is a group of products that are closely related because they function in a similar manner, are sold to the same customer groups, are marketed through the same types of outlet, or fall within given price ranges. For example, Nokia produces several lines of telecommunications products, Philips produces several lines of audio entertainment systems and Nike produces several lines of athletic shoes and clothings. We will examine the major product line decisions next.

Product line—A group of products that are closely related because they function in a similar manner, are sold to the same customer groups, are marketed through the same types of outlet, or fall within given price ranges.

Product line stretching: DaimlerChrysler introduced several smaller, lower-priced models, including Smart city-coupé, starting at €8405.64; Smart is the innovative brand for the sub-a segment in the DaimlerChrysler group.
SOURCE: MCC Smart GmbH, www.media.smart.com.

Product line-length decisions

The major product line decision involves *product line length* – the number of items in the product line. The line is too short if the manager can increase profits by adding items; the line is too long if the manager can increase profits by dropping items. Product line length is influenced by company objectives and resources. Companies that want to be positioned as full-line companies, or that are seeking high market share and market growth, usually carry longer lines. Companies that are keen on high short-term profitability generally carry shorter lines consisting of selected items. Another objective may be to allow upselling. For example, BMW seeks to move customers from its 3-series models to 5- and 7-series models. Still another objective might be to allow cross-selling: Hewlett-Packard sells printers as well as cartridges.

Over time, product line managers tend to add new products. However, as the manager adds items, several costs rise: design and engineering costs, inventory carrying costs, manufacturing changeover costs, order-processing costs, transportation costs, and promotional costs to introduce new items. Consequently, the company must plan product line growth carefully. It can systematically increase the length of its product line in two ways: by *stretching* its line and by *filling* its line. **Product line stretching** occurs when a company lengthens its product line beyond its current range. Figure 13.3 shows that the company can stretch its line downwards, upwards or both ways.

Product line stretching— Increasing the product line by lengthening it beyond its current range.

Figure 13.3 **Product-line stretching decisions**

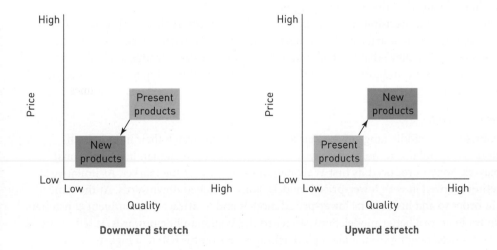

Downward stretch

Upward stretch

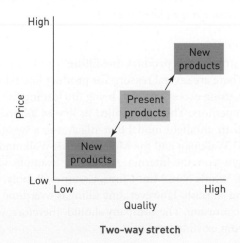

Two-way stretch

Downward stretch

Many companies initially locate at the upper end of the market and later stretch their lines downwards. A company may stretch downwards to plug a market hole that otherwise would attract a new competitor or to respond to a competitor's attack on the upper end. Or it may add low-end products because it finds faster growth taking place in the low-end segments.

Mercedes stretched downwards for all these reasons. Facing a slow-growth luxury car market and attacks by Japanese automakers on its high-end positioning, Mercedes successfully introduced its C-Class cars at €35,000 without harming its ability to sell other Mercedes for €100,000 or more. And in the joint venture with Switzerland's Swatch watchmaker, Mercedes launched the Smart microcompact car, priced from € 8,000 upwards.[15] Similarly, Compaq and IBM had to add less expensive personal computer lines to fend off competition from low-priced 'clones' and to take advantage of faster market growth in the lower end of the computer market.

Upward stretch

Companies at the lower end of the market may want to stretch their product lines *upwards*. Sometimes, companies stretch upwards in order to add prestige to their current products. They may be attracted by a faster growth rate or higher margins at the higher end, or they may simply want to position themselves as full-line manufacturers. Thus, Toyota, the leading Japanese auto company, introduced an up-market line – Lexus – and used an entirely new name rather than its own name. Other companies have included their own names in moving up-market. For example, Gallo introduced Ernest and Julio Gallo Varietals and priced these wines at more than twice the price of its regular wines.[16]

An upward stretch decision can be risky. The higher-end competitors not only are well entrenched, but also may strike back by entering the lower end of the market. Prospective customers may not believe that the newcomer can produce quality products. Finally, the company's salespeople and distributors may lack the talent and training to serve the higher end of the market.

Two-way stretch

Companies in the middle range of the market may decide to stretch their lines in both directions. Sony did this to hold off copycat competitors of its Walkman line of personal tape players. Sony introduced its first Walkman in the middle of the market. As imitative competitors moved in with lower-priced models, Sony stretched downwards. At the same time, in order to add lustre to its lower-priced models and to attract more affluent consumers keen to trade up to a better model, Sony stretched the Walkman line upwards. It sells more than 100 models, ranging from a plain playback-only version for €30 to a high-tech, high-quality €550 version that both plays and records. Using this two-way stretch strategy, Sony came to dominate the global personal tape player market.

Product line-filling decisions

Product line filling—

Increasing the product line by adding more items within the present range of the line.

An alternative to product line stretching is **product line filling** – adding more items within the present range of the line. There are several reasons for product line filling: reaching for extra profits, satisfying dealers, using excess capacity, being the leading full-line company, and plugging holes to keep out competitors. Thus, Sony filled its line by adding solar-powered and waterproof Walkmans and an ultralight model that attaches to a sweatband for exercisers, the Minidisc Walkman, the CD Walkman and the Memory Stick Walkman, which enables users to download tracks straight from the Internet. As another example, Cadbury's Dairy Milk line includes Fruit & Nut, Whole Nut, Mint Chips, Caramel, Bubbly, Crunchie Bits, Crispies, Short Cake Biscuit and Turkish. However, line filling is overdone if it results in cannibalisation and customer confusion. The company should, therefore, ensure that new items are *noticeably different* from existing ones.

Product-mix decisions

Some companies may offer not one but several lines of products which form a **product mix** or *product assortment*. For example, a cosmetics firm may have four main product lines in its product mix: cosmetics, jewellery, fashions and household items. Each product line may consist of sublines. For example, cosmetics beak down into lipstick, powder, nail varnish, eye-shadows and so on. Each line and subline may have many individual items. For example, eye-shadows contain a string of items, ranging from different colours to alternative application modes (e.g. pencil, roll-on, powder).

A company's product mix has four important dimensions: width, length, depth and consistency. For example, Unilever markets a fairly wide product mix consisting of many product lines, including paper, food, household cleaning, cosmetics and personal care products. Product mix *length* refers to the total number of items the company carries within its product lines. Product line *depth* refers to the number of versions offered of each product in the line. For Unilever offers different sizes and formulations (liquid, powder, tablet) of laundry detergent. Finally, the *consistency* of the product mix refers to how closely related the various product lines are in end use, production requirements, distribution channels or some other way. Unilever's packaged goods lines are consistent insofar as they are consumer products that go through the same distribution channels. The lines are less consistent insofar as they perform different functions for buyers.

These product-mix dimensions provide the handles for defining the company's product strategy. The company can increase its business in four ways:

1. It can add new product lines, thus widening its product mix. In this way, its new lines build on the company's reputation in its other lines.
2. The company can lengthen its existing product lines to become a more full-line company.
3. It can add more product versions of each product and thus deepen its product mix.
4. The company can pursue more product line consistency, or less, depending on whether it wants to have a strong reputation in a single field or in several fields.

Product mix (product assortment)—The set of all product lines and items that a particular seller offers for sale to buyers.

Branding strategy: building strong brands

Brands are viewed as *the* major enduring asset of a company, outlasting the company's specific products and facilities. John Stewart, co-founder of Quaker Oats, once said 'If this business were split up, I would give you the land and bricks and mortar, and I would keep the brands and trademarks, and I would fare better than you'. The CEO of McDonald's agrees. Consider a situation where every asset the company owns, every building and every piece of equipment were destroyed in a terrible natural disaster. McDonald's CEO argues that he would be able to borrow all the money to replace these assets very quickly because of the value of the brand. The brand is more valuable than the totality of all these assets![17]

Thus, brands are powerful assets that must be carefully developed and managed. In this section, we examine the key strategies for building and managing brands.

Brand equity

Brands are more than just names and symbols. Brands represent consumers' perceptions and feelings about products and its performance – everything that the product or service *means* to consumers. As one branding expert suggests, 'Ultimately, brands reside in the minds of consumers'.[18] Thus, the real value of a strong brand is its power to capture consumer preference and loyalty.

Brand equity—The value of a brand, based on the extent to which it has high brand loyalty, name awareness, perceived quality, strong brand associations, and other assets such as patents, trademarks and channel relationships.

Brands vary in the amount of power and value they have in the marketplace. Some brands are largely unknown to most buyers. Other brands have a high degree of consumer *brand awareness*. Still others enjoy *brand preference* – buyers select them over the others. Finally, some brands command a high degree of *brand loyalty*. A powerful brand has high **brand equity**. Brand equity is the positive differential effect that knowing the brand name has on customer response to the product or service. Brands have higher brand equity to the extent that they have higher brand loyalty, name awareness, perceived quality, strong brand associations and other assets such as patents, trademarks and channel relationships.[19] A measure of the brand's equity is the extent to which customers are willing to pay more for the brand. One study found that 72 per cent of customers would pay a 20 per cent premium for their brand of choice relative to the closest competing brand; 40 per cent said they would pay a 50 per cent premium.[20]

A brand with strong brand equity is a valuable asset. Companies have sought to put a value on their brands. *Brand valuation* is the process of estimating the total financial value of a brand. Measuring the actual equity of a brand name is difficult.[21] However, according to one estimate, the brand value of Coca-Cola is $69 billion, that of Microsoft is $65 billion, and IBM's is $53 billion. Other brands rating among the world's most valuable include General Electric, Nokia, Intel, Disney, Ford, McDonald's, and AT&T.[22] 'Brand equity has emerged over the past few years as a key strategic asset', observes a brand consultant. 'CEOs in many industries now see their brands as a source of control and a way to build stronger relationships with customers.'[23]

Because it is so hard to measure, companies usually do not list brand equity on their balance sheets. Although it is difficult to incorporate brand values in balance sheets, accounting standards (e.g. the UK Financial Reporting Standard, FRS 10, and its international equivalent, IAS 38) compel firms to put a value on their acquired brands on their balance sheets. Accounting for brands may pose a challenge to marketers in the new millennium, but given the recent mergers and acquisition trends in Europe, assessing how much brands are worth helps management to see the link between the money spent on acquiring a brand and the value created (see Marketing Insights 13.1).

Brand accounting makes sense as it gets managers to consider how they might manage the acquired brand as an asset that the company has paid, often handsomely, for.[24] For example, Germany's Mannesmann paid nearly £20 billion for the mobile phone brand Orange. Britain's Vodafone AirTouch acquired Mannesmann in 2000 for $190 billion. Volkswagen snapped up Rolls-Royce Motor Cars Ltd for £479 million. Unilever paid $20.3 billion for Bestfoods, the maker of Knorr soups and Hellmann's mayonnaise.

High brand equity provides a company with many competitive advantages. A powerful brand enjoys a high level of consumer brand awareness and loyalty, and the company will incur lower marketing costs relative to revenues. Because consumers expect stores to carry the brand, the company has more leverage in bargaining with retailers. Because the brand name carries high credibility, the company can more easily launch line and brand extensions, as when Lever Brothers leveraged its well-known Persil brand to introduce dishwashing detergent. Above all, a powerful brand offers the company some defence against fierce price competition.

Marketers need to manage their brands carefully to preserve brand equity. In order to maintain or improve brand awareness, perceived brand quality and usefulness, and positive brand associations over time, they need to work with R&D to provide a constant flow of improved and innovative products to satisfy customers' changing needs. Investment in skilful advertising and excellent trade and consumer service is also necessary. Some companies appoint 'brand equity managers' to guard their brands' images, associations and quality. They work to prevent brand managers from overpromoting brands in order to produce short-term profits at the expense of long-term brand equity.

Brands: what are they worth?

Given the importance of brand value, how do companies determine what their brands are worth? According to Jeremy Bullmore of WPP, while everyone agrees that brands are valuable, there is no consensus on how to value them. He adds: 'The only time you can be sure of the value of your brand is just after you have sold it.'

One of the most commonly quoted brand valuation studies is by Interbrand, the branding consultancy. Using publicly available financial and marketing information, Interbrand estimates the economic earnings – which is equal to the brand's future operating profits minus a capital and tax charge – for the world's best-known brands and translates those forecasts into brand valuations. Interbrand calculates the proportion of future earnings that is attributable to the brand, based on an assessment of the role played by brands in different markets, and applying a discount to reflect the amount of risk. The method of analysis means that private companies' brands where information is unavailable (e.g. Levi's, Lego, Mars) or firms where earnings are not generated in the accepted sense (e.g. Visa, MasterCard, the BBC) are omitted.

However, others argue that there are weaknesses in the Interbrand approach, claiming that it fails to measure what markets want to know: the future growth potential of the brand, including the potential impact of strategies such as brand extension.

According to Alec Rattray, marketing director at Landor Associates, one thing is simple and certain: there is no such thing as a static measure. The value of a brand is based on a number of dynamic variables including competitive set, category strength, differentiation, relevance, management ability, corporate strategy and existing intangible and tangible assets. Not only do these change regularly, but the focus on each one changes depending on the requirements of the business. Brand value is a relative measure, contingent on circumstances and perspective. Ultimately, brands are valued by their audiences, not by consultants.

So, what is the right way to value a brand? It very much depends on the firm's objective. Is it seeking to measure the disposal or acquisition value of the company, division, service or product? Is it seeking to allocate an appropriate marketing investment? Does it want to put its intangibles on the books? Does it simply want to know what difference the brand makes?

Depending on the question, there are two fundamentally different approaches. The first is shareholder value – a measure of the future growth potential of a company by understanding the contribution made by a brand or brands. This is generally expressed in terms of the potential effect on share price, earnings and/or sales, and

marketing insights

...13.1

is the conventional 'corporate' perspective. Calculating shareholder value is based on four measures: tangible and intangible assets – the meat and drink of accountants – and strategic robustness plus managerial capability. This second group is where sophistication lies. Measuring past performance provides little guidance as to future growth; leadership and vision is a more valid measure.

These measures must then be factored through an analysis of brand saliency in a specific category. For example, brands have a greater role to play in mobile as opposed to fixed-line telephony. This 'brand factor' must be based on empirical data. Databases such as Y&R's Brand Asset Valuator® and WPP's BrandZ are ideal for this type of rigorous contextualisation. Using BAV data, BrandEconomics™ has emerged as a significant advance in brand valuation. It correlates the proportion of intangible value with brand image tracking, to determine a relationship between brand strength and the earnings of the business.

The second approach to valuing brands is brand equity – a measure of the historical and present value a brand commands in shaping trial, preference and loyalty. This is the classic 'consumer' perspective. Calculating brand equity is based on the fundamentals of brand building – recognising that superior differentiation is a cypher for premium pricing and that superior relevance is highly correlated to market share. Differentiation and relevance are understood by consumers as special characteristics of function, performance, personality and authority. Hence, measuring how brands outperform their competitors against these characteristics – identifying brand equity – provides a yardstick for the brand's value.

As with shareholder value, you need a broad base of knowledge: what are the specific characteristics that shape purchase behaviour in a given sector? Through which services or channels are they best delivered and communicated?

Brand valuation is critical, but it is not a mystery. You determine what you want to measure and why. And you combine shareholder value and brand equity methodologies to make a robust measure.

SOURCES: Based on Alec Rattray, 'Measure for measure', *Financial Times, FT Creative Business* (9 July 2002), p. 15; see also Louella Miles, 'Brands of gold', *Marketing Business* (December/January 2000), pp. 18–21; 'Leaders of the pack', *Financial Times* (18 July 2000), p. 17; 'Brands bite back', *The Economist* (21 March 1998), p. 98.

Yet, behind every powerful brand stands a set of loyal customers. Therefore, the basic asset underlying brand equity is *customer equity* – the value of the consumer relationships that the brand creates. This suggests that the proper focus of marketing planning is that of extending *loyal customer lifetime value*, with brand management serving as an essential marketing tool.[25]

Branding poses challenging decisions to the marketer. Figure 13.4 shows the major branding decisions involving brand positioning, brand name selection, brand sponsorship and brand development. We will examine each of these in turn.

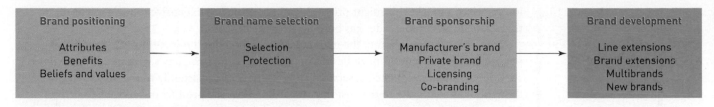

Figure 13.4 **Major brand strategy decisions**

Brand positioning

Marketers need to position their brands clearly in target customers' minds. But a brand is a complex symbol that can convey several levels of meaning:[26]

1. *Attributes.* A brand first brings to mind certain product attributes. For example, Mercedes suggests such attributes as 'well engineered', 'well built', 'durable', 'high prestige', 'fast', 'expensive' and 'high resale value'. The company may use one or more of these attributes in its advertising for the car. For years, Mercedes advertised 'Engineered like no other car in the world'. This provided a positioning platform for other attributes of the car.

2. *Benefits.* Customers do not buy attributes, they buy benefits. Therefore, attributes must be translated into functional and emotional benefits. For example, the attribute 'durable' could translate into the functional benefit 'I won't have to buy a new car every few years.' The attribute 'expensive' might translate into the emotional benefit 'The car makes me feel important and admired.' The attribute 'well built' might translate into the functional and emotional benefit 'I am safe in the event of an accident.'

3. *Values.* A brand also says something about the buyers' values. Thus Mercedes buyers value high performance, safety and prestige. A brand marketer must identify the specific groups of car buyers whose values coincide with the delivered benefit package.

4. *Culture.* A brand also represents a certain culture. The Mercedes represents 'German culture': high performance, efficient, high quality.

5. *Personality.* A brand also projects a personality. Motivation researchers sometimes ask 'If this brand were a person, what kind of person would it be?'. Consumers might visualise a Mercedes automobile as being a wealthy, middle-aged business executive. The brand will attract people whose actual or desired self-images match the brand's image.

All this suggests that a brand is a complex symbol. If a company treats a brand only as a name, it misses the point of branding. The challenge of branding is to develop a deep set of meanings or associations for the brand. Given the five levels of a brand's meaning, marketers must decide the level(s) at which they will position the brand and to promote the brand. It would be a mistake to promote only the brand's attributes. Remember, buyers are interested not so much in brand attributes as in brand benefits. Moreover, competitors can easily copy attributes. Or the current attributes may later become less valuable to consumers, hurting a brand that is tied too strongly to specific attributes.

Even promoting the brand on one or more of its benefits can be risky. Suppose Mercedes touts its main benefit as 'high performance'. If several competing brands emerge with as high or higher performance, or if car buyers begin placing less importance on performance as compared to other benefits, Mercedes will need the freedom to move into a new benefit positioning.

The most lasting and sustainable meanings of a brand are its core values and personality. They define the brand's essence. Thus Mercedes stands for 'high achievers and success'. The company must build its brand strategy around creating and protecting these values and personality. Although Mercedes has recently yielded to market pressures by introducing lower-priced models, this might prove risky. Marketing less expensive models might dilute the personality that Mercedes has built up over the decades.

When positioning a brand, the marketer should establish a mission for the brand and a vision of what the brand must be and do. A brand is the company's promise to deliver a specific set of features, benefits, services and experiences consistently to the buyers. It can be thought of as a contract to the customer regarding how the product or service will deliver value and satisfaction. The brand contract must be simple and honest. Sleep Inn, for example, offers clean rooms, low prices and good service but does not promise expensive furniture or large bathrooms. In contrast, Ritz-Carlton offers luxurious rooms and a truly memorable experience but does not promise low prices.

Brand name selection

Selecting the right name is a crucial part of the marketing process. A good name can add greatly to a product's success. However, finding the best brand name is a difficult task. It begins with a careful review of the product and its benefits, the target market and proposed marketing strategies.

Desirable qualities for a brand name include the following:

1. It should suggest something about the product's benefits and qualities. Examples are Pro-activ (a cholesterol-lowering margarine), Oasis (a refreshing fruit drink), Frisp (a light savoury snack) and TimeOut (a chocolate biscuit to go with coffee or tea breaks).

2. It should be easy to pronounce, recognise and remember. Short names help. Examples are Benecol (cholesterol-lowering dairy products), Dove (soap), Yale (security products) and Hula Hoops (potato crisps shaped like the name). But longer ones are sometimes effective, such as 'I Can't Believe It's Not Butter' margarine.

3. The brand name should be distinctive. Examples are Shell, Kodak and Virgin.

4. The name should translate easily (and meaningfully) into foreign languages. For example, in Chinese Ferrari is pronounced as 'fa li li', the Chinese symbols for which mean 'magic, weapon, pull, power', which flatter the brand. But accountancy firm Price Waterhouse was reported to have been translated as 'expensive water closet'.

Finding a name for a product designed for worldwide markets is not easy. Companies must avoid the pitfalls inherent in injudicious product naming.
SOURCE: Interbrand.

5. It should be capable of registration and legal protection. A brand name cannot be registered if it infringes on existing brand names. Also, brand names that are merely descriptive or suggestive may not be protectable. For example, the Miller Brewing Company registered the name Lite for its low-calorie beer and invested millions in establishing the name with consumers. But the courts later ruled that the terms *lite* and *light* are generic or common descriptive terms applied to beer and that Miller could not use the Lite name exclusively.[27]

Once chosen, the brand name must be registered with the appropriate Trade Marks Register, giving owners intellectual property rights and preventing competitors from using the same or a similar name (see Marketing Insights 13.2). Many firms try to build a brand name that will eventually become identified with the product category. Brand names such as Hoover, Kleenex, Levi's, Scotch Tape, Post-it Notes, Formica and Fiberglas have succeeded in this way. However, their very success may threaten the company's rights to the name. Many originally protected brand names, such as cellophane, aspirin, nylon, kerosene, linoleum, yo-yo, trampoline, escalator, thermos and shredded wheat, are now generic names that any seller can use.[28]

Brand sponsor

A manufacturer has four sponsorship options. The product may be launched as a **manufacturer's brand** (or national brand), as when Lever Brothers, Nestlé and IBM sell their output under their own manufacturer's brand names. Or the manufacturer may sell to intermediaries that give it a **private brand** (also called *retailer brand*, *distributor brand* or *store brand*). For example, Cott, a Canadian company, makes store-branded foods and drinks, and supplies to retailers worldwide. Although most manufacturers create their own brand names, others market **licensed brands**. For example, some clothing and fashion accessory sellers pay large fees to put the names or initials of fashion innovators such as Calvin Klein, Pierre Cardin and Gucci on their products. Finally, companies can join forces and **co-brand** a product.

Manufacturers' brands versus private brands

Manufacturers' brands have long dominated the retail scene. In recent times, however, an increasing number of supermarkets, department and discount stores, and appliance dealers have developed their own private brands. These private brands are often hard to establish and costly to stock and promote. However, intermediaries develop private labels because they can be profitable. They can often locate manufacturers with excess capacity that will produce the private label at a low cost, resulting in a higher profit margin for the intermediary. Private brands also give intermediaries exclusive products that cannot be bought from competitors, resulting in higher store traffic and loyalty. For example, Sainsbury's, the grocery retailer, offers its own brand of laundry detergents, called Novon, which is marketed alongside branded products produced by P&G and Lever Brothers.

In the so-called *battle of the brands* between manufacturers' and private brands, retailers have many advantages. They control what products they stock, where they go on the shelf and which ones they will feature in local circulars. Intermediaries can give their own store brands better display space and make certain they are better stocked. They price store brands lower than comparable manufacturers' brands, thereby appealing to budget-conscious shoppers, especially in difficult economic times.

As store brands improve in quality and as consumers gain confidence in their store chains, store brands will continue to pose a strong challenge to manufacturers' brands. The battle rages on. Winners are most likely to follow one simple rule – achieve success through delivering superior value to target customers. Ultimately, consumer franchise is the name of the game![29]

Manufacturer's brand (national brand)—A brand created and owned by the producer of a product or service.

Private brand (middleman, distributor or store brand)—A brand created and owned by a reseller of a product or service.

Licensed brand—A product or service using a brand name offered by the brand owner to the licensee for an agreed fee or royalty.

Co-brand—The practice of using the established brand names of two different companies on the same product.

marketing insights

13.2   Trademarks worth fighting for!

What's in a name? Quite a lot, brand loyalists might say. But what's in a slogan, a shape, a smell or a colour? Plenty that's worth fighting for, many might add. Philips' razors, Wall's ice-cream, Pampers' nappies, Wrigley's chewing-gum, Nestlé's confectionery, . . . the range of trademark cases passing before the European Court of Justice, the European Union's ultimate arbiter on trademark law, could hardly be more diverse.

Nestlé, the Swiss confectionery and food group, which makes KitKat, has already trademarked the phrase 'Have a Break, Have a KitKat'. But it has lost its battle to secure similar intellectual property rights over the simpler 'Have a Break' phrase. Back in 2002, its application to the Trade Mark Registry was turned down after objections by US-owned arch-rival Mars. The registry's hearing officer said that the mark was 'devoid of any distinctive character' and therefore lacked 'inherent distinctiveness'. Nestlé, however, appealed to the High Court, pointing to consumer research suggesting that use of the mark 'Have a Break' elicited the response 'Have a KitKat' from a substantial number of snack-munchers – and also that a chocolate bar called 'Have a Break' would be supposed to come from the makers of KitKat. But Mr Justice Rimer had regarded the survey exercise as 'somewhat pointless', acknowledging that many of those questioned associated the phrase 'Have a Break' with KitKat or were reminded of the chocolate bar. He added: 'The survey demonstrated, and could demonstrate, no more than that a high proportion of the public will make the association. It did not, and could not, show that "Have a Break" had acquired a distinctiveness as a result of its use as a mark.'

In April 2003, a preliminary opinion in the Wrigley's Doublemint case narrowed the extent to which brand names with a descriptive element can be protected. Under the EU's Community Trade Mark Regulation, names made up solely of descriptions are barred from registration. Nevertheless, back in 2001 Procter & Gamble succeeded in registering the Pampers 'Baby Dry' brand. Baby Dry's success, according to Francis Jacobs, Advocate-General (A-G), was because of its 'extreme ellipsis, unusual structure, resistance to any intuitive grammatical analysis' and the fact that it was an 'invented term'. In the case of Doublemint, 'whose features are . . . very considerably less marked', while the word 'doublemint' might not appear in any dictionary, 'its creation is essentially limited to removing the space between two words which may well be used together descriptively.'

What about the trademarking of shapes? Compared to names or slogans, 'shapes' has been a thorny area for intellectual property law, partly because a shape is often marketed in association with a brand name. 'It's often difficult to prove sufficient distinctiveness for a secondary mark [such as the shape]', said Elaine Rowley, a

...13.2

lawyer at Marks & Clerk, a trademark specialist. A long legal tussle between Philips and Remington over electric shaver designs finally provided guidance in 2002 for 'functional shapes'. Essentially, a company cannot monopolise an engineering design by registering it as a trademark. While the famous Coke bottle has long been trademarked, other cases – such as Unilever's Viennetta ice-cream dessert – are only now working their way through the court. Unilever, who makes Viennetta, claims that the fancily decorated block of ice-cream represents a distinctive shape. But lawyers say there is still confusion over the extent to which 'aesthetic shapes' can be trademarked. What is meant by 'distinctiveness'?

In the Viennetta case, a High Court judge said he was inclined to refuse registration of the ice-cream's shape as a trademark. First, although Viennetta was widely recognised by the public, it had not been shown that Unilever had used the shape to denote trade origin or that the public depended on the shape alone to denote trade origin. 'What has not been proved is that any member of the public would rely upon the appearance alone to identify the goods. They recognise it but do not treat it as a trademark', the judge suggested. Secondly, he said the shape had not acquired a 'distinctive character' because a small but significant proportion of the public confused other fancy ice-cream desserts with Viennetta: research submitted by Unilever suggested that 15 per cent of those questioned confused other products with Viennetta.

Trademark parameters in such areas as colour and smell are even more controversial. Colour is an area that is attracting a great deal of interest. In a recent Libertel case – where the Dutch group was trying to register a shade of orange for telecoms-related goods and services – the advocate-general decided that it could not be determined how the company planned to use the colour in relation to its services and products, and found that a colour in itself – unassociated with any other element or object – could not be a trademark. It looks like very broad registrations will face an uphill task.

As for smell, a German applicant – a Mr Sieckmann – was rebuffed by the court. He had attempted to register an olfactory mark, by outlining its chemistry, depositing a sample of the scent in a container, and describing it verbally as 'balsamically fruity with a slight hint of cinnamon'. But the court said his efforts failed to meet the registration requirement that a mark's representation be 'clear, precise, self-contained, easily accessible, intelligible, durable and objective'.

Certainly, trademark battles will rage on and the European Commission's efforts to harmonise trademark standards and build up a cohesive body of case law have some way to go. Meanwhile, be prepared for plenty of courtroom surprises!

SOURCES: Nikki Tait, 'Time to test the boundaries', *Financial Times, Special Report: Intellectual Property* (30 April 2003), p. II; Nikki Tait, 'Viennetta trademark case cuts no ice with judge', *Financial Times* (19 December 2002), p. 3; Nikki Tait, 'Nestlé loses battle over "Have a Break" trademark', *Financial Times* (3 December 2002), p. 4.

Licensing

Most manufacturers take years and spend millions to create their own brand names. However, some companies license names or symbols previously created by other manufacturers, names of celebrities, and characters from popular movies and books – for a fee, any of these can provide an instant and proven brand name. Clothing and accessories sellers pay large royalties to adorn their products – from blouses to ties and linens to luggage – with the names or initials of well-known fashion innovators such as Calvin Klein, Gucci, Tommy Hilfiger or Armani.

Sellers of children's products attach an almost endless list of character names to clothing, toys, school supplies, linens, dolls, lunch boxes, cereals and other items. The character names include such classics as Disney's Mickey and Minnie Mouse, Barbie, Scooby Doo, Winnie the Pooh and Sesame Street to the more recent Teletubbies, Pokémon, Powerpuff Girls and Harry Potter characters.

Corporate brand licensing— A form of licensing whereby a firm rents a corporate trademark or logo made famous in one product or service category and uses it in a related category.

The fastest-growing licensing category is **corporate brand licensing** – renting a corporate trademark or logo made famous in one category and using it in a related category. Some examples include Cosmopolitan underwear, swimwear and home furnishings, Royal Ascot ties, hats, cashmere socks and jewellery, and Porsche sunglasses and accessories.

Name and character licensing has become big business in recent years. More and more for-profit and non-profit organisations are licensing their names to generate additional revenues and brand recognition. Coca-Cola's licensing programme has met with extraordinary success. It consists of a department overseeing more than 320 licensees in 57 countries producing more than 10,000 products, ranging from baby clothes and boxer shorts to earrings and even a fishing lure shaped like a tiny Coke can. Even the Vatican engages in licensing: heavenly images from its art collection, architecture, frescoes and manuscripts are now imprinted on such earthy objects as T-shirts, ties, glassware, candles and ornaments.[30]

Co-branding

Although companies have been co-branding products for many years, there has been a recent resurgence in co-branded products. Co-branding occurs when two established brand names of different companies are used on the same product or service. Co-branding partners seek to mutually enhance each other's service or product brand through close association. For example, Kellogg's joined forces with ConAgra to co-brand Kellogg's Healthy Choice cereals. In most co-branding situations, one company licenses another company's well-known brand to use in combination with its own.

Co-branding offers many advantages. Because each brand dominates in a different category, the combined brands create broader consumer appeal and greater brand equity. Co-branding also allows companies to enter new markets with minimal risk or investment. For example, by licensing its Healthy Choice brand to Kellogg, ConAgra entered the breakfast segment with a solid product. In return, Kellogg could leverage the broad awareness of the Healthy Choice name in the cereal category.

Co-branding also has its limitations. If a company chooses the wrong partner, or the partner suffers a setback or bad publicity, the company will be tainted by the association. In addition, such relationships usually involve complex legal contracts and licenses. Co-branding partners must carefully coordinate their advertising, sales promotion and other marketing efforts. Finally, when co-branding, each partner must trust that the other will take good care of its brand.[31]

Brand development

A company has four choices when it comes to developing brands (see Figure 13.5). It can introduce *line extensions* (existing brand names extended to new forms, sizes and flavours of an existing product category), *brand extensions* (existing brand names extended to new product categories), *multibrands* (new brand names introduced in the same product category) or *new brands* (new brand names in new product categories).

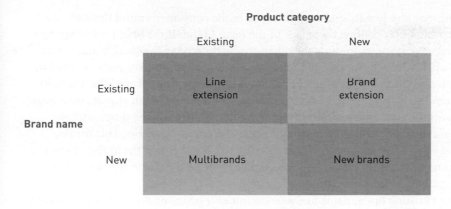

Product category

	Existing	New
Existing	Line extension	Brand extension
New	Multibrands	New brands

Brand name

Figure 13.5 **Brand development strategies**

Line extensions

Line extensions occur when a company introduces additional items in a given product category under the same brand name, such as new flavours, forms, colours, ingredients or package sizes. Thus, Danone has added several new flavours to its yoghurt line, as well as fat-free and large, family/economy-size varieties.

The vast majority of new-product activity consists of line extensions. A company introduces line extensions in order to meet consumers' desire for variety, utilise excess capacity, or simply command more shelf-space from resellers. Or it might recognise a latent consumer want and try to capitalise on it. However, line extensions involve some risks. An overextended brand might lose its specific meaning – some marketing strategists call this the 'line-extension trap'.[32] Heavily extended brands can also cause consumer confusion or frustration. A consumer buying cereal at a supermarket will be confronted by more than 150 brands, up to 30 different brand flavours and sizes of oatmeal alone. By itself, Quaker offers its original Quaker Oats, several flavours of Quaker instant oatmeal, and several dry cereals such as Oatmeal Squares, Toasted Oatmeal and Toasted Oatmeal-Honey Nut.

Another risk is that sales of an extension may come at the expense of other items in the line. A line extension works best when it takes sales away from competing brands, not when it 'cannibalises' the company's other items.[33]

Line extension—Using a successful brand name to introduce additional items in a given product category under the same brand name, such as new flavours, forms, colours, added ingredients or package sizes.

Brand extensions

A **brand extension** (or brand stretching) strategy is any effort to use a successful brand name to launch new or modified products in a new category. Swiss Army Brand sunglasses is a brand extension. Swatch spread from watches into telephones. And Honda stretched its company name to cover different products such as its cars, motorcycles, lawnmowers, marine engines and snowmobiles.

A brand-extension strategy offers many advantages. A well-regarded brand name helps the company enter new product categories more easily as it gives a new product instant recognition and faster acceptance. Sony puts its name on most of its new electronic products, creating an instant perception of high quality for each new product. Thus, brand extensions also save the high advertising cost usually required to familiarise consumers with a new brand name.

At the same time, a brand-extension strategy involves some risk. Brand extensions such as Bic pantyhose, Heinz pet food and Cadbury soup met early deaths. In each case, the brand name was not appropriate to the new product, even though it was well made and satisfying. Brand extensions fail if the established brand name is launched into a very different market from the original brand and target customers in the new market did not value the brand's associations. Would you consider buying Chanel galoshes? Or a Pepsi single malt whisky?

Brand extension—Using a successful brand name to launch a new or modified product in a new category.

A brand name may also lose its special positioning in the consumer's mind through overuse. The extension may confuse the image of the main brand. If the brand extension fails, it may harm consumer attitudes towards the other products carrying the same brand name. *Brand dilution* occurs when consumers no longer associate a brand with a specific product or even highly similar products. Business observers, for example, have questioned the 'elasticity' of the Virgin name. Richard Branson has extended the Virgin name, which appears on a huge range of disparate products, ranging from music and entertainment media shops, airlines, mobile phones and Internet services to personal financial services, cosmetics, cola drinks, vodka and bridal wear. They argue that Virgin runs the risk of overusing the brand's power of quality, innovation, value for money and fun, and its emotional 'take on the big bullies and give you something better' associations.

Transferring an existing brand name to a new customer segment or product group requires great care. The best result is one when the extension enhances the core brand and builds the sales of both current and new products. Companies that are tempted to transfer a brand name must research whether the brand's associations fit the new product.[34]

Multibrands

Multibranding offers a way to establish different features and appeal to different buying motives. It also allows a company to lock up more reseller shelf-space. Or the company may want to protect its major brand by setting up *flanker* or *fighter brands*. Seiko uses different brand names for its higher-priced watches (Seiko Lasalle) and lower-priced watches (Pulsar) to protect the flanks of its mainstream Seiko brand. Companies such as Lever Brothers, Nestlé, Mars and Procter & Gamble create individual brand identities for each of their products. Lever's line of laundry detergents – Persil, Surf, etc. – have distinct labels, with the corporate name hardly featured. Similarly, Procter & Gamble produces at least nine brands of laundry products. These manufacturers argue that a **multibrand strategy** – managing a stable of brand names within the same product category – permits finer segmentation of the market, with each brand name suggesting different functions or benefits appealing to different buying motives of different customer segments.

Some companies develop multiple brands, not for individual products, but for different families of products. For example, the Japanese electronics group Matsushita has opted to use **range branding** and developed separate range names for its audio product families – Technics, National, Panasonic and Quasar.

A major drawback of multibranding is that each brand might obtain only a small market share, and none may be very profitable. The company may end up spreading its resources over many brands instead of building a few brands to a highly profitable level. These companies should reduce the number of brands they sell in a given category and set up tighter screening procedures for new brands.

The multibranding approach contrasts with the **corporate branding** strategy. In corporate branding, the firm makes its company name the dominant brand identity across all of its products, as in the case of Mercedes-Benz, Philips and Heinz. The main advantages are economies of scale in marketing investments and wider recognition of the brand name. It also facilitates introduction of new products, especially when the corporate name is well established.

Other companies have used a **company and individual branding** approach. This focuses on both the corporate and individual brand names. Kellogg's (e.g. Cornflakes, Raisin Bran, Rice Krispies, Coco Pops, Nutri-Grain, etc.), Nestlé (KitKat, Nescafé, Coffee-Mate, etc.) and Cadbury's (e.g. Dairy Milk, Roses, Milk Tray) are supporters of this branding strategy.

New brands

Firms that favour a multibrand approach are likely to create a new brand to differentiate a new product, whether it is introduced into an existing or a new-product category. However,

Multibrand strategy— A brand strategy under which a seller develops two or more brands in the same product category.

Range branding strategy— A brand strategy whereby the firm develops separate product range names for different families of product.

Corporate branding strategy— A brand strategy whereby the firm makes its company name the dominant brand identity across all of its products.

Company and individual branding strategy— A branding approach that focuses on the company name and individual brand name.

for some companies, a new brand may be created because it is entering a new-product category for which none of the company's current brands seems appropriate. For example, Toyota established a separate family name – the Lexus – for its new luxury executive cars in order to create a distinctive identity for the latter and to position these well away from the traditional mass-market image of the 'Toyota' brand name. Alternatively, a company may be compelled to differentiate its new product, and a new brand is the best route to signal its identity. For example, Siemens' new line of upmarket, fashion mobile phones were launched in 2003 under a new brand name – Xelibri – to create a distinctive identity for these phones.

As with multibranding, offering too many brands can result in a company spreading its resources too thinly. And in some industries, such as consumer-packaged goods, consumers and retailers have become concerned that there are already too many brands, with too few differences between them. Thus, Lever Brothers, Procter & Gamble and other large consumer product marketers are now pursuing *megabrand* strategies – weeding out weaker brands and focusing their marketing dollars only on brands that can achieve the number-one or number-two market-share positions in their categories.

Managing brands

Companies must carefully manage their brands. First, the brand's positioning must be continuously communicated to consumers. Major brand marketers often spend huge amounts on advertising to create brand awareness and to build preference and loyalty. For example, General Motors spends nearly $820 million annually to promote its Chevrolet brands. McDonald's spends more than $660 million.[35]

Such advertising campaigns can help to create name recognition, brand knowledge and maybe even some brand preference. However, the fact is that brands are not maintained by advertising but by the *brand experience*. Today, customers come to know a brand through a wide range of contacts and touchpoints. These include advertising, but also personal experience with the brand, word of mouth, personal interactions with company people, telephone interactions, company Web pages and many others. Any of these experiences can have a positive or negative impact on brand perceptions and feelings. The company must put as much care into managing these touchpoints as it does into producing its ads.

The brand's positioning will not take hold fully unless everyone in the company lives the brand. Therefore the company needs to train its people to be customer-centred. Even better, the company should build pride in its employees regarding their products and services so that their enthusiasm will spill over to customers. Companies such as Lexus, Dell and Harley-Davidson have succeeded in turning all of their employees into enthusiastic brand builders. Companies can carry on internal brand building to help employees to understand, desire and deliver on the brand promise.[36] Many companies go even further by training and encouraging their distributors and dealers to serve their customers well.

All of this suggests that managing a company's brand assets can no longer be left only to brand managers. Brand managers do not have enough power or scope to do all the things necessary to build and enhance their brands. Moreover, brand managers often pursue short-term results, whereas managing brands as assets calls for longer-term strategy. Thus, some companies are now setting up brand asset management teams to manage their major brands. Canada Dry and Colgate-Palmolive have appointed *brand equity managers* to maintain and protect their brands' images, associations and quality, and to prevent short-term actions by over-eager brand managers from hurting the brand. Similarly, Hewlett-Packard has appointed a senior executive in charge of the customer experience in each of its two divisions, consumer and B2B. Their job is to track, measure and improve the customer experience with H-P products. They report directly to the presidents of their respective divisions.

Finally, companies need to periodically audit their brands' strengths and weaknesses.[37] They should ask: Does our brand excel at delivering benefits that consumers truly value? Is the brand properly positioned? Do all of our consumer touchpoints support the brand's positioning? Do the brand's managers understand what the brand means to consumers? Does the brand receive proper, sustained support?

The brand audit may turn up brands that need to be repositioned because of changing customer preferences or new competitors. Some cases may call for completely *rebranding* a product, service or company. The recent wave of corporate mergers and acquisitions has set off a flurry of corporate rebranding campaigns. A prime example is Diageo, created by the merger of Grand Metropolitan and Guinness. However, building a new image and re-educating customers can be a huge undertaking.

Additional product considerations

Product decisions and social responsibility

Product decisions have attracted much public attention in recent years. When making such decisions, marketers should consider carefully a number of public policy issues and regulations involving acquiring or dropping products, patent protection, product quality and safety and product warranties.

Regarding the addition of new products, national governments or competition authorities may prevent companies from adding products through acquisitions if the effect threatens to lessen competition. Companies dropping products must be aware that they have legal obligations, written or implied, to their suppliers, dealers and customers who have a stake in the discontinued product. Companies must also obey patent laws when developing new products. A company cannot make its product illegally similar to another company's established product.

In whichever country manufacturers market their products, they must comply with specific laws regarding product quality and safety which serve to protect consumers. For example, various Acts provide for the inspection of sanitary conditions in the meat- and poultry-processing industries. Safety legislation exists to regulate fabrics, chemical substances, automobiles, toys, drugs and poisons. Irrespective of whether laws exist to regulate company's actions, consumers today increasingly expect companies to behave ethically. A recent study of service industries suggests that consumers' ethical perceptions of service providers impact satisfaction levels: while unethical behaviour damages the supplier, ethical behaviour is simply expected.[38]

If consumers have been injured by a product that has been designed defectively, they can sue manufacturers or dealers. Product liability suits can lead to manufacturers paying victims awards that can run into millions of euros. Faulty products can cost the company money because of the need to recall and replace faulty merchandise. For example, in September 1999, Intel had to recall and scrap some one million motherboards because of a problem with Intel chips. The recall had cost Intel over $300 million (€357 million).[39] But some product defects can cost customers a great deal of anxiety or pain. Sagami Rubber Industries, a Japanese condom producer, had to withdraw from sale 850,000 multipack packets of its new polyurethane condoms (called Sagami Original) because invisible pinholes were found in the condoms. The recall cost the company $2.3 million, but imagine the misfortune awaiting unsuspecting users of the defective condoms![40]

International product decisions

International marketers face special product and packaging challenges. As discussed in Chapter 6, they must decide what products to introduce in which countries, and how much of the product to standardise or adapt for world markets. On the one hand, companies would like to standardise their offerings. Standardisation helps a company to develop a consistent worldwide image. It also lowers manufacturing costs and eliminates duplication of research and development, advertising and product design efforts. On the other hand, consumers around the world differ in their cultures, attitudes and buying behaviours. And markets vary in their economic conditions, competition, legal requirements and physical environments. Companies must usually respond to these differences by adapting their product offerings. Something as simple as an electrical outlet can create big product problems:

> Those who have travelled to Europe know the frustration of electrical plugs, different voltages, and other annoyances of international travel. . . . Philips, the electrical appliance manufacturer, has to produce 12 kinds of irons to serve just its European market. The problem is that Europe still lacks a universal [electrical] standard. The ends of irons bristle with different plugs for different countries. Some have three prongs, others two; prongs protrude straight or angled, round or rectangular, fat, thin and sometimes sheathed. There are circular plug faces, squares, pentagons and hexagons. Some are perforated and some are notched. One French plug has a niche like a keyhole; British plugs carry fuses.[41]

Packaging also presents new challenges for international marketers. Packaging issues can be subtle. For example, names, labels and colours may not translate easily from one country to another. Consumers in different countries also vary in their packaging preferences. Europeans like efficient, functional, recyclable boxes with understated designs. In contrast, the Japanese often use packages as gifts. Thus in Japan, Lever Brothers packages its Lux soap in stylish gift boxes. Packaging may even have to be tailored to meet the physical characteristics of consumers in various parts of the world. For instance, soft drinks are sold in smaller cans in Japan to fit the smaller Japanese hand better.

Companies may have to adapt their packaging to meet specific regulations regarding package design or label contents. For instance, some countries ban the use of any foreign language on labels; other countries require that labels be printed in two or more languages. Labelling laws vary greatly from country to country. Thus, although product and package standardisation can produce benefits, the international company must usually modify its offerings to the unique needs of specific international markets.

In summary, whether domestic or international, product strategy calls for complex decisions on product line, product mix, branding, packaging and service support strategy. These decisions must be made not only with a full understanding of consumer wants and competitors' strategies, but also with considerable sensitivity to the broader, particularly regulatory, environment affecting product, packaging and labelling.

Summary

A product is more than a simple set of tangible features. The concept of a *product* is complex and can be viewed on three levels. The *core product* consists of the core problem-solving benefit(s) that the customer seeks when they buy a product. The *actual product* exists around the core and includes the features, styling, design, quality level, brand name and packaging. The *augmented product* is the actual product plus the various services offered with it, such as warranty, free delivery, installation and maintenance.

We defined the product as anything that can be offered to a market for attention, acquisition, use or consumption that might satisfy a need or want. Marketable entities, such as physical objects, services, persons, places, organisations or ideas can all be thought of as products.

Products fall into two broad classes based on the types of buyers that use them. *Consumer goods* are sold to the final end-user for personal consumption. They are classified according to consumer shopping habits (convenience, shopping, speciality and unsought products). *Industrial goods* are bought by individuals or organisations for further processing or use in conducting a business. They are classified according to their cost and the way they enter the production process (materials and parts, capital items and supplies and services).

Marketers make decisions regarding their individual products, product lines and product mixes. Individual product decisions involve *product attributes*, *branding*, *packaging*, *labelling* and *product-support services*. *Product attributes* deliver tangible benefits such as the product quality, features, style and design. A *brand* identifies and differentiates goods or services through the use of a name or distinctive design element, resulting in long-term value known as *brand equity*. Branding decisions include selecting a brand name and determining a brand strategy. *Packaging* provides many benefits such as protection, economy, convenience and promotion. Package decisions often include designing *labels* which identify, describe and possibly promote the product. Companies also develop *product support services* that enhance customer service and satisfaction and safeguard against competitors.

Most companies offer a product line rather than a single product. A *product line* is a group of products that are closely related because of similar function, customers, channels of distribution or pricing. To occupy a gap that might be otherwise filled by a competitor, the company can increase its product line length by *stretching upwards* to a higher-priced segment, or *downwards* to a lower-priced segment, or by *stretching both ways*. Profits can sometimes be increased by *product line filling*, adding more items within the present range of the line. The set of product lines and items within these lines offered to customers make up the *product mix* which can be described according to its *width*, *length*, *depth* and *consistency*. These dimensions are the tools for developing the company's product strategy.

Some analysts see brands as *the* major enduring asset of a company. Brands are more than just names and symbols – they embody everything that the product or service *means* to consumers. *Brand equity* is the positive differential effect that knowing the brand name has on customer response to the product or service. A brand with strong brand equity is a very valuable asset. In building brands, companies need to make decisions about brand positioning, brand name selection, brand sponsorship and brand development. The most powerful *brand positioning* builds around strong consumer beliefs and values. *Brand name selection* involves finding the best brand name based on a careful review of product benefits, the target market, and proposed marketing strategies. A manufacturer has four *brand sponsorship* options: it can launch a *manufacturer's brand* (or national brand), sell to resellers who use a *private brand*, market *licensed brands* or join forces with another company to *co-brand* a product. A company also has four choices when it comes to developing brands. It can introduce *line extensions, brand extensions, multibrands* or *new brands* (new brand names in new product categories).

Companies must build and manage their brands carefully. The brand's positioning must be continuously communicated to consumers. Advertising can help but brands are not maintained by advertising but by the *brand experience*. Customers come to know a brand through a wide range of contacts and touchpoints. The company must put as much care into managing these touchpoints as it does into producing its ads. Thus, managing a company's brand assets can no longer be left only to brand managers. Some companies set up brand asset management teams to manage their major brands. Finally, companies must periodically audit their brands' strengths and weaknesses. In some cases, brands may need to be repositioned because of changing customer preferences or new competitors. Other cases may call for completely *rebranding* a product, service or company.

Marketers must consider two additional product issues. The first is *social responsibility*. These include public policy issues and regulations involving acquiring or dropping products, patent protection, product quality and safety, and product warranties. The second involves the special challenges facing international product marketers, including decisions about what products to introduce in what countries, whether to *standardise* the product and packaging, and whether to *adapt* it to local conditions.

Overall, developing products and brands is a complex and demanding task. Market-oriented firms create a differential advantage through evaluating the many issues surrounding product decisions and maintaining consistency with broad company objectives. Customer needs and wants invariably lie at the heart of sound product strategies.

Discussing the issues

1. What are the three levels at which a product may be viewed? In your answer, use product examples to show how these different levels may be applied to help product marketers define their product offering.

2. Various classes of consumer products differ in the ways that consumers buy them. Provide examples of the four types of consumer products and discuss how they differ in the way they are marketed.

3. Why are many people willing to pay more for branded products than for unbranded products? What does this say about the value of branding?

4. Coca-Cola started with one type of cola drink. Now we find Coke in nearly a dozen varieties. It seems that almost every major brand has been greatly extended, some even past the breaking point. Why do consumer-goods manufacturers extend their brands? What issues do these brand extensions raise for manufacturers, retailers and consumers?

5. Brand name and symbol licensing has become a multi-billion-dollar worldwide business. Compare brand extension by the brand owner with licensing a brand name for use by another company. What are the opportunities and risks of each approach?

6. In recent years, many European and US carmakers have tried to reposition many of their brands. Thinking about examples of such repositioning efforts, describe whether a brand has moved to a high-quality end of the market or moved down-market. How easy is it for carmakers to reposition their brands? What else could they do to change consumers' perceptions of their cars?

Applying the concepts

1. The 'core product' offered by automobile manufacturers is transportation. The major problem-solving benefit is how to get from one place to another quickly and safely. However, most automobile manufacturers differentiate their products with additional service benefits. The various service approaches are almost as varied as are the automobile manufacturers themselves. Examine the websites for Fiat (www.fiat.com), Renault (www.renault.com), Mercedes-Benz (www.mercedes.co.uk), Ford (www.ford.com), General Motors (www.gm.com), Honda (www.honda.com), Lexus (www.lexus.com) and Toyota (www.toyota.com). Look beyond the automobiles themselves and closely examine the manufacturers' services and service options.

   (a) What primary services do the various automobile manufacturers offer? Prepare a grid that compares each company to the others.
   (b) What services do the different companies appear to offer in common? What services do the various companies use to differentiate themselves from one another?
   (c) Do any of the sites suggest that a company understands the service–profit chain? Explain.
   (d) Do any of the auto companies employ interactive marketing with respect to the service component? Explain.
   (e) What role does the Internet play in the product/service strategies of the companies in question?

2. A strong brand is often considered by managers to be their company's most important asset. Interbrand, the branding consultancy, analyses economic earnings forecasts for the world's best-known brands and translate those forecasts into brand valuations (www.interbrand.com).

   (a) According to recent studies, Coca-Cola tops the list of the world's strongest brands, followed by Microsoft, IBM and GE. Why do these brands command so much respect?
   (b) What makes a strong brand? How would you measure brand equity?
   (c) What does it take a brand (like Coca-Cola) to become the number one brand in the world?
   (d) Identify the top ten brands in the world today. Examine their websites for indicators of brand strength. Based on your answers to question 2(b), draw a grid that evaluates each of the brands based on the characteristics you listed. Examine the information in your grid. Which company is superior based on your own evaluation?

References

1. Carmel Allen, 'Profit and gloss', *How to Spend It, Weekend FT* (October 2000), pp. 63–4; Birna Helgadottir, 'The glamazons are here', *Business FT Weekend Magazine* (29 July 2000), pp. 30–3; William Hall and John Willman, 'Success without a ripple', *Financial Times* (13 March 2000), p. 14.

2. See Philip Kotler, Irving J. Rein and Donald Haider, *Marketing Places: Attracting investment, industry, and tourism to cities, states, and nations* (New York: Free Press, 1993), pp. 202, 273; more information accessed online at www.ireland.travel.ie and www.ida.ie, August 2002.

3. See V. Rangan Kasturi, Sohel Karim and Sheryl K. Sandberg, 'Do better at doing good', *Harvard Business Review* (May–June 1996), pp. 42–54; Sue Adkins, *Cause Related Marketing: Who cares wins* (London: Butterworth Heinemann, 1999).

4. Philip Kotler, *Kotler on Marketing* (New York: Free Press, 1999), p. 17.

5. See Simon London, 'When quality is not enough', *Financial Times* (15 July 2002), p. 9.

6. Roland T. Rust, Anthony J. Zahorik and Timothy L. Keiningham, 'Return on quality (ROQ): making service quality financially accountable', *Journal of Marketing* (April 1995), pp. 58–70; Thomas J. Douglas and William Q. Judge, 'Total quality management implementation and competitive advantage', *Academy of Management Journal* (February 2001), pp. 158–69.

7. Gunilla Kines, 'A walk on the safe side', *The European Magazine* (24–30 April 1997), p. 12; Maria Werner, 'IKEA's design for thrifty, stylish living', *ibid.*, p. 15.

8. James MacKintosh, 'Fiat facelift ditches ugly cars', *Financial Times* (29 May 2003), p. 12.

9. Susan Lambert, *Form Follows Function* (London: Victoria and Albert Museum, 1993), p. 57.

10. See Robert Dwek, 'Apple pushes design to core of marketing', *Marketing Week* (24 January 2002), p. 20; for more on design, see Christopher Lorenz, *The Design Dimension* (Oxford: Blackwell, 1990); and Stephen Potter, Robin Roy, Claire H. Capon, Margaret Bruce, Vivien Walsh and Janny Lewis, *The Benefits and Costs of Investment in Design: Using professional design expertise in product, engineering and graphics projects* (Manchester: Open University/UMIST, September 1991).

11. For a discussion of the 'case for brands' and a defence against anti-globalisation claims that brands are instruments of consumer oppression, see 'The case for brands', *The Economist* (8 September 2001), p. 9; and 'Who's wearing the trousers' in 'Special Report: Brands', *ibid.*, pp. 27–9.

12. 'Freddy Heineken', *The Economist* (12 January 2002), p. 89.

13. Claire Irvin, 'EU calls time on labelling', *Marketing Business* (July/August 1999), p. 22.

14. Bro Uttal, 'Companies that serve you best', *Fortune* (7 December 1987), pp. 98–116; see also William H. Davidow, 'Customer service: the ultimate marketing weapon', *Business Marketing* (October 1989), pp. 56–64; Barry Farber and Joyce Wycoff, 'Customer service: evolution and revolution', *Sales and Marketing Management* (May 1991), pp. 44–51.

15. John Templeman, 'A Mercedes in every driveway?', *Business Week* (26 August 1996), pp. 38–40; Sam Pickens and Dagmar Mussey, 'Swatch taps Zurich shop to develop Euro car ads', *Advertising Age* (19 May 1997), p. 32.

16. See David A. Aaker, 'Should you take your brand to where the action is?', *Harvard Business Review* (September–October 1997), pp. 135–43.

17. 'McAtlas shrugged', *Foreign Policy* (May–June 2001), pp. 26–37.

18. See Philip Kotler, *Marketing Management*, 11th edn (Upper Saddle River, NJ: Prentice-Hall, 2003), p. 419.

19. David A. Aaker, *Managing Brand Equity* (New York: Free Press, 1991).

20. Scott Davis, *Brand Asset Management: Driving profitable growth through your brands* (San Francisco: Jossey-Bass, 2000); David C. Bello and Morris B. Holbrook, 'Does an absence of brand equity generalize across product classes?', *Journal of Business Research* (October 1995), p. 125.

21. See T.P. Barwise, C.J. Higson, J.A. Likierman and P.R. Marsh, *Accounting for Brands* (London: Institute of Chartered Accountants in England and Wales, 1990); Peter H. Farquhar, Julia Y. Han and Yuji Ijiri, 'Brands on the balance sheet', *Marketing Management* (Winter 1992), pp. 16–22; Kevin Lane Keller, 'Conceptualising, measuring, and managing customer-based brand equity', *Journal of Marketing* (January 1993), pp. 1–22.

22. Gerry Khermouch, 'The best global brands', *Business Week* (6 August 2001), pp. 50–64.

23. Andrew Pierce and Eric Almquist, 'Brand building may face a test', *Advertising Age* (9 April 2001), p. 22. Also see Don E. Schultz, 'Mastering brand metrics', *Marketing Management* (May–June 2002), pp. 8–9 and Kevin Lane Keller, *Strategic Brand Management: Building, measuring and managing brand equity* (Upper Saddle River, NJ: Prentice-Hall, 1997).

24. Peter Williams, 'Making the most of your assets', *Marketing Business* (March 1999), pp. 30–3.

25. Roland T. Rust, Katherine N. Lemon and Valerie A. Zeithaml, *Driving Customer Equity: How lifetime customer value is reshaping corporate strategy* (New York: Free Press, 2000).

26. Jean-Noel Kapferer, *Strategic Brand Management: New approaches to creating and evaluating brand equity* (London: Kogan Page, 1992), p. 38 ff.; Jennifer L. Aaker, 'Dimensions of brand personality', *Journal of Market Research* (August 1997), pp. 347–56.

27. Thomas M.S. Hemnes, 'How can you find a safe trademark?', *Harvard Business Review* (March–April 1995), p. 44.

28. For a discussion of legal issues surrounding the use of brand names, see Dorothy Cohen, 'Trademark strategy', *Journal of Marketing* (January 1986), pp. 61–74; 'Trademark woes: help is coming', *Sales and Marketing Management* (January 1988), p. 84; Jack Alexander, 'What's in a name? Too much, said the FCC', *Sales and Marketing Management* (January 1989), pp. 75–8.

29. Jeremy Braune, 'The brand bond', *Marketing Business* (October 1999), pp. 46–7; 'Branded goods (1). Shrinking to grow', *The Economist* (26 February 2000), pp. 100–4; Richard Tomkins, 'Manufacturers strike back', *Financial Times* (16 June 2000), p. 16.

30. See Richard Tomkins, 'Coke to branch out into clothing', *Financial Times* (18 July 2000), p. 31; Silvia Sansoni, 'Gucci, Armani, and . . . John Paul II?', *Business Week* (13 May 1996), p. 61; Bart A. Lazar, 'Licensing gives known brands new life', *Advertising Age* (16 February 1998), p. 8; and Laura Petrecca, '"Corporate Brands" put licensing in the spotlight', *Advertising Age* (14 June 1999), p. 1.

31. Tom Blackett and Robert Boad, *Co-branding: The science of alliance* (London: Macmillan, 1999).

32. Al Ries and Jack Trout, *Positioning: The battle for your mind* (New York: McGraw-Hill, 1981).

33. For more on line extensions, see Kevin Lane Keller and David A. Aaker, 'The effects of sequential introduction of line extensions', *Journal of Marketing* (February 1992), pp. 35–50; Srinivas K. Reddy, Susan L. Holak and Subodh Bhat, 'To extend or not to extend: success determinants of line extensions', *Journal of Marketing Research* (May 1994), pp. 243–62.

34. For more on the use of brand extensions and consumers' attitudes towards them, see Deborah Roedder John, Barbara Loken and Christopher Joiner, 'The negation impact of extensions: can flagship products be diluted?', *Journal of Marketing* (January 1998), pp. 19–32; Zeynep Gurrhan-Canli and Durairaj Maheswaran, 'The effects of extensions on brand name dilution and enhancement', *Journal of Marketing* (November 1998), pp. 464–73; Vanitha Swaminathan, Richard J. Fox and Srinivas K. Reddy, 'The impact of brand extension introduction on choice', *Journal of Marketing* (October 2001), pp. 1–15; Paul A. Bottomly and Stephen J.S. Holden, 'Do we really know how consumers evaluate brand extensions? Empirical generalizations based on secondary analysis of eight studies', *Journal of Marketing Research* (November 2001), pp. 494–500; and Kalpesh Kaushik Desai and Kevin Lane Keller, 'The effect of ingredient branding strategies on host brand extendibility', *Journal of Marketing* (January 2002), pp. 73–93.

35. 'Top 100 megabrands by total measured advertising spending', *Advertising Age* (16 July 2001), p. S2.

36. See Donald D. Tosti and Roger D. Stotz, 'Building your brand from the inside out', *Marketing Management* (July–August 2001), pp. 29–33.

37. See Kevin Lane Keller, 'The brand report card', *Harvard Business Review* (January 2000), pp. 147–57.

38. James L. Thomas, Scott J. Vitell, Faye W. Gilbert and Gregory M. Rose, 'The impact of ethical cues on customer satisfaction with service', *Journal of Retailing*, **78** (2002), pp. 167–73.

39. Tom Foremski, 'Intel says that recall could cost it $300m', *Financial Times* (11 May 2000), p. 46.

40. Susanna Voyle, 'Recall of faulty products may help imports', *Financial Times* (16 April 1998), p. 6.

41. See Philip Cateora, *International Marketing*, 8th edn (Homewood, IL: Irwin, 1993), p. 270; David Fairlamb, 'One currency – but 15 economies', *Business Week* (31 December 2001), p. 59.

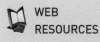

WEB RESOURCES

For additional classic case studies and Internet exercises, visit www.pearsoned.co.uk/kotler

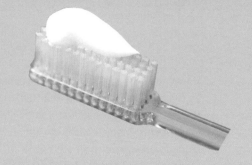

Concluding concepts 13
Colgate: one squeeze too many?

Colgate is the world's number one toothpaste company but they have their eye on another market – over the counter (OTC) drugs. What would you think of Colgate aspirin or Colgate antacid? Would you buy Colgate laxatives or Colgate dandruff shampoo? That is exactly what Colgate-Palmolive would like to know. Colgate wants to investigate the possibility of entering the over-the-counter (OTC) drugs market. Can it use its Colgate brand name, developed in the oral-care products market, in the OTC healthcare market?

Why does the OTC market interest Colgate? The first reason is market size. The worldwide OTC market annually accounts for over €50 billion in sales. It is the largest non-food consumer products industry, and it is growing at over 6 per cent annually.

Several trends are fuelling this rapid growth. Consumers are more sophisticated than they were and they increasingly seek self-medication rather than seeing a doctor. Companies are also switching many previously prescription-only drugs to OTC drugs. The companies can do this when they can show, based on extensive clinical tests, that the drug is safe for consumers to use without monitoring by a doctor. Moreover, OTC drugs tend to have very long product life-cycles. Medical researchers are also discovering new drugs or new uses or benefits of existing drugs. For example, researchers have found that the psyllium fibre used in some OTC natural laxatives is effective in controlling cholesterol.

Beyond the size and growth of the market, Colgate also knows that the OTC market can be extremely profitable. Analysts estimate that the average cost of goods sold for an OTC drug is only 29 per cent, leaving a gross margin of 71 per cent. Advertising and sales promotions are the largest expenditure categories for these products, accounting for an average of 42 per cent of sales. OTC drugs produce on average 11 per cent after-tax profit.

Because of the OTC market's attractiveness, Colgate conducted studies to learn the strength of its brand name with consumers. Colgate believes in the following equation: brand awareness + brand image = brand equity. Its studies found that Colgate was no. 1 in brand awareness, no. 2 in brand image and no. 2 in brand equity among OTC consumers in the US, even though it did not sell OTC products. The Tylenol brand name earned the number one spot in both brand image and brand equity. Similar studies among OTC consumers in major European markets supported Colgate's relatively strong brand equity position. Thus, Colgate's research shows that the OTC market is very large, is growing rapidly and is very profitable, and that Colgate has a strong brand equity position with OTC consumers. Most companies would find such a situation very attractive.

Colgate realises that entering the OTC market will not be easy. The company faces challenges in entering the OTC market:

> Colgate believes in the following equation: brand awareness + brand image = brand equity.

1. Its research suggests that the typical OTC product does not reach the break-even point for four years and does not recover development costs until the seventh year. OTC firms must therefore be correct in their product development decisions or they risk losing a great deal of money.

2. OTC drugs require a high level of advertising and promotion expenditures: 25 per cent of sales on year-round media alone. A firm must have substantial financial resources to enter this market.

3. The market is attractive so entering firms face stiff competition. The market has many competitors and is the least concentrated of any large consumer market. In Europe, no company has more than 3.5 per cent of the market and the top 15 companies account for only 25 per cent market share. Established companies like Bayer, Rhône-Poulenc Rorer, Sanofi, Boots, Boehringer Ingelheim and Warner-Lambert have strong sales forces and marketing organisations. They are strong financially and are willing to take competitors to court if they perceive any violations of laws or regulations. These firms also have strong research and development organisations that spin out new products. As governments squeeze state drug budgets, ethical drug companies have been aggressively working their way into the OTC market. There have been strings of acquisitions, ranging from Roche's purchase of Nicholas Laboratories to SmithKline Beecham's purchase of Stirling Winthrop from Kodak. Merck, America's leading drug company, has teamed up with Johnson & Johnson in the OTC market.

4. Because of the high and rising level of fixed costs, such as the costs of advertising and R&D, many smaller firms are leaving the industry or being acquired by larger firms. Many leading ethical drug companies' industry observers estimate that an OTC firm must have at least several hundred million dollars in sales. It needs this to cover fixed costs and to have the power to match big retailers. So, the OTC firms are growing larger and larger, and they are willing to fight aggressively for market share.

Given all these barriers to entry, you might wonder why Colgate would want to pursue OTC products, even if the industry is growing and profitable. Colgate has adopted a strategy that aims to make it the best global consumer products company. It believes that oral-care and OTC products are very similar. Both rely on their ingredients for effectiveness, are highly regulated and use similar marketing channels.

Colgate set up its Colgate Health Care Laboratories to explore product and market development opportunities in the OTC market. Colgate carried out a test market for a line of OTC products developed by its Health Care Laboratories. It test-marketed a wide line of OTC products, from a nasal decongestant to a natural fibre laxative, under the brand name Ektra. The predominantly white packages featured the Ektra name with the Colgate name in smaller letters below it.

Following the test market results, Colgate quietly established another test market to test a line of ten OTC healthcare products, all using the Colgate name as the brand name. The line includes aspirin-free pain reliever, ibuprofen, cold tablets, nighttime cold medicine, antacid, natural laxative and anti-dandruff shampoo. The test sought to establish how well the Colgate name would compete against established brands in each of the ten OTC product sectors.

Industry observers realise that the new line represents a significant departure from Colgate's traditional, high-visibility household goods and oral-care products. Responding to enquiries, Colgate suggests that: 'The Colgate name is already strong in oral hygiene, now we want to learn whether it can represent healthcare across the board. We need to expand into more profitable categories.'

Colgate will not talk specifically about its new line. Pharmacists, however, say that Colgate has blitzed the town with coupons and ads. Representatives have given away free tubes of toothpaste with purchases of the new Colgate products and have handed out coupons worth virtually the full price of the new products. If all that promotion was not enough, the manager of one store points out that Colgate has priced its line well below competing brands – as much as 20 per cent below in some cases. The same manager reports that the new products' sales are strong, but also adds 'With all the promotion they've done, they should be. They're cheaper, and they've got Colgate's name on them.'

Yet even if Colgate's test proves a resounding success, marketing consultants say expanding the new line could prove dangerous and, ultimately, more expensive than Colgate can imagine. 'If you put the Colgate brand name on a bunch of different products, if you do it willy-nilly at the lowest end, you're going to dilute what it stands for – and if you stand for nothing, you're worthless', observes a spokesperson from Lipincott and Margolies, a firm that handles corporate identity projects. Colgate might also end up alienating customers by slapping its name on so many products. If consumers are dissatisfied with one product, they might be dissatisfied with everything across the board.

Moreover, Colgate's new line moves far from its familiar turf. Although its new line is selling well, sales might not stay so strong without budget prices and a barrage of advertising and promotion. 'People are looking at it right now as a generic-style product', observes one store manager. 'People are really price conscious, and as long as the price is cheaper, along with a name that you can trust, people are going to buy that over others.'

Al Ries, chairman of Trout & Ries marketing consultants, questions whether any line extensions make sense – not only for Colgate, but also for other strong brand names. He says the reason Colgate has been able to break into the OTC drugs market is that other drugs have expanded and lost their niches. Mr Ries argues that Colgate and the traditional OTC medicine companies are turning their products into generic drugs instead of brands. They are losing 'the power of a narrow focus', he says. 'It reflects stupidity on the part of the traditional over-the-counter marketers. . . . If the traditional medicines maintained their narrow focus, they wouldn't leave room for an outsider such as Colgate.'

If Colgate is too successful, meanwhile, it also risks cannibalising its flagship product. Consultants note that almost all successful line extensions, and many not-so-successful ones, hurt the product from which they took their name. 'If Colgate made themselves to mean over-the-counter medicine, nobody would want to buy Colgate toothpaste', contends Mr Ries.

A Colgate spokesperson argues that Colgate could 'save tens of millions of dollars by not having to introduce a new brand name' for its new products. However, in doing so, it might also 'kill the goose that laid the golden egg'. Other marketing consultants believe that Colgate may be able to break into the market, but that it will take much time and money. 'They just don't bring a lot to the OTC party', one consultant indicates.

Although senior management at Colgate says that the company will continue to try to build share in its traditional cleanser and detergent markets, personal care is considered a stronger area. Leveraging a name into new categories can be tricky, requiring patience from sceptical retailers and fickle consumers. 'It isn't so much a question of where you can put the brand name', says one marketing consultant. 'It's what products the consumer will let you put the brand name on.'

Questions

1. What core product is Colgate selling when it sells toothpaste or the other products in its new line?
2. How would you classify these new products?

3. What implications does this classification have for marketing the new line?
4. What brand decisions has Colgate made? What kinds of product line decision? Are these decisions consistent?
5. How would you package the new products and what risks do you see in these packaging decisions?
6. Even if Colgate is successful in extending the brand into a range of OTC product markets in the US, to what extent will the company be able to repeat this success in its European markets?

SOURCES: Sean Brierley, 'Drug dependence', *Marketing Week* (14 November 1994), pp. 32–5; Paul Abrahams, 'A dose of OTC medicine for growth strategy', *Financial Times* (30 August 1994), p. 19; 'Hoffmann-La Roche: staying calm', *The Economist* (28 September 1991); David Pilling, 'Drug group wrestle with seismic shifts in business practices', *Financial Times Survey. Life Sciences and Pharmaceuticals* (6 April 2000), p. I; Ross Tiemen, 'Brand extensions: keep taking the tablets', *Financial Times* (15 April 2003); Neil Buckley, 'Overseas sales boost for Colgate', *Financial Times* (4 February 2004); Colgate Health Care Laboratories also cooperated in the development of this case.

Every invention is received by a cry of triumph which soon turns into a cry of fear.

BERTOLT BRECHT

New-product development and product life-cycle strategies

Chapter objectives

After reading this chapter, you should be able to:

- Explain how companies find and develop new-product ideas.
- List and define the steps in the new-product development process.
- Describe the stages of the product life-cycle.
- Explain how marketing strategy changes during a product's life-cycle.

Mini Contents List

◀ **SOURCE:** Microsoft Corporation.

Prelude case Nokia: game's on but not having fun!

Nokia has just fallen foul of the mayor of Rome after some stickers it distributed to promote its N-Gage gaming device ended up being plastered all over the city. Embarrassment was averted only when the Finnish company offered to pay for the costs of cleaning up. But stickers strewn across the monuments of the eternal city are not the only thing that Nokia, the world's leading maker of mobile phones, has struggled to shift. It has also had problems getting consumers excited about N-Gage, despite the massive marketing drive that has accompanied its first foray into the world of gaming consoles.

Nokia has set itself a target of selling 9 million of the devices worldwide in the first two years. But at its full-year results announcement, reporting a robust performance from its main handset business, Nokia disclosed that it had sold only about 600,000 N-Gage devices globally to retail outlets in its first three months. And the number of consumers who have bought the device is likely to be significantly lower. The handset maker conceded that sales of the device in Asia had been 'modest' and North American sales had failed to meet its expectations. The relatively bright spot was Europe, which had accounted for the majority of sales so far, with the UK performing well ahead of other markets, it said.

The N-Gage – a combination of gaming device and mobile phone – is failing to fly off the shelves.

But even the picture among leading retailers in Europe is at best mixed. The N-Gage – a combination of gaming device and mobile phone – is failing to fly off the shelves. At The Link, the UK cellphone retailer owned by Dixons Group, sales of the N-Gage are reported to have been hovering around a few hundred units a week across its network of more than 230 stores. 'Sales of N-Gage have been OK but unexciting', said Nick Wood, managing director of The Link.

Carphone Warehouse, Europe's largest mobile-phone retailer and probably Nokia's single biggest distributor of the N-Gage, has sold fewer than 50,000 of the devices across Europe since they reached its stores last October, according to senior staff at the company. Carphone has more than 1,100 stores in 11 countries across the continent, but well over half its N-Gage sales are understood to have come from the UK, supporting suggestions that demand for the device among mobile phone retailers in much of western Europe is failing to take off.

Anecdotal evidence appears to support this view. Michael Hultberg, deputy manager of the Game shop in Taby, north of Stockholm, said: 'It's not been successful so far. It might be the lack of games, and the fact that it's quite complex to change games'. Game has 40 outlets in Sweden.

Lacklustre initial sales at cellphone retailers come despite heavy subsidies from the cellular operators which, in some cases, have reduced the cost of the device to nothing for users who sign up to annual contracts. This is particularly disappointing for Nokia as it had been counting on strong subsidies from network operators to help buoy sales of the N-Gage. Indeed, many analysts following Nokia have argued that it is the mobile-phone retailers that will account for the lion's share of N-Gage sales since, without subsidies, it is just too expensive.

At an unsubsidised price, the N-Gage has been selling for up to €400. This compares with about €120 for Nintendo's Gameboy Advance SP, the world's dominant portable game console. In addition, the Gameboy boasts a catalogue of more than 700 games, compared with fewer than 20 games for the N-Gage so far. Retailers say Nokia needs to lower its price if it is to turn the N-Gage into a mainstream consumer proposition. Subsidies from operators can have only a limited impact on sales, they say, because the target market for the N-Gage is pre-paid mobile phones, where the subsidies tend to be minimal. On pre-paid tariffs in the UK, the N-Gage has typically sold for £150 (€250) or more. 'We will only see strong rises in sales volumes if we can get pre-paid prices below the £99 mark', said Mr Wood. 'At £99 on pre-pay it would be a very good seller. Nokia needs to bring the prices right down.'

The sales experience at Woolworths, the high-street retailer, appears to support this view. Woolworths said strong demand in the run-up to Christmas had forced it to order extra stock. It has been selling the device in conjunction with Orange, the mobile operator, at £129.99 including a free game – one of the lowest prices on pre-paid tariffs for the N-Gage in the UK. Orange has been one of the strongest supporters of the device, but even with its above-average subsidies, the mobile operator is thought to have sold only about 30,000 units across all its different retail channels in the UK, including almost 900 Woolworths stores.

To increase sales, some analysts believe, Nokia should consider following Nintendo's business model where it sells its Gameboy for a minimal margin but reaps its financial rewards from the huge market for games for its consoles. Ilkka Raiskinen, senior vice-president of games at Nokia, insists this is not a route that Nokia intends to take, arguing that the N-Gage can command a much higher price over traditional games consoles such as the

Gameboy because of its additional features, which include mobile telephony, Internet connectivity and the ability to play wireless multi-player games across devices. Most analysts readily support this view. But despite the additional features, they still believe the current price gap with the Gameboy is too great. Further, analysts argue that Nokia may be finding it difficult to generate strong sales of the N-Gage because of some intrinsic design flaws, such as a relatively short battery life or the inability to change game cartridges without removing the battery.

'What is a shame is that they did not take into account more feedback when it was first revealed in February 2003', said Ben Wood, analyst at Gartner, the technology research house. Mr Raiskinen responded that Nokia had learnt some valuable lessons about its strategy for N-Gage since launch, hinting that many of these lessons will feed through to improvements. 'We know where we have gaps', he said, pointing to areas such as its limited range of games, a lack of exclusive games for the N-Gage, and its distribution network in crucial markets such as the US. 'We have learnt a lot about the pricing dynamics and features that consumers value in a multi-function device.' Comments such as these, combined with lacklustre initial sales for the N-Gage, are fuelling speculation that Nokia is working on a successor that will incorporate improvements to some of its design flaws. Mr Raiskinen refused to comment apart from reiterating Nokia's long-term ambitions in the gaming market.

In terms of group financial performance, the N-Gage will have minimal impact next to annual global Nokia mobile-phone sales approaching 200 million units. But as Nokia targets several new markets for growth, its success or failure in the gaming arena may be highly symbolic.[1]

Questions

1. Given Nokia's dominance in the mobile-phone market, why do you think they have shifted their attention to games rather than develop new products for the mobile-communications market?

2. Nokia's N-Gage appears to be failing despite the company's leading position in the mobile-phone market. What are the reasons for its failure and how could it be rectified?

3. Nokia has clearly spent enormous sums in developing a product as radically new as the N-Gage. Where in the new-product development process did they go wrong? Is it the strategy that resulted in the development of the N-Gage that was wrong, the product concept, its features, the marketing mix that supported its launch, market testing, or what?

SOURCE: Christopher Brown-Humes and Robert Budden, 'Nokia tries to learn a new game', Financial Times (5 February 2004).

Introduction

In the previous chapter, we addressed decisions that marketers make in managing individual products or brands and entire product mixes. In this chapter, you will examine two additional product topics: developing new products and managing products through their life-cycles. New products are the lifeblood of an organisation. However, as the prelude case illustrates, new-product development is risky and many new products fail. The first part of this chapter therefore looks at the process for finding and growing successful new products. Once introduced, marketers want their products to enjoy a long and profitable life. In the second part of this chapter, we will see that products pass through several life-cycle stages and that each stage poses new challenges requiring different marketing strategies and tactics.

In competitive markets, the best and strongest firms sustain growth and maintain profitability over the longer term through successfully developing and launching a steady stream of new products or services. Firms must develop new products or services because of the rapid changes in customer tastes, technology and competition. Moreover, products have a finite life which is determined by the overall pace of new-product innovation taking place in the product market as well as by how well the marketing manager manages the brand during all stages of the product life-cycle. Introducing new products alone is therefore not sufficient. The firm must also know how to manage the new product as it goes through its life-cycle: that is, from its birth, through growth and maturity, to eventual demise as newer products come along that better serve consumer needs.

This product life-cycle presents two principal challenges. First, because all products eventually decline, the firm must find new products to replace ageing ones (the problem of *new-product development*). Second, the firm must be good at adapting its marketing strategies in the face of changing customer wants, technologies and competition (the problem of *product life-cycle strategies*). We look initially at the problem of finding and developing new products, and then at the challenge of managing them successfully over their life-cycles.

Innovation and new-product development strategy

Product innovation encompasses a variety of product development activities – product improvement, development of entirely new products, and extensions that increase the range or number of lines of product the firm can offer. Product innovations are not to be confused with **inventions**. The latter are new technologies or products which may or may not be commercialised and may or may not deliver benefits to customers. An **innovation** is defined as *an idea, service, product or piece of technology that has been developed and marketed to customers who perceive it as novel or new*. New-product development is an act of innovation which entails a process of identifying, creating and delivering new-product values or benefits that were not offered before in the marketplace.

A firm can obtain new products in two ways. One is through *acquisition* – by buying a whole company, a patent or a licence to produce someone else's product. Many large companies have decided to acquire existing brands rather than to create new ones because of the rising costs of developing and introducing major new products. The other route to obtaining new products is through **new-product development** in the company's own research-and-development department. By new products we mean original products, product improvements, product modifications and new brands that the firm develops through its own research-and-development efforts. In this chapter, we concentrate on new-product development – how businesses create and market new products.

Invention—A new technology or product that may or may not be commercialised and may or may not deliver benefits to customers.

Innovation—An idea, service, product or technology that has been developed and marketed to customers who perceive it as novel or new. It is a process of identifying, creating and delivering new-product or service values that did not exist before in the marketplace.

New-product development—The development of original products, product improvements, product modifications and new brands through the firm's own R&D efforts.

Risks and returns in new-product development

New product development is risky for a number of reasons, such as the following.

1. New-product development is an expensive affair. Pharmaceutical firms spend an average of £200 million or more to develop a new drug. This pales in comparison to what it costs firms like Sony to develop breakthrough consumer entertainment products – the company invested ¥200bn (€1.7bn) alone to develop the powerful semiconductor for the PlayStation2.[2]

2. New-product development takes time. Although companies can dramatically shorten their development time, in many industries such as pharmaceuticals, biotechnology, aerospace and food, new-product development cycles can be as long as 10–15 years. For example, the new-product launch cycle of consumer product firms such as Gillette may be anything from two to ten years. The uncertainty and unpredictability of market environments further raise the risks of commercialisation.

   Consider the following example. Swedish start-up firm Anoto, with backing from Ericsson, the mobile-phone company, launched a high-tech pen that allows users to send handwritten notes and hand-drawn pictures over the Internet and to mobile phones. Slightly fatter than a normal pen, Anoto's pen writes in normal ink, but contains a small camera, radio transmitter, rechargeable battery and ink cartridge. Special paper is used which contains millions of tiny dots that the pen's camera can see, drawing a virtual picture of the writing in its memory and transmitting this picture using radio technology, Bluetooth, to a mobile phone. From there, the picture is sent across the Internet to a recipient's email inbox or displayed on the screen of a mobile phone. Bluetooth is backed by computer and communications firms such as Microsoft, IBM, Intel and Nokia. Although all this sounds exciting, analysts point to the risks and uncertainty surrounding the exploitation of new technology. Although the technology is a clever idea, Anoto's pen could well become obsolete, being eclipsed by voice recognition as it takes off in the next 2–3 years. Or, it may be superseded by simpler, competing technologies such as Logitech's bionic personal digital pens which use optical sensors and tiny memory chips to record a person's writing and store it on a computer for safekeeping.[3]

3. Unexpected delays in development are also a problem. History is littered with grand pioneering engineering projects which have failed to satisfy the original expectations of bankers, investors and politicians. The £10 billion cost of the Channel tunnel, which opened on 6 May 1994, a year later than originally planned, was more than double the £4.8 billion forecast at the start of the project in 1987.

4. New products continue to fail at a disturbing rate. Recent studies put the new product failure rate of new consumer goods at 90 per cent in Europe and 90 per cent in the United States. Another study suggested that of the tens of thousands of new consumer food, beverage, beauty and healthcare products launched each year, only 40 per cent will be around five years later. Moreover, failure rates for new industrial products may be as high as 30 per cent. Still another estimates new-product failures to be as high as 95 per cent.[4]

Despite the risks, firms that learn to innovate well become less vulnerable to attacks by new entrants which discover new ways of delivering added value, benefits and solutions to customers' problems.

New-product development is risky. High-tech pens such as those recently pioneered by Anoto may be superseded by state-of-the-art devices like this Logitech® io ™ personal digital pen.
SOURCE: Logitech® io™.

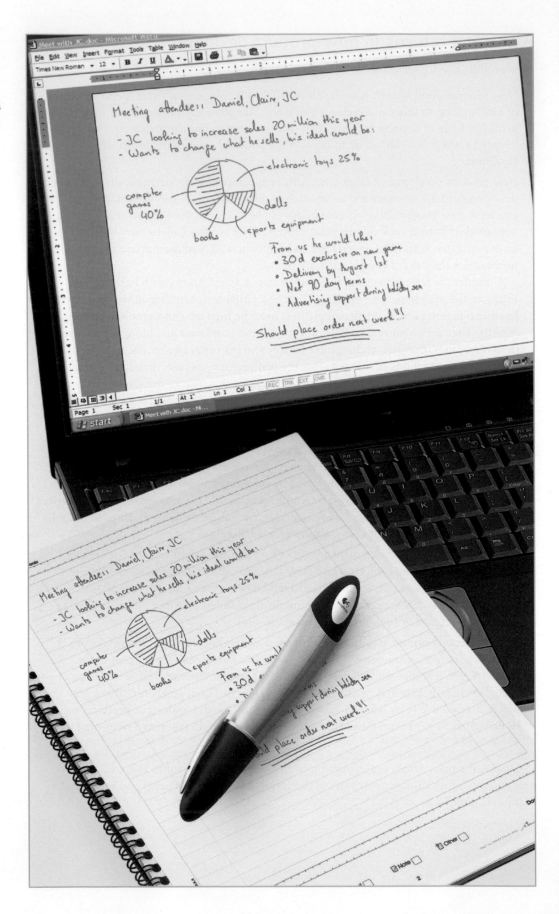

Why do new products fail?

Why do so many new products fail? There are several reasons. Although an idea may be good, the market size may have been overestimated. There just wasn't the demand for the product. Perhaps the actual product was not designed as well as it should have been. It may be a 'me too' product which is no better than products that are already established in the marketplace. Or maybe it was incorrectly positioned in the market, priced too high, or advertised and promoted badly. A high-level executive might push a favourite idea despite poor marketing research findings. Sometimes the costs of product development are higher than budgeted and sometimes competitors fight back harder than expected.

What influences new-product success?

Because so many new products fail, companies are anxious to learn how to improve their odds of new-product success. One way is to identify successful new products and find out what they have in common. Various studies suggest that new-product success depends on developing a *unique superior product*, one offering customers better quality, new features and higher value in use. Another key success factor is a *well-defined product concept* prior to development, in which the company carefully defines and assesses the target market, the product requirements and the benefits before proceeding. New products that are better than existing products at *meeting market needs* and delivering what customers really wanted invariably do well. Other success factors have also been suggested – senior management commitment, relentless commitment to innovation, smooth functioning and proficiency in executing the new-product development process.[5] Thus, successful commercialisation of new products requires a company to have a clear understanding of its consumers, markets and competitors and to develop products that deliver superior value to customers.

Successful new-product development may be an even bigger challenge in the future. Keen competition has led to increasing market fragmentation – companies must now aim at smaller market segments rather than the mass market, and this means smaller sales and profits for each product. New products must meet growing social and government constraints, such as consumer safety and environmental standards. The costs of finding, developing and launching new products will increase steadily due to rising manufacturing, media and distribution costs. Many companies that cannot afford the funds needed for new-product development will emphasise product modification and imitation rather than true innovation. Even when a new product is successful, rivals are so quick to copy it that the new product is typically fated to have only a short life.

So, companies face a problem – they must develop new products, but the odds weigh heavily against success. The solution lies in strong *new-product planning* and in setting up a systematic *new-product development process* for finding and growing new products. Top management must ultimately take the lead in setting the company-wide strategy and committing adequate resources to support product innovation.

Successful new-product development requires a company-wide effort. Successful innovative companies have more than a clearly articulated new-product strategy and consistent commitment of resources to new-product development. To ensure effective execution of new-product development, these companies have set up formal and sophisticated organisations for encouraging employees to excel in innovation and facilitating the new-product development process (see Marketing Insights 14.1). Let us now take a look at the major steps in the new-product development process.

New products that succeed
offer unique benefits that make
a difference for users.
SOURCE: Johnson and Johnson.
Agency: Liquorice.

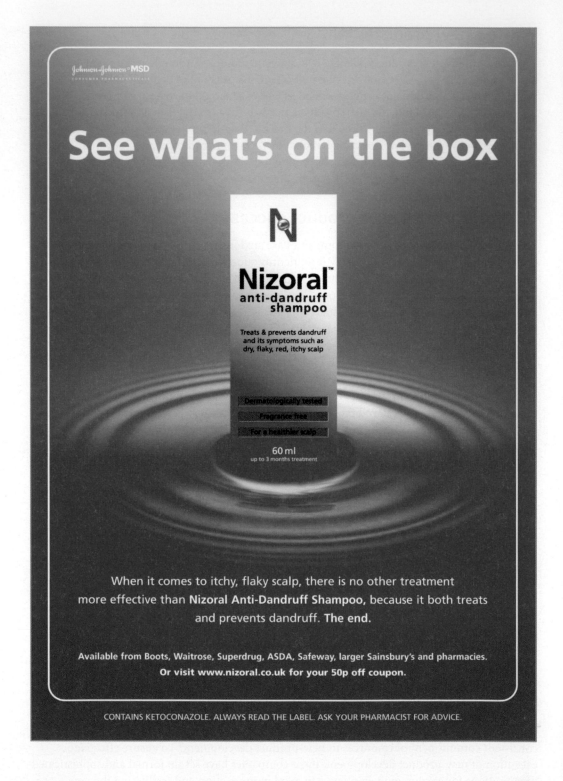

3M: champions of innovation

14.1

marketing insights

3M's emphasis on innovation is legendary. Every 3M ad carries the headline: 'Innovation: Working for You'. But at 3M, innovation is more than just an advertising pitch. 3M views innovation as its path to growth, and new products as its lifeblood. The company markets more than 50,000 products worldwide. These products range from sandpaper, adhesives and laser optical discs to contact lenses, heart–lung machines and futuristic synthetic ligaments; from coatings for boat hulls to hundreds of sticky tapes – Scotch tapes, masking tape, super-bonding tape, acid-free photo and document tape and even refastening, disposable nappy tape.

Each year 3M launches more than 200 new products. 3M's goal is to derive 30 per cent of each year's sales from products introduced within the previous four years. And, astonishingly, it usually succeeds. In 2002, a full third of its $16 billion (€13.2 billion) in sales came from products introduced within the past four years! It also earned the number-one spot on *Fortune*'s list of companies most admired for innovation.

3M's impressive record is due to several factors. At 3M, new-product development doesn't just happen. The company works hard to create an environment that supports innovation. It invests some 6 per cent of annual group sales in research and development – almost twice as much as the average company. To develop new products of the future quickly, senior management tolerates informal structures. Its Innovation Task Force seeks out and destroys corporate bureaucracy that might interfere with new-product progress. Hired consultants also help 3M to find ways to make employees more inventive.

3M's innovative culture encourages everyone to look for new products. The company's renowned '15 per cent rule' gives all employees space, allowing them to spend up to 15 per cent of their time 'bootlegging' – working on projects of personal interest, whether those projects directly benefit the company or not. When a promising idea comes along, 3M forms a venture team made up of the researcher who developed the idea and volunteers from manufacturing, sales, marketing and the legal department. The team nurtures the product and protects it from company bureaucracy. Team members stay with the product until it succeeds or fails and then return to their previous jobs. Some teams have tried three or four times before finally making a success of an idea. Each year, 3M awards Golden Step Awards to venture teams whose new products earned more than $2 million in domestic sales or $4 million in worldwide sales, within three years of introduction.

The company knows that it must try thousands of new-product ideas to hit one big jackpot. One well-worn slogan at 3M is 'You have to kiss a lot of frogs to find a prince.' 'Kissing frogs' often means making mistakes, but 3M accepts blunders and dead ends as a normal part of creativity and innovation. In fact, its philosophy seems to be 'if you aren't making mistakes, you're probably not doing anything'.

As it turns out, 'blunders' have turned into some of 3M's most successful products. There is the familiar story about the chemist who accidentally spilled a new chemical on her tennis shoes. Some days later, she noticed that the spots hit by the chemical had not become dirty. Eureka! The chemical eventually became Scotchgard fabric protector. They tell about the early scientist who had a deadly fear of shaving with a straight razor. Instead, he invented a very fine, waterproof sandpaper which he used to sand the stubble from his face each morning. This invention did not catch on as a shaving solution, but it became one of 3M's best-selling products – wet–dry sandpaper used for a wide variety of commercial and industrial applications.

Not least, there's the one about 3M scientist Spencer Silver who started out to develop a superstrong adhesive that didn't stick very well at all. He sent the apparently useless substance on to other 3M researchers to see if they could find something to do with it. Nothing happened for several years. Then Arthur Fry, another 3M scientist and a choir member, found that scraps of paper dabbed with Mr Silver's weak glue stuck nicely to pages marked out in his hymnal and later peeled off without damaging the hymnal. Eureka! Mr Fry's problem of marking places in his hymnal was solved. Thus were born 3M's ubiquitous Post-it notes, a product that is now one of the top-selling office supply products in the world!

It looks like 3M could easily amend its 'Innovation: Working for You' ad line to include 'and for 3M'. Still, there are limits. Some analysts question whether such a free-wheeling, no-questions-asked creative culture is appropriate, given the cost-reduction pressures of today's tougher economic times. In fact, 3M's CEO, Jim McNerney, is busily cutting costs and slimming down the company's workforce. He is also overhauling the 3M R&D organisation and culture, one in which even 3M old-timers agree that money hasn't always been spent wisely. According to one analyst, McNerney 'vows to take an organization of myriad product and research fiefdoms – which happens to be one of the most respected manufacturing concerns in the world – and hammer it into one shared corporate culture.' He is carefully examining where R&D dollars are spent and setting uniform performance standards and accountability across the company.

The risk is that the changing culture and organisational restructuring might stifle 3M's hallmark creativity. 'The most important thing about 3M – the single most important thing – is you get to do things your own way', says a senior 3M executive and 33-year veteran. McNerney understands the balancing act: efficiency versus hands-off R&D spending; accountability versus individual creative freedom. 'My job is to add scale in a fast-moving, entrepreneurial environment', he says. 'If I end up killing that entrepreneurial spirit, I will have failed.' For 3M, there is no room for complacency if it wants to remain a corporate superstar.

SOURCES: Quotes from Rick Mullin, 'Analysts rate 3M's new culture', *Chemical Week* (26 September 2001), pp. 39–40; and Michael Arndt, '3M: a lab for growth', *Business Week* (21 January 2002), pp. 50–1. Also, see Alison Maitland, '3M has succession taped', *Financial Times* (11 May 2000), p. 22; William H. Miller, 'New leader, new era' (November 2001), accessed online at **www.industryweek.com**; 'America's most admired companies', *Fortune* (4 March 2002), p. 75; for more information on 3M, visit **www.3m.com**.

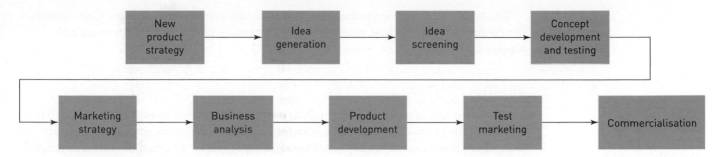

Figure 14.1 Steps in new product development

New-product development process

The new-product development process for finding and growing new products consists of nine main steps (see Figure 14.1).

New-product strategy

Effective product innovation is guided by a well-defined *new-product strategy*. The new-product strategy achieves four main goals: first, it gives direction to the new-product team and *focuses team effort*; second, it helps to *integrate* functional or departmental efforts; third, where understood by the new-product team, it allows tasks to be *delegated* to team members, who can be left to operate independently; and fourth, the very act of producing and getting managers to agree on a strategy requires *proactive*, not reactive, management, which increases the likelihood of a more thorough search for innovation opportunities.

Successful innovative companies place more emphasis upon the use of definitive strategy statements or a **product innovation charter** (PIC). The PIC draws managers' attention to the reasons or *rationale* behind the firm's search for innovation opportunities, the *product/market* and *technology* to focus on, the miscellaneous *goals* or *objectives* (market share, cash flow, profitability, etc.) to be achieved, and *guidelines* on the nature or level of innovativeness that will sell the new product.[6] The charter spells out the priority that managers should place on developing breakthrough products, changing existing ones and imitating competitors' products. Given that many or most new-product ideas are likely to be unsuitable for development, senior management has to establish specific criteria for new-product idea selection. Ideas are accepted based on the specific *strategic roles* the new products are expected to play. A new product's role might be to help the company maintain its industry position as an innovator, to defend a market-share position, or to get a foothold in a future new market. Or the new-product might help the company to take advantage of its special strengths or exploit technology in a new way.

Product innovation charter (PIC)—A new-product strategy statement formalising management's reasons or rationale behind the firm's search for innovation opportunities, the product/market and technology to focus upon, and the goals and objectives to be achieved.

Idea generation

The PIC should direct the systematic search for new-product ideas. **Idea generation** should be proactive and systematic rather than haphazard. This ensures that the company will find not only many ideas, but also ones that are good for its type of business. A company typically has to generate many ideas in order to find a few good ones. A recent survey of product managers found that of 100 proposed new-product ideas, 39 begin the product development process, 17 survive the development process, eight actually reach the marketplace and only one eventually reaches its business objectives. For pharmaceuticals companies, it can take some 6,000 to 8,000 starting ideas to produce one commercial success.[7]

Idea generation—The systematic search for new-product ideas.

To obtain a flow of new-product ideas, the company can tap many sources. Chief sources of new-product ideas include internal sources, customers, competitors, distributors and suppliers.

Internal sources

The company can find new ideas through its own formal research and development efforts. It can pick the brains of its executives, scientists, engineers, designers, manufacturing and salespeople. Some companies have established 'intrapreneurial' programmes that encourage employees to think up and develop new product ideas (see Marketing Insights 14.1). Formal or informal suggestion schemes can also be used to tap staff's ideas for improving production, products and services. Toyota claims that employees submit two million ideas annually – about 35 suggestions per employee – and that more than 85 per cent of these ideas are implemented.

Customers

Good new-product ideas also come from watching and listening to customers. The company can analyse customer questions and complaints to find new products that better solve consumer problems. It can conduct surveys or focus groups to learn about consumer needs and wants. Or company engineers or salespeople can meet with or work alongside customers to get suggestions and ideas. For example, companies such as Hewlett-Packard, Sony, Toyota and many other effective innovators are known to have their design engineers talk with final consumers to get ideas for new products.

Customers often create new products on their own, and companies can benefit by finding these products and putting them on the market. About one-third of all the software IBM leases for its computers is developed by outside users.[8] Indeed, studies of new industrial product development by Eric von Hippel has shown that the highest percentage of ideas originate with lead users – those customers who make the most advanced use of the company's products and who recognise the need for improvements before other customers do.[9]

Customers, however, may not always know their future needs and wants. If Philips had questioned consumers 30 years ago about what new audio technology they wanted, they would never have said a personal stereo – the idea would not have occurred to them. This is one of the reasons why Finnish mobile communications company Nokia employs a team of people around the world whose job is to think 10 years ahead and dream up ideas. They have to anticipate future needs before the consumer has even become aware of them. They must also predict the innovations of their rivals, so that the company can be one step ahead. Every so often, the ideas team hold focus groups for ordinary users and ask them what they want from their phones when they are on the move. The users are offered a handful of new ideas and their reactions are videoed. The team always pay attention to the quirky suggestions because there is often a lot of truth in them. The company also consults anthropologists to help unravel consumers' reactions, and these generate leads which give the team something to build on. It was anticipating needs before they exist that brought about Nokia's revolutionary 9000 Communicator, which was the world's first all-in-one mobile communications device – a fax, phone, digital diary, calculator and palm-top computer all rolled into one.[10]

Competitors

Competitors are another good source of new-product ideas. Companies watch competitors' ads and other communications to get clues about their new products. They can research competing competitors' products and services. For example, they can find out what customers like and dislike about competitors' products. Or they can buy competitors' new products, take them apart to see how they work, analyse their sales, and decide whether the company should bring out a new product of its own.

Distributors, suppliers and others

Resellers are close to the market and can pass along information about consumer problems and new-product possibilities. Suppliers can tell the company about new concepts, techniques and materials that can be used to develop new products. Other idea sources include trade magazines, shows and seminars, government agencies, advertising agencies, marketing research firms, university and commercial laboratories, science parks, and inventors. Companies may also turn to new-product consultants to find new ideas and problem solutions to serve customer needs better.

> For example, some years ago, Heineken of the Netherlands had to recall millions of bottles of its home-brewed Export beer due to contamination by glass particles. To avoid future such incidents, which are potentially very costly and damaging for the brand and the company, the brewer got its packaging research and development people to investigate potential solutions to the problem. They could not find anything they could buy off the shelf, so turned to the UK's PA Consulting Group, which looked at a variety of solutions, ranging from X-rays and gamma rays to nuclear magnetic resonance and ultrasonic techniques. PA eventually developed a solution inspired by a technique used by pharmaceutical firms to inspect vials. The consultants worked with a UK bottle-handling specialist and image-processing specialists to develop a system for Heineken. The safety innovation, as Heineken called it, underlined the importance of drawing inspiration from external parties to generate novel problem solutions.[11]

The search for new-product ideas should be systematic in order to ensure that many good ideas will surface, not sputter in and die. Top management can avoid these problems by installing an ideas management system that directs the flow of new ideas to a central point where they can be collected, reviewed and evaluated. The company may set up an ideas management system in a number of ways: appoint a respected senior person to be the company's ideas manager; create a multidisciplinary ideas management committee, consisting of people from R&D, engineering, purchasing, operations, finance, sales and marketing, who meet regularly and evaluate proposed new-product ideas; set up a freephone number for anyone who wants to volunteer new ideas to the ideas manager; encourage all of the company's stakeholders – employees, suppliers, distributors, dealers and so forth – to send their ideas to the ideas manager; and set up a formal recognition programme to reward those who contribute the best ideas.[12]

The ideas manager approach has two advantages. First, it helps foster an innovation-oriented company culture. It shows that top management supports, encourages and rewards innovation. Second, it yields a steady stream of ideas from which good ones will emerge. As the system matures, ideas will flow more freely. Importantly, companies that use such a formalised approach to finding new ideas will find that no longer will good ideas wither for the lack of a sounding-board or a senior product advocate.

YELLOW IS A SIGN OF IMPORTANCE.

That's why people with important business messages use our Post-it™ Notes adhesive note pads. Bright notes that stick virtually anywhere. To make sure your messages get noticed. Call 1-800-328-1684 for a free sample. Then get more Post-it Notes from a nearby stationer or retail store. And start getting the recognition you deserve.

Commercial Office Supply Division/3M

3M

Idea screening

The purpose of idea generation is to create a large number of ideas. The purpose of the succeeding stages is to *reduce* that number. The first idea-reducing stage is **idea screening**. The purpose of screening is to spot good ideas and drop poor ones as soon as possible. As product development costs rise greatly in later stages, it is important for the company to go ahead only with those product ideas that will turn into profitable products.

Most companies require their executives to write up new-product ideas on a standard form that can be reviewed by a new-product committee. The write-up describes the product, the target market and the competition, and makes some rough estimates of market size, product price, development time and costs, manufacturing costs and rate of return. The committee then evaluates the idea against a set of general criteria. Typically, the committee asks questions such as these: Is the product truly useful to consumers and society? Is this product good for our particular company? Does it mesh well with the company's objectives and strategies? Do we have the people, skills and resources to make it succeed? Does it deliver more value to customers than competing products? Is it easy to advertise and distribute? Many companies have well-designed systems for rating and screening new-product ideas.

Idea screening—Screening new-product ideas in order to spot good ideas and drop poor ones as soon as possible.

Concept development and testing

Attractive ideas must be developed into product concepts. It is important to distinguish between a *product idea*, a *product concept* and a *product image*. A **product idea** is an idea for a possible product that the company can see itself offering to the market. A **product concept** is a detailed version of the idea stated in meaningful consumer terms. A **product image** is the way consumers perceive an actual or potential product.

Concept development

DaimlerChrysler is getting ready to commercialise its experimental fuel-cell-powered electric car. This car's low-polluting fuel-cell system runs directly on methanol, which delivers hydrogen to the fuel cell with only water as a by-product. It is highly fuel efficient (75 per cent more efficient than petrol engines) and gives the new car an environmental advantage over standard internal combustion engine cars or today's super-efficient petrol–electric hybrid cars. DaimlerChrysler is currently road-testing its NECAR 5 (New Electric Car) subcompact prototype and plans to deliver the first fuel-cell cars to customers in 2004. Based on the tiny Mercedes A-Class, the car accelerates quickly, reaches speeds of 90 miles per hour, and has a 280-mile driving range, giving it a huge edge over battery-powered electric cars which travel only about 80 miles before needing 3–12 hours of recharging.[13]

DaimlerChrysler's task is to develop this new product into alternative product concepts, find out how attractive each concept is to customers and choose the best one. To increase the likelihood of concept acceptance, some firms involve the customer (or potential customer) in concept development – customers may, for example, be invited to the DaimlerChrysler's design reviews in the early stages of the new-product process. The following product concepts for the fuel-cell electric car might be created:

- *Concept 1.* A moderately priced subcompact designed as a second family car to be used around town. The car is ideal for running errands and visiting friends.
- *Concept 2.* A medium-cost sporty compact appealing to young people.

Product idea—An idea for a possible product that the company can see itself offering to the market.

Product concept—A detailed version of the new-product idea stated in meaningful consumer terms.

Product image—The way consumers perceive an actual or potential product.

- *Concept 3.* An inexpensive subcompact 'green' car appealing to environmentally conscious people who want practical transportation and low pollution.
- *Concept 4.* A high-end sports utility vehicle (SUV) appealing to those who love the space SUVs provide but lament the poor petrol mileage.

Concept testing

Concept testing—Testing new-product concepts with a group of target consumers to find out whether the concepts have strong consumer appeal.

Concept testing calls for testing new-product concepts with a group of target consumers. The concepts may be presented to consumers symbolically or physically. Here, in words, is *Concept 3*:

> An efficient, fun-to-drive, fuel-cell-powered electric subcompact car that seats four. This methanol-powered high-tech wonder provides practical and reliable transportation with virtually no pollution. It goes up to 90 miles per hour and, unlike battery-powered electric cars, it never needs recharging. It's priced, fully equipped, at €25,000.

For some concept tests, a word or picture description might be sufficient. However, a more concrete and physical presentation of the concept will increase the reliability of the concept test. Today, marketers are finding innovative ways to make product concepts more real to consumer subjects. For example, some are using virtual reality to test product concepts. Virtual reality programmes use computers and sensory devices (such as goggles or gloves) to simulate reality. For example, a designer of kitchen cabinets can use a virtual reality program to help a customer 'see' how his or her kitchen would look and work if remodelled with the company's products. Virtual reality is still in its infancy, but its applications are increasing daily.[14]

After being exposed to the concept, consumers may then be asked to react to it by answering the questions in Table 14.1. The answers will help the company decide which concept has the strongest appeal. For example, the last question asks about the consumer's intention to buy. Suppose 10 per cent of the consumers said they 'definitely' would buy and another 5 per cent said 'probably'. The company could project these figures to the population size of this target group to estimate sales volume. Concept testing offers a rough estimate of potential sales, but managers must view this with caution. The estimate is uncertain, largely because consumers do not always carry out stated intentions.[15] Potential customers may like the idea of the new product, but might not want to pay for one! It is still important to carry out such tests with product concepts so as to gauge customers' response as well as to identify

Table 14.1 Questions for fuel-cell-powered electric car concept test

1.	Do you understand the concept of a fuel-cell-powered electric car?
2.	Do you believe the claims about the car's performance?
3.	What are the main benefits of the fuel-cell-powered electric car compared with a conventional car?
4.	What are its advantages compared with a battery-powered electric car?
5.	What improvements in the car's features would you suggest?
6.	For what uses would you prefer a fuel-cell-powered electric car to a conventional car?
7.	What would be a reasonable price to charge for the car?
8.	Who would be involved in your decision to buy such a car? Who would drive it?
9.	Would you buy such a car? (Definitely, probably, probably not, definitely not)

aspects of the concept that are particularly liked or disliked by potential buyers. Feedback might suggest ways to refine the concept, thereby increasing its appeal to customers.

Marketing strategy development

Suppose DaimlerChrysler finds that Concept 3 for the fuel-cell-powered electric car tests best. The next step is to develop a **marketing strategy** for introducing this car to the market.

The **marketing strategy statement** consists of three parts. The first part describes the target market, the planned product positioning, and the sales, market share and profit goals for the first few years. Thus:

> The target market is younger, well-educated, moderate-to-high income individuals, couples or small families seeking practical, environmentally responsible transportation. The car will be positioned as more economical to operate, more fun to drive and less polluting than today's internal combustion engine cars or hybrid cars, and as less restricting than battery-powered electric cars which must be recharged regularly. The company will aim to sell 100,000 cars in the first year, at a loss of not more than €15 million. In the second year, the company will aim for sales of 120,000 cars and a profit of €25 million.

The second part of the marketing strategy statement outlines the product's planned price, distribution and marketing budget for the first year.

> The fuel-cell-powered electric car will be offered in three colours and will have optional air-conditioning and power-drive features. It will sell at a retail price of €20,000 – with 15 per cent off the list price to dealers. Dealers who sell more than 10 cars per month will get an additional discount of 5 per cent on each car sold that month. An advertising budget of €20 million will be split 50–50 between national and local advertising. Advertising will emphasise the car's fun and low emissions. During the first year, €150,000 will be spent on marketing research to find out who is buying the car and to determine their satisfaction levels.

The third part of the marketing strategy statement describes the planned long-run sales, profit goals and marketing mix strategy:

> The company intends to capture a 3 per cent long-run share of the total car market and realise an after-tax return on investment of 15 per cent. To achieve this, product quality will start high and be improved over time. Price will be raised in the second and third years if competition permits. The total advertising budget will be raised each year by about 10 per cent. Marketing research will be reduced to €60,000 per year after the first year.

Marketing strategy—The marketing logic by which the business unit hopes to achieve its marketing objectives.

Marketing strategy statement—A statement of the planned strategy for a new product that outlines the intended target market, the planned product positioning, and the sales, market share and profit goals for the first few years.

Business analysis

Business analysis—A review of the sales, costs and profit projections for a new product to find out whether these factors satisfy the company's objectives.

Once management has decided on its product concept and marketing strategy, it can evaluate the business attractiveness of the proposal. **Business analysis** involves a review of the sales, costs and profit projections for a new product to find out whether they satisfy the company's objectives. If they do, the product proceeds to the product development stage.

To estimate sales, the company looks at the sales history of similar products and conducts surveys of market opinion. It then estimates minimum and maximum sales to assess the range of risk. After preparing the sales forecast, management can estimate the expected costs and profits for the product, including marketing, R&D, manufacturing, accounting and finance costs. The company then uses the sales and costs figures to analyse the new product's financial attractiveness.

Product development

Product development—Developing the product concept into a physical product in order to ensure that the product idea can be turned into a workable product.

So far, for many new-product concepts, the product may have existed only as a word description, a drawing or perhaps a crude mock-up. If the product concept passes the business test, it moves into **product development**. Here, R&D or engineering develops the product concept into a physical product. The product development step, however, now calls for a large jump in investment. It will show whether the product idea can be turned into a workable product.

The R&D department will develop one or more physical versions of the product concept. R&D hopes to design a prototype that functions, is able to satisfy and excite consumers and can be produced quickly and at budgeted costs. Developing a successful prototype can take days, weeks, months or even years. Sometimes product design and development may pose a serious challenge for the firm and companies have to find ways to get round these obstacles.

Microsoft's 'TabletPC', launched in the UK in 2002, was heralded to be the 'next stage in the evolution of the PC'. Doing away with a keyboard, users should be able to operate the PC by speaking to it or writing on an electronic pad. But, there was a catch – the TabletPC had not been fully tuned to understand the English accent. Speech-recognition technology is still in its infancy and requires further development. Equally, the PC's ability to read handwriting was not up to scratch. Although the software has been refined by taking handwriting samples from 40,000 people in Reading, Manchester and Edinburgh, handwriting recognition technology will take a number of years to mature. Although the product has been launched, the problems faced by early users suggest that there are significant product development challenges to be overcome.[16]

Consider another example – the experience of Dentronic, a company spun off from Sweden's University of Umeå. Dentronic developed a new dental system called Decim, a composite for filling teeth that replaces mercury amalgam, which is a serious health hazard for dentists who have to handle it on a daily basis. Decim is better than other modern alternatives based on polymeric materials as it is longer lasting and has lower toxicity problems. However, the material, based on zirconium dioxide, requires a special combination of software and hardware systems to make up the filling. Unlike amalgam, it cannot be mixed as a paste in the surgery. Instead it involves advanced manufacturing techniques. A cast has to be made of the patient's tooth cavity as the model for CAD/CAM preparation of a corresponding inlay. The cast is captured by a special laser scanner, converted into a three-dimensional drawing, with manual adjustment of the chewing surface. A numerically controlled manufacturing unit automatically machines the inlay to shape, and, after polishing, it is cemented in place in the tooth, giving a perfect fit. Through an innovation network agency, IRC Northern Sweden, Dentronic secured the collaboration of a British software house as well as signed up with French ceramic materials supplier Norton Desmarquet which developed and manufactured exclusively for the company. Thanks to these external partners, Dentronic was able to surmount serious development and production problems which would have stalled the firm's efforts to commercialise its new non-toxic technology. Dentronic launched the Decim system under the brand name Denzir in Sweden in November 1999, followed by rapid international rollouts over 2000.[17]

When the prototypes are ready, they undergo rigorous functional tests under laboratory and field conditions to make sure that the product performs safely and effectively.

The prototype must have the required functional features and also convey the intended psychological characteristics. The fuel-cell-powered electric car, for example, should strike consumers as being well built, comfortable and safe. Management must learn what makes consumers decide that a car is well built. To some consumers, this means that the car has 'solid-sounding' doors. To others, it means that the car is able to withstand heavy impact in crash tests. Consumer tests are conducted, in which consumers test-drive the car and rate its attributes. For some products, prototyping and product development may involve both the key intermediaries that supply the product or service and the final consumer or end-user.

When designing products, the company should look beyond simply creating products that satisfy consumer needs and wants. Too often, companies design their new products without enough concern for how the designs will be produced. Companies may minimise production problems by adopting an approach towards product development called *design for manufacturability and assembly* (DFMA). Using this approach, companies work to fashion products that are *both* satisfying *and* easy to manufacture. This often results not only in lower costs but also in higher-quality and more reliable products.

Test marketing

If the product passes functional and consumer tests, the next step is **test marketing**, the stage at which the product and marketing programme are introduced into more realistic market settings.

Test marketing gives the marketer experience with marketing the product before going to the great expense of full introduction. It lets the company test the product and its entire marketing programme – positioning strategy, advertising, distribution, pricing, branding and packaging and budget levels. The company uses test marketing to learn how consumers and dealers will react to handling, using and repurchasing the product. The results can be used

Test marketing—The stage of new-product development where the product and marketing programme are tested in more realistic market settings.

to make better sales and profit forecasts. Thus a good test market can provide a wealth of information about the potential success of the product and marketing programme.

The amount of test marketing needed varies with each new product. Test marketing costs can be enormous. It takes time that may allow competitors to gain advantages. When the costs of developing and introducing the product are low or when management is already confident that the new product will succeed, the company may do little or no test marketing. Companies often do not test market simple line extensions, minor modifications of current products or copies of successful competitor products. However, when the new-product introduction requires a big investment, or when management is not sure of the product or marketing programme, the company may do a lot of test marketing.

The idea of test marketing also applies to new service products. For example, an airline company preparing to introduce a secure, cost-saving system of electronic ticketing may try out the new service first on domestic routes before rolling out the service to international flights. Or it might offer the ticketless system on its busiest routes and restrict the test to its most frequent travellers. The system's effectiveness and customers' acceptance and reactions can then be gauged prior to making the decision to extend the service to cover all of its domestic or global networks.

Whether or not a company decides to test market, and the amount of testing it does, depend on the cost and risk of introducing the product on the one hand, and on the testing costs and time pressures on the other. Although the costs of test marketing can be high, they are often small when compared to the costs of making a major mistake. A classic example is the Omo 'Power' fiasco. Unilever learned a costly lesson when it skipped formal test marketing of its revolutionary Omo 'Power' laundry detergent. It forged ahead with a £200 million Europe-wide launch in 1994. The company spent another £70 million on the withdrawal of the defective, clothing-annihilating detergent a year after its introduction.

When using test marketing, consumer-products companies usually choose one of three approaches – standard test markets, controlled test markets or simulated test markets.

Standard test markets

Using standard test markets, the company finds a small number of representative test cities, conducts a full marketing campaign in these cities and uses store audits, consumer and distributor surveys and other measures to gauge product performance. It then uses the results to forecast national sales and profits, to discover potential product problems and to fine-tune the marketing programme.

Standard market tests have some drawbacks. They can be costly and may take a long time – some last as long as three to five years. Moreover, competitors can monitor test-market results or even interfere with them by cutting their prices in test locations, increasing their promotion or even buying up the product being tested. Finally, test markets give competitors a look at the company's new product well before it is introduced nationally. Thus, competitors may have time to develop defensive strategies and may even beat the company's product to the market.

Despite these disadvantages, standard test markets are still the most widely used approach for major market testing. However, many companies today are shifting towards quicker and cheaper controlled and simulated test marketing methods.

Controlled test markets

Several research firms keep controlled panels of stores which have agreed to carry new products for a fee. The company with the new product specifies the number of stores and geographical locations it wants. The research firm delivers the product to the participating stores and controls shelf location, amount of shelf space, displays and point-of-purchase promotions, and pricing according to specified plans. Sales results are tracked to determine the impact of these factors on demand.

Controlled test-marketing systems like Nielsen's Scantrack and Information Resources Inc.'s (IRI) BehaviorScan track individual behaviour from the television set to the checkout counter. IRI maintains panels of shoppers in carefully selected markets.[18] It measures TV viewing in each panel household and can send special commercials to panel member television sets. Panel consumers buy from cooperating stores and show identification cards when making purchases.

Within test stores, IRI controls such factors as shelf placement, price and in-store promotions. Detailed electronic scanner information on each consumer's purchases is fed into a central computer, where it is combined with the consumer's demographic and TV viewing information and reported daily. Thus, BehaviorScan can provide store-by-store, week-by-week reports on the sales of new products being tested. And because the scanners record the specific purchases of individual consumers, the system also can provide information on repeat purchases and the ways in which different types of consumers are reacting to the new product, its advertising, and various other elements of the marketing programme.

Controlled test markets usually cost less than standard test markets and take less time than them (six months to a year). However, some companies are concerned that the limited number of small cities and panel consumers used by the research services may not be representative of their products' markets or target consumers. And, as in standard test markets, controlled test markets allow competitors to get a look at the company's new product. Nonetheless, experienced research firms can project test-market results to broader markets, while accounting for biases in the test markets used.

Simulated test markets

Companies also can test new products in a simulated shopping environment. The company or research firm shows, to a sample of consumers, ads and promotions for a variety of products, including the new product being tested. It gives consumers a small amount of money and invites them to a real or laboratory store, where they may keep the money or use it to buy items. The researchers note how many consumers buy the new product and competing brands. This simulation provides a measure of trial and the commercial's effectiveness against competing commercials. The researchers then ask consumers the reasons for their purchase or non-purchase. Some weeks later, they interview the consumer by phone to determine product attitudes, usage, satisfaction and repurchase intentions. Using sophisticated computer models, the researchers then project national sales from results of the simulated test market.

Recently, some marketers have begun to use interesting new high-tech approaches to simulated test market research, such as virtual reality and the Internet.

Virtual reality tools such as Simul-Shop can recreate shopping situations in which researchers can test consumers' reactions to such factors as product positioning, store layouts and package designs. Suppose a breakfast cereal marketer wants to test reactions to a new package design and store-shelf positioning. Using Simul-Shop on a standard desktop PC, test-shoppers begin their shopping with a screen showing the outside of a grocery store. They click to enter the virtual store and are guided to the appropriate store section. Once there, they scan the shelf, pick up various cereal packages, rotate them, study the labels and look around to see what is on the shelf behind them. About the only thing they can't do is open the box and taste the cereal. The virtual shopping trip includes full sound and video, along with a guide who directs users through the experience and answers their questions.

Other services such as Alternative Realities Corporation (ARC) offers a virtual reality amphitheatre called the VisionDome. The Dome offers 360 by 160 degrees of film projection, allowing as many as 40 people at one time to participate and interact in a virtual reality experience. When conducting research on, say, a car, customers can go into a VisionDome, see that car in three dimensions, look at it from every angle, sit in it and take it out for a test drive. Customers can immerse themselves totally in the product. They can configure that car exactly the way they want it.

Virtual reality as a research tool offers several advantages. One, it is relatively inexpensive. A virtual reality store can display an almost infinite variety of products, sizes, styles and flavours in response to consumers' desires and needs. The technique's interactivity allows marketers and consumers to work together via computer on new product designs and marketing programmes. Finally, virtual reality has great potential for international marketing research. With virtual reality, researchers can create virtual stores in each country and region where the new product will be launched, using the appropriate local products, shelf layouts and currencies. Once the stores are online, a product concept can be quickly tested across locations. Research results, revealing markets with the greatest opportunity for a successful launch, can be communicated to head-quarters electronically. Virtual reality research also has its limitations. Like any simulated shopping situation, it never quite matches the real thing. It is not clear how true test participants' responses are in a simulated experience.[19]

In general, simulated test markets overcome some of the disadvantages of standard and controlled test markets. They usually cost much less, can be run in eight weeks and keep the new product out of competitors' view. Yet, because of their small samples and simulated shopping environments, many marketers do not think that simulated test markets are as accurate or reliable as larger, real-world tests. Still, simulated test markets are used widely, often as 'pre-test' markets. Because they are fast and inexpensive, they can be run to assess quickly a new product or its marketing programme. If the pre-test results are strongly positive, the product might be introduced without further testing. If the results are very poor, the product might be dropped or substantially redesigned and retested. If the results are promising but indefinite, the product and marketing programme can be tested further in controlled or standard test markets.[20]

Test marketing new industrial products

Business marketers use different methods for test marketing their new products, such as product-use tests, trade shows, distributor/dealer display rooms, and standard or controlled test markets.

Product-use tests

Here the business marketer selects a small group of potential customers who agree to use the new product for a limited time. The manufacturer's technical people watch how these customers use the product. From this test the manufacturer learns about customer training and servicing requirements. After the test, the marketer asks the customer about purchase intent and other reactions. For some products, product-use tests may involve both the business customer and final or end-user.

Trade shows

These shows draw a large number of buyers who view new products in a few concentrated days. The manufacturer sees how buyers react to various product features and terms, and can assess buyer interest and purchase intentions.

Distributor and dealer display rooms

The new industrial product may be placed next to other company products and possibly competitors' products in the showrooms. This method yields preference and pricing information in the normal selling atmosphere of the product.

Standard or controlled test markets

These are used to measure the potential of new industrial products. The business marketer produces a limited supply of the product which is sold by the salespeople to customers in a limited number of geographical areas. The company gives the product full advertising, sales promotion and other marketing support. Such test markets let the company test the product and its marketing programme in real market situations.

Commercialisation

Test marketing gives management the information needed to make a final decision about whether to launch the new product. If the company goes ahead with **commercialisation** – that is, introducing the new product into the market – it will face high costs. It may have to spend, as in the case of a new consumer packaged good, between €10 million and €200 million for advertising, sales promotion and other marketing efforts in the first year. The company will have to build or rent a manufacturing facility. It must have sufficient funds to gear up production to meet demand. Failure to do so can leave an opening in the market for competitors to step in.

Commercialisation— Introducing a new product into the market.

> For example, when London-based electronics company Psion introduced its Series 5 palmtop organisers, the products were so popular that the firm could not meet demand initially. The backlog of orders was taking some four months to clear. Potentially, that left a gap in the handheld computer market for American and Japanese rivals, who built similar machines based on an operating system designed by US software giant Microsoft.

The company launching a new product must make four decisions.

When?

The first decision is introduction timing – whether the time is right to introduce the new product. If it cannibalises the sales of the company's other products, its introduction may be delayed. If it can be improved further, or if the economy is down, the company may wait until the following year to launch it.

Where?

The company must decide where to launch the new product. Should it be in a single location, or region, several regions, the national market or the international market? Few companies have the confidence, capital and capacity to launch new products into full national or international distribution. They will develop a planned market rollout over time. In particular, small companies may enter attractive cities or regions one at a time. Larger companies may quickly introduce new products into several regions or into the entire national market.

Companies such as Nokia, Unilever, Procter & Gamble and Colgate-Palmolive, with international distribution systems, may introduce new products through global rollouts. Colgate-Palmolive used a 'lead-country' strategy for its Palmolive Options shampoo and conditioner: it was first introduced in Australia, the Philippines, Hong Kong and Mexico, then rapidly rolled out into Europe, Asia, Latin America and Africa. However, international firms are increasingly introducing their new products in swift global assaults.

To whom?

Within the rollout markets, the company must target its distribution and promotion to customer groups who represent the best prospects. These prime prospects should have been profiled by the firm in earlier research and test marketing. For instance, Vertu, Nokia's 'retro-modern' mobile phone, with a sapphire face and a body available in platinum, white gold or stainless steel and sold at an astonishing £14,950, was targeted at movie stars and the super-rich kids. Generally, firms must fine-tune their targeting efforts, starting with the innovators, then looking especially for early adopters, heavy users and opinion leaders. Opinion leaders are particularly important as their endorsement of the new product has a powerful impact upon adoption by other buyers in the marketplace.

How?

The company also must develop an *action plan* for introducing the new product into the selected markets. It must spend the marketing budget on the marketing mix and various other activities.

For example, when Germany's Siemens unveiled its new fashion mobile phone brand, Xelibri, in 2003, the main thrust of Xelibri's launch strategy was to establish credibility as a fashion brand. Xelibri hosted the opening party of the London Fashion Week to which celebrities and opinion-leading editors and journalists of the fashion press were invited to celebrate 'Xelibri's birthday party'. This, together with other selected fashion events and a comprehensive PR campaign, drew huge media attention, including the support of fashion industry influencers, while creating high brand and product awareness among fashion-savvy people globally. David LaChapelle, the celebrated fashion photographer, was assigned to create pictures to emphasise Xelibri's fashionable, provocative image, consistent with its intended brand identity. Advertising was used to sustain the high brand awareness already created by the other communication tools; TV and cinema ads served to reinforce Xelibri's fashion statement. Being positioned as a fashion accessory, upmarket department stores like Selfridges in the UK and Peek & Cloppenburg in Germany,

Organising for new-product development

Many companies have traditionally organised their new-product development process into the orderly sequence of steps shown in Figure 14.1, starting with determining the new product strategy and ending with commercialisation. Under this **sequential product development** approach, one company department works individually to complete its phase of the development process before passing the new product on to the next department, as in a kind of relay race. The sequential process has its merits – it helps bring order and control to risky and complex new-product development projects. But the approach also can be fatally slow. In fast-changing, highly competitive markets, such slow-but-sure product development may result in product failures, lost sales and profits and crumbling market positions.

Today, 'speed to market' and reducing new-product development 'cycle time' have become pressing concerns to companies in all industries. One study, for example, found that a six-month delay in introducing a new product cut its lifetime profits by one-third. By contrast, spending 10 per cent over the development budget will reduce profits by only 2 per cent.[22]

In order to get their new products to market more quickly, many companies are adopting a faster, more flexible, team-oriented approach called **simultaneous product development**, or team-based or collaborative product development. Under this approach, company departments work closely together through cross-functional teams, overlapping the steps in the pro-duct development process to save time and increase effectiveness. Instead of passing the new product from department to department, the company assembles a team of people from various departments that stays with the new product from start to finish. These teams typically include people from the finance, marketing, design, manufacturing or operations, and legal departments, and even supplier and customer companies. Simultaneous development is more like a rugby match than a relay race – team members pass the new product back and forth as they move down-field towards the common goal of a speedy and successful new-product launch.

Top management gives the product development team general strategic direction but no clear-cut product idea or work plan. It challenges the team with stiff and seemingly contradictory goals – 'turn out carefully planned and superior new products, but do it quickly' – and then gives the team whatever freedom and resources it needs to meet the challenge. The team becomes a driving force that pushes the product forward. In a sequential process, a bottleneck at one phase can seriously slow or even halt the entire project. In the simultaneous approach, if one function hits snags, it works to resolve them while the team moves on.

However, the simultaneous approach has some limitations. Superfast product development can be riskier and more costly than the slower, more orderly sequential approach. It can often create increased organisational tension and confusion. Moreover, the company must take care that rushing a product to market does not adversely affect its quality – the objective is not merely to create products faster, but to create them *better* and faster. Despite these drawbacks, in rapidly changing industries facing increasingly shorter product life-cycles, the rewards of fast and flexible product development far exceed the risks. Companies that get new and improved products to the market faster than competitors gain a dramatic competitive edge. They can respond more quickly to emerging consumer tastes and charge higher prices for more advanced designs.[23]

Sequential product development—A new-product development approach in which one company department works individually to complete its stage of the process before passing the new product along to the next department and stage.

Simultaneous product development—An approach to developing new products in which various company departments work closely together, overlapping the steps in the product development process to save time and increase effectiveness.

Successful new-product development is not just about having a special organisational *structure* for new-product development. An innovative organisation must have, at its helm, *top management* that gives priority to new products, which are seen as the life-blood of the company. Their *vision* for innovation is clearly communicated to, and its *value shared* by, staff at all levels of the organisation. A clear *strategy* as guiding force, backed by top management support, ensures that teams consistently perform. Top management not only believes wholeheartedly in, but also devotes sufficient resources to, new-product development. A strongly innovative organisation is also committed to its people (*staff*), investing continually in helping them to acquire and maintain the necessary *skills* to meet the challenge of innovation. The organisation must also embrace the *product champions* who, against all the odds, strive to take projects to completion. They, in turn, rely on the *executive champion*, whose authority is invaluable in fighting off the political battles that interfere with new-product progress. Furthermore, information and communication *systems* are designed to facilitate learning and to ensure that information flows quickly to critical individuals responsible for making or implementing new-product development decisions. Real innovation is a risky activity, so firms must foster an *entrepreneurial culture* and *climate* for innovation, with planning, control and reward systems encouraging risk-taking as opposed to its avoidance. Last, but not least, to innovate effectively, firms must build customer-focused, functionally well-integrated organisations. In successful innovative firms, new-product development is seldom left to chance. There may be an element of luck underpinning successful commercialisation of innovations. Luck, unfortunately, is not easy to replicate. The lessons of strategic new-product planning and implementation, however, are.[24]

We have looked at the problem of finding and developing new products. Next, let us examine the problem of managing them over their life-cycle.

Product life-cycle strategies

Product life-cycle (PLC)— The course of a product's sales and profits over its lifetime. It involves five distinct stages: product development, introduction, growth, maturity and decline.

After launching the new product, the management challenge lies in making sure that the product enjoys a long and healthy life. The new product is not expected to sell for ever, but the company will want to recover a decent profit to cover all the effort and risk that went into launching it. Management is aware that each product will have a life-cycle, although the exact shape and length is not known in advance.

Figure 14.2 shows a typical **product life-cycle** (PLC), the course that a product's sales and profits take over its lifetime. The product life-cycle has five distinct stages:

1. *Product development* begins when the company finds and develops a new-product idea. During product development, sales are zero and the company's investment costs mount.

Figure 14.2 Sales and profits over the product's life from inception to demise

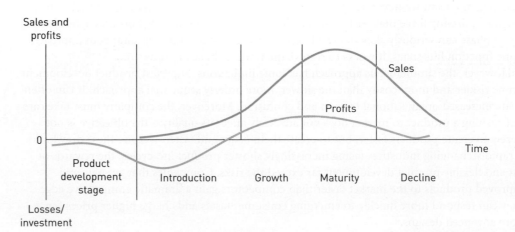

2. *Introduction* is a period of slow sales growth as the product is being introduced in the market. Profits are non-existent in this stage because of the heavy expenses of product introduction.

3. *Growth* is a period of rapid market acceptance and increasing profits.

4. *Maturity* is a period of slowdown in sales growth because the product has achieved acceptance by most potential buyers. Profits level off or decline because of increased marketing outlays to defend the product against competition.

5. *Decline* is the period when sales fall off and profits drop.

Not all products follow the product life-cycle. Some products are introduced and die quickly; others stay in the mature stage for a long, long time. Some enter the decline stage and are then cycled back into the growth stage through strong promotion or repositioning.

The PLC concept can describe a product class (petrol-engined cars), a product form (people-carrier) or a brand (the Ford Explorer). The PLC concept applies differently in each case. Product classes have the longest life-cycles. The sales of many product classes stay in the mature stage for a long time. Product forms, in contrast, tend to have the standard PLC shape. Product forms such as 'cream deodorants', the 'dial telephone' and 'cassette tapes' passed through a regular history of introduction, rapid growth, maturity and decline. A specific brand's life-cycle can change quickly because of changing competitive attacks and responses. For example, although teeth-cleaning products (product class) and toothpaste (product form) have enjoyed fairly long life-cycles, the life-cycles of specific brands have tended to be much shorter.

The PLC concept can also be applied to what are known as styles, fashions and fads. Their special life-cycles are shown in Figure 14.3. A **style** is a basic and distinctive mode of expression. For example, styles appear in British homes (Edwardian, Victorian, Georgian), clothing (formal, casual), and art (realistic, surrealistic, abstract). Once a style is invented, it may last for generations, coming in and out of vogue. A style has a cycle showing several periods of renewed interest.

A **fashion** is a currently accepted or popular style in a given field. For example, the more formal 'business attire' look of corporate dress of the 1980s and early 1990s has now given way to the 'business casual look' of today. Fashions tend to grow slowly, remain popular for a while, then decline slowly.

Fads are fashions that enter quickly, are adopted with great zeal, peak early and decline very fast. They last only a short time and tend to attract only a limited following. Fads often have a novel or quirky nature, as when people start buying Rubik's cubes, 'pet rocks' or yo-yos. Fads appeal to people who are looking for excitement, a way to set themselves apart or something to talk about to others. Fads do not survive for long because they normally do not satisfy a strong or lasting need or satisfy it well.[25] However, some products, like Ty Inc.'s Beanie Babies, may begin life as fads but later become sought-after products that fetch a high price. Beanie Babies were originally children's toys. The craze has now passed over to adults who now make up 70 per cent of collectors. They trade the 212-strong range of animals on the secondary market (Beanies that sold for a few euros can trade for thousands), take out insurance policies in case their Beanies are stolen, and write in for legal advice about how to split their collections if they get divorced![26]

Style—A basic and distinctive mode of expression.

Fashion—A current accepted or popular style in a given field.

Fads—Fashions that enter quickly, are adopted with great zeal, peak early and decline very fast.

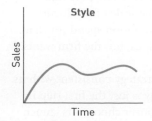
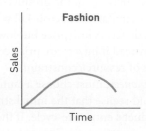
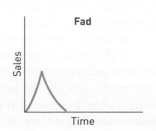

Figure 14.3 Marketers need to understand and predict style, fashion and fad

The PLC concept can be applied by marketers as a useful framework for describing how products and markets work. But using the PLC concept for forecasting product performance or for developing marketing strategies presents some practical problems.[27] For example, managers may have trouble identifying which stage of the PLC the product is in, pinpointing when the product moves into the next stage and determining the factors that affect the product's movement through the stages. In practice, it is difficult to forecast the sales level at each PLC stage, the length of each stage and the shape of the PLC curve.

Using the PLC concept to develop marketing strategy can also be difficult because strategy is both a cause and a result of the product's life-cycle. The product's current PLC position suggests the best marketing strategies, and the resulting marketing strategies affect product performance in later life-cycle stages. Yet when used carefully, the PLC concept can help in developing good marketing strategies for different stages in the product life-cycle.

We looked at the product development stage of the product life-cycle in the first part of the chapter. Now let us look at strategies for each of the other life-cycle stages.

Introduction stage

Introduction stage—The product life-cycle stage when the new product is first distributed and made available for purchase.

The **introduction stage** starts when the new product is first launched. Introduction takes time, and sales growth is apt to be slow. Well-known products such as instant coffee, personal computers and mobile telephones lingered for many years before they entered a stage of rapid growth.

In this stage, as compared to other stages, profits are negative or low because of the low sales and high distribution and promotion expenses. Much money is needed to attract distributors and build their inventories. Promotion spending is relatively high to inform consumers of the new product and get them to try it. Because the market is not generally ready for product refinements at this stage, the company and its few competitors produce basic versions of the product. These firms focus their selling on those buyers who are the readiest to buy – usually the higher-income groups. For radical product technologies, such as mobile telecommunications, business or professional users were the earliest targets.

A company might adopt one of several marketing strategies for introducing a new product. It can set a high or low level for each marketing variable, such as price, promotion, distribution and product quality. Considering only price and promotion, for example, management might *skim* the market *slowly* by launching the new product with a high price and low promotion spending. The high price helps recover as much gross profit per unit as possible, while the low promotion spending keeps marketing spending down. Such a strategy makes sense when the market is limited in size, when most consumers in the market know about the product and are willing to pay a high price (these consumers are typically called the 'innovators'), and when there is little immediate potential competition. If, however, most consumers in the limited market are unaware and know little about the innovation, and require educating and convincing, a high level of promotion spending is required. A high-price, high-promotion strategy also helps the firm to *skim rapidly* the price-insensitive end of the market in the early stages of the new product's launch.

On the other hand, a company might introduce its new product with a low price and heavy promotion spending (a *rapid penetration* strategy). This strategy promises to bring the fastest market penetration and the largest market share, and it makes sense when the market is large, potential buyers are price sensitive and unaware of the product, there is strong potential competition, and the company's unit manufacturing costs fall with the scale of production and accumulated manufacturing experience. A low-price but low-promotion spend (or *slow penetration* strategy) may be chosen instead if buyers are price conscious, but the firm wants to keep its launch costs down because of resource constraints.

A company, especially the *market pioneer*, must choose a launch strategy consistent with its intended product positioning. It should realise that the initial strategy is just the first step in a grander marketing plan for the product's entire life-cycle. If the pioneer chooses its launch strategy to make a 'killing', it will be sacrificing long-run revenue for the sake of short-run gain. As the pioneer moves through later stages of the life-cycle, it will have continuously to formulate new pricing, promotion and other marketing strategies. It has the best chance of building and retaining market leadership if it plays its cards correctly from the start.[28]

Growth stage

If the new product meets market needs or stimulates previously untapped needs, it will enter a **growth stage**, in which sales will start climbing quickly. The early adopters will continue to buy, and later buyers will start following their lead, especially if they hear favourable word-of-mouth. Attracted by the opportunities for profit, new competitors will enter the market. They will introduce new product features, improve on the pioneer's product and expand the market for the product. The increase in competitors leads to an increase in the number of distribution outlets, and sales jump just to build reseller inventories. Prices remain where they are or fall only slightly. Companies keep their promotion spending at the same or a slightly higher level. Educating the market remains a goal, but now the company must also meet the competition.

Profits increase during the growth stage, as promotion costs are spread over a large volume and as unit-manufacturing costs fall. The firm uses several strategies to sustain rapid market growth as long as possible. It improves product quality and adds new product features and models. It enters new market segments and tries to grow sales further by selling through new distribution channels. It shifts some advertising from building product awareness to building product conviction and purchase, and it lowers prices at the right time to attract more buyers.

In the growth stage, the firm faces a trade-off between high market share and high current profit. By spending a lot of money on product improvement, promotion and distribution, the company can capture a dominant position. In doing so, however, it gives up maximum current profit, which it hopes to make up in the next stage.

Growth stage—The product life-cycle stage at which a product's sales start climbing quickly.

Maturity stage

At some point, a product's sales growth will slow down and the product will enter a **maturity stage**. This maturity stage normally lasts longer than the previous stages, and it poses strong challenges to marketing management. Most products are in the maturity stage of the life-cycle, and, therefore, most of marketing management deals with the mature product.

The slowdown in sales growth results in many producers with many products to sell. In turn, this overcapacity leads to greater competition. Competitors begin to cut prices, increase their advertising and sales promotions, and raise their R&D budgets to find better versions of the product. These steps lead to a drop in profit. Some of the weaker competitors start dropping out of the industry, and the industry eventually contains only well-established competitors.

Although many products in the mature stage appear to remain unchanged for long periods, most successful ones stay alive through continually evolving to meet changing consumer needs. Product managers should do more than simply ride along with or defend their mature products – a good offensive is the best defence. They should stretch their imagination and look for new ways to innovate in the market (market development), or to modify the product (product development) and the marketing mix (marketing innovation).

Maturity stage—The stage in the product life-cycle where sales growth slows or levels off.

Market development

Here, the company modifies the market in order to increase the consumption of the current product. It repositions the brand and aims it at new users and market segments which the company is not currently serving, as when Johnson & Johnson targeted the adult market with its baby powder and shampoo. The company may want to reposition the brand to appeal to a larger or faster-growing segment, as Lucozade did when it introduced its new line of drinks aimed at younger users, not convalescents, the original target segment for the brand. The company must also look for ways to increase usage of the product among present customers. Amazon.com sends permission-based emails to regular customers, letting them know when their favourite authors or performers publish new books or CDs.

Product development

The company might try to modify the product by changing characteristics, such as quality, features or style, to attract new users and to inspire more usage. It might improve the product's quality and performance – its durability, reliability, speed or taste, for example. In an attempt to maintain its dominance of the world computer-games market, five years after the launch of PlayStation 1, Sony introduced PlayStation 2 (PS2), which offers a jump in performance and versatility. The PS2 incorporates two new semiconductor chips, the 'Emotion engine' 128-bit processor and the massively parallel 'Graphics Synthesiser', which give far richer and more detailed graphics than the first-generation machine. Its digital video disc (DVD) player also shows recorded films, and with a software upgrade, users can plug it into digital cable networks, transforming the PlayStation into a broadband Internet-access device that can download games, films and music produced by the company's other business divisions.[29]

The firm might add new features that expand the product's usefulness, safety or convenience. For example, Nokia keeps adding new functions to its line of mobile phones, the

Adding value to a product in the late stage of its product life-cycle is important. Swatch, eager to demonstrate their commitment to finding solutions to consumer problems, never cease to innovate.
SOURCE: Swatch AG.

mobile communications network operator Orange adds new services to trigger more usage of its network, and Sony keeps adding new features to its Walkman and Discman lines. Some firms may exploit technological innovations to revitalise the product as in the case of L'Oréal's new thickening shampoo for men. It's new 'Elvive for Men' shampoo contains Regenium–XY, a combination of one of hair's vital substances and a new active ingredient, which acts on the hair roots, strengthening and thickening the hair.

Finally, firms can improve the product's styling and attractiveness. Thus car manufacturers restyle their cars to attract buyers who want a new look. The makers of consumer food and household products frequently introduce new flavours, colours, ingredients or packages to revitalise consumer buying.

Marketing innovation

Marketers can also try to modify the marketing mix – improving sales by changing one or more marketing-mix elements. Price cuts attract new users and competitors' customers. Marketers can launch a better advertising campaign or use aggressive sales promotions – trade deals, discounts, premiums and contests. The company can also move into larger market channels, as Dell Computers did when it pioneered telephone selling of personal computers. Or they can use mass merchandisers, if these channels are growing.

Finally, the company can offer new or improved services to buyers or create unique and distinctive value propositions that deliver superior benefits to users. For example, not so long ago, many householders in the UK had little choice but to burn coal to keep their houses warm. But since 1947, when the coal industry was nationalised, the introduction of the 1956 Clean Air Act and the availability of cleaner, more convenient natural gas from the North Sea from the 1970s saw annual household consumption of coal in the UK fall from more than 38 million tonnes to 1.6 million tonnes by 2003. Today, over three-quarters of British homes are supplied with gas, while those that do not burn gas are more likely to heat their homes with oil or electricity than coal. However, CPL, the country's biggest coal merchant and manufacturer of smokeless fuel, argues that, despite the declining trend, there is still life in the sector. The product has changed – typically coal was delivered loose to homes in one-hundredweight sacks, but today CPL sells an increasing amount of four-kilogram bags of smokeless fuel from supermarkets and garage forecourts. The latter outlets are ideal for occasional users – they burn fuel not to warm up the home, but because they like the romantic atmosphere it creates. Burning coal is increasingly a lifestyle choice for many users, according to an industry spokesperson. So, never underestimate the potential for turning around any dying commodity! What next? Designer fuels, perhaps.[30]

Decline stage

The sales of most product forms and brands eventually dip. This is the **decline stage**. The decline may be slow, as in the case of oatmeal cereal, or rapid, as in the case of gramophone records. Sales may plunge to zero, or they may drop to a low level where they continue for many years.

Sales decline for many reasons, including technological advances, shifts in consumer tastes and increased competition. As sales and profits decline, some firms withdraw from the market. Those remaining may reduce the number of their product offerings. They may drop smaller market segments and marginal trade channels, or they may cut the promotion budget and reduce their prices further.

Carrying a weak product can be very costly to a firm, and not just in profit terms. There are many hidden costs. A weak product may take up too much of management's time. It often requires frequent price and inventory adjustments. It requires advertising and sales force attention that might be better used to make 'healthy' products more profitable or to create

Decline stage—The product life-cycle stage at which a product's sales decline.

14.2 Smile! Leica takes you back to the good old days

FT

The march of technology leaves its mark on many industries. Consumers' insatiable appetite for the latest gadget often rapidly obsoletes old technologies and companies' means of delivering consumer benefits. As the saying goes, 'New technology often kills old business.'

The same may be said of the camera industry. The global camera market is rushing towards digital domination. Sales of digital cameras overtook those of their traditional analogue peers in 2002 and are forecast to account for 63 per cent of the market by 2006. Some prophets of doom in the industry are even predicting the demise of film, used in box Brownies and their successors for more than a century. Asian production values mean the average shelf-life in the camera store for a new digital model is just six months; and a year or so later it is likely to be uneconomic or even impossible to repair for lack of spare parts. Such is the rate of change that one UK photography magazine recently mistakenly chose for its Camera of the Year award a digital camera no longer in production.

In the middle of this computerised maelstrom sits Leica, the German-based camera equipment and sports optics maker, which has just launched the Leica MP, a mechanical analogue camera that relies on design and manufacturing techniques harking back to the 1950s. Some might argue that a period of gloom in the world economy – with Leica's biggest markets, the US and Germany, particularly hard hit – is a dangerous time to fly in the face of the global trend towards digital photography. But Jean-Jacques Viau, marketing product manager, brushes aside such fears, describing the launch of the MP as 'a logical move'. He adds: 'For every action, there is a contrary reaction.'

Leica occupies a small upmarket niche and aims to show that smaller operators can thrive by rejecting mainstream trends and catering for that vocal minority more interested in precision instruments than in increasing electronic automation. As Mr Viau says: 'We could be the shelter for people who react to the changes of model every six months.' That shelter does not come cheap. The MP costs about £1,850 (€2,775) *excluding* the lens.

Unlike the more common single lens reflex cameras – where you look directly through the lens – rangefinders such as the MP have separate viewfinder and focusing devices. Leica may have invented 35 mm photography but it does not have the rangefinder market to itself. In recent years, it has been coming to terms with competitors using former German brand names, most of which have been snapped up by the Japanese.

...14.2

Cosina saw a gap in the market for a cheaper rangefinder and launched the Voigtlander Bessa range – at about a quarter of the price of a Leica. Other companies include Contax, owned by Japan's Kyocera; Konica; and Rollei, an independent German-based company. The resurgence of interest in back-to-basics cameras has been pronounced and has benefited Leica. It sold more than 16,000 rangefinder cameras in 2002, the most since 1968. Robert White, an independent retailer in the south of England, says: 'People are realising there's more to life than a piece of plastic. It's back to the good old days.'

For now, Leica may be bucking the mass digital trend but discerning photographers are snapping up its luxury analogue cameras. As digital dominance marches on, Hanns-Peter Cohn, Leica's chief executive, is far from complacent. Leica is reaping the rewards of its restructuring of the past five years, which has involved cutting its debt and reducing stock levels. The retail expertise of luxury goods manufacturer Hermes, which has a 31 per cent stake in Leica, has helped to position Leica as a luxury purchase. He sees this route as crucial. 'For the future, it's important that we have our own shops', he says. 'It started in Hamburg. Why not in central London, [or] in Madison Avenue, New York? And why not on one corner of the street a flagship Hermes store and on the other corner a little Leica shop? There are a lot of people all over the world who like to buy value, real value, and we have only one problem: to find them.'

SOURCES: Adapted from Ian Chapman, 'A camera focused on luxury', *Financial Times* (31 March 2003), p. 15; see also Scott Morrison, 'Consumer photography develops speedily', *Financial Times* (12 January 2004), p. 29; Amy Yee and Dan Roberts, 'Kodak hopes for digital boom', *Financial Times* (23 January 2004), p. 25.

new ones. A product's failing reputation can cause customer concerns about the company and its other products. The biggest cost may well lie in the future. Keeping weak products delays the search for replacements, creates a lopsided product mix, hurts current profits and weakens the company's foothold on the future.

For these reasons, companies need to pay more attention to their ageing products. The firm should identify those products in the decline stage by regularly reviewing sales, market shares, costs and profit trends. Then management must decide whether to maintain, harvest for cash or drop each of these declining products.

Management may decide to *maintain* its brand without change in the hope that competitors will leave the industry. For example, Procter & Gamble made good profits by remaining in the declining liquid soap business as others withdrew. Alternatively, management may decide to reposition the brand in the hope of moving it back into the growth stage of the product life-cycle. Or management may find new ways to revitalise the business, as in the case of Leica, the German-based camera equipment and sports optics maker which sought to buck the mass digital camera trend through targeting discerning photographers with a new line of upmarket, old-tech (analogue) equipment (see Marketing Insights 14.2).

Management may decide to harvest the product, which means reducing various costs (plant and equipment, maintenance, R&D, advertising, sales force) and hoping that sales hold up. If successful, harvesting will release cash and increase the company's profits in the short run. Or management may decide to drop the product from the line. It can sell it to another firm or simply liquidate it at salvage value. For example, declining real ale sales in the UK during the 1990s caused dozens of regional brewers to close down, while others including the country's largest brewers, Bass and Whitbread, sold off their brewing interests to foreign groups such as the Belgian Interbrew.[31] If the company plans to find a buyer for the declining product-business, it will not want to run down the product through harvesting.

Importantly, before divesting an old product, management should carefully consider whether the product or technology can be revived at all. As some firms have found, ditching old technologies completely can be a mistake, because technologies dismissed as yesterday's habit may turn out to be not such old hat after all.

> Consider the following examples. Clockwork, once a standard technology used to power clocks, watches and children's toys, was made obsolete by battery-powered gadgets. However, as the power needed by modern circuitry decreases, clockwork is becoming a feasible power source once more. Wind-up torches and radios are on sale and the US military is even considering hand-cranked satellite navigation devices and landmine detectors that would save soldiers from carrying bulky battery packs.
>
> Electronic devices containing valves, then transistors and finally microprocessors displaced mechanical components used in calculators some decades ago. Now, microscopic mechanical components are also staging a comeback. These are used in a new class of silicon chips which perform functions that electronic devices cannot, such as tiny silicon arms and levers that act as compact filters, timekeepers, optical switches and sensors.[32]

Table 14.2 summarises the key characteristics of each stage of the product life-cycle. The table also lists the marketing objectives and strategies for each stage.[33]

	Introduction	Growth	Maturity	Decline
Characteristics				
Sales	Low sales	Rapidly rising sales	Peak sales	Declining sales
Costs	High cost per customer	Average cost per customer	Low cost per customer	Low cost per customer
Profits	Negative	Rising profits	High profits	Declining profits
Customers	Innovators	Early adopters	Middle majority	Laggards
Competitors	Few	Growing number	Stable number beginning to decline	Declining number
Marketing objectives	Create product awareness and trial	Maximise market share	Maximise profit while defending market share	Reduce expenditure and milk the brand
Strategies				
Product	Offer a basic product	Offer product extensions, service, warranty	Diversify brand and models	Phase out weak items
Price	Use cost-plus	Price to penetrate market	Price to match or beat competitors	Cut price
Distribution	Build selective distribution	Build intensive distribution	Build more intensive distribution	Go selective: phase out unprofitable outlets
Advertising	Build product awareness among early adopters and dealers	Build awareness and interest in the mass market	Stress brand differences and benefits	Reduce to level needed to retain hard-core loyals
Sales promotion	Use heavy sales promotion to entice trial	Reduce to take advantage of heavy consumer demand	Increase to encourage brand switching	Reduce to minimal level

Table 14.2 Summary of product life-cycle characteristics, objectives and strategies

SOURCE: Philip Kotler, *Marketing Management: Analysis, planning, implementation, and control*, 11th edn, © 2003, p. 340. Reprinted by permission of Pearson Education, Inc., Upper Saddle River, NJ.

summary discussing the issues

Summary

An organisation's current products face limited life spans and must be replaced by newer products. But new products can fail – the risks of innovation are as great as the rewards. The key to successful innovation lies in a total-company effort, strong planning, a marketing focus and a *systematic new-product development process.*

We examined the new-product development process which covers nine stages. The process starts with determining the *new-product strategy*, which provides direction for the new-product development effort. Next, the company must find new-product ideas. *Idea generation* may stem from internal sources and from external sources, such as customers, competitors, distributors, suppliers and others. Next comes *idea screening*, which reduces the number of ideas based on the company's defined criteria. Ideas that pass the screening stage continue through product *concept development*, in which a detailed version of the new-product idea is stated in meaningful consumer terms. In the next stage, *concept testing*, new-product concepts are tested with a group of target consumers to determine whether the concepts have strong consumer appeal. Strong concepts proceed to *marketing strategy development*, in which an initial marketing strategy for the new product is developed from the product concept. In the *business analysis* stage, a review of the sales, costs and profit projections for the new product is undertaken to determine whether it is likely to satisfy the company's objectives. Positive results here move the concept into *product development*, which now calls for a large jump in investment. As the product becomes more concrete, it is subjected to functional and customer tests. If it passes these tests, the product moves to *test marketing*, at which the product and marketing programme are tested in a more realistic market setting. The company goes ahead with *commercialisation* if test-market results are positive. The purpose of each stage is to decide whether the idea should be further developed or dropped.

Each product has a *life-cycle* marked by a changing set of problems and opportunities. The sales of the typical product follow an S-shaped curve made up of five stages. The cycle begins with the *product development* stage when the company finds and develops a new-product idea. The *introduction stage* is marked by slow growth and low profits as the product is distributed to the market. If successful, the product enters a *growth stage*, which offers rapid sales growth and increasing profits. Next comes a *maturity stage*, when sales growth slows down and profits stabilise. The company seeks strategies to revitalise sales growth, including market, product and marketing-mix modification. Finally, the product enters a *decline stage*, in which sales and profits dwindle. Management must decide whether to maintain the brand, without change, hoping competitors will drop out of the market; harvest, by reducing costs and maintaining sales; or drop the product, selling it to another firm or liquidating it at salvage value.

Discussing the issues

1. Choose a familiar company and assume that you are responsible for generating new-product ideas. How would you structure your new-product development process? What might be the most valuable sources of new ideas? How would you stimulate the development of new ideas in this organisation?

2. What factors must new-product development managers consider when testing new-product ideas and concepts with potential customers? How might the Internet assist

marketers in their efforts to determine potential customers' attitudes and responses towards new-product ideas?

3. Imagine that you have just developed a revolutionary new games console that may eventually lead to an entirely new portable gaming activity. Propose a marketing strategy which you will present to potential investors. What factors should you consider to increase your chances of securing investors' interest in this new product?

4. Do you think that the product life-cycle concept is a useful marketing-planning tool? Why or why not?

5. Which product life-cycle stage, if any, is the most important? Which stage is the riskiest? Which stage offers the greatest profit potential? Which stage appears to require the greatest amount of 'hands-on' management? You may use practical examples to address these questions and to explain the thinking behind each of your answers.

Applying the concepts

1. Go to a grocery store you normally shop at. Make a list of 10 items that appear to be new products. If you prefer, you can visit an online retail store and perform the exercise. In either case, note any information provided by the store or product packaging concerning the new offering. Rate each product for its level of innovation: give a '10' score for extremely novel and highly innovative products and '1' for a very minor change such as an improved package or fragrance. How truly new or innovative are these products overall? Do you think companies are being too risk averse because 'pioneers are the ones who get shot'?

2. 'Danger, Will Robinson! Danger!' might be one of the most memorable phrases ever uttered by a robot. However, today, the phrase would more likely be 'Buy Me! Take Me Home!'. Who will offer the first practical, affordable home robot? NASA? Intel? Sony? Lego? Did you say Lego? Yes, the same little company that developed those great plastic building blocks has now developed several models of home robots (such as the R2-D2 model from *Star Wars*) that sell for as little as €250. These Lego model kits contain Lego pieces, light and touch sensors, gears and a minicomputer brick that forms the core of the system. The small, efficient robots already perform many hard-to-believe tasks (without complaining), and Lego is making daily upgrades. Copycat competitors have already begun a modification frenzy that will one day produce an awesome personal assistant. See www.lego.com, www.legomindstorms.com, www.lugnet.com and www.crynwr.com/lego-robotics for more information.

   (a) Who might the first customers be for a Lego robot? Explain.
   (b) Project the product life-cycle for this new product. Explain your thinking.
   (c) Outline a strategy for positioning this product away from the toy category and into the 'personal-device' category. What would be the most important aspect of this positioning strategy? What headline would you select for the first Lego robot advertisement? In what media would you advertise? Would you use the same headline ad? Explain.
   (d) Design a quick test-market study for the Lego robot. Where would you administer the test?
   (e) What other new products might complement Lego's robot line and how should Lego extend the robot concept into other products? Are these effective strategies for managing the robot line over its life-cycle? Explain.

References

1. Christopher Brown-Humes and Robert Budden, 'Nokia tries to learn a new game', *Financial Times* (5 February 2004), accessed at www.ft.com; see also 'Game strategists look to next wave', *Financial Times FT Creative Business* (2 December 2003), p. 15; additional information on global game console revenues and growth projections available at www.instat.com.

2. Michiyo Nakamoto and Tim Burt, 'Comment and analysis on consumer electronics', *Financial Times* (10 February 2003), p. 19; see also www.ft.com/sony for more information on Sony and its consumer entertainment business.

3. Fiona Harvey, 'High-tech ballpoint pen gets the message across', *Financial Times* (7 April 2000), p. 4.

4. Deloitte and Touche, 'Vision in manufacturing study', Deloitte Consulting and Kenan-Flagler Business School (6 March 1998); A.C. Nielsen, 'New product introduction – successful innovation/ failure: fragile boundary', A.C. Nielsen BASES and Ernst & Young Global Client Consulting (24 June 1999); Philip Kotler, *Kotler on Marketing* (New York: Free Press, 1999), p. 51; Robert G. Cooper, 'New product success in industrial firms', *Industrial Marketing Management*, **21** (1992), pp. 215–23; William Bolding, Ruskin Morgan and Richard Staelin, 'Pulling the plug to stop the new product drain', *Journal of Marketing Research* (February 1997), pp. 164–76; Eric Berggreb and Thomas Nacher, 'Why good ideas go bust', *Management Review* (February 2000), pp. 32–6; Eric Berggren, 'Introducing new products can be hazardous to your company: use the right new-solutions delivery tools', *The Academy of Management Executive* (August 2001), p. 92; and Bruce Tait, 'The failure of marketing "science"', *Brandweek* (8 April 2002), pp. 20–2.

5. For an excellent review, see Mitzie M. Montoya-Weiss and Roger Calantone, 'Determinants of new product performance: a review and meta-analysis', *Journal of Product Innovation Management*, **11** (1994), pp. 397–417. See also Don H. Lester, 'Critical success factors for new product development', *Research-Technology Management* (January–February 1998), pp. 36–43; Michael Song and Mark E. Parry, 'A cross-national comparative study of new product development processes: Japan and United States', *Journal of Marketing* (April 1997), pp. 1–18; Jerry Wind and Vijay Mahajan, 'Issues and opportunities in new product development', *Journal of Marketing Research* (February 1997), pp. 1–12; Robert G. Cooper and Elko J. Kleinschmidt, *New Product: The key factors in success* (Chicago, IL: American Marketing Association, 1990); Axel Johne and Patrician Snelson, *Successful Product Development: Lessons from American and British firms* (Oxford: Blackwell, 1990).

6. C. Merle Crawford, *New Products Management*, 4th edn (Boston, MA: Irwin, 1994), Ch. 3.

7. See Rosbeth Moss Kanter, 'Don't wait to innovate', *Sales and Marketing Management* (February 1997), pp. 22–4; Greg A. Steven and James Burley, '3,000 raw ideas equals 1 commercial success!', *Research-Technology Management* (May–June 1997), pp. 16–27.

8. See 'Listening to the voice of the marketplace', *Business Week* (21 February 1983), p. 90; Eric von Hipple, 'Get new products from consumers', *Harvard Business Review* (March–April 1982), pp. 117–22.

9. Eric von Hippel, 'Lead users: a source of novel product concepts', *Management Science* (July 1986), pp. 791–805.

10. Lisa Wirkkala, 'Sibelius? No, it's my mobile', *The European Magazine* (17–23 April 1997), p. 7.

11. Andrew Baxter, 'Heineken wins the battle of the tainted bottle', *Financial Times* (11 May 2000), p. 24.

12. Philip Kotler, *Kotler on Marketing* (New York: Free Press, 1999), pp. 43–4.

13. See 'DaimlerChrysler plans '04 launch of fuel cell car', *Ward's Auto World* (April 1999), p. 25; and William J. Cook, 'A Mercedes for the future', *U.S. News & World Report* (29 March 1999), p. 62; John McCormick, 'The future is not quite now', *Automotive Manufacturing & Production* (August 2000), pp. 22–4; 'DaimlerChrysler unveils NECAR 5 methanol-powered fuel cell vehicle', *Chemical Market Reporter* (13 November 2000), p. 5.

14. Raymond R. Burke, 'Virtual reality shopping: breakthrough in marketing research', *Harvard Business Review* (March–April 1996), pp. 120–31; Mike Hoffman, 'Virtual shopping', *Inc.* (July 1998), p. 88; Christopher Ryan, 'Virtual reality in marketing', *Direct Marketing* (April 2001), pp. 57–62; and Patrick Waurzyniak, 'Going virtual', *Manufacturing Engineering* (May 2002), pp. 77–88.

15. For more on product concept testing, see William L. Moore, 'Concept testing', *Journal of Business Research*, **10** (1982), pp. 279–94; David A. Schwartz, 'Concept testing can be improved – and here's how', *Marketing News* (6 January 1984), pp. 22–3.

16. Clayton Hirst and Leo Lewis, 'IT with an American accent', *Telegraph* (20 October 2002), p. 7; Paul Abrahams, 'Gates hopes Tablet will pep up PC market', *Financial Times* (7 November 2002), p. 3.

17. 'Taking the toxin out of teeth', *Innovation and Technology Transfer*, 1 (January 2000), pp. 7–8. More information on the Innovation Relay Centre, IRC Northern Sweden, can be obtained by visiting their website: www.uminovacenter.umu.se.

18. For information on BehaviorScan, visit www.behaviorscan.com.

19. Raymond R. Burke, 'Virtual shopping: breakthrough in marketing research', *Harvard Business Review* (March–April 1996), pp. 120–31; Tom Dellacave, Jr, 'Curing market research headaches', *Sales and Marketing Management* (July 1996), pp. 84–5; Brian Silverman, 'Get 'em while they're hot', *Sales and Marketing Management* (February 1997), pp. 47–8, 52; Tim Studt, 'VR speeds up car designs', *Research & Development* (March 1998), p. 74; Sara Sellar, 'The perfect trade show rep', *Sales & Marketing Management* (April 1999), p. 11.

20. For more on simulated test markets, see Kevin Higgins, 'Simulated test marketing winning acceptance', *Marketing News* (1 March 1985), pp. 15, 19; Howard Schlossberg, 'Simulated vs traditional test marketing', *Marketing News* (23 October 1989), pp. 1–2.

21. Based on information presented in 'Xelibri: A Siemens Mobile Adventure', a case study written by F. Clemens, H. Hedderich and H. Sassmann (under supervision of Lutz Kaufmann), WHU, Otto Beisheim Graduate School of Management, Vallendar, Germany, 2003. The case study is distributed by ECCH Collection, England and USA (for more information, visit: http://www.ecch.cranfield.ac.uk).

22. Don G. Reinertsen, 'The search for new product killers', *Electronic Business* (July 1983), pp. 62–6.

23. Hirotake Takeuchi and Ikujiro Nonaka, 'The new product development game', *Harvard Business Review* (January–February 1986), pp. 137–46; Bro Uttal, 'Speeding new ideas to market', *Fortune* (2 March 1987), pp. 62–5; Craig A. Chambers, 'Transforming new product development', *Research-Technology Management* (November–December 1996), pp. 32–8; Srikant Datar, Jordan C. Clark, Sundre Kekre, Surendra Rajiv and Kannan Srinivasan, 'Advantages of time-based new product development in a fast-cycle industry', *Journal of Marketing Research* (February 1997), pp. 36–49.

24. See Jerry Wind and Vijay Mahajan, 'Issues and opportunities in new product development', *Research-Technology Management* (May–June 1997), pp. 16–27; Vittorio Chiesa, Paul Coughlan and Chris A. Voss, 'Development of a technical innovation audit', *Journal of Product Innovation Management*, 13 (1996), pp. 105–36; Robert G. Cooper and Elko J. Kleinschmidt, 'Benchmarking the firm's critical success factors in new product development', *Journal of Product Innovation Management*, 12 (1995), pp. 374–91; Shona L. Brown and Kathleen M. Eisenhardt, 'Product development: past research, present findings, and future directions', *Academy of Management Review* (April 1995), p. 343.

25. See David Stipp, 'The theory of fads', *Fortune* (14 October 1996), pp. 49–52; John Grossmann, 'A follow-up on four fabled frenzies', *Inc.* (October 1994), pp. 66–7; Irma Zandl, 'How to separate trends from fads', *Brandweek* (23 October 2000), pp. 30–3.

26. 'You've Beanie had', *The Economist* (4 September 1999), p. 78.

27. See George S. Day, 'The product life cycle: analysis and applications issues', *Journal of Marketing* (Fall 1981), pp. 60–7; Chuck Ryan and Walter E. Rigg, 'Redefining the product life cycle: the five-element product wave', *Business Horizons* (September–October 1996), pp. 33–40.

28. For a discussion of how brand performance is affected by the product life-cycle stage at which the brand enters the market, see Venkatesh Shankar, Gregory S. Carpenter and Lekshman Krishnamurthi, 'The advantages of entry in the growth stage of the product life cycle: an empirical analysis', *Journal of Marketing Research* (May 1999), pp. 269–76; William Boulding and Markus Christen, 'First-mover disadvantage', *Harvard Business Review* (October 2001), pp. 20–1; and William T. Robinson and Sungwook Min, 'Is the first to market the first to fail? Empirical evidence for industrial goods businesses', *Journal of Marketing Research* (February 2002), p. 120.

29. 'In their dreams', *The Economist* (26 February 2000), pp. 99–100.

30. Andrew Taylor, '"Designer fuel" finds new role in the home', *Financial Times* (7 March 2003), p. 25.

31. 'Battling brewers', *The Economist* (18 March 2000), pp. 89–90; 'Brewer's droop', *The Business FT Weekend Magazine* (29 July 2000), pp. 34–6.

32. 'In praise of old technology', *The Economist* (17 April 1999), p. 22.

33. For a more comprehensive discussion of marketing strategies over the course of the product life-cycle, see Philip Kotler, *Marketing Management*, The Millennium Edition (Upper Saddle River, NJ: Prentice Hall, 2000), Ch. 10, pp. 303–16.

WEB RESOURCES

For additional classic case studies and Internet exercises, visit www.pearsoned.co.uk/kotler

Concluding concepts 14
Red Bull: waking a new market

Stimulation

Little did Austrian businessman Dietrich Mateschitz suspect when he visited Bangkok in the early 1980s that his trip would launch not only a new product but also a new product category. Mateschitz, international marketing director for Blendax, a German toothpaste producer, encountered Krating Daeng, a 'tonic syrup' that Red Bull Beverage Company had been marketing in Thailand for years. Mateschitz discovered that one glass of the product eliminated his jetlag.

Returning to Austria, Mateschitz began a three-year product development process that included the drink's image, packaging and marketing strategy. In 1987, he obtained the marketing rights to Red Bull (the translated Thai name) from the Thai company and launched his marketing strategy.

> Typical energy drinks, like Red Bull, contain about as much caffeine as a cup of coffee.

The product

Although marketers credit Red Bull with creating the 'energy drink' category, the pursuit of drinks to enhance performance and well-being is not new. Coca-Cola made similar claims in 1886 and Gatorade enhanced the performance of Florida University's Gators football team. In Britain, Lucozade helped pep up tired housewives in the 1980s and energise athletes in the 1990s.

Red Bull is a lightly carbonated energy drink that comes in slender aluminium cans. The label indicates that it has 110 calories, 0 grams of fat, 200 milligrams of sodium, 28 grams of carbohydrates, 27 grams of sugar, and less than 1 gram of protein. Ingredients include sucrose, glucose, sodium citrate, taurine, glucuronolactone, caffeine, inositol, niacinamide, calcium pantothenate, pyridoxine HCL, vitamin B_{12}, and artificial flavours and colours, all mixed in carbonated water.

Sounds delicious? Well, that is part of the problem. Each of an energy drink's ingredients has a specific purpose – but each also has its own taste, and in some cases an aftertaste. It's no easy matter to blend the ingredients to get the correct benefits for the consumer but also something the consumer will drink voluntarily.

Energy drinks sometimes include *amino acids* that are protein building blocks. Taurine, for example, is an important aid in the release of insulin and can prevent abnormal blood clotting. Because researchers have cited a deficiency of *vitamins and minerals* as being associated with

a lack of energy, beverage makers often include them in energy drinks. Niacin (vitamin B_3) works with other vitamins to metabolise carbohydrates. Riboflavin (vitamin B_{12}) helps combat anaemia and fatigue by helping to manufacture red blood cells.

Some drinks include *botanicals* such as ginkgo biloba, guarana and ginseng. Ginkgo biloba is purported to provide mental energy and 'sharpness' by stimulating blood flow to the brain. Finally, most energy drinks contain *caffeine*, an alkaloid stimulant that the body absorbs and circulates to all body tissues. Caffeine affects the central nervous system, the digestive tract, and the body's metabolism, boosting adrenaline levels to increase blood pressure and heart rate. Typical energy drinks, like Red Bull, contain about as much caffeine as a cup of coffee.

Packaging is also important. Some fruity energy beverages come in glass bottles, but many energy drinks that contain light-sensitive vitamins, like B_{12}, come in slender metal cans to prevent the vitamins from breaking down.

The marketing strategy

Mateschitz designed an unusual marketing strategy. 'We don't bring the product to the people', he argues, 'we bring people to the product.' Initially, when Red Bull entered the market, it used traditional beverage distributors. But as the product gained popularity, the company began to pursue a more focused distribution strategy. Red Bull sales representatives now approach a beverage distributor and insist that he or she sell only Red Bull and no other energy drink. If the distributor will not agree, Red Bull hires young people to load the product in vans and distribute it themselves.

The company divides the market into territories, with sales teams in each area responsible for developing distribution and targeted marketing plans. Each of the teams is equipped with a bespoke iPAQ pocket PC that they download to a Red Bull webpage using GPS-enabled mobile phones. The local team seeks to determine where people aged 16 to 29 are hanging out and what they find interesting. First, the sales team calls on popular clubs and bars that will offer the drink on-premise. As incentives, the team offers Red Bull coolers and other promotional items. Red Bull works with individual accounts rather than large chains because it has found that the process goes much faster due to the lack of bureaucracy. It has also found that young people in local hotspots are open to trying new things and help generate a 'buzz' about Red Bull. However, the company does not endorse all the new things people try, like mixing the product with vodka or tequila, and it has a FAQ section on its website, www.redbull.com, to counter the many rumours that have developed around the product.

Second, the sales team also opens off-premise accounts such as gyms, healthfood stores, and convenience stores near colleges. The product sells for about €2 in convenience stores. In addition, 'consumer educators' roam local streets and hand out free samples. The company has encouraged students to drive around with big Red Bull cans strapped to the tops of their cars and to throw Red Bull parties focused on weird themes.

Contrary to traditional promotion practice, Red Bull advertises only *after* it believes a local market is maturing. The company's philosophy is that media can reinforce but not introduce a brand. Thus, it builds demand even before it introduces the product at retail. Only about 19 per cent of the €100 million the brand spent on promotion in 2000 was for measured media. Red Bull spends about 35 per cent of sales on promotion. The company has also begun sponsoring extreme sporting events and extreme athletes.

Uncanny results

Does all this grassroots marketing work? In 2001, Red Bull sold 1.6 billion cans in 62 countries, up 80 per cent over 2000. In the United States, Red Bull entered the list of the top 10 carbonated beverage distributors with a mere 0.1 per cent market share – but its case volume grew 118 per cent over 2000 to 10.5 million cases. It now captures a 70 to 90 per cent share of the energy drink market.

With results like that, it did not take long for competitors to jump in. Pepsi bought South Beach Beverage Company (makers of the SoBe brand) and developed an energy drink it calls 'Adrenaline Rush'. Coca-Cola jumped in with KMX. Beermaker Anheuser-Busch joined in with a product it calls '180' to denote that it turns your energy around 180 degrees. In early 2000, another Thai company, Otsotspa, entered the fray with its own energy drink, called 'Shark'.

Mateschitz does not seem concerned about competition. He knows Red Bull has a tremendous head start and strong local marketing teams. He already has plans to enter Brazil and South Africa. However, Mateschitz does have a few concerns. 'It makes no sense to build a company on one product', he argues. So far, he has put the Red Bull brand on only one other product. LunAqua is a still water that the company claims it bottles only 13 times per year, during each full moon when the moon reaches its full 'energy level'. There is also a variety of LunAqua that contains caffeine. But Mateschitz knows that it will take more than just moon power to stay ahead of the competition in the energy drink market. You can bet he will be up all night, sipping Red Bull and developing new product ideas.

Also, while his eye is on global expansion, trouble is brewing closer to home. France and Denmark have banned the drink. The European Commission challenged an attempt by France to ban Red Bull because of its high level of caffeine and other products. However, the European Court of Justice upheld France's right to ban the drink.

The drink had been implicated in the death of Ross Cooney, a healthy 18-year-old student from Limerick in Ireland. The inquest said the teenager died of Sudden Adult Death Syndrome, but called for an enquiry into high-caffeine energy drinks.

Britain's Committee on Toxicity investigated Red Bull in 2001 and found it safe, although it advised pregnant women against drinking it and other high-caffeine drinks. However, it looks like Ireland will soon be following Denmark and France in banning the product. Will others follow?

Questions

1. Based on the information in the case, evaluate Red Bull's product development process. What process would you recommend as it considers developing new products?
2. At what stage of the product life-cycle are energy drinks as a category? What does this position imply for category competitors?
3. Do you believe there is a long-term market for functional foods and beverages like energy drinks? Why or why not?
4. Using the 'product-market expansion grid' presented in Chapter 2 (see Figure 2.3), recommend specific ideas for Red Bull in the areas of market penetration, product development, and market development.

SOURCES: David Jago, 'Global trends: hitting the shelves', *Prepared Foods* (June 2002), p. 9; 'Selling energy face value', *The Economist* (11 May 2002); 'Sales of Red Bull beverage in United States grow to 10.5 million cases', *Knight-Ridder/Tribine Business News* (14 March 2002), from the *Bangkok Post*; 'Shark UK launch to challenge Red Bull's dominance', *Marketing* (28 February 2002), p. 6; Kenneth Hein, 'A bull's market', *Brandweek* (28 May 2001), p. 21; David Noonan, 'Red Bull's good buzz', *Newsweek* (14 May 2001), p. 39; Laura A. Brandt, 'Energizing elixirs!', *Prepared Foods* (April 2001), p. 55; Jeff Cioletti, 'Boosting beverages', *Supermarket Business* (15 January 2001), p. 31; 'Red Bull staff speed up the process via orange route', *Computing* (27 November 2003); Maxine Frith, 'European court backs ban on Red Bull over health concerns', *The Independent* (7 February 2004).

Marketing services

> Economic competition is not war, but competition is mutual service.

EDWIN CANON

Chapter objectives

After reading this chapter, you should be able to:

- Define a *service*.
- Describe the characteristics that affect the marketing of services.
- Identify the additional marketing considerations that services require.
- Define service marketing strategies for improving firms' differentiation, quality and productivity.

Mini Contents List

◀ SOURCE: Wirtschafts Woche.
Agency: Juny von Matt/Spree;
Illustration: René Borst.

Prelude case Stena Line: sailing out of troubled waters

ANNA ACKFELDT*
Aston Business School, UK

Stena Line, the Swedish international transport and travel service company, is among the world's largest organisations for ferry traffic. With a modern fleet of 33 ships, Stena Line operates a network of 17 strategically located ferry routes in Scandinavia and around the UK. Annually, between these routes, some 12.6 million passengers travel with Stena Line, while nearly 1.1 million units of freight and 2.4 million cars are carried by its fleet.

Stena Line started out in 1962 as a small local company, when it launched the Gothenburg–Fredrikshaven route, followed by the Gothenburg–Kiel route in 1967. In 1980, Stena Line merged with its local competitor, Sessanlinjen, which gave it a local ferry monopoly in Gothenburg. This merger was the start of a rapid expansion programme which was sustained over the 1980s, mainly through the organic growth of ferry routes and introduction of new services. By 1987 Stena Line had become the seventh largest service export company in Sweden. However, by the 1990s, Stena Line had to face some critical decisions regarding its future.

> Stena Line has articulated a vision – to become its clients' first-choice operator for both travel and freight.

When Sweden became a member of the EU in 1995, one important consequence for Stena Line's operations was the abolition of the duty-free licences. On-board sales contributed approximately 45 per cent to Stena Line's profit, and the duty-free sales generated most of this profit. Mainly due to the high cost of alcohol and tobacco in the domestic market, for many passengers duty-free shopping on board was a reason to travel on short cruises on the Gothenburg–Fredrikshaven route. Competitively priced alcoholic beverages, gambling and entertainment on board and shopping in Denmark were also part of the motivation to travel with Stena Line.

It was expected that passenger numbers, revenue and profit margins would decrease when the duty-free licences were abolished. Also, the Scandinavian market was saturated and the rapid expansion and modernisation of the fleet had put pressure on the organisation's profitability and finances. Stena Line's response was to continue its geographic expansion into The Netherlands and the UK to counteract the expected losses in duty-free licences in Scandinavia. The company invested in new and larger vessels, added new routes and acquired more

competitors. The coordination and restructuring of the international acquisitions, subsequent rationalisation of the Scandinavian operations, and the effects of the recession in the early 90s almost took their toll. However, Stena Line continued to battle through these hard times.

Stena Line articulated a vision – to become its clients' first-choice operator for both travel and freight. To achieve this vision, it had to offer an attractive service – a route network where every route has an optimum geographical location and enjoys market-dominance and high traffic frequency. The fleet of vessels operating the routes must be modern, well maintained and adapted to suit well-defined customer groups. A wide range of products and services catering to the needs, wants and desires of well-defined customer groups needs to be provided. The service offered should be perceived by the customers as providing value for money and service delivery staff are seen to be friendly and positive. Staff policy has to create an attractive workplace where employees are motivated to deliver high-quality service.

Over time, the level of competition has also increased. Stena Line's main competitors have traditionally been other ferry companies, but low-price airlines, the English Channel tunnel and the bridge across Öresund have become direct competitors. Haulage companies, business travellers and holidaymakers now have more choices of transportation services. The challenge for Stena Line, therefore, is to continuously strive to improve the level of efficiency and to be more efficient than competitors in all spheres of their operation. In addition, the provision of excellent service is a key success factor in this highly competitive market.

As part of the aim to provide excellent service and products, the company recognises that a market-oriented approach is required. In recent years, customer relation management programmes, staff training and internal marketing strategies have been implemented throughout the organisation to complement the market-oriented strategy. An annual employee survey is conducted to measure employee attitudes towards their jobs and the organisation. Training and development courses are used as tools to increase the level of efficiency, knowledge and confidence of the employees. Internal marketing tools are used to communicate relevant and important information to employees.

Stena Line also recognises that individual business units should be given the autonomy to innovate and to implement their own strategies. Hence, Stena Line is a decentralised organisation with autonomous business units. Unit managers have the authority to do what it takes to achieve planned marketing and customer satisfaction objectives, providing these are consistent with wider corporate values. Operational managers and their teams are, in turn, empowered and held accountable for their tasks and to deliver results according to set objectives.

Stena Line's investments in service quality improvements, its service operations strategy and service delivery systems have started to pay off. By 2003, the net income per guest on board passenger ferries had increased by 5 per cent. Service quality and customer satisfaction ratings are also improving, with some routes even receiving more incoming letters of praise than complaints!

---

*Adapted from original case by Anna Ackfeldt with permission.

Questions

1. What constitutes the service offering for travellers with Stena Line and is this the same for truck drivers, business travellers and holidaymakers? In your answer, identify the tangible and intangible aspects of the service and the criteria that these different customer groups might consider when selecting Stena Line over alternative modes of transport.

2. What are the main aspects of the service that distinguish it from physical products?

3. What is internal marketing and why is this practice important to Stena Line? Discuss how the company's staffing policy, internal marketing strategy and customer relations programme affect service quality, customer satisfaction and profits.

Introduction

One of the major trends of recent years has been the phenomenal growth of services. This shift towards a service economy is largely attributed to rising affluence, more leisure time and the growing complexity of products that require servicing. Moreover, as companies find it harder to differentiate their physical products, they increasingly turn to service differentiation, seeking to win and retain customers through delivering superior services. The questions posed in the prelude case get us to think about the nature of the service offering. For example, there are the tangible aspects (e.g. a modern fleet, duty-free shops, restaurants) and intangible elements (entertainment value, friendliness of service staff, availability of ferry routes) of the total service experience. In this chapter, we will address the many aspects of service delivery that make service marketing different from marketing physical goods and the implications for service management.

Many developed countries have seen a dramatic increase in the importance of services to national economies and to the individual consumer.[1] In the major European countries, the US and Japan, more people are employed in services than in all other sectors of the economy put together. Both public and private sector services in these countries account for between 60 and 75 per cent of gross domestic output. In international trade, services make up a quarter of the value of all international trade.[2] In fact, a variety of service industries – from banking, insurance and communications to transportation, travel and entertainment – now account for well over 60 per cent of the economy in developed countries around the world. In some countries, service occupations have been forecast to contribute to all net job growth in the next five years.[3]

Service jobs include not only those in service industries – hotels, airlines, banks, law firms, telecommunications and others – but also those in product-based industries, such as corporate lawyers, medical staff and sales trainers. Product-based companies also market tangible goods with accompanying services. BMW and Ford offer more than just motor vehicles. Their offer also includes repair and maintenance services, warranty fulfilment, showrooms and other support services. Consumer services are marketed to individuals and households, while industrial services are those offered to business and other organisations.

The increase in demand for consumer and industrial services has been attributed to a number of factors. First, rising affluence has increased consumers' desire to contract out mundane tasks such as cleaning, cooking and other domestic activities, giving rise to a burgeoning convenience industry. Second, rising incomes and more leisure time have created greater demand for a whole array of leisure services and sporting activities. Third, higher consumption of sophisticated technologies in the home (e.g. home computers, multimedia entertainment equipment, security systems) has increased the need for specialist services to install and maintain them. In the case of business customers, more complex markets and technologies have triggered companies' need for the expertise and knowledge of service organisations, such as market research agencies, marketing and technical consultants. Furthermore, the rising pressure on firms to reduce fixed costs means that many are buying in services rather than incurring the overheads involved in performing specialised tasks in-house. The need to remain flexible has also led to firms hiring services that provide use without ownership. Finally, an increasing number of firms are keen to focus on their core competences. They are beginning to contract out non-core activities, such as warehousing and transportation, thus stimulating the growth of specialist business service organisations. All these developments have, in turn, led to a growing interest in the special problems of marketing services.

Service industries vary greatly. In most countries, the *government sector* offers services: for example, legal, employment, healthcare, military, police, fire and postal services, schools and regulatory agencies. The *private non-profit* sector offers services such as museums, charities, churches, colleges, foundations and hospitals. A large part of the *business organisations* sector includes profit-oriented service suppliers like airlines, banks, hotels, insurance companies, consulting firms, medical and law practices, entertainment companies, advertising and research agencies and retailers.

As a whole, selling services presents some special problems calling for special marketing solutions. Let us now examine the nature and special characteristics of service organisations that affect the marketing of services.

Nature and characteristics of a service

Defining services and the service mix

A **service** is any activity or benefit that one party can offer to another which is essentially intangible and does not result in the ownership of anything. Its production may or may not be tied to a physical product.

Activities such as renting a hotel room, depositing money in a bank, travelling on a ferry or an aeroplane, visiting a doctor, getting a haircut, having a car repaired, watching a professional sport, seeing a movie, having clothes cleaned at a dry cleaner and getting advice from a solicitor all involve buying a service. Service businesses are also popping up on the Internet. Everything from online betting and video replays of crucial scores of Manchester United to real-time stocks and shares information feeds are new services that people seem to be willing to pay for. According to the market research company Datamonitor, in 2002 the e-services market worldwide was worth some $1 billion, with Europe accounting for around 12 per cent of the global market for Internet-based customer service solutions.[4]

Generally, a company's offering to customers often includes some services. The service component can be a minor or a major part of the total offering. As such, there is rarely such a thing as a pure service or pure good. In trying to distinguish between goods and services, it may be more appropriate to consider the notion of a goods–service continuum, with offerings ranging from tangible-dominant to intangible-dominant (see Figure 15.1).

Firms can create a differential advantage by moving along the continuum, seeking to alter the balance of tangible and intangible elements associated with their offering. Five categories of offerings can be distinguished:

Service—Any activity or benefit that one party can offer to another which is essentially intangible and does not result in the ownership of anything.

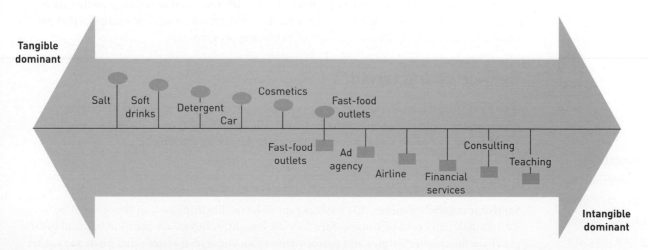

Figure 15.1 The tangible–intangible continuum for goods and services

1. The offering consists of a *pure tangible good*, such as soap, toothpaste or salt – no services accompany the product.

2. The offering consists of a *tangible good accompanied by one or more services* – the sales of technologically sophisticated products such as computers and cars are often dependent on the quality and availability of accompanying customer services (e.g. display rooms, delivery, repair and maintenance, user training programmes, installation advice and warranty fulfilment). In a sense, car manufacturers such as Mercedes and Ford are more service intensive than manufacturing intensive, with a rising proportion of their revenues coming from the financial services (e.g. leasing packages, purchase loans) they offer to buyers.

3. Many service providers also supply physical products along with their basic service. A *hybrid offer* consists of equal parts of goods and services. Examples include restaurants that provide both food and service, and retailers that supply a range of manufactured goods in relation to their special role as channel intermediaries.

4. A *service with accompanying minor goods* consists of a major service along with additional services and supporting goods. For example, British Airways and other airline passengers primarily buy transportation service, but the trip also includes some tangibles such as food, drinks, headphones and an airline magazine. The service also requires a capital-intensive good – an aircraft – but the primary offer is a service.

5. The offering is a *pure service*, consisting primarily of a service such as a haircut, babysitting or financial services.[5]

Because the service mix varies, it is difficult to generalise about services without further distinctions. One distinction is the nature of ownership – that is, whether they are private (e.g. warehousing and distribution firms, banks) or public (e.g. police, state-run hospitals) sector organisations. Another is the type of market – consumer (e.g. household insurance policy provider, retailer) or industrial (e.g. computer bureaux). Services can also involve high customer contact, where the service involves the customer's presence, as in the case of hairdressing and healthcare. Or there is low customer contact, as in dry cleaning and car repair, where the services are directed at objects. Services can be people-based (e.g. consultancies, education) or equipment-bound (e.g. automated car washes, vending machines, automatic cash dispensers). People-based services can be further distinguished according to whether they rely on highly professional staff, such as legal advisers and medical practitioners, or unskilled labour, such as window cleaning, porters and caretakers.

The wide variety of service offerings means that service providers must address the problems specific to their particular service in order to create and maintain a competitive advantage. Despite this variety across sectors, there are a number of characteristics that are unique to services that affect the design of marketing programmes.

Service characteristics

A company must consider five main service characteristics when designing marketing programmes: *intangibility*, *inseparability*, *variability*, *perishability* and *lack of ownership*. We will look at each of these characteristics in the following sections.[6]

Intangibility

Service intangibility means that services cannot be readily displayed, so they cannot be seen, tasted, felt, heard or smelt before they are bought. A buyer can examine in detail before purchase the colour, features and performance of an audio hi-fi system that he or she wishes to buy. In contrast, a person getting a haircut cannot see the result before purchase. Airline

Service intangibility—

A major characteristic of services – they cannot be seen, tasted, felt, heard or smelt before they are bought.

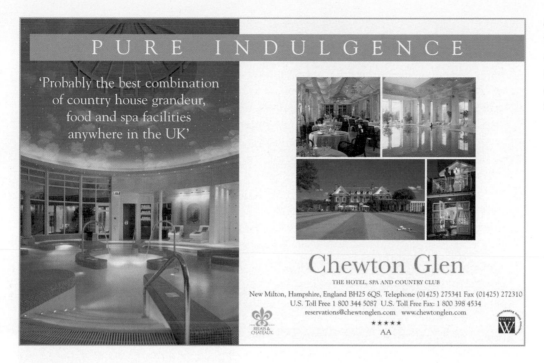

A hotel like Chewton Glen tangibilises its service offering by advertising the grandeur of its country house setting and its fine dining and spa facilities.
SOURCE: Chewton Glen.

passengers have nothing but a ticket and the promise that they and their luggage will arrive safely at the intended destination, hopefully at the same time.

Because service offerings lack tangible characteristics that the buyer can evaluate before purchase, uncertainty is increased. To reduce uncertainty, buyers look for 'signals' of service quality. They draw conclusions about quality from the place, people, equipment, communication material and price that they can see. Therefore, the service provider's task is to 'manage the evidence' – they try to 'tangibilise the service' or to provide concrete evidence of the benefits offered. Whereas product marketers are challenged to add intangibles (e.g. fast delivery, extended warranty, after-sales service) to their tangible offers, service marketers try to add tangible cues suggesting high quality to their intangible offers.[7]

Consider a bank that wants to convey the idea that its service is quick and efficient. It must make this positioning strategy tangible in every aspect of customer contact through a number of marketing tools. The *place* or bank's physical setting must suggest quick and efficient service: its exterior and interior should have clean lines; internal traffic flow should be planned carefully; and waiting lines should seem short. The bank's staff (i.e. *people*) should be busy and properly dressed. There should be a sufficient number of staff to manage the workload. The *equipment* – computers, photocopiers, desks – should look modern. The bank's *communication materials* should suggest efficiency, with clean and simple designs and carefully chosen words and photos that communicate the bank's positioning. The bank should choose a name and *symbol* for its service that suggest speed and efficiency. Because service intangibility increases purchase risk, buyers tend to be more influenced by word-of-mouth, which gives credibility to the service, than by advertising messages paid for by the service provider. As such, the service marketer (the bank in this case) should stimulate word-of-mouth communication by targeting opinion leaders who could be motivated to try its services, and satisfied customers who could be encouraged to recommend its service(s) to peers and friends. Its *pricing* for various services should be kept simple and clear. Although retail bank branches on high streets have traditionally served as conduits for delivering banking services to consumers, the problem presented by service intangibility is increasingly exacerbated by a fast-changing market environment.

Consider the challenges presented by the Internet and new wireless technology. The latter technologies are creating new virtual banks, and together with increasing deregulation, have opened the floodgates to non-banks, which are making inroads into traditional banking sectors. Until recently, retail banks had to have a physical presence close to the customer in the form of a branch network where financial transactions were done. Thanks to the Internet, digital television and mobile telephones, online and virtual banking are now a reality. Traditional banks face increasing pressure to ask what makes them visible in a virtual world. Financial transactions are for the most part intangible. And, as people do not see a credit card payment, touch a mortgage or feel a fund transfer, what features are there left in traditional banks to allow them to survive in the long run? Moreover, technology is making it easier for non-banks, like retailers, and new Internet banks, like Egg (UK) and UnoFirst (Spain), to enter the business. What makes banks special any more? As Bill Gates of Microsoft said: 'the world needs banking but it does not need banks'. In response to these challenges, traditional 'brick-and-mortar' banks are having to rethink their business. Much of the time, a bank's role is not as much about managing money, but processing information. It may be that, one day, they will be relegated to the back-room, providing systems for supermarkets, airlines or television channels. Or branches will be transformed from transaction to information and advisory centres. Those that fear the worst are fast expanding into offering new services. For example Finland's MeritaNordbanken now runs a virtual shopping mall and Spanish bank BBVA sells everything from books to groceries.[8]

Inseparability

Service inseparability—
A major characteristic of services – they are produced and consumed at the same time and cannot be separated from their providers, whether the providers are people or machines.

Physical goods are produced, put into inventory, distributed through multiple intermediaries, later sold to users and, still later, consumed. In contrast, services are first sold, then produced and consumed at the same time and in the same place. **Service inseparability** means that services cannot be separated from their providers, whether the providers are people or machines. If a service employee provides the service, then the employee is a part of the service. A rock concert is an example. The pop group or band is the service. It cannot deliver the service without the members of the band being present. A school or college teacher is a part of the education service provided and has to be present to deliver the service to students. Moreover, the rock group cannot deliver the service without the consumers (the audience) being present. A teacher cannot conduct the teaching session if there are no students attending class. Because the customer is also present as the service is produced, *provider–customer interaction* is a special feature of services marketing. Both the provider and the client affect the service outcome. How a doctor treats her patient or how a legal adviser relates to his client, for example, influences the client's judgement of the overall service delivered. The extent to which a teacher is able to develop a rapport with her students will influence the quality of their learning experience. Thus, it is important for service staff to be trained to interact well with clients.

A second feature of the inseparability of services is that other customers are also present or involved. The concert audience, students in the class, other passengers in a train, customers in a restaurant, all are present while an individual consumer is consuming the service. Their behaviour can determine the satisfaction that the service delivers to the individual customers. For example, an unruly crowd in the restaurant would spoil the atmosphere for other customers dining there and reduce satisfaction. The implication for management would be to ensure at all times that customers involved in the service do not interfere with each other's satisfaction.

Because of the simultaneity of service production and consumption, service providers face particular difficulty when demand rises. A goods manufacturer can make more, or mass-produce and stock up in anticipation of growth in demand. This is not possible for service operators like restaurants or a law firm. Service organisations have therefore to pay careful attention to managing growth, given the constraints. A high price is used to ration the limited supply of the preferred provider's service. Several other strategies exist for handling the problem of demand growth. First, the service provider can learn to work with larger groups, so that more customers are serviced simultaneously. For example, bigger sites or premises are used by retailers to accommodate larger numbers of customers, and a pop concert will cater for a larger audience if held in an open-air sports arena than in an enclosed concert hall. Second, the service provider can learn to work faster. Productivity can be improved by training staff to do tasks and utilise time more efficiently. Finally, a service organisation can train more service providers.

Variability

As services involve people in production and consumption, there is considerable potential for variability. **Service variability** means that the quality of services depends on who provides them, as well as when, where and how they are provided. As such, service quality is difficult to control. For example, some hotels have a reputation for providing better service than others. Within a given hotel, one registration-desk employee may be cheerful and efficient, whereas another, standing just a few metres away, may be unpleasant and slow.

The ability to satisfy customers depends ultimately on the behaviour of frontline service employees. A brilliant marketing strategy will achieve little if they do their job badly and deliver poor-quality service. Service firms can take several steps towards quality control.[9] First, they invest in good hiring and training procedures. Airlines, banks and hotels, for example, invest large sums of money in recruiting the right employees and training them to give good service. They train their front-line people so that they are empowered to take actions or do what is necessary to ensure that customers are treated well and to deal with customer complaints satisfactorily. However, training in many companies often boils down to little more than pep talks. In order for training to make a real difference to employees' behaviour, companies ensure that training focuses on helping employees to develop essential skills to do their jobs well. Consider the following example:

Service variability—A major characteristic of services – their quality may vary greatly depending on who provides them and when, where and how.

Denmark's ISS is one of the world's leading international commercial cleaning businesses. In an industry characterised by low-skilled workers and high staff turnover, ISS trains its staff relentlessly. Commercial cleaning involves far more than just running a vacuum cleaner over the carpet. ISS serves big clients – factories, hospitals and offices. To do this well and profitably, employees must do their job efficiently. This means conserving time and

> cleaning supplies, improving quality and avoiding accidents and injuries. This is difficult enough in ordinary office buildings. At hospitals, chemical plants and factories, the equipment and skills needed can be tricky. Employees must also be able to spot and deal instantly with idiosyncratic customers they come across in the job. In the first six months on the job, employees are given training in cleaning techniques, such as knowing which chemicals to use for specific stains and surfaces, and in safety. In the next six months, employees move on to applied economics – they learn to interpret clients' contracts, how profitable a contract is and how the client's profitability contributes to that of ISS's local branch. This is invaluable if the employee is promoted to team leader, which can occur after a year. Once employees become team leaders, they receive training on how to deal with customers, coach junior staff in the team and learn management techniques that will help them meet performance targets, based on both profitability and customer retention. All this training helps ISS staff to do their jobs well.

Knowing how to do something well and being motivated to do it are different things. The second step towards quality control is to motivate staff by providing employee incentives that emphasise and reward quality, such as employee-of-the-month awards or bonuses based on customer feedback.

> ISS relies on a number of mechanisms to motivate its staff. One is the use of teamwork and peer pressure to motivate employees to do their best. For example, although most of the clients can be handled by a single person, ISS groups its cleaners into two- or three-person hit-squads rather than sending one person to each site. The squad works together and travels from site to site. Although seemingly inefficient, the extra motivation more than offsets the costs. ISS also encourages employees to stay loyal to the firm by paying them a little more. Managers are sometimes asked not to compete on wage costs even if it means that the division will lose some bids. The company believes that by retaining staff, all the training it has invested is not wasted. As quality improves, the company continues to win new business, despite the higher costs. A major account won recently includes a contract to clean hotel rooms at Disneyland Paris.

A third mechanism to improve quality is by making service employees more visible and accountable to consumers – car dealerships can let customers talk directly with the mechanics working on their cars. A firm can check customer satisfaction regularly through suggestion and complaint systems, customer surveys and comparison shopping. When poor service is found, it is corrected.

In the case of ISS, management views contact between ISS supervisors and its clients' site managers as crucial. If clients are dissatisfied with the service, superiors get to know about it. In order to generate more contact with customers, ISS rescheduled many of its clients so that its teams overlap for half an hour or so with office workers, making it easier for clients to voice their complaints.[10]

Fourth, service firms can increase the consistency of employee performance by substituting equipment for staff (e.g. vending machines, automatic cash dispensers), and through standardising the service-performance process throughout the organisation. This is done by developing a service blueprint which delineates events and processes or job procedures in a flowchart, which alerts employees to potential fail points with the aim of ensuring activities are done properly (e.g. Walt Disney's theme parks, McDonald's restaurants and Club Med vacation resorts).

Perishability

Service perishability means that services cannot be stored for later sale or use. Some dentists and general practitioners charge patients for missed appointments because the service value existed only at that point and disappeared when the patient did not show up. The perishability of services is not a problem when demand is steady. However, when demand fluctuates, service firms often have difficult problems. For example, public transportation companies have to own much more equipment because of rush-hour demand than they would if demand were even throughout the day.

Service perishability—
A major characteristic of services – they cannot be stored for later sale or use.

Service firms can use several strategies for producing a better match between demand and supply. On the demand side, differential pricing – that is, charging different prices at different times – will shift some demand from peak periods to off-peak periods. Examples are cheaper early-evening movie prices, low-season holidays and reduced weekend train fares. Airline companies offer heavily discounted 'standby' tickets to fill unbooked seats. Or non-peak demand can be increased, as in the case of business hotels developing mini-vacation weekends for tourists.

Complementary services can be offered during peak times to provide alternatives to waiting customers, such as cocktail lounges to sit in while waiting for a restaurant table and automatic tellers in banks. Reservation systems can also help manage the demand level – airlines, hotels and doctors use them regularly.

On the supply side, firms can hire part-time employees to serve peak demand. Schools add part-time teachers when enrolment goes up, and restaurants call in part-time waiters and waitresses to handle busy shifts. Peak-time demand can be handled more efficiently by rescheduling work so that employees do only essential tasks during peak periods. Some straightforward tasks can be shifted to consumers (e.g. packing their own groceries). Or providers can share services, as when several hospitals share an expensive piece of medical equipment. Finally, a firm can plan ahead for future expansion, as when an airline company buys more wide-bodied jumbo jets in anticipation of future growth in international air travel or a theme park may buy surrounding land for later development. Service firms have to consider using any of the above strategies for achieving a better match between demand and supply. Some businesses have come up with novel solutions to perishability problems. Consider the following examples:

Services are perishable: empty seats at slack times cannot be stored for later use during peak periods.

Club Med operates hundreds of Club med 'villages' (resorts) around the world. Unsold rooms and airline packages mean lost revenues. In addition to relying on travel agents to sell last-minute packages, the company now uses email to notify people in its database early to midweek on rooms and air seats available for travel that weekend. These 'unsold inventory' are heavily discounted – typically 30 to 40 per cent below the standard package.[11]

The Dutch flower auctions in Holland provide an example of state-of-the-art auctions, where nearly 60 per cent of the world's cut flowers are sold annually. Because flowers are perishable, these auctions are designed for speed. Daily, millions of flowers are shipped to Amsterdam's Schiphol airport. They are swiftly taken to nearby auction centres. By the end of the day, over 34 million flowers and 3 million potted plants will have been purchased, covering some 60,000 transactions. Most of the flowers will then be rushed to the airport for immediate export. Over a 24-hour period, flowers are shipped to an auction centre, purchased by a wholesaler, sold to a retailer and bought by a New Yorker! The key to the process is to start with a high price set by the auctioneer, unlike the English auction in which bidders push the price up from below. The price then drops until a buyer signals he wants the goods. Each transaction takes only about four seconds. The speed is ideal for selling a large quantity of easily evaluated goods that are perishable and must be sold quickly. Since 1995, the auction houses have established an electronic system, allowing buying-at-a-distance. Online buyers can participate in several

auctions simultaneously and gain a better feel for pricing and supply.
The Dutch auction has been adopted by a number of e-businesses.
Intermodalex.com, for example, uses the system to lease container space
on oceangoing vessels. Container space, like flowers, is perishable and
is lost once the vessel casts off.[12]

Lack of ownership

When customers buy physical goods, such as cars and computers, they have personal access to the product for an unlimited time. They actually own the product. They can even sell it when they no longer wish to own it. In contrast, service products lack that quality of ownership. The service consumer often has access to the service for a limited time. An insurance policy is yours only when you have paid the premium and continue to renew it. A holiday is experienced and, hopefully, enjoyed, but after the event it remains ephemeral, unlike a product that the consumer owns after purchase. Because of the lack of ownership, service providers must make a special effort to reinforce their brand identity and affinity with the consumer using one or more of the following methods:

- They could reinforce the service brand identity and affinity with the customer. For example, SAS offers frequent travellers a ticketless Travel Pass, preloaded with 10, 20, 30 or an unlimited number of business-class flights to a choice of Scandinavian cities.

- They could offer incentives to consumers to use their service again, as in the case of frequent-flyer schemes promoted by British Airways and Travel Passes offered by Scandinavian Airlines.

- They could create membership clubs or associations to give a sense of belonging and ownership (e.g. British Airways' executive clubs for air travellers).

Where appropriate, service providers might turn the disadvantage of non-ownership into a benefit: for example, an industrial design consultant might argue that, by employing his or her expertise, the customer would actually be reducing costs, given that the alternative would be for that customer to employ a full-time designer with equally specialised knowledge. Paying for access to services rather than performing the activities in-house (e.g. warehousing) reduces capital cost, while also giving greater flexibility to a business.

Marketing strategies for service firms

Until recently, service firms lagged behind manufacturing firms in their use of marketing. Many service businesses are small (shoe repair shops, barber shops, dry cleaners) and often consider formal management and marketing techniques unnecessary or too costly. Some service organisations (e.g. schools, churches) were at one time so much in demand that they did not need marketing until recently. Others (e.g. legal, medical and accounting practices) believed that it was unprofessional to use marketing. However, successful service organisations recognise that the specific nature of services requires tailored marketing approaches and that traditional product-based marketing is unlikely to be effective if principles are transferred without adaptation. This does not mean that new marketing principles and theory should be developed for services, rather that the existing principles should be adapted to the service environment.[13]

Just like manufacturing firms, smart service businesses use marketing to create powerful brands which are positioned strongly in chosen target markets. Budget-priced airlines like Ryanair and easyJet position themselves as no-frills, low-cost carriers. Global data communications service provider NTT positions itself as a 'trusted partner' that can bring one-stop network solutions to western businesses operating in Asia. These and other service firms establish their positions through traditional marketing-mix activities.

However, because service firms differ from tangible products, they require additional marketing approaches. In a product business, products are fairly standardised and can sit on the shelves waiting for customers. But in a service business, the customer and front-line service employee interact to create the service. Thus service providers must work to interact effectively with customers to create superior value during service encounters. Effective interaction, in turn, depends on the skills of front-line service staff, and on the service production and support processes backing these employees.

The service–profit chain

Successful service companies focus their attention on both their employees and customers. They understand the *service–profit chain*, which links service firms' profits with employee and customer satisfaction. This chain consists of five links:[14]

1. Internal service quality – superior employee selection and training, a quality work environment and strong support for those dealing with customers, which results in . . .

2. Satisfied and productive service employees – more satisfied, loyal and hardworking employees, which results in . . .

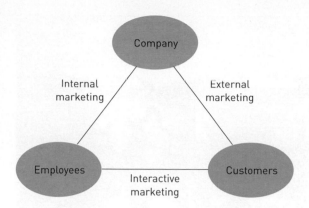

Figure 15.2 **Three types of marketing in service industries**

3. Greater service value – more effective and efficient customer value creation and service delivery, which results in . . .

4. Satisfied and loyal customers – satisfied customers who remain loyal, repeat purchase and refer other customers, which results in . . .

5. Healthy service profits and growth – superior service firm performance.

Therefore, reaching service profits and growth goals begins with taking care of those who take care of customers. All of this suggests that, in order to achieve favourable service outcomes, service marketing requires more than just traditional external marketing using the four Ps. Figure 15.2 shows that service marketing also requires both *internal marketing* and *interactive marketing*.

Internal marketing means that the service firm must invest heavily in employee quality and performance. It must effectively train and motivate its customer-contact employees and all the supporting service people to work as a *team* to provide customer satisfaction. For the firm to deliver consistently high service quality, everyone must practise a customer orientation. It is not enough to have a marketing department doing traditional marketing while the rest of the company goes its own way. Marketers must also encourage everyone else in the organisation to be customer-centred. In fact, internal marketing must *precede* external marketing. It makes little sense to advertise excellent service before the company's staff is ready, willing and able to provide it. Thus, the service organisation must orient its employees carefully, instil in them a sense of pride and motivate them by recognising and rewarding outstanding service deeds.

Interactive marketing means that perceived service quality depends heavily on the quality of the buyer–seller interaction. In product marketing, product quality often depends little on how the product is obtained. But in services marketing, especially in high-contact and professional services, service quality depends on both the service deliverer and the quality of the delivery. Effective service deliverer–customer interaction is important for achieving a satisfactory service transaction. Service marketers cannot assume that they will satisfy the customer simply by providing good technical service. This is because the customer judges service quality not just on *technical quality* (e.g. the success of the surgery, the tastiness of the food served in the restaurant), but also on its *functional quality* (e.g. whether the surgeon showed concern and inspired confidence, whether the waiter was friendly and polite). Also, each interaction is a 'moment of truth' for the provider, where not just the service encounter, but also the organisation, will be decisively judged by the customer. Thus, professionals cannot assume that they will satisfy the client simply by providing good technical service. They have to master interactive marketing skills or functions as well.[15]

Effective buyer–seller interaction may help to secure a satisfied customer. However, to retain customers over the long term, many service providers have to develop *relationship marketing* skills for managing customer relationships. The topic of relationship marketing is addressed in greater detail in Chapter 11.

Internal marketing— Marketing by a service firm to train and effectively motivate its customer-contact employees and all the supporting service people to work as a team to provide customer satisfaction.

Interactive marketing— Marketing by a service firm that recognises that perceived service quality depends heavily on the quality of buyer–seller interaction.

Shangri-la Hotels are renowned worldwide for their opulent hotels. But, as this ad suggests, deep down the hotel chain's success is due to their legendary service from warm, caring employees.
SOURCE: Shangri-La International Hotel Management Limited/TBWA Hong Kong.

At the new Kowloon Shangri-La much has changed, but the important things remain the same.

The award-winning Kowloon Shangri-La invites you to experience a new level of opulence in our beautifully renovated harbour-front hotel. The famous Lobby and Lobby Lounge are now more magnificent than ever. All 700 guestrooms and suites have been tastefully refurbished, and exciting new restaurant concepts have been introduced. But beneath it all, our soul remains the same, with breathtaking harbour views and legendary Shangri-La service from warm, caring people.

Kowloon Shangri-La, Hong Kong Tel: (852) 2721 2111, Fax: (852) 2723 8686, E-mail: ksl@shangri-la.com
For reservations, please call London (44 20) 8747 8485, your travel consultant or book on-line at www.shangri-la.com
AUSTRALIA • MAINLAND CHINA • HONG KONG SAR • FIJI ISLANDS • INDONESIA • MALAYSIA
MYANMAR • PHILIPPINES • SINGAPORE • TAIWAN • THAILAND • UNITED ARAB EMIRATES

Kowloon Shangri-La
HONG KONG

Today, as competition and costs increase, and as productivity and quality decrease, more marketing sophistication is needed. Service companies face three major marketing tasks: they want to increase their *competitive differentiation*, *service quality* and *productivity*.

Managing differentiation

In these days of intense price competition, service marketers often complain about the difficulty of differentiating their services from those of competitors. To the extent that customers view the service of different providers as similar, they care less about the provider than the price. Witness, for example, the recent growth in online banking. Customers are lured to bank online not only because of the advantages of 24-hour service but also because of the tempting deals (for example, higher savings rates or lower transaction costs) that the online banks can offer them. Similarly, budget airlines are mushrooming because many fliers care more about travel costs than service. Service providers therefore often use pricing to differentiate their offering. However, pricing strategies (e.g. price cuts) are quickly emulated by competitors. Furthermore, intense price competition erodes margins and does not create a sustainable differential advantage over the long term.

Service differentiation poses particular challenges. Service intangibility and inseparability mean that consumers rarely compare alternative service offerings in advance of purchase in the way that potential buyers of products do. Differences in the attractiveness or value of competing services are therefore not readily obvious to the potential buyer. However, services can be differentiated. The solution to price competition is to develop a differentiated *offer*, *delivery* or *image*. The offer can include *innovative features* that set one company's offer apart from its competitors' offers.

> For example, British Airways offered international business and first-class travellers a sleeping compartment, hot showers and cooked-to-order breakfasts. Virgin Atlantic Airways was among the first to introduce innovations such as in-flight movie menus, advance seating, air-to-ground telephone service and frequent-flyer awareness programmes to differentiate their offers. Following British Airways, Virgin Atlantic also introduced reclining business-class seats that convert into a bed. The ability to offer this extra luxury to business travellers put these two carriers into a dimension of comfort way beyond all other competitors. In addition, Virgin Upper Class cabin has a private area for its beauty and massage treatments.[16]

Unfortunately, service differentiation exposes a second problem – service innovations cannot be patented and are easily copied. Still, the service company that innovates regularly will usually gain a succession of temporary advantages over competitors. Moreover, an innovative reputation may help it keep customers who want to go with the best.

Third, the variability of services suggests that standardisation and quality are difficult to control. Consistency in quality is generally hard to obtain, but firms that are customer-oriented and have sound internal marketing schemes will increase their ability to differentiate their brand by offering superior-quality service *delivery*.

The service company can differentiate its service *delivery* in three ways: through *people*, *physical environment* and *process*. These are often referred to as the additional *three Ps* in service marketing.[17]

Because many services are provided by people, it is these people who can make a huge difference to customer satisfaction. The company can distinguish itself by having more able and reliable customer-contact people to deliver its service. The enthusiasm and smart appearance of front-line customer-contact staff also helps. More importantly, as mentioned earlier, the service business that selects the right people as well as emphasising internal marketing, combined with customer-focused staff training and education, can succeed in improving employee quality and performance that will sustain superiority in service delivery. Ultimately, the commitment and performance of front-line staff, backed by the support of people involved in the operational processes, are vital to the success of service production and delivery. In turn, these affect customer relationships and the organisation's success.

The firm can develop a superior physical environment in which the service product is presented and delivered. Hotels and restaurants, for example, will pay a great deal of attention to interior décor and ambience to project a superior service to target customers. Some retailers, such as The Body Shop and Harrods, have effectively managed the physical environment, giving very distinctive identities to their outlets.

Or it can design a superior delivery process. For example, banks offer their customers home banking as a better way to use banking services than by having to drive, park and wait in line. Service companies can choose among different service processes to deliver their service: restaurants can use different modes of delivery ranging from fast-food and self-service to buffet, silver or candle-light service. Alternatively, some service providers have learnt to exploit new technologies to differentiate the way in their services are provided. For example, British Airways introduced new speech recognition services to improve the efficiency of their customer flight enquiry and confirmation services, while making it easier and more pleasant for customers to access flight information (see Marketing Insights 15.1).

Finally, service intangibility and variability mean that a consistent service brand image is not easily built. Brand image also takes time to develop and cannot be copied by competitors. Service companies that work on distinguishing their service by creating unique and powerful images, through symbols or branding, will gain a lasting advantage over competitors with lack-lustre images. For example, the Ritz, Sheraton and Hard Rock Café all enjoy superior brand positioning which has taken years to develop. Organisations such as Lloyds Bank (which adopted the black horse as its symbol of strength), McDonald's (personified by its Ronald McDonald clown) and the International Red Cross have all differentiated their images through symbols. Amidst a technological revolution and rising competition, differentiation through branding has also become a priority for both traditional and mobile telecommunication service companies such as BT and Orange.

One has only to look at success stories like Orange to appreciate the value of superior brand recognition in the telecoms market. The mobile network operator has built one of Europe's strongest telecoms brands. When Orange was launched in 1995, the concept of branding in mobile phones was virtually non-existent. Rather, it was the handset manufacturers like Nokia, Ericsson and Motorola that had the greater brand recognition. Crucially, Orange created an interesting brand, which was about service to customers, not technology. Orange was, and still is, about lifestyle, freedom, choice and independence – the Orange proposition is a wirefree handset that could be used by anyone, to keep in touch any time, any place. The promise was something new, unconventional, special and optimistic, conveyed through advertising using visual images of birth and awakening. Orange became an offering with a distinctive brand name, a vision (the future), a look and a set of values which quickly captured the imagination of users. Within nine months of launch, the brand's spontaneous awareness soared ahead of the established mobile network operators, Vodafone and Cellnet. Over the years, Orange has also protected the brand name despite its involvement in partnerships and joint ventures around the world, while attracting a premium of £26 billion when acquired by France Télécom. How is it done? 'Developing the Orange brand is not rocket science', according to Hans Snook, chief executive of Orange. 'It's very simple. It's about treating people with respect and giving them what they want in ways they can understand. Brands are about values. . . . Brands are particularly important in telecommunications because when everything is the same, how you feel about a service is what makes you choose one over another.'[18]

British Airways: no long haul for callers!

marketing insights

Customers calling British Airways flight enquiries and confirmation services need no longer endure the endless choices, frustrations or delays typical of 'traditional' interactive voice recognition (IVR) systems. Instead they are greeted by Claire, the voice of the new speech recognition service. British and US-based customers use voice commands rather than keypads to negotiate their way through the system – keying in long flight numbers or destinations is a thing of the past.

Programmed to understand 47 different English accents and approximately 42 combinations for UK airports and terminals, Claire gives users a more human touch. It is also possible to interrupt her to get faster answers. 'The dialogue is crafted to guide callers through the system via a series of questions', explains Nick Applegarth, director for Europe at Nuance Communications, the California-based speech recognition software developer. By repeating the caller's request and asking for confirmation, Claire is approximately 95 per cent accurate. If the system cannot recognise the voice or question or if the flight is delayed, calls are automatically routed to a centre agent. 'It was important not only to make Claire "human" but related to the airline – the voice had to be clear, easy to understand and sound intelligent without putting callers off', says Mr Applegarth.

If not convinced by the faster and more personal service Claire offers, even the most ardent of sceptics might be persuaded by economic and efficiency statistics. Installed within 16 weeks, Claire achieved a 100 per cent return on investment within six months and call costs have dropped from £2 to 10p each. Since flight enquiry call times are shorter, more calls can be processed through the system, which routinely handles more than 12,000 enquiries per day from mobile phones and/or fixed lines.

But it is not all about money. It is also about helping customers intelligently, fast and efficiently to minimise their frustration and/or anxiety. British Airways believes that speech recognition can make a difference to the way in which it provides the services its customers need while making it easier and more pleasant to access information. In common with other airlines, BA has been hit by the industry-wide recession and is looking at ways of making its business more efficient. It considers speech recognition to be a mature, reliable technology which can be used to automate and therefore reduce costs on the approximately three million routine calls handled via its call centres each year.

Having successfully implemented Claire, British Airways is considering the possibility of using speech recognition on other services, making the time callers are 'on hold' more productive. The necessary personal information can be gathered while they are waiting and made available to agents when they take the call. Such

...15.1

a system would further release employees from routine tasks, ensuring their time is spent more productively and adding value to customers and the airline.

Whatever the future plans to use speech recognition, Paul Coby, chief information officer and head of IT at British Airways, does not believe in duplicating effort: 'Our golden rule is to build things once, so software created for our website BA.com can be used for voice recognition. When developing flight information for the website, we can use the same code and turn it into voice, which makes integrating online and voice services cost effective and easy. . . . To create Claire, we only had to do limited development work and buy the licences from Nuance and switching gear from Aspect Communications [a US call centre solutions provider].'

Mr Coby says customers will always want to talk to people for complex transactions and booking, or if they are not happy using speech recognition. 'This is a mature technology which is simple for the public to use and makes it easy for us to provide the services our customers need. People like being able to interrupt and move through the system to get routine information fast', he says.

SOURCES: A reproduction of Priscilla Awde, 'British Airways. Claire cuts the long haul for callers', *Financial Times FT-IT Review Speech Recognition 3* (16 April 2003), p. IV; article accessed online at **www.ft.com/ftit**, December 2003.

Managing service quality

One of the major ways a service firm can differentiate itself is by delivering consistently higher quality than its competitors. Like manufacturers before them, many service industries have now joined the customer-driven quality movement. In Scandinavian countries, and particularly Sweden, service quality management is a topic of national concern, with the government taking a lead role through initiatives such as the Swedish Customer Satisfaction Barometer. Elsewhere, such as in the UK, local authorities or councils are also facing increasing pressure to deliver higher quality services to the local communities they serve. Initiatives such as the 'Best Value programme' had been introduced and aimed at achieving continuous improvements in local council performance. Ongoing pressure exists to 'revolutionise' and 'modernise' the management of local community services and to focus on customer satisfaction. For the public, the ultimate test of a local authority is whether its services are any good. Importantly, for initiatives like Best Value to succeed, the councils involved have to improve their understanding of what their public values, to better involve the public in the services they receive and to enhance their 'power as consumers'. Radical though it may sound, the days of consumer power are here to stay. The search for value begins with the needs of people in the community, and then giving them the quality services they want and value.[19]

Top service companies recognise that outstanding quality gives them a potent competitive advantage that leads to superior sales and profit performance. True, offering greater service quality results in higher costs. However, investments usually pay off because greater customer satisfaction leads to increased customer retention and sales.[20]

The key is to exceed the customer's service quality expectations. As the chief executive at American Express puts it, 'Promise only what you can deliver and deliver more than you promise!'[21] Customers' service expectations are formed from past encounters and experiences, word-of-mouth and the firm's advertising. If *perceived service* of a given firm exceeds *expected service*, customers are apt to use the service provider again. Customer retention is, perhaps, the best measure of quality and reflects the firm's ability to hang on to its customers by consistently delivering value to them. Thus, where the manufacturer's quality target might be 'zero defects', the service provider's goal is 'zero customer *defections*'.

Therefore, to meet quality targets, the service provider needs to set quality goals through identifying the expectations of target customers concerning service quality. Unfortunately, quality in service industries is harder to define, judge or quantify than product quality. It is hard to quantify service quality because intangibility means that there are seldom physical dimensions, like performance, functional features or maintenance cost, which can be used as benchmarks and measured. It is harder to get agreement on the quality of a haircut than on that of a hair dryer, for instance. The inseparability of production and consumption means that service quality must be defined on the basis of both the process in which the service is delivered and the actual outcome experienced by the customer. Again, it is difficult to quantify standards or reference points against which service delivery process and performance outcomes are measured.

Despite the difficulty, service organisations can measure quality. In practice, the provider has to determine how customers of the service *perceive* quality. Studies suggest that customer assessments of service quality are the result of a comparison of what they expect with what they experience.[22] Any mismatch between the two is a 'quality gap'. There are a number of quality gaps that cause unsuccessful service delivery:

1. The gap between consumer expectations and management perception. Management might not correctly perceive what customers want. Mobile phone service providers might think that customers want sophisticated technology, but users may be more attracted to low price and simplicity.

2. The gap between management perception and service quality specification. Management might correctly perceive customers' wants but not set a performance standard. The restaurant manager may tell staff to deliver a 'fast' service to customers but does not specify this in minutes.

3. The gap between service quality specification and service delivery. Personnel might be poorly trained or are incapable or unwilling to meet the set standard. Or they may be working to conflicting standards, such as taking time to listen to customers and serving them quickly.

4. The gap between service delivery and external communications. The service provider's advertising and presentations by its sales representatives influence customers' expectations. A hotel brochure emphasises its wide range of guest services and beautiful bedrooms, but the guest arrives to find that the room he's been given is plain and tacky looking, while the very service he expects to use – the gym – is closed for maintenance until further notice. Here, external communications have distorted the customer's expectations.

5. The gap between perceived service and expected service. Customers may misperceive service quality. For example, the helpful clothing store attendant may follow the customer round the store, pointing to the 'new arrivals', while constantly asking the customer if she could assist him in choosing an item. The customer basically expects to be left to his own devices while he makes up his own mind. Although the store assistant is trying to show care, the customer will interpret this level of attention as a source of annoyance and irritation.

The service quality manager's goal is therefore to narrow the quality gap, taking into account that what is being measured is perceived quality, which is always a judgement by

Figure 15.3 Key determinants of
perceived service quality

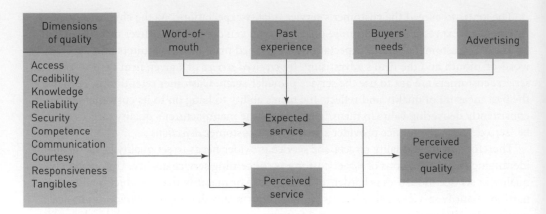

the customer. Hence, what the customer thinks is reality, is reality; quality is whatever the customer says it is.

To improve quality, service marketers have to identify the key determinants of service quality (that is, the key criteria customers use to judge quality), what target customers' expectations are, and how customers rate the firm's service in relation to these criteria against what they expected. We have already addressed issues surrounding the determination of customer expectations. Next, we look at the criteria that reflect service quality.

An important study highlights 10 key determinants of perceived service quality.[23] Figure 15.3 summarises these dimensions: *access* (is the service easy to get access to and delivered on time?); *credibility* (is the company credible and trustworthy?); *knowledge* (does the service provider really understand customers' needs?); *reliability* (how dependable and consistent is the service?); *security* (is the service low-risk and free from danger?); *competence* (are staff knowledgeable and in possession of the skills required to deliver good service?); *communication* (how well has the company explained its service?); *courtesy* (are staff polite, considerate and sensitive to customers?); *responsiveness* (are staff willing and quick to deliver the service?); and *tangibles* (do the appearance of staff, the physical environment and other tangible representations of the service reflect high quality?). The first five are concerned with the quality of the *outcome* of service provided, while the last five are related to the quality of the delivery *process*. By focusing on the dimensions that are important to customers, the service firm can ensure that customers' expectations are fully met.

To a large extent, aspects such as good understanding of customers' needs and the ability to provide consistent and dependable service are achieved through internal marketing and continual investment in employee quality and performance. The reputation and credibility of the service provider and customers' perceived risk are interrelated. If the consumer trusts the service provider, he or she expects that the service is free from danger or perceives little risk in using the service. Credibility can be improved through effective communication of service quality through advertising and/or satisfied customers. Access can be improved by having multi-site locations while waiting times can be reduced through synchronising supply and demand and/or tackling staff productivity problems.

Various studies have shown that well-managed service organisations share a number of common practices. These are summarised below.

1. Customer obsession. Top service companies are '*customer obsessed*'. They have a clear sense of their target customers and their needs. They have developed a distinctive strategy for satisfying customer needs that wins enduring customer loyalty.

2. Top management commitment. The best service organisations persistently show *top management commitment to quality*. Management at companies such as Marks & Spencer, American Express and McDonald's look not only at financial performance, but also at

service performance. They develop a quality culture that encourages and rewards personnel for good service delivery.

3. High service quality standards. The best service firms *set high service quality standards*. Swissair, for example, aims to have 96 per cent or more of its passengers rate its service as good or superior; otherwise, it takes action. The standards must be set *appropriately* high. A 98 per cent accuracy standard may sound good, but using this standard, 64,000 Federal Express packages would be lost each day, 10 words would be misspelt on each page, 400,000 prescriptions would be misfilled daily, and drinking water would be unsafe eight days a year. Top service companies do not settle merely for 'good' service, they offer 'breakthrough service', aiming at being 100 per cent defect-free.[24]

4. Monitoring systems. Top service firms monitor service performance. They *watch service performance closely* – both their own and that of competitors. They communicate their concerns about service quality to employees and provide performance feedback. They use methods such as comparison shopping, customer surveys, suggestion schemes and customer complaint programmes. During the past decade, many service companies have invested heavily to develop streamlined and efficient service delivery systems. They want to ensure that customers will receive consistently high-quality service in every service encounter.

5. Good service recovery. Customers like to see things right first time. Unlike product manufacturers, which can adjust their machinery and inputs until everything is perfect, service quality will always vary, depending on the interactions between employees and customers. Problems will inevitably occur. Mistakes are a critical part of every service. Hard as they try, even the best service companies can't prevent the occasional late delivery, burnt steak, or grumpy employee. The fact is, in services, often performed in the customer's presence, errors are inevitable. If things go wrong, customer complaints are an opportunity for companies to remedy poor service. *Good service recovery* can turn angry customers into loyal ones. In fact, good recovery can win more customer purchasing and loyalty than when things had gone well in the first place. When companies are responsive and deal with poor service promptly and effectively, they can win back customer confidence and loyalty. Therefore companies should take steps to recover from service mistakes when they do occur.[25]

Most firms, however, are bad at handling customer complaints, if indeed they deal with them at all. Leading firms, on the other hand, view customer care in service-recovery situations as a source of unrivalled competitive advantage. The first step is to empower front-line service employees – that is, to give them the authority, responsibility and incentives they need to recognise, care about and tend to customer needs. Such empowered employees can act quickly and effectively to keep service problems from resulting in lost customers.

They also establish effective complaint procedures to capture these opportunities. Because only a small minority of dissatisfied customers ever complain, the firm should proactively attract complaints from disenchanted customers. Channels of communication should be kept open to give customers access and to make it easy for them to offer feedback. Free telephone calls, regular follow-up of customer surveys and staff training all help. Customers themselves may use different channels of complaint: telephone, fax, letter, email or personal visit to the store. Companies also have systems and procedures installed to offer a high level of customer service and care in service-recovery situations, giving the company another chance to offer service and satisfaction to the dissatisfied customer.

Finally, service-conscious organisations develop a non-threatening culture – they do not penalise staff responsible for the 'mistake', in order to encourage them to analyse, resolve and learn from complaints. In addition to practising a 'no-blame policy', staff are rewarded for creating service-recovery opportunities.

6. Satisfying employees and customers. Well-managed service companies *satisfy employees as well as customers.* They believe that good employee relations will result in good customer relations. Management clearly defines and communicates service level targets so that, first, its employees know what service goals they must achieve, and second, its customers know what to expect to receive from their interaction with the service provider.

As mentioned earlier, management also executes internal marketing to create an environment of employee support and to reward good performance. Management regularly monitors employee job satisfaction. For example, the Danish-based international cleaning services giant ISS stresses good working relations and utilisation of human resources. Staff are encouraged to join trade unions. Total quality management is firmly upheld – staff are trained so that they can do their jobs well and derive satisfaction from them. Happy and satisfied customers yield happy employees. ISS has also gone to the extreme of moving into palatial new headquarters in a wooded country estate in northern Copenhagen – an absence of air-conditioning or dust-hugging carpets, together with soothing colours, reflect management's belief that scientific cleaning can help reduce staff illness.

Managing productivity

Rapidly rising costs put service firms under great pressure to increase service productivity. The problem is particularly acute where the service is labour intensive. Productivity can be improved in several ways, as follows.

1. The service providers can train current employees better, or they can hire new ones who will work harder or more skilfully for the same pay.

2. The service providers can increase the quantity of their service by giving up some quality (e.g. doctors having to handle more patients by giving less time to each).

3. The provider can 'industrialise the service' by adding equipment and standardising production, as in McDonald's production-line approach to fast-food retailing. Commercial dishwashing, jumbo jets and multiple-unit cinemas (i.e. cineplexes and megaplexes) all represent the use of technological advances to increase service output.

4. Service providers can also increase productivity by designing more effective services. How-to-quit-smoking clinics and health-and-fitness recommendations may reduce the need for expensive medical services later on.

5. Providers can also give customers incentives to substitute company labour with their own labour. For example, business firms that sort their own mail before delivering it to the post office pay lower postal rates. Self-service restaurants are another case in point. Pay-and-display facilities in car parks alleviate the need to employ attendants (as well as reducing waiting time).

6. Service providers can harness the power of technology to save time and costs and make service workers more productive. A well-designed website can allow customers to obtain buying information, narrow their purchase options or even make a purchase directly, saving service provider time. For example, personal computer buyers can visit the Dell website (www.Dell.com), review the characteristics of various Dell models, check out prices and organise their questions ahead of time. Even if they choose to call a Dell telesales representative rather than buying via the website, they are better informed and require less personal service.

However, companies must avoid pushing productivity so hard that doing so reduces perceived quality. Some productivity steps help standardise quality, increasing customer satisfaction. But other productivity steps lead to too much standardisation and can rob consumers of a customised service. Attempts to industrialise a service or to cut costs can make a service company more efficient in the short run, but reduce its longer-run ability to innovate, maintain service quality and flexibility, or respond to consumer needs and desires. In some cases, service providers accept reduced productivity in order to create more service differentiation or quality.[26]

In the final analysis, the key to superior service provision is to realise that customer service improvement cannot be made in isolation of the other activities of the business. The experience of Air France illustrates the need for service firms to tackle service quality issues in tandem with a wider drive to redress the shortcomings of a business.

Until recently, few would dispute that the quality of customer care at Air France left a lot to be desired. Besides the usual arrogance – knowing what's best for the customer – Air France had all the problems of indifferent service quality common under state ownership. However, in September 2002, the now semi-privatised operator became the first global airline to achieve certification for the quality of its service by SGS, the respected Swiss quality assurance group. Back in 1995, the airline's management team realised that, to turn around the company's fortune in the face of an aviation downturn, the company had to put the customer at the heart of their programme. They knew that satisfying customers took more than a smile and the enjoinder 'Have a nice day'. Some of the biggest causes of customer dissatisfaction were flight delays and poor responses from staff. The company had to undertake a 'root-and-branch' overhaul. Great efforts were expended to train call-centre staff and ground crew. Aircrew were integrated within the commercial business to improve their awareness of the link between passengers and profit. Customer feedback forms covering some 270,000 customers a year became an essential element of the company's new monitoring system. This included 'mystery customers' from an external company who make 1,300 checks a year on staff responses which are reported to the management. Air France's efforts have paid off. The benefits are clearly evident, in steadily improving punctuality, higher aircraft occupancy and continued profitability, despite the travails of the aviation sector worldwide.[27]

We have addressed strategies for handling the marketing problems that service organisations face. Importantly, to be successful, service firms must practise internal and interactive marketing, in addition to adopting an external marketing focus. The key lies in management's ability to develop a quality culture and to operationalise effectively an extended marketing mix that results in superior service differentiation and quality.

International services marketing

An Italian sportswear manufacturer calls her advertising agency in London to confirm plans for new billboards in Venezuela. A German tourist checks into her hotel room in New York – the hotel is owned by a Singaporean company and managed by an American firm. The Zürich branch of a Japanese bank participates in a debt offering for an aircraft-leasing company in

McDonald's branch in Riyadh, Saudi Arabia. The fast food chain customises its menus to reflect local tastes. McArabia Sandwiches are offered in its branches in the Middle East.
SOURCE: Associated Press/ Wide World Photos/Hasan Jamali.

Ireland. A British construction firm builds an airport in Japan, and an American insurance company sells its products in Germany. These are just a few examples of the thousands of service transactions that take place each day around the globe.

A lot of trade no longer involves putting things into a crate and sending them abroad on ships! More and more, the global economy is dominated by services. The World Trade Organisation estimates that commercial-service trade is now worth over one trillion euros, almost one-quarter of the value of trade in goods. Indeed, a variety of service industries – from banking, insurance and communications to transportation, travel and entertainment – now account for well over 60 per cent of the economy in developed countries around the world. The worldwide growth rate for services (16 per cent in the past decade) is almost double the growth rate of manufacturing.[28] The internationalisation of services is very apparent when one travels around the world. Service firms like Hertz, Avis, DHL, Deli France, McDonald's, Novotel, Holiday Inn, Ibis and many others are found all over the world. Indeed, there are so many McDonald's restaurants in Budapest that it looks as if you are in the US.[29]

Some industries have a long history of international operations. For example, the commercial banking industry was one of the first to grow internationally. Many banks had to provide global services in order to meet the foreign exchange and credit needs of their home-country clients wanting to sell overseas. The Dutch ABN AMRO Bank established the first foreign bank in Saudi Arabia in response to the demand from Moslem clients in the then Nederlandsch Indië (now Indonesia) to change money in the country on their pilgrimage to Mecca. In recent years, however, as the scope of international financing has broadened, many banks have become truly global operations. Germany's Deutsche Bank, for example, has branches in over 41 countries. Thus, for its clients around the world that wish to take advantage of growth opportunities created by German reunification, Deutsche Bank can raise money not just in Frankfurt, but also in Zürich, London, Paris and Tokyo.

Retailers are among the latest
service businesses to go global.
Here Asian shoppers buy
American products in a Dutch-
owned Makro store in Kuala
Lumpur, Malaysia.
SOURCE: Munshi Ahmed
Photography.

The travel industry also moved naturally into international operations. American hotel
and airline companies led the way, growing quickly in Europe and the Far East during the
economic expansion that followed World War II. Credit card companies soon followed –
the early worldwide presence of American Express has recently been matched by Visa and
MasterCard. Business travellers and holidaymakers like the convenience and they have now
come to expect that their credit cards will be honoured wherever they go.

Professional and business services industries such as accounting, management consulting
and advertising have only recently started operating on a worldwide scale. The international
growth of these firms followed the globalisation of the manufacturing companies they serve.
For example, increasingly globalised manufacturing firms have found it much easier to have
their accounts prepared by a single accounting firm, even when they operate in two dozen
countries. This paved the way for rapid international consolidation in the accounting industry
in the late 1980s, as seen in the merging of established accounting companies around the
world with America's 'Big Eight' to become the international 'Big Six' almost overnight.
Similarly, as their client companies began to employ global marketing and advertising
strategies, advertising agencies and other marketing services firms responded by globalising
their own operations.[30]

Retailers are among the latest service businesses to go global. As their home markets
become saturated with stores, retailers such as Carrefour, Makro, Wal-Mart, Tesco, H&M,
The Body Shop, Lush and others have all expanded into faster-growing markets in Europe
and Asia. European retailers are making similar moves. Carrefour of France is the leading
retailer in Brazil and Argentina. Asian shoppers now buy western products in Dutch-owned
Makro stores.[31]

As service industries go global, an interesting trend is emerging which poses unique
challenges and opportunities for service providers. The trend is one of outsourcing of
highly skilled professional services to overseas locations. The practice is being pursued
by an increasing number of companies to improve efficiency and to cut costs (see
Marketing Insights 15.2).

15.2 Office Tiger

marketing insights

Service industries are going global. Alongside this trend is one that looks set to herald a big change – the restructuring of affluent world economies. From software design and equity research to film animation and medical services, a new breed of skilled professionals are proving that geographic distance poses no obstacle to outsourcing even the highest-paid jobs to lower-cost overseas centres. Consider the following incident. Clutching her side in pain, a woman suspected of appendicitis was rushed to the Crozer-Chester hospital on the outskirts of Philadelphia. Within minutes of her arrival, the recommendation whether to operate or not was being made by a Harvard-trained specialist, reading her computer-aided tomography (CAT) scan from a computer screen 5,800 miles away in the Middle East. The woman had little time to ponder how much her life had become dependent on the forces of globalisation!

The trend, still only a trickle at present, may look to some like a temporary fad pursued by companies seeking to cut costs. But, whether an impending threat or not, the migration of so-called white-collar jobs has ascended the value chain from call-centre operators and back-office clerks to occupations such as investment analysts, accounting and medical, computer software and design specialists.

At the centre of this service revolution is India. Just as China is fast becoming the new workshop of the world for light manufacturing, India has cast its eye on the world's professional services. But we're talking about high-value outsourcing. Office Tiger, an outsourcing company with offices on the sixth floor of a pink stone shopping mall in Chennai, formerly known as Madras, is emerging as the virtual research arm of Wall Street. The business employs postgraduates, financial analysts and business planners. Their average age is 26. Mr Joseph Sigelman founded the company four years ago with Harvard Business School colleague Randy Altschuler, with $18 million of private equity funding. Currently, Office Tiger generates annual revenues of $20 million which is forecast to increase fivefold in three years.

With six of the top 12 investment banks as clients, Office Tiger is doubling its capacity in the Chennai arcade. Mr Sigelman himself has spent six years with three banks in London and New York. US banks have led the way in outsourcing to India procedures such as IT systems management and data transactions. According to Nasscom, India's IT lobby group, these pioneers have saved $8 billion in the past four years.

This new brand of outsourcing is driven by investment banks' efforts to cut costs as well as to overhaul research divisions following recent corporate scandals. Office Tiger's initial outsourcing contracts were limited to desktop publishing. Today, its portfolio includes complicated equity research. For example, one client is a European

...15.2

bank which asked the company to investigate 1,000 companies' pension-funding liabilities. Another is a US private equity group that has outsourced its quarterly tracking of fund-of-funds' underlying portfolio investments.

The foundation of Office Tiger's expertise is evident. Among its 1,000 staff, some 75 are PhDs while 300 have other postgraduate qualifications, many with backgrounds in domestic finance or business consultancy, often with foreign companies. One employee, Neeraj Sinha, once helped set up McKinsey's Indian offshore research centres. Others are equally enterprising. Shivakameswari Narayan, a law graduate from Harvard Business School (HBS), declined a job with her family's motorcycle business. She says 'I'm here to do what every HBS graduate wants to do: rise in a sunrise industry.' The most prized employees are headhunted while others have come to know Office Tiger by word-of-mouth or text message. Entry tests for employment are used; these are so rigorous that fewer than 5 per cent of applicants survive the first cut!

Employees are paid above (Indian) market rates, given their education and employment record. Starting salaries are unlikely to be less than 50,000 rupees ($1,000) a month, which is generous by domestic standards. A similar employee in Manhattan would earn at least $8,000 a month. Immediate cost-savings for a foreign client of 30–50 per cent are common for most Indian software and contact centre operations.

What about office culture? Office dress code is western business attire; women don't wear saris, the most formal dress in India, and male workers share ties with each other because not everyone owns one. Mr Altschuler explains that this way, the place feels like an investment bank and the staff can empathise with clients. Moreover, employees' hours are based on the US working day, meaning night-time in India. Another thing hasn't changed either – pressure remains intense. A third of Office Tiger's deadlines are less than one hour.

The signs are that companies like Office Tiger in India will take a bigger and growing slice of offshore financial service businesses in the next few years. Put bluntly by Tarun Das, head of the Confederation of Indian Industry, 'There is no economic limit to what can be outsourced to India. The only limit that we can see is a political backlash in the west against migration of jobs to India and elsewhere.'

SOURCES: Adapted and based on Khozem Merchant, 'Business is roaring at Office Tiger', *Financial Times* (20 August 2003), p. 15; see also Dan Roberts and Edward Luce, 'Service industries go global: skilled white-collar jobs are starting to migrate to lower-cost centres overseas', *Financial Times* (20 August 2003), p. 15; 'International:tough call for the US cost-centres. Outsourcing can lead to having too much of a good thing', FT.com site, 21 December 2003.

International expansion opportunities abound for service businesses, including even those that are traditionally viewed as basic public services. Consider the following example:

> Post offices are generally regarded as national entities serving communities' postal needs across local and regional centres. Most postal deliveries in the EU are made nationally and only 4 per cent are sent across borders. Postal operators in the EU have typically enjoyed monopolies over all national letter deliveries and parcels up to 350 g. With the move to full liberalisation in 2003, new measures introduced by the European Commission aim to open the letters market in member countries to more competition. There are trends towards the liberalisation of letter delivery around the world. Three operators from different countries – the UK's Post Office, Dutch-owned TNT Post Group (TPG) and Singapore Post – are joining forces to offer a global mail delivery service, in direct competition with national operators. The alliance partners pool their deliveries for letters and piggy-back on each other's infrastructure in order to build a global network. TPG's global network was built up following its acquisition of Australian parcel and logistics company TNT in 1996, while Singapore Post will give the venture a strong Asian base. Although representing a small proportion of mail sent, the market for international mail, currently valued at £4.4 billion (€7.21 billion), is expected to grow. Whereas volume of personal letters is declining due to emails and faxes, the business mailshot market is growing. There are therefore tremendous opportunities for national postal service operators who are quick to take advantage of the increased commercial freedom brought by market liberalisation to expand their operations abroad.[32]

The rapidly expanding international marketplace provides many attractive opportunities for service firms. It also creates some special challenges, however. Service companies wanting to operate in other countries are not always welcomed with open arms. Whereas manufacturers usually face straightforward tariff, quota or currency restrictions when attempting to sell their products in another country, service providers are likely to face more subtle barriers. In some cases, rules and regulations affecting international services firms reflect the host country's traditions. In others, they appear to protect the country's own fledgling service industries from large global competitors with greater resources. In still other cases, however, the restrictions seem to have little purpose other than to make entry difficult for foreign service firms.

> Most of the industrialised nations want their banks, insurance companies, construction firms and other service providers to be allowed to move people, capital and technology around the globe unimpeded. Instead they face a bewildering complex of national regulations, most of them designed to guarantee jobs for local competitors. A Turkish law, for example, forbids international accounting firms to bring capital into the country to set up offices

> and requires them to use the names of local partners, rather than prestigious international ones, in their marketing. To audit the books of a multinational company's branch in Buenos Aires, an accountant must have the equivalent of a high-school education in Argentinian geography and history. India is perhaps the most [difficult] big economy in the world [to enter] these days . . . New Delhi prevents international insurance companies from selling property and casualty policies to the country's swelling business community or life insurance to its huge middle class.[33]

Clearly, service organisations face many difficulties when seeking to enter foreign markets. In recognition of the problems, recent rounds of the General Agreement on Tariffs and Trade (GATT) (see Chapter 6) have extended international trade rules to cover services in addition to manufactured goods. In time, new service agreements are expected to ease the barriers that limit such trade. Thus, despite the difficulties in international service marketing, the trend towards growth of global service companies will continue, especially in banking, telecommunications and professional services. Today, service firms are no longer simply following their manufacturing customers. Instead, many are taking the lead in international expansion.

Summary

Marketing has been broadened in recent years to cover services.

As we move towards a *world service economy*, marketers need to know more about marketing services. *Services* are products that consist of activities, benefits or satisfactions offered for sale that are essentially intangible. Services are characterised by five key characteristics. First, services are *intangible* – they cannot be seen, tasted, felt, heard or smelt. Services are *inseparable* from their service providers. Services are *variable* because their quality depends on the service provider as well as the environment surrounding the service delivery. Services are also *perishable*. As a result they cannot be stored, built up or back-ordered. Finally, service products often *do not result in* the *ownership* of anything. Each characteristic poses problems and requires strategies. Marketers have to find ways to make the service more tangible; to increase the productivity of providers who are inseparable from their products; to standardise the quality in the face of variability; and to improve demand shifts and supply capacities in the face of service perishability. In addition to the four Ps marketing approach, service organisations have to manage three additional Ps: *people*, *physical evidence* and *processes*.

Successful service companies focus attention on *both* customers and employees. They understand the *service–profit chain*, which links service firm profits with employee and customer satisfaction. Services marketing strategy calls not only for external marketing, but also for *internal marketing* to motivate employees, and for *interactive marketing* to create service delivery skills among service providers.

To succeed, service marketers have to excel in creating *competitive differentiation* and in managing service *quality* and *service productivity*. Service organisations can develop differentiated offerings, delivery or image. Service quality is tested at each service encounter. To maintain high service quality, managers have to determine *service quality* dimensions and identify *customers' expectations of service quality*. The gaps that exist between customers' expectations of service quality and the service quality experienced determine customer satisfaction.

Well-managed service organisations also reflect the following common practices: *customer obsession*, *top management commitment*, *high quality standards*, thorough *systems for monitoring service performance* and *customer complaints (good service recovery)* and *satisfying employees as well as customers*.

With their costs rising rapidly, service firms face great pressure to increase service productivity through hiring and fostering more skilful workers through *better selection and training*, *making quantity–quality trade-offs*, *'industrialising' the service*, *creating more effective services*, *substituting customer labour for service providers' labour* and *harnessing the power of technology*.

Finally, we addressed the marketing challenges facing service providers in international markets.

Discussing the issues

1. What are the primary differences between products and services? Use examples to illustrate the differences. Give examples of hybrid offers.

2. How might service organisations deal with the intangibility, inseparability, variability and perishability of the service they provide? In your answer, show how these characteristics impact the organisation's marketing approach.

3. Wresting an apology from an airline for a delayed flight or persuading your telecom service provider that it has overcharged is often easier said than done. Many firms do not have easy channels for customers to register complaints. How important is it for firms to have established procedures for capturing customer complaints? Suggest ways in which firms could improve their capacity to deal with customer complaints and convert dissatisfied customers into satisfied customers through effective service-recovery.

4. What are internal and interactive marketing? Give examples of how service firms or organisations might use these concepts to enhance their service–profit chain.

5. Globalisation presents both opportunities and challenges to service firms. Identify service sectors that are increasingly internationalising or globalising. What do you think are the greatest challenges facing firms within these sectors? Show how service management concepts such as the service–profit chain, internal marketing and interactive marketing should be applied to enhance service quality and delivery outcomes for international service organisations.

Applying the concepts

1. The core service in the airline industry is transportation. The 'problem-solving' benefit for the customer is travel from one place to another. To differentiate their services, airlines provide many additional benefits. If you intend to fly from one country to another within Europe you might consider KLM Royal Dutch Airlines, British Airways or Lufthansa. Review the websites of these airlines and complete the table to evaluate their services.

	KLM Royal Dutch Airlines www.klm.com	British Airways www.british-airways.com	Lufthansa www.lufthansa.com
Many destinations?			
Attractive frequent-flyer programme?			
Other service features			
Evidence of service quality			
Evidence of competitive positioning strategy			
Ways customers can give feedback to company at site			

(a) How would you classify airlines using consumer product categories: convenience, shopping, speciality or unsought products?

(b) Which airline brand name best conveys a quality image to you?

(c) How does each airline differentiate itself from the others: KLM? British Airways? Lufthansa?

(d) Which airline would you choose for your European travel? Why?

2. Perishability is very important in the airline industry: unsold seats are gone for ever, and too many unsold seats mean large losses. With computerised ticketing, airlines can easily use pricing to deal with perishability and variations in demand.

(a) Call a travel agent or use an online service that is accessible to check airline fares. Get prices on the same route for 60 days in advance, two weeks, one week and today. Is there a clear pattern to the fares?

(b) When a store is overstocked on ripe fruit, it may lower the price to sell out quickly. What are airlines doing to their prices as the seats get close to 'perishing'? Why? What would you recommend as a pricing strategy to increase total revenues?

References

1. D.F. Burgess, 'Is trade liberalisation in the service sector in the national interest?', *Oxford Economic Papers*, **47**, 1, 1995, pp. 60–78; Ian N. Lings and Roger F. Brooks, 'Implementing and measuring effectiveness of internal marketing', *Journal of Marketing Management*, **14** (1998), pp. 325–51.

2. 'The manufacturing myth', *The Economist* (19 March 1994), pp. 98–9; Ronald Henkoff, 'Service is everybody's business', *Fortune* (27 June 1994), pp. 48–60.

3. See Henkoff, op. cit.; Adrian Palmer and Catherine Cole, *Services Marketing: Principles and practice* (Upper Saddle River, NJ: Prentice Hall, 1995), pp. 56–60; Valerie Zeithaml and Mary Jo Bitner, *Services Marketing* (New York: McGraw-Hill, 1996), pp. 8–9; and Michael van Biema and Bruce Greenwald, 'Managing our way to higher service-sector productivity', *Harvard Business Review* (July–August 1997), pp. 87–95.

4. Philip Manchester, 'A golden opportunity for internet-based services', FT-IT Review E-Business: Services, *Financial Times* (3 May 2000), p. XVI.

5. For more on definitions and classifications of services, see Christopher H. Lovelock, *Services Marketing*, 3rd edn (Upper Saddle River, NJ: Prentice Hall, 1996) and John E. Bateson, *Managing Services Marketing: Text and readings* (Hinsdale, IL: Dryden Press, 1989).

6. See Leonard L. Berry, 'Services marketing is different', *Business* (May–June 1980), pp. 24–30; Karl Albrecht, *At America's Service* (Homewood, IL: Dow-Jones-Irwin, 1988); William H. Davidow and Bro Uttal, *Total Customer Service: The ultimate weapon* (New York: Harper & Row, 1989).

7. See Theodore Levitt, 'Marketing intangible products and product intangibles', *Harvard Business Review* (May–June 1981), pp. 94–102.

8. Trevor Watkins, 'The marketing hybrid: Financial services in Europe', *Marketing Insights* (October–December 2002), pp. 11–13; see also Christopher Brown-Humes, 'Internet banking. Clients engaged in revolution', in Financial Times Survey: Finland, *Financial Times* (10 July 2000), p. VI; James Mackintosh, 'The bank is dead . . .', in FT Life on the Net, Chapter 8, p. 14, *Financial Times* (5 September 2000); John Wilmon, 'Branch equity', *Financial Times* (7 July 2000), p. 18. For an excellent survey of online finance, see 'A survey of online finance. The virtual threat', *The Economist* (20 May 2000). Further details are available from www.ft.com/lifeonthenet.

9. For more discussion, see James L. Heskett, 'Lessons in the service sector', *Harvard Business Review* (March–April 1987), pp. 122–4; E. Gummesson, *Quality Management in Service Organisations* (New York: International Service Quality Association, St John's University, 1993).

10. 'Service with a smile', *The Economist* (25 April 1998), pp. 85–6.

11. Carol Krol, 'Case study: Club Med uses e-mail to pitch unsold, discount packages', *Advertising Age* (14 December 1998), p. 40.

12. Eric van Heck, 'The cutting edge in auctions', *Harvard Business Review* (March–April 2000), p. 189; John-Paul Flintoff, 'Pay and bouquet', *The Business FT Weekend Magazine* (16 September 2000), pp. 24–5.

13. Leslie de Chernatony and Malcolm McDonald, *Creating Powerful Brands in Consumer, Services and Industrial Markets*, 2nd edn (Oxford: Butterworth-Heinemann, 1998).

14. See James L. Heskett, Thomas O. Jones, Gary W. Loveman, W. Earl Sasser, Jr, and Leonard A. Schlesinger, 'Putting the service–profit chain to work', *Harvard Business Review* (March–April 1994), pp. 164–74; and James L. Heskett, W. Earl Sasser, Jr, and Leonard A. Schlesinger, *The Service Profit Chain: How leading companies link profit and growth to loyalty, satisfaction, and value* (New York: Free Press, 1997). Also see Eugene W. Anderson and Vikas Mittal, 'Strengthening the satisfaction–profit chain', *Journal of Service Research* (November 2000), pp. 107–20.

15. For more reading on internal and interactive marketing, see Christian Gronroos, 'A service quality model and its marketing implications', *European Journal of Marketing*, 18, 4 (1984), pp. 36–44; Christian Gronroos, 'Internal marketing – theory and practice', in T.M. Bloch, G.D. Upah and V.A. Zeithaml (eds), *Services Marketing in a Changing Environment* (American Marketing Association, 1985); see also Neeru Malhotra and A. Mukherjee, 'Analysing the commitment–service quality relationship: a comparative study of retail banking call centres and branches', *Journal of Marketing Management* 19 (2003), pp. 941–71; Ian N. Lings, 'Balancing internal and external market orientation', *Journal of Marketing Management* 15 (1999), pp. 239–63; Richard J. Varey, 'A model of internal marketing for building and sustaining a competitive advantage', *Journal of Marketing Management*, 11 (January/February/April 1995), pp. 41–54.

16. Amon Cohen, 'Bed time at Virgin', *Financial Times* (24 July 2000), p. 19.

17. B.H. Booms and M.J. Bitner, 'Marketing strategies and organisational structures for service firms', in J. Donnelly and W.R. Gearoge (eds), *Marketing of Services* (Chicago: American Marketing Association, 1981), pp. 47–51.

18. Peter Purton, 'Telcos reinvent their businesses' and 'The virtual telco', FT Telecoms Survey, *Financial Times* (21 June 2000), pp. v and vi respectively; Joia Shillingford, 'How to build a telecoms brand', Financial Times Survey, *ibid.*, p. vi.

19. Alan Pike, 'The search for value in town halls', *Financial Times* (12 February 1998), p. 10.

20. See Joseph Cronin, Jr and Steven A. Taylor, 'Measuring service quality: a re-examination and extension', *Journal of Marketing* (July 1992), pp. 55–68; David Ballantyne, Martin Christopher and Adrian Payne, 'Improving the quality of services marketing: service (re)design is the critical link', *Journal of Marketing Management* (January/February/April 1995), pp. 7–24; Valerie A. Zeithaml,

Leonard L. Berry and A. Parasuraman, 'Services competitiveness: an Anglo-US study', *Business Strategy Review*, **8**, 1 (1997), pp. 7–22.

21. John Paul Newport, 'American Express: service that sells', *Fortune* (20 November 1989), p. 20; Frank Rose, 'Now quality means service too', *Fortune* (22 April 1991), pp. 97–108.

22. C. Gronroos, *Strategic Management and Marketing in the Service Sector* (Bromley: Chartwell-Bratt, 1985), pp. 38–40; see also A. Parasuraman, Valarie A. Zeithaml and Leonard L. Berry, 'A conceptual model of service quality and its implications for future research', *Journal of Marketing*, **49** (Fall 1985), pp. 41–50; Valerie Zeithaml, Leonard L. Berry and A. Parasuraman, *Delivering Service Quality: Balancing customer perceptions and expectations* (New York: Free Press, 1990); A. Parasuraman, Valerie Zeithaml and Leonard Berry, 'Reassessment of expectations as a comparison standard in measuring service quality: implications for further research', *Journal of Marketing*, **58** (January 1994), pp. 111–24; Michael K. Brady and J. Joseph Crorin, Jr, 'Some new thoughts on conceptualizing perceived service quality', *Journal of Marketing*, **65** (July 2001), pp. 34–49.

23. Parasuraman *et al.*, 'A conceptual model', op. cit.; Leonard L. Berry and A. Parasuraman, *Marketing Services: Competing through quality* (New York: Free Press, 1991), p. 16.

24. See James L. Heskett, W. Earl Sasser, Jr and Christopher W.L. Hart, *Service Breakthroughs* (New York: Free Press, 1990).

25. See Erika Rasmusson, 'Winning back angry customers', *Sales & Marketing Management* (October 1997), p. 131; Stephen S. Tax, Stephen W. Brown and Murali Chandrashekaran, 'Customer evaluations of service complaint experiences: Implications for relationship marketing', *Journal of Marketing* (April 1998), pp. 60–76; Stephen W. Brown, 'Practicing best-in-class service recovery', *Marketing Management* (Summer 2000), pp. 8–9; James G. Maxham III, 'Service recovery's influence on consumer satisfaction, positive word-of-mouth, and purchase intentions', *Journal of Business Research* (October 2001), p. 11; and David E. Bowen, 'Internal service recovery: developing a new construct', *Measuring Business Excellence* (2002), p. 47.

26. See Leonard A. Schlesinger and James L. Heskett, 'The service-driven service company', *Harvard Business Review* (September–October 1991), pp. 72–81; and Michael van Biema and Bruce Greenwald, 'Managing our way to higher service-sector productivity', *Harvard Business Review* (July–August 1997), pp. 87–95.

27. Ross Tieman, 'Customer service. Secret of competitive advantage', *Financial Times Special Report FT Management: Customer Relations* (19 March 2003), p. II.

28. Tom Hayes, 'Services go international', *Marketing News* (14 March 1994), pp. 14–15; 'Schools brief: trade winds', *The Economist* (8 November 1997), pp. 124–5; 'Trade in services', *The Economist* (5 February 2000), pp. 95–6.

29. For an international perspective on services marketing management, see Hans Kasper, Piet van Helsdingen and Wouter de Vries, Jr, *Services Marketing Management* (Chichester: Wiley, 1999).

30. Michael R. Czinkota and Ilkka A. Ronkainen, *International Marketing*, 2nd edn (Chicago, IL: Dryden, 1990), p. 679.

31. Barney Jopson, 'Soft-soaping the consumer', *Financial Times* (27 February 2003), p. 13; Nicholas George, 'Fashions and costs cut to a better fit', *Financial Times* (7 March 2003), p. 13; Andrew Ward, 'An octopus in the shopping trolley', *Financial Times* (11 January 2003), p. 9; Tony Lisanti, 'Europe's abuzz over Wal-Mart', *Discount Stores News* (3 May 1999), p. 11; 'Top 200 global retailers', *Stores* (January 1998), pp. S5–S12.

32. See Louella Miles, 'Let the battle commence', *Marketing Business* (September 2000), pp. 16–18; Thorold Barker, 'Post Office set for global alliance', *Financial Times* (9 March 2000), p. 25.

33. Lee Smith, 'What's at stake in the trade talks', *Fortune* (27 August 1990), pp. 76–7.

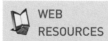

WEB RESOURCES

For additional classic case studies and Internet exercises, visit www.pearsoned.co.uk/kotler

Concluding concepts 15
The Ritz

The Ritz is not just a hotel, it is style, sophistication, wealth, all mixed with fun and gaiety. Since Irving Berlin wrote 'Putting on the Ritz' legions of artists, from Ella Fitzgerald to Judy Garland, have taken up the refrain. Whole albums are still dedicated to the theme that rose in the 1920s but from London to Boston, from Bali to Bahrain, the Ritz retains its glitter. The latest place to savour is the Ritz-Carlton Berlin on the central Potsdamer Platz – offering a special introductory price per room of only €165! The hotel chain achieved this repeated success by continuing to try hard at catering for the needs of the most demanding customers of all – the rich.

The Ritz is now part of the Ritz-Carlton chain of luxury hotels that caters to the top 5 per cent of corporate and leisure travellers. The company's 'Credo' sets lofty customer service goals: 'The Ritz-Carlton Hotel is a place where the genuine care and comfort of our guests is our highest mission. We pledge to provide the finest personal service and facilities for our guests who will always enjoy a warm, relaxed yet refined ambience. The Ritz-Carlton experience enlivens the senses, instils well-being, and fulfils even the unexpressed wishes and needs of our guests.' The company's Web page concludes: 'Here a calm settles over you. The world, so recently at your door, is now at your feet.'

> Staff learn that anyone who receives a customer complaint *owns* that complaint until it's resolved.

The Credo is more than just words on paper – Ritz-Carlton delivers on its promises. In surveys of departing guests, some 95 per cent report that they've had a truly memorable experience. In fact, at Ritz-Carlton, exceptional service encounters have become almost commonplace. Take the experiences of Nancy and Harvey Heffner of Manhattan, who stayed at the Ritz-Carlton Naples, in Naples, Florida (recently rated the best hotel in the United States, fourth best in the world, by *Travel & Leisure* magazine). As reported in the *New York Times*:

'The hotel is elegant and beautiful', Mrs Heffner said, 'but more important is the beauty expressed by the staff. They can't do enough to please you.' When the couple's son became sick last year in Naples, the hotel staff brought him hot tea with honey at all hours of the night, she said. When Mr Heffner had to fly home on business for a day and his return flight was delayed, a driver for the hotel waited in the lobby most of the night.

Such personal, high-quality service has also made the Ritz-Carlton a favourite among conventioneers. 'They not only treat us like kings when we hold our top-level meetings in their hotels, but we just never get any complaints', comments one convention planner. 'Perhaps the biggest challenge a planner faces when recommending the Ritz-Carlton at Half Moon Bay to the boss, board and attendees is convincing them that meeting there truly is work', says another. 'The . . . first-rate catering and service-oriented convention services staff [and] the Ritz-Carlton's ambiance and beauty – the elegant, Grand Dame-style lodge, nestled on a bluff between two championship golf courses overlooking the Pacific Ocean – makes a day's work there seem anything but.'

In 1992, Ritz-Carlton became the first hotel company to win the Malcolm Baldrige National Quality Award. Since its incorporation in 1983, the company has received virtually every major award that the hospitality industry bestows. More importantly, service quality has resulted in high customer retention: more than 90 per cent of Ritz-Carlton customers return. And despite its hefty room rates, the chain enjoys a 70 per cent occupancy rate, almost nine points above the industry average.

Most of the responsibility for keeping guests satisfied falls to Ritz-Carlton's customer-contact employees. Thus, the hotel chain takes great care in selecting its personnel. 'We want only people who care about people', notes the company's vice president of quality. Once selected, employees are given intensive training in the art of coddling customers. New employees attend a two-day orientation, in which top management drums into them the '20 Ritz-Carlton Basics'. Basic number one: 'The Credo will be known, owned, and energized by all employees.'

Employees are taught to do everything they can never to lose a guest. 'There's no negotiating at Ritz-Carlton when it comes to solving customer problems', says the quality executive. Staff learn that *anyone* who receives a customer complaint *owns* that complaint until it's resolved (Ritz-Carlton Basic number 8). They are trained to drop whatever they're doing to help a customer – no matter what they're doing or what their department. Ritz-Carlton employees are empowered to handle problems on the spot, without consulting higher-ups. Each employee can spend up to €2,000 to redress a guest grievance, and each is allowed to break from his or her routine for as long as needed to make a guest happy. 'We master customer satisfaction at the individual level', adds the executive. 'This is our most sensitive listening post . . . our early warning system.' Thus, while competitors are still reading guest comment cards to learn about customer problems, Ritz-Carlton has already resolved them.

Ritz-Carlton instils a sense of pride in its employees. 'You serve', they are told, 'but you are not servants.' The company motto states, 'We are ladies and gentlemen serving ladies and gentlemen'. Employees understand their role in Ritz-Carlton's success. 'We might not be able to afford a hotel like this,' says employee Tammy Patton, 'but we can make it so people who can afford it will want to keep coming here.'

And so they do. When it comes to customer satisfaction, no detail is too small. Customer-contact people are taught to greet guests warmly and sincerely, using guest names when possible. They learn to use the proper language with guests – phrases such as *good morning, certainly, I'll be happy to, welcome back*, and *my pleasure*, never *Hi* or *How's it going*? The Ritz-Carlton Basics urge employees to escort guests to another area of the hotel rather than pointing out directions, to answer the phone within three rings and with a 'smile', and to take pride and care in their personal appearance. As the general manager of the Ritz-Carlton Naples, puts it, 'When you invite guests to your house, you want everything to be perfect.'

Ritz-Carlton recognizes and rewards employees who perform feats of outstanding service. Under its 5-Star Awards program, outstanding performers are nominated by peers and managers, and winners receive plaques at dinners celebrating their achievements. For on-the-spot recognition, managers award Gold Standard Coupons, redeemable for items in the gift shop and free weekend

stays at the hotel. Ritz-Carlton further rewards and motivates its employees with events such as Super Sports Day, an employee talent show, luncheons celebrating employee anniversaries, a family picnic, and special themes in employee dining rooms. As a result, Ritz-Carlton's employees appear to be just as satisfied as its customers are. Employee turnover is less than 30 per cent a year, compared with 45 per cent at other luxury hotels.

Ritz-Carlton's success is based on a simple philosophy: to take care of customers, you must first take care of those who take care of customers. Satisfied employees deliver high service value, which then creates satisfied customers. Satisfied customers, in turn, create sales and profits for the company.

Questions

1. Most people see a Ritz-Carlton hotel as a swanky building on a prime site, such as London's Piccadilly, but is the structure the essence of the hotel chain's success?
2. What accounts for the Ritz-Carlton's continued success?
3. Even the Ritz does not charge €2,000 to stay, so how can the company justify allowing employees to spend 'up to €2,000 to redress a guest grievance'?
4. What are the key determinants of the service quality perceived by the Ritz-Carlton's customers?
5. To serve its globe-hopping customers the hotel chain has to provide the same level of service 'from London to Boston, from Bali to Bahrain'. What are the barriers to offering services that are 'the same' or of 'the same quality' within so many cultures? How can such uniform service quality be achieved?

SOURCES: Quotes and other information from Edwin McDowell, 'Ritz-Carlton's keys to good service', *New York Times* (31 March 1993), p. D1; Howard Schlossberg, 'Measuring customer satisfaction is easy to do – until you try', *Marketing News* (26 April 1993), pp. 5, 8; Ginger Conlon, 'True Romance', *Sales & Marketing Management* (May 1996), pp. 85–90; 'The Ritz-Carlton, Half Moon Bay', *Successful Meetings* (November 2001), p. 40; *Wall Street Journal* (20 June 2002), p. D1; N.V. Henderson, 'Ritz-Carlton Las Vegas captures AAA Five Diamond Award within months of opening', *Business Wire* (17 November 2003); *Wall Street Journal*, 'Ritz-Carlton tops Four Seasons' (27 August 2003); *AP Worldstream*, 'New Ritz-Carlton opens on Berlin's central Potsdamer Platz' (11 January 2004); 'Putting on the Ritz: Capital sings Irving Berlin', *Capital* (1992); www.ritzcarlton.com (February 2004).

Price: value plus a reasonable sum for the
wear and tear of conscience in demanding it.

AMBROSE PIERCE

Price

Chapter 16 Pricing

IN PART SIX WE COVER an element of the marketing mix that is both easy and
expensive to manipulate – price.

Price cutting is an easy way to attract customers quickly, but a poor route to long-
term market success. The reason is that giving a 10 per cent price cut to a customer
can mean taking a 50 per cent cut in profits. The industrialist Philip Armour
explained that businesses often resort to price-cutting: 'Anybody can cut prices,
but it takes brains to make a better article.'

Many internal and external pressures influence the price decision, from internal
costs to government legislation. The examination of these in **Chapter 16** leads to
value-based pricing, where a customer's perception of price, rather than costs, drives
price. We then look at pricing strategies under a variety of situations, such as when
launching a product, when changing prices and when pricing within a product range.

DOLMIO

£1.39

Promotional Price 27.8p per 100g.
Promotional Price £2.89 per kg.

Solero EXOTIC

3x
3x

£1.99

Promotional Price 34.95p per 100ml.
Promotional Price £3.51 per kg.

THIN crispy Pepperoni

£1.99

KIEVS GARLIC BUTTER
2 CHICKEN BREAST
Valley
Sun Valley

£1.99

BUY ONE GET ONE FREE

Excludes R.O.I. While stocks last.
Maximum 3 deals per customer.
Offers end 19.05.01.

Iceland.co.uk

Are we doing a deal or are we doing a deal...

Buy sheep, sell deer.

ANON

Pricing

Chapter objectives

After reading this chapter, you should be able to:

- Identify and define the internal and external factors affecting pricing decisions.
- Contrast general approaches to setting prices.
- Describe pricing strategies for imitative and new products and know when to use them.
- Explain how pricing is influenced by the product mix and show how companies determine a set of prices that maximises the profits of the total product mix.
- Discuss how companies adapt prices to meet different market circumstances and opportunities.
- Discuss the key issues relating to initiating and responding to price changes.

Mini Contents List

Prelude case The Oresund Bridge: over or under, down and out, again and again

MARIA DEL MAR SOUZA FONTAN
Aston Business School, UK

This time it was supposed to be different. Governments have no problem commissioning grand projects that go under or over the sea, but they do have problems in keeping costs down and getting people to use the facility. Within a year of being opened it looked like the Oresund Bridge, which crosses the Oresund Straits between Copenhagen in Denmark and Malmö in Sweden, was going the way of similar attempts to join up bits of land.

There is a pattern in the joining of conspicuous bits of land:

1. The idea is so obvious that people start thinking about joining them long before the technology. Some designs for an Oresund Bridge date from 1886 and Napoleon planned to attack Britain using a tunnel under the English Channel.

2. Governments take over the prestige project that suffers cost overruns.

3. Too few people use the construction to cover its cost.

4. Some form of regular subsidy is sought.

> Some designs for an Oresund Bridge date from 1886 and Napoleon planned to attack Britain using a tunnel under the English Channel.

The poor management structure during the construction of the Channel Tunnel linking England and France resulted in a two-year delay and a cost that reached €11 billion compared with the originally estimated €4.7 billion. Forecasts of the level of traffic using the tunnel were too optimistic, resulting in financial problems for Eurotunnel, the Channel Tunnel's operator. London & Continental, the consortium awarded the contract to build and operate the high-speed railway between London and the Channel Tunnel, was also in trouble, the number of passengers between London, Paris and Brussels being 50 per cent below forecasts. Eurotunnel is now seeking wide-ranging changes to the way the tunnel is funded to overcome 'fundamental structural problems in the cross-channel rail industry'. Basically, not enough people use the tunnel. Cross-channel travel is up but advanced ferries and luxurious ferries are biting increasingly into the market and people are increasingly using low-cost easyJet and Ryanair. A particular change in the market is the number of passengers who fly and then hire a car rather than shipping their own.

Embarrassing as they are, the Channel Tunnel's problems were minor compared with Japan's recent bridge building. Inaugurated in 1998, the Akashi Kaikyo Bridge is the longest suspension bridge in the world. It crosses the Akashi Straits and connects the city of Kobe to Awaji Island, and cost ¥800 billion (€8.5 billion). However, spectacular as it is to behold, locals and Japanese taxpayers wonder what it is for. Authorities claimed that some 37,000 cars would use the bridge each day, although only 100–200 a day ever used the ferry between Kobe and Awaji Island. The bridge was to bring all manner of economic opportunities to the residents of Awaji and the equally impoverished island of Shikoku. Although a great aesthetic and engineering success, people still do not want to go to Awaji. After an initial burst of enthusiasm, daily use remains little above the numbers who used the ferry.

Shortly after opening, it looked like the Oresund bridge-cum-tunnel was going the same way as its predecessors. Not only was its use far below forecast but also it looked like its use could go even lower. Novo Nordisk, a Danish drug firm that moved its HQ to Malmö to take advantage of the 'bridge effect', urged its Danish staff to limit their trips to Malmö by working more from home. Swedish furniture chain IKEA went even further and banned its employees from using the bridge on company business. They are told to make the crossing using the ferry. The ferry is a lot slower than the bridge but also a lot less expensive.

The Danish and Swedish governments initiated the Oresund Bridge project in 1991. The aim was to build a fixed link across the Oresund Region, which comprises Zealand, Lolland-Falster and Bornholm, on the Danish side, as well as Scania and Sweden. The construction of this bridge was to provide stronger and more intense cooperation regarding economy, education, research and culture between the two nations, as well as constituting the link to the European mainland for Sweden. In July 2000, the €1.5 billion bridge-cum-tunnel opened to traffic. The investment was to be recouped from the thousands of cars crossing the bridge every day. The link is changing local life. More Swedes are visiting the cafés and galleries of Copenhagen although Malmö does not seem so attractive to the Danes.

Economic reality is proving to be well short of expectations. Peaking at 20,000 crossings a day soon after opening, traffic fell to 6,000. Seventy-five per cent more people cross the straits than did before the construction but numbers are way below target. An advertising campaign aims to attract more people to use the bridge but price seems to be the problem. With many fewer cars

Exhibit 16.1 Oresund Bridge typical pricing (€)

Vehicle type	Length	Basic price	4-trip card	10-trip card	Business rate 7,501–10,000 trips (per trip)
Motorcycle	–	17	34	104	–
Private	Up to 6 m	32	64	192	12.10
Private	Up to 9 m	64	128	192	26.89
Lorries	9 m to 12 m	82.80	–	–	38.31

than expected crossing the bridge, the Danish and Swedish governments have to find a route to a better possible return on investment, by changing their pricing strategy.

There are currently two types of fares, depending on whether drivers pay at the toll station or whether they sign an agreement which offers discounts for frequent travellers. Motorists who cross the bridge only a few times a year will pay 'the cash price', whilst those who use the bridge regularly will be in position to benefit considerably from a subscription agreement (Exhibit 16.1). Following the tradition when bits of land are attempts to overcome 'fundamental structural problems' faced by the bridge, the Danish tax minister is proposing a tax deduction for people to cummute across the bridge in order to encourage greater use.[1]

Questions

1. Why do you think the forecasts for national or international prestige projects, including the Anglo-French Concorde, Britain's Millennium Dome and Humber Bridge, are so far off target? Is price *the* problem?

2. Since it looks like these prestige projects will never cover their costs, never mind produce a financial return on investment made, what criteria should be used in evaluating pricing alternatives?

3. Suggest an alternative pricing schedule for the Oresund Bridge, giving the reasons for your pricing decision.

Introduction

Companies today face a fierce and fast-changing pricing environment. The recent economic downturn has put many companies in a 'pricing vice'. One analyst sums it up this way: 'They have virtually no pricing power. It's impossible to raise prices, and often, the pressure to slash them continues unabated. The pricing pinch is affecting business across the spectrum of manufacturing and services – everything from chemicals and autos to hoteliers and phone services.'[2] It seems that almost every company is slashing prices, and that is hurting their profits.

Yet, cutting prices is often not the best answer. Reducing prices unnecessarily can lead to lost profits and damaging price wars. It can signal to customers that price is more important than the brand. Instead, companies should 'sell value, not price'.[3] They should persuade customers that paying a higher price for the company's brand is justified by the greater value it delivers. Most customers will gladly pay a fair price in exchange for real value. The challenge is to find the price that will let the company make a fair profit by harvesting the customer value it creates. According to one pricing expert, pricing involves 'harvesting your profit potential'.[4] If effective product development, promotion and distribution sow the seeds of business success, effective pricing is the harvest. Firms successful at creating customer value with the other marketing mix activities must still capture some of this value in the prices they earn. Yet, despite its importance, many firms do not handle pricing well.

In this chapter, we will focus on the problem of setting prices and the development of pricing strategies and programmes. First, we define price and evaluate the internal and external factors that marketers must consider when setting prices. Next, we examine general pricing approaches. Finally, we address pricing strategies available to marketers – new-product pricing strategies, product mix pricing strategies, price adjustment strategies based on buyer and situational factors, and price reaction strategies.

What is price?

All products and services have a price, just as they have a value. Many non-profit and all profit-making organisations must also set prices, be they for crossing some water (as in the prelude case) or the price of Madonna's Brixton Academy comeback celebration-cum-concert tickets for those who cannot get them officially. *Pricing* is controversial and goes by many names:

> Price is all around us. You pay *rent* for your apartment, *tuition* for your education and a *fee* to your physician or dentist. The airline, railway, taxi and bus companies charge you a *fare*; the local utilities call their price a *rate*; and the local bank charges you *interest* for the money you borrow . . . The guest lecturer charges an *honorarium* to tell you about a government official who took a *bribe* to help a shady character steal *dues* collected by a trade association. Clubs or societies to which you belong may make a special *assessment* to pay unusual expenses. Your regular lawyer may ask for a *retainer* to cover her services. The 'price' of an executive is a *salary*, the price of a salesperson may be a *commission* and the price of a worker is a *wage*. Finally, although economists would disagree, many of us feel that *income taxes* are the price we pay for the privilege of making money.[5]

In the narrowest sense, **price** is the amount of money charged for a product or service. More broadly, price is the sum of all the values that consumers exchange for the benefits of having or using the product or service. In the past, price has been the major factor affecting buyer choice. This is still the case in poorer countries, among less affluent groups and with commodity products. However, non-price factors have become more important in buyer-choice behaviour in recent decades.

Historically, prices were set by negotiation between buyers and sellers. Through bargaining, they would arrive at an acceptable price. Individual buyers paid different prices for the same products, depending on their needs and bargaining skills. By contrast, fixed-price policies – setting *one* price for *all* buyers – is a relatively modern idea that evolved with the development of large-scale retailing at the end of the nineteenth century. F.W. Woolworth and other retailers advertised a 'strictly one-price policy' because they carried so many items and had so many employees.

Now, some 100 years later, the Internet promises to reverse the fixed pricing trend and take us back to an era of **dynamic pricing** – charging different prices depending on individual customers and situations. The Internet, corporate networks and wireless communications are connecting sellers and buyers as never before. Websites such as Compare.Net and PriceScan.com allow buyers to compare products and prices quickly and easily. Online auction sites such as eBay.com and Amazon.com Auctions make it easy for buyers and sellers to negotiate prices on thousands of items – from refurbished computers to antique tin trains. Sites like Priceline even let customers set their own prices. At the same time, new technologies allow sellers to collect detailed data about customers' buying habits, preferences and even spending limits, so they can tailor their products and prices.[6]

Price is the only element in the marketing mix that produces revenue; all other elements represent costs. Price is also one of the most flexible elements of the marketing mix. Unlike product features and channel commitments, price can be changed quickly. At the same time, pricing and price competition is the number one problem facing many marketers. Yet, many companies do not handle pricing well. One frequent problem is that companies are too quick to cut prices in order to gain a sale rather than convincing buyers that their products or services are worth a higher price. Other common mistakes are: pricing that is too cost-oriented rather than customer-value oriented; prices that are not revised often enough to reflect market changes; pricing that does not take the rest of the marketing mix into account; and prices that are not varied enough for different products, market segments and buying occasions.

Price—The amount of money charged for a product or service, or the sum of the values that consumers exchange for the benefits of having or using the product or service.

Dynamic pricing—Charging different prices depending on individual customers and situations.

Factors to consider when setting prices

A company's pricing decisions are affected both by internal company factors and by external environmental factors (see Figure 16.1).[7]

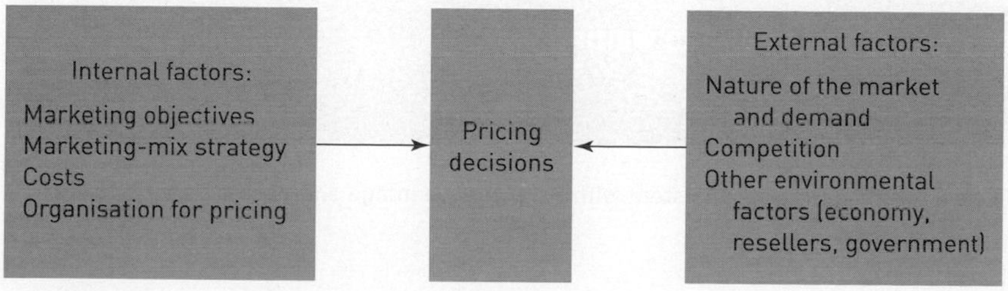

Figure 16.1 **Factors affecting price decisions**

Internal factors affecting pricing decisions

Internal factors affecting pricing include the company's marketing objectives, marketing-mix strategy, costs and organisation.

Marketing objectives

Before setting price, the company must decide on its strategy for the product. If the company has selected its target market and positioning carefully, then its marketing-mix strategy, including price, will be fairly straightforward. For example, when Toyota decided to produce its Lexus cars to compete with European luxury cars in the higher-income segment, this required charging a high price. Sleep Inn and Travelodge position themselves as motels that provide economical rooms for budget-minded travellers, a position that requires charging a low price. Thus pricing strategy is largely determined by past decisions on market positioning.

At the same time, the company may seek additional objectives. A firm that has clearly defined its objectives will find it easier to set price. Examples of common objectives are *survival*, *current profit maximisation*, *market-share maximisation* and *product-quality leadership*.

Companies set *survival* as their fundamental objective if they are troubled by too much capacity, heavy competition or changing consumer wants. To keep a factory going, a company may set a low price through periods of low demand, hoping to increase prices when demand

Marketing objectives: the price that BMW has set for its new 6 Series Coupé is consistent with its exclusive image and positioning – a car you've waited long enough for will not come 'cheap'.

SOURCE: BMW (GB) Ltd. *Agency*: WCRS/Saatchi and Saatchi.

recovers. In the public sector, such as with Britain's Millennium Dome, *survival* became the issue when government tired of demands for subsidy. In this case, profits are less important than survival. As long as their prices cover variable costs and some fixed costs, they can stay in business.[8] However, survival is only a short-term objective. In the long run, the firm must learn how to add value or face extinction.

Many companies use *current profit maximisation* as their pricing goal. They estimate what demand and costs will be at different prices and choose the price that will produce the maximum current profit, cash flow or return on investment. In all cases, the company wants current financial results rather than long-run performance. Other companies want to obtain *market-share leadership*. They believe that the company with the largest market share will enjoy the lowest costs and highest long-run profit. To become the market-share leader, these firms set prices as low as possible.

A variation of this objective is to pursue a specific *market-share gain*. Say the company wants to increase its market share from 10 per cent to 15 per cent in one year. It will search for the price and marketing programme that will achieve this goal.

> Digital television transmission is set to make the current analogue television as outdated as 16 mm cine film or vinyl albums. It produces cinema-quality pictures while cramming hundreds of channels through the wavebands needed for a dozen analogue transmissions. Seeing its mould-breaking potential, satellite television company BSkyB was determined to fight for market leadership of digital television transmission. BSkyB's consortium of BT, HSBC and Matsushita subsidised its TV set-top converters by €1 billion, almost giving them away although they cost over €500 each to produce.

In pricing its set-top boxes below cost, BSkyB aims to increase its market share and long-term profitability by considering the long-term cash flows that result from the customer's subscription. In this case the income will come from access charges to BSkyB's channels.

A company might decide that it wants to achieve *product-quality leadership*. This normally calls for charging a high price to cover such quality and the high cost of R&D:

> For example, Jaguar's limited edition XJ220 sold for £400,000 (€600,000) each, but had wealthy customers queuing to buy one. Pitney Bowes pursues a product-quality leadership strategy for its fax equipment. While Sharp, Canon and other competitors fight over the low-price fax machine market with machines selling at around €600, Pitney Bowes targets large corporations with machines selling at about €6,000. As a result, it captured some 45 per cent of the large-corporation fax niche. Less exotically, at the height of the 1990s baked bean price wars, Heinz's strategy was to set the price at 2p above the price of supermarket own-label baked beans. As retailers slashed prices, so did Heinz. At one point, retailers' cheapest can of beans cost as little as 3 pence. Heinz realised that this was crazy. So, it decided to price up rather than down. The company invested in the quality of the product; it added ring-pull ends on the cans for easy opening and reinvested in TV advertising. Heinz's market share went up.[9]

A company might also use price to attain other more specific objectives. It can set prices low to prevent competition from entering the market or set prices at competitors' levels to stabilise the market:

> Leading UK grocery retailers Sainsbury and Tesco used 'Essentials' and 'Everyday super value range' campaigns to counter the attack of discounters Aldi and Netto on the UK market. Originally projected to take 20 per cent of the grocery market by 2000, forecasters later predicted the discounters would take only 12 per cent.[10]

Prices can be set to keep the loyalty and support of resellers or to avoid government intervention. Prices can be reduced temporarily to create excitement for a product or to draw more customers into a retail store. One product may be priced to help the sales of other products in the company's line. Thus pricing may play an important role in helping to accomplish the company's objectives at many levels.

Non-profit and public organisations may adopt a number of other pricing objectives. A university aims for *partial cost recovery*, knowing that it must rely on private funds or endowments and public grants to cover the remaining costs. A non-profit hospital may aim for *full cost recovery* in its pricing. A non-profit theatre company may price its productions to fill the maximum number of theatre seats. A social service agency may set a *social price* geared to the varying income situations of different clients.

Marketing-mix strategy

Price is only one of the marketing-mix tools that a company uses to achieve its marketing objectives. Price decisions must be coordinated with product design, distribution and promotion decisions to form a consistent and effective marketing programme. Decisions made for other marketing-mix variables may affect pricing decisions. For example, producers using many resellers that are expected to support and promote their products may have to build larger reseller margins into their prices. The decision to position the product on high-performance quality will mean that the seller must charge a higher price to cover higher costs.

Companies often make their pricing decisions first and then base other marketing-mix decisions on the prices that they want to charge. Here, price is a crucial product-positioning factor that defines the product's market, competition and design. The intended price determines what product features can be offered and what production costs can be incurred.

Many firms support such price-positioning strategies with a technique called **target costing**, a potent strategic weapon. Target costing reverses the usual process of first designing a new product, determining its cost and then asking 'Can we sell it for that?'. Instead, it starts with a target cost and works back:

Target costing—A technique to support pricing decisions, which starts with deciding a target cost for a new product and works back to designing the product.

> When starting up, Swatch surveyed the market and identified an unserved segment of watch buyers who wanted 'a low-cost fashion accessory that also keeps time'. Armed with this information about market needs, Swatch set out to give consumers the watch they wanted at a price they were willing to pay, and it managed the new product's costs accordingly. Like most watch buyers, targeted consumers were concerned about precision, reliability and durability. However, they were also concerned about fashion and affordability.

Target costing: by managing costs carefully, Swatch was able to create a watch that offered just the right blend of fashion and function at a price consumers were willing to pay.
SOURCE: Courtesy of Swatch Ltd.

To keep costs down, Swatch designed fashionable simpler watches that contained fewer parts and that were constructed from high-tech but less expensive materials. It then developed a revolutionary automated process for mass-producing the new watches and exercised strict cost controls throughout the manufacturing process. By managing costs carefully, Swatch was able to create a watch that offered just the right blend of fashion and function at a price consumers were willing to pay. As a result of its initial major success, consumers have placed increasing value on Swatch products, allowing the company to introduce successively higher-priced designs.[11]

Other companies de-emphasise price and use other marketing-mix tools to create *non-price* positions. Often, the best strategy is not to charge the lowest price, but rather to differentiate the marketing offer to make it worth a higher price.

London's City Airport and the airlines that fly from there do not compete on price. Instead they offer the retailing, speed of processing and convenience wanted by frequent-flying executives. In this case less means more. City's compact terminal has no burger bars, no video arcades and no air bridges.

Gucci's very strong image and reputation as a prestigious brand mean that customers are willing to pay for the fashion house's expensive fragrances.
SOURCE: Advertising Archives.

> Surveys show that City Airport's regular users prefer using the aircraft's own stairs and braving the English weather rather than wait, hunched under luggage racks while air bridges are connected.[12]

Thus the marketer must consider the total marketing mix when setting prices. If the product is positioned on non-price factors, then decisions about quality, promotion and distribution will strongly affect price. If price is a crucial positioning factor, then price will strongly affect decisions made about the other marketing-mix elements. Even so, marketers should remember that buyers rarely buy on price alone. Instead, they seek product and service offerings that give them the best value in terms of benefits received for the price paid.

Costs

Costs set the floor for the price that the company can charge for its product. The company wants to charge a price that both covers all its costs for producing, distributing and selling the product, and delivers a fair rate of return for its effort and risk. A company's costs may be an important element in its pricing strategy. Many companies work to become the 'low-cost producers' in their industries. Companies with lower costs can set lower prices that result in greater sales and profits.

Types of cost

Fixed costs—Costs that do not vary with production or sales level.

A company's costs take two forms, fixed and variable. **Fixed costs** (also known as overheads) are costs that do not vary with production or sales level. For example, a company must pay

670

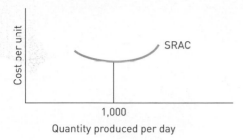

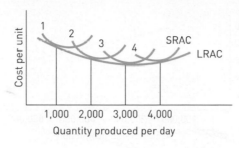

Figure 16.2 **Cost per unit at different levels of production**

A. Cost behaviour in a fixed-size plant

B. Cost behaviour over different-sized plants

each month's bills for rent, heat, interest and executive salaries, whatever the company's output. In many industries, such as airlines, fixed costs dominate. If an airline has to fly a sector with few passengers on board it can only save on the 15 per cent of its costs accounted for by cabin crew and passenger service. All other costs, including flight crew (7 per cent), fuel (15 per cent) and maintenance (10 per cent), are fixed.[13]

Variable costs vary directly with the level of production. Each personal computer produced involves a cost of computer chips, wires, plastic, packaging and other inputs. These costs tend to be the same for each unit produced, their total varying with the number of units produced.

Total costs are the sum of the fixed and variable costs for any given level of production. Management wants to charge a price that will at least cover the total production costs at a given level of production. The company must watch its costs carefully. If it costs the company more than competitors to produce and sell its product, the company will have to charge a higher price or make less profit, putting it at a competitive disadvantage.

Costs at different levels of production

To price wisely, management needs to know how its costs vary with different levels of production. For example, consider Roberts, a maker of high-quality radios owned by the Irish domestic appliance company, Glen Dimplex. Glen Dimplex seeks to add new and innovative products to the Roberts range. It builds a plant to produce 1,000 Roberts luxury travel clocks per day. Figure 16.2A shows the typical short-run average cost curve (SRAC). It shows that the cost per clock is high if Roberts' factory produces only a few per day. But as production moves up to 1,000 clocks per day, average cost falls. This is because fixed costs are spread over more units, with each one bearing a smaller fixed cost. Roberts can try to produce more than 1,000 clocks per day, but average costs will increase because the plant becomes inefficient. Workers have to wait for machines, the machines break down more often and workers get in each other's way.

If Roberts believed it could sell 2,000 clocks a day, it should consider building a larger plant. The plant would use more efficient machinery and work arrangements. Also, the unit cost of producing 2,000 units per day would be lower than the unit cost of producing 1,000 units per day, as shown in the long-run average cost (LRAC) curve (Figure 16.2B). In fact, a 3,000-capacity plant would be even more efficient, according to Figure 16.2B. But a 4,000 daily production plant would be less efficient because of increasing diseconomies of scale – too many workers to manage, paperwork slows things down and so on. Figure 16.2B shows that a 3,000 daily production plant is the best size to build if demand is strong enough to support this level of production.

Costs as a function of production experience

Suppose Roberts runs a plant that produces 3,000 clocks per day. As Roberts gains experience in producing hand-held clocks, it learns how to do it better. Workers learn short-cuts and become more familiar with their equipment. With practice, the work becomes better

Variable costs—Costs that vary directly with the level of production.

Total costs—The sum of the fixed and variable costs for any given level of production.

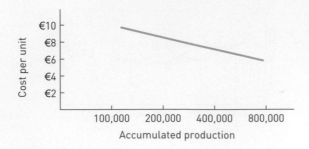

Figure 16.3 Cost per unit as a function of accumulated production: the experience curve

Experience curve (learning curve)—The drop in the average per-unit production cost that comes with accumulated production experience.

organised and Roberts finds better equipment and production processes. With higher volume, Roberts becomes more efficient and gains economies of scale. As a result, average cost tends to fall with accumulated production experience. This is shown in Figure 16.3.[14] Thus the average cost of producing the first 100,000 clocks is €10 per clock. When the company has produced the first 200,000 clocks, the average cost has fallen to €9. After its accumulated production experience doubles again to 400,000, the average cost is €7. This drop in the average cost with accumulated production experience is called the **experience curve** (or **learning curve**).

If a downward-sloping experience curve exists, this is highly significant for the company. Not only will the company's unit production cost fall; it will fall faster if the company makes and sells more during a given time period. But the market has to stand ready to buy the higher output. And to take advantage of the experience curve, Roberts must get a large market share early in the product's life-cycle. This suggests the following pricing strategy. Roberts should price its clocks low; its sales will then increase and its costs will decrease through gaining more experience, and then it can lower its prices further.

Some companies have built successful strategies around the experience curve. For example, during the 1980s, Bausch & Lomb consolidated its position in the soft contact lens market by using computerised lens design and steadily expanding its one Soflens plant. As a result, its market share climbed steadily to 65 per cent. Yet a single-minded focus on reducing costs and exploiting the experience curve will not always work. Experience curves became somewhat of a fad during the 1970s and, like many fads, the strategy was sometimes misused. Experience-curve pricing carries some serious risks. The aggressive pricing might give the product a cheap image. The strategy also assumes that competitors are weak and not willing to fight it out by meeting the company's price cuts. Finally, while the company is building volume under one technology, a competitor may find a lower-cost technology that lets it start at lower prices than the market leader, who still operates on the old experience curve.

Organisational considerations

Management must decide who within the organisation should set prices. Companies handle pricing in a variety of ways. In small companies, prices are often set by top management rather than by the marketing or sales departments. In large companies, pricing is typically handled by divisional or product line managers. In industrial markets, salespeople may be allowed to negotiate with customers within certain price ranges. Even so, top management sets the pricing objectives and policies, and it often approves the prices proposed by lower-level management or salespeople. In industries in which pricing is a key factor (such as in aerospace, steel and oil), companies will often have a pricing department to set the best prices or help others in setting them. This department reports to the marketing department or top management. Others who have an influence on pricing include sales managers, production managers, finance managers and accountants.

External factors affecting pricing decisions

Pricing decisions are affected by external factors such as the nature of the market and demand, competition and other environmental elements.

The market and demand

Whereas costs set the lower limit of prices, the market and demand set the upper limit. Both consumer and industrial buyers balance the price of a product or service against the benefits of owning it. Thus, before setting prices, the marketer must understand the relationship between price and demand for its product. In this section, we explain how the price–demand relationship varies for different types of market and how buyer perceptions of price affect the pricing decision. We then discuss methods for measuring the price–demand relationship.

Pricing in different types of market

The seller's pricing freedom varies with different types of market. Economists recognise four types of market, each presenting a different pricing challenge.

Under **pure competition**, the market consists of many buyers and sellers trading in a uniform commodity such as wheat, copper or financial securities. No single buyer or seller has much effect on the going market price. A seller cannot charge more than the going price because buyers can obtain as much as they need at the going price. Nor would sellers charge less than the market price because they can sell all they want at this price. If price and profits rise, new sellers can easily enter the market. In a purely competitive market, marketing research, product development, pricing, advertising and sales promotion play little or no role. Thus sellers in these markets do not spend much time on marketing strategy.

Under **monopolistic competition**, the market consists of many buyers and sellers that trade over a range of prices rather than a single market price. A range of prices occurs because sellers can differentiate their offers to buyers. Either the physical product can be varied in quality, features or style or the accompanying services can be varied. Each company can create a quasi-monopoly for its products because buyers see differences in sellers' products and will pay different prices for them. Sellers try to develop differentiated offers for different customer segments and, in addition to price, freely use branding, availability, advertising and personal selling to set their offers apart. For example, Ty's Beanie Babies have cultivated a distinctive appeal that has both stimulated demand and seen the price of some Beanies rocket.[15]

Under **oligopolistic competition**, the market consists of a few sellers that are highly sensitive to each other's pricing and marketing strategies. The product can be uniform (steel, aluminium) or non-uniform (cars, computers). There are few sellers because it is difficult for new sellers to enter the market. Each seller is alert to competitors' strategies and moves. If a steel company slashes its price by 10 per cent, buyers will quickly switch to this supplier. The other steel makers must respond by lowering their prices or increasing their services. An oligopolist is never sure that it will gain anything permanent through a price cut. In contrast, if an oligopolist raises its price, its competitors might not follow this lead. The oligopolist would then have to retract its price increase or risk losing customers to competitors.

In a **pure monopoly**, the market consists of one seller. The seller may be a government monopoly (a postal service), a private regulated monopoly (a power company) or a private non-regulated monopoly (Microsoft Windows). Pricing is handled differently in each case. A government monopoly can pursue a variety of pricing objectives: set price below cost because the product is important to buyers who cannot afford to pay full cost; set price either to cover costs or to produce good revenue; or set price quite high to slow down consumption or to protect an inefficient supplier. In a regulated monopoly, the government permits the company to set rates that will yield a 'fair return', one that will let the company maintain and expand its operations as needed. Non-regulated monopolies are free to price at what the

Pure competition—A market in which many buyers and sellers trade in a uniform commodity – no single buyer or seller has much effect on the going market price.

Monopolistic competition— A market in which many buyers and sellers trade over a range of prices rather than a single market price.

Oligopolistic competition— A market in which there are a few sellers that are highly sensitive to each other's pricing and marketing strategies.

Pure monopoly—A market in which there is a single seller – it may be a government monopoly, a private regulated monopoly or a private non-regulated monopoly.

market will bear. However, they do not always charge the full price for a number of reasons: a desire not to attract competition, a desire to penetrate the market faster with a low price, or a fear of government regulation.

Consumer perceptions of price and value

In the end, the consumer will decide whether a product's price is right. When setting prices, the company must consider consumer perceptions of price and how these perceptions affect consumers' buying decisions. Pricing decisions, like other marketing-mix decisions, must be buyer-oriented.

When consumers buy a product, they exchange something of value (the price) to get something of value (the benefits of having or using the product). Effective, buyer-oriented pricing involves understanding how much value consumers place on the benefits they receive from the product and setting a price that fits this value. These benefits can be actual or perceived. For example, calculating the cost of ingredients in a meal at a fancy restaurant is relatively easy. But assigning a value to other satisfactions such as taste, environment, relaxation, conversation and status is very hard. And these values will vary both for different consumers and in different situations.

> Functional confectionery, such as Clorets or Fisherman's Friend, offers tangible problem solutions that customers value. These products may cost little more to make than conventional sugar-based confectionery, such as Polo Mints or Rowntree's Fruit Pastilles, but customers value their physical performance. Makers of these products do not rely on consumers' perception of their brand's value, but convey the products on the pack and by promotions. For instance, the flavour, strength and packaging of Hall's Mentho-Lyptus is fine-tuned for local markets but remains true to its core benefit: throat soothing.

Thus the company will often find it hard to measure the values that customers will attach to its product. But consumers do use these values to evaluate a product's price. If customers perceive that the price is greater than the product's value, they will not buy the product. If consumers perceive that the price is below the product's value, they will buy it, but the seller loses profit opportunities.

Marketers must therefore try to understand the consumer's reasons for buying the product and set the price according to consumer perceptions of the product's value. Because consumers vary in the values they assign to different product features, marketers often vary their pricing strategies for different segments. They offer different sets of product features at different prices. For example, Philips offers €250 small 41 cm portable TV models for consumers who want basic sets and €1,200 68 cm 100-Hz Nicam stereo models loaded with features for consumers who want the extras.

Analysing the price–demand relationship

Each price the company might charge leads to a different level of demand. The relation between the price charged and the resulting demand level is shown in the demand curve in Figure 16.4A. The demand curve shows the number of units that the market will buy in a given time period at different prices that might be charged. In the normal case, demand and price are inversely related: that is, the higher the price, the lower the demand. Thus the company would sell less if it raised its price from P_1 to P_2. In short, consumers with limited budgets will probably buy less of something if its price is too high.

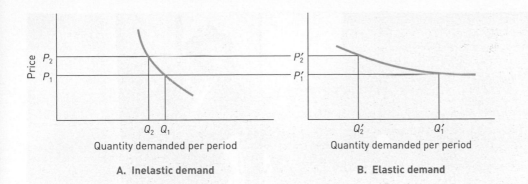

Figure 16.4 Inelastic and elastic demand

A. Inelastic demand

B. Elastic demand

In the case of prestige goods, the demand curve sometimes slopes upward. Consumers think that higher prices mean more quality.

> When Gibson Guitars lowered its prices to compete more effectively with Japanese rivals like Yamaha and Ibanez the result was not what they expected. Gibson found that its instruments didn't sell as well at lower prices. 'We had an inverse [price–demand relationship]', noted Gibson's chief executive officer. 'The more we charged, the more product we sold.' Gibson's slogan promises: 'The world's finest musical instruments'. It turns out that low prices simply aren't consistent with 'Gibson's century-old tradition of creating investment-quality instruments that represent the highest standards of imaginative design and masterful craftsmanship'.[16]

However, even for prestige products, if the price is too high, demand will reduce.

Most companies try to measure their demand curves by estimating demand at different prices. The type of market makes a difference. In a monopoly, the demand curve shows the total market demand resulting from different prices. If the company faces competition, its demand at different prices will depend on whether competitors' prices stay constant or change with the company's own prices. Here, we will assume that competitors' prices remain constant. Later in this chapter, we will discuss what happens when competitors' prices change.

In measuring the price–demand relationship, the market researcher must not allow other factors affecting demand to vary. For example, if Philips increased its advertising at the same time that it lowered its television prices, we would not know how much of the increased demand was due to the lower prices and how much was due to the increased advertising. The same problem arises if a holiday weekend occurs when the lower price is set – more gift-giving over some holidays causes people to buy more portable televisions. Economists show the impact of non-price factors on demand through shifts in the demand curve rather than movements along it.

Price elasticity of demand

Marketers also need to know **price elasticity** – how responsive demand will be to a change in price. Consider the two demand curves in Figure 16.4. In Figure 16.4A, a price increase from P_1 to P_2 leads to a relatively small drop in demand from Q_1 to Q_2. In Figure 16.4B, however, a similar price increase leads to a large drop in demand from Q_1' to Q_2'. If demand hardly changes with a small change in price, we say the demand is *inelastic*. If demand changes greatly, we say the demand is *elastic*. The price elasticity of demand is given by the following formula:

Price elasticity—A measure of the sensitivity of demand to changes in price.

The demand curve sometimes slopes upward: Gibson was surprised to learn that its high-quality instruments didn't sell as well at lower prices.
SOURCE: Courtesy of Gibson Guitar.

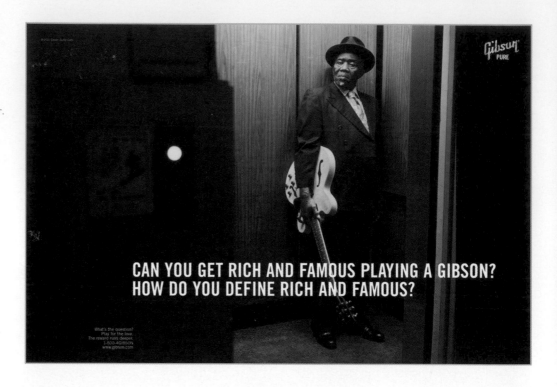

CAN YOU GET RICH AND FAMOUS PLAYING A GIBSON?
HOW DO YOU DEFINE RICH AND FAMOUS?

$$\text{Price elasticity of demand} = \frac{\text{\% change in quantity demanded}}{\text{\% change in price}}$$

Suppose demand falls by 10 per cent when a seller raises its price by 2 per cent. Price elasticity of demand is therefore −5 (the minus sign confirms the inverse relation between price and demand) and demand is elastic. If demand falls by 2 per cent with a 2 per cent increase in price, then elasticity is −1. In this case, the seller's total revenue stays the same: that is, the seller sells fewer items, but at a higher price that preserves the same total revenue. If demand falls by 1 per cent when the price is increased by 2 per cent, then elasticity is −½ and demand is inelastic. The less elastic the demand, the more it pays for the seller to raise the price.

What determines the price elasticity of demand? Buyers are less price sensitive when the product they are buying is unique or when it is high in quality, prestige or exclusiveness. They are also less price sensitive when substitute products are hard to find or when they cannot easily compare the quality of substitutes. Finally, buyers are less price sensitive when the total expenditure for a product is low relative to their income or when another party shares the cost.[17]

If demand is elastic rather than inelastic, sellers will consider lowering their price. A lower price will produce more total revenue. This practice makes sense as long as the extra costs of producing and selling more do not exceed the extra revenue. At the same time, most firms want to avoid pricing that turns their products into commodities. In recent years, forces such as deregulation and the instant price comparisons afforded by the Internet and other technologies have increased consumer price sensitivity, turning products ranging from telephones and computers to new automobiles into commodities in consumers' eyes. Marketers need to work harder than ever to differentiate their offerings when a dozen competitors are selling virtually the same product at a comparable or lower price. More than ever, companies need to understand the price sensitivity of their customers and prospects and the trade-offs people are willing to make between price and product characteristics.

Action	Regular price	10% discount	Percentage change
Sales			
Price (€)	1.00	0.90	
Sales volume	100	105	
Sales value (€)	100.00	94.50	(5.5)
Cost of goods sold			
Unit cost (€)	0.50	0.50	
Sales (units)	100	105	
Cost (€)	50.00	52.50	5.0
Gross profit	50.00	42.00	(16.0)
Other trading expenses	40.00	40.00	0.0
Net profit	10.00	2.00	(80.0)
Return on sales (%)	10.0	2.1	

Table 16.1 How discounts influence sales and profits

Price influence on profits

Increasing *sales volume* in items sold is the driving force behind much marketing activity. There are good reasons for this: increased sales show success and a growing company, increased market share shows competitive success and, if sales do not match production, capacity will be underused or customers disappointed.

Unfortunately, when price is used to increase sales volume, *sales value* – the proceeds from sales – may reduce. *Sales value* and *sales volume* do not always move hand in hand. A company that increases sales by 5 per cent by cutting prices by 10 per cent increases sales volume but reduces sales value, as the example in Table 16.1 shows.

Gross profit is the difference between net proceeds from sales and the cost of goods sold. The costs are the variable costs incurred each time a product is made. They typically include raw materials, labour, energy and so on. The interplay between gross profit and price is dramatic. The once popular idea of 'everyday low prices' increased sales volumes and value, but not always by enough to cover lost margins. The example in Table 16.1 shows that the 10 per cent price cut has much more impact on *gross profits* than do sales.

Net profit is the surplus remaining after all costs have been taken. The gross profit shows the contribution made to the company by each unit sold, but neglects many other trading expenses incurred by a company. These included fixed costs like rates and staff, and strategic expenditure like research and development. Interest paid on debts is sometimes not included because this depends upon the capital structure of the company. The fixed cost means that *net profit* is more volatile than *gross profit* (see Table 16.1). This sensitivity encourages companies to convert some of their fixed costs into variable ones: for example, hiring trucks rather than buying them.

Net profit—The difference between the income from goods sold and all expenses incurred.

Return on sales (or *margin*) measures the ratio of profit to sales:

$$\text{Return on sales} = \frac{\text{Net profit}}{\text{Sales}}$$

This is useful in comparing businesses over time. During a four-year period a company may find both sales and net profit increasing, but are profits keeping pace with sales? In Table 16.1 the 10 per cent price promotion gives an increase in sales volume, but a big reduction in return on sales. The interplay between price, sales, profits and investment makes these and other ratios central to marketing decision making and control. Marketing Insights 16.1 introduces *Economic Value Added* (EVA), a measure that has become increasingly important in recent years.

16.1 ## Economic Value Added

Return on capital employed (ROCE)

Some companies, such as grocery chains, have low returns on sales but are profitable. They achieve this because the critical measure is return on capital employed. This is the product of return on sales (ROS) and the speed at which assets are turned over (the activity ratio):

$$\text{ROCE} = \text{ROS} \times \text{ACTIVITY} = \frac{\text{NP}}{\text{Sales}} \times \frac{\text{Sales}}{\text{Assets}}$$

By turning over its assets four times each year, a supermarket can achieve a 20 per cent return on capital employed although its return on sales is only 5 per cent, while an exclusive clothes shop has very high margins but turns its assets over slowly.

$$\text{Supermarket ROCE} = \frac{5}{100} \times \frac{100}{25} = 20 \text{ per cent}$$

$$\text{Clothes shop ROCE} = \frac{40}{100} \times \frac{100}{300} = 13.3 \text{ per cent}$$

These are powerful ratios that can define how a company can do business. Aldi, the German discount grocery chain, succeeds with margins half those of many grocers. Its margins are very low (2–3 per cent), but it keeps its return on capital employed high by high stock turnover and keeping its other assets low.

There are two benefits from increasing asset turnover: improved return on capital employed, and reduced fixed costs. The firm that hires trucks rather than buying them reduces its fixed costs and, therefore, its sensitivity to volume changes. Also, by reducing its assets it increases its activity ratio and return on capital employed. Increased asset turnover is one of the direct benefits of just-in-time (JIT) and lean manufacturing. JIT cuts down the assets tied up in stock, and improves quality while lean manufacturing reduces investment in plant.

Capital cost covered (C^3)

Assets cost money and return on capital costs takes that into account. It is a powerful tool because it combines three critical business ratios:

$$C^3 = \text{ROS} \times \text{ACTIVITY} \times \text{CAPITAL EFFICIENCY}$$

$$= \frac{\text{NP}}{\text{Sales}} \times \frac{\text{Sales}}{\text{Assets}} \times \frac{\text{Assets}}{\text{Cost of capital}}$$

The cost of capital is the average cost of debt and shareholder equity. For a supermarket the figure is 10 per cent per year. With assets of €25 million, the cost of capital is €25m × 0.10 = €2.5m, giving:

marketing insights

$$C^3 = \frac{5}{100} \times \frac{100}{25} \times \frac{25}{2.5} = \frac{NP}{CC} = 2.0$$

...16.1

In other words, the net profit is double the capital cost – the company is healthy. This ratio is more discriminating than the familiar distinction between profit and loss. If the capital cost covered is below zero, a firm is making a loss. A capital cost covered above zero indicates a profit. However, capital cost covered between zero and 1 shows that a firm is in profit but not adding value – its profit does not cover its cost of capital.

Economic Value Added (EVA)

EVA makes a direct comparison between the cost of capital and net profits. It is a simple idea that has hugely increased the value of companies using it. Many leading companies see EVA as a way of examining the value of their investments and strategy.

The supermarket's EVA is:

EVA = Net profit − Cost of capital = 5 − 2.5 = €2.5m

Profit, economic value added and capital cost covered are related concepts: profit shows how a company's trading is going, economic value added shows a company's wealth creation in monetary terms, while capital cost covered gives the rate of wealth creation.

Category	C^3	EVA	NP	Economic state
I	>1	>0	>0	A profitable company which is adding economic value
II	0–1	<0	>0	A company whose profits do not cover the cost of capital
III	<0	<0	<0	A loss-making company

The supermarket is a clear category I company. This contrasts with the clothes store whose capital, at 16.25 per cent, is more expensive because the clothes market is cyclical and fashion-dependent. Assets of €300 million give a capital cost of €48.75 million.

	C^3	EVA (€m)	NP (€m)	Category
Supermarket	2.0	2.5	5	I
Clothes store	0.8	(9.5)	40	II

Many of the *dot bombs* (dotcom companies that went bust) never strayed beyond being category III companies, never making any net profits (NP < 0) after having a high advertising spend with low margins and sales volume.

SOURCES: Ross Tieman, 'Innovation and business agility is vital to success', *Special Report FT Management: Customer Relations. Financial Times* (19 May 2003), p. II; Neil Buckley, 'Potential cost of selling it cheap every day', *Financial Times* (24 March 1994), p. 17; 'Valuing companies: a star to sail by?', *The Economist* (2 August 1997), pp. 61–3.

Competitors' costs, prices and offers

Another external factor affecting the company's pricing decisions is competitors' costs and prices, and possible competitor reactions to the company's own pricing moves. A consumer who is considering the purchase of a Canon camera will evaluate Canon's price and value against the prices and values of comparable products made by Nikon, Minolta, Pentax and others. In addition, the company's pricing strategy may affect the nature of the competition it faces. If Canon follows a high-price, high-margin strategy, it may attract competition. A low-price, low-margin strategy, however, may stop competitors or drive them out of the market.

Canon needs to benchmark its costs against its competitors' costs to learn whether it is operating at a cost advantage or disadvantage. It also needs to learn the price and quality of each competitor's offer. Once Canon is aware of competitors' prices and offers, it can use them as a starting point for its own pricing. If Canon's cameras are similar to Nikon's, it will have to price close to Nikon or lose sales. If Canon's cameras are not as good as Nikon's, the firm will not be able to charge as much. If Canon's products are better than Nikon's, it can charge more. Basically, Canon will use price to position its offer relative to the competition.

Other external factors

When setting prices, the company must also consider other factors in its external environment. *Economic conditions* can have a strong impact on the firm's pricing strategies.[18] Economic factors such as boom or recession, inflation and interest rates affect pricing decisions because they affect both the costs of producing a product and consumer perception of the product's price and value. The company must also consider what impact its prices will have on other parties in its environment. How will *resellers* react to various prices? The company should set prices that give resellers a fair profit, encourage their support and help them to sell the product effectively. The *government* is another important external influence on pricing decisions. Finally, *social concerns* may have to be taken into account. In setting prices, a company's short-term sales, market share and profit goals may have to be tempered by broader societal considerations.

General pricing approaches

The price that the company charges will be somewhere between one that is too low to produce a profit and one that is too high to produce any demand. Figure 16.5 summarises the primary considerations in setting price. Product costs set a floor to the price; consumer perceptions of the product's value set the ceiling. The company must consider competitors' prices and other external and internal factors to find the best price between these two extremes.

Companies set prices by selecting a general pricing approach that includes one or more of these three sets of factors – costs, consumer perception and competitors' prices. We will examine the following approaches: the *cost-based approach* (cost-plus pricing, break-even analysis and target profit pricing); the *buyer-based approach* (perceived-value pricing); and the *competition-based approach* (going-rate and sealed-bid pricing).

Figure 16.5 Primary considerations in price settings

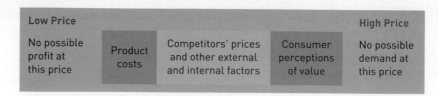

Low Price				High Price
No possible profit at this price	Product costs	Competitors' prices and other external and internal factors	Consumer perceptions of value	No possible demand at this price

Cost-based pricing

Cost-plus pricing

The simplest pricing method is **cost-plus pricing** – adding a standard mark-up to the cost of the product. Construction companies, for example, submit job bids by estimating the total project cost and adding a standard mark-up for profit. Lawyers, accountants and other professionals typically price by adding a standard mark-up to their costs. Some sellers tell their customers they will charge cost plus a specified **mark-up**: for example, aerospace companies price this way to the government.

To illustrate *mark-up* pricing, suppose a toaster manufacturer had the following costs and expected sales:

Variable cost	€10
Fixed cost	€300,000
Expected unit sales	50,000

Then the manufacturer's cost per toaster is given by:

$$\text{Unit cost} = \text{Variable cost} + \frac{\text{Fixed costs}}{\text{Unit sales}} = €10 + \frac{€300,000}{50,000} = €16$$

Now suppose the manufacturer wants to earn a 20 per cent mark-up on sales. The manufacturer's mark-up price is given by:

$$\text{Mark-up price} = \frac{\text{Unit cost}}{1.0 - \text{desired return on sales}} = \frac{€16}{1.0 - 0.2} = €20$$

The manufacturer would charge dealers €20 a toaster and make a profit of €4 per unit. The dealers, in turn, will mark up the toaster. If dealers want to earn 50 per cent on sales price, they will mark up the toaster to €40 (€20 + 50 per cent of €40). This number is equivalent to a *mark-up on cost* of 100 per cent (€20/€20).

Does using standard mark-ups to set prices make logical sense? Generally, no. Any pricing method that ignores demand and competitors' prices is not likely to lead to the best price. Suppose the toaster manufacturer charged €20 but sold only 30,000 toasters instead of 50,000. Then the unit cost would have been higher, since the fixed costs are spread over fewer units and the realised percentage mark-up on sales would have been lower. Mark-up pricing works only if that price actually brings in the expected level of sales. Moreover, what if the firm's costs are too high compared to competitors' costs?

> Brio, the Swedish toy producer and the largest toy distributor in Scandinavia, have seen a major drop in both profits and sales for its toys, in recent years. While the Brio brand symbolizes a high quality toy, robust enough to become a family heirloom to be passed down from brother to sister and to the next generation, parents see Brio toys as being far too expensive. Besides, these days, parents can buy basic toy products of the same quality from supermarket chains and furniture retailers like Ikea, who are churning out their own private-label wooden toys, notably train sets, at a fraction the price Brio charges. Brio realizes that in its quest to fulfil its vision of 'the good toy',

Cost-plus pricing—Adding a standard mark-up to the cost of the product.

Mark-up/mark-down—The difference between selling price and cost as a percentage of selling price or cost.

> the company had ignored the question of whether parents were able to afford to buy it. The company had placed too much emphasis on the value (premium) of the toys and not enough on their cost![19]

Still, mark-up pricing remains popular for a number of reasons. First, sellers are more certain about costs than about demand. By tying the price to cost, sellers simplify pricing – they do not have to make frequent adjustments as demand changes. Second, when all firms in the industry use this pricing method, prices tend to be similar and price competition is thus minimised. Third, many people feel that cost-plus pricing is fairer to both buyers and sellers. Sellers earn a fair return on their investment, but do not take advantage of buyers when buyers' demand increases.

Break-even analysis and target profit pricing

Break-even pricing (target profit pricing)—Setting price to break even on the costs of making and marketing a product; or setting price to make a target profit.

Another cost-oriented pricing approach is **break-even pricing** or a variation called **target profit pricing**. The firm tries to determine the price at which it will break even or make the target profit it is seeking. Target pricing is used by General Motors, which prices its cars to achieve a 15–20 per cent profit on its investment. This pricing method is also used by public utilities, which are constrained to make a fair return on their investment. Target pricing uses the concept of a *break-even chart*, which shows the total cost and total revenue expected at different sales volume levels. Figure 16.6 shows a break-even chart for the toaster manufacturer discussed here. Fixed costs are €300,000 regardless of sales volume. Variable costs are added to fixed costs to form total costs, which rise with volume. The total revenue curve starts at zero and rises with each unit sold. The slope of the total revenue curve reflects the price of €20 per unit.

The total revenue and total cost curves cross at 30,000 units. This is the *break-even volume*. At €20, the company must sell at least 30,000 units to break even: that is, for total revenue to cover total cost. Break-even volume can be calculated using the following formula:

$$\text{Break-even volume} = \frac{\text{Fixed cost}}{\text{Price} - \text{Variable cost}} = \frac{€300,000}{€20 - €10} = 30,000$$

If the company wants to make a target profit, it must sell more than 30,000 units at €20 each. Suppose the toaster manufacturer has invested €1,000,000 in the business and wants to set a price to earn a 20 per cent return or €200,000. In that case, it must sell at least 50,000 units at €20 each. If the company charges a higher price, it will not need to sell as many toasters to achieve its target return. But the market may not buy even this lower volume at the higher price. Much depends on the price elasticity and competitors' prices.

Figure 16.6 Break-even chart for determining target price

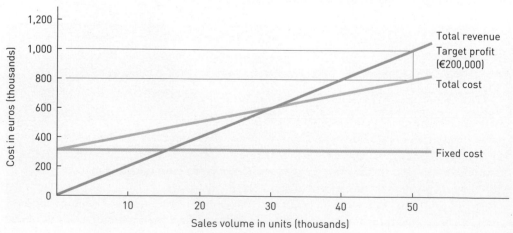

(1) Price (€)	(2) Unit demand needed to break even (000)	(3) Expected unit demand at given price (000)	(4) Total revenues = (1) × (3) (€000)	(5) Total cost* (€000)	(6) Profit = (4) − (5) (€000)
14	75	71	994	1,010	−16
16	50	67	1,072	970	102
18	37.5	60	1,080	900	180
20	30	42	840	720	120
22	25	23	506	530	−24

Table 16.2 Break-even volume and profits at different prices

*Assumes a fixed cost of €300,000 and a constant unit variable cost of €10.

The manufacturer should consider different prices and estimate break-even volumes, probable demand and profits for each. This is done in Table 16.2. The table shows that as price increases, break-even volume drops (column 2). But as price increases, demand for the toasters also falls off (column 3). At the €14 price, because the manufacturer clears only €4 per toaster (€14 less €10 in variable costs), it must sell a very high volume to break even. Even though the low price attracts many buyers, demand still falls below the high break-even point and the manufacturer loses money. At the other extreme, with a €22 price, the manufacturer clears €12 per toaster and must sell only 25,000 units to break even. But at this high price, consumers buy too few toasters and profits are negative. The table shows that a price of €18 yields the highest profits. Note that none of the prices produces the manufacturer's target profit of €200,000. To achieve this target return, the manufacturer will have to search for ways to lower fixed or variable costs, thus lowering the break-even volume.

Airbus Industries base their forecasts for their superjumbo A3XX on the superior breakeven that it will offer airlines who buy it. Although much larger than its major competitor, the Boeing B747–400, the A3XX operating cost means that it breaks even at a fraction of its total capacity.[20]

Aircraft	Boeing 747–400	Airbus A3XX
Passenger capacity	413	555
Break-even: passengers	290	323
Profitable seats: beyond break-even	123	232
Break-even: percentage of capacity	70%	58%

Value-based pricing

An increasing number of companies are basing their prices on the product's perceived value. **Value-based pricing** uses buyers' perceptions of value, not the seller's cost, as the key to pricing. Value-based pricing means that the marketer cannot design a product and marketing programme and then set the price. Price is considered along with the other marketing-mix variables *before* the marketing programme is set.

Figure 16.7 compares cost-based pricing with value-based pricing. Cost-based pricing is product driven. The company designs what it considers to be a good product, totals the costs

Value-based pricing— Setting price based on buyers' perceptions of product values rather than on cost.

Figure 16.7 Cost-based versus value-based pricing

SOURCE: *The Strategy and Tactics of Pricing*, 3rd edn by Thomas T. Nagle and Reed K. Holden (2002), p. 4. Reprinted by permission of Pearson Education, Inc., Upper Saddle River, NJ 07458.

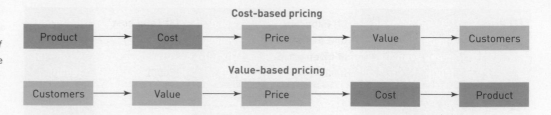

of making the product and sets a price that covers costs plus a target profit. Marketing must then convince buyers that the product's value at that price justifies its purchase. If the price turns out to be too high, the company must settle for lower mark-ups or lower sales, both resulting in disappointing profits.

Value-based pricing reverses this process. The company sets its target price based on customer perceptions of the product value. The targeted value and price then drive decisions about product design and what costs can be incurred. As a result, pricing begins with analysing consumer needs and value perceptions and a price is set to match consumers' perceived value:

> Consider Thorn selling its 10W 2D energy-saving electric light bulbs to a hotel manager. The SL18 costs far more to make than a conventional 60-watt tungsten light bulb, so a higher price has to be justified. Value pricing helps by looking at the hotel manager's total cost of ownership rather than the price of electric light bulbs. The life-cycle costs of the manager using a tungsten bulb for the 1,000 hours that they last includes the price of the bulb (60c), the labour cost of replacing it (50c) and electricity (€4.80). The life-cycle cost of the tungsten bulb is therefore €5.90. The Thorn 10W 2D bulb uses a sixth of the electricity of a conventional bulb and lasts eight times longer. Its life-cycle cost must therefore be compared with the cost of owning eight tungsten bulbs: 8 × €5.90 = €47.20. To work out the value of the Thorn bulb, its cost of ownership is also considered: changing the bulb 50c and electricity €6.40 (one-sixth the electricity costs of eight tungsten bulbs). The maximum value-based price of the Thorn bulb to the hotel manager is therefore:
>
> Maximum value-based price = competitor's cost of ownership – own operating costs
>
> = €47.20 – (€6.40 + 50c)
>
> = €40.30
>
> Using this evidence, Thorn can argue that it is worth the hotel manager paying a lot more than 60c to buy the energy-saving bulb. It is unrealistic to think that the manager would pay the full €40.30, but based on these figures, the actual price of €10.00 for the Thorn energy-saving bulb looks very reasonable. At first sight it seems hard to justify replacing a 60c tungsten bulb with a €10.00 energy-saving one, but value-based pricing shows the hotel manager is saving €30.00 by doing so. The value-based pricing using life-cycle costs can be used to justify paying a premium price on products, from low-energy light bulbs to airliners.[21]

A company using perceived-value pricing must find out what value buyers assign to different competitive offers. However, measuring perceived value can be difficult. Sometimes consumers are asked how much they would pay for a basic product and for each benefit added to the offer. Or a company might conduct experiments to test the perceived value of different product offers. If the seller charges more than the buyers' perceived value, the company's sales will suffer. Many companies overprice their products and their products sell poorly. Other companies underprice. Underpriced products sell very well, but they produce less revenue than they would if prices were raised to the perceived-value levels.

In recent years, several companies have adopted **value pricing** strategies – offering just the right combination of quality and good service at a fair price. In many cases, this has involved the introduction of less expensive versions of established brand-name products such as Travelodge and Holiday Express budget hotels. In other cases, such as IKEA and Wal-Mart, value pricing has involved redesigning existing brands in order to offer more quality for a given price or the same quality for less.

In many business-to-business marketing situations, the pricing challenge is to find ways to maintain the company's *pricing power* – its power to maintain or even raise prices without losing market share. To retain pricing power – to escape price competition and to justify higher prices and margins – a firm must retain or build the value of its marketing offer. This is especially true for suppliers of commodity products, which are characterised by little differentiation and intense price competition. In such cases, many companies adopt *value-added* strategies. Rather than cutting prices to match competitors, they attach value-added services to differentiate their offers and thus support higher margins.

An important type of value pricing at the retail level is *everyday low pricing (EDLP)*. EDLP involves charging a constant, everyday low price with few or no temporary price promotions and special sales. The king of EDLP is Wal-Mart, who practically defined the concept. Except for a few sale items every month, Wal-Mart promises everyday low prices on everything it sells.[22] These constant prices eliminate week-to-week price uncertainty and can be contrasted to the 'high–low' pricing of promotion-oriented competitors. In *high–low pricing*, the retailer charges higher prices on an everyday basis but runs frequent promotions to lower prices temporarily on selected items below the EDLP level.

Retailers adopt EDLP for many reasons, the most important of which is that constant sales and promotions are costly and have eroded consumer confidence in the credibility of everyday shelf prices. Consumers also have less time and patience for such time-honoured traditions as watching for supermarket specials and clipping coupons. However, to offer everyday low prices, a company must first have everyday low costs. If not, the company could not make money at the lower prices that it charges for the products that it sells.

Value pricing—Offering just the right combination of quality and good service at a fair price.

Competition-based pricing

Consumers will base their judgements of a product's value on the prices that competitors charge for similar products. Here, we discuss two forms of competition-based pricing: *going-rate pricing* and *sealed-bid pricing*.

Going-rate pricing

In **going-rate pricing**, the firm bases its price largely on *competitors*' prices, with less attention paid to its *own* costs or to demand. The firm might charge the same as, more, or less than its chief competitors. In oligopolistic industries that sell a commodity such as steel, paper or fertiliser, firms normally charge the same price. The smaller firms follow the leader: they change their prices when the market leader's prices change, rather than when their own demand or costs change. Some firms may charge a bit more or less, but they hold the amount

Going-rate pricing—Setting price based largely on following competitors' prices rather than on company costs or demand.

of difference constant. Thus, minor petrol retailers usually charge slightly less than the big oil companies, without letting the difference increase or decrease.

> Going-rate pricing applies to complex products as well as commodities. Fierce competition between aerospace producers cut world aircraft prices by a fifth between 1996 and 1998. Manfred Bischoff, chief executive of Daimler-Benz's Dasa, cites Boeing as the chief culprit. 'There is a crumbling of prices in certain markets', he says. 'The price is dictated by Boeing. We are followers in this case.'[23]

Although it gives firms little control of their revenue, going-rate pricing can be quite popular. When demand elasticity is hard to measure, firms feel that the going price represents the collective wisdom of the industry concerning the price that will yield a fair return. They also feel that holding to the going price will prevent harmful price wars.

Sealed-bid pricing

In sealed-bid pricing, a firm bases its price on how it thinks competitors will price rather than on its own costs or on demand. Would-be suppliers can submit only one bid and cannot know the other bids. Sealed-bid auctions, where buyers submit secret bids, have always been common in business-to-business (B2B) marketing and some consumer markets, such as Scottish house buying. Governments also often use this method to procure supplies.

Until the advent of the Internet, haggling (one-to-one negotiations) and a non-negotiable price had grown to dominate pricing. Auctions existed in specialised markets, such as commodities, some specialised financial services, fine art and antiques. Now, led by eBay.com, online auctions for Beanie Babies and much more have become one of the most influential Internet innovations. Whereas conventional auctions needed the market to gather for an auction or have simultaneous telephone contact, the Internet's global reach and simultaneity are putting auctions at the centre of trading. If forecasters are correct, auctions are set to become an increasingly common part of everyone's life. B2B is currently the dominant form but consumer-based auctions, both B2C and C2C, are now running at an estimated €20 billion a year. Because of the growth in popularity of auctions, especially with the growth of the Internet, companies should be aware of the array of auction-type pricing procedures. Here, we discuss sealed-bid pricing as a form of auction-type pricing as well as address recent developments in auction-type pricing.

In the late nineteenth century the French economist Léon Walras likened the entire pricing mechanism to the operation of a 'Walrasian auctioneer' who calls out a price, sees how many buyers and sellers there are and, if they do not balance, makes adjustments until demand equals supply. In the non-negotiable price setting that dominated C2C markets, the 'adjustments' take place over time to match supply and demand. In auctions, as in haggling where buyers and sellers negotiate a price or walk away, prices are set during each transaction. Economists see auctions as an efficient way of matching supply and demand but they do introduce uncertainty into transactions. The sellers do not know the price they will receive and buyers have no guarantee of making a purchase. One of the most common forms of auction, sealed-bid pricing, is an example.

First-price sealed-bid pricing occurs in two ways. Potential buyers may be asked to submit sealed bids, and the item is awarded to the buyer who offers the highest price. Conversely, firms may have to bid for a contract to supply goods or services that is awarded to the contender with the lowest price.

First-price sealed-bid pricing—Potential buyers submit sealed bids, and the item is awarded to the buyer who offers the best price.

Company's bid (€)	Profit if bid wins (€) (1)	Assumed probability of bid winning (2)	Expected profit (€) (3) = (1) × (2)
9,500	100	0.81	81
10,000	600	0.36	216
10,500	1,100	0.09	99
11,000	1,600	0.01	16

Table 16.3 Effects of different bids on expected profit

In sealed-bid pricing, a firm bases its bid price on how it thinks competitors will bid. To win a contract, a contender has to price below other firms. Yet the firm cannot set its price below a certain level. It cannot price below cost without harming its position. In contrast, the higher the company sets its price above its costs, the lower its chance of getting the contract.

The net effect of the two opposite pulls can be described in terms of the *expected profit* of the particular bid (see Table 16.3). Suppose a bid of €9,500 would yield a high chance (say, 0.81) of getting the contract, but only a low profit (say, €100). The expected profit with this bid is therefore €81. If the firm bid €11,000, its profit would be €1,600, but its chance of getting the contract might be reduced to 0.01. The expected profit would be only €16. Thus the company might bid the price that would maximise the expected profit. According to Table 16.3, the best bid would be €10,000, for which the expected profit is €216.

Using expected profit as a basis for setting price makes sense for the large firm that makes many bids. In playing the odds, the firm will make maximum profits in the long run. But a firm that bids only occasionally or needs a particular contract badly will not find the expected-profit approach useful. The approach, for example, does not distinguish between a €100,000 profit with a 0.10 probability and a €12,500 profit with a 0.80 probability. Yet the firm that wants to keep production going would prefer the second contract to the first.

In **English auctions** the price is raised successively until only one bidder remains. This is the most common auction form, familiar from scenes of rare items, be it a Van Gogh or a pair of Madonna's pants, being sold by one of the great auction houses, such as Sotheby's or Christie's. These have joined eBay as providers of online auctions aimed at its network of regular dealers (sothebys.com) or, for smaller collectables ($100 to $100,000), at consumers (sothebys.amazon.com). One of the largest European operators, qxl.com, operates both B2C and C2C while on holidayauctions.net customers can bid for bargain late-break holidays.

English auction—Price is raised successively until only one bidder remains.

In **Dutch auctions** prices start high and are lowered successively until someone buys. These auctions originated in the Dutch wholesale flower markets. B2B online traders, such as Bidbusiness.co.uk and construauction.com, use both English and Dutch auctions to sell industrial products.

Dutch auction—Prices start high and are lowered successively until someone buys.

In **collective buying** increasing numbers of customers agree to buy as prices are lowered to the final bargain. The more customers join in, the lower the price becomes until a minimum demand is met. Letsbuyit.com and adabra.com offer each auction over a limited period for each option, then move on to the next batch. These sites often offer batches of products, say several items of kitchen equipment that are most suited to B2B markets.

Collective buying—An increasing number of customers agree to buy as prices are lowered to the final bargain price.

In a **reverse auction** customers name the price that they are willing to pay for an item and seek a company willing to sell. In pioneering their online service priceline.com takes advantage of two major trends: first, most industries being in a continual state of excess capacity and, second, customers being 'brand neutral' if they can get a good deal. Most of Priceline's business is in travel services and mortgages but it is moving into life insurance, groceries and second-hand goods.

Reverse auction—Customers name the price that they are willing to pay for an item and seek a company willing to sell.

Although economists see auctions as close to Adam Smith's 'invisible hand' that drives markets, there are few cool hands at auctions. Major art auctions are social, newsworthy and

Build your own holidays and save a fortune. More and more travellers are doing just that by using online services like Priceline.
SOURCE: www.priceline.com.

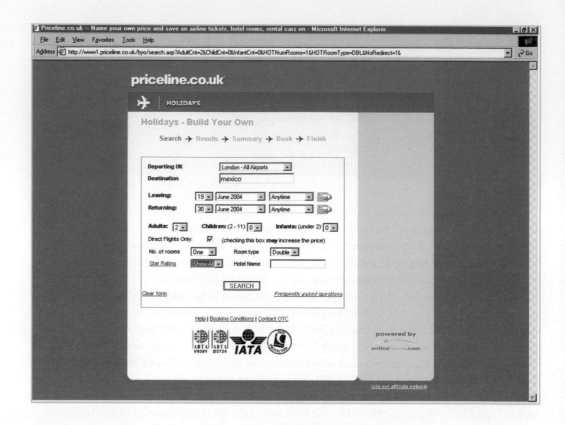

exciting events. Jim Rose, of QXL, has no doubt about why online auctions are similarly popular: 'They're fun, they're entertaining, and people describe it as "winning" something rather than "buying" it.' The 'winner's curse' is very apparent in some South-east Asian markets where to 'win', contenders pay more than high street prices. And how many people can attend an auction and not walk away with something they had no intention of buying! The **second-price sealed bid** method can reduce some of the stress. In this, sealed bids are submitted but the buyer pays a price equal to the second-best bid.[24]

Second-price sealed bid— Sealed bids are submitted but the contender placing the best bid pays only the price equal to the second-best bid.

We have explored the many internal and external factors that affect a company's pricing decisions and examined general approaches to setting prices. Next, we will look at the complex dynamics of pricing and the dynamic pricing strategies available to marketers. Price setting involves balancing conflicting interests and can be used to achieve a range of objectives. Even more, a company does not set a single price, but rather a *pricing structure* that covers different items in its line. This pricing structure changes over time as products move through their life-cycles. The company adjusts product prices to reflect changes in costs and demand, and to account for variations in buyers and situations. As the competitive environment changes, the company considers when to initiate price changes and when to respond to them.

New-product pricing strategies

Pricing strategies usually change as the product passes through its life-cycle. The introductory stage is especially challenging. We can distinguish between pricing a product that imitates existing products and pricing an innovative product that is patent protected.

A company that plans to develop an imitative new product faces a product-positioning problem. It must decide where to position the product versus competing products in terms of

Price

High   Low

High	Premium strategy	Good-value strategy
Low	Overcharging strategy	Economy strategy

Quality

Figure 16.8 **Four price-positioning strategies**

quality and price. Figure 16.8 shows four possible positioning strategies. First, the company might decide to use a *premium pricing* strategy – producing a high-quality product and charging the highest price. At the other extreme, it might decide on an *economy pricing* strategy – producing a lower-quality product, but charging a low price. These strategies can coexist in the same market as long as the market consists of at least two groups of buyers, those who seek quality and those who seek price. Thus, Tag-Heuer offers very high-quality sports watches at high prices, whereas Casio offers digital watches at almost throwaway prices.[25]

The *good-value* strategy represents a way to attack the premium pricer. A leading grocery chain always uses the **strapline**: 'Good food costs less at Sainsbury's'. If this is really true and quality-sensitive buyers believe the good-value pricer, they will sensibly shop at Sainsbury's and save money – unless the premium product offers more status or snob appeal. Using an *overcharging* strategy, the company overprices the product in relation to its quality. In the long run, however, customers are likely to feel 'taken'. They will stop buying the product and will complain to others about it. Thus this strategy should be avoided.[26]

Strapline—A slogan often used in conjunction with a brand's name, advertising and other promotions.

Companies bringing out an innovative, patent-protected product face the challenge of setting prices for the first time. They can choose between two strategies: *market-skimming pricing* and *market-penetration pricing*.

Market-skimming pricing

Many companies that invent new products initially set high prices to 'skim' revenues layer by layer from the market, a strategy called **market-skimming pricing**.

Market-skimming pricing— Setting a high price for a new product to skim maximum revenues layer by layer from the segments willing to pay the high price; the company makes fewer but more profitable sales.

> Maaväl was launched in Sweden at Skr12 (€1.40), more than twice the price of ordinary yoghurt. Developed by Scotia and a consortium of 1,300 Swedish farmers, Maaväl contains Olibra, a 'nutriceutical' made of a patent combination of palm oil extract, oat oil and water. It encourages the small intestine to release chemicals that tell the brain that enough has been eaten, giving a 'prolonged feeling of fullness'. The high price indicates the product's uniqueness and special properties, and allows quicker recovery of development costs. Similar value-added, functional foods have proved profitable. Finland's Rasio has seen its share price increase tenfold since it launched Benecol, a cholesterol-lowering margarine. The success stimulated follow-ups with Benecol 'cream cheese type spread' and yogurt drink, and Flora pro.activ, a 'me-too' from Van den Bergh Foods.[27]

Consider another example – Intel. When Intel first introduces a new computer chip, it charges the highest price it can, given the benefits of the new chip over competing chips. It sets a price that makes it *just* worthwhile for some segments of the market to adopt computers containing the chip. As initial sales slow down and as competitors threaten to introduce similar chips, Intel lowers the price to draw in the next price-sensitive layer of customers.[28]

Market-penetration pricing

Market-penetration pricing—Setting a low price for a new product in order to attract large numbers of buyers and a large market share.

Rather than setting a high initial price to skim off small but profitable market segments, some companies use **market-penetration pricing**. They set a low initial price in order to *penetrate* the market quickly and deeply – to attract a large number of buyers quickly and win a large market share. The high sales volume results in falling costs, allowing the company to cut its price even further. For example, Dell used penetration pricing to sell high-quality computer products through lower-cost mail-order channels. Its sales soared when IBM, Compaq, Apple and other competitors selling through retail stores could not match their prices. The Bank of Scotland and Winterthur of Switzerland used their Direct Line, Privilege and Churchill subsidiaries to grab profits and share in the motor insurance market by selling direct to consumers at market-penetrating prices. The high volume results in lower costs that, in turn, allow the discounters to keep prices low.[29]

Several conditions favour setting a low price. First, the market must be highly price sensitive, so that a low price produces more market growth. Second, production and distribution costs must fall as sales volume increases. Finally, the low price must help keep out the competition and the penetration pricer must maintain its low-price position– otherwise the price advantage may be only temporary. For example, Dell faced difficult times when IBM and Compaq established their own direct distribution channels. However, competitive market-penetration pricing to gain share can be withering. Almost all the US's leading Internet service providers, including Mindspring, PSINet, Earthlink, BBN and Netcom, are losing money as they fight for market share and new customers.[30]

Product-mix pricing strategies

The strategy for setting a product's price often has to be changed when the product is part of a product mix. In this case, the firm looks for a set of prices that maximises the profits on the total product mix. Pricing is difficult because the various products have related demand and costs, and face different degrees of competition. Five *product-mix pricing* situations are summarised in Table 16.4.

Table 16.4 Product-mix pricing strategies

Product line pricing	Optional-product pricing	Captive-product pricing	By-product pricing	Product-bundle pricing
Setting price steps between product line items	Pricing optional or accessory products sold with the main product	Pricing products that must be used with the main product	Pricing low-value by-products to get rid of them	Pricing bundles of products sold together

Product line pricing

Companies usually develop product lines rather than single products. For example, Merloni's sells Indesit, Ariston and Scholte appliances with price and status ascending in that order. There are full ranges of Indesit to Ariston appliances, from washing machines to freezers, covering the first two price bands, while Scholte sells expensive built-in kitchen equipment. In **product line pricing**, management must decide on the price steps to set between the various products in a line.

The price steps should take into account cost differences between the products in the line, customer evaluations of their different features, and competitors' prices. If the price difference between two successive products is small, buyers will usually buy the more advanced product. This will increase company profits if the cost difference is smaller than the price difference. If the price difference is large, however, customers will generally buy the less advanced products.

In many industries, sellers use well-established *price points* for the products in their line. Thus record stores might carry CDs at five price levels: budget, mid-line, full-line and imports, ascending in price and with discounted special promotions on current chart albums. The customer will probably associate low- to high-quality recordings with the first three price points. Even if the prices are raised a little, people will normally buy CDs at their own preferred price points. The seller's task is to establish perceived quality differences that support the price differences.

> **Product line pricing**—Setting the price steps between various products in a product line based on cost differences between the products, customer evaluations of different features, and competitors' prices.

Optional-product pricing

Many companies use **optional-product pricing** – offering to sell optional or accessory products along with their main product. For example, a Toyota Yaris customer may choose to add satellite navigation, a CD autochanger or a roof spoiler. Pricing these options is a sticky problem. Car companies have to decide which items to include in the base price and which to offer as options. BMW's basic cars once came famously under-equipped. Typically the 318i is about €20,000, but the customer then has to pay extra for a radio (prices vary), electric windows (€350), sun roof (€900) and security system (€550). The basic model is stripped of so many comforts and conveniences that most buyers reject it. They pay for extras or buy a better-equipped version. More recently, however, American and European carmakers have been forced to follow the example of the Japanese carmakers and include in the basic price many useful items previously sold only as options. The advertised price now often represents a well-equipped car.

> **Optional-product pricing**—The pricing of optional or accessory products along with a main product.

Captive-product pricing

Companies that make products that must be used along with a main product are using **captive-product pricing**. Examples of captive products are razors, camera film, video games and computer software. Producers of the main products (razors, cameras, video game consoles and computers) often price them low and set high mark-ups on the supplies. Thus Gillette sells low-priced razors, but makes money on the replacement blades. Polaroid prices its instant cameras low (€40 for a Barbie Cam) because it makes its money on specialised films they need (€10). And Nintendo sells its game consoles at low prices but makes money on video game titles. In fact, whereas Nintendo's margins on its consoles run at a mere 1–5 per cent, margins on its game cartridges run close to 45 per cent. Video game sales contribute more than half the company's profits. Similarly, Sony and Microsoft recently dropped the prices of their PlayStation2 and Xbox game consoles by one-third despite the fact that the original prices were already set below cost. Despite losses on the game console, Sony makes

> **Captive-product pricing**—Setting a price for products that must be used along with a main product, such as blades for a razor and film for a camera.

Captive-product pricing:
Nintendo sells game consoles at
reasonable prices and makes
money on video game titles.
SOURCE: Courtesy of Nintendo
America, Inc. *agency*: Leo Burnett.

more than 60 per cent of its operating profit from the sale of PlayStation2 and its accompanying games.[31]

In the case of services, this strategy is called **two-part pricing**. The price of the service is broken into a *fixed fee* plus a *variable usage rate*. Thus a telephone company charges a monthly rate – the fixed fee – plus charges for calls beyond some minimum number – the variable usage rate. Amusement parks charge admission plus fees for food and some rides. The service firm must decide how much to charge for the basic service and how much for the variable usage. The fixed amount should be low enough to induce usage of the service, and profit can be made on the variable fees.

Two-part pricing—
A strategy for pricing
services in which price is
broken into a fixed fee plus
a variable usage rate.

By-product pricing

By-products—Items
produced as a result of the
main factory process, such
as waste and reject items.

By-product pricing—Setting
a price for by-products in
order to make the main product's price more competitive.

In producing processed meats, petroleum products, chemicals and other products, there are often **by-products**. If the by-products have no value and if getting rid of them is costly, this will affect the pricing of the main product. Using **by-product pricing**, the manufacturer will seek a market for these by-products and should accept any price that covers more than the cost of storing and delivering them. This practice allows the seller to reduce the main product's price to make it more competitive. By-products can even turn out to be profitable. For example, many lumber mills have begun to sell bark chips and sawdust profitably as decorative mulch for home and commercial landscaping.

Product-bundle pricing

Using **product-bundle pricing**, sellers often combine several of their products and offer the bundle at a reduced price. Thus theatres and sports teams sell season tickets at less than the cost of single tickets; hotels sell specially priced packages that include room, meals and entertainment; computer makers include attractive software packages with their personal computers, and Internet service providers sell packages that include Web access, Web hosting, email and an Internet search programme. Price bundling can promote the sales of products that consumers might not otherwise buy, but the combined price must be low enough to get them to buy the bundle.

In other cases, *product-bundle pricing* is used to sell more than the customer really wants. Obtaining a ticket to a rock event is sometimes difficult, but tickets to international concerts bundled with flights, accommodation, etc., are often widely available.[32]

Product-bundle pricing—Combining several products and offering the bundle at a reduced price.

Price-adjustment strategies

Companies usually adjust their basic prices to account for various customer differences and changing situations. Table 16.5 summarises seven price-adjustment strategies: *discount and allowance pricing, segmented pricing, psychological pricing, promotional pricing, value pricing, geographical pricing* and *international pricing*.

Discount and allowance pricing

Most companies adjust their basic price to reward customers for certain responses, such as early payment of bills, volume purchases and off-season buying. These price adjustments – called *discounts* and *allowances* – can take many forms.

A **cash discount** is a price reduction to buyers who pay their bills promptly. A typical example is '2/10, net 30', which means that although payment is due within 30 days, the buyer can deduct 2 per cent if the bill is paid within 10 days. The discount must be granted to all buyers meeting these terms. Such discounts are customary in many industries and help to improve the sellers' cash situation and reduce bad debts and credit-collection costs.

A **quantity discount** is a price reduction to buyers who buy large volumes. A typical example is Pilot Hi-Tecpoint pens from Staples Office Supplies at €6 for a pack of three, €10 for six and €18 for 12. Wine merchants often give '12 for the price of 11' and Makro, the trade

Cash discount—A price reduction to buyers who pay their bills promptly.

Quantity discount—A price reduction to buyers who buy large volumes.

Table 16.5 Price adjustment strategies

Discount and allowance pricing	Segmented pricing	Psychological pricing	Value pricing	Promotional pricing	Geographical pricing	International pricing
Reducing prices to reward customer responses such as paying early or promoting the product	Adjusting prices to allow for differences in customers, products and locations	Adjusting prices for psychological effect	Adjusting prices to offer the right combination of quality and service at a fair price	Temporarily reducing prices to increase short-run sales	Adjusting prices to account for the geographical location of customers	Adjusting prices in international markets

warehouse, automatically gives discounts on any product bought in bulk. Discounts provide an incentive to the customer to buy more from one given seller, rather than from many different sources. Price does not always decrease with the quantity purchased. More often than realised, people pay a **quantity premium**, a surcharge paid by buyers who purchase high volumes of a product.

> In Japan it often costs more per item to buy a 12-pack of beer or sushi than smaller quantities because the larger packs are more giftable and therefore less price sensitive. Quantity surcharges can also occur when the product being bought is in short supply or in sets – for example, several seats together at a 'sold-out' rock concert or sports event – and some small restaurants charge a premium to large groups. Similarly, in buying antiques, it costs more to buy six complete place settings of cutlery than a single item. In this case the price will continue to increase with volume, eight place settings costing more than six, and 12 place settings costing more than eight.[33]

A **trade discount** (also called a **functional discount**) is offered by the seller to trade channel members that perform certain functions, such as selling, storing and record keeping. Manufacturers may offer different functional discounts to different trade channels because of the varying services they perform, but manufacturers must offer the same functional discounts within each trade channel.

A **seasonal discount** is a price discount to buyers who buy merchandise or services out of season. For example, lawn and garden equipment manufacturers will offer seasonal discounts to retailers during the autumn and winter to encourage early ordering in anticipation of the heavy spring and summer selling seasons. Hotels, motels and airlines will offer seasonal discounts in their slower selling periods. Seasonal discounts allow the seller to keep production steady or stabilise capacity utilisation during the entire year.

Allowances are another type of reduction from the list price. For example, **trade-in allowances** are price reductions given for turning in an old item when buying a new one. Trade-in allowances are most common in the car industry, but are also given for other durable goods. **Promotional allowances** are payments or price reductions to reward dealers for participating in advertising and sales-support programmes.

In stable markets, price adjustments have traditionally been relatively infrequent changes made as part of a strategy marketing or promotional programme. The Internet is changing that. In online trading, the ink on sticker prices often has no time to dry. Prices can change from hour to hour and from customer to customer. Marketing Insights 16.2 looks at these new pricing dynamics.

Segmented pricing

Companies will often adjust their basic prices to allow for differences in customers, products and locations. In **segmented pricing**, the company sells a product or service at two or more prices, even though the difference in prices is not based on differences in costs. Segmented pricing takes several forms:

1. *Customer-segment pricing.* Different customers pay different prices for the same product or service. Museums, for example, will charge a lower admission for young people, the unwaged, students and senior citizens. In many parts of the world, tourists pay more to see museums, shows and national monuments than do locals.

Quantity premium— A surcharge paid by buyers who purchase high volumes of a product.

Functional discount (trade discount)—A price reduction offered by the seller to trade channel members that perform certain functions, such as selling, storing and record keeping.

Seasonal discount—A price reduction to buyers who buy merchandise or services out of season.

Trade-in allowance—A price reduction given for turning in an old item when buying a new one.

Promotional allowance—A payment or price reduction to reward dealers for participating in advertising and sales-support programmes.

Segmented pricing—Pricing that allows for differences in customers, products and locations. The differences in prices are not based on differences in costs.

Back to the future: pricing on the Web

At one time all prices were negotiated. The Web seems to be taking us back – into a new age of fluid pricing. 'Potentially, [the Internet] could push aside stickier prices and usher in an era of dynamic pricing', says *Business Week* writer Robert Hof, 'in which a wide range of goods would be priced according to what the market will bear – instantly, constantly.' Here's how.

Lower prices, higher margins

Web buying and selling can lower costs. Thanks to their Internet connections, buyers and sellers around the world can connect at almost no cost. Reduced inventory and distribution costs add to the savings. For example, by selling online and making its computers to order, Dell Computer reduces inventory costs and eliminates retail mark-ups. It passes on its savings as 'lowest price per $ for performance'.

Tailor offers to individuals

Web merchants can target prices to specific customers. For example, Amazon.com can assess each visitor's 'click-stream', the way the person navigates the website, then tailor products and prices to that shopper's behaviour. If visitors behave like a price-sensitive shopper, they may be offered a lower price. The Internet also lets sellers give some customers access to special prices. For example, CDnow emails a special website address with lower prices to certain buyers. If you don't know the secret address, you pay full price.

Change prices according to changes in demand or costs

With printed catalogues, such as Lands' End or Hawkshead, a price is a price until the next catalogue is printed. In contrast, online sellers can change prices hourly. This allows sellers to adjust to changing costs, offer promotions on slow-moving and unsold items or nudge prices upwards on hot-selling goods. Lastminute.com, the opportunistic dotcom, helps the leisure sector sell unbooked hotel rooms and unsold entertainment tickets and to fill flights close to their sell-by date. Many business marketers use their extranets, the private networks that link them with suppliers and customers, to get a precise handle on inventory, costs and demand at any given moment and adjust prices instantly.

marketing insights

...16.2 Negotiate prices online

Want to sell that antique pickle jar? Post it on eBay, the world's biggest online flea market. Want to dump that excess stock? Try adding an auction feature to your own website. Sharper Image claims it's getting 40 per cent of retail for excess goods sold via its online auction site, compared with only 20 per cent from liquidators.

Get instant price comparisons from thousands of vendors

Web shoppers can quickly compare information about products and vendors almost anywhere. Online comparison guides, such as Compare.Net, Kelkoo and PriceScan, give product and price comparisons at the click of a mouse. Compare.Net lets consumers do side-by-side comparison of items, provides a smart tips sections and an online glossary giving helpful tips and product information to aid in consumers' buying decision. Other sites offer intelligent shopping agents. MySimon, for instance, takes a buyer's criteria for a camcorder or collectable, then routes through sellers' sites to find the best match at the best price.

Negotiate lower prices

With market information and access comes buyer power. In addition to simply finding the vendor with the best price, customers armed with price information can often negotiate lower prices.

> UTC tried something new. Instead of haggling with dozens of individual vendors to secure printed circuit boards for various subsidiaries worldwide, it put the contract out on FreeMarkets, an online marketplace for industrial goods. Bids poured in from 39 suppliers, saving UTC over €11 million off its initial €27 million estimate.

Will dynamic pricing sweep the marketing world? 'Not entirely', says Hof. 'It takes a lot of work to haggle – which is why fixed prices happened in the first place.' However, he continues, 'Pandora's E-box is now open, and pricing will never be the same.'

SOURCES: Quotes and extracts from Robert D. Hof, 'Going, going, gone', *Business Week* (12 April 1999), pp. 30–2; Robert D. Hof, 'The buyer always wins', *Business Week* (22 March 1999), pp. EB26–EB28; and Stephen Manes, 'Off-Web dickering', *Forbes* (5 April 1999), p. 134. Also see Michael Krauss, 'Web offers biggest prize in product pricing game', *Marketing News* (6 July 1998), p. 8; Hazel Ward, 'Top of the shops', *e.business* (April 2000), pp. 69–71; Chris Nuttall, 'Lastminute becomes last word in travel', *Financial Times* (20 November 2003), p. 25; and Michael Rappa, 'Managing the digital enterprise. Case study: mySimon', available at http://digitalenterprise.org/cases/mysimon.html, accessed 18 February 2004.

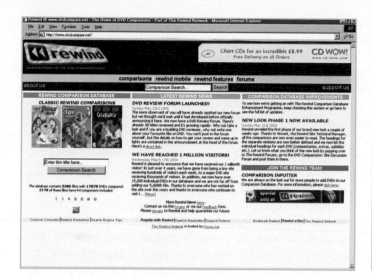

Buying a sports utility vehicle, a DVD player or even a toe ring? Online shopping guides like Compare.Net and Pricescan.com enable buyers to make side-by-side comparisons of product features and prices at the click of a mouse.
SOURCE: (left) Dvdcompare.net/rewind.com; (right) Pricescan.com Inc.

2. *Product-form pricing.* Different versions of the product are priced differently, but not according to differences in their costs. For instance, the Dutch company Skil prices its 6434II electric drill at €100, which is €60 more than the price of its 6400H. The 6434H is more powerful and has more features, yet this extra power and features cost only a few more euros to build in.

3. *Location pricing.* Different locations are priced differently, even though the cost of offering each location is the same. For instance, theatres vary their seat prices because of audience preferences for certain locations, and EU universities charge higher tuition fees for non-EU students.

4. *Time pricing.* Prices vary by the season, the month, the day and even the hour. Public utilities vary their prices to commercial users by time of day and weekend versus weekday. Telephone companies offer lower 'off-peak' charges, electricity costs less at night and resorts give seasonal discounts.

For segmented pricing to be an effective strategy, certain conditions must exist. The market must be segmentable and the segments must show different degrees of demand. Members of the segment paying the lower price should not be able to turn round and resell the product to the segment paying the higher price. Competitors should not be able to undersell the firm in the segment being charged the higher price. Nor should the costs of segmenting and watching the market exceed the extra revenue obtained from the price difference. Of course, the segmented pricing must also be legal. Most importantly, segmented prices should reflect real differences in customers' perceived value. Otherwise, in the long run, the practice should not lead to customer resentment and ill will.

Psychological pricing

Price says something about the product. For example, many consumers use price to judge quality. A €100 bottle of perfume may contain only €3 worth of scent, but some people are willing to pay the €100 because this price indicates something special.

In using **psychological pricing**, sellers consider the psychology of prices and not simply the economics. For example, one study of the relationship between price and quality perception of cars found that consumers perceive higher-priced cars as having higher quality.[34] By the

Psychological pricing—
A pricing approach that considers the psychology of prices and not simply the economics; the price is used to say something about the product.

same token, higher-quality cars are perceived as even higher priced than they actually are. When consumers can judge the quality of a product by examining it or by calling on past experience with it, they use price less to judge quality. When consumers cannot judge quality because they lack the information or skill, price becomes an important quality signal. Psychological pricing is particularly apparent in airport duty-free shops where people buy expensive items in unfamiliar categories. In such outlets, exquisite malt whiskies are often sold inexpensively but inexperienced buyers are attracted by grandly packaged and overpriced blended whiskies.

Reference prices—Prices that buyers carry in their minds and refer to when they look at a given product.

Another aspect of psychological pricing is **reference prices** – prices that buyers carry in their minds and refer to when looking at a given product. The reference price might be formed by noting current prices, remembering past prices or assessing the buying situation. Sellers can influence or use these consumers' reference prices when setting price. For example, a company could display its product next to more expensive ones in order to imply that it belongs in the same class. Department stores often sell women's clothing in separate departments differentiated by price: clothing found in the more expensive department is assumed to be of better quality. Companies also can influence consumers' reference prices by stating high manufacturer's suggested prices, by indicating that the product was originally priced much higher or by pointing to a competitor's higher price.

Even small differences in price can suggest product differences. Consider a stereo priced at €400 compared to one priced at €399. The actual price difference is only €1, but the psychological difference can be much greater. For example, some consumers will see the €399 as a price in the €300 range rather than the €400 range. Whereas the €399 is more likely to be seen as a bargain price, the €400 price suggests more quality. Complicated numbers, such as €347.41, also look less appealing than rounded ones, such as €350. Some psychologists argue that each digit has symbolic and visual qualities that should be considered in pricing. Thus, 8 is round and even and creates a soothing effect, whereas 7 is angular and creates a jarring effect.[35]

Promotional pricing

Promotional pricing— Temporarily pricing products below the list price, and sometimes even below cost, to increase short-run sales.

With **promotional pricing**, companies will temporarily price their products below list price and sometimes even below cost. Promotional pricing takes several forms. Supermarkets and department stores will price a few products as *loss leaders* to attract customers to the store in the hope that they will buy other items at normal mark-ups. Sellers will also use *special-event pricing* in certain seasons to draw in more customers. Thus linens are promotionally priced every January to attract weary Christmas shoppers back into the stores. Manufacturers will sometimes offer *cash rebates* to consumers who buy the product from dealers within a specified time; the manufacturer sends the rebate directly to the customer. Rebates have recently been popular with carmakers and producers of durable goods and small appliances.

Some manufacturers offer *low-interest financing*, *longer warranties* or *free maintenance* to reduce the consumer's 'price'. This practice has recently become a favourite of the car industry. The seller may simply offer *discounts* from normal prices to increase sales and reduce stocks. Some manufacturers may even offer 'zero-financing' in moves to capture customers.

Mitsubishi, the Japanese carmaker that is 37 per cent owned by DaimlerChrysler, is in dire straits. Much of its problems in the US, however, may be of its own making. To lure young, low-income buyers to its newly-launched line of mini-cars, Mitsubishi used 'zero, zero, zero' financing: no money down, no interest payments, and no repayment of principal for the first year. For Mitsubishi, this was one ZERO too many. The company racked up huge losses as its young, impecunious buyers failed – surprise, surprise – to start to make payments when their year was up.[36]

Promotional pricing, therefore, can have adverse effects. Moreover, used too frequently and copied by competitors, price promotions can create 'deal-prone' customers who wait until brands go on sale before buying them. Equally, constantly reduced prices can erode a brand's value in the eyes of customers. Marketers sometimes use price promotions as a quick fix instead of sweating through the difficult process of developing effective longer-term strategies for building their brands. In fact, one observer notes that price promotions can be downright addicting to both the company and the customer: 'Price promotions are the brand equivalent of heroin: easy to get into but hard to get out of. Once the brand and its customers are addicted to the short-term high of a price cut it is hard to wean them away to real brand building. . . . But continue and the brand dies by 1000 cuts.'[37]

The frequent use of promotional pricing can also lead to industry price wars. Such price wars usually play into the hands of only one or a few competitors – those with the most efficient operations. For example, until recently, the computer industry avoided price wars. Computer companies, including IBM, Hewlett-Packard and Compaq, showed strong profits as their new technologies were snapped up by eager consumers. When the market cooled, however, many competitors began to unload PCs at discounted prices. In response, Dell, the industry's undisputed low-cost leader, started a price war that only it could win.

In mid-2000, Dell declared a brutal price war just as the industry slipped into its worst slump ever. The result was nothing short of a rout. While Dell chalked up $361 million (€429.6 million) in profits the following year, the rest of the industry logged $1.1 billion (€1.31 billion) in losses. Dell's edge starts with its direct-selling approach. By taking orders straight from customers and building machines to order, Dell avoids paying retailer markups, getting stuck with unsold PCs, and keeping costly inventories. For example, at any given moment, Dell's warehouses hold just four days of stock, compared with 24 days for competitors. That gives it a gigantic edge in a market where the price of chips, drives, and other parts typically falls 1 per cent a week. Moreover, Dell has mastered supply chain management. It requires suppliers to use sophisticated software that wires them straight into Dell's factory floor, allowing Dell's plants to replenish supplies only as needed throughout the day. That software alone saved Dell $50 million in the first six months of use. Since launching the price war, the price of a Dell computer has dropped more than 18 per cent, leaving competitors with few effective weapons. IBM has responded by outsourcing its PC production and sales. And H-P and Compaq merged in hopes of finding strength in numbers. Says Michael Dell, 'When we sell these products, we make money. When our competitors sell them, they lose money.'[38]

The point is that promotional pricing can be an effective means of generating sales in certain circumstances but can be damaging if taken as a steady diet.

Geographical pricing

A company must also decide how to price its products to customers located in different parts of the country or the world. Should the company risk losing the business of more distant customers by charging them higher prices to cover the higher shipping costs? Or should the company charge all customers the same prices regardless of location? We will look at five **geographical pricing** strategies for the following hypothetical situation:

Geographical pricing— Pricing based on where customers are located.

> Tromsø a.s. is a Norwegian paper products company selling to customers all over Europe. The cost of freight is high and affects the companies from whom customers buy their paper. Tromsø wants to establish a geographical pricing policy. It is trying to determine how to price a Nkr1,000 order to three specific customers: Customer A (Oslo), Customer B (Amsterdam) and Customer C (Barcelona).

FOB-origin pricing—A geographic pricing strategy in which goods are placed free on board a carrier; the customer pays the freight from the factory to the destination.

One option is for Tromsø to ask each customer to pay the shipping cost from the factory to the customer's location. All three customers would pay the same factory price of Nkr1,000 (€806), with Customer A paying, say, Nkr100 for shipping; Customer B, Nkr150; and Customer C, Nkr250. Called **FOB-origin pricing**, this practice means that the goods are placed *free on board* (hence, *FOB*) a carrier. At that point the title and responsibility pass to the customer, who pays the freight from the factory to the destination.

Because each customer picks up its own cost, supporters of FOB pricing feel that this is the fairest way to assess freight charges. The disadvantage, however, is that Tromsø will be a high-cost firm to distant customers. If Tromsø's main competitor happens to be in Spain, this competitor will no doubt outsell Tromsø in Spain. In fact, the competitor would outsell Tromsø in most of southern Europe, whereas Tromsø would dominate the north.

Uniform delivered pricing— A geographic pricing strategy in which the company charges the same price plus freight to all customers, regardless of their location.

Uniform delivered pricing is the exact opposite of FOB pricing. Here, the company charges the same price plus freight to all customers, regardless of their location. The freight charge is set at the average freight cost. Suppose this is Nkr150. Uniform delivered pricing therefore results in a higher charge to the Oslo customer (who pays Nkr150 freight instead of Nkr100) and a lower charge to the Barcelona customer (who pays Nkr150 instead of Nkr250). On the one hand, the Oslo customer would prefer to buy paper from another local paper company that uses FOB-origin pricing. On the other hand, Tromsø has a better chance of winning over the Spanish customer. Other advantages of uniform delivered pricing are that it is fairly easy to administer and it lets the firm advertise its price nationally.

Zone pricing—A geographic pricing strategy in which the company sets up two or more zones. All customers within a zone pay the same total price; the more distant the zone, the higher the price.

Zone pricing falls between FOB-origin pricing and uniform delivered pricing. The company sets up two or more zones. All customers within a given zone pay a single total price; the more distant the zone, the higher the price. For example, Tromsø might set up a Scandinavian zone and charge Nkr100 freight to all customers in this zone, a northern European zone in which it charges Nkr150 and a southern European zone in which it charges Nkr250. In this way, the customers within a given price zone receive no price advantage from the company. For example, customers in Oslo and Copenhagen pay the same total price to Tromsø. The complaint, however, is that the Oslo customer is paying part of the Copenhagen customer's freight cost. In addition, even though they may be within a few miles of each other, a customer just barely on the south side of the line dividing north and south pays much more than one that is just barely on the north side of the line.

Basing-point pricing—A geographic pricing strategy in which the seller designates some city as a basing point and charges all customers the freight cost from that city to the customer location, regardless of the city from which the goods are actually shipped.

Using **basing-point pricing**, the seller selects a given city as a 'basing point' and charges all customers the freight cost from that city to the customer location, regardless of the city from which the goods are actually shipped. For example, Tromsø might set Oslo as the basing point and charge all customers Nkr100 plus the freight from Oslo to their locations. This means that a Copenhagen customer pays the freight cost from Oslo to Copenhagen, even though the goods may be shipped from Tromsø. Using a basing-point location other than the factory raises the total price for customers near the factory and lowers the total price for customers far from the factory.

If all sellers used the same basing-point city, delivered prices would be the same for all customers and price competition would be eliminated. Industries such as sugar, cement, steel and cars used basing-point pricing for years, but this method has become less popular today. Some companies set up multiple basing points to create more flexibility: they quote freight charges from the basing-point city nearest to the customer.

Finally, the seller that is anxious to do business with a certain customer or geographical area might use **freight-absorption pricing**. Using this strategy, the seller absorbs all or part of the actual freight charges in order to get the desired business. The seller might reason that if it can get more business, its average costs will fall and more than compensate for its extra freight cost. Freight-absorption pricing is used for market penetration and to hold on to increasingly competitive markets.

Freight-absorption pricing— A geographic pricing strategy in which the company absorbs all or part of the actual freight charges in order to get the business.

International pricing

Companies that market their products internationally must decide what prices to charge in the different countries in which they operate. In some cases, a company can set a uniform worldwide price. For example, Airbus sells its jetliners at about the same price everywhere, whether in the United States, Europe or a Third World country. However, most companies adjust their prices to reflect local market conditions and cost considerations.

The price that a company should charge in a specific country depends on many factors, including economic conditions, competitive situations, laws and regulations, and development of the wholesaling and retailing system. Consumer perceptions and preferences may also vary from country to country, calling for different prices. Or the company may have different marketing objectives in various world markets, which require changes in pricing strategy. For example, Sony might introduce a new product into mature markets in highly developed countries with the goal of quickly gaining mass-market share – this would call for a penetration pricing strategy. In contrast, it might enter a less developed market by targeting smaller, less price-sensitive segments – in this case, market-skimming pricing makes sense.

Costs play an important role in setting international prices. Travellers abroad are often surprised to find that goods, which are relatively inexpensive at home, may carry outrageously higher price tags in other countries. A pair of Levi's selling for $30 (€35) in the US goes for about $63 in Tokyo and $88 in Paris. A McDonald's Big Mac selling for a modest $2.25 in the US costs $5.75 in Moscow. A Britney Spears CD sells for $15.99 in the US, but costs about $20 in the UK. Conversely, a Gucci handbag going for only $60 in Milan, Italy, fetches $240 in the US. In some cases, such price escalation may result from differences in selling strategies or market conditions. In most instances, however, it is simply a result of the higher costs of selling in foreign markets – the additional costs of modifying the product, higher shipping and insurance costs, import tariffs and taxes, costs associated with exchange-rate fluctuations and higher channel and physical distribution costs.[39]

For example, Campbell found that its distribution costs in the UK were 30 per cent higher than in the US. US retailers typically purchase soup in large quantities – 48-can cases of a single soup by the dozens, hundred or carloads. In contrast, English grocers purchase soup in small quantities – typically in 24-can cases of *assorted* soups. Each case must be hand-packed for shipment. To handle these small orders, Campbell had to add a costly extra wholesale level to its European channel. The smaller orders also mean that English retailers order two or three times as often as their US counterparts, bumping up billing and order costs. These and other factors caused Campbell to charge much higher prices for its soups in the UK.[40] Thus international pricing presents some special problems and complexities that are discussed in more detail in Chapter 6.

Price changes

After developing their price structures and strategies, companies often face situations in which they must initiate price changes or respond to price changes by competitors.

Initiating price changes

In some cases, the company may find it desirable to initiate either a price cut or a price increase. In both cases, it must anticipate possible buyer and competitor reactions.

Initiating price cuts

Several situations may lead a firm to consider cutting its price. One such circumstance is excess capacity. In this case, the firm needs more business and cannot get it through increased sales effort, product improvement or other measures. It may drop its *follow-the-leader pricing* – charging about the same price as its leading competitor – and aggressively cut prices to boost sales. But as the airline, construction equipment and other industries have learned in recent years, cutting prices in an industry loaded with excess capacity may lead to price wars as competitors try to hold on to market share.

Another situation leading to price changes is falling market share in the face of strong price competition. Several industries – cars, consumer electronics, cameras, watches and steel, for example – lost market share to Japanese competitors who offered high-quality products at lower prices than Western competitors. In response, defending companies resorted to more aggressive pricing to hold on to their markets.

A company may also cut prices in a drive to dominate the market through lower costs. Either the company starts with lower costs than its competitors or it cuts prices in the hope of gaining market share that will further cut costs through larger volume. Bausch & Lomb used an aggressive low-cost, low-price strategy to become an early leader in the competitive soft contact-lens market.

Initiating price increases

In contrast, many companies have had to *raise* prices in recent years. They do this knowing that customers, dealers and even their own sales force may resent the price increases. Yet a successful price increase can greatly increase profits. For example, if the company's profit margin is 3 per cent of sales, a 1 per cent price increase will increase profits by 33 per cent if sales volume is unaffected.

A considerable factor in price increases is cost inflation. Rising costs squeeze profit margins and lead companies to make regular rounds of price increases. Companies often raise their prices by more than the cost increase in anticipation of further inflation. Another factor leading to price increases is over-demand: when a company cannot supply all its customers' needs, it can raise its prices, ration products to customers or both.

Companies can increase their prices in a number of ways to keep up with rising costs. Dropping discounts and adding higher-priced units to the line can raise prices almost invisibly. Or prices can be pushed up openly. Companies have learned to take care when passing price increases on to customers. The price increases should be supported with a company communication programme telling customers why prices are being increased. The company sales force should help customers find ways to economise.

Where possible, the company should consider ways to meet higher costs or demand without raising prices. For example, it can shrink the product instead of raising the price, as confectionery manufacturers do. It can substitute less expensive ingredients or remove certain product features, packaging or services. Or it can 'unbundle' its products and services, removing and separately pricing elements that were formerly part of the offer. IBM, for example, now offers training and consulting as separately priced services.

Buyer reactions to price changes

Whether the price is raised or lowered, the action will affect buyers, competitors, distributors and suppliers, and may interest government as well. Customers do not always interpret prices in a straightforward way. They may view a price *cut* in several ways. For example, what would you think if Sony were suddenly to cut its DVD prices in half? You might think that these DVDs are about to be replaced by newer models or that they have some fault and are not selling well. You might think that Sony is in financial trouble and may not stay in the business long enough to supply future parts. You might believe that quality has been reduced. Or you might think that the price will come down even further and that it will pay to wait and see.

Similarly, a price *increase*, which would normally lower sales, may have some positive meanings for buyers. What would you think if Sony *raised* the price of its latest DVD model? On the one hand, you might think that the item is very 'hot' and may be unobtainable unless you buy it soon. Or you might think that the recorder is unusually good value. On the other hand, you might think that Sony is greedy and charging what the traffic will bear.

Competitor reactions to price changes

A firm considering a price change has to worry about the reactions of its competitors as well as its customers. Competitors are most likely to react when the number of firms involved is small, when the product is uniform and when the buyers are well informed.

How can the firm figure out the likely reactions of its competitors? If the firm faces one large competitor and if the competitor tends to react in a set way to price changes, that reaction can be easily anticipated. But if the competitor treats each price change as a fresh challenge and reacts according to its self-interest, the company will have to figure out just what makes up the competitor's self-interest at the time.

The problem is complex because, like the customer, the competitor can interpret a company price cut in many ways. It might think that the company is trying to grab a larger market share, that the company is doing poorly and trying to boost its sales or that the company wants the whole industry to cut prices to increase total demand.

When there are several competitors, the company must guess each competitor's likely reaction. If all competitors behave alike, this amounts to analysing only a typical competitor. In contrast, if the competitors do not behave alike – perhaps because of differences in size, market shares or policies – then separate analyses are necessary. However, if some competitors will match the price change, there is good reason to expect that the rest will also match it.

Responding to price changes

Here we reverse the question and ask how a firm should respond to a price change by a competitor. The firm needs to consider several questions: Why did the competitor change the price? Was it to make more market share, to use excess capacity, to meet changing cost conditions or to lead an industry-wide price change? Is the price change temporary or

Figure 16.9 Assessing and responding to a competitor's price cut

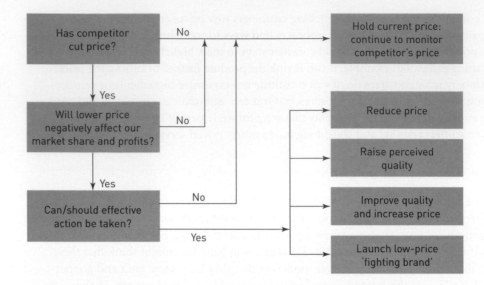

permanent? What will happen to the company's market share and profits if it does not respond? Are other companies going to respond? What are the competitor's and other firms' responses to each possible reaction likely to be?

Besides these issues, the company must make a broader analysis. It has to consider its own product's stage in the life-cycle, its importance in the company's product mix, the intentions and resources of the competitor and the possible consumer reactions to price changes. The company cannot always make an extended analysis of its alternatives at the time of a price change, however. The competitor may have spent much time preparing this decision, but the company may have to react within hours or days. About the only way to cut down reaction time is to plan ahead for both possible price changes and possible responses from the competitor.

Figure 16.9 shows the ways in which a company might assess and respond to a competitor's price cut. Once the company has determined that the competitor has cut its price and that this price reduction is likely to harm company sales and profits, it might simply decide to hold its current price and profit margin. The company might believe that it will not lose too much market share or that it would lose too much profit if it reduced its own price. It might decide that it should wait and respond when it has more information on the effects of the competitor's price change. For now, it might be willing to hold on to good customers, while giving up the poorer ones to the competitor. The argument against this holding strategy, however, is that the competitor may get stronger and more confident as its sales increase and the company might wait too long to act.

By keeping the appeal of their products ahead of the competition and keeping costs down, Nokia has not only maintained profitability but increased its market share of the mobile phone market. According to Jorma Ollila, Nokia's chief executive: 'There was a belief among some in the market that new players entering the marketplace would disrupt the formula, but that has not happened.'[41]

If the company decides that effective action can and should be taken, it might make any of the following four responses.

1. *Reduce price.* The leader might drop its price to the competitor's price. It may decide that the market is price sensitive and that it would lose too much market share to the lower-priced competitor. Or it might worry that recapturing lost market share later would be too hard. Cutting price will reduce the company's profits in the short run. Some companies might also reduce their product quality, services and marketing communications to retain profit margins, but ultimately this will hurt long-run market share. The company should try to maintain its quality as it cuts prices.

2. *Raise perceived quality.* Like Nokia, a company might maintain its price but strengthen the perceived value of its offer. It could improve its communications, stressing the relative quality of its product over that of the lower-price competitor. The firm may find it cheaper to maintain price and spend money to improve its perceived quality than to cut price and operate at a lower margin.

3. *Improve quality and increase price.* The company might increase quality and raise its price, moving its brand into a higher price position. The higher quality justifies the higher price, which in turn preserves the company's higher margins. Or the company can hold the price on the current product and introduce a new brand at a higher price position.

4. *Launch low-price 'fighting brand'.* One of the best responses is to add lower-price items to the line or to create a separate lower-price brand. This is necessary if the particular market segment being lost is price sensitive and will not respond to arguments of higher quality. Thus, when attacked on price by Fuji, Kodak introduced low-priced Funtime film. When challenged on price by store brands and other low-priced entrants, Nestlé turned a number of its brands into fighting brands, including Fussell's condensed milk. In response to price pressures, Miller cut the price of its High Life brand by 20 per cent in most markets and sales jumped 9 per cent in less than a year.[42]

Pricing strategies and tactics form an important element of a company's marketing mix. In setting prices, companies must carefully consider a great many internal and external factors before choosing a price that will give them the greatest competitive advantage in selected target markets. However, companies are not usually free to charge whatever prices they wish. Several laws restrict pricing practices and a number of ethical considerations affect pricing decisions. Pricing strategies and tactics also depend upon the way that we pay for things. Increasingly, what we spend does not depend on how much money we have on us or how much we earned that week. These days our money is rarely something we see or feel; it is the electronic transmission of data between files within banks or on the Internet:

Increasingly, people pay, for even small transactions, by credit card, debit card, prepaid smart cards or e-cash. People and companies are also turning to trading their skills and produce without using money. A plumber may do a job for you if you will mow his lawn for a week and babysit one night. But, if the plumber does not want anything you can provide, he could turn to clubs that trade credits. The plumber does the job for you, but he can use his credits to get goods or services from someone else.

Today, institutions like London's Capital Barter Corporation (CBC) orchestrate third-party deals for companies that offer their services for trade credits rather than cash. CBC's deals range from a £15 (€22) restaurant meal to a £15,000 stock of computers. The most popular items are airline tickets, photocopiers and computers. Barter is not just for small deals between small

firms – Lufthansa, Playtex and US Networks have all had deals worth
€2 million or more. CBC and other barter companies, including The Bartering
Company and Eurotrade, debit and credit their members' accounts in 'trade
pounds'. Each member has a credit limit depending upon the size of the
company and the tradability of its products.

And there is the Internet now which has its own money. New e-payment
formats, including iClickCharge and Opass, cost retailers little and allow
'micropayments' down to €0.001. There are also creative variants like
PayTrust that specialises in the electronic payment of subscribers' household
bills. Most exotic of all is e-gold, where customers fund their online accounts
by buying gold or other precious metals. Once purchased, this libertarian
commodity is free of currency, purchases being paid for in units of weight
of the metals.[43]

Summary

Despite the increased role of non-price factors in the modern marketing process, *price*
remains an important element in the marketing mix. Many internal and external factors
influence the company's pricing decisions. *Internal factors* include the firm's *marketing
objectives*, *marketing-mix strategy*, *costs* and *organisation for pricing*.

The pricing strategy is largely determined by the company's *target market and
positioning objectives*. Common pricing objectives include survival, current profit
maximisation, market-share leadership and product-quality leadership.

Pricing decisions affect and are affected by product design, distribution and promotion
decisions. Hence, they must be carefully coordinated with the other *marketing-mix*
decisions when designing the marketing programme.

Costs set the floor for the company's price – the price must cover all the costs of
making and selling the product, plus a fair rate of return. Management must decide who
within the *organisation* is responsible for setting price. Top management usually sets
pricing policies, but some pricing authority may be delegated to lower-level managers,
including salespeople, production, finance and accounting managers.

External factors that influence pricing decisions include the nature of the market and
demand; competitors' prices and offers; and factors such as the economy, reseller needs
and government actions. The seller's pricing freedom varies with different types of
market. Pricing is especially challenging in markets characterised by monopolistic
competition oligopoly.

In the end, the consumer weighs the price against the perceived values of using the
product – if the price exceeds the sum of the values, consumers will not buy the product.
Consumers differ in the values they assign to different product features, and marketers
often vary their pricing strategies for different price segments. When assessing the
market and demand, the company estimates the demand curve, which shows the
probable quantity purchased per period at alternative price levels. The more *inelastic*
the demand, the higher the company can set its price. *Demand* and *consumer value
perceptions* set the ceiling for prices.

Consumers also compare a product's price to the prices of *competitors'* products. The company can select one or a combination of three general pricing approaches: the *cost-based approach* (cost-plus pricing, break-even analysis and target profit pricing); the *value-based approach* (value-based pricing); and the *competition-based approach* (going-rate, sealed-bid pricing or auctions). With the advent of the Internet, online auctions look like becoming an increasingly common means of price setting.

Pricing is a dynamic process. Companies design a *pricing structure* that covers all their products. They change this structure over time and adjust it to account for different customers and situations. Pricing strategies usually change as a product passes through its life-cycle. There are several price-quality strategies for introducing an imitative product. In pricing innovative new products, a company can follow a *skimming policy* by initially setting high prices to 'skim' the maximum amount of revenue from various segments of the market. Or it can use *penetration pricing* by setting a low initial price to win a large market share.

When the product is part of a product mix, the firm searches for a set of prices that will maximise the profits from the total mix. The company decides on *price steps* for items in its product line and on the pricing of *optional products*, *captive products*, *by-products* and *product bundles*.

Companies apply a variety of *price-adjustment strategies* to account for differences in consumer segments and situations: *discount and allowance pricing*, *segmented pricing*, *psychological pricing*, *promotional pricing*, *value pricing*, *geographical pricing* and *international pricing*.

When a firm considers initiating a *price change*, it must consider customers' and competitors' reactions. Customers' perception of the price change influences their reactions. Competitors' reactions flow from a set reaction policy or a fresh analysis of each situation. The firm initiating the price change must also anticipate the probable reactions of suppliers, intermediaries and government. The firm that faces a price change initiated by a competitor must try to understand the competitor's intent as well as the likely duration and impact of the change. When facing a competitor's price change, the company might sit tight, reduce its own price, raise perceived quality, improve quality and raise price, or launch a fighting brand.

Discussing the issues

1. A health and leisure club in a major city has seen its membership renewal rate fall at a rate of 10 per cent per year for the past three years. Assume you are the managing director of the club. You are faced with a dilemma. On one hand, you are under great pressure to raise new membership and renewal subscription fees to compensate for falling revenues. However, you suspect that higher subscription rates will make matters worse. On the other hand, you might seek to attract new customers and retain existing club members by reducing new subscription and renewal rates. What internal and external pricing factors should you consider before you make your decision? Explain.

2. List and critically discuss the general approaches to pricing. Select examples of products that you regularly use. Notice the price of each of these items. For each item, state the main benefits you are looking for in using the product. Does the price communicate the total benefits sought? Does the product's price suggest good value? Do you think the manufacturer or retailer is overcharging or undercharging consumers for the product?

Why or why not? What pricing approach do you think is most appropriate for setting the price for these products?

3. Like Amazon.com and Egg, the Internet bank, many e-commerce operations offer prices well below those in the high street or retail outlets and are making huge losses. What are the Internet businesses hoping to achieve with their aggressive pricing? Is their price advantage likely to be maintained? Some companies are adopting the concept of dynamic pricing on the Internet. How is dynamic pricing used on the Internet and what are the benefits for e-commerce operations?

4. Companies often adjust their basic prices to allow for differences in customers, products and locations. Use examples to illustrate the various forms of price adjustment strategies. In your answer, discuss where relevant the advantages and disadvantages of specific price adjustment strategies.

5. Assume that you are the manager of a consumer electronics and home entertainment department store. Formulate rules that govern (a) initiating a price cut, (b) initiating a price increase, (c) a negative reaction from buyers to a price change by your company, (d) a competitor's response to your price change, and (e) your response to a competitor's price change. In your answer, explain the assumptions underlying your proposed rules.

Applying the concepts

1. Conduct a pricing survey of computer printers, including home, office and portable printers offered by different companies (e.g. Hewlett-Packard, Epson, Canon, Océ, Xerox as well as retailer own-brands). Where possible, visit the retail stores or the websites of the retail stores and companies concerned to get more information.

   (a) What patterns do you detect for the pricing of different brands and types of printers (e.g. home, office, portable, basic, advanced)? Are there differences in pricing at different locations (e.g. retail versus direct/online)?

   (b) What pricing approaches appear to be used by different companies and their retailers?

   (c) What internal and external factors are important to consider when deciding a pricing strategy in this industry?

2. Visit the online shopping sites of major retailers in Europe and the US and compare the prices of identical products for sale in both areas. (Examples to choose are CDs by European and American artists sold by Amazon.com in the US and the same CDs sold by their European operations, such as Amazon.co.uk.) How different are the prices and to what extent do the prices reflect the country of origin of the products? What are the barriers to the prices being forced to converge by people shopping online across borders? How do the prices compare with high-street prices and those from online price comparison websites?

References

1. 'A not-so-popular Nordic bridge', *The Economist* (7 October 2000), p. 61; 'Asia: the bridge to nowhere in particular', *The Economist* (4 April 1998), p. 42; Robert Wright, 'Eurotunnel in traffic volume downturn', *Financial Times* (21 January 2004); 'Oresundsbro Konsortiet report operating result of DKK686m', *Nordic Business Report* (4 March 2003); 'Danish minister proposes tax relief for Oresund commuter', *Nordic Business Report* (6 June 2003); www.bridgepros.com/project/Oresund%20Bridge/. For prices and traffic information see www.oresundsbron.com.

2. Dean Foust, 'Raising prices won't fly', *Business Week* (3 June 2002), p. 34.

3. Philip Kotler, *Marketing Management*, 11th edn (Upper Saddle River, NJ: Prentice Hall, 2003), p. 470.

4. Thomas T. Nagle and Reed K. Holden, *The Strategy and Tactics of Pricing*, 3rd edn (Upper Saddle River, NJ: Prentice Hall, 2002), p. 1.

5. See David J. Schwartz, *Marketing Today: A basic approach*, 3rd edn (New York: Harcourt Brace Jovanovich, 1981), pp. 270–3.

6. See Amy E. Cortese, 'Good-bye to fixed pricing?', *Business Week* (4 May 1998), pp. 71–84; Robert D. Hof, 'The buyer always wins', *Business Week* (22 March 1999), pp. EB26–EB28; Robert D. Hof, 'Going, going, gone', *Business Week* (22 April 1999), pp. 30–2; and Michael Vizard, Ed Scannell and Dan Neel, 'Suppliers toy with dynamic pricing', *InfoWorld* (14 May 2001), p. 28.

7. For a discussion of factors affecting pricing decisions, see Thomas T. Nagle and Reed K. Holden, *The Strategy and Tactics of Pricing*, 2nd edn (Upper Saddle River, NJ: Prentice Hall, 2002), Ch. 1; Margaret C. Campbell, '"Why did you do that?" The important role of inferred motive in perceptions of price fairness', *Journal of Product & Brand Management*, **8**, 2 (1999), pp. 145–53; Thomas C. Lawton, 'The limits of price leadership: Needs-based positioning strategy and the long-term competitiveness of Europe's low fare airlines', *Long Range Planning*, **32**, 6 (1999), pp. 573–86.

8. 'Millennium Dome: doomed', *The Economist* (16 September 2000), p. 37.

9. Maggie Urry, 'United Biscuit's biggest breakfast plan', *Financial Times* (22 August 2003), p. 21; Norton Paley, 'Fancy footwork', *Sales and Marketing Management* (July 1994), pp. 41–2.

10. Helen Slingsby, 'Discounters lose at their own game', *Marketing Week* (23 September 1994), pp. 21–2; Neil Buckley, 'Sainsbury launch price war campaign', *Financial Times* (10 October 1994), p. 8.

11. See Timothy M. Laseter, 'Supply chain management: the ins and outs of target costing', *Purchasing* (12 March 1998), pp. 22–5. Also the Swatch Web page at www.swatch.com; Archie Lockamy III and Wilbur I. Smith, 'Target costing for supply chain management: criteria and selection', *Industrial Management & Data Systems*, **100**, 5 (2000), pp. 210–18; Melanie Wells, 'On his watch', *Forbes* (18 February 2002), pp. 93–4.

12. David Humphries, 'Niche airports for high-flyers', *How To Spend It* (London: Financial Times, 2000), pp. 8–10.

13. Yann Cochennec, 'The profitability problem', *Interavia* (June 2000), pp. 26–31.

14. Here accumulated production is drawn on a semi-log scale, so that equal distances represent the same percentage increase in output. For further work on experience curves see Stuart Chambers and Robert Johnston, 'Experience curves in services: macro and micro level approaches', *International Journal of Operations & Production Management*, **20**, 7 (2000), pp. 842–59; G.J. Steven, 'The learning curve: from aircraft to spacecraft?', *Management Accounting*, **77**, 5 (1999), pp. 64–5.

15. 'You've beanie had', *The Economist* (4 September 1999), p. 78; also see Beaniex.com, a Beanies website where you can get a royal blue elephant called Peanut for a cool $5,200 (€5,900)!

16. Joshua Rosenbaum, 'Guitar maker looks for a new key', *Wall Street Journal* (11 February 1998), p. B1; www.gibson.com (December 2004).

17. Nagle and Holden, *Strategy and Tactics of Pricing*, op. cit., Ch. 4.

18. For an operable example of this, see Kai Kristenson and Hans Jorn Juhl, 'Pricing and correspondence to market conditions: some Danish evidence', *European Journal of Marketing*, **24**, 5 (1989), pp. 50–5.

19. Nicholas George, 'Brio's toy trains hit the buffers', *Financial Times* (29 August 2003), p. 10.

20. Kevin Done, 'Building the superjumbo', *Financial Times* (2 November 2000), p. 21; Rebecca Hoar, 'Fight for the skies', *EuroBusiness* (May 2000), pp. 68–72.

21. Values taken from 'Energy-saving light bulbs', *Which?* (May 1993), pp. 8–10; also see 'Low energy light bulbs', *Which?* (October 1999).

22. See Mike Troy, 'Kmart: 2. Drop EDLP – continue promoting the value message', *DSN Retailing Today* (11 March 2002), p. 33; and Laura Heller, 'Simple messages reinforce EDLP', *DSN Retailing Today* (10 June 2002), p. 129.

23. Graham Bowley, 'Aircraft prices down a fifth, says Dasa', *Financial Times* (21 January 1998), p. 27; Oliver Sutton, 'What's in a price hike?', *Interavia* (December 1998), pp. 36–8.

24. 'The heyday of the auction', *The Economist* (24 July 1999), pp. 79–80; 'The price is right', *The Economist* (29 July 2000), p. 24; 'Bidding to win', *e.Business* (May 2000), pp. 36–49; Stuart Derrick, 'Putting a price on Europe', *e.Business* (December 2000), pp. 57–9.

25. John Parry, 'Times are changing for Tag-Heuer', *The European* (11–17 November 1994), p. 32; Ian Fraser, 'Don't crack under the pressure', *European Business* (June 1994), pp. 66–8. For more discussion see Kenneth N. Thompson and Barbara J. Coe, 'Gaining sustainable competitive advantage: selecting a perceived value price', *Pricing Strategy & Practice*, **5**, 2 (1997), pp. 70–9; Charles R. Duke, 'Matching appropriate pricing strategy with markets and objectives', *Journal of Product & Brand Management*, **3**, 2 (1994), pp. 15–27.

26. Bridget Williams, *The Best Butter in the World: A history of Sainsbury's* (London: Ebury, 1994).

27. Daniel Green, 'Yogurt may yield fat profit', *Financial Times* (9 January 1998), p. 16; Anna-Maija Tanttu, 'Spreading the benefits of science', *The European Magazine* (17 April 1997), pp. 10–11. For a study of pricing innovations see Biren Prasad, 'Analysis of pricing strategies for new product introduction', *Pricing Strategy & Practice*, **5**, 4 (1997), pp. 132–41; Ronald E. Goldsmith and Stephen J. Newell, 'Innovativeness and price sensitivity: managerial, theoretical and methodological issues', *Journal of Product & Brand Management*, **6**, 3 (1997), pp. 163–74.

28. David Kirkpatrick, 'Intel goes for broke', *Fortune* (16 May 1994), pp. 62–8; Andy Reinhardt, 'Pentium: the next generation', *Business Week* (12 May 1997), pp. 42–3; David Kirkpatrick, 'Intel's amazing profit machine', *Fortune* (17 February 1996), pp. 60–72.

29. Ralph Atkins, 'A certain lack of drive', *Financial Times* (25 November 1994), p. 18. For another example see Kay Atwal, 'New tactics cut soap giants down to size', *Marketing Week*, **19**, 25 (1996), p. 20.

30. Nicholas Denton, 'Higher costs in line for Internet users', *Financial Times* (13 February 1998), p. 4.

31. Seanna Browder, 'Nintendo: at the top of its game', *Business Week* (9 June 1997), pp. 72–3; N'Gai Croal, 'Game Wars 5.0', *Newsweek* (28 May 2001), pp. 65–6; 'Console competition lowers opening price points', *DSN Retailing Today* (25 March 2002), p. 18; and Khanh T.L. Tran, 'Microsoft to spend $2 billion on Xbox videogame', *Wall Street Journal* (21 May 2002), p. D5.

32. David Greenaway, Geoffrey Reed and Refaat Hassan, 'By-products and effective protection', *Journal of Economic Studies*, **21**, 6 (1994), pp. 31–6. 'Scrap tyre "cooking" becomes an economically viable proposition', *Professional Engineering*, **12**, 22 (1999), p. 9. Nagle and Holden, op cit., pp. 244–7; Stefan Stremersch and Gerard J. Tellis, 'Strategic bundling of products and prices: a new synthesis for marketing', *Journal of Marketing Research* (January 2002), pp. 55–72.

33. S.M. Widrick, 'Measurement of incidence of quantity surcharge among selected grocery products', *Journal of Consumer Affairs* (Summer 1979); Yiorgos Zotos and Steven Lysonski, 'An exploration of the quantity surcharge concept in Greece', *European Journal of Marketing*, **27**, 10 (1993), pp. 5–18; John Kay, 'Waldfogel's unwanted gift', *Financial Times* (13 December 2000), p. 20.

34. Gary M. Erickson and Johnny K. Johansson, 'The role of price in multi-attribute product evaluations', *Journal of Consumer Research* (September 1985), pp. 195–9.

35. For more reading on reference prices and psychological pricing, see Robert M. Schindler and Patrick N. Kirby, 'Patterns of right-most digits used in advertised prices: implications for nine-ending effects', *Journal of Consumer Research* (September 1997), pp. 192–201; Michel Wedel and Peter S.H. Leeflang, 'A model for the effects of psychological pricing in Gabor–Granger price studies', *Journal of Economic Psychology*, **19**, 2 (1998), pp. 237–60; Dhruv Grewal, Kent B. Monroe, Chris Janiszewski and Donald R. Lichtenstein, 'A range theory of price perception', *Journal of Consumer Research* (March 1999), pp. 353–68; Ana María Angulo, José María Gil, Azucena Gracia and Mercedes Sánchez, 'Hedonic prices for Spanish red quality wine', *British Food Journal*, **102**, 7 (2000), pp. 481–93; Tridib Mazumdar and Purushottam Papatla, 'An investigation of reference price segments', *Journal of Marketing Research* (May 2000), pp. 246–58; Indrajit Sinha and Michael Smith, 'Consumers' perceptions of promotional framing of price', *Psychology & Marketing* (March 2000), pp. 257–71; and Tulin Erdem, Glenn Mayhew and Baohong Sun, 'Understanding reference-price shoppers: a within- and across-category analysis', *Journal of Marketing Research* (November 2001), pp. 445–57.

36. 'Japanese carmakers: the also-rans', *The Economist* (21 February 2004), pp. 73–4.

37. Tim Ambler, 'Kicking price promotion habit is like getting off heroin – hard', *Marketing* (27 May 1999), p. 24. Also see Robert Gray, 'Driving sales at any price?', *Marketing* (11 April 2002), p. 24.

38. Adapted from Andrew Park and Peter Burrows, 'Dell, the conqueror', *Business Week* (24 September 2001), pp. 92–102. See also Andy Serwer, 'Dell does domination', *Fortune* (21 January 2002), pp. 70–5; and Gary McWilliams, 'Dell Computer's Kevin Rollins becomes a driving force', *Wall Street Journal* (4 April 2002), p. B6.

39. David Wickers and Rob Ryan, 'America the booty full', *Sunday Times Travel* (14 November 1999), pp. 1–2; Peggy Hollinger, 'Britons pay most for popular Christmas presents, survey finds', *Financial Times* (17 November 2000), p. 7; 'Smuggling: the Belgian job', *The Economist* (8 May 1999), pp. 26–7. For a theoretical analysis of parallel imports, see B. Rachel Yang, Reza H. Ahmadi and Kent B. Monroe, 'Pricing in separable channels: the case of parallel imports', *Journal of Product & Brand Management*, **7**, 5 (1998), pp. 433–40.

40. Philip R. Cateora, *International Marketing*, 7th edn (Homewood, IL: Irwin, 1990), p. 540; see also S. Tamer Cavusgil, 'Pricing for global markets', *Columbia Journal of World Business* (Winter 1996), pp. 66–78.

41. Greg McIvor, 'Nokia shrugs off price pressure', *Financial Times* (13 February 2000), p. 29; Jaanis Kerkis, 'Talk of the worlds', *Financial Times Weekend Magazine* (9 October 1999), pp. 15–18.

42. Jonathon Berry and Zachary Schiller, 'Attack of the fighting brands', *Business Week* (2 May 1994), p. 125.

43. Motoka Rich, 'Abracadabra! It's the barter magicians', *Financial Times* (1–2 October 1994), p. 4; Michael Lindemann, 'Germany flexible at last on credit cards', *Financial Times* (11 November 1994), p. 3; 'Bill payment on the Internet: for whom the bill tolls', *The Economist* (4 September 1999), p. 103; 'E-money revisited', *The Economist* (22 July 2000), p. 106; 'E-cash 2.0', *The Economist* (19 February 2000), p. 77; Simon Jenkins, *The Year 1000* (London: Abacus, 2000).

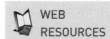

WEB RESOURCES

For additional classic case studies and Internet exercises, visit www.pearsoned.co.uk/ kotler

Concluding concepts 16
easyJet: easy come, easy go

Michael O'Leary, the ebullient chief executive of Ryanair, takes some beating. Not only has he created Europe's leading low-cost airline, but also in a market that attracts flamboyant extroverts Michael O'Leary puts Virgin's Sir Richard Branson in the shade. To announce the opening of two additional bases at Rome Ciampina and Barcelona-Girona, he turned up dressed as the Pope. His pronouncements were as exuberant as his look. He announced he had overtaken British Airways in the previous month's short-haul traffic and declared Ryanair would double in size during the next decade, overtaking Europe's existing short-haul market leaders Air France, British Airways and Lufthansa.

'We make money with falling air fares. And we make stinking piles of money with rising fares. . . . We could be a monster, it's scary', declares Mr O'Leary. While regular airlines whined about the impact of 9–11, Ryanair's market share and cash mountain grew. 'With our business model', he proclaimed, 'we will soon be offering to fly people across Europe for free.'

If you get it right, the low-cost formula is a route to high rewards in an airline industry better known for chronic loss makers. It has worked for 20 years for Southwest Airlines in the US, the original low-cost pioneer. By 2003, Ryanair had established itself as one of the world's most profitable airlines. It trades on a racy forward price/earnings ratio of more than 36, a level normally reserved for growth companies, not airlines.

Others follow Ryanair's business model. With easyJet, Stelios Hajiloannou, the son of a wealthy Greek ship-owner, is challenging Ryanair and is extending his pricing model to hire cars, with easyCar. All these low-cost operations use a dynamic pricing model that matches price and demand minute buy minute. Book an easyCar Mercedes early and most days you will get an excellent deal. However, as the booking date approaches prices can go up and down to achieve the best return. Mr Hajiloannou now intends to extend the idea to cinemas where prices will vary hugely to match supply and demand. On the run-up to the 2004 Oscars, he was in Hollywood to broker a deal with film companies to get the flexibility he wants.

Established airlines are responding differently to the low-cost challenge. British Airways sold their low-cost airline, Go, after years of heavy losses but in the hope of making 'a small profit' in the year of the sale. According to their new chef executive, Rod Eddington, the new team at BA decided that Go does not fit in with his vision of running a profitable (high-cost) full-service airline. There have been enough casualties along the way to show that the low-cost model is far from being a one-way bet, however. In the UK collapse, KLM's did not run smoothly, and in the US a fatal crash ruined highly successful ValuJet.

Virgin Express, Sir Richard Branson's Brussels and Nasdaq-listed attempt at setting up a no-frills carrier, provided further proof of the pitfalls waiting for operators that fail to control their costs. Its losses are still mounting. In contrast to its fast-growing rivals, it retrenching by cutting routes and selling aircraft.

'In this business it's low-cost that wins', says Mr O'Leary. 'Ninety-nine per cent of people want the cheapest price. They don't want awards for the in-flight magazine or the best coffee. The brand, who cares? It has to be safe, on time and cheap. It's a bus service, it's transport.'

It is not all easy flying for established low-cost airlines, either. easyJet's high aircraft utilisation rate makes it especially vulnerable to delays; it may face difficulties protecting its name and branding; the business is subject to strong seasonal variations; it may not meet its growth targets; rapid growth may be difficult to manage; it will incur significant costs acquiring additional aircraft; it is exposed to fuel price fluctuations; and there are the well-publicised problems with landing charges at Luton airport, its main hub.

Whatever the risks put forward by careful investment bankers, most aviation analysts believe that it is easyJet and Ryanair that are the likely low-cost winners. Both airlines solely operate simple fleets and keep operations simple by offering no free food. Ray Webster, easyJet chief executive, says there are important differences between easyJet and Ryanair. Whereas Dublin-based Ryanair has flourished during much of its first decade using older second-hand aircraft, easyJet has chosen to use new

> To announce the opening of two additional bases, Ryanair's CEO dressed up as the Pope.

aircraft, believing in the cost advantages to be gained from lower maintenance needs, the ability to achieve high utilisation levels, quick turnaround times and greater reliability of service.

Ryanair has been ruthless about offering the lowest fares available, and a vital part of its strategy is to fly to secondary airports with much lower charges. It has also been expanding its network to more leisure destinations. By contrast, easyJet uses more main airports that people want to use and that attract higher-paying business passengers as well as leisure travellers. As a result, easyJet is seeking to add greater depth to the network by using the growing fleet to increase frequencies rather than destinations. Because it started later than Ryanair, easyJet has also been able to avoid using travel agents as a key way of keeping distribution costs low.

Mr O'Leary is just as devoted a believer in the power of the Internet to cut sales and marketing costs, but says that at Ryanair these savings are still feeding through to the bottom line, whereas they have already been booked at easyJet. The Web also gives an 'amazing capacity to fill our aircraft very quickly and we can sell with very little advertising', says Mr O'Leary, who is planning to add more routes next year to secondary airports, where the costs are low. 'There is a huge floating population in London that just wants to fly somewhere. If you make it very cheap they just go for a weekend anyway', he says. Publicly he pours scorn on his rivals' strategies, but perhaps even Ryanair would be forced to admire the easyJet low-cost toilet strategy.

Both airlines are adding new Boeing 737 aircraft at a rapid pace to meet forecast growth rates. In the easyJet case, they order the aircraft with one toilet removed in order to cram in one more seat. 'There are no free meals or free drinks on board. If people have to pay, they consume less. There is less waste, the cabin crew themselves can do the clean up. We don't have to stock the galleys and clean the aircraft at the airport. And people use the toilets less, so we can take one out.'

Having failed to take on the low-cost airlines at their own game, the established airlines are using their powerful political influence to hobble the new competition. Legislation forcing airlines to pay fixed penalties for delays will be particularly painful to the low-cost operators with little margin to cover fines and high utilisation that gives them less time to make up for delays.

Ryanair is particularly hit by the European Commission's upholding a complaint that they illegally received incentives granted by Belgium's Walloon government to encourage the airline to fly from Charleroi airport. Ryanair may repay €4m of concessions it received in cut-price landing fees and handling charges.

While Ryanair still reels from the Charleroi judgement, two more complaints hit the European Commission's desk, this time about two deals with French regional airports: Strasbourg and Pau. They expect additional complaints from Italy and Germany to follow.

The battle is not all one-sided. Ryanair's Michael O'Leary said the airline will soon be launching a series of 'state aid' complaints against flag-carrier airlines. The Assembly of European Regions has also complained that the European Commission's decision is 'a direct threat to the existence of European airports'. They explain that low-cost airlines have had 'enormous impact' on regional development, particularly tourism and small business. Giving the power back to the flag-carriers in their major airports will further concentrate activities and visitors in a few congested hubs, like Heathrow and Orly. Commenting on the failure of a fellow low-cost airline, a Ryanair spokesman said 'The fall of Air Littoral is a direct consequence of misguided French Government policy, which seeks to promote and protect the high fare airline Air France, while denying ordinary consumers choice, competition and access to low fares.' Wolfgang Kurth, chef executive of Germany's Hapag-Lloyd Express and president of the newly formed European Low Fares Airline Association (ELFAA), states their case. Low-cost airlines have 'enabled large numbers of consumers to travel at a fraction of the cost, allowed previously unprofitable airports to become viable and profitable entities, and also have benefited regional development and the growth of tourism.'

Questions

1. What is stimulating the growth of budget airlines and what explains the economics behind Michael O'Leary's claim that Ryanair could soon be flying people around Europe for free?
2. What allows Europe's new budget airlines to keep their costs down and which operator has the advantage?
3. Does the Internet have a distinct role in the budget airlines' operations?
4. How does the European Commission's claim that Charleroi priced their landing fees and handling charges too low for Ryanair square with ELFAA's claim that it is low-cost airlines that have allowed regional airports to thrive profitably? How do you think the regional airports arrived at their fees and charges?

5. What is the likely impact of easyJet's style on pricing when applied to cinemas? Could a similar pricing approach apply in other circumstances when price and demand do not match, such as major sporting events, rock concerts and inner-city parking?

SOURCES: Kevin Done, 'Budget airlines lured by hope of sky high profits', *Financial Times* (11 November 2000), p. 20; Kevin Done, 'Ryanair reveals expansion plans', *Financial Times* (5 December 2003); Kevin Done, 'Regions braced for Ryanair fallout', *Financial Times* (29 January 2004); Mary Watkins, 'Brussels outlaws Ryanair subsidy', *Financial Times* (3 February 2004); Kevin Done, 'Ryanair faces more complaints on airport subsidies', *Financial Times* (5 February 2004); Joanna Chung, 'EasyJet issues upbeat challenge to Ryanair', *Financial Times* (6 February 2004); www.easyjet.com; www.ryanair.co.uk. By pricing a car on www.easycar.com you will get a table that clearly shows how the hire charges adjust with supply and demand.

Promise, large promise, is the soul of an advertisement.

DR JOHNSON (WRITER AND LEXICOGRAPHER)

Promotion

IN PART SEVEN WE COVER the third element of the marketing mix – promotion. We show how organisations communicate with their various target markets.

Being able to design and develop a product or service that has all the features that attract customers is one thing. Getting the message across to them and ultimately capturing or retaining a customer is quite a different matter; consequently, marketers must learn how to communicate effectively with their customers. **Chapter 17** shows how to do this and gives an overview of the types of marketing communication or the promotion mix. There is no one best communication tool or approach to use; rather, marketers must employ a combination of tools and carefully coordinate their strategies for each in order to deliver a clear, consistent and compelling message about the organisation and its products.

Chapter 18 addresses three mass communication tools – advertising, sales promotion and public relations efforts. We see how they help to achieve different types of response from consumers. Furthermore, we explore the opportunities and the barriers facing marketers seeking to communicate to customers worldwide.

Moving on from the discussion of indirect, non-personal forms of communication, **Chapter 19** examines the role of direct marketing, including both face-to-face and non-personal communications, to reach target customers. Personal communications – that is, the use of a sales force to reach the firm's customers – is increasingly seen as a source of value creation, not just as order takers. Through them, customer relationships can be forged and sustained. In addition, there are non-personal, direct marketing tools such as telephones, televisions, mail, catalogues and computers that have become important media for communicating messages as well as selling products and services to customers. These communications channels can help organisations not only to reach specific target markets quickly, but also to interact and do business with customers. As Chapter 4 has covered in more detail firms' use of the Internet and online marketing techniques to reach customers directly, Chapter 19 will address other forms of direct, non-personal marketing.

Beat your gong and sell your candies.

CHINESE PROVERB

CHAPTER seventeen

Integrated marketing communication strategy

Chapter objectives

After reading this chapter, you should be able to:

- Name and define the four tools of the marketing communications mix.
- Discuss the process and advantages of integrated marketing communications.
- Outline the steps in developing effective marketing communications.
- Explain the methods for setting the promotion budget and factors that affect the design of the promotion mix.

Mini Contents List

◀ SOURCE: DoH/Crown copyright.

Prelude case Cadbury's Dairy Milk: staying at the top of the chocolate tree

FT

The past year has not been an easy one for the UK's confectionery companies. There was the long hot summer, concerns over obesity, and the continuing fight for market share in a slow-growing market. But, boosted by its flagship Dairy Milk brand, Cadbury Schweppes, for now at least, has emerged victorious in the chocolate wars. Revenue at Cadbury Trebor Bassett, the group's UK confectionery arm, rose 13 per cent thanks to the Dairy Milk line, following its biggest product relaunch ever in 2003. This saw its smaller brands – Cadbury's Caramel and Wispa – moved into the Dairy Milk stable, where they were renamed Dairy Milk Caramel and Dairy Milk Bubbly, while adding new variants such as Dairy Milk with Mint Chips.

The relaunch came after a strategic review following the integration of Trebor Bassett in 2001. '[The number of] brands became a business issue – there were too many small brands which we couldn't sustain amid media inflation. Consumers were also confused', Louise Cooke, the group's marketing director says. 'We decided that, both from a business and consumer perspective, there was a better way to do this.'

> Britons consume about 10 kg each of chocolate a year – amounting to three to four chocolate bars per person per week.

At around £4bn, the UK chocolate market is one of the largest in Europe. Britons consume about 10 kg each of chocolate a year, and while this is less than the Swiss and the Irish, it still amounts to three to four chocolate bars per person per week, says the Biscuit Cake Chocolate and Confectionery Association. Consumers look for variety, dipping into 10 to 15 products, but can only maintain strong relationships with a limited number of brands.

After quantitative market research, Cadbury decided that it needed to cut its number of brands, but also noted that the consumer's relationship with the Cadbury brand was very strong. 'The important thing is to offer people the product variety in the brand that they love', says Cooke. Hence the move to rebrand Wispa, launched in the 1980s to compete against Rowntree's Aero, and Caramel. The relaunch also included the redesign of the Dairy Milk packaging, emphasising the Cadbury purple, and the creation of new displays for the large supermarkets. Briefing the sales force and getting them to sell the 'Dairy Milk story' to retailers was also key.

But what of the communications? The Dairy Milk relaunch was accompanied by low-key marketing, with Cadbury preferring to emphasise the role played by product design and sales in its success. 'The first thing you look at is the structure of the brand, then the product, then execution. Communication is the last thing', according to Cooke.

Cadbury is planning more advertising later in 2004, but until now, apart from its Coronation Street sponsorship which promotes assorted chocolate offerings, it has been limited to a TV campaign for Dairy Milk Caramel plus direct mailing for Caramel devotees, and an outdoor campaign for Dairy Milk variants Mint Chips and Turkish.

Compared with Nestlé Rowntree and Masterfoods whose market shares are 22.1 per cent and 26.7 per cent respectively in 2003, Cadbury leads with 28.4 per cent. It is in the enviable position of consumers associating the company name closely with chocolate. It also has history on its side, with the Dairy Milk brand having been around since 1905.

While Cadbury may be at the top of the chocolate tree now, will this continue, and what of its competitors? Observers note that with Masterfoods' reputation for innovation, and Nestlé pushing to revitalise its brands, the fight for market share is likely to become even fiercer. Arnaud Langlois, analyst at JP Morgan detects real momentum at Cadbury, especially after the integration with Trebor Bassett: '[They are] supported by an improved distribution platform, increased media investment and point of sale [promotional] activity. Cadbury's products have gained shelf space – you can see Cadbury products more than ever.'[1]

Questions

1. To what extent do you agree with Louise Cooke's view that 'The first thing you look at is the structure of the brand, then the product, then execution. Communication is the last thing.' What role does communication play in building brands in general, and in supporting the relaunch of Dairy Milk?
2. Consider the major forms of communication used in the Dairy Milk relaunch. Critically evaluate the communication mix adopted by the company.
3. What factors must be considered to ensure that the firm's communication strategy serves to maintain strong consumer relationships with its flagship Dairy Milk brand?

SOURCE: adapted from EmikoTerazone, 'Cadbury hits a purple patch', FT Creative Business (2 March 2004).

Introduction

Modern marketing calls for more than just developing a good product, pricing it attractively, and making it available to target customers. Companies must also *communicate* with current and prospective customers, and what they communicate should not be left to chance. Just as good communication is important in building and maintaining any kind of relationship, it is a critical element in a company's efforts to build customer relationships.

To communicate well, companies often hire advertising agencies to develop effective ads, sales promotion specialists to design sales-incentive programmes, direct-marketing specialists to develop databases and interact with customers and prospects by mail and telephone, and public relations firms to develop corporate images. They train their salespeople to be friendly, helpful and persuasive. For most companies, the question is not *whether* to communicate, but *how much to spend* and *in what ways*. All of their communications efforts must be blended into a consistent and coordinated communications programme.

A modern company has to communicate with its intermediaries, consumers and various publics. Its intermediaries communicate with their consumers and publics. Consumers have word-of-mouth communication with each other and with other publics. Meanwhile, each group provides feedback to every other group. The company therefore has to manage a complex marketing communications system (see Figure 17.1).

A company's total marketing communications mix – also called its **promotion mix** – consists of the specific blend of advertising, personal selling, sales promotion, public relations and direct marketing tools that the company uses to pursue its advertising and marketing objectives. Let us define the five main promotion tools:

- **Advertising**. Any paid form of non-personal presentation and promotion of ideas, goods or services by an identified sponsor.
- **Personal selling**. Personal presentation by the firm's sales force for the purpose of making sales and building customer relationships.
- **Sales promotion**. Short-term incentives to encourage the purchase or sale of a product or service.
- **Public relations**. Building good relations with the company's various publics by obtaining favourable publicity, building up a good 'corporate image', and handling or heading off unfavourable rumours, stories and events.
- **Direct marketing**. Direct connections with carefully targeted individual consumers both to obtain an immediate response and to cultivate lasting customer relationships – the use of telephone, mail, fax, email, the Internet and other tools to communicate directly with specific consumers.[2]

Each category in the promotions mix involves specific tools. For example, advertising includes print, radio and television broadcast, outdoor and other forms. Personal selling includes sales presentations, fairs and trade shows, and incentive programmes. Sales promotion includes activities such as point-of-purchase displays, premiums, discounts, coupons, competitions, speciality advertising and demonstrations. Direct marketing includes catalogues, telephone marketing, fax, kiosks, the Internet and more. Thanks to technological breakthroughs, people can now communicate through traditional media (newspapers, radio, telephone, television) as well as through newer types of media (fax machines, mobile phones, computers). The new technologies have encouraged more companies to move from mass communication to more targeted communication and one-to-one dialogue.

At the same time, communication goes beyond these specific promotion tools. The product's design, its price, the shape and colour of its package, and the stores that sell it – *all* communicate something to buyers. Thus, although the promotion mix is the company's

Promotion mix—The specific mix of advertising, personal selling, sales promotion and public relations that a company uses to pursue its advertising and marketing objectives.

Advertising—Any paid form of non-personal presentation and promotion of ideas, goods or services by an identified sponsor.

Personal selling—Personal presentation by the firm's sales force for the purpose of making sales and building customer relationships.

Sales promotion—Short-term incentives to encourage purchase or sales of a product or service.

Public relations—Building good relations with the company's various publics by obtaining favourable publicity, building up a good 'corporate image', and handling or heading off unfavourable rumours, stories and events. Major PR tools include press relations, product publicity, corporate communications, lobbying and counselling.

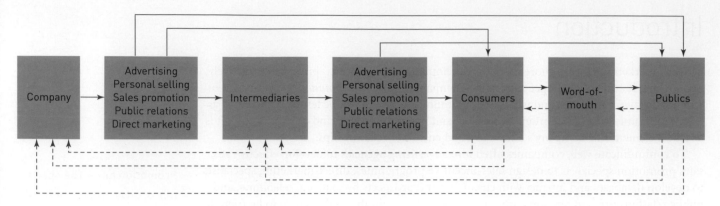

Figure 17.1 **The marketing communications system**

primary communication activity, the entire marketing mix – promotion *and* product, price and place – must be coordinated for greatest communication impact.

In this chapter, we begin by examining the rapidly changing marketing communications environment, the concept of integrated marketing communications and the communication process. Next, we discuss the factors that marketing communicators must consider in shaping an overall communications mix. Finally, we summarise the legal, ethical and social responsibility issues in marketing communications.

In Chapter 18, we look at *mass-communication tools* – advertising, sales promotion and public relations. Chapter 19 examines the *sales force* and *direct marketing* as communication and promotion tools.

Integrated marketing communications

During the past several decades, companies around the world have perfected the art of mass marketing – selling highly standardised products to masses of customers. In the process, they have developed effective mass-media advertising techniques to support their mass-marketing strategies. These companies routinely invest huge sums of money in the mass media, reaching tens of millions of customers with a single ad. However, in the twenty-first century, marketing managers face some new marketing communications realities.

The changing communications environment

Two major factors are changing the face of today's marketing communications. First, as mass markets have fragmented, marketers are shifting away from mass marketing. More and more, they are developing focused marketing programmes designed to build closer relationships with customers in more narrowly defined micromarkets. Second, vast improvements in information technology are speeding the movement towards segmented marketing. Today's information technology helps marketers to keep closer track of customer needs – more information is available about customers at the individual and household levels than ever before. New technologies also provide new communications avenues for reaching smaller customer segments with more tailored messages.

The shift from mass marketing to segmented marketing has had a dramatic impact on marketing communications. Just as mass marketing gave rise to a new generation of mass-media communications, so the shift towards one-to-one marketing is spawning a new generation of more specialised and highly targeted communications efforts.[3]

Photographed at Swissôtel The Stamford, Singapore

You've just checked into
a Swissôtel.

Not coincidentally,
stress and tension have checked out.

Promises kept. At Swissôtel, we work hard to earn our reputation for reliability, promising not only to meet your expectations, but to exceed them. See what a pleasure business can be at Swissôtel. You will feel better for it, we promise.

swissôtel
Hotels & Resorts

Asia • Australia • Europe • North America • South America
Swissôtel is managed by Raffles International Limited

Visit our website at www.swissotel.com

The Swissôtel promise – comfort, relaxation, peace-of-mind as a result of the brand's reliability – is central to the Hotel's communication strategy, no doubt subtly captured in this ad.
SOURCE: Raffles International Hotels and Resorts.

Given this new communications environment, marketers must rethink the roles of various media and promotion-mix tools. Mass-media advertising has long dominated the promotion mixes of consumer-product companies. For example, in 2003, media advertising represented 40.5 per cent of global marketing spend, followed by sales promotion (20.5 per cent), PR and sponsorships (15.4 per cent), direct mail (14.0 per cent) and interactive marketing (7.7 per cent). However, although television, magazines and other mass-media remain very important, their dominance is declining. Companies are not giving up on mass-media advertising, but are seeking ways to get better value for money.[4]

For example, Unilever's Comfort Refresh, a clothing and fabric deodorant spray, is advertised in the women's lavatories of clubs and pubs, because its target audience of young females, who use it to remove the smell of cigarette smoke from their clothing, are more likely to be out partying than sitting at home watching television for hours at a time. Refresh also sponsors a TV series that appeals to young females. In keeping with the assumption that the company can no longer expect to communicate efficiently with consumers through a mere 30-second TV commercial, when the company launched Comfort Easy Iron spray, product demonstrations were staged in shopping malls across the country. Unilever is also increasing its use of outdoor poster advertising in brand-building campaigns for product launches (see Marketing Insights 17.1).[5]

Market fragmentation has resulted in media fragmentation – in an explosion of more focused media that better match today's targeting strategies. Beyond the traditional mass-media

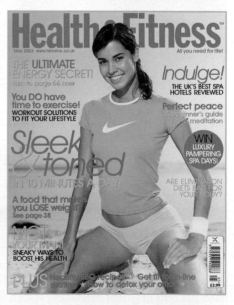

The new media environment: the relatively few mass magazines of past decades have been replaced today by thousands of magazines targeting special-interest audiences (see bottom three magazines). Add to these own-brand glossies (see top three magazines) with their own targeted and captive audiences.

SOURCE: Asda, © New Crane Ltd., Profile Pursuit Ltd., BBC Worldwide, F1 Racing, Health and Fitness.

Outdoor campaigns staying 'cool' after all this time

As advertisers seek new and dramatic ways of reaching mass audiences, outdoor campaigns are undergoing a revival. Although still in their infancy, digital technologies such as plasma screens and wireless networks for projecting moving images on to walls on airport lounges, bus shelters and metro stations may, given time, promise new and dramatic ways of capturing audience attention. Already, 'Transvision', 6 m × 3 m light emitting diode (LED) screens, pioneered by outdoor media owner Maiden Outdoor, are found next to train indicator boards in London's Victoria, Waterloo and Euston stations, serving a diet of advertising messages as well as news, sports and weather updates from the BBC. LED posters were also fitted to London buses in a promotion Viacom Outdoor ran for Nike. Adshell, part of the Clear Channel media group, even created sensory experiences by embedding the sound of puppies barking in a bus shelter campaign for *101 Dalmatians* and the smell of oranges in another shelter ad for the drink Tango.

At £20,000 upwards a screen compared with £1,000 for a conventional wood or metal panel, digital outdoor ads, however, are unlikely to consign traditional posters to the scrap yard. And who can dispute the power of good old-fashioned paper and paste? More than 100 years ago, it was outdoor advertising that shouldered Unilever's brand-building campaign for Sunlight soap, as the now celebrated images of Victorian children began to adorn the arches of railway bridges, shop fronts and the gable ends of houses.

According to Keith Weed, chairman of Lever Fabergé, Unilever's UK operating company for home and personal care products, and owner of household brands such as Persil, Dove and Lynx, the company is increasing its use of outdoor advertising in the years ahead. The reason for this is the belief that big brands have to reach mass audiences – big brands need the 'oxygen' of a mass consumer audience, and even more so in today's ultra-noisy marketing environment. The £15m launch of Lever Fabergé's Dove new moisturising shampoo back in January 2002 illustrates the point. In order to dominate attention at the launch, Dove turned to outdoor which gave greater control and allowed more effective targeting of the 16–34 age group, who are relatively light TV viewers.

The campaign presented a simple, powerful proposition that was tested in situ to ensure maximum impact when the campaign broke. The campaign outperformed category averages, with awareness reaching a whopping 76 per cent, compared to a cosmetics and toiletries average of 44 per cent. The outdoor visuals spearheaded a campaign that was extended across all the media channels, including in-store

...17.1

displays. They were also used to support the sales effort which exceeded a target figure of 10 per cent market share in 10 weeks.

Mass media tools like outdoor campaigns have plenty of mileage left in them. One reason is their ability to deliver mass audience impact at an affordable rate in an increasingly fragmented, multi-media environment. According to advertising agency J Walter Thompson, consumers, on average, are exposed weekly to 350 posters, 250 TV ads, 3 cinema ads, 150 radio commercials and 400 press ads and inserts. However, the constant bombardment of ad messages is matched by a rising level of ad avoidance. Pan-European media buyer CIA reckons that almost 50 per cent of European TV viewers are trying to avoid ad breaks. True, the digital revolution, spearheaded by television and the Internet, is supposed to create multi-channel outlets delivering highly targeted advertising campaigns with ever-greater returns on marketing investment. But multi-channel television has meant an increasingly fragmented audience and declining audience share. To reach the same number of people today compared with five years ago takes seven times as many ad spots. Moreover, the growth in Internet take-up is now tailing off and ad revenues are growing only moderately from what is a very low base. Even so, online advertising must compete for a share of the noise on the internet; and, e-mails must compete for attention with dozens of other messages, ranging from faxes and voicemail to telephone messages and letters.

Although certain products and services may benefit from the new, fragmented media landscape, there is a growing feeling that these cannot deliver by themselves the mass audience impact that consumer brands need. Outdoor advertising stands out as one of the few media with the potential to grab everyone's attention and to deliver big impact. In the foreseeable future, cutting-edge technology could transform the face of outdoor campaigns. Using wireless technology, imagine the possibilities: posters can be 'fired' into position; content could be changed at the press of a key; or screen messages could be directed towards specific audiences identified by their mobile phones. While television is the biggest mass medium today, the great outdoors is set to play an increasingly important role in communicating the promise of brands.

SOURCES: Adapted from Alan Cane, 'Signs of the times', *Financial Times Creative Business* (28 January 2003), p.11; based upon a article by Keith Weed, 'The great outdoors', *Financial Times Creative Business* (9 July 2002), p.6.

channels, advertisers are making increased use of new, highly targeted media, ranging from highly focused speciality magazines and cable or satellite television channels to CD catalogues and websites on the Internet, to airport kiosks and floor decals in supermarket aisles. Many companies are diverting marketing spending to interactive marketing (online communication and sponsorship, websites and extranets, email marketing and interactive digital TV), which can be focused more effectively on individual consumer and trade segments. In all, companies are doing less *broadcasting* and more *narrowcasting*.

Feel the difference moisturisation makes to your hair.

Hair contains 10% water. Water that's essential to keep hair beautiful. New Dove Moisturising Shampoo contains 1/4 moisturising milk. It moisturises deep inside at every wash and leaves hair bouncy and noticeably softer. New Dove Moisturising Milk Shampoo, available for normal, dry, greasy and coloured hair.

Lever has successfully used outdoor advertising to support its brand-building campaigns. In the 1880s, ads like this Sunlight Soap campaign adorned the arches of Victorian railway bridges, shop fronts and the gable ends of houses. Today, Lever continues to rely on outdoor advertising as in the launch of its Dove hair-care range in 2002.
SOURCE: Reproduced with kind permission of Lever Fabergé from originals in Unilever Archives.

The need for integrated marketing communications

The shift from mass marketing to targeted marketing, and the corresponding use of a richer mixture of communication channels and promotion tools, poses a problem for marketers. Customers do not distinguish between message sources the way marketers do. In the consumer's mind, advertising messages from different media such as television, magazines or online sources blur into one. Messages delivered via different promotional approaches all become part of a single overall message about the company. Conflicting messages from these different sources can result in confused company images and brand positions.

All too often, companies fail to integrate their various communications channels. The result is a hodgepodge of communications to consumers. Mass-media advertisements say one thing, a price promotion sends a different signal, a product label creates still another message, company sales literature says something altogether different, and the company's website seems out of sync with everything else.

The problem is that these communications often come from different company sources. Advertising messages are planned and implemented by the advertising department or advertising agency. Personal selling communications are developed by sales management. Other functional specialists are responsible for public relations, sales promotion, direct marketing, online sites and other forms of marketing communication.

Recently, such functional separation has been a major problem for many companies and their Internet communications activities. Many companies first organised their new Web communications operations into separate groups or divisions, isolating them from mainstream marketing activities. However, although some companies have compartmentalised the new communication tools, customers won't. Customers may do a bit of Web-surfing to find out about companies' products or services, but this does not mean that they no longer pay attention to TV or magazine ads or take any notice of firms' sales promotion campaigns.[6]

To be sure, the Internet promises exciting marketing communications potential. However, marketers trying to use the Web alone to build brands face many challenges. One limitation is that the Internet does not build mass brand awareness. The Web simply cannot match the impact of World Cups, Olympic Games or Six Nations Rugby, where tens of millions of people see the same 30-second Nokia or Nike ad at the same time. Instead, it is like having millions of private conversations. Using the Web, it is hard to establish universal meanings – such as 'Nokia Connecting People' or 'Just do it' that are at the heart of brand recognition and brand value.

Thus, if treated as a special case, the Internet – or any other marketing communication tool – can be a *dis*integrating force in marketing communications. Instead, all the communication tools must be carefully integrated into the broader marketing communications mix.

> For example, supermarket chain Sainsbury's used seamlessly integrated offline and online communications to promote its 'Sainsbury's To You' home delivery service. A consistent message was used to promote a consistent offer of £5 (€7) off the customer's first online shop via online and offline advertising, the Sainsbury's website, emailouts and in-store events. Although it seems obvious, according to John Baker, head of digital services at media agency Proximity London, it is not uncommon to find the online agency saying they will offer a discount of £5 to shop online, and the offline ad saying £10 off.[7]

Integrated marketing communications—

The concept under which a company carefully integrates and coordinates its many communications channels to deliver a clear, consistent, and compelling message about the organisation and its products.

In the past, no one person was responsible for thinking through the communication roles of the various promotion tools and coordinating the promotion mix. Members of various departments often differ in their views on how to split the promotion budget. The sales manager would rather hire a few more salespeople than spend a few hundred thousand euros more on a single television commercial. The public relations manager feels that he or she can do wonders with some money shifted from advertising to public relations. Today, however, more companies are adopting the concept of **integrated marketing communications** (IMC). Under this concept, as illustrated in Figure 17.2, the company carefully integrates and coordinates its many communications channels to deliver a clear, consistent and compelling

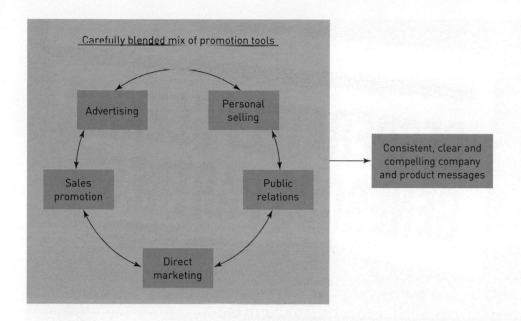

Figure 17.2 **Integrated marketing communications**

message about the organisation and its products.[8] It builds a strong brand identity in the marketplace by tying together and reinforcing all the company's messages, positioning and images, and identity, coordinating these across all its marketing communications venues. It means that your PR materials say the same thing as your direct mail campaign, and your advertising has the same 'look and feel' as your website.

IMC calls for recognising all contact points where the customer may encounter the company, its products and its brands. Each *brand contact* will deliver a message, whether good, bad or indifferent. The company works out the roles that the various promotional tools will play and the extent to which each will be used to deliver a consistent and positive message at all contact points. It carefully coordinates the promotional activities and the timing of when major campaigns take place. It keeps track of its promotional expenditures by product, promotional tool, product life-cycle stage and observed effect in order to improve future use of the promotion-mix tools. Finally, to implement integrated marketing communications, some companies appoint a marketing communications director – or *marcom manager* – who has overall responsibility for the company's communications efforts. Essentially, in order for the firm's external communications to be integrated effectively, it must first integrate its internal communications activities.

Integrated marketing communications produce better communications consistency and greater sales impact. They place the responsibility in someone's hands – where none existed before – to unify the company's image as it is shaped by thousands of company activities. They lead to a total marketing communication strategy aimed at showing how the company and its products can help customers solve their problems.

A view of the communication process

Integrated marketing communications involve identifying the target audience and shaping a well-coordinated promotional programme to elicit the desired audience response. Too often, marketing communications focus on overcoming immediate awareness, image or preference problems in the target market. This approach to communication is too shortsighted. Today, marketers are moving towards viewing communications as *managing the customer relationship over time*, that is, during the pre-selling, selling, consumption and post-consumption stages.

Because customers differ, communications programmes need to be developed for specific segments, niches and even individuals. Importantly, given the new interactive communications technologies, companies must ask not only 'How can we reach our customers?' but also 'How can we find ways to let our customers reach us?'.

Thus, the communication process should start with an audit of all the potential interactions that target customers may have with the product and company. For example, someone buying a new personal computer may talk to others, see television commercials, read articles and advertisements in newspapers and magazines, visit various websites and try out computers in one or more stores. The marketer needs to assess the influence that each of these communications experiences will have at different stages of the buying process. This understanding helps marketers to allocate their communication budget more effectively and efficiently.

To communicate effectively, marketers need to understand how communication works. Communication involves the nine elements shown in Figure 17.3. Two of these elements are the major parties in a communication – the *sender* and the *receiver*. Another two are the major

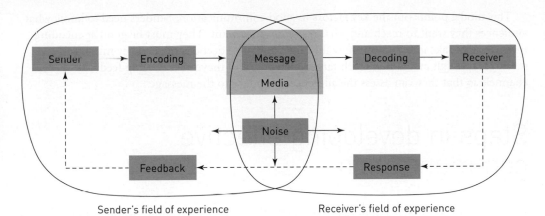

Figure 17.3 Elements in the communication process

Sender's field of experience   Receiver's field of experience

communication tools – the *message* and the *media*. Four more are primary communication functions – *encoding, decoding, response* and *feedback*. The last element is *noise* in the system. We will explain each of these elements using an ad for Ericsson mobile phones.

■ *Sender.* The *party sending the message* to another party – in this case, Ericsson.

■ *Encoding.* The process of *putting the intended message or thought into symbolic form* – Ericsson's advertising agency assembles words and illustrations into an advertisement that will convey the intended message.

■ *Message.* The *set of words, pictures or symbols* that the sender transmits – the actual Ericsson mobile phone ad.

■ *Media.* The *communication channels* through which the message moves from sender to receiver – in this case, the specific magazines that Ericsson selects.

■ *Decoding.* The process by which the receiver *assigns meaning to the symbols* encoded by the sender – a consumer reads the Ericsson mobile phone ad and interprets the words and illustrations it contains.

■ *Receiver.* The *party receiving the message* sent by another party – the consumer or business customer who reads the Ericsson mobile phone ad.

■ *Response.* The reactions of the receiver after being exposed to the message – any of hundreds of possible responses, such as the customer is more aware of the attributes of the Ericsson mobile phone, actually buys the mobile phone advertised, or does nothing.

■ *Feedback.* The part of the *receiver's response communicated back to the sender* – Ericsson's research shows that consumers like and remember the ad, or consumers write or call the company praising or criticising the ad or its products.

■ *Noise.* The *unplanned static or distortion* during the communication process, which results in the receiver getting a different message from the one the sender sent – for example, the customer is distracted while reading the magazine and misses the Ericsson mobile phone ad or its key points.

For a message to be effective, the sender's encoding process must mesh with the receiver's decoding process. Thus, the best messages consist of words and other symbols that are familiar to the receiver. The more the sender's field of experience overlaps with that of the receiver, the more effective the message is likely to be. Marketing communicators may not always *share* their consumers' field of experience. For example, an advertising copywriter from one social stratum might create an ad for consumers from another stratum – say, blue-collar workers or wealthy business executives. However, to communicate effectively, the marketing communicator must understand the consumer's field of experience.

This model points out the key factors in good communication. Senders need to know what audiences they want to reach and what responses they want. They must be good at encoding messages that take into account how the target audience decodes them. They must send messages through media that reach target audiences and they must develop feedback channels so that they can assess the audience's response to the message.

Steps in developing effective communication

We now examine the steps in developing an effective integrated communications and promotion programme. The marketing communicator must identify the target audience, determine the communication objectives, design a message, choose the media through which to send the message, and collect feedback to measure the promotion's results. Let us address each of these steps in turn.

Identifying the target audience

A marketing communicator starts with a clear target audience in mind. The audience may be potential buyers or current users, those who make the buying decision or those who influence it. The audience may be individuals, groups, special publics or the general public. The target audience will heavily affect the communicator's decisions on *what* will be said, *how* it will be said, *when* it will be said, *where* it will be said and *who* will say it.

Determining the communication objectives

Once the target audience has been defined, the marketing communicator must decide what response is sought. Of course, in many cases, the final response is *purchase*. But purchase is the result of a long process of consumer decision making. The marketing communicator needs to know where the target audience now stands and to what state it needs to be moved. To do this, he or she must determine whether or not the customer is ready to buy.

The target audience may be in any of six **buyer-readiness stages** – the stages that consumers normally pass through on their way to making a purchase. These stages are *awareness, knowledge, liking, preference, conviction* and *purchase* (see Figure 17.4). They can be described as a *hierarchy of consumer response stages*. The purpose of marketing communication is to move the customer along these stages and ultimately to achieve final purchase.

Buyer-readiness stages—
The stages that consumers normally pass through on their way to purchase, including awareness, knowledge, liking, preference, conviction and purchase.

Awareness

The marketing communicator's target market may be totally unaware of the product, know only its name or know one or a few things about it. If most of the target audience is unaware, the communicator tries to build awareness, perhaps starting with just name recognition. This process can begin with simple messages that repeat the company or product name. For

Figure 17.4 **Buyer readiness stages**

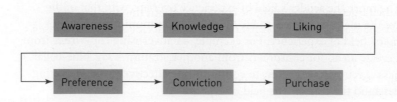

730

example, when Orange introduced its mobile phone network, it began with an extensive 'teaser' advertising campaign to create name familiarity. Initial ads for Orange created curiosity and awareness by emphasising the brand name, but not the service.

Knowledge

The target audience might be aware of the existence of the company or of the product, but not know much more. The company needs to learn how many people in its target audience have little, some or much knowledge about its offering. At launch, Orange ads created knowledge by informing potential buyers of the company's service and innovative features.

Liking

Assuming target audience members *know* the product, how do they *feel* about it? Once potential buyers knew about Orange, the company's marketers would want to move them along to the next stage – to develop favourable feelings about the brand. If the audience looks unfavourably on the brand, the communicator has to find out why, and then resolve the problems identified before developing a communications campaign to generate favourable feelings.

Preference

The target audience might *like* the product, but not *prefer* it to others. In this case, the communicator must try to build consumer preference by promoting the product's quality, value and other beneficial features. The communicator can check on the campaign's success by measuring the audience's preferences again after the campaign. If Orange finds that many potential customers like its service offering but prefer other mobile phone operators' brands, it will have to identify those areas where its offerings are not as good as competing deals and where they are better. It must then promote its advantages to build preference among prospective clients, while redressing its weaknesses.

Conviction

A target audience might *prefer* the product, but not develop a *conviction* about buying it. Thus some customers may prefer Orange to other mobile phone network brands, but may not be absolutely sure that it is what they should subscribe to. The communicator's job is to build conviction that the offering is the best one for the potential buyer. A combination of the promotion-mix tools should be used to create preference and conviction. Advertising can be used to extol the advantages offered by the brand. Press releases and public relations activities would be used to stress the brand's specific features, such as its innovativeness or performance.

Direct marketing tools could be used or dealer salespeople could also be encouraged to educate potential buyers about the product or service options, value for the price and after-sale service.

Purchase

Finally, some members of the target audience might be convinced about the product, but not quite get around to making the *purchase*. Potential buyers might decide to wait for more information or for the economy to improve. The communicator must lead these consumers to take the final step. Actions might include offering special promotional prices, rebates or premiums. Salespeople might call or write to selected customers, inviting them to visit the sales outlet for a special demonstration or product trial.

In discussing buyer readiness stages, we have assumed that buyers pass through *cognitive* (awareness, knowledge), *affective* (liking, preference, conviction), and *behavioural* (purchase) stages, in that order. This '*learn–feel–do*' sequence is appropriate when buyers have high involvement with a product category and perceive brands in the category to be highly differentiated, such as the purchase of a car. But consumers often follow other sequences. For example, they might follow a '*do–feel–learn*' sequence for high-involvement products with little perceived differentiation, such as a central heating system. Still a third sequence is the '*learn–do–feel*' sequence, where consumers have low involvement and perceive little differentiation, as is the case when they buy a product such as salt.

Furthermore, marketing communications alone cannot create positive feelings and purchases for the product. So, for example, Orange must provide superior value to potential buyers. In fact, outstanding marketing communications can actually speed the demise of a poor product. The more quickly potential buyers learn about the poor product, the faster they become aware of its faults. Thus, good marketing communications call for 'good deeds followed by good words'. Nonetheless, by understanding consumers' buying stages and their appropriate sequence, the marketer can do a better job of planning communications.

Designing a message

Having defined the desired audience response, the communicator turns to developing an effective message. Ideally, the message should get *Attention*, hold *Interest*, arouse *Desire* and obtain *Action* (a framework known as the AIDA model). In practice, few messages take the consumer all the way from awareness to purchase, but the AIDA framework suggests the desirable qualities of a good message.

In putting the message together, the marketing communicator must decide what to say (*message content*) and how to say it (*message structure and format*).

Message content

Rational appeals—Message appeals that relate to the audience's self-interest and show that the product will produce the claimed benefits; examples are appeals of product quality, economy, value or performance.

Emotional appeals—Message appeals that attempt to stir up negative or positive emotions that will motivate purchase; examples are fear, guilt, shame, love, humour, pride and joy appeals.

The communicator has to figure out an appeal or theme that will produce the desired response. There are three types of appeal: rational, emotional and moral. **Rational appeals** relate to the audience's self-interest. They show that the product will produce the desired benefits. Examples are messages showing a product's quality, economy, value or performance. Thus, in its ads, Mercedes offers automobiles that are 'engineered like no other car in the world', stressing engineering design, performance and safety.

Emotional appeals attempt to stir up either positive or negative emotions that can motivate purchase. Communicators may use positive emotional appeals such as love, humour, pride, promise of success and joy. Consider the following examples:

> British Telecom's 'Make someone happy with a phone call' and 'It's good to talk' campaigns stir a bundle of strong emotions. Ad campaigns for Häagen-Dazs equate ice-cream with pleasure (foreplay, to be precise): one classic ad tells consumers how 'It is the *intense* flavour of the finest ingredients combined with *fresh* cream that is essentially Häagen-Dazs', and is followed by the strapline: 'Now it's on everybody's lips'.[9]

Communicators can also use negative emotional appeals, such as fear, guilt and shame appeals in order to get people to do things they should (brush their teeth, invest in a pension plan, buy new tyres) or to stop doing things they shouldn't (smoke, drink too much, eat fatty foods). For example, a recent Crest ad invoked mild fear when it claimed 'There are some

A GOOD NIGHT'S
SLEEP MEANS A
GOOD DAY AHEAD

A BED THAT'S HAND MADE SPECIFICALLY FOR YOU IS AN
INVESTMENT THAT PAYS OFF EVERY MORNING OF YOUR LIFE.

SAVOIR BEDS
SINCE 1905

For a brochure telephone 020 7486 2222 *www.savoirbeds.co.uk*

Advertisers can use humour and appeal to consumers' sensory pleasures as seen in this ad by Savoir Beds.
SOURCE: Savior Beds.
Agency: Large, Smith and Walford Partnership.

things you just can't afford to gamble with' (cavities). So did Michelin tyre ads that featured cute babies and suggested 'Because so much is riding on your tyres'.[10]

Moral appeals are directed to the audience's sense of what is 'right' and 'proper'. They are often used to urge people to support social causes such as a cleaner environment, better race relations, equal rights for women and aid to the disadvantaged.

Message structure

The communicator must decide *how* to say it. This requires the communicator to handle three message-structure issues. The first is whether to draw a conclusion or to leave it to the audience. Early research showed that drawing a conclusion was usually more effective where the target audience is less likely to be motivated or may be incapable of arriving at the appropriate conclusion. More recent research, however, suggests that in many cases where the targets are likely to be interested in the product, the advertiser is better off asking questions to

Moral appeals—Message appeals that are directed to the audience's sense of what is right and proper.

stimulate involvement and motivate customers to think about the brand, and then letting them come to their own conclusions.

The second message structure issue is whether to present a one-sided argument (mentioning only the product's strengths), or a two-sided argument (touting the product's strengths while also admitting its shortcomings). Usually, a one-sided argument is more effective in sales presentations – except when audiences are highly educated or likely to hear opposing claims or when the communicator has a negative association to overcome. The third message-structure issue is whether to present the strongest arguments first or last. Presenting them first gets strong attention, but may lead to an anticlimactic ending.[11]

Two-sided arguments can be used to good effect in communicating basic product benefits. SOURCE: NESCAFÉ®; GOLD BLEND®, DECAF®, Courtesy Société des Produits Nestlé S.A., trademark owners.

To us caffeine is like this day.

If you take it away, a year is still a year, you still grow a bit older and a bit wiser. It's the same with caffeine. When we at Nescafé take it away from our beans, our decaffeinated coffees still have the great flavour and fresh aroma of our regular coffees.

Message format

The communicator also needs a strong *format* for the message. In a print ad, the communicator has to decide on the headline, copy, illustration and colour. To attract attention, advertisers can use novelty and contrast, eye-catching pictures and headlines, distinctive formats, message size and position, and colour, shape and movement. If the message is to be carried over the radio, the communicator has to choose words, sounds and voices. The 'sound' of an announcer promoting banking services should be different from one promoting quality furniture.

If the message is to be transmitted on television or conveyed in person, then all these elements plus body language have to be planned. Presenters plan their facial expressions, gestures, dress, posture and even hairstyle. If the message is carried on the product or its package, the communicator has to watch texture, scent, colour, size and shape. For example, colour plays an important communication role in food preferences.

> When consumers sampled four cups of coffee that had been placed next to brown, blue, red and yellow containers (all the coffee was identical, but the consumers did not know this), 75 per cent felt that the coffee next to the brown container tasted too strong; nearly 85 per cent judged the coffee next to the red container to be the richest; nearly everyone felt that the coffee next to the blue container was mild; and the coffee next to the yellow container was seen as weak.

Thus, if a coffee company wants to communicate that its coffee is rich, it should probably use a red container along with label copy boasting the coffee's rich taste.[12]

Even when an individual is exposed to a message, he or she may pay no attention to the message because it is either boring or irrelevant. The communicator increases the chances of the message attracting the attention of the target audience by taking into consideration the following factors:

- The message must have a practical value to the target audience because individuals are in the market for the product (for example, advertising pension schemes to undergraduates is a waste of time as they are likely to find such policies irrelevant to them for the time being).

- The message must interest the target group.

- The message must communicate new information about the product or brand. Consumers pay more attention to new messages.

- The message must reinforce or help to justify the buyer's recent purchase decisions – if you have recently bought a personal computer, it is likely that you will notice or your attention will be quickly drawn to ads for the PC (the phenomenon is called cognitive dissonance reduction).

- The message must be presented in such a way as to make an impact. As explained above, this objective can be achieved by paying attention to message formats and stressing creativity in the way the copy, artwork/illustrations and physical layout or presentation are delivered.

While advertisers' basic aim is to get their ads noticed, they must be sensitive to, and comply with, codes of practice operated by the industry watchdogs or country regulators. Messages should create maximum impact but without causing public offence and irritation.

Message format: to attract attention, advertisers can use distinctive formats, novelty and eye-catching pictures, as in this award-winning Volkswagen ad.
SOURCE: Reproduced by kind permission of Volkswagen of America, Inc. and Arnold Worldwide, *Photographer*: © Steve Bronstein.

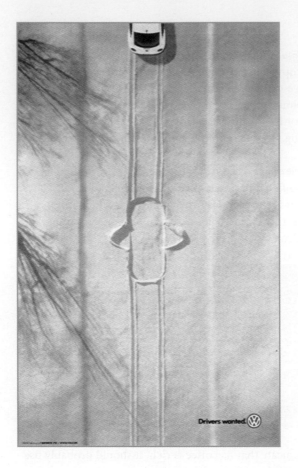

For example, in Spain, the Madrid agency responsible for a direct marketing campaign for Fiat's Cinquento car sent out love letters to 50,000 young mothers. A second batch of letters was then sent to these women revealing the Cinquento as the secret admirer. Rather than this being seen as an amusing piece of junk mail, it caused a storm of protest. The Spanish Women's Institute denounced the campaign: apparently, some women were so troubled by the letters, they were scared to leave the house. For most of the time, people are prepared to enjoy a light-hearted puzzle. But in this case, the intrigue, though interesting, only stretched so far. There is a fine dividing line between attracting and irritating consumers. Then, there are the bad taste ads and ones using 'shock tactics' which can also do much damage. In the UK, one RSPCA (Royal Society for the Prevention of Cruelty to Animals) campaign drew attention to the plight of horses exported for consumption by using a harrowing image of a dead pony hanging from a hook. Although the advertising watchdog, the ASA, had no intention to frustrate the worthy efforts of the RSPCA, it upheld public complaints of the visual image used in the ad which was deemed misleading and grossly offensive.

Choosing media

The communicator must now select *channels of communication*. There are two broad types of communication channel: *personal* and *non-personal*.

Personal communication channels

In **personal communication channels,** two or more people communicate directly with each other. They might communicate face to face, over the telephone or mobile phone, through the mail or even through an Internet 'chat'. Personal communication channels are effective because they allow for personal addressing and feedback.

Some personal communication channels are controlled directly by the company. For example, salespeople contact buyers in the target market. Other personal communications about the product may reach buyers through channels not directly controlled by the company. These might include independent experts – consumer advocates, consumer buying guides and others – making statements to target buyers. Or they might be neighbours, friends, family members and associates talking to target buyers. This last channel, known as **word-of-mouth influence**, has considerable effect in many product areas.

Personal influence carries great weight for products that are expensive, risky or highly visible. For example, buyers of cars and major appliances often go beyond mass-media sources to seek the opinions of knowledgeable people. Companies can take steps to put personal communication channels to work for them. For example, they can create *opinion leaders* – people whose opinions are sought by others – by supplying certain people with the product on attractive terms. This is also called **buzz marketing** – cultivating opinion leaders and getting them to spread information about a product or service to others in their communities. They could work through community members such as local radio personalities, heads of local organisations or community leaders. They can also use influential people in their advertisements or develop advertising that has high 'conversation value'.

> For example, the Mini USA unit of BMW North America used buzz marketing to kick-start demand for its new retro-style Mini Cooper in the USA. The Mini USA unit is now bucking car advertising tradition by using unconventional tactics. To launch the return of the Mini, 'we wanted to be as different as we could because the car is so different than anything out there', says a Mini marketer. As a result, there is no national television advertising. Instead, BMW generated buzz for the Mini in less conventional ways. For example, the 'Mini Ride' display touring the United States, which includes an actual Mini, looks like a children's ride. The car is also being promoted on the Internet, in ads painted on city buildings and on baseball-type cards handed out at auto shows. To intrigue passers-by, BMW put Minis on top of sport utilities and drove them around 24 cities. In addition, BMW is selling unusual Mini-brand items – including remote-control cars, watches and cuckoo clocks – on its website. The country's 70 dealers – top BMW dealers who agreed to build separate Mini showrooms – have been deluged with orders, practically assuring that the 20,000 cars available in the United States will quickly be sold. The campaign attracted more than 50,000 people who expressed interest in buying the car by registering at www.miniusa.com. Not a bad response, considering that

Personal communication channels—Channels through which two or more people communicate directly with each other, including face to face, person to audience, over the telephone, or through the mail.

Word-of-mouth influence—Personal communication about a product between target buyers and neighbours, friends, family members and associates.

Buzz marketing—Cultivating opinion leaders and getting them to spread information about a product or service to others in their communities.

interest was built from the ground up through buzz marketing. Until a few years ago, fewer than 2 per cent of Americans apparently had even heard of the original Mini.[13]

Non-personal communication channels

Non-personal communication channels are media that carry messages without personal contact or feedback. They include major media, atmospheres and events. Important **media** consist of print media (newspapers, magazines, direct mail), broadcast media (radio, television), display media (billboards, signs, posters) and online and electronic media (online services, websites, CDs, DVDs). **Atmospheres** are designed environments that create or reinforce the buyer's leanings towards buying a product. Thus lawyers' offices and banks are designed to communicate confidence and other factors that might be valued by their clients. **Events** are occurrences staged to communicate messages to target audiences. For example, public relations departments arrange press conferences, grand openings, shows and exhibits, public tours and other events to communicate with specific audiences.

Non-personal communication affects buyers directly. In addition, using mass media often affects buyers indirectly by causing more personal communication. Communications first flow from television, magazines and other mass media to opinion leaders and then from these opinion leaders to others. Thus opinion leaders step between the mass media and their audiences and carry messages to people who are less exposed to media. This suggests that mass communicators should aim their messages directly at opinion leaders, letting them carry the message to others. For example, pharmaceutical firms direct their new drugs promotions at the most influential doctors and medical experts first – the 'thought leaders' in the profession; if they are persuaded, their opinions have an impact upon the new product's acceptance by others in the field. Thus opinion leaders extend the influence of the mass media. Or they may alter the message or not carry the message, thus acting as gatekeepers.

Selecting the message source

In either personal or non-personal communication, the message's impact on the target audience is also affected by how the audience views the communicator. The credibility and attractiveness of the **message source** – the company, the brand name, the spokesperson for the brand, or the actor in the ad who endorses the product – must therefore be considered.

Messages delivered by highly credible sources are more persuasive. Pharmaceutical firms want doctors to tell about their products' benefits because doctors rank high on expertise in their field, so they have high credibility. Many food companies promote to doctors, dentists and other healthcare experts to motivate these professionals to recommend their products to patients. For example, for years, Sensodyne Toothpaste has promoted the product in dental surgeries, and ads use endorsements by dental practitioners to persuade target users to adopt the brand. But, to remain credible, the source must be perceived by the target audience as being an expert where the product is concerned, and trustworthy: that is, objective and honest in his or her opinion of the benefits claimed for the product.

Marketers also use celebrity endorsers – top athletes, well-known film stars, fashion models and even cartoon characters – to deliver their brand messages. Michael Owen, Paul Gascoigne and Gary Lineker have all spoken for Walkers crisps, while Tiger Woods stands behind Nike, Tag Heuer and a dozen other brands.

However, companies must be careful when selecting celebrities to represent their brands. Picking the wrong spokesperson can result in embarrassment and a tarnished image. Nike found this out when it entrusted its good name to the care of Kobe Bryant who was trialled

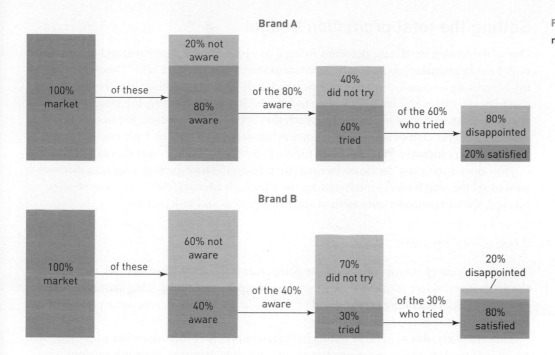

Figure 17.5 **Feedback measurements for two brands**

for sexual assault. Pepsi and Kodak faced similar embarrassment when their spokesperson, boxer Mike Tyson, was accused of beating his wife and was later jailed for rape.

Collecting feedback

After sending the message, the communicator must research its effect on the target audience. This involves asking the target audience members whether they remember the message, how many times they saw it, what points they recall, how they felt about the message, and their past and present attitudes towards the product and company. The communicator would also like to measure behaviour resulting in the message – how many people bought a product, talked to others about it or visited the store.

Figure 17.5 shows an example of feedback measurement for two hypothetical brands. Looking at Brand A, we find that 80 per cent of the total market is aware of it, that 60 per cent of those aware of it have tried it, but that only 20 per cent of those who tried it were satisfied. These results suggest that although the communication programme is creating *awareness*, the product fails to give consumers the *satisfaction* they expect. Therefore, the company should try to improve the product while staying with the successful communication programme. In contrast, only 40 per cent of the total market is aware of Brand B, only 30 per cent of those aware of Brand B have tried it, but 80 per cent of those who have tried it are satisfied. In this case, the communication programme needs to be stronger to take advantage of the brand's power to obtain satisfaction.

Setting the total promotion budget and mix

We have looked at the steps in planning and sending communications to a target audience. But how does the company decide on the total *promotion budget* and its division among the major promotional tools to create the *promotion mix*? By what process does it blend the tools to create integrated marketing communications? We now look at these questions.

Setting the total promotion budget

One of the hardest marketing decisions facing a company is how much to spend on promotion. John Wanamaker, an American department store magnate, once said: 'I know that half of my advertising is wasted, but I don't know which half. I spent \$2 million for advertising, and I don't know if that is half enough or twice too much.' It is not surprising, therefore, that industries and companies vary widely in how much they spend on promotion. Promotion spending may be 20–30 per cent of sales in the cosmetics industry and only 2 or 3 per cent in the industrial machinery industry. Within a given industry, both low and high spenders can be found.

How does a company decide on its promotion budget? There are four common methods used to set the total budget for advertising: the affordable method, the percentage-of-sales method, the competitive-parity method and the objective-and-task method.[14]

Affordable method

Affordable method—Setting the promotion budget at the level management thinks the company can afford.

A common 'rule-of-thumb' used by many companies is the **affordable method**: they set the promotion budget at the level they think the company can afford. They start with total revenues, deduct operating expenses and capital outlays, and then devote some portion of the remaining funds to advertising.

Unfortunately, this method of setting budgets completely ignores the effect of promotion on sales. It tends to place advertising last among spending priorities, even in situations where advertising is critical to the firm's success. It leads to an uncertain annual promotion budget, which makes long-range market planning difficult. Although the affordable method can result in overspending on advertising, it more often results in underspending.

Percentage-of-sales method

Percentage-of-sales method—Setting the promotion budget at a certain percentage of current or forecast sales or as a percentage of the sales price.

In the **percentage-of-sales method**, marketers set their promotion budget at a certain percentage of current or forecast sales. Or they budget a percentage of the unit sales price. Automotive companies usually budget a fixed percentage for promotion based on the planned car price. Fast-moving consumer goods companies usually set it at some percentage of current or anticipated sales.

The percentage-of-sales method has advantages. It is simple to use and helps managers think about the relationship between promotion spending, selling price and profit per unit. The method supposedly creates competitive stability because competing firms tend to spend about the same percentage of their sales on promotion.

Despite these claimed advantages, however, there is little to justify the method. It wrongly views sales as the *cause* of promotion rather than as the *result*.[15] The budget is based on availability of funds rather than on opportunities. It may prevent the increased spending sometimes needed to turn around falling sales. It fails to consider whether a higher or lower level of spending would be more profitable. Because the budget varies with year-to-year sales, long-range planning is difficult. Finally, the method does not provide any basis for choosing a *specific* percentage, except what has been done in the past or what competitors are doing.

Competitive-parity method

Competitive-parity method—Setting the promotion budget to match competitors' outlays.

Other companies use the **competitive-parity method**, setting their promotion budgets to match competitors' outlays. They watch competitors' advertising or get industry promotion-spending estimates from publications or trade associations, and then set their budgets based on the industry average.

Two arguments support this method. First, competitors' budgets represent the collective wisdom of the industry. Second, spending what competitors spend helps prevent promotion wars. Unfortunately, neither argument is valid. There are no grounds for believing that the competition has a better idea of what a company should be spending on promotion than does the company itself. Companies differ greatly in terms of market opportunities and profit margins, and each has its own special promotion needs. Finally, there is no evidence that budgets based on competitive parity prevent promotion wars.

Objective-and-task method

The most logical budget-setting method is the **objective-and-task method**, whereby the company sets its promotion budget based on what it wants to accomplish with promotion. The method entails (1) defining specific promotion objectives, (2) determining the tasks needed to achieve these objectives, and (3) estimating the costs of performing these tasks. The sum of these costs is the proposed promotion budget.

The objective-and-task method forces management to spell out its assumptions about the relationship between amount spent and promotion results. But it is also the most difficult method to use. Managers have to set sales and profit targets and then work back to what tasks must be performed to achieve desired goals. Often it is hard to figure out which specific tasks will achieve specific objectives. For example, suppose Philips wants 95 per cent awareness for its new DVD player model during the six-month introductory period. What specific advertising messages and media schedules would Philips need in order to attain this objective? How much would these messages and media schedules cost? Philips management must consider such questions, even though they are hard to answer. By comparing the campaign cost with expected profit gains, the financial viability of the promotions campaign can be determined.

The main advantage of this method is that it gets managers to define their communication objectives, how each objective will be met using selected promotion tools and the financial implications of alternative communication programmes.

Objective-and-task method—Developing the promotion budget by (1) defining specific objectives, (2) determining the tasks that must be performed to achieve these objectives, and (3) estimating the costs of performing these tasks. The sum of these costs is the proposed promotion budget.

Setting the promotion mix

The concept of integrated marketing communications suggests that it must blend the promotion tools carefully into a coordinated *promotion mix*. But how does the company determine what mix of promotion tools it will use?

Companies are always looking for ways to improve promotion by replacing one promotion tool with another that will do the same job more economically. Many companies have replaced a portion of their field sales activities with telephone sales and direct mail. Other companies have increased their sales promotion spending in relation to advertising to gain quicker sales.

Designing the promotion mix is even more complex when one tool must be used to promote another. Thus when British Airways decides to offer Air Miles for flying with the company (a sales promotion), it has to run ads to inform the public. When Lever Brothers uses a consumer advertising and sales promotion campaign to back a new washing powder, it has to set aside money to promote this campaign to the resellers to win their support.

Many factors influence the marketer's choice of promotion tools. We now look at these factors.

The nature of each promotion tool

Each promotion tool has unique characteristics and costs. Marketers must understand these characteristics in selecting the promotion mix. Let us examine each of the major tools.

Advertising

The many forms of advertising make it hard to generalise about its unique qualities. However, several qualities can be noted:

- Advertising can reach masses of geographically dispersed buyers at a low cost per exposure. For example, TV advertising can reach huge audiences.

- Beyond its reach, large-scale advertising by a seller says something positive about the seller's size, popularity and success.

- Because of advertising's public nature, consumers tend to view advertised products as standard and legitimate – buyers know that purchasing the product will be understood and accepted publicly.

- Advertising enables the seller to repeat a message many times, and lets the buyer receive and compare the messages of various competitors.

- Advertising is also very expressive, allowing the company to dramatise its products through the artful use of visuals, print, sound and colour.

- On the one hand, advertising can be used to build up a long-term image for a product (such as Mercedes-Benz car ads). On the other hand, advertising can trigger quick sales (as when department stores like Debenhams and Selfridges advertise a weekend sale).

Advertising also has some shortcomings:

- Although it reaches many people quickly, advertising is impersonal and cannot be as persuasive as company salespeople.

- Advertising is only able to carry on a one-way communication with the audience, and the audience does not feel that it has to pay attention or respond.

- In addition, advertising can be very costly. Although some advertising forms, such as newspaper and radio advertising, can be done on smaller budgets, other forms, such as network TV advertising, require very large budgets.

Personal selling

Personal selling is the most effective tool at certain stages of the buying process, particularly in building up buyers' preferences, convictions and actions. Compared to advertising, personal selling has several unique qualities:

- It involves personal interaction between two or more people, so each person can observe the other's needs and characteristics and make quick adjustments.

- Personal selling also allows all kinds of relationships to spring up, ranging from a matter-of-fact selling relationship to a deep personal friendship. The effective salesperson keeps the customer's interests at heart in order to build a long-term relationship.

- Finally, with personal selling the buyer usually feels a greater need to listen and respond, even if the response is a polite 'no thank you'.

These unique qualities come at a cost, however. A sales force requires a longer-term commitment than does advertising – advertising can be turned on and off, but sales force size is harder to change. Personal selling is also the company's most expensive promotion tool, costing companies several hundred euros on average per sales call.

Sales promotion

Sales promotion includes a wide assortment of tools – coupons, contests, price reductions, premium offers, free goods and others – all of which have many unique qualities:

With personal selling, the customer feels a greater need to listen and respond, even if the response is a polite 'no thank you'.
SOURCE: Jon Feingersh Stock Boston.

- They attract consumer attention and provide information that may lead to a purchase.

- They offer strong incentives to purchase by providing inducements or contributions that give additional value to consumers.

- Moreover, sales promotions invite and reward quick response. Whereas advertising says 'buy our product', sales promotion offers incentives to consumers to 'buy it now'.

Companies use sales promotion tools to create a stronger and quicker response. Sales promotion can be used to dramatise product offers and to boost sagging sales. Sales promotion effects are usually short-lived, however, and are often not as effective as advertising or personal selling in building long-run brand preference. To be effective, marketers must carefully plan the sales promotion campaign and offer target customers genuine value.

Public relations

Public relations or PR offers several unique qualities. It is all those activities that the organisation does to communicate with target audiences which are not directly paid for.

- PR is very believable: news stories, features, sponsorships and events seem more real and believable to readers than ads do.

- Public relations can reach many prospects who avoid salespeople and advertisements, since the message gets to the buyers as 'news' rather than as a sales-directed communication.

- Like advertising, PR can dramatise a company or product. The Body Shop is one of the few international companies that have used public relations as a more effective alternative to mass TV advertising.

Marketers tend to underuse public relations or to use it as an afterthought. Yet a well-thought-out public relations campaign used with other promotion-mix elements can be very effective and economical.

Direct marketing

Although there are many forms of direct marketing – direct mail, telemarketing, electronic marketing, online marketing and others – they all share four distinctive characteristics.

- Direct marketing is non-public as the message is normally addressed to a specific person.
- Direct marketing is immediate as messages can be prepared very quickly.
- Direct marketing can be customised, so messages can be tailored to appeal to specific customers.
- Direct marketing is interactive: it allows a dialogue between the communicator and the consumer, and messages can be altered depending on the consumer's response.

Thus, direct marketing is well suited to highly targeted marketing efforts and to building one-to-one customer relationships.

Promotion mix strategies

Push strategy—A promotion strategy that calls for using the sales force and trade promotion to push the product through channels. The producer promotes the product to wholesalers, the wholesalers promote to retailers, and the retailers promote to consumers.

Pull strategy—A promotion strategy that calls for spending a lot on advertising and consumer promotion to build up consumer demand. If the strategy is successful, consumers will ask their retailers for the product, the retailers will ask the wholesalers, and the wholesalers will ask the producers.

Marketers can choose from two basic promotion mix strategies – *push* promotion or *pull* promotion. Figure 17.6 contrasts the two strategies. The relative emphasis on the specific promotion tools differs for push and pull strategies. A **push strategy** involves 'pushing' the product through distribution channels to final consumers. The firm directs its marketing activities (primarily personal selling and trade promotion) towards channel members to induce them to carry the product and to promote it to final consumers. Using a **pull strategy**, the producer directs its marketing activities (primarily advertising and consumer promotion) towards final consumers to induce them to buy the product. If the pull strategy is effective, consumers will then demand the product from channel members, who will in turn demand it from producers. Thus under a pull strategy, consumer demand 'pulls' the product through the channels.

Some small industrial-goods companies use only push strategies; some direct-marketing companies use only pull. However, most large companies use some combination of both. For example, Lever Brothers uses mass-media advertising to pull consumers to its products and a large sales force and trade promotions to push its products through the channels.

In recent years, consumer-goods companies have been decreasing the pull portions of their promotion mixes in favour of more push. There are a number of reasons behind this shift in

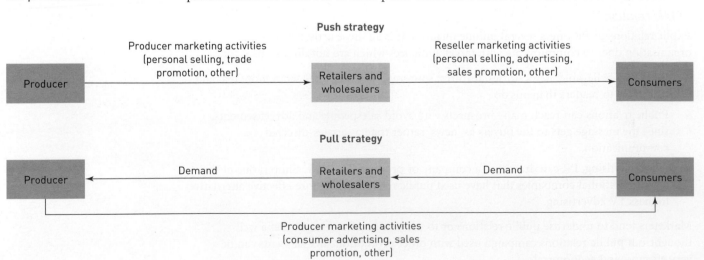

Figure 17.6 **Push versus pull promotion strategy**

promotion strategy. One is the rising cost of mass-media campaigns. Many firms have also found advertising less effective in recent years. Companies are increasing their segmentation efforts and tailoring their marketing programmes more narrowly, making national advertising less suitable than localised retailer promotions. In these days of heavy brand extensions and me-too products, many companies are finding it difficult to feature meaningful product differentiations in advertising. Instead, they differentiate their brands through price reductions, premium offers, coupons and other promotions aimed at the trade.

The growing strength of retailers is also a key factor influencing the shift from pull to push. Big retail chains in Europe have greater access now than ever before to product sales and profit information. They have the power to demand and get what they want from suppliers. And what they want is margin improvements – that is, more push. Mass advertising bypasses them on its way to the consumers, but push promotion benefits them directly. Consumer promotions give retailers an immediate sales boost and cash from trade allowances pads retailer profits. So, manufacturers are compelled to use push promotions just to obtain good shelf space and advertising support from their retailers.

However, reckless use of push promotion leads to fierce price competition and a continual spiral of price slashing and margin erosion, leaving less money to invest in the product R&D, packaging and advertising that is required to improve and maintain long-run consumer preference and loyalty. Robbing the advertising budget to pay for more sales promotion could mortgage a brand's long-term future for short-term gains. While push strategies will remain important, particularly in packaged-goods marketing, companies that find the best mix between the two – consistent advertising to build long-run brand value and consumer preference and sales promotion to create short-run trade support and consumer excitement – are most likely to win the battle for loyal and satisfied customers.[16]

Factors in designing promotion mix strategies

Companies consider many factors when designing their promotion mix strategies, including the type of product/market, buyer-readiness stage and the product life-cycle stage.

Type of product/market

The importance of different promotional tools varies between consumer and business markets (see Figure 17.7). Consumer-goods companies usually put more of their funds into advertising, followed by sales promotion, personal selling and then public relations. Advertising is relatively more important in consumer markets because there are a larger number of buyers, purchases tend to be routine, and emotions play a more important role in the purchase-decision process. In contrast, industrial-goods companies put most of their

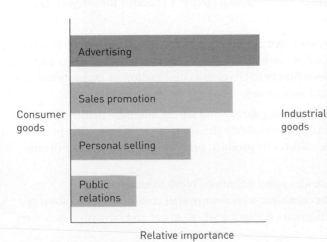

Figure 17.7 Relative importance of promotion tools in consumer versus industrial markets

funds into personal selling, followed by sales promotion, advertising and public relations. In general, personal selling is used more heavily with expensive and risky purchases, and in markets with fewer and larger sellers.

Although advertising is less important than sales calls in business markets, it still plays an important role. Advertising can build product awareness and knowledge, develop sales leads and reassure buyers. Similarly, personal selling can add a lot to consumer-goods marketing efforts. It is simply not the case that 'salespeople put products on shelves and advertising takes them off'. Well-trained consumer-goods salespeople can sign up more dealers to carry a particular brand, convince them to give more shelf space and urge them to use special displays and promotions.

Buyer-readiness stage

The effects of the promotional tools vary for the different buyer-readiness stages. Advertising, along with public relations, plays the leading role in the awareness and knowledge stages, more important than that played by 'cold calls' from salespeople. Customer liking, preference and conviction are more affected by personal selling, which is closely followed by advertising. Finally, closing the sale is mostly done with sales calls and sales promotion. Clearly, advertising and public relations are the most cost-effective at the early stages of the buyer decision process, while personal selling, given its high costs, should focus on the later stages of the customer buying process.

Product life-cycle stage

The effects of different promotion tools also vary with stages of the product life-cycle. In the introduction stage, advertising and public relations are good for producing high awareness, and sales promotion is useful in getting early trial. Personal selling efforts must be geared to persuading the trade to carry the product. In the growth stage, advertising and public relations continue to be powerful influences, whereas sales promotion can be reduced because fewer incentives are needed. In the mature stage, sales promotion again becomes important relative to advertising. Buyers know the brands and advertising is needed only to remind them of the product. In the decline stage, advertising is kept at a reminder level, public relations is dropped and salespeople give the product only a little attention. Sales promotion, however, might continue strong in order to stimulate trade and prop up sales.

Integrating the promotion mix

Having set the promotion budget and mix, the company must now take steps to see that all of the promotion mix elements are smoothly integrated. Here is a checklist for integrating the firm's marketing communications.

■ *Analyse trends – internal and external – that can affect your company's ability to do business.* Look for areas where communications can help the most. Determine the strengths and weaknesses of each communications function. Develop a combination of promotional tactics based on these strengths and weaknesses.

■ *Audit the pockets of communications spending throughout the organisation.* Itemise the communications budgets and tasks and consolidate these into a single budgeting process. Reassess all communications expenditures by product, promotional tool, stage of the life-cycle, and observed effect.

■ *Identify all contact points for the company and its brands.* Work to ensure that communications at each point are consistent with your overall communications strategy and that your communications efforts are occurring when, where and how your *customers* want them.

■ *Team up in communications planning.* Engage all communications functions in joint planning. Include customers, suppliers and other stakeholders at every stage of communications planning.

■ *Create compatible themes, tones and quality across all communications media.* Make sure each element carries your unique primary messages and selling points. This consistency achieves greater impact and prevents the unnecessary duplication of work across functions.

■ *Create performance measures that are shared by all communications elements.* Develop systems to evaluate the combined impact of all communications activities.

■ *Appoint a director responsible for the company's persuasive communications efforts.* This move encourages efficiency by centralising planning and creating shared performance measures.[17]

Socially responsible marketing communication

In shaping its promotion mix, a company must be aware of the large body of legal and ethical issues surrounding marketing communications. Most marketers work hard to communicate openly and honestly with consumers and resellers. Still, abuses may occur, and public policy makers have developed a substantial body of laws and regulations to govern advertising, personal selling, sales promotion and direct marketing activities. In this section, we discuss the issues regarding advertising, sales promotion and personal selling. Issues concerning direct marketing will be addressed in Chapter 19.

Advertising and sales promotion

By law, companies must avoid false or deceptive advertising. Advertisers must not make false claims, such as suggesting that a product cures something when it does not. They must avoid ads that have the capacity to deceive, even though no one may actually be deceived. A car cannot be advertised as getting 45 km per gallon unless it does so under typical conditions, and a diet bread cannot be advertised as having fewer calories simply because its slices are thinner.

Sellers must avoid bait-and-switch advertising or deceptive sales promotions that attract buyers under false pretences. For example, a large retailer advertised a dishwashing machine at €250. However, when consumers tried to buy the advertised machine, the seller downplayed its features, placed faulty machines on showroom floors, understated the machine's performance and took other actions in an attempt to switch buyers to a more expensive machine. Such actions are both unethical and illegal.

International advertisers must also observe local rules. For example, in the United States, direct-to-consumer advertising is allowed for prescription drugs. Pharmaceutical firm Eli Lilly uses magazine advertisements to boost public awareness of its $2.4 billion (€2.7 billion) per year anti-depressant, Prozac (see Marketing Insights 17.2). Heavy consumer promotion pushed up sales of cholesterol-lowering drugs, such as Bristol-Myers Squibb's Pravachol, Warner-Lambert's Lipitor and Merck's Zocor.[18] By contrast, in Europe, such advertisements are illegal. Prescription drugs can be promoted only in medical journals and other publications where qualified physicians are presumed to browse.

A company's trade promotion activities are also closely regulated. For example, in some countries, sellers cannot favour certain customers through their use of trade promotions. They must make promotional allowances and services available to all resellers on proportionately equal terms.

marketing insights

17.2 Promoting health on the Internet: for whose eyes only?

Health is the number one reason people log on to the Internet. So what? Well, for a start, European governments are facing uncharted waters where legislating for drug promotions is concerned. They are finding it impossible to impose national rules upon what is essentially a borderless medium – the Internet.

Eli Lilly, the US pharmaceuticals company, makes the world's best-selling anti-depressant – Prozac. If you log on to the Internet, you can visit their website at **www.prozac.com**. The website allows you to take a test to see whether you are depressed. Try it and one can see why EU heads are having their minds blown in a regulatory minefield. Click and you can learn more about depression and a few other illnesses. Viewers have the opportunity to scan material about Prozac. Useful tips are just another click away – such as how to take control of the predicament, maximising the patient's recovery and caring for a loved one suffering from depression. If you like, you can even send a page to a friend!

Herein lies the problem. Throughout Europe, promotion of prescription drugs to the general public is illegal. That applies as much to the Internet as it does to television, radio or print media. Unlike in the US, promotions of these products can only be targeted at medical professionals, not prospective patients. True, a few words in fine print appear on the first page to remind viewers that 'This information is intended for U.S. residents only.'! But who's to stop European residents from scanning the material and what can authorities do if residents ignore the somewhat discreet warning?

Regulators have tried banning websites. For example, the UK regulatory body, the Medicines Control Agency, banned websites set up by Biogen and Schering, manufacturers of beta-interferon, a drug for treating multiple sclerosis, which is under-utilised (and expensive) in Britain. The sites were campaigning for greater access by patients to the drug, but were deemed 'promotional' by the regulator.

Pharmaceutical firms see e-communication as a golden opportunity to strike up a dialogue with potential patients. There really is no stopping now. Companies are deciphering how best to exploit the new medium. Corporate websites typically bore customers with reams of information about their medicines. And most patients are unlikely to tap into individual companies to fish out information about their illness. Rather, more and more firms are using (more often than not, sponsoring) third parties that run disease-specific sites, like **diabetes.com**, **mybackpain.com**, **sleepeasy.com** and **what have you.com** to reach potential customers.

The regulatory loophole is a catalyst for pharmaceutical companies to redefine their communication spheres. According to a spokesperson for consultancy firm Booz, Allen

& Hamilton, the issue is who owns consumers' eyeballs. Drug firms would have to rethink ways to own the consumer, within the legal confines. Meanwhile, more and more pharmaceutical companies are exploiting the loophole in a regulatory vacuum.

Finally, if you've passed the test (i.e. clinically, you're far from depressed), give a sigh of relief! Log out, be happy and keep those spirits up!

SOURCES: 'Advertising drugs. Pill pushers', *The Economist* (9 August 1997), pp. 62–3; David Pilling, 'Prozac online lifts drug sector spirits', *Financial Times* (3–4 June 2000), p. 15; insights gained from the Eli Lilly and Company website (14 September 2000), at http://www.prozac.com.

Beyond simply avoiding legal pitfalls, such as deceptive or bait-and-switch advertising, companies can invest in communications to encourage and promote socially responsible programmes and actions. For example, earth-moving equipment manufacturer Caterpillar is one of several companies and environmental groups forming the Tropical Forest Foundation, which is working to save the great Amazon rainforest. It uses advertising to promote the cause and its involvement. The *Financial Times* has run several FT lunch/evening meal promotions, in conjunction with participating restaurants in the UK, to raise money for the charity Save the Children.

Personal selling

A company's salespeople must follow the rules of 'fair competition'. Some countries have enacted deceptive sales acts that spell out what is not allowed. For example, salespeople may not lie to consumers or mislead them about the advantages of buying a product. To avoid bait-and-switch practices, salespeople's statements must match advertising claims.

In business-to-business selling, salespeople may not offer bribes to purchasing agents or to others who can influence a sale. They may not obtain or use technical or trade secrets of competitors through bribery or industrial espionage. And salespeople must not disparage competitors or competing products by suggesting things that are not true.

No doubt, the laws governing sales and marketing practices differ across countries. Thus, international marketers must be fully aware of the laws and regulations governing sales and marketing communications practices, and how they differ across the countries in which they operate, when designing cross-border communications programmes. Beyond understanding and abiding by these laws and regulations, companies should ensure that they communicate honestly and fairly with consumers and resellers.

Summary

Modern marketing calls for more than just developing a good product, pricing it attractively and making it available to target customers. Companies must also *communicate* with current and prospective customers, and what they communicate should not be left to chance. For most companies, the question is not *whether* to communicate, but *how much to spend* and *in what ways*.

In this chapter, we defined the company's total *marketing communications mix* – also called *promotion mix* – as the specific blend of *advertising*, *personal selling*, *sales promotion*, *public relations* and *direct marketing* tools that the company uses to pursue its advertising and marketing objectives. Advertising includes any paid form of non-personal presentation and promotion of ideas, goods or services by an identified sponsor. Personal selling is any form of personal presentation by the firm's sales force for the purpose of making sales and building customer relationships. Firms use sales promotion to provide short-term incentives to encourage the purchase or sale of a product or service. Public relations focuses on building good relations with the company's various publics by obtaining favourable unpaid publicity. Finally, firms seeking immediate response from targeted individual customers use direct marketing tools to communicate with customers.

We addressed nine elements of the communication process and how the process works: the *sender* and *receiver* are the two main parties in a communication; the *message* and *media* are the major communication tools; *encoding*, *decoding*, *response* and *feedback* are the major functions performed; and *noise* is the unplanned distortion during the process.

This chapter also identified major changes in today's marketing communications environment. First, recent shifts in marketing strategy from mass marketing to targeted or one-on-one marketing, coupled with advances in computers and information technology, have had a dramatic impact on marketing communications. Although still important, the mass media are giving way to a profusion of smaller, more focused media. Companies are doing less *broadcasting* and more *narrowcasting*. As marketing communicators adopt richer but more fragmented media and promotion mixes to reach their diverse markets, they risk creating a communication hodgepodge for consumers. To prevent this, more companies are adopting the concept of *integrated marketing communications*, which calls for carefully integrating all sources of company communication to deliver a clear and consistent message to target markets.

To integrate its external communications effectively, the company must first integrate its internal communications activities. The company then works out the roles that the various promotional tools will play and the extent to which each will be used. It carefully coordinates the promotional activities and the timing of when major campaigns take place. Finally, to help implement its integrated marketing strategy, the company appoints a *marketing communications director* who has overall responsibility for the company's communications efforts.

Next, we outlined the steps involved in developing effective marketing communication. In preparing marketing communications, the communicator's first task is to *identify the target audience* and its characteristics. Next, the communicator has to define the response sought, whether it be *awareness*, *knowledge*, *liking*, *preference*, *conviction* or *purchase*. Then a *message* should be constructed with an effective content and structure. *Media* must be selected, for both personal and non-personal communication. Finally, the communicator must collect *feedback* by watching how much of the market becomes aware, tries the product and is satisfied in the process.

We moved on to explain the methods for setting the promotion budget, promotion mix strategies and the factors that affect the design of the promotion mix. The most popular approaches are to spend what the company can afford, to use a percentage of sales, to base promotion on competitors' spending, or to base promotion on an analysis and costing of the communication objectives and tasks.

The company has to divide the *promotion budget* among the major tools to create the *promotion mix*. Companies can pursue a *push* or a *pull* promotional strategy, or a combination of the two. The best blend of promotion tools depends on the type of product/market, the buyer's readiness stage and the product life-cycle stage.

Finally, people at all levels of the organisation must be aware of the many legal and ethical issues surrounding marketing communications today. Companies must work hard and proactively at communicating openly, honestly and agreeably with their customers and resellers.

Discussing the issues

1. The shift from mass marketing to targeted marketing, and the corresponding use of a richer mixture of promotion tools and communication channels, poses problems for many marketers. Using all of the promotion-mix elements suggested in the chapter, propose a plan for integrating marketing communications for the following:

   ■ A boutique that sells smart, casual attire aimed at young professional men and women.
   ■ The launch of Nokia's latest N-gage, a portable gaming system.
   ■ A university's Business Studies department seeking to attract more overseas students on a masters level degree programme.
   ■ A campaign to raise millions of euros to support development and emergency projects in less developed countries in Africa and Asia.
   ■ A local zoo, museum, theatre or civic event.

2. The Internet promises exciting marketing communications potential. However, when mismanaged, it can also serve as a disintegrating force in marketing communications. Explain. How can disintegration be avoided? Where possible, draw on examples of firms' Internet-based communications to support your discussion.

3. The marketing communicator can use one or more types of appeals or themes to produce a desired response.

   (a) What are these types of appeals?
   (b) When should each be used?
   (c) Provide an example of each of type of appeal using three different magazine ads.

4. Michael Jordan, Tiger Woods, Jeff Gordon and numerous well-known athletes have had a huge impact on advertising and endorsements. Explain the positive and negative consequences of using celebrity sports figures to promote a company's products or services. What impact does the use of sports celebrity endorsers have on the average person? Is this different from the impact of other types of celebrity endorsers?

5. Consider a small consumer-goods company that has historically set the promotion budget as a percentage of anticipated sales.

   (a) Make out a case for changing the method, indicating your preferred method, and explain why.

(b) What would be the most appropriate promotional mix strategy (push or pull) for the company?

(c) Should it balance the two (push and pull) strategies? Explain.

Applying the concepts

1. Think of a nationally advertised product or service that has been running an advertising message for a while. Go to a bookshop, a newsagent and/or the library and seek out magazines and other relevant print media that may contain print advertising for the brand you have selected. Where possible, get a copy of the ads from current and back issues of the magazines and the printed material you have accessed. Now examine the ads closely.

(a) How consistent are the message content, structure and format?

(b) Which response(s) do you think the campaign is seeking: awareness, knowledge, liking, preference, conviction or purchase?

(c) Do you think the ad campaign is successful in achieving the desired response? Why or why not?

2. Manufacturers of today's highly complicated computer products face a difficult task in determining how to promote their products effectively. The rapid pace of technological change in the market means that tomorrow's computers will probably be as different from today's as today's laptops are from yesterday's old 'punched card' machines. Consumers do not respond well to the detailed descriptions that are often needed to explain complex technological features and differences. So, how do producers tell consumers in plain terms what they need to know about new generations of products without boring them? The answer may be as close as the computer company's website. Experts predict that more and more consumers will be surfing the Web for product information and that fewer will rely on traditional information sources. Select five computer manufacturers and examine their websites for more information on new personal computer and handheld computer products. For example, you can visit Sharp (www.sharp.com), IBM (www.ibm.com), NEC Computer Systems (www.nec.com), Casio (www.casio.com), Apple (www.apple.com), Dell (www.dell.com) or Sony (www.sony.com).

(a) How are the marketing communications at the selected websites different from those found in traditional advertising media? Compare and critique the online versus traditional (offline) forms of marketing communication. Assess the advantages and disadvantages of each form. Which of the two forms is more effective? Explain.

(b) Compare the websites you have accessed. Which of the websites is the most effective? Explain.

(c) After reviewing each site, pick a product that you might like to own (such as a laptop or handheld computer). Based solely on the information provided at the websites that you have accessed, which company and product most grabs your attention and purchasing interest? Critique your information-gathering experience. What information was most useful? How could the communication be improved? Would you be willing to purchase the product via the Internet? Why or why not?

References

1. Adapted from EmikoTerazono, 'Cadbury hits a purple patch', *FT Creative Business*, *FT.com* (2 March 2004), accessed at http://news.ft.com.

2. For these and other definitions, see Peter D. Bennett, *Dictionary of Marketing Terms* (Chicago, IL: American Marketing Association, 1995).

3. See James R. Ogdan, *Developing a Creative and Innovative Integrated Marketing Communications Plan* (Upper Saddle River, NJ: Prentice Hall, 1998).

4. Louisa Hearn, 'The tide is turning', *Financial Times Creative Business* (16 December 2003), pp. 4–5.

5. Richard Tomkins, 'End of spin and grin', *Financial Times* (2 June 2000), p. 16.

6. Don E. Schultz, 'New media, old problem: keep Marcom integrated', *Marketing News* (29 March 1999), p. 11.

7. David Murphy, 'The integrated approach', *Marketing Business* (May 2003), pp. 15–19.

8. Don E. Schultz, 'The inevitability of integrated communications', *Journal of Business Research* (November 1996), pp. 139–46; Don E. Schultz, Stanley I. Tannenbaum and Robert F. Lauterborn, *Integrated Marketing Communication* (Chicago, IL: NTC, 1992), Ch. 3 and 4. Also see Ogdan, op. cit.; and David Picton and Amanda Broderick, *Integrated Marketing Communications*, 2nd edn (New York: Financial Times Management, 2004).

9. 'Repent, ye sinners, repent', *The Economist* (24 April 1993), pp. 87–8; *Financial Times* (16 March 1992), p. 9.

10. For more on fear appeals, see Punam Anand Keller and Lauren Goldberg Block, 'Increasing the persuasiveness of fear appeals: the effect of arousal and elaboration', *Journal of Consumer Research* (March 1996), pp. 448–59.

11. For more on message content and structure, see Leon G. Schiffman and Leslie Lazar Kanuk, *Consumer Behavior*, 6th edn (Upper Saddle River, NJ: Prentice Hall, 1997), Ch. 10 and 12; Alan G. Sawyer and Daniel J. Howard, 'Effects of omitting conclusions in advertisements to involved and uninvolved audiences', *Journal of Marketing Research* (November 1991), pp. 467–74; Cornelia Pechmann, 'Predicting when two-sided ads will be more effective than one-sided ads: the role of correlational and correspondent inferences', *Journal of Marketing* (November 1992), pp. 441–53.

12. Philip Kotler, *Marketing Management: Analysis, planning, implementation and control*, 10th edn (Upper Saddle River, NJ: Prentice Hall, 2000), p. 559.

13. Adapted from Jean Halliday, 'Creating max buzz for new BMW Mini', *Advertising Age* (17 June 2002), p. 12.

14. For more on setting promotion budgets, see J. Thomas Russell and W. Ronald Lane, *Kleppner's Advertising Procedure*, 15th edn (Upper Saddle River, NJ: Prentice-Hall, 2002), pp. 145–9; and Kissan Joseph and Vernon J. Richardson, 'Free cash flow, agency costs, and the affordability method of advertising budgeting', *Journal of Marketing* (January 2002), pp. 94–107.

15. David Allen, 'Excessive use of the mirror', *Management Accounting* (June 1996), p. 12; Laura Petrecca, '4A's will study financial returns on ad spending', *Advertising Age* (April 1997), pp. 3, 52; Dana W. Hayman and Don E. Schultz, 'How much should you spend on advertising?', *Advertising Age* (26 April 1999), p. 32.

16. Louis Therrien, 'Brands on the run', *Business Week* (April 1993), pp. 26–9; Karen Herther, 'Survey reveals implications of promotion trends for the 90's', *Marketing News* (1 March 1993), p. 7; David Short, 'Advertisers come out to spend again', *The European* (12–18 August 1994), p. 21.

17. Based on Matthew Gonring, 'Putting integrated marketing communications to work today', *Public Relations Quarterly* (Fall 1994), pp. 45–8. Also see Philip Kotler, *Marketing Management*, 11th edn (Upper Saddle River, NJ: Prentice Hall, 2003), pp. 583–4.

18. 'Pill pushers', *The Economist* (9 August 1997), pp. 62–3.

WEB RESOURCES

For additional classic case studies and Internet exercises, visit www.pearsoned.co.uk/kotler

Concluding concepts 17
Absolut Vodka: Samantha and the Hunk on the Level

PONTUS ALENROTH, ROBERT BJORNSTROM, JOAKIM ERIKSSON AND THOMAS HELGESSON*
Halstad University, Sweden.

With sales in 126 markets globally, Absolut Vodka is now the third largest spirit in the world. V&S of Stockholm, Sweden, is the international brand owner and manufacturer of ABSOLUT VODKA as well as Plymouth Gin, Danzka Vodka Level Vodka, ABSOLUT CUT and Fris Vodka. Absolut's market showing is surprising given it comes from Sweden, a country with highly restrictive licensing laws that do not allow spirits to be advertised. However, in the last two decades, Absolut has grown from being a little-known brand made in a country with no reputation in the spirits market to the world's leading premium brand of vodka.

> The Absolut bottle is considered a masterpiece in glass design.

When Lars Olsson Smith, Sweden's 'King of Vodka', introduced a new kind of 'Absolut Rent Brännvin' (Absolutely Pure Vodka) in 1879, little did he realise it would become the world's leading premium vodka a century later. In the nineteenth century the self-made spirits tycoon introduced a revolutionary rectification/continuous distillation method, which is still used in producing Absolut Vodka. The result was a clear, high-quality vodka, free from dangerous and bad-tasting by-products. As its label shows, Absolut Vodka trades on its heritage:

ABSOLUT
Country of Sweden

VODKA

This superb vodka
was distilled from grain grown
in the rich fields of Sweden.
It has been produced by the famous
old distilleries of Shus
in accordance with more than
400 years of Swedish tradition.
Vodka has been sold under the name
Absolut since 1879.

ABSOLUT MAGIC.

The bottle continues to be the centrepiece in campaigns like 'ABSOLUT MAGIC'. This ad reinforces the vodka's aura of exclusiveness, timelessness and sheer magic.

Absolut's website (www.absolut.com) allows every aspect of the label's claims to be explored.

Despite its long traditions, Absolut Vodka's success was late in coming. In 1979, Vin & Sprit (now called V&S), the Swedish state-owned alcohol monopoly, decided to export the vodka to the US. After objections from American authorities, the name Absolutely Pure Vodka was changed to Absolut Vodka. Consultants had surveyed the US spirits market and found 'a clearly discernible consumer trend towards "white spirits" [such as vodka, gin and white rum] as opposed to "brown spirits" [brandy, whisky and dark rum]; white spirits are seen as being purer and healthier'. V&S had no marketing or product design experience, so it employed outside teams of marketing and management experts to create a product for the newly discovered market.

The design of the bottle was recognised at an early stage as crucial to success. Absolut's Gunnar Broman had the idea when he saw some eighteenth-century medicine bottles in a Stockholm antique shop. The bottles were elegant, different, simple and very Swedish. In reality, vodka was sold as a medicine in similar bottles during the eighteenth and nineteenth centuries. Broman argued his case for more than a year until the bottle was finally approved and the manufacturing problems were overcome. The resulting Absolut bottle was very different from that of competitors. It was considered a masterpiece in glass design: a timeless shape with fine lines and the exceptionally clear glass that distinguish Absolut from other premium vodkas.

Absolut's acceptance in the US market did not come easy. When Absolut's team first presented their ideas to New York agency NW Ayer, some of the agency's staff were thrilled but most shook their heads, thinking 'who wants to drink a vodka from Sweden anyway?'. But, after many meetings, they agreed on the theme of 'Absolut Country of Sweden Vodka'. The bottle should be made of clear glass with silver text on it. They tested their idea by putting their bottles among the other big brands to see how it looked.

One of the people working with the Absolut account, Myron Poloner, fell in love with the bottle. He could sit and watch the 'medicine bottle' for hours and one night it struck him. The bottle should have no label at all. You should be able to see right through it. The vodka should be a premium vodka for well-educated people with a high income who could afford to eat out. They liked to hold parties at their home and to show off.

Attempts to sell the idea to US distributors met with the same cool reaction as the early meetings with the ad agency. 'Who has ever heard of a Swedish vodka? And it doesn't have a label. It'll disappear on the shelf. It will never sell!'

Carillon Importers Ltd, based in Manhattan, had a different view. Carillon's leader, Al Singer, accepted 'the challenge' the moment he saw the product. However, the company had only one salesman, Michel Roux, but he was to play a leading role in the success of Absolut Vodka. Singer did not want to work with a big New York agency,

preferring instead Martin Landey Arlow. Landey and Singer also wanted to change the bottle, making it taller and with a thicker bottom. One day, as a joke, one of Broman's employees put a coin on the bottle's shoulder. The Americans loved it, so his staff decided to create a seal. They tried shields, swords, guns, naked women, men's heads, etc. Broman's office was coincidentally located in Absolut's founder Lars Olsson Smith's old house. While there he thought, why not put 'The king of vodka's' head on the seal? The president of Vin & Sprit, Lars Lindmark, decided that the ABSOLUT VODKA letters should be blue for the 80 proof bottles and red for the 100 proof ones. And so the bottle changed to that we know today.

Unfortunately, Martin Landey had to stop acting for Carillon because of a conflict of interest with another, more profitable client in the spirits business. TBWA, another New York agency, heard about Carillon, contacted Singer and got the account. Geoff Hayes and Graham Turner were assigned to Absolut. One evening Hayes was sketching while watching TV. Trying to find a symbol of purity and simplicity, he made a halo. Soon his floor was covered with different ad-ideas, all with a humorous twist. The next day, he showed his ads to Turner. They changed the name for the Absolut Purity ad to Absolut Perfection. Absolut Heaven showed the bottle with wings. Fifteen minutes later they had a dozen different Absolut 'something' ads.

The Absolut, Carillon and TBWA staff loved the idea. 'All advertising should centre around the bottle, the product should not be identified with any particular lifestyle, and the approach should have a timeless yet contemporary feel to it.' Every advertisement has two features in common: the depiction of an Absolut bottle and a two- or three-word caption beginning with the word 'Absolut'. It hit the US market in 1979 and Absolut soon became the biggest-selling imported vodka brand.

The innovative way of marketing Absolut contrasted directly with that of the established brands. As David Wachsman points out, the advertising of spirits in the United States used 'one of three formats: a roomful of exceedingly happy people, a celebrity holding a glass, or old-fashioned settled family life'. Then came 'Absolut Perfection' and hundreds of different ads.

Absolut Vodka is a highly premium-priced vodka and therefore has an aura of up-market exclusiveness. Considering the target market and the early magazine ads (Absolut Perfection, etc.), a tie-up with the arts world was inevitable. The first step in this direction was taken in 1985 when the New York cult pop artist Andy Warhol was commissioned to paint the Absolut Vodka bottle. Today Absolut cooperates with artists and designers in all the contemporary arts. 'The purity and clarity' of the product, says Göran Lundquist, the then President of The Absolut Company (now V&S Absolut Spirits), a part of the V&S Group, is a 'timeless source of inspiration' (the current President of V&S Absolut Spirits and CEO of the V&S Group is Bengt Baron). There are now over 3,000 works in the Absolut collection. All feature some aspect of the bottle or its label. Like other very successful campaigns, the marketing is so sensational that the product receives a huge amount of free media exposure. In Absolut's case this has even occurred in markets, like Sweden, that did not allow alcohol advertising.

Absolut's unconventional marketing has generated demand for its ads – the advertising agency receives thousands of requests for ad reprints. The ads have become a modern icon. Besides winning the Effie and the Kelly awards, Absolut was honoured with an induction into America's Marketing Hall of Fame. That seal of approval confirmed Absolut's success and impact on the American lifestyle, especially since the only other brands that have received such an honour are Coke and Nike. 'Absolut Art' is also achieving international recognition. Warhol's and other key US works, together with others specially commissioned from French artists Bosser and Delprat, were shown at Paris's prestigious Lavignes-Bastille Gallery. From there, the exhibition moved to London's Royal College of Art, where new works by British artists, including Peter Blake, were added. The exhibition then travelled to Berlin, Munich and Milan. Over 350 artists and fashion designers have now produced Absolut ads. Their cult status is reflected in home3.swipenet.se and www.absolutad.org, websites dedicated to Absolut art.

An ingenious bottle and creative marketing played a crucial part in the Absolut saga, but V&S's distribution partnership was also crucial to its success. However, Absolut had to bid farewell to Carillon, its original distributor in 1995 and teamed up with Seagrams. After a long and fruitful relationship, Absolut had outgrown Carillon. In 2001, following the sale of the spirit division of Seagrams, V&S set up its New York based, American subsidiary. The Absolut Spirits Company which is the importer of ABSOLUT in the USA. At the same time, V&S formed a new distribution set-up for the US with Future Brands, a joint venture between V&S and Jim Beam Brands.

The Absolut Akademi aims to create 'a competitive edge through people': 'The goal is to build a quality culture around a quality product.' Another tool in marketing is the *Absolut Reflexions* magazine, which is distributed in all markets. Used as a PR tool, *Absolut Reflexions* spreads news of the brand, its advertising and activities to consumers all over the world.

V&S followed its Absolut's success in the US with attacks on the European, Asian and Pacific markets. Compared with the United States, the European market is slow growing, fragmented and conservative. Europe has many leisure drinking cultures, but these vary from region to region and there are well-established traditions everywhere. Except for countries where vodka is the national drink, the European vodka market is underdeveloped. Vodka is drunk by only 4 per cent of consumers in Europe, compared to 21 per cent of Americans. To repeat its American success, Absolut will need clever and innovative strategies tailored specifically for each of Europe's submarkets. V&S is bullish about Absolut's chances in Europe. 'We have built up a wide experience of operating abroad and we are confident we can meet the competition', says V&S's Margareta Nyström. The company believes that wherever there is a demand for premium vodka, Absolut Vodka is the optimal choice. 'Absolut Vodka proves itself time and time again as more than just a fine vodka: it's an idea. And nothing can stop an idea whose time has come.'

After years as a challenger in the spirits market, Absolut is the leading brand that many are following. V&S are defending its position by extending its product range by acquisition and new product launches. Early 2004 saw the launch of Level Vodka in the US. V&S's Carl Horton, president and chief executive of The Absolut Spirits Company, explains: 'Level is our long-awaited entry into the vibrant super-premium vodka segment.' Level aims for a perfect balance of smoothness and character, which is achieved by a unique combination of two distillation methods: 'One taste and consumers will see it's a completely new level of vodka.'

While attacking the super-premium market with Level Vodka, V&S combined the iconic brand with the equally icon *Sex in the City* series. In a campaign reminiscent of the impact of the early Absolut ads, in the 'Hop, Skip and a Week' episode of *Sex in the City*, Samantha Jones makes a deal for her latest lover to appear in a fictional ABSOLUT HUNK ad where he is nude but for a suggestively placed Absolut Vodka bottle. Absolut paid nothing for the 'product placement', but both *Sex in the City* and Absolut gained hugely from the publicity surrounding the 'appearance'. Fiction became reality as the ABSOLUT HUNK ad appeared all over New York City, including on a huge Times Square billboard. ABSOLUT HUNK is now the new 'it' drink in New York bars.

---

*The authors wrote the original case 'Absolut Vodka: Absolutely Successful' on which this case is based.

Questions

1. What is the foundation of Absolut Vodka's success? Is It the vodka, the bottle, the distribution or the promotion?

2. How does Absolut's marketing build upon American trends in the late 1980s and early 1990s? Is Absolut a fashion product that will decline with the trends?

3. Do you believe that Absolut Vodka 'is an idea whose time has come' and that nothing can stop its success?

4. V&S's European campaign uses ads in the same style as those that have been so successful in the United States. Do you think the US approach will work in other regions?

5. Since Absolut Vodka is such a lifestyle product, would you recommend that V & S should extend the brand into other markets in the same way as Virgin has extended into video games, PCs, cola and vodka?

6. Absolut's successful advertising has benefited greatly from the publicity it generated. Can advertising campaigns be designed to create such media attention or is their success just good fortune?

SOURCES: Adapted from the following: Andrew Edgecliff-Johnson, 'Drinks disposal leave Seagram with hangover', *Financial Times* (20 November 2000), p. 36; John Thornhill, 'Trying to make selling spirits seriously easy', *Financial Times* (1 September 2000), p. 16; 'Level Vodka to launch nationally in 2004', *Business Wire* (6 November 2003); *The Irish Times,* 'Drink ads box clever' (23 August 2003); www.absolut.com;for ABSOLUT HUNK ad and cocktail ingredients visit ez-entertainment.net/features/absolut.htm.

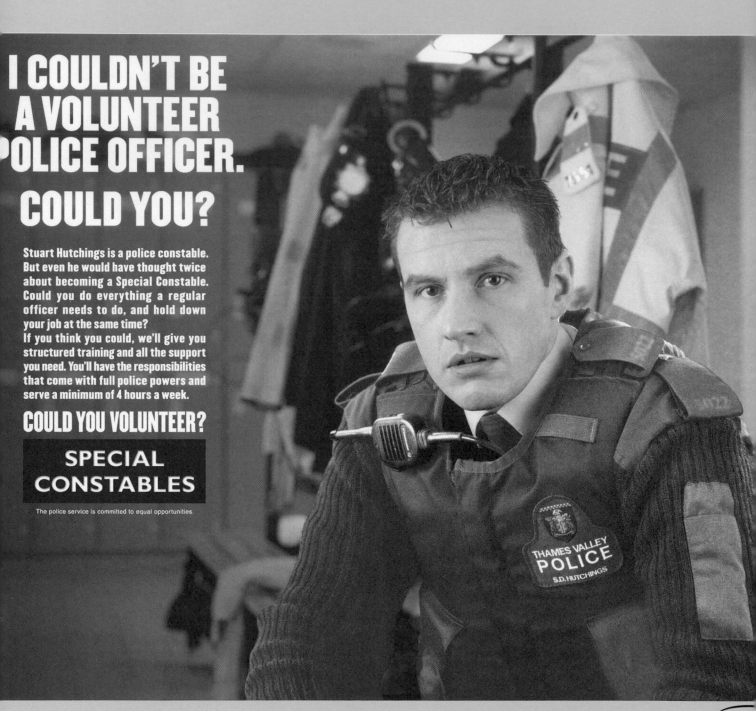

I COULDN'T BE A VOLUNTEER POLICE OFFICER.

COULD YOU?

Stuart Hutchings is a police constable. But even he would have thought twice about becoming a Special Constable. Could you do everything a regular officer needs to do, and hold down your job at the same time? If you think you could, we'll give you structured training and all the support you need. You'll have the responsibilities that come with full police powers and serve a minimum of 4 hours a week.

COULD YOU VOLUNTEER?

SPECIAL CONSTABLES

The police service is committed to equal opportunities.

0845 608 3000   www.policecouldyou.co.uk   Home O

It is far easier to write ten passable sonnets than to write an advertisement that will take in a few thousand of the uncritical buying public.

ALDOUS HUXLEY

CHAPTER

eighteen

Advertising, sales promotion and public relations

Chapter objectives

After reading this chapter, you should be able to:

■ Define the roles of advertising, sales promotion and public relations in the promotion mix.
■ Describe the main decisions involved in developing an advertising programme.
■ Explain how sales promotion campaigns are developed and implemented.
■ Explain how companies use public relations to communicate with their publics.

Mini Contents List

◀ SOURCE: Home Office/Crown copyright.

Prelude case   Procter & Gamble: feeling the heat

Applying pressure

Consumer products giant Procter & Gamble has felt pressure in recent years as shareholders expressed their concerns over what they saw as the company's sometimes lacklustre performance. Shareholders and stock-market analysts pressed the company to develop new products to beef up its stable of long-term successes like Pampers, Tide and Crest, which were competing in mature, saturated markets.

> P&G designed ThermaCare for the temporary relief of minor muscle and joint aches and pain associated with over-exertion, over-use, strains, sprains and arthritis.

The company responded with a wave of new products. Some, like Dryel, a home dry-cleaning product, and Fit, a rinse for fruit and vegetables, failed to register with consumers. Others, however, like Crest Whitestrips, a tooth-whitening system launched in 2000, reached the company's new-product goal of $200 million (€165.3 million) in first-year sales. Such successes are not enough, however – P&G has to keep the new products coming if it is to reach its goals of 4 to 6 per cent annual sales growth and double-digit earnings growth.

Pain relief

To meet its ambitious growth goals, P&G developed a new-ventures unit, staffed with employees whose job was to develop new-product ideas and then pass them on to the appropriate business unit for development. The new-ventures unit examined the $3.3 billion pain-relief market to see whether the company had any skills that it might apply to that market. It already knew much about this market due to its previous marketing of Aleve pain reliever (since sold to Bayer). Further, from its work on Pampers, Charmin and Bounty, the company also had excellent knowledge in paper technology.

Merging these two capabilities, P&G's researchers developed the idea of the 'external analgesic' – a product that consumers could use externally to provide long-lasting warmth to specific areas of the body where they experienced pain. After seven years of consumer and scientific testing, in early 2002 P&G announced that it would launch ThermaCare HeatWraps.

P&G designed ThermaCare for the temporary relief of minor muscle and joint aches and pain associated with over-exertion, over-use, strains, sprains and arthritis. Women could also use the product for temporary relief of minor menstrual cramping and associated back pain. The HeatWraps were portable, air-activated, disposable (single-use), self-heating devices that provided a continuous low-level therapeutic heat (104°F or 40°C) for up to eight hours.

The HeatWrap was a small pad that resembled a very thin diaper and came in shapes designed for the lower or upper back, the neck or arm, and the abdomen. When the consumer opened the package, the HeatWrap was exposed to air. Inside the wrap were a series of oval-shaped heat discs that contained a mixture of naturally heat-generating materials: iron, carbon, sodium chloride, sodium thiosulphate and water. The air penetrated a perforated film that controlled oxygen permeability. The iron in the heat discs began to oxidise, and the chemical process generated the heat. The process was basically the same one that manufacturers of hand warmers had used for years. However, P&G had found a way to use its paper technology to sustain and control the heat-generating reaction.

Doctors and pharmacists recommended that people who experienced muscle pain due to exercising should first apply packs for up to 20 minutes at a time, three to four times per day for one to two days, accompanied with a pain reliever, such as aspirin or aspirin-like products. They recommended that the patient should then use heat therapy.

P&G recommended that consumers wear the HeatWrap for at least three hours and up to eight hours, repeating the process each day for up to seven days. Users could wear the HeatWraps under their clothing and go about their normal routines. Consumers were warned that they should not use the HeatWraps with other externally applied medications like lotions or ointments due to the risk of a skin reaction. When finished with the HeatWrap, consumers could dispose of it in the household rubbish, as all materials in the products were environmentally compatible.

Wrapping it up

P&G's marketers were excited about what they saw as a breakthrough product. The company planned to price the product at $6.99 (€5.79) per box at retail, producing a 25 per cent profit margin for retailers, well above the margin for other pain-relief products. The package contained either two wraps in the back size or three wraps in the neck, arm or abdomen sizes.

The company planned to concentrate on US sales during the first year. It decided to allocate up to $90 million for an integrated, promotional campaign to introduce ThermaCare. If successful, the new product would be introduced into P&G's major European markets in the second year. To design the campaign, P&G hired D'Arcy Masius Benton & Bowles, an advertising agency it had used for many years.

The agency knew that a breakthrough product needed a breakthrough promotion programme. After all, P&G was offering a unique product that presented consumers with many new concepts at the same time. Consumers would not be familiar with the product or how it worked. How could the advertising and promotion keep consumers from just shrugging and taking another pain pill? How could it educate consumers about what ThermaCare was, what it did, and how it was different from other pain-relief strategies? How could it help P&G make ThermaCare a household name? Will the advertising and promotion be different for the European market?[1]

Questions

1. What are possible target audiences for ThermaCare? In what buyer-readiness stages will these target audiences be?
2. What issues will the advertising agency face in designing messages for the selected target audiences? What message 'theme' or 'headline' summarises the positioning that you'd recommend for ThermaCare?
3. What recommendations would you make to P&G and D'Arcy to help them develop an integrated promotion strategy for ThermaCare in the US and European markets? Be sure to deal with the issues of setting the overall promotion mix, selecting a message source, and collecting feedback.

Introduction

In Chapter 17, we looked at overall integrated marketing communications planning. In this chapter, we will explore the mass-communication tools – advertising, sales promotion and public relations. These are also largely non-personal forms of communication and promotion. Personal selling and other direct forms of marketing communication are discussed in Chapter 19.

Companies must do more than offer good products or services. As we gather from the prelude case, firms must inform consumers about product or service benefits and carefully position these in consumers' minds. To do this, they must skilfully use the mass-promotion tools of *advertising*, *sales promotion* and *public relations*. In this chapter, we dig more deeply into each of these tools.

Advertising

Advertising can be traced back to the very beginnings of recorded history. Archaeologists working in the countries around the Mediterranean Sea have dug up signs announcing various events and offers. The Romans painted walls to announce gladiator fights, and the Phoenicians painted pictures promoting their wares on large rocks along parade routes. A Pompeii wall painting praised a politician and asked for votes. During the Golden Age in Greece, town criers announced the sale of cattle, crafted items and even cosmetics. An early 'singing commercial' went as follows: 'For eyes that are shining, for cheeks like the dawn. For beauty that lasts after girlhood is gone. For prices in reason, the woman who knows will buy her cosmetics from Aesclyptos.'

Modern advertising, however, is a far cry from these early efforts. At constant 2002 prices, advertising expenditure in 2003 was estimated at US $78.7 billion in Europe, US $154.5 billion in the US, US $64.5 in Asia Pacific and, globally, spending stood at some US $500 billion. According to ZenithOptimedia, global ad spend is set to rise by 4.7 per cent in 2004.[2] Global firms such as the consumer goods giant Unilever spent nearly €4 billion on advertising in 2002, making it the biggest advertiser in the world. The company recognises that when it is fighting for consumers' hearts and minds in a cluttered world, message impact and reach are vital, with advertising becoming more important than ever. As a senior marketer at Unilever Bestfoods says, 'We aren't going to see the death of advertising, nor the death of TV advertising, although over time, more and more of our budgets will be going into other media.'[3]

Advertising—Any paid form of non-personal presentation and promotion of ideas, goods or services by an identified sponsor.

We define **advertising** as any paid form of non-personal presentation and promotion of ideas, goods or services through mass media such as newspapers, magazines, television or radio by an identified sponsor.

Although advertising is used mostly by business firms, it is also used by a wide range of not-for-profit organisations, professionals and social agencies to communicate their causes to various target publics. Advertising is a good way to inform and persuade, whether the purpose is to sell Nokia mobile phones worldwide or to encourage smokers to give up the habit. Advertising is used in order to stimulate a response from the target audience. The response may be perceptual in nature: for example, the consumer develops specific views or opinions about the product or brand, or these feelings are altered by the ad. The response could be behavioural: for instance, the consumer buys the product or increases the amount that he or she buys.

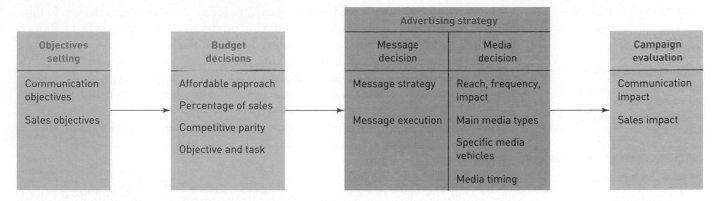

Figure 18.1 **Main advertising decisions**

Important decisions in advertising

Marketing management must make four important decisions when developing an advertising programme (see Figure 18.1): setting advertising objectives, setting the advertising budget, developing advertising strategy and evaluating advertising campaigns.

Setting advertising objectives

The first step is to set **advertising objective**. These objectives should be based on decisions about the target market, positioning and marketing mix, which define the job that advertising must achieve in the total marketing programme.

An advertising objective is a specific communication task to be accomplished with a specific target audience during a specific period of time. Advertising objectives can be classified by primary purpose – whether the aim is to inform, persuade or remind. Table 18.1 lists examples of each of these objectives.

Advertising objective—
A specific communication task to be accomplished with a specific target audience during a specific period of time.

Table 18.1 **Possible advertising objectives**

Informative advertising
- Telling the market about a new product
- Suggesting new uses for a product
- Informing the market of a price change
- Explaining how the product works

- Describing available services
- Correcting false impressions
- Reducing customers' fears
- Building a company image

Persuasive advertising
- Building brand preference
- Encouraging switching to your brand
- Changing customer perceptions of product attributes

- Persuading customers to purchase now
- Persuading customers to receive a sales call

Reminder advertising
- Reminding customers that the product may be needed in the near future
- Reminding customers where to buy the product

- Keeping the product in customers' minds during off-seasons
- Maintaining top-of-mind product awareness

Informative advertising— Advertising used to inform consumers about a new product or feature and to build primary demand.

Persuasive advertising— Advertising used to build selective demand for a brand by persuading consumers that it offers the best quality for their money.

Comparison advertising (knocking copy)— Advertising that compares one brand directly or indirectly to one or more other brands.

Informative advertising is used heavily when introducing a new product category. In this case, the objective is to build primary demand. Thus producers of DVD players first informed consumers of the image quality and convenience benefits of the new product.

Persuasive advertising becomes more important as competition increases. Here, the company's objective is to build selective demand. For example, when DVD players become established and accepted, Sony begins trying to persuade consumers that its brand offers the best quality for their money.

Some persuasive advertising has become **comparison advertising**, in which a company directly or indirectly compares its brand with one or more other brands:

> For example, in its classic comparative campaign, Avis, the car rental company, positioned itself against market-leading Hertz by claiming 'We're number two, so we try harder.' In the UK, Korean carmaker Hyundai sought to raise awareness of its cars with a series of light-hearted efforts: 'Even a kettle has a longer guarantee than Rover.' Another example is the claims and counter-claims between airline companies regarding who offers the widest and longest seats in business-class flight cabins. Virgin Atlantic's recent ad campaign for its new Upper Class Suite reminds business class travellers that its fully flat bed measures at least 7 and a half inches longer and up to 13 inches wider than BA's Club World seat, hence making it 'the biggest boy in business class.'

There are potential dangers in using comparison advertising. As often happens with comparison advertising, both sides complain that the other's ads are misleading. The approach is legal in the United Kingdom and the US, but its use is banned in a number of European countries. Belgium and Germany regard it as tantamount to unfair competition. For example, a relatively innocuous Carlsberg commercial with the tagline 'Probably the best lager in the world' could not be run in those countries because it implicitly identifies products offered by rivals. Similarly, Avis's 'We try harder' ad would not have been allowed in Germany because, although nobody is named, Hertz is presumed to be the only real competitor.

Efforts continue to harmonise EU rules on comparative advertising across the EU. Meanwhile, advertisers in the region must remain sensitive to individual country codes of practice and legislation. This style of communication will probably always exist in one form or another, as most advertising is essentially comparative – after all, the aim of the advertiser is to persuade the consumer to respond to one product offering rather than another.[4]

Reminder advertising— Advertising used to keep consumers thinking about a product.

Reminder advertising is important for mature products as it keeps consumers thinking about the product. Expensive Coca-Cola ads on television are often designed to remind people about Coca-Cola, not merely to inform or persuade them. Advertisers might also seek to assure existing customers that they have made the right choice. For example, car firms might use reinforcement advertising that depicts satisfied owners enjoying some special feature of their new car.

Setting the advertising budget

After determining its advertising objectives, the company next sets its *advertising budget* for each product. Four commonly used methods for setting promotion budgets were discussed in Chapter 17. Here we describe some specific factors that should be considered when setting the advertising budget:

Comparative advertising: longer and wider seat-cum-flatbed – in this ad, Virgin Atlantic explains why its new Upper Class Suite is heads and shoulders above rival BA's Club World seat.

SOURCE: Virgin Atlantic.

- *Stage in the product life-cycle.* A brand's advertising budget often depends on its stage in the product life-cycle. New products typically need large advertising budgets to build awareness and to persuade consumers to try the products. In contrast, mature brands usually require lower budgets as a percentage of sales.

- *Market share.* Market share also impacts the amount of advertising needed. Because building the market or taking share from competitors requires larger advertising spending than does simply maintaining current share, low-share brands usually need more advertising spending as a percentage of sales.

- *Competition and clutter.* In a market with many competitors and high advertising clutter, a brand must be advertised more heavily to be noticed above the noise in the market.

- *Advertising frequency.* When many repetitions are needed to present the brand's message to consumers, the advertising budget must be larger.

- *Product differentiation.* Undifferentiated brands – those that closely resemble other brands in their product class (coffee, laundry detergents, chewing gum, beer, soft drinks) – may require heavy advertising to set them apart. When the product differs greatly from those of competitors, advertising can be used to point out the differences to consumers.

No matter what method is used, setting the advertising budget is no easy task. How does a company know whether it is spending the right amount? Some critics maintain that large consumer packaged-goods firms tend to overspend on advertising, while industrial companies generally underspend on advertising. They also claim that, on the one hand, the large consumer companies use lots of image advertising extensively without really knowing its effects. They overspend as a form of 'insurance' against not spending enough. On the other hand, business advertisers tend to rely too heavily on their sales forces to bring in orders. They underestimate the power of company and product image in pre-selling to industrial customers. Thus they do not spend enough on advertising to build customer awareness and knowledge.

Some companies have built sophisticated statistical models to determine the relationship between promotional spending and brand sales, and to help determine the 'optimal investment' across various media. Still, because so many factors affect advertising effectiveness, some controllable and others not, measuring the results of advertising spending remains an inexact science. In most cases, managers must rely on large doses of judgement along with more quantitative analysis when setting advertising budgets.[5]

Developing advertising strategy

Advertising strategy covers two major elements: creating the advertising messages and selecting the advertising media. In the past, companies viewed media planning as secondary to the message-creation process. Many companies also developed messages and media independently. The creative department first created the advertisements, then the media department selected the best media for carrying these advertisements to the desired target audiences. Separation of the functions often caused friction between 'creatives' and media planners.

Today, however, media fragmentation, soaring media costs and more focused target marketing strategies have promoted the importance of the media planning function. In some cases, an advertising campaign might begin with a good message idea followed by the choice of appropriate media. In other cases, however, a campaign might begin with a good media opportunity, followed by advertisements designed to take advantage of that opportunity. Increasingly, companies are realising the benefits of planning these two important activities jointly. More and more advertisers are orchestrating a closer harmony between their messages and the media that deliver them. Media planning is no longer an after-the-fact complement to a new ad campaign. Media planners are now working more closely than ever with creatives to allow media selection to help shape the creative process, often before a single ad is written. In some cases, media people are even initiating ideas for new campaigns.

Among the more noteworthy ad campaigns based on tight media-creative partnerships is the pioneering campaign for Absolut vodka, marketed by Seagram.

The Absolut team and its ad agency meet once each year with a slew of magazines to set Absolut's media schedule. The team first goes through the 800 produced ads, which all run frequently in a copy rotation, and, if needed, the agency's creative department then creates the media-specific ads. The result is a wonderful assortment of very creative ads for Absolut, tightly targeted to audiences of the media in which they appear. For example, an 'Absolut Bravo' ad in playbills has roses adorning a clear bottle, whereas business magazines contain an 'Absolut Merger' foldout. In some cases, the creatives even developed ads for magazines not yet on the schedule, such as a clever 'Absolut Centerfold' ad for *Playboy* magazine. The ad portrayed a clear, unadorned playmate bottle ('11-inch bust, 11-inch waist, 11-inch hips'). In all, Absolut has developed more than 800 ads for the almost two-decade-old campaign. At a time of soaring media costs and cluttered communication channels, a closer cooperation between creative and media people has paid off handsomely for Absolut. Largely as a result of its breakthrough advertising, Absolut now captures a sizeable share of the global vodka market.[6]

Creating the advertising message

No matter how big the budget, advertising can succeed only if commercials gain attention and communicate well.

The changing message environment

Good advertising messages are especially important in today's costly and cluttered advertising environment. The average consumer has numerous television channels and radio stations and thousands of magazines to choose from. Add the countless radio stations, and a continuous barrage of catalogues, direct-mail and online ads and out-of-home media. Consumers are bombarded with ads at home, at work and at all points in between!

ABSOLUT VODKA: media planners work with creatives to design ads targeted to specific media audiences. 'ABSOLUT BRAVO' appears in theatre playbills. 'ABSOLUT CHICAGO' targets the Windy City.

SOURCE: Reproduced by permission of V&S Vin & Spirit AB (publ). ABSOLUT country of Sweden logo, ABSOLUT ABSOLUT bottle design and ABSOLUT calligraphy are trademarks owned by V&S Vin & Spirit AB, copyright © 2003 V&S Vin & Spirit AB (publ).

If all this advertising clutter bothers some consumers, it also causes big problems for advertisers – it is very costly. Network TV advertisers could pay tens to hundreds of thousands of euros for a 30-second slot during a popular prime-time TV programme. Also, their ads are sandwiched in with a clutter of other commercials, announcements and network promotions in any viewing hour.

Until recently, television viewers were very much a captive audience for advertisers. Viewers had only a few channels to choose from. But with the growth in cable and satellite TV, video cassette recorders, DVDs and remote-controlled technologies, today's audience have many more options. They can avoid ads by watching commercial-free channels. With remote control, they can instantly turn off the sound during a commercial or 'zap' around the channels to see what else is on.

Just to gain and hold attention, today's advertising messages must be better planned, more imaginative, more innovative, more entertaining and more rewarding to consumers. Creative strategy, even intentionally controversial ads, will play an increasingly important role in helping advertisers break through the clutter and gain attention for their products.

Message strategy

The first step in creating effective advertising messages is to decide what general message will be communicated to consumers – to plan the *message strategy*. Generally, the purpose of advertising is to get target consumers to think about or react to the product or company in a certain way. People will respond only if they believe they will benefit from doing so. Thus, developing an effective message strategy usually begins with identifying target customer *benefits* that can be used as advertising appeals. Ideally, advertising message strategy follows directly from the company's broader positioning strategy.

Message strategy statements tend to be plain, straightforward outlines of benefits and positioning points that the advertiser wants to stress. The advertiser must develop a compelling *creative concept* – or '*big idea*' – that will bring the message strategy to life in a distinctive and memorable way. At this stage, simple message ideas become great ad campaigns. Usually, a copywriter and art director will team up to generate many creative concepts, hoping that one of these concepts will turn out to be the big idea. The creative concept may emerge as a visualisation, a phrase or a combination of the two.[7]

How should advertising planners evaluate advertising messages? Generally, the creative concept should guide the choice of specific appeals to be used in an ad campaign. Advertising appeals should have three characteristics. First, they should be *meaningful*, pointing out benefits that make the product more desirable or interesting to target customers. Second, appeals must be *believable*. This objective is difficult because many consumers doubt the truth of advertising in general. One study found that a full one-third of the public rates advertising messages as 'unbelievable'.[8] Advertisers also argue that the most meaningful and believable benefits may not be the best ones to feature. Consumer scepticism is not surprising since many ads sell the notion that the product is bigger, better, brighter or far longer-lasting than rival offerings. However, more recently, a number of companies have adopted a different tack, using advertising that stresses honesty in selling to consumers.

For example, Ikea and Guinness acknowledge that their service or product is not perfect, and then turn these 'failures' into winning advertising copy. The culture of honesty is seen in Guinness's attempt to advertise one of the most annoying things about drinking stout – the long pouring time. Drinkers get fed up waiting for Guinness to be poured. The company therefore decided to tackle this in its popular ad campaign using the strapline, 'Good things come to those who wait'. In the case of Ikea, one bold campaign in the UK tells people the truth about Ikea stores. The ad features a tattooed giant who shouts about the furniture store's long queues, its lack of assistants and the hassle of self-assembly. The ad is honest by suggesting that Ikea is not about service. Customers are therefore spared all that 'better, bigger, brighter' advertising hype and told the truth and why Ikea is like it is. So far, Ikea thinks that it is working and business remains buoyant, so much so that the retailer continues to open more stores in the country, which happens to be one way to deal with the fruits of its success – its hellishly overcrowded stores.[9]

Appeals should also be *distinctive* in terms of telling consumers how the product is different from or better than competing brands. For example, the most meaningful benefit of owning a wristwatch is that it keeps accurate time, yet few watch ads feature this benefit. Instead, based on the distinctive benefits they offer, watch advertisers might select any of a number of advertising themes. For years, Timex has been the affordable watch that 'Takes a lickin' and keeps on tickin'.' In contrast, Swatch has featured style, fun and fashion, whereas Rolex stresses luxury and status. Advertisers should therefore pre-test each ad to determine that it has the maximum impact, believability and appeal.

Message execution

The advertiser now has to turn the 'big idea' into an actual ad execution that will capture the target market's attention and their interest. The impact of the message depends not only on *what* is said, but also on *how* it is said. The creative people must find the best style, tone, words and format for executing the message. Any message can be presented in different *execution styles*, such as the following:

- *Slice of life*. This style shows one or more people using the product in a normal setting (e.g. the classic Persil laundry detergent commercials which show the role of the mother who knows she can rely on Persil to keep her family's washing clean, white and bright).

- *Lifestyle*. This style shows how a product fits in with a particular lifestyle. For example, the UK 'After Eight' mints advertisement (elegant dinner party in a period house) appeals to aspirations more than anything else.

- *Fantasy*. This style creates a fantasy around the product or its use. For instance, many ads are built around dream themes. Gap introduced a perfume named Dream. Ads show a woman sleeping blissfully and suggest that the scent is 'the stuff that clouds are made of'.

- *Mood or image*. This style builds a mood or image around the product, such as beauty, love or serenity. No claim is made about the product except through suggestion. Timotei shampoo employs the mood for nature and simplicity – a strategy that has worked successfully in many countries across the globe.

- *Musical*. The ad is built around a song or some well-known music, so that emotional responses to the music are associated with the product. For example, one of the most famous ads in history was a Coca-Cola ad built around the song 'I'd like to teach the world to sing'.

- *Personality symbol*. This style creates a character that represents the product. The character might be *animated* (e.g. Shreik for Hewlett-Packard office systems) or *real* (e.g. Gary Lineker for Walkers' Crisps; David Beckham for Marks & Spencer's DB07 boys' clothing range).

■ *Technical expertise.* This style shows the company's expertise in making the product. Thus DaimlerChrysler promotes its investment in intelligent technologies to build tomorrow's energy-efficient automobiles, and Volkswagen-Audi cars imply superiority with the advertising slogan 'Vorsprung durch Technik'.

■ *Scientific evidence.* This style presents survey or scientific evidence that the brand is better or better liked than one or more other brands. For years, Crest toothpaste has used scientific evidence to convince buyers that Crest is better than other brands at fighting cavities. In Elida Gibbs' relaunch of the skin-care brand Pond's, the advertisement referred to the 'Pond's Institute' where women were shown having their skin analysed, the ad emphasising the brand's scientific problem-solving qualities.

DaimlerChrysler promotes its energy-efficient, intelligent technologies as alternative drive systems of the future.
SOURCE: DaimlerChrysler AG Stuttgart/Auburn Hills.

Just what the environment needs from a car. Water.

If nature had one wish, what do you think it would be? A car that doesn't produce exhaust?
We thought so too. That's why our hydrogen powered Fuel Cell vehicles only emit water.
In fact, as they've proven in recent road tests, they may well be the alternative drive systems of
the future. At DaimlerChrysler Research we're developing these intelligent technologies today.
For the automobiles of tomorrow.

To find out more about 'Energy for the Future' visit www.daimlerchrysler.com

DAIMLERCHRYSLER
Answers for questions to come.

The world's fastest soft top.*

The new BMW Z4

www.bmw.co.uk
Tel. 0800 325 600

The Ultimate
Driving Machine

*Unfolds in 10 seconds flat.

Impressive as the new BMW Z4's fully automatic soft top is, it would be remiss not to mention its 6-cylinder, 231 bhp engine, capable of 0-62 mph in 5.9 seconds or the new Driving Dynamics Control system that makes the Z4 even more responsive.

The new BMW Z4 from £26,655. Model featured BMW Z4 3.0 with optional wheels £31,565. The Official Fuel Economy Figures range for Z4. Extra Urban 42.8 – 38.7mpg (6.6 – 7.3 l/100km). Urban 22.6 – 20.9 mpg (12.5 – 13.5 l/100km). Combined 31.7 – 29.7mpg (8.9 – 9.5 l/100km). CO_2 emissions 216 – 231 g/km. For information regarding financial services availab e to business users, please contact your local BMW Dealer.

This ad. for the new BMW Z4 fully automatic soft top shows the impact of an efficient copy – the message is concise, conveying a simple, yet compelling and meaningful benefit.

SOURCE: BMW (GB) Ltd. *Agency:* WCRS/Saatchi and Saatchi.

■ *Testimonial evidence or endorsement.* This style features a highly believable or likeable source endorsing the product. It could be ordinary people saying how much they like a given product or a celebrity presenting the product.

The advertiser must also choose a *tone* for the ad. Positive tones that evoke happiness, feelings of achievement, fun and excitement tend to be more effective than negative tones. By contrast, negative appeals that evoke fear may discourage viewers from looking at the advertisement, and so would be counterproductive. The advertiser not only has to use ad appeals that can break through the commercial clutter, but also has to avoid appeals that take attention away from the message.

The advertiser must also use memorable and attention-getting *words* in the ad.

> For example, rather than claiming simply that 'a BMW is a well-engineered car', BMW uses more creative and high-impact phrasing: 'The ultimate driving machine'. Instead of saying that Häagen-Dazs is 'a good tasting ice-cream', its ads say that it is 'Our passport to indulgence: passion in a touch, perfection in a cup, summer in a spoon, one perfect moment'. It's not that 'Philishave gives optimum shaving satisfaction due to its high quality and advanced technology'.

> Rather, use the shaver 'For a better, closer shave'. And Stella Artois is not simply a high-priced, high-quality beer, but instead, 'Stella Artois (is) – reassuringly expensive'.

Finally, *format* elements make a difference in an ad's impact as well as in its cost. A small change in ad design can make a big difference in its effect. The *illustration* is the first thing the reader notices – it must be strong enough to draw attention. Next, the *headline* must effectively entice the right people to read the copy. Finally, the *copy* – the main block of text in the ad – must be simple but strong and convincing.

Importantly, all the elements – style, tone, words, format – must effectively work together. Even then, fewer than 50 per cent of the exposed audience will notice even a truly outstanding ad; about 30 per cent will recall the main point of the headline; about 25 per cent will remember the advertiser's name; and fewer than 10 per cent will have read most of the copy. Less than outstanding ads, unfortunately, will not achieve even these results.

Selecting advertising media

The advertiser must next decide upon the media to carry the message. The main steps in media selection are: (1) deciding on *reach*, *frequency* and *impact*; (2) choosing among chief *media types*; (3) selecting specific *media vehicles*; and (4) deciding on *media timing*.

Deciding on reach, frequency and impact

Reach—The percentage of people in the target market exposed to an ad campaign during a given period.

To select media, the advertiser must decide what reach and frequency are needed to achieve advertising objectives. **Reach** is a measure of the *percentage* of people in the target market who are exposed to the ad campaign during a given period of time. For example, the advertiser might try to reach 70 per cent of the target market during the first three months of the campaign. **Frequency** is a measure of how many *times* the average person in the target market is exposed to the message. For example, the advertiser might want an average exposure frequency of three. The advertiser must also decide on the desired **media impact** – the qualitative value of a message exposure through a given medium. For example, for products that need to be demonstrated, messages on television may have more impact than messages on radio because television uses sight and sound. The same message in a national newspaper may be more believable than in a local weekly.

Frequency—The number of times the average person in the target market is exposed to an advertising message during a given period.

Media impact—The qualitative value of an exposure through a given medium.

In general, the more reach, frequency and impact the advertiser seeks, the higher the advertising budget will have to be.

Choosing among chief media types

The media planner has to know the reach, frequency and impact of each of the major media types. The major media types are newspapers, television, direct mail, radio, magazines, outdoor and the Internet. As shown in Table 18.2, each medium has advantages and limitations.

How do advertisers select appropriate media from the range of media available? Media planners consider many factors when making their media choices. The *media habits of target consumers* will affect media choice and advertisers look for media that reach target consumers effectively. So will the *nature of the product*: for example, fashions are best advertised in colour magazines and car performance is best demonstrated on television. Different *types of message* may require different media: for instance, a message announcing a big sale tomorrow will require radio or newspapers; a message with a lot of technical data might require magazines or direct mailings or an online ad and website. *Cost* is also an important consideration in media choice: whereas network television is very expensive, newspaper or

Medium	Advantages	Limitations
Newspapers	Flexibility; timeliness; local market coverage; broad acceptance; high believability	Short life; poor reproduction quality; small pass-along audience
Television	Good mass-market coverage; low cost per exposure; combines sight, sound and motion; appealing to the senses	High absolute cost; high clutter; fleeting exposure; less audience selectivity
Radio	Good local acceptance; high geographic and demographic selectivity; low cost	Audio presentation only; low attention (the 'half-heard' medium); fleeting exposure; fragmented audience
Magazines	High geographic and demographic selectivity; credibility and prestige; high-quality reproduction; long life; good pass-along readership	Long ad purchase lead time; high cost; some waste circulation; no guarantee of position
Direct mail	High audience selectivity; flexibility; no ad competition within the same medium; allows personalisation	Relatively high cost per exposure; 'junk mail' image
Outdoor	Flexibility; high repeat exposure; low cost; low message competition; good positional selectivity	No audience selectivity; creative limitations
Internet	High selectivity; low cost; immediacy; interactive capabilities	Small, demographically skewed audience; relatively low impact; audience controls exposure

Table 18.2 Profiles of major media forms

radio advertising costs much less but also reaches fewer consumers. The media planner looks at both the total cost of using a medium and the cost per 1,000 exposures – the cost of reaching 1,000 people using the medium.

Media impact and cost must be re-examined regularly. For a long time, television and magazines dominated in the media mixes of national advertisers, with other media often neglected. Recently, however, as network television costs soar and audiences shrink, many advertisers are looking for new ways to reach consumers. The move towards micromarketing strategies, focused more narrowly on specific consumer groups, has also fuelled the search for new media to replace or supplement network television. As a result, advertisers are increasingly shifting larger portions of their budgets to media that cost less and target more effectively.

Three media benefiting greatly from the shift are outdoor advertising, cable television and digital satellite television systems. Billboards have undergone a resurgence in recent years. Gone are the ugly eyesores of the past; in their place we now see cleverly designed, colourful attention grabbers. Outdoor advertising provides an excellent way to reach important local consumer segments at a fraction of the cost per exposure of other major media. Cable television and digital satellite systems are also gaining importance. Such systems allow narrow programming formats such as all sports, all news, nutrition, arts, gardening, cooking, travel, history and others that target select groups. Advertisers can take advantage of such 'narrowcasting' to 'rifle in' on special market segments rather than use the 'shotgun' approach offered by network broadcasting.

Outdoor, cable and satellite media seem to make good sense. But, increasingly, ads are popping up in far less likely places. In their efforts to find less costly and more highly targeted ways to reach consumers, advertisers have discovered a dazzling collection of 'alternative media' ranging from parking lot tickets and park benches to petrol pumps and public toilets.

Selecting specific media vehicles

Media vehicles—Specific media within each general media type, such as specific magazines, television shows or radio programmes.

The media planner must now choose the best **media vehicles** – that is, specific media within each general media type. In most cases, there is an incredible number of choices. For radio and television, and in any one country, there are numerous stations and channels to choose from, together with hundreds, even thousands, of programme vehicles – the particular programmes or shows where the commercial should be broadcast. Prime-time programmes are the favourites, but costs escalate with the popularity of the programme.

In the case of magazines, the media planner must look up circulation figures and the costs of different ad sizes, colour options, ad positions and frequencies for specific magazines. Each country has its own high- or general-circulation magazines (for example, radio and TV guides) which reach general audience groups. There is also a vast selection of special-interest publications that enable advertisers to reach special groups of audiences (for example, business magazines to reach business executives). The planner selects the media that will do the best job in terms of selectively reaching the target customer group. Then he or she must evaluate each magazine on factors such as credibility, status, reproduction quality, editorial focus and advertising submission deadlines. The media planner ultimately decides which vehicles give the best reach, frequency and impact for the money. With increasing emphasis on improving efficiency, some companies are seeking new ways to boost their media buying power. For example, Sony has adopted a new approach in Europe based on the barter system (see Marketing Insights 18.1).

Media planners have to compute the cost per 1,000 persons reached by a vehicle. For example, if a full-page, four-colour advertisement in a monthly business *magazine* costs £30,000 and its readership is 3 million people, the cost of reaching each group of 1,000 persons is about £10. The same advertisement in a regional trade magazine may cost only £20,000 but reach only 1 million persons, giving a cost per 1,000 of about £20. The media planner would rank each magazine by cost per 1,000 and favour those magazines with the lower cost per 1,000 for reaching target consumers. Additionally, the media planner considers the cost of producing ads for different media. Whereas newspaper ads may cost very little to produce, flashy television ads may cost millions. Media costs vary across different countries, so care must be taken not to generalise the figures.

Thus the media planner must balance media cost measures against several media impact factors. First, the planner should balance costs against the media vehicle's *audience quality*. For a personal digital assistant (PDA) ad, business magazines would have a high-exposure value; magazines aimed at new parents or woodwork enthusiasts would have a low-exposure value. Second, the media planner should consider *audience attention*. Readers of fashion magazines such as *Vogue*, for example, typically pay more attention to ads than do readers of business magazines. Third, the planner should assess the vehicle's *editorial quality*. For example, the *Financial Times* and *The Economist* are more credible and prestigious than tabloid newspapers such as the *News of the World* or weeklies and celebrity magazines such as *Hello!* and *Now*.

Deciding on media timing

The advertiser must also decide how to schedule the advertising over the course of a year. Suppose sales of a product peak in December and drop in March. The firm can vary its advertising to follow the seasonal pattern, to oppose the seasonal pattern, or to be the same all year. Most firms do some seasonal advertising. Some do *only* seasonal advertising: for example, many department stores advertise – usually their seasonal sales – in specific periods

Why pay with hard cash? Bartering will do!

18.1

FT

marketing insights

Bartering comes into its own when times are hard. As many businesses are seeking to cut costs, especially in marketing and promotion, one of the consumer sector's leading advertisers decided to introduce a system of bartering in Europe. Sony, the electronics and entertainment giant, aims to barter everything from television sets and personal computers to video and music releases in return for advertising exposure on TV, radio, cinema, posters and the Internet and in newspapers and magazines. Recently, Sony appointed OMD Europe, the media buying agency, to handle Sony's €300m (£189m) account across more than 20 countries including Britain, France and Germany. Hilary Jeffrey, general manager of OMD UK, believes that despite the worldwide advertising downturn, Sony can near-double the weight of its official media budget by being 'more creative about the value of its assets to audience providers'.

Although many broadcasters do not like the notion of bartering – it is seen as opening the floodgates to more overt forms of advertiser-funded programming – the system is accepted practice in many markets, such as the US. In the 1950s, Unilever and Procter & Gamble directly funded the emerging TV soap opera genre in order to provide a mass-market vehicle for its advertisements, a trend that many contemporary advertisers note with envy. Advertiser-funded programming is not unknown in Europe but Sony is the first leading company in Europe to be openly in favour of bartering. Arguably, as both a kit and content company, it is uniquely placed to exploit the bartering trend.

Its appointment of OMD – whose media buying account will for the first time bring together consumer electronics, movies/films, videos and recording stars such as Jennifer Lopez, Bruce Springsteen and Sade – not only 'provides significant efficiencies in the very near term' but also helps 'to leverage the weight of our joint advertising activities', according to Paul Burger, president of Sony Music Entertainment Europe. OMD says Sony recognises that hard cash is still an important element of the media buying business but believes that money should be just the beginning of the negotiation process. 'What we are telling audience providers such as newspapers and TV stations is that Sony has far more to give than simply money, as can be seen from even a cursory asset-audit', says Ms Jeffrey. 'By bartering the latest Lopez release or *Men In Black 2* DVD-video, we intend to make the budget work very hard for the client in whatever market we happen to be.'

In addition to providing media owners such as TV stations and newspaper publishers with products and services, OMD says it recognises that media owners, too, have assets to barter. The agency will try to instigate swapping deals where, say, the use of a newly released Sony video such as *Spiderman* 'buys' access to a media company's spin-off website or magazine portfolio. OMD will also investigate product

...18.1

placement deals where Sony hardware gets star billing in nominated TV shows. Although product placement, or undue prominence for commercial products, is strictly prohibited on British shows by the Independent Television Commission Code, the ITC says the notion of bartering would be permissible in Britain as long as programme content was not directly affected.

OMD Europe, a subsidiary of Omnicom Group, the world's largest marketing and corporate communications company, also has experience of bartering in eastern Europe, where broadcasters are short of both up-to-date equipment and programming. 'In Poland, where there has long been a shortage of quality content, a number of our clients have been able to provide good quality, off-the-shelf programmes in return for free air time', says Ms Jeffrey.

One of the biggest exponents of US companies' use of bartering has been the James Bond films. Although it is the astonishing level of overt product placement in the films that has received most of the attention, it is the behind-the-scenes bartering of products, in return for promotion and advertising before and after release, that arguably has been even more important to their commercial success.

Sony, meanwhile, already has long-term plans for more direct bargaining power in the media arena, including becoming a programme-maker in its own right. 'The prospect of Sony's having more direct control on the audience-delivering process by literally making [its] own programmes and 'selling' them to broadcasters in return for free advertising exposure is by no means out of the question', says Ms Jeffrey.

SOURCE: Adapted from Virginia Matthews, 'The decline of hard cash', *Financial Times* (28 October 2002), p. 21.

in the year, such as Christmas, Easter and summer. Advertisers can also ensure greater efficiency in running their TV campaigns – in terms of the number of television impacts and their price – by shifting TV campaigns into cheaper months.

According to advertising spot cost-checker, Media Audits, the fast-moving consumer good company Kimberly-Clark achieved 6.4 per cent of value above what its spend would normally buy through focusing its UK TV budgets in the months of January and December, rather than initiating campaigns in more expensive months such as October and November. By contrast, food company Kraft acquired 4.2 per cent less value by concentrating its campaigns in more expensive periods. While Media Audits acknowledges that some companies are limited in their ability to use the cheaper months, it believes that 60–70 per cent of them should be in a good position to exploit seasonal differences in pricing.[10]

Finally, the advertiser has to choose the pattern of the ads. **Continuity** means scheduling ads evenly within a given period. **Pulsing** means scheduling ads unevenly over a given time period. Thus 52 ads could be either scheduled at one per week during the year or pulsed in several bursts. The idea is to advertise heavily for a short period to build awareness that carries over to the next advertising period. Those who favour pulsing feel that it can be used to achieve the same impact as a steady schedule, but at a much lower cost. However, some media planners believe that although pulsing achieves minimal awareness, it sacrifices depth of advertising communications.

Recent advances in technology have had a substantial impact on the media planning and buying functions. Today, for example, new computer software applications called *media optimisers* allow media planners to evaluate vast combinations of television programmes and prices. Such programmes help advertisers to make better decisions about which mix of networks, programmes, and day parts will yield the highest reach per ad euro.

> **Continuity**—Scheduling ads evenly within a given period.
>
> **Pulsing**—Scheduling ads unevenly, in bursts, over a certain time period.

Evaluating advertising

The advertising programme should regularly evaluate both the communication impact and the sales effects of advertising. Measuring the communication effects of an ad or **copy testing** tells whether the ad is communicating well. Copy testing can be done before or after an ad is printed or broadcast. Before the ad is placed, the advertiser can show it to consumers, ask how they like it, and measure recall or attitude changes resulting from it. After the ad is run, the advertiser can measure how the ad affected consumer recall or product awareness, knowledge and preference.

But what sales are caused by an ad that increases brand awareness by 20 per cent and brand preference by 10 per cent? The sales effects of advertising are often harder to measure than the communication effects. Sales are affected by many factors besides advertising – such as product features, price and availability. Despite the difficulty of accounting for sales, advertising effects must be monitored. Figure 18.2 shows the levels of communication effect that advertisers are likely to monitor and measure with respect to a campaign:

> **Copy testing**—Measuring the communication effect of an advertisement before or after it is printed or broadcast.

- The change in brand awareness is determined by the number of customers who were previously *unaware* of the brand and the number who *notice* the advertisement and are now *aware* of the brand, or by the difference in the number of customers who are aware that the brand exists before and after the campaign. If there has been little increase or

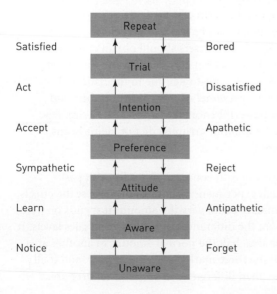

> **Figure 18.2** Advertising: measuring communications and sales effectiveness

even a decline in brand awareness, the advertiser has to determine whether the reason is the poor impact achieved by the communications campaign or that customers *forget* because of poor recall or inadequate advertising investment.

■ The nature of consumers' attitudes towards a brand can be ascertained before and after a campaign. An informative ad allows consumers to *learn* more about product/brand benefits. If the message is poorly targeted, or conveys an undesirable or unbelievable message, consumers are *antipathetic* towards the brand. They do not develop any liking for the product. Advertisers may have to redesign the copy to generate greater interest among customers or improve message content in order to enhance the level of comprehension of brand benefits among target customers.

■ Consumers who are *sympathetic* towards advertised brand benefits would manifest their favourable response in the form of stated brand preference. Similarly, before-and-after (the campaign) studies would enable changes in consumer brand preference to be determined. Reasons for brand *rejection* should be identified so that communication weaknesses can be redressed.

■ An advertising campaign may be used to turn preference among customers into more definite *intention* to buy. Again, this response can be measured and changes in the level of buying intent may be determined.

■ It is usually difficult to measure the sales effect of a campaign. Questions such as 'What sales are caused by an ad that increases brand awareness by 20 per cent and brand preference by 10 per cent?' are not easy to answer. Sales or *trials* are affected by many factors besides advertising, such as product features, price and availability. One way to measure the sales effect of advertising is to compare past sales with past advertising expenditures. Another way is through experiments. For example, to test the effects of different advertising levels, Pizza Hut could vary the amount it spends on advertising in different market areas and measure the differences in resulting sales levels. It could spend the normal amount in one market area, half the normal amount in another area, and twice the normal amount in a third area. If the three market areas are similar, and if all other marketing efforts in the area are the same, then the differences in sales in the three cities could be related to advertising level. More complex experiments could be designed to include other variables, such as differences in the ads or media used.

■ If the customer is *satisfied* with the brand he or she has bought, this will lead to *repeat* purchase on another buying occasion. The extent to which advertising or a specific 'reminder' campaign affects repeat purchase is difficult to measure because of the difficulty of separating out the immediate and long-term effects of advertising. 'Before-and-after' type studies and controlled experiments can be used, nonetheless, to detect changes in purchase and usage frequency. Again, advertisers should obtain consumer feedback to increase their understanding of the impact of communications on repeat purchase. Advertising may not be blamed for non-repeat sales due to the nature of product consumption: for example, consumers get *bored* with the same product and want variety. In this case, advertising is not powerful enough to arrest that desire. Few of us would relish the thought of surviving on an uninterrupted diet of Heinz beans, Heinz soup and Heinz sausages all year round!

One way to measure the sales effect of advertising is to compare past sales with past advertising expenditures. Another way is through experiments. For example, to test the effects of different advertising spending levels, the company could vary the amount it spends on advertising in different market areas and measure the differences in the resulting sales levels. It could spend the normal amount in one market area, half the normal amount in another area and twice the normal amount in a third area. If the three market areas are similar, and if all other marketing efforts in the area are the same, then differences in sales in the three areas could be related to advertising level. More complex experiments could be designed to include other variables, such as difference in the ads or media used.

Other advertising considerations

In developing advertising strategies and programmes, the company must address two additional questions. First, how will it organise the advertising function – who will perform the advertising tasks? Second, how will the company adapt its advertising strategies and programmes to the complexities of international markets?

Organising for advertising

Different organisations handle advertising in different ways. In small and medium-sized companies, advertising might be handled by someone in the sales or marketing department. Large companies might set up advertising departments whose job it is to set the advertising budget, work with the ad agency and handle dealer displays and other advertising not done by the agency. Most companies, small or large, tend to use outside advertising agencies because they offer several advantages.

There are disadvantages in relinquishing the advertising function to an outside agency: loss of total control of the advertising process, a reduction in flexibility, conflicts arising when the agency dictates working practices, and client inability to exercise control or coordination. Despite the potential problems, however, most firms find that they benefit from employing the specialised expertise of agencies.

How does an advertising agency work? Advertising agencies were started in the mid-to-late nineteenth century by salespeople and brokers who worked for the media and received commission for selling advertising space to companies. As time passed, the salespeople began to help customers prepare their ads. Eventually they formed agencies and grew closer to the advertisers than to the media. Today's agencies employ specialists who can often perform advertising tasks – research, creative work – better than the company's own staff. Agencies bring an outside point of view to solving a company's problems, along with years of experience from working with different clients and situations. Thus, even companies with strong advertising departments of their own use advertising agencies.

Some ad agencies are huge – McCann-Erickson has a worldwide annual gross income of nearly $1.9 billion on billings (the dollar amount of advertising placed for clients) of almost $18 billion. In recent years, many agencies have grown by gobbling up other agencies, thus creating huge agency holding companies. An 'agency mega-group' such as WPP Group, includes several large advertising, public relations and promotion agencies with a combined worldwide gross income of $8 billion on billings exceeding $75 billion.[11]

Most large agencies have staff and resources to handle all phases of an ad campaign for their clients, from creating a marketing plan to developing campaigns and preparing, placing and evaluating ads. Agencies usually have four departments: creative, which develops and produces ads; media, which selects media and places ads; research, which studies audience characteristics and wants; and business, which handles the agency's business activities. Each account is supervised by an account executive and people in each department are usually assigned to work on one or more accounts.

Ad agencies have traditionally been paid through commission and fees. Higher commissions are paid to the well-recognised agencies for their ability to place more advertisements in media. However, both advertisers and agencies are becoming more and more unhappy with the commission system. Larger advertisers complain that they have to pay more for the same services received by smaller ones simply because they place more advertising. Advertisers also believe that the commission system drives agencies away from low-cost media and short advertising campaigns. Agencies, on the other hand, are unhappy because they perform extra services for an account without getting more pay. The commission formula also tends to overlook important emerging media such as the Internet. There have been vast changes in how ad agencies reach consumers, using methods that go beyond network TV or magazine advertising. As a result, new agency payment methods may now include anything from fixed retainers or straight hourly fees for labour to incentives keyed to performance of the agencies' ad campaigns or some combination of these.

Another trend is affecting the agency business. Many agencies have sought growth by diversifying into related marketing services. These new diversified agencies offer a one-stop shop – a complete list of integrated marketing and promotion services under one roof, including advertising, sales promotion, marketing research, public relations and direct and online marketing. Some have added marketing consulting, television production and sales training units in an effort to become full 'marketing partners' to their clients.

However, many agencies are finding that advertisers do not want much more from them than traditional media advertising services plus direct marketing, sales promotion and sometimes public relations. Thus, many agencies have recently limited their diversification efforts in order to focus more on traditional services or their core expertise. Some have even started their own 'creative boutiques' – smaller and more independent agencies that can develop creative campaigns for clients free of large-agency bureaucracy.

International advertising decisions

We have discussed advertising decisions in general. International advertisers face many complexities not encountered by domestic advertisers. When developing advertising for international markets, a number of basic issues must be considered.

Standardisation or differentiation

The most basic issue concerns the degree to which global advertising should be adapted to the unique characteristics of various country markets. Some large advertisers have attempted to support their global brands with highly standardised worldwide advertising, with campaigns that work as well in Bangkok as they do in Budapest. For example, Coca-Cola's Sprite brand uses standardised appeals to target the world's youth. Gillette's ads for its Sensor Excel for Women are almost identical worldwide, with only minor adjustments to suit the local culture. Ericsson, the Swedish telecommunications giant, spent $100 million on a standardised global television campaign with the tag line 'make yourself heard,' which featured Agent 007, James Bond.

Standardisation produces many benefits, such as lower advertising costs, greater coordination of global advertising efforts and a more consistent worldwide company or product image. However, standardisation also has drawbacks. Most importantly, it ignores the fact that country markets, not just across the continents but also within supposedly 'harmonised' trading communities, such as the European Union, differ greatly in their cultures, demographics and economic conditions. Pan-European advertising, for example, is complicated because of the EU's cultural diversity as reflected in the differences in circumstances, language, traditions, music, beliefs, values and lifestyles among member nations. Ironically, the English have more in common with the Australians, who live on the opposite side of the globe, than with the Germans or the French, their closer neighbours. Cultural differences also exist across Asian countries (Japanese and Indonesian consumers are as alike as the Germans and Italians), as they do among emerging European markets. For example, the three Baltic countries – Estonia, Latvia and Lithuania – are far from being a common market, each having different languages, currencies and consumer habits.

Although advertising messages might be standardised, their executions cannot be, as culture invariably dominates communications.[12] Indeed, a survey of pan-European brand managers showed that a majority believe it is difficult to standardise advertising execution.[13] Thus, most international advertisers 'think globally, but act locally'. They develop global advertising *strategies* that make their worldwide advertising efforts more efficient and consistent. Then they adapt their advertising *programmes* to make them more responsive to consumer needs and expectations within local markets. In many cases, even when a standard message is used, execution styles are adapted to reflect local moods and consumer expectations.

Successful standardised advertising is most likely to work for capital goods or business-to-business marketing, where targets are more homogeneous in their needs and buy the product for the same reasons. For example, whether for a European, Asian or American construction company, the purchase of bulldozers is influenced by similar economic factors (for example, productivity, lifetime cost of running the equipment, parts delivery). Consumer-goods advertising is less amenable to cross-cultural standardisation. However, considerable similarities are found in segments, such as the world's rich to whom lifestyle goods and brands like Mont Blanc, Cartier and Hugo Boss appeal. Similarly, youth culture across the globe may be targeted with a common message. Brands such as Nike, Pepsi and Jeep are advertised in much the same way globally; Jeep has created a worldwide brand image of ruggedness and reliability; Nike urges Americans, Africans, Asians and Europeans alike to 'Just do it'; Pepsi uses a standard appeal to target the world's youth.

Centralisation or decentralisation

Global advertisers are concerned with the degree to which advertising decision making and implementation should be centralised or decentralised. Five key factors influence the choice between centralisation and decentralisation of the responsibility for international advertising decisions and implementation:

1. *Corporate and marketing objectives*. A company whose global marketing objectives dominate over domestic objectives is likely to centralise advertising and communications decisions.

2. *Product uniformity*. The more similar the product or service marketed across different countries, the greater the feasibility of a uniform approach, which allows for centralised management of advertising.

3. *Product appeal*. Underpinning the product's appeal are the reasons why customers use the product, which may differ among different cultures, whatever the demographic or psychographic characteristics of consumers. Golf club membership is a status purchase in Singapore; in the United Kingdom it is a moderate leisure activity, without such a label of exclusivity attached. Where underlying appeals vary significantly, decentralised decision making makes better sense.

4. *Cultural sensitivities*. Where a product's usage and appeal are culture-bound in terms of the local attitudes towards consumption, habits and preferences, as in the case of drinks and food products, more decentralisation is necessary.

5. *Legal constraints*. Individual country rules and regulations affect advertising decisions and their implementation. Decentralisation of responsibility to tap local wisdom and knowledge makes sense where strict country regulations apply. In the European Union, until real 'harmonisation' is achieved, cross-border advertisers must remain alert to subtle differences in nations' rules and codes of practice in order to avoid costly mistakes.

HSBC prides itself as 'the world's local bank' using a standardised message to reinforce its global strengths.
SOURCE: HSBC Holdings plc.
Agency: Lowe Worldwide.
Photographer: Richar Pullar.

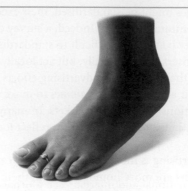

INDIA

Married

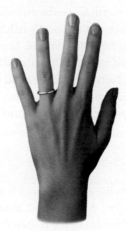

CANADA

Married

Never underestimate the importance of local knowledge.

Where a wedding ring goes is just something you grow up knowing when you're a local.

At HSBC, we have banks in more countries than anyone else. And each one is staffed by local people.

We have offices in 79 countries and territories; Europe, Asia-Pacific, the Americas, the Middle East, and Africa. Being local enables them to offer insights into financial opportunities and create service initiatives that would never occur to an outsider.

It means our customers get the kind of local knowledge and personal service that you'd expect of a local bank.

And a level of global knowledge and widely sourced expertise that you wouldn't.

HSBC
The world's local bank

The modes used by firms vary. Some organisations exert tight control from the centre and executionary changes for local culture and conditions are closely monitored. Some corporations grant local management some degree of freedom to develop advertising within broad strategic guidelines, but with central directives on agencies and media buying groups. Yet others may give local management total autonomy in both strategy determination and local implementation of advertising strategies.

Worldwide advertising media

The international media comprise an extensive mix:

- *Newspapers.* Faster and more efficient circulation is possible with new technologies, such as satellite printing, which allows advertising copy to be sent by satellite to the printers. Many international newspapers (e.g. *International Herald Tribune, Financial Times, Asahi Shimbun, Wall Street Asian, Wall Street Journal*) are printed simultaneously in more than one country. In general, there have been enormous developments in local and global press, and more newspapers have gone global to reach specific audiences.

- *Magazines.* There are some national and international journals which carry ads that target regional, international or global customers (e.g. *Fortune, Newsweek, Time, The Economist*). Women's magazines, such as *Cosmopolitan, Elle, Vogue* and *Harper's Bazaar*, are printed in different editions for readers in different target countries/regions.

- *Professional and technical magazines.* In Europe alone, there are more than 15,000 titles, and the number is rising yearly.

- *Cinema.* This is a relatively popular medium for reaching younger viewers, such as teenagers. In developing and less developed nations, cinema remains important.

- *Television.* There are few country markets where television is not available or where advertising is not carried via that medium. Satellite and cable opportunities have expanded enormously and accelerated the use of TV for international advertising. A few stations – notably CNN, NBC Super Channel and Eurosport – are well-recognised international media channels. Other international TV channels include Dow Jones's European Business News, BBC Worldwide and NBC's CNBC.

- *Outdoor advertising and transport advertising.* This medium is used throughout the world. In the western developed markets, advertisers are expanding their repertoire of outside media (e.g. park benches, trucks, taxis, bus stop shelters). This medium is used as an alternative in cases where the product category cannot be advertised on TV, as in the case of tobacco and alcoholic products. In some countries, such as India and the People's Republic of China, outdoor advertising has become more important.

- *Interactive communication media.* Interactive systems, such as videotext and pay-TV, have gained importance as cable TV continues to develop. Not only is the Internet a new channel for advertising, so are novelties such as TiVo, which allow viewers to store and play back TV programmes in real time. Interactive TV services are also emerging that increasingly give viewers control over what they watch and when they watch it, fragmenting further the mass television audience.

- *Radio.* As a medium for international advertising, radio is constrained by availability in the sense that most commercial radio is regional. Radio Luxembourg, the international European station, transmits ads in several languages and reaches the whole of Europe.

- *Place-based media.* This is a worldwide development and advertisers are increasingly deploying the medium to reach audiences wherever they happen to be – at work, the fitness centre, the supermarket, airports and in the aeroplane.

- *Trade fairs and exhibitions.* These can be costly, but are useful media for international communications.

- *Sponsorship.* Sponsorship of sports or arts events, like the Olympic Games and the soccer World Cup, offers vast audience reach. Such global audiences are rare and the effectiveness of the initiatives is not always easy to measure.

- *Other media.* Point-of-sale materials are not easy to reproduce internationally. Invariably, they have to be adapted to local conditions, specifically the language, regulations and distribution outlets. Direct mail is used in many countries, but it is primarily a local technique. As postal services vary from country to country, including within the EU, the medium has yet to be applied internationally. Nonetheless, credit card companies that have an international customer database can exploit this medium for worldwide communications. Add to this online media such as the Internet which is growing in importance for organisations seeking to reach a global audience (Chapter 4 discusses online marketing in greater detail).

Media planning, buying and costs

International media planning is more complicated than local media planning as the media situation differs from country to country. To plan effectively, international advertisers require high-quality, reliable cross-country media and audience research data. In some countries, there is inadequate media research. Moreover, research techniques and measurement standards vary greatly across countries, making cross-country comparisons of media research data almost impossible. Unless reliable inter-country comparisons can be made, international advertisers will find it difficult to evaluate and quantify international media effectiveness. In the EU, the European Association of Advertising Agencies has been working to bring together data to help pan-European media researchers. Recent pan-European research projects, funded jointly by advertisers, agencies and print and TV media, have generated data that help media planners go some way towards building more effective campaigns across Europe as well as in individual territories.[14]

Prices and preference for certain media also may vary greatly across countries. One survey suggests that, in the Scandinavian countries, print media dominate as an advertising medium, with two in three consumers polled voicing positive attitudes towards print advertising; only one in five held the same opinion of TV advertising. The preference for the printed word has important implications for advertising media choice.[15] Another report suggests that at least 40 of the top 50 pan-European advertisers have consolidated their media buying into a single network in order to get cheaper prices. Nonetheless, cultural differences remain in buying preferences. For example, in Italy, the number of spots advertisers tend to buy (also called the average advertising weight) is much higher than in the rest of Europe. According to one source, cultural differences stem from what planners feel 'happy' with, rather than rational reasons, often resulting in local resistance to centralised or standardised approaches. Hence, it is difficult to standardise pan-European media strategies. If the Marketing Director at HQ were to tell her Italian operation that it is running advertising weights that are two-and-a-half times higher than that run by the firm's other European operations, she will literally have to take on the Italian marketing team.[16]

Thus, firms that advertise their products in different country markets must select the media to use based on a consideration of their target groups and the budget available and must adapt their media strategy based on the media scene and relative media cost-effectiveness in different countries.

International advertising regulations

Countries also differ in the extent to which they regulate advertising practices. Many countries have extensive systems of laws restricting how much a company can spend on advertising, the media used, the nature of advertising claims and other aspects of the advertising programme. In recent years, much discussion in Europe has centred on laws governing marketing to children and the advertising of tobacco and alcohol.

In Sweden, Norway and Denmark, TV advertising to children under 12 is banned. To play it safe, McDonald's advertises itself in Sweden as a family restaurant. Advertising to children is also restricted in Belgium, Ireland, Holland and Austria, and is under consideration in Italy and Poland. Greece bans TV ads for toys before 10 p.m.

As regards tobacco advertising, the European Commission requires its member states to ban all tobacco promotion by 2006. These bans are being phased in gradually: tobacco ads via cinema, radio, posters and direct mail were banned in July 2001, followed by print in 2002 and sponsorship in 2003. Worldwide sponsorships such as Formula One are expected to go after 2006.

For alcohol advertising, Sweden and Finland impose strict limitations, while France is the most restrictive – all forms of alcohol advertising are banned. Denmark and the UK are calling for health warnings to be placed on packaging. Germany, too, is calling for stricter regulations.

However, a ruling in the European Court of Justice in March 2001, in a case brought by the owners of *Gourmet* magazine against a Swedish ban on alcohol advertising, suggested that such bans pose a barrier to trade within the EU. The ruling recognises that governments can restrict alcohol advertising if done in the interests of public health. The *Gourmet* case was subsequently referred back to the Swedish court to decide if the alcohol ban was proportional to the protection of public health, or whether the government could have achieved the same effect with less restrictive measures. Nonetheless, the ruling is expected to pave the way for many companies to challenge and overturn national advertising bans in the years ahead.[17]

The Internal Market Commission continues to resolve the patchwork of national advertising regulations in order to bring order into the EU's multi-billion-euro advertising industry. Cross-border advertising will develop further with the advent of online interactive media and electronic commerce. However, cultural and regulatory differences mean that advertising campaigns can never be truly pan-European. Thus although advertisers may develop standardised strategies to guide their overall advertising efforts, specific advertising programmes and executions are usually adapted to meet local cultures and customs, media characteristics and advertising regulations.

Having discussed advertising in the previous sections, let us now examine sales promotion.

Sales promotion

Sales promotion consists of short-term incentives, in addition to the basic benefits offered by the product or service, to encourage the purchase or sale of a product or service. Whereas advertising offers reasons to buy a product or service, sales promotion offers reasons that would achieve immediate sales. It seeks to motivate the customer to buy *now*.

Sales promotion includes a wide variety of promotion tools designed to stimulate earlier or stronger market response. These tools are used by many organisations – manufacturers,

Sales promotion—Short-term incentives to encourage purchase or sales of a product or service.

Consumer promotion—Sales promotion designed to stimulate consumer purchasing, including samples, coupons, rebates, prices-off, premiums, patronage rewards, displays, and contests and sweepstakes.

Trade (or retailer) promotion—Sales promotion designed to gain reseller support and to improve reseller selling efforts, including discounts, allowances, free goods, cooperative advertising, push money, and conventions and trade shows.

Business promotion—Sales promotion designed to generate business leads, stimulate purchase, reward business customers and motivate the salesforce.

Sales force promotion—Sales promotion designed to motivate the sales force and make sales force selling efforts more effective, including bonuses, contests and sales rallies.

distributors, retailers, trade associations and non-profit institutions – and may be targeted towards the consumer or final buyer, business customers, the trade or retailer and the company's sales force. **Consumer promotions** include money-off, coupons, premiums, contests and others. **Trade promotions** range from special discounts, free goods and loyalty bonuses to training. **Business promotions** include many of the same tools used for consumer or trade promotions such as conventions and trade shows, as well as sales contests. **Sales force promotions** include bonuses, commissions, free gifts and competitions.

Rapid growth of sales promotion

Several factors have contributed to the rapid growth of sales promotion, particularly in consumer markets. First, inside the company, product managers face greater pressures to increase their current sales, and promotion is increasingly viewed as an effective short-run sales tool. In mature markets, manufacturers are striving to maintain market share through a balance between longer-term 'share-of-voice' gained from advertising and shorter-term incentives for the consumer. Second, externally, the company faces more competition, and competing brands are less differentiated. Increasingly, competitors are using sales promotion to help differentiate their offers. Third, advertising efficiency has declined because of rising costs, media clutter and legal restraints. Sales promotion used in conjunction with other communications, such as direct mail, can offer a more cost-effective route to reach target consumers. Fourth, consumers have become more deal-oriented and ever-larger retailers are demanding more deals from manufacturers. Finally, developments in information technology, the reduction in data storage and retrieval costs, and the increased sophistication of targeting techniques have facilitated implementation and enabled more effective measurement and control of sales promotion efforts.

The growing use of sales promotion has resulted in *promotion clutter*, similar to advertising clutter. Consumers who are continually bombarded with promotions are increasingly 'tuning out' promotions, weakening their ability to trigger immediate purchase. Manufacturers are now searching for ways to rise above the clutter, such as offering larger coupon values, creating more dramatic point-of-purchase displays or developing more creative sales promotion campaigns that stand out from the crowd.

In developing a sales promotion programme, a company must set sales promotion objectives and then select the best tools for accomplishing these objectives.

Setting sales promotion objectives

Sales promotion objectives vary widely. Let us take *consumer promotions* first. Sellers may use consumer promotions to: (1) increase short-term sales; (2) help build long-term market share; (3) entice consumers to try a new product; (4) lure consumers away from competitors' products; (5) encourage consumers to 'load up' on a mature product; or (6) hold and reward loyal customers.

Objectives for *trade promotions* include: (1) motivating retailers to carry new items and more stock; (2) inducing them to advertise the product and give it more shelf space; and (3) persuading them to buy ahead.

For the *sales force*, objectives may be to: (1) get more sales force support for current or new products; or (2) stimulate salespeople to sign up new accounts.

Sales promotions are usually used together with advertising, personal selling or other promotion mix tools. Consumer promotions are usually advertised and can add excitement and pulling power to ads. Trade and sales force promotions support the firm's personal selling process.

Objectives, however, should be measurable. Rather than stating that the promotion aims to increase sales, the objective should be specific about the level of increase, who the main targets are and whether increased sales are expected to come from new triallists or from current consumers who are loading up or bringing forward their purchase.

In general, sales promotions should be **consumer relationship building**. Rather than creating only short-term sales volume or temporary brand switching, sales promotions should help to reinforce the product's position and build long-term relationships with customer relationships. Increasingly, marketers are avoiding the 'quick fix', price-led promotions in favour of promotions designed to build brand equity.

Even price promotions can be designed to build customer relationships. Examples include all the 'frequency marketing programmes', 'loyalty card schemes' and 'clubs' that have mushroomed in recent years.

Consumer relationship-building promotions—Sales promotions that promote the product's positioning and include a selling message along with the deal.

> For example, the health and beauty retailer Body Shop International introduced the 'Love your body membership' as part of the move to recover its sales in the US. The Body Shop US loyalty card scheme operates on a different model from the high-street loyalty cards familiar to many UK consumers. It has an initial charge of US $10 (£5.90), which entitles the holder to a 10 per cent discount for one year, together with a free birthday gift and other gifts, according to how much the card holder spent. In the UK, the company introduced The Body Shop People card, which is free on application and offers the choice of savings on particular purchases or a donation of an equivalent amount to charities nominated by the group.[18]

If properly designed, every sales promotion tool has the potential to build consumer relationships.

Sales promotions have certain limitations. Sellers need to recognise that new triers at whom their promotions are targeted consist of consumers of the product category, loyal users of another brand and users who frequently switch brands. Sales promotions often attract the last group – *brand switchers* – because non-users and users of other brands do not always notice or act on a promotion. Brand switchers are looking mostly for low price or good value. Sales promotions are unlikely to turn them into loyal brand users. Moreover, when a company uses price promotion for a brand too much of the time, consumers begin to think of it as a cheap brand. Or many consumers will buy the brand only when there is a special offer. Most analysts believe that sales promotion activities do not build long-term consumer preference and loyalty, as does advertising. Instead, they only boost short-term sales that cannot be maintained over the long run. Marketers therefore rarely use sales promotion for dominant brands because it would do little more than subsidise current users.[19]

Despite the dangers, many consumer packaged-goods companies continue to use sales promotions. These marketers assert that sales promotions benefit manufacturers by letting them adjust to short-term changes in supply and demand and to differences in customer segments. Sales promotions encourage consumers to try new products instead of always staying with their current ones. They lead to more varied retail formats, such as the everyday-low-price store or the promotional-pricing store, which give consumers more choice. Finally, sales promotions lead to greater consumer awareness of prices, and consumers themselves enjoy the satisfaction of taking advantage of price specials.[20]

Major sales promotion tools

Many tools can be used to accomplish sales promotion objectives. The promotion planner should consider the type of market, the sales promotion objectives, the competition and the cost-effectiveness of each tool. Descriptions of the main consumer and trade promotion tools follow.

Consumer promotion tools

The main consumer promotion tools include samples, coupons, cash refunds, price packs, premiums, advertising specialities, patronage rewards, point-of-purchase displays and demonstrations, and contests, sweepstakes and games.

Samples are offers of a trial amount of a product. Sampling is the most effective, but most expensive, way to introduce a new product. Consumer packaged-goods marketers tend to use sampling as part of their promotion strategy. Some samples are free; for others, the company charges a small amount to offset its cost. The sample might be delivered door to door, sent by mail, handed out in a store, attached to another product or featured in an ad.

Coupons are certificates that give buyers a saving when they purchase specified products. They can stimulate sales of a mature brand or promote early trial of a new brand. However, when used excessively, they result in coupon clutter and a decline in redemption rates. Thus, most major consumer goods companies are issuing fewer coupons and targeting them more carefully. They are also cultivating new outlets for distributing coupons, such as supermarket shelf dispensers, electronic point-of-sale coupon printers or through 'paperless coupon systems' that dispense personalised discounts to targeted buyers at the checkout counter in stores.

Cash refund offers (or **rebates**) are like coupons except that the price reduction occurs after the purchase rather than at the retail outlet. The consumer sends a 'proof of purchase' to the manufacturer, which then refunds part of the purchase price by mail.

Price packs or reduced prices offer consumers savings off the regular price of a product. The reduced prices are marked by the producer directly on the label or package. Price packs can be single packages sold at a reduced price (such as two for the price of one) or two related products banded together (such as a toothbrush and toothpaste). Price packs are very effective – even more so than coupons – in stimulating short-term sales.

Premiums are goods offered either free or at low cost as an incentive to buy a product. A premium may come inside the package (in-pack) or outside the package (on-pack) or through the mail. Premiums are sometimes mailed to consumers who have sent in a proof of purchase, such as a box top. A *self-liquidating premium* is a premium sold below its normal retail price to consumers who request it.

Advertising specialities are useful articles imprinted with an advertiser's name and given as gifts to consumers. Typical items include pens, calendars, key rings, matches, shopping bags, T-shirts, caps and coffee mugs. **Patronage rewards** are cash or other awards offered for the regular use of a certain company's products or services. For example, airlines offer 'frequent flyer plans', awarding points for miles travelled that can be turned in for free airline trips. Hotels have adopted 'honoured guest' plans that award points to users of their hotels. And supermarkets and retailers issue 'reward points' which translate into cash-off for certain company products.

Point-of-purchase (POP) promotions include displays and demonstrations that take place at the point of purchase or sale. Unfortunately, many retailers do not like to handle the hundreds of displays, signs and posters they receive from manufacturers each year. Manufacturers have responded by offering better POP materials, tying them in with television or print messages, and offering to set them up.

Competitions, sweepstakes, lotteries and games give consumers the chance to win something, such as cash, trips or goods, by luck or through extra effort. A *competition* calls for consumers to submit an entry – a jingle, slogan, guess or suggestion – to be judged by a panel that will select the best entries. A *sweepstake* calls for consumers to submit their names for a draw. For a *lottery*, consumers buy tickets which enter their names into a draw. A *game* presents consumers with something, such as bingo numbers or missing letters, every time they buy, which may or may not help them win a prize. A sales contest urges dealers and sales force to increase their efforts, with prizes going to the top performers.

Samples—Offers to consumers of a trial amount of a product.

Coupons—Certificates that give buyers a saving when they purchase a product.

Cash refund offers (rebates)—Offers to refund part of the purchase price of a product to consumers who send a 'proof of purchase' to the manufacturer.

Price packs—Reduced prices that are marked by the producer directly on the label or package.

Premiums—Goods offered either free or at low cost as an incentive to buy a product.

Advertising specialities—Useful articles imprinted with an advertiser's name, given as gifts to consumers.

Patronage rewards—Cash or other awards for the regular use of a certain company's products or services.

Point-of-purchase (POP) promotions—Displays and demonstrations that take place at the point of purchase or sale.

Competitions, sweepstakes, lotteries and games—Promotions that offer customers the chance to win something – cash, goods or trips – by luck or extra effort.

Sales promotions in Europe

The sales promotion industry is relatively more developed in the United Kingdom than in the other EU member states. Supermarket retailing in the United Kingdom is dominated by a few key players and decisions regarding acceptance of manufacturers' sales promotion activities are centralised. Cost-effectiveness is increased as the sales promotion handling house is able to use the retailing groups' own administrative processes.

Cultural differences affect consumers' acceptance of different sales promotion techniques. An incentive that is desirable in one country may have little appeal in another. Household items, especially electrical goods, are very popular in Germany. Beach towels, sunglasses and T-shirts are more popular in Spain and Portugal, while in France, it is pens, lighters and watches. In Italy, brand association is important – if the merchandise features a designer name, a recognised brand name or a football club, the chances are that it will be well received.

Like advertising, sales promotion techniques also face different legal constraints across Europe. In the UK, sales promotion activities are relatively free from legal constraints. Other countries like Poland, Hungary and the Czech Republic have relatively liberal policies on promotions and incentives. By contrast, legal controls are stricter in Belgium, Germany, France and, notably so, in Norway. In Belgium, for example, retailers are not allowed to offer discounts of more than 33 per cent – a rule that prevents them from running 'buy-one-get-one-free' offers. In France, Belgium, Spain, Portugal, Italy, Luxembourg, Greece and Ireland, retailers are also not allowed to entice customers into their shops by offering sales below cost – that is, selling at a loss.

An important part of the European Commission's efforts to build a single market is to reduce the myriad different national barriers to sales promotions through the introduction of new rules to free up restrictive regulations. Arguably, liberalising promotional offers – currently worth more than €40bn a year across the EU – would boost the retail sector. In essence, the Commission's radical reforms include scrapping all limits on promotional discounts, free gifts and promotional offers, better information on promotional games to be provided to participating consumers, and the harmonising of rules on promotional games such as scratch cards across the EU.

Countries that favour tighter promotional legislation claim they have consumers' interests at heart, as restrictions on promotional offers are an important way of protecting consumers from unscrupulous retailers. Proponents of greater liberalisation, however, argue that increased regulation makes it more difficult for consumers as less information is made available. The Commission believes that there is urgent need to break down the barriers to marketing goods across the EU. Doing so will serve consumer interests as well as prevent unfair trade practices.[21]

However, the extent to which directives can truly protect consumers is now a hotly debated issue as sellers turn increasingly to the Web to market products and services. Consider the following example:

> When Amazon, the online book seller, opened online outlets in Germany, it offered all publications postage free. Cabinet Stewart, a lobbyist group representing the European Promotional Marketing Alliance (EPMA), in favour of retention of sales promotion techniques as practised in the UK, points to the contradiction posed by online sellers that engage in cross-border marketing activities. Is the free postage to be deemed a discount, which in this case exceeds the 3 per cent factor allowed by German law? Even if this is illegal, few German consumers are likely to object. And how can legislators possibly

check all incoming online transactions? And is there a basis for prosecution? According to the lobbyist group, when it comes to electronic commerce, decisions about legality of sales promotions could be based upon the 'country-of-origin' and 'mutual recognition' approach. This means promotions deemed legal in the source country should automatically be accepted in other member states. Clearly, EU legislators in the 21st century face a 'doublethink' – in holding the view that it is their right to protect 'home' consumers from overly persuasive marketing tactics (e.g. the manipulative evils of discounts and premiums), they have apparently ignored the common knowledge that e-commerce is truly a borderless, global phenomenon. Little can be done, for now, to deny consumers the pleasure of endless 'illegal' promotional offers over the Internet.[22]

For now, the European Commission continues in its efforts to free up restrictive regulations on sales promotions across the enlarged EU. Until true harmonisation is achieved, marketers must remain sensitive and adapt accordingly to national constraints. Even if sales promotion rules are harmonised and pan-European campaigns are used, the cultural, linguistic and climatic differences across countries mean that such campaigns, based on a central or core theme, will have to be adapted to favour conditions in each territory.

Ingenuity can help agencies to create pan-European sales promotions, with only slight adaptations in each country.

Promotional Campaigns Group (PCG) ran a campaign for Iomega, aimed at encouraging customers to buy multipacks of Zip 100 disks rather than single items. The promotion gets customers to 'Win all the stuff you buy today! When purchasing a multipack of Zip disks.' The mechanics of the promotion were adapted to comply with different rules in France, Germany and the UK, where the campaigns were run. In France, scratch cards were inserted into promotional multipacks with on-pack stickers. In the UK, instant-win scratch cards were issued by check-out staff, or customers could enter into a free prize draw. In Germany, retailers ran a competition involving a leaflet entry to win their day's purchases. In each participating country, the promotional campaign was deemed highly successful, with retailers recording sales increase.[23]

Trade promotion tools

Trade promotion can persuade retailers or wholesalers to carry a brand, give it shelf space, promote it in advertising and push it to consumers. Shelf space is so scarce these days that manufacturers often have to offer price discounts, allowances, buy-back guarantees or free goods to retailers and wholesalers to get on the shelf and, once there, to stay on it.

Manufacturers use several trade promotion tools. Many of the tools used for consumer promotions – contests, premiums, displays – can also be used as trade promotions. Alternatively, the manufacturer may offer a straight **discount** off the list price on each case

Discount—A straight reduction in price on purchases during a stated period of time.

purchased during a stated period of time (also called a *price-off*, *off-invoice* or *off-list*). The offer encourages dealers to buy in quantity or to carry a new item. Dealers can use the discount for immediate profit, for advertising or for price reductions to their customers.

Manufacturers may also offer an **allowance** (usually so much off per case) in return for the retailer's agreement to feature the manufacturer's products in some way. An *advertising allowance* compensates retailers for advertising the product. A *display allowance* compensates them for using special displays.

Manufacturers may offer *free goods*, which are extra cases of merchandise, to intermediaries that buy a certain quantity or that feature a certain flavour or size. They may offer *push incentives* – cash or gifts to dealers or their sales force to 'push' the manufacturer's goods. Manufacturers may give retailers free *speciality advertising items* that carry the company's name, such as pens, pencils, coffee mugs, calendars, paperweights, matchbooks and memo pads.

Allowance—(1) Reduction in price on damaged goods. (2) Promotional money paid by manufacturers to retailers in return for an agreement to feature the manufacturer's product in some way.

Business promotion tools

Companies spend huge sums of money each year on promotion to industrial customers. These business promotions are used to generate business leads, stimulate purchases, reward customers and motivate salespeople. Business promotion includes many of the same tools used for consumer or trade promotions. Here, we focus on two of the main business promotion tools – conventions and trade shows, and sales contests.

Conventions and trade shows

Many companies and trade associations organise conventions and trade shows to promote their products. Firms selling to the industry show their products at the trade show. Vendors receive many benefits, such as opportunities to find new sales leads, contact customers, introduce new products, meet new customers, sell more to present customers and educate customers with publications and audiovisual materials.

Trade shows also help companies reach many prospects not reached through their sales forces. A high proportion of a trade show's visitors see a company's salespeople for the first time at a show. Business managers face several decisions, including which trade shows to participate in, how much to spend on each trade show, how to build dramatic exhibits that attract attention, and how to follow up on sales leads effectively.[24]

Sales contests

A *sales contest* is a contest for salespeople or dealers to urge their sales force to increase their efforts over a given period. Sales contests motivate and recognise good company performers, who may receive trips, cash prizes or other gifts. Sales contests work best when they are tied to measurable and achievable sales objectives (such as finding new accounts, reviving old accounts or increasing account profitability) and when employees believe they have an equal chance of winning. Otherwise, employees will not take up the challenge.

Developing the sales promotion programme

The marketer must make several other decisions in order to define the full sales promotion programme. First, the marketer must decide on the *size of the incentive*. A certain minimum incentive is necessary if the promotion is to succeed; a larger incentive will produce more sales response. The marketer must ensure that the promotion genuinely offers extra value and incentives to targets. Importantly, the promotion must not be misleading, and the firm must have the ability to honour redemptions. If not, the campaign could backfire, exposing the firm to bad publicity which damages its reputation and brand image.

The household appliance company Hoover ran a sales promotion offering consumers two free return flights to Europe or America if they bought any of its vacuum cleaners, washing machines or other household appliances worth more than £100 (€164). Unfortunately, the company (and no fewer than the three sales promotions agencies, which were involved in originating and costing the promotion) had miscalculated. As it happened, most consumers bought cheap vacuum cleaners that cost as little as £120 while the cheapest pair of return air tickets to New York cost over three times that amount. The firm received as many as 200,000 applications for free flights within the first 10 months of the campaign, but managed to issue only about 6,000 tickets within that same period. Although the travel agents, hired by Hoover, were also alleged to be unfairly dissuading consumers from taking up the offer, angry customers waited adamantly for their tickets. Maytag, Hoover's parent company, had to come up with a rescue package to honour Hoover's commitment to customers. Hundreds of disgruntled consumers were awarded sums of over £450 in compensation. The fiasco had cost Hoover well over £48 million, but in the UK, Hoover's name became a sick joke to millions of consumers and the company also attracted column inches of bad publicity.[25]

The marketer must also set *conditions for participation*. Incentives might be offered to everyone or only to select groups. Conditions, such as the proof of purchase or closing date of the offer, must be clearly stated. The marketer must then decide how to *promote and distribute the promotion* programme itself. A money-off coupon could be given out in a package, at the store, by mail or in an advertisement. Each distribution method involves a different level of reach and cost. Increasingly, marketers are blending several media into a total campaign concept.

The *length of the promotion* is also important. If the sales promotion period is too short, many prospects (who may not be buying during that time) will miss it. If the promotion runs for too long, the deal will lose some of its 'act now' force.

The marketer also must decide on the *response mechanism*: that is, the redemption vehicle to be used by the customer who takes part in the promotion. Immediate reward – for example, a price reduction, or a free gift attached to the product on offer – often yields a higher response. If the incentive requires further action to be taken by the consumer – for instance, to make another purchase or to collect the required number of tokens in promotion packs and then post these off to claim a gift or free product – the redemption rate can be reduced.

Whenever possible, sales promotion tools should be *pre-tested* to find out whether they are appropriate and of the right incentive size. Consumer sales promotions can be pre-tested quickly and inexpensively. For example, consumers can be asked to rate or rank different possible promotions, or promotions can be tried on a limited basis in selected geographic areas.

Companies should prepare implementation plans for each promotion, covering lead time and sell-off time. *Lead time* is the time necessary to prepare the programme before launching it. *Sell-off time* begins with the launch and ends when the promotion ends.

Evaluation is also very important. Many companies fail to evaluate their sales promotion programmes, while others evaluate them only superficially. The most common evaluation method is to compare sales before, during and after a promotion. Suppose a company has a

6 per cent market share before the promotion, which jumps to 10 per cent during the promotion, falls to 5 per cent right after and rises to 7 per cent later on. The promotion seems to have attracted new triers and more buying from current customers. After the promotion, sales fall as consumers use up their stocks. The long-run rise to 7 per cent means that the company gained some new users. If the brand's share had returned to the old level, then the promotion would have changed only the *timing* of demand rather than the *total* demand.

Consumer research would also show the kinds of people who responded to the promotion and what they did after it ended. *Surveys* can provide information on how many consumers recall the promotion, what they thought of it, how many took advantage of it and how it affected their buying. Sales promotions can also be evaluated through *experiments* that vary factors such as incentive value, timing, duration and distribution method.

Clearly, sales promotion plays an important role in the total promotion mix. To use it well, the marketer must define the sales promotion objectives, select the best tools, design the sales promotion programme, pre-test and implement the programme, and evaluate the results. Moreover, sales promotion must be coordinated carefully with other promotion mix elements within the integrated marketing communications programme.

Public relations

Another important mass-promotion technique is **public relations**. This concerns building good relations with the company's various publics by obtaining favourable publicity, building up a good 'corporate image' and handling or heading off unfavourable rumours, stories and events. Public relations (PR) departments perform any or all of the following functions:

- *Press relations or press agency.* Creating and placing newsworthy information in the news media to attract attention to a person, product or service.
- *Product publicity.* Publicising specific products.
- *Public affairs.* Building and maintaining local, national and international relations.
- *Lobbying.* Building and maintaining relations with legislators and government officials to influence legislation and regulation.
- *Investor relations.* Maintaining relationships with shareholders and others in the financial community.
- *Development.* Public relations with donors or members of non-profit organisations to gain financial or volunteer support.

Public relations—Building good relations with the company's various publics by obtaining favourable publicity, building up a good 'corporate image', and handling or heading off unfavourable rumours, stories and events. Major PR tools include press relations, product publicity, corporate communications, lobbying and counselling.

Public relations is used to promote products, people, places, ideas, activities, organisations and even nations. Trade associations have used public relations to rebuild interest in declining commodities such as eggs, apples, milk and potatoes. Even nations have used public relations to attract more tourists, foreign investment and international support. Companies can use PR to manage their way out of crisis, as in the case of Johnson & Johnson's masterly use of public relations to save Tylenol from extinction after its product-tampering scare.

The role and impact of public relations

Public relations can have a strong impact on public awareness at a much lower cost than advertising can. The company does not pay for the space or time in the media. Rather, it pays for staff to develop and circulate information and to manage events. If the company develops an interesting story, it could be picked up by several different media, having the same effect as advertising that would cost millions of euros. It would have more credibility than advertising.

Despite its potential strengths, public relations is often described as a marketing stepchild because of its limited and scattered use. The public relations department is usually located at corporate headquarters. Its staff is so busy dealing with various publics – stockholders, employees, legislators, city officials – that public relations programmes to support product marketing objectives may be ignored. Moreover, marketing managers and public relations practitioners do not always talk the same language. Many public relations practitioners see their job as simply communicating. In contrast, marketing managers tend to be much more interested in how advertising and public relations affect sales and profits.

This situation is changing, however. Although public relations still captures only a small portion of the overall marketing budgets of most firms, PR is playing an increasingly important brand-building role as more and more businesses view good public relations as a powerful brand-building tool. In fact, two well-known marketing consultants have concluded that advertising doesn't build brands, PR does. They provide the following advice, which points to the potential power of public relations as a first step in brand building:

> Just because a heavy dose of advertising is associated with most major brands doesn't necessarily mean that advertising built the brands in the first place. The birth of a brand is usually accomplished with [public relations], not advertising. Our general rule is [PR] first, advertising second. [Public relations] is the nail, advertising the hammer. [PR] creates the credentials that provide the credibility for advertising. . . . Anita Roddick built The Body Shop into a major international brand with no advertising at all. Instead, she travelled the world on a relentless quest for publicity. . . . Until recently Starbucks Coffee Co. didn't spend a hill of beans on advertising, either. In 10 years, the company spent less than $10 million (€8.2 million) on advertising, a trivial amount for a brand that delivers annual sales of $1.3 billion. Wal-Mart Stores became the world's largest retailer . . . with very little advertising. . . . In the toy field, Beanie Babies became highly successful . . . and on the Internet, Yahoo!, Amazon.com, and Excite became powerhouse brands, [all] with virtually no advertising.[26]

In their book *The Fall of Advertising and the Rise of PR*, the consultants Al and Laura Ries assert that the era of advertising is over, and that public relations is quietly becoming the most powerful marketing communications tools. Although most marketers don't go this far, the point is a good one. Advertising and public relations should work hand in hand to build and maintain brands.

Major public relations tools

PR professionals use several tools. One essential tool is *news*. PR professionals find or create favourable news about the company and its products or people. Sometimes news stories occur naturally. At other times, the PR person can suggest events or activities that would create news.

Speeches also create product and company publicity. Increasingly, company executives must field questions from the media or give talks at trade associations or sales meetings. These events can either build or hurt the company's image.

Another common PR tool is *special events*, ranging from news conferences, press tours, grand openings and firework displays to laser shows, hot-air balloon releases, multimedia presentations and star-studded spectaculars, or educational programmes designed to reach

The birth of a brand is often accomplished with public relations, not advertising. For example, Beanie Babies have been highly successful with virtually no advertising.
SOURCE: The Image Works.

and interest target publics. Richard Branson, the chief executive of Virgin Group, offers a good example of a practitioner who has perfected the art of deploying both speeches and special events for self- and corporate promotion.

Public relations people also prepare *written materials* to reach and influence their target markets. These materials include annual reports, brochures, articles and company newsletters and magazines.

Audiovisual materials, such as films, slide-and-sound programmes and video and audio cassettes, are being used increasingly as communication tools.

Corporate-identity materials also help create a corporate identity that the public immediately recognises. Logos, stationery, brochures, signs, business forms, business cards, buildings, uniforms and even company cars and trucks make effective marketing tools when they are attractive, distinctive and memorable.

Finally, companies might improve public goodwill by contributing money and time to *public service activities*: campaigns to raise funds for worthy causes – for example, to fight illiteracy, support the work of a charity, or assist the aged and handicapped – help to raise public recognition.

Sponsorship is any vehicle through which corporations gain public relations exposure. Corporate sponsorships have become an important promotional tool for companies looking to lift their brand image, or introduce new product lines or services. Worldwide spending on sponsorships totalled $24bn in 2002, an annual increase of 3.4 per cent, according to IEG, a Chicago-based research company, while in the US the figure totalled almost $10bn. Some companies have used sponsorship as a strategic promotional tool to build brand image or launch new products and services. Witness, for example, Samsung, which has successfully joined a small but distinguished band of Olympic sponsors. By focusing its sponsorship activities on a few premium global events such as the Olympics, the company turned the Samsung name into a desirable global brand (see Marketing Insights 18.2).

marketing insights

18.2   Samsung's cool 'matrix' values

In what has proved to be one of Samsung's more audacious marketing coups, the Korean group managed to snatch the sponsorship of the two sequels to the hit movie *The Matrix* from the jaws of Nokia. The Finnish handset manufacturer had been the official sponsor of the first *Matrix* movie in 1999, and the Nokia phone had played a very visible part in the narrative as the entrance and exit points for the characters beaming themselves into the eponymous virtual reality mindset.

But by the time the second film, *The Matrix Reloaded*, came out earlier in 2003 [2003], the phones in the characters' hands were carrying a Samsung logo. 'I am a big fan of *The Matrix*', says Eric Kim, head of Samsung's global marketing operations. 'When I first saw that movie, I loved it. Not only because it was cool and had action and was futuristic, but it's also very philosophical. And it fits with our brand perfectly. The target audience was young – in their 20s and 30s – and it conveyed a very cool lifestyle message.'

At the time *The Matrix Reloaded* was being made, Samsung was working in partnership with AOL Time Warner on an instant messaging phone; Kim used the relationship to get in touch with Warner Studios. Samsung spent a reported $100 m to sponsor the movie, along with General Motors' Cadillac, the beer brand Heineken and Coca-Cola's PowerAde. 'I pursued that deal very aggressively', says Kim.

Sporting events account for a bulk of the sponsorship market, but entertainment deals including film and television have become a growth area. 'As a follower brand [one trying to catch a market leader], Samsung needed different and unique sponsorships. With *The Matrix Reloaded* it has clearly had great returns in terms of visibility and alignment with the brand', says Raman Mangalorkar at consultancy AT Kearney.

However, some corporate marketing executives warn that product placement in films may not be for everyone. '[Product placement] is very difficult to exploit', says Keld Strudahl, head of marketing and global sponsorship at brewer Carlsberg. He adds that the costs tend to be too high and the returns remain unclear. Apart from buying the right to place a product, sponsorships only become effective when they are packaged with other promotions including marketing and new product lines, which adds to the bill. Carlsberg has focused on sport and has emphasised its long-term involvement in certain events. 'Having a long-term relationship is one of the main criteria. We're not interested in one-off events', says Strudahl. He also notes that the bigger the event, the better the returns.

To that end, the Olympics have played a large part in Samsung's strategy, and its involvement has spanned several years. 'The Olympics are the premier global event, and the sponsors are major global brands like Coca-Cola, McDonald's and so on', says

...18.2

Kim. 'For us to be part of that small, distinguished crowd gave us instant credibility. Although we didn't have the heritage of Coca-Cola, we were being accepted as a global brand.'

Samsung's sponsorship of the 1998 Winter Games was the first by a Korean company. Since then it has been a wireless sponsor on a number of occasions, providing mobiles, pagers and two-way radios for Olympic participants. In 2002, for the Salt Lake City Winter Games, Samsung created one of its most famous images – the haunting 'Snow Woman' – who appeared in a series of surreal sport-themed advertisements.

Kim says that Samsung evaluates its brand position each year with a multi-country survey which measures consumer awareness and preference. For a company trying to reach consumers in Europe and the US, a worldwide event like the Olympic Games has served its purpose of improving its image. However, Kim is acutely aware that the main challenge for marketers is to turn consumer awareness into affinity and the need to link that to product sales. For the 2004 summer Olympic Games in Athens, Samsung's strategy is shifting slightly, says Kim. It's not just about getting noticed, but creating a sense of loyalty and attachment in the audience. Hence the focus will be on highly emotive events – for example, Samsung has become one of only two sponsors of the torch relay that marks the start of the Games. 'Until now the emphasis was on creating an appropriate level of awareness. Now we think we have achieved that our next goal is to achieve relevance and preference', Kim says.

SOURCES: Based on Maija Pesola and Emiko Terazono, 'Fun and games', *Financial Times FT Creative Business* (9 September 2003), p. 11; see also Maija Pesola, 'Goodbye South Korea. Hello World', *ibid.*, p. 10.

A company's *website* can also be a good public relations vehicle. Consumers and members of other publics can visit the site for information and entertainment. Websites can also be ideal for handling crisis situations. As more and more people look to the Net for information, a 'web' of opportunity now unfolds for public relations.

Company websites are now used to post testimonials from satisfied buyers, to make new product announcements and to allow the organisation to respond publicly to events, particularly crises, swiftly and to a broad audience at relatively low cost. The direct-to-consumer nature of corporate websites means that firms' PR departments and their agencies have greater control over the message to be communicated. In the pre-Web era, firms would rely on journalists to write 'stories' about the organisation, its product or an employee to make the organisation or event newsworthy and to win credibility.

One of the most important benefits of using company websites for public relations is a greater control of message consistency. Publicity material can be used to support sales, where appropriate. For example, since an online press release is going straight to the consumer, rather than journalists, links to sales or customer enquiries can be made and consumers' response can be attained instantaneously.

Public relations involves many functions beyond product publicity, including public affairs, lobbying and investor relations. For example, most company websites feature special sections for current and potential investors – like this one from Ericsson.
SOURCE: www.ericsson.com.

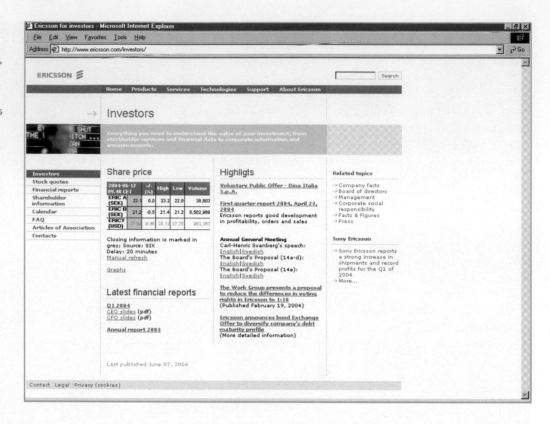

The Internet may change the fundamentals of public relations work. However, the Internet is not a substitute for journalists and their high-impact editorials. The firm's online PR efforts have to be supplemented with direct and face-to-face communications with journalists and other opinion-formers.[27]

Main public relations decisions

As with the other promotion tools, in considering when and how to use product public relations, management should set PR objectives, choose the PR messages and vehicles, implement the PR plan and evaluate the results.

Setting public relations objectives

The *objectives* for public relations are usually defined in relation to the types of news story to be communicated, the communication objectives to be achieved (for instance, awareness creation, knowledge dissemination, generation of specific publicity for target groups) and the specific target audiences.

Choosing public relations messages and vehicles

Message themes for the public relations exercise should be aligned with the organisation's PR objectives. In some cases the choice of PR messages and tools will be clear-cut. In others, the organisation has to create the news rather than find it by sponsoring noteworthy events. Creating events is especially important in publicising fund-raising drives for non-profit organisations. In the past, fund-raisers have created a large set of special events, ranging from art exhibits, auctions and dinners, to marathons, walkathons and swimathons.

Implementing the public relations plan

The PR campaign must be implemented with care. For example, a *great* story is easy to place, but, unfortunately, most stories are not earth shattering and would not get past busy editors. Thus PR professionals have to acquire a good feel for what media editors want to feature in their papers and magazines as well as establish good relationships with them. They view media editors as a market to be satisfied so that editors will continue to use their stories.

Evaluating public relations results

Public relations results are difficult to measure because PR is used with other promotion tools and its impact is often indirect. Ideally, the company should measure the change in product awareness, knowledge and attitude resulting from the publicity campaign. Assessing the change requires measuring the before-and-after-the-campaign levels of these measures. Finally, sales and profit impact, if obtainable, is the best measure of public relations effort. If advertising and sales promotion were also stepped up during the period of the PR campaign, their contribution has to be considered.

Increasingly, companies, particularly high-media-profile organisations such as banks, food, chemicals and pharmaceuticals firms, invest in longer-term media tracking to help public relations managers to design and implement more effective PR programmes. They employ specialist media analysis and evaluation agencies or PR consultants to conduct in-depth media analyses which include coverage in both electronic and print media, and identify issues and public perceptions about the organisation's reputation, products and services and those of their competitors, as well as tracking legislative initiatives. They generate 'management intelligence' to determine the effectiveness of an organisation's PR activities and to help forward planning of communications and customer/public relationship building, including how management should react in a crisis management situation.

> For example, the charity organisation Barnardo's conducted media content analyses to identify if the public's perception of Barnardo's was consistent with the modern aspects of Barnardo's work. The charity was concerned that people still thought of Barnardo's as an outfit that runs orphans' homes, whereas the last one closed in the early 1980s, and they are now tackling modern childcare issues. By systematically tracking all reference to Barnardo's work currently in the press, the organisation found that the analyses proved that its initial strategy was working. When Shell UK faced adverse publicity over the disposal of its defunct oil rig, Brent Spar, Shell hired experts to provide in-depth analyses of media coverage and public opinion. The information helped the company deliver a strategic counter-attack once management understood the issues embedded in the crisis: who the opposition was and the nature of its agenda.[28]

Finally, like the other communications tools, public relations should be blended smoothly with other promotion activities within the company's overall integrated marketing communications effort.

Summary

Companies must do more than deliver good products and services – they have to inform customers about product benefits and carefully position these in customers' minds. To do this, they must skilfully employ mass-promotions to target specific buyers. The three mass-promotion tools are *advertising*, *sales promotion* and *public relations*.

Advertising – the use of paid media by a seller to inform, persuade and remind target audiences about its products or organisation – is a strong promotion tool which takes many forms and has many uses. *Sales promotion* covers a wide variety of short-term purchasing incentives – coupons, premiums, contests, buying allowances – designed to stimulate final and business consumers, the trade and the company's own sales force. In many countries, sales promotion spending has been growing faster than advertising spending in recent years. *Public relations* – gaining favourable publicity and creating a favourable company image – is the least used of the major promotion tools, although it has great potential for building consumer awareness and preference.

Advertising decision making involves decisions about the objectives, the budget, the message, the media and, finally, the evaluation of results. Advertisers should set clear *objectives* as to whether the advertising is supposed to inform, persuade or remind buyers. The advertising *budget* can be based on what is affordable, on a percentage of sales, on competitors' spending, or on the objectives and tasks. *Message decisions* involve planning the message strategy and executing it effectively. The *media decision* involves defining reach, frequency and impact goals, choosing major media types, selecting media vehicles, and deciding on media timing. Finally, *evaluation* calls for evaluating the communication and sales effects of advertising before, during and after the advertising is placed.

Companies that advertise their products in different country markets can apply the basic principles relating to domestic advertising, but they must take into account the complexities involved in international advertising. They must address the similarities and differences in customer needs and buying behaviour, as well as cultural, socio-economic, political and regulatory environments across country markets, which will affect the decision to standardise or differentiate advertising strategies and executions.

Sales promotions call for setting sales promotion objectives (in general, sales promotions should be *consumer relationship building*), selecting tools, developing, pre-testing and implementing the sales promotion programme. Marketers use consumer promotion tools (*samples, coupons, cash refunds, price packs, premiums, advertising specialities, patronage rewards, point-of-purchase promotions, contests, sweepstakes, games*), trade promotion tools (*discounts, allowances, free goods, push money*) and business promotion tools (*conventions, trade shows, sales contests*) as well as decide on issues such as the size of the incentive, the conditions for participation, how to promote and distribute the promotion package and the duration of the promotion. After the sales promotion process is completed, the company evaluates the results.

Organisations use *public relations* to obtain favourable publicity, to build up a good 'corporate image' and to handle or head off unfavourable rumours, stories and events. Public relations involves setting PR objectives, choosing PR messages and vehicles, implementing the PR plan and evaluating PR results. To accomplish these goals, PR professionals use a variety of tools, such as *news, speeches* and *special events*. Or they communicate with various publics through *written, audiovisual* and *corporate identity materials*, and contribute money and time to *public service activities*.

Discussing the issues

1. Until recently, television viewers were considered the captive audience for advertisers. How has this changed? To what extent will the changes in consumer television viewing habits impact advertising? What actions should advertisers consider to regain the consumer audience?

2. Advertisers must develop compelling creative concepts or big ideas that will bring their message strategies to life in a distinctive way. Look at some magazine advertisements. Find what you perceive to be compelling creative concepts. Identify specific appeals being used in these ads and comment on what you think the advertisers are trying to accomplish with these ads.

3. Sales promotions are short-term incentives to trigger sales. How might companies use these tools for customer relationship building? Critically evaluate the role of sales promotion as a customer relationship building tool.

4. Companies often run advertising, sales promotion and public relations efforts at the same time. Can their efforts be separated? Discuss how a company might evaluate the effectiveness of each element in this mix.

5. The Internet is the latest public relations frontier. Web users now routinely share their experiences and problems with a company's products, service, prices and warranties on electronic bulletin boards and chat rooms and at various websites. What kinds of special public relations problems and opportunities does the Internet present to today's marketers? How can companies use their own websites to deal with these problems and opportunities? Find examples of companies that use their websites as public relations tools. Critique each website on its content, effectiveness and capacity to act as a proactive public relations tool.

Applying the concepts

1. Buy a Sunday paper and sort through the colour advertising and coupon inserts. Find examples that combine advertising, sales promotion and/or public relations. For instance, a manufacturer may run a full-page ad that also includes a coupon and information on its sponsorship of a charity event.

   (a) Do you think these approaches using multiple tools are more or less effective than a single approach? Why?
   (b) Try to find ads from two direct competitors. Are these brands using similar promotional tools in similar ways?

2. Log into the websites of tobacco companies such as Philip Morris (www.philipmorris.com), RJ Reynolds (www.rjrt.com), BAT (www.bat.com) or Brown and Williamson (www.brownandwilliamson.com). Navigate to the tobacco area. You may encounter links to news about the tobacco industry, documents containing harsh criticisms from anti-smoking lobbies, as well as a host of other pro- and anti-tobacco material. RJ Reynolds tells you that 'it manufactures products that have significant and inherent health risks' though it still urges you to report and protest about 'unfair' anti-smoking bans. On its website, Philip Morris admits that 'cigarette smoking is addictive'. Others, like Brown and Williamson, enable you to link to their 'courthouse' section so you can keep an exact count of the legal

assaults upon the company. For years tobacco firms like Philip Morris have operated under a siege mentality, closing themselves off from the questions and criticisms coming from the outside world. Recently, however, this culture has slowly begun to change, with companies facing increasing pressure to change their image. However, being a responsible corporate citizen and changing the company's culture, products and image will not be easy.

(a) What public relations issues do cigarette manufacturers such as BAT, Philip Morris and RJ Reynolds face?

(b) What kind of public relations advantages does admission of tobacco's health risks create? What problems?

(c) Outline a public relations programme for gaining public trust and shareholder interest.

References

1. Stuart Elliott, 'Things heat up for P&G', NYTimes.com (12 February 2002), p. 1; 'Procter & Gamble', *Drug Store News* (10 September 2001), p. 19; Cliff Peale, 'P&G hopes ThermaCare is a blockbuster', *Cincinnati Enquirer*, Cincinnati.com (22 July 2001); 'ThermaCare Therapeutic HeatWraps', *New Product Bulletin, American Pharmaceutical Association*, 2001; www.ThermaCare.com (August 2002).

2. Stephanie Kirchgaessner and Gautum Malkani, 'Champagne season may not be far away', *Financial Times* (29 October 2003), p. 27; Louisa Hearn, 'The tide is turning', *Financial Times FT Creative Business* (16 December 2003), pp. 4–5; for more details on advertising expenditure by country and medium, see 'Advertising expenditure by country and medium' in *European Marketing Pocket Book 2004* (Henley-on-Thames: NTC Publications, 2004).

3. 'Hundreds of brands, billions to spend', *Financail Times FT Creative Business* (25 February 2003), pp. 2–3.

4. See Patricia Nacimiento, 'Germany: higher court takes new view on comparative advertising', *International Commercial Litigation* (July/August 1998), p. 47; John Shannon, 'Comparative ads call for prudence', *Marketing Week* (22 May 1999), p. 32.

5. See Andrew Ehrenberg, Neil Barnard and John Scriven, 'Justifying our advertising budgets', *Marketing & Research Today* (February 1997), pp. 38–44; Dana W. Hayman and Don E. Schultz, 'How much should you spend on advertising?', *Advertising Age* (26 April 1999), p. 32; J. Thomas Russell and W. Ronald Lane, *Kleppner's Advertising Procedure*, 15th edn (Upper Saddle River, NJ: Prentice Hall, 2002), pp. 145–9; and Kissan Joseph and Vernon J. Richardson, 'Free cash flow, agency costs, and the affordability method of advertising budgeting', *Journal of Marketing* (January 2002), pp. 94–107.

6. Lynne Roberts, 'New media choice: Absolut Vodka', *Marketing* (9 April 1998), p. 12; Eleftheria Parpis, 'TBWA: Absolut', *Adweek* (9 November 1998), p. 172; and the Q&A section at www.absolutvodka.com (March 2000).

7. See also the classic text by Judith Corstjens, *Strategic Advertising: A practitioner's handbook* (Oxford: Heinemann Professional Publishing, 1990).

8. See Faye Rice, 'How to deal with tougher customers', *Fortune* (3 December 1990), pp. 38–48.

9. Emma Halls, 'Roll up to the truth zone', *The Times* (7 July 2000), p. 30.

10. Alastair Ray, 'Time to sort out big local differences', *Financial Times FT Creative Business* (9 September 2003), p. 6.

11. Information on advertising agency income and billings obtained online at http://adage/dataplace (August 2002); for more information on European advertising income see *European Marketing Pocket Book 2004*, op. cit.

12. Greg Harris, 'Factors influencing the international advertising practices of multinational companies', *Management Decision*, 34, 6 (1996), pp. 5–11; Nikolaos Papavassiliou and Vlasis Stathakopoulos, 'Standardization versus adaptation of international advertising strategies: towards a framework', *European Journal of Marketing*, 31, 7 (1997), pp. 504–27.

13. J.N. Kapferer and Eurocom, 'How global are global brands?', ESOMAR Seminar on the Challenge of Branding Today and in the Future, Brussels, 28–30 October 1992.

14. Boris Kaz, 'Researching the pan-European media market', *Admap* (July–August 1996), pp. 31–2; John Shannon, 'Research boost for pan-Euro TV', *Marketing Week* (19 April 1996), p. 29.

15. John Shannon, 'TV ads struggle in Scandinavia', *Marketing Week* (20 September 1996), p. 26.

16. Alastair Ray, op. cit.

17. Deborah Hargreaves, 'Peeling back promotion barriers', *Financial Times* (2 April 2001), p. 14; James Curtis, 'Legal muscles from Brussels', *Marketing Business* (September 2000), pp. 44–5; 'Coca-Cola rapped for running competition in India', AdAgeInternational.com (February 1997); David Short and Hilary Clarke, 'Undoing the patchwork of advertising laws', *The European* (16–22 May 1996), p. 25; for more on EU legislation visit http://europa.eu.int/eur-lex/en/.

18. Alison Smith, 'Body Shop in trial of loyalty card scheme', *Financial Times* (22 January 2004), p. 20.

19. Louise O'Brien and Charles Jones, 'Do rewards really create loyalty?', *Harvard Business Review* (May–June 1995), pp. 75–82; Graham R. Dowling and Mark Uncles, 'Do customer loyalty programs really work?', *Sloan Management Review* (Summer 1997), pp. 71–82.

20. See John Philip Jones, 'The double jeopardy of sales promotions', *Harvard Business Review* (September–October 1990), pp. 145–52.

21. Francesco Guerrera, 'Brussels to free up retail regulations', *Financial Times* (22 August 2002), p. 6; Francesco Guerrera and Adam Jones, 'EU bargains over sales promotions', *Financial Times* (22 August 2002), p. 6.

22. Mandy Thatcher, 'Abroad beyond', *Marketing Business* (February 2000), pp. 42–4; the EPMA comprises three organisations – The British Promotional Merchandise Association (BPMA), The European Federation of Sales Promotion (EFSP) and The Institute of Sales Promotion (ISP); further details from: Cabinet Stewart European Affairs, Rue d'Arlon 40, Brussels.

23. Mandy Thatcher, op. cit.

24. Richard Szathmary, 'Trade shows', *Sales and Marketing Management* (May 1992), pp. 83–4; Srinath Gopalakrishna, Gary L. Lilien, Jerome D. Williams and Ian Sequeira, 'Do trade shows pay off?', *Journal of Marketing* (July 1995), pp. 75–83; Ben Chapman, 'The trade show must go on', *Sales & Marketing Management* (June 2001), p. 22.

25. Mandy Thatcher, 'Back to basics', *Marketing Business* (September 2000), pp. 32–4; Natalie Cheary, 'Hoover fails to shake off free flights horror', *Marketing Week* (1 May 1997), p. 22.

26. Al Ries and Laura Ries, 'First do some publicity', *Advertising Age* (8 February 1999), p. 42. Also see Al Ries and Laura Ries, *The Fall of Advertising and the Rise of PR* (New York: HarperBusiness, 2002).

27. Steve Jarvis, 'How the Internet is changing the fundamentals of publicity', *Marketing News* (17 July 2000), pp. 6–7; Carlos Grande and Caroline Daniel, 'The high and lows of online shopping', *Financial Times* (16 May 2000), p. 9.

28. Jo-Anne Walker, 'News analysis', *Marketing Week* (24 November 1996), p. 39.

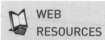

WEB RESOURCES

For additional classic case studies and Internet exercises, visit www.pearsoned.co.uk/kotler

Concluding concepts 18
Ninety per cent of spend wasted!

DAVID BOWEN*

If half the money spent on advertising is wasted, at least 90 per cent of the money spent on brand sites is flushed away. Why?

The principal reason is that brand-builders have failed to realise just how different the Web is from other media. In particular, it is hopeless at soundbites. Brand-builders want to get across short messages by osmosis and association – nothing awkward like logic. The Web is just too literal and too sophisticated: it is marvellous for explaining the intricacies of the Martian landscape, or offering a choice of 2m books, but it falls down badly when trying to sell you a bar of chocolate or a bottle of vodka.

> The most common mistake is to spend a little and get nothing.

Let us start with the vodka – ABSOLUT VODKA. Its site (www.absolut.com) epitomises this failure to get to grips with the medium. It is possibly the most elaborate brand-building site on the Web, and probably the biggest waste of money. I see a group of clever Swedes sitting around wondering if they can create a 'multimedia experience that truly conveys our brand values'. The result is a sub-daytime TV experience, with naff music, stilted voiceovers and pretty pictures trying to dress up desperately thin content. A few advertisements, cocktail recipes and some truly embarrassing features: try the 'Night out' in the ABSOLUT VANILLA section for a good cringe. This site is worthless because it is pointless. If you are going to spend a lot of money on a branding site, give it a job.

It is interesting to contrast national offerings from the same company to see what a difference this makes. Take Coca-Cola. Most of its national sites (accessible from www.coke.com) contain what has become a standard mix of TV ads, games, screensavers and the like – soft content that has hardly moved on in the last five years and reflects a depressing lack of imagination. By contrast, MyCokeMusic.com, part of the UK offering, is a branding site with a purpose. Here you can download a track for £0.80 (€1.33) or an album for £6.40, or stream a track (that is, listen to it once) for £0.01. Coca-Cola sponsors the UK charts so the site fits perfectly with its image and, best of all, generates revenue.

Alternatively, look at the Guinness site (www.guinness.com). It asks on the home page where you are. Say you are in the US and you get a standard branding site, with ads (including an archive), product and company information, and a small store where you can buy a T-shirt but not a drink – all a bit ho-hum really. However, tell it you are in the UK, and you will find a site hung on the company's rugby sponsorship. Here is a sophisticated Fantasy Rugby game linked to the Six Nations tournament. I will be amazed if it is not a success.

Weetabix, the cereal company, has a site (www.weetabix.co.uk) that is sometimes useful, sometimes not. When it is supporting a cereal packet competition, it is essential. However, when there are no competitions, it is just another branding site – pleasant enough but pointless!

Guinness, Coke and Weetabix are lucky (or clever): they have seen ways of using the Web to support their overall promotional activity. But what do you do if you have no such hook? A good starting point is to follow Mars's lead with the Mars Bar. There is no Mars Bar site, but how many companies have such nerve? We have a product; therefore, we *must* have a website. OK, but make sure you get the right balance between money spent and effectiveness.

The most common mistake is to spend a little and get nothing. Hershey has a site for its KitKat (www.kitkatbar.com) that consists of one page with a slogan: 'White and dark chocolate now available at your favourite retailer'. The only link in the main area is to an Ad Alert, a pop-up window warning that this website 'may be trying to sell you something'. Well, at least it is cheap – but why not go the Mars Bar route and spend the money in the pub instead?

The Americans call the Mars Bar a Milky Way, and it does have a site (www.milkyway.com). While much more elaborate than KitKat's, it is still thin: a list of ingredients, two television ads, some history, recipes and a product locator (put in your zip code and find a retailer). Some of these are marginally useful, especially if you want to turn your Milky Way into pink mousse tart, but how many people would really look on the Web for a retailer that sells a common confectionery? Or go online to watch a telly ad? I am not singling Milky Way out – it is one of thousands with a similarly dull mix.

If you spend a little more, and apply some imagination, the Web can start to make some sense. The British KitKat site (www.kitkat.co.uk) shows the possible effects of investment. In common with many brand sites, it consists of a cartoon world, with invitations to click here and there to find various goodies. The navigation is vague, a deliberate ruse to keep visitors on the site as long as possible. Nevertheless, after a few clicks I found two downloadable items that will appeal to some: an Asteroids game and the Breakmate, a device that lets you say when you next want a break, and triggers a pop-up window at the time you specify. It may not be very exciting, but at least it fits the bar's 'Have a break . . .' slogan and leaves a branded gizmo sitting on a visitor's desktop.

Online games can work too. They do not have to be complex to be engaging. My children and I have wasted a few happy hours playing Air Hockey at the Mini UK site (www.mini.co.uk); it is remarkably like Pong, which I used to play in the Seventies. The games on the US Twizzlers site (www.twizzlers.com) are even simpler: try the surprisingly tricky Seeing Red word puzzle. If you do want something more sophisticated, locate – if you can – the table football game at Coke UK (www.cocacola.co.uk): too clever for me, but my son likes it.

Given the plethora of such games and other diversions, these sites will flourish only if they get a loyal following – which leads me on to a site for which I have a special fondness. Acdoco is a North of England-based manufacturer of specialist cleaning products. Its site (www.acdo.co.uk) also has the 'world's longest-running online soap', called The Laundorama. This semi-animated cartoon is very silly, and aimed firmly at students. The company sees it as a way of competing with the giants without pouring money into television ads. Does it work? Well, it has been going since April 1998: someone must think it does. At least – thank heavens – it is different.

Questions

1. How do Web-based communications differ from the other elements of the communications mix?
2. What are the websites mentioned trying to achieve?
3. Why does David Bowen draw a distinction between most of the websites he details in the case and those that explain the intricacies of the Martian landscape (www.marsrovers.jpl.nasa.gov) or offer a choice of two million books (www.amazon.com)?
4. Does it matter or not if 'half the money spent on advertising is wasted' or '90 per cent of money spent on brand sites is flushed away'?
5. How can marketers evaluate the return on the money they spend upon brand sites and other advertising?

---

* David Bowen works for the website effectiveness consultancy Bowen Craggs & Co (www.bowencraggs.com). This case is based on his article, 'In search of a mission', *Financial Times* (5 February 2004) © David Bowen.

Everyone lives by selling something.

ROBERT LOUIS STEVENSON

Personal selling and direct marketing

Chapter objectives

After reading this chapter, you should be able to:

- Discuss the role of a company's salespeople in creating value for customers and building customer relationships.
- Identify and explain the major sales force management steps.
- Discuss the personal selling process, distinguishing between transaction-oriented marketing and relationship marketing.
- Define direct marketing and discuss its benefits to customers and companies.
- Identify and discuss the major forms of direct marketing.

Mini Contents List

- Prelude case – MD Foods AMBA: rethinking its sales force strategy and structure
- Introduction
- Personal selling
- Managing the sales force
- The personal selling process
- Marketing Insights 19.1 – Cross-cultural selling: in search of universal values
- Direct marketing
- Benefits and growth of direct marketing
- Customer databases and direct marketing
- Marketing Insights 19.2 – Database growth: a wealth of information, but a poverty of customer attention
- Forms of direct marketing
- Summary
- Concluding concepts 19 – Britcraft Jetprop: whose sale is it anyhow?

◀ SOURCE: Avon Cosmetics Ltd.

Prelude case MD Foods AMBA: rethinking its sales force strategy and structure

MD Foods AMBA, owned by over 8,000 Danish farmers, is Denmark's largest dairy cooperative. Production facilities are spread across the country. Through MD Foods International (MDI), MD operates its production and distribution facilities in England. Cooperative arrangements with counterparts such as Arla in Sweden and Arla's sales force in Finland enabled MD to establish a strong presence in the Scandinavian markets. In milk tonnage terms, MD is now the fourth largest dairy in Europe. MD also has sales subsidiaries in England, France, Germany, Greece, Italy, Poland, Norway, Sweden and the Middle East.

> A number of important changes have occurred in the European market environment in the past decade.

Europe's dairy industry is dominated by national producers. Generic products are typically marketed by product type, such as brie, feta, camembert and so forth, which are internationally known. MD faces increasing competition not only from national and local producers but also from international companies with a track record in product development and branding.

A number of important changes have occurred in the European market environment in the past decade. These include the withdrawal of EU subsidies to the export of dairy products to non-EU countries in 1996, the increasing concentration of food retailers in Europe and the increasing centralisation in retailers' buying decision making as well as product mix planning. MD accounts for a third of total EU exports of feta cheese. The end of subsidies to exports to markets such as the Middle East has had a big impact on MD's profits, putting heavy pressure on the company to shift milk used for feta production to other products (such as milk powders and yellow cheeses) for EU customers.

Apart from deciding which product group(s) to emphasise, another major problem confronting MD is how to develop a more effective sales and marketing structure to compete cost-effectively in these market situations.

In the past, MD has based its sales organisation on geographical and national considerations. Moreover, the focus of the sales force was on individual stores rather than retail chains or key accounts. With the emerging retail concentration and centralisation of buying and planning functions in customers' organisations, MD recognises the need to respond to these pressures and to consider the options for managing the sales function, from analysing sales to managing key accounts. The time was right for dramatic action.

A key opportunity arose when one customer – a large international retailer – introduced the idea of key account management to MD. This one customer's European turnover from MD exceeded the turnover of many of MD's subsidiaries, making it more important than some of MD's geographic markets. MD decided to introduce key account management in its sales and marketing organisations, starting in Denmark, where retail concentration is high and MD has a dominant market position. Essentially, three key account managers were appointed to serve specific key accounts, divided into FDB, the Danish cooperative; DS, a private retail group together with Aldi, part of a German retail group; and other retailers. The key account managers worked as a team with three trade managers (who have in-store marketing and space management expertise) in relation to the specific key accounts. The Sales Director coordinated the key account managers, while the trade managers reported to the national trade marketing manager. In this way, MD could achieve optimisation of the sales force, while also ensuring that know-how is shared through coordination of trade marketing.

The organisational change piloted in Denmark was later introduced in Sweden, but reactions from both MD's subsidiary and major Swedish retailers were less positive. At headquarters, MD is contemplating what steps to take next. What should MD's sales force strategy and organisational structure for sales be? Should the key account management format be applied in other markets? Should the key account managers be responsible for the sales force assigned to their key account? Existing sales forces also vary in size, from 15 to four people. Large sales forces dealing with stores with more autonomous management see to tasks such as sales, merchandising, displays, placing signs and posters and new campaigns. Smaller sales forces serve the highly centralised retailers and handle merchandising and displays. New developments must also take into account different workloads, skills and career developments for sales forces and key account managers serving different retailers and geographic markets. What will satisfy customer and employee requirements? Finally, can the new structure that is evolved be successfully applied to MD's operations across Europe?[1]

Questions

1. Why does MD Foods rely on a sales force to sell its products?
2. What are the key considerations that MD Foods needs to take into account in setting its sales force's objectives, strategy, structure and compensation? Identify the trade-offs involved in each of these decisions.
3. What are the key challenges facing MD Foods in developing and implementing an organisational structure that will satisfy both customers and employees (sales force, marketing and key account managers)? Recommend and justify a strategy for MD Foods.

SOURCE: Based on Mogéns Bjerre, 'MD Foods AMBA: a new world of sales and marketing', in *Understanding Marketing: A European Casebook* Celia Philips, Ad Pruyn and Marie-Paule Kestemont (eds), pp. 30–41, reproduced with permission, © John Wiley & Sons Ltd, Chichester, UK, 2000.

Introduction

The questions in the prelude case reflect some of the critical issues that management must address when determining sales force strategy and structure. Indeed, the decisions called for are relevant not only for MD Foods, as in the prelude case, but also for any firm that uses a sales force to help it market its goods and services.

In the previous two chapters, you learned about integrated marketing communication (IMC) and three specific elements of the marketing communications mix – advertising, sales promotion and publicity. This chapter is about the final two IMC elements – *personal selling* and *direct marketing*. Both involve direct connections with customers aimed towards building customer-unique value and lasting relationships.

Personal selling is the interpersonal arm of marketing communications in which the sales force interacts with customers and prospects to make sales and build relationships. Direct marketing consists of direct connections with carefully targeted consumers to both obtain an immediate response and cultivate lasting customer relationships. Actually, direct marketing can be viewed as more than just a communications tool. In many ways, it constitutes an overall marketing *approach* – a blend of communications and distribution channels all rolled into one. As you read on, remember that although this chapter examines personal selling and direct marketing as separate tools, they must be carefully integrated with other elements of the marketing communication mix.

Personal selling

Robert Louis Stevenson once noted that 'everyone lives by selling something'. We are all familiar with the sales forces used by business organisations to sell products and services to customers around the world. Sales forces are found in non-profit as well as profit organisations. Churches use membership committees to attract new members. Hospitals and museums use fund-raisers to contact donors and raise money. In the first part of this chapter, we examine the role of personal selling in the organisation, sales force management decisions and the personal selling process.

The nature of personal selling

Selling is one of the oldest professions in the world. The people who do the selling go by many names: *salespeople, sales representatives, account executives, sales consultants, sales engineers, field representatives, agents, district managers, marketing representatives* and *account development reps*, to name a few.

When someone says 'salesperson', what image comes to mind? Perhaps it's the stereotypical 'travelling salesman' – the fast-talking, ever-smiling peddler who travels his territory foisting his wares on reluctant customers. Such stereotypes, however, are sadly out of date. Today, most professional salespeople are well-educated, well-trained men and women who work to build long-term, value-producing relationships with their customers. They succeed not by taking customers in but by helping them out – by assessing customer needs and solving customer problems.

Consider Airbus, the aerospace company that markets commercial aircraft. It takes more than a friendly smile and a firm handshake to sell expensive computer systems. Selling high-tech aircraft that each cost tens of millions of euros is complex and challenging. A single big sale can run into billions of euros. Airbus salespeople head up an extensive team of company sales specialists – sales and service technicians, financial analysts, planners, engineers – all dedicated to finding ways to satisfy airline customer needs. The salespeople begin by becoming experts on the airlines. They find out where each airline wants to grow, when it wants to replace planes and details of its financial situation. The team runs Airbus and rival planes through computer systems, simulating the airline's routes, cost per seat and other factors to show that their planes are most efficient. Then the high-level negotiations begin. The selling process is nerve-rackingly slow – it can take two to three years from the first sales presentation to the day the sale is announced. Sometimes top executives from both the airline and the company are brought in to close the deal. After getting the order, salespeople must stay in almost constant touch to keep track of the account's equipment needs and to make certain the customer stays satisfied. Success depends on building solid, long-term relationships with customers, based on performance and trust.

Salesperson—An individual acting for a company by performing one or more of the following activities: prospecting, communicating, servicing and information gathering.

The term **salesperson** covers a wide range of positions. At one extreme, a salesperson might be largely an *order taker*, such as a department store salesperson standing behind the counter. At the other extreme are the *order getters*, salespeople whose job demands the *creative selling* of products and services ranging from appliances, industrial equipment or aeroplanes to insurance, advertising or consulting services. Other salespeople engage in *missionary selling*, whereby they are not expected or permitted to take an order, but only build goodwill or educate buyers. An example is a salesperson for a pharmaceutical company who calls on doctors to educate them about the company's drug products and to urge them to prescribe these products to their patients. In this chapter, we focus on the more creative types of selling and on the process of building and managing an effective sales force.[2]

The role of the sales force

Personal selling is the interpersonal arm of the promotion mix. Advertising consists of one-way, non-personal communication with target consumer groups. In contrast, personal selling involves two-way personal communication between salespeople and individual customers – whether face to face, by telephone, through videoconferences or by other means. As such, personal selling can be more effective than advertising in more complex selling situations. Salespeople can probe customers to learn more about their problems. They can adjust the marketing offer to fit the special needs of each customer and can negotiate terms of sale. They can build long-term personal relationships with key decision makers.

The role of personal selling varies from company to company. Some firms have no salespeople at all – for example, organisations that sell only through mail-order catalogues or through manufacturers' representatives, sales agents or brokers. In most firms, however, the sales force plays a major role. In companies that sell business products, such as ABB or DuPont, the salespeople may be the only contact. To these customers, the sales force *is* the

CONTINUING THE TRADITION OF

SHANGRI-LA HOSPITALITY

SHANGRI-LA
HOTELS and RESORTS

For reservations at Asia's finest luxury hotels, please call London (44 20) 8747 8485,
your travel consultant, any Shangri-La or Traders hotel or book on-line at www.shangri-la.com
AUSTRALIA • MAINLAND CHINA • HONG KONG SAR • FIJI ISLANDS • INDONESIA • MALAYSIA • MYANMAR • PHILIPPINES • SINGAPORE • TAIWAN • THAILAND • UNITED ARAB EMIRATES

company. In consumer product companies, such as Adidas and Unilever, which sell through intermediaries, final consumers rarely meet salespeople or even know about them. Still, the sales force plays an important behind-the-scenes role. It works with wholesalers and retailers to gain their support and to help them to be more effective in selling the company's products.

The sales force serves as the critical link between a company and its customers. In many cases, salespeople serve both masters – the seller and the buyer. First, they *represent the company to customers*. They find and develop new customers and communicate information about the company's products and services. They sell products by approaching customers, presenting their products, answering objections, negotiating prices and terms, and closing sales. In addition, they provide customer service and carry out market research and intelligence work.

At the same time, salespeople *represent customers to the company*, acting inside the firm as a 'champions' of customers' interests and managing buyer–seller relationships. Thus, the salesperson often acts as an '*account manager*' who manages the relationship between the seller and buyer. Salespeople relay customer concerns about company products and actions back to those who can handle them. They learn about customer needs and work with others in the company to develop greater customer value. The old view was that salespeople should worry about sales and the company should worry about profit. However, the current view holds that salespeople should be concerned with more than just producing sales – they should work with others in the company to produce *customer satisfaction* and *company profit*.

As companies move towards a stronger market orientation, their sales forces are becoming more market focused and customer oriented. Today, organisations expect salespeople to look at sales data, measure market potential, gather market intelligence and develop marketing strategies and plans. They should know how to orchestrate the firm's efforts towards delivering customer value and satisfaction. A market-oriented rather than a sales-oriented sales force will be more effective in the long run. Beyond winning new customers and making sales, it will help the company to create long-term, profitable relationships with customers. As such, the company's sales team can be a central force in an organisation's relationship marketing programme. Relationship marketing is discussed in greater detail in Chapter 11.

Managing the sales force

Sales force management— The analysis, planning, implementation and control of sales force activities. It includes setting sales force objectives; designing sales force strategy; and recruiting, selecting, training, supervising and evaluating the firm's salespeople.

We define **sales force management** as the analysis, planning, implementation and control of sales force activities. It includes setting sales force objectives, designing sales force strategy and structure, recruiting, selecting, training, compensating, supervising and evaluating the firm's salespeople. The primary sales force management decisions are shown in Figure 19.1. Let us take a look at each of these decisions next.

Setting sales force objectives

Companies set different objectives for their sales forces. Salespeople usually perform one or more of the following tasks:

- *Prospecting*. Finding and developing new customers.
- *Communicating*. Communicating information about the company's products and services.
- *Selling*. Selling products by approaching customers, presenting their products, answering objections and closing sales.
- *Servicing*. Providing services to customers (e.g. consulting on problems, providing technical assistance, arranging finance).
- *Information gathering*. Carrying out market research and intelligence work, and filling out sales call reports.

Figure 19.1 Major steps in sales force management

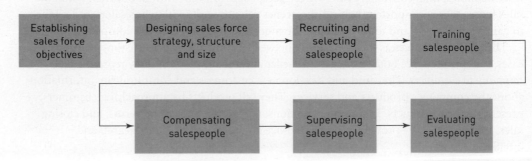

812

Some companies are very specific about their sales force objectives and activities. For example, a company may advise its salespeople to spend 80 per cent of their time with current customers and 20 per cent with prospects, and 85 per cent of their time on current products and 15 per cent on new products. The company believes that if such norms are not set, salespeople tend to spend almost all of their time selling current products to current accounts and neglect new products and new prospects.

Designing sales force strategy and structure

Marketing managers face several sales force strategy and design questions. How should salespeople and their tasks be structured? How big should the sales force be? Should salespeople sell alone or work in teams with other people in the company? Should they sell in the field or by telephone? How should salespeople be compensated? And how should performance be rewarded where selling tasks are shared across members within the sales team? We address these issues below.

Sales force strategy

Every company competes with other firms to get orders from customers. Thus it must base its strategy on an understanding of the customer buying process. A company can use one or more of several sales approaches to contact customers. An individual salesperson can talk to a prospect or customer in person or over the phone, or make a sales presentation to a buying group. Similarly, a sales *team* (such as a company executive, a salesperson and a sales engineer) can make a sales presentation to a buying group. In *conference selling*, a salesperson brings resource people from the company to meet with one or more buyers to discuss problems and opportunities. In *seminar selling*, a company team conducts an educational seminar about state-of-the-art developments for a customer's technical people.

Often, the salesperson has to act as an account manager who arranges contacts between people in the buying and selling companies. Because salespeople need help from others in the company, selling calls for teamwork. Others who might assist salespeople include top management, especially when big sales are at stake; technical people who provide technical information to customers; customer service representatives who provide installation, maintenance and other services to customers; and office staff, such as sales analysts, order processors and secretaries.

Once the company decides on a desirable selling approach, it can use either a direct or a contractual sales force. A *direct* (or *company*) *sales force* consists of full- or part-time employees who work exclusively for the company. This sales force includes *inside salespeople*, who conduct business from their offices via telephone or visits from prospective buyers, and *field salespeople*, who travel to call on customers. A *contractual sales force* consists of manufacturers' reps, sales agents or brokers who are paid a commission based on their sales.

Sales force structure

Sales force strategy influences the structure of the sales force. A company can divide up sales responsibilities along any of several lines. The decision is simple if the company sells only one product line to one industry with customers in many locations. In that case the company would use a *territorial sales force structure*. If the company sells many products to many types of customer, it might need either a *product sales force structure*, a *customer sales force structure*, or a combination of the two.

Territorial sales force structure

In the **territorial sales force structure**, each salesperson is assigned to an exclusive geographic area and sells the company's full line of products or services to all customers in that territory.

Territorial sales force structure—A sales force organisation that assigns each salesperson to an exclusive geographic territory in which that salesperson carries the company's full line.

This organisation clearly defines the salesperson's job and fixes accountability. It also increases the salesperson desire to build local business relationships that, in turn, improve selling effectiveness. Finally, because each salesperson travels within a small geographic area, travel expenses are relatively small.

Product sales force structure

Product sales force structure—A sales force organisation under which salespeople specialise in selling only a portion of the company's products or lines.

Salespeople must know their products, a task that is not easy if the company's products are numerous, unrelated and technically complex. This, together with the growth of product management, has led many companies to adopt a **product sales force structure**, in which the sales force sells along product lines. For example, Kodak uses different sales forces for its film products and its industrial products. The film products sales force deals with simple products that are distributed intensively, whereas the industrial products sales force deals with complex products that require technical understanding.

The product structure can lead to problems, however, if a given customer buys many of the company's products. For example, a hospital supply company may have several product divisions, each with a separate sales force. Several salespeople might end up calling on the same hospital on the same day. This means that they travel over the same routes and wait to see the same customer's purchasing agents. These extra costs must be measured against the benefits of better product knowledge and attention to individual products.

Customer sales force structure

Customer sales force structure—A sales force organisation under which salespeople specialise in selling only to certain customers or industries.

More and more companies are using a **customer sales force structure**, whereby they organise the sales force along customer or industry lines. Separate sales forces may be set up for different industries, for serving current customers versus finding new ones, and for large accounts versus regular accounts.

Organising its sales force around customers can help a company to become more customer focused. For example, giant ABB, the Swiss-based industrial equipment maker, changed from a product-based to a customer-based sales force. The new structure resulted in a stronger customer orientation and improved service to clients:

> David Donaldson sold boilers for ABB. After 30 years, Donaldson sure knew boilers, but he didn't know much about the broad range of other products offered by ABB's Power Plant division. Customers were frustrated because as many as a dozen ABB salespeople called on them at different times to peddle their products. Sometimes representatives even passed each other in customers' lobbies without realising that they were working for the same company. ABB's bosses decided that this was a poor way to run a sales force. So, David Donaldson and 27 other power plant salespeople began new jobs. [Donaldson] now also sells turbines, generators, and three other product lines. He handles six major accounts . . . instead of a [mixed batch] of 35. His charge is to know the customer intimately and sell him the products that help him operate productively. Says Donaldson: 'My job is to make it easy for my customer to do business with us . . . I show him where to go in ABB whenever he has a problem.' The president of ABB's power plant businesses [adds]: 'If you want to be a customer-driven company, you have to design the sales organisation around individual buyers rather than around your products.'[3]

Complex sales force structures

When a company sells a wide variety of products to many types of customer over a broad geographical area, it often combines several types of sales force structure. Salespeople can be specialised by customer and territory, by product and territory, by product and customer, or by territory, product and customer. A salesperson might then report to one or more line and staff managers. No single structure is best for all companies and situations. Each organisation should select a structure that best serves the needs of its customers and fits its overall marketing strategy.

Sales force size

Once the company has set its strategy and structure, it is ready to consider *sales force size*. Salespeople constitute one of the company's most productive – and most expensive – assets. Therefore, increasing their number will increase both sales and costs.

The past few years have seen a reduction in sales force size. Advances in selling technology, such as selling on the Internet or the use of account management software, make salespeople more efficient in handling customers and can even replace salespeople altogether.[4]

Many companies use some form of **workload approach** to set sales force size. The company groups accounts according to size, account status or other factors related to the amount of effort required to maintain them. It then determines the number of salespeople needed to call on them the desired number of times. The logic is as follows. Suppose we have 1,000 Type-A accounts each requiring 36 calls per year, and 2,000 Type-B accounts each requiring 12 calls per year. In this case, the sales force's *workload*, as defined by the number of calls it must make per year, is 60,000 calls (36,000 + 24,000). Suppose our average salesperson can make 1,000 calls a year. The company thus needs 60 salespeople (60,000/1,000).

> **Workload approach**—An approach to setting sales force size, whereby the company groups accounts into different size classes and then determines how many salespeople are needed to call on them the desired number of times.

Other sales force strategy and structure issues

Sales management also have to decide who will be involved in the selling effort and how various sales and sales support people will work together.

Outside and inside sales forces

The company may have an **outside sales force** (or field sales force), an **inside sales force** or both. Outside salespeople travel to call on customers, whereas inside salespeople conduct business from their offices via telephone or visits from prospective buyers.

To reduce time demands on their outside sales forces, many firms have increased the size of their inside sales team, which includes technical support people, sales assistants and telemarketers. Technical support people provide technical information and answers to customers' questions. Sales assistants provide clerical back-up for outside salespeople. They call ahead and confirm appointments, conduct credit checks, follow up on deliveries and answer customers' queries when salespeople cannot be reached. Telemarketers use the phone to find new leads and qualify prospects for the field sales force or to sell and service accounts directly.

The inside sales force frees salespeople to spend more time selling to major accounts and finding major new prospects. Depending on the complexity of the product and customer, a telemarketer can make 20–30 decision-maker contacts a day, compared to the average of four that an outside salesperson can make. For many types of product and selling situation, **telemarketing** can be as effective as a personal sales call, but much less expensive. For example, whereas a typical personal sales call can cost well over £200, a routine industrial telemarketing call costs between £5 and £20 depending on the complexity of the call.

Just as telemarketing is changing the way that many companies go to market, the Internet offers explosive potential for restructuring sales forces and conducting sales operations. More

> **Outside sales force**—Outside salespeople (or field sales force) who travel to call on customers.
>
> **Inside sales force**— Salespeople who service the company's customers and prospect from their offices via telephone or visits from prospective customers.
>
> **Telemarketing**—Using the telephone to sell directly to consumers.

and more companies are now using the Internet to support their personal selling efforts, ranging from selling and training salespeople to conducting sales meetings and servicing accounts. Electronic negotiations are also taking root, with more and more organisations using the Web to conduct sales negotiations.

> Take an extreme example which is found in the soccer world. Managers of some of the world's biggest football clubs – including Manchester United, Eindhoven, Olympique Marseille, Inter Milan and the entire Brazilian first division – have negotiated transfers of players using a private (members-only) business-to-business (B2B) site, run by InterClub (developed by the German consultancy realTech and communications systems company InterClubNet). Similar marketplaces are being developed with other big-money sports such as ice hockey and basketball.

E-negotiation has its merits. For a start, the emails last for ever. The *durability* of emails enables negotiators to keep track of negotiations with each of the half-dozen or more companies involved at the same time. A second advantage is the *instant record-keeping* that e-negotiations entail. Although the telephone is cheaper and faster and can convey more information than a quick email, there are distinct advantages for negotiators using email or electronic sites. The negotiations can be done at lower cost and at a time that is convenient for the parties involved.

Sceptics, not surprisingly, argue that negotiations are more likely to go well if conducted face to face. There is only so much that one can accomplish in an exchange through keyboards and screens. Proponents, however, note that e-negotiations can be facilitated by the brief getting-to-know-you telephone call. And there is nothing to stop the negotiators from breaking the ice by swapping photographs and personal details before negotiations commence. Moreover, not all electronic negotiations take place between strangers, and e-negotiations can go well when the parties involved already know each other.

However, the durability and immediacy of emails mean that each piece of correspondence must be re-read and double-checked to minimise confusion, misunderstanding and embarrassment. It is much more difficult for the negotiator to retract information or 'emotions' once he or she has 'hit the send button'. Experts urge e-negotiators to heed the lessons learnt by every Victorian letter-writer – the best policy is: 'when in doubt, leave it overnight'. There is no better filter to apply to an angry note than a good night's sleep.[5]

Team selling

Team selling—Using teams of people from sales, marketing, production, finance, technical support, and even upper management to service large, complex accounts.

As products become more complex, and as customers grow larger and more demanding, a single salesperson simply can't handle all of a large customer's needs. Instead, most companies are now using **team selling** to service large, complex accounts. Companies are finding that sales teams can unearth problems, solutions and sales opportunities that no individual salesperson could. Such teams might include people from any area or level of the selling firm – sales, marketing, technical and support services, R&D, engineering, operations, finance and others. In team selling situations, the salesperson shifts from 'soloist' to 'orchestrator' who helps coordinate a whole-company effort to build profitable relationships with key customers.[6]

Team selling does have its pitfalls. Selling teams can confuse and overwhelm customers who are used to working with only one salesperson. Salespeople who are used to having customers all to themselves may have trouble learning to work with and trust others on a team. Finally, difficulties in evaluating individual contributions to the team selling effort can create some sticky compensation issues.

Key account management

Continuing relationships with large customers dominate the activities of many sales organisations. For makers of fast-moving consumer goods such as Procter & Gamble, Unilever and Danone, the relationship is with major retailers such as Tengelmann, Carrefour, Tesco or Ahold. The importance of these retailers has changed the way marketing as a whole is being organised. *Account managers* often orchestrate the relationship with a single retailer, although some will manage several smaller retailers or a group of independent outlets. Any major retailer will probably always be carrying major manufacturers' brands, so the account manager's role is one of increasing the profitability of sales through the channel. In this arrangement a great deal of sales promotions effort and advertising is customised for retailers that want exclusive lines or restrict the sort of promotions that they accept.

The situation is very similar in industrial sales organisations when a supplier has to sell components, raw materials, supplier or capital equipment in the concentrated markets described in Chapter 7. Even when a prospect is not a client, there are regular contacts at all levels between the organisations. When the client or prospect is particularly important, key account managers are responsible. These aim for a mutually beneficial relationship between the seller and buyer. The buyer benefits from traceability of supplies, smart purchasing, and lean supply and facilities management, while the seller gains market knowledge and profitable sales.

In most companies, account managers are like brand managers in not having formal or informal teams working for them. This means the key account managers compete for the resources to serve their client. Their role is to maintain smooth but creative relationships between the buying and selling teams.[7]

Recruiting and selecting salespeople

At the heart of any successful sales force operation is the recruitment and selection of good salespeople. The performance difference between an average salesperson and a top salesperson can be substantial. In a typical sales force, the top 30 per cent of the salespeople might bring 60 per cent of the sales. Thus careful salesperson selection can greatly increase overall sales force performance.

Beyond the differences in sales performance, poor selection results in costly turnover. When a salesperson quits, the costs of finding and training a new salesperson, plus the costs of lost sales, can be very high. Also, a sales force with many new people is less productive than one with a stable membership.[8]

What are the traits of a good salesperson?

Selecting salespeople would not be a problem if the company knew what traits spell surefire sales success. If it knew that good salespeople were outgoing, aggressive and energetic, for example, it could simply check applicants for these characteristics. Many successful salespeople, however, are also bashful, soft-spoken and laid back.

One survey suggests that good salespeople have a lot of enthusiasm, persistence, initiative, self-confidence and job commitment. They are committed to sales as a way of life and have a strong customer orientation. Another study suggests that good salespeople are independent and self-motivated and are excellent listeners. Still another study advises that salespeople should be a friend to the customer as well as persistent, enthusiastic, attentive and, above all, honest. They must be internally motivated, disciplined, hard working and able to build strong relationships with customers. Still other studies suggest that good salespeople are team players, not loners.[9]

When recruiting, companies should analyse the sales job itself and the characteristics of the most successful salespeople to identify the traits needed by a successful salesperson in their industry. Does the job require a lot of planning and paperwork? Does it call for much travel? Will the salesperson face a lot of rejections? Will the salesperson be working with high-level buyers? The successful sales candidate should be suited to these duties.

Recruiting procedures and selection

After management has decided on needed traits, it must *recruit* the desired candidate. The human resources department looks for applicants by getting names from current salespeople, using employment agencies and placing classified ads. Another source is to attract top salespeople from other companies. Proven salespeople need less training and can be immediately productive.

Recruiting will attract many applicants, from which the company must select the best. The selection procedure can vary from a single informal interview to lengthy testing and interviewing. Many companies give formal tests to sales applicants. Tests typically measure sales aptitude, analytical and organisational skills, personality traits and other characteristics.[10] Test results count heavily in companies such as IBM, Prudential, Procter & Gamble and Gillette. Gillette, for example, claims that tests have reduced turnover by 42 per cent and that test scores have correlated well with the later performance of new salespeople. But test scores provide only one piece of information in a set that includes personal characteristics, references, past employment history and interviewer reactions.[11]

Training salespeople

New salespeople may spend anything from a few weeks or months to a year or more in training. The average initial training period is four months. Then, most companies provide continuous sales training via seminars, sales meetings and the Web throughout the salesperson's career. Training programmes have several goals. Salespeople need to know and identify with the company, so most companies spend the first part of the training programme describing the company's history and objectives, its organisations, its financial structure and facilities, and its chief products and markets. Because salespeople also need to know the company's products, sales trainees are shown how products are produced and how they work. They also need to know the characteristics of competitors and customers, including distributors, so the training programme teaches them about competitors' strategies and about different types of customer and their needs, buying motives and buying habits. Because salespeople must know how to make effective presentations, they are trained in the principles of selling. Finally, salespeople need to understand field procedures and responsibilities. They learn how to divide time between active and potential accounts and how to use an expense account, prepare reports and route communications effectively.

Compensating salespeople

To attract salespeople, a company must have an attractive compensation plan. These plans vary greatly both by industry and by companies within the same industry. Compensation is made up of several elements – a fixed amount, a variable amount, expenses and fringe benefits. The fixed amount, usually a salary, gives the salesperson some stable income. The variable amount, which might be commissions or bonuses based on sales perfomance, rewards the salesperson for greater effort. Expense allowances, which repay salespeople for job-related expenses, let salespeople undertake needed and desirable selling efforts. Fringe benefits, such as paid vacations, sickness or accident benefits, pensions and life insurance, provide job security and satisfaction.

Management must decide what *mix* of these compensation elements makes the most sense for each sales job. Different combinations of fixed and variable compensation give rise to four

Companies spend hundreds of millions of euros to train their salespeople in the art of selling.
SOURCE: Digital Vision Limited.

basic types of compensation plans – straight salary, straight commission, salary plus bonus and salary plus commission.

The sales force compensation plan can both motivate salespeople and direct their activities. If sales management wants salespeople to emphasise new account development, it might pay a bonus for opening new accounts. Thus, the compensation plan should direct the sales force towards activities that are consistent with overall marketing objectives.

Table 19.1 shows how a company's compensation plan should reflect its overall marketing strategy. If the overall marketing strategy is to grow rapidly and gain market share, the compensation plan should be to reward high sales performance and new-account development. In contrast, if the marketing goal is to maximise profitability of current accounts, the compensation plan might contain a larger base salary component, with additional incentives based on current account sales and customer satisfaction. In fact, more and more companies are moving away from high-commission plans that may drive salespeople to make short-term grabs for business. They may even ruin a customer relationship because they were pushing too hard to close a deal. Instead, companies are designing compensation plans that reward salespeople for building customer relationships and growing the long-run value of each customer.[12]

Supervising salespeople

New salespeople need more than a territory, compensation and training – they need *supervision*. Through supervision, the company *directs* and *motivates* the sales force to do a better job.

Table 19.1 The relationship between overall marketing strategy and sales force compensation

	STRATEGIC GOAL		
	To gain market share rapidly	To solidify market leadership	To maximise profitability
Ideal salesperson	■ An independent self-starter	■ A competitive problem solver	■ A team player ■ A relationship manager
Sales focus	■ Deal making ■ Sustained high effort	■ Consultative selling	■ Account penetration
Compensation role	■ To capture accounts ■ To reward high performance	■ To reward new and existing account sales	■ To manage the product mix ■ To encourage team selling ■ To reward account management

SOURCE: Adapted from Sam T. Johnson, 'Sales compensation: In search of a better solution', *Compensation & Benefits Review* (November–December 1993), pp. 53–60. Copyright © 1998 American Management Association, New York, http://www.amanet.org.

Directing salespeople

How much should sales management be involved in helping salespeople manage their territories? It depends on everything from the company's size to the experience of its sales force.

Developing customer targets and call norms

Companies vary in how closely they supervise their salespeople. Many help their salespeople in identifying customer targets and setting call norms. Companies often specify how much time their sales force should spend prospecting for new accounts and set other time management priorities. If left alone, many salespeople will spend most of their time with current customers, which are better-known quantities. Moreover, whereas a prospect may never deliver any business, salespeople can depend on current accounts for some business. Therefore, unless salespeople are rewarded for opening new accounts, they may avoid new-account development.

Using sales time efficiently

Companies also direct salespeople in how to use their time efficiently. One tool is the *annual call schedule* which shows which customers and prospects to call on in which months and which activities to carry out. Activities include taking part in trade shows, attending sales meetings and carrying out marketing research. Another tool is *time-and-duty analysis*. In addition to time spent selling, the salesperson spends time travelling, waiting, eating, taking breaks and doing administrative chores. Figure 19.2 shows how salespeople spend their time. Because of the tiny portion of the day most sales staff actually spend selling or negotiating and talking face to face with potential customers, companies must look for ways to save time. This can be done by getting salespeople to use phones instead of travelling, simplifying record-keeping forms, finding better call and routing plans, and supplying more and better customer information.

Many firms have adopted sales force automation systems, computerised sales force operations for more efficient order-entry transactions, improved customer service and better

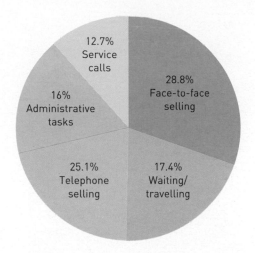

Figure 19.2 **How salespeople spend their time**
SOURCE: Reprinted with permission from Dartnell Corporation, 30th Sales Force Compensation Survey, copyright © 1998 by Dartnell Corporation, 360 Hiatt Drive, Palm Beach Gardens, FL 33418. All rights reserved. For more information on our customer service products please call 1-800-621-5463 or visit our website at www.dartnellcorp.com.

salesperson decision-making support. Salespeople use computers to profile customers and prospects, analyse and forecast sales, manage accounts, schedule sales calls, enter orders, check inventories and order status, prepare sales and expense reports, process correspondence and carry out many other activities. Sales force automation not only lowers sales force calls and improves productivity; it also improves the quality of sales management decisions.

Perhaps the fastest-growing sales force technology tool is the Internet. As more and more organisations and individuals embrace Internet technology, salespeople are using the Internet regularly in their daily selling activities. The most common uses include gathering competitive information, monitoring customer websites and researching industries and specific customers. As more and more companies provide their salespeople with Web access, experts expect continued growth in sales force Internet usage.[13]

Motivating salespeople

Beyond directing salespeople, sales managers must also motivate them. Some salespeople will do their best without any special urging from management. To them, selling may be the most fascinating job in the world. But selling can also be frustrating. Salespeople usually work alone, and they must sometimes travel away from home. They may face aggressive, competing salespeople and difficult customers. They sometimes lack the authority to do what is needed to win a sale and may thus lose large orders that they have worked hard to obtain. Therefore, salespeople often need special encouragement to do their best.

Management can boost sales force morale and performance through its organisational climate, sales quota and positive incentives.

Organisational climate
Organisational climate reflects the feeling that salespeople have about their opportunities, value and rewards for good performance. Some companies treat salespeople as if they are not very important, and performance suffers accordingly. Other companies treat their salespeople as valued contributors and allow virtually unlimited opportunity for income and promotion. Not surprisingly, these companies enjoy higher sales force performance and less turnover.

Sales quotas
Many companies motivate their salespeople by setting **sales quotas** – standards stating the amount they should sell and how sales should be divided among the company's products. Compensation is often related to how well salespeople meet their quotas.

Sales quotas—Standards set for salespeople, stating the amount they should sell and how sales should be divided among the company's products.

Positive incentives

Companies also use various positive incentives to increase sales force effort. *Sales meetings* provide social occasions, breaks from routine, chances to meet and talk with 'company brass', and opportunities to air feelings and to identify with a larger group. Companies also sponsor *sales contests* to spur the sales force to make a selling effort above what would normally be expected. Other incentives include honours, merchandise and cash awards, trips and profit-sharing plans.

Evaluating salespeople

So far we have described how management communicates what salespeople should be doing and how it motivates them to do it. This process requires good feedback, which means getting regular information from salespeople to evaluate their performance.

Sources of information

Management gets information about its salespeople in several ways. The most important source is the *sales report*, including weekly or monthly work plans and longer-term territory marketing plans. The *work plan* describes intended calls and routing, which provide management with information on the salespeople's whereabouts, and provides a basis for comparing plans and performance. The *annual territory marketing plan* outlines how new accounts will be built and sales from existing accounts increased.

Salespeople also write up their completed activities on *call reports* and turn in *expense reports* for which they are partly or wholly repaid. Additional information comes from personal observation, customers' letters and complaints, customer surveys and talks with other salespeople.

Formal evaluation of performance

Using sales force reports and other information, sales management *formally evaluates* members of the sales force. Formal evaluation forces management to develop and communicate clear standards for judging performance. Management must also obtain well-rounded information about each salesperson. Formal evaluation provides salespeople with constructive feedback which helps them to improve future performance and to motivate them to perform well.

We have looked at the key issues surrounding sales force management – designing and managing the sales force. Next we turn to the actual personal selling process.

The personal selling process

Personal selling is an ancient art that has spawned a large literature and many principles. Effective salespeople operate on more than just instinct – they are highly trained in methods of territory analysis and customer management. Effective companies take a *customer-oriented approach* to personal selling. They train salespeople to identify customer needs and to find solutions. This approach assumes that customer needs provide sales opportunities, that customers appreciate good suggestions and that customers will be loyal to salespeople who have their long-term interests at heart. By contrast, those companies that use a *sales-oriented approach* rely on high-pressure selling techniques. They assume that the customers will not buy except under pressure, that they are influenced by a slick presentation and that they will not be sorry after signing the order (and that, even if they are, it no longer matters).

Steps in the selling process

Most training programmes view the **selling process** as consisting of several steps that the salesperson must master (see Figure 19.3). These steps focus on the goal of getting new customers and obtaining orders from them. However, many salespeople spend much of their time maintaining existing accounts and building long-term customer relationships. We will address the relationship aspect of the personal selling process in a later section.

Selling process—The steps that the salesperson follows when selling, which include prospecting and qualifying, pre-approach, approach, presentation and demonstration, handling objections, closing and follow-up.

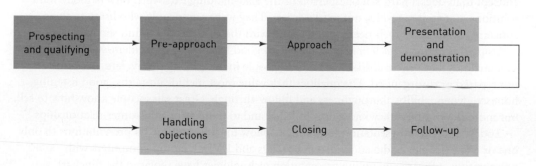

Figure 19.3 **Major steps in effective selling**

Prospecting and qualifying

Prospecting—The step in the selling process in which the salesperson identifies qualified potential customers.

The first step in the selling process is **prospecting** – identifying qualified potential customers. The salesperson must approach many prospects to get just a few sales. Although the company supplies some leads, salespeople need skill in finding their own. They can ask current customers for referrals. They can build referral sources, such as suppliers, dealers, non-competing salespeople and bankers. They can join organisations to which prospects belong, or can engage in speaking and writing activities that will draw attention. They can search for names in newsletters or directories and use the telephone and post to track down leads. Or they can drop in unannounced on various offices (a practice known as 'cold calling').

Salespeople need to know how to *qualify* leads: that is, how to identify the good ones and screen out the poor ones. Prospects can be qualified by looking at their financial ability, volume of business, special needs, location and possibilities for sales growth.

Pre-approach

Pre-approach—The step in the selling process in which the salesperson learns as much as possible about a prospective customer before making a sales call.

Before calling on a prospect, the salesperson should learn as much as possible about the organisation (what it needs, who is involved in the buying) and its buyers (their characteristics and buying styles). This step is known as the **pre-approach**. The salesperson can consult standard industry and online sources, acquaintances and others to learn about the company. The salesperson should set *call objectives*, which may be to qualify the prospect, to gather information or to make an immediate sale. Another task is to decide on the best approach, which might be a personal visit, a phone call or a letter. The best timing should be considered carefully because many prospects are busiest at certain times. Finally, the salesperson should give thought to an overall sales strategy for the account.

Approach

Approach—The step in the selling process in which the salesperson meets and greets the buyer to get the relationship off to a good start.

During the **approach** step, the salesperson should know how to meet and greet the buyer, and get the relationship off to a good start. This step involves the salesperson's appearance, his or her opening lines and the follow-up remarks. The opening lines should be positive to build goodwill from the beginning of the relationship. This opening might be followed by some key questions to learn more about the customer's needs, or by showing a display or sample to attract the buyer's attention and curiosity. As in all stages of the selling process, listening to the customer is crucial.

Presentation and demonstration

Presentation—The step in the selling process in which the salesperson tells the product 'story' to the buyer, showing how the product will make or save money for the buyer.

The **presentation** is that step in the selling process where the salesperson tells the product 'story' to the buyer, presenting customer benefits and showing how the product solves the customer's problems. The problem-solver salesperson fits better with today's marketing concept than does a hard-sell salesperson or the glad-handing extrovert. Buyers today want solutions, not smiles; results, not razzle-dazzle. They want salespeople who listen to their concerns, understand their needs and respond with the right products and services.

Using this *need-satisfaction approach* calls for good listening and problem-solving skills.[14] The qualities that buyers dislike most in salespeople include being pushy, late, deceitful, and unprepared or disorganised. The qualities they value most include empathy, good listening, honesty, dependability, thoroughness and follow-through. Great salespeople know how to sell, but more importantly, they know how to listen and to build strong customer relationships.[15]

Today, advanced presentation technologies allow for full multimedia presentations to only one or a few people. Audio and video discs (CDs and DVDs), laptop computers with presentation software and online presentation technologies have replaced the flipchart.

Handling objections

Customers almost always have objections during the presentation or when asked to place an order. The problem can be either logical or psychological, and objections are often unspoken. In **handling objections**, the salesperson should use a positive approach, seek out hidden objections, ask the buyer to clarify any objections, take objections as opportunities to provide more information, and turn the objections into reasons for buying. Every salesperson should be trained in the skills of handling objections.

Closing

After handling the prospect's objections, the salesperson now tries to close the sale. Some salespeople do not get around to **closing** or do not handle it well. They may lack confidence, feel guilty about asking for the order or fail to recognise the right moment to close the sale. Salespeople should know how to spot closing signals from the buyer, including physical actions, comments and questions. For example, the customer might sit forward and nod approvingly or ask about prices and credit terms. Salespeople can use one of several closing techniques. They can ask for the order, review points of agreement, offer to help write up the order, ask whether the buyer wants this model or that one, or note that the buyer will lose out if the order is not placed now. The salesperson may offer the buyer special reasons to close, such as a lower price or an extra quantity at no charge.

Follow-up

The last step in the selling process – **follow-up** – is necessary if the salesperson wants to ensure customer satisfaction and repeat business. Right after closing, the salesperson should complete any details on delivery time, purchase terms and other matters. The salesperson should then schedule a follow-up call when the initial order is received to make sure there is proper installation, instruction and servicing. This visit would reveal any problems, assure the buyer of the salesperson's interest and reduce any buyer concerns that might have arisen since the sale.

International selling

The typical sales process can be applied in international selling. However, intercultural trade always requires special efforts in tailoring sales and negotiation approaches (see Marketing Insights 19.1).

Personal selling and customer relationship management

The principles of personal selling as described are *transaction oriented*, in that their aim is to help salespeople close a specific sale with a customer. But in many cases, the company is not seeking simply a sale: it has targeted a major customer that it would like to win and keep. The company would like to show the customer that it has the capabilities to serve the customer over the long haul, in a mutually profitable relationship. The sales force usually plays an important role in building and managing long-term customer relationships.

More companies today are moving away from transaction marketing, with its emphasis on making a sale. Instead, they are practising **relationship marketing**, which emphasises maintaining profitable long-term relationships with customers by creating superior customer value and satisfaction. They realise that, when operating in maturing markets and facing stiffer competition, it costs a lot more to wrest new customers from competitors than to keep current ones.

Today's large customers favour suppliers who can sell and deliver a coordinated set of products and services to many locations, and who can work closely with customer teams to

In the sales presentation, the salesperson tells the product story to the buyers.
SOURCE: Walter Hodges and Tony Stone Images. Reproduced courtesy of GettyOne.

Handling objections—The step in the selling process in which the salesperson seeks out, clarifies and overcomes customer objections to buying.

Closing—The step in the selling process in which the salesperson asks the customer for an order.

Follow-up—The last step in the selling process, in which the salesperson follows up after the sale to ensure customer satisfaction and repeat business.

Relationship marketing—The process of creating, maintaining and enhancing strong, value-laden relationships with customers and other stakeholders.

19.1 ## Cross-cultural selling: in search of universal values

Face-to-face selling is the least easily controlled part of international marketing. Academics and consultants have drawn up numerous lists of 'do's and don'ts' based on examining negotiations within particular cultures. Increasingly, international marketers are turning to both culture-specific negotiation studies and general cultural research in an attempt to understand the cultural values that influence negotiation behaviour and how best to adapt their selling styles.

One popular tool is the Geert Hofstede 'five universal values' framework for defining national culture. These five aspects are as follows.

■ *Time orientation*. This is a culture's sense of immediacy. Generally, Asians have longer time orientations than western cultures and tend to spend a longer time establishing a personal relationship at the start of the negotiation process. It is one reason why western business people found *karaoke* sessions rewarding when negotiating with Japanese and Korean executives! Because the relationship is the *content* of the negotiation, and the basis of the longer-term benefits derived from the deal, as opposed to the short-term aspects of the deal in progress, the 'relationship approach' will better fit Asian cultures than it would western cultures. The lesson: when selling to someone with a long-term orientation culture, expect to spend more time on forming the client relationship, rather than merely focusing on the contract.

■ *Aversion to uncertainty*. The level of risk that negotiators will bear is partly a function of the level of uncertainty that they are used to in their culture. For countries where people reflect a higher tolerance of ambiguity, such as the UK and Denmark, the salesperson may spend less time probing the buyer's needs before closing the deal. In countries such as France, where people have lower tolerance of uncertainty, the French salesperson may take longer to clarify exactly what it is that the customer needs.

■ *Acceptance of unequal power*. The level of inequality that people expect and accept in their jobs and lives – also called 'power distance' by Hofstede – also affects negotiation style. In high power distance cultures, subordinates would only approach high-level superiors with a problem of great importance. By contrast, in low power distance cultures, staff at a lower level in the corporate hierarchy are more accustomed to being treated like equals by their superiors, with whom they feel they can discuss matters directly. So, when negotiating with a buyer used to weighting status heavily, the seller organisation should ensure that salesperson seniority matches that of the buyer.

...19.1

- *Individualism or collectivism*. This reflects the person's level of independence and degree of freedom. The US and UK are generally regarded as individualistic societies which value freedom and independence. In collectivistic cultures, such as Japan and China, people's sense of value is derived from belonging to a group. Consequently, negotiators influenced by the latter culture may take more time and effort to reach consensus and closure.

- *Masculinity and femininity*. Achievement and possessions reflect masculine values, while the social environment and helping others tap femininity. People tend to lie along the masculinity–femininity continuum. In masculine cultures, exemplified by Austria in Hofstede's study, salespeople use an assertive style, which can be off-putting if applied in feminine cultures, such as Denmark. The latter would place more emphasis on partnership to achieve both parties' desired outcomes. Those in the middle of this continuum would value the establishment of good relationships with clients as much as hard facts and contractual details.

The five universal values offer a base for addressing cross-cultural settings in international selling and the need for adaptation of the selling approach. However, neither Hofstede nor advocates of his model suggest that successful international negotiation comes from following the old adage 'when in Rome, do as the Romans do'. Rather, the experts argue that negotiators do not negotiate with someone from their own culture in the same way that they negotiate with someone from another culture. So, knowing how Swedish people negotiate with each other seldom gives much help in predicting how they will negotiate with their Japanese counterpart. Moreover, as an increasing proportion of international executives are educated abroad or have broad overseas experience, they may adapt their cultural styles to show familiarity with their foreign negotiators' cultural values. Imagine a German salesperson adopting the French 'win–win' approach when negotiating with her French client and the French client using 'win–lose' techniques typically associated with German negotiation style. The key, therefore, lies not so much in *mimicking* the foreign client's cultural values, but in subtle *adaptation* to fit the other negotiator's style.

SOURCES: Geert Hofstede, *Culture's Consequences: Comparing values, behaviors, institutions and organizations across nations*, 2nd edn (London: Sage Publications, 2003); Anne Macquin and Dominique Rouziés, 'Selling across the culture gap', *Financial Times*, FT Mastering Global Business, Part Seven (1997), pp. 10–11; Geert Hofstede, *Cultures and Organisations: Software of the mind* (London: McGraw-Hill, 1991); Sergey Frank, 'Global negotiating', *Sales and Marketing Management* (May 1992), pp. 64–9; J.C. Morgan and J.J. Morgan, *Cracking the Japanese Market* (New York: Free Press, 1991).

improve products and processes. For these customers, the first sale is only the beginning of the relationship.

Unfortunately, many companies are not set up for these developments. They often sell their products through separate sales forces, each working independently to close sales. Their technical people may not be willing to lend time to educate a customer. Their engineering, design and manufacturing people may have the attitude that 'it's our job to make good products and the salesperson's to sell them to customers'. However, the more successful companies recognise that winning and keeping accounts requires more than making good products and directing the sales force to close lots of sales. It requires a carefully coordinated, whole-company effort to create value-laden, satisfying relationships with important customers.

Relationship marketing is based on the premise that important accounts need focused and ongoing attention. Studies have shown that the best salespeople are those who are highly motivated and good closers, but more than this, they are customer-problem solvers and relationship builders. Salespeople working with key customers must do more than call when they think a customer might be ready to place an order. They also study the account and understand its problems. They call or visit frequently, work with the customer to help solve the customer's problems and improve its business, and take an interest in customers as people.

Companies may take care of customers by offering them gifts, free entertainment or corporate hospitality. Freebies, such as a calendar or a fountain pen carrying the supplier's logo, are usually accepted by clients without a second thought. A nice dinner merely to build client relations or to keep in touch with a valued customer rarely raises an eyebrow. Corporate entertaining or hospitality is an expected part of business life. Some managers argue that corporate entertaining serves a purpose. The idea is to get the client out for a good time and to make them feel good about the company in the hope that the client will receive the company's sales representatives ahead of the competition. Furthermore, a night at the theatre or opera, with a ticket for an accompanying partner, is useful when overseas visitors need to be entertained in the evening. Weekend outings for clients and potential customers allow the company to buy a little of a contact's private time to talk about business. In some business cultures (e.g. Japan, Malaysia, Thailand and most countries in the Far East), offering and accepting hospitality is part of work and often seen as a way of establishing relationships.

However, corporate hospitality can be costly. At top sporting events – such as the football Cup Final at Wembley, or a day at Epsom for the horse racing – the cost could be astronomical. It costs something upwards of £1,500 per head to entertain at the Wimbledon men's tennis finals. And don't ask what a meal for four in a Tokyo geisha club would amount to. Nevertheless, businesses will spend that amount of money if they have big international customers coming into the city to talk over deals that are worth millions of pounds. So, when does an all-expenses-paid golfing trip, a free weekend in Paris or a case of finest Moët & Chandon stop being part of corporate life and begin to look like sleaze? What should businesspeople do when faced with freeloading opportunities? In the absence of clear corporate or standard guidelines, how would managers decide whether a gift, meal or trip is acceptable or sleazy?

Some experts offer the following simple guidelines:

1. The first test is the 'means test'. It draws the line at entertainment 'way beyond the level the person would normally be able to afford themselves'. It also depends on the level of superiority or importance of the individual. A steak in a wine bar at lunchtime is not beyond the means of most ordinary managers. However, if you want to talk business with the CEO of a big company, you may have to meet him in more expensive surroundings.

2. The second test is the 'wow test'. When you open an envelope containing an invitation, you may say 'how nice' (or you may groan and say 'I suppose I had better be there!'). However, if you find yourself saying 'Wow!', then you had better think twice.

3. The third test is the *reciprocity test*. It is worthwhile occasionally to check that entertaining is reciprocal – suppliers buy you lunch, but you also buy them lunch back sometimes. That way, the relationship does not become too oppressive.

Some companies have no qualms about offering or receiving freebies, whereas some actively discourage all employees from accepting hospitality. Companies must therefore set guidelines for their managers and employees on where to draw the line. However, if you're in doubt about the morality or ethics of an offer, follow the experts' advice on where to draw the line: look at whether a mention of the hospitality arrangement – meal, trip or gift – in the press would cause embarrassment; try the 'means' test; do the *wow* test.[16]

The importance of relationship marketing is now widely recognised. Companies find that they earn a higher return from resources invested in retaining customers than from money spent to attract new ones. Increasingly, companies also recognise the importance of establishing strategic partnerships with valued customers, making skilled relationship marketing essential.

Direct marketing

Many of the marketing and promotion tools that we've examined in previous chapters were developed in the context of *mass marketing:* targeting broad markets with standardised messages and offers distributed through intermediaries. Today, however, with the trend towards more narrowly targeted or one-to-one marketing, many companies are adopting *direct marketing,* either as a primary marketing approach or as a supplement to other approaches. Increasingly, companies are using direct marketing to reach carefully targeted customers more efficiently and to build stronger, more personal, one-to-one relationships with them. In this section, we explore the exploding world of direct marketing.

Direct marketing consists of direct communications with carefully targeted individual customers to obtain an immediate response and cultivate lasting customer relationships. Direct marketers communicate directly with customers, often on a one-to-one, interactive basis. Using detailed databases, they tailor their marketing offers and communications to the needs of narrowly defined segments or even individual buyers. Beyond brand and image building, they usually seek a direct, immediate and measurable consumer response. For example, Dell Computer interacts directly with customers, by telephone or through its website, to design built-to-order systems that meet customers' individual needs. Buyers order directly from Dell, who quickly and efficiently delivers the new computers to their homes or offices.

Direct marketing—Direct communications with carefully targeted individual customers to obtain an immediate response.

The new direct-marketing model

Early direct marketers – catalogue companies, direct mailers and telemarketers – gathered customer names and sold their goods mainly through the post and by telephone. Today, fired by rapid advances in database technologies and new marketing media – especially the Internet and other electronic channels – direct marketing has undergone a dramatic transformation.

Direct marketing can take the form of direct distribution – as marketing channels that contain no intermediaries. In previous chapters, we have also included direct marketing as one element of the marketing communications mix – as an approach for communicating directly with customers. In fact, direct marketing is both these things. Most companies still use direct marketing as a supplementary channel or medium for marketing their goods. Thus, companies such as Nokia and Lexus market mostly through mass-media advertising and their dealer networks but also supplement these channels with direct marketing. Their direct marketing includes promotional materials mailed directly to prospective buyers and their Web pages which provide customers with information about various models, financing (in the case of Lexus) and dealer locations. Similarly, many department stores and banks sell the majority of their merchandise or services off their 'bricks and mortar' outlets as well as directly through telemarketing and their websites.

However, for many companies today, direct marketing is more than just a supplementary channel or medium. For these companies, direct marketing – especially Internet marketing and e-commerce – constitutes a new and complete model for doing business. More than just another marketing channel or advertising medium, this new *direct model* is rapidly changing the way companies think about building relationships with customers.

Whereas most companies use direct marketing and the Internet as supplemental approaches, firms employing the direct model use it as the *only* approach. Examples include Dell, online bookseller Amazon.com, CoShopper.com, a Norwegian Internet shopping company, Framfab, the Swedish Internet consultancy, and Direct Line, the UK-based insurance company. This direct model has proved highly successful, not just for these companies, but for the fast-growing number of other companies that employ it. Many strategists have hailed direct marketing as the new marketing model of the next millennium.

For companies like Nokia, direct marketing and the Web supplement other marketing efforts.
SOURCE: Nokia (**www.nokia.com**).

Benefits and growth of direct marketing

Whether used as a complete business model or as a supplement to a broader integrated marketing mix, direct marketing brings many benefits to both buyers and sellers. As a result, direct marketing has grown very rapidly.

The benefits of direct marketing

Direct marketing benefits buyers in many ways. First, it is *convenient*. From the comfort of their homes or offices, customers can browse mail catalogues or sellers' websites at any time of the day or night. Buying is *easy* and *private*. Customers confront fewer buying hassles and do not have to face salespeople or open themselves up to persuasion and emotional pitches. Business customers can learn about available products and services without waiting for and tying up time with salespeople.

Direct marketing often gives shoppers greater product *access* and *selection*. For example, the world's the limit for the Web. Cyberstores such as Amazon, CDNow and others can offer an almost unlimited selection compared to the more meagre assortments of counter-parts in the bricks-and-mortar world. Beyond a broader selection of sellers and products, online and Internet channels also give buyers access to a wealth of comparative *information*, information about companies, products and competitors, at home and around the globe. Good websites often provide more information in more useful forms than even the most solicitious salesclerk can. Amazon.com and CDNow, for example, offer best-seller lists and reviews.

Finally, direct marketing – especially online buying – is *interactive* and *immediate*. Customers can often interact with the sellers by phone or on the seller's website to create exactly the configuration of information, products or services they desire, then order them on the spot. Furthermore, the Internet and other forms of direct marketing give customers a greater measure and sense of control. For example, a rising proportion of car buyers 'shop online', arming themselves with information about car models and dealer costs before showing up at a dealership.

Direct marketing also yields many benefits to sellers. First, direct marketing is a powerful tool for *customer relationship building*. Using database marketing, today's marketers can target small groups or individual consumers, tailor offers to individual needs and promote these offers through personalised communications. Direct marketing can also be timed to reach prospects at just the right moment. For example, Nestlé's baby food division maintains a database of new parents and mails them six personalised packages of gifts and advice at key stages in the baby's life. And, because they reach more interested consumers at the best times, direct marketing materials receive higher readership and response. Direct marketing also permits easy testing of alternative media and messages.

Because of its one-to-one, interactive nature, the Internet is an especially potent direct-marketing tool. Direct marketing also gives sellers access to buyers that they could not reach through other channels. For example, the Internet provides access to *global* markets that might otherwise be out of reach.

Finally, direct marketing can offer sellers a *low-cost*, *fast* and *efficient* alternative for reaching their markets. For example, direct marketing has grown rapidly in B2B marketing, partly in response to the ever-increasing costs of marketing through the sales force. When personal sales calls cost several hundred euros per contact, they should be made only when necessary and to high-potential customers and prospects. Lower cost-per-contact media – such as telemarketing, direct mail and company websites – often prove more cost-effective in reaching and selling to more prospects and customers.[17]

The growth of direct marketing

As a result of these advantages to both buyers and sellers, direct marketing has become the fastest growing form of marketing. Sales through traditional direct-marketing channels (telephone marketing, direct mail, catalogues, direct-response television, and others) have been growing rapidly. During 1997–2002, the annual rate of growth in spending on conventional direct marketing channels (e.g. direct mail) outstripped that for mass-marketing channels such as advertising. Total direct marketing expenditure in Europe as a whole grew from €31,725 million (at current prices) in 1997 to €46,330 million by 2002.[18]

Customer databases and direct marketing

Customer database—An organised collection of comprehensive data about individual customers or prospects, including geographic, demographic, psychographic and buying behaviour data.

Effective direct marketing begins with a good customer database. A **customer database** is an organised collection of comprehensive data about individual customers or prospects, including geographic, demographic, psychographic and buying behaviour data. The database can be used to locate good potential customers, tailor products and services to the special needs of targeted consumers, and maintain long-term customer relationships. *Database marketing* is the process of building, maintaining and using customer databases and other databases (products, suppliers, resellers) for the purpose of contacting and transacting with customers.

Although many companies are now building and using customer databases for targeting marketing communications and selling efforts at the individual customer, data protection regulations in some countries may slow down growth in database marketing practices. For example, usage in the United States and the United Kingdom is far more widespread, with data laws being much more open compared to the rest of Europe. But the international race is on to exploit database marketing and few businesses can afford to ignore this important vehicle for competitive success. As Tom Peters comments in *Thriving on Chaos*, 'A market has never bought things. Customers buy things. That's why database marketing's ability to target the individual customer in the crowded marketplace is so valuable.'[19]

Many companies confuse a customer mailing list with a customer database. The former is simply a set of names, addresses and telephone numbers. A customer database contains much more information. In business-to-business marketing, the salesperson's customer profile might contain information such as the products and services that the customer has bought, past volumes and prices, key contacts (and their ages, birthdays, hobbies and favourite foods), competitive suppliers, status of current contracts, estimated customer expenditures for the next few years, and assessments of competitive strengths and weaknesses in selling and servicing the account.

In consumer marketing, the customer database might contain a customer's demographics (age, income, family members, birthdays), psychographics (activities, interests and opinions), buying behaviour (past purchases, buying preferences) and other relevant information. Companies must distinguish between *transaction-based* and *custom-built* marketing databases. Transactional databases are put in by an accounts department for the purpose of sending invoices/bills out and getting money back. By contrast, custom-built databases focus on what the firm's marketing people need to know to serve and satisfy customers profitably and better than the competition can – for example, the most cost-effective way to reach target customers, the net worth of a transaction, customers' requirements and lifetime values, lapsed customers and why they departed, why competitors are making inroads and where. Armed with the information in their databases, these companies can identify small groups of customers to receive fine-tuned marketing offers and communications.

Companies use their databases in many ways. They can use a database to identify prospects and generate sales leads by advertising products or offers. Or they can use the database to profile customers based on previous purchasing and to decide which customers should receive particular offers. Databases can help the company to deepen customer loyalty – companies can build customers' interest and enthusiasm by remembering buyer preferences and by sending appropriate information, gifts, or other materials. The database can help a company make attractive offers of product replacements, upgrades, or complementary products, just when customers might be ready to act.

For example, Mars, a market leader in pet food as well as confectionery, maintains an exhaustive pet database. In Germany, the company has compiled the names of virtually every German family that owns a cat. It obtained these names by contacting veterinarians, via its Katzen-Online.de website, and by offering the public a free booklet titled 'How to Take Care of Your Cat'. People who request the booklet fill out a questionnaire, providing their cat's name, age, birthday, and other information. Mars then sends a birthday card to each cat in Germany each year, along with a new cat food sample and money-saving coupons for Mars brands. The result is a lasting relationship with the cat's owner.

The Halifax Bank in the UK offers another example of how the effective deployment of customer databases and implementation of database management systems might lead to more intelligent selling. Halifax uses a sophisticated customer relationship management software system called 'interaction advisor' to enable front-line staff in the bank's contact centres and branches, as well as its interactive voice response systems and banking kiosks, to analyse key customer information and present optimal product offers to individual customers. The database system enables Halifax to use real-time cross-sell offers to 750 of its branch banks, meaning that sales representative can manage their customers in a more personal and profitable way. As customers interacted with Halifax through the contact centre or bank branch, the interaction advisor updates customer information and 'learns' to continuously adjust product offers and services to fit customer needs and behaviour. Halifax acknowledges that, in the past, cross-selling resulted in sales agents suggesting product offers that customers already possessed or did not need. Using the 'interaction advisor', sales agents are now able to make offers that are timely and relevant, improving customer satisfaction and increasing revenue opportunities. Moreover, by following sales prompts generated by its sophisticated database management system, the bank had achieved an increase of between 10 and 15 per cent in sales leads, with nearly half of these leads resulting in a sale.[20]

Hence, a rich customer database allows the company to build profitable new business by locating good prospects, anticipating customer needs, cross-selling products and services and rewarding loyal customers. But many companies are sceptical about the returns on investment in databases. The recent growth in companies' customer databases has led to nothing more than information overload, making it increasingly difficult to grab customers' attention (see Marketing Insights 19.2).

Like many other marketing tools, database marketing requires a special investment. Companies must invest in computer hardware, database software, analytical programme,

Loyal customers are made, not born. More and more companies are seeking to create and maintain better relationships with customers. Ads like this one draw companies' attention to CRM software tools for communicating and managing relationships with customers. SOURCE: SAP Global Marketing. *Agency*: OgilvyOne Worldwide.

CRM FOR THE SKEPTICAL. AND THE ACCOUNTABLE.

mySAP CRM GENERATES REAL ROI. AND WE HAVE THE PROOF.

Over two thousand companies have chosen mySAP™ Customer Relationship Management to reduce front-end costs, increase cross-selling, and improve net cash flow. With results like these — real, quantifiable results — it's no surprise that SAP is the fastest-growing CRM provider in the world. Skeptics, cynics and naysayers, please visit sap.com/crm/roi for your free ROI reports, prepared in collaboration with an independent third party, which detail real customer results. Then get ready to become believers.

THE BEST-RUN BUSINESSES RUN SAP

Database growth: a wealth of information, but a poverty of customer attention

19.2

marketing insights

Massachusetts-based consultant Richard Winter knows better than anyone that companies are accumulating data at a rapid rate, but he found hoarding on a massive scale. '[Database growth] is accelerating beyond previous expectations. Not only in size but also in workload [and] complexity of data and usage', he says. In a 2001 survey conducted by his firm, Winter Corporation, three-quarters of the databases covered held less than one terabyte (1,000 gigabytes). Three years later, his survey showed more than 90 per cent exceeded this. At the top of the pile was France Télécom with 29.2 terabytes – equivalent to over six times the printed collection of the Library of Congress!

While companies that sell the software (Oracle, International Business Machines, Teradata, Sybase, Microsoft) and hardware (Hewlett-Packard, IBM, Sun Microsystems, Hitachi, EMC), on which very large databases are built, welcome this acceleration of database growth, it isn't always good news for the companies that purchase the software. At sixth place on the Winter Corporation list, for example, comes Kmart, the retailer that filed for Chapter 11 protection from its creditors in 2003. A whopping 12.6 terabytes of data – covering stocks, sales, customers and suppliers – was not enough to save Kmart from bankruptcy.

Any fool can build a big database. But data have little value on their own; they are useful only when they are turned into information. Modern, relational databases are designed to facilitate this through their sheer capacity to analyse and query rows and columns of data – 496bn rows in the case of AT&T, the US telecommunications group. The trick is building a database robust and flexible enough for its intended purpose. Even so, more information does not mean more and better actions! The human capacity to absorb information remains unchanged. Kmart had lots of data and may even have been successful at turning them into information. But it failed to grab customers' attention. The reason? Information overload. As Herbert Simon, the late economist, psychologist and Nobel laureate, wrote: 'What information consumes is rather obvious: it consumes the attention of its recipients. . . . Hence a wealth of information creates a poverty of attention.'

The unprecedented competition for customer attention is one of the most pressing issues. Take email. Cheap, immediate and easy to customise, it was the ideal channel for one-to-one marketing – the use of customer data to build enduring relationships. Yet over 2003, the sheer volume of email – solicited and unsolicited – has led many consumers to install 'spam' filters. Not surprisingly, as uncovered by a 2003 survey conducted by Jupiter Research, the technology research company, 59 per cent of marketers were experiencing lower response rates to their email marketing

...19.2

campaigns as a result of filters. Even messages that get through are increasingly viewed with suspicion. The latest wave of online fraud, or 'phishing', involving faked emails appearing to come from financial institutions, has put everyone on their guard. Add to this the millions of consumers who have signed up to a 'do not call' phone register, putting them off-limits to telemarketers. In addition, thanks to the rise of personal video recorders, TV viewers can now skip over advertisements and watch a programme uninterrupted. In each case – email, telemarketing, TV advertising – consumers are responding to information overload by rationing their attention. Herbert Simon would not have been surprised.

All this leaves marketers with a dilemma. Their substantial investments in database and related technologies are designed to facilitate direct, personalised communication and sales. Yet an increasingly small proportion of these messages is being heard. Marketing gurus offer two varieties of solution.

'Viral marketing' proponents argue that companies can get their message across by securing the attention of trendsetters and opinion leaders whose voices are always heard: do not build relationships, build a buzz. The other wing says that relationship between companies and customers need to be taken to the next level. Customers need to be co-opted so they take a direct role in creating a product. Only then can a company be sure of getting their attention. An advocate of this way of thinking is Shawn Fanning, creator of Napster, the music file-sharing site that attracted a community of 40 m users before it was shut down by the record industry.

There is no single 'right way', however, to capture the valuable attention of customers. One-to-one marketing, viral marketing, Napster-style co-creation of value – each has its place. Arguably, the most successful companies are those that find an attention-grabbing formula and keep it to themselves. On the Winter's list is Wal-Mart, the world's largest retailer. Wal-Mart uses data not to engender one-to-one relationships with customers but to offer prices so crushingly low that customers pay attention. But just how Wal-Mart does this is one piece of information that remains a secret.

SOURCES: Adapted from Simon London, 'Choked by a data surfeit', *Financial Times* (29 January 2004), p. 17; see also Tom Davenport and John Beck, *The Attention Economy* (Maidenhead: McGraw-Hill, 2003) and C.K. Prahalad and Venkat Ramaswamy, *The Future of Competition: Co-creating unique value with customers* (Boston: Harvard Business School Publishing, 2004).

communication links and skilled personnel. The database system must be user-friendly, fit for its intended purpose and available to various marketing groups, including those in product and brand management, new-product development, advertising and promotion, direct mail, telemarketing, Web marketing, field sales, order fulfilment and customer service. A well-managed database should lead to sales gains that will more than cover its costs [21]

Forms of direct marketing

The major forms of direct marketing include personal selling, telephone marketing, direct-mail marketing, catalogue marketing, direct-response television (DRTV) marketing and online shopping. Many of these techniques were first developed in the United States, but have become increasingly popular in Europe. In the EU, some forms of direct marketing – notably direct mail and telemarketing – are forecast to grow. In practice, however, the impact of a unified Europe has been limited by the labyrinth of legislation across the Union, which means that certain direct marketing techniques are feasible in some countries but not others.

> For example, telemarketing is more widely practised in the UK and the Netherlands than in Germany and is virtually non-existent in countries such as Belgium, Sweden and Finland. Differences in postal systems, standards and rates across countries pose problems for pan-European direct-mailing programmes. Direct mail is strong in countries with efficient and inexpensive postal systems (e.g. the UK, Sweden) and weak where the post is slow and delivery unreliable (e.g. Spain, Italy). Even etiquette is a problem. The bright, brash American-style direct-mail methods used in the UK would be considered anything but courteous in France. On the other hand, the flowery phrases of a formal letter in France would definitely be *de trop* in the UK.

We have already examined personal selling in depth earlier in this chapter and looked closely at online marketing in Chapter 4. Here, we will examine the other direct marketing forms.

Telephone marketing

Telephone marketing or **telemarketing** uses the telephone to sell directly to consumers. It has become a major direct marketing tool. Marketers use *outbound* telephone marketing to generate and qualify sales leads, and sell directly to consumers and businesses. Calls may also be for research, testing, database building or appointment making, as a follow-up to a previous contact, or as part of a motivation or customer-care programme.

Marketers use *inbound* freephone numbers to receive orders from television and print ads, direct mail or catalogues. Marketers also use inbound telephone calls to receive customer enquiries and complaints.

In Europe, telemarketing is more established in the UK and Netherlands than in Germany, which has the toughest telemarketing laws. For example, in Germany the consent of the prospects or consumers is required before they can be contacted. If someone buys a shovel from a garden centre in winter, even if they gave their name and telephone number, the centre cannot telephone them in the spring with a special offer on bulbs because that would be illegal. Contrast the situation in Holland, where, for example, before an election, political parties are permitted to ring voters to gain their support.[22]

When properly designed and targeted, telemarketing provides many benefits, including purchasing convenience and increased product and service information.[23] However, the recent explosion in unsolicited telephone marketing has annoyed many consumers who object to

Telemarketing—Using the telephone to sell directly to consumers.

'junk phone calls' that pull them away from the dinner table or clog up their answering machines. Laws or self-regulatory measures have been introduced in different countries in response to complaints from customers. At the same time, some consumers may appreciate the genuine and well-presented offers they receive by telephone.

Direct-mail marketing

Direct-mail marketing—
Direct marketing through single mailings that include letters, ads, samples, foldouts and other 'salespeople on wings' sent to prospects on mailing lists.

Direct-mail marketing involves sending an offer, announcement, reminder or other item to a person at a particular address. Using highly selected mailing lists, direct marketers send out millions of mail pieces each year – letters, ads, brochures, samples, video- and audio-tapes, CDs, and other 'salespeople with wings'. Direct mail expenditure per capita varies across the major EU countries, but in general, direct-mail spend per head is disproportionately higher than that spent on telemarketing and, in a majority of cases, represents well over half of the total direct marketing expenditure per capita. The only exception is the UK where telemarketing expenditure per capita (€79.9) exceeded that for direct mail (€61.0) in 2001.[24]

Direct mail is well suited to direct, one-on-one communication. It permits high target-market selectivity, can be personalised, is flexible and allows easy measurement of results. Whereas the cost per 1,000 people reached is higher than with mass media such as television or magazines, the people who are reached are much better prospects – direct-mail marketers target individuals according to their personal suitability to receive particular offerings and promotions. Direct mail has proved very successful in promoting all kinds of products, from books, magazine subscriptions and insurance to gift items, clothing, gourmet foods, consumer packaged goods and industrial products. Direct mail is also used heavily by charities, such as Oxfam and Action Aid, which rely on correspondence selling to persuade individuals to donate to their charity.[25]

The direct-mail industry constantly seeks new methods and approaches. For example, videotapes and CDs are now among the fastest-growing direct-mail media. Used in conjunction with the Internet, CDs offer an affordable way to drive traffic to Web pages personalised for a specific market segment or a specific promotion. They can also be used to demonstrate computer-related products. For example, Sony sent out a CD that allowed PC users to demo its VAIO portable notebook on their own computers.[26]

Until recently, all direct mail was paper-based and handled by postal and telegraphic services and other mail carriers. Recently, however, fax mail, email and voice mail have become popular. These new forms deliver direct mail at incredible speeds, compared to the post office's 'snail mail' pace. Yet, much like mail delivered through traditional channels, they may be resented as 'junk mail' if sent to people who have no interest in them. For this reason, direct marketers must carefully identify their targets to avoid wasting huge sums of money or the recipient's time.

Catalogue marketing

Catalogue marketing—
Direct marketing through print, video or electronic catalogues that are mailed to select customers, made available in stores or presented online.

Catalogue shopping once started almost as explosively as the Internet, though few of us might remember this. Cataloguers' sales pitch was remarkably similar too – no need to struggle to the store, vast choice, lower prices. Today, the growth in catalogue shopping has slowed but catalogues are increasingly used by store retailers, which see them as an additional medium for cultivating sales. Most consumers enjoy receiving catalogues and will sometimes even pay to get them. Many catalogue marketers are now even selling their catalogues at bookstores and magazine stands. Many business-to-business marketers also rely heavily on catalogues.

Rapid advances in technology, however, along with the move to personalised one-to-one marketing, have resulted in dramatic changes in **catalogue marketing**. With the stampede

Web-based catalogues: most catalogue companies now present merchandise and take orders over the Internet.

SOURCES: (left) 3 Suisses France (**www.3suisses.fr**); (right) La Redoute (**www.redoute.co.uk**).

to the Internet, more and more catalogues are going electronic. Many traditional print or mail-order catalogue firms have added Web-based catalogues to their marketing mixes and a variety of new, Web-only cataloguers have emerged. For example, Web-based sales account for 10 per cent of the turnover at Quelle, the German mail-order company. Quelle expects half of the group's sales to come via the Net within the next five years. Other mail-order companies such as 3 Suisses and La Redoute in France, and Lands' End anticipate at least 15 per cent of sales to be generated online by 2005.[27]

However, the Internet has not yet killed off printed catalogues – far from it. Web catalogues currently generate only about 13 per cent of all catalogue sales. Printed catalogues remain the primary medium and many former Web-only companies have created printed catalogues to expand their business.[28]

Along with the benefits, however, Web-based catalogues also present challenges. Whereas a print catalogue is intrusive and creates its own attention, Web catalogues are passive and must be marketed. It is much more difficult to attract new customers with a Web catalogue. And the online cataloguers have to use advertising, linkage and other means to drive traffic to their sites. Thus, even cataloguers who are sold on the Web are not likely to abandon their print catalogues completely.

Direct-response television marketing

Direct-response television marketing (DRTV) takes one of two main forms. The first is *direct-response advertising*. Direct marketers air television spots, 60 or 120 seconds long, that persuasively describe a product or service and give customers a freephone number for ordering. Direct-response television advertising can also be used to build brand awareness, convey brand/product information, generate sales leads and build a customer database.

Television viewers may encounter longer, 30-minute advertising programmes, or 'infomercials', for a single product, during which the features or virtues of a product are discussed by 'experts' before an audience. These are selling programmes which are presented in an entertaining manner to attract the target audience. Direct response TV commercials are usually cheaper to make and the media purchase is less costly. Moreover, results are easily measured as, unlike branding campaigns, direct-response ads always include a toll-free

Direct-response television marketing (DRTV)—The marketing of products or services via television commercials and programmes which involve a responsive element, typically the use of a freephone number that allows consumers to phone for more information or to place an order for the goods advertised.

number or a Web address, making it easier for marketers to gauge whether consumers are paying attention to their messages.

For years, infomercials have been associated with somewhat questionable pitches for juicers and other kitchen gadgets, get-rich-quick schemes, and nifty ways to stay in shape without working very hard at it. In recent years, however, a number of large companies have begun using infomercials to sell their wares over the phone, refer customers to retailers, send out coupons and product information, or attract buyers to their websites. Organisations ranging from mail order (e.g. Sounds Direct), leisure (e.g. Scandinavian Seaways) and financial services (e.g. Direct Line, AA Insurance Services) to cars (e.g. Daewoo, Fiat), fast-moving consumer goods (e.g. Britvic, Martini, McVitie's) and government departments (e.g. the British army, US navy) have been using DRTV marketing. DRTV marketing has also been used by charities and fund-raising campaigners to persuade viewers to offer donations or volunteer services. Examples include the 'Live Aid' campaign that captured the imagination of millions of people across the globe, 'Children in Need' and many other international fund-raising events.[29]

In recent years, direct-response TV advertising is giving way to interactive TV (iTV). Advertisers, from a range of sectors, including cars, travel, telecommunications and financial services, are actively using iTV to deliver more complex messages and information to target viewers. Audiences are encouraged to interact with the company's ads through an impulse response format which invites them to press the 'red button' on the remote control device for more information.

> For example, Vodafone has used iTV to explain the services on offer via what feels like a Vodafone live service. Viewers appear to pay more attention during interactive TV commercial breaks. MTV ran a classic arcade game – Pong – during the ad breaks on its channels in 2002 and invited viewers to play. Players accumulated points but those who switched channels lost their scores. Nickelodeon ran the Sabina Magic Spell game which offered a prize for viewers who could recall the sequence in which icons appeared in order to keep viewers tuned in during the peak viewing time and to reduce channel-hopping. The channel reported a drop in the proportion of viewers 'zapping' from 33 per cent to 20 per cent over a four-week period. Advertisers who use iTV state that interactivity follows similar rules to direct-response TV. While ads aired during daytime and peak times generate more response, those shown during lower-rating programmes were also consistently successful. Some advertisers argue that pressing the red button is more effective than a telephone call to action. Yet others have found that the rate of response via interactive TV was nine times higher than via a phone number.[30]

Home-shopping channels, another form of direct-response television marketing, are TV programmes or entire channels dedicated to selling goods and services. The programmes offer bargain prices on products ranging from jewellery, lamps, collectible dolls and clothing, to power tools and consumer electronics – usually obtained by the home-shopping channel at close-out prices. The presentation of products is upbeat and a theatrical atmosphere is created, often with the help of celebrity guests, and up-to-date information can be given on product availability, creating further buying excitement. QVC and other TV shopping channels are now operating in Europe. These compete with large European electronic home-shopping businesses such as TV Shop. TV Shop operates across Europe, of which Germany is the biggest market. While infomercials account for some 60 per cent of the firm's turnover, its activities are wide ranging. It produces commercial videos and TV programmes, operates a Swedish shopping channel, and runs electronic shopping malls as well as other Internet-based sales operations in Europe.

Access to TV shopping channels has been restricted to homes with satellite or cable TV. In Europe, the Netherlands, Belgium, Luxembourg and Germany lead in terms of household penetration of cable systems. However, over the next few years, the reach of TV shopping channels will increase as the cable and satellite market grows. TV shopping channel operators believe that countries such as the United Kingdom, France, Spain and Italy, with a lower level of satellite and cable penetration, offer great potential for growth.[31]

Integrated direct marketing

Too often, a company's individual direct marketing efforts are not well integrated with one another or with other elements of its marketing and promotion mixes. For example, a firm's media advertising may be handled by the advertising department working with a traditional advertising agency. Meanwhile, its direct mail and catalogue business activities may be handled by direct marketing specialists while its website is developed and operated by an outside Internet firm. Even within a given direct marketing campaign, too many companies use a 'one-shot' approach to reach and sell a prospect or a single vehicle in multiple stages to trigger purchases.

A more powerful approach is **integrated direct marketing**, which involves using multiple-vehicle, multiple-stage campaigns to improve response. Whereas a direct-mail piece alone might generate a 2 per cent response, adding a website and freephone number can raise the response rate by 50 per cent to a 3 per cent response. A well-designed outbound telemarketing effort might multiply the response rate by 500 per cent. Suddenly a 2 per cent response has grown to 15 per cent or more by adding interactive marketing channels to a regular mailing.

More elaborate integrated direct-marketing campaigns can be used. Consider the following multimedia, multistage marketing campaign:

Paid ad with a response channel	→	Direct mail	→	Outbound telemarketing	→	Face-to-face sales call

Here, the paid ad to target customers creates product awareness and stimulates enquiries. The company immediately sends direct mail to those who enquire. Within a few days, the company follows up with a phone call seeking an order. Some prospects will order by phone or via the firm's website; others might request a face-to-face sales call. In such a campaign, the marketer seeks to improve response rates and profits by adding media and stages that contribute more to additional sales than to additional costs.

Public policy and ethical issues in direct marketing

Direct marketers and their customers usually enjoy mutually rewarding relationships. Occasionally, however, a darker side emerges. The aggressive and sometimes shady tactics of a few direct marketers can bother or harm consumers, giving the entire industry a black eye. Abuses range from simple excesses that irritate consumers to instances of unfair practices or even outright deception and fraud. The direct marketing industry has also faced growing concerns about invasion-of-privacy issues.[32]

Integrated direct marketing—Direct marketing campaigns that use multiple vehicles and multiple stages to improve response rates and profits.

Irritation, unfairness, deception and fraud

Direct marketing excesses sometimes annoy or offend consumers. Most of us dislike direct-response TV commercials that are too loud, too long and too insistent. Especially bothersome are dinner-time or late-night phone calls. Beyond irritating consumers, some direct marketers have been accused of taking unfair advantage of impulsive or less sophisticated buyers. TV shopping shows and programme-long 'infomercials' seem to be the worst culprits. They feature smooth-talking hosts, elaborately staged demonstrations, claims of drastic price reductions, 'while they last' time limitations, and unequalled ease of purchase to inflame buyers who have low sales resistance.

Worse yet, so-called 'heat merchants' design mailings and write copy intended to mislead buyers. Other direct marketers pretend to be conducting research surveys when they are actually asking leading questions to screen or persuade consumers. Fraudulent schemes, such as investment scams or phoney collections for charity, have also multiplied in recent years. Crooked direct marketers can be hard to catch: direct marketing customers often respond quickly, do not interact personally with the seller, and usually expect to wait for delivery. By the time buyers realise that they have been duped, the thieves are usually somewhere else, plotting new schemes.

Invasion of privacy

Invasion of privacy is perhaps the toughest public policy issue now confronting the direct marketing industry. These days, it seems that almost every time consumers order products by mail or telephone, enter a sweepstake, apply for a credit card or take out a magazine subscription, or order products by mail, telephone or the Internet, their names are entered into some company's already bulging database. Using sophisticated computer technologies, direct marketers can use these databases to 'microtarget' their selling efforts.

Consumers benefit from such database marketing if they receive more offers that are closely matched to their interests. However, many critics worry that marketers may know *too* much about consumers' lives, and that they may use this knowledge to take unfair advantage of consumers. At some point, they claim, the extensive use of databases intrudes on consumer privacy.

For example, they ask, should telecom network operators be allowed to sell marketers the names of customers who frequently call the freephone numbers of, say, catalogue companies? Should a credit card company such as Mastercard, Visa or American Express be allowed to make data on its millions of cardholders available to merchants who accept its card? Is it right for credit bureaux to compile and sell lists of people who have recently applied for credit cards – people who are considered prime direct-marketing targets because of their spending behaviour?

In their drives to build databases, companies sometimes get carried away. For example, Microsoft caused substantial privacy concerns when it introduced its Windows 95 software. It used a 'Registration Wizard' which allowed users to register their new software online. However, when users went online to register, without their knowledge Microsoft 'read' the configurations of their PCs to learn about the major software products running on each customer's system. When users learned of this invasion, they protested loudly and Microsoft abandoned the practice.[33] Such access to and use of information has caused much concern and debate among companies, consumers and public policy makers.

The direct marketing industry in a number of countries is addressing issues of ethics and public policy. For example, in the United Kingdom, faced with the threat of legislation, including wider EU directives, the industry has adopted tougher self-regulation measures to restrain unsavoury practices and to bring the 'cowboys' into line. In many countries, consumer privacy has become a major regulatory issue. To build consumer confidence in shopping direct, associations for businesses practising interactive and database marketing have launched consumer privacy rules. These rules generally require that their members adhere to a carefully developed set of consumer privacy rules: members must notify customers when any personal information is rented, sold or exchanged with others; they must also honour consumer requests to 'opt out' of information exchanges with other marketers or not to receive mail, telephone or other solicitations again; and to honour consumer requests to remove their names from the company's database, when they do not wish to receive mail or telephone offers at home. Similarly, new regulations based on the new European Union Directive on Privacy and Electronic Communications, which came into force in October 2003, seek to outlaw spam. Companies will be required to ask customers to 'opt-in' to receiving emails, failing which they can be penalised for breaking the rules.[34]

Direct marketers know that, left untended, unethical conduct will lead to increasingly negative consumer attitudes, lower response rates, and calls for more restrictive legislation. More importantly, most direct marketers want the same things that consumers want: honest and well-designed marketing offers targeted only towards consumers who will appreciate and respond to them. Direct marketing is just too expensive to waste on consumers who don't want it.

Mass marketers have typically tried to reach millions of buyers with a single product and a standard message communicated via the mass media. Consequently, most mass-marketing communications were one-way communications directed *at* consumers rather than two-way communications *with* consumers. Today, many companies are turning to direct marketing in an effort to reach carefully targeted customers more efficiently and to build stronger, more personal, one-to-one relationships with them.

Summary

Personal selling and direct marketing are both direct tools for communicating with and persuading current and prospective customers. Selling is the interpersonal arm of the communications mix. To be successful in personal selling, a company must first build and then manage an effective sales force. Firms must also be good at direct marketing, the process of forming one-to-one connections with customers. Today, many companies are turning to direct marketing in an effort to reach carefully targeted customers more efficiently and to build stronger, more personal, one-to-one relationships with them.

People who do the selling are called by a variety of names, including salespeople, sales representatives, account executives, sales consultants, sales engineers, agents, district managers and marketing representatives. Regardless of their titles, members of the sales force play a key role in modern marketing organisations.

Most companies use salespeople, and many companies assign them the key role in the marketing mix. For companies selling business products, the firm's salespeople work directly with customers. Often, the sales force is the customer's only direct contact with the company and, therefore, may be viewed by customers as representing the company itself. In contrast, for consumer product companies that sell through intermediaries, consumers usually do not meet salespeople or even know about them. But the sales force works behind the scenes, dealing with wholesalers and retailers to obtain their support and helping them become effective in selling the firm's products.

As an element of the marketing mix, the sales force is very effective in achieving certain marketing objectives and carrying out such activities as prospecting, communicating, selling and servicing, and information gathering. But with companies becoming more market oriented, a market-focused sales force also works to produce *customer satisfaction* and *company profit.* To accomplish these goals, the sales force needs skills in marketing analysis and planning in addition to the traditional selling skills.

The high cost of the sales force calls for an effective *sales management process* consisting of six steps: setting sales force objectives; designing sales force strategy, structure, size and compensation; recruiting and selecting; training; supervising; and evaluating.

In designing a sales force, sales management must address issues such as what type of sales force structure will work best (territorial, product, customer or complex structured); how large the sales force should be; who should be involved in the selling effort; and how its various sales and sales-support people will work together (inside or outside and team selling). Sales management must also decide how the sales force should be compensated in terms of salary, commissions, bonuses, expenses and fringe benefits.

To hold down the high costs of hiring the wrong people, salespeople must be *recruited* and *selected* carefully. In recruiting salespeople, a company may look to job duties and the characteristics of its most successful salespeople to suggest the traits it wants in its sales force. *Training* programmes familiarise new salespeople not only with the art of selling, but with the company's history, its products and policies, and the characteristics of its market and competitors. All salespeople need *supervision*, and many need continuous encouragement in view of the many decisions they have to make and the many frustrations they invariably face. Periodically, the company must *evaluate* their performance to help them do a better job. Salespeople evaluation relies on information regularly gathered through sales reports, personal observations, customers' letters and complaints, customer surveys and conversations with other salespeople.

The art of selling involves a seven-step *selling process*: *prospecting and qualifying*, *pre-approach*, *approach*, *presentation and demonstration*, *handling objections*, *closing* and *follow-up*. These steps help marketers close a specific sale and, as such, tend to be *transaction-oriented*. However, a seller's dealings with customers should be guided by the larger concept of *relationship marketing*. The company's sales force should help to orchestrate a whole-company effort to develop profitable long-term relationships with key customers based on superior customer value and satisfaction.

Next, we address direct marketing which consists of direct connections with carefully targeted individual consumers to both obtain an immediate response and cultivate lasting customer relationships. Using detailed databases, direct marketers tailor their offers and communications to the needs of narrowly defined segments or even individual buyers.

For buyers, direct marketing is convenient, easy to use and private. It gives them ready access to a wealth of products and information, at home and around the globe. Direct marketing is also immediate and interactive, allowing buyers to create exactly the configuration of information, products or services they desire, then order them on the spot. For sellers, direct marketing is a powerful tool for building customer relationships. Using database marketing, today's marketers can target small groups or individual consumers, tailor offers to individual needs, and promote these offers through personalised communications. It also offers them a low-cost, efficient alternative for reaching their markets. As a result of these advantages to both buyers and sellers, direct marketing has become a fast-growing form of marketing.

We identified the main forms of direct marketing – *personal selling*, *telephone marketing*, *direct-mail marketing*, *catalogue marketing*, *direct-response television marketing* and *online marketing*. We discuss personal selling in the first part of this chapter and examined online marketing in detail in Chapter 4. *Telephone marketing* consists of using the telephone to sell directly to consumers. *Direct-mail marketing* consists of the company sending an offer, announcement, reminder or other item to a person at a specific address. Recently, three new forms of mail delivery have become popular – *fax mail*, *email* and *voice mail*. Some marketers rely on *catalogue marketing*, or selling through catalogues mailed to a select list of customers or made available in stores. *Direct-response television marketing* has two forms: *direct-response advertising* or *infomercials*, and *home shopping channels*. *Online marketing*, discussed in Chapter 4, involves online channels and e-commerce, which electronically link consumers with sellers.

Finally, direct marketers have to address a variety of public policy and ethical issues. Direct marketers and their customers have typically forged mutually rewarding relationships. However, there remains a potential for customer abuse, ranging from irritation and unfair practices to deception and fraud. There also have been growing concerns about invasion of privacy, perhaps the most difficult public policy issue currently facing the direct marketing industry.

Discussing the issues

1. One of the most pressing issues that sales managers face is how to structure salespeople and their tasks. Evaluate the methods described in the text. For each method, provide (a) a brief description of its chief characteristics, (b) an example of how it is used, and (c) a critique of its effectiveness.

2. Telemarketing and Web-based selling provide marketers with opportunities to reach customers at work and in their homes. Critique each of these approaches, discussing the

advantages and disadvantages of each. Provide an example of product or service marketing that uses each approach and discuss how the selling process works in these examples.

3. List and briefly describe the steps involved in the personal selling process. Which step do you think is most difficult for the average salesperson? Which step is the most critical to successful selling? Which step do you think is usually done most correctly? Explain each of your choices.

4. Make a list of products or services that you have purchased via direct marketing channels. What were the factors that influenced your decision to buy direct? If these products or services could also be purchased from a reseller or retail outlet, would the buying experience be different? How?

5. Companies that know about individual customer needs and characteristics can customise their offers, messages, delivery modes and payment methods to maximise customer value and satisfaction. Select an organisation that operates within each of the following sectors: (a) home insurance, (b) computers, (c) charity, (d) automotive, and (e) personal finance. What information should these organisations keep in their customer databases? Where would they get this information? How might they use the databases? How much would it cost to build such databases?

Applying the concepts

1. Helen Adolph was excited about her new job as a personal communication consultant for Nokia (www.nokia.com), the giant phone producer that captures a quarter of the global market and half the profits. Rivals such as Ericsson (www.ericsson.com), Siemens (www.siemens.com), Samsung (www.samsung.com) and Motorola (www.motorola.com) have vowed to make things tougher for Nokia in the years ahead. For more information about these manufacturers, please visit their websites. They've developed new designs, communications applications and strategic alliances between hardware and software makers in an effort to lure fickle consumers away from Nokia.

   (a) Adolph is attempting to sell Nokia's latest model of personal communication device to Shell Oil in the UK (several thousand phones). What sales strategy and plan should Adolph recommend? In your answer, consider the advantages and disadvantages of Nokia's product.

   (b) Would you recommend that Nokia employ individual selling or team selling? Explain.

   (c) Which step of the sales process do you think will be most critical to Adolph's success?

   (d) What could Adolph do to establish a strong relationship with local Shell representatives?

2. Watch a satellite or cable television shopping channel or tune into a television shopping show. Where feasible, you might surf the Internet and 'tour' a specialist retailer's site. Or you might sample Virgin's radio station by clicking on icons, accessing features such as playlists and DJ biographies.

   (a) How are the TV shows attempting to reach target buyers? Do they mix product lines (e.g. fine china with sports equipment) or do they target more carefully?

   (b) How do online communications attempt to reach target buyers?

   (c) What are the main differences in the way the TV shopping channels and Internet retailers attempt to evoke a response from target consumers?

References

1. Based on Mogens Bjerré, 'MD Foods AMBA: a new world of sales and marketing', in Celia Phillips, Ad Pruyn and Marie-Paule Kestemont (eds), *Understanding Marketing: A European casebook* (Chichester, UK: © John Wiley & Sons Ltd, 2000), pp. 30–41. Reproduced with permission.

2. See David Jobber and Geoff Lancaster, *Selling and Sales Management*, 6th edn (Harlow: FT/Prentice-Hall, 2003).

3. Charles Fleming and Leslie Lopez, 'The corporate challenge – no boundaries: ABB's dramatic plan is to recast its structure along global lines', *Wall Street Journal* (28 September 1998), p. R16; further information can be accessed online at www.abb.com; see also Emin Babakus, David W. Cravens, Ken Grant, Thomas N. Ingram and Raymond W. LaForge, 'Investigating the relationships among sales, management control, sales territory design, salesperson performance, and sales organisation effectiveness', *International Journal of Research in Marketing*, **13**, 2 (October 1996), pp. 345–60.

4. Melinda Ligos, 'The incredible shrinking sales force', *Sales and Marketing Management* (December 1998), p. 15.

5. Amaya Guillerma, 'A league of their own', *Connectis* (Issue 5, October 2000), p. 22; 'Negotiating by e-mail', *The Economist* (8 April 2000), p. 85.

6. Richard C. Whiteley, 'Orchestrating service', *Sales and Marketing Management* (April 1994), pp. 29–30.

7. For more discussion of key account management, see Peter Cheverton, *Key Account Management*, 2nd edn (London: Kogan Page, 2001) and Malcolm McDonald, Beth Rogers and Diana Woodburn, *Key Customers: How to manage them profitably* (Oxford: Butterworth-Heinemann, 2000).

8. Thomas R. Wotruba and Pradeep K. Tyagi, 'Met expectations and turnover in direct selling', *Journal of Marketing* (July 1991), pp. 24–35; and Chad Kaydo, 'Overturning turnover', *Sales and Marketing Management* (November 1997), pp. 50–60.

9. Erika Rasmusson, 'The 10 traits of top salespeople', *Sales and Marketing Management* (August 1999), pp. 34–7; Andy Cohen, 'The traits of great sales forces', *Sales and Marketing Management* (October 2000), pp. 67–72.

10. See Robert G. Head, 'Systemizing salesperson selection', *Sales and Marketing Management* (February 1992), pp. 65–8; 'To test or not to test', *Sales and Marketing Management* (May 1994), p. 86.

11. See 'To test or not to test', *Sales and Marketing Management* (May 1994), p. 86; Elena Harris, 'Reduce recruiting risks', *Sales and Marketing Management* (May 2000), p. 18; and Erin Stout, 'Recruiting and hiring for less', *Sales and Marketing Management* (May 2002), p. 61.

12. Geoffrey Brewer, 'Brain power', *Sales and Marketing Management* (May 1997), pp. 39–48; Don Peppers and Martha Rogers, 'The money trap', *Sales and Marketing Management* (May 1997), pp. 58–60; Don Peppers and Martha Rogers, 'The price of customer service', *Sales and Marketing Management* (April 1999), pp. 20–1; Erin Stout, 'Is your pay plan on target?', *Sales and Marketing Management* (January 2002), p. 18.

13. Amy J. Morgan and Scott A. Inks, 'Technology and the sales force: increasing acceptance of sales force automation', *Industrial Marketing Management* (July 2001), pp. 463–72; Eilene Zimmerman, 'Casting the net wide', *Sales and Marketing Management* (April 2002), pp. 50–6; Melinda Ligos, 'Point, click and sell', *Sales and Marketing Management* (May 1999), pp. 51–6.

14. Stephen B. Castleberry and C. David Shepherd, 'Effective interpersonal listening and personal selling', *Journal of Personal Selling and Sales Management* (Winter 1993), pp. 35–49; John F. Yarbrough, 'Toughing it out', *Sales and Marketing Management* (May 1996), pp. 81–4.

15. Betsey Cummings, 'Do customers hate salespeople?', *Sales and Marketing Management* (June 2001), pp. 44–51; Rosemary P. Ramsey and Ravipreet S. Sohi, 'Listening to your customers: the impact of perceived salesperson listening behavior on relationship outcomes', *Journal of Academy of Marketing Science* (Spring 1997), pp. 127–37.

16. Diane Summers, 'Hitching a ride on the corporate gravy train', *Financial Times* (24 October 1994), p. 7.

17. Emma Charlton, 'Business-to-business online exchanges. A case of first come, first served', FT-IT Review, Manufacturing in the Internet age, *Financial Times* (1 November 2000), p. II; Andrew Baxter,

'Internet heralds new era of collaboration', *ibid.*, p. V; additional information on B2B exchanges accessed at www.ft.com/ftit.

18. Based on statistics presented in 'Pan-European: Media. Direct Marketing expenditure', *The European Marketing Pocket Book* (Henley-on-Thames: World Advertising Research Centre (WARC), 2004), p. 34; for direct-marketing statistics in the US, visit www.the-dma.org/cgi/; see also 'Hi ho, hi ho, down the data mine we go', *The Economist* (23 August 1997), pp. 55–6.

19. Tom Peters, *Thriving on Chaos* (New York: Knopf, 1987).

20. David Murphy, 'The truth about CRM', *Marketing Business* (February 2004), pp. 29–33; for further information about customer database management and CRM systems, visit www.crm-forum.com; www.crmcommunity.com; see also the FT online supplement to explore the challenges involved in setting up CRM projects, available at www.ft.com/understandingcrm, accessed on 26 February 2004.

21. For more discussion of database marketing principles and practices, see Alan Tapp, *Principles of Direct and Database Marketing* (Harlow: FT/Prentice-Hall, 2000).

22. A. Burnside, 'Calling the shots', *Marketing* (25 January 1990), p. 40; Anne Massey, 'Ring my bell', *Marketing Business* (June 1992), pp. 35–9; Kevin R. Hopkins, 'Dialing into the future', *Business Week* (28 July 1997), p. 90.

23. See Martin Everett, 'Selling by telephone', *Sales and Marketing Management* (December 1993), pp. 75–9; John F. Yarbrough, 'Dialing for dollars', *Sales and Marketing Management* (January 1997), pp. 61–7.

24. 'Pan-European: Media. Direct Marketing expenditure per capita', *The European Marketing Pocket Book* (Henley-on-Thames: World Advertising Research Centre (WARC), 2004), p. 35. Figures for the US can be found in *Economic Impact: U.S. Direct Marketing Today Executive Survey*, Direct Marketing Association, 2002. Also see Cara B. Dipasquale, 'Direct-mail sector staying the course', *Advertising Age* (11 March 2002), p. 16.

25. Tony Coad, 'Distinguishing marks', *Marketing Business* (October 1992), pp. 12–14.

26. Hallie Mummert, 'The year's best bells and whistles', *Target Marketing* (November 2000), pp. TM3–TM5; and Susan Reda, 'Software package seeks to revive CD-ROMs as consumer marketing technology', *Stores* (November 2000), pp. 66–70.

27. Constance Legrand, 'A marriage made in cyber-heaven', *Connectis* (October 2000), pp. 40–1.

28. 'DMA study shows the Internet generates 13 per cent of catalog sales', DMA press release (4 June 2001), accessed online at www.the-dma.org/cgi/disppressrelease?article=102++++++.

29. See Martin Croft, 'Right to reply', *Marketing Week* (12 April 1996), pp. 37–42; Paul Gander, 'Tele vision', *Marketing Week* (23 August 1996), pp. 29–34; David Reed, 'Double vision', *Marketing Week* (17 April 1997), pp. 59–62.

30. Alastair Ray, 'Press the red button', *Marketing Business* (April 2003), pp. 29–30; Bill Clash, 'Beyond the red button', accessed at www.partnersin.tv/benefits.asp.

31. For more information on satellite and cable household penetration rates in European countries, see *The European Marketing Pocket Book 2004* (Henley-on-Thames: World Advertising Research Centre (WARC), 2004). See also Frank Rose, 'The end of TV as we know it', *Fortune* (23 December 1996), pp. 58–68; Elizabeth Lesly and Robert D. Hof, 'Is digital convergence for real?', *Business Week* (23 June 1997), pp. 42–3.

32. See Katie Muldoon, 'The industry must rebuild its image', *Direct* (April 1995), p. 106.

33. 'Hi ho, hi ho, down the data mine we go', op. cit.; John Hagel III and Jeffrey F. Rayport, 'The coming battle for customer information', *Harvard Business Review* (January–February 1997), pp. 53–65.

34. 'EU rules aim to outlaw spam', *Marketing Business* (May 2003), p. 4; see also www.informationcommissioner.gov.uk for more information on the British government's Information Commissioner's powers to investigate companies that send spam.

WEB RESOURCES

For additional classic case studies and Internet exercises, visit www.pearsoned.co.uk/kotler

Concluding concepts 19
Britcraft Jetprop: whose sale is it anyhow?*

On 14 April 1997, Bob Lomas, sales administration manager at Britcraft Civil Aviation (BCA), received a telephone call from Wing Commander Weir, the air attaché for the United Kingdom in a European nation. The wing commander had found out that the national air force (NAF) of the European nation (hereafter Country) was looking for a lighter, utility/transport aircraft to replace its ageing freight/transport aircraft for intra-European operations. The air attaché thought the Britcraft Jetprop, BCA's top-selling aircraft, was a suitable candidate.

Britcraft Aviation

Britcraft Aviation is owned by Britcraft Group Ltd, a British company with global engineering interests. Before being bought by Britcraft, BCA was a differently named independent company, known for designing and producing many famous military aircraft in the past. Military and executive aircraft were sold by Britcraft Military Aviation (BMA) and Britcraft Executive Aviation (BEA), located at a different site from that of the civil division.

The Jetprop's major rival was a similar aircraft made by Fokker, a Dutch company that was Britcraft's main competitor. The Jetprop was designed as a regional airliner, particularly for developing countries. Unlike the Fokker, the Jetprop was a low-winged aircraft, with an unobstructed passenger area, which gave it aerodynamic, structural and maintenance advantages. All components used on auxiliary services were selected for proven reliability, long overhaul life and ease of provisioning, enabling the aircraft to achieve the primary design objective of low maintenance costs and high operator utilisation. The aircraft was fully fail-safe, whereby any failure due to fatigue developed sufficiently slowly for it to be detected during routine inspection before it became dangerous. The Jetprop also gave short take-off and landing (STOL) performance from semi-prepared runways. The primary design objectives remained the main selling features of the aircraft.

Sales organisation

BCA's sales organisation, which covered civil and military sales, was responsible for selling the Jetprop. A number of these sales became VIP transports for heads of state. Each year, markets were analysed and a list was made of the most likely sales prospects for the coming 12 months. Area sales managers received 'designated

areas' comprising several prospective customers grouped geographically. There were exceptions due to special relationships that a salesperson had developed in the past. With time, new prospects were added to the designated areas.

Doug Watts, whose designated area included the air forces of Malaysia, Thailand, Zaïre (now the Democratic Republic of Congo) and Germany, was the area sales manager eventually responsible for the NAF prospect. Like several other area sales managers, he had joined Britcraft after a distinguished career in the UK's Royal Air Force (RAF). A few area sales managers without RAF experience had previously worked in the company's technical departments. The Sales Department had a very high status in the company, occupying a series of ground-floor offices at the front of the Jetprop factory.

> The aircraft was fully fail-safe, and gave short take-off and landing performance.

The sales engineers were all technically qualified, a number having postgraduate degrees. They were responsible for providing technical support to the Sales Department and did considerable routine work associated with the sales effort. Although they were not working directly for the area sales managers, their work usually related to one part of the world, requiring frequent contact with one or two people in the Sales Department, which was located close to the Sales Engineering Department.

Ian Crawford, the marketing director of Britcraft, worked at Britcraft's HQ in London. He was responsible for marketing for the whole of Britcraft Aviation in the United Kingdom and overseas. He also managed Britcraft Aviation's regional executives – senior executives strategically based to cover all the world's markets.

The opening phase

After receiving the telephone call from Wing Commander Weir, Bob Lomas circulated news of the prospect. Doug Watts took overall responsibility for it. Although BCA had agents in the Country, these had either not heard of the NAF requirement or failed to tell the company about it. BCA therefore made direct contact with the national

---

*This case is based on in-company records and documents. For this reason the identity of the buyer and the seller and the names of the people in the case are disguised.

authorities in the Country. Following a visit to Herr Hans Schijlter, the defence secretary, Bob Lomas sent copies of the standard Jetprop military brochure directly to the Ministry of Defence. Lieutenant Colonel Schemann, junior defence secretary, acknowledged its receipt. The next contact made was with Lieutenant General Baron von Forster, defence attaché to the Country's embassy in London, whom Bob Lomas had met at the Hanover Air Show. The general confirmed the NAF's interest in new equipment and asked for details of the Jetprop to pass on to the authorities.

On 6 July, Air Commodore Netherton informed John Upton of Britcraft that the NAF probably had a requirement for a state VIP aircraft. The retired RAF air commodore had lived in the capital of the Country for eight years, where he had been responsible for the Queen's Flight. He founded Eilluft AG, a group that dominated civil aircraft maintenance and light aircraft operations in the Country. He was an *ad hoc* agent for the prospective sale of Britcraft's fighter aircraft. As an accredited agent for BMA, he became an agent in the Country for BCA. The sales organisations of BEA, which produced the Britcraft executive jet for VIPs, and BCA were told of the sales opportunity.

In response, Geoff Lancaster, deputy sales manager of BCA, sent copies of the Jetprop brochure to Air Commodore Netherton to pass on to the prospective customer. As the air commodore was not familiar with the Jetprop, a letter enclosed with the brochures outlined some of the selling points (e.g. the size of the accommodation, low price, full galley and toilet facilities, uses short airfields, available credit terms) that he could use. The letter also mentioned that the Country's minister of defence had recently flown in a Jetprop of the Queen's Flight and was favourably impressed.

On 10 July, Air Commodore Netherton met the officer in charge of the Operations Requirements Branch of the NAF, who confirmed plans to replace several types of transport aircraft. Simultaneously, Wing Commander Weir contacted Ron Hill, the executive director of marketing for BCA, requesting the company to contact the Long Term Planning Department of the NAF directly about its requirement. Major Graff or, alternatively, Colonel Beauers and Lieutenant Colonel Horten, were suitable contacts there.

Work in Iran prevented Ron Hill from attending a meeting arranged on behalf of Doug Watts by Brian Cowley, the Jetprop sales manager. Instead, Steve Williams, his executive assistant, took his place. The discussions – between Steve Williams, Air Commodore Netherton, Major Graff (the officer in command of reequipment evaluations) and Lieutenant Colonel Horten (the second in command of the Planning Department) – went well. They noted that the Jetprop was among the

replacements considered. Fokker had, however, already demonstrated its aircraft, which many in the NAF favoured. The final requirement would be for two or three general transport aircraft plus possibly one for the paratroop training school at NAF-Graz. A Short Skyvan had already given a demonstration as a paradrop aircraft and the Canadians wanted to demonstrate their aircraft.

The Jetprop's demonstration to the NAF would be on 20 October. Major Graff asked for further evidence to support the Jetprop. The advantages of the Jetprop over the Fokker aircraft were highlighted, which were lack of bonding and spot welding, no pneumatics, fail-safe design, progressive maintenance and rough-airfield performance. During the visit they met briefly with Colonel Beauers, the officer commanding the Long Term Planning Department, whom Air Commander Netherton had known well for a number of years, but who was soon to move to NATO HQ. After the meeting the air commodore expressed the hope that, provided the presentation in October went well and the NAF wanted the aircraft, the political people would agree to the purchase. He added that the sale of the paradrop aircraft seemed likely to depend upon support from Colonel Smit, the commanding officer of NAF-Graz, while the main issue, he thought, would be the aircraft's ability to operate safely, fully loaded for a parachute-training mission, from the NAF-Graz airstrip, which was grass and only 650 metres long.

Following the visit, Ernie Wentworth, a senior sales engineer, managed the technical selling effort. Through the Sales Department customer specifications engineer, the Production Planning Department was asked for a delivery schedule and the Estimating Department was requested to cost the aircraft. Other technical departments also became involved in supplying cost and performance evaluations. The Contracts Department would finally negotiate a price for the package of aircraft, spares, guarantees, and after-sales services required.

Major Graff later requested details of the take-off and landing performance of the Jetprop at NAF-Graz. Since it was marginal, Air Commodore Netherton concluded that the only course was to convince the airfield's commanding officer to extend the runway.

Before the scheduled demonstration took place, a number of the NAF personnel – Lt Col Horten (chief of Plans and Studies), Lt Col Wabber (chief of Pilot Training), Major Bayer and Major Graff (Plans and Studies) – were invited to attend the UK's biennial Farnborough Air Show where they were entertained by Britcraft. The meeting progressed well. Nine NAF officers visited BCA for the demonstration of the Jetprop in October, including officers from NAF Planning, Plans and Studies, Avionics, Technical Section, Supply/Spares and HQ Transport.

During the visit, technical specialists looked after most of the NAF officers, while the Long Term Planning Department people discussed contractual details. Prices for the basic version and additional options – strengthened floor for cargo operations, and large freight door – were also presented. The cost of avionics, spares and other equipment that allowed the aircraft to perform a wide variety of roles would be additional.

On the whole, the demonstration and presentation went very well, although Major von Betterei, 'from whom it was difficult even to wring a smile', was evidently 'Fokker oriented'. Air Commodore Netherton and he had been able to talk separately with the senior officer present, with whom they had a 'long and useful discussion about compensation'.

The second phase

Compensation or offset is an increasingly common part of large international sales. It usually involves a provision being made for the vendor or the vendor's country to buy goods from the customer's country. The discussion with Colonel Zvinek, of NAF Planning, Plans and Studies, during the demonstration marked the first occasion when offset appeared accompanying the NAF's procurement of transport aircraft.

The BEA advised the BCA that the offset was critical. In the past, the BEA had lost to the French, who offered very high offset, in the sale of two executive jet aircraft to the NAF. Meanwhile, BMA warned BCA not to use any of the compensation it had already earmarked for a possible sale of military trainer aircraft.

Air Commodore Netherton sought clarification from Herr Maximilian, an under-secretary in the Ministry of Economic Affairs, who was responsible for advising the Country's ministerial committee on offset. Herr Maximilian said offset had recently been between 60 and 70 per cent of the value of a contract and had been completed by the delivery date of the last aircraft. He felt that ideally the work should relate directly to the major project being considered, but should not involve the manufacture of main subassemblies such as wings, airframes or engines. He concluded by saying that negotiations were the responsibility of the vendor alone, who should not increase prices as a result of the required activities.

Soon after his visit to Herr Maximilian, the NAF gave the replacement top priority with a schedule for finalising the requirement in March 1998, signing of letter of intent by mid-1998, contract and deposit payment in late 1998 and delivery and full payment in 1999.

Colonel Zvinek, who originally doubted the Jetprop, was converted since the demonstration, together with all the other important NAF officers concerned. All that was necessary was to assemble an acceptable offset.

Some time passed with little further progress being made with the sale. It became evident that Fokker was offering a very substantial offset, aided by its shareholding in Baden GmbH, which owned Nationale Flugzeugwerke AG (NFW), the Country's largest airframe manufacturer, and which already manufactured Fokker parts.

Early in 1998, Kevin Murphy, the contracts manager for BCA, sent a firm proposal to Colonel Zvinek, with the Sales Engineering Department offering new performance and weight information that showed Jetprop in a better light.

Some days later an urgent email came from Roger Woods of Britcraft, who had met Colonel Horten at a cocktail party in the capital, noting that Fokker's exceptional offset looked like losing Britcraft the deal. Air Commodore Netherton talked to Colonel Horten and then confirmed that the offset was 'not big business'. Further, Messrs Jones and Bedwell of BMA, who were in the Country at that time negotiating a large offset deal with the Ministry of Economic Affairs, found that 'offset would not really be involved on such a small order'.

In a subsequent meeting in April 1998, Major Graff informed Air Commodore Netherton that there was a feeling that the Jetprop was inferior to the Fokker on several technical grounds and the price of €13,930,000 compared unfavourably with the Fokker offer. The total cost, including the price of spares, was more than the amount budgeted. A new formal offer of €13,230,000, entailing a reduction in the number of roles the aircraft had to perform, went to the Country before the end of April.

At the Paris Air Show on 13 June, Doug Watts met Major Graff who emphasised that the offset was important, and that the NAF wanted to change the aircraft specifications and a new quotation would be necessary. Steve Williams had left Britcraft, so Geoff Lancaster took over negotiations. Wing Commander Weir was contacted who said he would probably be able to help in arranging some offset deal, but added that diplomatic circles generally felt that it was 'Britain's turn' to obtain a contract.

On 16 July Geoff Lancaster, Major Graff and Air Commodore Netherton visited Herr Maximilian at the Ministry of Economic Affairs. Four alternative offset arrangements were discussed:

1. Bought-out equipment for the Jetprop could be purchased from the Country's firms.

2. Basic aircraft could be flown to the Country to be finished and new avionics fitted by a NAF contractor.

3. Britcraft's vendors could subcontract work into the Country.

4. The Country's industry could build a future batch of Jetprops.

Herr Maximilian's response to the suggestion was not enthusiastic. He underlined his government's concern about offset being related directly to the contract or involving the NAF or the government. He quoted that, in the recent sale of two Boeing aircraft to the Country's national airline, Boeing had agreed to place €30,000,000 of work with the Country's industry in the first year and €150,000,000 over the next 10 years. The figures suggested that the offset was far more than the price of the two aircraft.

After leaving the ministry, Geoff Lancaster told Major Graff the consequence of further delay in placing a firm order. Delays would reduce the likelihood of Britcraft being able to supply at the original price. Several customers were also on the verge of signing contracts for Jetprops. Major Graff worried about the delay, but said there was little he could do. His recommendations for purchase would go on to General Petsch, which would constitute the official NAF requirements. They would then go through a sequence of decision-makers: the air force adviser, the defence secretary, Hans Schijlter, who would examine the report closely but not consider offset, and the minister of defence, the Prime Minister and the minister for economic affairs, would make the final decision. Before Geoff Lancaster left the Country it was agreed to arrange for a group of NAF officers to visit Schiller Aviation, an independent airline which had recently bought some Jetprops. Air Commodore Netherton escorted the group on the visit and later reported that the airline was 'very complimentary' about the aircraft and Britcraft support.

The offset

In an attempt to arrange the necessary offset, several channels were investigated. A team of Britcraft design and production engineers investigated what work could be 'put out' to subcontractors in the Country. Negotiations with a number of companies did not come to fruition. Eventually, a company, Coles & Turf, offered to buy €45,000,000 worth of the Country's goods for a commission of 10 per cent. Britcraft felt that the commission rate requested left no room for them to make a profit on the contract, and eventually got Coles & Turf to agree to €15,000,000 of offset.

On 16 October there came a blow to the NAF deal. A Brazilian operator signed a contract with BCA for six aircraft. This meant that the NAF aircraft would be from the more expensive batch 15 rather than the original

batch 14 and would cost more – €14,700,000. The NAF reluctantly accepted the price increase and signed a letter of intent in November. Roden AG agreed to accept €4,500,000 worth of specified subcontract work.

As April approached, a team at Britcraft was preparing to make a trip to the Country for final negotiations and contract signing. A day before they were due to leave, Dick Drake, the commercial director, received an email from the Country's authorities. It read:

> Department of Economic Affairs urgently expect more precision about your commitment and also a sensible increase of work for national industry. It is quite obvious that the 10 per cent offset is absolutely unsatisfactory. A reply is expected by 29 April.

A copy of the message went to Air Commodore Netherton, to which Dick Drake added:

> It is virtually certain that it will be necessary for me to reply on Friday that we regret we are unable to increase our commitment and the only other offset is that which they already know about from the aero-engine supplier. However, before replying, I would like to know whether Weir still believes it is Britain's turn.

Questions

1. Trace the stages in the buying process and how the Country's interests changed from one stage to the next. Why were the Country's interests changing and was Britcraft keeping pace with the changes?
2. How well did the strengths of the Jetprop match the needs of the NAF?
3. Identify the players in the buying centre and gauge their role and influence. How well did Britcraft manage the complexity of the buying centre and their diverse needs?
4. Discriminate between the sales roles of the people in Britcraft.
5. Did Britcraft's structure help or hinder its sales campaign? How could it be changed for the better?
6. What were Britcraft's main failings and strengths? Do you think it will win the sale or is it too out of touch with the needs of the NAF and the Country's government? What could it do at this late stage? Is it still 'Britain's turn'?

To open a shop is easy; to keep it open is an art.

CONFUCIUS (PHILOSOPHER)

Place

PART eight

Chapter 20 Managing marketing channels

THE FINAL PART of this text addresses the fourth element of the marketing mix – place. It will help you to understand the decisions and actions that companies take in order to bring products and services to customers. It also considers how new information and communication technologies are transforming distribution and retailing functions.

How products and services are delivered to customers for final usage or consumption can make a difference to how customers perceive the quality and value of the overall offering. Speed of delivery, guaranteed supply and availability, convenience to shoppers and so forth can enhance buyer–seller relationships and increase customer satisfaction. Consequently, firms are increasingly paying greater attention to how they manage their distribution or marketing channels to deliver goods and services that customers want at the right time, right place and right price. In **Chapter 20**, our final chapter, we address channel organisations and the functions they perform and show how firms can build more cost-effective routes to serving and satisfying their target markets.

> Keep your shop and your shop
> will keep you.
>
> THOMAS FULLER

Managing marketing channels

Chapter objectives

After reading this chapter, you should be able to:

- Explain why companies use marketing channels and discuss the functions these channels perform.
- Discuss how channel members interact and how they organise to perform the work of the channel.
- Identify the major channel alternatives open to a company and how companies select, motivate and evaluate channel members.
- Discuss the nature and importance of retailers, wholesalers and physical distribution.
- Explain integrated logistics, including how it may be achieved and its benefits to the company.

Mini Contents List

- Prelude case – Dell Corporation
- Introduction
- Supply chains and the value delivery network
- The nature and importance of marketing channels
- Channel behaviour and organisation
- Marketing Insights 20.1 – Mail Box Etc: signed, sealed and delivered
- Channel design decisions
- Channel management decisions
- Marketing logistics and supply chain management
- Channel trends
- Marketing Insights 20.2 – Retail giants: coming to terms with the global marketplace
- Summary
- Concluding concepts 20 – Pieta luxury chocolates

◄ SOURCE: H&M.

Prelude case Dell Corporation

What if a manufacturing company didn't need to have any inventory? Imagine the reduction to cost structure that could be achieved by simply getting rid of the need to carry huge amounts of finished goods on its books – and eliminating the nail-biting stress of waiting until those goods are sold. For Michael Dell, founder and CEO of Austin, Texas-based Dell Corporation, very little imagination is required. He has built a company with annual revenues in excess of $40bn entirely around a vision whereby manufacturing of an individual item does not begin until it has been ordered by a customer. Every single Dell product has an end user's name on it before it even leaves the factory.

> Every single Dell product has an end user's name on it before it even leaves the factory.

Visiting a Dell factory gives you an idea of just how effective Michael Dell has been in executing this supply chain management philosophy. At the company's Irish factory near Limerick, for example, there are 40 doors at one end of the factory that deliver the parts needed to build a variety of products – including desktop computers and servers – and 40 doors at the other end of the factory where the finished goods are dispatched to be delivered to customers. The company never holds more than four hours' worth of parts inventory at any time – and Dell is not even considered to have acquired the parts until the moment they are offloaded from a truck and brought into the factory. The same process is used in Dell operations throughout the world, including the company's showcase factory at its US headquarters in Austin.

After the parts are unloaded, the process of building individual, custom-made systems begins. All the parts that are needed for the assembly of a given system are placed in a plastic box that passes along a conveyor belt and is then routed to an assembler. Each part is scanned – along with a label denoting the name, address and details of the buyer (including the specifications of the system that has been ordered) – so that individual parts are associated with individual systems sold to individual buyers. This means that if a problem with a given part is discovered at any point, the company knows exactly which systems contain that part and can notify the owners about the need for a fix. In addition, it means that if a buyer reports problems, Dell's technical support system can pull up the details of what was installed in the system at the factory, when it was assembled, and by whom.

Over the past year, Dell has started to build products other than desktop, server and notebook computer systems using this method of manufacturing – and recently changed its corporate name (from Dell Computer Corporation to Dell Corporation) to reflect this fact. It is all part of the 'Dell model' that Michael Dell says is just as applicable to manufacturing computer printers, handheld computers and MP3 players as it is to a personal computer. 'If we look across the whole $800bn IT market, we see that there is a kind of standardisation and commoditisation occurring across many different product areas, so we have tried to understand what the best opportunities are for us to deliver value', he said in a recent interview. Mr Dell also said that the direct manufacturing model gave his company an unparalleled insight into the kinds of product areas that his company should move into – as well as those from which it should retreat. 'One of the magic abilities of any great product company is to understand technologies and customer requirements and come up with the perfect combination to solve a problem', said Mr Dell, although he admits that customers sometimes do not realise that they have a problem that technology can solve. 'The customer is not likely to come and say they need a new metallic compound used in the construction of their notebook computer, but they may tell us they need a computer that is really light and rugged. Where some companies fall down is that they get enamoured with the idea of inventing things – and sometimes what they invent is not what people need.' He said that by using the Dell model, he knows very quickly when a product isn't going to sell. 'When we launch a new product, we know within 48 hours whether or not it's going to work', he says. 'We had a Web PC that didn't turn out so well. But if you have no experiments, then you have no success. Occasionally, you just miss.'

Mr Dell concluded that by having a sales, manufacturing and distribution model where the maximum possible number of variables are under its control, the company has been in a position to grow significantly during the recent economic downturn. 'We have a fortunate situation in our business', he said. 'To the extent that there are tensions in the economy, we tend to be a more attractive choice. We have done well in tough economies – and we have a very efficient system that works well in many different economic environments.'

Questions

1. Taking the case of computer products, identify the supply chain for the distribution of these products and explain the channel service needs of customers. To what extent are store- and non-store-based distribution channels alike or different in terms of the channel functions they perform?
2. What are the advantages and disadvantages of the 'Dell model' of sales, manufacturing and distribution?
3. How might Dell sustain its competitive advantage in an increasingly competitive and mature market place? What channel strategies should it consider to enhance its value delivery network? Justify.

SOURCE: This case is a reproduction of Geof Wheelwright, 'Bytes to order', *Financial Times, FT Understanding supply chain execution* (26 November 2003), p. 15.

Introduction

In this chapter, we will examine the last of the marketing mix tools — place. Firms rarely work alone in bringing value to customers. Instead, most are only a single link in a larger supply chain or distribution channel. As such, an individual firm's success depends not only on how well it performs but also on how well its *entire marketing channel* competes with competitors' channels. For example, Mercedes can make the world's best cars but still not do well if its dealers perform poorly in sales and service against the dealers of Ford, Toyota, BMW or Honda. In order to bring value to customers, Mercedes must choose its channel partners carefully and practise sound partner relationship management.

In the first part of this chapter, we address the basics of marketing channel design and channel partner relationship management. Then we will look more deeply into the two major intermediary channel functions, retailing and wholesaling. We investigate the characteristics of different kinds of retailers and wholesalers, the marketing decisions they make and trends for the future. You'll see that the retailing and wholesaling landscapes are changing rapidly to match explosive changes in markets and technology.

Specifically, in this chapter, we examine the following questions concerning marketing channels:

- What is the nature of marketing channels?
- How do channel firms organise to do the work of the channel?
- What problems do companies face in designing and managing their channels?
- What role does physical distribution play in attracting and satisfying customers?
- How are marketing channels changing and what are their implications for marketers?

Most firms cannot bring value to customers by themselves. Instead, they must work closely with other firms in a larger value delivery network. Let us take a look at what is meant by a value delivery network.

Supply chains and the value delivery network

Producing a product or service and making it available to buyers requires building relationships not just with customers, but also with key suppliers and resellers in the company's *supply chain*. This supply chain consists of upstream and downstream partners, including suppliers, intermediaries and even intermediaries' customers.

Upstream from the manufacturer or service provider is the set of firms that supply the raw materials, components, parts, information, finances and expertise needed to create a product or service. Marketers, however, have traditionally focused on the 'downstream' side of the supply chain – on the *marketing channels* or *distribution channels* that look forward towards the customer. Marketing channel partners such as wholesalers and retailers form a vital connection between the firm and its target consumers.

Both upstream and downstream partners may also be part of other firms' supply chains. But it is the unique design of each company's supply chain that enables it to deliver superior value to customers. An individual firm's success depends not only on how well *it* performs but also on how well its entire supply chain and marketing channel competes with competitors' channels.

The term *supply chain* may be too limited – it takes a *make-and-sell* view of the business. It suggests that raw materials, productive inputs and factory capacity should serve as the starting point for market planning. A better term would be *demand chain* because it suggests a *sense-and-respond* view of the market. Under this view, planning starts with the needs of target customers, to which the company responds by organising resources with the goal of building profitable customer relationships.

Even a demand chain view of a business may be too limited, because it takes a step-by-step linear view of purchase–production–consumption activities. With the advent of the Internet, however, companies are forming more numerous and complex relationships with other firms. For example, companies such as Toyota, Mercedes and Ford manage numerous supply chains. They also sponsor or transact on many B2B websites and online purchasing exchanges as needs arise. Like these companies, many large companies today are engaged in building and managing a continuously evolving *value delivery network*.

Value delivery network— A network made up of the company, suppliers, distributors and customers who 'partner' with each other to improve the performance of the entire system.

A **value delivery network** is made up of the company, suppliers, distributors and ultimately customers who 'partner' with each other to improve the performance of the entire system. For example, Palm, the leading manufacturer of handheld devices, manages a whole community of suppliers and assemblers of semiconductor components, plastic cases, LCD displays and accessories, of offline and online resellers, and of 45,000 complementors who have created over 5,000 applications for the Palm operating systems. All of these diverse partners must work effectively together to bring superior value to Palm's customers.

This chapter focuses on marketing channels – on the downstream side of the value delivery network. However, it is important to remember that this is only part of the full value network. To bring value to customers, companies need upstream supplier partners just as they need downstream channel partners. To provide banking services, for example, HSBC buys equipment and supplies such as automated teller machines (ATMs), printed deposit slips and computers. To make its services available to customers and obtain information about customer transactions, the bank maintains a distribution channel consisting of company-owned bank branches and websites as well as thousands of ATMs owned by other banks. Increasingly, marketers are participating in and influencing their company's upstream activities as well as its downstream activities. More than marketing channel managers, they are becoming full network managers.

The nature and importance of marketing channels

Marketing channel (distribution channel)— A set of interdependent organisations involved in the process of making a product or service available for use or consumption by the consumer or industrial user.

Few producers sell their goods directly to the final users. Instead, most use third parties or intermediaries to bring their products to market. They try to forge a **marketing channel** (or **distribution channel**) – a set of interdependent organisations involved in the process of making a product or service available for use or consumption by the consumer or business user.[1] The channel of distribution is therefore all those organisations through which a product must pass between its point of production and consumption.[2]

A company's channel decisions directly affect every other marketing decision. The company's pricing depends on whether it uses mass merchandisers or high-quality speciality stores. The firm's sales force and advertising decisions depend on how much persuasion, training and motivation the dealers or resellers need. Whether a company develops or acquires certain new products may depend on how well those products fit the abilities of its channel members.

Companies often pay too little attention to their distribution channels, however, sometimes with damaging results. In contrast, many companies have used imaginative distribution systems to *gain* a competitive advantage. For example, the creative and imposing distribution system created by FedEx made it a leader in the small-package delivery industry. Amazon.com pioneered the delivery of books via the Internet. And Dell Corporation revolutionised its industry by selling personal computers directly to consumers rather than through retail stores. As we saw in the prelude case, an effective supply chain management model lay at the very heart of Dell's success.

Distribution channel decisions often involve long-term commitments to other firms. For example, companies such as BMW, Nokia or McDonald's can easily change their advertising, pricing or promotion programmes. They can scrap old products and introduce new ones as market tastes demand. But when they set up distribution channels through contacts with franchises, independent dealers or large retailers, they cannot readily replace these channels with company-owned stores if conditions change. Therefore, management must design its channels carefully, with an eye on tomorrow's likely selling environment as well as today's.

How channel members add value

Why do producers give some of the selling job to intermediaries? After all, doing so means giving up some control over how and to whom the products are sold. The use of intermediaries results from their greater efficiency in making goods available to target markets. Through their contacts, experience, specialisation and scale of operation, intermediaries usually offer the firm more than it can achieve on its own.

Figure 20.1 shows how using intermediaries can provide economies. Part A shows three manufacturers, each using direct marketing to reach three customers. This system requires nine different contacts. Part B shows the three manufacturers working through one distributor, which contacts the three customers. This system requires only six contacts. In this way, intermediaries reduce the amount of work that must be done by both producers and consumers.

From the economic system's point of view, the role of marketing intermediaries is to convert the assortments of products made by producers into the assortments wanted by consumers. Producers make narrow assortments of products in large quantities, but consumers want broad assortments of products in small quantities. In the marketing channels, intermediaries buy the large quantities of many producers and break them down into the smaller quantities and broader assortments wanted by consumers. As such, intermediaries play an important role in matching supply and demand.

The concept of marketing channels is not limited to the distribution of tangible products. Producers of services and ideas also face the problem of making their output available to target populations. Hotels, banks, airlines and other service providers take great care to make

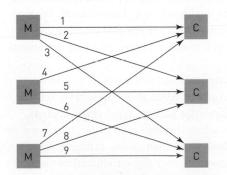

A. Number of contacts without a distributor
$$M \times C = 3 \times 3 = 9$$
M = Manufacturer   C = Customer

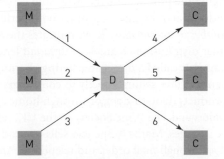

B. Number of contacts with a distributor
$$M + C = 3 + 3 = 6$$
D = Distributor

Figure 20.1 How a marketing intermediary reduces the number of channel transactions and raises economy of effort

their services conveniently available to target customers. Social service organisations and agencies develop 'education delivery systems' and 'healthcare delivery systems' for reaching sometimes widely dispersed populations. Hospitals must be located to serve various patient populations, and schools must be located close to the children who need to be taught. Communities must locate their fire stations to provide rapid response to fires and polling stations must be placed where people can vote conveniently.

In making products and services available to consumers, channel members add value by bridging the major time, place and possession gaps that separate goods and services from those who would use them. Members of the marketing channel perform many key functions. Some help to complete transactions:

- *Information*. Gathering and distributing marketing research and intelligence information about actors and forces in the marketing environment needed for planning and facilitating exchange.
- *Promotion*. Developing and spreading persuasive communications about an offer.
- *Contact*. Finding and communicating with prospective buyers.
- *Matching*. Shaping and fitting the offer to the buyer's needs, including such activities as manufacturing, grading, assembling and packaging.
- *Negotiation*. Reaching an agreement on price and other terms of the offer, so that ownership or possession can be transferred.

Others help to fulfil the completed transactions:

- *Physical distribution*. Transporting and storing goods.
- *Financing*. Acquiring and using funds to cover the costs of the channel work.
- *Risk taking*. Assuming the risks of carrying out the channel work.

The question is not *whether* these functions need to be performed, but rather *who* is to perform them. To the extent that the manufacturer performs these functions, its costs go up and its prices have to be higher. At the same time, when some of these functions are shifted to intermediaries, the producer's costs and prices may be lower, but the intermediaries must charge more to cover the costs of their work. In dividing the work of the channel, the various functions should be assigned to the channel members who can add the most value for the cost.

Number of channel levels

Companies can design their marketing channels to make products and services available to customers in different ways. Each layer of marketing intermediaries that performs some work in bringing the product and its ownership closer to the final buyer is a **channel level**. Because the producer and the final consumer both perform some work, they are part of every channel. The *number of intermediary levels* indicates the *length* of a channel. Figure 20.2A shows several consumer distribution channels of different lengths.

Channel 1, called a **direct-marketing channel**, has no intermediary levels. It consists of a manufacturer selling directly to consumers. For example, Avon and Tupperware sell their products door-to-door or through home and office sales parties. Wine clubs, such as Laithwaites and The Wine Society in the UK, sell their wines through mail order, telephone or at their websites. Marks & Spencer sells its products through its own stores, offline and online, as well as through mail order and telephone. And a university may deliver education on its campus or through distance (or off-campus) learning.

The remaining channels in Figure 20.2A are *indirect*-marketing channels containing one or more intermediaries. Figure 20.2B shows some common business distribution channels. The

Channel level—A layer of intermediaries that performs some work in bringing the product and its ownership closer to the final buyer.

Direct-marketing channel— A marketing channel that has no intermediary levels.

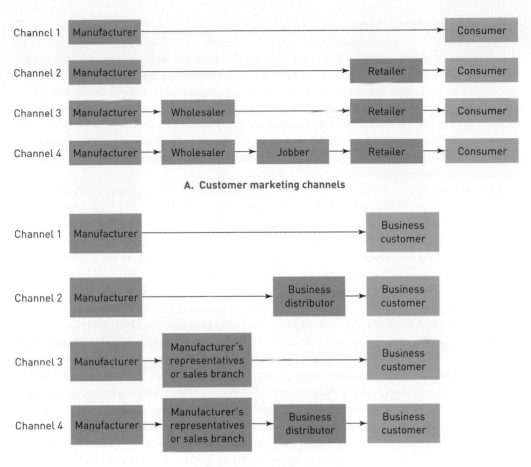

Figure 20.2 **Consumer and business marketing channels**

business marketer can use its own sales force to sell directly to business customers. Or it can sell to various types of intermediaries, who in turn sell to these customers. Consumer and business marketing channels with even more levels are sometimes found, but less often. From the producer's point of view, a greater number of levels means less control and greater channel complexity. Moreover, all of the institutions in the channel are connected by several types of *flows*. These include the *physical flow* of products, the *flow of ownership*, the *payment flow*, the *information flow* and the *promotion flow*. These flows can make even channels with only one or a few levels very complex. The types of intermediary channel will be discussed in greater detail in a later section.

Channel behaviour and organisation

Distribution channels are more than simple collections of firms tied together by various flows. They are complex behavioural systems in which people and companies interact to accomplish individual, company and channel goals. Some channel systems consist only of informal interactions among loosely organised firms, while others consist of formal interactions guided by strong organisational structures. Moreover, channel systems do not stand still – new types of intermediary surface and whole new channel systems evolve. Here we look at channel behaviour and at how members organise to do the work of the channel.

Channel behaviour

A marketing channel consists of firms that have banded together and are dependent on each other to achieve a common goal. For example, a Peugeot dealer depends on the manufacturer to design cars that meet consumer needs. In turn, Peugeot depends on the dealer to attract consumers, persuade them to buy Peugeot cars, and service cars after the sale. The Peugeot dealer also depends on the other dealers to provide good sales and service that will uphold the reputation of Peugeot and its dealer body. In fact, the success of individual Peugeot dealers depends on how well the entire Peugeot marketing channel competes with the channels of other car manufacturers.

Each channel member plays a specialised role in the channel. For example, Philips' role is to produce consumer electronics products that consumers will like and to create demand through national, regional and worldwide advertising. The role of the specialist shops, department stores and other independent outlets that stock and sell Philips' products is to display these items in convenient locations, to answer buyers' questions, to close sales and to provide a good level of customer service. The channel will be most effective when each member is assigned the tasks it can do best.

Ideally, because the success of individual channel members depends on overall channel success, all channel firms should work together smoothly to secure healthy margins or profitable sales. They should understand and accept their roles, coordinate their activities and cooperate to attain overall channel goals. By cooperating, they can more effectively sense, serve and satisfy the target market. Unfortunately, individual channel members rarely take such a broad view. Cooperating to achieve overall channel goals sometimes means giving up individual company goals. Although channel members are dependent on one another, they often act alone in their own short-term best interests. They often disagree on the roles that each should play – that is, on who should do what and for what rewards. Such disagreements over goals, roles and rewards generate **channel conflict**. Conflict can occur at two levels.

Horizontal conflict is conflict among firms at the same level of the channel. For instance, Peugeot dealers in a particular geographic territory may complain that the other dealers in the territory steal sales from them by pricing too low or by selling outside their assigned territories.

Vertical conflict is more common and refers to conflicts between different levels of the same channel. For example, some personal computer manufacturers created conflict with their high street dealers when they opened online stores to sell PCs directly to customers. Dealers, not surprisingly, complained. To resolve the conflict, manufacturers had to develop communication campaigns to educate dealers on how online efforts would assist dealers rather than hurt sales.

Some conflict in the channel takes the form of healthy competition.

Channel conflict—
Disagreement among marketing channel members on goals and roles – who should do what and for what rewards.

Over the past five years, the toy company Lego opened a number of concept stores including licensed children's-wear stores, airport and other shopping stores throughout Europe, park stores in the UK, Denmark and the US, and United Nations-themed stores in the US. Lego management argued that the concept stores are about investing time and effort in inspiring high-street retailers – about setting a standard of retail innovation which ordinary retailers alone would not be able to achieve. Far from being inspired, many of Lego's current retailers objected to the potential impacts on their own businesses. Many were concerned about having to cut price to compete with the stores. Some felt they had been undervalued or devalued as Lego stockists. Lego management were quick to reassure disgruntled channel members that the stores that offer a 'new retail experience' will not at all threaten customer traffic in the conventional retail outlets. The 'Lego store' is about building and sustaining a superior standard for the brand, which in turn promotes the esteem of the company's products for *all* Lego retailers. According to the company, Lego sales within a 50-mile radius of Legoland UK lifted after opening the park store. Lego product sales have risen above industry trends since its Minneapolis store opened. Besides, Lego's strategy has been to build an armoury of retailing experiences which would be transferred to its retail customers through franchise operations. Essentially, both manufacturer and retailer can satisfy consumers more effectively through building upon Lego's tradition for quality, heritage and innovation.

Such competition can be good for the channel – without it, the channel could become passive and non-innovative. But severe or prolonged conflict can disrupt channel effectiveness and cause lasting harm to channel relationships. Companies should manage channel conflict to keep it from getting out of hand.

For the channel as a whole to perform well, each channel member's role must be specified and channel conflict must be managed. The channel will perform better if it includes a firm, agency or mechanism that has the power to assign roles, secure channel cooperation and manage conflict. Let us take a look at how channel members organise to do the work of the channel.

Channel organisation

Historically, marketing channels have been loose collections of independent companies, each showing little concern for overall channel performance. These *conventional distribution channels* have lacked strong leadership and power, often resulting in damaging conflict and poor performance. One of the biggest recent channel developments has been the emergence of *vertical marketing systems* that provide channel leadership.

Vertical marketing systems

Figure 20.3 contrasts the two types of channel arrangement.

A **conventional distribution channel** consists of one or more independent producers, wholesalers and retailers. Each is a separate business seeking to maximise its own profits, even at the expense of profits for the system as a whole. No channel member has much control over the other members and no formal means exists for assigning roles and resolving channel conflict. In contrast, a **vertical marketing system** (VMS) consists of producers, wholesalers and retailers acting as a unified system. One channel member owns the others, has contracts with them, or wields so much power that they must all cooperate. The VMS can be dominated by the producer, wholesaler or retailer.

We now look at the three main types of VMS shown in Figure 20.4. Each type uses a different means for setting up leadership and power in the channel.

Corporate VMS

A **corporate VMS** combines successive stages of production and distribution under single ownership. Coordination and conflict management are attained through regular

---

Conventional distribution channel—A channel consisting of one or more independent producers, wholesalers and retailers, each a separate business seeking to maximise its own profits, even at the expense of profits for the system as a whole.

Vertical marketing system (VMS)—A distribution channel structure in which producers, wholesalers and retailers act as a unified system. One channel member owns the others, has contracts with them, or has so much power that they all cooperate.

Corporate VMS—A vertical marketing system that combines successive stages of production and distribution under single ownership – channel leadership is established through common ownership.

Figure 20.3 A conventional
marketing channel versus a
vertical marketing system

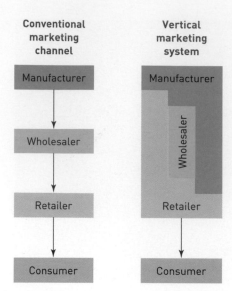

Figure 20.4 Main types of
vertical marketing system

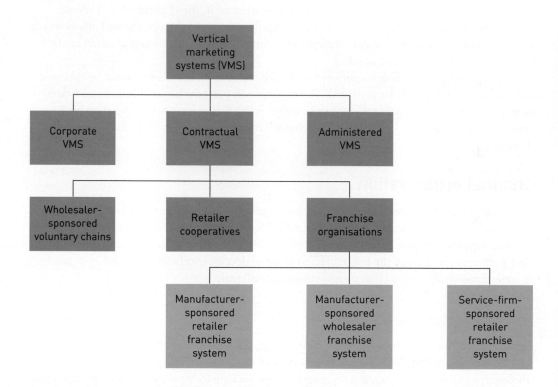

organisational channels. Petrol distribution through chains of petrol stations owned by the oil company is an example of delivery and control achieved by such a system. Breweries that sell beer through public houses under their ownership provide another example. Fashion retailers have also taken advantage of corporate VMS.

By controlling the entire distribution chain, Spanish clothing chain Zara turned into the world's fastest-growing fashion retailer. The secret to Zara's success is its control over almost every aspect of the supply chain, from design and production to its own worldwide distribution network. Zara makes 40 per cent of its own fabrics and produces more than half of its own clothes, rather than relying on a hodgepodge of slow-moving suppliers. New styles take shape in Zara's own design centres, supported by real-time sales data. New designs feed into Zara manufacturing centres, which ship finished products directly to 450 Zara stores in 30 countries, saving time, eliminating the need for warehouses and keeping inventories low. Effective vertical integration makes Zara faster, more flexible and more efficient than international competitors such as Gap, Benetton and Sweden's H&M. Zara can make a new line from start to finish in just three weeks, so a look seen on TV can be in Zara stores within a month, versus an industry average of nine months. And Zara's low costs let it offer midmarket chic at downmarket prices. The company's stylish but affordable offerings have attracted a cult following, and the company's sales have more than doubled to some €2.3 billion in the past five years.[3]

Contractual VMS

A **contractual VMS** consists of independent organisations at different levels of production and distribution who join together through contracts to obtain more economies or sales impact than each could achieve alone. Coordination and conflict management are attained through the legal arrangements agreed among channel members. There are three types of contractual VMS: wholesaler-sponsored voluntary chains, retailer cooperatives and franchise organisations.

In **wholesaler-sponsored voluntary chains**, wholesalers organise voluntary chains of independent retailers to help them compete with large chain organisations. The wholesaler develops a programme in which independent retailers standardise their selling practices and achieve buying economies that let the group compete effectively with chain organisations.

In **retailer cooperatives**, a group of independent retailers band together to own wholesale operations jointly, or to conduct joint wholesaling and possibly production. The Swiss Migros, with its dozen or so cooperatives, and the UK's Cooperative Societies take advantage of group buying and promotion economies through setting up such marketing arrangements. Members buy most of their goods through the retailer co-op and plan their advertising jointly. Profits are passed back to members in proportion to their purchases.

The **franchise** organisation is the most common of the three types of contractual relationship. In a franchise relationship, the franchiser links several stages in the production–distribution system. The franchiser typically provides a brand identity and start-up, marketing and accounting assistance as well as management know-how to the franchisee. In return, the franchiser gets some form of compensation, such as an initial fee and a continuing royalty payment, lease fees for equipment and a share of the profits. For example, the Hong Kong clothing group Esprit Holdings is built on a highly streamlined channel model under which it buys from third-party suppliers in China and sells to franchisees in its target markets throughout Europe, the USA and Asia, thereby minimising its own overheads.[4] Franchising has been a fast-growing retailing form in recent years. Almost every kind of business has been franchised – from hotels and fast-food restaurants to dental and garden maintenance services, from wedding consultants and domestic services to funeral homes and fitness centres.

Franchising offers a number of benefits to both the franchiser and the franchisee. The main advantages for the franchiser are as follows:

- The franchiser secures fast distribution for its products and services without incurring the full costs of setting up and running its own operations. Franchising also enables the franchiser to expand a successful business more rapidly than by using its own capital.

Contractual VMS—A vertical marketing system in which independent firms at different levels of production and distribution join together through contracts to obtain more economies or sales impact than they could achieve alone.

Wholesaler-sponsored voluntary chains—Voluntary chains of independent retailers organised by the wholesaler to help them compete with large chain organisations.

Retailer cooperatives—Contractual vertical marketing systems in which retailers organise a new, jointly owned business to carry on wholesaling and possibly production.

Franchise—A contractual association between a manufacturer, wholesaler or service organisation (a franchiser) and independent businesspeople (franchisees) who buy the right to own and operate one or more units in the franchise system.

- The franchiser gets very highly motivated management as the franchisees are working for themselves rather than a salary.

- The contractual relationship ensures that franchisees operate to and maintain franchisers' standards.

The main advantages for franchisees are as follows:

- They are buying into a proven system if selling an established brand name (e.g. Esprit, McDonald's, Shell, The Body Shop, Interflora).

- They can start a business with limited capital and benefit from the experience of the franchiser. This way they reduce the costs and risks of starting a new business.

- Franchisees also get the benefits of centralised purchasing power – since the franchisers will buy in bulk for the franchisees.

- They get instant expertise in operational issues such as advertising, promotions, accounts and legal matters, and can rely on franchisers' help should things go wrong.

Franchise systems have several disadvantages:

- Franchisers invariably have to forfeit some control when operating through franchisees.

- The franchisees may not all perform exactly to franchisers' operating standards, and inconsistencies in service levels can tarnish the brand name.

- Franchisees may not always have a good deal, in that they have to work extremely hard to meet sales and financial targets to make the business pay, and although they have already paid their initial fee, they have to meet continuing management services or royalty payments.

There are three forms of franchise. The first form is the *manufacturer-sponsored retailer franchise system*, as found in the car industry. BMW, for example, licenses dealers to sell its cars; the dealers are independent businesspeople who agree to meet various conditions of sales and service. Shell, the oil company, adopts a franchising system on many of its petrol forecourts in countries around the world. The French designer garden furniture company Jardin en Plus has relied greatly on franchising to expand into other European markets.

The second type of franchise is the *manufacturer-sponsored wholesaler franchise system*, as found in the soft-drinks industry. Coca-Cola, for example, licenses bottlers (wholesalers) in various markets, which buy Coca-Cola syrup concentrate and then carbonate, bottle and sell the finished product to retailers in local markets. The third franchise form is the *service-firm-sponsored retailer franchise system*, in which a service firm licenses a system of retailers to bring its service to consumers. Examples are found in the car rental business (Hertz, Avis, Europcar), the fast-food service business (Deli France, McDonald's), the hotel business (Holiday Inn, Ramada Inn), and business-to-business services (see Marketing Insights 20.1).

The fact that most consumers cannot tell the difference between contractual and corporate VMSs shows how successfully the contractual organisations compete with corporate chains.

Administered VMS—
A vertical marketing system that coordinates successive stages of production and distribution, not through common ownership or contractual ties, but through the size and power of one of the parties.

Administered VMS

An **administered VMS** coordinates successive stages of production and distribution, not through common ownership or contractual ties, but through the size and power of one or a few dominant channel members. Manufacturers of a top brand can obtain strong trade cooperation and support from resellers. For example, in the fast-moving consumer-goods market, companies like Nestlé, Unilever and Procter & Gamble can command unusual cooperation from resellers regarding displays, shelf space, promotions and price policies. In the consumer electronics sector, Sony can obtain a great deal of trade support from retail stores for its top-selling brands. Similarly, large retailers like IKEA and Wal-Mart can exert strong influence on the manufacturers that supply the products they sell. Consider IKEA.

Mail Box Etc: signed, sealed and delivered

20.1

FT

marketing insights

Imagine you run a small business or you work from home. Wouldn't it be useful to have one person who takes care of all of your document printing, photocopying, packing, packaging, shipping and mailing needs? Indeed, for a growing number of businesses, the answer to this question is 'yes'. Many small and medium-sized companies are seeking to use a 'one-stop shop' that takes away the hassle by coordinating all these activities as well as providing a mail/parcel pick-up and delivery service any time of day. Mail Box Etc (MBE) offers just the solution.

Mail Box Etc hopes to have more of its one-stop-shops, where people can rent mail boxes, print out documents and do their photocopying, springing up on UK high streets soon – and it sees franchising as the way to do it. MBE has a total of 4,500 centres around the world, and is part of UPS, the world's largest package deliverer. The business began 23 years ago in the US – where it has recently been rebranded as 'The UPS Store'. It also has arms in Canada, Italy and elsewhere, operating under different master franchisers.

In Britain, it has 72 high street outlets, and it is looking to expand that number to about 300 main centres. 'We will eventually have a network that will be useable by the majority of the UK population', says Chris Gillam, managing director of MBE in the UK. 'It may include outlets in supermarkets and elsewhere, using a model that is slightly different from the current one.'

MBE specialises in three main areas. It rents out mail boxes, from which people can collect their mail or parcels at any time of the day or night, and it also operates a mail forwarding service. It operates a packing and shipping service that finds the appropriate carrier for a particular job. And the company also provides a photocopying and documents service.

MBE's customers tend to be small and medium-sized businesses, says Mr Gillam – and he points to the increasing number of people who run their own businesses or work from home for all or part of the week as a target market. Mr Gillam says he does not normally seek out potential franchisees – they tend to have an idea about going into franchising, perhaps developed through their bank or accountant, and then find out about Mail Boxes through the franchising press. MBE says its franchisees come from various walks of life – some have moved from financial services backgrounds, and others from sectors as diverse as catering and the armed services.

Although the company likes its new franchisees to have some previous experience in sales or management, it says this is not essential because it provides its own training. Mr Gillam – who is also on the governing board of the British Franchise Association – says one of the great benefits of franchising is that people can get a foothold in an area of business in which they have had no previous experience. Still,

...20.1

the start-up investment for a new MBE centre is some £85,000. About one-third of that is usually provided by the franchisee as liquid cash, while the rest is often borrowed through high street banks. A further working capital provision of between £10,000 and £20,000 is then needed, depending on the part of the country where the business is being set up. And once the new franchise is up and running, the links are maintained. 'We can do a great deal more in ongoing support and improved marketing', Mr Gillam says. MBE is appointing a new advertising agency and providing marketing materials to its franchisees. 'A lot of our business is aimed at small business', he adds. 'So we help franchisees come up with marketing material aimed at particular sectors.'

Those targeted sectors include solicitors and the hotel business. Once the franchisees have the information, they can then use their own databases to target suitable new clients. If, eventually, a franchisee wishes to leave the business – the franchise agreements are for 10 years – MBE also provides help in finding a new franchisee to take over. 'It's a bit like cradle to the grave', Mr Gillam jokes.

SOURCE: Lydia Adetunji, 'Mail Box Etc: New network of one-stop-shops', *Financial Times Special Report: Franchising* (4 June 2003), p. II.

In just over four decades, IKEA, the privately owned Swedish furniture and home furnishings group, grew from a single store in Sweden's backwoods to become one of the most successful international retailers in the world. By 2004, it had 165 stores in 25 countries around the world, excluding some 21 franchises, taking over €11.3 billion of sales in the year to 31 August 2003. Traditionally, selling furniture was a fragmented affair, shared between department stores and small family-owned shops. All sold expensive products and delivered up to two or three months after a customer's order. IKEA, however, sells most of its furniture as knocked-down kits for customers to take home and assemble themselves. IKEA also trims costs to a minimum while still offering products that are durable and distinguished by design and quality. It does this by using global sourcing, working with key suppliers around the world that can supply high-quality raw materials at low prices. In return these suppliers get technical advice and leased equipment from the company. IKEA's designers also work closely with manufacturers to find smart ways to reduce product costs from the outset. Other savings come from the huge economies of scale from operating in cheap out-of-town stores and from enormous production runs made possible by selling the same furniture all around the world. IKEA's success also means success for its suppliers. But they must operate to IKEA's terms and enable the global firm to fulfil its promise of quality merchandise at low cost to customers worldwide.[5]

Firms can secure fast distribution for their products and services without incurring the full costs of setting up and running their own operations. Here, The Body Shop has successfully relied on franchising to expand its business rapidly.
SOURCE: The Body Shop International plc.

Horizontal marketing systems

Another channel development is the **horizontal marketing system**, in which two or more companies at one level join together to follow a new marketing opportunity. By combining their capital, production capabilities or marketing resources, companies can accomplish more than any one company working alone.

Companies might join forces with competitors or non-competitors.[6] They might work with each other on a temporary or permanent basis, or they may even create a separate company. Such channel arrangements also work well globally. For example, because of its excellent coverage of international markets, Nestlé jointly sells General Mills's cereal brands in markets outside North America. Coca-Cola and Nestlé formed a joint venture to market ready-to-drink coffee and tea worldwide. Coke provides worldwide experience in marketing and distributing beverages, and Nestlé contributes two established brand names – Nescafé and Nestea.

Horizontal marketing system—A channel arrangement in which two or more companies at one level join together to follow a new marketing opportunity.

Figure 20.5 Hybrid marketing channel

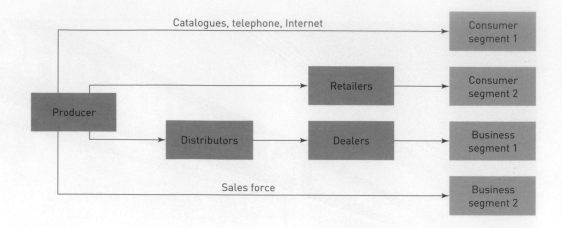

Hybrid marketing systems

In the past, many companies used a single channel to sell to a single market or market segment. Today, with the proliferation of customer segments and channel possibilities, more and more companies have adopted *multi-channel distribution systems* – often called **hybrid marketing channels**. Such multi-channel marketing occurs when a single firm sets up two or more marketing channels to reach one or more customer segments.

Figure 20.5 shows a hybrid channel system. In the figure, the producer sells directly to consumer segment 1 using direct-mail catalogues, telemarketing and the Internet and reaches consumer segment 2 through retailers. It sells indirectly to business segment 1 through distributors and dealers, and to business segment 2 through its own sales force.

Sony maintains a wide distribution coverage by adopting a hybrid marketing system. For example, Sony sells its consumer products through exclusive retail outlets such as the Sony Centres, through mass merchandisers like electrical chain stores (e.g. Comet, Dixons) and catalogue shops (e.g. Index, Argos) and by using direct marketing channels, such as electronic and mail-order catalogues.

Multi-channel distribution systems offer many advantages to companies facing large and complex markets. With each new channel, the company expands its sales and market coverage, and gains opportunities to tailor its products and services to the specific needs of diverse customer segments. But such hybrid channel systems are harder to control, and they generate conflict as more channels compete for customers and sales. For example, when IBM began selling personal computers directly to customers at low prices through catalogues and telemarketing and its own website, many of its dealers cried 'unfair competition' and threatened to drop the IBM line or give it less emphasis. Many outside salespeople felt they were being undercut by the new 'inside channels'.[7]

Changing channel organisation

Changes in technology and the explosive growth of direct and online marketing are having a profound impact on the nature and design of marketing channels. One major trend is towards **disintermediation** – a big term with a clear message and important consequences. Disintermediation means that more and more product and service producers are bypassing intermediaries and going directly to final buyers, or that radically new types of channel intermediaries are emerging to displace traditional ones.

Thus, in many industries, traditional intermediaries are dropping by the wayside. For example, companies like Dell Computer sell directly to final buyers, eliminating retailers from their marketing channels. E-commerce merchants are growing rapidly in number and size, displacing traditional bricks-and-mortar retailers. Today, consumers can buy flowers, books,

Hybrid marketing channels—Multi-channel distribution, as when a single firm sets up two or more marketing channels to reach one or more customer segments. A variety of direct and indirect approaches are used to deliver the firm's goods to its customers.

Disintermediation— The elimination of a layer of intermediaries from a marketing channel or the displacement of traditional resellers by radically new types of intermediaries.

videos, CDs, toys, household products, groceries, clothes, consumer electronics and many other goods and services without ever visiting a store.

Disintermediation presents problems and opportunities for both producers and intermediaries. To avoid being swept aside, traditional intermediaries must find new ways to add value in the supply chain. To remain competitive, product and service producers must develop new channel opportunities, such as the Internet and other direct channels. However, developing these new channels often brings them into direct competition with their established channels, resulting in conflict. To ease this problem, companies often look for ways to make going direct a plus for both the company and its channel partners.

Going direct is rarely an all-or-nothing proposition. For example, to trim costs and add business, Hewlett-Packard opened three direct-sales websites: Shopping Village (for consumers), HP Commerce Centre (for businesses buying from authorised resellers) and Electronic Solutions Now (for existing contract customers). However, to avoid conflicts with its established reseller channels, HP forwards all its Web orders to resellers, who complete the orders, ship the products and get the commissions. In this way, HP gains the advantages of direct selling but also boosts business for resellers.[8]

Channel design decisions

We now look at several channel decisions facing manufacturers. In designing marketing channels, manufacturers struggle between what is ideal and what is practical. A new firm usually starts by selling in a limited market area. Deciding on the *best* channels might not be a problem: the problem might simply be how to convince one or a few good intermediaries to handle the line.

If successful, the new firm might branch out to new markets through existing intermediaries. In smaller markets, the firm might sell directly to retailers; in larger markets, it might sell through distributors. In one part of the country, it might grant exclusive franchises; in another, it might sell through all outlets willing to handle the merchandise. In one country it might use international sales agents; in another, it might partner a local firm. Or it might add a Web store that sells directly to hard-to-reach customers. In this way, channel systems often evolve to meet market opportunities and conditions. However, for maximum effectiveness, channel analysis and decision making should be more purposeful. Designing a channel system calls for:

- Analysing customer service needs
- Defining the channel objectives and constraints
- Identifying the major channel alternatives
- Evaluating those alternatives.

Analysing customer service needs

We noted earlier that marketing channels are part of the overall *customer value delivery network* in which each channel member adds value for the customer. Thus designing the marketing channel starts with finding out what consumers want from the channel. Do customers want to buy from nearby locations or are they willing to travel to more distant, centralised locations? Would they rather buy in person or over the phone, through the mail or via the Internet? Do they value immediate delivery or are they willing to wait? Do they want breadth of assortment or do they prefer specialisation? Do customers want many add-on services (delivery, credit, repairs, installation) or will they obtain these elsewhere? The faster the delivery, the greater the assortment provided, and the more add-on services supplied, the greater the channel's service level.

However, providing the fastest delivery, greatest assortment and most comprehensive services may not be possible or practical. The company and its channel members may not have the resources or skills needed to provide all the desired services. Also, providing higher levels of service results not only in higher costs for the channel, but also in higher prices for consumers. The company must balance consumer service needs against the feasibility and costs of meeting these needs as well as customer price preferences. Generally, customers tend to make trade-offs between service quality and other purchase dimensions, such as price. The success of discount retailing – on and off the Web – shows that consumers are often willing to accept lower service levels in exchange for lower prices.

Setting channel objectives

Channel objectives should be stated in terms of targeted levels of customer service. The company can usually identify several segments wanting different levels of channel service. The company should decide which segments to serve and the best channels to use in each case. The company should aim to minimise the total channel cost of meeting customer service requirements.

The company's channel objectives are also influenced by the nature of the company, its products, its marketing intermediaries, competitors and the environment. For example, companies selling perishable products require more direct marketing to avoid delays and too much handling. The company's size and financial situation determine which marketing functions it can handle itself and which it must give to intermediaries. In some cases, a company may want to compete in or near outlets that carry competitors' products. Thus companies may want their brands to be displayed next to competing brands: in town or city centres, Burger King wants to locate near McDonald's; Sony, Panasonic and Philips audio and video systems all compete for floor space in similar retail outlets; Nestlé and Mars confectionery brands want to be positioned side by side, and aggressively compete for shelf space, in the same grocery outlets. In other cases, producers may avoid the channels used by competitors. Avon, for example, decided not to compete with other cosmetics makers for scarce positions in retail stores and, instead, set up a profitable door-to-door selling operation in the home and overseas markets. Finally, *environmental factors*, such as economic conditions and legal constraints, affect channel design decisions. For example, in a depressed economy, producers want to distribute their goods in the most economical way, using shorter channels and dropping unneeded services that add to the final price of the goods.

Identifying major alternatives

When the company has defined its channel objectives, it should next identify its major channel alternatives in terms of the *types* and *number* of intermediaries to use and the *responsibilities* of each channel member.

Types of channel alternatives

A number of options exist:

- *Direct marketing*. A number of direct marketing approaches can be used, ranging from direct-response selling via advertisements in print media, on radio or television, by mail order and catalogues to telephone and Internet selling. These methods are discussed in Chapter 19.
- *Sales force*. The company can sell directly through its own sales force or deploy another firm's sales force. Alternatively, a contract sales force might be used. The use of a company's direct sales force to sell to customers is discussed in Chapter 19.

■ *Intermediaries*. **Intermediaries** are independent organisations that will carry out a number of activities. They include *wholesalers* and *retailers* who buy, take title to and resell the firm's goods. We will first address the nature of wholesalers.

Wholesalers

Wholesalers engage in wholesaling activity – selling goods and services to those buying for resale or business use. But why would a producer use wholesalers rather than selling directly to retailers or consumers? Quite simply, wholesalers add value by performing one or more of the following channel functions:

■ *Selling and promoting*. Wholesalers' sales forces help manufacturers reach many small customers at a low cost. The wholesaler has many contacts and is often more trusted by the buyer than the distant manufacturer.

■ *Buying and assortment building*. Wholesalers can select items and build assortments needed by their customers, thereby saving the consumers a considerable amount of work.

■ *Bulk-breaking*. They save their customers money by buying in huge lots and breaking bulk (breaking large lots into small quantities).

■ *Warehousing*. Wholesalers hold inventories, thereby reducing the inventory costs and risks of suppliers and customers.

■ *Transportation*. Wholesalers can provide quicker delivery to buyers because they are closer than the producers.

■ *Financing*. They finance their customers by giving credit, and they finance their suppliers by ordering early and paying bills on time.

■ *Risk bearing*. Wholesalers absorb risk by taking title and bearing the cost of theft, damage, spoilage and obsolescence.

■ *Market information*. They give information to suppliers and customers about competitors, new products and price developments.

■ *Management services and advice*. Wholesalers often help retailers train their sales assistants, improve store layouts and displays, and set up accounting and inventory control systems.

There are many types of wholesaler (see Table 20.1). They fall into three major groups: *merchant wholesalers, brokers and agents* and *manufacturers' sales branches and offices*.

Merchant wholesalers include two broad types: full-service wholesalers and limited-service wholesalers. *Full-service wholesalers* provide a full set of services, whereas *limited-service wholesalers* offer fewer services to their suppliers and customers. The several different types of limited-service wholesalers perform varied specialised functions in the distribution channel.

Brokers and **agents** differ from merchant wholesalers. First, they do not take title to goods, and perform only a few functions. Like merchant wholesalers, they generally specialise by product line or customer type. A broker brings buyers and sellers together and assists in negotiation. Agents represent buyers or sellers on a permanent basis. Manufacturers' agents, also called manufacturers' representatives, are a common type of agent wholesaler.

The third type of wholesaling is that done in manufacturers' sales branches and offices by sellers or buyers themselves rather than through independent wholesalers.

Retailers

Although wholesalers play an important channel role, **retailers** are also critical intermediaries as they provide the final link between the consumer and provider. *Non-store retailing* has been growing much faster than has store retailing. Non-store retailing includes selling to final consumers through direct mail, catalogues, telephone, home TV shopping shows, home and office parties, door-to-door contact, vending machines, online services and the Internet, and

Intermediaries—Distribution channel firms that help the company find customers or make sales to them, including wholesalers and retailers that buy and resell goods.

Wholesaler—A firm engaged primarily in selling goods and services to those buying for resale or business use.

Merchant wholesaler—Independently owned business that takes title to the merchandise it handles.

Broker—A wholesaler who does not take title to goods and whose function is to bring buyers and sellers together and assist in negotiation.

Agent—A wholesaler who represents buyers or sellers on a relatively permanent basis, performs only a few functions, and does not take title to goods.

Retailers—Businesses whose sales come primarily from retailing.

Table 20.1 Major types of wholesalers

Type	Description
Merchant wholesalers	Independently owned businesses that take title to the merchandise they handle. In different trades they are called *jobbers*, *distributors* or *mill supply houses*. Include full-service wholesalers and limited-service wholesalers.
Full-service wholesalers	Provide a full line of services: carrying stock, maintaining a sales force, offering credit, making deliveries and providing management assistance. There are two types:
Wholesale merchants	Sell primarily to retailers and provide a full range of services. *General-merchandise wholesalers* carry several merchandise lines, whereas *general-line wholesalers* carry one or two lines in greater depth. *Speciality wholesalers* specialise in carrying only part of a line. Examples are healthfood wholesalers and seafood wholesalers.
Industrial distributors	Sell to manufacturers rather than to retailers. Provide several services, such as carrying stock, offering credit and providing delivery. May carry a broad range of merchandise, a general line or a speciality line.
Limited-service wholesalers	Offer fewer services than full-service wholesalers. Limited-service wholesalers are of several types:
Cash-and-carry wholesalers	Carry a limited line of fast-moving goods and sell to small retailers for cash. Normally do not deliver. For example, a small fish store retailer may drive to a cash-and-carry fish wholesaler, buy fish for cash and bring the merchandise back to the store.
Truck wholesalers (or truck jobbers)	Perform primarily a selling and delivery function. Carry a limited line of semi-perishable merchandise (such as milk, bread, snack foods), which they sell for cash as they make their rounds to supermarkets, small groceries, hospitals, restaurants, factory cafeterias and hotels.
Drop shippers	Do not carry inventory or handle the product. On receiving an order, they select a manufacturer, who ships the merchandise directly to the customer. The drop shipper assumes title and risk from the time the order is accepted to its delivery to the customer. They operate in bulk industries, such as coal, lumber and heavy equipment.
Rack jobbers	Serve grocery and drug retailers, mostly in non-food items. They send delivery trucks to stores, where the delivery people set up toys, paperbacks, hardware items, health and beauty aids, or other items. They price the goods, keep them fresh, set up point-of-purchase displays and keep inventory records. Rack jobbers retain title to the goods and bill the retailers only for the goods sold to consumers.
Producers' cooperatives	Owned by farmer members and assemble farm produce to sell in local markets. The co-op's profits are distributed to members at the end of the year. They often attempt to improve product quality and promote a co-op brand name.
Mail-order wholesalers	Send catalogues to retail, industrial and institutional customers. Maintain no outside sales force. Orders are filled and sent by mail, truck or other transportation.
Brokers and agents	Do not take title to goods. Their main function is to facilitate buying and selling, for which they earn a commission on the selling price. Generally, they specialise by product line or customer types.
Brokers	Their chief function is bringing buyers and sellers together and assisting in negotiation. They are paid by the party who hired them, and do not carry inventory, get involved in financing or assume risk. Examples are food brokers, real estate brokers, insurance brokers and security brokers.
Agents	Represent either buyers or sellers on a more permanent basis than brokers do. There are several types:
Manufacturers' agents	Represent two or more manufacturers of complementary lines. A formal written agreement with each manufacturer covers pricing, territories, order handling, delivery service and

Table 20.1 (cont'd)

Type	Description
	warranties, and commission rates. Often used in such lines as clothing, furniture and electrical goods. Most manufacturers' agents are small businesses, with only a few skilled salespeople as employees. They are hired by small manufacturers who cannot afford their own field sales forces, and by large manufacturers who use agents to open new territories or to cover territories that cannot support full-time salespeople.
Selling agents	Have contractual authority to sell a manufacturer's entire output. The manufacturer either is not interested in the selling function or feels unqualified. The selling agent serves as a sales department and has significant influence over prices, terms and conditions of sale.
Purchasing agents	Generally have a long-term relationship with buyers and make purchases for them, often receiving, inspecting, warehousing and shipping the merchandise to the buyers. They provide helpful market information to clients and help them obtain the best goods and prices available.
Commission merchants	Take physical possession of products and negotiate sales. Normally, they are not employed on a long-term basis. Used most often in agricultural marketing by farmers who do not want to sell their own output and do not belong to producers' cooperatives. The commission merchant takes a truckload of commodities to a central market, sells it for the best price, deducts a commission and expenses and remits the balance to the producer.
Manufacturers' and retailers' branches and offices	Wholesaling operations conducted by sellers or buyers themselves rather than through independent wholesalers. Separate branches and offices can be dedicated to either sales or purchasing: ■ *Sales branches and offices* are set up by manufacturers to improve inventory control, selling and promotion. Sales branches carry inventory. Sales offices do not carry inventory. ■ *Purchasing offices* perform a role similar to that of brokers or agents but are part of the buyer's organisation. Retailers tend to set up purchasing offices in major market centres.

other direct retailing approaches. We discussed traditional, non-store or direct-marketing channels in Chapter 19, while Chapter 4 addressed online marketing tools. In this chapter, we will focus on store retailing.

Retail stores come in all shapes and sizes, and new retail types keep emerging. Generally, they can be distinguished by the amount of service they offer, the breadth and depth of their product lines, the relative prices charged and how they are organised.

Amount of service Different products require *different amounts of service* and *customer service preferences* vary. **Self-service retailers** cater for customers who are willing to perform their own 'locate–compare–select' process to save money. Self-service is the basis of all discount operations and is typically used by sellers of convenience goods (e.g. supermarkets) and nationally branded, fast-moving shopping goods (e.g. discount stores). **Limited-service retailers**, such as department stores, provide more sales assistance because they carry more shopping goods about which customers need information. **Full-service retailers**, such as speciality stores and up-market department stores, assist customers in every phase of the shopping process. They usually carry more speciality goods, for which customers like to be 'waited on'. They provide more services, resulting in much higher operating costs, which are invariably passed along to customers as higher prices.

Product line Retailers vary in the *length and breadth of their product assortments*. A **speciality store** carries a narrow product line with a deep assortment within that line. Examples are

Self-service retailers— Retailers that provide few or no services to shoppers; shoppers perform their own locate–compare–select process.

Limited-service retailers— Retailers that provide only a limited number of services to shoppers.

Full-service retailers— Retailers that provide a full range of services to shoppers.

Speciality store—A retail store that carries a narrow product line with a deep assortment within that line.

stores selling fashion wear, outdoor leisure garments, cosmetics, books or flowers (e.g. Naf-Naf, Rohan, The Body Shop, Foyles, Interflora). Today, speciality stores are flourishing for several reasons. The increasing use of market segmentation, market targeting and product specialisation has resulted in a greater need for specialist stores that focus on specific products and segments.

In contrast, **department stores** carry a wide variety of product lines. Examples of well-known department stores are Harrods and Harvey Nichols (in the United Kingdom), Takashimaya and Isetan (in Japan and south-east Asia), Saks and Bloomingdale (in the United States), El Corte Ingles (in Spain), Galeries Lafayette (in France) and Karlstadt (in Germany). In recent years, department stores have been squeezed between more focused and flexible speciality stores on the one hand, and more efficient, low-priced discounters on the other. In response, many have added promotional pricing to meet the discount threat. Others have increased the use of store brands and single-brand 'boutiques' and 'designer shops' (such as Dolce and Gabana, Salvatore Ferragamo or DKNY shops within department stores) to compete with speciality stores. Still others are trying mail-order, telephone or Web selling. Service, invariably, remains the key differentiating factor.

Convenience stores are small stores that carry a limited line of high-turnover convenience goods. Typical examples are Happy Shopper, Spar, Mace and VG stores. These are located near residential areas and remain open for long hours. In countries where retail laws are more relaxed and there is less restriction in store opening hours, convenience stores may be open seven days a week. They satisfy an important consumer need in a niche segment – shoppers in this segment use convenience stores for emergency or 'fill-in' purchases outside normal hours or when time is short, and they are willing to pay for the convenience of location and opening hours.

In the UK, analysts believe that the convenience store market could grow between 30 and 60 per cent between 2003 and 2007. The sector is fragmented, boasting 50,000 stores, with independently owned outlets accounting for more than 40 per cent of sales. More and more people appear to prefer to visit their local (neighbourhood) convenience store to do top-up shopping because they do not have time every day to browse endless supermarket shelves to find lunch or dinner. The major supermarket chain stores are responding to this trend.

Britain's number one grocery retailer Tesco has become the second biggest convenience retailer, behind the Co-operative Group, who owns Alldays, through its purchase of 862 T&S stores in October 2002. Rebranded Tesco Express, these stores could change the pattern of grocery retailing in the country. Tesco also operates a partnership with Esso and runs some 100 stores on the petrol retailer's forecourts. Meanwhile, rival Sainsbury is aiming to grab a larger slice of the growing UK convenience store market with plans to open 100 or more stores at Shell petrol filling stations over 2003–2006, in addition to its existing 52 stand-alone 'Local' convenience stores network. According to Sainsbury, measured by sales per square foot, 11 of its top 20 performing stores were local, neighbourhood stores and three of them were on Shell forecourts. As opportunities for large store expansion out-of-town in the UK are declining because of planning restrictions, we will witness more and more marriages between petrol retailers and supermarkets.[9]

Supermarkets are the most frequently shopped type of retail store. Today, however, they are facing slow sales growth because of an increase in competition from convenience stores,

Department store—A retail organisation that carries a wide variety of product lines – typically clothing, home furnishings and household goods; each line is operated as a separate department managed by specialist buyers or merchandisers.

Convenience store—A small store located near a residential area that is open long hours seven days a week and carries a limited line of high-turnover convenience goods.

Supermarkets—Large, low-cost, low-margin, high-volume, self-service stores that carry a wide variety of food, laundry and household products.

discount food stores and superstores. Thus, supermarkets have to make improvements to attract more customers. In the battle for 'share of stomachs', some of the larger supermarkets, for example, have moved up-market, providing in-store bakeries, gourmet deli counters and fresh seafood departments. Others are cutting costs, establishing more efficient operations and lowering prices in order to compete more effectively with food discounters. As we saw earlier, some like Tesco and Sainsbury are seeking to widen their presence in the local store market.

Superstores are much larger than regular high street supermarkets and offer a large assortment of routinely purchased food products, non-food items and services, ranging from dry cleaning, post offices and film developing and photo finishing, to cheque cashing, petrol forecourts and self-service car-washing facilities. Superstores are located out of town, frequently in retail parks, with vast free car parks. The 1990s saw the explosive growth of superstores that are actually giant speciality stores, the so-called **category killers**. They feature stores the size of aircraft hangars that carry a very deep assortment of branded products belonging to a particular line, with a knowledgeable staff. Category killers have been prevalent in a wide range of categories, including books, toys, electronics, furniture, home improvement products, sporting goods and even pet supplies.

Another superstore variation, **hypermarkets**, are even bigger, perhaps as large as six football fields. They carry an even larger assortment of routinely purchased food and packaged goods and non-food items such as clothing, furniture and household appliances. Carrefour, the number one grocery retailer in France, opened the world's first 'hypermarché' at Ste-Geneviève-des-Bois, near Paris, in 1963. Since then, the concept quickly took off in France and the company now operates hundreds of these giant stores in Europe, South America and Asia. Other examples of hypermarkets include Real in Germany, Pyrca in Spain and Meijers in the Netherlands. Although hypermarkets have dominated in some countries, such as France, Italy and the Netherlands, the concept has enjoyed mixed success in the UK. Those that tried in the UK – Sainsbury's Savacentres, Asda and Tesco Extra – invested heavily to make the stores look nice and to offer additional facilities such as crèches, cafés and carefully designed car parks.[10]

Relative prices   Retailers can also be classified according to the prices they charge. Most retailers charge regular prices and offer normal-quality goods and customer service. Others offer higher-quality goods and services at higher prices. The retail stores that feature low prices are discount stores and off-price retailers.

A **discount store** sells standard merchandise at lower prices by accepting lower margins and selling higher volume. Examples include the German Aldi, the Danish Netto, the French Carrefour, and Matalan and Peacock in the UK. The early discount stores cut expenses by offering few services and operating in warehouse-like facilities in low-rent, heavily travelled districts. In recent years, facing intense competition from other discounters and department stores, many discount retailers have 'traded up'. They have improved décor, added new lines and services and opened suburban branches, which have led to higher costs and prices.

When the major discount stores traded up, a new wave of **off-price retailers** moved in to fill the low-price, high-volume gap. Ordinary discounters buy at regular wholesale prices and accept lower margins to keep prices down. In contrast, off-price retailers buy at less-than-regular wholesale prices and charge consumers less than retail. One type of off-price retailer is the factory outlet. **Factory outlets** sometimes group together in *factory outlet malls* and *value-retail centres*, where dozens of outlet stores offer prices 30–50 per cent below retail on a wide range of items. Whereas outlet shopping centres consist primarily of manufacturers' outlets, value-retail centres combine manufacturers' outlets with off-price retail stores and department store clearance outlets. Factory outlet stores have recently taken off. Even retailers such as Marks & Spencer now offer a mix of slow-selling stock, ranges from the

---

Superstore—A store around twice the size of a regular supermarket that carries a large assortment of routinely purchased food and non-food items and offers such services as dry cleaning, post offices, film developing, photo finishing, cheque cashing, petrol forecourts and self-service car-washing facilities.

Category killers—A modern 'breed' of exceptionally aggressive 'off-price' retailers that offer branded merchandise in clearly defined product categories at heavily discounted prices.

Hypermarkets—Huge stores that combine supermarket, discount and warehouse retailing; in addition to food, they carry furniture, appliances, clothing and many other products.

Discount store—A retail institution that sells standard merchandise at lower prices by accepting lower margins and selling at higher volume.

Off-price retailer—Retailer that buys at less-than-regular wholesale prices and sells at less than retail.

Factory outlet—Off-price retailing operation that is owned and operated by a manufacturer and that normally carries the manufacturer's surplus, discontinued or irregular goods.

Bullring: standing in the heart of Birmingham, Britain's second largest city, the Bullring shopping centre is one of Europe's largest and most innovative shopping destinations, housing two major department stores, Selfridges and Debenhams, and well over 140 shops, restaurants and bars. New shopping concepts like this offer a brand new experience for shoppers.
SOURCE: (both) Birmingham Photo Library/Jonathan Berg.

previous season and items specifically manufactured for factory outlets. A growing number of factory outlets typically feature designer brands such as Versace, Donna Karan, Esprit and Calvin Klein, causing department stores to protest to the manufacturers of these brands.[11]

Another off-price retail format is the **warehouse club** (also known as **wholesale club** or **membership warehouse**), which operates in huge, draughty, warehouse-like facilities and offers few frills. Customers themselves must wrestle furniture, heavy appliances and other large items to the checkout line. Such clubs make no home deliveries. The policy is 'cash and carry' as they accept no credit cards, but they do offer ultra-low prices and surprise deals on selected branded goods. For example, the German-owned Makro operates vast warehouses across Europe, selling food, beverages, wines and spirits, confectionery, household goods, clothes and other assortments to members – consumers and trade (resellers/retailers) who pay a membership fee. Warehouse clubs saw tremendous growth over the 1980s, but growth has slowed considerably in the 1990s as a result of increasing competition among warehouse store chains and effective reactions by supermarkets and discount stores.

Organisational approach   Although many retail stores are independently owned, an increasing number are banding together under some form of corporate or contractual organisation. The major types of retail organisations include *corporate chains, voluntary chains* and *retailer cooperatives, franchise organisations* and *merchandising conglomerates*.

Chain stores are two or more outlets that are commonly owned and controlled. Their size allows them to buy in large quantities at lower prices and gain promotional economies. They can hire specialists to deal with pricing, promotion, merchandising, inventory control and sales forecasting.

The great success of corporate chains caused many independents to band together in one of two forms of contractual associations. One is the *voluntary chain* – a wholesaler-sponsored group of independent retailers that engages in group-buying and common merchandising. The other form of contractual association is the *retailer cooperative* – a group of independent retailers that band together to set up a jointly owned, central wholesale operation and conduct joint merchandising and promotion efforts. These organisations give independents the buying and promotion economies they need to meet the prices of corporate chains.

Another form of contractual retail organisation is a franchise. The main difference between franchise organisations and other contractual systems (voluntary chains and retail cooperatives) is that franchise systems are normally based on some unique product or service, on a method of doing business, or on the trade name, goodwill or patent that the franchiser has developed. Franchising, which we discussed in an earlier section, has been prominent in fast food, fashion clothing, video stores, health and fitness centres, haircutting, vehicle hire, hotels and dozens of other product and service areas.

Finally, *merchandising conglomerates* are corporations that combine several different retailing forms under central ownership. Examples include Arcadia and the Kingfisher Group. Arcadia operates Principles (middle- to upmarket clothing for professional men and women), Dorothy Perkins (middle-market apparel for younger females), Top Shop (high fashion, mid-priced clothing for the young, trendy segment), and Evans (larger-sized clothing or outsizes for the older female). The Kingfisher Group owns numerous speciality chains and variety chain stores, including B&Q (do-it-yourself, DIY store), Comet (electrical and home appliances), Superdrug (discount toiletries), Charlie Brown's (vehicle spare parts and accessories), and Woolworth's (general merchandise and variety store). Diversified retailing, which provides superior management systems and economies that benefit all the separate retail operations, is likely to increase in the new millennium.

We have discussed the types of channel members. Next we look at decisions concerning the number of channels to use.

Warehouse club (wholesale club, membership warehouse)—Off-price retailer that sells a limited selection of brand-name grocery items, appliances, clothing and a hodgepodge of other goods at deep discounts to members who pay annual membership fees.

Number of marketing intermediaries

Companies must also decide on *channel breadth* – the number of channel members to use at each level. Three strategies are available: intensive distribution, exclusive distribution and selective distribution. Producers of convenience products and common raw materials typically seek **intensive distribution** – a strategy whereby they stock their products in as many outlets as possible. These goods must be available where and when consumers want them. For example, sweets, chewing gum, disposable razors, soft drinks and other similar items are sold in myriad outlets to provide maximum brand exposure and consumer convenience. Nestlé, Bic, Coca-Cola and many consumer-goods companies distribute their products in this way.

By contrast, some producers purposely limit the number of intermediaries handling their products. The extreme form of this practice is **exclusive distribution**, in which the producer gives only a limited number of dealers the exclusive rights to distribute its products in their territories. Exclusive distribution is often found in the distribution of luxury cars (e.g. Rolls-Royce, Jaguar) and prestige clothing for men and women (e.g. Giorgio Armani, Prada, Yves St Laurent). By granting exclusive distribution, the manufacturers gain strong selling support from the outlet and more control over dealer prices, promotion, credit and services. Exclusive distribution also enhances brand image and allows for higher mark-ups.

Between intensive and exclusive distribution lies **selective distribution** – the use of more than one, but fewer than all of the intermediaries that are willing to carry a company's products. Most electronic products, furniture and small household appliance brands are distributed in this manner. For example, Miele, Whirlpool and AEG sell their major appliances through dealer networks and selected large retailers. By using selective distribution, they do not have to spread their efforts over many outlets, including many marginal ones. They can develop good working relationships with selected channel members and expect a better-than-average selling effort. Selective distribution gives producers good market coverage with more control and less cost than does intensive distribution.

Responsibilities of channel members

The producer and its intermediaries need to agree on the terms and responsibilities of each channel member. They should agree on price policies, conditions of sale, territorial rights and specific services to be performed by each party. The producer should establish a list price and a fair set of discounts for intermediaries. It must define each channel member's territory, taking care where it places new resellers. Mutual services and duties need to be spelled out carefully, especially in franchise and exclusive distribution channels.

Evaluating the main alternatives

Once a company has identified several channel alternatives, it has to select the one that will best satisfy its long-run objectives. The firm must evaluate each alternative against *economic*, *control* and *adaptive* criteria.

Using economic criteria, the company compares the likely profitability of different channel alternatives. It estimates the sales that each channel would produce and the costs of selling different volumes through each channel. The company must also consider control issues. Using intermediaries usually means giving them some control over the marketing of the product, and some intermediaries take more control than others. Other things being equal, the company prefers to keep as much control as possible. Finally, the company must apply adaptive criteria. Channels often involve long-term commitments, yet the company wants to keep the channel flexible so that it can adapt to environmental changes. Thus, to be considered, a channel involving long-term commitment should be greatly superior on economic or control grounds.

Intensive distribution— Stocking the product in as many outlets as possible.

Exclusive distribution— Giving a limited number of dealers the exclusive right to distribute the company's products in their territories.

Selective distribution— The use of more than one, but less than all of the intermediaries that are willing to carry the company's products.

Designing international distribution channels

International marketers face many additional complexities in designing their channels. Each country has its own unique distribution system that has evolved over time and changes very slowly. For instance, in food and drinks retailing, contract distributors play a more important role in the delivery of goods from producer to retailer in the United Kingdom than in countries such as Germany, France, Spain and Italy. Also, multiple retailer dominance of the grocery market is more pervasive in the United Kingdom than in the latter countries. Thus global marketers must usually adapt their channel strategies to the existing structures within each country.

International logistics are becoming an increasingly important area for global businesses whose inbound supply movements are shifting from domestic sources to global ones, and whose outbound supplies face an equally international trade flow. Sophisticated computer-based technologies, such as computer-integrated logistics (CIL), are used to enable international companies and logistics service providers to manage the supply chain and specific logistics functions. International logistics place even greater demands on good integration of logistics operations and systems between the suppliers, manufacturer and others involved in moving supplies or goods along the supply chain across national borders.

In some overseas markets, the distribution system is complex and hard to penetrate, consisting of many layers and large numbers of intermediaries. For example, in Japan, the distribution system encompasses a wide range of wholesalers, agents, brokers and retailers, differing more in number than in function from their European or American counterparts.[12]

Many western firms have had great difficulty breaking into the closely knit, tradition-bound Japanese distribution network. For example, when the French retail group Carrefour entered the Japanese market in December 2000, it faced hostility from wholesalers. Carrefour's pricing demands and refusal to accept the multi-layered supply system sometimes left it struggling to maintain stocks.[13] However, Japan's archaic 'Large Scale Retail Law', which controlled planning permission for new stores and opening hours to protect small retailers from new high-street competitors, has been deregulated. Retailing law reforms have enabled

The Japanese distribution system has remained remarkably traditional. A profusion of tiny retail shops are supplied by an even greater number of small wholesalers.
SOURCE: Stock Boston/Charles Gupton.

foreign retailers, ranging from Boots and The Body Shop to IKEA and Toys 'R' Us, to break the links between the manufacturers and the high-street stores.[14]

At the other extreme, distribution systems in developing countries may be scattered and inefficient, or altogether lacking. For example, although China and India each contain hundreds of millions of people, these markets are much smaller than the population numbers suggest. Their inadequate distribution systems mean that most companies can profitably access only the small portion of the population living in the most affluent cities.[15]

Thus international marketers face a wide range of channel alternatives. Designing efficient and effective channel systems between and within various country markets poses a difficult challenge.

Channel management decisions

Once the company has reviewed its channel alternatives and decided on the best channel design, it must implement and manage the chosen channel. Channel management calls for selecting and motivating individual channel members and evaluating their performance over time.

Selecting channel members

Producers vary in their ability to attract qualified marketing intermediaries. Some producers have no trouble signing up channel members. In some cases, the promise of exclusive or selective distribution for a desirable product will draw plenty of applicants. At the other extreme are producers that have to work hard to line up enough qualified intermediaries. When household group Reckitt launched its new 'green' detergent brand, Down to Earth, in the UK market, access was restricted to one supermarket chain – Tesco. The Belgian firm Ecover managed to acquire sole rights for distribution in Asda stores and in Sainsbury, Safeway and the Co-op when it launched its radical 'green' detergents at the height of green consumerism in the United Kingdom. Many small food and grocery producers that own marginal brands often have difficulty getting retailers to carry their products.

When selecting intermediaries, the company should determine what characteristics distinguish the better ones. It will want to evaluate the channel members' years in business, other lines carried, growth and profit record, level of cooperation and reputation. If the intermediaries are sales agents, the company will want to evaluate the number and character of other lines carried and the size and quality of the sales force. If the intermediary is a retail store that wants exclusive or selective distribution, the company will want to evaluate the store's customers, location and future growth potential.

Managing and motivating channel members

Channel members must be continuously motivated to do their best. The company must sell not only *through* the intermediaries, but *to* and *with* them. More advanced companies see their intermediaries as first-line customers and partners. They practise strong *partner relationship management (PRM)* to forge long-term partnerships with channel members. This creates a marketing system that meets the needs of both the company *and* its partners.

In managing its channels, a company must convince distributors that they can succeed better by working together as a part of a cohesive value delivery system.[16] Thus, manufacturers such as Unilever and P&G work together with grocery retailers to create superior value for final consumers. They jointly plan merchandising goals and strategies, inventory levels and advertising and promotion plans. Similarly, construction equipment manufacturer JCB and automobile producers such as Ford and Toyota have to work closely with their dealers to help them to be successful in selling the company's products.

Many companies are now installing high-tech partner relationship management systems to coordinate their whole-channel marketing efforts. Just as they use customer relationship management (CRM) software systems to help manage relationships with important customers, companies can now use PRM software to help recruit, train, organise, manage, motivate and evaluate relationships with channel partners.[17]

Evaluating channel members

The producer must regularly check channel member performance against agreed targets such as sales quotas, average inventory levels, customer delivery time, treatment of damaged and lost goods, cooperation in company promotion and training programmes, and services to the customer. The company should recognise and reward intermediaries that are performing well. Those which are underperforming should be helped, remedial actions should be taken or, as a last resort, the intermediary should be replaced. The firm must periodically 'requalify' its intermediaries and prune the weak performers, allowing only the best ones to carry its products.

Finally, manufacturers need to be sensitive to their dealers. Those who treat their dealers poorly risk not only losing their support, but also causing legal problems. Disputes with dealers are counterproductive. The key to profitable channel management lies in creating win–win outcomes for all in the value delivery network – a mutually beneficial relationship that yields cooperation, not conflict, among channel participants will invariably result in higher channel performance.

Marketing logistics and supply chain management

In today's global marketplace, selling a product is sometimes easier than physically getting it to customers. Companies must decide on the best way to store, handle and move their products and services, so that they are available to customers in the right assortments, at the right time and in the right place. Physical distribution and logistics effectiveness will have a significant impact on both customer satisfaction and company costs. A poor distribution system can destroy an otherwise good marketing effort. Here we consider the nature and importance of *marketing logistics*, goals of the *logistics system*, *major logistics functions*, *choosing transportation modes* and the importance of *integrated logistics management*.

The nature and importance of marketing logistics

To some managers, physical distribution means only trucks and warehouses. But modern logistics is much more than this. **Physical distribution** or **marketing logistics** involves planning, implementing and controlling the physical flow of materials, final goods and related information from points of origin to points of consumption to meet customer requirements at a profit. In short, it involves getting the right product to the right customer in the right place at the right time.[18]

Traditional physical distribution has typically started with products at the plant and tried to find low-cost solutions to get them to customers. However, today's marketers prefer *customer-centred logistics* thinking which starts with the marketplace and works backwards to the factory or even to sources of supply. Marketing logistics addresses not only *outbound*

Physical distribution (marketing logistics)—The tasks involved in planning, implementing and controlling the physical flow of materials and final goods from points of origin to points of use to meet the needs of customers at a profit.

Figure 20.6 Supply chain
management

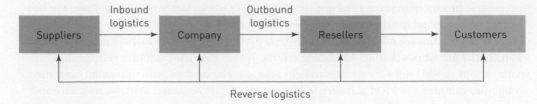

Reverse logistics

distribution (moving products from the factory to customers), but also *inbound distribution* (moving products and materials from suppliers to the factory) and *reverse distribution* (moving broken, unwanted or excess products returned by consumers and resellers). In short, it involves entire *supply chain management* – managing upstream and downstream value-added flows of materials, final goods and related information among suppliers, the company, resellers and final consumers, as shown in Figure 20.6. Thus the logistics manager's task is to coordinate the whole channel physical distribution system – the activities of suppliers, purchasing agents, marketers, channel members and customers. These activities include forecasting, purchasing, production planning, order processing, inventory management, warehousing and transportation planning.

Companies today are placing greater emphasis on logistics for several reasons:

■ Customer service and satisfaction have become the cornerstones of marketing strategy in many businesses, and distribution is an important customer service element. Companies can gain a powerful competitive advantage by using improved logistics to give customers faster delivery, better service or lower prices.

■ Improved logistics can yield tremendous cost savings to both the company and its customers. About 15 per cent of an average product's price is accounted for by shipping and transport alone.

■ The explosion in product variety has created a need for improved logistics management. For example, 100 years ago, a typical grocery store carried only 200–300 items. The store manager could keep track of this inventory on about 10 pages of notebook paper stuffed in a shirt pocket. Today, the average store carries a bewildering stock of 10,000 to 20,000 items. Ordering, shipping, stocking and controlling such a variety of products presents a sizeable logistics challenge.

■ Finally, improvements in information technology have created opportunities for improving distribution efficiency. The increased use of sophisticated supply chain management software, Web-based logistics systems, point-of-sale scanners, uniform product codes, satellite tracking and electronic transfer of order and payment data, enables companies to manage the flow of goods, information and finances through the supply chain quickly and efficiently.

Goals of the logistics system

The starting point for designing a marketing logistics system is to study the service needs of customers. Some companies state their logistics objective as providing maximum customer service at the least cost. Unfortunately, no logistics system can *both* maximise customer service *and* minimise distribution costs. Maximum customer service implies rapid delivery, large inventories, flexible assortments, liberal returns policies and a host of other services – all of which raise distribution costs. In contrast, minimum distribution cost implies slower delivery, small inventories and larger shipping lots – which represent a lower level of overall customer service.

The goal of the marketing logistics system should be to provide *a targeted level of customer service at the least cost*. The company must first research the importance of various distribution services that customers require and then set desired service levels for each segment. The objective is to maximise *profits*, not sales. Therefore, the company must weigh the benefits of providing higher levels of service against the costs. Some companies offer less service than their competitors and charge a lower price. Other companies offer more service and charge higher prices to cover higher costs.

Major logistics functions

Given a set of logistics objectives, the company is ready to design a logistics system that will minimise the cost of attaining these objectives. The major logistics functions are warehousing, inventory management and transportation.

Warehousing

Most companies must store their tangible goods while they wait to be sold. To ensure they can meet orders speedily, they must have stock available. A storage function is needed because production and consumption cycles rarely match. For example, a lawnmower manufacturer might produce all year long and store up its products for the heavy spring and summer buying season. The storage function overcomes differences in needed quantities and timing.

A company must decide on *how many* and *what types* of warehouses it needs, and *where* they will be located. The company might use storage warehouses, which store goods for moderate to long periods. Or they may use **distribution centres**, which are designed to move goods rather than just store them. They are large and highly automated warehouses designed to receive goods from various plants and suppliers, take orders, fill them efficiently, and deliver goods to customers as quickly as possible.

Distribution centre—A large, highly automated warehouse designed to receive goods from various plants and suppliers, take orders, fill them efficiently, and deliver goods to customers as quickly as possible.

Like almost everything else these days, warehousing has seen dramatic changes in technology in recent years. Older, multi-storey warehouses with outdated materials-handling methods are steadily being replaced by newer, single-storey *automated warehouses* with advanced, computer-controlled materials-handling systems requiring few employees. Computers and scanners read orders and direct lift trucks, electric hoists or robots to gather goods, move them to loading docks and issue invoices.

In the European market, more and more producers of industrial and consumer goods are looking to incorporate pan-European distribution networks to provide consistently high standards of service and flexibility. For example, in the face of stiff competition in mainland European markets, British steel producer Corus set up regional distribution centres from which to serve customers across Europe. At the same time, it implemented new IT systems that linked production plants, distribution operators and customers, thus improving service efficiency.[19]

Inventory management

Inventory levels also affect customer satisfaction. The major problem is to maintain the delicate balance between carrying too much inventory and carrying too little. Carrying too much inventory results in excessive inventory carrying costs and stock obsolescence. With too little stock, the firm risks not having products when customers want to buy. Stock-outs lead to costly emergency shipments or production, customer dissatisfaction or lost sales as unserved customers switch to a competitor. Hence, in managing inventory, firms must balance the costs of carrying larger inventories against resulting sales and profits.

Today, many companies have greatly reduced their inventories and related costs through *just-in-time* (JIT) logistics systems. Through such systems, producers and retailers carry only small inventories of parts or merchandise, often only enough for a few days of operations. New stock arrives at the factory or retail outlet exactly when needed, rather than being stored in inventory until being used. JIT systems require accurate forecasting along with fast,

frequent and flexible delivery, so that new supplies will be available when needed. However,
these systems result in substantial savings in inventory carrying and handling costs.

Transportation

The choice of transportation carriers affects the pricing of products, delivery performance
and condition of the goods when they arrive – all of which will affect customer satisfaction.
In shipping goods to its warehouses, dealers and customers, the company can choose among
five transportation modes: road, rail, water, pipeline and air. For digital products, firms can
use an alternative distribution mode – the Internet.

Road

Trucks are highly flexible in their routing and time schedules. They are efficient for short
hauls of high-value merchandise. In the EU, the bulk of goods traded is moved by road
vehicles. According to the Conference of European Transport Ministers (CEMT), transport
volumes in the EU have risen by more than 50 per cent in the last 20 years.[20] The gradual
deregulation and removal of restrictive practices in the road transport market in the EU has
led to an increase in intra-EU haulage competition, with a downward pressure on rates. Also,
there is increasingly greater freedom for international hauliers to transport goods between
destinations within one country, resulting in greater efficiency in the use of trucks.

Rail

Railroads are one of the most cost-effective modes for shipping large amounts of bulk
products – coal, sand, minerals, farm and forest products – over long distances. The EU's
efforts to speed up the development of rail freight and combined road/rail transport services
throughout Europe – including the opening up of networks in eastern Europe – are pushing

rail transport much more firmly into the general distribution spotlight. However, collaboration and standardisation among Europe's railways is necessary to reinforce rail's presence on main cross-border routes.[21]

Water

In countries favourably served by coastal and inland waterways, a large amount of goods can be moved by ships and barges. Although the cost of water transportation is very low for shipping bulky, low-value, non-perishable products such as sand, coal, grain, oil and metallic ores, water transportation is the slowest mode and is affected by the weather. In the EU, waterways' share of freight transport volume is low compared to rail and roads. Its full potential, however, can only be realised through harmonisation of European shipping and port policies and pricing systems, and continued attempts to remove restrictive and unhelpful legislation.

Pipeline

Pipelines are a specialised means of shipping raw commodities such as petroleum, natural gas and chemicals from sources to markets. Most pipelines are used by their owners to ship their own products.

Air

Although the use of air carriers tends to be restricted to low-bulk goods, they are becoming more important as a transportation mode. Air-freight rates are much higher than rail or truck rates, but air freight is ideal when speed is needed or distant markets have to be reached. Among the most frequently air-freighted products are perishables (fresh fish, cut flowers) and high-value, low-bulk items (technical instruments, jewellery). Air freight is advantageous as it reduces inventory levels, packaging costs and the number of warehouses needed.

Internet

The *Internet* carries digital products from producer to customer via satellite, cable modem or telephone wire. Software firms, the media, music companies and education all make use of the Internet to transport digital products. While these firms primarily use traditional transportation to distribute CDs, newspapers and more, the Internet holds the potential for lower product distribution costs.

In choosing a transportation mode for a product, shippers must balance many considerations: speed, dependability, availability, cost, capability and others. Thus, if a shipper needs speed, air and truck are the prime choices. If the goal is low cost, then water or pipeline might be best. In practice, firms may rely on a combination of transportation methods which would best enable them to meet logistics objectives cost-effectively.

Logistics information management

Companies manage their supply chains through information. Channel partners often link up to share information and to make better joint logistics decisions. From a logistics perspective, information flows such as customer orders, billing, inventory levels and even customer data are closely linked to channel performance. Information can be shared and managed in many ways – by mail or telephone, through salespeople, via the Internet, or through *electronic data interchange (EDI)*, the computerised exchange of data between organisations. Retailers such as Tesco and Wal-Mart, for example, maintain EDI links with their major suppliers.[22] Benetton, the Italian company, gained a competitive advantage in the past through its management of total supply or throughput time. It uses direct feedback from its franchised outlets to monitor sales trends, links this information into its computer-aided design and manufacturing system and, making use of its highly flexible manufacturing processes, quickly produces (even small quantities) to order.[23] These companies aim to design simple, accessible, fast and accurate processes for capturing, processing and sharing channel information.

In some cases, suppliers might actually be asked to generate orders and arrange deliveries for their customers. Large retailers are having to work closely with major suppliers to set up *vendor-managed inventory (VMI)* systems or *continuous inventory replenishment* systems.[24] Using VMI, the customer shares real-time data on sales and current inventory levels with the supplier. The supplier then takes full responsibility for managing inventories and deliveries. Some retailers even go so far as to shift inventory and delivery costs to the supplier. To work, however, such systems require close cooperation between the buyer and seller.[25]

Integrated logistics management

Integrated logistics management—A physical distribution concept that recognises the need for a firm to integrate its logistics system with those of its suppliers and customers. The aim is to maximise the performance of the entire distribution system.

Today, companies are increasingly adopting the concept of **integrated logistics management**. This concept recognises that providing better customer service and trimming distribution costs require *teamwork*, both inside the company and among all the marketing channel organisations. Inside the company, the various functional departments must work closely together to maximise the company's own logistics performance. Outside, the company must integrate its logistics system with those of its suppliers and customers to maximise the performance of the entire distribution system.

Cross-functional teamwork inside the company

In most companies, responsibility for various logistics activities is assigned to many different functional units – marketing, sales, finance, manufacturing, purchasing. Too often, each function tries to optimise its own logistics performance without regard for the activities of the other functions. However, transportation, inventory, warehousing and order-processing activities interact, often in an inverse way. For example, lower inventory levels reduce inventory carrying costs. But they may also reduce customer service and increase costs from stock-outs, backorders, special production runs and costly fast-freight shipments. Because distribution activities involve strong trade-offs, decisions by different functions must be coordinated to achieve superior overall logistics performance.

Thus the goal of integrated logistics management is to harmonise all of the company's distribution decisions. Close working relationships among functions can be achieved in several ways. Some companies have created permanent logistics committees made up of managers responsible for different physical distribution activities and for setting policies for improving overall logistics performance.

Companies can also create management positions that link the logistics activities of functional areas. Many companies have created 'supply managers', who manage all of the supply chain activities for each of their product categories. Some have a senior executive for logistics with cross-functional authority.[26] Finally, companies can employ sophisticated, system-wide supply chain management software, now available from Oracle, Eqos, Ariba and other software providers.[27] The important thing is that the company coordinates its logistics and marketing activities to create high market satisfaction at a reasonable cost.

Building logistics partnerships

Companies must do more than improve their own logistics. They must also work with other channel members to improve whole-channel distribution. The members of a distribution channel are linked closely in delivering customer satisfaction and value. One company's distribution system is another company's supply system. The success of each channel member depends on the performance of the entire supply chain. For example, a big supermarket like

Asda (owned by Wal-Mart) can charge the lowest prices at retail only if its entire supply chain – consisting of thousands of merchandise suppliers, transport companies, warehouses and service providers – operates at maximum efficiency.

Today, smart companies coordinate their logistics strategies and build strong partnerships with suppliers and customers to improve customer service and reduce channel costs. Many companies have created *cross-functional, cross-company teams*. Other companies partner through *shared projects*. For example, some of the larger retailers – such as Selfridges and House of Fraser – are working with suppliers on in-store programmes. Retailers can allow key suppliers to use their stores as a testing ground for new merchandising programmes. The suppliers spend time at the test stores watching how their product sells and how customers relate to it. They then create programmes specially tailored to the retail outlet and its customers.

Today, more and more companies are also beginning to exploit information technology and the Internet to develop sophisticated electronic, business-to-business (B2B) market-places, where companies can build collaborative global procurement, trading or supply chain networks. One example is Covisint, the automotive industry B2B exchange and Web portal launched by General Motors, Daimler-Chrysler and Ford in late 2000, which claimed around 135,000 users across 96 countries by 2004. In February 2004 the privately held portal was acquired by Compuware Corporation, which plans to expand the Web portal used by the automotive industry to other industries, including healthcare and financial services. Other examples of B2B exchanges include ChemConnect in the chemicals and plastics industry, GlobalNetXchange in retailing and MyAircraft.com in the aerospace industry.[28]

Today, as a result of logistics partnerships, many companies have switched from *anticipatory-based distribution systems* to *response-based distribution systems*.[29] In anticipatory distribution, the company produces the amount of goods called for by a sales forecast, holding stocks at various supply points such as the plant, distribution centres and retail outlets, and reordering automatically when its order point is reached. A response-based distribution system, in contrast, is *customer-triggered*. The producer continuously builds and replaces stock as orders arrive. It produces what is currently selling.

For example, in the global motor car industry, manufacturers are coming under increasing pressure to increase the speed of customer response, while also tailoring products to consumer needs, in order to strengthen customer loyalty. Toyota, Ford and GM are all trying out the concept of BTO (build-to-order) or OTD (order-to-delivery). BTO is a system pioneered by Dell. When a customer goes online or calls a freephone number to order his personal computer, Dell assembles the tailored product and ships it to the customer within days. A car is far more complex than a PC, but many car manufacturers believe that they can reduce order-to-delivery time to less than two weeks compared to the three or more months that purchasers currently have to wait. Essentially, a customer will pick her preferred package and, within seconds, the transaction reaches a central database which checks that the order meets an approved design; the car is then scheduled for assembly, based on the earliest date the parts can be shipped. The system should reduce the transaction cost, while taking costs out of the inventory process. The 'dream' is for customers to get all but the most unusual packages within a matter of days![30]

Third-party logistics

Third-party logistics (3PL) provider—An independent logistics provider that performs any or all of the functions required to get its client's product to market.

Most businesses perform their own logistics function, but a growing number of firms outsource some or all of their logistics to **third-party logistics (3PL) providers** such as UPS Worldwide Logistics, DHL, FedEx Logistics and Emory Global Logistics. Such integrated logistics companies perform any or all of the functions required to get their clients' product to market. Advance computers and communications make it possible for companies to outsource much more than the simple delivery of physical goods, creating a wide range of

Companies can outsource many of their complex logistics processes to specialists like DHL who deliver one-stop logistic services ranging from transportation and warehousing to IT-based solutions and logistics financing and consulting.
SOURCE: DHL Worldwide Network/Jung von Matt.

services including inventory holding and after-sales services. Supply chain outsourcing is evolving from delivery of simple third-party logistics (3PL) through provision of management services (4PL) into full-blown, totally integrated logistics provision (ILP).

For example, DHL and UPS provide clients with coordinated, single-source logistics services including supply chain management, customised information technology, inventory control, warehousing, transportation management, customer service and fulfilment, and freight auditing and control.[31]

Companies outsource supply chain functions for several reasons. First, because getting the product to market is their main focus, these providers can often do it more efficiently and at lower cost. According to one study, outsourcing typically results in 15–30 per cent cost savings. Second, outsourcing logistics frees a company to focus more intensely on its core business.[32] Finally, integrated logistics companies understand increasingly complex logistics environments. This can be especially helpful to companies attempting to expand their global market coverage. For example, companies distributing their products across Europe face a bewildering array of environmental restrictions that affect logistics, including packaging standards, truck size and weight limits, and noise and emission pollution controls. By outsourcing its logistics, a company can gain a complete pan-European distribution system without incurring the costs, delays and risks associated with setting up its own system.

Channel trends

We have examined the major channel and logistics decisions facing managers. Finally, let us look at the major changes occurring in distribution channels.

Retailing and wholesaling trends

Retailing trends

Retailers operate in a harsh and fast-changing environment, which offers threats as well as opportunities. For example, in many countries, the industry suffers from chronic overcapacity, resulting in fierce competition for customers. Consumer demographics, lifestyles and shopping patterns are changing rapidly, as are retailing technologies. To be successful, then, retailers will have to choose target segments carefully and position themselves strongly. They will have to take the following retailing developments into account as they plan and execute their competitive strategies.

New retail forms and shortening retail life-cycles

New retail forms continue to emerge to meet new situations and consumer needs, but the life-cycle of new retail forms is getting shorter.[33] Department stores took about 100 years to reach the mature stage of the life-cycle; more recent forms, such as warehouse stores, reached maturity in about 10 years. In such an environment, seemingly solid retail positions can crumble quickly.

Many retailing innovations are partially explained by the **wheel of retailing** concept. According to this concept, many new types of retailing forms begin as low-margin, low-price, low-status operations. They challenge established retailers that have become 'fat' by letting their costs and margins increase. The new retailers' success leads them to upgrade their facilities, carry higher-quality merchandise and offer more services. In turn, their costs increase, forcing them to increase their prices. Eventually, the new retailers become like the conventional retailers they replaced. The cycle begins again when still newer types of retailer

Wheel of retailing—
A concept of retailing which states that new types of retailer usually begin as low-margin, low-price, low-status operations, but later evolve into higher-priced, higher-service operations, eventually becoming like the conventional retailers they replaced.

evolve with lower costs and prices. The wheel of retailing concept seems to explain the initial success and later troubles of department stores, supermarkets and discount stores, and the recent success of off-price and no-frills retailers.[34] Thus retailers cannot sit back with a successful formula. To thrive, they must keep adapting and reshaping their business accordingly.

While the wheel of retailing explains the evolution and development of new types of retail store, the concept of the **retailing accordion** can be used to explain the intermittent changes in the depth of retailers' merchandise or the breadth of their operations. Typically, retailers begin by selling a wide assortment of products. They are followed by retailers offering a narrower or more specialised range of products, which in turn are eventually superseded by broad-line mass merchandisers. The theory suggests that retailers pass through a *general–specific–general cycle*. It adequately tapped the evolution of the American retail scene, where the nineteenth-century general stores gave way to the twentieth-century specialist retailers, which were then superseded by the postwar mass merchandisers. The accordion concept may be used to describe the more recent *specific–general–specific cycle* of retailing observed in some sectors.

Retailing accordion— A phenomenon describing how the width of retailers' product assortment or operations shifts over time: there tends to be a general–specific–general cycle. However, it is possible that many retailing businesses evolve along a specific–general–specific cycle.

> For instance, some retailers begin by selling a narrow range or special type of goods, as in a grocery store that carries mainly food, drinks and convenience items. As sales expand, the store manager tends to add new merchandise, such as household goods, stationery, cosmetics and non-prescription drugs, to his or her portfolio. As it grows further, extra services and amenities – for example, delicatessen, fresh-fish-and-seafood counter, in-store bakery, credit card and cheque facilities – are added. This is the path reflected by large supermarkets, which started as narrow-line grocery retailers, stretching out over the years into broad-line superstores. More recently, further growth in edge-of-town superstores is slowing down and out-of-town shopping centres are reaching saturation point. Some of the larger supermarkets are moving back into the high streets. In the UK, Sainsbury's and Tesco reintroduced small town-centre formats, Metro and Central respectively, which are able to trade more profitably now than they could 10 years ago through the supermarkets' increased buying power and efficiency.[35]

Growth of non-store retailing

Although most retailing still takes place the old-fashioned way across countertops in stores, consumers now have an array of alternatives, including mail order, television, phone and online shopping. Although such advances may threaten some traditional retailers, they offer exciting opportunities for others. Most store retailers are now actively exploring direct retailing channels. In fact, more online retailing is conducted by 'click-and-brick' retailers than by 'click-only' retailers. For example, office-supply retailer Office Depot is now the world's biggest online retailer after Amazon.com.[36]

Retail convergence

Today's retailers are increasingly selling the same products at the same prices to the same consumers in competition with a wider variety of other retailers. For example, any consumer can buy CDs at about the same price from any or all of a dozen different types of retailers – speciality music stores, discount music stores, electronics superstores, general merchandise discount stores, video-hire outlets and any of dozens of websites. And when it comes to brand-name appliances, department stores, discount stores, off-price retailers, electronics superstores and a slew of websites all compete for the same customers.

This merging of consumers, products, prices and retailers is called *retail convergence*:[37] it is the coming together of shoppers, goods and prices. Customers of all income levels are shopping at the same stores, often for the same goods. Old distinctions such as discount store, speciality store and department store are losing significance: the successful store must match a host of rivals on selection, service and price.

Such convergence means greater competition for retailers and greater difficulty in differentiating offerings. The competition between chain superstores and smaller, independently owned stores has become particularly heated. Because of their bulk buying power and high sales volume, chains can buy at lower costs and thrive on smaller margins. The arrival of a superstore can quickly force nearby independents out of business. For example, Wal-Mart in the UK and Germany has been accused of destroying smaller independents in neighbouring towns.

Yet the news is not all bad for smaller companies. Many small, independent retailers are thriving. They are finding that sheer size and marketing muscle are often no match for the personal touch that small stores can provide or the speciality niches that small stores fill for a devoted customer base.

The rise of mega-retailers

The rise of huge mass merchandisers and speciality superstores, the formation of vertical marketing systems and buying alliances, and a rash of retail mergers and acquisitions have created a core of superpower mega-retailers. In the grocery sector, for example, the battle for global power among the 80 large supermarket groups in Europe has created a superleague of fewer than 10 heavyweight retailers including Wal-Mart, Carrefour, Metroag, Tesco, Ahold, Groupe Casino, Sainsbury's and Delhaize.

Through their superior information systems and buying power, these giant retailers are able to offer better merchandise selections, good service and strong price savings to consumers. As a result, they grow even larger by squeezing out their smaller, weaker competitors. The mega-retailers also are shifting the balance of power between retailers and producers. A relative handful of retailers now control access to enormous numbers of consumers, giving them the upper hand in their dealings with manufacturers.

The growing importance of retail technology

Retail technologies are becoming critically important as competitive tools. Progressive retailers are using computers to produce better forecasts, control inventory costs, order electronically from suppliers, send email between stores, and even sell to customers within stores. They are adopting checkout scanning systems, online transaction processing, electronic funds transfer, electronic data interchange, in-store television and improved merchandise-handling systems.

Perhaps the most startling advances in retailing technology concern the ways in which today's retailers are connecting with customers. In the past, retailers connected with their customers through stores, through their salespeople, through the brands and packages they sold, and through direct mail and advertising in the mass media. But today, life is more complex. There are dozens of new ways to attract and engage consumers. Indeed, even if one omits the obvious – the Web – retailers are still surrounded by technical innovations that promise to redefine the way they and manufacturers interact with customers. Consider touch-screen kiosks, electronic shelf labels and signs, handheld shopping assistants, smart cards, self-scanning systems, virtual reality displays and intelligent agents. So, if we ask the question, 'Will technology change the way retailers interface with customers in the future?', the answer has got to be yes.[38]

Global expansion of retailers

Retailers with unique formats and strong brand positioning are increasingly moving into other countries. Many are expanding internationally to escape mature and saturated home markets. Over the years, several giant US retailers – McDonald's, KFC, Gap, Toys 'R' Us, Wal-Mart – have become prominent in countries around the world as a result of their great marketing prowess. However, European and Asian retailers are ahead of the US when it comes to global expansion. Only 18 per cent of the top US retailers operate globally, compared to 40 per cent of European retailers and 31 per cent of Asian retailers. Among the European retailers that have gone global are Britain's Tesco and Marks & Spencer, Italy's Benetton, France's Carrefour hypermarkets and Sweden's Hennes & Mauritz and IKEA home furnishing stores.[39]

> Marks & Spencer, which started out as a penny bazaar in 1884, grew into a chain of variety stores over the decades and now has a thriving string of over 150 franchised stores around the world, which sell mainly its private-label clothes, including Brooks Brothers. It also runs a major food business. IKEA's well-constructed but fairly inexpensive furniture has proven very popular in countries across the world, where shoppers often spend an entire day in an IKEA store. Europe's largest fashion retailer, Hennes & Mauritz, has 945 stores in 18 countries and plans to accelerate the pace of its global expansion with the opening of another 140 new stores over 2004. And French discount retailer Carrefour, the world's second largest retailer after Wal-Mart, has embarked on an aggressive mission to extend its role as a leading international retailer.[40]

Although many retailers appear to have caught globalisation fever, not all have done well. Despite the enthusiasm, retailers have found that store retailing is proving difficult to transfer across national frontiers. UK retailers Dixons, Habitat, Mothercare and Next have been forced to retreat from the US. Even Italy's Benetton, a past master at internationalisation, had to close hundreds of US stores in the early 1990s. And, as Carrefour and Wal-Mart found, entry into foreign markets is not trouble-free (see Marketing Insights 20.2).

Trends in wholesaling

As the wholesaling industry moves into the twenty-first century, it faces considerable challenges. The industry remains vulnerable to one of the most enduring trends of the last decade – fierce resistance to price increases and the winnowing out of suppliers who are not adding value based on cost and quality. Progressive wholesalers constantly watch for better ways to meet the changing needs of their suppliers and target customers. They recognise that, in the long run, their only reason for existence comes from adding value by increasing the efficiency and effectiveness of the entire marketing channel. To achieve this goal, they must constantly improve their services and reduce their costs.

The distinction between large retailers and large wholesalers continues to blur. There are retailers that operate formats such as wholesale clubs and hypermarkets that perform many wholesale functions. In return, many large wholesalers are setting up their own retailing operations. A prime example of this type of *hybrid* operator is the cash-and-carry self-service wholesaler Makro, which in one sense is a limited-service wholesaler, selling primarily to the trade – that is, to small shopkeepers/retailers. In another sense, Makro is also a large retailer in

Retail giants: coming to terms with the global marketplace

20.2

As major store retailers within national boundaries have consolidated into corporate giants and domestic markets have become ever more crowded, the big players have been crossing borders for growth opportunities. However, store retailing is a business that is proving difficult to transfer across national frontiers. Even for those whose international businesses are well advanced, including Carrefour and Wal-Mart, getting things right in international markets is not easy.

First, consider the French retailer Carrefour. Like other foreign retailers, from food to luxury goods, Carrefour was drawn to the ¥143,000 billion (€1,290 billion) Japanese retail market by its consumers' high disposable incomes and declining land prices. Carrefour has 9,600 stores in 30 countries worldwide. Emboldened by its success in other countries, Carrefour entered Japan in 2000 and now operates seven outlets in the world's second largest retail market.

However, from the very beginning, the retail group had misread consumers and alienated wholesalers. Consumers turned away on finding low-priced Japanese fare that jarred with their expectations of French delicacies at lavish prices. It faced hostility from wholesalers with its pricing demands and refusal to accept their multi-layered distribution system, leaving the retailer often struggling to maintain stocks.

Following this troubled entry, Carrefour's superstores now offer French products and cluster food items to suit Japanese tastes. They offer cut-portions of fruit and a wider range of ready-to-eat meals. They now have relations with second-tier suppliers who are often blocked by the cartel-like structure of the Japanese wholesale system. Expansion is also now focused more on western Japan where lower prices are more likely to attract shoppers than in Tokyo. Nonetheless, while the French retail group is looking to recover from its troubled entry into Japan, whatever the future for Carrefour, competitors are already responding to opportunities in this market. Wal-Mart and Tesco have entered Japan and local market-leaders like Aeon are slashing prices and expanding aggressively with new super-store formats. The question is whether Carrefour can do it alone – some of their teething problems could have been avoided had they taken the conventional route and entered through a joint venture partner or acquisition. Being too aggressive and arrogant at the beginning, Carrefour must now accept that some things work better in Japan the Japanese way.

Carrefour is not alone. The problems facing the world's largest retailer, America's Wal-Mart, when it entered the German market are instructive. Through its acquisition of the Wertkauf hypermarket in 1997 and Interspar in 1998, Wal-Mart Germany became the country's fourth largest hypermarket chain. Although this move initially sent shockwaves through the European retail industry, the German venture

marketing insights

895

...20.2 was proving to be performing poorly, losing $200–300 million (€224–333 million) a year.

Volker Barth, head of Wal-Mart Germany, acknowledges that they did make mistakes. The most serious one was disregarding the German food retailing distribution structure. To control the distribution to stores, the company centralised procurement rather than left it to suppliers. This resulted in delivery chaos and stock-out rates as high as 20 per cent compared with a 7 per cent average for the industry. Although sizeable, with 10 per cent of the hypermarket sector, Wal-Mart Germany had less than 2 per cent of the food retail market. It lacked the purchasing muscle to dictate to suppliers and distributors, unlike Edeka and Rewe with a combined market share of 30 per cent. Moreover, in a sector already dominated by hard discounters, Wal-Mart's 'low-price message' was nothing new. Rivals quickly matched its price cuts. High renovation costs and the complexity of Germany's planning and social regulations have also delayed planned refurbishment of stores, with many remaining unattractive or in the wrong locations. Poor-quality staff and sloppy customer service at its Interspar stores have not helped either.

Wal-Mart also acknowledged misjudging corporate culture. Filling the top positions at the German stores with US expatriates prompted an exodus of German managers, which denied the group local expertise. Wal-Mart's losses in Germany may be reconcilable, given the venture is in its infancy. IKEA waited eight years until its US store eventually went into profit.

For now, both Carrefour and Wal-Mart continue to follow their global expansion paths. But one thing's for certain – to succeed they have to blend their products and services, quality and prices to suit local tastes. And management has to be responsive to new ideas and local systems of doing business. As a spokesperson for an Asian retail conglomerate noted, 'We considered alliances with Wal-Mart and Carrefour but they both had an attitude that their way was best. So we chose Tesco instead because we were impressed by how open its management was to new ideas.'

SOURCES: Bayan Rahman, 'Carrefour begins a new era in Japan', *Financial Times* (6 October 2003), p. 26; Andrew Ward, 'An octopus in the shopping trolley', *Financial Times* (11 January 2002), p. 9; Fraser Nelson, 'Grocers must play their cards right', *The Times* (1 September 1999), p. 9; 'Shopping all over the world', *The Economist* (19 June 1999), pp. 83–9; Bertrand Benoit, 'Wal-Mart finds German failures hard to swallow', *Financial Times* (12 October 2000), p. 25; Peggy Hollinger and Chris Tighe, 'C&A was forced down market and now out', *Financial Times* (16 June 2000), p. 3; Ian Bickerton, 'A victim of fashion', *Financial Times* (27 June 2000), p. 18; Peggy Hollinger, 'A shopping market stacked with difficulties', *Financial Times* (2 August 2000), p. 19.

that many of the 'trade visitors' who purchase goods from its warehouse are not resellers but individuals bulk-buying for personal consumption.[41]

Wholesalers will continue to increase the services they provide to retailers – retail pricing, cooperative advertising, marketing and management information reports, accounting services, online transactions and others. Rising costs on the one hand, and the demand for increased services on the other, will put the squeeze on wholesaler profits. Wholesalers who do not find efficient ways to deliver value to their customers will soon drop by the wayside. However, the increased use of computerised, automated and Web-based systems will help wholesalers to contain the costs of ordering, shipping and inventory holding, boosting their productivity.

Finally, facing slow growth in their domestic markets and the trend towards globalisation, many large wholesalers are going global, thus creating new challenges for the wholesaling industry worldwide. To survive, players must learn to adapt to their changing environment. Like their customers – the resellers or retailers, whose success relies on their ability to capture and retain customers by offering better value than the competition can – wholesalers must consistently add to that value-creation process. For all channel partners, wholesalers and retailers alike, nothing happens until a sale takes place, until customers buy. And there are no long-term rewards unless these customers come back for more!

Summary

Producing a product or service and making it available to buyers requires building relationships not just with customers, but also with key suppliers and resellers in the company's *supply chain*. Marketers have traditionally focused on the distribution or *marketing channels* that look forward towards the customer. A company's channel decisions directly affect every other marketing decision. Each channel system creates a different level of revenues and costs, and reaches a different segment of target customers. Most producers try to forge a *marketing channel* – a set of interdependent organisations involved in the process of making a product or service available for use or consumption by the consumer or business user. Through their contacts, experience, specialisation and scale of operation, intermediaries usually offer the firm more than it can achieve on its own.

Marketing channels perform many key functions: *information gathering and dissemination*, *communication and promotion*, *contact work*, *matching offers to buyers' needs*, *negotiation*, *physical distribution*, *financing*, and *risk taking*.

The channel is most effective when each member is assigned the tasks it can do best and all members work together smoothly. They should understand and accept their roles, coordinate their goals and activities and cooperate to attain overall channel goals. In recent years, new types of channel organisation have appeared that provide stronger leadership for assigning roles and managing conflict, leading to improved performance.

Each firm needs to identify alternative ways to reach its market. These vary from direct selling to using one, two, three or more intermediary *channel levels*. Marketing channels face continuous change. Three of the most important trends are the growth of *vertical*, *horizontal* and *multi-channel* or *hybrid marketing systems*. These trends affect channel cooperation, conflict and competition.

Channel design begins with assessing customer channel-service needs and company channel objectives and constraints. The company then identifies the main channel alternatives in terms of the *types* of intermediary, the *number* of intermediaries and the *channel responsibilities* of each.

There are many types of channel intermediary, ranging from wholesalers, brokers and agents to retailers. *Wholesaling* includes all the activities involved in selling goods or services to those who are buying for the purpose of resale or for business use. Wholesalers perform many functions, including selling and promoting, buying and assortment building, bulk-breaking, warehousing, transporting, financing, risk bearing, supplying market information and providing management services and advice.

Wholesalers fall into three groups: *merchant wholesalers* take possession of the goods; *agents* and *brokers* do not take possession of the goods but are paid a commission for aiding buying and selling; and *manufacturers' sales branches and offices* are wholesaling operations conducted by non-wholesalers to bypass the wholesalers.

Retailers perform activities involved in selling goods and services directly to final consumers for their personal, non-business use. Retailers can be classified as *store retailers* and *non-store retailers*. They can be further classified by the *amount of service* they provide (e.g. self-service, limited service or full service); *product line sold* (e.g. speciality store, department store, supermarket, convenience store, superstores); and their *relative price emphasis* (e.g. discount store, category killer, off-price retailers). Today, many retailers are banding together in corporate and contractual *retail organisations* (e.g. corporate chains, voluntary chains and retailer cooperatives, franchise organisations and merchandising conglomerates).

Each channel alternative must be evaluated according to economic, control and adaptive criteria. Channel management calls for selecting, motivating and periodically evaluating qualified intermediaries. The company must sell not only *through* the intermediaries, but *to* and *with* them. The key is to forge long-term partnerships with their channel partners to create a marketing system that meets the needs of both the manufacturer and the partners. Companies operating in different geographic markets can apply the key principles of channel management, but must adapt approaches to the conditions in international markets.

More business firms are now paying attention to *physical distribution* or *marketing logistics*. Marketing logistics involves coordinating the activities of the entire *supply chain* – inbound, outbound and reverse distribution – to maximise value to customers. No logistics system can both maximise customer service and minimise distribution costs. The goal of logistics management is to provide a *targeted* level of service at the least cost. The major logistics functions include *warehousing*, *inventory management*, *transportation* and *logistics information management*.

Increasingly, companies adopt the *integrated logistics concept* as they recognise that improved logistics requires teamwork in the form of close working relationships across functional areas inside the company and across various organisations in the supply chain. Companies achieve logistics harmony among functions by creating cross-functional logistics teams, integrative supply manager positions and senior-level logistics executives with cross-functional authority. Channel partnerships can take the form of cross-company teams, shared projects and information-sharing systems. Today, some companies are outsourcing their logistics functions to third-party logistics providers to reduce costs, increase efficiency and gain faster and more effective access to global markets.

Discussing the issues

1. Explain the purpose of a company's supply chain. Is the term 'supply chain' too limited for today's business activities? Using examples, explain what you understand to be a firm's value delivery network and to what extent it is different from a supply chain.

2. What is disintermediation? Give an example other than those discussed in the chapter. What opportunities and problems does disintermediation present for traditional retailers? Explain.

3. In only the past few years, online retailing has boomed.

   (a) How will retailers going online change the competitive balance between retailers, direct and catalogue marketers, wholesalers and manufacturers?

(b) What are the major advantages of online retailing? The pitfalls?

(c) What do you predict will be the future of online retailing?

4. List and describe each of the channel functions that have been traditionally assigned to wholesalers.

(a) How will wholesalers have to change to meet the threat of increasing competition from large retailers?

(b) What type of wholesaler is best equipped to compete and evolve in the next decade? Explain.

5. Many European and US retailers are seeking to expand globally.

(a) What key factors might govern successful international expansion?

(b) Thinking of examples of local retailers, explain which of these might be well positioned for global expansion.

(c) How will online retailing affect global retail expansion?

(d) Study Sweden's IKEA home furnishing stores (www.ikea.com). Why has IKEA been so successful in expanding into overseas markets?

Applying the concepts

1. You probably have heard of an extranet. An extranet occurs when a company opens part of its own internal network (or intranet) to trusted suppliers, distributors and other selected external business partners. Via such extranets, a company can communicate quickly and efficiently with its partners, complete transactions and share data. A supplier might analyse the customer's inventory needs. Partners might swap customer lists for interrelated products and services or share purchasing systems to gain savings through more efficient purchasing. These 'virtual partners' communicate in nanoseconds about shifting supply and demand situations, customer requests and opportunities, and just-in-time inventory needs. Purchase processing times can be reduced from weeks to minutes at enormous cost savings, which can then be passed along to consumers.

(a) What role will extranets play in distribution decisions for retailers, wholesalers and manufacturers?

(b) Discuss the potential dangers and benefits of an extranet system.

(c) How might outsourcers employ the extranet concept (if at all)? What types of activities and information might be shared on such extranets? What might be their advantages and disadvantages?

2. Virtual retailing is touted to have a bright future, thanks to consumer demand for more and more service and customisation. Through virtual retailing, a seller comes directly into your home, at your convenience, and allows you to design your own personalised product and shopping experience. This sounds great – no high-pressure salespeople and no congested car parks. At a virtual retail site, you can take as much or as little time as you like to make up your own mind. And virtual retailing has made mass customisation a reality. Select a product (e.g. clothing, shoes, spectacles) and identify a company whose website allows you to customise its products. Visit the website of the company you have selected.

(a) How does virtual retailing compare with traditional shopping formats? What are the major advantages and disadvantages for consumers?

(b) Try to design your own product. Discuss the pros and cons of your experience. How would this experience be different from buying in a retail store? Would you be willing to purchase the item you designed? Why or why not?

References

1. Louis Stern and Adel I. El-Ansary, *Marketing Channels*, 5th edn (Upper Saddle River, NJ: Prentice Hall, 1996), p. 3.

2. For alternative levels of definition of a channel of distribution, see Michael J. Baker, *Macmillan Dictionary of Marketing and Advertising*, 2nd edn (London: Macmillan, 1990), pp. 47–8.

3. 'Business floating on air', *The Economist* (19 May 2001), pp. 56–7; Richard Heller, 'Galician beauty', *Forbes* (28 May 2001), p. 98; and Miguel Helft, 'Fashion fast forward', *Business 2.0* (May 2002), p. 60.

4. Angela Mackay, 'Esprit celebrates its anniversary in style', *Financial Times* (19 September 2003), p. 31.

5. Christopher Brown-Humes, 'An empire built on a flat-pack', *Financial Times* (24 November 2003), p. 12; for more information on IKEA's vision, latest facts and figures and press releases, visit www.ikea.com.

6. This has been called 'symbiotic marketing'. For further reading, see Lee Adler, 'Symbiotic marketing', *Harvard Business Review* (November–December 1966), pp. 59–71; P. 'Rajan' Varadarajan and Daniel Rajaratnam, 'Symbiotic marketing revisited', *Journal of Marketing* (January 1986), pp. 7–17; Gary Hamel, Yves L. Doz and C.D. Prahalad, 'Collaborate with your competitors and win', *Harvard Business Review* (January–February 1989), pp. 133–9.

7. For more discussion on the challenges that multi-channel formats pose for companies, see Matt Hobb and Hugh Wilson, 'The multi-channel challenge', *Marketing Business* (February 2004), pp. 12–15; information also accessed at www.cranfield.ac.uk/som/ccarm/multichannel where you can download the IBM/Cranfield white paper 'Optimising multi-channel performance'.

8. Rochelle Garner, 'Mad as hell', *Sales and Marketing Management* (June 1999), pp. 55–9.

9. Astrid Wendlandt, 'Sainsbury to build on deal with Shell', *Financial Times* (3 June 2003), p. 25; Alison Smith, 'Tesco steals a march on local rivals', *Financial Times* (31 October 2002), p. 25.

10. Sarah Cunningham, 'The seduction of the hyper-sensitive Brits', *The Times* (19 June 1999), pp. 28–9; Matthew Barbour, 'Rolling in the aisles at Tesco', *The Times* (19 June 1999), p. 29.

11. Howard Banks, 'The malling of Europe', *Forbes* (22 February 1999), p. 66; Peggy Hollinger, 'M&S moves into factory outlets', *Financial Times* (13 July 2000), p. 25.

12. Subhash C. Jain, *International Marketing Management*, 3rd edn (Boston: PWS-Kent Publishing, 1990), pp. 489–91; Emily Thornton, 'Revolution in Japanese retailing', *Fortune* (7 February 1994), pp. 143–7; 'Ever-shorter channels – wholesale industry restructures', *Focus Japan* (July–August 1997), pp. 3–4.

13. Bayan Rahman, 'Carrefour begins a new era in Japan', *Financial Times* (6 October 2003), p. 26.

14. Bayan Rahman, 'The Japanese face of Boots', *Financial Times* (4 October 2000), p. 15.

15. See Philip Cateora, *International Marketing*, 7th edn (Homewood, IL: Irwin, 1990), pp. 570–1; Dexter Roberts, 'Blazing away at foreign brands', *Business Week* (12 May 1997), p. 58.

16. For more on channel relationships, see James A. Narus and James C. Anderson, 'Rethinking distribution', *Harvard Business Review* (July–August 1996), pp. 112–20; James C. Anderson and James A. Narus, *Business Market Management* (Upper Saddle River, NJ: Prentice Hall, 1999), pp. 276–88; Jonathon D. Hibbard, Nirmalya Kumar and Louis W. Stern, 'Examining the impact of destructive acts in marketing channel relationships', *Journal of Marketing Research* (February 2001), pp. 45–61; and Stavros P. Kalafatis, 'Buyer–seller relationships among channels of distribution', *Industrial Marketing Management* (April 2002), pp. 215–28.

17. See Heather Harreld and Paul Krill, 'Channel management', *InfoWorld* (8 October 2001), pp. 46–52; and Barbara Darrow, 'Comergent revs up PRM', *Crn* (8 April 2002), p. 60.

18. For further reading to gain insights into the practical challenges facing firms when managing logistics and the supply chain, see Martin Christopher and Helen Perk, *Marketing Logistics*, 2nd edn (Oxford: Butterworth-Heinemann, 2002).

19. Michael Terry, 'Drive for greater efficiency', *Financial Times* (3 September 1992), p. IV.

20. Tom Todd, 'The new ground rules', *EuroBusiness* (May 1994), pp. 43–4.

21. 'Rays of hope and prophecies of doom', *EuroBusiness* (May 1994), pp. 46–7.

22. Judy Strauss and Raymond Frost, *E-Marketing*, 2nd edn (Upper Saddle River, NJ: Prentice Hall, 2001), p. 193.

23. Martin Christopher, 'From logistics to competitive advantage', *Marketing Business* (August 1989), pp. 20–1.

24. See Robert E. Danielson, 'CPFR: Improving your business without being limited by technology', *Apparel Industry Magazine* (February 2000), pp. 56–7; and Ben A. Chaouch, 'Stock levels and delivery rates in vendor-managed inventory programs', *Production and Operations Management* (Spring 2001), pp. 31–44.

25. For a discussion of practical applications and implementation of supply chain systems and software, see FT supplement, 'Understanding supply chain execution', *Financial Times* (26 November 2003); information also accessible at www.ft.com/supplychainexecution.

26. Shlomo Maital, 'The last frontier of cost reduction', *Across the Board*, **31**, 2 (February 1994), pp. 51–2.

27. 'Understanding supply chain execution', *Financial Times* (26 November 2003); information also accessible at www.ft.com/supplychainexecution; also see Lara L. Sowinski, 'Supply chain management and logistics software', *World Trade* (February 2001), pp. 34–6; Marc L. Songini, 'PeopleSoft pushes CRM, supply chain software', *Computerworld* (6 May 2002), p. 19; and Amy Rogers, 'Supply chain players toss a few barbs as competition heats up', *Crn* (22 April 2002), pp. 29–30.

28. Sean Michael Kerner, 'Compuware buys auto industry play Covisint', *Ecommerce* (5 February 2004), accessed at http://www.internetnews.com/ec-news/article.php/3309311, 11 March 2004; Ellen Messmer, 'Compuware to acquire Covisint B2B exchange', *Network World Fusion* (5 February 2004), accessed at http://www.nwfusion.com/news/2004/0205covisint.html, 9 March 2004; Michael Rappa, 'ChemConnect', *Managing the Digital Enterprise* (16 July 2003), accessed at http://digitalenterprise.org/cases/chemconnect.html; Carlos Grande, 'Exchange of the big brands', *Financial Times* (21 July 2000), p. 16; Andrew Edgecliffe-Johnson, 'Top 50 consumer groups go online', *Financial Times* (17 March 2000), p. 36; 'Seller beware', *The Economist* (4 March 2000), pp. 85–6; Nikki Tait, 'Part suppliers to examine e-commerce', *Financial Times* (4 April 2000), p. 34.

29. For a general discussion of improving supply chain performance, see Marshall L. Fisher, 'What is the right supply chain for your product?', *Harvard Business Review* (March–April 1997), pp. 105–16.

30. 'Car making', *The Economist* (26 August 2000), pp. 68–70.

31. Phil Manchester, 'Outsourcing: Keeping check on a vital partnership', FT Understanding supply chain execution, *Financial Times* (26 November 2000), pp. 4–5.

32. Martha Celestino, 'Choosing a third-party logistics provider', *World Trade* (July 1999), pp. 54–6.

33. For more discussion on emerging models of retailing, see 'Reinventing the store', *The Economist* (22 November 2003), pp. 89–91.

34. Don E. Schultz, 'Another turn of the wheel', *Marketing Management* (March–April 2002), pp. 8–9; Malcolm P. McNair and Eleanor G. May, 'The next revolution of the retailing wheel', *Harvard Business Review* (September–October 1978), pp. 81–91; Eleanor G. May, 'A retail odyssey', *Journal of Retailing* (Fall 1989), pp. 356–67; Stephen Brown, 'The wheel of retailing: past and future', *Journal of Retailing* (Summer 1990), pp. 143–9.

35. S.C. Hollander, 'Notes on the retail accordion', *Journal of Retailing*, **42**, 2 (1966), p. 24; Neil Buckley, 'Still shopping as the margins drop', *Financial Times* (4 August 1994), p. 15; Cathy Hart, 'The retail accordion and assortment strategies: an exploratory study', *International Review of Retail Distribution and Consumer Research*, **9** (April 1999), pp. 111–26.

36. Charles Haddad, 'Office Depot's E-Diva', *Business Week* (6 August 2001), pp. EB22–EB24; and Meryl Davids Landau, 'Sweet revenge', *Chief Executive* (May 2002), pp. 58–62.

37. Excerpt adapted from Alice Z. Cuneo, 'What's in store?', *Advertising Age* (25 February 2002), pp. 1, 30–1.

38. Marshall L. Fisher, Ananth Raman and Anna Sheen McClelland, 'Rocket science retailing is almost here: are you ready?', *Harvard Business Review* (July–August 2000), pp. 115–24; Regina Fazio Maruca, 'Retailing: confronting the challenges that face bricks-and-mortar stores', *Harvard Business Review* (July–August 1999), pp. 159–68.

39. 'Global retailing in the connected economy', *Chain Store Age* (December 1999), pp. 69–82; 'Top 200 global retailers', *Stores* (October 2000), pp. G6–G15; Joseph H. Ellis, 'Global retailing's winners and losers', *Chain Store Age* (December 1997), pp. 27–9.

40. Nicholas George, 'Hennes to accelerate global expansion', *Financial Times* (30 January 2004), p. 31; and 'H&M to expand small store concept', *Financial Times* (7 March 2003), p. 27; Tim Craig, 'Carrefour: at the intersection of global', *Dsn Retailing Today* (18 September 2000), p. 16. Additional information from Richard Tomlinson, 'Who's afraid of Wal-Mart?', *Fortune* (26 June 2000), pp. 186–96; and www.carrefour.com, July 2002.

41. *Cash and Carry Outlets* (Hampton, Middlesex: Keynote Publications, 1992).

WEB RESOURCES

For additional classic case studies and Internet exercises, visit www.pearsoned.co.uk/kotler

Concluding concepts 20
Pieta luxury chocolates

Peter Abel, the young managing director of his family's firm, was pleased with the way he had revitalised the firm after he took over 10 years ago. Since being formed in 1923, Pieta had sold its luxury Belgian chocolates through its own small shops. It had a high reputation within the trade and many devoted customers. It was the country's largest luxury chocolate manufacturer, but until Peter took over, the company had stagnated. In his opinion, Pieta should be more like other leading family firms such as Cadbury, Ferrero and Mars.

When he took over, he launched the company into new ventures. Franchising widened distribution to some small shops which now had corners devoted to Pieta's range. He felt these did not compete with Pieta's own shops because the franchisees were CTNs (confectioners, tobacconists and newsagents), where people made many impulse purchases. These contrasted with Pieta's shops, which people visited to make purchases for a special occasion or as an indulgence. Other distribution channels that were developed included own-label to Marks & Spencer in the UK, direct mailing for special occasions, and exporting (see Exhibit 20.1).

There were some new Pieta shops and 20 per cent of the old ones were refurbished. The refurbishment rate was slower than he would have liked, for he knew that

> Pieta had been Belgium's largest luxury chocolate manufacturer, but the company had stagnated.

many of the shops were poorly located, cluttered and overcrowded. The well-sited shops often had queues trailing out of their doors when they were busy, but most did not do so well. The company had not kept pace with changes in shopping and geodemographics. Most of Pieta's shops were on secondary sites in declining industrial towns. Other new channel opportunities, such as 'shop-in-shop' outlets and international expansion, had also been largely ignored.

However, the product range was now wider. The chocolate market was seasonal, so the shops sold ice-creams to help summer sales. The outlets also carried a range of greetings cards and Pieta gift vouchers to make them more of a one-stop shop. Soon he would be introducing countlines aimed at the mass market (countlines are wrapped bars, such as KitKat, or small bags of products such as M&Ms).

As a result of his efforts, Peter was able to present a dynamic set of results to his family shareholders (see Exhibit 20.2). He was angry to find that some shareholders were not as supportive as they had been. Some worried about the company's reputation being spoilt by it becoming less exclusive. Others were anxious about the new injection of equity he was requesting. He thought it odd that the strategy they had supported and backed financially two years ago was now in question. He reminded them how well the firm had done despite the tough economic climate over the last few years (see Exhibit 20.3). The

Exhibit 20.1 **Channel performance**

Year	Sales tonnage					
	Own shops	CTN franchise	M&S own label	Direct mail	Export	Number of own shops
1994	6,049	1	3	3	3	128
1995	7,203	92	255	136	11	130
1996	8,351	392	661	167	24	130
1997	9,933	1,002	636	172	149	132
1998	11,845	1,303	462	205	184	138
1999	14,753	1,259	868	205	167	148
Gross margin (%)	55	45	37	35	33	
Net profit (%)	6	14	7	3	(6)	

Exhibit 20.2 Company performance (Bfr m)

Year	Sales	Gross profit	Net profit	Net assets	Equity	Debt
1989	2,262	1,285	282	1,218	809	409
1990	2,222	1,215	308	1,305	885	420
1991	2,783	1,568	387	1,503	1,043	460
1992	3,461	1,961	636	1,896	1,241	655
1993	4,270	2,405	723	2,373	1,488	885
1994	5,653	3,005	779	2,931	1,735	1,196
1995	7,091	4,066	951	3,425	2,002	1,423
1996	8,821	4,696	793	4,228	2,217	2,011
1997	10,887	5,803	975	4,749	2,661	2,088
1998	12,826	6,891	1,123	6,201	2,594	3,607
1999	15,551	9,064	1,372	7,515	3,113	4,402

Exhibit 20.3 Economic performance

Year	Retail Price Index	CTN Price Index	Cost of Living Index	Cost of debt (%)	Cost of equity (%)
1989	100	100	100	11	13
1990	108	107	109	9	12
1991	133	121	117	11	17
1992	151	131	128	14	18
1993	175	155	148	16	23
1994	208	191	184	17	28
1995	238	223	213	17	21
1996	271	257	251	12	20
1997	310	285	274	13	26
1998	345	297	311	16	23
1999	389	351	360	16	25

company was now more professional than it had ever been. He had just introduced a new tier of senior people to manage the day-to-day operations of the company. These were not family members, but were bright and very well qualified and had broad experience within the industry. With them in place he would have more time to think about and initiate other ways of developing the company.

Questions

1. Comment on Abel's expansion strategy and Pieta's performance since he took over.
2. Argue the case for further expansion wanted by Abel.
3. What is the scope for channel innovation in the industry?

4. How is Abel's strategy endangering Pieta's future performance and brand image? What, if anything, has Abel been neglecting?
5. Track the changes in C^3 (capital cost covered) and EVA (economic value added) for Pieta over the last ten years. Marketing Insights 16.1 shows how to do this.
6. Comment on the C^3 and EVA trends and compare them with the impression given by the growth in profits and sales. What strategies of Abel's explain the performance that the C^3 and EVA reveal? Should the trend be changed and, if so, how could it be changed?

SOURCE: From company records. All dates, figures and names have been changed for commercial reasons.

GLOSSARY

Accessibility—The degree to which a market segment can be reached and served.

Actionability—The degree to which effective programmes can be designed for attracting and serving a given market segment.

Actual product—A product's parts, quality level, features, design, brand name, packaging and other attributes that combine to deliver core product benefits.

Adapted marketing mix—An international marketing strategy for adjusting the marketing-mix elements to each international target market, bearing more costs but hoping for a larger market share and return.

Administered VMS—A vertical marketing system that coordinates successive stages of production and distribution, not through common ownership or contractual ties, but through the size and power of one of the parties.

Adoption process—The mental process through which an individual passes from first hearing about an innovation to final adoption.

Adoption—The decision by an individual to become a regular user of the product.

Advertising objective—A specific communication task to be accomplished with a specific target audience during a specific period of time.

Advertising specialities—Useful articles imprinted with an advertiser's name, given as gifts to consumers.

Advertising—Any paid form of non-personal presentation and promotion of ideas, goods or services by an identified sponsor.

Affordable method—Setting the promotion budget at the level management thinks the company can afford.

Agent—A wholesaler who represents buyers or sellers on a relatively permanent basis, performs only a few functions, and does not take title to goods.

Allowance—(1) Reduction in price on damaged goods. (2) Promotional money paid by manufacturers to retailers in return for an agreement to feature the manufacturer's product in some way.

Alternative evaluation—The stage of the buyer decision process in which the consumer uses information to evaluate alternative brands in the choice set.

Annual plan—A short-term plan that describes the company's current situation, its objectives, the strategy, action programme and budgets for the year ahead, and controls.

Approach—The step in the selling process in which the salesperson meets and greets the buyer to get the relationship off to a good start.

Aspirational group—A group to which an individual wishes to belong.

Atmospheres—Designed environments that create or reinforce the buyer's leanings towards consumption of a product.

Attitude—A person's consistently favourable or unfavourable evaluations, feelings and tendencies towards an object or idea.

Augmented product—Additional consumer services and benefits built around the core and actual products.

Available market—The set of consumers who have interest, income and access to a particular product or service.

B2B (business-to-business) e-commerce—Using B2B trading networks, auction sites, spot exchanges, online product catalogues, barter sites and other online resources to reach new customers, serve current customers more effectively and obtaining buying efficiencies and better prices.

B2C (business-to-consumer) e-commerce—The online selling of goods and services to final consumers.

Balance sheet—A financial statement that shows assets, liabilities and net worth of a company at a given time.

Basing-point pricing—A geographic pricing strategy in which the seller designates some city as a basing point and charges all customers the freight cost from that city to the customer location, regardless of the city from which the goods are actually shipped.

Behavioural segmentation—Dividing a market into groups based on consumer knowledge, attitude, use or response to a product.

Belief—A descriptive thought that a person holds about something.

Benchmarking—The process of comparing the company's products and processes to those of competitors or leading firms in other industries to find ways to improve quality and performance.

Benefit segmentation—Dividing the market into groups according to the different benefits that consumers seek from the product.

Brand equity—The value of a brand, based on the extent to which it has high brand loyalty, name awareness, perceived quality, strong brand associations, and other assets such as patents, trademarks and channel relationships.

Brand extension—Using a successful brand name to launch a new or modified product in a new category.

Brand image—The set of beliefs that consumers hold about a particular brand.

Brand—A name, term, sign, symbol or design, or a combination of these, intended to identify the goods or services of one seller or group of sellers and to differentiate them from those of competitors.

Break-even pricing (target profit pricing)—Setting price to break even on the costs of making and marketing a product; or setting price to make a target profit.

Broker—A wholesaler who does not take title to goods and whose function is to bring buyers and sellers together and assist in negotiation.

Business analysis—A review of the sales, costs and profit projections for a new product to find out whether these factors satisfy the company's objectives.

Business buying process—The decision-making process by which business buyers establish the need for purchased products and services, and identify, evaluate and choose among alternative brands and suppliers.

Business market—All the organisations that buy goods and services to use in the production of other products and services, or for the purpose of reselling or renting them to others at a profit.

Business portfolio—The collection of businesses and products that make up the company.

Business promotion—Sales promotion designed to generate business leads, stimulate purchase, reward business customers and motivate the salesforce.

Buyer—The person who makes an actual purchase.

Buyer-readiness stages—The stages that consumers normally pass through on their way to purchase, including awareness, knowledge, liking, preference, conviction and purchase.

Buying centre—All the individuals and units that participate in the business buying-decision process.

Buzz marketing—Cultivating opinion leaders and getting them to spread information about a product or service to others in their communities.

By-product pricing—Setting a price for by-products in order to make the main product's price more competitive.

By-products—Items produced as a result of the main factory process, such as waste and reject items.

C2B (consumer-to-business) e-commerce—Online exchanges in which consumers search out sellers, learn about their offers, and initiate purchases, sometimes even driving transaction terms.

C2C (consumer-to-consumer) e-commerce—Online exchanges of goods and information between final consumers.

Capital items—Industrial goods that partly enter the finished product, including installations and accessory equipment.

Captive-product pricing—Setting a price for products that must be used along with a main product, such as blades for a razor and film for a camera.

Cash cows—Low-growth, high-share businesses or products; established and successful units that generate cash that the company uses to pay its bills and support other business units that need investment.

Cash discount—A price reduction to buyers who pay their bills promptly.

Cash refund offers (rebates)—Offers to refund part of the purchase price of a product to consumers who send a 'proof of purchase' to the manufacturer.

Catalogue marketing—Direct marketing through print, video or electronic catalogues that are mailed to select customers, made available in stores or presented online.

Category killers—A modern 'breed' of exceptionally aggressive 'off-price' retailers that offer branded merchandise in clearly defined product categories at heavily discounted prices.

Causal research—Marketing research to test hypotheses about cause-and-effect relationships.

Channel conflict—Disagreement among marketing channel members on goals and roles – who should do what and for what rewards.

Channel level—A layer of intermediaries that performs some work in bringing the product and its ownership closer to the final buyer.

Click-and-mortar companies—Traditional brick-and-mortar companies that have added e-marketing to their operations.

Click-only companies—The so-called dotcoms which operate only online without any brick-and-mortar market presence.

Closed-end questions—Questions that include all the possible answers and allow subjects to make choices among them.

Closing—The step in the selling process in which the salesperson asks the customer for an order.

Co-brand—The practice of using the established brand names of two different companies on the same product.

Cognitive dissonance—Buyer discomfort caused by postpurchase conflict.

Collective buying—An increasing number of customers agree to buy as prices are lowered to the final bargain price.

Commercialisation—Introducing a new product into the market.

Communication adaptation—A global communication strategy of fully adapting advertising messages to local markets.

Company and individual branding strategy—A branding approach that focuses on the company name and individual brand name.

Comparison advertising (knocking copy)—Advertising that compares one brand directly or indirectly to one or more other brands.

Competitions, sweepstakes, lotteries and games—Promotions that offer customers the chance to win something – cash, goods or trips – by luck or extra effort.

Competitive advantage—An advantage over competitors gained by offering consumers greater value, either through lower prices or by providing more benefits that justify higher prices.

Competitive strategies—Strategies that strongly position the company against competitors and that give the company the strongest possible strategic advantage.

Competitive-parity method—Setting the promotion budget to match competitors' outlays.

Competitor analysis—The process of identifying key competitors; assessing their objectives, strategies, strengths and weaknesses, and reaction patterns; and selecting which competitors to attack or avoid.

Competitor-centred company—A company whose moves are mainly based on competitors' actions and reactions; it spends most of its time tracking competitors' moves and market shares and trying to find strategies to counter them.

Competitor intelligence—Information gathered that informs on what the competition is doing or is about to do.

Complex buying behaviour—Consumer buying behaviour in situations characterised by high consumer involvement in a purchase and significant perceived differences among brands.

Concentrated marketing—A market-coverage strategy in which a firm goes after a large share of one or a few submarkets.

Concept testing—Testing new-product concepts with a group of target consumers to find out whether the concepts have strong consumer appeal.

Confused positioning—A positioning error that leaves consumers with a confused image of the company, its product or a brand.

Consumer buying behaviour—The buying behaviour of final consumers – individuals and households who buy goods and services for personal consumption.

Consumer market—All the individuals and households who buy or acquire goods and services for personal consumption.

Consumer product—A product bought by final consumers for personal consumption.

Consumer promotion—Sales promotion designed to stimulate consumer purchasing, including samples, coupons, rebates, prices-off, premiums, patronage rewards, displays, and contests and sweepstakes.

Consumer-oriented marketing—A principle of enlightened marketing which holds that a company should view and organise its marketing activities from the consumers' point of view.

Consumer relationship-building promotions—Sales promotions that promote the product's positioning and include a selling message along with the deal.

Consumerism—An organised movement of citizens and government agencies to improve the rights and power of buyers in relation to sellers.

Continuity—Scheduling ads evenly within a given period.

Contract manufacturing—A joint venture in which a company contracts with manufacturers in a foreign market to produce the product.

Contractual VMS—A vertical marketing system in which independent firms at different levels of production and distribution join together through contracts to obtain more economies or sales impact than they could achieve alone.

Convenience product—A consumer product that the customer usually buys frequently, immediately, and with a minimum of comparison and buying effort.

Convenience store—A small store located near a residential area that is open long hours seven days a week and carries a limited line of high-turnover convenience goods.

Conventional distribution channel—A channel consisting of one or more independent producers, wholesalers and retailers, each a separate business seeking to maximise its own profits, even at the expense of profits for the system as a whole.

Copy testing—Measuring the communication effect of an advertisement before or after it is printed or broadcast.

Core product—The problem-solving services or core benefits that consumers are really buying when they obtain a product.

Core strategy—The identification of a group of customers for whom the firm has a differential advantage, and then positioning itself in that market.

Corporate brand licensing—A form of licensing whereby a firm rents a corporate trademark or logo made famous in one product or service category and uses it in a related category.

Corporate branding strategy—A brand strategy whereby the firm makes its company name the dominant brand identity across all of its products.

Corporate VMS—A vertical marketing system that combines successive stages of production and distribution under single ownership – channel leadership is established through common ownership.

Corporate website—A site set up by a company on the Web, which carries information and other features designed to answer customer questions, build customer relationships and generate excitement about the company, rather than to sell the company's products or services directly. The site handles interactive communication initiated by the consumer.

Cost-plus pricing—Adding a standard mark-up to the cost of the product.

Countertrade—International trade involving the direct or indirect exchange of goods for other goods instead of cash. Forms include barter compensation (buyback) and counterpurchase.

Coupons—Certificates that give buyers a saving when they purchase a product.

Culture—The set of basic values, perceptions, wants and behaviours learned by a member of society from family and other important institutions.

Cultural environment—Institutions and other forces that affect society's basic values, perceptions, preferences and behaviours.

Current marketing situation—The section of a marketing plan that describes the target market and the company's position in it.

Customer-centred company—A company that focuses on customer developments in designing its marketing strategies and on delivering superior value to its target customers.

Customer-centred company—A company that focuses on customer developments in designing its marketing strategies and on delivering superior value to its target customers.

Customer database—An organised collection of comprehensive data about individual customers or prospects, including geographic, demographic, psychographic and buying behaviour data.

Customer delivered value—The difference between total customer value and total customer cost of a marketing offer – 'profit' to the customer.

Customerisation—Leaving it to the individual customers to design the marketing offering – allowing customers to be prosumers rather than only consumers.

Customer lifetime value—The amount by which revenues from a given customer over time will exceed the company's costs of attracting, selling and servicing that customer.

Customer sales force structure—A sales force organisation under which salespeople specialise in selling only to certain customers or industries.

Customer satisfaction—The extent to which a product's perceived performance matches a buyer's expectations. If the product's performance falls short of expectations, the buyer is dissatisfied. If performance matches or exceeds expectations, the buyer is satisfied or delighted.

Customer value analysis—Analysis conducted to determine what benefits target customers value and how they rate the relative value of various competitors' offers.

Customer value delivery system—The system made up of the value chains of the company and its suppliers, distributors and ultimately customers, who work together to deliver value to customers.

Customer value—The consumer's assessment of the product's overall capacity to satisfy his or her needs.

Cycle—The medium-term wavelike movement of sales resulting from changes in general economic and competitive activity.

Decider—The person who ultimately makes a buying decision or any part of it – whether to buy, what to buy, how to buy, or where to buy.

Deciders—People in the organisation's buying centre who have formal or informal powers to select or approve the final suppliers.

Decision-and-reward systems—Formal and informal operating procedures that guide planning, budgeting, compensation and other activities.

Decision-making unit (DMU)—All the individuals who participate in, and influence, the consumer buying-decision process.

Decline stage—The product life-cycle stage at which a product's sales decline.

Deficient products—Products that have neither immediate appeal nor long-term benefits.

Demands—Human wants that are backed by buying power.

Demarketing—Marketing to reduce demand temporarily or permanently – the aim is not to destroy demand, but only to reduce or shift it.

Demographic segmentation—Dividing the market into groups based on demographic variables such as age, sex, family size, family life cycle, income, occupation, education, religion, race and nationality.

Demography—The study of human populations in terms of size, density, location, age, sex, race, occupation and other statistics.

Department store—A retail organisation that carries a wide variety of product lines – typically clothing, home furnishings and household goods; each line is operated as a separate department managed by specialist buyers or merchandisers.

Derived demand—Business demand that ultimately comes (derives) from the demand for consumer goods.

Descriptive research—Marketing research to better describe marketing problems, situations or markets, such as the market potential for a product or the demographics and attitudes of consumers.

Desirable products—Products that give both high immediate satisfaction and high long-run benefits.

Differentiated marketing—A market-coverage strategy in which a firm decides to target several market segments and designs separate offers for each.

Direct investment—Entering a foreign market by developing foreign-based assembly or manufacturing facilities.

Direct marketing—Direct communications with carefully targeted individual customers to obtain an immediate response.

Direct-mail marketing—Direct marketing through single mailings that include letters, ads, samples, fold-outs and other 'salespeople on wings' sent to prospects on mailing lists.

Direct-marketing channel—A marketing channel that has no intermediary levels.

Direct-response television marketing (DRTV)—The marketing of products or services via television commercials and programmes which involve a responsive element, typically the use of a freephone number that allows consumers to phone for more information or to place an order for the goods advertised.

Discount store—A retail institution that sells standard merchandise at lower prices by accepting lower margins and selling at higher volume.

Discount—A straight reduction in price on purchases during a stated period of time.

Disintermediation—The elimination of a layer of intermediaries from a marketing channel or the displacement of traditional resellers by radically new types of intermediaries.

Dissonance-reducing buying behaviour—Consumer buying behaviour in situations characterised by high involvement but few perceived differences among brands.

Distribution centre—A large, highly automated warehouse designed to receive goods from various plants and suppliers, take orders, fill them efficiently, and deliver goods to customers as quickly as possible.

Dogs—Low-growth, low-share businesses and products that may generate enough cash to maintain themselves, but do not promise to be large sources of cash.

Durable product—A consumer product that is usually used over an extended period of time and that normally survives many uses.

Dutch auction—Prices start high and are lowered successively until someone buys.

Dynamic pricing—Charging different prices depending on individual customers and situations.

E-business or electronic business—The use of electronic platforms – intranets, extranets and the Internet – to conduct a company's business.

Economic environment—Factors that affect consumer buying power and spending patterns.

Electronic commerce—A general term for a buying and selling process that is supported by electronic means.

Electronic Data Interchange (EDI)—Custom-built systems that link the computer systems of major buyers to their suppliers to enable them to coordinate their activities more closely.

Electronic marketing—The marketing side of e-commerce – company efforts to communicate about, promote and sell products and services over the Internet.

Embargo—A ban on the import of a certain product.

Emotional appeals—Message appeals that attempt to stir up negative or positive emotions that will motivate purchase; examples are fear, guilt, shame, love, humour, pride and joy appeals.

Emotional selling proposition (ESP)—A non-functional attribute that has unique associations for consumers.

Engel's laws—Differences noted over a century ago by Ernst Engel in how people shift their spending across food, housing, transportation, health care, and other goods and services categories as family income rises.

English auction—Price is raised successively until only one bidder remains.

Enlightened marketing—A marketing philosophy holding that a company's marketing should support the best long-run performance of the marketing system; its five principles are consumer-oriented marketing, innovative marketing, value marketing, sense-of-mission marketing and societal marketing.

Environmental management perspective—A management perspective in which the firm takes aggressive actions to affect the publics and forces in its marketing environment rather than simply watching it and reacting to it.

Environmental sustainability—A third environmentalism wave in which companies seek to produce profits for the company while sustaining the environment.

Environmentalism—An organised movement of concerned citizens and government agencies to protect and improve people's living environment.

Ethnic segmentation—Offering products or marketing approaches that recognise the special strengths or needs of an ethnic community.

Events—Occurrences staged to communicate messages to target audiences; examples are news conferences and grand openings.

Exchange controls—Government limits on the amount of its country's foreign exchange with other countries and on its exchange rate against other currencies.

Exchange—The act of obtaining a desired object from someone by offering something in return.

Exclusive distribution—Giving a limited number of dealers the exclusive right to distribute the company's products in their territories.

Experience curve (learning curve)—The drop in the average per-unit production cost that comes with accumulated production experience.

Experimental research—The gathering of primary data by selecting matched groups of subjects, giving them different treatments, controlling related factors and checking for differences in group responses.

Exploratory research—Marketing research to gather preliminary information that will help to better define problems and suggest hypotheses.

Export department—A form of international marketing organisation that comprises a sales manager and a few assistants whose job is to organise the shipping out of the company's goods to foreign markets.

External audit—A detailed examination of the markets, competition, business and economic environment in which the organisation operates.

Externalities—Activities or facilities that are external to an organisation but affect its performance.

Factory outlet—Off-price retailing operation that is owned and operated by a manufacturer and that normally carries the manufacturer's surplus, discontinued or irregular goods.

Fads—Fashions that enter quickly, are adopted with great zeal, peak early and decline very fast.

Family life-cycle—The stages through which families might pass as they mature over time.

Fashion—A current accepted or popular style in a given field.

Financial intermediaries—Banks, credit companies, insurance companies and other businesses that help finance transactions or insure against the risks associated with the buying and selling of goods.

First-price sealed-bid pricing—Potential buyers submit sealed bids, and the item is awarded to the buyer who offers the best price.

Fixed costs—Costs that do not vary with production or sales level.

FOB-origin pricing—A geographic pricing strategy in which goods are placed free on board a carrier; the customer pays the freight from the factory to the destination.

Focus group—A small sample of typical consumers under the direction of a group leader who elicits their reaction to a stimulus such as an ad or product concept.

Follow-up—The last step in the selling process, in which the salesperson follows up after the sale to ensure customer satisfaction and repeat business.

Forecasting—The art of estimating future demand by anticipating what buyers are likely to do under a given set of conditions.

Fragmented industry—An industry characterised by many opportunities to create competitive advantages, but each advantage is small.

Franchise—A contractual association between a manufacturer, wholesaler or service organisation (a franchiser) and independent businesspeople (franchisees) who buy the right to own and operate one or more units in the franchise system.

Freight-absorption pricing—A geographic pricing strategy in which the company absorbs all or part of the actual freight charges in order to get the business.

Frequency—The number of times the average person in the target market is exposed to an advertising message during a given period.

Full-service retailers—Retailers that provide a full range of services to shoppers.

Functional discount (trade discount)—A price reduction offered by the seller to trade channel members that perform certain functions, such as selling, storing and record keeping.

Gatekeepers—People in the organisation's buying centre who control the flow of information to others.

Gender segmentation—Dividing a market into different groups based on sex.

General need description—The stage in the business buying process in which the company describes the general characteristics and quantity of a needed item.

Geodemographics—The study of the relationship between geographical location and demographics.

Geographic segmentation—Dividing a market into different geographical units such as nations, states, regions, counties, cities or neighbourhoods.

Geographical pricing—Pricing based on where customers are located.

Global firm—A firm that, by operating in more than one country, gains R&D, production, marketing and financial advantages that are not available to purely domestic competitors.

Global industry—An industry in which the strategic positions of competitors in given geographic or national markets are affected by their overall global positions.

Global marketing—Marketing that is concerned with integrating or standardising marketing actions across different geographic markets.

Global organisation—A form of international organisation whereby top corporate management and staff plan worldwide manufacturing or operational facilities, marketing policies, financial flows and logistical systems. The global operating unit reports directly to the chief executive, not to an international divisional head.

Going-rate pricing—Setting price based largely on following competitors' prices rather than on company costs or demand.

Government market—Governmental units – national and local – that purchase or rent goods and services for carrying out the main functions of government.

Growth stage—The product life-cycle stage at which a product's sales start climbing quickly.

Habitual buying behaviour—Consumer buying behaviour in situations characterised by low consumer involvement and few significant perceived brand differences.

Handling objections—The step in the selling process in which the salesperson seeks out, clarifies and overcomes customer objections to buying.

Horizontal marketing system—A channel arrangement in which two or more companies at one level join together to follow a new marketing opportunity.

Human need—A state of felt deprivation.

Human want—The form that a human need takes as shaped by culture and individual personality.

Hybrid marketing channels—Multi-channel distribution, as when a single firm sets up two or more marketing channels to reach one or more customer segments. A variety of direct and indirect approaches are used to deliver the firm's goods to its customers.

Hypermarkets—Huge stores that combine supermarket, discount and warehouse retailing; in addition to food, they carry furniture, appliances, clothing and many other products.

Idea generation—The systematic search for new-product ideas.

Idea screening—Screening new-product ideas in order to spot good ideas and drop poor ones as soon as possible.

Implausible positioning—Making claims that stretch the perception of the buyers too far to be believed.

Income segmentation—Dividing a market into different income groups.

Individual marketing—Tailoring products and marketing programmes to the needs and preferences of individual customers.

Industrial product—A product bought by individuals and organisations for further processing or for use in conducting a business.

Industry—A group of firms which offer a product or class of products that are close substitutes for each other. The set of all sellers of a product or service.

Inelastic demand—Total demand for a product that is not much affected by price changes, especially in the short run.

Influencer—A person whose view or advice influences buying decisions.

Influencer—A person whose views or advice carries some weight in making a final buying decision; they often help define specifications and also provide information for evaluating alternatives.

Information search—The stage of the buyer decision process in which the consumer is aroused to search for more information; the consumer may simply have heightened attention or may go into active information search.

Informative advertising—Advertising used to inform consumers about a new product or feature and to build primary demand.

Initiator—The person who first suggests or thinks of the idea of buying a particular product or service.

Innovation—An idea, service, product or technology that has been developed and marketed to customers who perceive it as novel or new. It is a process of identifying, creating and delivering new-product or service values that did not exist before in the marketplace.

Innovative marketing—A principle of enlightened marketing which requires that a company seek real product and marketing improvements.

Inside sales force—Salespeople who service the company's customers and prospect from their offices via telephone or visits from prospective customers.

Institutional market—Schools, hospitals, nursing homes, prisons and other institutions that provide goods and services to people in their care.

Integrated direct marketing—Direct marketing campaigns that use multiple vehicles and multiple stages to improve response rates and profits.

Integrated logistics management—A physical distribution concept that recognises the need for a firm to integrate its logistics system with those of its suppliers and customers. The aim is to maximise the performance of the entire distribution system.

Integrated marketing communications—The concept under which a company carefully integrates and coordinates its many communications channels to deliver a clear, consistent, and compelling message about the organisation and its products.

Intensive distribution—Stocking the product in as many outlets as possible.

Interactive marketing—Marketing by a service firm that recognises that perceived service quality depends heavily on the quality of buyer–seller interaction.

Intermediaries—Distribution channel firms that help the company find customers or make sales to them, including wholesalers and retailers that buy and resell goods.

Internal audit—An evaluation of the firm's entire value chain.

Internal marketing—Marketing by a service firm to train and effectively motivate its customer-contact employees and all the supporting service people to work as a team to provide customer satisfaction.

Internal records information—Information gathered from sources within the company to evaluate marketing performance and to detect marketing problems and opportunities.

International division—A form of international marketing organisation in which the division handles all of the firm's international activities. Marketing, manufacturing, research, planning and specialist staff are organised into operating units according to geography or product groups, or as an international subsidiary responsible for its own sales and profitability.

Internet (the Net)—A vast public web of computer networks connecting users of all types all around the world to each other and to a large 'information repository'. The Internet makes up one big 'information highway' that can dispatch bits at incredible speeds from one location to another.

Internet exchanges—Web-based bazaars, often shared by buyers, where suppliers bid against requirements posted on the Internet.

Introduction stage—The product life-cycle stage when the new product is first distributed and made available for purchase.

Invention—A new technology or product that may or may not be commercialised and may or may not deliver benefits to customers.

Joint ownership—A joint venture in which a company joins investors in a foreign market to create a local business in which the company shares joint ownership and control.

Joint venturing—Entering foreign markets by joining with foreign companies to produce or market a product or service.

Leading indicators—Time series that change in the same direction but in advance of company sales.

Learning—Changes in an individual's behaviour arising from experience.

Licensed brand—A product or service using a brand name offered by the brand owner to the licensee for an agreed fee or royalty.

Licensing—A method of entering a foreign market in which the company enters into an agreement with a licensee in the foreign market, offering the right to use a manufacturing process, trademark, patent, trade secret or other item of value for a fee or royalty.

Life-cycle segmentation—Offering products or marketing approaches that recognise the consumer's changing needs at different stages of their life.

Lifestyle—A person's pattern of living as expressed in his or her activities, interests and opinions.

Limited-service retailers—Retailers that provide only a limited number of services to shoppers.

Line extension—Using a successful brand name to introduce additional items in a given product category under the same brand name, such as new flavours, forms, colours, added ingredients or package sizes.

Long-range plan—A plan that describes the principal factors and forces affecting the organisation during the next several years, including long-term objectives, the chief marketing strategies used to attain them and the resources required.

Macroenvironment—The larger societal forces that affect the whole microenvironment – demographic, economic, natural, technological, political and cultural forces.

Management contracting—A joint venture in which the domestic firm supplies the management know-how to a foreign company that supplies the capital; the domestic firm exports management services rather than products.

Manufacturer's brand (national brand)—A brand created and owned by the producer of a product or service.

Market—The set of all actual and potential buyers of a product or service.

Market-centred company—A company that pays balanced attention to both customers and competitors in designing its marketing strategies.

Mark-up/mark-down—The difference between selling price and cost as a percentage of selling price or cost.

Market challenger—A runner-up firm in an industry that is fighting hard to increase its market share.

Market follower—A runner-up firm in an industry that wants to hold its share without rocking the boat.

Market leader—The firm in an industry with the largest market share; it usually leads other firms in price changes, new product introductions, distribution coverage and promotion spending.

Market nicher—A firm in an industry that serves small segments that the other firms overlook or ignore.

Market positioning—Arranging for a product to occupy a clear, distinctive and desirable place relative to competing products in the minds of target consumers. Formulating competitive positioning for a product and a detailed marketing mix.

Market segment—A group of consumers who respond in a similar way to a given set of marketing stimuli.

Market segmentation—Dividing a market into distinct groups of buyers with different needs, characteristics or behaviour, who might require separate products or marketing mixes.

Market targeting—The process of evaluating each market segment's attractiveness and selecting one or more segments to enter.

Market-penetration pricing—Setting a low price for a new product in order to attract large numbers of buyers and a large market share.

Market-skimming pricing—Setting a high price for a new product to skim maximum revenues layer by layer from the segments willing to pay the high price; the company makes fewer but more profitable sales.

Marketing—A social and managerial process by which individuals and groups obtain what they need and want through creating and exchanging products and value with others.

Marketing audit—A comprehensive, systematic, independent and periodic examination of a company's environment, objectives, strategies and activities to determine problem areas and opportunities, and to recommend a plan of action to improve the company's marketing performance.

Marketing channel (distribution channel)—A set of interdependent organisations involved in the process of making a product or service available for use or consumption by the consumer or industrial user.

Marketing concept—The marketing management philosophy which holds that achieving organisational goals depends on determining the needs and wants of target markets and delivering the desired satisfactions more effectively and efficiently than competitors do.

Marketing control—The process of measuring and evaluating the results of marketing strategies and plans, and taking corrective action to ensure that marketing objectives are attained.

Marketing environment– The actors and forces outside marketing that affect marketing management's ability to develop and maintain successful relationships with its target customers.

Marketing implementation—The process that turns marketing strategies and plans into marketing actions in order to accomplish strategic marketing objectives.

Marketing information system (MIS)—People, equipment and procedures to gather, sort, analyse, evaluate and distribute needed, timely and accurate information to marketing decision makers.

Marketing intelligence—Everyday information about developments in the marketing environment that helps managers prepare and adjust marketing plans.

Marketing intermediaries—Firms that help the company to promote, sell and distribute its goods to final buyers; they include physical distribution firms, marketing-service agencies and financial intermediaries.

Marketing management—The art and science of choosing target markets and building profitable relationships with them.

Marketing mix—The set of controllable tactical marketing tools – product, price, place and promotion – that the firm blends to produce the response it wants in the target market.

Marketing offer—Some combination of products, services, information, or experiences offered to a market to satisfy a need or want.

Marketing process—The process of (1) analysing marketing opportunities; (2) selecting target markets; (3) developing the marketing mix; and (4) managing the marketing effort.

Marketing research—The function that links the consumer, customer and public to the marketer through information that is used to identify and define marketing opportunities and problems, to generate, refine and evaluate marketing actions, to monitor marketing performance, and to improve understanding of the marketing process.

Marketing services agencies—Marketing research firms, advertising agencies, media firms, marketing consulting firms and other service providers that help a company to target and promote its products to the right markets.

Marketing strategy statement—A statement of the planned strategy for a new product that outlines the intended target market, the planned product positioning, and the sales, market share and profit goals for the first few years.

Marketing strategy—The marketing logic by which the business unit hopes to achieve its marketing objectives.

Marketing website—A site on the Web created by a company to interact with consumers for the purpose of moving them closer to a purchase or other marketing outcome. The site is designed to handle interactive communication initiated by the company.

Mass customisation—Preparing individually designed products and communication on a large scale.

Mass marketing—Using almost the same product, promotion and distribution for all consumers.

Materials and parts—Industrial products that enter the manufacturer's product completely, including raw materials and manufactured materials and parts.

Maturity stage– The stage in the product life-cycle where sales growth slows or levels off.

Measurability—The degree to which the size, purchasing power and profits of a market segment can be measured.

Media—Non-personal communications channels including print media (newspapers, magazines, direct mail), broadcast media (radio, television), and display media (billboards, signs, posters).

Media impact—The qualitative value of an exposure through a given medium.

Media vehicles—Specific media within each general media type, such as specific magazines, television shows or radio programmes.

Membership groups—Groups that have a direct influence on a person's behaviour and to which a person belongs.

Merchant wholesaler—Independently owned business that takes title to the merchandise it handles.

Message source—The company, the brand name, the salesperson of the brand, or the actor in the ad who endorses the product.

Microenvironment—The forces close to the company that affect its ability to serve its customers – the company, market channel firms, customer markets, competitors and publics, which combine to make up the firm's value delivery system.

Micromarketing—A form of target marketing in which companies tailor their marketing programmes to the needs and wants of narrowly defined geographic, demographic, psychographic or behavioural segments.

Mission statement—A statement of the organisation's purpose – what it wants to accomplish in the wider environment.

Modified rebuy—A business buying situation in which the buyer wants to modify product specifications, prices, terms or suppliers.

Monopolistic competition—A market in which many buyers and sellers trade over a range of prices rather than a single market price.

Moral appeals—Message appeals that are directed to the audience's sense of what is right and proper.

Motive (drive)—A need that is sufficiently pressing to direct the person to seek satisfaction of the need.

Multibrand strategy—A brand strategy under which a seller develops two or more brands in the same product category.

Multiple niching—Adopting a strategy of having several independent offerings that appeal to several different subsegments of customer.

Natural environment—Natural resources that are needed as inputs by marketers or that are affected by marketing activities.

Need recognition—The first stage of the buyer decision process in which the consumer recognises a problem or need.

Net profit—The difference between the income from goods sold and all expenses incurred.

New product—A good, service or idea that is perceived by some potential customers as new.

New task—A business buying situation in which the buyer purchases a product or service for the first time.

New-product development—The development of original products, product improvements, product modifications and new brands through the firm's own R&D efforts.

Niche marketing—Adapting a company's offerings to more closely match the needs of one or more subsegments where there is often little competition.

Non-durable product—A consumer product that is normally consumed in one or a few uses.

Non-personal communication channels—Channels that carry messages without personal contact or feedback, including media, atmospheres and events.

Non-tariff trade barriers—Non-monetary barriers to foreign products, such as biases against a foreign company's bids or product standards that go against a foreign company's product features.

Objective-and-task method—Developing the promotion budget by (1) defining specific objectives, (2) determining the tasks that must be performed to achieve these objectives, and (3) estimating the costs of performing these tasks. The sum of these costs is the proposed promotion budget.

Observational research—The gathering of primary data by observing relevant people, actions and situations.

Occasion segmentation—Dividing the market into groups according to occasions when buyers get the idea to buy, actually make their purchase, or use the purchased item.

Off-price retailer—Retailer that buys at less-than-regular wholesale prices and sells at less than retail.

Oligopolistic competition—A market in which there are a few sellers that are highly sensitive to each other's pricing and marketing strategies.

Online advertising—Advertising that appears while consumers are surfing the Web, including banner and ticker ads, interstitials, skyscrapers and other forms.

Open trading networks—Huge e-marketspaces in which B2B buyers and sellers find each other online, share information and complete transactions efficiently.

Open-end questions—Questions that allow respondents to answer in their own words.

Operating control—Checking ongoing performance against annual plans and taking corrective action.

Operating statement (profit-and-loss statement or income statement)—A financial statement that shows company sales, cost of goods sold and expenses during a given period of time.

Opinion leaders—People within a reference group who, because of special skills, knowledge, personality or other characteristics, exert influence on others.

Optional-product pricing—The pricing of optional or accessory products along with a main product.

Order-routine specification—The stage of the business buying process in which the buyer writes the final order with the chosen supplier(s), listing the technical specifications, quantity needed, expected time of delivery, return policies and warranties.

Outside sales force—Outside salespeople (or field sales force) who travel to call on customers.

Overpositioning—A positioning error referring to too narrow a picture of the company, its product or a brand being communicated to target customers.

Packaging—The activities of designing and producing the container or wrapper for a product.

Packaging concept—What the package should be or do for the product.

Patronage rewards—Cash or other awards for the regular use of a certain company's products or services.

Penetrated market—The set of consumers who have already bought a particular product or service.

Percentage-of-sales method—Setting the promotion budget at a certain percentage of current or forecast sales or as a percentage of the sales price.

Perception—The process by which people select, organise and interpret information to form a meaningful picture of the world.

Performance review—The stage of the business buying process in which the buyer rates its satisfaction with suppliers, deciding whether to continue, modify or drop them.

Personal communication channels—Channels through which two or more people communicate directly with each other, including face to face, person to audience, over the telephone, or through the mail.

Personal influence—The effect of statements made by one person on another's attitude or probability of purchase.

Personal selling—Personal presentation by the firm's sales force for the purpose of making sales and building customer relationships.

Personality—A person's distinguishing psychological characteristics that lead to relatively consistent and lasting responses to his or her own environment.

Persuasive advertising—Advertising used to build selective demand for a brand by persuading consumers that it offers the best quality for their money.

Physical distribution (marketing logistics)—The tasks involved in planning, implementing and controlling the physical flow of materials and final goods from points of origin to points of use to meet the needs of customers at a profit.

Physical distribution firms—Warehouse, transportation and other firms that help a company to stock and move goods from their points of origin to their destinations.

Place—All the company activities that make the product or service available to target customers.

Planned obsolescence—A strategy of causing products to become obsolete before they actually need replacement.

Pleasing products—Products that give high immediate satisfaction but may hurt consumers in the long run.

Point-of-purchase (POP) promotions—Displays and demonstrations that take place at the point of purchase or sale.

Political environment—Laws, government agencies and pressure groups that influence and limit various organisations and individuals in a given society.

Portfolio analysis—A tool by which management identifies and evaluates the various businesses that make up the company.

Postpurchase behaviour—The stage of the buyer decision process in which consumers take further action after purchase based on their satisfaction or dissatisfaction.

Potential market—The set of consumers who profess some level of interest in a particular product or service.

Pre-approach—The step in the selling process in which the salesperson learns as much as possible about a prospective customer before making a sales call.

Premiums—Goods offered either free or at low cost as an incentive to buy a product.

Presentation—The step in the selling process in which the salesperson tells the product 'story' to the buyer, showing how the product will make or save money for the buyer.

Price elasticity—A measure of the sensitivity of demand to changes in price.

Price packs—Reduced prices that are marked by the producer directly on the label or package.

917

Price—The amount of money charged for a product or service, or the sum of the values that consumers exchange for the benefits of having or using the product or service.

Primary data—Information collected for the specific purpose at hand.

Primary demand—The level of total demand for all brands of a given product or service – for example, the total demand for motor cycles.

Private brand (middleman, distributor or store brand)—A brand created and owned by a reseller of a product or service.

Private trading networks (PTNs)—B2B trading networks that link a particular seller with its own trading partners.

Problem recognition—The first stage of the business buying process in which someone in the company recognises a problem or need that can be met by acquiring a good or a service.

Product adaptation—Adapting a product to meet local conditions or wants in foreign markets.

Product—Anything that can be offered to a market for attention, acquisition, use or consumption that might satisfy a want or need. It includes physical objects, services, persons, places, organisations and ideas.

Product-bundle pricing—Combining several products and offering the bundle at a reduced price.

Product concept—A detailed version of the new-product idea stated in meaningful consumer terms.

Product concept—The idea that consumers will favour products that offer the most quality, performance and features, and that the organisation should therefore devote its energy to making continuous product improvements.

Product development—Developing the product concept into a physical product in order to ensure that the product idea can be turned into a workable product.

Product idea—An idea for a possible product that the company can see itself offering to the market.

Product image—The way consumers perceive an actual or potential product.

Product innovation charter (PIC)—A new-product strategy statement formalising management's reasons or rationale behind the firm's search for innovation opportunities, the product/market and technology to focus upon, and the goals and objectives to be achieved.

Product invention—Creating new products or services for foreign markets.

Product life-cycle (PLC)—The course of a product's sales and profits over its lifetime. It involves five distinct stages: product development, introduction, growth, maturity and decline.

Product line filling—Increasing the product line by adding more items within the present range of the line.

Product line pricing—Setting the price steps between various products in a product line based on cost differences between the products, customer evaluations of different features, and competitors' prices.

Product line stretching—Increasing the product line by lengthening it beyond its current range.

Product line—A group of products that are closely related because they function in a similar manner, are sold to the same customer groups, are marketed through the same types of outlet, or fall within given price ranges.

Product mix (product assortment)—The set of all product lines and items that a particular seller offers for sale to buyers.

Product position—The way the product is defined by consumers on important attributes – the place the product occupies in consumers' minds relative to competing products.

Product quality—The ability of a product to perform its functions; it includes the product's overall durability, reliability, precision, ease of operation and repair, and other valued attributes.

Product sales force structure—A sales force organisation under which salespeople specialise in selling only a portion of the company's products or lines.

Product specification—The stage of the business buying process in which the buying organisation decides on and specifies the best technical product characteristics for a needed item.

Product-support services—Services that augment actual products.

Production concept—The philosophy that consumers will favour products that are available and highly affordable, and that management should therefore focus on improving production and distribution efficiency.

Profitable customer—A person, household or company whose revenues over time exceed, by an acceptable amount, the company's costs of attracting, selling and servicing that customer.

Promotion mix—The specific mix of advertising, personal selling, sales promotion and public relations that a company uses to pursue its advertising and marketing objectives.

Promotion—Activities that communicate the product or service and its merits to target customers and persuade them to buy.

Promotional allowance—A payment or price reduction to reward dealers for participating in advertising and sales-support programmes.

Promotional pricing—Temporarily pricing products below the list price, and sometimes even below cost, to increase short-run sales.

Proposal solicitation—The stage of the business buying process in which the buyer invites qualified suppliers to submit proposals.

Prospecting—The step in the selling process in which the salesperson identifies qualified potential customers.

Psychographic segmentation—Dividing a market into different groups based on social class, lifestyle or personality characteristics.

Psychographics—The technique of measuring lifestyles and developing lifestyle classifications; it involves measuring the chief AIO dimensions (activities, interests, opinions).

Psychological pricing—A pricing approach that considers the psychology of prices and not simply the economics; the price is used to say something about the product.

Public relations—Building good relations with the company's various publics by obtaining favourable publicity, building up a good 'corporate image', and handling or heading off unfavourable rumours, stories and events. Major PR tools include press relations, product publicity, corporate communications, lobbying and counselling.

Public—Any group that has an actual or potential interest in or impact on an organisation's ability to achieve its objectives.

Pull strategy—A promotion strategy that calls for spending a lot on advertising and consumer promotion to build up consumer demand. If the strategy is successful, consumers will ask their retailers for the product, the retailers will ask the wholesalers, and the wholesalers will ask the producers.

Pulsing—Scheduling ads unevenly, in bursts, over a certain time period.

Purchase decision—The stage of the buyer decision process in which the consumer actually buys the product.

Pure competition—A market in which many buyers and sellers trade in a uniform commodity – no single buyer or seller has much effect on the going market price.

Pure monopoly—A market in which there is a single seller – it may be a government monopoly, a private regulated monopoly or a private non-regulated monopoly.

Push strategy—A promotion strategy that calls for using the sales force and trade promotion to push the product through channels. The producer promotes the product to wholesalers, the wholesalers promote to retailers, and the retailers promote to consumers.

Qualified available market—The set of consumers who have interest, income, access and qualifications for a particular product or service.

Qualitative research—Exploratory research used to uncover consumers' motivations, attitudes and behaviour. Focus-group interviewing, elicitation interviews and repertory grid techniques are typical methods used in this type of research.

Quality—The totality of features and characteristics of a product or service that bear on its ability to satisfy stated or implied needs.

Quantitative research—Research which involves data collection by mail or personal interviews from a sufficient volume of customers to allow statistical analysis.

Quantity discount—A price reduction to buyers who buy large volumes.

Quantity premium—A surcharge paid by buyers who purchase high volumes of a product.

Question marks—Low-share business units in high-growth markets that require a lot of cash in order to hold their share or become stars.

Quota—A limit on the amount of goods that an importing country will accept in certain product categories; it is designed to conserve on foreign exchange and to protect local industry and employment.

Range branding strategy—A brand strategy whereby the firm develops separate product range names for different families of product.

Rational appeals—Message appeals that relate to the audience's self-interest and show that the product will produce the claimed benefits; examples are appeals of product quality, economy, value or performance.

Reach—The percentage of people in the target market exposed to an ad campaign during a given period.

Reference groups—Groups that have a direct (face-to-face) or indirect influence on the person's attitudes or behaviour.

Reference prices—Prices that buyers carry in their minds and refer to when they look at a given product.

Relationship marketing—The process of creating, maintaining and enhancing strong, value-laden relationships with customers and other stakeholders.

Reminder advertising—Advertising used to keep consumers thinking about a product.

Resellers—The individuals and organisations that buy goods and services to resell at a profit.

Retailer cooperatives—Contractual vertical marketing systems in which retailers organise a new, jointly owned business to carry on wholesaling and possibly production.

Retailers—Businesses whose sales come primarily from retailing.

Retailing accordion—A phenomenon describing how the width of retailers' product assortment or operations shifts over time: there tends to be a general–specific–general cycle. However, it is possible that many retailing businesses evolve along a specificgeneral–specific cycle.

Reverse auction—Customers name the price that they are willing to pay for an item and seek a company willing to sell.

Role—The activities a person is expected to perform according to the people around him or her.

Sales force management—The analysis, planning, implementation and control of sales force activities. It includes setting sales force objectives; designing sales force strategy; and recruiting, selecting, training, supervising and evaluating the firm's salespeople.

Sales force promotion—Sales promotion designed to motivate the sales force and make sales force selling efforts more effective, including bonuses, contests and sales rallies.

Sales promotion—Short-term incentives to encourage purchase or sales of a product or service.

Sales quotas—Standards set for salespeople, stating the amount they should sell and how sales should be divided among the company's products.

Salesperson—An individual acting for a company by performing one or more of the following activities: prospecting, communicating, servicing and information gathering.

Salutary products—Products that have low appeal but may benefit consumers in the long run.

Sample—A segment of the population selected for market research to represent the population as a whole.

Samples—Offers to consumers of a trial amount of a product.

Seasonal discount—A price reduction to buyers who buy merchandise or services out of season.

Seasonality—The recurrent consistent pattern of sales movements within the year.

Second-price sealed bid—Sealed bids are submitted but the contender placing the best bid pays only the price equal to the second-best bid.

Segment marketing—Adapting a company's offerings so they more closely match the needs of one or more segments.

Segmented pricing—Pricing that allows for differences in customers, products and locations. The differences in prices are not based on differences in costs.

Selective attention—The tendency of people to screen out most of the information to which they are exposed.

Selective demand—The demand for a given brand of a product or service.

Selective distortion—The tendency of people to adapt information to personal meanings.

Selective distribution—The use of more than one, but less than all of the intermediaries that are willing to carry the company's products.

Selective retention—The tendency of people to retain only part of the information to which they are exposed, usually information that supports their attitudes or beliefs.

Self-concept—Self-image, or the complex mental pictures that people have of themselves.

Self-service retailers—Retailers that provide few or no services to shoppers; shoppers perform their own locate–compare–select process.

Selling concept—The idea that consumers will not buy enough of the organisation's products unless the organisation undertakes a large-scale selling and promotion effort.

Selling process—The steps that the salesperson follows when selling, which include prospecting and qualifying, pre-approach, approach, presentation and demonstration, handling objections, closing and follow-up.

Sense-of-mission marketing—A principle of enlightened marketing which holds that a company should define its mission in broad social terms rather than narrow product terms.

Sequential product development—A new-product development approach in which one company department works individually to complete its stage of the process before passing the new product along to the next department and stage.

Served market (target market)—The part of the qualified available market that the company decides to pursue.

Service inseparability—A major characteristic of services – they are produced and consumed at the same time and cannot be separated from their providers, whether the providers are people or machines.

Service intangibility—A major characteristic of services – they cannot be seen, tasted, felt, heard or smelt before they are bought.

Service perishability—A major characteristic of services – they cannot be stored for later sale or use.

Service variability—A major characteristic of services – their quality may vary greatly depending on who provides them and when, where and how.

Service—Any activity or benefit that one party can offer to another which is essentially intangible and does not result in the ownership of anything.

Services—Activities, benefits or satisfactions that are offered for sale.

Shopping product—A consumer product that the customer, in the process of selection and purchase, characteristically compares with others on such bases as suitability, quality, price and style.

Simultaneous product development—An approach to developing new products in which various company departments work closely together, overlapping the steps in the product development process to save time and increase effectiveness.

Single-source data systems—Electronic monitoring systems that link consumers' exposure to television advertising and promotion (measured using television meters) with what they buy in stores (measured using store checkout scanners).

Social classes—Relatively permanent and ordered divisions in a society whose members share similar values, interests and behaviours.

Societal marketing concept—The idea that the organisation should determine the needs, wants and interests of target markets and deliver the desired satisfactions more effectively and efficiently than competitors in a way that maintains or improves both the consumer's and society's well-being.

Societal marketing—A principle of enlightened marketing which holds that a company should make marketing decisions by considering consumers' wants, the company's requirements, consumers' long-run interests and society's long-run interests.

Specialised industry—An industry where there are many opportunities for firms to create competitive advantages that are huge or give a high pay-off.

Speciality product—A consumer product with unique characteristics or brand identification for which a significant group of buyers is willing to make a special purchase effort.

Speciality store—A retail store that carries a narrow product line with a deep assortment within that line.

Stalemate industry—An industry that produces commodities and is characterised by a few opportunities to create competitive advantages, with each advantage being small.

Standardised marketing mix—An international marketing strategy for using basically the same product, advertising, distribution channels and other elements of the marketing mix in all the company's international markets.

Stars—High-growth, high-share businesses or products that often require heavy investment to finance their rapid growth.

Statistical demand analysis—A set of statistical procedures used to discover the most important real factors affecting sales and their relative influence; the most commonly analysed factors are prices, income, population and promotion.

Status—The general esteem given to a role by society.

Straight product extension—Marketing a product in a foreign market without any change.

Straight rebuy—A business buying situation in which the buyer routinely reorders something without any modifications.

Strapline—A slogan often used in conjunction with a brand's name, advertising and other promotions.

Strategic business unit (SBU)—A unit of the company that has a separate mission and objectives and that can be planned independently from other company businesses. An SBU can be a company division, a product line within a division, or sometimes a single product or brand.

Strategic control—Checking whether the company's basic strategy matches its opportunities and strengths.

Strategic group—A group of firms in an industry following the same or a similar strategy.

Strategic plan—A plan that describes how a firm will adapt to take advantage of opportunities in its constantly changing environment, thereby maintaining a strategic fit between the firm's goals and capabilities and its changing market opportunities.

Style—A basic and distinctive mode of expression.

Subculture—A group of people with shared value systems based on common life experiences and situations.

Substantiality—The degree to which a market segment is sufficiently large or profitable.

Supermarkets—Large, low-cost, low-margin, high-volume, self-service stores that carry a wide variety of food, laundry and household products.

Superstore—A store around twice the size of a regular supermarket that carries a large assortment of routinely purchased food and non-food items and offers such services as dry cleaning, post offices, film developing, photo finishing, cheque cashing, petrol forecourts and self-service car-washing facilities.

Supplier search—The stage of the business buying process in which the buyer tries to find the best vendors.

Supplier selection—The stage of the business buying process in which the buyer reviews proposals and selects a supplier or suppliers.

Suppliers—Firms and individuals that provide the resources needed by the company and its competitors to produce goods and services.

Supplies and services—Industrial products that do not enter the finished product at all.

Survey research—The gathering of primary data by asking people questions about their knowledge, attitudes, preferences and buying behaviour.

SWOT analysis—A distillation of the findings of the internal and external audits which draws attention to the critical organisational strengths and weaknesses and the opportunities and threats facing the company.

Systems buying—Buying a packaged solution to a problem and without all the separate decisions involved.

Target costing—A technique to support pricing decisions, which starts with deciding a target cost for a new product and works back to designing the product.

Target market—A set of buyers sharing common needs or characteristics that the company decides to serve.

Target marketing—Directing a company's effort towards serving one or more groups of customers sharing common needs or characteristics.

Tariff—A tax levied by a government against certain imported products. Tariffs are designed to raise revenue or to protect domestic firms.

Team selling—Using teams of people from sales, marketing, production, finance, technical support, and even upper management to service large, complex accounts.

Technological environment—Forces that create new technologies, creating new product and market opportunities.

Telemarketing—Using the telephone to sell directly to consumers.

Territorial sales force structure —A sales force organisation that assigns each salesperson to an exclusive geographic territory in which that salesperson carries the company's full line.

Test marketing—The stage of new-product development where the product and marketing programme are tested in more realistic market settings.

Third-party logistics (3PL) provider—An independent logistics provider that performs any or all of the functions required to get its client's product to market.

Time-series analysis—Breaking down past sales into their trend, cycle, season and erratic components, then recombining these components to produce a sales forecast.

Total costs—The sum of the fixed and variable costs for any given level of production.

Total customer cost—The total of all the monetary, time, energy and psychic costs associated with a marketing offer.

Total customer value—The total of the entire product, services, personnel and image values that a buyer receives from a marketing offer.

Total market demand—The total volume of a product or service that would be bought by a defined consumer group in a defined geographic area in a defined time period in a defined marketing environment under a defined level and mix of industry marketing effort.

Total quality management (TQM)—Programmes designed to constantly improve the quality of products, services, and marketing processes.

Trade (or retailer) promotion—Sales promotion designed to gain reseller support and to improve reseller selling efforts, including discounts, allowances, free goods, cooperative advertising, push money, and conventions and trade shows.

Trade-in allowance—A price reduction given for turning in an old item when buying a new one.

Transaction—A trade between two parties that involves at least two things of value, agreed-upon conditions, a time of agreement and a place of agreement.

Trend—The long-term, underlying pattern of sales growth or decline resulting from basic changes in population, capital formation and technology.

Two-part pricing—A strategy for pricing services in which price is broken into a fixed fee plus a variable usage rate.

Underpositioning—A positioning error referring to failure to position a company, its product or brand.

Undifferentiated marketing—A market-coverage strategy in which a firm decides to ignore market segment differences and go after the whole market with one offer.

Uniform delivered pricing—A geographic pricing strategy in which the company charges the same price plus freight to all customers, regardless of their location.

Unique selling proposition (USP)—The unique product benefit that a firm aggressively promotes in a consistent manner to its target market. The benefit usually reflects functional superiority: best quality, best services, lowest price, most advanced technology.

Unsought product—A consumer product that the consumer either does not know about or knows about but does not normally think of buying.

User—The person who consumes or uses a product or service.

Users—Members of the organisation who will use the product or service; users often initiate the buying proposal and help define product specifications.

Value analysis—An approach to cost reduction in which components are studied carefully to determine whether they can be redesigned, standardised or made by less costly methods of production.

Value chain—A major tool for identifying ways to create more customer value.

Value delivery network—A network made up of the company, suppliers, distributors and customers who 'partner' with each other to improve the performance of the entire system.

Value marketing—A principle of enlightened marketing which holds that a company should put most of its resources into value-building marketing investments.

Value positioning—A range of positioning alternatives based on the value an offering delivers and its price.

Value pricing—Offering just the right combination of quality and good service at a fair price.

Value-based pricing—Setting price based on buyers' perceptions of product values rather than on cost.

Variable costs—Costs that vary directly with the level of production.

Variety-seeking buying behaviour—Consumer buying behaviour in situations characterised by low consumer involvement, but significant perceived brand differences.

Vertical marketing system (VMS)—A distribution channel structure in which producers, wholesalers and retailers act as a unified system. One channel member owns the others, has contracts with them, or has so much power that they all cooperate.

Viral marketing—The Internet version of word-of-mouth marketing – e-mail messages or other marketing events that are so infectious that customers will want to pass them on to friends.

Volume industry—An industry characterised by few opportunities to create competitive advantages, but each advantage is huge and gives a high pay-off.

Warehouse club (wholesale club, membership warehouse)—Off-price retailer that sells a limited selection of brand-name grocery items, appliances, clothing and a hodgepodge of other goods at deep discounts to members who pay annual membership fees.

Web communities—Websites upon which members can congregate online and exchange views on issues of common interest.

Webcasting (push programming)—The automatic downloading of customised information of interest to recipients' PCs, affording an attractive channel for delivering Internet advertising or other information content.

Wheel of retailing—A concept of retailing which states that new types of retailer usually begin as low-margin, low-price, low-status operations, but later evolve into higher-priced, higher-service operations, eventually becoming like the conventional retailers they replaced.

Wholesaler—A firm engaged primarily in selling goods and services to those buying for resale or business use.

Wholesaler-sponsored voluntary chains—Voluntary chains of independent retailers organised by the wholesaler to help them compete with large chain organisations.

Word-of-mouth influence—Personal communication about a product between target buyers and neighbours, friends, family members and associates.

Workload approach—An approach to setting sales force size, whereby the company groups accounts into different size classes and then determines how many salespeople are needed to call on them the desired number of times.

Zone pricing—A geographic pricing strategy in which the company sets up two or more zones. All customers within a zone pay the same total price; the more distant the zone, the higher the price.

SUBJECT INDEX

COMPANY INDEX